P9-DJL-872

Strategic Management

STRATEGIC MANAGEMENT

An Integrated Approach

THIRD EDITION

Charles W. L. Hill

UNIVERSITY OF WASHINGTON

Gareth R. Jones

TEXAS A & M UNIVERSITY

HOUGHTON MIFFLIN COMPANY BOSTON TORONTO

GENEVA, ILLINOIS PALO ALTO PRINCETON, NEW JERSEY

For Jennifer, Nicholas, and Julia

G.R.J.

For Alexandra, Elizabeth, Charlotte, and Michelle

C.W.L.H.

Associate Editor: *Susan M. Kahn*
Associate Production/Design Coordinator: *Jennifer Waddell*
Senior Manufacturing Coordinator: *Priscilla Bailey*
Marketing Manager: *Robert D. Wolcott*

Cover design and image by Beth Santos.

Printed in the U.S.A.

Library of Congress Catalog Card Number: 94-76508

ISBN: 0-395-70943-1

Exam copy ISBN: 0-395-71675-6

56789-RM-98-97-96

Brief Contents

Contents

Preface

The increasing support for and acceptance of an integrated approach to strategic management, that which we pioneered in the first two editions of *Strategic Management*, has led us to build on and expand this approach for the third edition. To increase its value, we have continued to utilize feedback from users of the last two editions of our book. We still provide comprehensive and up-to-date coverage of the burgeoning strategic management literature while keeping the text readable. We have written or collected a new set of strategic management cases and developed a new interactive teaching approach to enhance the students' learning experience. Finally, we have extended and refined the learning features present in the text and in the teaching materials that accompany *Strategic Management*.

COMPREHENSIVE AND UP-TO-DATE COVERAGE

Competitive Advantage

Recognizing the continuing research thrust toward exploring the sources of competitive advantage both domestically and globally, we have integrated recent research on the building blocks of competitive advantage into our text. The third edition of *Strategic Management* contains two new chapters (Chapters 4 and 5) that focus on the four building blocks of competitive advantage—efficiency, quality, innovation, and customer responsiveness—and we explore how an organization builds strengths in these areas through its functional-, business-, and corporate-level strategy. In addition, we have reorganized the chapters on strategy implementation to show how organizational design can be used to build competitive advantage. This new focus has enabled us to give a more comprehensive and integrated picture of the strategic management process.

Global Dimension of Strategy

We have also increased our emphasis on the global dimension of strategy. Our chapter on global issues has been moved up and now comes directly after business-level strategy. This change has allowed us to relate better to the value-creation process. Furthermore, almost all the chapters contain new material on the global dimension of strategy. In the chapter on analyzing the environment, for example, there is a new discussion of the global environment, whereas the chapter on matching strategy to structure probes the strategy-structure relationship in

a global context. The global strategy chapter itself has been extensively revised and updated to incorporate all recent research and thinking.

Other Changes in the Third Edition

To stay abreast of the field and respond to requests and suggestions from the users of the previous edition we have made several other additions or changes in content. They include the following:

- A discussion of strategic leadership, strategic intent, cognitive biases, and their impact on decision making (Chapter 1)
- Increased coverage of ethics and social responsibility (Chapter 2)
- Coverage of Porter's "competitive advantage of nations" framework (Chapter 3)
- Thorough coverage of the four building blocks of competitive advantage—efficiency, quality, innovation, and customer responsiveness (Chapters 4 and 5)
- Integrated coverage of total quality management and time-based competition (Chapter 5)
- A discussion of how to pursue simultaneously both a low-cost and a differentiation strategy (Chapter 6)
- New and expanded treatment of acquisitions, new ventures, and restructuring (Chapter 10)
- New organization of the strategy implementation chapters, with a stronger focus on global organizational design (Chapters 11, 12, and 13)

While each chapter has been thoroughly revised and updated, we have been careful to preserve the balanced and integrated nature of our account of the strategic management process. Moreover, as we added new material, we deleted less current or less important concepts and information to ensure that students would concentrate on the core concepts and issues in the field. We have paid close attention to retaining the book's readability.

STRATEGIC MANAGEMENT CASES

The thirty-one cases that we have selected for this edition will appeal, we are certain, to students and professors alike, both because these cases are intrinsically interesting and because of the number of strategic management issues they illuminate. The organizations discussed in the cases range from large, well-known ones, for which students can do library research in order to update the information, to small, entrepreneurial businesses that illustrate the uncertainty and challenge of the strategic management process. In addition, the selection includes many international cases, and most of the other cases contain some element of global strategy.

Only two cases in our selection are unchanged from the last edition of *Strategic Management*—the perennial favorites, Nucor and Hanson PLC. We have written or updated another twelve cases of our own for this edition: the Computer Industry, Compaq, the Rise of IBM, the Fall of IBM, the Global Auto Industry in 1994, Toyota in 1994, General Motors, Boeing, Blockbuster Video, Kodak, Philips NV, and Philips versus Sony. We feel that our entire selection is unrivaled in breadth and depth, and we are grateful to the case authors who have contributed to this edition. They include the following:

Sexton Adams
University of North Texas
Frank C. Barnes
University of North Carolina, Charlotte
M. Edgar Barrett
American Graduate School of International Management
Robert A. Blumenthal
University of Washington
James W. Bronson
Washington State University
Brad Brown
University of Virginia
Tim Craig
University of Victoria
John Dunkelberg
Wake Forest University
Tom Goho
Wake Forest University
Barbara Gottfried
Bentley College
Adelaide Griffin
Texas Woman's University
Alan N. Hoffman
Bentley College
Stephen Jenner
California State University—Dominguez Hills
Javad Kargar
North Carolina Central University
Joseph Lampel
New York University
Karen D. Loch
Georgia State University
Patricia P. McDougal
Georgia Institute of Technology
Stewart C. Malone
University of Virginia
Paul Miesing
State University of New York at Albany
Mike W. Peng
University of Washington
Susan Peters
Texas A&M University
Valerie J. Porciello
Bentley College
Michael Porter
Harvard Business School
Richard Reed
Washington State University
Brian Shaffer
University of Kentucky
Jamal Shamsie
New York University
Teri Shanander
University of Kentucky
Melissa A. Schilling
University of Washington
Debra L. Sottolano
State University of New York at Albany
Rebecca Wayland
Harvard Business School

NEW INTERACTIVE TEACHING APPROACH

Besides integrating recent research and global concerns into our discussion, in the third edition, we have striven to enhance the book's value for students in two other major ways. We have increased our use of real-world examples and have developed some new interactive learning features designed to increase students' understanding of strategic management concepts.

Each chapter of the book begins with an **all-new opening case**, followed by discussion questions, which can be used to stimulate class discussion. Every chapter also contains several detailed **Strategy in Action boxes**, which provide graphic examples of the real-world implications of strategic management theory.

At the end of each chapter, after the chapter summary, we have added two new exercises that we find to be very useful in kindling students' interest in the course material. The first is an **Article File**, which requires students to seek out an example of a company that has been dealing with the issues discussed in the chapters. For instance, students are asked to locate and research a company pursuing a low-cost or a differentiation strategy, and to describe this company's strategy, its advantages and disadvantages, and the core competencies required to pursue it. Students' presentations of their findings lead to lively class discussions.

The second exercise is the **Strategic Management Project.** Students, in small groups, choose a company to study for the whole semester and then analyze the company using the series of questions provided at the end of every chapter. For example, students might select Ford Motor Co. and, using the series of chapter questions, collect information on Ford's top managers, mission, ethical

position, domestic and global strategy and structure, and so on. Eventually, students would write a case study of their company and present it to the class at the end of the semester. Normally, we also have students present one or more of the cases in the book early in the semester, but in our classes we now treat the students' own projects as the major class assignment and their case presentations as the climax of the semester's learning experience.

We have found that our new interactive approach to teaching strategic management appeals to students. It also greatly improves the quality of their learning experience. Our new approach is more fully discussed in the Instructor's Resource Manual.

TEACHING AND LEARNING AIDS

Taken together, the teaching and learning features of *Strategic Management* provide a package that is unsurpassed in its coverage and that supports the integrated approach, which we have taken throughout the book. Further details for using the supplementary materials can be found in the Instructor's Resource Manual.

For the Instructor

- The **Instructor's Resource Manual**, which users liked so much in the first two editions of *Strategic Management,* has been refined and expanded. As usual, for each case we offer a *comprehensive teaching note,* which gives a complete analysis of case issues. In addition, for each book chapter we provide a *synopsis,* a list of *teaching objectives,* a *comprehensive lecture outline,* and *answers to discussion questions*. Each of the new chapter opening cases also has a corresponding *teaching note* to help guide class discussion. Furthermore, the lecture outlines include summaries of the material in the *Strategy in Action* boxes.
- A new **Test Bank** (in the Instructor's Resource Manual), created for the third edition, offers a set of comprehensive true/false and multiple-choice questions, and the answers to them, for each chapter in the book. An *electronic version* of the Test Bank allows instructors to generate and change tests easily on the computer.
- A package of **color transparencies** accompanies the book. These include nearly all the art found in the text.
- A **videotape** pertaining to several of the cases and some of the concepts in the text is available to instructors. It helps highlight many issues of interest and can be used to spark class discussion.

For the Student

- A new **Moody's Company Data disk set** is available as a supplement. The disks contain complete financial data on most of the large, well-known companies that are the subjects of the cases in *Strategic Management*. With these data, students or instructors can perform strategic and financial analyses.
- **Micromatic**, second edition, is a computer-based simulation that introduces students to tools and concepts of today's business world, such as spreadsheet calculations, "what-if" scenarios, financial analysis, and competitive analysis.
- **Policy Expert** includes four computer tools—business calculator, ratio analysis, portfolio models, and environmental scan—that assist students in analyzing actual businesses or cases in a strategic management text.

ACKNOWLEDGMENTS

This book is the product of far more than two authors. We wish to thank again the case authors for allowing us to use their materials, and Susan Peters for writing the new Test Bank. We also want to thank the Departments of Management at the University of Washington and Texas A & M University for providing the setting and atmosphere in which the book could be written, and the students of these universities who reacted to and provided input for many of our ideas. In addition, the following reviewers gave us valuable suggestions for improving the manuscript from its original version to its current form:

Ken Armstrong
Anderson University
Kunal Banerji
West Virginia University
Glenn Bassett
University of Bridgeport
Thomas H. Berliner
The University of Texas at Dallas
Geoffrey Brooks
Western Oregon State College
Gene R. Conaster
Golden State University
Steven W. Congden
Ithaca College
Catherine M. Daily
Ohio State University
Helen Deresky
SUNY—Plattsburgh
Mark Fiegener
Oregon State University
Isaac Fox
Washington State University
Eliezer Geisler
Northeastern Illinois University
Gretchen Gemeinhardt
University of Houston
Lynn Godkin
Lamar University
Robert L. Goldberg
Northeastern University
Graham L. Hubbard
University of Minnesota
Tammy G. Hunt
University of North Carolina at Wilmington
W. Grahm Irwin
Miami University
Marios Katsioloudes
University of South Carolina Coastal Carolina College
Geoffrey King
California State University—Fullerton
Rico Lam
University of Oregon
Robert J. Litschert
Virginia Polytechnic Institute and State University
Franz T. Lohrke
Louisiana State University
Lance A. Masters
California State University—San Bernãdino
Charles Mercer
Drury College
Van Miller
University of Dayton
Joanna Mulholland
West Chester University of Pennsylvania
Paul R. Reed
Sam Houston State University
Rhonda K. Reger
Arizona State University
Malika Richards
Indiana University
Ronald Sanchez
University of Illinois
Joseph A. Schenk
University of Dayton
Brian Shaffer
University of Kentucky
Barbara Spencer
Clemson University
Lawrence Steenberg
University of Evansville
Ted Takamura
Warner Pacific College
Bobby Vaught
Southwest Missouri State
Robert P. Vichas
Florida Atlantic University
Daniel White
Drexel University

Finally, thanks are due to our families for their patience and support during the revision process. We especially thank our wives, Alexandra Hill and Jennifer George, for their ever increasing support and affection.

I INTRODUCTION TO STRATEGIC MANAGEMENT

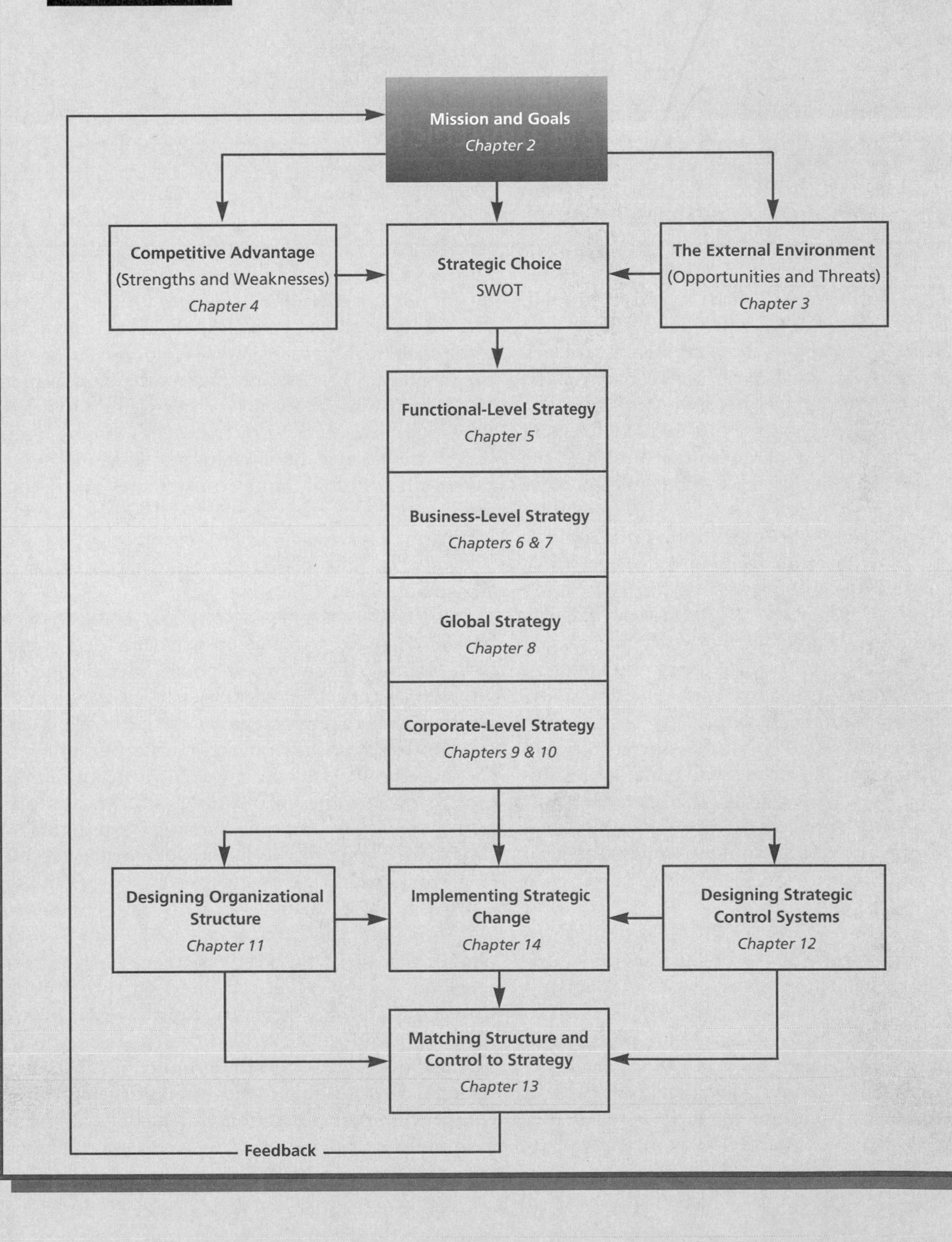

1 The Strategic Management Process

1.1 OPENING CASE: SOUTHWEST AIRLINES

For most of the last fifteen years, the U.S. airline industry has been one of the least attractive to be in. Between 1978 and 1993, when the industry was deregulated, twenty-nine new airlines entered it. This rapid increase in airline carrying capacity led to a situation of overcapacity. As more and more airlines chased passengers, they lowered fares to gain them; fares fell to levels barely sufficient to keep the airlines profitable. Since 1978 the industry has twice engaged in an intense price war: from 1981 to 1983 and from 1990 to 1993. Competition grew so fierce during these two periods that in 1982 the whole industry lost $700 million, and between 1990 and 1992 it lost a staggering $7.1 billion—more than it had made during its previous fifty years.

Yet despite the hostile environment, one company, Southwest Airlines, not only remained consistently profitable, but actually improved its performance while its competitors were wallowing in red ink. Southwest is a regional airline with a major presence in Texas. In 1992, when all the other major U.S. airlines lost money, Southwest reported a sharp jump in its net profit—to $105.5 million on revenues of $1.68 billion, up from $26.9 million on revenues of $1.31 billion in 1991.

Two factors have made Southwest profitable: its low costs and the loyalty of its customers. Its low costs stem from a number of sources. Southwest offers a no-frills approach to customer service. No meals are served on board and there are no first class seats. Southwest does not subscribe to the big reservation computers used by travel agents because it deems the booking fees too costly. The airline flies only one type of aircraft, the fuel-efficient Boeing 737, which keeps training and maintenance costs down. A major asset, too, is its very productive work force. Southwest employees say that they are willing to work hard because they feel appreciated by the top management. As one flight attendant put it, "You don't want to let Herb down." Herb Kelleher, the CEO, has been known to help flight attendants serve drinks and maintenance engineers service planes. In addition, Southwest operates a generous stock option plan that extends to all employees. As a result, employees own about 10 percent of the airline's stock, which gives them a further incentive to work hard.

Southwest's customer loyalty also comes from a number of sources. Its low-cost structure lets Southwest offer its customers low prices. This builds loyalty, which is further strengthened by the airline's reputation as the most reliable carrier in the industry. Southwest has the quickest turnaround time in the industry; its ground crew needs just fifteen minutes to turnaround an incoming aircraft and prepare it for departure, thus, helping keep flights on time. The company also has a well-earned reputation for listening to its customers. For example, when five Texas medical students who commuted weekly to an out-of-state medical school complained that the flight got them to class fifteen minutes late, Southwest moved the departure time up fifteen minutes. Furthermore, Southwest's focused route structure—it serves just fifteen states, mostly in the South—has helped it build a substantial regional presence and avoid some of the cutthroat competition that the nationwide airlines have had to grapple with. [1]

Discussion Questions

1. What does the success of Southwest Airlines tell you about the relative importance of factors specific to the industry and to the company in explaining a company's performance?

2. What is the basis of Southwest's competitive advantage? How might it lose that advantage?

1.2 INTRODUCTION

A central objective of strategic management is to find out why some organizations succeed while others fail. For example, in the airline industry, what distinguishes the successes such as Southwest from failures such as Continental? Why has Southwest consistently outperformed the industry, whereas Continental has found itself in bankruptcy court twice within a decade? Similarly, in the computer industry, why are Digital Equipment and IBM, once regarded as two of the world's most successful computer companies, now deemed failures, whereas companies such as Dell Computer and Compaq Computer are considered successes? Or in the retail industry, why have former giants like Sears and J. C. Penney fallen on hard times, and relative newcomers like The Gap, Toys Я Us, and The Limited, become industry stars? The material contained in this book enables you to answer such questions. It can help you understand why some organizations succeed and others fail, why success may turn into failure (as seems to have happened at IBM and Digital), and how a failing organization can regain success (as Chrysler has done twice in the last fifteen years).

We explain how three broad factors determine a company's success: the industry where it is based, the country (or countries) where it is located, and its own resources, capabilities, and strategies (see Figure 1.1). You will learn why some industries are more profitable than others and see how being based in an attractive industry can help a company achieve success. For example, during the last two decades, companies in the airline industry have been much less profitable than those in the pharmaceutical industry.

Figure 1.1
The Determinants of Company Performance

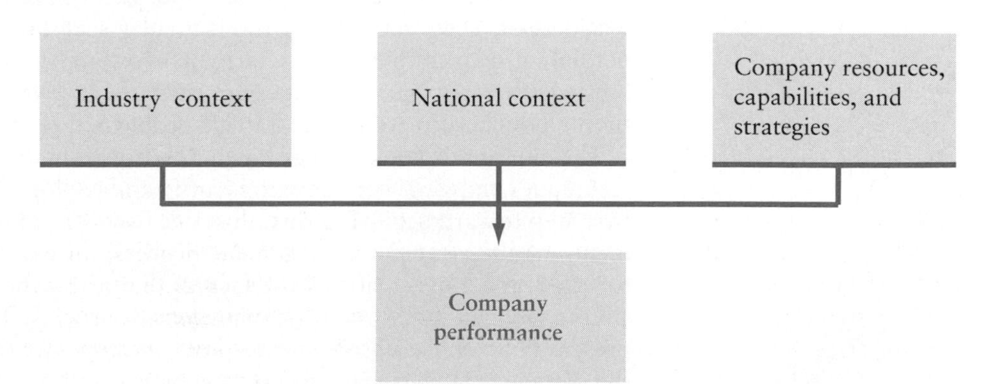

We also discuss how the national context of a country influences the competitiveness of companies based within that nation. National context is important because in many industries the marketplace has become a global one, where companies from many countries are competing head-to-head around the world. In such global markets, some companies find it easier to succeed because they are located in countries that have a competitive advantage in certain industries. To illustrate, many of the world's most successful automobile and consumer electronics companies are based in Japan, many of the most successful pharmaceutical companies are based in the United States and Switzerland, and many of the most successful financial services companies are based in the United States and Britain. We examine the reasons that such patterns of national competitive advantage emerge and explore their implications for the success or failure of individual enterprises.

However, the third factor—a company's resources, capabilities, and strategies—is by far the strongest determinant of success or failure.[2] Thus some companies manage to thrive even in very hostile industries, where the average level of profitability is low. Southwest Airlines, profiled in the Opening Case, exemplifies such a company. Southwest's success is due to the fact that its resources, capabilities, and strategies have enabled it to achieve a low-cost position and build customer loyalty. These accomplishments have protected Southwest from the price wars that have ravaged the airline industry for most of the last decade. Similarly, poor companies exist in some very profitable industries. Although the pharmaceutical industry as a whole has been very profitable for the last twenty years, the profitability of individual companies within the industry varies widely. Some companies, such as Merck, have consistently outperformed other companies, such as Squibb Corp. and Warner-Lambert, by a wide margin. We explain why there is so much variance in performance among companies operating within the same industry and the same national context.

Understanding the roots of success and failure is not an empty academic exercise. Such understanding brings a better appreciation of the strategies that can increase the probability of success and reduce the probability of failure. Accordingly, much of this book is devoted to describing the pros and cons of various strategies. Many of these strategies are generic—that is, they apply to all organizations, large or small, manufacturing or service, and profit-seeking or not-for-profit. For even a small not-for-profit organization, such as a local theater or church charity, has to make decisions about how best to generate revenues, given the environment in which it is based and the organization's own strengths and weaknesses. These strategic decisions involve such factors as analyzing the competition. The local church-run charity has to compete with other charities for the limited resources that individuals are prepared to give to charitable causes. Identifying how best to do so is a strategic problem.

The aim of this book is to give you a thorough understanding of the analytical techniques and skills necessary to identify and exploit strategies successfully. The first step toward achieving this objective involves an overview of the main elements of the strategic management process, an examination of how they fit together, and a discussion of the factors that affect the quality of strategic decisions generated by the strategic management process. That is the function of the present chapter. In subsequent chapters, we consider the individual elements of the strategic management process in greater detail.

1.3 WHAT IS STRATEGY?

The Traditional Approach

Reflecting the military roots of strategy, *The American Heritage Dictionary* defines **strategy** as "the science and art of military command as applied to the overall planning and conduct of large-scale combat operations."[3] The *planning* theme remains an important component of most management definitions of strategy. For example, Harvard's Alfred Chandler defined strategy as "the determination of the basic long-term goals and objectives of an enterprise, and the adoption of courses of action and the allocation of resources necessary for carrying out these goals."[4] Implicit in Chandler's definition is the idea that strategy involves *rational* planning. The organization is depicted as choosing its goals, identifying the courses of action (or strategies) that best enable it to fulfill its goals, and allocating resources accordingly. Similarly, James B. Quinn of Dartmouth College has defined strategy as "the pattern or plan that integrates an organization's major goals, policies, and action sequences into a cohesive whole."[5] Along the same lines, William F. Glueck defined strategy as "a unified, comprehensive, and integrated plan designed to ensure that the basic objectives of the enterprise are achieved."[6]

The case of Royal Dutch/Shell Group, discussed in Strategy in Action 1.1, is a good example of how strategic planning works and how superior planning can result in a competitive advantage. The scenario-based planning used at Shell is designed to educate general managers about the complex and dynamic nature of the company's environment. As a result of using this planning process, during the early 1980s Shell's managers anticipated the crash in oil prices that subsequently occurred during 1986. By 1986 Shell had taken steps to ensure that it would remain profitable if oil prices crashed. In contrast, most of its competitors were operating under the illusion that oil prices would remain strong during the 1980s.

A New Approach

For all their appeal, planning-based definitions of strategy have evoked criticism. As Henry Mintzberg of McGill University has pointed out, the planning approach incorrectly assumes that an organization's strategy is always the outcome of rational planning.[8] According to Mintzberg, definitions of strategy that stress the role of planning ignore the fact that strategies can emerge from within an organization without any formal plan. That is to say, even in the absence of intent, strategies can emerge from the grassroots of an organization. Indeed, strategies are often the emergent response to unforeseen circumstances. Mintzberg's point is that strategy is more than what a company intends or plans to do; it is also what it actually does. With this in mind, Mintzberg has defined strategy as *"a pattern in a stream of decisions or actions,"*[9] the pattern being a product of whatever **intended strategies** (planned) are actually realized and of any **emergent** (unplanned) **strategies.** The scheme proposed by Mintzberg is illustrated in Figure 1.2.

Mintzberg's argument is that emergent strategies are often successful and may be more appropriate than intended strategies. Richard Pascale has described how this was the case for the entry of Honda Motor Co. into the U.S. motorcycle market.[10] When a number of Honda executives arrived in Los Angeles from Japan in 1959 to establish an American subsidiary, their original aim (intended strategy) was to focus on selling 250 cc and 350 cc machines to confirmed motorcycle enthusiasts, rather than 50 cc Honda Cubs, which were a big hit in

STRATEGY IN ACTION 1.1

Strategic Planning at Royal Dutch/Shell

Royal Dutch/Shell Group, the world's largest oil company, is well known for its addiction to strategic planning. Despite the fact that many management gurus and CEOs now consider strategic planning an anachronism, Shell is convinced that long-term strategic planning has served the company well. Part of the reason for this success is that at Shell planning does not take the form of complex and inflexible ten-year plans generated by a team of corporate strategists far removed from operating realities. Rather, planning involves the generation of a series of "what if" scenarios whose function is to try to get general managers at all levels of the corporation to think strategically about the environment in which they do business.

The strength of Shell's scenario-based planning system was perhaps most evident during the early 1980s. At that time the price of a barrel of oil hovered at around $30. With exploration and development costs running at an industry average of about $11 per barrel, most oil companies were making record profits. Moreover, industry analysts were generally bullish; many were predicting that oil prices would increase to around $50 per barrel by 1990. Shell, however, was mulling over a handful of future scenarios, one of which included the possibility of a breakdown of the OPEC oil cartel's agreement to restrict supply, an oil glut, and a drop in oil prices to $15 per barrel. In 1984 Shell instructed the managers of its operating companies to indicate how they would respond to a $15 per barrel world. This "game" set off some serious work at Shell exploring the question, "What will we do if it happens?"

By early 1986 the consequences of the "game" included efforts to cut exploration costs by pioneering advanced exploration technologies, massive investments in cost-efficient refining facilities, and a process of weeding out the least-profitable service stations. All this planning occurred at a time when most oil companies were busy diversifying outside the oil business rather than trying to improve the efficiency of their core operations. As it turned out, the price of oil was still $27 per barrel in early January 1986. But the failure of the OPEC cartel to set new production ceilings, new production from the North Sea and Alaska, and declining demand due to increased conservation efforts had created a growing oil glut. In late January the dam burst. By February 1 oil was priced at $17 per barrel, and by April the price was $10 per barrel.

Because Shell had already visited the $15 per barrel world, it had gained a head start over its rivals in its cost-cutting efforts. As a result, by 1989 the company's average oil and gas exploration costs were less than $2 per barrel, compared with an industry average of $4 per barrel. Moreover, in the crucial refining and marketing sector, Shell made a net return on assets of 8.4 percent in 1988, more than double the 3.8 percent average of the other oil majors: Exxon, BP, Chevron, Mobil, and Texaco.[7]

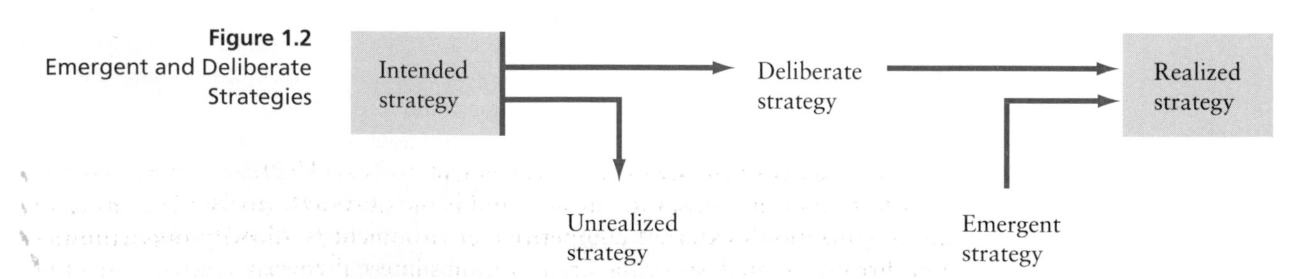

Figure 1.2
Emergent and Deliberate Strategies

Source: Reprinted from "Strategy Formation in an Adhocracy," by Henry Mintzberg and Alexandra McHugh, published in *Administrative Science Quarterly*, Vol. 30, No. 2, June 1985, by permission of *Administrative Science Quarterly*.

Japan. Their instinct told them that the Honda 50s were not suitable for the U.S. market, where everything was bigger and more luxurious than in Japan.

However, sales of the 250 cc and 350 cc bikes were sluggish, and the bikes themselves were plagued by mechanical failure. It looked as if Honda's strategy was going to fail. At the same time the Japanese executives were using the Honda 50s to run errands around Los Angeles, attracting a lot of attention. One day they got a call from a Sears, Roebuck buyer who wanted to sell the 50 cc bikes to a broad market of Americans who were not necessarily already motorcycle enthusiasts. The Honda executives were hesitant to sell the small bikes for fear of alienating serious bikers who might then associate Honda with "wimp" machines. In the end they were pushed into doing so by the failure of the 250 cc and 350 cc models. The rest is history. Honda had stumbled onto a previously untouched market segment that was to prove huge: the average American who had never owned a motorbike. Honda had also found an untried channel of distribution: general retailers rather than specialty motorbike stores. By 1964 nearly one out of every two motorcycles sold in the United States was a Honda.

The conventional explanation of Honda's success is that the company redefined the U.S. motorcycle industry with a brilliantly conceived *intended* strategy. The fact was that Honda's intended strategy was a near disaster. The strategy that *emerged* did so not through planning but through unplanned action taken in response to unforeseen circumstances. Nevertheless, credit should be given to the Japanese management for recognizing the strength of the emergent strategy and for pursuing it with vigor.

The critical point demonstrated by the Honda example is that—in contrast to the view that all strategies are planned—successful strategies can emerge within an organization without prior planning often is response to unforeseen circumstances. As Mintzberg has noted, strategies can take root in all kinds of strange places, virtually wherever people have the capacity to learn and the resources to support that capacity. In practice, the strategies of most organizations are probably a combination of the intended and the emergent. The message for management is that it needs to recognize the process of emergence and to intervene when appropriate, killing off bad emergent strategies but nurturing potentially good ones. To make such decisions, however, managers must be able to judge the worth of emergent strategies. They must be able to think strategically.

1.4 A MODEL OF THE STRATEGIC MANAGEMENT PROCESS

The strategic management process can be broken down into five different components, illustrated in Figure 1.3. You might want to think of Figure 1.3 as a plan of the book, for it also shows how the different chapters relate to the different components of the strategic management process. The five components are (1) selection of the corporate mission and major corporate goals; (2) analysis of the organization's external competitive environment to identify **opportunities** and **threats**; (3) analysis of the organization's internal operating environment to identify the organization's **strengths** and **weaknesses**; (4) the selection of strategies that build on the organization's strengths and correct its weaknesses in order to take advantage of external opportunities and counter external threats; and (5)

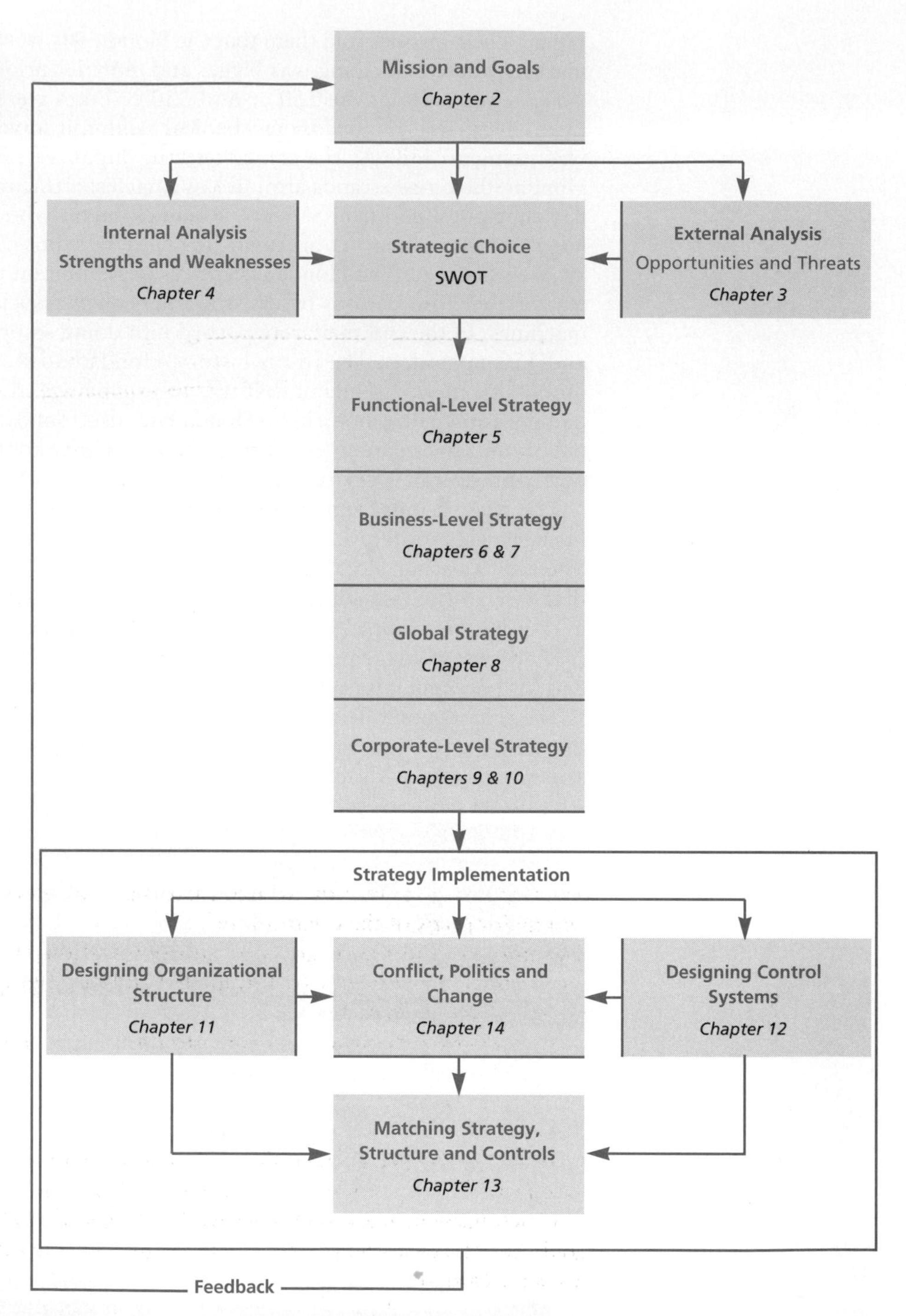

Figure 1.3 Components of the Strategic Management Process

strategy implementation. The task of analyzing the organization's external and internal environment and then selecting an appropriate strategy is normally referred to as **strategy formulation.** In contrast, **strategy implementation** typically involves designing appropriate organizational structures and control systems to put the organization's chosen strategy into action.

The traditional approach has been to stress that each component illustrated in Figure 1.3 constitutes a *sequential* step in strategic management. In the traditional view, each *cycle* of the process begins with a statement of the corporate mission and major corporate goals. The mission statement is followed by external analysis, internal analysis and strategic choice. The strategy making ends with the design of the organizational structure and control systems necessary to implement the organization's chosen strategy. In practice, however, that sequence is likely to hold true only for formulating and implementing *intended* strategies.

As noted earlier, emergent strategies arise from within the organization without prior planning—that is, without going through the steps illustrated in Figure 1.3 in a sequential fashion. However, top management still has to evaluate emergent strategies. Such evaluation involves comparing each emergent strategy with the organization's goals, external environmental opportunities and threats, and the organization's internal strengths and weaknesses. The objective is to assess whether the emergent strategy fits the organization's needs and capabilities. In addition, Mintzberg stresses that an organization's capability to produce emergent strategies is a function of the kind of corporate culture fostered by the organization's structure and control systems.

In other words, the different components of the strategic management process are just as important from the perspective of emergent strategies as they are from the perspective of intended strategies. The essential differences between the strategic management process for intended and for emergent strategies are illustrated in Figure 1.4. The formulation of intended strategies is basically a top-down process, whereas the formulation of emergent strategies is a bottom-up process.

Mission and Major Goals

The first component of the strategic management process is defining the **mission** and **major goals** of the organization. This topic is covered in depth in Chapter 2. The mission and major goals of an organization provide the context within which intended strategies are formulated and the criteria against which emergent strategies are evaluated.

The mission sets out why the organization exists and what it should be doing. For example, the mission of a national airline might be defined as satisfying the needs of individual and business travelers for high-speed transportation at a reasonable price to all the major population centers of North America.

Major goals specify what the organization hopes to fulfill in the medium to long term. Most profit-seeking organizations operate with a hierarchy of goals, in which maximizing stockholder wealth is placed at or near the top. Secondary goals are objectives judged necessary by the company if it is to maximize stockholder wealth. For example, General Electric operates with a secondary goal of being first or second in every major market in which it competes. This secondary goal reflects the belief at General Electric that building market share is the best way to achieve the primary goal of maximizing stockholder wealth. Similarly, a major goal of Coca-Cola has been to put a Coke within an arm's reach of every consumer in the world. If Coca-Cola achieves this goal, superior stockholder returns are likely to follow. Not-for-profit organizations typically have a more diverse set of goals.

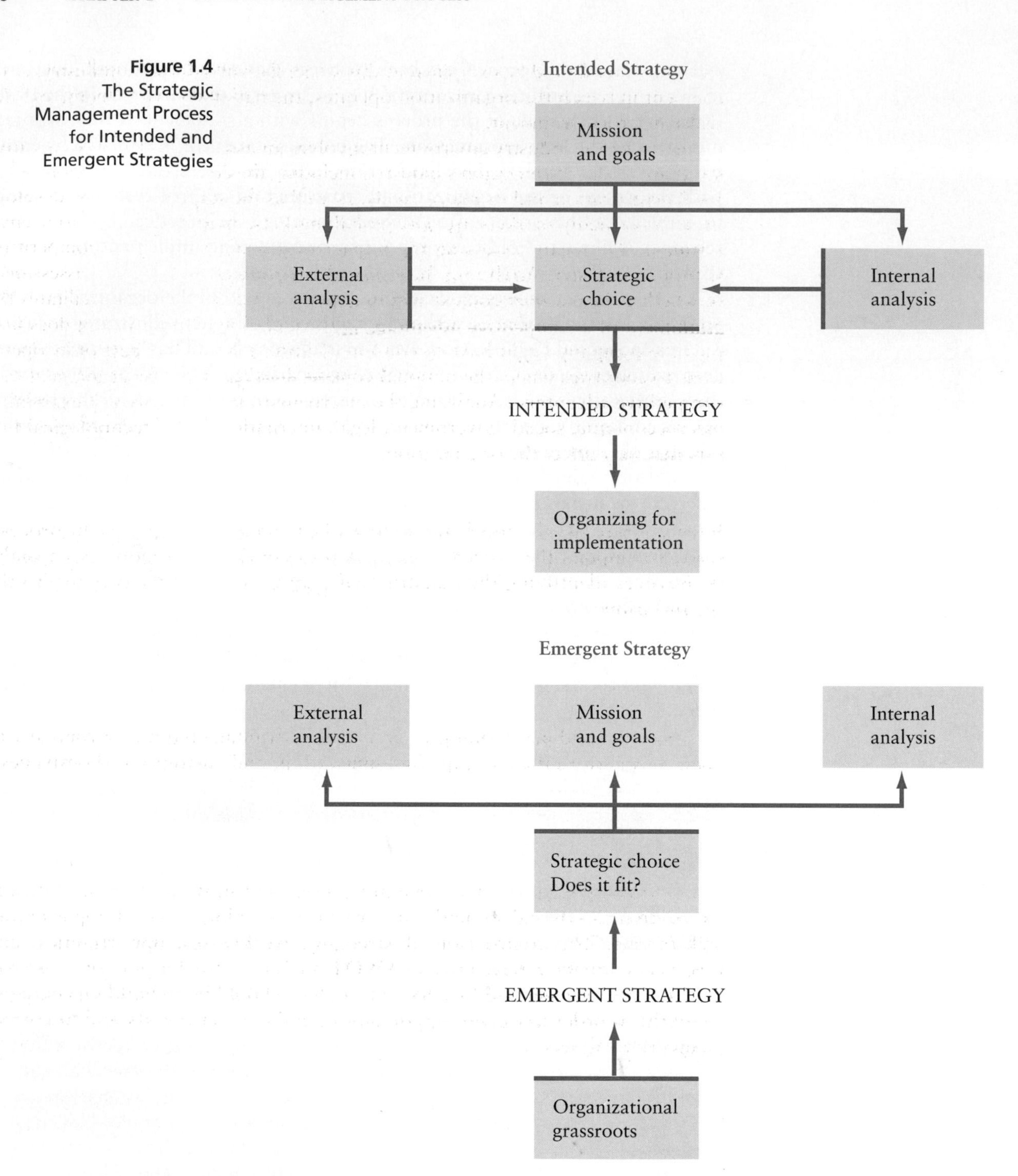

Figure 1.4 The Strategic Management Process for Intended and Emergent Strategies

External Analysis

The second component of the strategic management process is the analysis of the organization's external operating environment. This topic is covered in detail in Chapter 3. The objective of external analysis is to identify strategic *opportunities* and *threats* in the organization's operating environment. Three interrelated

environments should be examined at this stage: the immediate, or industry, environment in which the organization operates, the national environment, and the wider macroenvironment.

Analyzing the industry environment involves an assessment of the competitive structure of the organization's industry, including the competitive position of the focal organization and its major rivals, as well as the stage of industry development. Since many markets are now global markets, analyzing the industry environment also means assessing the impact of globalization upon competition within an industry. Analyzing the national environment requires an assessment of whether the national context within which a company operates facilitates the attainment of a competitive advantage in the global marketplace. If it does not, then the company might have to consider shifting a significant part of its operations to countries where the national context does facilitate the attainment of a competitive advantage. Analyzing the macroenvironment consists of examining macroeconomic, social, government, legal, international, and technological factors that may affect the organization.

Internal Analysis

Internal analysis, the third component of the strategic management process, serves to pinpoint the *strengths* and *weaknesses* of the organization. Such analysis involves identifying the quantity and quality of resources available to the organization. These issues are considered in Chapter 4, where we probe the sources of competitive advantage. We look at how companies attain a competitive advantage, and we discuss the role of distinctive competencies (unique company strengths), resources, and capabilities in building and sustaining a company's competitive advantage. One conclusion that we reach in Chapter 4 is that building and maintaining a competitive advantage requires a company to achieve superior efficiency, quality, innovation, and customer responsiveness. Company strengths lead to superiority in these areas, whereas company weaknesses translate into inferior performance.

Strategic Choice

The next component involves generating a series of strategic alternatives, given the company's internal strengths and weaknesses and its external opportunities and threats. The comparison of strengths, weaknesses, opportunities, and threats is normally referred to as a **SWOT** analysis.[11] The purpose of the strategic alternatives generated by a SWOT analysis should be to build on company strengths in order to exploit opportunities and counter threats and to correct company weaknesses. To choose among the alternatives generated by a SWOT analysis, the organization has to evaluate them against each other with respect to their ability to achieve major goals. The strategic alternatives generated may encompass functional-level, business-level, corporate-level, and global strategies. The process of strategic choice requires the organization to identify the set of functional-level, business-level, corporate-level, and global strategies that would best enable it to survive and prosper in the fast-changing and globally competitive environment which characterizes most modern industries.

Functional-Level Strategy Competitive advantage stems from a company's ability to attain superior efficiency, quality, innovation, and customer responsiveness—a point made in Chapter 4. In Chapter 5, we examine the different func-

tional-level strategies that can be employed to achieve these four crucial aims. By functional-level strategies, we mean strategies directed at improving the effectiveness of functional operations within a company, such as manufacturing, marketing, materials management, research and development, and human resources.

For example, the Opening Case points out how much of Southwest Airlines' efficiency derives from a productive work force. In turn, this high productivity is partly a result of Southwest's human relations strategy, including the decision to give employees an ownership stake in the company through stock options. Chapter 5 considers many of the modern operations management strategies directed primarily at the functional-level—for instance, total quality management (TQM), flexible manufacturing systems, just-in-time (JIT) inventory systems, and techniques for reducing the cycle time in new product development.

Business-Level Strategy The business-level strategy of a company encompasses the overall competitive theme that a company chooses to stress, the way it positions itself in the marketplace to gain a competitive advantage, and the different positioning strategies that can be used in different industry settings. The various strategic options available are discussed in Chapter 6. We review the pros and cons of three generic business-level strategies: a strategy of **cost leadership**, a strategy of **differentiation**, and a strategy of **focusing** on a particular market niche. Southwest Airlines clearly pursues a low-cost strategy: the overall competitive theme that the company has chosen to stress is low cost.

In Chapter 7, we build on Chapter 6 to consider the relationship between business-level strategy and industry structure. We concentrate on the different strategic options confronting companies in radically different industry settings, such as the benefits and drawbacks of establishing a first-mover advantage in a newly formed or embryonic industry. We also discuss the role of market signaling, price leadership, and product differentiation for sustaining a competitive advantage in mature industries, and explore the different strategic options that a company can choose from in a declining industry.

Global Strategies In today's world of global markets and global competition, achieving a competitive advantage and maximizing company performance increasingly require a company to expand its operations outside its home country. Accordingly, a company must consider the various global strategies it can pursue. In Chapter 8, we assess the benefits and costs of global expansion, and examine four different strategies—multidomestic, international, a global, and transnational—that a company can adopt to compete in the global marketplace. In addition, that chapter explores the benefits and costs of strategic alliances between global competitors, the different entry modes that can be used to penetrate a foreign market, and the role of host-government policies in influencing a company's choice of global strategy.

Corporate-Level Strategy We deal with the issue of corporate-level strategy in Chapters 9 and 10. An organization's corporate-level strategy must answer this question: What businesses should we be in to maximize the long-run profitability of the organization? For many organizations, competing successfully often involves **vertical integration**—either backward into the production of inputs for the company's main operation or forward into the disposal of outputs

from the operation. Beyond this, companies that succeed in establishing a sustainable competitive advantage may find that they are generating resources *in excess* of their investment requirements within their primary industry. For such organizations, maximizing long-run profitability may entail **diversification** into new business areas. Accordingly, in Chapter 9, we look closely at the costs and benefits of different diversification strategies. In addition, we examine the role of **strategic alliances** as alternatives to diversification and vertical integration. In Chapter 10, we review the different vehicles that companies use to achieve vertical integration and diversification, including **acquisitions** and **new ventures**. We also consider how diversified companies can **restructure** their portfolio of businesses in order to improve company performance.

Strategy Implementation

In this book, we break down the topic of strategy implementation into four main components; (1) designing appropriate organizational structures, (2) designing control systems, (3) matching strategy, structure, and controls, and (4) managing conflict, politics, and change.

Designing Organizational Structure To make a strategy work, regardless of whether it is intended or emergent, the organization needs to adopt the correct structure. The main options are discussed in Chapter 11. Designing a structure entails allocating task responsibility and decision-making authority within an organization. The issues covered include how best to divide an organization into subunits, how to distribute authority among the different levels of an organization's hierarchy, and how to achieve integration between subunits. The options reviewed include whether an organization should function with a tall or a flat structure, how centralized or decentralized decision-making authority should be, the extent to which an organization should be divided into semiautonomous subunits (that is, divisions or departments), and the different mechanisms available to integrate those subunits.

Designing Control Systems Besides choosing a structure, an organization must also establish appropriate organizational control systems. It must decide how best to assess the performance and control the actions of subunits. The options range from market and output controls to bureaucratic and control through organizational culture, all of which we tackle in Chapter 12. An organization also needs to decide what kind of reward and incentive systems to set up for employees. Chapter 12 reviews those options as well.

Matching Strategy, Structure, and Controls If it wants to succeed, a company must achieve a *fit* among its strategy, structure, and controls. Chapter 13 focuses on the various means toward this end. Since different strategies and environments place different demands on an organization, they call for different structural responses and control systems. For example, a strategy of cost leadership demands that an organization be kept simple (so as to reduce costs) and that controls stress productive efficiency. On the other hand, a strategy of differentiating a company's product by unique technological characteristics generates a need for integrating the company's activities around its technological core and for establishing control systems that reward technical creativity.

Managing Conflict, Politics, and Change Although in theory the strategic management process is characterized by *rational* decision making, in practice organizational politics plays a key role. Politics is endemic to organizations. Different subgroups (departments or divisions) within an organization have their own agendas, and typically, these conflict. Thus departments may compete with each other for a bigger share of an organization's finite resources. Such conflicts may be resolved as much by the relative distribution of power between subunits as by a rational evaluation of relative need. Similarly, individual managers often engage in contests with each other over what the correct policy decisions are. Power struggles and coalition building are major consequences of such conflicts and clearly play a part in strategic management. Strategic change tends to bring such power struggles to the fore, since by definition change entails altering the established distribution of power within an organization. In Chapter 14, we analyze the sources of organizational power and conflict, and we consider how organizational power and conflict can cause organizational inertia, which can inhibit strategic change. In addition, we examine how an organization can manage conflicts to fulfill its strategic mission and implement change.

The Feedback Loop

The feedback loop in Figure 1.3 indicates that strategic management is an ongoing process. Once a strategy is implemented, its execution must be monitored to determine the extent to which strategic objectives are actually being achieved. This information passes back to the corporate level through feedback loops. At the corporate level, it is fed into the next round of strategy formulation and implementation. It serves either to reaffirm existing corporate goals and strategies or to suggest changes. For example, when put into practice, a strategic objective may prove to be too optimistic, and so the next time more conservative objectives are set. Alternatively, feedback may reveal that strategic objectives were attainable but implementation was poor. In that case, the next round in strategic management may concentrate more on implementation. Because feedback is an aspect of organizational control, it is considered in detail in Chapter 12.

1.5 CRITICISMS OF FORMAL PLANNING SYSTEMS

The model of the strategic management process described in the previous section might be called a **fit model** of strategy formulation and implementation. Its central purpose is to identify strategies that *align, fit*, or *match* a company's resources and capabilities to the demands of the environment in which the company operates. To put it another way, its aim is to match company strengths and weaknesses with environmental opportunities and threats. According to this model, the low-cost strategy pursued by Southwest Airlines and the different actions that support that strategy are good because they fit the extremely cost-competitive environment in which Southwest operates.

Originally developed at Harvard Business School during the 1960s, the fit model of strategy is most closely associated with the name of Kenneth Andrews.[12] Since the 1960s, it has been widely accepted as the model for how

companies should formulate and implement strategies. Consequently, it is pertinent to ask whether this model actually works and whether the process outlined in the previous section helps companies establish a competitive advantage. On balance, the research evidence seems to indicate that such planning systems do help companies make better strategic decisions, but the evidence is far from compelling and disputed by many. For example, of fourteen studies reviewed in a survey by Lawrence Rhyne, eight found varying degrees of support for the hypothesis that strategic planning improves company performance, five found no support for the hypothesis, and one reported a negative relationship between planning and performance.[13]

Moreover, in recent years informed observers have increasingly questioned the use of formal planning systems as an aid to strategic decision making. Thomas J. Peters and Robert H. Waterman, authors of the bestseller *In Search of Excellence*, are among those who have raised doubts about the usefulness of formal planning systems.[14] Similarly, Mintzberg's revision of the concept of strategy suggests that *emergent* strategies may be just as successful as the *intended* strategies which are the outcome of formal planning. Recently, Mintzberg has roundly criticized proponents of the fit model for failing to recognize this.[15] Furthermore, business history is filled with examples of companies that have made poor decisions on the basis of supposedly comprehensive strategic planning.[16] For example, Exxon's decisions to diversify into electrical equipment and office automation and to offset shrinking U.S. oil reserves by investing in shale oil and synthetic fuels resulted from a 1970s planning exercise that was overly pessimistic about the demand for oil-based products. Exxon foresaw ever higher prices for oil and predicted sharp falls in demand as a result. But, oil prices actually tumbled during the 1980s, invalidating one of the basic assumptions of Exxon's plan. In addition, Exxon's diversification failed because of poor acquisitions and management problems in office automation.

Five explanations can be offered as to why formal strategic planning systems based on the fit model do not produce better results. We consider four of them here and take up the fifth, which focuses on decision-making biases among managers, in the next section. The four explanations are as follows: (1) planning equilibrium, (2) planning under uncertainty, (3) ivory tower planning, and (4) strategic intent versus strategic fit.

Planning Equilibrium

For a valuable management technique such as formal planning to be a source of competitive advantage, some companies must have the technique while others do not. In such circumstances, we might expect those with the technique to outperform those lacking it. However, once everybody has the technique, it levels the playing field. A technique used by every company can no longer be a source of competitive advantage. In such a situation, we say that the technique is in equilibrium. Because almost all large companies currently have some kind of formal strategic planning process, a condition of planning equilibrium exists. It would be surprising, then, to find that planning is a source of competitive advantage. However, it follows from the same logic that the company that *does not* plan may put itself at a competitive disadvantage. Thus planning may be necessary to earn average profits, but it will not by itself allow a company to earn the above-average profits associated with competitive advantage.

Planning Under Uncertainty

One reason for the poor reputation of strategic planning is that many executives, in their initial enthusiasm for planning techniques during the 1960s and 1970s, forgot that the future is inherently unpredictable. As at Exxon, a common problem was that executives often assumed that it was possible to forecast the future accurately. But in the real world, the only constant is change. Even the best-laid plans can fall apart if unforeseen contingencies occur. The recognition that in an uncertain world the future cannot be forecast with sufficient accuracy led Royal Dutch/Shell to pioneer the scenario approach to planning discussed in the Strategy in Action 1.1. Rather than try to forecast the future, Shell's planners attempt to model the company's environment and then use that model to predict a range of possible scenarios. Executives are then asked to devise strategies to cope with the different scenarios. The objective is to get managers to understand the dynamic and complex nature of their environment and to think through problems in a strategic fashion.

The scenario approach to planning seems to have spread quite rapidly among large companies. According to one survey, by the mid 1980s over 50 percent of the *Fortune* 500 companies used scenario planning methods.[17] Although a detailed evaluation of the pros and cons of scenario planning has yet to appear, recent work by Paul Schoemaker of the University of Chicago seems to suggest that scenario planning does expand people's thinking, and as such it may lead to better plans, as seems to have occurred at Royal Dutch/Shell. However, Schoemaker cautions that forcing planners to consider extreme scenarios that are unbelievable can discredit the approach and cause resistance on the planners' part.

Ivory Tower Planning

A serious mistake made by many companies in their initial enthusiasm for planning has been to treat planning as an exclusively top management function. This *ivory tower* approach can result in strategic plans formulated in a vacuum by planning executives who have little understanding or appreciation of operating realities. As a consequence, they formulate strategies that do more harm than good. For example, when demographic data indicated that houses and families were shrinking, planners at General Electric's appliance group concluded that smaller appliances were the wave of the future. Because the planners had little contact with homebuilders and retailers, they did not realize that kitchens and bathrooms were the two rooms that were not shrinking. Nor did they appreciate that working women wanted big refrigerators to cut down on trips to the supermarket. The result was that General Electric wasted a lot of time designing small appliances for which there was only limited demand.

The ivory tower concept of planning can also lead to tensions between planners and operating personnel. The experience of General Electric's appliance group is again illuminating. Many of the planners in this group were recruited from consulting firms or from top-flight business schools. Many of the operating managers took this pattern of recruitment to mean that corporate executives did not deem them smart enough to think through strategic problems for themselves. Out of this impression grew an us-versus-them state of mind, which quickly escalated into hostility. As a result, even when the planners were right, operating managers would not listen to them. In the 1970s the planners correctly recognized the importance of the globalization of the appliance market and the emerging Japanese threat. However, operating managers, who then saw Sears Roebuck and Company as the competition, paid them little heed.

Correcting the ivory tower approach to planning involves recognition that, to succeed, strategic planning must comprise managers at all levels of the corporation. It is important to understand that much of the best planning can and should be done by operating managers. They are the ones closest to the facts. The role of corporate-level planners should be that of facilitators, who help operating managers do the planning.

Strategic Intent Versus Strategic Fit

The strategic fit model of planning has been criticized by C. K. Prahalad of the University of Michigan and Gary Hamel of London Business School. In a series of influential articles, Prahalad and Hamel have attacked the fit model as being too static and limiting.[18] They argue that adopting the fit model to strategy formulation leads to a mindset in which management focuses too much on the degree of fit between the *existing* resources of a company and *current* environmental opportunities, and not enough upon building *new* resources and capabilities to create and exploit *future* opportunities. Strategies formulated via the fit model, say Prahalad and Hamel, tend to be more concerned with today's problems than tomorrow's opportunities. As a result, companies that rely exclusively on the fit approach to strategy formulation are unlikely to be able to build and maintain a competitive advantage. This is particularly true in a dynamic competitive environment, where new competitors are continually arising and new ways of doing business are constantly being invented.

As Prahalad and Hamel note, again and again, U.S. companies using the fit approach have been surprised by the ascent of foreign competitors that initially seemed to lack the resources and capabilities needed to make them a real threat. This happened to Xerox, which ignored the rise of Canon and Ricoh in the photocopier market until they had become serious global competitors; to General Motors, which initially ignored the threat posed by Toyota and Honda in the 1970s; and to Caterpillar Inc., which ignored the threat posed by Komatsu to its heavy earth-moving business until it was almost too late to respond.

The secret of the success of companies like Toyota, Canon, and Komatsu, according to Prahalad and Hamel, is that they all had bold ambitions, which outstripped their existing resources and capabilities. All wanted to achieve global leadership, and they set out to build the resources and capabilities that would enable them to attain this goal. Consequently, the top management of these companies created an obsession with winning at all levels of the organization and then sustained that obsession over a ten- to twenty-year quest for global leadership. It is this obsession that Prahalad and Hamel refer to as **strategic intent**. At the same time, they stress that strategic intent is more than simply unfettered ambition. They argue that strategic intent also encompasses an active management process, which includes: "focusing the organization's attention on the essence of winning; motivating people by communicating the value of the target; leaving room for individual and team contributions; sustaining enthusiasm by providing new operational definitions as circumstances change; and using intent consistently to guide resource allocations."[19]

Thus underlying the concept of strategic intent is the notion that strategy formulation should involve setting ambitious goals, which stretch a company, and then finding ways to build the resources and capabilities necessary to attain those goals.

Although Prahalad and Hamel aptly criticize the fit model, they note that in practice the two approaches to strategy formulation are not mutually exclusive. All the components of the strategic management process that we discussed in the previous section are important. Managers do have to analyze the external environment to identify opportunities and threats. They do have to analyze the company's resources and capabilities to identify strengths and weaknesses. They need to be familiar with the range of functional-level, business-level, corporate-level, and global strategies that are available to them. And they need to have an appreciation for the structures required to implement different strategies. What Prahalad and Hamel seem to be saying is that the strategic management process should begin with challenging goals—such as attaining global leadership. Then, throughout the process the emphasis should be on finding ways (strategies) to develop the resources and capabilities necessary to achieve these goals, rather than on exploiting existing strengths to take advantage of existing opportunities. The difference between strategic fit and strategic intent, therefore, may just be one of emphasis. Strategic intent is more internally focused and is concerned with building new resources and capabilities. Strategic fit focuses more on matching existing resources and capabilities to the external environment.

Strategy in Action 1.2 describes how Eastman Kodak's Imaging Sector is trying to apply the concept of strategic intent to its strategic management of technology. The Kodak example does seem to suggest that the concept of strategic intent is internally focused. Although there is nothing wrong with this—indeed, an internal focus is desirable—some critics of Prahalad and Hamel's approach, such as Michael Porter, wonder whether the result might not be a failure to analyze the external environment in sufficient depth.[20]

1.6 PITFALLS IN STRATEGIC DECISION MAKING

Even the best-designed strategic planning systems will fail to produce the desired results if strategic decision makers fail to use the information at their disposal effectively. There is in fact a good deal of evidence that many managers are poor strategic decision makers.[23] The reasons have to do with two related psychological phenomena: cognitive biases and groupthink. We discuss each of them in turn and then consider techniques for improving decision making.

Cognitive Biases

The rationality of human decision makers is bounded by our own cognitive capabilities. We are not supercomputers, and it is difficult for us to absorb and process large amounts of information effectively. As a result, we tend to fall back on certain rules of thumb, or heuristics, when making decisions. Many of these rules of thumb are actually quite useful, since they help us to make sense out of a complex and uncertain world. However, sometimes they also lead to severe and **systematic errors** in the decision making process.[24] (Systematic errors are errors that appear time and time again). These systematic errors seem to arise from a series of **cognitive biases** in the way that human decision makers process information and reach decisions. Because of cognitive biases, many managers end up making poor strategic decisions.

STRATEGY IN ACTION 1.2

Eastman Kodak Applies Strategic Intent to the Management of Technology

Kodak first began to make the concept of strategic intent operational in late 1989, after the publication of Hamel and Prahalad's *Harvard Business Review* article on the concept.[21] To date, the concept has been taken furthest in Kodak's Imaging Sector. The company's largest and oldest business sector, in 1990 it represented 59 percent of Kodak's total $19 billion in revenues and 57 percent of the earnings from operations.

Kodak sees the concept of strategic intent as referring to the desired state of the company. For Kodak, this desired state is to be the world leader in imaging. The strategic question for Kodak is how to become such a leader. To this end, Kodak has identified the competitive skills that it must have just to survive in tomorrow's global markets and the core competencies that will be required to build a competitive advantage in those markets.

The competitive skills identified by Kodak include the following:

1. *Customer focus*: the ability to identify and serve customer needs
2. *Cycle time*: the ability to rapidly develop new products that serve customer needs
3. *Manufacturing*: the ability to raise manufacturing quality and lower manufacturing costs
4. *Alliances*: the ability to gain access to critical technology through strategic alliances
5. *Benchmarking*: the ability to measure Kodak's skills against those of other competitors

Kodak is now formulating strategies that will enable it to build these kinds of competitive skills. For example, the company has introduced a total quality management program (TQM) in an attempt to improve manufacturing quality and cut costs.

As for core competencies, these refer to the skills of a company that provide the basis for its competitive advantage. Kodak has focused on its technical core competencies, and identified two types of technology that underlie them: *strategic* technologies and *enabling* technologies. Strategic technologies are technologies that Kodak must be a world leader in because they are the source of competitive advantage. Enabling technologies are necessary for success but do not have to be controlled internally. A strategic technology for Kodak is silver halide materials technology. Silver halide is the critical element in photography, the powerful light-sensitive catalyst in the imaging process. Kodak has pioneered the development of a process to produce new types of silver halide crystals, which significantly enhance the sharpness of color photographs. This process, which is proprietary to Kodak, gives the company a potential competitive advantage in the global marketplace. An enabling technology for Kodak is the technology used to measure small amounts of dye on silver halide grains. This technology is essential to manufacture reproducible silver halide emulsions used in the photographic process, but the technology itself is not the source of competitive advantage. With the distinction between strategic and enabling technologies in mind, Kodak is now allocating resources to upgrade its strategic technologies, such as the silver halide materials technology, to ensure that they are the best in the world. Simultaneously, the company is trying to ensure that its enabling technologies are as good as any used by competitors.[22]

Figure 1.5 presents five well-known cognitive biases. These biases have been verified repeatedly in laboratory settings, so we can be reasonably sure that they exist and that we are all prone to them.[25] The **prior hypothesis bias** refers to the fact that decision makers who have strong prior beliefs about the relationship between two variables tend to make decisions on the basis of these beliefs, even when presented with evidence that their beliefs are wrong. Moreover, they tend to seek and use information that is consistent with their prior beliefs, while

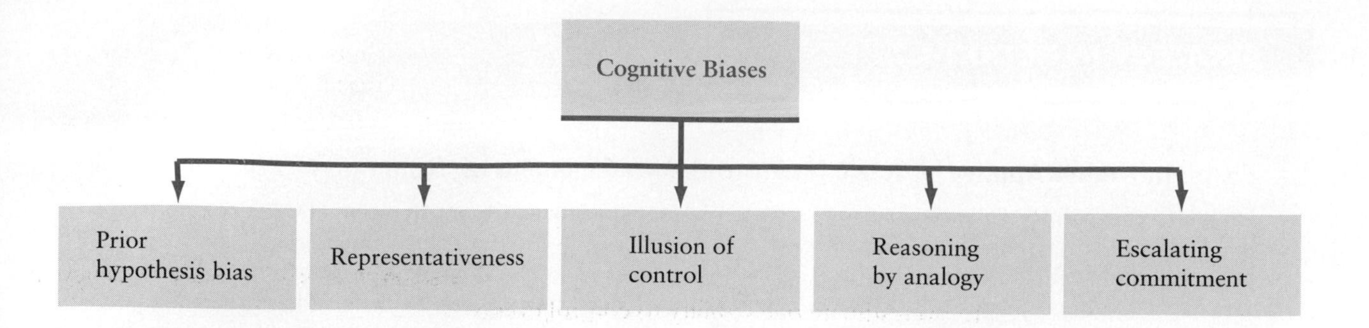

Figure 1.5
Five Well-Known Cognitive Biases

ignoring information that contradicts these beliefs. To put this bias in a strategic context, it suggests that a CEO who has a strong prior belief that a certain strategy makes sense might continue to pursue that strategy, despite evidence that it is inappropriate or failing.

Another well-known cognitive bias is referred to as **escalating commitment.**[26] Escalating commitment occurs when decision makers, having already committed significant resources to a project, commit even more resources if they receive feedback that the project is failing. This may be an irrational response; a more logical response would be to abandon the project and move on, (that is, to "cut your losses and run"), rather than escalate commitment. Feelings of personal responsibility for a project apparently induce decision makers to stick with a project, despite evidence that it is failing. One of the most famous examples of escalating commitment is U.S. policy toward the Vietnam War. President Lyndon B. Johnson's reaction to information that U.S. policy in Vietnam was failing was to commit ever more resources to the war.[27] To draw on a business example, during the 1960s and 1970s the response of large U.S. steel makers to cost-efficient competition from minimills and foreign steelmakers was to increase their investments in the technologically obsolete steelmaking facilities they already possessed, rather than invest in new cutting-edge technology.[28] This was irrational; investments in such obsolete technology would never enable them to become cost efficient.

The bias of **reasoning by analogy** involves the use of simple analogies to make sense out of complex problems. U.S. policy toward Vietnam in the 1960s, for example, was guided by the analogy of falling dominoes. U.S. policymakers believed that if Vietnam fell to the communists the rest of Southeast Asia would also fall. The danger of using such analogies is that by oversimplifying a complex problem they can mislead. For example, several companies have relied on the analogy of a three-legged stool to justify diversifying into business areas of which they had little prior knowledge. The analogy suggests that a stool with fewer than three legs—and by extension, a company that is active in fewer than three different businesses—is unbalanced. Chrysler applied this analogy to justify its decision in the mid 1980s to diversify into the aerospace industry by acquiring Gulfstream, a manufacturer of executive jets. Five years later Chrysler admitted that the diversification move had been a mistake and divested itself of this activity.

Representativeness is a bias rooted in the tendency to generalize from a small sample, or even a single vivid anecdote. Generalizing from small samples, however, violates the statistical law of large numbers, which says that it is inappropriate to generalize from a small sample, let alone from a single case. An

interesting example of representativeness occurred after World War II, when the CEO of Montgomery Ward, Seawell Avery, shelved plans for national expansion to meet competition from Sears because he believed that a depression would follow the war. He based his belief on the fact that there had been a depression after World War I. As it turned out, there was no depression, and Sears went on to become a nationwide retailer, whereas Montgomery Ward did not. Avery's mistake was to generalize from one postwar experience and assume that depressions always follow wars.

The final cognitive bias is referred to as the **illusion of control.** It is the tendency to overestimate one's ability to control events. Top-level managers seem to be particularly prone to this bias. Having risen to the top of an organization, they tend to be overconfident about their ability to succeed. According to Richard Roll, such overconfidence leads to what he has termed the **hubris hypothesis** of takeovers.[29] Roll argues that senior managers are typically overconfident about their abilities to create value by acquiring another company. Hence, they end up making poor acquisition decisions, often paying far too much for the companies they acquire. Subsequently, servicing the debt taken on to finance such an acquisition makes it all but impossible to make money from the acquisition.

Groupthink

The biases just discussed are individual biases. However, most strategic decisions are made by groups, not individuals. Thus the group context within which decisions are made is clearly an important variable in determining whether cognitive biases will operate to adversely affect the strategic decision-making processes. The psychologist Irvin Janis has argued that many groups are characterized by a process known as **groupthink** and that as a result many groups do make poor strategic decisions.[30] Groupthink occurs when a group of decision makers embarks on a course of action without questioning underlying assumptions. Typically, a group coalesces around a person or policy. It ignores or filters out information that can be used to question the policy and develops after-the-fact rationalizations for its decision. Thus commitment is based on an emotional, rather than an objective, assessment of the correct course of action. The consequences can be poor decisions.

This phenomenon may explain, at least in part, why companies often make poor strategic decisions in spite of sophisticated strategic management. Janis traced many historical fiascoes to defective policymaking by government leaders who received social support from their in-group of advisers. For example, he suggested that President John F. Kennedy's inner circle suffered from groupthink when the members of this group supported the decision to launch the Bay of Pigs invasion of Cuba, even though available information showed that it would be an unsuccessful venture and would damage U.S. relations with other countries.

Janis has observed that groupthink-dominated groups are characterized by strong pressures toward uniformity, which make their members avoid raising controversial issues, questioning weak arguments, or calling a halt to softheaded thinking. An interesting example of groupthink in a business context, the acquisition of Howard Johnson by the Imperial Group, is highlighted in Strategy in Action 1.3. Note that in this case groupthink seemed to exacerbate a number of other cognitive biases, including the illusion of control and prior hypothesis bias.

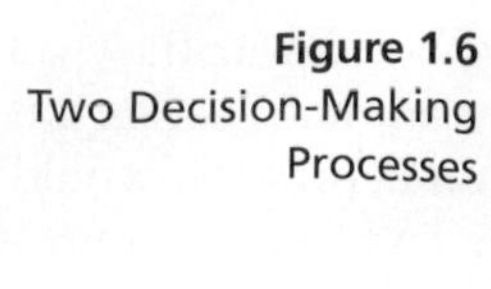

Figure 1.6
Two Decision-Making Processes

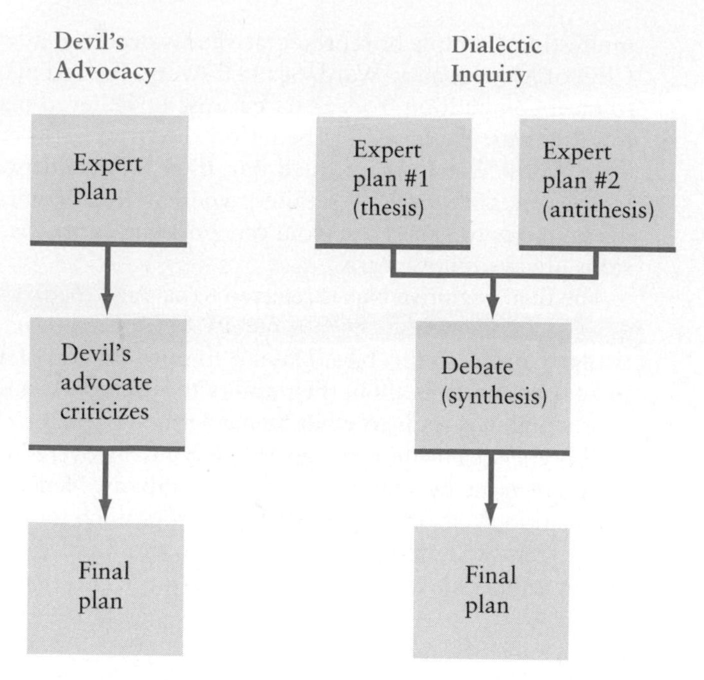

Techniques for Improving Decision Making

The existence of cognitive biases and groupthink raises the issue of how to bring critical information to bear on the decision mechanism so that strategic decisions made by the company are realistic and based on thorough evaluation. Two techniques known to counteract groupthink and cognitive biases are devil's advocacy and dialectic inquiry.

Devil's advocacy and **dialectic inquiry** have been proposed as two means of guarding against the weaknesses of the expert approach.[32] *Devil's advocacy* involves the generation of both a plan and a critical analysis of the plan. One member of the decision-making group acts as the devil's advocate, bringing out all the reasons that might make the proposal unacceptable. In this way, decision makers can become aware of the possible perils of recommended courses of action. *Dialectic inquiry* is more complex, for it involves the generation of a plan (a thesis) and a counterplan (an antithesis). According to R. O. Mason, one of the early proponents of this method in strategic management, the plan and the counterplan should reflect plausible but conflicting courses of action.[33] Corporate decision makers consider a debate between advocates of the plan and counterplan. The purpose of the debate is to reveal problems with definitions, recommended courses of action, and assumptions. As a result, corporate decision makers and planners are able to form a new and more encompassing conceptualization of the problem, which becomes the final plan (a synthesis).

Each of the two decision-making processes is illustrated in Figure 1.6. If either of those processes had been used in the Imperial case, very likely a different (and probably better) decision would have been made. However, there is considerable dispute over which of the two methods is better.[34] Researchers have come to conflicting conclusions, and the jury is still out on this issue. From a practical point of view, however, devil's advocacy is probably the easier method to implement because it involves less commitment in terms of time than dialectic inquiry.

STRATEGY IN ACTION 1.3

Imperial's acquisition of Howard Johnson: A Case of Groupthink

When Britain's Imperial Group acquired Howard Johnson Co. in 1979, Imperial was the third largest tobacco company in the world, after British American Tobaccos and Philip Morris Companies, Inc. In the 1970s it began a diversification program designed to reduce its dependence on the declining tobacco market. Part of this program included a plan to acquire a major U.S. company. Imperial spent two years scanning the United States for a suitable acquisition opportunity. It was seeking an enterprise in a high-growth industry that had a high market share, a good track record, and good growth prospects and that could be acquired at a reasonable price. Imperial scanned more than 30 industries and 200 different companies before deciding on Howard Johnson.

When Imperial announced plans to buy Howard Johnson for close to $500 million in 1979, its shareholders threatened rebellion. They were quick to point out that at $26 per share Imperial was paying double what Howard Johnson had been worth only six months earlier, when share prices stood at $13. The acquisition hardly seemed to be at a reasonable price. Moreover, the motel industry was entering a low- rather than a high-growth phase, and growth prospects were poor. Besides, Howard Johnson did not have a good track record. Imperial ignored shareholder protests and bought the lodging chain. Five years later, after persistent losses, Imperial was trying to divest itself of Howard Johnson. The acquisition had been a complete failure.

What went wrong? Why, after a two-year planning exercise, did Imperial buy a company that so patently did not fit its own criteria? The answer would seem to lie not in the planning, but in the quality of strategic decision making. Imperial bought Howard Johnson in spite of its planning, not because of it. What happened at Imperial was that the CEO decided independently that Howard Johnson was a good buy. A rather authoritarian figure who was overly confident about his ability (a case of hubris), the CEO surrounded himself with subordinates who agreed with him. In a clear sign that groupthink was at work, once he had made his choice his advisers concurred with his judgment and shared in developing rationalizations for it. No one questioned the decision itself, even though information was available to show that it was flawed. Instead, strategic planning was used to justify a decision that in practice did not conform with strategic objectives.[31]

1.7 STRATEGIC MANAGERS AND STRATEGIC LEADERSHIP

Up to this point we have not discussed the role that managers play in formulating and implementing strategy. The first half of this section examines the strategic role of managers at different levels within an organization; the second half focuses on leadership.

Levels of Strategic Management

In most modern organizations, one finds two types of managers: **general managers** and **functional managers**. General managers are individuals who bear responsibility for the overall performance of the organization or for one of its major self-contained divisions. Their overriding concern is for the health of the

total organization under their direction. Functional managers, on the other hand, bear responsibility for specific business functions, such as personnel, purchasing, production, sales, customer service, and accounts. Thus their sphere of authority is generally confined to one organizational activity, whereas strategic managers oversee the operation of the whole organization. This responsibility puts general managers in the unique position of being able to direct the total organization in a strategic sense.

A typical multibusiness company has three main levels of management: the corporate level, the business level, and the functional level (see Figure 1.7). General managers are found at the first two of these levels, but their strategic roles differ, depending on their sphere of responsibility. Functional managers too have a strategic role, though of a different kind. We now look at each of the three levels and the strategic roles assigned to managers within them.

Corporate Level The corporate level of management consists of the chief executive officer (CEO), other senior executives, the board of directors, and corporate staff. These individuals occupy the apex of decision making within the organization. The CEO is the main general manager at this level. His or her strategic role is *to oversee* the development of strategies for the total organization. Typically, this role involves defining the mission and goals of the organization, determining what businesses it should be in, allocating resources among the different business areas, formulating and implementing strategies that span individual businesses, and providing leadership for the rest of the organization.

For example, consider General Electric. The company is involved in a wide range of businesses, including lighting equipment, major appliances, motor and

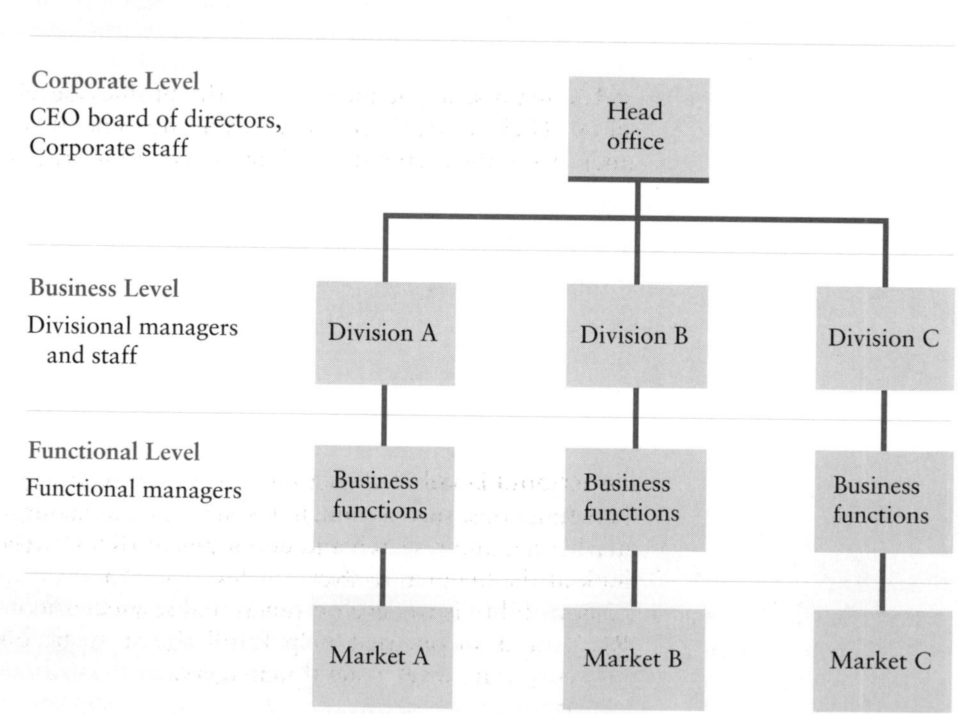

Figure 1.7 Levels of Strategic Management

transportation equipment, turbine generators, construction and engineering services, industrial electronics, medical systems, aerospace, and aircraft engines. The main strategic responsibilities of its CEO, Jack Welch, include setting overall strategic objectives, allocating resources among the different business areas, deciding whether the firm should divest itself of any of the businesses, and determining whether it should acquire any new ones. In other words, it is up to Welch to develop strategies that span individual businesses. He is concerned with building and managing the corporate portfolio of businesses. It is not his specific responsibility, however, to develop strategies for competing in the individual business areas, such as aerospace or major appliances. The development of such strategies is the responsibility of business-level strategic managers.

Besides overseeing resource allocation and managing the divestment and acquisition processes, corporate-level general managers also provide a link between the people who oversee the strategic development of a firm and those who own it (stockholders). Corporate-level general managers, and particularly the CEO, can be viewed as the guardians of stockholder welfare. It is their responsibility to ensure that corporate strategies pursued by the company are consistent with maximizing stockholder wealth. If they are not, then ultimately the CEO is likely to be called to account by the stockholders.

Business Level In a multibusiness company, the business level consists of the heads of individual business units within the organization and their support staff. In a single-industry company, the business and corporate levels are the same. A business unit is an organizational entity that operates in a distinct business area. Typically, it is self-contained and has its own functional departments (for example, its own finance, buying, production, and marketing departments). Within most companies, business units are referred to as **divisions**. General Electric, for example, has more than 100 divisions, one for each business area that the company is active in.

The main strategic managers at the business level are the heads of the divisions. Their strategic role is to translate general statements of direction and intent from the corporate level into concrete strategies for individual businesses. Thus while corporate-level general managers are concerned with strategies that span individual businesses, business-level managers are concerned with strategies that are specific to a particular business. As noted earlier, at General Electric the corporate level has committed itself to the objective of being first or second in every business in which the corporation competes. However, it is up to the general managers who head each division to work out for their business the details of a strategy that is consistent with this objective.

Functional Level Functional managers bear responsibility for specific business functions, such as human resources, manufacturing, materials management, marketing, and research and development (R&D). They are not in a position to look at the big picture. Nevertheless, they have a major strategic role, for their responsibility is to develop functional strategies in manufacturing, marketing, R&D, and so on, that help fulfill the strategic objectives set by business- and corporate-level general managers. In the case of General Electric's major appliance business, for instance, manufacturing managers are responsible for

developing manufacturing strategies consistent with the corporate objective of being first or second in that industry. Moreover, functional managers provide most of the information that makes it possible for business- and corporate-level general managers to formulate realistic and attainable strategies. Indeed, because they are closer to the customer than the typical general manager, functional managers may themselves generate important strategic ideas, which subsequently become major strategies for the company. Thus it is important for general managers to listen closely to the ideas of their functional managers. An equally great responsibility for managers at the functional level involves strategy implementation—the execution of corporate- and business-level decisions.

Strategic Leadership

One of the key strategic roles of managers, whether they are general or functional managers, is to provide strategic leadership for their subordinates. *Strategic leadership* refers to the ability to articulate a strategic vision for the company and to motivate others to buy into that vision. An enormous amount has been written about leadership, and it is beyond the scope of this book to review this complex topic in detail. However, a few key characteristics of good leaders have been identified by several authors, and we discuss them here.[35] These characteristics are (1) vision, eloquence, and consistency, (2) commitment, (3) being well informed, (4) a willingness to delegate and empower, and (5) political astuteness.

Vision, Eloquence, and Consistency One of the key tasks of leadership is to give the organization a sense of direction. Strong leaders seem to have a vision of where the organization should go. Moreover, they are eloquent enough to be able to communicate this vision to others within the organization in terms that can energize people, and they consistently articulate their vision until it becomes part of the culture of the organization.[36] John F. Kennedy and Martin Luther King, Jr., are both examples of visionary leaders. Both had a vision of a fairer society and both were able to communicate it eloquently to people, using evocative language that energized the audience. Think of the impact of Kennedy's phrase "Ask not what your country can do for you, ask what you can do for your country" and of King's "I have a dream" speech. Both also consistently emphasized their vision in speech after speech. Examples of strong business leaders include Jack Welch of General Electric, Lee Iacocca, formerly of Chrysler, Herb Kelleher of Southwest Airlines (see Opening Case 1.1), and Steve Jobs, formerly of Apple Computer, who is profiled in Strategy in Action 1.4. As Strategy in Action 1.4 demonstrates, Jobs gave Apple Computer a clear strategic vision, which formed the basis for much of the company's success.

Commitment A strong leader is someone who demonstrates commitment to his or her particular vision. Often this involves leadership by example. For illustration, consider the case of Nucor's CEO, Ken Iverson. Nucor is a very efficient steelmaker with perhaps the lowest cost structure in the steel industry. The company has turned in twenty years of profitable performance in an industry where most companies have lost money. It has done so by relentlessly focusing on cost minimization, which starts with Iverson himself. Iverson answers his

STRATEGY IN ACTION 1.4

Steve Jobs as a Visionary Leader

Along with Steve Wozniak, Steve Jobs was the cofounder of Apple Computer, the pioneer in the market for personal computers. It is generally acknowledged that Jobs did not understand the inner workings of personal computers. The actual design for Apple's first personal computers is credited to Wozniak. But as Wozniak also said, "It never crossed my mind to sell computers. It was Steve who said . . . 'Let's hold them up in the air and sell a few.'" Jobs insisted that the computer be "light and trim, well designed in muted colors." Jobs also pushed his engineers to "make machines that will not frighten away a skittish clientele."

What was visionary about Jobs's leadership was his evangelical zeal to show people the future potential for the product. Jobs envisaged a world in which there would be a personal computer on every desk. He compared the computer to the telephone in its significance for ordinary people. Jobs set out to create and conquer a very large market before anyone else realized that the potential existed. He acted as a missionary, both to potential consumers (Jobs is credited with selling hundreds of thousands, possibly millions, of Americans on the new technology) and to employees within Apple. Under Jobs's leadership, Apple in its early days was more of a cult than a company, dedicated to transforming the world by making the new technology available to everyone. The employees who were converted by Jobs's vision, as most were, worked with a furious energy to help produce this technology. The result was one of the most successful business start-ups in American business history.

However, as Apple became well established and as the industry gained respectability, Jobs's weaknesses began to overshadow his visionary leadership. Jobs may have been a visionary, but he also gained a reputation for being ambitious to the point of megalomania and intolerant of people who did not live up to his often unreasonably high expectations. As a result, over time Jobs alienated more and more people at Apple. When the board of directors finally removed him from day-to-day management in 1985, he had few supporters left in the company. Jobs left Apple shortly thereafter and began to try to recreate his vision through NeXT, Inc.[38]

own phone, employs only one secretary, drives an old car, flies coach, and is proud of being one of the lowest-paid CEOs in the *Fortune* 500. This kind of commitment is a powerful signal to employees within Nucor that Iverson is serious about doing everything possible to minimize costs. It earns Iverson the respect of Nucor employees, which in turn makes them more willing to work hard. Similarly, as noted in the Opening Case, Herb Kelleher, the CEO of Southwest Airlines, has a reputation for helping his flight attendants and maintenance crews with their work. This commitment earns Kelleher the respect of Southwest employees, who are therefore willing to work hard for him.

Being Well Informed Good leaders do not operate in a vacuum. Rather, they develop a network of formal and informal sources that keep them well informed about what is going on within their company. They develop backchannel ways of finding out what is going on within the organization so that they do not have to rely on formal information channels. This is wise, since formal channels can be captured by special interests within the organization or by gatekeepers, who may misrepresent the true state of affairs within the company to the leader. People like Kelleher at Southwest, who are constantly interacting with

their employees at all levels within the organization, are better able to build informal information networks than leaders who closet themselves away in a remote corporate headquarters and never interact with lower-level employees.

Willingness to Delegate and Empower Good leaders are skilled delegators. They recognize that unless they do delegate they can quickly become overloaded with responsibilities. They also recognize that empowering subordinates to make decisions is a good motivation tool. Delegating also makes sense when it results in decisions being made by those who must implement them. At the same time, good leaders recognize that they need to maintain control over certain key decisions. Thus, although they will delegate many decisions to lower-level employees, they will not delegate the decisions that they judge to be of critical importance to the future success of the organization under their leadership.

Political Astuteness Edward Wrapp has noted that good general managers tend to be politically astute.[37] By this he means three things. First, good general managers play the power game with skill, preferring to build consensus for their ideas rather than use their authority to force ideas through. They act as members or leaders of a coalition rather than as dictators. Second, good general managers often hesitate to commit themselves publicly to detailed strategic plans or precise objectives, since in all probability the emergence of unexpected contingencies will require adaptation. Thus a successful general manager might commit the organization to a particular vision, such as minimizing costs or boosting product quality, without stating precisely how or when this will be achieved. It is important to note that good general managers often have precise private objectives and strategies that they would like to see the organization pursue. However, they recognize the futility of public commitment, given the likelihood of change and the difficulties of implementation.

Third, Wrapp claims that good general managers possess the ability to push through programs in a piecemeal fashion. They recognize the futility of trying to push total packages or strategic programs through the organization, since significant objections to at least part of such programs are likely to arise. Instead, the successful general manager is willing to take less than total acceptance in order to achieve modest progress toward a goal. The successful general manager tries to push through his or her ideas in a piecemeal fashion, so that they appear as incidentals to other ideas, though in fact they are part of a larger program or hidden agenda that moves the organization in the direction of the manager's objectives.

1.8 SUMMARY OF CHAPTER

The chapter provides an overview of the strategic management process and examines some of the factors that influence the quality of strategic decisions generated by that process. Besides identifying the main components of the strategic management process, it points out several flaws in traditional planning systems and the harmful effect that cognitive biases and groupthink can have on the quality of strategic decision making. The role played by strategic leaders in the strategic decision-making process is discussed and the characteristics of strong leaders identified.

The key points of this chapter are as follows:

1. A central objective of strategic management is to identify why some organizations succeed while others fail.
2. The success of a company depends on three broad factors—the industry in which it is based, the country (or countries) in which it is located, and its own resources, capabilities, and strategies.
3. Traditional definitions of *strategy* stress that an organization's strategy is the outcome of a rational *planning* process. Mintzberg's revision of the concept suggests that strategy can *emerge* from within an organization in the absence of any prior intentions.
4. The major components of the strategic management process include defining the mission and major goals of the organization; analyzing the external and internal environments of the organization; choosing strategies that align, or *fit,* the organization's strengths and weaknesses with external environmental opportunities and threats; and adopting organizational structures and control systems to implement the organization's chosen strategy.
5. Strategic planning often fails because executives do not plan for uncertainty and because ivory tower planners lose touch with operating realities.
6. Prahalad and Hemal have criticized the fit model of strategy on the ground that it focuses too much on the degree of fit between existing resources and current opportunities, and not enough on building new resources and capabilities to create and exploit future opportunities.
7. *Strategic intent* refers to an obsession with achieving an objective that stretches the company and requires it to build new resources and capabilities.
8. In spite of systematic planning, companies may adopt poor strategies if their decision-making processes are vulnerable to groupthink and if individual cognitive biases are allowed to intrude into the decision-making process.
9. Techniques for enhancing the effectiveness of strategic decision making include devil's advocacy and dialectic inquiry.
10. General managers are individuals who bear responsibility for the overall performance of the organization or for one of its major self-contained divisions. Their overriding strategic concern is for the health of the total organization under their direction.
11. Functional managers are individuals who bear responsibility for a particular business function. Although they are not in a position to see the big picture, they do have a number of important strategic responsibilities.
12. The key characteristics of good leaders include vision, eloquence, and consistency; commitment; being well informed; a willingness to delegate and empower; and political astuteness.

Discussion Questions

1. What do we mean by *strategy?*
2. What are the strengths of formal strategic planning? What are its weaknesses?

3. Evaluate the 1987 Iran-Contra affair from a strategic decision-making perspective. Do you think different decisions would have been made if the Reagan administration had used a dialectic inquiry or a devil's advocacy approach when making strategic decisions? Was the sale of arms to Iran the result of an intended or an emergent strategy?
4. Evaluate President Bill Clinton against the leadership characteristics discussed in the text. On the basis of this comparison, do you think that President Clinton is a good strategic leader.

Article File 1

At the end of every chapter in this book, you will find an Article File task. The task requires you to search newspapers or magazines in the library for an example of a real company that satisfies the task question or issue. Your first article file task is as follows:

Find an example of a company that has recently changed its strategy. Identify whether this change was the outcome of a formal planning process or whether it was an emergent response to unforeseen events occurring in the company's environment.

Strategic Management Project: Module 1

To give you a practical insight into the strategic management process, we provide a series of strategic modules—one at the end of every chapter in this book. Each module asks you to collect and analyze information relating to the material discussed in that chapter. By completing these strategic modules, you will gain a clearer idea of the overall strategic management process. The first step in this project is to pick a company to study. We recommend that you focus on the same company throughout the book. Remember also, that we will be asking you for information about the corporate and international strategy of your company, as well as its structure. We strongly recommend that you pick a company for which such information is likely to be available.

There are two approaches that can be used to select a company to study, and your instructor will tell you which one to follow. The first approach is to pick a well-known company that has a lot of information written about it. For example, large publicly held companies such as IBM, Microsoft, and Southwest Airlines are routinely covered in the business and financial press. By going to the library at your university, you should be able to track down a great deal of information on such companies. Many libraries now have electronic data search facilities such as *ABI/Inform*, *The Wall Street Journal Index*, the *F&S Index*, and *Nexis*. These enable you to identify any article that has been written in the business press on the company of your choice within the last few years. If you do not have electronic data search facilities at your university, we suggest that you ask your librarian about data sources. A number of nonelectronic data sources are available. For example, *F&S Predicasts* publishes an annual list of articles relating to major companies that appeared in the national and international business

press. You will also want to collect full financial information on the company that you pick. Again, this can be accessed from electronic data bases such as *Compact Disclosure*. Alternatively, your library might have the annual financial reports, 10-K filings, or proxy statements pertaining to the company you pick. Again, ask your librarians, they are the best source of information.

A second approach is to pick a smaller company in your city or town to study. Although small companies are not routinely covered in the national business press, they may be covered in the local press. More importantly, this approach can work well if the management of the company will agree to talk to you *at length* about the strategy and structure of the company. If you happen to know somebody in such a company or if you yourself have worked there at some point, this approach can be very worthwhile. However, we *do not* recommend this approach unless you can get a *substantial* amount of guaranteed access to the company of your choice. If in doubt, ask your instructor before making a decision. The key issue is to make sure that you have access to enough interesting information to complete the organizational design modules.

Assignment

Your assignment for Strategic Management Project, Module #1, is to choose a company to study and to obtain enough information about that company to carry out the following instructions and answer the questions asked.

1. Give a short account of the history of the company, and trace the evolution of its strategy over time. Try to determine whether the strategic evolution of your company is the product of intended strategies, emergent strategies, or some combination of the two.
2. Identify the mission and major goals of the company.
3. Do a preliminary analysis of the internal strengths and weaknesses of the company and of the opportunities and threats that it faces in its environment. On the basis of this analysis, identify the strategies that you think the company should pursue. (Note: you will need to perform a much more detailed analysis later in the book.)
4. Who is the CEO of the company? Evaluate the CEO's leadership capabilities.

Endnotes

1. B. O'Brien "Flying on the Cheap," *Wall Street Journal*, October 26, 1992, A1. B. O'Reilly "Where Service Flies Right," *Fortune*, August 24, 1992, pp. 116–117. A. Salpukas "Hurt in Expansion, Airlines Cut Back and May Sell Hubs," *Wall Street Journal*, April 1, 1992, pp. A1, C8.
2. Research evidence suggests that firm level effects account for most of the variance in profit rates across industries, and that industry effects are relatively unimportant. See R. P. Rumelt "How Much Does Industry Matter?" *Strategic Management Journal*, 12 (1991), 167–186.
3. *The American Heritage Dictionary of the English Language* 3rd ed. (Boston: Houghton-Mifflin, 1992).
4. Alfred Chandler, *Strategy and Structure: Chapters in the History of the American Enterprise* (Cambridge, Mass.: MIT Press, 1962).
5. James B. Quinn, *Strategies for Change: Logical Incrementalism* (Homewood, Ill.: Irwin, 1980).
6. William F. Glueck, *Business Policy and Strategic Management* (New York: McGraw-Hill, 1980).
7. "According to Plan," *Economist*, July 22, 1989, pp. 60–63. Arie P. de Geus, "Planning as Learning," *Harvard Business Review* (March–April 1988), 70–74. Pierre Wack, "Scenarios: Uncharted Waters Ahead," *Harvard Business Review* (September–October 1985), 73–89. Toni Mack, "It's Time to

Take Risks," *Forbes* October 6, 1986, pp. 125–133.

8. Henry Mintzberg, "Patterns in Strategy Formulation," *Management Science*, 24 (1978), 934–948.
9. Ibid. Italics added.
10. Richard T. Pascale, "Perspectives on Strategy: The Real Story Behind Honda's Success," *California Management Review*, 26, (1984), 47–72.
11. K. R. Andrews, *The Concept of Corporate Strategy* (Homewood, Ill.: Dow Jones Irwin, 1971). H. I. Ansoff, *Corporate Strategy* (New York: McGraw-Hill, 1965). C. W. Hofer and D. Schendel, *Strategy Formulation: Analytical Concepts* (St. Paul, Minn.: West, 1978).
12. Andrews, *The Concept of Corporate Strategy*.
13. Lawrence C. Rhyne, "The Relationship of Strategic Planning to Financial Performance," *Strategic Management Journal*, 7 (1986), 423–436.
14. Thomas J. Peters and Robert H. Waterman, *In Search of Excellence* (New York: Harper & Row, 1982).
15. Henry Mintzberg, "The Design School: Reconsidering the Basic Premises of Strategic Management," *Strategic Management Journal*, 11, (1990), 171–196.
16. For some examples, see S. Tilles, "How to Evaluate Corporate Strategy," *Harvard Business Review*, 41 (1963), 111–121. Also see "The New Breed of Strategic Planner," *Business Week*, September 17, 1984, pp. 62–68.
17. P. J. H. Schoemaker, "Multiple Scenario Development: Its Conceptual and Behavioral Foundation," *Strategic Management Journal*, 14, 1993, 193–213.
18. See G. Hamel and C. K. Prahalad, "Strategic Intent," *Harvard Business Review*, (May–June 1989), 63–76; and C. K. Prahalad and G. Hamel, "The Core Competence of the Organization," *Harvard Business Review*, (May–June 1990) 79–91.
19. Hamel and Prahalad, "Strategic Intent," p. 64.
20. M. E. Porter, "Towards a Dynamic Theory of Strategy," *Strategic Management Journal*, 12 (1991), pp. 95–118.
21. Hamel and Prahalad, "Strategic Intent," p. 64.
22. E. P. Przybyowicz and T. W. Faulkner, "Kodak Applies Strategic Intent to the Management of Technology," *Research Technology Management*, (January–February 1993), 31–38.
23. For a review of the evidence see C. R. Schwenk, "Cognitive Simplification Processes in Strategic Decision Making," *Strategic Management Journal*, 5 (1984), 111–128; and K. M. Eisenhardt and M. Zbaracki, "Strategic Decision Making," *Strategic Management Journal*, Special Issue, 13 (1992), 17–37.
24. The original statement of this phenomenon was made by A. Tversky and D. Kahneman, "Judgment Under Uncertainty: Heuristics and Biases," *Science*, 185 (1974), 1124–1131.
25. Schwenk, "Cognitive Simplification Processes," pp. 111–128.
26. B. M. Staw, "The Escalation of Commitment to a Course of Action," *Academy of Management Review*, 6 (1981), 577–587.
27. Ibid.
28. M. J. Tang, "An Economic Perspective on Escalating Commitment," *Strategic Management Journal*, 9, 1988, 79–92.
29. R. Roll, "The Hubris Hypotheses of Corporate Takeovers," *Journal of Business*, 59 (1986), 197–216.
30. Irvin L. Janis, *Victims of Groupthink*, 2nd ed. (Boston: Houghton Mifflin, 1982).
31. The story ran on an almost daily basis in the *Financial Times* of London during the autumn of 1979.
32. See R. O. Mason, "A Dialectic Approach to Strategic Planning," *Management Science*, 13 (1969), 403–414; R. A. Cosier and J. C. Aplin, "A Critical View of Dialectic Inquiry in Strategic Planning," *Strategic Management Journal*, 1 (1980), 343–356; and I. I. Mintroff and R. O. Mason, "Structuring III—Structured Policy Issues: Further Explorations in a Methodology for Messy Problems," *Strategic Management Journal*, 1 (1980), 331–342.
33. Mason, "A Dialectic Approach," pp. 403–414.
34. D. M. Schweiger and P. A. Finger, "The Comparative Effectiveness of Dialectic Inquiry and Devil's Advocacy," *Strategic Management Journal* 5 (1984), 335–350.
35. For a summary of recent research on strategic leadership, see D. C. Hambrick, "Putting Top Managers Back into the Picture," *Strategic Management Journal*, Special Issue, 10 (1989), 5–15.
36. N. M. Tichy and D. O. Ulrich, "The Leadership Challenge: A Call for the Transformational Leader," *Sloan Management Review*, (Fall 1984), 59–68. F. Westley and H. Mintzberg, "Visionary Leadership and Strategic Management," *Strategic Management Journal*, Special Issue, 10 (1989), 17–32.
37. E. Wrapp, "Good Managers Don't Make Policy Decisions," *Harvard Business Review*, (September–October 1967), 91–99.
38. Sources: Westley and Mintzberg, "Visionary Leadership," pp. 17–32. J. Cocks, "The Updated Book of Jobs," *Time*, January 3, 1983, pp. 25–27. B. Utta, "Behind the Fall," *Fortune*, October 14, 1985, pp. 20–24.

2 Mission and Goals

2.1 OPENING CASE: ALLEGIS CORPORATION

In the early 1980s Dick Ferris, the CEO of United Air Lines, had a vision of the future in which United Air Lines was one component of a "worldwide door-to-door travel service." Ferris believed that a company that provided flight, rental car, and hotel services could realize significant synergies. He spoke with zeal about a future in which travel agents around the world would sit in front of their computer screens, coordinating reservations for his airline, his hotels, and his rental cars.

Assembling the assets for this travel empire had begun in 1970 with the purchase of Westin Hotel Company. Under Ferris's leadership, United Air Lines bought The Hertz Corp. from RCA in 1985 for $587 million. In March 1987 United bought Hilton International for $980 million. At the same time United Air Lines officially changed its name to Allegis Corporation in a symbolic attempt to emphasize the company's rebirth as an integrated travel operation.

The problem with this strategy was that it did not have the support of two major stakeholder groups: the company's airline pilots and stockholders. Ferris's difficulties with the pilots began in mid 1985, when he demanded wage and productivity concessions from the pilots' union, the Air Line Pilots Association of United Air Lines (ALPA), in order to compete with low-cost carriers such as People Express and Continental. He succeeded in getting the pilots to accept his demands, but only after a twenty-nine-day strike that soured management-labor relations and produced a $92 million quarterly loss. Then, in April 1985, ALPA offered to buy the airline for $4.5 billion. According to F. C. Dubinsky, ALPA chairman at United, the bid was motivated by the pilots' fear that "the airline is no longer the focus of the company. The management is a hotel management team. We want to return to our core business." The bid was refused by corporate leadership.

While these events were unfolding, a number of corporate raiders were beginning to take an interest in the company. In March 1987 Allegis stock was trading in the $55 to $60 range. According to stock analysts and many institutional investors, at that price the stock was grossly undervalued. Several investment experts judged that the company would be worth at least $100 per share if its operations were sold separately. Buoyed by such estimates, real estate mogul Donald Trump was the first raider to surface. He purchased 5 percent of the stock. After issuing several statements critical of Ferris, Trump sold his stake, but not before he had "talked up" the company's stock price and made a profit of $50 million on the transaction. Then in May 1987 Coniston Partners, an investment fund, disclosed that it had purchased 13 percent of Allegis stock. Coniston's intention was to remove the board of directors and sell off the company's constituent businesses.

Ferris's reaction to the takeover bids from ALPA and Coniston was to initiate two takeover defenses. First, as part of a $15-billion jet order, Allegis provided The Boeing Co. with new-issue convertible notes valued at $700 million. Should a single investment entity purchase more than 40 percent of Allegis stock, the interest rates on the notes would increase drastically, thereby severely raising the costs of any hostile takeover attempt. This tactic, however, failed to reassure the majority of Allegis stockholders, who were becoming increasingly dissatisfied with Ferris. In response, the Allegis board suggested a massive

recapitalization plan that would immediately repay stockholders $60 per share in cash and leave them with stock worth an estimated $28 per share. The drawback, though, was that the plan would add more than $3 billion to the $2.4 billion in long-term debt already on the company's balance sheet. Such a debt load would have been perilous in the competitive airline industry, and the resulting interest payments might have wiped out profits.

Ultimately, the Allegis board could not countenance piling up heavy debt to salvage a master plan that shareholders disliked. Nor could it support a CEO who had so clearly alienated both Wall Street investors and many of the company's employees. Consequently, in June 1987 the board ousted Dick Ferris; repudiated his travel supermarket strategy; announced that Hertz, Westin, and Hilton International would all be sold; decided to consider selling a major stake in United Air Lines to its employees; and announced plans to change the company's name back to United Air Lines. In effect, after supporting Dick Ferris through two difficult years, the board reversed itself under pressure from employees and stockholders. Coniston and ALPA responded by dropping their takeover bids. In the view of both parties, the board was now proposing to do what they had wanted all along.[1]

Discussion Questions

1. What does the story of Dick Ferris and Allegis tell you about the link between strategy formulation and stakeholders' demands?
2. Why do you think that pilots and stockholders of Allegis did not support Ferris's diversification strategy?

2.2 OVERVIEW

Allegis failed to satisfy the interests of two of its major constituencies, or stakeholders: its stockholders and its employees. As a consequence, CEO Dick Ferris, the architect of Allegis's strategy, lost his job. To avoid the problems that Allegis faced, companies can and should identify and incorporate the claims of various stakeholder groups into strategic decision making. In this chapter, we consider how they can proceed toward this end.

The corporate mission statement is the first key indicator of how an organization views the claims of its stakeholders. Its purpose is to set the organizational context within which strategic decisions will be made—in other words, to give an organization strategic focus and direction. All strategic decisions flow from the mission statement. Typically, the **mission statement** defines the organization's business, states its vision and goals, and articulates its main philosophical values.[2] In examining how organizations formulate such statements, we concentrate on these three main components.

Figure 2.1 gives an example of a mission statement—that of Weyerhaeuser Co., the largest U.S. forest products company. Although this statement does not define Weyerhaeuser's business, it clearly articulates the company's vision and philosophical values. Most of the items listed under "Our Strategies" are actually major goals of the company.

After examining how to construct a mission statement, we consider a company's various **stakeholders**: individuals or groups, either within or outside the organization, that have some claim on it (see Figure 2.2). Their interests must be taken into account when a mission statement is formulated. (Note that various stakeholder groups are explicitly recognized in Weyerhaeuser's mission statement in Figure 2.1). Then we look closely at one particularly important stakeholder group, *stockholders,* and we analyze how stockholders can and do

Figure 2.1
Weyerhaeuser's Mission Statement

Our Vision

The best forest products company in the World.

Our Strategies

We shall achieve our vision by: Making Total Quality the Weyerhaeuser way of doing business. > Relentless pursuit of full customer satisfaction. > Empowering Weyerhaeuser people. > Leading the industry in forest management and manufacturing excellence. Producing superior returns for our shareholders.

Our Values

Customers. We listen to our customers and improve our products to meet their present and future needs.

People. Our success depends upon high-performing people working together in a safe and healthy workplace where diversity, development, and teamwork are valued and recognized.

Accountability. We expect superior performance and are accountable for our actions and results. Our leaders set clear goals and expectations, are supportive, and provide and seek frequent feedback.

Citizenship. We support the communities where we do business, hold ourselves to the highest standards of ethical conduct and environmental responsibility, and communicate openly with Weyerhaeuser people and the public.

Financial Responsibility. We are prudent and effective in the use of the resources entrusted to us.[3]

Reprinted from "The Company Mission as a Strategic Tool," by John Pearce III, Sloan Management Review, Spring 1982, p. 22, by permission of publisher.

influence the corporate mission and hence corporate strategies. The chapter closes with a look at the *ethical dimension* of strategic decisions and at the relationship between ethics and stakeholder welfare.

2.3 DEFINING THE BUSINESS

The first component of a mission statement is a clear definition of the organization's business. Essentially, defining the business involves answering these questions: "What is our business? What will it be? What should it be?"[4] The answers vary, depending on whether the organization is a single-business or a diversified enterprise. A **single-business** enterprise is active in just one main business area. For example, U.S. Steel in the 1950s was involved just in the production of steel. By the 1980s, however, U.S. Steel had become USX Corporation, a diversified company with interests in steel, oil and gas, chemicals, real estate, transportation, and the production of energy equipment. For USX, the process of defining itself is complicated by the fact that to a large extent the concern of a multibusiness enterprise is *managing businesses*. Thus the business definition of USX involves different issues than did the definition of U.S. Steel. In this section, the problem of how to define the business of a single-business company is considered first. Discussion of how best to define the business of a diversified enterprise follows.

Figure 2.2
The Relationship Between the Mission, Stakeholders, and Strategies

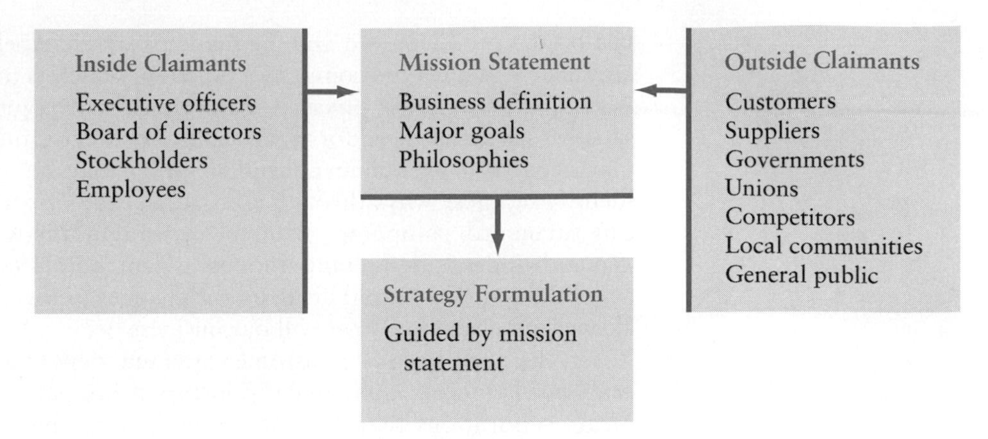

Source: Reprinted from "The Company Mission as A Strategic Tool," by John Pearce III, *Sloan Management Review*, Spring 1982, page 22, by permission of the publisher.

A Single-Business Company

To answer the question, What is our business? Derek F. Abell has suggested that a company should define its business in terms of three dimensions: who is being satisfied (what customer groups), what is being satisfied (what customer needs), how are customer needs being satisfied (by what skills or distinctive competencies)?[5] Figure 2.3 illustrates these three dimensions.

Abell's approach stresses the need for a **consumer-oriented** rather than a **product-oriented** business definition. A product-oriented business definition focuses

Figure 2.3:
Abell's Framework for Defining the Business

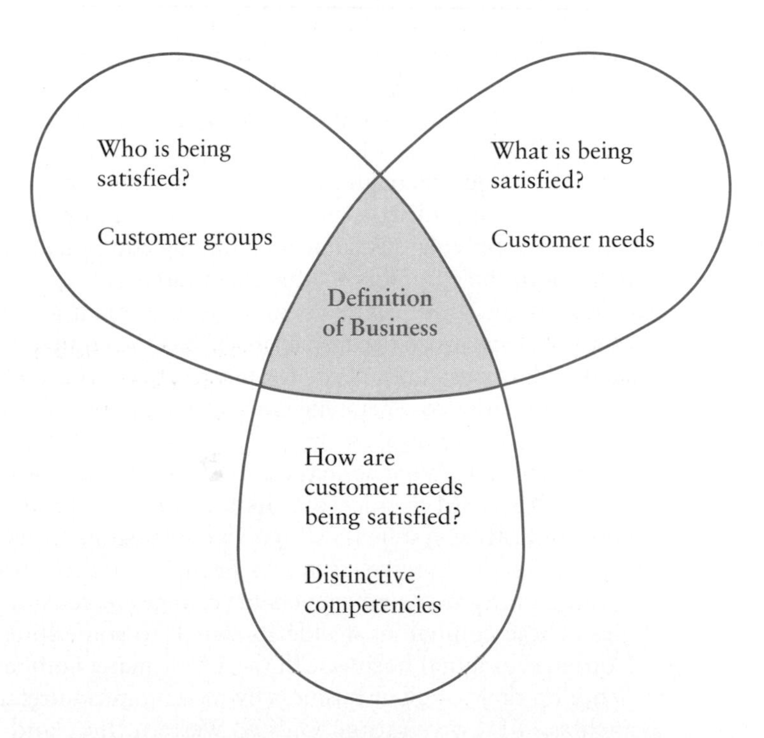

Source: Derek F. Abell, *Defining the Business: The Starting Point of Strategic Planning* (Englewood Cliffs, N.J.: Prentice-Hall, 1980), p. 17.

just on the products sold and the markets served. Abell maintains that such an approach obscures the company's function, which is to satisfy consumer needs. A product is only the physical manifestation of applying a particular skill to satisfy a particular need for a particular consumer group. In practice, the particular need of a particular consumer group may be served in different ways. Identifying these ways through a broad, consumer-oriented business definition can safeguard companies from being caught unawares by major shifts in demand. Indeed, by helping anticipate demand shifts, Abell's framework can assist companies in capitalizing on the changes in their environment. It can help answer the question, What will our business be?

Yet, the need to take a customer-oriented view of a company's business has often been ignored. Consequently, history is littered with the wreckage of once-great corporations that did not define their business or that defined it incorrectly. These firms failed to see what their business would become, and ultimately they declined. Theodore Levitt described the fall of the once mighty U.S. railroads in terms of their failure to define their business correctly:

> The railroads did not stop growing because the need for passenger and freight transportation declined. That grew. The railroads are in trouble today not because the need was filled by others (cars, trucks, airplanes, even telephones), but because it was not filled by the railroads themselves. They let others take customers away from them because they assumed themselves to be in the railroad business rather than in the transportation business. The reason they defined their industry wrong was because they were railroad oriented instead of transport oriented; they were product oriented instead of customer oriented.[6]

If the railroads had used Abell's framework, they might have anticipated the impact of technological change and decided that their business was transportation. In that case, they might have transferred their early strength in rail into dominance in today's diversified transport industry. But most railroads stuck to a product-oriented definition of their business and went bankrupt.

In contrast, for a long time IBM correctly foresaw what its business would be. Originally, IBM was a leader in the manufacture of typewriters and mechanical tabulating equipment using punch-card technology. However, IBM defined its business as providing a means for information processing and storage, rather than just supplying mechanical tabulating equipment and typewriters. Given this definition, the company's subsequent moves into computers, software systems, office systems, and printers seem logical. It might also be argued that IBM's current problems arose because in the 1980s the company lost sight of the fact that increasingly consumer needs for information processing and storage were being satisfied by low-cost personal computers, and not the mainframe computers produced by its core business.

The question, What should our business be? can also be answered using Abell's framework. IBM decided that its business should be computers, word processors, and office systems—all natural extensions of its original business. Other companies do not see as much promise in their original business, perhaps because of negative and irreversible changes in consumer needs and in technologies. These companies decide to switch to something else and diversify away from their original business. In the 1960s many companies reduced their dependence on their original business by moving into unrelated areas. Conglomerates such as ITT Corporation, Gulf & Western, Inc., and Textron were a result of this diversification movement.[7]

A Diversified Company

A diversified company faces special problems when trying to define its business because it actually operates several businesses. In essence, the corporate business is often one of *managing a collection of businesses*. For example, USX, formerly U.S. Steel, is still known primarily for its steel interests. A consumer-oriented definition of USX's steel interests might be something like this: "USX seeks to satisfy customers' needs for a high-strength construction and fabricating material." However, USX is, in fact, a diversified company, which in 1986 generated only 33 percent of its revenues from steel. The rest came from oil and gas, chemicals, real estate, transportation, and energy equipment. Clearly, the consumer-oriented definition given above applies only to the company's steel operations; it does not suffice as a definition of its *corporate* businesses.

In a diversified enterprise, the question, What is our business? must be asked at two levels: the business level and the corporate level. At the business level, such as USX's steel operations, the focus should be on a consumer-oriented definition. But at the corporate level, management cannot simply aggregate the various business definitions, for doing so will lead to an imprecise and confusing statement. Instead, the corporate business definition should focus on how the corporate level *adds value* to the constituent businesses of the company. That is, the mission statement should identify the contribution that the corporate level makes to the efficient operation of business units. It should indicate why those business units are better off as part of the corporation than as free-standing entities.

The issue of how the corporate level might add value to the constituent business units of a diversified company is explored in depth in Chapter 9, when we review corporate-level strategies. Suffice it to say here that if the corporate headquarters of a diversified company cannot identify how it improves the efficiency of business units within the company, those business units may be better off on their own. Indeed, the realization that in many cases the corporate level does *not* add value to the constituent business units of the company was behind the divestment trend of the 1980s and early 1990s. During that period we witnessed the breakup and downsizing of many of the old conglomerates—such as Gulf & Western, ITT, and Textron—that had been built up through diversified acquisitions in the 1960s and 1970s.[8]

2.4 VISION AND MAJOR GOALS

The second component of a company's mission statement, the detailing of its vision and major corporate goals, is a formal declaration of what the company is trying to achieve. The spelling out of the vision and major goals gives direction to the corporate mission statement and helps guide the formulation of strategy.

Strategic Intent, Vision, and Goals

In Chapter 1 we introduce the concept of **strategic intent**, recently popularized by Gary Hamel and C. K. Prahalad. As you may recall, underlying this concept is the notion that managers should set ambitious goals that stretch a company. Often, the vision presented in a company's mission statement articulates the company's strategic intent. Thus, Weyerhaeuser's vision, proclaimed in its mission statement, is to be "the best forest products company in the world." This is Weyerhaeuser's strategic intent. Another example, appears in Figure 2.4, the

Figure 2.4
Philip Morris's Mission Statement

Our Mission is to be the most successful consumer packaged goods company in the world. We pursue our mission by:

1. Maintaining the highest quality of people.
2. Protecting and building our brand franchises.
3. Growing profitable new business with line extensions, new products, geographic expansion, acquisitions, and joint ventures and strategic alliances.
4. Maximizing productivity and synergy in all businesses at all times.
5. Making total quality management a reality in every aspect of our everyday operations.
6. Managing with a global perspective.[9]

mission statement of Philip Morris Companies, Inc. This company's vision, or its strategic intent, is to be "the most successful consumer packaged goods company in the world." Both Philip Morris and Weyerhaeuser have adopted ambitious visions, which are likely to stretch their respective organizations.

Beyond articulating their vision, many companies also state other major goals in their mission statement. These goals specify how a company intends to go about attaining its strategic intent. So, for example, the Weyerhaeuser mission statement tells the company that it intends to attain its vision by focusing on total quality, empowering its employees, and striving to satisfy customers. The Philip Morris statement makes plain the company's intent to achieve its vision by maximizing productivity and synergy and stressing total quality management. Both companies list other specific goals. All these goals shape the choice of strategies. The goal of maximizing productivity, for instance, indicates that when Philip Morris reviews its strategic options, it will favor strategies that increase its productivity.

Maximizing Stockholder Wealth

Although most profit-seeking organizations operate with a variety of major corporate goals, within a *public* corporation—at least in theory—all these goals should be directed toward one end: maximizing stockholder wealth. Stockholders provide a company with capital and in exchange expect an appropriate return on their investment. A company's stockholders are its legal owners. Consequently, the overriding goal of most corporations is to maximize stockholder wealth, which involves increasing the long-run returns earned by stockholders from owning shares in the corporation. This is stated explicitly in Weyerhaeuser's mission statement, which notes that a major goal of the company is to "produce superior returns for our shareholders."

Stockholders receive returns in two ways: from dividend payments and from capital appreciation in the market value of a share (that is, by increases in stock market prices). A company can best maximize stockholder returns by pursuing

strategies that maximize its own return on investment (ROI), which is a good general indicator of a company's efficiency. The more efficient a company is, the better its future prospects look to stockholders and the greater is its ability to pay dividends. Furthermore, higher ROI leads to greater demand for a company's shares. Demand bids up the share price and leads to capital appreciation.

The Short-Term Problem

As management theorist Peter F. Drucker and many others have pointed out, there is danger in emphasizing only ROI. An overzealous pursuit of ROI can misdirect managerial attention and encourage some of the worst management practices, such as maximizing short-run rather than long-run ROI. A short-run orientation favors such action as cutting expenditures judged to be nonessential in that span of time—for instance, expenditures for research and development, marketing, and new capital investments. Although decreasing current expenditure increases current ROI, the resulting underinvestment, lack of innovation, and poor market awareness jeopardize long-run ROI. Yet despite these negative consequences, managers do make such decisions because the adverse effects of a short-run orientation may not materialize and become apparent to stockholders for several years. By that time the management team responsible may have moved on, leaving others to pick up the pieces.

In a now famous *Harvard Business Review* article, Robert H. Hayes and William J. Abernathy argue that the widespread focus on short-run ROI has been a major factor in the long-run loss of international competitiveness by U.S. companies.[10] MIT economist Lester Thurow likewise faults the short-run orientation of many American businesses for some of their problems. Thurow claims that many U.S. companies are unwilling to make long-run investments for fear of depressing their short-run ROI. He cites declining expenditures for research and development and reduced innovative activity within American enterprises as evidence of this orientation.[11] Similarly, after a detailed study of productivity problems in American industry, the MIT Commission on Industrial Productivity concluded that the short time horizons of many American corporations placed them at a competitive disadvantage vis-à-vis their foreign competitors.[12] One of the consequences of short-term horizons in America, according to the MIT Commission, was the U.S. loss of leadership in the videocassette recorder industry to Japanese companies. The videocassette recorder was pioneered in the 1950s by the U.S.-based Ampex Corporation, primarily for use in the broadcasting industry. Ampex did try to produce a consumer variant of the product for a mass market but pulled out in 1970, when it decided it could not afford the R&D investment. Similarly, RCA, which also tried to develop a consumer videocassette recorder, pulled out in 1975 in the face of high development costs and manufacturing problems. This left the field open for Sony and Matsushita, both of which had been investing heavily during the 1970s to develop their own technology. Today the videocassette market is a multibillion-dollar market dominated by Matsushita. No American company competes in this market.

As Strategy in Action 2.1 recounts, a similar story of short-term behavior seems to be emerging in the market for active matrix liquid crystal displays (AM-LCDs). The AM-LCD technology, too, was originally developed in the United States, but the market is now dominated by Japanese companies.

STRATEGY IN ACTION 2.1

How a Short-Term Orientation May Have Cost the United States Leadership in the Market for Active Matrix Liquid Crystal Displays

Active matrix liquid crystal displays (AM-LCDs) are the flat-top color displays used in laptop and notebook personal computers. In addition to computer displays, the screens are also critical components in camcorders, medical instruments, high-definition television, auto dashboards, aerospace instruments, factory control devices and instrumentation for the military. Although production was just getting off the ground in 1990, with sales of $250 million worldwide, forecasts suggest worldwide sales of $1 billion in 1994 and $10 billion plus by the year 2000.

The AM-LCD technology was pioneered during the 1960s at two U.S. companies, RCA and Westinghouse, but, neither succeeded in commercializing it. One reason was that corporate management at both companies balked at the development costs and long payback periods involved and cut funding. The principal Westinghouse researcher, Jim Fergason, subsequently left the company and set up a venture to manufacture AM-LCDs. However, few U.S. companies were willing to utilize the technology, and Fergason found it difficult to raise sufficient venture capital. Ultimately, Fergason's venture failed.

With no large U.S. company undertaking primary AM-LCD research, it was left to the Japanese to emerge as the major producers of AM-LCDs. By 1990 Sharp, NEC and Toshiba now dominated the market, with 95 percent of worldwide production. Unlike their major American competitors, these Japanese firms made massive investments in AM-LCD research and production facilities during the 1980s. Sharp alone reportedly spent more than $1 billion on developing the technology during the 1980s and plans to spend $640 million more during the 1991–1995 period.

Although a number of small U.S. companies are involved in this business, they tend to focus on highly specialized niches (for instance, supplying the Defense Department) and have made investments only to support limited production. Except for IBM, which has a joint venture with Toshiba in Japan to manufacture AM-LCDs, no major U.S. company has a presence in this industry, and no U.S. company is capable of mass production. The principal reason seems to be that the massive capital expenditures required to produce AM-LCD screens have deterred U.S. companies from entering the business, as have the high risks involved. The risks have become much greater, given the Japanese lead in the technology and the long payback period for any investments. (Japanese executives talk about five or six years' losses as the "cost" of entering this business.) Few American companies are willing to invest in an industry where Japanese companies are already well ahead. In addition, the production process is a particularly difficult one to master, for even the smallest contaminant in the production process, such as dust, can damage a display. It is estimated that 60 percent of AM-LCDs coming off Japanese production lines are defective and have to be scrapped. Thus the combination of high capital costs, high risks and a difficult production process have deterred many major U.S. companies from entering the market.[13]

Secondary Goals

To guard against short-run behavior, Drucker suggests that companies adopt a number of secondary goals in addition to ROI. These goals should be designed to balance short-run and long-run considerations. Drucker's list includes secondary goals relating to these areas: (1) market share, (2) innovation, (3) productivity, (4) physical and financial resources, (5) manager performance and development, (6) worker performance and attitude, and (7) social responsibility. Although such secondary goals need not be part of a mission statement, many of the most important ones are.

Even if a company does not recognize secondary goals explicitly, it must recognize them implicitly through a commitment to long-run profitability. Take Hewlett-Packard, one of the companies that Thomas J. Peters and Robert H. Waterman cite as being an "excellent" company.[14] The following quotation from Hewlett-Packard's mission statement clearly expresses the importance of an orientation toward maximizing long-run profitability and can serve as a model:

> In our economic system, the profit we generate from our operations is the ultimate source of the funds we need to prosper and grow. It is the one absolutely essential measure of our corporate performance over the **long term**. Only if we continue to meet our profit objective can we achieve our other corporate objectives.[15]

2.5 CORPORATE PHILOSOPHY

The third component of a mission statement is a summing up of the corporate philosophy: the basic beliefs, values, aspirations, and philosophical priorities that the strategic decision makers are committed to and that guide their management of the company. It tells how the company intends to do business and often reflects the company's recognition of its social and ethical responsibility (ethics are discussed in a later section of this chapter). Thus a statement of corporate philosophy can have an important impact on the way a company conducts itself.

Many companies establish a philosophical creed to emphasize their own distinctive outlook on business. A company's creed forms the basis for establishing its corporate culture (an issue considered in Chapter 12). The creed of Lincoln Electric Co., for instance, states that productivity increases should be shared primarily by customers and employees through lower prices and higher wages. This belief distinguishes Lincoln Electric from many other enterprises and, by all accounts, is acted on by the company in terms of its specific strategies, objectives, and operating policies.[16]

Another company whose philosophy is famous is health care giant Johnson & Johnson. Its credo, reproduced in Figure 2.5, expresses Johnson & Johnson's belief that the company's first responsibility is to the doctors, nurses, and patients who use J&J products. Next come its employees, the communities in which these employees live and work, and finally the stockholders. The credo is prominently displayed in every manager's office; and according to the Johnson & Johnson managers, the credo guides all important decisions.

Strong evidence of the credo's influence was apparent in the company's response to the Tylenol crisis. In 1982 seven people in the Chicago area died after taking Tylenol capsules that had been laced with cyanide. Johnson & Johnson immediately withdrew all Tylenol capsules from the U.S. market, at an estimated cost to the company of $100 million. At the same time the company embarked on a comprehensive communication effort involving 2,500 Johnson & Johnson employees and targeted at the pharmaceutical and medical communities. By such means, Johnson & Johnson successfully presented itself to the public as a company that was willing to do what was right, regardless of the cost. As a consequence, the Tylenol crisis enhanced rather than tarnished Johnson & Johnson's image. Indeed, because of its actions, the company was able to regain its status as a market leader in painkillers in a matter of months.[17]

Figure 2.5
Johnson & Johnson's Credo

Our Credo

We believe our first responsibility is to the doctors, nurses, and patients,
to mothers and fathers and all others who use our products and service
In meeting their needs everything we do must be of high quality.
We must constantly strive to reduce our costs
in order to maintain reasonable prices.
Customers orders must be serviced promptly and accurately.
Our suppliers and distributors must have an opportunity
to make a fair profit.

We are responsible to our employees,
the men and women who work with us throughout the world.
Everyone must be considered as an individual.
We must respect their dignity and recognize their merit.
They must have a sense of security in their jobs.
Compensation must be fair and adequate,
and working conditions clean, orderly and safe.
Employees must feel free to make suggestions and complaints.
There must be equal opportunity for employment, development
and advancement for those qualified.
We must provide competent management,
and their actions must be just and ethical.

We are responsible to the communities in which we live and work
and to the world community as well.
We must be good citizens support good works and charities
and bear our fair share of taxes.
We must encourage civic improvements and better health and educat
We must maintain in good order
the property we are privileged to use,
protecting the environment and natural resources.

Our final responsibility is to our stockholders.
Business must make a sound profit.
We must experiment with new ideas.
Research must be carried on, innovative programs developed
and mistakes paid for.
New equipment must be purchased, new facilities provided
and new products launched.
Reserves must be created to provide for adverse times.
When we operate according to these principles,
the stockholders should realize a fair return.

Johnson & Johnson

Source: Courtesy of Johnson & Johnson's

2.6 CORPORATE STAKEHOLDERS

Stakeholders and the Mission Statement

Stakeholders are individuals or groups that have some claim on the company. They can be divided into **internal claimants** and **external claimants.**[18] Internal claimants are stockholders and employees, including executive officers and board members. External claimants are all other individuals and groups affected by the company's actions. Typically, they comprise customers, suppliers, governments, unions, competitors, local communities, and the general public.

All stakeholders can justifiably expect that the company will attempt to satisfy their particular demands. Stockholders provide the enterprise with capital and in exchange expect an appropriate return on their investment. Employees provide labor and skills and in exchange expect commensurate income and job satisfaction. Customers want value for money. Suppliers seek dependable buyers. Governments insist on adherence to legislative regulations. Unions demand benefits for their members in proportion to their contributions to the company. Rivals seek fair competition. Local communities want companies that are responsible citizens. The general public seeks some assurance that the quality of life will be improved as a result of the company's existence.

A company has to take these claims into account when formulating its strategies, or else stakeholders may withdraw their support. Stockholders may sell their shares, employees leave their jobs, and customers buy elsewhere. Suppliers are likely to seek more dependable buyers, whereas governments can prosecute the company. Unions may engage in disruptive labor disputes, and rivals may respond to unfair competition by anticompetitive moves of their own or by filing antitrust suits. Communities may oppose the company's attempts to locate its facilities in their area, and the general public may form pressure groups, demanding action against companies that impair the quality of life. Any of these reactions can have a disastrous impact on an enterprise.

A mission statement enables a company to incorporate stakeholder claims into its strategic decision making and thereby reduce the risk of losing stakeholder support. The mission statement thus becomes the company's formal commitment to a stakeholder group; it carries the message that its strategies will be formulated with the claims of those stakeholders in mind. We have already discussed how stockholder claims are incorporated into the mission statement when a company decides that its primary goal is maximizing long-run profitability. Any strategies that the company generates should reflect this major corporate goal. Similarly, the mission statement should recognize additional stakeholder claims, in its secondary goals and philosophy.

Stakeholder Impact Analysis

A company cannot always satisfy the claims of all stakeholders. The claims of different groups may conflict, and in practice few organizations have the resources to manage all stakeholders. For example, union claims for higher wages can conflict with consumer demands for reasonable prices and stockholder demands for acceptable returns. Often the company must make choices. To do so, it must identify the most important stakeholders and give highest priority to pursuing strategies that satisfy their needs. Stakeholder impact analysis can provide such identification. Typically, stakeholder impact analysis involves the following steps:

1. Identifying stakeholders
2. Identifying stakeholders' interests and concerns
3. As a result, identifying what claims stakeholders are likely to make on the organization
4. Identifying the stakeholders that are most important from the organization's perspective
5. Identifying the resulting strategic challenges[19]

Such an analysis enables the company to identify the stakeholders most critical to its survival and allows it to incorporate their claims into the mission statement explicitly. From the mission statement, stakeholder claims then feed down into the rest of the strategy formulation process. For example, if community involvement is identified as a critical stakeholder claim, it must be incorporated in the mission statement, and any strategies that conflict with it must be rejected.

2.7 CORPORATE GOVERNANCE AND STRATEGY

Corporate mission statements generally give a great deal of attention to satisfying stockholders' demands. As providers of capital and legal owners of the corporation, stockholders play a unique role. Ultimately, one of the major goals of an enterprise is to give its stockholders a good rate of return on their investment. In the case of most publicly held corporations, however, stockholders delegate the job of controlling the company and determining strategies to corporate managers, who become the agents of the stockholders.[20] Accordingly, corporate managers should pursue strategies that are in the best interest of the stockholders and maximize stockholder wealth. Although many managers do pursue strategies that maximize stockholder wealth, not all act in this fashion.

Management Goals Versus Stockholder Goals

Why should managers want to pursue other strategies than those consistent with maximizing stockholder wealth? The answer depends on the personal goals of professional managers. Many writers have argued that managers are motivated by desires for status, power, job security, income, and the like.[21] By virtue of their position within the company, certain managers, such as the CEO, can use their authority and control over corporate funds to satisfy these desires. For example, CEOs might use their position to invest corporate funds in various perks that enhance their status—executive jets, lavish offices, and expense-paid trips to Hawaii—rather than investing those funds in ways that increase stockholder wealth. Economists have termed such behavior **on-the-job consumption.**[22] A prime example of someone who appeared to engage in excessive on-the-job consumption, Ross Johnson, the former CEO of RJR Nabisco, is profiled in Strategy in Action 2.2.

Besides engaging in on-the-job-consumption, CEOs, along with other senior managers, might satisfy their desires for greater income by awarding themselves excessive pay increases. Many critics of American industry claim that this has now become an endemic problem among U.S. companies. They point out that CEO pay has been increasing far more rapidly in recent years than the pay of average Americans. For example, between 1980 and 1992 the average pay of an engineer doubled, from $28,486 to $58,240, while the average pay of 1,000

STRATEGY IN ACTION 2.2

Ross Johnson and the RJR Airforce: A Case of on-the-job Consumption

Ross Johnson was the CEO at RJR Nabisco, one of America's largest food and tobacco products concerns, from 1984 until late 1989, when the company was acquired in a $26-billion leveraged buyout engineered by Kohlberg, Kravis, Roberts & Co. During his tenure at RJR Nabisco, Johnson worked hard to earn a reputation as one of the most profligate CEOs in corporate America. The symbol of Johnson's excess was the "RJR Airforce"—a fleet of ten top-of-the-line corporate jets and thirty-six pilots that were constantly at the call of Johnson and his chief lieutenants—whether it was to go to a business meeting in Washington, a shopping trip in New York, or an RJR-sponsored golf tournament in California. Johnson's favorite corporate jets were the Gulfstream G4s. At $21 million apiece, they appealed to his sense of fun and desire for comfort. They were also large enough to allow his German shepherd dog—who appeared on the passenger manifest when he traveled with Johnson as "A. Shepherd"—to roam around a bit.

To house the RJR Airforce, Johnson ordered a new hangar area to be built at Atlanta's Charlie Brown Airport. The original plans called for $12 million to be spent. The money didn't go into the hangar itself, but into an adjacent three-story reception building, which Johnson had built. With 20,000 square feet of space, tinted windows, a stunning three-story atrium, and Italian marble floors, the building was rightly referred to as the "Taj Mahal of corporate hangars." When the architects presented the original plans to Johnson, they were understandably nervous. After all, although Johnson had given them instructions to make the building state-of-the-art, this was going to cost $12 million. Johnson looked over the drawings, listened to the architects, and made his recommendation: add another 7,000 square feet. As a grateful vendor who was involved in the project later commented, "It was the only company I ever worked for without a budget."[23]

CEOs of large companies surveyed by *Business Week* increased sixfold, from $624,996 to $3,842,247.[24] In 1991 the average American CEO earned 85 to 100 times as much as the average American worker. By comparison, in Japan the average CEO earns 17 times as much as the average worker, while in Germany the average CEO earns 23 to 25 times as much.[25] (For more data comparing CEO compensation in the United States to that in other countries, see Figure 2.6.)

What particularly rankles the critics is the sheer size of some CEO pay packages and their apparent lack of relationship to company performance.[26] In 1992, for example, Tony O'Reilly, the CEO of H. J. Heinz, received $115.3 million in salary and stock options, and Roberto Goizueta, the CEO of Coca-Cola, received $101.1 million. Although both Heinz and Coca-Cola have done reasonably well under the leadership of O'Reilly and Goizueta, many critics felt that the size of these pay awards was out of all proportion to the achievement of the CEOs. Perhaps more disturbing was the case of Stephen Wolf, the CEO of UAL, the parent company of United Air Lines. In 1992 Wolf received salary and stock options worth $17.1 million, despite the fact that the return from holding UAL stock over the previous three years had fallen by 26 percent.[27]

A further concern is that in trying to satisfy the desires for status, security, power, and income, the CEO might grow the company through diversification. Although such growth may do little to enhance the company's profitability, and thus stockholder wealth, it increases the size of the empire under the CEO's control, and by

Figure 2.6: Average Remuneration of CEOs of Companies With $250 Million in Sales in 11 Countries

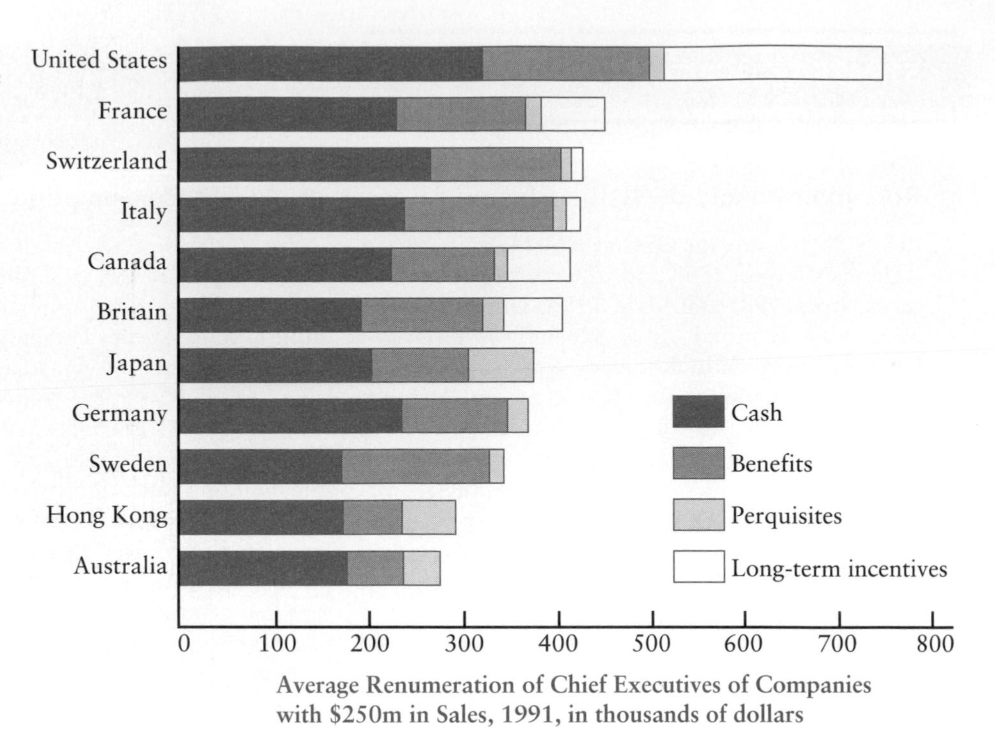

Data for 1991. Source: Towers Perrin.

extension, the CEO's status, power, security, and income (there is a strong relationship between company size and CEO pay).[28] To quote Carl Icahn, one of the most renowned corporate raiders of the 1980s,

> make no mistake, a strongly knit corporate aristocracy exists in America. The top man, what's more, usually finds expanding his power more important than rewarding owners (stockholders). When Mobil and USX had excess cash, did they enrich shareholders? Of course not. They bought Marcor and Marathon—disastrous investments, but major increases in the size of the manor.[29]

Thus, instead of maximizing stockholder wealth, some senior managers may trade long-run profitability for greater growth through diversification. Figure 2.7 graphs profitability against a company's growth rate. A company that does not grow is probably missing out on some profitable opportunities.[30] A growth rate of G_0 in Figure 2.7 is not consistent with maximizing profitability ($P_1 < P_{max}$). A moderate growth rate of G_1, on the other hand, does allow a company to maximize profits, producing profits equal to P_{max}. Achieving a growth rate in excess of G_1, however, requires diversification into areas that the company knows little about. Consequently, it can only be achieved by sacrificing profitability (that is, past G_1 the investment required to finance further growth does not produce an adequate return, and the company's profitability declines). Yet G_2 may be the growth rate favored by an "empire building" CEO, for it will increase his power, status, and income. At this growth rate profits are only equal to P_2. Because $P_{max} > P_2$, a company growing at this rate is clearly not maximizing its profitability, and hence the wealth of its stockholders. However, a growth rate of G_2 may be consistent with attaining managerial goals of power, status, and income.

Figure 2.7
The Tradeoff Between Profitability and Growth Rate

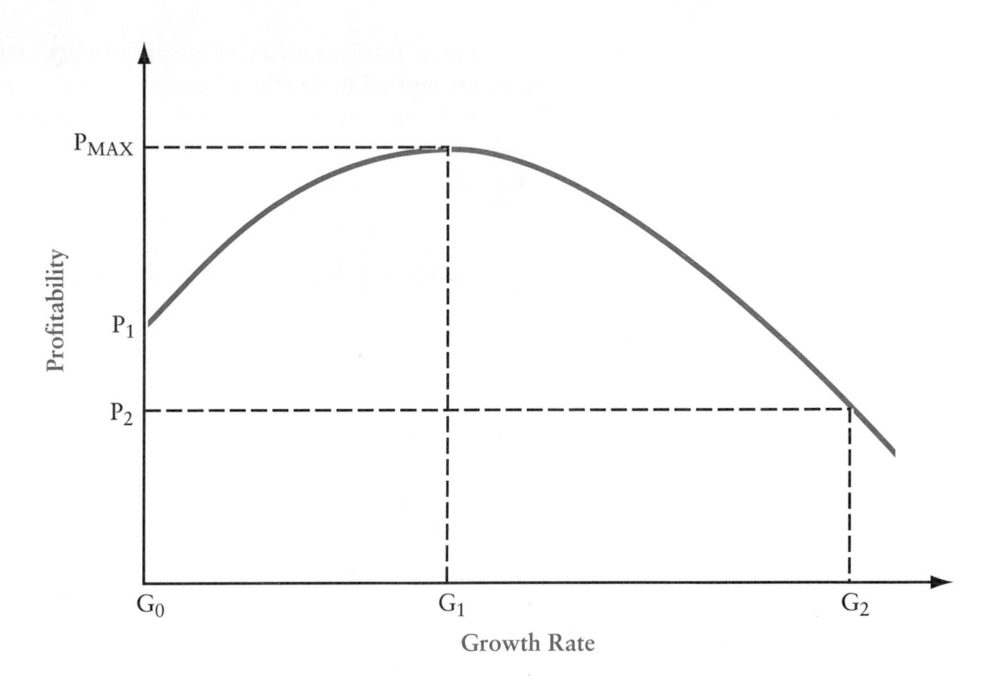

It must be stressed that by no means do all managers behave in the way just outlined. Indeed, many are good stewards who consciously act to increase stockholder wealth. However, given that some managers put their own interests first, the problem facing stockholders is how to govern the corporation so that managerial desires for on-the-job consumption, excessive salaries, or empire-building diversification are held in check. In addition, there is a need for mechanisms that allow stockholders to remove incompetent or ineffective managers. A number of **governance mechanisms** perform this function, including stockholder meetings, the board of directors, stock-based compensation schemes, the takeover market, and leveraged buyouts.

Stockholder Meetings

The constitution of most publicly held corporations specifies that companies should hold stockholder meetings at least once a year. These meetings provide a forum in which stockholders can voice their approval or discontent with management. In theory, at such meetings stockholders can propose resolutions that, if they receive a majority of stockholder votes, can shape management policy, limit the strategies management can pursue, and remove and appoint key personnel. In practice, though, until quite recently stockholder meetings functioned as little more than rubber stamps for management resolutions. Stockholders must finance their own challenges and, in many cases, meet stiff regulations limiting the number of proxy votes they can solicit. Thus proposing resolutions critical of management was normally deemed too expensive and difficult to be worthwhile. Rather, it was understood that stockholders could best show dissatisfaction with a company by selling their shares.

However, the emergence of powerful institutional investors as major stockholders has brought changes. By 1992 the stock holdings of all institutional

investors—pension funds, mutual funds, insurance companies, banks, brokers, and dealers—amounted to nearly 60 percent of all corporate stock.[31] The significance of the growing concentration of stock in institutional hands is that institutions can no longer sell their shares without pushing down the price and taking a loss on the transaction. Jose Arau, principal investment officer for the California Public Employees Retirement System, one of the nation's largest institutional investors, has observed: "In the past you could always vote with your feet, but if you hold a thousand stocks, it's tough to do that."[32]

The lack of room to sell is putting pressure on institutions to show their dissatisfaction with management by voting against certain management proposals or backing proposals that are critical of management. As a result, institutions are banding together to put pressure on management teams that are perceived as being incompetent or pursuing strategies inconsistent with maximizing long-run returns. For example, in 1992 and 1993 institutional fund managers played a major role behind the scenes in pressuring outside directors on corporate boards to remove the following CEOs: Richard Robinson at American Express, John Akers at IBM, Robert Stempel at General Motors, and Ken Olson at Digital.

The Role of the Board

Stockholder interests are looked after within the company by the board of directors. Board members are directly elected by stockholders, and under corporate law the board represents the stockholders' interests in the company. Thus the board can be held legally accountable for the company's actions. Its position at the apex of decision making within the company allows the board to monitor corporate strategy decisions and ensure that they are consistent with stockholder interests. If the board's sense is that corporate strategies are not in the best interest of stockholders, it can apply sanctions such as voting against management nominations to the board of directors or submitting their own nominees. In addition, the board has the legal authority to hire, fire, and compensate corporate employees, including, most importantly, the CEO.[33] In the case of Allegis Corporation, discussed in the Opening Case, one factor that led to the dismissal of CEO Dick Ferris was that his strategies lost the support of the Allegis board.

The typical board comprises a mix of insiders and outsiders. Inside directors are required because they have valuable information about the company's activities. Without such information the board cannot adequately perform its monitoring function. But since insiders are full-time employees of the company, their interests tend to be aligned with those of management. Hence, outside directors are needed to bring objectivity to the monitoring and evaluation processes. Outside directors are not full-time employees of the company. Many of them are full-time professional directors who hold positions on the boards of several companies. The need to maintain a reputation as competent outside directors gives them an incentive to perform their tasks as objectively and effectively as possible.[34]

Critics charge that inside directors may be able to dominate the outsiders on the board. Insiders can use their position within the management hierarchy to exercise control over the content of company-specific information that the board receives. Consequently, they can present information in a way that puts management in a favorable light. In addition, insiders have the advantage of intimate knowledge of the company's operations. Because superior knowledge and control over information are sources of power (see Chapter 12), insiders may be better positioned to influence boardroom decision making than outsiders. The

board may become the captive of insiders and merely rubber-stamp management decisions, instead of guarding stockholder interests. A board dominated by insiders may pursue strategies consistent with the interests of management rather than of stockholders.

Some critics contend that many boards are dominated by the company CEO.[35] To support this view, they point out that both inside and outside directors are often the personal nominees of the CEO. The typical inside director is subordinate to the CEO in the company's hierarchy and therefore unlikely to criticize the boss. Since outside directors are frequently the CEO's nominees as well, they can hardly be expected to evaluate the CEO objectively. Thus the loyalty of the board may be biased toward the CEO and not the stockholders. This problem has prompted management gurus such as Peter Drucker to comment that the one thing all boards have in common is that they do not function.

Nevertheless, there are signs that many corporate boards are moving away from merely rubber-stamping top-management decisions and are beginning to play a much more active governance role. The catalyst has been an increase in the number of lawsuits filed by stockholders against board members. The trend started in 1985, when a Delaware court ruled that the directors of Trans Union Corporation had been too quick to accept a takeover bid. The court held the directors personally liable for the difference between the offer they accepted and the price the company might have fetched in a sale. The directors then agreed to make up the $23.5 million difference. Since that ruling, a number of major lawsuits have been filed by stockholders against board members. These include suits directed against board members at Holly Farms, Northrop Corp., Lincoln Savings & Loan, Lotus Development Corp., and RJR Nabisco.[36]

Spurred on by the threat of legal action, an increasing number of boards have started to assert their independence from company management in general and from corporate CEOs in particular. In recent years boards of directors have engineered the removal or resignation of CEOs at a number of major U.S. corporations including American Express, Digital Equipment, General Motors, and IBM. Another trend of some significance is the increasing tendency for outside directors to be made chairman of the board. By 1997, according to the estimates from the National Association of Corporate Directors, 40 to 50 percent of big companies will name an outside director as chairman, up from less than half of that figure in 1990.[37] Such appointments limit the ability of corporate insiders, and particularly the CEO, to exercise control over the board. It was notable that the removal of Robert Stempel as the CEO of General Motors followed the appointment of an outside director, John Smale, as chairman of the GM board.

Stock-Based Compensation Schemes

To get around the problem of captive boards, stockholders have urged many companies to introduce stock-based compensation schemes for their senior executives. These schemes are designed to align the interests of managers with those of stockholders. In addition to their regular salary, senior executives are given stock options in the firm. Stock options give managers the right to buy the company's shares at a predetermined price, which may often turn out to be less than the market price of the stock. The idea behind stock options is to motivate managers to adopt strategies that increase the share price of the company, for in doing so they will also increase the value of their stock options.

For example, in November 1992 Michael Eisner, the CEO of The Walt Disney Company, exercised stock options that he had been granted some years earlier, when Disney's stock was trading far below its November 1992 market value. His profit from exercising these options was a staggering $197 million. Although critics call such rewards excessive, it should be remembered that under Eisner's leadership Disney's stockholders have reaped substantial benefits. Indeed, had the stock price fallen rather than risen during Eisner's tenure, his stock options would have been worthless. As a counterpoint, consider the case of Paul Lego, CEO of Westinghouse. In 1991 Lego was granted the option to buy 700,000 shares in Westinghouse at $22.28 each. However, by mid 1992 Westinghouse stock was trading at under $17 per share, making his options worthless. Shortly afterward Lego resigned as CEO, following pressure from the board, without being able to exercise any of his stock options.[38]

Studies seem to confirm that stock-based compensation schemes for senior executives—such as stock options—can align management and stockholder interests. For instance, one study found that managers were more likely to consider the effects of their acquisition decisions on stockholder wealth if they themselves were significant shareholders.[39] According to another study, managers who were significant stockholders were less likely to pursue diversification strategies that would maximize the size of the company rather than its profitability.[40] For all their attractions, stock-based compensation schemes have yet to be universally adopted by American companies, although the practice is spreading rapidly. Some critics also argue that the schemes do not always have the desired effect, since stock compensation plans can harm stockholders by diluting their interests and unjustifiably rewarding management for improvements in stock prices. Critics note that stock price increases are often due to an improving economy rather than managerial effort, and they ask why management should be rewarded for such increases. In addition, when stock prices are falling because of factors outside the company's control, such as an economic slump, executives may see the value of their stockholdings decline rapidly. Under such circumstances, stock-based compensation schemes give managers little incentive to align their goals with those of stockholders in general.

The Takeover Constraint and Corporate Raiders

If the board is loyal to management rather than to stockholders or if the company has not adopted stock-based compensation schemes, then, as suggested earlier, management may pursue strategies and take actions inconsistent with maximizing stockholder wealth. Stockholders, however, still have some residual power, for they can always sell their shares. If they start doing so in large numbers, the price of the company's shares will decline. If the share price falls far enough, the company might be worth less on the stock market than the book value of its assets, at which point it may become a takeover target.

The risk of being bought out is known as the **takeover constraint.** The takeover constraint effectively limits the extent to which managers can pursue strategies and take actions that put their own interests above those of stockholders. If they ignore stockholder interests and the company is bought out, senior managers typically lose their independence and probably their jobs as well. So the threat of takeover can constrain management action. The experience of Allegis Corporation, presented in the Opening Case, is one example of this process.

In recent years the threat of takeover has often been enforced by **corporate raiders.** The corporate raider phenomenon emerged in a big way during the late

1970s and early 1980s. Corporate raiders are individuals or institutions that buy up large blocks of shares in companies that they think are pursuing strategies inconsistent with maximizing stockholder wealth. They argue that if these companies pursued different strategies, they could create more wealth for stockholders. Raiders buy stock in a company either to take over the business and run it more efficiently or to precipitate a change in the top management, replacing the existing team with one more likely to maximize stockholder welfare.

Raiders, of course, are motivated not by altruism but by gain. If they succeed in their takeover bid, they can institute strategies that create value for stockholders—including themselves. Even if a takeover bid fails, raiders can still earn millions, for their stockholdings will typically be bought out by the defending company for a hefty premium. Called **greenmail**, this source of gain has stirred much controversy and debate about its benefits.

Poison Pills and Golden Parachutes

One response by management to the threat posed by takeovers has been to create so-called **poison pills**. The purpose of a poison pill is to make it difficult for a raider to acquire a company. The poison pill devised by Household International in 1985 is typical. The Household board of directors unilaterally changed the company's constitution. In response to any takeover bid involving a premium over market value of less than $6 billion, stockholders could not sell their stock without the prior permission of the board. At that time Household had a market value of less than $2 billion, so the constitution change effectively gave the board the ability to reject any takeover attempt that offered less than $8 billion for Household. Because no raiders in their right mind would offer $8 billion for a company valued at less than $2 billion, the tactic essentially nullified the takeover constraint with regard to Household.

The right of companies to create poison pills has been challenged on several occasions in court by stockholders who object to the unilateral restrictions imposed by management on their right to sell stock to a prospective acquirer. To date the courts have tended to side with management (the right of Household's board to issue restrictions was upheld by a Delaware court). However, there are many examples of stockholders at stockholder meetings introducing resolutions that effectively limit the ability of a company to devise a poison-pill defense, so it remains to be seen just how successful and widespread this tactic is going to be.

Another response to the threat posed by takeovers has been the increasing use of *golden parachute contracts*. Golden parachutes are severance contracts that handsomely compensate top-level managers for the loss of their jobs in the event of a takeover. These contracts came into being because of fears that takeover threats were forcing managers to focus on maximizing short-term earnings in an attempt to boost the company's current stock price, thereby reducing the risk of takeover at the expense of long-run investments in R&D and new capital equipment. Managers also complained that the threat of takeover diminished their willingness to fund risky but potentially profitable investments. Advocates of golden parachute contracts argue that by reducing managers' concerns about losing their jobs, the contracts encourage managers to focus on long-run investments and take necessary risks. In addition, because they lessen worry about job loss, golden parachute contracts make it more likely that top management will review takeover proposals objectively, taking stockholder interests into account when deciding how to respond.

For these reasons, golden parachute contracts, when used properly, can be beneficial. On the other hand, some stockholders see golden parachutes as little more than an "insurance against incompetence" or as a "reward for failure," and they argue that managers should not be rewarded for losing their job.[41] One way of ensuring that this does not occur while still preserving the beneficial aspects of golden parachute contracts may be to link the payment of a golden parachute to the premium earned by stockholders in the event of a takeover bid.

Leveraged Buyouts

A dramatic feature of the 1980s was the rapid growth in the number of leveraged buyouts (LBOs). The LBO is a special kind of takeover. Whereas in a typical takeover a raider buys enough stock to gain control of a company, in an LBO a company's own executives are often (but not always) among the buyers. The management group undertaking an LBO typically raises cash by issuing bonds and then uses that cash to buy the company's stock. Thus LBOs involve a swap of equity for debt. In effect, the company replaces its stockholders with creditors (bondholders), transforming the corporation from a public into a private entity. However, often the same institutions that were major stockholders before an LBO are major bondholders afterward. The difference is that as stockholders they were not guaranteed a regular dividend payment from the company; as bondholders they do have such a guarantee.

During the 1980s the total number and value of LBOs undertaken in the United States increased dramatically. The total value of the 76 LBOs undertaken in 1979 was $1.4 billion (in 1988 dollars). In comparison, the total value of the 214 LBOs undertaken in 1988 exceeded $77 billion—nearly one-third of the value of all mergers and acquisitions in the United States.[42] Since then, however, the LBO business in the United States has slowed to a crawl, with only a handful of transactions being executed each year. Its demise, though, may be only temporary. Takeovers tend to go in cycles, and it is quite possible that the next time the United States undergoes a merger boom there will also be a boom in LBOs.

Supporters of the LBO technique, most notably Michael Jensen, claim that the LBO should be viewed as yet another governance mechanism that keeps management discretion in check.[43] Jensen's theory is that LBOs solve many of the problems created by imperfect corporate governance mechanisms. According to Jensen, a major weakness and source of waste in the public corporation is the conflict between stockholders and managers over the payout of free cash flow. He defines **free cash flow** as cash flow in excess of that required to fund all investment projects with positive net present values when discounted at the relevant cost of capital. Since free cash flow is by definition cash that cannot be profitably reinvested within the company, Jensen argues that it should be distributed to stockholders, but he notes that managers resist such distributions of surplus cash. Instead, for reasons discussed earlier, they tend to invest such cash in growth-maximizing or empire-building strategies.

Jensen sees LBOs as a solution to this problem. Although management does not have to pay out dividends to stockholders, it must make regular debt payments to bondholders or face bankruptcy. Thus, according to Jensen, the debt used to finance an LBO helps limit the waste of free cash flow by compelling managers to pay out excess cash to service debt rather than spending it on empire-building projects with low or negative returns, excessive staff, indulgent perquisites, and other organizational inefficiencies. Furthermore, Jensen sees

debt as a way of motivating managers to seek greater efficiencies; high debt payments can force managers to slash unsound investment programs, reduce overhead, and dispose of assets that are more valuable outside the company. The proceeds generated by these restructurings can then be used to reduce debt to more sustainable levels, creating a leaner, more efficient, and more competitive organization.

Not all commentators are as enthusiastic about the potential of LBOs as Jensen. The Secretary of Labor in the Clinton administration, Robert Reich, who had taught political economy and management at Harvard's John F. Kennedy School of Government, is one of the most vocal critics of LBOs.[44] Reich sees two main problems with LBOs. First, he argues that the necessity of paying back large loans forces management to focus on the short term and cut back on long-term investments, particularly in R&D and new capital spending. The net effect is likely to be a decline in the competitiveness of LBOs. Second, Reich believes that the debt taken on to finance an LBO significantly increases the risk of bankruptcy. The strong economy of the 1980s may have obscured this fact. Reich cites a study by the Brookings Institution, which examined the effects of a recession similar in severity to the one that rocked the United States in 1974 and 1975. The Brookings computer simulation revealed that, given the levels of corporate debt prevailing in the late 1980s, one in ten U.S. companies would succumb to bankruptcy.

2.8 STRATEGY AND ETHICS

Many strategic questions have an ethical dimension.[45] The reason for this is simple. Any action taken by a company inevitably affects the welfare of its stakeholders: employees, suppliers, customers, stockholders, the local communities in which it does business, and the general public. While a proposed strategy may enhance the welfare of some stakeholder groups, it may harm others. For example, faced with falling demand and excess capacity, a steel producer may decide to close down a steelmaking facility that is the major source of employment in a small town. Although this action might be consistent with maximizing stockholder wealth, it could also result in thousands of people losing employment and the death of a small town. Is such a decision ethical? Is it the right thing to do, considering the likely impact on employees and the community in which they live? Managers must balance these competing benefits and costs. They must decide whether to proceed with the proposed strategy in the light of their assessment not only of its economic benefits, but also of its ethical implications, given the potentially adverse effect on some stakeholder groups.

The Purpose of Business Ethics

The purpose of business ethics, as a discipline, is not so much to teach the difference between right and wrong, as to give people the tools for dealing with moral complexity, so that they can identify and think through the moral implications of strategic decisions.[46] Most of us already have a good sense of what is right and wrong. We already know that it is wrong to lie, cheat, and steal. We know that it is wrong to take actions that put the lives of others at risk. Such moral values are instilled into us at an early age through formal and informal socialization.

The problem, however, is that although most managers rigorously adhere to such moral principles in their private life, some fail to apply them in their professional life, occasionally with disastrous consequences.

The history of Manville Corporation illustrates such failure. (Strategy in Action 2.3 offers another example, that of Jack-in-the-Box). Two decades ago Manville (then Johns Manville) was solid enough to be included among the giants of American industry. By 1989 80 percent of the equity of Manville was owned by a trust representing people who had sued the company for liability in connection with one of its principal former products, asbestos. More than forty years ago information began to reach the medical department of Johns Manville—and through them the company's managers—suggesting that inhalation of asbestos particles was a major cause of asbestosis, a fatal lung disease. Manville's managers suppressed the research. Moreover, as a matter of company policy, they apparently decided to conceal the information from affected employees. The company's medical staff collaborated in the cover-up. Somehow managers at Manville had persuaded themselves that this was the right course of action rather than taking steps to improve working conditions and finding safer ways to handle asbestos. They calculated that the cost of improving working conditions was greater than the cost of health insurance to cover those who became ill, and so the best "economic" decision was to conceal information from employees.[47]

The key to understanding the Manville story is the realization that the men and women at Manville who participated in the coverup were not amoral monsters, but just ordinary people, like you and me. Most of them would probably never dream of breaking the law or of physically harming anyone. And yet they consciously made a decision that led directly to great human suffering and death. How could this happen? What seemed to have occurred was that the decision to suppress information was considered on purely economic grounds. Its moral dimension was ignored. Somehow the managers involved at Manville were able to convince themselves that they were engaged in making a rational business decision which should be subjected to an economic cost-benefit analysis. Ethical considerations never entered into this calculation. Such behavior is possible only in an environment where business decisions are viewed as having no ethical component. But as the Manville example shows, business decisions *do* have an ethical component.

The task of business ethics, therefore, is to make two central points (1) that business decisions do have an ethical component and (2) that managers must weigh the ethical implications of strategic decisions before choosing a course of action. Had managers at Manville been trained to think through the ethical implications of their decision, it is unlikely that they would have chosen the same course of action.

Shaping the Ethical Climate of an Organization

To foster awareness that strategic decisions have an ethical dimension, a company must establish a climate that emphasizes the importance of ethics. This requires at least three steps. First, top managers have to use their leadership position to incorporate an ethical dimension into the values that they stress. At Hewlett-Packard, for example, Bill Hewlett and David Packard, the company's founders, propagated a set of values known as The HP Way. These values, which shape the way business is conducted both within and by the corporation, have an important ethical component. Among other things, they stress the need for

STRATEGY IN ACTION 2.3

The Jack-in-the-Box Poisonings: A Case of Questionable Ethics?

In early January 1993 hospitals in the Seattle area began to notice a dramatic rise in the number of cases of *E. coli* bacterial infections. The *E. coli* bacteria are found in undercooked meat. The symptoms of infection include severe fever, diarrhea, and vomiting. In the case of young people, the infection can be life threatening. Most of the victims of this outbreak were young, and many were in very serious condition. Epidemiologists quickly found a common element in all but a handful of cases: most of the victims had eaten hamburgers at local Jack-in-the-Box restaurants shortly before falling ill.

Foodmaker, the parent company of Jack-in-the-Box, was quick to issue a statement denying that the meat served in its restaurants was undercooked. At the same time it blamed the outbreak on a batch of bad meat that had been delivered from a supplier. The supplier responded by placing blame on Jack-in-the-Box. While Foodmaker and its supplier traded insults, the number infected had risen to 200 and several children were seriously ill. Then Washington State health inspectors revealed that local Jack-in-the-Box restaurants were cooking meat at 140 degrees Fahrenheit, 15 degrees below the 155-degree Washington State standard that had been in force since March 1992. Foodmaker responded by claiming that it had never received notification of the increase in Washington State standards to 155 degrees. However, when Health Department officials came up with a copy of the notification that had been sent to local Jack-in-the-Box restaurants, Foodmaker changed its position. According to Robert Nugent, president of Jack-in-the-Box, the company had received the notification but the vice president whose responsibility it was to notify local area restaurants had not done so. Jack-in-the-Box indicated that it would take disciplinary action against the vice president, whom they refused to name.

Meanwhile, the number of children infected had soared to 450, one had died, several were in a coma, and a number of others were in critical condition. At this stage Jack-in-the-Box offered to pay the hospital costs for those infected. But there was a catch: in return for paying medical costs, the company's lawyers asked the parents of the infected children to sign forms waiving their rights to subsequently file a lawsuit against Jack-in-the-Box. This request was greeted with outrage, and Jack-in-the-Box once more had to shift its position. This time the company agreed to pay full hospital costs without requiring any waivers of the right to file lawsuits.

By mid February 1993 the worst of the outbreak was over. However, for Foodmaker the impact was only just becoming apparent. Nationwide sales at Jack-in-the-Box restaurants had plunged 35 percent in the first two weeks of February, the company's stock price had lost 30 percent of its value, and the company had announced that it had put on hold plans to open up eighty-five new Jack-in-the-Box restaurants in 1993. What seems to have hurt Jack-in-the-Box most was not the outbreak itself, but the company's repeated attempts to shift responsibility for the outbreak to others, and its cynical attempt to link the offer of financial help to victims with lawsuit waivers. As a result, Jack-in-the-Box came out of the crisis with its reputation tarnished and its sales slumping—in contrast to Johnson & Johnson, which, because of its very different conduct, came out of the Tylenol crisis with its reputation for ethical behavior enhanced.[48]

confidence in and respect for people, open communication, and concern for the individual employee. Had they been operational at Manville, these values would have helped managers there avoid their catastrophic mistake.

Second, ethical values must be incorporated into the company's mission statement. As noted earlier, Johnson & Johnson's credo, presented in Figure 2.5, helped the company respond to the Tylenol crisis in an ethical manner. Third, ethical values must be acted on. Top managers have to implement hiring, firing,

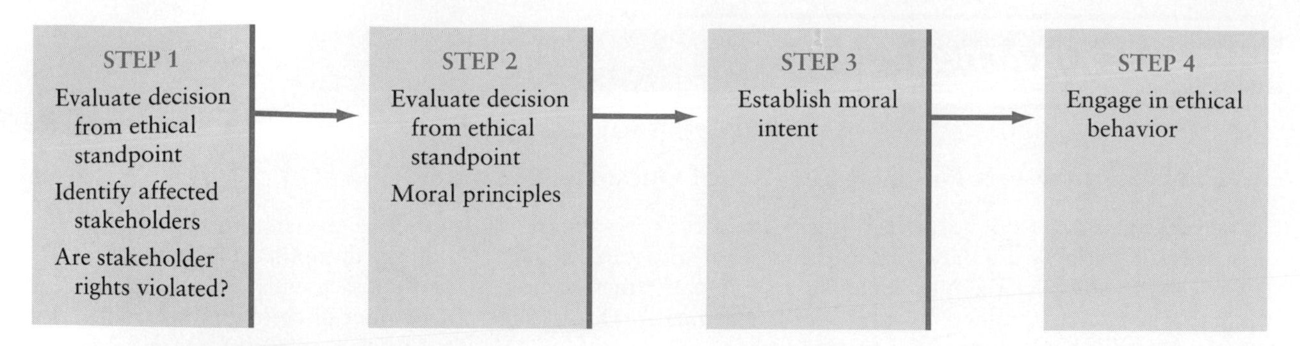

Figure 2.8
A Model of Ethical Decision Making

and incentive systems that explicitly recognize the importance of adhering to ethical values in strategic decision making. At Hewlett-Packard, for example, it has been said that although it is difficult to lose your job (because of the concern for individual employees), nothing gets you fired more quickly than violating the ethical norms of the company as articulated in The HP Way.[49]

Thinking Through Ethical Problems

Besides establishing the right kind of ethical climate in an organization, managers must be able to think through the ethical implications of strategic decisions in a systematic way. A number of different frameworks have been suggested as aids to the decision-making process. The four-step model shown in Figure 2.8 is a compilation of the various approaches recommended by several authorities on this subject.[50]

In step 1—evaluating a proposed strategic decision from an ethical standpoint—managers must identify which stakeholders the decision would affect and in what ways. Most importantly, they need to determine if the proposed decision would violate the rights of any stakeholders. The term *rights* refers to the fundamental entitlements of a stakeholder. For example, one might argue that the right to information about health risks in the workplace is a fundamental entitlement of employees. It is also an entitlement that Manville ignored.

Step 2 involves judging the ethics of the proposed strategic decision, given the information gained in step 1. This judgment should be guided by various moral principles that should not be violated. The principles might be those articulated in a corporate mission statement or other company documents (such as Hewlett-Packard's The HP Way). In addition, there are certain moral principles that we have adopted as members of society—for instance, the prohibition on stealing—and these should not be violated. The judgment at this stage will also be guided by the decision rule that is chosen to assess the proposed strategic decision. Although long-run profit maximization is rightly the decision rule that most companies stress, this decision rule should be applied subject to the constraint that no moral principles are violated.

Step 3, establishing moral intent, means that the company must resolve to place moral concerns ahead of other concerns in cases where either the rights of stakeholders or key moral principles have been violated. At this stage input from top management might be particularly valuable. Without the proactive encouragement of top managers, middle-level managers might tend to place the narrow economic interests of the company before the interests of stakeholders. They might do so in the often erroneous belief that top managers favor such an approach.

Step 4 requires the company to engage in ethical behavior. Clearly, Johnson & Johnson fulfilled this requirement during the Tylenol poisoning scare by pulling all of its product off retail store shelves at great cost to the company.

Corporate Social Responsibility

Corporate social responsibility is the sense of obligation on the part of companies to build certain social criteria into their strategic decision making. The concept implies that when companies evaluate decisions from an ethical perspective, there should be a presumption in favor of adopting courses of action that enhance the welfare of society at large. The goals selected might be quite specific: to enhance the welfare of communities in which a company is based, improve the environment, or empower employees to give them a sense of self worth.

In its purest form, social responsibility can be supported for its own sake simply because it is the right way for a company to behave. Less pure but perhaps more practical are the arguments that socially responsible behavior is in a company's self-interest. Economic actions have social consequences affecting a company's outside claimants. Therefore, to retain the support of these claimants, it must take those social consequences into account when formulating strategies. Otherwise it may generate ill will and opposition. For example, if a community perceives a company as having an adverse impact on the local environment, it may block the company's attempts to build new facilities in the area.

A prime example of a company that is committed to being socially responsible is the British retailer, Body Shop International, whose CEO, Anita Roddick, has become an energetic spokesperson for the importance of social responsibility. Body Shop competes in the international cosmetics and toiletries market but offers unique products based on natural ingredients. None of its products are tested on animals, contain artificial ingredients or are elaborately packaged. The products appeal to consumers who are concerned about animal rights and the environment. Body Shop purchases many of the ingredients for its products from Third World producers, and pays them well. It also plows money back into the communities where its suppliers are based to support a variety of health and educational projects. Far from hurting the company, this commitment to social responsibility has helped propel it from a single store in 1976 to a global enterprise with $1.5 billion in revenues in 1992. According to Roddick:

> You can run a business differently from the way most businesses are run, you can share your prosperity with employees, and empower them without being in fear of them. You can rewrite the book in terms of how a company interacts with the community, on third world trade, global responsibility, and the role of educating customers and shareholders, and you can do all this and still play the game according to the City (the British version of Wall Street), still raise money, delight the Institutions and give shareholders a wondrous return on their investment.[51]

Roddick's point, is that being socially responsible does not harm business. Indeed, judging from Body Shop's success, exactly the opposite may often be the case. Still, there are those who argue that a company has no business pursuing social goals. Nobel laureate Milton Friedman, for one, insists that social responsibility considerations should not enter into the corporate strategic decision process:

> What does it mean to say that the corporate executive has a social responsibility in his capacity as a businessman? If this statement is not pure rhetoric, it must mean that he is to act in some way that is not in the interests of his employers. For example . . . that he is to make expenditures on reducing pollution beyond the amount that is in the best interests of the corporation or that is required by law in order to contribute to the social objective of improving the environment. . . . Insofar as his actions in accord with his social responsibility reduce returns to stockholders, he is spending their money. Insofar as his actions raise the price to customers, he is spending the customers' money. Insofar as the actions lower the wages of some employees, he is spending their money.[52]

Friedman's position is that a business has only one kind of responsibility: to use its resources for activities that increase its profits, so long as it stays within the rules of the game, which is to say, so long as it engages in open and free competition without deception or fraud.

On the other hand, Edward H. Bowman of the University of Pennsylvania's Wharton School argues that social responsibility is actually a sound investment strategy —a view consistent with the experience of The Body Shop.[53] He maintains that a company's social behavior affects the price of its stock; thus socially responsible policy can also benefit a company's important inside claimants, the stockholders. According to Bowman, many investors see companies that are not socially responsible as riskier investments. Moreover, many institutional investors, such as churches, universities, cities, states, and mutual funds, pay attention to corporate social behavior and thus influence the market for a company's stock.

Evidence can certainly be found in favor of Bowman's arguments. For example, the withdrawal of American assets from South Africa by companies such as IBM and General Motors in 1986 can at least in part be attributed to a desire to create a favorable impression with investors. At that time, for social or political reasons, many investors were selling any stock they held in companies that maintained a substantial presence in South Africa. Similarly, Union Carbide saw its market value plunge more than 37 percent in 1984, in the aftermath of the gas leak at its Bhopal plant in India (which killed 2000 people and left 150,000 seriously injured) and subsequent revelations concerning poor safety procedures at many Union Carbide plants. For Union Carbide, the consequence was a takeover bid from GAF Corporation (which ultimately failed), extended litigation, and a negative image problem.

2.9 SUMMARY OF CHAPTER

The primary purpose of this chapter is to identify various factors that constitute the organizational context within which strategies are formulated. Normally, these factors are explicitly recognized through the corporate mission statement. The mission statement thus sets the boundaries within which strategies must be contained. Specifically, the following points are made:

1. The mission statement is the starting point of strategic management. It sets the context within which strategies are formulated.
2. The mission statement contains three broad elements: a definition of the company's business, a statement of the major goals of the corporation (including vision), and a statement of corporate philosophy.

3. For a single-business company, defining the business involves focusing on consumer groups to be served, consumer needs to be satisfied, and the technologies by which those needs can be satisfied. This amounts to a consumer-oriented business definition.
4. For a diversified company, defining the business involves focusing on the value that the corporate level adds to the constituent businesses of the company.
5. A company's major corporate goal should reflect concern for the welfare of the company's owners—its stockholders. Maximizing long-run profits is the major goal consistent with maximizing stockholder wealth.
6. To avoid adverse short-run consequences of an overzealous focus on profitability, a company needs to adopt a number of secondary goals that balance short-run and long-run considerations.
7. A company's corporate philosophy makes clear how the company intends to do business. A statement of this philosophy reflects the company's basic values, aspirations, beliefs, and philosophical priorities.
8. Every company has its stakeholders—individuals who have some claim on the organization. They can be divided into inside and outside claimants. The company needs to recognize their claims in its mission statement, for if it does not, it may lose their support.
9. Stockholders are among a company's most important internal claimants. If stockholder wealth is not maximized, the company runs the risk of becoming a takeover target. Companies sometimes fall into this trap because of managerial desires for on-the-job consumption, empire-building diversification strategies, and excessive pay increases.
10. A number of governance mechanisms serve to limit the ability of managers to pursue strategies and take actions that are at variance with maximizing stockholder wealth. These include stockholder meetings, the board of directors, stock-based compensation schemes, and the threat of a takeover.
11. Many strategic decisions have an ethical dimension. Any action by a company inevitably has an impact on the welfare of its stakeholders.
12. The purpose of business ethics is not so much to teach the difference between right and wrong, but to give people the tools for dealing with moral complexity—for identifying and thinking through the moral implications of strategic decisions.

Discussion Questions

1. Why is it important for a company to take a consumer-oriented view of its businesses? What are the possible shortcomings of such a view?
2. What are the strategic implications of a focus on short-run returns? Discuss these implications in terms of the impact on product innovation, marketing expenditure, manufacturing, and purchasing decisions.
3. Are corporate raiders a positive or negative influence on the U.S. economy? How can companies reduce the risk of a takeover?
4. "Companies should always behave in an ethical manner, whatever the economic cost." Discuss this statement.

Article File 2

Find an example of a company that ran into trouble because it failed to take into account the rights of one of its stakeholder groups when making an important strategic decision.

Strategic Management Project: Module 2

This module deals with the relationships your company has with its major stakeholder groups. With the information you have at your disposal, perform the tasks and answer the questions listed:

1. Find out whether your company has a formal mission statement. Does this statement define the business, identify major goals, and articulate the corporate philosophy?
2. If your company lacks a mission statement, what do you think its mission statement should be like?
3. If your company has a mission statement, do you see it as appropriate, given the material discussed in this chapter?
4. Identify the main stakeholder groups in your company. What claims do they place on the company? How is the company trying to satisfy those claims?
5. Evaluate the performance of the CEO of your company from the perspective of (a) stockholders, (b) employees, (c) customers, and (d) suppliers. What does this evaluation tell you about the ability of the CEO and the priorities that he or she is committed to?
6. Try to establish whether the governance mechanisms that operate in your company do a good job of aligning the interests of top managers with those of stockholders.
7. Pick a major strategic decision made by your company in recent years and try to think through the ethical implications of that decision. In the light of your review, do you think that the company acted correctly?

Endnotes

1. Kenneth Labich, "How Dick Ferris Blew It," *Fortune*, July 6, 1987, pp. 42–46. Jodi Klein, "The Lack of Allegiance at Allegis," *Business & Society Review* (Spring 1988), 30–33. James Ellis, "The Unraveling of an Idea," *Business Week*, June 22, 1987, pp. 42–43.
2. Derek F. Abell, *Defining the Business: The Starting Point of Strategic Planning* (Englewood Cliffs, N.J.: Prentice-Hall, 1980). K. Andrews, *The Concept of Corporate Strategy* (Homewood, Ill.: Dow Jones Irwin, 1971). John A. Pearce, "The Company Mission as a Strategic Tool," *Sloan Management Review* (Spring 1982), 15–24.
3. Source: Weyerhaeuser Co., Annual Report,.
4. These three questions were first proposed by P. F. Rucker. See P. F. Drucker, *Management—Tasks, Responsibilities, Practices* (New York: Harper & Row, 1974), pp. 74–94.
5. Abell, *Defining the Business*, p. 17.
6. Theodore Levitt, "Marketing Myopia," *Harvard Business Review* (July–August 1960), 45–56.
7. F. J. Weston and S. K. Mansinghka, "Tests of the Efficiency Performance of Conglomerate Firms," *Journal of Finance*, 26 (1971), 919–935.
8. For details see Jeffrey R. Williams, Betty Paez, and Leonard Sanders, "Conglomerates Revisited," *Strategic Management Journal*, 9 (1988), 403–414.

9. Philip Morris Company, Annual Report and Accounts, 1992.
10. Robert H. Hayes and William J. Abernathy, "Managing Our Way to Economic Decline," *Harvard Business Review* (July–August 1980), 67–77.
11. Lester C. Thurow, *The Zero Sum Solution* (New York: Simon and Schuster, 1985), 69–89.
12. Michael L. Dertouzos, Richard K. Lester, and Robert M. Solow, *Made in America* (Cambridge, Mass.: MIT Press.
13. Sources: "Flat Out in Japan," *The Economist*, February 1, 1992, pp. 79–80. H. Nomura, "IBM, Apple Fight LCD Screen Tariffs: US Decision Forcing Assembly Offshore," *Nikkei Weekly*, October 26, 1992. A. Tanzer, "The New Improved Color Computer," *Forbes*, July 23, 1990, pp. 276–280.
14. Thomas J. Peters and Robert H. Waterman, *In Search of Excellence* (New York: Harper & Row, 1982).
15. Excerpt from Hewlett-Packard's Mission Statement. Courtesy of Hewlett-Packard Company.
16. M. D. Richards, *Setting Strategic Goals and Objectives* (St. Paul, Minn.: West, 1986).
17. For details see "Johnson & Johnson (A)," *Harvard Business School Case* #384–053, Harvard Business School.
18. Pearce, "The Company Mission," pp. 15–24.
19. I. C. Macmillan and P. E. Jones, *Strategy Formulation: Power and Politics* (St. Paul, Minn.: West, 1986).
20. M. C. Jensen and W. H. Meckling, "Theory of the Firm: Managerial Behavior, Agency Costs and Ownership Structure," *Journal of Financial Economics*, 3 (1976), 305–360.
21. For example, see R. Marris, *The Economic Theory of Managerial Capitalism* (London: Macmillan, 1964), and J. K. Galbraith, *The New Industrial State* (Boston: Houghton Mifflin, 1970).
22. E. F. Fama, "Agency Problems and the Theory of the Firm," *Journal of Political Economy*, 88 (1980), 375–390.
23. Bryan Burrough and John Helyar, *Barbarians at the Gate* (New York: Harper & Row, 1990).
24. John A. Byrne and Chuck Hawkins, "Executive Pay: The Party Ain't Over Yet," *Business Week*, April 26, 1993, pp. 56–64.
25. George Will, "CEOs Aren't Paid for Performance," *Seattle Times*, September 1, 1991, p. 1.
26. For studies that look at the determinants of CEO pay, see M. C. Jensen and K. J. Murphy, "Performance Pay and Top Management Incentives," *Journal of Political Economy*, 98 (1990), 225–264; and Charles W. L. Hill and Phillip Phan, "CEO Tenure as a Determinant of CEO Pay," *Academy of Management Journal*, 34 (1991), 707–717.
27. Byrne and Hawkins, "Executive Pay," pp. 56–64.
28. See Jensen and Murphy, "Performance Pay," pp. 225–254, and Hill and Phan, "CEO Tenure," pp. 707–717.
29. Carl Icahn, "What Ails Corporate America—And What Should Be Done?" *Business Week*, October 27, 1986, p. 101.
30. E. T. Penrose, *The Theory of the Growth of the Firm* (London: Macmillan, 1958).
31. "America's Investment Famine," *Economist*, June 27, 1992, pp. 89–90.
32. Quoted in Christopher Power and Vick Cahan, "Shareholders Aren't Just Rolling Over Anymore," *Business Week*, April 27, 1987, pp. 32–33.
33. O. E. Williamson, *The Economic Institutions of Capitalism* (New York: Free Press, 1985).
34. E. F. Fama, "Agency Problems and the Theory of the Firm," *Journal of Political Economy*, 88, (1980, 375–390.
35. M. L. Mace, *Directors: Myth and Reality* (Cambridge, Mass.: Harvard University Press, 1971. S. C. Vance, *Corporate Leadership: Boards of Directors and Strategy* (New York: McGraw Hill, 1983).
36. Michele Galen, "A Seat on the Board Is Getting Hotter," *Business Week*, July 3, 1989, pp. 72–73.
37. Gilbert Fuchsberg, "Chief Executives See Their Power Shrink," *Wall Street Journal*, March 15, 1993, p. B1, B3.
38. John Byrne, "If CEO Pay Makes You Sick, Don't Look at Stock Options," *Business Week*, April 13, 1992, pp. 34–35.
39. W. G. Lewellen, C. Eoderer, and A. Rosenfeld, "Merger Decisions and Executive Stock Ownership in Acquiring Firms," *Journal of Accounting and Economics*, 7 (1985), 209–231.
40. C. W. L. Hill and S. A. Snell, "External Control, Corporate Strategy, and Firm Performance," *Strategic Management Journal*, 9 (1988), pp. 577–590.
41. H. Singh and F. Harianto, "Management-Board Relationships, Takeover Risk, and the Adoption of Golden Parachutes," *Academy of Management Journal*, 32 (1989), pp. 7–24.
42. "Whose Firm? Whose Money?" *Economist*, May 5, 1990, Survey: Punters or Proprietors? pp. 7–8.
43. See Michael C. Jensen, "Agency Costs of Free Cash Flow, Corporate Finance, and Takeovers," *American Economic Review* (1986), 323–329; and Michael C. Jensen, "The Eclipse of the Public Corporation," *Harvard Business Review* (September–October 1989), Vol. 76, pp. 61–74.
44. Robert B. Reich, "Leveraged Buyouts: America Pays the Price," *New York Times Magazine*, January 29, 1989, pp. 32–40.
45. R. Edward Freeman and Daniel Gilbert. *Corporate Strategy and the Search for Ethics* (Englewood Cliffs, N.J.: Prentice-Hall, 1988).
46. Robert C. Solomon. *Ethics and Excellence* (Oxford University Press, 1992).
47. Saul W. Gellerman, "Why Good Managers Make Bad Ethical Choices," *Ethics in Practice: Managing the Moral Corporation*, ed. Kenneth R. Andrews (Harvard Business School Press, 1989).
48. Sources: Benjamin Holden. "Foodmaker Delays Expansion Plans in Wake of Food-Poisoning Outbreak," *Wall Street Journal*, February 16, 1993, p. B10. Benjamin Holden. "Foodmaker, Struggling After Poisonings, Breaks with Its Public Relations Firm," *Wall Street Journal*, February 12, 1993, p. A4.
49. Kirk O. Hanson and Manuel Velasquez, "Hewlett-Packard Company: Managing Ethics and Values," in *Corporate Ethics: A Prime Business Asset*. The Business Roundtable, February 1988.
50. For example, see R. Edward Freeman and Daniel Gilbert, *Corporate Strategy and the Search for Ethics* (Englewood Cliffs, N.J.: Prentice-Hall, 1988). Thomas Jones, "Ethical Decision Making by Individuals in Organizations," *Academy of Management Review*, 16 (1991), 366–395. J. R. Rest, *Moral Development: Advances in Research and Theory* (New York: Praeger, 1986).
51.
52. Milton Friedman, "A Friedman Doctrine: The Social Responsibility of Business Is to Increase Its Profits," *New York Times Magazine*, September 13, 1970, p. 33.
53. Edward D. Bowman. "Corporate Social Responsibility and the Investor," *Journal of Contemporary Business* (Winter 1973), 49–58.

II THE NATURE OF COMPETITIVE ADVANTAGE

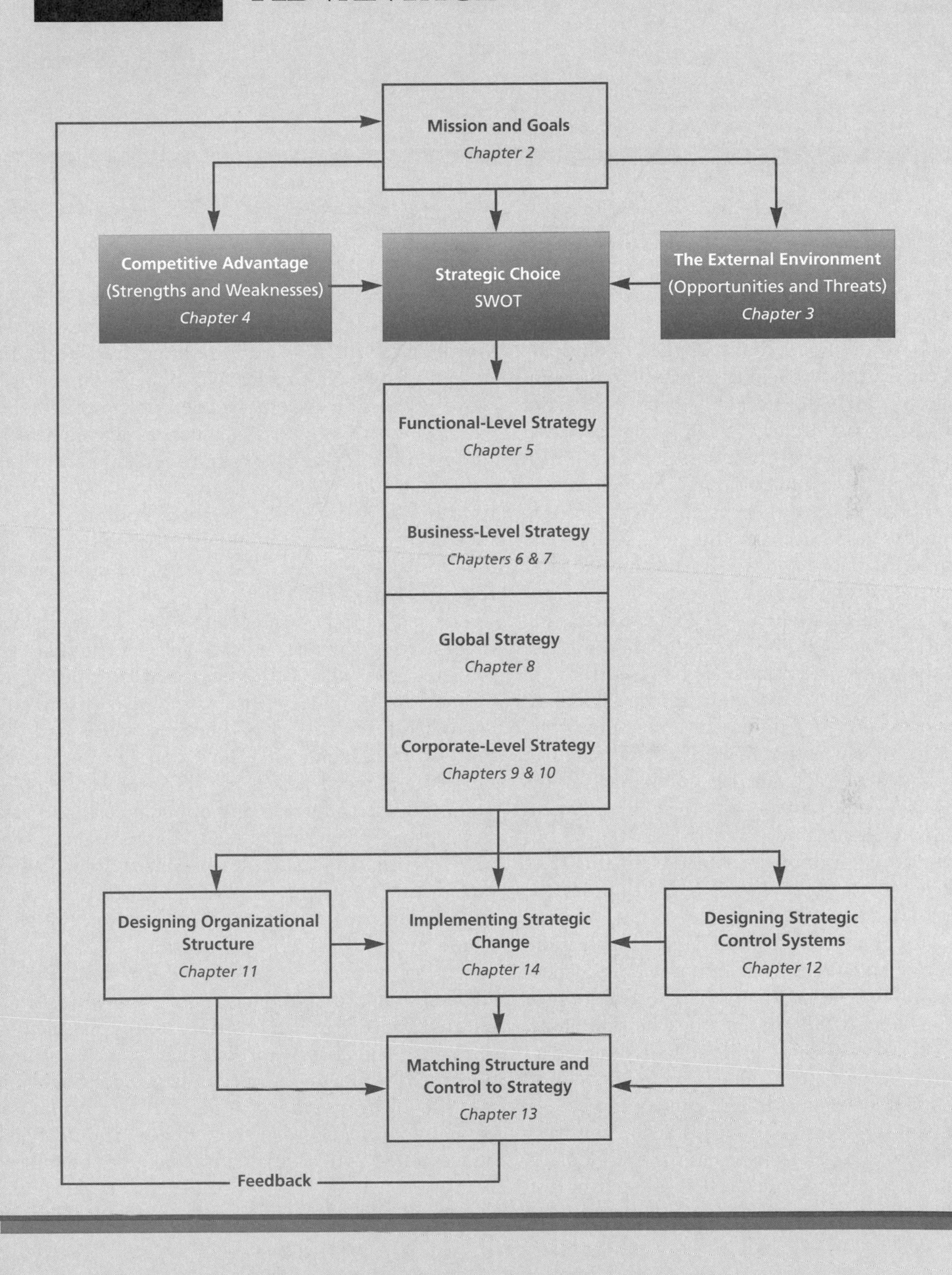

3 The External Environment

3.1 OPENING CASE: WANG LABORATORIES

Founded in 1951 by a Chinese immigrant, An Wang, in the 1970s Wang Laboratories, Inc. was one of a small group of companies that managed to outsmart IBM and carve a profitable niche for itself in the computer industry. In Wang's case the niche was word processing. Back in the early 1970s Wang developed its own proprietary word-processing software, which it loaded on its own minicomputers, which ran on Wang's proprietary operating system. Word processing terminals were connected to these minicomputers. The terminals replaced typewriters and moved letter and document writing into a new era.

A story is told that when An Wang was touring the United Nations building a secretarial pool broke out into spontaneous applause as he passed. "I am the secretaries' friend" he explained to his companion, "I have freed them from the tyranny of the typewriter." And so it was that Wang Labs became one of the high-technology miracle companies of the 1970s. By 1988 the company employed 31,500 people worldwide, generated revenues of over $3 billion, made $92.7 million in after-tax profits, and was ranked 143 on the *Fortune* 500 list of industrial companies. By August 1992, however, the company had filed for Chapter 11 bankruptcy protection. Revenues had fallen to $1.9 billion and employment to under 8,000. The company had lost a total of $1.9 billion since 1988 and its stock market value, which once stood at $5.6 billion, had slumped to $70 million. Wang's stock, which traded at $42.50 in 1982, was now trading at 37.5 cents a share.

The reason for Wang's fall was that the company lost touch with changes going on in the marketplace. Just as it outflanked IBM in the 1970s, so it in turn was outflanked by a host of personal computer and software companies in the mid 1980s. As personal computers gained in popularity, and as inexpensive word-processing software became available, the demand for Wang's expensive minicomputer-based word-processing system declined precipitously. For example, one long-time Wang user explained how he scrapped his $400,000 Wang minicomputer, which had cost $100,000 per year to service, and replaced it with a network of 25 personal computers for a total cost of under $100,000. Faced with this kind of low-cost competition, Wang's market collapsed in the latter half of the 1980s.

The sad aspect of the Wang story, however, was that the company turned down an opportunity to get into the personal computer industry during its infancy. In March 1984 the company considered a partnership with Apple Computer, which had just released the Macintosh. The objective was to combine Wang's word-processing software with Apple's graphical user interface and applications, and take market share from the MS-DOS–based systems, such as IBM's original PC. Apple's president, John Sculley, recognizing the value of Wang's word-processing application, was reportedly very keen on the deal. Apple even talked about licensing its Macintosh operating system to Wang, which would have enabled Wang to manufacture PCs. However, Wang rejected the proposal. According to internal memos, senior managers at Wang felt that "office automation is *our* business—Apple could decide to move in and use Wang to enter the market. . . . Apple is a young, volatile, ego-driven company. Should Wang be associated with such an unpredictable company?" Wang also scoffed at word-processing programs developed by the likes of WordStar and WordPerfect.

As a $2 billion company, Wang failed to see small start-ups such as WordPerfect as viable competitors. In addition, Wang was reportedly reluctant to sell its software separately from its hardware. The company felt that if it sold its word-processing software separately, no one would buy its hardware. This might have been true, but today no one buys either its software or hardware, whereas companies like WordPerfect have far surpassed Wang in sales.[1]

Discussion Questions

1. What does the story of Wang tell companies about the importance of scanning the external environment?
2. With hindsight, what steps could Wang have taken that might have averted the disaster that befell the company in the early 1990s?

3.2 OVERVIEW

As we noted in Chapter 1, two of the primary determinants of organizational performance are the industry environment in which a company competes and the country (or countries) in which it is located. Both of these factors are aspects of the company's **external environment.** Some companies do well partly because their external environment is extremely attractive. Others do poorly because their external environment is hostile. In this chapter, we consider the influence of the company's industry environment and national context on its competitive advantage.

A major theme in this chapter is that to succeed a company must either fit its strategy to the industry environment in which it operates, or be able to reshape the industry environment to its advantage through its chosen strategy. Companies typically fail when their strategy no longer fits the environment in which they operate (see Figure 3.1). The story of Wang Labs, presented in the Opening Case, exemplifies these processes. The early success of Wang Labs stemmed from the demand for word-processing applications that the company's pioneering innovations had generated. In the process, Wang created a whole new niche in the computer industry—a niche that it dominated. In other words, Wang's innovations reshaped the industry environment to its advantage, creating a new niche in which there was a close fit between Wang's strategy and customer demands. Later, however, Wang lost sight of competitive changes taking place in the industry environment. It failed to appreciate the threat that the rise of cheap personal computers and word-processing software presented to its position. Indeed, the evidence suggests that Wang failed to see personal computers and the related software applications as direct competitors. This failure proved to be a fatal mistake. By the mid 1980s there was a lack of fit between the environment in which Wang operated and the company's strategy. Wang had lost touch with the changes taking place in the market niche that it had created. Other companies were better able to meet the demands of customers for word-processing software and hardware, and Wang fell by the wayside. Wang might have survived had it taken a conscious decision in the early 1980s to move into personal computers and related word-processing applications. Such a strategy would have fitted the new environment created by the personal computer revolution, but Wang failed to appreciate this fact, and consequently went bankrupt.

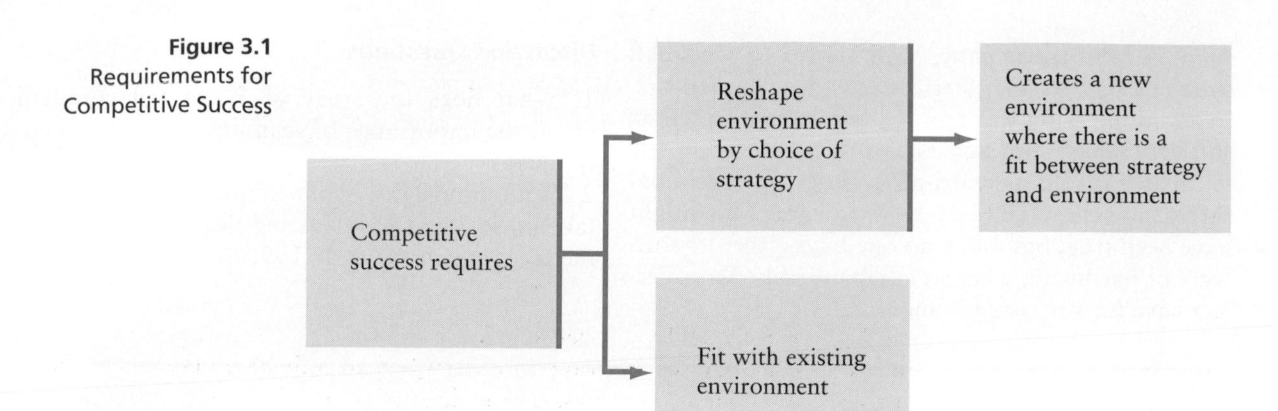

Figure 3.1
Requirements for Competitive Success

If companies are to avoid the mistakes that Wang made, they must understand the forces that drive competition in the industry in which they are operating. Otherwise they have little hope of either pursuing strategies that fit the existing industry environment or identifying strategies that might reshape the industry environment to their advantage. Against this background, the objective of this chapter is to discuss a number of models that can assist managers in analyzing the environment. The models provide a framework that can be used to identify environmental **opportunities** and **threats**. Opportunities arise when environmental trends create the potential for a company to achieve a competitive advantage. For example, the advances in microprocessor technology during the 1960s created the opportunity for Wang to build affordable minicomputers, which could be used to run word-processing applications. Similarly, the continuing advances in microprocessor technology during the 1970s created the opportunity for companies to build inexpensive personal computers—an opportunity that Apple, IBM, and Compaq all took advantage of, but Wang ignored. Threats arise when environmental trends endanger the integrity and profitability of a company's business. In this sense, the rise of personal computers amounted to more than a missed opportunity for Wang; it also constituted a threat.

We begin with a discussion of a model for analyzing the industry environment. Next we consider the competitive implications that arise when groups of companies within an industry pursue similar strategies. We then examine the nature of industry evolution and discuss in detail how the globalization of the world economy is affecting the competitive forces at work in an industry environment. Finally, we assess the impact of national context on competitive advantage. By the end of the chapter, you should be familiar with the main factors that managers have to take into account when analyzing a company's external environment for opportunities and threats.

3.3 THE FIVE FORCES MODEL

An **industry** can be defined as a group of companies offering products or services that are close substitutes for each other. Close substitutes are products or services that satisfy the same basic *consumer* needs. For example, the metal and

plastic body panels used in automobile construction are close substitutes for each other. Despite different production technologies, auto supply companies manufacturing metal body panels are in the same basic industry as companies manufacturing plastic body panels. They are serving the same consumer need, the need of auto assembly companies for body panels.

The task facing managers is to analyze competitive forces in an industry environment in order to identify the opportunities and threats confronting a company. Michael E. Porter of the Harvard School of Business Administration has developed a framework that helps managers in this analysis.[2] Porter's framework, known as the **five forces model** appears in Figure 3.2. This model focuses on five forces that shape competition within an industry: (1) the risk of new entry by potential competitors, (2) the degree of rivalry among established companies within an industry, (3) the bargaining power of buyers, (4) the bargaining power of suppliers, and (5) the closeness of substitutes to an industry's products.

Porter argues that the stronger each of these forces, the more limited is the ability of established companies to raise prices and earn greater profits. Within Porter's framework, a strong competitive force can be regarded as a threat since it depresses profits. A weak competitive force can be viewed as an opportunity, for it allows a company to earn greater profits. Because of factors beyond a company's direct control, such as industry evolution, the strength of the five forces may change through time. In such circumstances, the task facing strategic managers is to recognize opportunities and threats as they arise and to formulate appropriate strategic responses. In addition, it is possible for a company, through its choice of strategy, to alter the strength of one or more of the five forces to its advantage. This is part of the subject matter of the following chapters. In this chapter, we focus on understanding the impact that each of the five forces has on a company.

Figure 3.2
The Five Forces Model

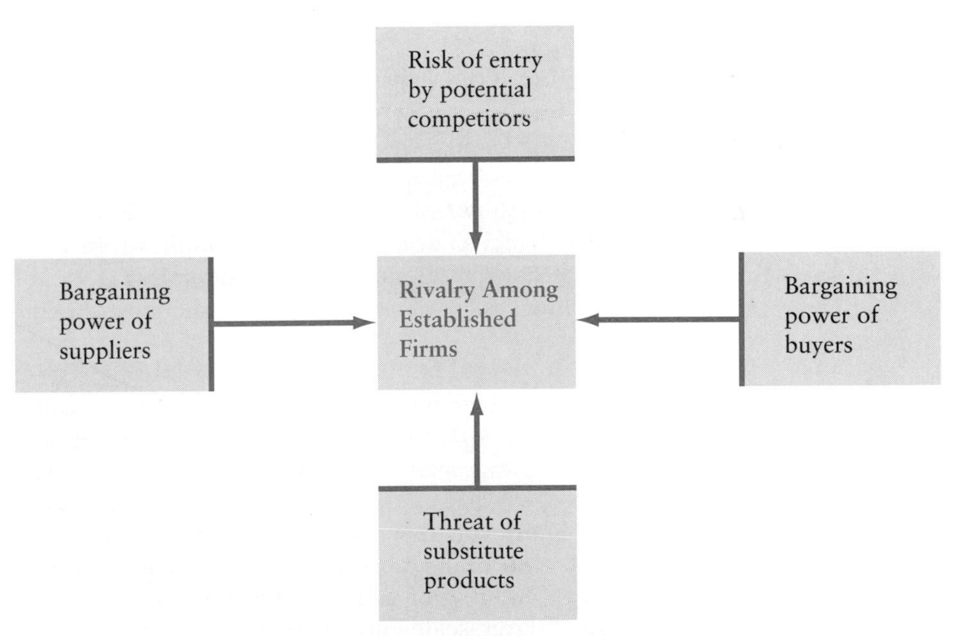

Source: Adapted and reprinted by permission of *Harvard Business Review*. An exhibit from "How Competitive Forces Shape Strategy" by Michael E. Porter (March–April 1979).

Potential Competitors

Potential competitors are companies that currently are not competing in an industry but have the capability to do so if they choose. American Telephone & Telegraph Co., for example, was regarded as a potential competitor in the personal computer industry in the early 1980s, for it had the technology, sales force, and capital necessary to manufacture and sell PCs. AT&T, in fact, did enter the industry in 1985, although it subsequently failed to secure a strong market position. Established companies try to discourage potential competitors from entering, since the more companies enter an industry, the more difficult it becomes for established companies to hold their share of the market and to generate profits. Thus a high risk of entry by potential competitors represents a threat to the profitability of established companies. On the other hand, if the risk of new entry is low, established companies can take advantage of this opportunity to raise prices and earn greater returns.

The strength of the competitive force of potential rivals is largely a function of the height of barriers to entry. The concept of barriers to entry implies that there are significant costs to joining an industry. The greater the costs that potential competitors must bear, the greater are the barriers to entry. High entry barriers keep potential competitors out of an industry even when industry returns are high. The classic work on barriers to entry was done by economist Joe Bain, who identified three main sources of barriers to new entry: brand loyalty, absolute cost advantages, and economies of scale.[3]

Brand Loyalty Brand loyalty is buyers' preference for the products of established companies. A company can create brand loyalty through continuous advertising of brand and company names, patent protection of products, product innovation through company research and development programs, an emphasis on high product quality, and good after-sales service. Significant brand loyalty makes it difficult for new entrants to take market share away from established companies. Thus it reduces the threat of entry by potential competitors since they may see the task of breaking down well-established consumer preferences as too costly.

Absolute Cost Advantages Lower absolute costs give established companies an advantage that is difficult for potential competitors to match. Absolute cost advantages can arise from superior production techniques. These techniques can be due to past experience, patents, or secret processes; control of particular inputs required for production, such as labor, materials, equipment, or management skills; or access to cheaper funds because existing companies represent lower risks than established companies. If established companies have an absolute cost advantage, then again the threat of entry decreases.

Economies of Scale Economies of scale are the cost advantages associated with large company size. Sources of scale economies include cost reductions gained through mass-producing a standardized output, discounts on bulk purchases of raw-material inputs and component parts, the spreading of fixed costs over a large volume, and scale economies in advertising. If these cost advantages are significant, then a new entrant faces the dilemma of either entering on a small scale and suffering a significant cost disadvantage or taking a very large risk by entering on a large scale and bearing significant capital costs. A further risk of large-scale entry is that the increased supply of products will depress prices and result in vigorous retaliation by established companies. Thus, when established companies have economies of scale, the threat of entry is reduced.

If established companies have built brand loyalty for their products, have an

STRATEGY IN ACTION 3.1

Barriers to Entry into the Commercial Jet Aircraft Industry

Currently, there are only three major players in the global commercial jet aircraft industry; Airbus Industrie, Boeing, and McDonnell Douglas. The existence of so few players can be explained in part, by the barriers to entering this industry. These entry barriers derive from the enormous costs and risks associated with developing a new jet airliner and from the scale economies enjoyed by incumbent companies.

Regarding development costs, McDonnell Douglas spent $1.5 billion on development and tooling for its MD-11 wide-bodied jetliner, introduced in the late 1980s, and it has calculated that the development costs for the proposed MD-12 airliner, which will compete with Boeing's 747, will be of the order on $5 billion. Given such enormous development costs, in order to break even a company has to capture a significant share of world demand. In the case of the MD-11, for example, McDonnell Douglas will have to sell more than 200 aircraft to break even, a figure that represents 13 percent of predicted industry sales for that type of aircraft between 1990 and the year 2000. For an aircraft such as the MD-12, it may take 400 to 500 units to break even. Consequently, it can take ten to fourteen years of production before an aircraft reaches its break-even point—and this on top of the five to six years of negative cash flows that have to be borne during development. Such high development costs and risks act as a deterrent to new entry; they raise entry barriers.

As for scale economies, worldwide consensus is that there are significant economies of scale in aircraft production. Most importantly, experience-based cost economies on the average lower the unit cost of producing a particular jet aircraft by about 20 percent every time accumulated output is doubled. Hence companies with established operations will have a significant cost advantage over any new entrants. Indeed, it has been estimated that companies achieving only half the market share required to break even face a 20 percent unit cost disadvantage compared with those whose market share exceeds the break-even point. Thus incumbents such as Boeing, which have been producing models such as the 747 and 737 for years, have a substantial cost advantage vis-à-vis potential new entrants.

Yet despite the major barriers to entering this industry, Airbus did successfully enter during the 1980s—the first company to do so since the early 1960s. Today Airbus has a market share that is second only to Boeing's. However, Airbus is an unusual case, for the company received substantial subsidies from the governments of Germany, France, Spain, and Britain to help it overcome the industry's entry barriers.[5]

absolute cost advantage with respect to potential competitors, or have significant scale economies, then the risk of entry by potential competitors is greatly diminished. When this risk is low, established companies can charge higher prices and earn greater profits than would have been possible otherwise. Clearly, then, it is in the interest of companies to pursue strategies consistent with these aims. Indeed, empirical evidence suggests that the height of barriers to entry is the most important determinant of profit rates in an industry.[4] Examples of industries where entry barriers are considerable include pharmaceuticals, household detergents, and commercial jet aircraft. In the first two cases, product differentiation achieved through substantial expenditures for research and development and for advertising has built brand loyalty, making it difficult for new companies to enter these industries on a significant scale. So successful have the differentiation strategies of Procter & Gamble and Unilever been in household detergents that these two companies dominate the global industry. In the case of the commercial jet aircraft industry, which is discussed in depth in Strategy in Action 3.1, the barriers to entry are primarily due to scale economies.

Rivalry Among Established Companies

The second of Porter's five competitive forces is the extent of rivalry among established companies within an industry. If this competitive force is weak, companies have an opportunity to raise prices and earn greater profits. But if it is strong, significant price competition, including price wars, may result from the intense rivalry. Price competition limits profitability by reducing the margins that can be earned on sales. Thus intense rivalry among established companies constitutes a strong threat to profitability. The extent of rivalry among established companies within an industry is largely a function of three factors: (1) industry competitive structure, (2) demand conditions, and (3) the height of exit barriers in the industry.

Competitive Structure Competitive structure refers to the number and size distribution of companies in an industry. Different competitive structures have different implications for rivalry. Structures vary from **fragmented** to **consolidated**. A fragmented industry contains a large number of small or medium-sized companies, none of which is in a position to dominate the industry. A consolidated industry is dominated by a small number of large companies or, in extreme cases, by just one company (a monopoly). Fragmented industries range from agriculture, video rental, and health clubs, to real estate brokerage and suntanning parlors. Consolidated industries include aerospace, automobiles, and pharmaceuticals. The most common competitive structure in the United States is a consolidated structure—what economists call an *oligopoly*.[6] The range of structures and their different characteristics are illustrated in Figure 3.3.

Many fragmented industries are characterized by low entry barriers and commodity-type products that are hard to differentiate. The combination of these traits tends to result in boom-and-bust cycles. Low entry barriers imply that whenever demand is strong and profits are high there will be a flood of new entrants hoping to cash in on the boom. The explosion in the number of video stores, health clubs, and suntanning parlors during the 1980s, exemplifies this situation. Often the flood of new entrants into a booming fragmented industry creates excess capacity. Once excess capacity develops, companies start to cut prices in order to utilize their spare capacity. The difficulty companies face when trying to differentiate their products from those of competitors can worsen this tendency. The result is a price war, which depresses industry profits, forces some companies out of business, and deters potential new entrants. For example, after a decade of expansion and booming profits, many health clubs are now finding that they have to offer large discounts in order to hold on to their membership. In general, the more commodity-like an industry's product, the more vicious will

Figure 3.3
The Continuum of Industry Structures

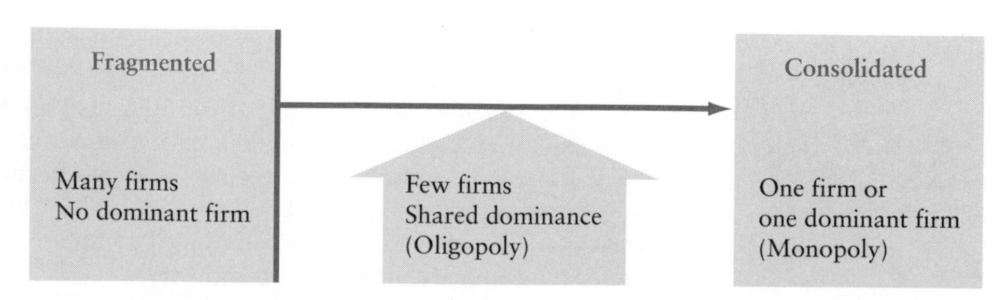

be the price war. This bust part of the cycle continues until overall industry capacity is brought into line with demand (through bankruptcies), at which point prices may stabilize again.

A fragmented industry structure, then, constitutes a threat rather than an opportunity. Most booms will be relatively short-lived because of the ease of new entry and will be followed by price wars and bankruptcies. Since differentiation is often difficult in these industries, the best strategy for a company to pursue in such circumstances may be one of cost minimization. This strategy allows a company to rack up high returns in a boom and survive any subsequent bust.

The nature and intensity of competition for consolidated industries are much more difficult to predict. The one certainty about consolidated industries is that the companies are interdependent—that is, the competitive actions of one company directly affect the profitability of others in the industry. For example, the introduction by General Motors' of cut-rate financing to sell cars in 1986 had an immediate negative impact on the sales and profits of Chrysler Corp. and Ford Motor Co., which then had to introduce similar packages in order to protect their market share.

Thus, in a consolidated industry, the competitive action of one company directly affects the market share of its rivals, forcing a response from them. The consequence of such competitive interdependence can be a dangerous competitive spiral, with rival companies trying to undercut each other's prices, pushing industry profits down in the process. The fare wars that have racked the airline industry in recent years provide a good example of this. When demand for airline travel fell during 1990 as the U.S. economy slipped into a recession, airlines started cutting prices to try to maintain their passenger loads. When one airline serving a particular route cut its prices, its competitors would soon follow. The result was a particularly severe downward price spiral. So intense did price competition become that between 1990 and 1992 the industry lost a staggering $7.1 billion, more than had been made during its previous fifty years, and some long-established carriers, such as Pan American World Airways, disappeared into bankruptcy.

Clearly, the interdependence of companies in consolidated industries and the possibility of a price war constitute a major threat. Companies often seek to reduce this threat by following the price lead set by a dominant company in the industry. However, companies must be careful, for explicit price-fixing agreements are illegal, although tacit agreements are not. (A tacit agreement is one arrived at without direct communication. Instead, companies watch and interpret each other's behavior. Normally, tacit agreements involve following the price lead set by a dominant company.)[7] However, tacit price-leadership agreements often break down under adverse economic conditions, as is beginning to occur in the beer industry. For most of the 1980s Anheuser-Busch was the acknowledged price leader in this industry. The resulting absence of price competition helped keep industry profits high. However, slow growth in beer consumption during the late 1980s and early 1990s put pressure on the earnings of all beer majors and persuaded Miller Brewing Company—a division of Philip Morris—and Adolph Coors Co. to break ranks and institute a policy of deep and continuous discounting for most of their beer brands. In 1990 market leader Anheuser-Busch announced that it would start offering similar discounts in order to protect its sales volume. Thus, after the breakdown of a tacit price-leadership agreement, the beer industry seems to be sliding toward a price war.

More generally, when price wars are a threat, companies compete on nonprice factors such as product quality and design features. This type of competition constitutes an attempt to build brand loyalty and minimize the likelihood of a price war. The effectiveness of this strategy, however, depends on how easy it is to differentiate the industry's product. Although some products (such as cars) are relatively easy to differentiate, others (such as airline travel) are essentially commodities that are very difficult to differentiate.

Demand Conditions Industry demand conditions are another determinant of the intensity of rivalry among established companies. Growing demand tends to moderate competition by providing greater room for expansion. Demand grows when the market as a whole is growing through the addition of new consumers or when existing consumers are purchasing more of an industry's product. When demand is growing, companies can increase revenues without taking market share away from other companies. Thus growing demand gives a company a major opportunity to expand operations.

Conversely, declining demand results in more competition as companies fight to maintain revenues and market share. Demand declines when consumers are leaving the marketplace or when each consumer is buying less. When demand is declining, a company can attain growth only by taking market share away from other companies. Thus declining demand constitutes a major threat, for it increases the extent of rivalry between established companies. The issue of what determines demand conditions is discussed in more detail later in the chapter, when we consider industry evolution.

Exit Barriers Exit barriers are a serious competitive threat when industry demand is declining. Exit barriers are economic, strategic, and emotional factors that keep companies competing in an industry even when returns are low. If exit barriers are high, companies can become locked into an unfavorable industry. Excess productive capacity can result. In turn, excess capacity tends to lead to intensified price competition, with companies cutting prices in an attempt to obtain the orders needed to utilize their idle capacity.

Common exit barriers include the following:

1. Investments in plant and equipment that have no alternative uses and cannot be sold off. If the company wishes to leave the industry, it has to write off the book value of these assets.
2. High fixed costs of exit, such as severance pay to workers who are being made redundant.
3. Emotional attachments to an industry, as when a company is unwilling to exit from its original industry for sentimental reasons.
4. Strategic relationships between business units. For example, within a multi-industry company, a low-return business unit may provide vital inputs for a high-return business unit based in another industry. Thus the company may be unwilling to exit from the low-return business.
5. Economic dependence on the industry, as when a company is not diversified and so relies on the industry for its income.

The experience of the steel industry illustrates the adverse competitive effects of high exit barriers.[8] A combination of declining demand and new low-cost sources of supply created overcapacity in the global steel industry during the late

1980s. American companies, with their high-cost structure, were on the sharp end of this decline. Demand for American steel fell from a 1977 peak of 160 million tons to 70 million tons in 1986. The outcome was excess capacity amounting to an estimated 45 million tons in 1987, or 40 percent of total productive capacity. In order to try to utilize this capacity, many steel companies slashed their prices. As a consequence of the resulting price war, industry profits were low, and several of the majors, including LTV Steel Company and Bethlehem Steel, faced bankruptcy.

Since the steel industry was characterized by excess capacity for most of the 1980s, why did companies not reduce that capacity? The answer is that many tried to, but the costs of exit slowed this process and prolonged the associated price war. For example, in 1983 USX shut down 16 percent of its raw steel-making capacity at a cost of $1.2 billion. USX had to write off the book value of these assets; they could not be sold. In addition, it had to cover pensions and insurance for 15,400 terminated workers. Given such high exit costs, companies such as USX have remained locked into this unprofitable industry. The effect of impeded exit has been more intense price competition than might have been the case otherwise. Thus high exit barriers, by slowing the speed with which companies leave the industry, threaten the profitability of all companies within the steel industry.

Interactions Among Factors The extent of rivalry among established companies within an industry is a function of competitive structure, demand conditions, and exit barriers. Particularly within a consolidated industry, the interaction of these factors determines the extent of rivalry. For example, the environment of a consolidated industry may be favorable when demand growth is high. Under such circumstances, companies might seize the opportunity to adopt price-leadership agreements. However, when demand is declining and exit barriers are high, the probable emergence of excess capacity is likely to cause to price wars. Thus, depending on the interaction between these various factors, the *extent* of rivalry among established companies in a consolidated industry might constitute an opportunity or a threat. These issues are summarized in Table 3.1.

Table 3.1
Demand Conditions and Exit Barriers as Determinants of Opportunities and Threats in a Consolidated Industry

		Demand conditions	
		Demand decline	Demand growth
Exit barriers	High	High threat of excess capacity and price wars	Opportunities to raise prices through price leadership and to expand operations
	Low	Moderate threat of excess capacity and price wars	Opportunities to raise prices through price leadership to expand operations

The Bargaining Power of Buyers

The third of Porter's five competitive forces is the bargaining power of buyers. Buyers can be viewed as a competitive threat when they force down prices or when they demand higher quality and better service (which increase operating costs). Alternatively, weak buyers give a company the opportunity to raise prices and earn greater returns. Whether buyers are able to make demands on a company depends on their power relative to that of the company. According to Porter, buyers are most powerful in the following circumstances:

1. When the supply industry is composed of many small companies and the buyers are few in number and large. These circumstances allow the buyers to dominate supply companies.
2. When the buyers purchase in large quantities. In such circumstances, buyers can use their purchasing power as leverage to bargain for price reductions.
3. When the supply industry depends on the buyers for a large percentage of its total orders.
4. When the buyers can switch orders between supply companies at a low cost, thereby playing off companies against each other to force down prices.
5. When it is economically feasible for the buyers to purchase the input from several companies at once.
6. When the buyers can use the threat to supply their own needs through vertical integration as a device for forcing down prices.[9]

An example of an industry whose buyers are powerful is the auto component supply industry. The suppliers of auto component are numerous and typically small in scale. Their customers, the auto manufacturers, are large in size and few in number. Chrysler, for example, does business with nearly 2,000 different component suppliers and normally contracts with a number of different companies to supply the same part. The auto majors have used their powerful position to play off suppliers against each other, forcing down the price they have to pay for component parts and demanding better quality. If a component supplier objects, then the auto major uses the threat of switching to another supplier as a bargaining tool. Additionally, to keep component prices down, both Ford and General Motors have used the threat of manufacturing a component themselves rather than buying it from auto component suppliers. Buyers in the health care industry are also gaining power, and Strategy in Action 3.2 discusses this development.

The Bargaining Power of Suppliers

The fourth of Porter's competitive forces is the bargaining power of suppliers. Suppliers can be viewed as a threat when they are able to force up the price that a company must pay for input or reduce the quality of goods supplied, thereby depressing the company's profitability. Alternatively, weak suppliers give a company the opportunity to force down prices and demand higher quality. As with buyers, the ability of suppliers to make demands on a company depends on their power relative to that of the company. According to Porter, suppliers are most powerful in the following circumstances:

1. When the product that suppliers sell has few substitutes and is important to the company.
2. When the company's industry is not an important customer to the suppliers. In such instances, the suppliers' health does not depend on the company's industry, and suppliers have little incentive to reduce prices or improve quality.

STRATEGY IN ACTION 3.2

The Changing Relationship Between Buyers and Suppliers in the Health Care Industry

For decades pharmaceutical companies, as major suppliers of critical health care products, have been in the driver's seat in the health care industry. Pharmaceutical companies such as Merck, Pfizer, Glaxo, and Ciba-Geigy spent hundreds of millions of dollars annually to develop new drugs. Although this is a risky process with a low probability of success, the companies that do develop new drugs with important medical applications have historically been in a very powerful position. Companies can patent drugs, which prohibits competitors from producing and marketing products based on the same chemical compound for a seventeen-year period. Protected by patents, pharmaceutical companies have been able to charge high prices. Since the prescribers of drugs, doctors, do not pay for the drug, they have had no reason to concern themselves with prices. Instead, they have been more concerned with medical benefits to patients. As for the patients, since their insurance companies often end up paying for drug prescriptions, they too have not had a strong incentive to focus on drug prices. Consequently, there has been very little pressure on drug prices in the pharmaceutical industry. During the 1980s and early 1990s, for example, drug prices in the United States rose at two to three times the annual inflation rate. In 1992 they rose at an annual rate of 5.7 percent—significantly faster than the 2.9 percent inflation rate.

There are signs that this situation is changing and powerful buyers are beginning to limit the ability of pharmaceutical companies to raise drug prices. Two factors are at work here. The first is the rise of health maintenance organizations (HMOs). HMOs were started in an attempt to control health care costs. Subscribers to HMOs sacrifice freedom of choice as to health care provider for lower insurance costs. HMOs have proved attractive to companies, which have found that it is often cheaper to provide employees with health care coverage through HMOs than through conventional health insurance. As one aspect of their effort to control costs, HMOs negotiate directly with pharmaceutical companies on behalf of all their doctors for attractive prices on key drugs. The larger purchasing power of HMOs, along with their concern about drug prices, which individual doctors have never had, is starting to have an effect on drug prices.

On their own HMOs would probably not be able to limit drug prices. A key drug may have only one supplier, and that puts HMOs at a disadvantage. After all, an HMO can hardly deny a seriously ill patient access to a potentially life saving drug simply because it costs too much. What is starting to happen, however, is that drug companies are introducing metoo drugs to compete with the patented drugs of competitors. Metoo drugs differ chemically from the pioneer's product and therefore are not covered by a patent, but they offer similar medical benefits. For example, three companies are now marketing very similar antidepressant drugs: SmithKline Beecham offers Paxil; Eli Lilly & Co, Prozac; and Pfizer, Zoloft (Eli Lilly's Prozac was the pioneer). The shift to metoo drugs is occurring because pharmaceutical companies have made so many major medical breakthroughs during the last few decades that there are very few promising areas for research left. So in order to maintain their historic growth rates, they are increasingly looking to metoo drugs.

From an HMO's perspective, the recent emergence of metoo drugs suddenly gives it a choice. Thus, for example, if Eli Lilly refuses to reduce the price for Prozac, an HMO can always threaten to use a substitute such as Paxil. Indeed, in early 1993 SmithKline Beecham's stated strategy for Paxil was to price it 13 percent below Prozac. The fact that health providers now have a choice, and the apparent willingness of pharmaceutical companies to start price discounting, is beginning to change the power relationship in the health care industry. Although HMOs, the major buyers of drugs, historically had little clout with the drug companies, their power is increasing. If the trend continues, the result is likely to be more intense competition and lower drug prices and profits in the pharmaceutical industry, but also lower costs for HMOs.[10]

3. When suppliers' respective products are differentiated to such an extent that it is costly for a company to switch from one supplier to another. In such cases, the company depends on its suppliers and cannot play them off against each other.
4. When, to raise prices, suppliers can use the threat of vertically integrating forward into the industry and competing directly with the company.
5. When buying companies cannot use the threat of vertically integrating backward and supplying their own needs as a means to reduce input prices.[11]

For a long time the airlines exemplified an industry whose suppliers were powerful. In particular, the airline pilots and aircraft mechanics unions, as suppliers of labor, were in a very strong position with respect to the airlines. The airlines depended on union labor to fly and service their aircraft. Because of labor agreements and the probability of damaging strikes, nonunion labor was not regarded as a feasible substitute. The unions used this position to raise pilots' and mechanics' wages above the level that would have prevailed in more competitive circumstances, like those currently found in the industry. This situation persisted until the early 1980s, when the resulting high-cost structure of the airline industry was driving many airlines into bankruptcy. The airlines then used the threat of bankruptcy to break union agreements and drive down labor costs, often by as much as 50 percent.

The Threat of Substitute Products

The final force in Porter's model is the threat of substitute products—the products of industries that serve similar consumer needs as those of the industry being analyzed. For example, companies in the coffee industry compete indirectly with those in the tea and soft-drink industries. (All three industries serve consumer needs for drinks.) The prices that companies in the coffee industry can charge are limited by the existence of substitutes such as tea and soft drinks. If the price of coffee rises too much relative to that of tea or soft drinks, then coffee drinkers will switch from coffee to those substitutes. This phenomenon occurred when unusually cold weather destroyed much of the Brazilian coffee crop in 1975–1976. The price of coffee rose to record highs, reflecting the shortage, and consumers began to switch to tea in large numbers.

The existence of close substitutes presents a strong competitive threat, limiting the price a company can charge and thus its profitability. However, if a company's products have few close substitutes (that is, if substitutes are a weak competitive force), then, other things being equal, the company has the opportunity to raise prices and earn additional profits. Consequently, its strategies should be designed to take advantage of this fact.

The Role of the Macroenvironment

So far we have treated industries as self-contained entities, yet in practice they are embedded in a wider **macroenvironment**. That is, the broader economic, technological, demographic, social, and political environment (see Figure 3.4). Changes in the macroenvironment can have a direct impact on any one of the five forces in Porter's model, thereby altering the relative strength of these forces and with it, the attractiveness of an industry. We briefly consider the impact that each aspect of these macroenvironmental forces can have on an industry's competitive structure.

Figure 3.4 The Role of the Macroenvironment

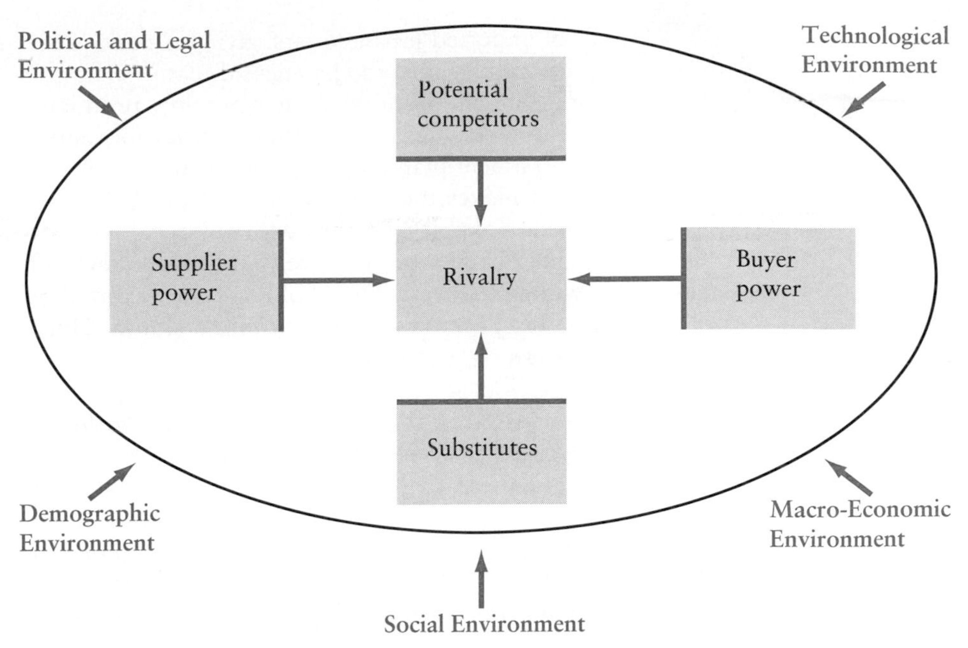

The Macroeconomic Environment The state of the macroeconomic environment determines the general health and well-being of the economy. This in turn affects a company's ability to earn an adequate rate of return. The four most important macroeconomic indicators in this context are the growth rate of the economy, the interest rates, currency exchange rates, and inflation rates.

Because it leads to an expansion in consumer expenditure, economic growth tends to produce a general easing of competitive pressures within an industry. This gives companies the opportunity to expand their operations. Because economic decline leads to a reduction in consumer expenditure, it increases competitive pressures. Economic decline frequently causes price wars in mature industries.

The level of interest rates can determine the level of demand for a company's products. Interest rates are important whenever consumers routinely borrow money to finance their purchase of these products. The most obvious example is the housing market, where the mortgage rate directly affects demand, but interest rates also have an impact on the sale of autos, appliances, and capital equipment, to give just a few examples. For companies in such industries, rising interest rates are a threat and falling rates an opportunity.

Currency exchange rates define the value of different national currencies against each other. Movement in currency exchange rates has a direct impact on the competitiveness of a company's products in the global marketplace. For example, when the value of the dollar is low compared with the value of other currencies, products made in the United States are relatively inexpensive and products made overseas are relatively expensive. A low or declining dollar reduces the threat from foreign competitors while creating opportunities for increased sales overseas. For example, the fall in the value of the dollar against the Japanese yen that occurred between 1985 and 1993, when the dollar/yen exchange rate declined from \$1 = Y240 to \$1 = Y105, has sharply increased the

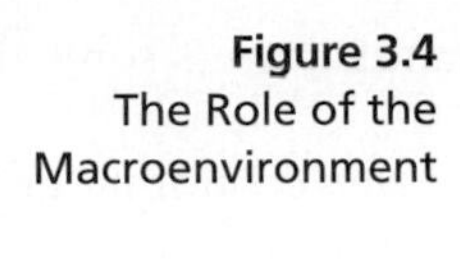

price of imported Japanese cars, giving American car manufacturers some degree of protection against the Japanese threat.

Inflation can destabilize the economy, producing slower economic growth, higher interest rates, and volatile currency movements. If inflation keeps increasing, investment planning becomes hazardous. The key characteristic of inflation is that it makes the future less predictable. In an inflationary environment, it may be impossible to predict with any accuracy the real value of returns that can be earned from a project five years hence. Such uncertainty makes companies less willing to invest. Their holding back in turn depresses economic activity and ultimately pushes the economy into a slump. Thus high inflation is a threat to companies.

The Technological Environment Since World War II, the pace of technological change has accelerated, unleashing a process that has been called a "perennial gale of creative destruction."[12] Technological change can make established products obsolete overnight. At the same time it can create a host of new product possibilities. Thus it is both creative and destructive—both an opportunity and a threat. One of the most important impacts of technological change is that it can affect barriers to entry and as a result, radically reshape industry structure. For example, the Opening Case shows Wang Laboratories, Inc. strong hold on the word-processing market during the 1970s. However, technological change during the early 1980s—the development of cheap personal computers—effectively lowered the barriers to entering the word-processing market. The result was entry by software companies such as WordPerfect and Microsoft, whose word-processing programs could be run on cheap personal computers. Ultimately, this technologically driven development led to the Wang's bankruptcy.[13]

The Social Environment Like technological change, social change creates opportunities and threats. One of the major social movements of the 1970s and 1980s was the trend toward greater health consciousness. Its impact has been immense, and companies that recognized the opportunities early have often reaped significant gains. Philip Morris, for example, capitalized on the growing health trend when it acquired Miller Brewing Company and then redefined competition in the beer industry with its introduction of low-calorie beer (Miller Lite). Similarly, Pepsico was able to gain market share from its archrival, The Coca-Cola Company, by introducing diet colas and fruit-based soft drinks first. At the same time the health trend has created a threat for many industries. The tobacco industry, for example, is now in decline as a direct result of greater consumer awareness of the health implications of smoking. Similarly, the sugar industry has seen sales decrease as consumers have decided to switch to artificial sweeteners.

The Demographic Environment The changing composition of the population is another factor that can create both opportunities and threats. For example, as the baby-boom generation of the 1960s has moved through the population, it has created a host of opportunities and threats. Currently, baby boomers are getting married and creating an upsurge in demand for the consumer appliances normally bought by couples marrying for the first time. Thus companies such as Whirlpool Corporation and General Electric Co. are looking to capitalize on the predicted upsurge in demand for washing machines, dish-

washers, spin dryers, and the like. The other side of the coin is that industries oriented toward the young, such as the toy industry, have seen their consumer base decline in recent years.

The Political and Legal Environment Political and legal factors also have a major effect on the level of opportunities and threats in the environment. One of the most significant trends in recent years has been the move toward deregulation. By eliminating many legal restrictions, deregulation has lowered barriers to entry and opened a number of industries to intense competition. The deregulation of the airline industry in 1979, for example, created the opportunity to establish low-fare carriers—an opportunity that Texas Air, People Express, and others tried to capitalize on. At the same time the increased intensity of competition created many threats, including, most notably, the threat of prolonged fare wars, which have repeatedly thrown the airline industry into turmoil during the last decade.

For the future, fears about the destruction of the ozone layer, acid rain, and global warming may be near the top of the political agenda in the 1990s. Given these concerns, governments seem increasingly likely to enact tough environmental regulations to limit air pollution. Rather than resisting this trend, companies should try to take advantage of it. For example, back in 1974, when ozone depletion was still a theory, E. I. du Pont de Nemours & Co. decided to start research into substitutes for ozone-damaging chlorofluorocarbons (CFCs), widely used in aerosols, air conditioners, and refrigeration equipment. At the same time, Du Pont made a pledge to phase out production of CFCs if they were shown to be a threat to public health. In March 1988, in response to NASA data, Du Pont honored that commitment and promised to phase out production of CFCs within ten years. Although Du Pont stands to lose $600 million per year from the sales of CFCs, since the mid 1970s the company's research has yielded three viable alternatives to CFCs, each of which is now produced commercially. Thus, by anticipating regulations and undertaking appropriate action, Du Pont is now well positioned to take a large share of the market for CFC substitutes when CFCs are phased out of use in the late 1990s.

3.4 STRATEGIC GROUPS WITHIN INDUSTRIES

The Concept of Strategic Groups

So far we have said little about how companies in an industry might differ from each other and what implications the differences might have for the opportunities and threats that they face. In practice, companies in an industry often differ from each other with respect to factors such as distribution channels used, market segments served, product quality, technological leadership, customer service, pricing policy, advertising policy, and promotions. Within most industries, it is possible to observe groups of companies in which each member follows the same basic strategy as other companies in the group but a strategy different from the one followed by companies in other groups. These groups of companies are known as **strategic groups.**[14]

Normally, a limited number of groups capture the essence of strategic differences between companies within an industry. For example, in the pharmaceutical

industry two main strategic groups stand out (see Figure 3.5).[15] One group, which includes such companies as Merck, Eli Lilly, and Pfizer, is characterized by heavy R&D spending and a focus on developing new proprietary blockbuster drugs. The companies in this *proprietary group* are pursuing a high- risk/high-return strategy. It is a high-risk strategy because basic drug research is difficult and expensive. Bringing a new drug to market can cost $100–200 million in R&D money and a decade of research and clinical trials. The strategy is also a high-return one because a single successful drug can be patented, giving the innovator a seventeen-year monopoly on its production and sale. This lets the innovator charge a very high price for the patented drug, allowing the company to earn millions, if not billions of dollars, over the lifetime of the patent. (For example, in 1992 Glaxo earned $3.44 billion in revenues from a single drug—the antidepressant Zantal).

The second strategic group might be characterized as the *generic drug* group. This group of companies, which includes Marion Labs, ICN Pharmaceuticals, and Carter Wallace, focuses on the manufacture of generic drugs—low-cost copies of drugs pioneered by companies in the proprietary group whose patents have now expired. The companies in this group are characterized by low R&D spending and an emphasis on price competition. They are pursuing a low-risk, low-return strategy. It is low risk because they are not investing millions of dollars in R&D. It is low return because they cannot charge high prices.

Implications of Strategic Groups

The concept of strategic groups has a number of implications for industry analysis and the identification of opportunities and threats. First, a company's immediate competitors are those in its strategic group. Since all the companies in a strategic group are pursuing similar strategies, consumers tend to view the products of such enterprises as being direct substitutes for each other. Thus a major threat to a company's profitability can come from within its own strategic group.

Second, different strategic groups can have a different standing with respect to each of Porter's five competitive forces. In other words, the risk of new entry by potential competitors, the degree of rivalry among companies within a group, the bargaining power of buyers, the bargaining power of suppliers, and the competitive force of substitute products can all vary in intensity among different strategic groups within the same industry.

For example, in the pharmaceutical industry, companies in the proprietary group have historically been in a very powerful position vis-à-vis buyers because their products are patented. Besides, rivalry within this group has been limited to competition to be the first to patent a new drug (so-called patent races). Price competition has been rare, although, as indicated in Strategy in Action 3.2, there are signs that this might be changing. Without price competition, companies in this group have been able to charge high prices and earn very high profits. In contrast, companies in the generic group have been in a much weaker position vis-à-vis buyers since they lack patents for their products and since buyers can choose between very similar competing generic drugs. Moreover, price competition between the companies in this group has been quite intense, reflecting the lack of product differentiation. Thus companies within this group have earned somewhat lower returns than companies in the proprietary group.

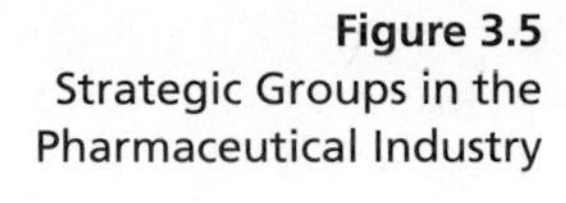
Figure 3.5 Strategic Groups in the Pharmaceutical Industry

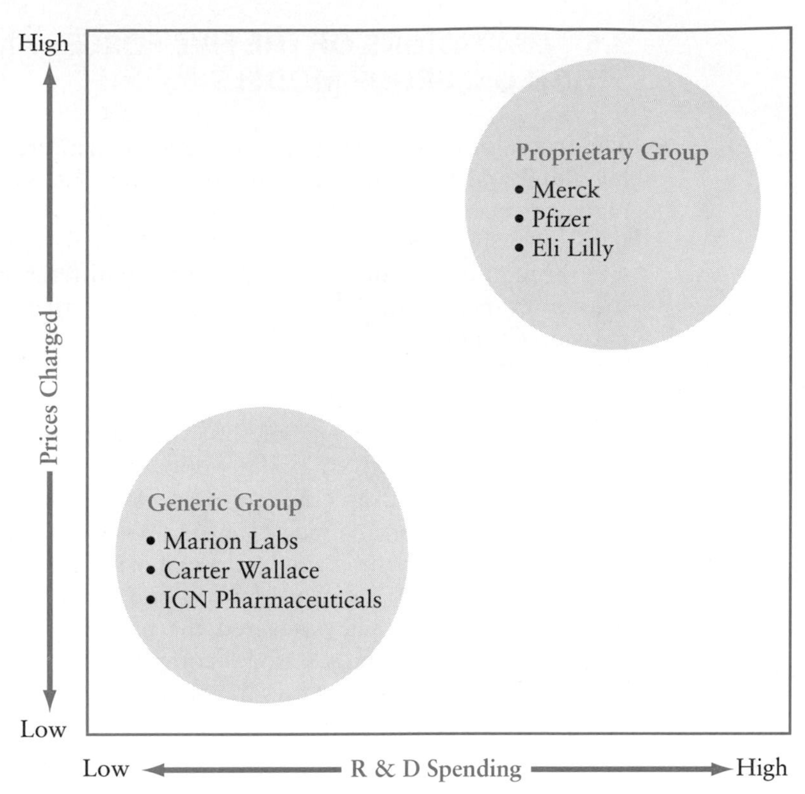

It follows that some strategic groups are more desirable than others, for they have a lower level of threats and greater opportunities. Managers must evaluate whether their company would be better off competing in a different strategic group. If the environment of another strategic group is more benign, then moving into that group can be regarded as an opportunity.

Yet this opportunity is rarely without costs, mainly because of **mobility barriers** between groups. Mobility barriers are factors that inhibit the movement of companies between groups in an industry. They include both the barriers to entry into a group and the barriers to exit from a company's existing group. For example, Marion Labs would encounter mobility barriers if it attempted to enter the proprietary group in the pharmaceutical industry. These mobility barriers would arise from the fact that Marion lacks the R&D skills possessed by companies in the proprietary group, and building these skills would be an expensive proposition. Thus a company contemplating entry into another strategic group must evaluate the height of mobility barriers before deciding whether the move is worthwhile.

Mobility barriers also imply that companies within a given group may be protected to a greater or lesser extent from the threat of entry by companies based in other strategic groups. If mobility barriers are low, then the threat of entry from companies in other groups may be high, effectively limiting the prices companies can charge and the profits they can earn without attracting new competition. If mobility barriers are high, then the threat of entry is low, and companies within the protected group have an opportunity to raise prices and earn higher returns without attracting entry.

3.5 LIMITATIONS OF THE FIVE FORCES AND STRATEGIC GROUP MODELS

The five forces and strategic group models constitute very useful ways of thinking about and analyzing the nature of competition within an industry. However, managers need to be aware of their shortcomings. Both models (1) present a static picture of competition which slights the role of innovation and (2) de-emphasize the significance of individual company differences while overemphasizing the importance of industry and strategic group structure as determinants of company profit rates.

Static Models in a Dynamic World

Over any reasonable length of time, in many industries competition can be viewed as a process driven by innovation.[16] Companies that pioneer new products, processes, or strategies can often earn enormous profits. This prospect gives companies a strong incentive to seek innovative products, processes, and strategies. Consider, for example, the explosive growth of Apple Computer, Toys Я Us, Dell Computer, or Wal-Mart. In one way or another, all these companies were innovators. Apple pioneered the personal computer, Dell pioneered a whole new way of selling personal computers (by mail order), Toys Я Us pioneered a new way of selling toys (through large discount warehouse-type stores), and Wal-Mart pioneered the low-price discount superstore concept.

Successful innovation can revolutionize industry structure. In recent decades one of the most common consequences of innovation has been to lower the fixed costs of production, thereby reducing barriers to entry and allowing new, and smaller, enterprises to compete with large established organizations. Take the steel industry as an example. Two decades ago the industry was populated by large, integrated steel companies such as US Steel, LTV, and Bethlehem Steel. The industry was a typical oligopoly, dominated by a small number of large producers, in which tacit price collusion was practiced. Then along came a series of efficient minimill producers such as Nucor and Chaparral Steel, which utilized a new technology—electric arc furnaces. Over the last twenty years they have revolutionized the structure of the industry. What was once a consolidated industry is now much more fragmented and price competitive. The successor company to US Steel, USX, now has only a 15 percent market share, down from 55 percent in the mid 1960s, and both Bethlehem and LTV have been through Chapter 11 bankruptcy proceedings. In contrast, as a group the minimills now hold over 30 percent of the market, up from 5 percent twenty years ago. Thus the minimill innovation has reshaped the nature of competition in the steel industry.[17] A five forces model applied to the industry in 1970 would look very different from a five forces model applied in 1995.

The steel industry is hardly unique in this respect. Even more dramatic changes have been taking place in the computer industry, where a whole host of companies that did not even exist a decade ago—companies like Compaq Computer, Dell Computer, Sun Microsystems, and Silicon Graphics—have been grabbing market share from established producers such as IBM, Digital Equipment, and Wang Labs, all of whom have lost money in recent years. Fifteen years ago no one could have predicted this, but today the revolution that Apple Computer started when it introduced its first personal computer—a revolution that itself was the product of profound technological change—has completely transformed

the structure of the computer industry. As a result, a five forces analysis and strategic group map of the computer industry done in 1980 would look completely different from one done in 1995.

In his most recent work, Michael Porter, the propagator of the five forces and strategic group concepts, has explicitly recognized the role of innovation in revolutionizing industry structure. Porter now talks of innovations as "unfreezing" and "reshaping" industry structure. His view seems to be that after a period of turbulence triggered off by innovation the structure of an industry once more settles down into a fairly stable pattern. Once the industry stabilizes in its new configuration, the five forces and strategic group concepts can once more be applied.[18] This view of the evolution of industry structure is often referred to as *punctuated equilibrium*.[19] The punctuated equilibrium view holds that long periods of equilibrium, when an industry's structure is stable, are punctuated by periods of rapid change when industry structure is revolutionized by innovation. Thus there is an unfreezing and refreezing process.

Figure 3.6 shows what punctuated equilibrium might look like for one key dimension of industry structure—competitive structure. From time T_0 to T_1 the competitive structure of the industry is a stable oligopoly, with a few companies sharing the market. At time T1 a major new innovation is pioneered by either an existing company or a new entrant. The result is a period of turbulence between T1 and T2. After a while, however, the industry settles down into a new state of equilibrium, but now the competitive structure is far more fragmented. Note that the opposite could have happened: the industry could have become more consolidated, although this seems to be less common. In general, innovations seem to lower barriers to entry, allow more companies into the industry, and as a result lead to fragmentation rather than consolidation.

Figure 3.6
Punctuated Equilibrium and Competitive Structure

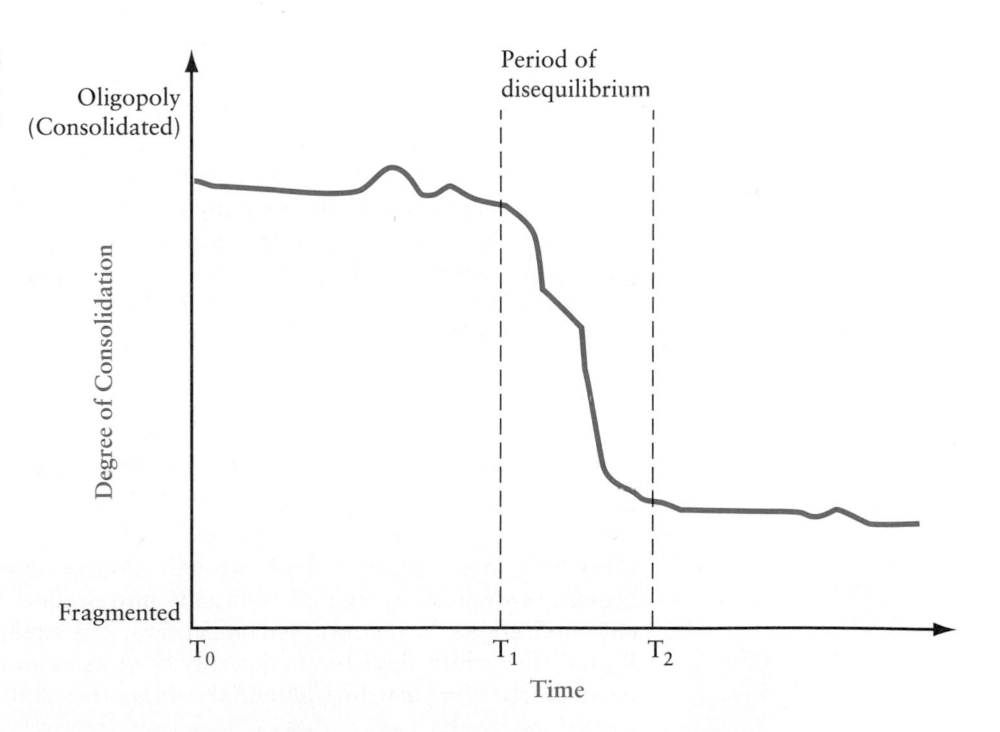

The punctuated equilibrium model of industry evolution makes a good deal of sense. It implies that the five forces and strategic group models are applicable while the industry is in a steady state but not while it is undergoing radical restructuring due to innovation or some other discontinuity. (Deregulation of an industry is another example of a discontinuity.) Because the five forces and strategic group models are static they cannot adequately capture what occurs during such periods of rapid change, but they are certainly useful tools for analyzing industry structure during periods of stability. It should be noted, however, that some experts in this field question the validity of the punctuated equilibrium approach. For example, in a recent book, Richard D'Avani has argued that many industries are **hypercompetitive.**[20] Hypercompetitive industries are characterized by permanent and ongoing innovation (the computer industry is often cited as an example of a hypercompetitive industry). In such industries, industry structure is constantly being revolutionized by innovation; there are no periods of equilibrium. When this is the case, one might argue that the five forces and strategic group models are of limited value since they represent no more than snapshots of a moving picture.

Industry Structure and Company Differences

The second criticism of the five force and strategic group models is that they overemphasize the importance of industry structure as a determinant of company performance and underemphasize the importance of differences between companies within an industry or strategic group. As we point out in the next chapter, there can be enormous variance in the profit rates of individual companies within an industry. Recent research by Richard Rumelt, for example, suggests that industry structure explains only about 10 percent of the variance in profit rates across companies, the implication being that individual company differences explain much of the remainder.[21] Other studies have put the variance explained closer to 20 percent, which is still not a large figure.[22] Similarly, a growing number of studies have found only very weak evidence of a link between strategic group membership and company profit rates, despite the fact that the strategic group model predicts a strong link.[23] Collectively, these studies suggest that the individual resources and capabilities of a company are far more important determinants of its profitability than is the industry or strategic group of which the company is a member. Although these findings do not make the five forces and strategic group models irrelevant, they do mean that the models have limited usefulness. A company will not be profitable just because it is based in an attractive industry or strategic group; much more is required, as we discuss in Chapters 4 and 5.

3.6 COMPETITIVE CHANGES DURING INDUSTRY EVOLUTION

Over time most industries pass through a series of well-defined stages, from growth through maturity and eventually into decline. These stages have different implications for the form of competition. The strength and nature of each of Porter's five competitive forces typically changes as an industry evolves.[24] This is particularly true regarding potential competitors and rivalry, and we focus on

these two forces in our discussion. The changes in the strength and nature of these forces give rise to different opportunities and threats at each stage of an industry's evolution. The task facing managers is to *anticipate* how the strength of each force will change with the stage of industry development and to formulate strategies that take advantage of opportunities as they arise and that counter emerging threats.

The **industry life cycle model** is a useful tool for analyzing the effects of industry evolution on competitive forces. The model is similar to the product life cycle model discussed in the marketing literature. Using the industry life cycle model, we can identify five industry environments, each linked to a distinct stage of an industry's evolution: (1) an embryonic industry environment, (2) a growth industry environment, (3) a shakeout environment, (4) a mature industry environment, and (5) a declining industry environment (see Figure 3.7).

Embryonic Industries

An *embryonic* industry is one that is just beginning to develop (for example, personal computers in 1980). Growth at this stage is slow because of such factors as buyers' unfamiliarity with the industry's product, high prices due to the inability of companies to reap any significant scale economies, and poorly developed distribution channels. Barriers to entry at this stage in an industry's evolution tend to be based on access to key technological know-how rather than cost economies or brand loyalty. If the core know-how required to compete in the industry is complex and difficult to grasp, barriers to entry can be quite high and incumbent companies will be protected from potential competitors. Rivalry in embryonic industries is based not so much on price as upon educating customers, opening up distribution channels, and perfecting the design of the product. Such rivalry can be intense, and the company that is the first to solve design problems often has the opportunity to develop a significant market position. An embryonic industry may also be the creation of one company's innovative efforts, as happened with personal computers (Apple), vacuum cleaners

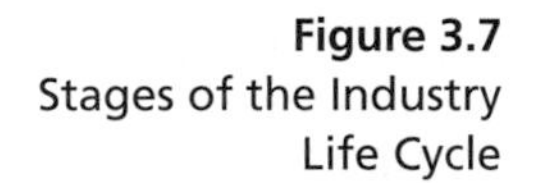

Figure 3.7
Stages of the Industry Life Cycle

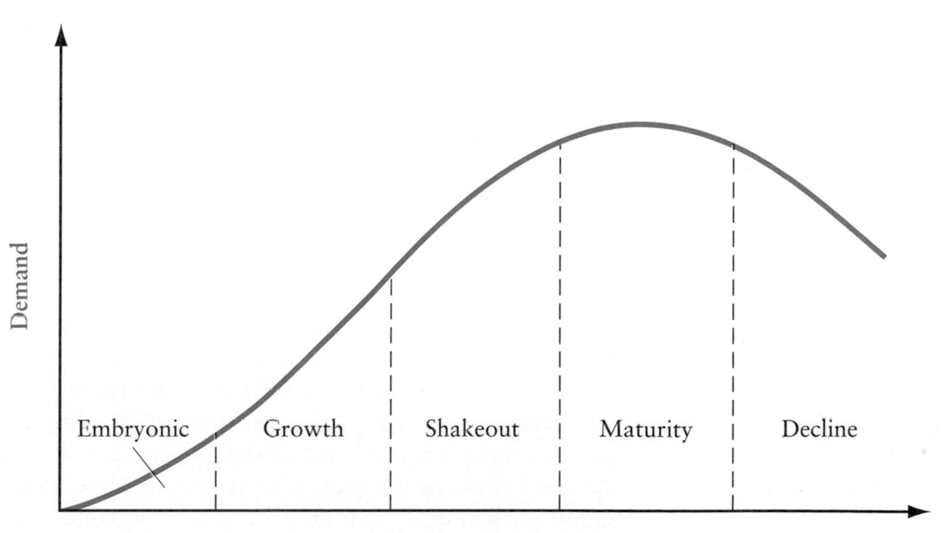

(Hoover), and photocopiers (Xerox). In such circumstances, the company has a major opportunity to capitalize on the lack of rivalry and build up a strong hold on the market.

Growth Industries

Once demand for the industry's product begins to take off, the industry develops the characteristics of a growth industry. In a *growth* industry, first-time demand is expanding rapidly as many new consumers enter the market. Typically, an industry grows when consumers become familiar with the product, when prices fall because experience and scale economies have been attained, and when distribution channels develop. The personal computer industry was in the growth stage for most of the 1980s and early 1990s. To illustrate, in the United States 55,000 personal computers were sold in 1981. By 1984 the figure had risen to 7.5 million, and by 1992 it was 20 million.

Normally, the importance of control over technological knowledge as a barrier to entry diminishes by the time an industry enters its growth stage. Because few companies have yet achieved significant scale economies or differentiated their product sufficiently to guarantee brand loyalty, other barriers to entry tend to be low as well. Consequently, the threat from potential competitors generally is highest at this point. Paradoxically, though, high growth usually means that new entrants can be absorbed into an industry without a marked increase in competitive pressure.

During an industry's growth stage, rivalry tends to be low. Rapid growth in demand enables companies to expand their revenues and profits without taking market share away from competitors. A company has the opportunity to expand its operations. In addition, a strategically aware company takes advantage of the relatively benign environment of the growth stage to prepare itself for the intense competition of the coming industry shakeout.

Industry Shakeout

Explosive growth of the type experienced by the personal computer industry in the 1980s and early 1990s cannot be maintained indefinitely. Sooner or later the rate of growth slows, and the industry enters the shakeout stage. In the *shakeout* stage, demand approaches saturation levels. In a saturated market, there are few potential first-time buyers left. Most of the demand is limited to replacement demand.

As an industry enters the shakeout stage, rivalry between companies becomes intense. What typically happens is that companies that have become accustomed to rapid growth during an industry's growth phase continue to add capacity at rates consistent with past growth. Managers use historic growth rates to forecast future growth rates, and they plan expansions in productive capacity accordingly. As an industry approaches maturity, however, demand no longer grows at historic rates. The consequence is the emergence of excess productive capacity. This condition is illustrated in Figure 3.8, where the solid curve indicates the growth in demand over time and the broken curve indicates the growth in productive capacity over time. As you can see, past point t_1, the growth in demand slows as the industry becomes mature. However, capacity continues to grow until time t_2. The gap between the solid and the broken lines signifies excess capacity. In an attempt to utilize this capacity, companies often cut prices.

Figure 3.8
Growth in Demand and Capacity

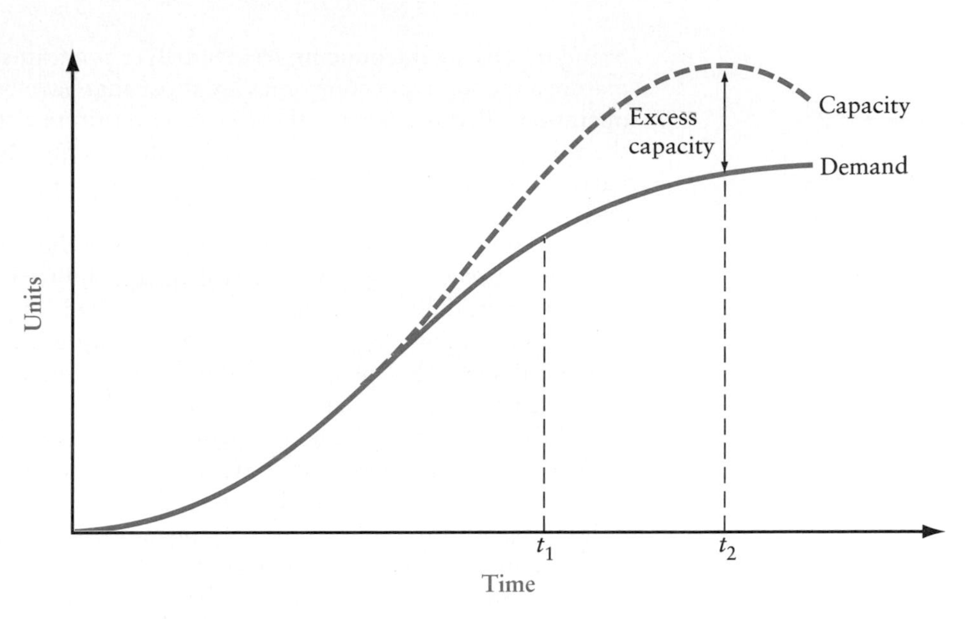

The result can be an intense price war, which drives many of the most inefficient companies into bankruptcy. This is itself enough to deter any new entry.

An example of what can occur took place in the semiconductor industry during the mid 1980s. In 1983 there were twenty plants in operation worldwide producing dynamic random-access memories (DRAMs). Propelled by strong market growth and optimistic predictions, by early 1985 the number of plants had more than doubled. By mid 1985, however, there was a significant unanticipated slowdown in the growth rate of the market. As a consequence, by the end of 1985, from 30 to 40 percent of industry DRAM capacity was standing idle. Overcapacity triggered fierce price cutting and the withdrawal of several incumbent producers. As a result, by 1987 the number of plants producing DRAMs had fallen 30 percent from the 1985 high. Interestingly enough, however, since this shakeout the DRAM market has once more resumed its rapid growth. The market is not yet mature so a further shakeout is due some time in the future. The 1985–1986 shakeout just gave a foretaste of what the future may bring.

Mature Industries

The shakeout stage ends when the industry enters its *mature* stage. In a mature industry, the market is totally saturated and demand is limited to replacement demand. During this stage, growth is low or zero. What little growth there is comes from population expansion bringing new consumers into the market.

As an industry enters maturity, barriers to entry increase and the threat of entry from potential competitors decreases. As growth slows during the shakeout, companies can no longer maintain historic growth rates merely by holding on to their market share. Competition for market share develops, driving down prices. Often the result is a price war, as happened in the airline industry during the 1988–1992 shakeout. To survive the shakeout, companies begin to focus both on costs minimization and on building brand loyalty. The airlines, for example, tried to cut operating costs by hiring nonunion labor and to build

brand loyalty by introducing frequent-flyer programs. By the time an industry matures, the surviving companies are those that have brand loyalty and low-cost operations. Because both of these factors constitute a significant barrier to entry, the threat of entry by potential competitors is greatly diminished. High entry barriers in mature industries give companies the opportunity to increase prices and profits.

As a result of the shakeout, most industries in the maturity stage have consolidated and become oligopolies. In the airline industry, for example, because of the shakeout, the top five companies controlled 80 percent of the industry in 1992, up from only 50 percent in 1984. In mature industries, companies tend to recognize their interdependence and try to avoid price wars. Stable demand gives them the opportunity to enter into price-leadership agreements. The net effect is to reduce the threat of intense rivalry among established companies, thereby allowing greater profitability. However, as noted earlier, the stability of a mature industry is always threatened by further price wars. A general slump in economic activity can depress industry demand. As companies fight to maintain their revenues in the face of declining demand, price-leadership agreements break down, rivalry increases, and prices and profits fall. The periodic price wars that occur in the airline industry seem to follow this pattern. A similar pattern now seems to be developing in the U.S. brewing industry, which is profiled in Strategy in Action 3.3.

Declining Industries

Eventually, most industries enter a decline stage. In the *decline* stage, growth becomes negative for a variety of reasons, including technological substitution (for example, air travel for rail travel), social changes (greater health consciousness hitting tobacco sales), demographics (the declining birthrate hurting the market for baby and child products), and international competition (low-cost foreign competition pushing the American steel industry into decline). Within a declining industry, the degree of rivalry among established companies usually increases. Depending on the speed of the decline and the height of exit barriers, competitive pressures can become as fierce as in the shakeout stage.[26] The main problem in a declining industry is that falling demand leads to the emergence of excess capacity. In trying to utilize this capacity, companies begin to cut prices, thus sparking a price war. As noted earlier, the American steel industry has experienced these problems because of the attempt of steel companies to utilize their excess capacity. The same problem occurred in the airline industry in the 1990–1992 period, as companies cut prices to ensure that they would not be flying with half-empty planes (that is, that they would not be operating with substantial excess capacity). Exit barriers play a part in adjusting excess capacity. The greater the exit barriers, the harder it is for companies to reduce capacity and the greater is the threat of severe price competition.

Variations on the Theme

It is important to remember that the industry life cycle model is a generalization. In practice, industry life cycles do not always follow the pattern illustrated in Figure 3.7. In some cases, growth is so rapid that the embryonic stage is skipped altogether, as happened in the personal computer industry. In other instances, industries fail to get past the embryonic stage. Industry growth can be revitalized after long periods of decline, either through innovations or through social changes. For example, the health boom brought the bicycle industry back to life

STRATEGY IN ACTION 3.3

Competition in a Mature Industry: The U.S. Beer Industry

Consumption of beer has been essentially flat in the U.S. since the early 1980s. Between 1960 and 1980 U.S. beer consumption increased from 90 million barrels to 175 million barrels per annum. Since then it has hardly shifted. A major reason for this seems to be growing awareness of the dangers of alcohol abuse, along with tougher drinking-and-driving laws. Faced with a maturing market, the major U.S. brewers have responded by purchasing smaller regional brewers and by aggressive marketing in key regions. Their rationale has been that growth can only be maintained through consolidation. Thus in 1992 the top three beer companies in the United States (Anheuser-Busch, Miller, and Coors) accounted for 77 percent of the total market, up from 60 percent only a decade earlier. In becoming larger, the major brewers have gained from substantial economies of scale. As their per-barrel costs decline, the big three have been able to funnel more money into marketing and distribution, which has given them a clear advantage vis-à-vis smaller regional breweries.

However, such a strategy is now becoming increasingly difficult to maintain in the face of strategic moves by a number of second-tier brewers, such as The Stroh Brewery Co. and G. Heileman Brewing Co. Both of these companies have benefited by emphasizing their regional focus in marketing campaigns and by low pricing. For example, in Washington State, Heileman owns Rainer Beer, a Seattle-based regional brewery. All of Rainer's advertising stresses its local roots in Seattle, and never mentions the fact that the company is owned by Heileman. In response, during the late 1980s Miller and Coors both started to discount as they tried to gain share from the regionals. However, the tactic hurt Anheuser-Busch as much as the regionals. Anheuser-Busch responded by cutting its own prices, and the result has been a marked increase in the intensity of price competition in the U.S. brewing industry and a commensurate decline in company profit rates. For the major brewing companies, the problem now is that consumers and retailers have become accustomed to price discounting. Thus it is proving very difficult for them to disengage from what is essentially a no-win strategy.[25]

after a long period of decline. The time span of the different stages can also vary significantly from industry to industry. Some industries can stay in maturity almost indefinitely if their products become basic necessities of life, as is the case for the automobile industry. Others skip the mature stage and go straight into decline. That is essentially what occurred in the vacuum tube industry. Vacuum tubes were replaced by transistors as a major component in electronic products while the industry was still in its growth stage. Still other industries may go through not one but several shakeouts before they enter full maturity. As our example of DRAM chips illustrates, this seems to be happening in the semiconductor industry.

3.7 GLOBALIZATION AND INDUSTRY STRUCTURE

A fundamental change is occurring in the world economy. The term *global shift* has been coined by one author to capture the essence of the change.[27] We seem to be witnessing the globalization of production and of markets. With regard to the **globalization of production**, it has been observed that increasingly individual

companies are dispersing parts of their production process to different locations around the globe to take advantage of national differences in the cost and quality of factors of production (that is, labor, energy, land, and capital). The objective is to lower costs and boost profits. Consider General Motors' (GM) Pontiac Le Mans. Based on a comparison of relative factor costs and quality, GM has dispersed many of the different activities that go to make up the Le Mans to different locations around the globe. As a result, of the $20,000 paid to GM for a Le Mans, about $6,000 goes to South Korea, where the Le Mans is assembled, $3,500 goes to Japan for advanced components (engines, transaxles, and electronics), $1,500 to Germany, where the Le Mans was designed, $800 to Taiwan, Singapore, and Japan for small components, $500 to Britain for advertising and marketing services, and about $100 to Ireland for data-processing services. The remaining $7,600 goes to GM and to the lawyers, bankers, and insurance agents that GM uses in the United States. The point is that GM is trying to lower its overall costs by dispersing its various productive activities to the optimal location for performing a given activity, wherever in the world that may be.[28]

As for the **globalization of markets**, it has been argued that we are moving away from an economic system in which national markets are distinct entities, isolated from each other by trade barriers and barriers of distance, time, and culture, and toward a system in which national markets are merging into one huge global marketplace. According to this view, the tastes and preferences of consumers in different nations are beginning to converge on some global norm. Thus in many industries it is no longer meaningful to talk about the German market, the American market, or the Japanese market—there is only the global market. The global acceptance of Coca-Cola, Levi blue jeans, the Sony Walkman and McDonald's hamburgers exemplifies this trend.[29] On the other hand, it is important not to push this view too far. As you will see in Chapter 8, where we discuss this issue in depth, very significant differences in consumer tastes and preferences between national markets still remain in many industries. These differences frequently require that marketing strategies and product features be customized to local conditions. Nevertheless, there is no doubt that more global markets exist today than at any previous period in history.

The Causes of Global Shift

Two factors underlie the trend toward the increasing globalization of markets and production. Since the end of World War II, barriers to the free flow of goods, services, and capital between countries have decreased, and dramatic changes have occurred in communication, information, and transportation technologies.

In the aftermath of World War II, the advanced industrial nations of the West committed themselves to the goal of removing barriers to the free flow of goods, services, and capital between nations. The goal of removing barriers to the free flow of goods was enshrined in an international treaty known as the General Agreement on Tariffs and Trade (GATT). Under the umbrella of the GATT, in the half century since World War II there has been a significant lowering of barriers to the free flow of goods.

The result of the GATT has been to facilitate the globalization of markets and production. The lowering of trade barriers has allowed companies to view the

world, rather than a single country, as their market. It has also made it increasingly possible to base individual production activities at the optimal locations for them, serving the world market from those locations. Thus a company might design a product in one country, produce component parts in two other countries, assemble the product in yet another country, and then export the finished product around the world.

If the lowering of trade barriers made the globalization of markets and production a theoretical possibility, technological change has transformed this into a tangible reality. Since the end of World War II, major advances have taken place in communications, information processing and transportation technology. Perhaps the single most important innovation has been the development of the microprocessor, which underlies many of the recent advances in communications technology. Over the last thirty years global communications have been revolutionized by developments in satellite and optical fiber technology. Satellites and optical fibers can carry hundreds of thousands of signals simultaneously. Both of these technologies rely on the microprocessor to encode, transmit, and decode the vast amount of information that flows along the electronic highway.

These technological innovations have dramatically lowered the real costs of information processing and communication over the last two decades. Lower costs in turn, have made it possible for companies to manage globally dispersed production systems. Indeed, a worldwide communications network has become essential to the functioning of many companies. For example, Texas Instruments, the U.S. electronics company, has approximately fifty plants located in some nineteen countries. It operates a satellite-based communications system to coordinate, on a global scale, its production planning, cost accounting, financial planning, marketing, customer service, and personnel management. The system consists of more than 300 remote job-entry terminals, 8,000 inquiry terminals, and 140 mainframe computers, which are linked to the system. The system enables managers in TI's worldwide operations to send vast amounts of information to each other instantaneously and to effect tight coordination among the company's different plants and activities.[30]

Besides communications and information-processing technology, the development of commercial jet aircraft has helped knit together the worldwide operations of many international businesses. By jetliner, it takes a day at most for an American manager to travel to her company's European or Asian operations, greatly increasing her ability to oversee a globally dispersed production system.

Technological innovation has also facilitated the globalization of markets. Low-cost jet travel has resulted in the mass movement of people between countries. This has helped reduce the cultural distance between countries and has laid the ground for some convergence of consumer tastes and preferences. At the same time global communications networks and global media are helping to create a worldwide culture. U.S. television networks such as CNN, MTV, and HBO can now be received in many countries around the world, and Hollywood films are shown the world over. In any society the media is one of the main conveyers of culture, and as global media develop, something akin to a global culture is likely to develop as well. The logical end result of this process will be the emergence of global markets for consumer products. Indeed, the first signs that this is beginning to occur are already apparent. It is now as easy to find a McDonald's restaurant in Tokyo as it is in New York; to buy a Sony

Walkman in Rio as it is in Berlin; and to buy Levi blue jeans in Paris as it is in San Francisco.

The Consequences of Global Shift

The trend toward the globalization of production and the globalization of markets has several important implications for competition within an industry. First, it is crucial for companies to recognize that industry boundaries do not stop at national borders. Because many industries are becoming global in scope, actual and potential competitors exist not only in a company's home market, but also in other national markets. Companies that scan just their home market can be caught unprepared by the entry of efficient foreign competitors. Thus, for example, the U.S. auto companies erroneously perceived the threat of entry into the U.S. auto market to be low and were unprepared for the onslaught of Japanese competition that began in the late 1970s. The globalization of markets and production and the resulting growth of world trade, foreign direct investment and imports all imply that companies around the globe are finding their home markets under attack from foreign competitors. This is true in Japan, where Eastman Kodak has taken market share in the film industry away from Fuji in recent years, in the United States, where Japanese automobile firms have challenged the U.S. trio of GM, Ford, and Chrysler, and in Western Europe, where the once dominant Dutch company, Philips, has seen its market share in the consumer electronics industry taken by Japan's JVC, Matsushita, and Sony.

Second, the shift from national to global markets during the last twenty years has intensified competitive rivalry in industry after industry. National markets that were once consolidated oligopolies, dominated by three or four companies and subjected to relatively little foreign competition, have been transformed into segments of fragmented global industries, where a large number of companies battle each other for market share in country after country. This rivalry has driven down profit rates and made it all the more critical for companies to maximize their efficiency, quality, customer responsiveness, and innovative ability. The painful restructuring and downsizing that has been going on at companies such as General Motors and Kodak is as much a response to the increased intensity of global competition as it is to anything else. It should be noted, however, that not all global industries are fragmented. Many remain consolidated oligopolies, except that now they are consolidated global, rather than national, oligopolies. One such industry, the global tire industry, is discussed in Strategy in Action 3.4.

Third, as competitive intensity has increased, so has the rate of innovation. Companies strive to gain an advantage over their competitors by pioneering new products, processes, and ways of doing business. The result has been to compress product life cycles and make it vital for companies to stay on the leading edge of technology. In regard to highly competitive global industries, where the rate of innovation is accelerating, the criticism that Porter's five forces model is too static may be particularly relevant.

Finally, it should be noted that even though globalization has increased both the threat of entry and the intensity of rivalry within many formerly protected national markets, it has also created enormous opportunities for companies based in those markets. The steady decline in trade barriers has opened up many

STRATEGY IN ACTION 3.4

Competitive Interdependence in the Global Tire Industry

The globalization of production and markets has transformed many formerly consolidated national industries into fragmented global ones. However, other global industries remain consolidated oligopolies—for example, the global tire industry. In 1992 the global tire industry served a $48 billion worldwide market. Five companies controlled 66 percent of the market, with the big three—Michelin of France, Bridgestone of Japan, and Goodyear of the United States—accounting for 20 percent, 16.5 percent and 16 percent of global market share, respectively.

Like many other consolidated industries selling a commodity type of product, the global tire industry has been characterized by competitive interdependence and periodic price wars. The one variant has been the use of price discounting in a selective way to maintain dominance in home markets. The first instance of such price discounting occurred in the early 1980s, when the industry was in the process of becoming a global entity. Michelin used its strong European profits to support competitive price cutting in the North American market, which was dominated by Goodyear. Goodyear could have retaliated by cutting its North American prices, but because only a small amount of Michelin's worldwide business was in North America, Michelin had little to lose from a North American price war. Goodyear, on the other hand, would have sacrificed profits in its largest market. Therefore, Goodyear struck back by cutting prices and expanding its operations in Europe. The action forced Michelin to slow down its attack on Goodyear's North American market and to think again about the costs of taking market share away from Goodyear.

After the competitive price cutting of the early 1980s, something approaching tacit price collusion seemed to operate: both Goodyear and Michelin refrained from cutting prices in each other's home market. By the early 1990s, however, the tacit price collusion had broken down. The global industry was in the grip of a vicious price war, triggered by two events. First, Japan's Bridgestone had acquired Firestone, and in the process established itself as the number two player in the industry. The rise of Bridgestone threatened the fragile truce between Goodyear and Michelin. Second, the global auto industry experienced a serious business slump in the early 1990s. The tire industry, as a major supplier to the auto industry, found its prices under pressure from auto companies, which were quite willing to play tire manufacturers off against each other in order to gain lower prices. Faced with slumping sales and excess capacity, the tire companies had little choice but to start discounting on price. Once again, though, there was a regional bias to their discounting. Bridgestone used its Japanese profits to try and subsidize aggressive pricing in Europe. Michelin responded by cutting its prices sharply in Europe in an effort to keep the Japanese company from gaining market share there. The end result was that tire prices were bid down in Europe and profits slumped. At the same time, both Michelin and Bridgestone initiated aggressive pricing in North America in an attempt to take share away from Goodyear. Goodyear was forced to respond in kind, and prices also plunged in the North American market. Consequently, both Goodyear and Michelin lost money in 1991 and 1992, while Bridgestone saw almost all of its Japanese profits wiped out by the losses borne by its North American and European subsidiaries.[31]

once protected markets to companies based outside them. Thus, for example, in recent years U.S. companies have accelerated their investments in the nations of Eastern Europe, Latin America, and Southeast Asia as they try to take advantage of growth opportunities in those areas.

3.9 NATIONAL CONTEXT AND COMPETITIVE ADVANTAGE

As noted in Chapter 1, the national context of a country influences the competitiveness of companies based within it. Despite the globalization of production and markets, many of the most successful companies in certain industries are still clustered in a small number of countries. For example, many of the world's most successful biotechnology and computer companies are based in the United States, many of the world's most successful consumer electronics companies are based in Japan, and many of the world's most successful chemical and engineering companies are based in Germany. This suggests that the national context within which a company is based may have an important bearing on the competitive position of that company in the global marketplace.

Companies need to understand how national context can affect competitive advantage, for then they will be able to identify (1) where their most significant competitors are likely to come from and (2) where they might want to locate certain productive activities. Thus, seeking to take advantage of U.S. expertise in biotechnology, many foreign companies have set up research facilities in U.S. locations such as San Diego, Boston, and Seattle, where U.S. biotechnology companies tend to be clustered. Similarly, in an attempt to take advantage of Japanese success in consumer electronics, many U.S. electronics companies have set up research and production facilities in Japan, often in conjunction with Japanese partners.

Economic theory stresses that **factor conditions**—the cost and quality of factors of production—are a prime determinant of the competitive advantage that certain countries might have in certain industries. Factors of production include **basic factors,** such as land, labor, capital, and raw materials, and **advanced factors** such as technological know-how—managerial sophistication, and physical infrastructure (that is, roads, railways, and ports). The competitive advantage that the United States enjoys in biotechnology might be explained by the presence of certain advanced factors of production—for example, technological know-how—in combination with some basic factors, which might be a pool of relatively low-cost venture capital that can be used to fund risky start-ups in industries such as biotechnology.

Of course, factor conditions alone are only part of the story. In a study of competitive advantage, Michael Porter identified other elements of national context that play an important role. According to Porter, there are four basic determinants of a nation's competitive position in certain industries: factor conditions, industry rivalry, demand conditions, and related and supporting industries (see Figure 3.9). He argues that a country will have a competitive advantage in a particular industry under the following conditions:

1. The country has the right mix of basic and advanced factors of production to support that industry.
2. Intense rivalry between local companies in that industry has forced them to be efficient.
3. Strong local demand conditions have helped foster a strong local industry, while demanding consumers have forced companies to become more efficient.
4. Related and supporting industries are also internationally competitive, thus providing companies in the focal industry with low-cost and high-quality inputs and complementary products.[32]

Figure 3.9
The Determinants of National Competitive Advantage

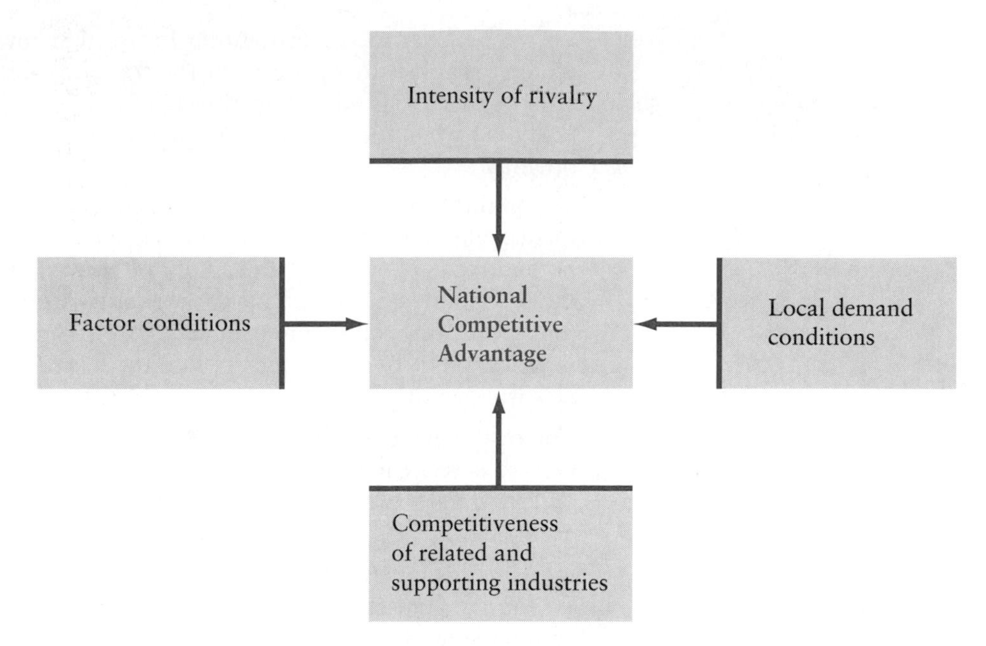

As an example, consider the U.S. computer hardware industry (personal computers, workstations, minicomputers, and mainframes). The existence of a world-class industry in the United States can be explained by the presence of advanced factors of production in the form of technological know-how; an intense rivalry among myriad competing computer companies; a strong local demand for computers (more personal computers have been sold in the United States than in the rest of the world combined); and internationally competitive supporting industries, such as the computer software and microprocessor industries.

Perhaps the most important implication of Porter's framework is the message that it carries about the attractiveness of certain locations for performing certain productive activities. For instance, many Japanese computer companies have moved much of their R&D activity to the United States so that they can benefit from the international competitiveness of the United States in this industry. Most U.S. financial service companies have substantial operations in London so that they can take advantage of London's central position in the world financial services industry. And many international textile companies have design operations in Italy so that they can take advantage of Italian style and design know-how. In all these cases, companies are trying to build a competitive advantage by establishing critical productive activities in the optimal location, as defined by the various elements highlighted in Porter's framework. This is an issue we discuss in depth in Chapter 8.

3.9 SUMMARY OF CHAPTER

This chapter details a framework that managers can use to analyze the external environment of their company, enabling them to identify opportunities and threats. The following major points are made in the chapter:

1. For a company to succeed, either its strategy must fit the environment in which the company operates, or the company must be able to reshape this environment to its advantage through its choice of strategy. Companies typically fail when their strategy no longer fits the environment in which they operate.
2. The main technique used to analyze competition in the industry environment is the five forces model. The five forces, (a) the risk of new entry by potential competitors, (b) the extent of rivalry among established firms, (c) the bargaining power of buyers, (d) the bargaining power of suppliers, and (e) the threat of substitute products. The stronger each of these forces, the more competitive is the industry and the lower is the rate of return that can be earned in that industry.
3. The risk of entry by potential competitors is a function of the height of barriers to entry. The higher the barriers to entry, the lower is the risk of entry and the greater are the profits that can be earned in the industry.
4. The extent of rivalry among established companies is a function of an industry's competitive structure, demand conditions, and barriers to exit. Strong demand conditions moderate the competition among established companies and create opportunities for expansion. When demand is weak, intensive competition can develop, particularly in consolidated industries with high exit barriers.
5. Buyers are most powerful when a company depends on them for business but they themselves are not dependent on the company. In such circumstances, buyers are a threat.
6. Suppliers are most powerful when a company depends on them for business but they themselves are not dependent on the company. In such circumstances, suppliers are a threat.
7. Substitute products are the products of companies based in industries serving consumer needs similar to the needs served by the industry being analyzed. The more similar the substitute products are to each other, the lower is the price that companies can charge without losing customers to the substitutes.
8. Most industries are composed of strategic groups. Strategic groups are groups of companies pursuing the same or a similar strategy. Companies in different strategic groups pursue different strategies.
9. The members of a company's strategic group constitute its immediate competitors. Since different strategic groups are characterized by different opportunities and threats, it may pay a company to switch strategic groups. The feasibility of doing so is a function of the height of mobility barriers.
10. The five forces and strategic group models have been criticized for presenting a static picture of competition that de-emphasizes the role of innovation. Innovation can revolutionize industry structure and completely change the strength of different competitive forces.
11. The five forces and strategic group models have been criticized for de-emphasizing the importance of individual company differences. A company will not be profitable just because it is based in an attractive industry or strategic group; much more is required.

12. Industries go through a well-defined life cycle, from an embryonic stage, through growth, shakeout, and maturity, and eventually into decline. Each stage has different implications for the competitive structure of the industry, and each stage gives rise to its own set of opportunities and threats.
13. A fundamental change is occurring in the world economy: the globalization of production and of markets, or global shift. The consequences of global shift include more intense rivalry, more rapid innovation, and shorter product life cycles.
14. There is a link between national context and the competitive advantage of a company in the global economy.

Discussion Questions

1. Under what environmental conditions are price wars most likely to occur in an industry? What are the implications of price wars for a company? How should a company try to deal with the threat of a price war?
2. Discuss Porter's five forces model with reference to what you know about the U.S. airline industry. What does the model tell you about the level of competition in this industry?
3. How do you think the trend toward greater globalization is likely to impact upon the nature and intensity level of competition in the U.S. airline market?
4. Identify a growth industry, a mature industry, and a declining industry. For each industry, identify the following: (a) the number and size distribution of companies, (b) the nature of barriers to entry, (c) the height of barriers to entry, and (d) the extent of product differentiation. What do these factors tell you about the nature of competition in each industry? What are the implications for a company in terms of opportunities and threats?
5. Assess the impact of macroenvironmental factors on the likely level of enrollment at your university over the next decade. What are the implications of these factors for the job security and salary level of your professors?

Article File 3

Find an example of an industry that has become more competitive in recent years. Identify the reasons for the increase in competitive pressure.

Strategic Management Project: Module 3

This module requires you to analyze the industry environment in which your company is based. With the information you have at your disposal, perform the tasks and answer the questions listed:

1. Apply the five forces model to the industry in which your company is based. What does this model tell you about the nature of competition in the industry?
2. Are there any changes taking place in the macroenvironment that might have an impact, either positive or negative, on the industry in which your company is based? If so, what are these changes and how will they affect the industry?
3. Identify any strategic groups that might exist in the industry. How does the intensity of competition differ across the strategic groups you have identified?
4. How dynamic is the industry in which your company is based? Is there any evidence that innovation is reshaping competition or has done so in the recent past?
5. In what stage of its life cycle is the industry in which your company is based? What are the implications of this for the intensity of competition both now, and in the future?
6. Is your company based in an industry that is becoming more global? If so, what are the implications of this for competitive intensity?
7. Analyze the impact of national context as it pertains to the industry in which your company is based. Does national context help or hinder your company in achieving a competitive advantage in the global marketplace?

Endnotes

1. Sources: P. Andrews, "Wrong Turns on the Road to PCdom Come Back to Haunt Wang," *Seattle Times*, August 25, 1992, p. D3. B. Ziegler, "Once Booming Wang Laboratories Failed to Heed the Changing Market," *Seattle Times*, August 23, 1992, p. C6. W. M. Bulkeley, and J. R. Wilkes, "Steep Slide: Filing in Chapter 11, Wang Sends Warning to High Tech Circles," *Wall Street Journal*, August 19, 1992, p. A1.
2. Michael E. Porter, *Competitive Strategy* (New York: Free Press, 1980).
3. J. E. Brian, *Barriers to New Competition* (Cambridge, Mass.: Harvard University Press, 1956). For a review of the modern literature on barriers to entry, see R. J. Gilbert, "Mobility Barriers and the Value of Incumbency," in *Handbook of Industrial Organization*, ed. R. Schmalensee and R. D. Willig (Amsterdam: North Holland, 1989), I.
4. Most of this information on barriers to entry can be found in the industrial organization economics literature. See especially Bain, *Barriers to New Competition*; M. Mann, "Seller Concentration, Barriers to Entry and Rates of Return in 30 Industries," *Review of Economics and Statistics*, 48 (1966) 296–307; W. S. Comanor and T. A. Wilson, "Advertising, Market Structure and Performance," *Review of Economics and Statistics*, 49 (1967), 423–440; and Gilbert, "Mobility Barriers and the Value of Incumbency."
5. Sources: M. L. Dertouzos, R. K. Lester, and R. M. Solow, *Made in America* (Cambridge, Mass.: MIT Press, 1989). "The Jumbo War," *Economist*, June 15, 1991, pp. 65–66; "Dissecting Airbus," *Economist*, February 16, 1991, pp. 51–52.
6. For a review of the theory of oligopoly, see C. Shapiro, "Theories of Oligopoly Behavior," in *Handbook of Industrial Organization*, ed. R. Schmalensee and R. D. Willig (Amsterdam: North Holland, 1989), I.
7. For discussion of tacit agreements, see T. C. Schelling, *The Strategy of Conflict*, (Cambridge, Mass.: Harvard University Press, 1960).
8. For details see D. F. Barnett, and R. W. Crandall, *Up From the Ashes* (Washington, D.C.: Brookings Institution and F. Koelbel, "Strategies for Restructuring the Steel Industry," *Metal Producing*, 33 (1986), 28–33.
9. Michael E. Porter, *Competitive Strategy* (New York: Free Press, 1980).
10. Sources: E. Tanouye, "Drug Prices Get a Dose of Market Pressure," *Wall Street Journal*, March 11, 1993, B1. C. G. McLaughlin, "Market Responses to HMOs: Price Competition or Rivalry?" *Inquiry*, 25 (1988), 207–218.
11. Porter, *Competitive Strategy.*
12. The phrase was originally coined by J. Schumpeter, *Capitalism, Socialism and Democracy* (London: Macmillan, 1950), p. 68.
13. See M. Gort and J. Klepper, "Time paths in the Diffusion of Product Innovations," *Economic Journal* (September 1982), 630–653. Looking at the history of forty-six different products, Gort and Klepper found that the length of time before other companies entered the markets created by a few inventive companies declined from an average of 14.4 years for products introduced before 1930 to 4.9 years for those introduced after 1949.

14. The development of strategic group theory has been a strong theme in the strategy literature. Important contributions include R. E. Caves and Michael E. Porter, "From Entry Barriers to Mobility Barriers," *Quarterly Journal of Economics* (May 1977), 241–262; K. R. Harrigan, "An Application of Clustering for Strategic Group Analysis," *Strategic Management Journal,* 6 (1985), 55–73; K. J. Hatten and D. E. Schendel, "Heterogeneity Within an Industry: Firm Conduct in the U.S. Brewing Industry, 1952–71," *Journal of Industrial Economics,* 26 (1977), 97–113; and Michael E. Porter, "The Structure Within Industries and Companies' Performance," *Review of Economics and Statistics,* 61 (1979), 214–227.
15. For details on the strategic group structure in the pharmaceutical industry, see K. Cool and I. Dierickx, "Rivalry, Strategic Groups, and Firm Profitability," *Strategic Management Journal,* 14 (1993), 47–59.
16. This perspective is associated with the Austrian school of economics. The perspective goes back to Schumpeter. For a recent summary of this school and its implications for strategy, see R. Jacobson, "The Austrian School of Strategy," *Academy of Management Reviews,* 17 (1992), 782–807.
17. D. F. Barnett and R. W. Crandall, *Up from the Ashes.*
18. Michael E. Porter, *The Competitive Advantage of Nations* (New York: Free Press, 1990).
19. The term *punctuated equilibrium* is borrowed from evolutionary biology. For a detailed explanation of the concept, see M. L. Tushman, W. H. Newman, and E. Romanelli, "Convergence and Upheaval: Managing the Unsteady Pace of Organizational Evolution," *California Management Review,* 29 29–44; and C. J. G. Gersick, "Revolutionary Change Theories: A Multilevel Exploration of the Punctuated Equilibrium Paradigm," *Academy of Management Review,* 16 (1991), 10–36.
20. Richard D'Avani, *Hypercompetition* (New York: Free Press, 1994).
21. Richard P. Rumelt, "How Much Does Industry Matter?" *Strategic Management Journal,* 12 (1991) 167–185.
22. See R. Schmalensee, "Inter-Industry Studies of Structure and Performance," *Handbook of Industrial Organization,* ed. R. Schmalensee and R. D. Willig (Amsterdam: North Holland, 1989), I.
23. For example, see K. Cool and D. Schendel, "Strategic Group Formation and Performance: The Case of the U.S. Pharmaceutical Industry 1932–1992," *Management Science* (September 1989), 1102–1124.
24. Charles W. Hofer has argued that life cycle considerations may be the most important contingency when formulating business strategy. See Charles W. Hofer, "Towards a Contingency Theory of Business Strategy," *Academy of Management Journal,* 18 (1975), 784–810. There is also empirical evidence to support this view. See C. R. Anderson and C. P. Zeithaml, "Stages of the Product Life Cycle, Business Strategy, and Business Performance," *Academy of Management Journal,* 27 (1984), 5–24; and D. C. Hambrick and D. Lei, "Towards an Empirical Prioritization of Contingency Variables for Business Strategy," *Academy of Management Journal,* 28 (1985), 763–788.
25. Standard and Poor's Industry Surveys, *Food, Beverage and Tobacco,* November 5, 1992.
26. The characteristics of declining industries have been summarized by K. R. Harrigan, "Strategy Formulation in Declining Industries," *Academy of Management Review,* 5 (1980), 599–604.
27. P. Dicken, *Global Shift* (New York: Guilford Press, 1992).
28. Robert B. Reich, *The Work of Nations* (New York: Knopf, 1991).
29. Theodore Levitt, "The Globalization of Markets," *Harvard Business Review* (May–June 1983), 92–102.
30. Dicken, *Global Shift.*
31. Sources: "The Tyre Industry's Costly Obsession with Size," *Economist,* June 8, 1991, pp. 65–66. "A Bridge Too Far," *Financial World,* June 9, 1992, pp. 52–54.
32. Porter, *Competitive Advantage.*

4 Competitive Advantage: Resources, Capabilities, and Competencies

4.1 OPENING CASE: MARKS & SPENCER

Marks & Spencer (M&S) is a British retailing institution. Founded in 1884 by Michael Marks, a Polish Jew who had emigrated to England, the company has been a national chain since the early 1900s. By 1926 the company had a branch in every major town in the country and had become Britain's largest retailer, a position it still holds in 1994. Primarily a supplier of clothing and foodstuffs, M&S is one of the world's most profitable retailers. In 1992 M&S's 280 United Kingdom stores had sales of $7.5 billion. M&S accounted for 15 percent of all retail clothing sales in the United Kingdom, and 4.6 percent of all food sales. According to the *Guinness Book of Records*, in 1991 the company's flagship store at Marble Arch in London had a turnover of $3,700 per square foot—more than any other department store in the world.

The secret of the company's success lies in the way it follows some key strategic principles, many of which were already well established by the 1920s. M&S provides a selective range of clothing and food items aimed at rapid turnover. The firm sells all its products under its own St. Michael label. M&S offers high quality products at moderate rather than low prices. This combination of high quality and reasonable price encourages customers to associate M&S with value for money, and the firm's ability to deliver this combination consistently over the years has built up enormous customer goodwill in Britain. So strong is M&S's reputation among British consumers that the company does no advertising in that market—a major source of cost saving.

To achieve the combination of moderate prices and high quality, M&S works very closely with its suppliers, many of whom have been selling a major portion of their output to M&S for generations. The focus on quality is reinforced by M&S's practice of having its technical people work closely with suppliers on product design. Suppliers are more than willing to respond to the firm's demands, for they know that M&S is loyal to its suppliers and as it grows so do they. The sales volume generated by M&S's strategy of providing only a selective range of clothing and food enables M&S's suppliers to realize substantial economies of scale from large production runs. These cost savings are then passed on to M&S in the form of lower prices. In turn, M&S passes on part of the savings to the consumer.

Crucial to M&S's effectiveness is a clear focus on the customer. The tone is set by top management. Each senior manager makes a habit of wearing M&S clothes and eating M&S food. Thus managers develop an understanding of what it is that customers want and like about M&S products; by staying close to the customer they can improve the quality and design of the products they offer. The customer focus is reinforced at the store level by store managers who monitor sales volume and quickly identify lines that are selling and those that are not. Then store managers can transmit this information to suppliers, which have the capacity to quickly modify their production, increasing the output of lines that are selling well and reducing the output of lines that are not moving.

Another central feature of M&S is its pioneering approach to human relations. Long before it became fashionable to do so, M&S had developed a commitment to the well-being of its employees. M&S has always viewed itself as a family business with a broad responsibility for the welfare of its employees. M&S

offers employees medical and pension plans that provide benefits that are well above the industry average. The company pays its employees at a rate that is well above the industry average, and it makes a practice of promoting employees from within, rather than hiring from outside. Furthermore, there are a series of in-store amenities for employees, including subsidized cafeterias, medical services, recreation rooms and hairdressing salons. The reward for M&S is the trust and loyalty of its employees and, ultimately, high employee productivity.

Also vital is the company's commitment to simplifying its operating structure and strategic control systems. M&S has a very flat hierarchy; there is little in the way of intervening management layers between store managers and top management. The firm utilizes just two profit margins, one for foodstuff and one for clothing. This practice reduces bureaucracy and frees its store managers from worrying about pricing issues. Instead, they are encouraged to focus on maximizing sales volume. A store's performance is assessed by its sales volume. Control is achieved partly through formal budgetary procedures, and partly through an informal probing process, in which top management drops in unannounced at stores and quizzes managers there about the store. In a typical year, just about every store in Britain will receive at least one unannounced visit from top management. This keeps store managers on their toes and constantly alert to the need to provide the kind of value-for-money products that customers have come to associate with M&S.[1]

Discussion Questions

1. What do you think is the source of Marks & Spencer's competitive advantage?
2. Marks & Spencer has managed to maintain its competitive advantage in British retailing for over fifty years. Why, do you think, have rival firms found Marks & Spencer's competitive position so difficult to attack?

4.2 OVERVIEW

In Chapter 3, we discuss the elements of the external environment that determine an industry's attractiveness and examine how industry structure explains why some industries are more profitable than others. However, industry structure is not the only force that acts upon company profits. As we note in Chapter 1, within any given industry some companies are more profitable than others. For example, in the global auto industry, Toyota has consistently outperformed General Motors for most of the last twenty years. In the steel industry, Nucor has consistently outperformed US Steel. In the U.S. retail clothing industry, The Gap has consistently outperformed JC Penney's, while in the British retail clothing industry, as detailed in the Opening Case, Marks & Spencer has consistently outperformed its competitors for over half a century. The question, therefore, is why, within a given industry, do some companies do better than others? Put another way, what is the basis of competitive advantage?

Marks and Spencer provides some clues as to the sources of competitive advantage, that is, a company's ability to outperform its competitors. In the Opening Case, you saw how the competitive advantage of Marks & Spencer in the British retailing industry was based on its consistent ability to deliver high quality clothing and food products at a reasonable price (to deliver value for money). How does M&S achieve this? First, its strategy of offering only a limited product selection and focusing on volume lets its suppliers realize efficiency gains from scale economies. These gains, which result in lower costs, are passed on to M&S in the form of lower input prices. Second, M&S manages its relationship with suppliers to encourage them to focus on product quality and to be responsive to M&S's

needs. Third, the customer focus at M&S ensures that the company is responsive to customer demands. Fourth, the trust and commitment that M&S's human relations policy generates among M&S employees is translated into high employee productivity, which in turn helps lower M&S's costs and increases customer responsiveness. Fifth, the lack of a company bureaucracy helps lower M&S's costs by removing overheads. Finally, the enormous customer goodwill that M&S has generated in Britain enables the company to operate without advertising, which again lowers costs.

Thus we might conclude that M&S's competitive advantage comes from an ability to lower costs through **high efficiency**, provide consistently **high quality products**, and be **responsive to customer needs**. We might also argue that the company's success can be traced in part to the fact that it was a strategic **innovator** in the retail industry. It was the first nationwide retail operation in Britain, the first to adopt the strategy of selling a limited selection of high-quality merchandise, the first to adopt progressive human relations policies, and the first to build long-term cooperative relationships with its suppliers.

As you will see in this chapter, **efficiency, quality, innovation, and customer responsiveness** can be regarded as the four main building blocks, or dimensions, of competitive advantage. Companies that have achieved a competitive advantage typically excel on at least one of these four main dimensions. In turn, these dimensions are the product of an organization's competencies, resources, and capabilities. In this chapter, we examine how an organization seeks to build competitive advantage by developing competencies, resources, and capabilities to create superior efficiency, quality, innovation, and customer responsiveness. We then discuss three critical questions. First, once it is obtained, what factors influence the durability of competitive advantage? Second, why do successful companies lose their competitive advantage? Third, how can companies avoid competitive failure and sustain their competitive advantage over time? Whereas companies like M&S have enjoyed a long-run competitive advantage, the competitive advantage enjoyed by other companies is often short-lived. IBM's competitive advantage in the personal computer industry, for example, lasted only about two years before it was battered by low-priced clones and speedier innovators such as Compaq. Recent business history is littered with the wreckage of once great companies like IBM, Sears, and General Motors, which have lost their competitive edge and are striving to regain it. In this chapter, we provide a framework for answering these questions.

4.3 COMPETITIVE ADVANTAGE: LOW COST AND DIFFERENTIATION

We say that a company has a **competitive advantage** when its profit rate is higher than the average for its industry. Profit rate is normally defined as some ratio, such as return on sales (ROS) or return of assets (ROA). Table 4.1 gives the 1992 return on sales and return on assets of twenty-five U.S. companies in the computer industry. As you can see, 1992 was a bad year for the computer industry. The average ROS for the industry in 1992 was –0.8 percent and the average ROA was 0.6 percent. Yet some companies clearly did much better than the average—among them Apple Computer, AST Research, Dell Computer, and

Table 4.1
1992 Profit Rates in the Computer Industry

Company	Sales $ million	ROS (%)	ROA (%)
IBM	65,096	–8	–6
Hewlett-Packard	16,427	3	4
Digital Equipment	14,027	–20	–25
Unisys	8,422	4	5
Apple Computer	7,078	7	13
Compaq Computer	4,132	5	7
Sun Microsystems	3,682	5	6
Pitney Bowes	3,460	3	2
Seagate Technology	2,889	2	3
Amdahl	2,554	0	0
Conner Peripherals	2,273	5	6
Tandem Computers	2,058	–2	–2
Wang Laboratories	1,910	–19	–33
Storage Technology	1,512	1	1
Intergraph	1,182	1	1
Quantum	1,128	4	9
Data General	1,127	–6	–7
Gateway 2000	1,107	6	26
SCI Systems	1,945	0	1
Maxtor	1,039	1	2
AST Research	951	7	12
Western Digital	940	–8	–14
Dell Computer	890	6	9
Silicon Graphics	867	–14	–16
Cray Research	798	–2	–1
Average		–0.8	0.6

Gateway 2000, all with respectable profit rates. These companies had a competitive advantage in 1992. On the other hand, there were a number of other companies that did much worse than average, including some of the big names in the computer industry such as Digital Equipment, IBM, and Wang Laboratories. These companies were at a competitive disadvantage.

The most basic determinant of a company's profit rate is its gross profit margin (Π), which is simply the difference between total revenues (TR) and total costs (TC), divided by total costs:

$$\Pi = (TR - TC)/TC$$

To put it another way,

$$\Pi = \{(\text{Unit Price} * \text{Unit Sales}) - (\text{Unit Cost} * \text{Unit Sales})\} / (\text{Unit Cost} * \text{Unit Sales}).$$

It follows that for a gross profit margin to be higher than the average for the industry one of the following must be occurring:

- The company's *unit price must be higher* than that of the average company and its unit cost must be equivalent to that of the average company.
- The company's *unit cost must be lower* than that of the average company and its unit price must be equivalent to that of the average company.
- The company must have *both* a lower unit cost and a higher unit price than the average company.

Thus, to achieve a competitive advantage, a company must either have lower costs than its competitors, or it must differentiate its product in some way so that it can charge a higher price than its competitors, or it must do both simultaneously.

When a company charges a higher unit price than the industry average, it is engaging in **premium pricing**. For a consumer to be prepared to pay a premium price, the company must be adding value to the product, from the consumer's perspective, in a way that competitors are not. Adding value requires **differentiating** the product from those offered by competitors along one or more dimensions, such as quality, design, delivery time, and after-sales services and support. More precisely, it means achieving superior performance on dimensions such as these.

Building on these basic ideas, Michael Porter has referred to **low cost** and **differentiation** as **generic business-level strategies**.[2] That is, the strategies represent the two fundamental ways of trying to obtain a competitive advantage in an industry. A low-cost strategy is based on doing everything possible to lower unit costs. A differentiation strategy is based on doing everything possible to differentiate products from those offered by competitors in order to be able to charge a premium price. In the computer industry, for example, the competitive advantage enjoyed by Apple in 1992 was based on differentiation (see Table 4.1). Apple had a unique proprietary operating system and a strong brand name, both of which enable the company to differentiate itself from its competitors. On the other hand, the competitive advantage of Gateway 2000, Dell, and AST Research was based upon low cost. All these companies were low-cost manufacturers of IBM-compatible personal computers (clones). As a result, they were able to charge a low price for their products.

We say more about Porter's views in Chapter 6, when we discuss business-level strategy in depth. For now, our task is to identify those factors that enable a company to attain a low-cost and/or differentiation position and thus achieve a competitive advantage.

4.4 THE GENERIC BUILDING BLOCKS OF COMPETITIVE ADVANTAGE

As noted earlier, four factors build competitive advantage: efficiency, quality, innovation, and customer responsiveness. They are the generic building blocks of competitive advantage (Figure 4.1). These factors are generic in the sense that they represent four basic ways of lowering costs and achieving differentiation that any company can adopt, regardless of its industry or the products or services it produces. Although these factors are discussed separately below, it should be noted that they are all highly interrelated. Thus, for example, superior quality can lead to superior efficiency, while innovation can enhance efficiency, quality, and customer responsiveness.

Figure 4.1
Generic Building Blocks of Competitive Advantage

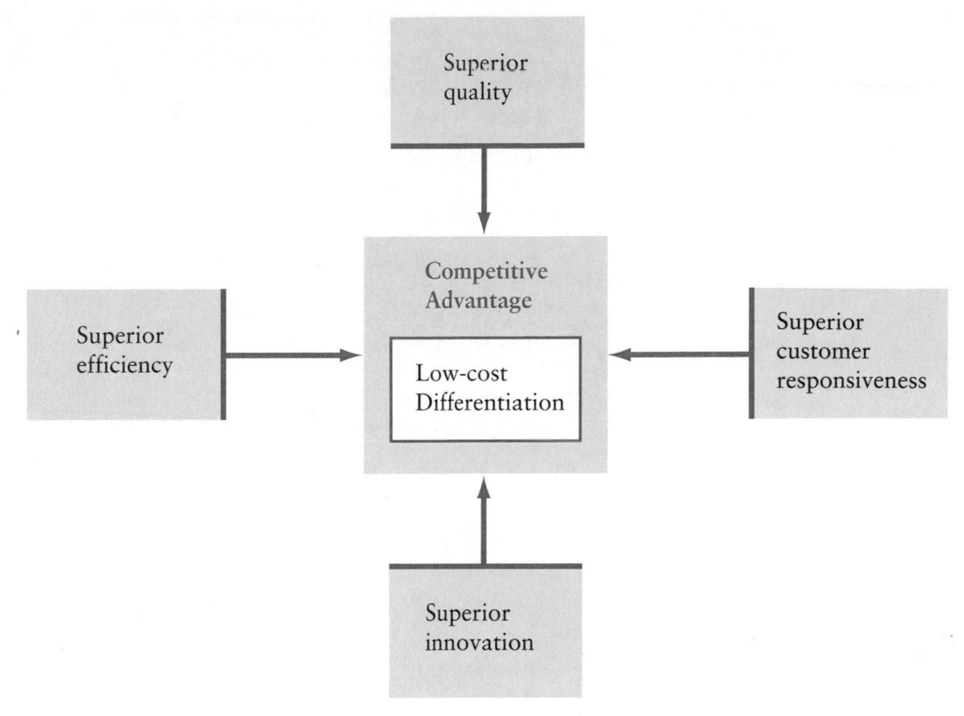

Efficiency

A company is a device for transforming inputs into outputs. Inputs are basic factors of production such as labor, land, capital, management, technological know-how, and so on. Outputs are the goods and services that a company produces. Efficiency is measured by the cost of inputs required to produce a given output. The more efficient a company, the lower is the cost of inputs required to produce a given output. Thus efficiency helps a company attain a low-cost competitive advantage. In the Opening Case, you saw how Marks & Spencer's ability to reduce the cost of inputs through its relationship with suppliers, its ability to do without advertising, its lack of bureaucracy, and its high employee productivity all underlay its ability to offer consumers high quality goods at a reasonable price. That is, they all underlay M&S's cost-based competitive advantage.

One of the keys to achieving high efficiency is to utilize inputs in the most productive way possible. The most important component of efficiency for most companies is employee productivity, which is usually measured by output per employee. Holding all else constant, the company with the highest employee productivity in an industry will typically have the lowest costs of production. In other words, that company will have a cost-based competitive advantage. For example, Marks & Spencer, because of its human resources strategy and lack of a corporate bureaucracy, has a very productive work force. In turn, this helps lower M&S's costs vis-à-vis those of its competitors, thereby giving the company a competitive advantage. Another example is given in Table 4.2. It details the hours that it takes to assemble a motor vehicle, on average, in Japanese-owned automobile plants in Japan, Japanese-owned automobile plants in North America, American-owned automobile plants in North America, and European-owned plants in Europe. A quick glance at these figures suggests that, in general, Japanese-owned auto plants have a cost-based competitive advantage that

Table 4.2
Assembly Plant Characteristics for Volume Producers

Performance	Japanese in Japan	Japanese in North America	American in North America	All Europe
Employee Productivity (hours per vehicle)	16.8	21.2	25.1	36.2
Quality (Defects/ 100 vehicles)	60	65	82.3	97

Source: Adapted with the permission of Rawson Associates, an imprint of Macmillan Publishing Company from *The Machine That Changed the World* by James P. Womack, Daniel T. Jones and Daniel Roos. Copyright © 1990 James P. Womack,. Daniel T. Jones, Daniel Roos, and Donna Sammons Carpenter.

comes from their higher employee productivity. Of course, in turn this translates into market share. In the United States, for example, Japanese automobile companies hold about 27 percent of the market for cars, up from 20 percent a decade ago.

The interesting issue, of course, is how to achieve high productivity and efficiency. In later chapters, we examine in detail how a company achieves high productivity and efficiency (and quality, innovation, and customer responsiveness). For now, we just note that to achieve high productivity and efficiency a company must adopt the appropriate strategy, structure, and control systems.

Quality

Quality products are goods and services that are reliable in the sense that they do the job they were designed for and do it well. This concept applies whether we are talking about a Toyota automobile, a St. Michael's shirt sold at Marks & Spencer's, or the customer service department of a bank.

The impact of high product quality on competitive advantage is twofold.[3] First, providing high-quality products creates a brand name reputation for a company's products. In turn, this enhanced reputation allows the company to charge a higher price for its products. In the automobile industry, for example, Japanese companies like Toyota not only have had a productivity-based cost advantage over their U.S. and European competitors, they could also charge a higher price for their cars because of the higher quality of their products (see Table 4.2). Thus, compared with a company like General Motors, Toyota has had both lower costs and the ability to charge higher prices. As a result, Toyota has operated with a much bigger profit margin than GM.

The second impact of quality on competitive advantage comes from the greater efficiency, and hence lower unit costs brought about by higher product quality. The major effect here is through the impact of quality on productivity. Higher product quality means that less employee time is wasted making defective products or providing substandard services and less time has to be spent fixing mistakes. This translates into higher employee productivity and lower unit costs. Thus high product quality not only lets a company charge higher prices for its product; it also lowers costs (Figure 4.2).

The importance of quality in building competitive advantage has increased dramatically in recent years. Indeed, so crucial is the emphasis placed on quality

by many companies that achieving high product quality can no longer be viewed as just one way of gaining a competitive advantage. In many industries, it has become an absolute imperative for survival.

Innovation

Innovation can be defined as anything new or novel about the way a company operates or the products it produces. Thus innovation includes advances in the kinds of products, production processes, management systems, organizational structures, and strategies developed by a company. Viewed this way, Marks & Spencer's pioneering relationship with its employees, Toy Я Us's discounting strategy in the retail toy business, Toyota's lean production system for manufacturing automobiles, and Sony's development of the Walkman can all be viewed as innovations, for they all involve a company doing something novel.

Innovation is perhaps the single most important building block of competitive advantage. As noted in Chapter 3, in the long run, competition can be viewed as a process driven by innovation. Although not all innovations succeed, those that do can be a major source of competitive advantage. The reason is that, by definition, successful innovation gives a company something **unique**—something that its competitors lack (until they imitate the innovation). This uniqueness may allow a company to differentiate itself from its rivals and charge a premium price for its product. Alternatively, it may allow a company to reduce its unit costs far below those of competitors.

As with efficiency and quality, we explore the issue of innovation more fully later in the book. For the moment, a few examples can highlight the importance of innovation. Marks & Spencer, profiled in the Opening Case, pioneered three major innovations in the British retailing industry: building long-term relationships with its suppliers, instituting advanced human relations practices, and offering a limited range of merchandise. These innovations help M&S to lower its costs relative to those of competitors offering products of a similar quality. Thus M&S's current cost-based competitive advantage derives in part from the fact that it was an innovator.

More generally, there are numerous examples of companies that have pioneered new products and reaped major rewards from their innovations. Consider Xerox's development of the photocopier, Intel's development of new microprocessors such as the 386, 486, and now the Pentium chip, Hewlett-Packard's development of the laser printer, Nike's development of high-tech athletic shoes, Bausch & Lomb's development of contact lenses, and Sony's development of the Walkman. All these product innovations helped build a competitive advantage for the pioneering companies. In each case, the company, by

Figure 4.2
The Impact of Quality on Profits

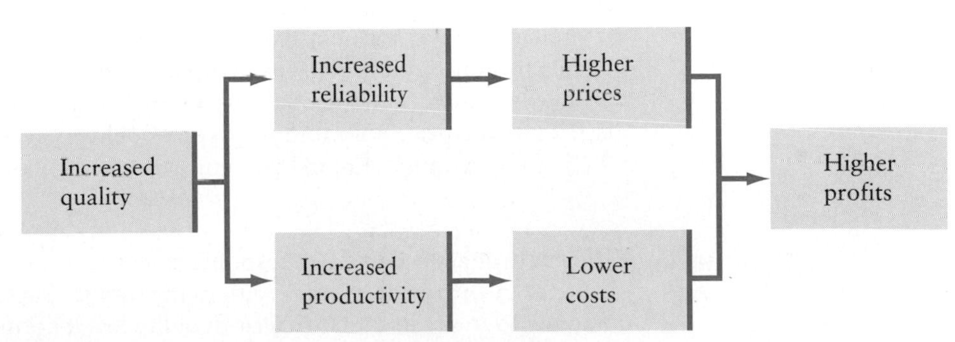

virtue of being the sole supplier of a new product, could charge a premium price for it. By the time competitors succeeded in imitating the innovator, the innovating company had built up such strong brand loyalty that its position proved difficult for the imitators to attack. Thus Sony is still known for its Walkman and Hewlett-Packard for its laser printers.

Customer Responsiveness

To achieve customer responsiveness, a company must give its customers exactly what they want when they want it. Consequently, a firm must do everything possible to identify customer needs and to satisfy them. Among other things, achieving superior customer responsiveness involves giving customers value for money. Steps taken to improve the efficiency of a company's production process and the quality of its output are consistent with this goal. In addition, satisfying customer needs may require the development of new products with features that existing products lack. In other words, *achieving superior efficiency, quality, and innovation are all part of achieving superior customer responsiveness.*

Another factor that stands out in any discussion of customer responsiveness is the need to **customize** goods and services to the unique demands of individual customers. For example, the proliferation of different types of soft drinks and beers in recent years can be viewed partly as a response to this trend. Automobile companies, too, have become more adept at customizing cars to the demands of individual customers. For instance, following the lead of Toyota, the Saturn division of General Motors builds cars to order for individual customers, letting them choose from a wide range of colors and options.

An aspect of customer responsiveness that has drawn increasing attention is **customer response time**[4]—the time that it takes for a good to be delivered or a service to be performed. For a manufacturer of machinery, response time is the time that it takes to fill customer orders. For a bank, it is the time it takes to process a loan or the time that customer must stand in line to wait for a free teller. And for a supermarket, it is the time that customers must stand in checkout lines. Customer survey after customer survey has shown slow response time to be a major source of customer dissatisfaction.[5] The way in which Citicorp changed its loan practices to reduce the time it took to process mortgage applications illustrates how reducing response time can build competitive advantage (see Strategy in Action 4.1).

Besides quality, customization, and response time, other sources of enhanced customer responsiveness are superior design, superior service, and superior after-sales service and support. All these factors enhance customer responsiveness and allow a company to differentiate itself from its less responsive competitors. In turn, differentiation enables a company to build brand loyalty and to charge a premium price for its products. For example, consider how much more people are prepared to pay for next-day delivery of express mail, as opposed to delivery in three to four days. In 1994 a two-page letter sent by overnight Express Mail within the United States cost about $9.95, compared with 29 cents for regular mail. Thus the price premium for express delivery (reduced response time) was $9.66, or a premium of 3,331 percent over the regular price!

Summary

Efficiency, quality, customer responsiveness, and innovation are all important elements in obtaining a competitive advantage. Superior efficiency enables a company to lower its costs; superior quality lets it both charge a higher price and

STRATEGY IN ACTION 4.1

How Citicorp Used Time-Based Competition to Build a Competitive Advantage

During the 1980s Citicorp moved from being a small player in the mortgage lending industry to being a major force. In 1982 mortgage originations from Citicorp were running at an annual rate of $756 million. By 1987 the annual rate had increased to $14.8 billion. Moreover, although Citicorp still accounted for only 3.3 percent of all mortgage originations in the United States in 1987, it could claim 37 percent more originations than its largest competitor, H. F. Ahmanson.

At the heart of Citicorp's success has been a strategy that achieves superior customer responsiveness by emphasizing quick response time and highly competent mortgage officers. Citicorp also realized that the borrower is only one of the customers that the lender must serve. The real estate agent is also a customer. The borrower often asks the agent which lending institution in the area has money at the most attractive rates. Which lending institution is the real estate agent going to recommend? Citicorp reasoned that what real estate agents want is to close a deal as quickly as possible. Therefore, they will recommend lending institutions that are quick at processing loan applications and staffed by responsive and competent loan officers.

Traditionally, loan applications take about forty-five days to approve, give or take two weeks. As anyone who has purchased real estate knows, these forty-five days can be a stressful and uncertain time. The stress is compounded when late in the approval process an ill-prepared mortgage company requires more documentation or clarification from the borrower. Against this background, Citicorp decided to reduce the time taken to approve a loan to just fifteen days. To achieve this goal, it created a program called MortgagePower. Real estate agents pay an annual subscription fee of $2,500 to join MortgagePower. The real estate agents then qualify their buyers for Citicorp in return for a half-point to one-and-a-half point discount and the promise of a loan decision within fifteen days. The agent can do whatever is allowed by state regulations with the discount—either give it all to the buyer or, in some states, keep the discount by charging the buyer a fee for arranging the financing. As already noted, the results for Citicorp have been dramatic.[6]

lower its costs; superior customer responsiveness allows it to charge a higher price; and superior innovation can lead to higher prices or lower unit costs. (Figure 4.3). Together, these four factors create a low-cost or differentiation advantage for a company, which brings above average profits and enables it to outperform its competitors.

4.5 DISTINCTIVE COMPETENCIES, RESOURCES, AND CAPABILITIES

A distinctive competency refers to a unique strength that allows a company to achieve superior efficiency, quality, innovation, or customer responsiveness (see Figure 4.4).[7] A firm with a distinctive competency can charge a premium price for its products or achieve substantially lower costs than its rivals. Consequently, it can earn a profit rate substantially above the industry average.

For example, Caterpillar has a distinctive competency in after-sales service and support. Caterpillar builds heavy construction equipment. As this equipment is very expensive, the last thing construction contractors want is to have it

Figure 4.3
The Impact of Efficiency, Quality, Customer Responsiveness, and Innovation on Unit Costs and Prices

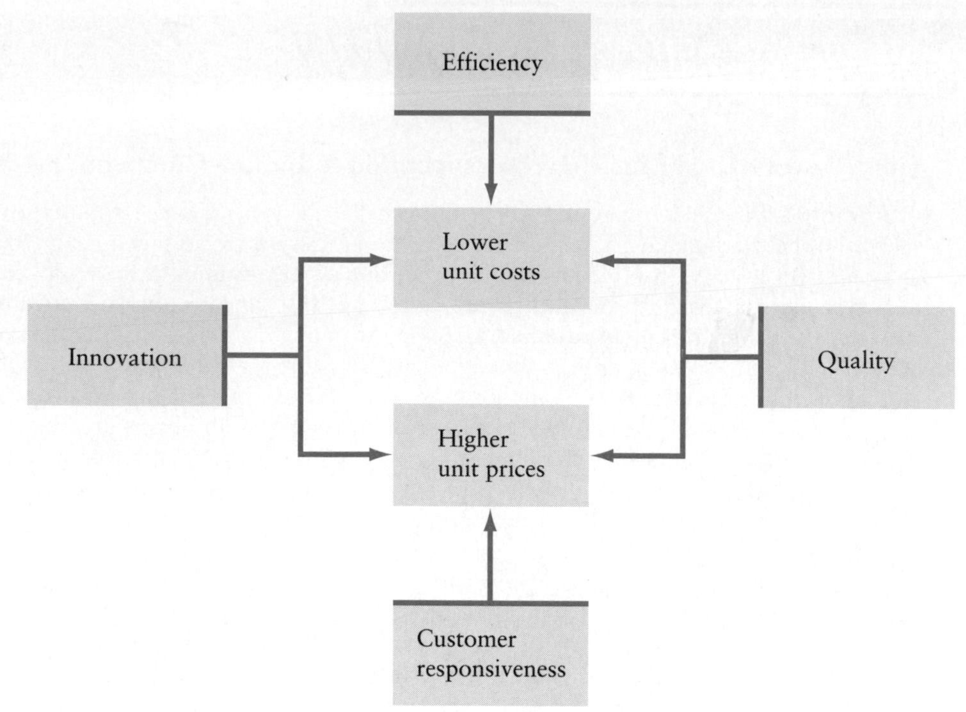

sit idle due to breakdowns. Caterpillar's response has been an after-sales service and support network that is second to none in its industry. The company can get a spare part and service personnel to any point in the world in twenty-four hours. Thus Caterpillar's distinctive competency in after-sales service and support has enabled it to achieve superior customer responsiveness, which in turn allows Caterpillar to charge a premium price for its products. Similarly, it can be argued that Toyota has distinctive competencies in the development and operation of manufacturing processes. Toyota has pioneered a whole range of manufacturing techniques, such as just-in-time inventory systems, self-managing teams, and reduced setup times for complex equipment. These competencies have helped Toyota attain superior efficiency and product quality, which are the basis of its competitive advantage in the global automobile industry.[8]

Resources and Capabilities

The distinctive competencies of an organization arise from two complementary sources: its **resources** and **capabilities**.[9] Resources refer to the financial, physical, human, technological, and organizational resources of the company. These can be divided into **tangible resources** (land, buildings, plant, and equipment) and **intangible resources** (brand names, reputation, patents, and technological or marketing know-how). To give rise to a distinctive competency a company's resources must be both *unique* and *valuable*. A unique resource is one that no other company has. For example, Polaroid's distinctive competency in instant photography was based on a unique intangible resource: the technological know-how involved in instant film processing. This know-how was protected from imitation by a thicket of patents. A resource is valuable if it in some way helps create strong demand for the company's products. Thus Polaroid's techno-

STRATEGY IN ACTION 4.2

How EMI Lost Its Leadership Position in CAT Scanners: A Tale of Good Resources but Poor Capabilities

When it was introduced in the 1970s, the computerized tomography scanner was touted as the greatest advance in radiology since the discovery of x-rays in 1895. CAT scanners generate cross-sectional views of the human body. They were invented by Godfrey Hounsfield, a senior research engineer at the British company, EMI, who subsequently won a Nobel Prize for his achievement. As a result of Hounsfield's achievement, EMI initially had sole possession of a unique and valuable intangible resource: the technological know-how needed to make CAT scanners. However, EMI lacked the capability to successfully exploit that resource in the marketplace. Specifically, it lacked the marketing skills required to educate potential consumers about the benefits of the product, and it lacked the after-sales service and support skills necessary to successfully market such a technologically complex product. As a result, eight years after introducing the CAT scanner, EMI was no longer in the CAT scanner business while an imitator, General Electric, had become the market leader. Even though it had a unique and valuable intangible resource (technological know-how), EMI's lack of capability to exploit that resource meant that it was unable to establish a distinctive competency and generate high profits.[11]

logical know-how was valuable because it created strong demand for its photographic products.

Capabilities refer to a company's skills at coordinating its resources and putting them to productive use. These skills reside in an organization's routines, that is, in the way a company makes decisions and manages its internal processes in order to achieve organizational objectives. More generally, a company's capabilities are the product of its organizational structure and control systems. These specify how and where decisions are made within a company, the kind of behaviors the company rewards, and the company's cultural norms and values. (We discuss how organizational structure and control systems help a company obtain capabilities in Chapters 11 and 12.) It is important to keep in mind that capabilities are, by definition, intangible. They reside not so much in individuals as in the way individuals interact, cooperate, and make decisions within the context of an organization.[10]

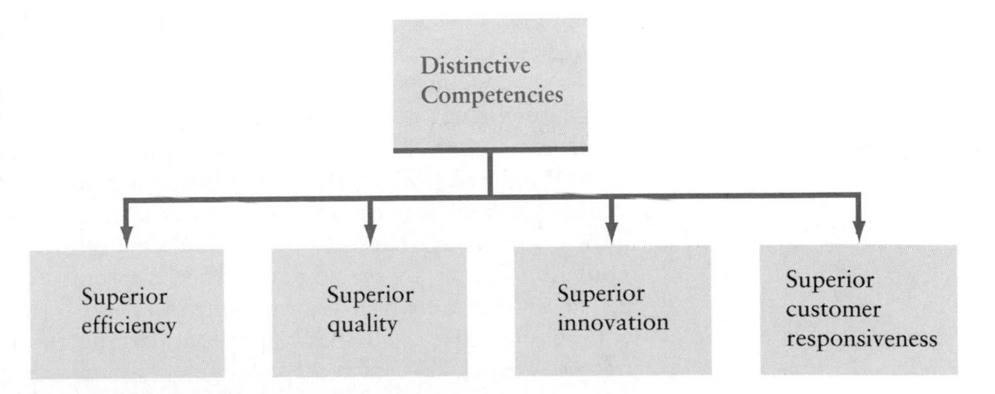

Figure 4.4
The Relationship Between Distinctive Competencies and the Building Blocks of Competitive Advantage

The distinction between resources and capabilities is critical to understanding what generates a distinctive competency. A company may have unique and valuable resources, but unless it has the capability to use those resources effectively it may not be able to create or sustain a distinctive competency. The story of EMI's failure to exploit the computerized axial tomography scanner (CAT), summarized in Strategy in Action 4.2, shows how a match of resources and capabilities is vital to building a competitive advantage.

It is also important to recognize that a company may not need unique and valuable resources to establish a distinctive competency so long as it has capabilities that no competitor possesses. For example, the steel minimill operator Nucor is widely acknowledged to be the most cost-efficient steelmaker in the United States. Nucor's distinctive competency in low-cost steelmaking, however, does not come from any unique and valuable resources. Nucor has the same resources (plant, equipment, skilled employees, know-how) as many other minimill operators. What distinguishes Nucor is its unique capability to manage its resources in a highly productive way. Specifically, Nucor's structure, control systems, and culture promote efficiency at all levels within the company.

In sum, for a company to have a distinctive competency it must at a minimum have either (1) a unique and valuable resource and the capabilities (skills) necessary to exploit that resource (as illustrated by Polaroid) or (2) a unique capability to manage common resources (as exemplified by Nucor). A company's distinctive competency is strongest when it possesses *both* unique and valuable resources, and unique capabilities to manage those resources.

Strategy and Competitive Advantage

The primary objective of strategy is to achieve a competitive advantage. Attaining this goal demands a two-pronged effort. A company needs to pursue strategies that build on its existing resources and capabilities (its competencies), as well as strategies that build additional resources and capabilities (that is, develop new competencies) and thus enhance the company's long-run competitive position.[12] Figure 4.5 illustrates the relationship between a firm's strategies and its resources and capabilities. It is important to note that by *strategies* we mean *all* types of strategy—functional-level strategies, business-level strategies, corporate-level strategies, international strategies, or, more typically, some combination of them. We discuss the various strategies available to a company in detail throughout the next six chapters. What needs stressing here is that successful strategies often either build on a company's existing distinctive competencies or help a company develop new ones.

The history of The Walt Disney Company during the 1980s exemplifies the need to pursue strategies that build on a firm's resources and capabilities. In the early 1980s Disney suffered a string of poor financial years. This culminated in a 1984 management shakeup, when Michael Eisner was appointed CEO. Four years later Disney's sales had increased from $1.66 billion to $3.75 billion, its net profits from $98 million to $570 million, and stock market valuation from $1.8 billion to $10.3 billion. What brought about this transformation was the company's deliberate attempt to exploit its existing resources and capabilities more aggressively. These resources and capabilities comprised Disney's enormous film library, its brand name, and its in-house filmmaking skills, particularly in animation. Under Eisner, many old Disney classics were re-released, first in movie theaters, and then on video, earning the company millions in the process. Disney also started a cable television channel, the Disney Channel, to

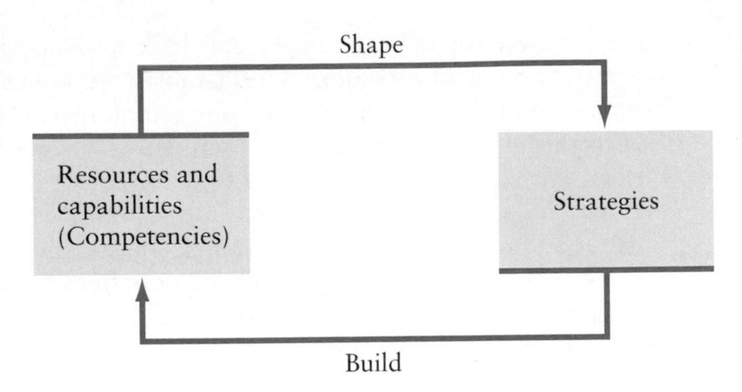

Figure 4.5
The Relationship Between Strategies and Resources and Capabilities

utilize this library and capitalize on the firm's brand name. In addition, under Eisner the filmmaking arm of Disney flourished, first with a string of low-budget box-office hits under the Touchstone label and then with the reintroduction of the product that had originally made Disney famous, the full-length animated feature. Putting together its brand name and in-house animation capabilities, Disney produced three major box-office hits in four years: *The Little Mermaid, Beauty and the Beast,* and *Aladdin.*[13] In sum, Disney's transformation was based primarily upon strategies that exploited the company's existing resource base.

Other companies that have successfully exploited their resources and capabilities to create profitable opportunities include 3M, which has exploited its distinctive competency in sticky tape to create businesses as diverse as Post-it Notes, pressure-sensitive tapes, and coated abrasives, and Honda, which has exploited its distinctive competency in the design and manufacture of high-powered lightweight engines to move from producing motorcycles to producing cars, lawn mowers, and four-wheel off-road buggies. By the same token, some of the most striking strategic failures of recent years have involved companies that have strayed too far from their distinctive competencies. For example, Exxon, which has distinctive competencies in oil exploration, extraction, and refining, spent much of the 1970s diversifying into areas such as office automation equipment, where it had no capabilities. The effort failed and Exxon sold off these diversified businesses during the 1980s.

As for the process of building resources and capabilities through strategies, consider Xerox Corp. During the late 1970s its market share in the photocopier business slumped by 50 percent because its main Japanese competitors, Canon and Ricoh, were paying close attention to their distinctive competencies whereas Xerox was not. As a result, by the early 1980s Canon and Ricoh were selling high-quality and technologically superior copiers at a price that was approximately equivalent to Xerox's. To recapture its lost market share, Xerox had to fundamentally rethink the way it did business. It launched a series of functional-level strategies designed to improve quality and product design, eliminate unnecessary inventory, and reduce new product development time (cycle time). In essence, the goal of these strategies was to develop the kind of resources and capabilities that had enabled Canon and Ricoh to take market share away from Xerox. So successful was Xerox in this process that it became the first major U.S. company to recapture market share from Japanese competitors. Its share of the U.S. copier market increased from a low of 10 percent in 1985 to 18 percent in 1991.[14] Xerox's renaissance, in other words, was built upon the successful implementation of functional-level strategies to build new distinctive competencies.

The Role of Luck

A number of scholars have argued that luck plays a critical role in determining competitive success and failure.[15] In its most extreme version, the luck argument devalues the importance of strategy altogether. Instead, it states that in the face of uncertainty some companies just happened to pick the correct strategy. Put another way, they just happened to develop or possess the right kind of resources and capabilities by accident rather than design.

Although luck may be the reason for a company's success in particular cases, it is an unconvincing explanation for the persistent success of a company. Recall our argument that the generic building blocks of competitive advantage are superior efficiency, quality, innovation, and customer responsiveness. Keep in mind also that competition is a process in which companies are continually trying to outdo each other in their ability to achieve high efficiency, quality, innovation, and customer responsiveness. Consequently, it is possible to imagine a company getting lucky and coming into possession of resources that allow it to achieve excellence on one or more of these dimensions; but it is difficult to imagine how *sustained* excellence on any of these four dimensions could be produced by anything other than conscious effort, that is, by strategy. Luck may indeed play a role in success, and Strategy in Action 4.3 discusses the lucky beginnings of Microsoft Corp. However, to argue that success is entirely a matter of luck is to strain credibility.

4.6 THE DURABILITY OF COMPETITIVE ADVANTAGE

The question that we now need to address is how long will a competitive advantage last once it has been created? In other words, what is the durability of a competitive advantage, given that other companies are also seeking to develop distinctive competencies that will give them a competitive advantage? The answer depends on three factors: the height of **barriers to imitation**, the capability of competitors, and the general dynamism of the industry environment.

Barriers to Imitation

Barriers to imitation are factors that make it difficult for a competitor to copy a company's distinctive competencies. Since distinctive competencies allow companies to earn superior profits, competitors want to imitate them. However, the greater the barriers to such imitation, the more sustainable is a company's competitive advantage.[17] It is important to note at the outset that ultimately almost any distinctive competency can be imitated by a competitor. The critical issue is *time*. The longer it takes competitors to imitate a distinctive competency, the greater the opportunity that the company has to build a strong market position and *reputation* with consumers, which is then difficult for competitors to attack. Moreover, the longer it takes to achieve an imitation, the greater is the opportunity for the imitated company to improve on its competency, or build other competencies, thereby staying one step ahead of the competition.

Imitating Resources The easiest distinctive competencies for prospective rivals to imitate tend to be those based on possession of unique and valuable *tangible* resources, such as buildings, plant, and equipment. Such resources are visible to competitors and can often be purchased on the open market. For

STRATEGY IN ACTION 4.3

How Microsoft's Luck Helped It Dominate the Computer Software Industry

The product that launched Microsoft into its leadership position in the software industry was MS-DOS, the operating system for IBM and IBM-compatible personal computers. The original DOS program, however, was not developed by Microsoft but by a company called Seattle Computer, where it was known as Q-DOS (which stood for "quick and dirty operating system"). What occurred was that when IBM was looking for an operating system to run its original PC, it contacted a number of software companies, including Microsoft, asking them whether they could develop such a system. IBM did not, however, get in touch with Seattle Computer. Bill Gates, as a player in the emerging Seattle computer community, knew that Seattle Computer had already developed a disk operating system. Gates borrowed $50,000 from his father, a senior partner in a prominent Seattle law firm. He then went to see the CEO of Seattle Computer and offered to purchase the rights to the company's Q-DOS system. He did not, of course, tell them that IBM was looking for a disk operating system. Since Seattle Computer was short of cash, the CEO quickly agreed. Gates renamed the system MS-DOS, upgraded it somewhat, and licensed it to IBM. The rest, as they say, is history.

So was Microsoft lucky? Of course it was. It was lucky that Seattle Computer had not heard about IBM's request. It was lucky that IBM approached Microsoft. It was lucky that Gates knew about Seattle Computer's operating system. And it was lucky that Gates had a father wealthy enough to lend him $50,000 on short notice. On the other hand, to attribute all of Microsoft's subsequent success to luck would be wrong. While MS-DOS gave Microsoft a tremendous head start in the industry, it did not guarantee that Microsoft would continue to enjoy the kind of worldwide success that it has. Microsoft had to build the appropriate set of resources and capabilities required to produce a continual stream of innovative software, which is precisely what Gates did with the cash generated from MS-DOS.[16]

example, if a company's competitive advantage is based on sole possession of efficient-scale manufacturing facilities, competitors may move fairly quickly to establish similar facilities. Thus, although Ford gained a competitive advantage over General Motors in the 1920s by being the first to adopt an assembly line manufacturing technology to produce automobiles, General Motors quickly imitated that innovation, competing away Ford's distinctive competence in the process. A similar process is occurring in the auto industry, at present, as companies try to imitate Toyota's famous production system, which formed the basis for much of its competitive advantage during the 1970s and 1980s. GM's Saturn plant, for instance, is GM's attempt to replicate Toyota's production system.

Intangible resources can be more difficult to imitate. This is particularly true of brand names. Brand names are important because they symbolize a company's reputation. In the heavy earth-moving equipment industry, for example, the Caterpillar brand name is synonymous with high quality and superior after-sales service and support. Similarly, the St. Michael's brand name used by Marks & Spencer symbolizes high-quality but reasonably priced clothing. Customers will often display a preference for the products of such companies because the brand name is an important guarantee of high quality. Although competitors might like to imitate well-established brand names, the law prohibits them from doing so.

Marketing and technological know-how are also important intangible resources. Unlike brand names, however, company-specific marketing and technological know-how can be relatively easy to imitate. In the case of marketing know-how, the movement of skilled marketing personnel between companies may facilitate the general dissemination of know-how. For example, in the 1970s Ford was acknowledged as the best marketer among the big three U.S. auto companies. In 1979 Ford lost a lot of its marketing know-how to Chrysler when its most successful marketer, Lee Iacocca, joined Chrysler after being fired by Henry Ford III following "personal disagreements." Iacocca subsequently hired many of Ford's top marketing people to work with him at Chrysler. More generally, successful marketing strategies are relatively easy to imitate because they are so visible to competitors. Thus Coca-Cola quickly imitated Pepsico's Diet Pepsi brand with the introduction of its own brand, Diet Coke. In a similar example, recently Compaq Computer imitated Dell Computer's successful marketing strategy of selling personal computers through mail order.

With regard to technological know-how, in theory, the patent system should make technological know-how relatively immune to imitation. Patents give the inventor of a new product a seventeen-year exclusive production agreement. Thus, for example, pharmaceutical giant Merck patented a cholesterol-reducing drug that is marketed under the brand name Mevacor. Approved by the FDA in August 1987, Mevacor generated sales of $430 million in 1988 and annual sales of over $1 billion in 1992. However, whereas it is relatively easy to use the patent system to protect a chemical compound from imitation, this is not true of many other inventions. In electrical and computer engineering, for example, it is often possible to "invent around" patents. Thus, although EMI took out patents on the CAT scanner, General Electric was able to use its reverse engineering skills to figure out how the CAT scanner worked (see Strategy in Action 4.2). It then developed a product that was very similar to EMI's CAT scanner and performed the same basic function; but it was not identical and therefore did not violate EMI's patent. More generally, a recent study found that 60 percent of patented innovations were successfully invented around in four years.[18] This suggests that, in general, distinctive competencies based on technological know-how can be relatively short-lived.

Imitating Capabilities Imitating a company's capabilities tends to be more difficult than imitating its tangible and intangible resources, chiefly because a company's capabilities are often invisible to outsiders. Since capabilities are based on the way in which decisions are made and processes managed deep within a company, by definition, it is hard for outsiders to discern the nature of a company's internal operations. Thus, for example, outsiders may have trouble identifying precisely why 3M is so successful at developing new products or why Nucor is such an efficient steel producer.

On its own, however, the invisible nature of capabilities would not be enough to halt imitation. In theory, competitors could still gain insights into how a company operates by hiring people away from that company. However, a company's capabilities rarely reside in a single individual. Rather, they are the product of how numerous individuals interact within a unique organizational setting. It is possible that no one individual within a company may be familiar with the totality of a company's internal operating routines and procedures. In such cases, hiring people away from a successful company in order to imitate its key capabilities may not be helpful.

For illustration, consider the way in which a football team works. The success of a team is not the product of any one individual but of how individuals work together as a team. It is the product of an unwritten or tacit understanding between the players of the team. Therefore, the transfer of a star player from a winning to a losing team may not be enough to improve the performance of the losing team. However, suppose that you buy the whole team. This is what almost happened in 1993, to the German subsidiary of General Motors. It had to obtain an injunction from the German government to prevent Ignacio Lopez de Arriortua, the former GM vice president of operations and the new CEO of Volkswagen, from poaching forty of GM's managers by offering them very high salaries. His intent was to take all the managers who were expert in low-cost production to Volkswagen, which is desperately trying to reduce its costs to compete with the Japanese. Clearly, he was trying to imitate GM's new-found competency in efficiency by buying GM's capabilities through buying its managers.

To sum up, since resources are easier to imitate than capabilities, a distinctive competency based on a company's unique capabilities is probably more durable (less imitable) than one based on its resources. It is more likely to form the foundation for a long-run competitive advantage.

Capability of Competitors

According to work by Pankaj Ghemawat, a major determinant of the capability of competitors to rapidly imitate a company's competitive advantage is the nature of the competitors' prior strategic commitments.[19] By **strategic commitment**, Ghemawat means a company's commitment to a particular way of doing business—that is, to developing a particular set of resources and capabilities. Ghemawat's point is that once a company has made a strategic commitment it will find it difficult to respond to new competition if doing so requires a break with this commitment. Therefore, when competitors already have long-established commitments to a particular way of doing business, they may be slow to imitate an innovating company's competitive advantage. Its competitive advantage will thus be relatively durable.

The U.S. automobile industry offers an example. From 1945 to 1975 the industry was dominated by the stable oligopoly of General Motors, Ford, and Chrysler, all of whom geared their operations to the production of large cars. In other words, their resources and capabilities were committed to the production of large cars. When the market shifted from large cars to small, fuel-efficient ones during the late 1970s, the U.S. companies lacked the resources and capabilities required to produce these cars. Their prior commitments had built the wrong kind of skills for this new environment. As a result, foreign producers, and particularly the Japanese, stepped into the market breach by providing compact, fuel-efficient, high-quality and low-cost cars. The failure of U.S. auto manufacturers to react quickly to the distinctive competency of Japanese auto companies gave the latter time to build a strong market position and brand loyalty, which are now proving difficult to attack.

Industry Dynamism

A dynamic industry environment is one that is changing rapidly. We examined the factors that determine the dynamism and intensity of competition in an industry in Chapter 3 when we discussed the external environment. What needs noting now is that the most dynamic industries tend to be those with a very high

rate of product innovation—for instance, the consumer electronics industry and the personal computer industry. In dynamic industries, the rapid rate of innovation means that product life cycles are shortening and that competitive advantage can be very transitory. A company that has a competitive advantage today may find its market position outflanked tomorrow by a rival's innovation.

In the personal computer industry, for example, the rapid increase in computing power during the last two decades has contributed to a high degree of innovation and environment turbulence. Reflecting the persistence of innovation, in the late 1970s and early 1980s Apple Computer had an industry-wide competitive advantage due to its innovation. Then in 1982 the advantage was seized by IBM with its introduction of its first personal computer. By the mid 1980s, however, IBM had lost its competitive advantage to high power "clone" manufacturers such as Compaq, which had beaten IBM in the race to be the first to introduce a computer based upon Intel's 386 chip. In turn, in the late 1980s and early 1990s Compaq subsequently lost its competitive advantage to companies like Dell, which pioneered new low-cost ways of delivering computers to consumers (mail order) and were able to undercut Compaq's price. Now Dell is finding it very difficult to hold on to its competitive advantage in the face of rapid imitation of its strategy by rivals, including Compaq and Gateway 2000, which are also selling computers via mail order.

Summary

The durability of a company's competitive advantage depends on three factors: the height of barriers to imitation, the capability of competitors to imitate its innovation, and the general level of dynamism in the industry environment (see Figure 4.6). When barriers to imitation are low, capable competitors abound, and the environment is very dynamic, with innovations being developed all the time, then competitive advantage is likely to be transitory. Such conditions are currently typical in the consumer electronics and personal computer industries. On the other hand, even within such industries, companies can build a more enduring competitive advantage if they are able to make investments that build barriers to imitation. Apple Computer has built a competitive advantage based on the combination of a proprietary disk operating system and an intangible image (as noted earlier, intangible resources are difficult to imitate). The resulting brand

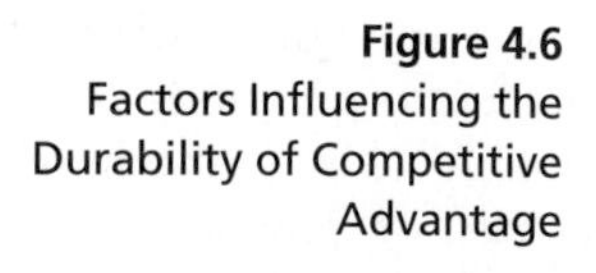

Figure 4.6
Factors Influencing the Durability of Competitive Advantage

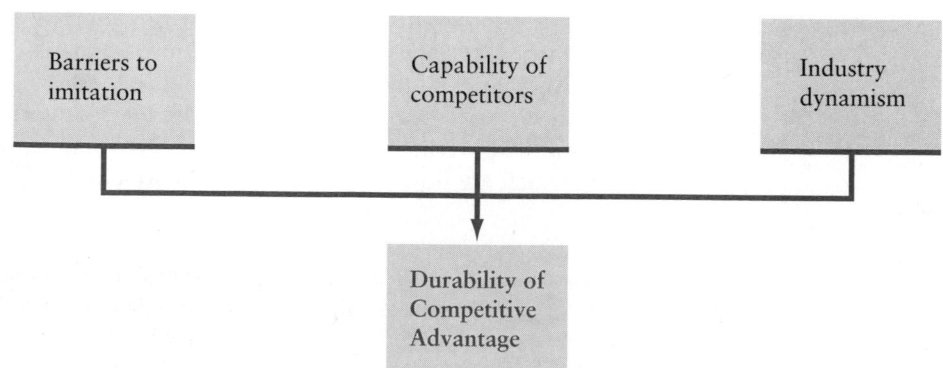

loyalty has enabled Apple to carve out a fairly secure niche in an industry where competitive advantage has otherwise proven to be very fleeting.

4.7 WHY DO COMPANIES FAIL?

In this section we take the issue of why a company might lose its competitive advantage one step further and ask, Why do companies fail? We define a failing company as one whose profit rate is substantially lower than the average profit rate of its competitors. A company can lose its competitive advantage but still not fail. It may just earn average profits. Failure implies something more drastic. Failing companies typically earn low or negative profits; in other words, they are at a competitive disadvantage.

The question, Why do companies fail? is particularly pertinent since some of the most successful companies of the twentieth century now seem to be at a competitive disadvantage. Companies like IBM, Sears, General Motors, American Express, and Digital Equipment, which were once held up as examples of managerial excellence, have all registered large losses in recent years. We explore three related reasons for failure: inertia, prior strategic commitments, and the Icarus paradox.

Inertia

The inertia argument is that companies find it difficult to change their strategies and structures in order to adapt to changing competitive conditions.[20] IBM is a classic example of this problem. For thirty years it was widely viewed as the world's most successful computer company. Then, in the space of a few short years, its success turned into a disaster, with a loss of $5 billion in 1992 leading to layoffs of more than 100,000 employees. IBM's troubles were caused by a dramatic decline in the cost of computing power as a result of innovations in microprocessors. With the advent of powerful low-cost microprocessors, the locus of the computer market shifted from mainframes to small, low-priced personal computers. This left IBM's huge mainframe operations with a much diminished market. Even though IBM had, and still has, a significant presence in the personal computer market, it had failed to shift the focus of its efforts away from mainframes and toward personal computers. This failure spelled disaster for one of the most successful companies of the twentieth century.

Why do companies like IBM find it so difficult to adapt to new environmental conditions? One factor that seems to stand out is the role of an organization's capabilities in causing inertia. Earlier in the chapter, we argue that organizational capabilities can be a source of competitive advantage; their downside, however, is that they are difficult to change. Recall that capabilities are the way a company makes decisions and manages its processes. IBM always emphasized close coordination between different operating units and favored decision processes that stressed consensus among interdependent operating units as a prerequisite for a decision to go forward.[21] This capability was a source of advantage for IBM during the 1970s, when coordination among its worldwide operating units was necessary to develop, manufacture, and sell complex mainframes. But the slow-moving bureaucracy that it had spawned was a source of failure in the 1990s, when organizations had to adapt readily to rapid environmental change.

Capabilities are difficult to change because a certain distribution of power and influence is embedded within the established decision-making and management processes of an organization. Those who play key roles in a decision-making process clearly have more power. It follows that changing the established capabilities of an organization means changing its existing distribution of power and influence, and those whose power and influence would diminish resist such change. Proposals for change trigger turf battles. This power struggle and the political resistance associated with trying to alter the way in which an organization makes decisions and manages its process—that is, trying to change its capabilities—bring on inertia. This is not to say that companies cannot change. However, because change is so often resisted by those who feel threatened by it, in most cases, change has to be crisis induced. By then the company may already be failing, as happened at IBM.

Prior Strategic Commitments

Ghemawat has argued that a company's prior strategic commitments not only limit its ability to imitate rivals, but may also cause competitive disadvantage.[22] IBM, for instance, had made major investments in the mainframe computer business. As a result, when the market shifted, it was stuck with significant resources that were specialized to that particular business. The company had manufacturing facilities geared to the production of mainframes, research organizations that were similarly specialized, and a mainframe sales force. Since these resources were not well suited to the newly emerging personal computer business, IBM's current difficulties were in a sense inevitable. Its prior strategic commitments locked IBM into a business that was shrinking. Shedding these resources was bound to cause hardship for all organization stakeholders.

The Icarus Paradox

In a recent book, Danny Miller postulated that the roots of competitive failure can be found in what he termed the Icarus paradox.[23] Icarus is a figure in Greek mythology who made himself a pair of wings to escape from an island where he was being held prisoner. He flew so well that he went higher and higher, ever closer to the sun, until the heat of the sun melted the wax that held his wings together and he plunged to his death in the Aegean Sea. The paradox is that his greatest asset, his ability to fly, caused his demise. Miller argues that the same paradox applies to many once successful companies. According to Miller, many companies become so dazzled by their early success that they believe more of the same type of effort is the way to future success. As a result, however, a company can become so specialized and inner-directed that it loses sight of market realities and the fundamental requirements for achieving a competitive advantage. Sooner or later this leads to failure.

Miller identifies four major categories among the rising and falling companies. The "craftsmen," such as Texas Instruments and Digital Equipment Corp. (DEC) achieved early success through engineering excellence. But then the companies became so obsessed with engineering details that they lost sight of market realities. (The story of DEC's demise is summarized in Strategy in Action 4.4.) Then there are the "builders," for instance, Gulf & Western and ITT. Having built successful, moderately diversified companies, they then became so enchanted with diversification for its own sake that they continued to diversify far beyond the point at which it was profitable to do so. Miller's third group are

STRATEGY IN ACTION 4.4

How DEC's Success Sowed the Seeds of Its Own Downfall

DEC's original success was founded on the minicomputer, a cheaper, more flexible version of its mainframe cousins that Ken Olsen and his brilliant team of engineers invented in the 1960s. Olsen and his staff improved their original minis until they absolutely could not be beaten for quality and reliability. In the 1970s their VAX series of minicomputers was widely regarded as the most reliable computers ever produced. DEC was rewarded by high profit rates. However, buoyed by its own success, DEC turned into an engineering monoculture. Its engineers became idols; its marketing and accounting staff were barely tolerated. Component specs and design standards were all that senior managers understood. Technological fine tuning became such an obsession that the needs of customers for smaller, more economical, user-friendly computers were ignored. DEC's personal computers, for example, bombed because they were so out of touch with the needs of consumers. DEC, in other words, blinded by its own early success, had failed to remain responsive to its customers, and by the early 1990s DEC was a company in deep trouble.[24]

the "pioneers" like Wang Labs. Enamored of their own originally brilliant innovations, they continued to search for additional brilliant innovations, but ended up producing novel but completely useless products. The final category comprises the "salesmen," exemplified by Procter & Gamble and Chrysler. They became so convinced of their ability to sell anything that they paid scant attention to product development and manufacturing excellence and as a result spawned a proliferation of bland, inferior products.

4.8 AVOIDING FAILURE AND SUSTAINING COMPETITIVE ADVANTAGE

How can a company avoid the traps that have snared so many once successful companies, such as IBM, DEC, Sears, General Motors, and others? How can it build a sustainable competitive advantage? We do not give a complete answer here as much of the remaining text deals with these issues. However, a number of key points can be made at this juncture.

Focus on the Building Blocks of Competitive Advantage

First, maintaining a competitive advantage requires a company to continue focusing on the four generic building blocks of competitive advantage—efficiency, quality, innovation, and customer responsiveness—and to develop distinctive competencies that contribute to superior performance in these areas. One of the messages of Miller's Icarus paradox is that many successful companies become unbalanced in their pursuit of distinctive competencies. DEC, for example, focused on engineering quality at the expense of almost everything

else including, most importantly, customer responsiveness. Other companies forget to focus on any distinctive competency. This was certainly the case at ITT, where an empire-building CEO, Harold Geneen, focused on diversification but lost sight of the need to focus on achieving excellence in efficiency, quality, innovation, and customer responsiveness at the level of business units within ITT.

Best Industrial Practice and Benchmarking

One of the best ways to develop distinctive competencies that contribute toward superior efficiency, quality, innovation, and customer responsiveness is to identify **best industrial practice** and to adopt it. Only by so doing will a company be able to build and maintain the resources and capabilities that underpin excellence in efficiency, quality, innovation, and customer responsiveness. What constitutes best industrial practice is an issue that we discuss in some depth in Chapter 5. However, identifying best industrial practice involves tracking the practice of other companies, and perhaps the best way to do so is through **benchmarking.** This is the process of measuring the company against the products, practices, and services of some of the most efficient global competitors. For example, when Xerox was in trouble in the early 1980s, it decided to institute a policy of benchmarking as a way of identifying how to improve the efficiency of its operations. Xerox benchmarked L.L. Bean for distribution procedures, Deere & Company for central computer operations, Procter & Gamble for marketing, and Florida Power & Light for total quality management processes. By the early 1990s Xerox was benchmarking 240 functions against comparable areas in other companies. This process has been credited with helping Xerox dramatically improve the efficiency of its operations.[25]

Overcoming Inertia

A further reason for failure is an inability to adapt to changing conditions because of organizational inertia. Overcoming the barriers to change within an organization is one of the key requirements for maintaining a competitive advantage, and we devote a whole chapter, Chapter 14, to this issue. Suffice it to say here that identifying barriers to change is an important first step. Once this step is taken, implementing change requires good leadership, the judicious use of power, and appropriate changes in organizational structure and control systems. All these issues are discussed later in the book.

4.9 SUMMARY OF CHAPTER

The principal objective of this chapter is identifying the basis of competitive advantage—identifying why, within a given industry, some companies outperform others. Competitive advantage is the product of at least one of the following: superior efficiency, superior quality, superior innovation, and superior customer responsiveness. Achieving superiority here requires that a company develop appropriate distinctive competencies, which in turn are a product of the kind of resources and capabilities that a company possesses. The chapter also examines issues related to the durability of competitive advantage. This durability is determined by the height of barriers to imitation, the capability of competitors to imitate a company's advantage, and the general level of environmental turbulence.

Finally, the discussion of why companies fail and what they can do to avoid failure indicates that failure is due to factors such as organizational inertia, prior strategic commitments, and the Icarus paradox. Avoiding failure requires that a company constantly try to upgrade its distinctive competencies in accordance with best industrial practice and that it take steps to overcome organizational inertia. The main points made in this chapter can be summarized as follows:

1. To achieve a competitive advantage a company must lower its costs, differentiate its product so that it can charge a higher price, or do both simultaneously.
2. The four generic building blocks of competitive advantage are efficiency, quality, innovation, and customer responsiveness.
3. Superior efficiency enables a company to lower its costs; superior quality allows it both to charge a higher price and to lower its costs; and superior customer service lets it charge a higher price. Superior innovation can lead to higher prices, particularly in the case of product innovations; or it can lead to lower unit costs, particularly in the case of process innovations.
4. Distinctive competencies are the unique strengths of a company. Valuable distinctive competencies enable a company to earn a profit rate that is above the industry average.
5. The distinctive competencies of an organization arise from its resources and capabilities.
6. Resources refer to the financial, physical, human, technological, and organizational assets of a company.
7. Capabilities refer to a company's skills at coordinating resources and putting them to productive use.
8. In order to achieve a competitive advantage, companies need to pursue strategies that build on the existing resources and capabilities of an organization (its competencies), and they need to formulate strategies that build additional resources and capabilities (develop new competencies).
9. The durability of a company's competitive advantage depends on the height of barriers to imitation, the capability of competitors, and environmental dynamism.
10. Failing companies typically earn low or negative profits. Three factors seem to contribute to failure—organizational inertia in the face of environmental change, the nature of a company's prior strategic commitments, and the Icarus paradox.
11. Avoiding failure requires a constant focus on the basic building blocks of competitive advantage, identification and adoption of best industrial practice, and overcoming inertia.

Discussion Questions

1. What are the main implications of the material discussed in this chapter for strategy formulation?

2. When is a company's competitive advantage most likely to endure over time?
3. Which is more important in explaining the success and failure of companies, strategizing or luck?

Article File 4

Find an example of a company that has sustained its competitive advantage for more than ten years. Identify the source of the competitive advantage and describe why it has lasted so long.

Strategic Management Project: Module 4

This module deals with the competitive position of your company. With the information you have at your disposal, perform the tasks and answer the questions listed:

1. Identify whether your company has a competitve advantage or disadvantage in its primary industry. (Its primary industry is the one in which it has the most sales.)
2. Evaluate your company against the four generic building blocks of competitive advantage: efficiency, quality, innovation, and customer responsiveness. How does this help you understand the performance of your company relative to its competitors?
3. What are the distinctive competencies of your company?
4. What role have prior strategies played in shaping the distinctive competencies of your company? What has been the role of luck?
5. Do the strategies currently pursued by your company build on its distinctive competencies? Are they an attempt to build new competencies?
6. What are the barriers to imitating the distinctive competencies of your company?
7. Is there any evidence that your company finds it difficult to adapt to changing industry conditions? If so, why do you think this is the case?

Endnotes

1. Sources: J. Thornhill, "A European Spark for Marks," *Financial Times*, July 13, 1992, p. 8. Marks and Spencer, Ltd. (A). *Harvard Business School Case* #91–392–089. J. Marcom, "Blue Blazers and Guacamole," *Forbes*, November 25, 1991, pp. 64–68. M. Evans, "Marks & Spencer Battles On," *Financial Post*, December 11, 1989, p. 32.
2. Michael E. Porter, *Competitive Advantage* (New York: Free Press, 1985).
3. See D. Garvin, "What Does Product Quality Really Mean," *Sloan Management Review*, 26 (Fall 1984), 25–44; P. B. Crosby, *Quality is Free* (Mentor, 1980); and A. Gabor, *The Man Who Discovered Quality* (Times Books, 1990).
4. G. Stalk and T. M. Hout, *Competing Against Time* (New York: Free Press, 1990).
5. Ibid.
6. R. Guenther, "Citicorp Shakes Up the Mortgage Market,"

Wall Street Journal, November 13, 1988, p. B1. "Mortgage Lenders Lavish New Attention on Real Estate Agents," *Savings Institutions* (February 1988), 82.

7. C. K. Prahalad and G. Hamel, "The Core Competence of the Corporation," *Harvard Business Review* (May–June 1990), 79–91.
8. M. Cusumano, *The Japanese Automobile Industry* (Cambridge, Mass.: Harvard University Press, 1989).
9. The material in this section relies on the so-called resource-based view of the firm. For summaries of this perspective, see J. B. Barney, "Firm Resources and Sustained Competitive Advantage," *Journal of Management*, 17 (1991), 99–120; J. T. Mahoney and J. R. Pandian, "The Resource-Based View Within the Conversation of Strategic Management," *Strategic Management Journal*, 13 (1992), 363–380; R. Amit and P. J. H. Schoemaker, "Strategic Assets and Organizational Rent," *Strategic Management Journal*, 14 (1993), 33–46; and M. A. Peteraf, "The Cornerstones of Competitive Advantage: A Resource-Based View," *Strategic Management Journal*, 14 (1993), 179–191.
10. For a discussion of organizational capabilities, see R. R. Nelson and S. Winter, *An Evolutionary Theory of Economic Change* (Cambridge, Mass.: Belknap Press, 1982).
11. See EMI and The CT Scanner (A) and (B). *Harvard Business School Cases* #383–194 and 383–195.
12. R. M. Grant, *Contemporary Strategic Analysis* (Cambridge, Mass.: Blackwell, 1991).
13. "Disney's Magic," *Business Week*, March 9, 1987. "Michael Eisner's Hit Parade," *Business Week*, February 1, 1988.
14. D. Kearns, "Leadership Through Quality," *Academy of Management Executive*, 4 (1990), 86–89. J. Sheridan, "America's Best Plants," *Industry Week*, October 15, 1990, pp. 27–40.
15. The classic statement of this position was made by A. A. Alchain, "Uncertainty, Evolution, and Economic Theory," *Journal of Political Economy*, 84 (1950), 488–500.
16. Stephen Manes and Paul Andrews, *Gates* (New York: Simon & Schuster 1993).
17. As with resources and capabilities, so the concept of barriers to imitation is also grounded in the resource-based view of the firm. For details see R. Reed and R. J. DeFillippi, "Causal Ambiguity, Barriers to Imitation, and Sustainable Competitive Advantage," *Academy of Management Review*, 15 (1990), 88–102.
18. E. Mansfield, "How Economists See R&D," *Harvard Business Review*, (November–December 1981), 98–106.
19. P. Ghemawat, *Commitment: The Dynamic of Strategy* (New York: Free Press, 1991).
20. M. T. Hannah and J. Freeman, "Structural Inertia and Organizational Change," *American Sociological Review*, 49 (1984), 149–164.
21. See IBM Corporation. *Harvard Business School Case* #180–034.
22. Ghemawat, *Commitment.*
23. D. Miller, *The Icarus Paradox* (HarperBusiness, 1990).
24. Ibid.
25. D. Kearns, "Leadership Through Quality," *Academy of Management Executive*, 4 (1990), 86–89.

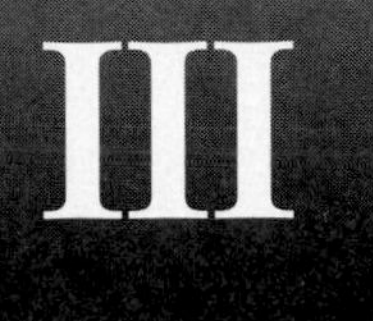

III STRATEGIES

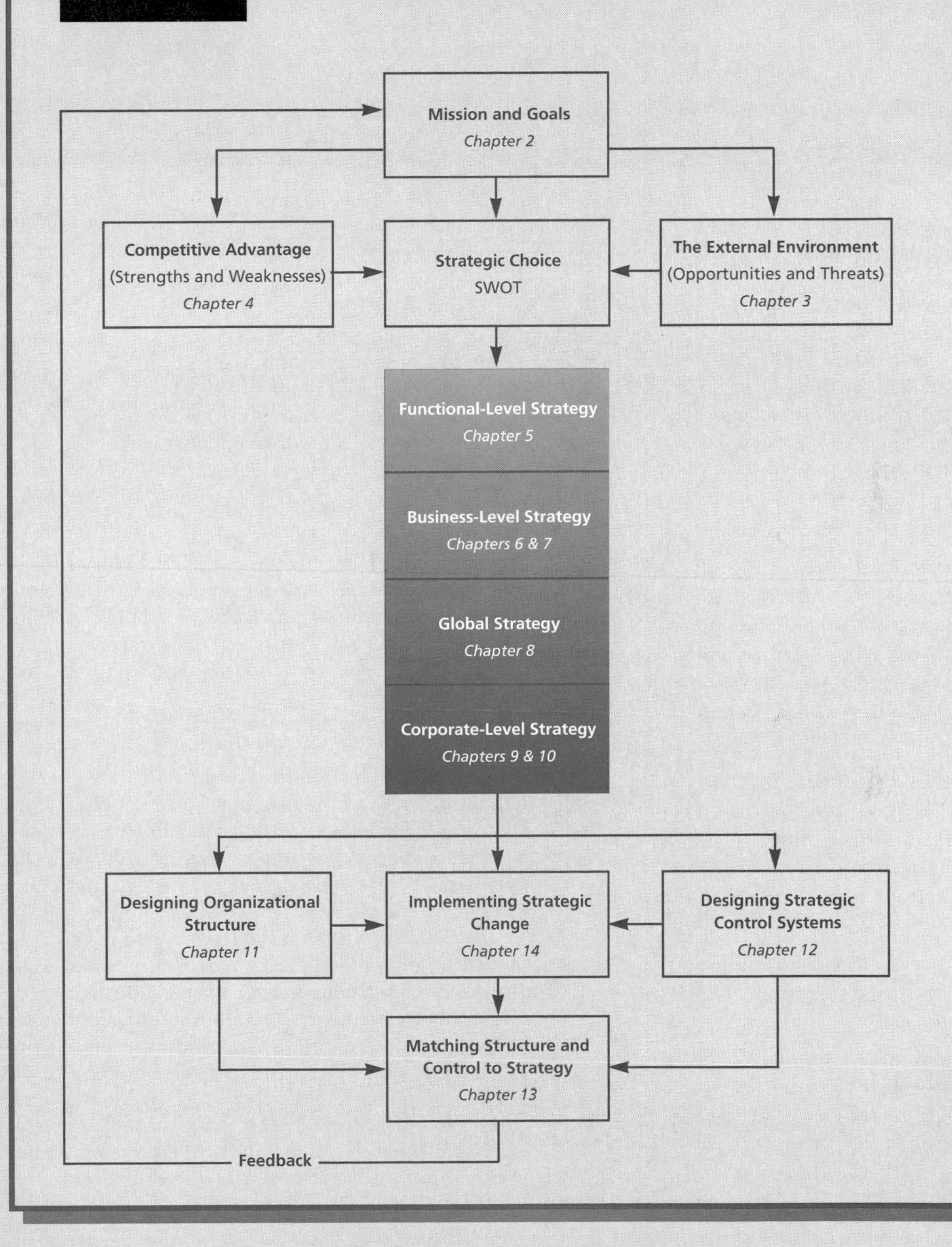

5 Building Competitive Advantage Through Functional-Level Strategies

5.1 OPENING CASE: XEROX CORP.

In 1960 Xerox Corp. shipped its first 914 copier, beginning one of the most successful new-product introductions in history. For the next fifteen years Xerox dominated the photocopier market. However, by 1980 the company was facing problems. Two Japanese companies, Canon and Ricoh, had emerged as significant global competitors, they were selling high-quality copiers at a price equivalent to Xerox's cost for producing comparable products. Because of relatively high costs and prices, Xerox's market share had fallen by half and its return on assets had slumped to 8 percent.

Xerox learned firsthand how far it had fallen behind when it began to produce and market a copier in the United States that had been designed by its Japanese affiliate, Fuji-Xerox. Xerox found that the reject rate for Fuji-Xerox parts was only a fraction of the reject rate for American-produced parts. Visits to Fuji-Xerox revealed another important truth: quality in manufacturing does not increase costs; it decreases costs by reducing the number of defective products and service costs.

These developments forced Xerox to rethink the way it did business. In 1982 the company launched the first of a series of initiatives that over the next decade transformed the way it ran its operations. In 1981 Xerox had more than 5,000 individual suppliers worldwide. The Xerox management realized that by consolidating the company's worldwide supply base it could achieve three goals:

1. By simplifying the purchasing process, it could cut overhead in the purchasing area.
2. By having a single supplier produce a single part for all of Xerox's worldwide operations, it would enable the supplier to achieve economies of scale in production; these cost savings could be passed on to Xerox in the form of lower prices.
3. By cutting down the number of suppliers, Xerox would find it easier to work with its suppliers to improve the quality of component parts.

Toward this end, in 1982 Xerox created "commodity teams," which included buyers, engineers, costing experts, and quality control personnel. Their first task was to decrease Xerox's supplier base from over 5,000 to under 500; they reduced it to 325 suppliers. Because the consolidation of suppliers simplified the purchasing process, overhead rates fell from 9 percent of total costs for materials in 1982 to about 3 percent by 1992.

Next, Xerox launched a quality training effort with its suppliers. Its goal was to reduce the number of defective parts coming from suppliers to under 1,000 per million. At that time some suppliers had defect rates as high as 25,000 per million parts. The company soon met its quality goal of 1,000 defects per million parts. Indeed, by 1992 the defect rate for parts was under 300 per million.

In 1983 Xerox introduced its Leadership Through Quality program. Groups were formed throughout the company, from top management down to the factory floor. Each group received training in quality improvement programs. Emphasis was placed on identifying quality shortfalls, determining the root causes of poor quality, developing solutions, and implementing them. The training program began with the top-tier groups and then cascaded down throughout the organization, spreading worldwide to some 100,000 employees.

In 1985 and 1986 Xerox began to focus on its new-product development process. One goal was to design products that, while customized to market conditions in different countries, also contained a large number of globally standardized parts. Another goal was to reduce the time it took to design new products and bring them to market. To achieve these goals, Xerox established multifunctional, multinational new-product development teams. Each team managed the design, component sources, manufacturing, distribution, and follow-up customer service on a worldwide basis. The use of design teams cut as much as one year from the overall product development cycle and saved millions of dollars.

One consequence of the new approach to product development was the 5100 copier. This was the first product designed jointly by Xerox and Fuji-Xerox for the worldwide market. The 5100 is manufactured in U.S. plants. It was launched in Japan in November 1990 and in the United States the following February. The 5100's global design reportedly reduced the overall time-to-market and saved the company more than $10 million in development costs.

In 1989 Xerox calculated that it could eliminate $1 billion in inventory and $200 million in inventory-related costs by linking worldwide customer orders more closely with production. It formed a multinational organization called Central Logistics and Assets Management, whose aim is to achieve tight integration between individual customer orders and plant production levels, thereby reducing the need to hold excessive inventory to serve demand.

As a result of all these steps, Xerox's position improved markedly during the 1980s. Thanks to its improved quality, lower costs and shorter product development time, Xerox was able to regain market share from its Japanese competitors and to boost its profits and revenues. Xerox's share of the U.S. copier market increased from a low of 10 percent in 1985 to 18 percent in 1991.[1]

Discussion Questions

1. Identify how the changes that Xerox undertook after 1980 helped the company to improve its efficiency, quality, innovation, and customer responsiveness.
2. To what extent were the changes undertaken by Xerox after 1980 the result of functions working together to achieve a common goal?

5.2 OVERVIEW

In Chapter 4, we discuss the central role played by efficiency, quality, innovation, and customer responsiveness in building and maintaining a competitive advantage. In this chapter, we examine the role of functional-level strategies in achieving efficiency, quality, innovation, and customer responsiveness. Functional-level strategies are strategies directed at improving the effectiveness of functional operations within a company, such as manufacturing, marketing, materials management, research and development, and human resources. Even though these strategies may be focused on a given function, as often as not they embrace two or more functions and require close cooperation among functions to attain company-wide efficiency, quality, innovation, and customer responsiveness goals.

For example, the Opening Case describes how Xerox utilized functional-level strategies to capture market share back from Canon and Ricoh. Xerox increased its efficiency by rationalizing its supply base and implementing materials management strategies that reduced inventory holding costs. It raised product quality by working closely with suppliers to improving quality and by utilizing its human resource management function to launch its company-wide 1983 Leadership Through Quality program. Moreover, Xerox increased both its customer responsiveness and innovative ability by reorganizing its new-product development

process to reduce product development time; it also customized its product to conditions prevailing in different national markets.

To explore the issue of functional-level strategies further, we begin this chapter by looking at the concept of the value chain. It offers us a framework for understanding the roles played by different functions within a company in achieving superior efficiency, quality, innovation, and customer responsiveness. Then we consider in detail the contribution that the different functional-level strategies can make toward achieving superior efficiency, quality, innovation, and customer responsiveness.

5.3 THE VALUE CHAIN

The value a company creates is measured by the amount that buyers are willing to pay for a product or service. A company is profitable if the value it creates exceeds the cost of performing value-creation functions, such as procurement, manufacturing, and marketing. To gain a competitive advantage, a company must either perform value-creation functions at a lower cost than its rivals or perform them in a way that leads to differentiation and a premium price. That is, it must pursue the strategies of low cost or differentiation discussed in Chapter 4.

The value-creation process can be illustrated with reference to a concept called the value chain, popularized by Michael Porter.[2] The form of the value chain is given in Figure 5.1. As you can see, the value chain is divided between primary activities and support activities. Each activity adds value to the product. **Primary activities** have to do with the physical creation of the product, its marketing and delivery to buyers, and its support and after-sales service. In this chapter, we consider the primary activities involved in the physical creation of the product under the heading of **manufacturing** and those involved in marketing, delivery, and after-sales service under the heading of **marketing.**

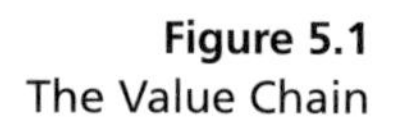

Figure 5.1
The Value Chain

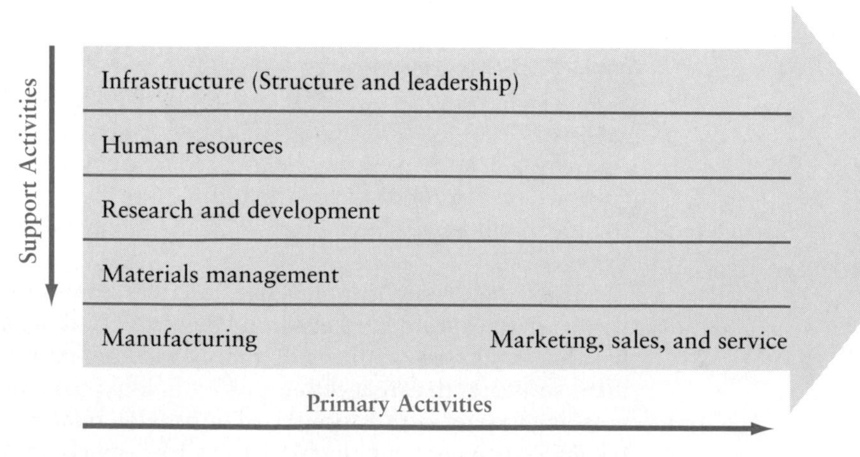

Adapted and reprinted with the permission of The Free Press, an imprint of Simon & Schuster from *Competitive Advantage: Creating and Sustaining Superior Performance* by Michael E. Porter. Copyright © 1985 by Michael E. Porter.

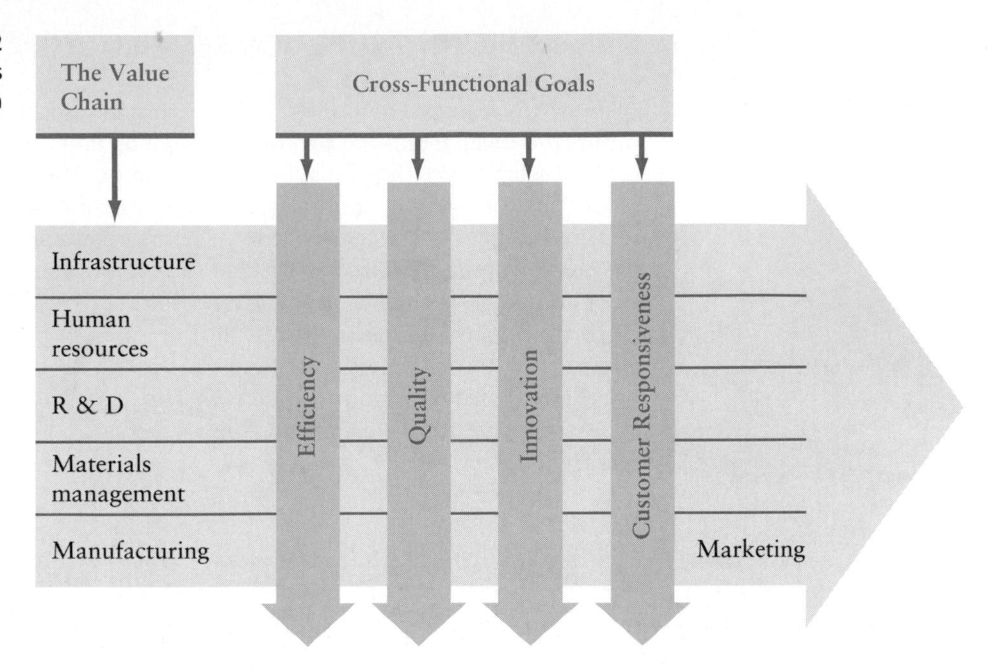

Figure 5.2
Cross-Functional Goals and the Value Chain

Support activities are the functional activities that allow the primary activities of manufacturing and marketing to take place. The **materials management** function controls the transmission of physical materials through the value chain, from procurement through operations and into distribution. The efficiency with which this is carried out can lower the cost of value creation. In addition, an effective materials management function can monitor the quality of inputs into the manufacturing process. This results in an increase in the quality of a company's outputs, thereby facilitating premium pricing. The **R&D** function develops new product and process technologies. Technological developments can lower manufacturing costs and result in the creation of more attractive products that demand a premium price. Thus R&D can affect primary manufacturing and marketing activities, and through them value creation. The **human resource** function ensures that the company has the right mix of skilled people to perform its value-creation activities effectively.

The final support activity is the **company infrastructure,** which has a somewhat different character from the other support activities. Infrastructure is the company-wide context within which all the other value-creation activities take place; it includes the company's organizational structure, control systems, and culture. Since top management can exert considerable influence in shaping these aspects of a company, top management should also be viewed as part of the infrastructure. Indeed, as we repeatedly emphasize in this chapter, top management, through strong leadership, can consciously shape the infrastructure of a company, and through that the performance of all other value-creation activities that take place within it.

An important point to note is that achieving the goals of superior efficiency, quality, innovation, and customer responsiveness requires strategies that embrace several distinct value-creation activities. Indeed, these goals can be regarded as *goals that cut across the different value-creation functions of a company*. As Figure 5.2 illustrates, attaining these goals demands substantial cross-functional integration.

5.4 ACHIEVING SUPERIOR EFFICIENCY

A company can be viewed as a device for transforming inputs into outputs. Inputs are basic factors of production such as labor, land, capital, management, technological know-how, machinery, and so on. Outputs are the goods and services that a company produces. Efficiency is measured by the cost of inputs required to produce a given output. The more efficient a company, the lower is the cost of inputs required to produce a given output. Put another way, an efficient company has higher **productivity** than its rivals, and therefore, lower costs. Here we review the various steps that companies can take to boost their efficiency and, accordingly, lower their unit costs. Before moving on, however, we must stress one key point: *achieving superior quality plays a major role in achieving superior efficiency*. We delay discussion of how to achieve superior quality until the next section.

Economies of Scale, Learning Effects, and the Experience Curve

One way of achieving superior efficiency is by gaining economies of scale and learning effects. Both of these concepts underlie a phenomenon referred to as the experience curve. Before discussing the experience curve, however, we must consider economies of scale and learning effects.

Economies of Scale Economies of scale are unit-cost reductions associated with a large scale of output. One source of economies of scale is the ability to spread fixed costs over a large production volume. Fixed costs are costs that must be incurred to produce a product whatever the level of output; they include the costs of purchasing machinery, the costs of setting up machinery for individual production runs, and the costs of advertising and R&D. Spreading fixed costs over a large volume of output lets a company reduce unit costs. Another source of scale economies is the ability of companies producing in large volumes to achieve a greater division of labor and specialization. Specialization, in turn, is said to have a favorable impact on employee productivity, mainly because it enables individuals to become very skilled at performing a particular task.

The classic example of such economies is Ford's Model T automobile. The world's first mass-produced car, the Model T Ford was introduced in 1923. Until 1923 Ford had made cars using an expensive hand-built "craft production" method. By introducing mass-production techniques, the company achieved greater division of labor (that is, splitting assembly into small, repeatable tasks) and specialization, which boosted employee productivity. It was also able to spread the fixed costs of developing an automobile and setting up production machinery over a large volume of output. As a result of these economies, the cost of manufacturing a car at Ford fell from $3,000 to less than $900 (in 1958 dollars).[3]

As in the Model T case, so in many other situations scale economies lower costs. Du Pont, for example, was able to reduce the cost of rayon fiber from 53 cents per pound to 17 cents per pound in less than two decades mainly through scale economies. But these economies do not continue indefinitely. Indeed, most experts agree that after a certain **minimum efficient scale (MES)** of output is reached there are few, if any, additional scale economies to be had from expanding volume.[4] (Minimum efficient scale refers to the minimum plant size necessary to gain significant economies of scale.) In other words, as shown in Figure 5.3, the long-run unit cost curve of a company is L-shaped. At outputs beyond MES in Figure 5.3, additional cost reductions are hard to come by.

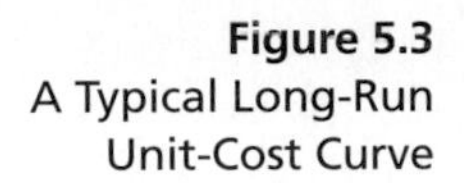
Figure 5.3
A Typical Long-Run Unit-Cost Curve

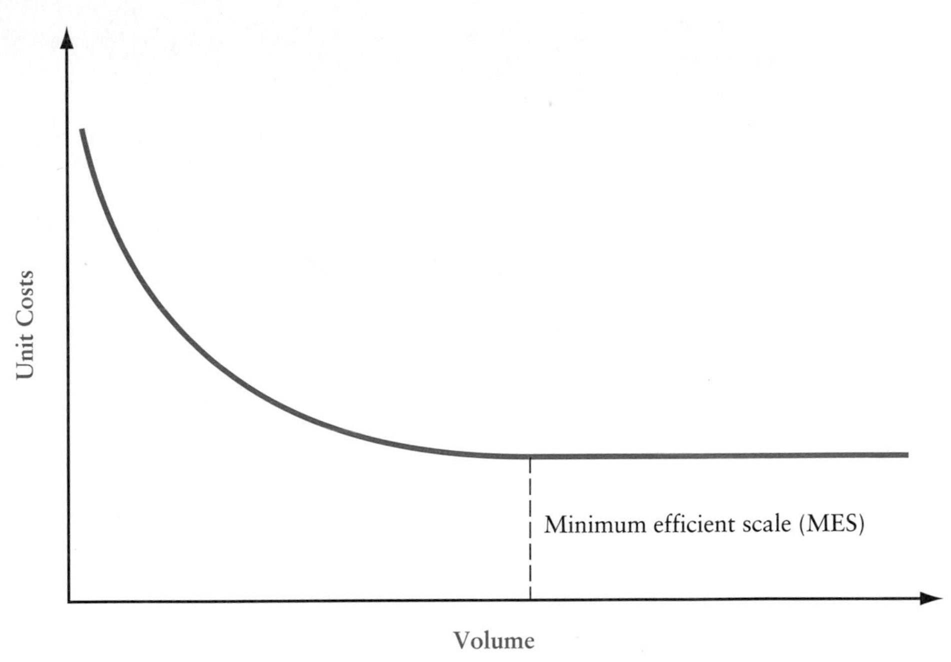

Learning Effects Learning effects are cost savings that come from learning by doing. Labor, for example, learns by repetition how best to carry out a task. In other words, labor productivity increases over time, and unit costs fall as individuals learn the most efficient way to perform a particular task. Equally important, in new manufacturing facilities management typically learns how best to run the new operation. Hence, production costs decline because of increasing labor productivity and management efficiency.

Learning effects tend to be more significant in situations where a technologically complex task is repeated, since there is more to learn. Thus learning effects will be more significant in an assembly process involving 1,000 complex steps than in an assembly process involving 100 simple steps. No matter how complex the task, however, learning effects typically die out after a limited period of time. Indeed, it has been suggested that they are really important only during the start-up period of a new process and cease after two or three years.[5]

The Experience Curve The experience curve refers to systematic unit-cost reductions that have been observed to occur over the life of a product.[6] According to the experience curve concept, unit manufacturing costs for a product typically decline by some characteristic amount each time *accumulated* output of the product is doubled (accumulated output is the total output of a product since its introduction). The relationship was first observed in the aircraft industry, where it was found that each time accumulated output of airframes was doubled unit costs declined to 80 percent of their previous level.[7] Thus the fourth airframe typically cost only 80 percent of the second airframe to produce, the eighth airframe only 80 percent of the fourth, the sixteenth only 80 percent of the eighth, and so on. The outcome of this process is a relationship between unit manufacturing costs and accumulated output similar to that illustrated in Figure 5.4.

Economies of scale and learning effects underlie the experience curve phenomenon. Put simply, as a company increases the accumulated volume of its

Figure 5.4
A Typical Experience Curve

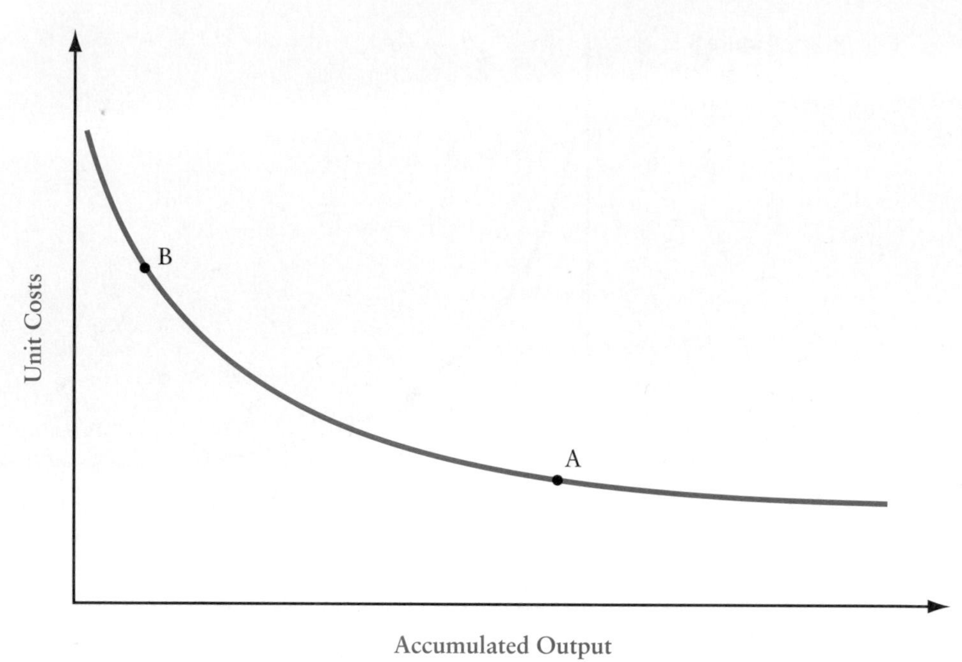

output over time, it is able to realize both economies of scale (as volume increases) and learning effects. Consequently, unit costs fall with increases in accumulated output.

The strategic significance of the experience curve is clear. It suggests that increasing a company's product volume and market share will also bring cost advantages over the competition. Thus company A in Figure 5.4, because it is further down the experience curve, has a clear cost advantage over company B. The concept is perhaps most important in those industries where the production process involves the mass production of a standardized output (for example, the manufacture of semiconductor chips). If a company wishes to become more efficient, and thereby attain a low-cost position, it must try to ride down the experience curve as quickly as possible. This involves constructing efficient scale manufacturing facilities even before the company has the demand, and the aggressive pursuit of cost reductions from learning effects. The company might also need to pursue an aggressive marketing strategy, cutting prices to the bone and stressing heavy sales promotions in order to build up demand, and hence accumulated volume, as quickly as possible. Once down the experience curve, because of its superior efficiency, the company is likely to have a significant cost advantage over its competitors. For example, it has been argued that the early success of Texas Instruments was based on exploiting the experience curve (see Strategy in Action 5.1 for details); that Japanese semiconductor companies aggressively used such tactics to ride down the experience curve and gain a competitive advantage over their U.S. rivals in the market for DRAM chips;[8] and that one reason Matsushita came to dominate the global market for VHS videotape recorders is that it based its strategy on the experience curve.[9]

However, the company furthest down the experience curve must not become complacent about its cost advantage. Strategy in Action 5.1 explains how obsession with the experience curve at Texas Instruments may have cost the company dearly in the end. More generally, there are three reasons why companies should

not become complacent about their efficiency-based cost advantages derived from experience effects. First, since neither learning effects nor economies of scale go on forever, the experience curve is likely to bottom out at some point; indeed, it must do so by definition. When this occurs, further unit-cost reductions from learning effects and economies of scale will be hard to come by. Thus, in time, other companies can catch up with the cost leader. Once this happens, a number of low-cost companies can have cost parity with each other. In such circumstances, establishing a sustainable competitive advantage must involve other strategic factors besides the minimization of production costs by utilizing existing technologies—factors such as better customer responsiveness, product quality, or innovation.

Second, cost advantages gained from experience effects can be made obsolete by the development of new technologies. For example, the price of television picture tubes followed the experience curve pattern from the introduction of television in the late 1940s until 1963. The average unit price dropped from $34 to $8 (in 1958 dollars) in that time. The advent of color television interrupted the experience curve. Manufacturing picture tubes for color televisions required a new manufacturing technology, and the price for color TV tubes shot up to $51 by 1966. Then the experience curve reasserted itself. The price dropped to $48 in 1968, $37 in 1970, and $36 in 1972.[10] In short, technological change can alter the rules of the game, requiring that former low-cost companies take steps to reestablish their competitive edge.

A further reason for avoiding complacency is that high volume does not necessarily give a company a cost advantage. Some technologies have different cost functions. For example, the steel industry has two alternative manufacturing technologies: an integrated technology, which relies on the basic oxygen furnace, and a minimill technology, which depends on the electric arc furnace. As illustrated in Figure 5.5, the minimum efficient scale (MES) of the electric arc furnace is located at relatively low volumes, whereas the MES of the basic oxygen furnace is located at relatively high volumes. Even when both operations are producing at their most efficient output levels, steel companies with basic oxygen furnaces *do not* have a cost advantage over minimills.

Consequently, the pursuit of experience economies by an integrated company using basic oxygen technology may not bring the kind of cost advantages that a naive reading of the experience curve phenomenon would lead the company to expect. Indeed, in recent years integrated companies have not been able to get enough orders to run at optimum capacity. Hence their production costs have been considerably higher than those of minimills.[11] More generally, as we discuss next, in many industries new flexible manufacturing technologies hold out the promise of allowing small manufacturers to produce at unit costs comparable to those of large assembly-line operations.

Flexible Manufacturing (Lean Production) and Efficiency

Central to the concept of economies of scale is the idea that the best way to achieve high efficiency, and hence low unit costs, is through the mass production of a standardized output. The tradeoff implicit in this idea is one between unit costs and product variety. Producing greater product variety from a factory implies shorter production runs, which in turn implies an inability to realize economies of scale. That is, increasing product variety makes it difficult for a company to increase its manufacturing efficiency and thus reduce its unit costs. According to this logic, the way to increase efficiency and drive down unit costs

is to limit product variety and produce a standardized product in large volumes (see Figure 5.6a).

This view of manufacturing efficiency has been challenged by the rise of flexible manufacturing technologies. The term **flexible manufacturing technology**—

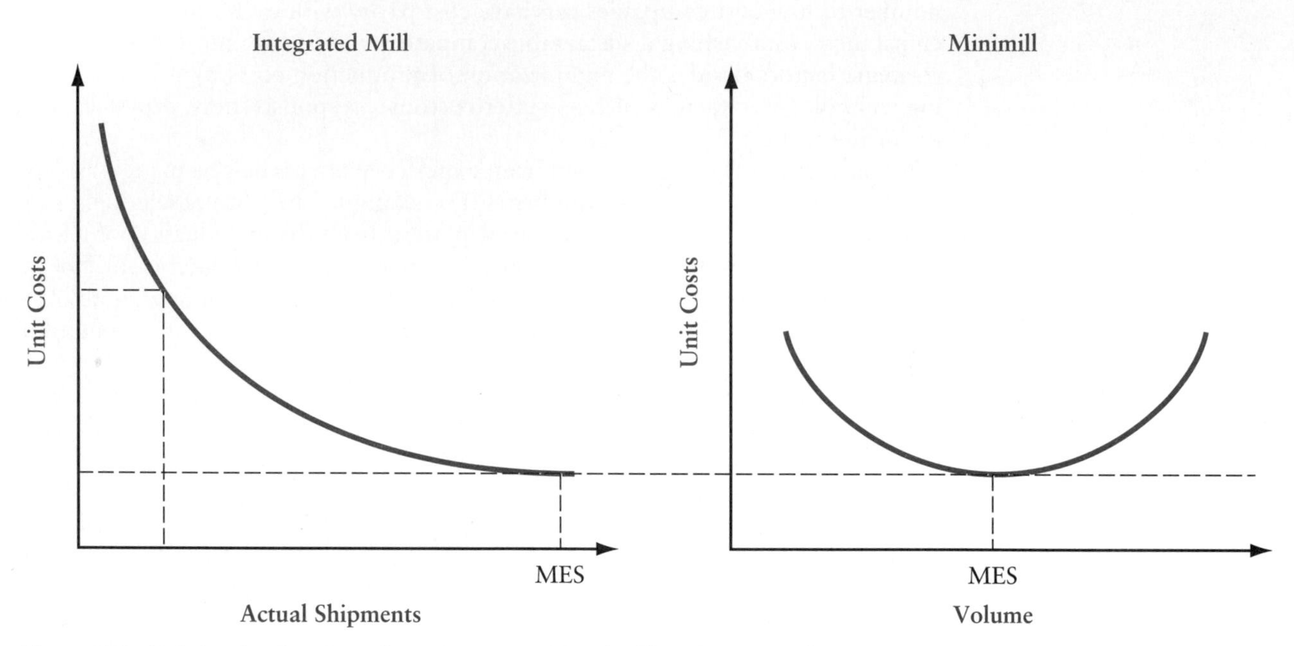

Figure 5.5 Unit Production Costs in an Integrated Steel Mill and a Minimill

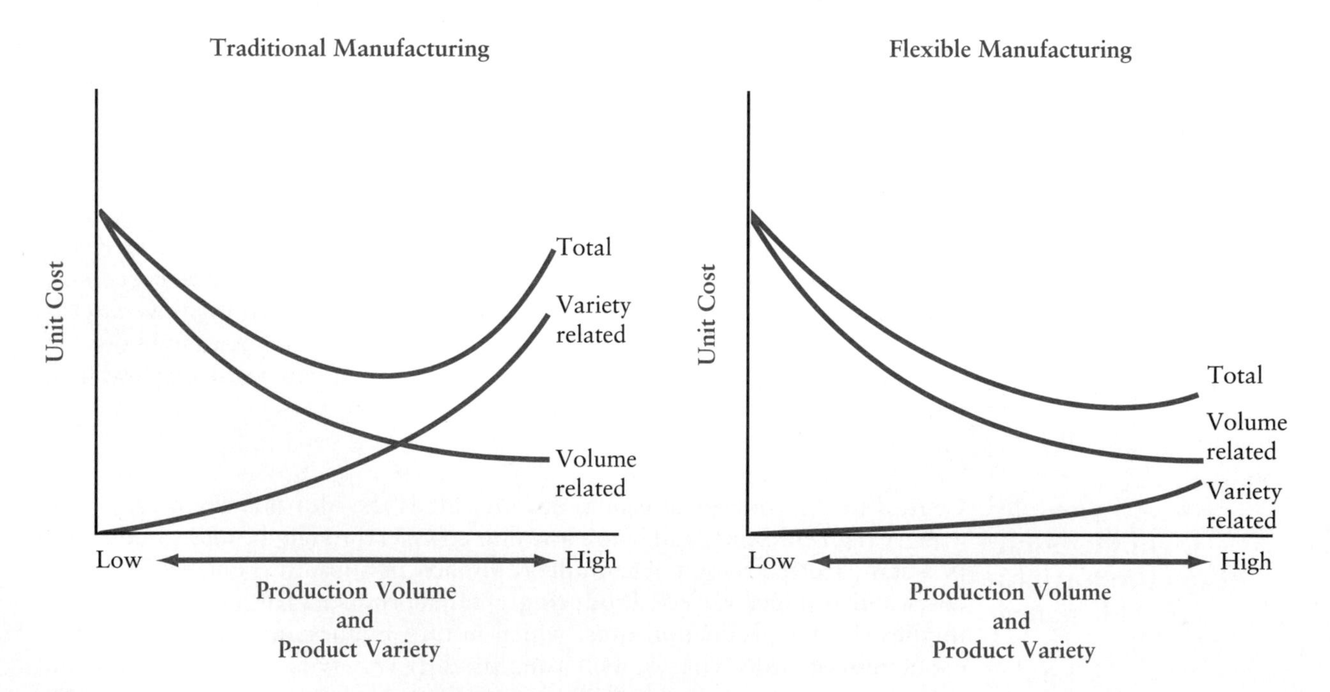

Figure 5.6 The Tradeoff Between Costs and Product Variety

Source: Adapted from G. R. Jones and J. E. Butler, "Costs, Revenues, and Business-Level Strategy," *Academy of Management Review,* 13 (1988), 208.

STRATEGY IN ACTION 5.1

How the Experience Curve Helped and Then Hindered Texas Instruments

Texas Instruments (TI) was an early user of the experience curve concept. TI was a technological innovator, first in silicon transistors, and then in semiconductors. The company discovered that with every doubling of accumulated production volume of a transistor or semiconductor, unit costs declined to 73 percent of their previous level. Building on this insight, when TI first produced a new transistor or semiconductor, it would slash the price of the product to stimulate demand. Its goal was to drive up the accumulated volume of production and so drive down costs through the realization of experience curve economies. As a result, during the 1960s and 1970s TI hammered its competitors in transistors and moved on to prevail in semiconductors, and ultimately in hand-held calculators and digital watches. Indeed, for the twenty years up until 1982 TI enjoyed rapid growth, with sales quadrupling between 1977 and 1981 alone.

However, after 1982 things began to go wrong for TI. The company's single-minded focus on cost reductions, an outgrowth of its strategic reliance on the experience curve, left TI with a poor understanding of consumer needs and market trends. Competitors such as Casio and Hewlett-Packard began to make major inroads into TI's hand-held calculator business by focusing on additional features that consumers demanded, rather than cost and price. TI was slow to react to this trend and lost substantial market share as a result. In the late 1970s TI also decided to focus on semiconductors for watches and calculators—where it had gained substantial cost economies based on the experience curve—rather than develop metal-oxide semiconductors for computer memories and advanced semiconductors. With the growth in minicomputers and personal computers in the early 1980s, however, the market shifted toward high-power metal-oxide semiconductors. Consequently, TI soon found itself outflanked by Intel and Motorola. Thus, although TI's focus on realizing experience curve economies initially benefited the company, later on it seems to have contributed a myopia that cost the company dearly.[12]

or **lean production**, as this technology is often called—covers a range of manufacturing technologies designed to (1) reduce setup times for complex equipment, (2) increase the utilization of individual machines through better scheduling, and (3) improve quality control at all stages of the manufacturing process.[13] Flexible manufacturing technologies allow the company to produce a wider variety of end products at a unit cost that at one time could only be achieved through the mass production of a standardized output (see Figure 5.6b). Indeed, recent research suggests that the adoption of flexible manufacturing technologies may actually increase efficiency and lower unit costs relative to what can be achieved by the mass production of a standardized output.[14]

Flexible manufacturing technologies vary in their sophistication and complexity. One of the most famous examples of a flexible manufacturing technology, Toyota's production system, is relatively unsophisticated, but it has been credited with making Toyota the most efficient auto company in the global industry. Toyota's flexible manufacturing system was developed by one of the company's engineers, Ohno Taiichi. After working in Toyota for five years and visiting Ford's U.S. plants, Ohno became convinced that the mass production philosophy for making cars was flawed. He saw numerous problems with the mass production system, including three major drawbacks. First, long production runs

created massive inventories, which had to be stored in large warehouses. This was expensive, both because of the cost of warehousing, and because inventories tied up capital in unproductive uses. Second, if the initial machine settings were wrong, long production runs resulted in the production of a large number of defects (that is, waste). And third, the mass production system was unable to accommodate consumer preferences for product diversity.

Ohno looked for ways to make shorter production runs economical. He developed a number of techniques designed to reduce setup times for production equipment (a major source of fixed costs). By using a system of levers and pulleys, he was able to reduce the time required to change dies on stamping equipment from a full day in 1950 to three minutes by 1971. This made small production runs economical, which in turn allowed Toyota to respond better to consumer demands for product diversity. Small production runs also eliminated the need to hold large inventories, thereby reducing warehousing costs. Furthermore, small product runs and the lack of inventory meant that defective parts were only produced in small numbers and entered the assembly process immediately. This reduced waste and made it easier to trace defects to their source and fix the problem. In sum, Ohno's innovations enabled Toyota to produce a more diverse product range at a lower unit cost than was possible with conventional mass production.[15]

Flexible machine cells are another common flexible manufacturing technology. A flexible machine cell is a grouping of various types of machinery, a common materials handler, and a centralized cell controller (computer). Each cell normally contains four to six machines capable of performing a variety of operations. The typical cell is dedicated to the production of a family of parts or products. The settings on machines are computer controlled. This allows each cell to switch quickly between the production of different parts or products.

Improved capacity utilization and reductions in work-in-progress (that is, stockpiles of partly finished products) and waste are major efficiency benefits of flexible machine cells. Improved capacity utilization arises from the reduction in setup times and from the computer-controlled coordination of production flow between machines, which eliminates bottlenecks. The tight coordination between machines also reduces work-in-progress. Reductions in waste arise from the ability of computer-controlled machinery to identify how to transform inputs into outputs while producing a minimum of unusable waste material. Given all these factors, whereas free-standing machines might be in use 50 percent of the time, the same machines when grouped into a cell can be used more than 80 percent of the time and produce the same end product with half the waste. This increases efficiency and results in lower costs.

The efficiency benefits of installing flexible manufacturing technology can be dramatic. For example, following the introduction of a flexible manufacturing system, General Electric's locomotive operations reduced the time it took to produce locomotive motor frames from sixteen days to sixteen hours, Similarly, after it introduced a flexible manufacturing system, Fireplace Manufacturers, one of the country's largest fireplace businesses, reduced scrap left over from the manufacturing process by 60 percent, increased inventory turnover threefold, and raised labor productivity by more than 30 percent.[16]

Besides improving efficiency and lowering costs, flexible manufacturing technologies let companies customize products to the unique demands of small consumer groups—at a cost that at one time could only be achieved by

mass-producing a standardized output. Thus they help a company increase its customer responsiveness.

Marketing Strategy and Efficiency

Marketing strategy—the position that a company takes with regard to pricing, promotion, advertising, product design, and distribution—can play a major role in boosting a company's efficiency. Some of the steps leading to greater efficiency are fairly obvious. For example, we have already discussed how riding down the experience curve to gain a low-cost position can be facilitated by aggressive pricing, promotions, and advertising—all of which are the task of the marketing function. However, there are other aspects of marketing strategy that have a less obvious but no less important impact on efficiency. Perhaps the most important is the relationship between **customer defection rates** and unit costs.[17]

Customer defection rates are the percentage of a company's customers that defect every year to competitors. Defection rates are determined by customer loyalty, which in turn is a function of the ability of a company to satisfy its customers. Because acquiring a new customer entails certain one-time fixed costs for advertising, promotions, and the like, there is a direct relationship between defection rates and costs. The longer a company holds on to a customer, the greater is the volume of customer-generated unit sales that can be set against these fixed costs, and the lower the average unit cost of each sale. Thus lowering customer defection rates allows a company to achieve substantial cost economies. This is illustrated in Figure 5.7, which shows that high defection rates imply high average unit costs (and vice-versa).

One consequence of the relationship summarized in Figure 5.7 is a relationship, illustrated in Figure 5.8, between the length of time that a customer stays with the

Figure 5.7
The Relationship Between Average Unit Costs and Customer Defection Rates

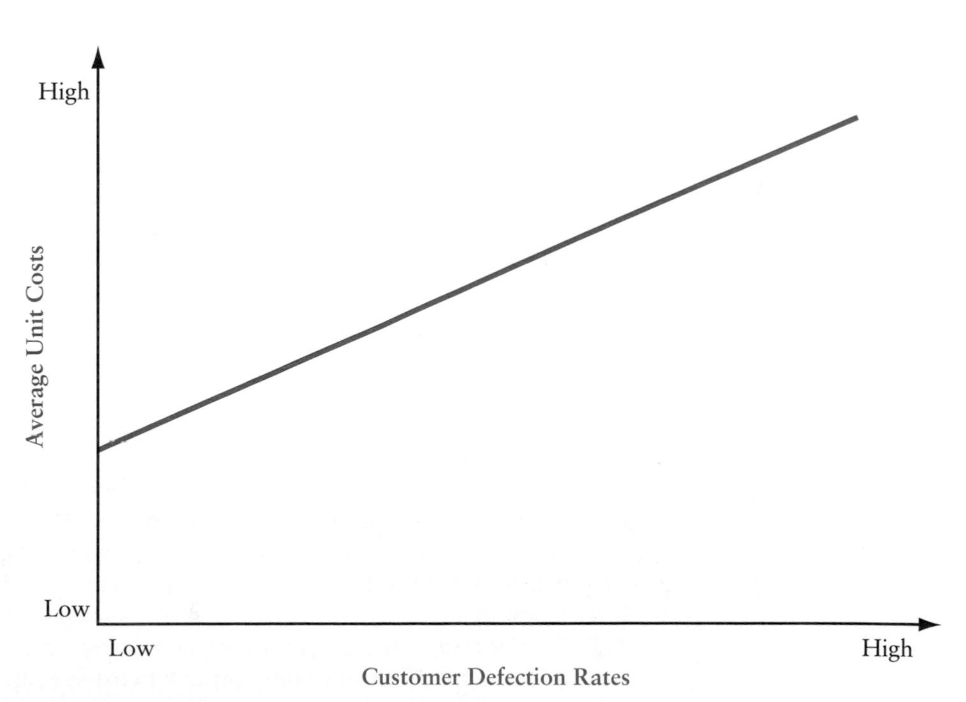

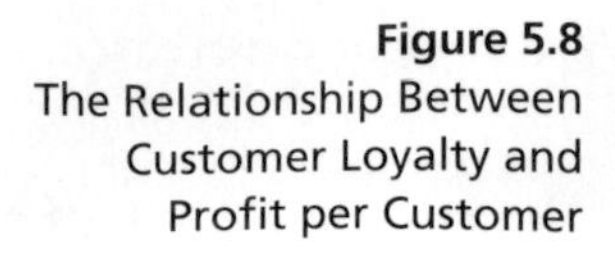
Figure 5.8
The Relationship Between Customer Loyalty and Profit per Customer

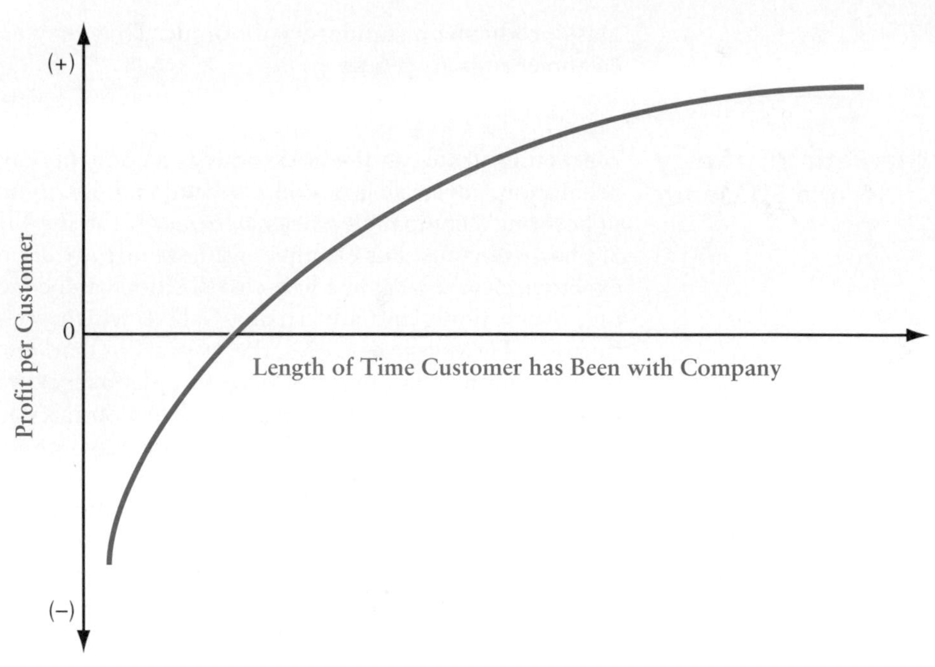

company and profit per customer. Because of the fixed costs of acquiring new customers, serving customers that stay with the company only for a short time before switching to competitors can often yield a negative profit. However, the longer a customer stays with the company, the more the fixed costs of acquiring that customer can be spread out over repeat purchases, which boosts the profit per customer. Thus, as shown in Figure 5.8, there is a positive relationship between the length of time that a customer stays with a company and profit per customer.

For an example of this phenomenon, consider the credit card business.[18] In 1990 most credit card companies spent an average of $51 to recruit a customer and set up a new account. These costs came from the advertising required to attract new customers, from credit checks required for each customer, and from the mechanics of setting up an account and issuing a card. These one-time fixed costs can only be recouped if a customer stays with the company for at least two years. Moreover, when customers stay a second year, they tend to increase their use of the credit card, which raises the volume of revenues generated by each customer over time. As a result, the average profit per customer in the credit card business increases from minus $51 in year 1 (that is, a loss of $51) to $44 in year 3 and $55 in year 6.

Another economic benefit of long-time customer loyalty is the free advertising that customers provide for a company. Loyal customers do a lot of talking, and they can dramatically increase the volume of business through referrals. A striking example of this is the British retailer Marks & Spencer, profiled in the Opening Case of Chapter 4. As you may recall, Marks & Spencer has generated such customer loyalty that it does not need to do any advertising in Britain—a major source of cost saving.

The key message, then, is that reducing customer defection rates and building customer loyalty can be a major source of cost saving. Because it leads to lower

unit costs, reducing customer defection rates by just 5 percent can increase profits per customer anywhere from 25 percent to 85 percent depending on the industry. For example, a 5 percent reduction in customer defection rates leads to the following increases in profits per customer over the average customer life: a 75 percent increase in profit per customer in the credit card business; a 50 percent increase in profit per customer in the insurance brokerage industry; a 45 percent increase in profit per customer in the industrial laundry business, and a 35 percent increase in profit per customer in the computer software industry.[19]

But how can a company reduce customer defection rates? It can do so by building brand loyalty, which in turn requires that the company be responsive to the needs of its customers. We consider the issue of customer responsiveness later in the chapter. For now, note that a central component of developing a strategy to reduce defection rates is to spot customers who do defect, find out why they defected, and act on that information so that other customers do not defect for similar reasons in the future. To take these measures, the marketing function must have information systems capable of tracking customer defections.

Materials Management Strategy, JIT, and Efficiency

The contribution of materials management to boosting the efficiency of a company can be just as dramatic as the contribution of manufacturing and marketing. Materials management encompasses the activities necessary to get materials to a production facility, through the production process, and out through a distribution system to the end user.[20] The potential for reducing costs through more efficient materials management is enormous. For the average manufacturing enterprise, materials and transportation costs account for between 50 percent and 70 percent of revenues. Even a small reduction in these costs can have a substantial impact on profitability. According to one estimate, for a company with revenues of $1 million, a return on investment rate of 5 percent, and materials costs that amount to 50 percent of sales revenues, increasing total profits by $15,000 would require either a 30 percent increase in sales revenues or a 3 percent reduction in materials costs.[21] In a saturated market, it would be much easier to reduce materials costs by 3 percent than to increase sales revenues by 30 percent. The Opening Case provides another example of the cost savings obtainable through more efficient materials management: by reorganizing its global materials management function, Xerox hoped to reduce its total inventory by $1 billion and its annual inventory holding costs by $200 million.

Improving the efficiency of the materials management function typically requires the adoption of **just-in-time (JIT)** inventory systems. The basic philosophy behind JIT is to economize on inventory holding costs by having materials arrive at a manufacturing plant just in time to enter the production process, and not before. The major cost saving comes from increasing inventory turnover, which reduces inventory holding costs, such as warehousing and storage costs. For example, Ford's switch to JIT systems in the early 1980s reportedly brought the firm a huge one-time saving—$3 billion. At Ford minimal inventory now turns over nine times a year instead of the former six, while carrying costs have been reduced by one-third.

More recently, the JIT concept has been adopted by a number of service companies, often with great success. For example, Wal-Mart, the nation's fastest-

growing general retailer, uses JIT systems to replenish the stock in its stores at least twice a week. Many stores receive daily deliveries. The typical competitor—Kmart or Sears—replenishes its stock every two weeks. Compared with these competitors, Wal-Mart can maintain the same service levels with one-fourth the inventory investment, which is a major source of cost saving. Thus faster inventory turnover has helped Wal-Mart achieve an efficiency-based competitive advantage in the retailing industry.[22]

The drawback of JIT systems is that they leave a firm without a buffer stock of inventory. Although buffer stocks of inventory are expensive to store, they can help tide a firm over shortages on inputs brought about by disruption among suppliers (for instance, a labor dispute at a key supplier). Buffer stocks can also help a firm respond quickly to increases in demand. However, there are ways around these limitations. For example, to reduce the risks linked to dependence on just one supplier for an important input, it might pay the firm to source inputs from multiple suppliers.

R&D Strategy and Efficiency

The role of superior research and development in helping a company achieve greater efficiency is twofold. First, the R&D function can boost efficiency by designing products that are easy to manufacture. By cutting down on the number of parts that make up a product, R&D can dramatically decrease the required assembly time, which translates into higher employee productivity and lower unit costs. For example, after Texas Instruments redesigned an infrared sighting mechanism that it supplies to the Pentagon, the company found that it had reduced the number of parts from 47 to 12, the number of assembly steps from 56 to 13, the time spent fabricating metal from 757 minutes per unit to 219 minutes per unit, and unit assembly time from 129 minutes to 20 minutes. The result was a substantial decline in manufacturing costs. It should be noted that design for manufacturing requires close coordination between the manufacturing and R&D functions of the company. This is best achieved by cross-functional teams that contain manufacturing and R&D personnel, so that they can work on the problem jointly.

The second way in which the R&D function can help a company to achieve greater efficiency is by pioneering process innovations. A process innovation is an innovation in the way production processes operate that improves the efficiency of those processes. Process innovations have often been a major source of competitive advantage. For example, in the automobile industry, Toyota's competitive advantage is based partly on the company's invention of new flexible manufacturing processes, which dramatically reduced setup times. This enabled Toyota to obtain efficiency gains associated with flexible manufacturing systems years ahead of its competitors.

Human Resources Strategy and Efficiency

Employee productivity is one of the key determinants of an enterprise's efficiency and cost structure. The more productive the employees, the lower will be the unit costs. The challenge for a company's human resource function is to devise ways to increase employee productivity. It has three main choices: training employees; organizing the work force into self-managing teams; and linking pay to performance.

Employee Training Individuals are a major input into the production process. A company that employs individuals with higher skills is likely to be more efficient than one employing less skilled personnel. Individuals who are more skilled can perform tasks faster and more accurately and are more likely to learn the complex tasks associated with many modern production methods than individuals with lesser skills. Training can upgrade employee skill levels, bringing the firm productivity-related efficiency gains.[23]

Indeed, the work done by the MIT Commission on Industrial Productivity indicates that one major source of the competitive advantage that many Japanese companies have over their European and U.S. rivals is their commitment to improving the skill level of their employees through ongoing training programs.[24] These training programs have four main components. First, rotating employees through various departments lets them acquire general skills. For example, all new workers hired at Sanyo, the Japanese electronics company, must spend time in sales and in rotations between research and manufacturing. Second, many Japanese companies have extensive off-the-job training. Of Sanyo's 30,000 employees, 10,000 pass through the Sanyo Corporate Educational Training Center each year, with every person spending at least three days at the center. Third, many Japanese companies encourage their employees to develop skills through correspondence courses, whose costs the employers often reimburse on completion of the program. Finally, participation in team activities focused on improving company performance results in a general upgrading of employee skill levels. Non-Japanese companies that wish to enhance the skills of their employees might consider taking similar steps.

Self-Managing Teams Self-managing teams are a relatively recent phenomenon in American industry. Few companies used them until the mid 1980s, but since then they have spread rapidly. The growth of flexible manufacturing cells, which group workers into teams, has undoubtedly facilitated the spread of self-managing teams. The typical team comprises five to fifteen employees who produce an entire product or subassembly. Team members learn all team tasks and rotate from job to job. A more flexible work force is one result. Team members can fill in for absent coworkers. Teams also take over managerial duties such as work and vacation scheduling, ordering materials, and hiring new members. The greater responsibility thrust on team members and the empowerment it implies are seen as motivators. (**Empowerment** is the process of giving lower-level employees decision-making power.) People often respond well to being given greater autonomy and responsibility. Performance bonuses linked to team production and quality targets work as an additional motivator.

The net effect of introducing self-managing teams is reportedly an increase in productivity of 30 percent or more and a substantial increase in product quality. Further cost savings arise from eliminating supervisors and creating a flatter organizational hierarchy. Perhaps the most potent combination is that of self-managing teams and flexible manufacturing cells. The two seem designed for each other. For example, after the introduction of flexible manufacturing technology and work practices based on self-managing teams in 1988, a General Electric plant in Salisbury, North Carolina, increased productivity by 250 percent compared with GE plants that produced that same products in 1984.[25] Still, teams are no panacea; unless they are integrated with flexible manufacturing technology, self-managing teams may fail to live up to their potential.

Pay for Performance People work for money, so it is hardly surprising that linking pay to performance can help increase employee productivity. However, the issue is not quite as simple as just introducing incentive pay systems; it is also important to define what kind of performance is to be rewarded and how. Some of the most efficient companies in the world, mindful that cooperation among employees is necessary to realize productivity gains, do *not* link pay to individual performance. Instead they link pay to group or team performance. For example, at Nucor, which is widely viewed as one of the most efficient steelmakers in the world, the work force is divided into teams of thirty or so. Bonus pay, which can amount to 30 percent of base pay, is linked to the ability of the team to meet productivity and quality goals. This creates a strong incentive for individuals to cooperate with each other in pursuit of team goals; that is, it facilitates teamwork.

Infrastructure and Efficiency

The infrastructure sets the context within which all other value-creation activities take place. It follows that the infrastructure can help in achieving efficiency goals. Above all, the infrastructure can foster a company-wide commitment to efficiency and promote cooperation among different functions in pursuit of efficiency goals.

A company-wide commitment to efficiency can be built through top management leadership. The leadership task is to articulate a vision that recognizes the need for all functions of the company to focus on improving their efficiency. It is not enough just to improve the efficiency of manufacturing, or marketing, or R&D. Achieving superior efficiency requires a company-wide commitment to this goal, and this can be articulated only by top management.

A further leadership task is to facilitate cross-functional cooperation needed to achieve superior efficiency. For example, designing products that are easy to manufacture requires that manufacturing and R&D personnel communicate, integrating JIT systems with production scheduling requires close communication between material management and manufacturing, designing self-managing teams to perform manufacturing functions requires close cooperation between human resources and manufacturing, and so on.

Summary: Achieving Superior Efficiency

Table 5.1 summarizes the primary roles that the various functions must take in order to achieve superior efficiency. Bear in mind that achieving superior efficiency is not something that can be tackled on a function by function basis. It requires an organization-wide commitment and an ability to ensure close cooperation among functions. Top management, by exercising leadership and influencing the infrastructure, plays a major role in this process.

5.5 ACHIEVING SUPERIOR QUALITY

As noted in Chapter 4, achieving superior quality gives a company two advantages. The enhanced reputation for quality lets the company charge a premium price for its product, and the elimination of defects from the manufacturing process increases efficiency and hence lowers costs. In this section, we examine

Table 5.1
The Primary Roles of Different Value-Creation Functions in Achieving Superior Efficiency

Value-Creation Function	Primary Roles
Infrastructure	(1) Provide company-wide commitment to efficiency
	(2) Facilitate cooperation between functions
Manufacturing	(1) Where appropriate, pursue experience curve-based cost economies
	(2) Implement flexible manufacturing systems
Marketing	(1) Where appropriate, adopt aggressive marketing to ride down the experience curve
	(2) Limit customer defections by building brand loyalty
Material Management	(1) Implement JIT systems
R&D	(1) Design products for ease of manufacture
	(2) Seek process innovations
Human Resources	(1) Institute training programs to build skills
	(2) Implement self-managing teams
	(3) Implement pay for performance

the means a company can use to achieve superior quality. The main management concept utilized to enhance quality is total quality management (TQM). TQM is a management philosophy that focuses on improving the quality of a company's products and services and stresses that all company operations should be oriented toward this goal. A company-wide philosophy, it requires the cooperation of all the different functions if it is to be successfully implemented. We first consider the total quality management concept and then discuss the various steps needed to implement TQM programs. Throughout, we highlight the roles that different functions must play in this process.

The TQM Concept

The total quality management (TQM) concept was first developed by a number of American consultants, including W. Edwards Deming, Joseph Juran, and A. V. Feigenbaum.[26] Originally, these consultants won few converts in the United States. In contrast, the Japanese embraced them enthusiastically and even named their premier annual prize for manufacturing excellence after Deming. The philosophy underlying TQM, as articulated by Deming, is based on the following five-step "chain reaction":

1. Improved quality means that costs decrease because of less rework, fewer mistakes, fewer delays, and better use of time and materials.
2. As a result, productivity improves.
3. Better quality leads to higher market share and allows the company to raise prices.
4. This increases the company's profitability and allows it to stay in business.
5. Thus the company creates more jobs.[27]

Deming has identified fourteen steps that should be part of any TQM program. These are summarized in Table 5.2. (Deming has continually changed

these points in line with his belief in the importance of continuous quality improvement; those given below are the latest—1990—version.) In essence, Deming urges a company to have a definite strategic plan for where it is going and how it is going to get there. He argues that management should embrace the philosophy that mistakes, defects, and poor-quality materials are not acceptable and should be eliminated. Quality of supervision should be improved by allowing more time for supervisors to work with employees and giving them appropriate skills for the job. Furthermore, management should create an environment in which employees will not fear reporting problems or recom-

Table 5.2
Deming's 14 Points to Quality

1. Create constancy of purpose toward improvement of product and service, with the aim of becoming competitive, staying in business, and providing jobs.
2. Adopt the new philosophy. We are in a new economic age. Western management must awaken to the challenge, learn its responsibilities, and take on leadership for change.
3. Cease dependence on inspection to achieve quality. Eliminate the need for inspection on a mass basis by building quality into the product in the first place.
4. End the practice of awarding business on the basis of price tag. Instead, minimize total cost.
5. Improve constantly and forever the system of production and service, to improve quality and productivity and thus constantly decrease costs.
6. Institute training on the job.
7. Institute leadership. The aim of leadership should be to help people, machines, and gadgets do a better job. Management leadership, as well as leadership of production workers, needs overhauling.
8. Drive out fear, so that everyone may work effectively for the company.
9. Break down barriers between departments. People in research, design, sales, and production must work as a team, to foresee problems in production and in use that may be encountered with the product or service.
10. Eliminate slogans, exhortations, and targets for the work force asking for zero defects and new levels of productivity. Such exhortations only create adversarial relationships. The bulk of the causes of low quality and low productivity belong to the system and thus lie beyond the power of the work force.
11. (a) Eliminate work standards on the factory floor; substitute leadership
    (b) Eliminate management by objective, management by numbers, and numerical goals; substitute leadership.
12. (a) Remove barriers that rob the hourly workers of their right to pride of workmanship. The responsibility of supervisors must be changed from sheer numbers to quality.
    (b) Remove barriers that rob people in management and in engineering of their right to pride of workmanship.
13. Institute a vigorous program of education and self-improvement.
14. Put everybody in the company to work to accomplish the transformation. The transformation is everybody's job.

Source: From *The Man Who Discovered Quality* by Andrea Gabor. Copyright © 1990 by Andrea Gabor. Reprinted by permission of Times Books, a division of Random House, Inc.

STRATEGY IN ACTION 5.2

Some Examples of the Impact of TQM Programs on Quality

- In 1987 Motorola's semiconductor business was producing 6,000 defects per million parts. By 1992 this figure had been reduced to 40 per million.[30]
- Since the company first adopted an aggressive TQM program in 1978, the number of defects reported by customers in Hitachi's software business have dropped from 100 per thousand computers, to less than 2 per thousand by 1992.[31]
- In 1978 Yokogawa Hewlett-Packard (YHP) adopted a TQM program. At that time the defect rate in its soldering process was 4,000 parts per million. By 1982 YHP had reduced its defect rate to 3 parts per million. Over the same time period employee productivity rose 91 percent, costs fell by 42 percent, and profits increased by 177 percent.[32]
- When Xerox first introduced a TQM program in conjunction with its suppliers in 1983, its suppliers were producing about 25,000 defective parts per million. By 1992 the defect rate on parts from suppliers was under 300 per million.[33]

mending improvements. Deming also believes that work standards should be defined not only as numbers or quotas, but should include some notion of quality to promote the production of defect-free output. He argues that management has the responsibility to train employees in new skills to keep pace with changes in the work place and that achieving better quality requires the commitment of everyone in the company.

It took the rise of Japan to the top rank of economic powers to alert Western business to the importance of the TQM concept. Since the early 1980s TQM practices have spread rapidly throughout Western industry. Strategy in Action 5.2 offers some examples of the impact that TQM programs can have on quality. However, despite such instances of spectacular success, TQM practices are still not universally accepted. A 1992 study by the American Quality Foundation found that only 20 percent of U.S. companies regularly review the consequences of quality performance, compared with 70 percent of Japanese companies.[28] Another study by Arthur D. Little, of 500 American companies using TQM found that only 36 percent believed that TQM was increasing their competitiveness.[29] A prime reason for this, according to the study, was that many companies had not fully understood or embraced the TQM concept.

Implementing TQM

Among companies that have successfully adopted TQM, certain imperatives stand out. We discuss them in the order in which they are usually tackled in companies implementing TQM programs, and we highlight the role that the various functions play in regard to each precept. What cannot be stressed enough, however, is that implementing TQM requires close cooperation among *all* functions in the pursuit of the common goal of improving quality. Strategy in Action 5.3 at the end of this section describes the efforts of a service company to put TQM into practice and the benefits it has gained.

Build Organizational Commitment to Quality There is evidence that TQM will do little to improve the performance of a company unless it is embraced by

everyone in the organization.[34] As you recall from the Opening Case, when Xerox launched its quality program in 1983, its first step was to educate its entire work force, from top management down, in the importance and operation of the TQM concept. It did so by forming groups, beginning with a group at the top of the organization that included the CEO. The top group was the first to receive basic TQM training. Each member of this group was then given the task of training a group at the next level in the hierarchy, and so on down throughout the organization until all 100,000 employees had received basic TQM training. Both top management and the human resource function of the company can play a major role in this process. Top management has the responsibility of exercising the leadership required to make a commitment to quality an organization-wide goal. The human resource function must take on responsibility for company-wide training in TQM techniques.

Focus on the Customer TQM practitioners see a focus on the customer as the starting point, and indeed, the raison d'être, of the whole quality philosophy.[35] The marketing function, because it provides the primary point of contact with the customer, should play a major role here. It needs to identify what the customers want from the good or service that the company provides; what the company actually provides to customers; and the gap between what customers want and what they actually get, which could be called the *quality gap*. Then, together with the other functions of the company, it needs to formulate a plan for closing the quality gap.

Find Ways to Measure Quality Another imperative of any TQM program is to create some metric that can be used to measure quality. This is relatively easy in manufacturing companies, where quality can be measured by criteria such as defects per million parts. It tends to be more difficult in service companies, but with a little creativity suitable metrics can be devised. For example, one of the metrics that Florida Power & Light uses to measure quality is meter reading errors per month. Another is the frequency and duration of power outages. L.L. Bean, the Freeport, Maine, mail-order retailer of outdoor gear, uses the percentage of orders that are correctly filled as one of its quality metrics. For some banks, the key metrics are the number of customer defections per year and the number of statement errors per thousand customers. The common theme that runs through all of these examples is identifying what quality means from a customer's perspective and devising a method to gauge this. Top management should take primary responsibility for formulating different metrics to measure quality, but to succeed in this effort, it must receive input from the various functions of the company.

Set Goals and Create Incentives Once a metric has been devised, the next step is to set a challenging quality goal and to create incentives for reaching that goal. An example of a challenging goal, given in the Opening Case, is Xerox's initial goal of reducing defective parts from 25,000 per million to 1,000 per million. One way of creating incentives to attain such a goal is to link rewards, like bonus pay and promotional opportunities to the goal. Thus, within many companies that have adopted self-managing teams, the bonus pay of team members is determined in part by their ability to attain quality goals. The task of setting goals and creating incentives is one of the key tasks of top management.

Solicit Input from Employees Employees can be a vital source of information regarding the sources of poor quality. Therefore, some framework must be established for soliciting employee suggestions as to the improvements that can be made. Quality circles—which are meetings of groups of employees—have often been used to achieve this goal. Other companies have utilized self-managing teams as forums for discussing quality improvement ideas. Whatever the forum, soliciting input from lower-level employees requires that management be open to receiving, and acting on, bad news and criticism from employees. According to Deming, one problem with American management is that it has grown used to "killing the bearer of bad tidings."[36] But, he argues, managers who are committed to the quality concept must recognize that bad news is a gold mine of information.[36]

Identify Defects and Trace Them to Source Product defects occur mostly in the production process. TQM preaches the need to identify defects during the work process, trace them to their source, find out what caused them, and make corrections so that they do not recur. Manufacturing and materials management typically have primary responsibility for this task.

To uncover defects, Deming advocates the use of statistical procedures to pinpoint variations in the quality of goods or services. Deming views variation as the enemy of quality.[37] Once variations have been identified, they must be traced to their source and eliminated. One technique that helps greatly in tracing defects to their source is reducing lot sizes for manufactured products. With short production runs, defects show up immediately in the production process. Consequently, they can be quickly traced to the source and the problem can be fixed. Reducing lot sizes also means that when defective products are produced, their number will not be large, thus decreasing waste. Flexible manufacturing techniques, discussed earlier, can be used to reduce lot sizes without raising costs. Consequently, adopting flexible manufacturing techniques is an important aspect of a TQM program.

Just-in-time (JIT) inventory systems also play a part. Under a JIT system, defective parts enter the manufacturing process immediately; they are not warehoused for several months before use. Hence defective inputs can be quickly spotted. The problem can then be traced to the supply source and corrected before more defective parts are produced. Under a more traditional system, the practice of warehousing parts for months before they are used may mean that large numbers of defects are produced by a supplier before they enter the production process.

Supplier Relations A major source of poor-quality finished goods are poor-quality component parts. To decrease product defects, a company has to work with its suppliers to improve the quality of the parts they supply. The primary responsibility in this area falls on the materials management function, since it is the function that interfaces with suppliers.

Supplier relations are discussed in the Opening Case on Xerox. Xerox worked closely with its suppliers to get them to adopt TQM programs. The result was a reduction in the defect rate on component parts from 25,000 per million in 1982 to under 300 per million by 1992. As already noted, too, JIT systems are required for high quality. A company must work closely with its suppliers if it is going to introduce a JIT system to manage material flows from them.

To implement JIT systems with suppliers and to get suppliers to adopt their own TQM programs, two steps are necessary. First, the supply base has to be rationalized so that the number of suppliers is reduced to manageable proportions. Xerox, for example, reduced its supply base from 5,000 to 325. Second, there is a need to commit to building a cooperative long-term relationship with the suppliers that remain. Asking suppliers to invest in JIT and TQM systems is asking them to make major investments that tie them to the company. For example, in order to fully implement a JIT system, the company may ask a supplier to relocate its manufacturing plant so that it is next door to the company's assembly plant. Suppliers are likely to be hesitant about making such investments unless they feel that the company is committed to an enduring, long-term relationship with them.

Design for Ease of Manufacture The more assembly steps a product requires, the more opportunities there are for making mistakes. Designing products with fewer parts should make assembly easier and result in fewer defects. Both R&D and manufacturing need to be involved in designing products that are easy to manufacture.

Break Down Barriers Between Functions Implementing TQM requires organization- wide commitment and substantial cooperation among functions. R&D has to cooperate with manufacturing to design products that are easy to manufacture, marketing has to cooperate with manufacturing and R&D so that customer problems identified by marketing can be acted on, human resource management has to cooperate with all of the other functions of the company in order to devise suitable quality-training programs, and so on. The issue of

Table 5.3
The Role of Different Functions in Achieving Superior Quality

Value-Creation Function	Primary Role
Infrastructure (Leadership)	(1) Provide leadership and commitment to quality
	(2) Find ways to measure quality
	(3) Set goals and create incentives
	(4) Solicit input from employees
	(5) Encourage cooperation between functions
Manufacturing	(1) Shorten production runs
	(2) Trace defects to source
Marketing	(1) Focus on the customer
	(2) Provide customer feedback on quality
Materials Management	(1) Rationalize suppliers
	(2) Help suppliers implement TQM
	(3) Trace defects to suppliers
R&D	(1) Design products that are easy to manufacture
Human Resources	(1) Institute TQM training programs
	(2) Organize employees into quality teams

STRATEGY IN ACTION 5.3

TQM at Intermountain Health Care

Intermountain Health Care is a nonprofit chain of twenty-four hospitals operating in Idaho, Utah, and Wyoming. Intermountain first adopted TQM for certain sections of its system in the mid 1980s, and in 1990 it adopted TQM systemwide. The goal of TQM was to find and eliminate inappropriate variations in medical care, provide the patient with better health care, and in the process, reduce costs. The starting point was to identify variations in practice across physicians, particularly with regard to the cost and success rate of treatments. These data were then shared among physicians within the Intermountain system. The next step was for the physicians to use the data to eliminate poor practices and generally upgrade the quality of medical care.

The outcome has been quite striking. One of the early results of this process was an attempt by Intermountain's hospital in Salt Lake City to lower the rate of postoperative wound infections. Before the effort began in 1985, the hospital's postoperative infection rate was 1.8 percent—0.2 points below the national average, but still unacceptably high from a TQM perspective. By using a bedside computer system to make sure that antibiotics were given to patients two hours before surgery, the hospital halved the infection rate, to 0.9 percent, within a year. Since then the postoperative infection rate has dropped further still, to 0.4 percent, compared with the national average of 2 percent. Since the average postoperative infection adds $14,000 to a hospital bill, this constitutes a big cost saving.

Intermountain is now focusing on dozens of problems, including situations in which the wrong type or dose of medication is given, the top cause of poor medical care. Intermountain expects its efforts in this area to quickly eliminate at least 60 percent of such mistakes and to reduce its medical costs by as much as $2 million a year per hospital.[38]

achieving cooperation among subunits within a company is explored in Chapter 11. What needs stressing at this point is that ultimately it is the responsibility of top management to ensure that such cooperation occurs.

Summary: Achieving Superior Quality

The primary role played by the different value-creation functions in achieving quality is summarized in Table 5.3. As the table makes clear, achieving TQM requires the adoption of strategies that cut across functions. Note the major role played by the infrastructure, and particularly by top management. Top management has the task of setting the context within which implementation of TQM programs occurs. This includes building an organization-wide commitment to quality and encouraging cooperation between functions in the pursuit of superior quality.

5.6 ACHIEVING SUPERIOR INNOVATION

In many ways innovation is the single most important building block of competitive advantage. Successful innovation of products or processes gives a company something unique that its competitors lack. This uniqueness may allow a com-

pany to charge a premium price or lower its cost structure below that of its rivals. Competitors, however, will try to imitate successful innovations. Often they will ultimately succeed, although high barriers to imitation can slow it down. Therefore, maintaining a competitive advantage requires a continuing commitment to innovation.

Many companies have built up a track record for successful innovation. Among them are Du Pont, which has produced a steady stream of successful innovations such as cellophane, nylon, Freon (used in all air conditioners), and Teflon (nonstick pans); Sony, whose successes include the Walkman and the compact disk; Merck, the drug company that during the 1980s produced seven major new drugs; 3M, which has applied its core competency in tapes and adhesives to developing a wide range of new products; and Intel, which to date at least, has consistently managed to lead in developing innovative new microprocessors to run personal computers.

The High Failure Rate of Innovation

Although innovation can be a source of competitive advantage, its failure rate is very high. One study that looked at product innovations estimated that only about 12 to 20 percent of new products actually generate profit when they get to the marketplace.[39] The remaining 80 to 88 percent fail. Two well-publicized failures were AT&T's losses, amounting to several billion dollars, on its failed venture in the personal computer industry and Sony's failure to establish the Betamax format in the video player and recorder market.

Four main reasons have been advanced to explain why so many new products fail to generate an economic return. The first reason is uncertainty. Developing new products is risky since no one can predict the demand. Although good market research can reduce the risks of failure, it cannot eradicate them altogether.

The second reason frequently cited is poor commercialization—a condition that occurs when there is an intrinsic demand for a new technology, but the technology is not well adapted to consumer needs. For instance, many of the early personal computers failed to sell because you needed to be a computer programmer to use them. It took Steve Jobs at Apple Computer to understand that if the technology could be made user-friendly, there would be an enormous market for it. Hence the original personal computers marketed by Apple incorporated little in the way of radically new technology, but they made existing technology accessible to the average person.

A third reason for failure is that companies often make the mistake of marketing a technology for which there is not enough demand. The Anglo-French supersonic jetliner, Concorde, is a salient example. A miracle of high technology, the Concorde can carry 140 passengers at twice the speed of sound, reducing the trans-Atlantic flight time by 60 or 70 percent. However, only eight Concordes were ever sold. At the price that it cost to produce the aircraft, there was little demand for it. Thus the whole venture was a costly mistake.

Finally, companies fail when they are slow to get their products to market. The longer the time between initial development and final marketing—that is, the slower the "cycle time"—the more likely it is that someone else will beat the firm to market and gain a first-mover advantage. By and large, slow innovators update their products less frequently than fast innovators. Consequently, they can be perceived as technical laggards relative to the fast innovators. In the automobile industry, General Motors has suffered from being a slow innovator. Its

STRATEGY IN ACTION 5.4

How a Slow Cycle Time Cost Apollo Computer the Lead in the Market for Workstations

In 1980 Apollo Computer created the market for engineering computer workstations. (Workstations are high-powered free-standing minicomputers.) Apollo was rewarded with rapid growth and a virtual monopoly. Its first serious competitor, Sun Microsystems, did not introduce a competing product until 1982. However, by 1988 Apollo had lost its lead in the workstation market to Sun. While Apollo was generating revenues of $600 million in 1988, Sun's revenues were over $1 billion. Between 1984 and 1988 Sun's revenues from workstations grew at an annual rate of 100 percent a year, compared with Apollo's annual growth rate of 35 percent.

The cause of Apollo's slower growth was slow cycle time. In the computer industry, innovations in microprocessor technology are proceeding at a furious pace. To stay abreast of new microprocessor technology, any manufacturer of computers must be continually updating its product. While Sun had succeeded in introducing a new product every twelve months, and doubling the power of its workstations every eighteen months on the average, Apollo's product development cycle had stretched out to over two years. As a result, Apollo's products were regularly superseded by the more technologically advanced products introduced by Sun, and Apollo was falling further and further behind. Consequently, while Sun had increased its market share from 21 percent to 33 percent between 1985 and 1988, Apollo's fell from 41 percent to under 20 percent. In 1989, facing mounting problems, Apollo was acquired by Hewlett-Packard.[40]

product development cycle has been about five years, compared with two to three years at Honda, Toyota, and Mazda, and three to four years at Ford. Because they are based on five-year-old technology and design concepts, by the time GM cars reach the market they are already out-of-date compared with the cars of faster innovators. Another example of the consequences of slow innovation, the demise of Apollo Computer at the hands of Sun Microsystems, is given in Strategy in Action 5.4.

Building Competencies in Innovation

Companies can take a number of steps in order to build a competency in innovation, and avoid failure. Five of the most important steps seem to be (1) building skills in basic and applied scientific research; (2) achieving close integration between R&D and marketing; (3) achieving close integration between R&D and manufacturing; (4) an ability to minimize time to market; and (5) good project management.[41]

Building Skills in Basic and Applied Research Building skills in basic and applied research requires the employment of research scientists and engineers and the establishment of a work environment that fosters creativity. A number of top companies try to achieve this by setting up university-style research facilities, where scientists and engineers are given time to work on their own research projects, in addition to projects that are linked directly to ongoing company research. At Hewlett-Packard, for example, the company labs are open to

engineers around the clock. Hewlett-Packard even encourages its corporate researchers to devote 10 percent of company time to exploring their own ideas—and does not penalize them if they fail. Similarly, at 3M there is the "15 percent rule," which allows researchers to spend 15 percent of the workweek researching any topic that they want to investigate, as long as there is the potential of a payoff for the company. The most famous outcome of this policy is the ubiquitous yellow Post-it Notes. The idea for them evolved from a researcher's desire to find a way to keep the bookmark from falling out of his hymn book. Post-it Notes are now a major 3M consumer business, with 1988 revenues of around $300 million.

Integrating R&D and Marketing A company's customers can be one of its primary sources of new product ideas. Identification of customer needs, and particularly unmet needs, can set the context within which successful product innovation takes place. As the point of contact with customers, the marketing function of a company can provide valuable information here in this regard. Moreover, integration of R&D and marketing are crucial if a new product is to be properly commercialized. Without integration of R&D and marketing, a company runs the risk of developing products for which there is little or no demand, such as the Concorde.

The case of Techsonic Industries illustrates the benefits of integrating R&D and marketing. This Alabama company manufactures depth finders—electronic devices used by fishermen to measure the depth of water beneath a boat and to track their prey. Techsonic had weathered nine new-product failures in a row before 1985. Then the company decided to interview sportspeople across the country to identify what it was they needed. They discovered an unmet need for a depth finder with a gauge that could be read in bright sunlight; so that is what Techsonic developed. In the year after the $250 depth finder hit the market, Techsonic's sales tripled to $80 million and its market share surged to 40 percent.[42]

Integrating Manufacturing and R&D Successful innovation also requires close integration between manufacturing and R&D. The critical task is to design products that are easy to manufacture, for that lowers manufacturing costs and leaves less room for making mistakes. Thus, designing for manufacturing can lower costs and increase product quality.

Integrating R&D and manufacturing can also help lower development costs and speed products to market. If a new product is not designed with manufacturing capabilities in mind, it may prove too difficult to build, given existing manufacturing technology. In that case, the product will have to be redesigned, and both overall development costs and the time it takes to bring the product to market may increase significantly. For example, making design changes during product planning could increase overall development costs by 50 percent and add 25 percent to the time it takes to bring the product to market.[43]

Reducing Time to Market As the case of Apollo Computer in Strategy in Action 5.4 illustrates, reducing time to market is a key competitive dimension. Companies that are slow on this dimension will lose technological leadership to their swifter competitors. It is the fast-cycle competitor that captures first-mover advantages and ensures that its product is always on the cutting edge of technology.

One of the key requirements for reducing time to market is to achieve cross-functional integration among R&D, manufacturing, and marketing. For an example, consider what occurred after Intel Corporation introduced its 386 microprocessor in 1986. A number of companies, including IBM and Compaq, were racing to be the first to introduce a 386-based personal computer. Compaq beat IBM by six months and gained a major share of the high-power market. Compaq succeeded mainly because it utilized a cross-functional team to develop the product. The team included engineers (R&D) and marketing, manufacturing, and finance people. Each function worked in parallel rather than sequentially. While engineers were designing the product, manufacturing people were setting up the manufacturing facilities, marketing people were working on distribution and planning marketing campaigns, and the finance people were working on project funding. The net effect of this type of approach can be to reduce the time it takes to get a product from the drawing board to the marketplace by over 50 percent when compared with sequential development.[44]

Project Management Project management is the overall management of the innovation process, from generation of the original concept, through development, and into final production and shipping. Project management requires three important skills: the ability to encourage as much idea generation as possible; the ability to select among competing projects at an early stage of development so that the most promising receive funding and potential costly failures are killed off; and the ability to minimize time to market. The concept of the development funnel, illustrated in Figure 5.9, can be used to summarize what is required to build these skills.[45]

As Figure 5.9 shows, the development funnel is divided into three phases. The objective in phase 1 is to widen the mouth of the tunnel to encourage as much idea generation as possible. To this end, a company should solicit input from all its functions, as well as from customers, competitors, and suppliers. The need to achieve integration between marketing and R&D, discussed earlier, can be placed in this context.

At gate 1 the funnel narrows. Here ideas are reviewed by a cross-functional team of managers who were not involved in the original concept development. Those concepts that are ready to proceed then move on to phase 2 of the funnel,

Figure 5.9
The Development Funnel

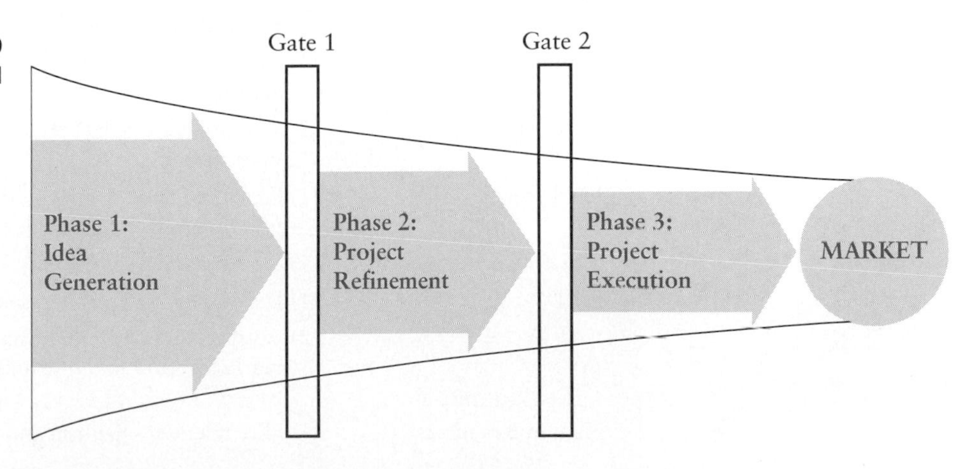

which is where the details of the project proposal are worked out. Note that gate 1 is *not* a go/no-go evaluation point. At this screen, ideas may be sent back for further concept development and then resubmitted for evaluation.

During phase 2, which typically lasts only one or two months, the data and information developed during phase 1 are put into a form that will enable senior management to evaluate proposed projects against competing projects. The next big selection point, gate 2, is a go/no-go evaluation point. Senior managers are brought in to review the various projects under consideration and to select those that seem likely winners. Any project selected at this stage to go forward will be funded and staffed, the expectation being that it will be carried through to market introduction. In phase 3, the project development proposal is executed by a cross-functional team in order to ensure that time to market is minimized.

Summary: Achieving Superior Innovation

The primary role that the various functions play in achieving superior innovation is summarized in Table 5.4. The table makes two matters clear. First, top management must bear primary responsibility for overseeing the whole development process. This entails both managing the development funnel and facilitating cooperation between functions. Second, while R&D plays a central role in the innovation process, the effectiveness of R&D in developing new products and processes depends on its ability to cooperate with marketing and manufacturing.

5.7 ACHIEVING SUPERIOR CUSTOMER RESPONSIVENESS

To achieve superior customer responsiveness a company must give customers what they want when they want it—so long as the company's long-term profitability is not compromised in the process. The more responsive a company is

Table 5.4
The Role of Various Functions in Achieving Superior Innovation

Value-Creation Function	Primary Role
Infrastructure	(1) Overall project management (i.e., managing the development function)
	(2) Facilitating cross-functional cooperation
Manufacturing	(1) Cooperating with R&D on designing products that are easy to manufacture
	(2) Working with R&D on developing process innovations
Marketing	(1) Providing market information to R&D; working with R&D on developing new products
Materials Management	(1) No primary responsibility
R&D	(1) Developing new products and processes
	(2) Cooperating with other functions, particularly marketing and manufacturing, in the development process
Human Resources	(1) Hire talented scientists and engineers

to the needs of its customers, the greater the brand loyalty that the company can command. In turn, strong brand loyalty may allow a company to charge a premium price for its products or enable it to sell more goods and services to customers. Either way, the company that is responsive to its customers' needs will have a competitive advantage.

Achieving superior customer responsiveness involves giving customers value for money, and steps taken to improve the efficiency of a company's production process and the quality of its output should be consistent with this aim. In addition, giving customers what they want may require the development of new products that have features not incorporated in existing ones. In other words, *achieving superior efficiency, quality, and innovation are all part of achieving superior customer responsiveness.* There are two other prerequisites for attaining this goal. The first is to focus on the company's customers and their needs, and the second, to find ways to better satisfy those needs.

Customer Focus

A company cannot be responsive to its customers' needs unless it knows what those needs are. Thus the first step to building superior customer responsiveness is to motivate the whole company to focus on the customer. The means to this end are leadership, shaping employee attitudes, and mechanisms for bringing customers into the company.

Leadership Customer focus must start at the top of the organization. A commitment to superior customer responsiveness involves attitudinal changes throughout a company that can ultimately be built only through strong leadership. A mission statement (see Chapter 2) that puts customers first is one way to send a clear message to employees within the company about the desired focus. Another way is the top management's own actions. For example, as you recall from the Opening Case in Chapter 4, the British retailer, Marks & Spencer is noted for its customer focus. The effort to stay close to the customer starts with the top managers, who wear M&S clothes, eat M&S food, and regularly visit M&S stores. Similarly, Tom Monaghan, the founder of Domino's Pizza, stays close to the customer by visiting as many stores as possible every week, running some deliveries himself, insisting that other top managers do the same, and eating Domino's pizza regularly.[46]

Employee Attitudes Achieving a superior customer focus requires that all employees see the customer as the focus of their activity. Leadership alone is not enough to attain this goal. All employees must be trained to focus on the customer, whether their function is marketing, manufacturing, R&D, or accounting. The objective should be to make employees think of themselves as customers—to put themselves in the customers' shoes. At that point, employees will be better able to identify ways to improve the quality of a customer's experience with the company.

To reinforce this mindset, incentive systems within the company should reward employees for satisfying customers. For example, senior managers at the Four Seasons hotel chain, who pride themselves on their customer focus, like to tell the story of Roy Dyment, a doorman in Toronto who neglected to load a departing guest's briefcase into his taxi. The doorman called the guest, a lawyer,

in Washington D.C., and found that he desperately needed the briefcase for a morning meeting. Dyment hopped on a plane to Washington and returned it—without first securing approval from his boss. Far from punishing Dyment for making a mistake and for not checking with management before going to Washington, the Four Seasons responded by naming Dyment Employee of the Year.[47] This action sent a powerful message to Four Seasons employees about the importance of satisfying customer needs.

Bringing Customers into the Company "Know thy customer" is one of the keys to achieving superior customer responsiveness. Knowing the customer not only requires that employees think like customers themselves; it also demands that they listen to what their customers have to say, and, as much as possible, bring them into the company. While this may not involve physically bringing customers into the company, it does mean bringing in customers' opinions by soliciting feedback from customers on the company's goods and services and by building information systems that communicate the feedback to the relevant people.

For an example, consider mail-order clothing retailer, Lands' End. Through its catalog and customer service telephone operators, Lands' End actively solicits comments from its customers about the quality of its clothing and the kind of merchandise they want Lands' End to supply. Indeed, it was customers' insistence that prompted the company to move into the clothing segment. Lands' End used to supply equipment for sailboats through mail-order catalogs. However, it received so many requests from customers to include outdoor clothing in its offering that it responded by expanding the catalog to fill this need. Soon clothing became the main business and Lands' End dropped the sailboat equipment. Today the company still pays close attention to customer requests. Every month a computer printout of customer requests and comments is given to managers. This feedback helps the company to fine-tune the merchandise it sells. Indeed, frequently new lines of merchandise are introduced in response to customer requests.[48]

Now many companies are trying to actively bring customers into their new product development process. You have already seen an example of this effort in the section on innovation: Techsonic's development of depth finders. Another example is Boeing's new 777 jetliner, the design of which was finalized only after intensive consultations with potential airline customers.[49]

Satisfying Customer Needs

Once a focus on the customer has been achieved, the next task is to satisfy the customer needs that have been identified. As already noted, efficiency, quality, and innovation all are crucial to satisfying those needs. Beyond that, companies can provide a higher level of satisfaction if they customize the product, as much as possible, to the requirements of individual customers and if they minimize the time it takes to respond to customer demands.

Customization Customization involves varying the features of a good or service to tailor it to the unique needs of groups of customers or, in the extreme case, individual customers. It used to be thought that customization raised

costs. However, the development of flexible manufacturing technologies has made it possible to produce a far greater variety of products than previously without suffering a substantial cost penalty. Companies can now customize their products to a much greater extent than was feasible 10–15 years ago. The following examples illustrate the effects of flexible manufacturing technologies:

- Panasonic Bicycle Company of Japan is able to turn out more than 11,000 variations of bicycle designs according to each customer's body height, size, and color preferences—all without any downtime in the factory.
- Ingersoll Milling Machine Company can produce 25,000 part designs, mostly in lots of one, and many one-of-a-kind designs to support its world dominance in the market for specialized production machinery.
- Because of its flexible production systems, Toshiba can manufacture nine different word processors on the same assembly line and twenty different varieties of laptop computer on an adjacent line, with only a limited increase in unit costs relative to manufacturing a single product.[50]

The trend toward customization has fragmented many markets, particularly consumer markets, into ever smaller niches. An example of this occurred in Japan in the early 1980s. At that time Honda dominated the motorcycle market in Japan. Second-placed Yamaha decided to go after Honda's lead. In 1981 it announced the opening of a new factory that, when operating at full capacity, would make Yamaha the world's largest manufacturer of motorcycles. Honda responded by proliferating its product line and stepping up its rate of new product introduction. At the start of what became known as the "motorcycle wars," Honda had 60 motorcycles in its product line. Over the next eighteen months Honda rapidly increased its model range to 113 models, customizing them to ever smaller niches. Honda was able to accomplish this without bearing a significant cost penalty because it was a flexible manufacturer. The flood of Honda's customized models pushed Yamaha out of much of the market, effectively stalling its bid to overtake Honda.[51]

Response Time Giving customers what they want *when they want it* requires speed of response to customer demands. To gain a competitive advantage, a company must often respond to consumer demands very quickly. The response time is important whether it relates to a furniture manufacturer's delivery of a product once it has been ordered, a bank's processing of a loan application, an automobile manufacturer's delivery of a spare part for a car that broke down, or the wait in a supermarket checkout line. We live in a fast-paced society, where time is a valuable commodity. Companies that can satisfy customer demands for rapid response can build brand loyalty and set a higher price for the product or service.

Increased speed lets a company charge a significant premium, as the mail delivery industry illustrates. The whole air express niche of the mail delivery industry is based on the notion that customers are often willing to pay considerably more for overnight Express Mail, as opposed to regular mail. Another example of the value of rapid response is Caterpillar, the manufacturer of heavy-earth moving equipment, which can get a spare part to any point in the world within twenty-four hours. Since downtime for heavy construction equipment is very costly, Caterpillar's ability to respond quickly in the event of equipment

malfunction is of prime importance to its customers. As a result, many of them have remained loyal to Caterpillar despite the aggressive low-price competition from Komatsu of Japan.

In general, reducing response time requires (1) a marketing function that can quickly communicate customer requests to manufacturing, (2) manufacturing and materials management functions that can quickly adjust production schedules in response to unanticipated customer demands, and (3) information systems that can help manufacturing and marketing in this process. Strategy in Action 5.5 provides a detailed example of the role that materials management and information systems can play in achieving superior customer responsiveness. Note that the combination of flexible manufacturing systems, just-in-time inventory systems, and information systems is needed for a quick response to customer demands.

Summary: Achieving Superior Customer Responsiveness

Table 5.5 summarizes the steps that the different functions must take if a company is to achieve superior customer responsiveness. Although marketing plays the critical role in helping a company attain this goal, primarily because it represents the point of contact with the customer, Table 5.5 shows that the other functions also have major roles to perform. Moreover, like achieving superior efficiency, quality, and innovation, achieving superior customer responsiveness requires top management to lead in building a customer orientation within the company.

Table 5.5
The Primary Role of Different Functions in Achieving Superior Customer Responsiveness

Value-Creation Function	Primary Role
Infrastructure	(1) Through leadership by example, build a company-wide commitment to customer responsiveness
Manufacturing	(1) Achieve customization by implementing flexible manufacturing
	(2) Achieve rapid response through flexible manufacturing
Marketing	(1) Know the customer
	(2) Communicate customer feedback to appropriate functions
Materials Management	(1) Develop logistics systems capable of responding quickly to unanticipated customer demands (JIT)
R&D	(1) Bring customers into the product development process
Human Resources	(1) Develop training programs that make employees think of themselves as customers

STRATEGY IN ACTION 5.5

How Materials Management and Information Systems Help Bose Improve Its Customer Responsiveness

The Massachusetts-based Bose Corp. manufactures some of the world's best-known high-fidelity speakers. Indeed, Bose speakers are bestsellers in Japan, the world leader in consumer electronics. Bose attributes much of its success to a tightly coordinated materials management function, which allows it to respond quickly to customer demands. Bose purchases most of the electronic and nonelectronic components that go into its speakers from independent suppliers. Roughly 50 percent of its purchases are from foreign suppliers, mostly in the Far East. Bose's problem is to coordinate this globally dispersed supply chain so that materials holding and transportation costs can be minimized. Component parts must arrive at Bose's Massachusetts assembly plant *just in time* to enter the production process, and not before. Yet, Bose has to remain responsive to customer demands, most of which usually means responding quickly to increased demand for certain speakers. If Bose fails to respond quickly, it can lose a big order to competitors. Since Bose does not want to hold extensive inventories at its Massachusetts plant, its supply chain must respond rapidly to increased demand for component parts.

The responsibility for coordinating the supply chain to minimize transportation and inventory-holding costs, yet ensure a fast response to customer demands falls on Bose's materials management function. It achieves coordination through a sophisticated logistics operation. Most of Bose's imports from the Far East come by ships to the West Coast and then go by train across North America to its Massachusetts plant. Most of the company's exports also move by ocean freight, although Bose will use air freight if goods are needed in a hurry.

To control this supply chain, Bose has established a relationship with W. N. Procter, a Boston-based freight forwarder and customs broker. Procter handles customs clearance and shipping from suppliers to Bose. It also offers Bose up-to-the minute electronic data interchange (EDI) capabilities, which give Bose the information needed to track parts as they move through the global supply chain. The EDI system is known as ProcterLink. When a shipment leaves a supplier, it goes into ProcterLink. From that point on Bose can track the supplies as they move across the globe toward Massachusetts. Thus Bose can fine-tune its production scheduling so that supplies enter the production process just in time. Because Procter is electronically tied into the U.S. customs system, it can electronically clear freight as much as five days before a ship arrives at a U.S. port or hours before an international air freight shipment touches down. Such early clearance can save several days in getting goods to Bose's manufacturing plant.

Just how well the system can work was illustrated recently when one Japanese customer doubled its order for Bose speakers. Bose had to gear up its manufacturing in a hurry, but many of the components were stretched out across long distances. By using ProcterLink, Bose was able to locate the needed parts in its supply chain. It then broke them out of the normal delivery chain and moved them by air freight to get them to the manufacturing line in time for the accelerated schedule. As a result, Bose was able to meet the request of its Japanese customer.[52]

5.8 SUMMARY OF CHAPTER

This chapter discusses the role that functional-level strategies play in achieving efficiency, quality, innovation, and customer responsiveness, reviews in detail the different steps that lead to this end, and makes the following main points:

1. To gain a competitive advantage, a company must either perform value-creation functions at a lower cost than its rivals or perform them in a way that leads to differentiation.
2. Superior quality plays a major role in achieving superior efficiency.
3. A company can increase efficiency through a number of steps. These include exploiting experience-based cost economies; adopting flexible manufacturing technologies; reducing customer defection rates; implementing just-in-time systems; getting the R&D function to design products that are easy to manufacture; upgrading the skills of employees through training; introducing self-managing teams; linking pay to performance; building a company-wide commitment to efficiency through strong leadership; and designing structures that facilitate cooperation among different functions in pursuit of efficiency goals.
4. Superior quality can help a company both to lower its costs and to differentiate its product and charge a premium price.
5. Achieving superior quality demands an organization-wide commitment to quality and a clear focus on the customer. It also requires metrics to measure quality goals and incentives that emphasize quality; input from employees regarding ways in which quality can be improved; a methodology for tracing defects to their source and correcting the problems that produce them; rationalization of the company's supply base; cooperation with the suppliers that remain to implement TQM programs; products that are designed for ease of manufacturing; and substantial cooperation among functions.
6. The failure rate with regard to new-product introductions is high due to factors such as uncertainty, poor commercialization, and slow cycle time.
7. To achieve superior innovation, a company must build skills in basic and applied research; closely integrate R&D and marketing; closely integrate R&D and manufacturing; minimize time to market; and ensure good project management.
8. To achieve superior customer responsiveness often requires that the company achieve superior efficiency, quality, and innovation.
9. To achieve superior customer responsiveness a company needs to give customers what they want when they want it. It must ensure a strong customer focus, which can be attained through leadership; train employees to think like customers and bringing customers into the company through superior market research; customize the product to the unique needs of individual customers or customer groups; and respond quickly to customer demands.

Discussion Questions

1. How are the four generic building blocks of competitive advantage related to each other?
2. What role can top management play in helping a company achieve superior efficiency, quality, innovation, and customer responsiveness?
3. In the long run, will adoption of TQM practices give a company a competitive advantage, or will it be required just to achieve parity with competitors?

4. In what sense might innovation be called the single most important building block of competitive advantage?

Article File 5

Find an example of a company that is widely regarded as an excellent company. Identify the source of its excellence and relate it to the material discussed in this chapter. Pay particular attention to the role played by the various functions in building excellence.

Strategic Management Project: Module 5

This module deals with the ability of your company to achieve superior efficiency, quality, innovation, and customer responsiveness. With the information you have at your disposal, answer the questions and perform the tasks listed:

1. Is your company pursuing any of the efficiency-enhancing practices discussed in this chapter?
2. Is your company pursuing any of the quality-enhancing practices discussed in this chapter?
3. Is your company pursuing any of the practices designed to enhance innovation discussed in this chapter?
4. Is your company pursuing any of the practices designed to increase customer responsiveness discussed in this chapter?
5. Evaluate the competitive position of your company in the light of your answers to questions 1–4. Explain what, if anything, the company needs to do to improve its competitive position.

Endnotes

1. Sources: R. Howard, "The CEO as Organizational Architect," *Harvard Business Review* (September–October 1992) 106–123. D. Kearns, "Leadership Through Quality," *Academy of Management Executive*, 4 (1990) 86–89. M. E. McGrath and R. W. Hoole, "Manufacturing's New Economies of Scale," *Harvard Business Review* (May–June 1992) 94–102. T. Rohan, "In Search of Speed," *Industry Week*, September 3, 1990, pp. 78–82. J. Sheridan, "America's Best Plants," *Industry Week*, October 15, 1990, pp. 27–40. J. Sheridan, "Suppliers: Partners in Prosperity," *Industry Week*, March 1990.
2. Michael E. Porter, *Competitive Advantage* (New York: Free Press, 1985).
3. W. J. Abernathy and K. Wayne, "Limits of the Learning Curve," *Harvard Business Review* (September–October 1974) pp. 109–119.
4. For example, see F. M. Scherer, A. Beckenstein, E. Kaufer, and R. D. Murphy, *The Economies of Multiplant Operations* (Cambridge Mass.: Harvard University Press, 1975).
5. G. Hall and S. Howell, "The Experience Curve from an Economist's Perspective," *Strategic Management Journal*, 6 (1985), 197–212
6. Boston Consulting Group, *Perspectives on Experience* (Boston: Boston Consulting Group, 1972); Hall and Howell, "The Experience Curve," pp. 197–212; and W. B. Hirschmann, "Profit from the Learning Curve," *Harvard Business Review* (January–February 1964), 125–139.
7. A. A. Alchian, "Reliability of Progress Curves in Airframe Production," *Econometrica*, 31 (1963), 679–693.
8. M. Borrus, L. A. Tyson, and J. Zysman, "Creating Advantage: How Government Policies Create Trade in the Semi-Conductor Industry," *Strategic Trade Policy and the New*

International Economics." ed. P. R. Krugman (Cambridge, Mass.: MIT Press, 1986).

9. S. Ghoshal and C. A. Bartlett, 1988. "Matsushita Electrical Industrial (MEI) in 1987," Harvard Business School Case #388–144.
10. Abernathy and Wayne, "Limits of the Learning Curve," pp. 109–119.
11. D. F. Barnett and R. W. Crandall, *Up From the Ashes: The Rise of the Steel Minimill in the United States* (Washington, D.C.: Brookings Institution, 1986).
12. G. Stalk and T. M. Hout, *Competing Against Time* (New York: Free Press, 1990). D. Miller, *The Icarus Paradox* (New York: HarperBusiness, 1990).
13. See P. Nemetz and L. Fry, "Flexible Manufacturing Organizations: Implications for Strategy Formulation," *Academy of Management Review,* 13 (1988), 627–638; N. Greenwood, *Implementing Flexible Manufacturing Systems* (New York: Halstead Press, 1986); and J. P. Womack, D. T. Jones, and D. Roos, *The Machine That Changed the World* (New York: Rawson Associates, 1990).
14. Womack, Jones, and Roos, *The Machine That Changed the World.*
15. Sources: M. A. Cusumano, *The Japanese Automobile Industry* (Cambridge, Mass.: Harvard University Press, (1989); Ohno Taiichi, *Toyota Production System* (Cambridge, Mass.: Productivity Press, (1980); Womack, Jones, and Roos, *The Machine That Changed the World.*
16. Sources: J. D. Goldhar and D. Lei, "The Shape of Twenty-First Century Global Manufacturing," *Journal of Business Strategy* (March/April, 1991), 37–41. "Factories that Turn Nuts into Bolts," *U.S. News and World Report,* July 14, 1986, pp. 44–45. J. Kotkin, "The Great American Revival," Inc. (February 1988), pp. 52–63.
17. F. F. Reichheld and W. E. Sasser, "Zero Defections: Quality Comes to Service," *Harvard Business Review* (September–October 1990), 105–111.
18. The example comes from Reichheld and Sasser, "Zero Defections," 105–111.
19. Ibid, pp. 105–111.
20. R. Narasimhan and J. R. Carter, "Organization, Communication and Coordination of International Sourcing," *International Marketing Review,* 7 (1990) 6–20.
21. H. F. Busch, "Integrated Materials Management," IJDP & MM, 18 (1990) 28–39.
22. Stalk and Hout, *Competing Against Time.*
23. A. Sorge and M. Warner, "Manpower Training, Manufacturing Organization, and Work Place Relations in Great Britain and West Germany," *British Journal of Industrial Relations,* 18 (1980), 318–333. R. Jaikumar, "Postindustrial Manufacturing," *Harvard Business Review* (November–December 1986), 72–83.
24. M. L. Dertouzos, R. K. Lester, and R. M. Solow, *Made in America* (Cambridge, Mass.: MIT Press, 1989).
25. J. Hoerr, "The Payoff from Teamwork," *Business Week,* July 10, 1989, pp. 56–62.
26. For general background information, see "How to Build Quality," *Economist*, September 23, 1989, pp. 91–92; A. Gabor, *The Man Who Discovered Quality* (New York: Penguin, 1990); and P. B. Crosby, *Quality is Free* (New York: Mentor, 1980).
27. W. E. Deming, "Improvement of Quality and Productivity Through Action by Management," *National Productivity Review*, 1 (Winter 1981–1982), 12–22.
28. J. Bowles, "Is American Management Really Committed to Quality?" *Management Review* (April 1992), 42–46.
29. O. Port and G. Smith, "Quality," *Business Week*, November 30, 1992, pp. 66–75.
30. L. Therrien, "Spreading the Message," *Business Week*, October 25, 1991, p. 60.
31. N. Gross, "Rails That Run on Software," *Business Week*, October 25, 1991, p. 84.
32. These data came from personal interviews conducted by Charles Hill in Japan during the summer of 1992.
33. Kearns, "Leadership Through Quality," pp. 86–89. J. Sheridan, "America's Best Plants," *Industry Week*, October 15, 1990, pp. 27–40.
34. Bowles, "Is American Management Really Committed to Quality?" pp. 42–46.
35. Gabor, *The Man Who Discovered Quality*.
36. Deming, "Improvement of Quality and Productivity," pp. 12–22.
37. W. E. Deming, *Out of the Crisis* (Cambridge, Mass.: MIT Center for Advanced Engineering Study, 1986).
38. J. F. Siler and S. Atchison, "The Rx at Work in Utah," *Business Week*, October 25, 1991, p. 113.
39. See work by Edwin Mansfield and his associates, for example, Edwin Mansfield, "How Economists See R&D," *Harvard Business Review* (November–December 1981), 98–106; and Edwin Mansfield, J. Rapoport, J. Schnee, S. Wagner, and M. Hamburger, *Research and Innovation in the Modern Corporation* (New York: Norton, 1971).
40. Stalk and Hout, *Competing Against Time*. B. Buell and R. D. Hof, "Hewlett–Packard Rethinks Itself," *Business Week*, April 1, 1991, pp. 76–79.
41. K. B. Clark and S. C. Wheelwright, *Managing New Product and Process Development* (New York: Free Press, 1993).
42. P. Sellers, "Getting Customers to Love You," *Fortune*, March 13, 1989, pp. 38–42.
43. O. Port, "Moving Past the Assembly Line," *Business Week Special Issue. Reinventing America*, (1992), 177–180.
44. Stalk and Hout, *Competing Against Time*.
45. K. B. Clark and S. C. Wheelwright, *Managing New Product and Process Development*, (New York: Free Press, 1993).
46. Sellers, "Getting Customers to Love You," pp. 38–42.
47. Ibid., pp. 38–42.
48. S. Caminiti, "A Mail Order Romance: Lands' End Courts Unseen Customers," *Fortune*, March 13, 1989, pp. 43–44.
49. K. West, "Boeing 2000," *Seattle Times*, October 21, pp. A7, A10, A11.
50. Sources: Goldhar and Lei, "The Shape of Twenty-first Century Global Manufacturing," pp. 37–41. "Factories that Turn Nuts into Bolts," pp. 44–45. Kotkin, "The Great American Revival," pp. 52–63.
50. Patricia Nemetz, "Flexible Manufacturing Strategies, Technologies, and Structures: A Contingency Based Empirical Analysis" (Ph.D. diss. University of Washington, 1990).
51. Stalk and Hout, *Competing Against Time*.
52. P. Bradley, "Global Sourcing Takes Split-second Timing," *Purchasing*, July 20, 1989, pp. 52–58.

6 Business-Level Strategy

6.1 OPENING CASE: LIZ CLAIBORNE, INC.

Designer Liz Claiborne founded her company in 1976 with the help of three partners. By 1990 her company had over $2 billion in sales yearly and its stock had become a Wall Street favorite. The secret of the company's success was based on Liz Claiborne's decision to focus on the rapidly growing professional women's clothing segment of the market. By 1976 women were entering the work force in rapidly increasing numbers, but relatively few companies were producing clothes for this segment—and they were very high-priced firms like Ellen Tracy, Donna Karan, and Ann Klein. Liz Claiborne decided to find out what kinds of clothing professional women wanted; then she used her considerable talents to create a design team to focus on providing attractively designed clothing for professional women at reasonable prices. In doing so, she tapped an unmet customer need and the result was dramatic as sales boomed.

To protect its image, Liz Claiborne sold her clothing through established retailers, like Macy's, Bloomingdale's, and Dillard's. Retailers were required to buy at least $50,000 worth of her collection, and the company controlled the way its suits and dresses were sold in each store—for example, the way clothes were hung and displayed. This attention to detail was part of her strategy of focusing on the upscale professional clothing niche. To promote its growth, the company then started to find new outlets for its clothes and opened a chain of Liz Claiborne boutiques and factory outlet stores. The Liz Claiborne team also used its design skills to produce a line of men's sportswear clothing and to develop new products like perfume, shoes, and accessories. By 1988 the Liz Claiborne name had become famous.

However, by 1990 that the company's growth had slowed. The company was in trouble. Competitors, recognizing the niche pioneered by Liz Claiborne had begun to offer their own lines of professional women's clothing. Expensive designers like Ann Klein and Donna Karan had new lines of cheaper clothing, priced to compete directly with Liz Claiborne. In addition, low-cost manufacturers had begun to produce clothing lines that undercut her prices, often using Liz Claiborne look-alike designs. This competition from both the top and the bottom end of the market took sales away from the company.

Another problem for Liz Claiborne came from the retail end. Many of the company's best customers, retailers like Macy's, were in deep financial difficulty and were cutting back on purchases to reduce their debt. At the same time, cost-conscious consumers were buying more and more clothing from stores like Casual Corner and JC Penney, and even discount stores like Kmart and Wal-Mart, which do not sell the Liz Claiborne line but the low-priced lines of competitors. As customers switched both to cheaper stores and to cheaper lines, Liz Claiborne's sales suffered.

Given this deteriorating situation, the company moved quickly to change its strategy. Jerry Chazen, who replaced Liz Claiborne as CEO of the company on her retirement, decided to broaden the company's product line and produce low-cost lines of clothing. To do so and at the same time protect the Liz Claiborne brand name, he bought Russ Togs, a clothing maker which produces three brands of women's clothing: Crazy Horse, The Villager, and Red Horse. As part of the company's new strategy, each of these clothing makers' lines will be redesigned and tar-

geted at a different price range in the women's clothing market. For example, Russ Togs, a sportswear line, is to be upgraded and will sell a new line of clothing for 20 to 30 percent less than the Liz Claiborne line. Moreover, this clothing will be sold through discount merchandisers like Wal-Mart and in low-priced department stores like Sears and JC Penney. In this way, the Liz Claiborne company will begin to serve the general women's clothing market, and not just the professional women's clothing niche.[1]

Top management hopes that this new strategy will bolster the company's sagging sales and lead to a new period of growth and expansion. They believe that there is wide scope for the company to take its existing design skills and capabilities and to apply these in new market segments. However, the company will now be going head-to-head with low-cost producers and will have to find new ways to reduce its costs in order to be able to compete. In 1993 its stock fell to $18, an all-time low, and analysts are uncertain about the company's future in an industry that is well known for the speed at which companies rise and fall.

Discussion Questions

1. What factors led to Liz Claiborne's success?
2. What changes has the company recently made in its strategy? Why?

6.2 OVERVIEW

As the Liz Claiborne case suggests, this chapter examines how a company can compete effectively in a business or industry and scrutinizes the various strategies that it can adopt to maximize competitive advantage and profitability. Chapter 3, on the industry environment, provides concepts for analyzing industry opportunities and threats. Chapters 4 and 5 discuss how a company can gain a competitive advantage and how distinctive competencies are built at the functional level in order to gain a competitive advantage. The purpose of this chapter is to consider the business-level strategies that a company can use to exploit its competitive advantage and compete effectively in an industry.

6.3 FOUNDATIONS OF BUSINESS-LEVEL STRATEGY

In Chapter 2, we discuss Derek F. Abell's view of the process of business definition as involving decisions about (1) customer needs, or what is to be satisfied, (2) customer groups, or who is to be satisfied, and (3) distinctive competencies, or how customer needs are to be satisfied.[2] These three decisions are at the heart of business-level strategy choice because they provide the source of a company's competitive advantage over its rivals and determine how the company will compete in a business or industry. Consequently, we need to look at the ways in which companies can gain a competitive advantage at the business level.

Customer Needs and Product Differentiation

Customer needs are anything that can be satisfied by means of the characteristics of a product or service. **Product differentiation** is the process of creating a competitive advantage by designing products—goods and services—to satisfy customer needs. All companies must differentiate their products to a certain degree in order to attract customers and satisfy some minimal level of customer

needs. However, some companies differentiate their products to a much greater degree than others, and this difference can give them a competitive edge.

Some companies offer the customer a low-priced product without engaging in much product differentiation. Others seek to create something unique about their products so that they satisfy customer needs in ways that other products cannot. The uniqueness may relate to the physical characteristics of the product, such as quality or reliability, or it may lie in the product's appeal to customers' psychological needs, such as the need for prestige or status.[3] Thus a Japanese car may be differentiated by its reputation for reliability, and a Corvette or a Porsche may be differentiated by its ability to satisfy customers' status needs.

Customer Groups and Market Segmentation

Market segmentation may be defined as the way a company decides to group customers, based on important differences in their needs or preferences, in order to gain a competitive advantage.[4] In general, a company can adopt three alternative strategies toward market segmentation.[5] First, it may choose not to recognize that different groups of customers have different needs and may adopt the approach of serving the average customer. Second, a company may choose to segment its market into different constituencies and develop a product to suit the needs of each group. For example, in a recent catalog, Sony offered twenty-four different 19-inch color television sets, each targeted at a different market segment. Similarly, many automobile companies produce a wide range of different car and light truck models, aimed at particular segments of the market. Third, a company can choose to recognize that the market is segmented but concentrate on servicing only one market segment, or niche.

Why would a company want to make complex product/market choices and create a different product tailored to each market segment rather than create a single product for the whole market? The answer is that the decision to provide many products for many market niches allows a company to satisfy customer needs better. As a result, customer demand for the company's products rises and generates more revenue than would be the case if the company offered just one product for the whole market.[6] Sometimes, however, the nature of the product or the nature of the industry does not allow much differentiation—for example, bulk chemicals or cement.[7] In these cases, there is little opportunity for obtaining a competitive advantage through product differentiation and market segmentation because there is little opportunity for serving customer needs and customer groups in different ways. Instead, price is the main criterion used by customers to evaluate the product, and the competitive advantage lies with the company that has superior efficiency and can provide the lowest-priced product.

Deciding on Distinctive Competencies

The third issue in business-level strategy is to decide what distinctive competencies to pursue to satisfy customer needs and groups.[8] In this context, **distinctive competencies** are the means by which a company attempts to satisfy customer needs and groups in order to obtain a competitive advantage. As we discuss in Chapter 4, there are four ways in which companies can obtain a competitive advantage: through achieving superior efficiency, quality, innovation, and customer responsiveness. In making business strategy choices, a company must decide how to organize and combine its distinctive competencies to gain a competitive advantage. The source of these distinctive competencies is examined at length in Chapter 5.

6.4 CHOOSING A GENERIC COMPETITIVE STRATEGY AT THE BUSINESS LEVEL

Companies pursue a business-level strategy to gain a competitive advantage that allows them to outperform rivals and achieve above-average returns. They can choose from three generic competitive approaches: **cost leadership, differentiation,** and **focus.**[9] These strategies are called **generic** because all businesses or industries can pursue them regardless of whether they are manufacturing, service, or not-for-profit enterprises. Each of the generic strategies results from a company making consistent choices on product, market, and distinctive competencies—choices that reinforce each other. Table 6.1 summarizes the choices appropriate for each generic strategy.

Cost-Leadership Strategy

A company's goal in pursuing a cost-leadership or low-cost strategy is to outperform competitors by doing everything it can to produce goods or services at a cost lower than theirs. Two advantages accrue from this strategy. First, because of its lower costs, the cost leader is able to charge a lower price than its competitors yet make the same level of profit as they do. If companies in the industry charge similar prices for their products, the cost leader makes a higher profit than its competitors because of its lower costs. Second, if industry rivalry increases and companies start to compete on price, the cost leader will be able to withstand competition better than the other companies because of its lower costs. For both these reasons, cost leaders are likely to earn above-average profits. But how does a company become the cost leader? It achieves this position by means of the product/market/distinctive-competency choices that it makes to gain a low-cost competitive advantage. Table 6.1 outlines these strategic choices.

Strategic Choices The cost leader chooses a low level of product differentiation. Differentiation is expensive; if the company expends resources to make its products unique, then its costs rise.[10] The cost leader aims for a level of differentiation not markedly inferior to that of the differentiator (a company that competes by spending resources on product development), but a level obtainable at

Table 6.1 Product/Market/Distinctive-Competency Choices and Generic Competitive Strategies

	Cost leadership	Differentiation	Focus
Product differentiation	Low (principally by price)	High (principally by uniqueness)	Low to high (price or uniqueness)
Market segmentation	Low (mass market)	High (many market segments)	Low (one or a few segments)
Distinctive competency	Manufacturing and materials management	Research and development, sales and marketing	Any kind of distinctive competency

low cost.[11] The cost leader does not try to be the industry leader in differentiation; it waits until customers want a feature or service before providing it. For example, a cost leader does not introduce stereo sound in television sets. It adds stereo sound only when it is obvious that consumers want it.

The cost leader also normally ignores the different market segments and positions its product to appeal to the average customer. The reason the cost leader makes this choice is that developing a line of products tailored to the needs of different market segments is an expensive proposition. A cost leader normally engages in only a limited amount of market segmentation. Even though no customer may be totally happy with the product, the fact that the company normally charges a lower price than its competitors attracts customers to its products.

In developing distinctive competencies, the overriding goal of the cost leader must be to develop competencies that enable it to increase its efficiency and lower its costs compared with its rivals. The development of distinctive competencies in manufacturing and materials management is central to achieving this goal. Companies pursuing a low-cost strategy may attempt to ride down the experience curve so that they can lower their manufacturing costs. Achieving a low-cost position may also require that the company develop skills in flexible manufacturing and adopt efficient materials-management techniques. (As you may recall, Table 5.1 outlines the ways in which a company's functions can be used to increase efficiency.) Consequently, the manufacturing and materials-management functions are the center of attention in the cost-leadership company, and the other functions shape their distinctive competencies to meet the needs of manufacturing and materials management.[12] For example, the sales function may develop the competency of capturing large, stable sets of customer orders. In turn, this allows manufacturing to make longer production runs and so achieve scale economies and reduce costs. The human resource function may focus on instituting training programs and compensation systems that lower costs by enhancing employee productivity. And the research and development function may specialize in process improvements to lower the costs of manufacture. The way in which Nissan developed its midsize car, the Altima, discussed in Strategy in Action 6.1, illustrates how a company decides to pursue a cost-leadership strategy.

The cost leader gears all its strategic product/market/distinctive-competency choices to the single goal of squeezing out every cent of costs to provide a competitive advantage. A company like Heinz is another excellent example of a cost leader. Beans and canned vegetables do not permit much of a markup. The profit comes from the large volume of cans sold (each can having only a small markup). Therefore the H. J. Heinz Company goes to extraordinary lengths to try to reduce costs—by even one-twentieth of a cent per can—because this will lead to large cost savings and thus bigger profits over the long run. As you will see in the chapters in Part IV on strategy implementation, another source of cost savings in pursuing cost leadership is the design of the organization structure to match this strategy, since structure is a major source of a company's costs. As we discuss in Chapter 12, a low-cost strategy usually implies tight production controls and rigorous use of budgets to control the production process.

Advantages and Disadvantages The advantages of each generic strategy are best discussed in terms of Porter's five forces model introduced in Chapter 3.[14] The five forces involve threats from competitors, powerful suppliers, power-

STRATEGY IN ACTION 6.1

Nissan's New Cost-Leadership Strategy

Nissan, the Japanese automaker, had watched its U.S. sales slide 35 percent from their peak in 1985. The reason? The quality and design of its car simply did not keep up with those of other Japanese competitors, such as Honda, Mazda, and Toyota. While these companies had been innovators in introducing stylish new rounded car designs and new cars like the Miata and the Previa for new market segments, Nissan plodded along with its boxy Stanzas and Maximas, which were at least as expensive as the cars of its rivals. As sales and profits declined, the company realized in 1991 that it needed to rethink its U.S. strategy. As part of a company-wide shakeup, Nissan appointed Earl J. Hesterberg as vice president and general manager of the U.S. Nissan Division and gave him wide authority to turn the U.S. division's fortunes around.[13]

Recognizing that Nissan was now far behind its rivals in terms of its reputation for product innovation and design, Hesterberg decided on a new strategy for introducing the new Nissan midsize car: a cost-leadership strategy. The midsize cars of Nissan's rivals—the Toyota Camry, Honda Accord, and Mazda 626—had increased steadily in size and price with each new model. A well-equipped Camry or Accord, for example, had a sticker price of more than $19,000. Hesterberg decided that Nissan would not increase the size of its car, and hence would keep its cost and price low. Nissan's designers were instructed to aim for a car that would be cheap to produce but be of a quality comparable to that of other Japanese manufacturers' cars. The result was the Nissan Altima, whose four-door base model version lists for $13,000 and the better-equipped one costs thousands less than the Camry or Accord. Nissan kept costs low by deliberately restricting the number of different models of the Altima. Customers have only two basic choices, the base version or the better-equipped version.

Another part of Hesterberg's strategy was to concentrate most of Nissan's marketing budget—over $100 million—on the Altima and the Nissan Quest, its new minivan, and to focus on building a large market share for these cars in order to build sales revenues. In its marketing, Nissan was careful to emphasize the value of the Altima by comparing its quality with Toyota's Lexus, which costs over four times as much.

The results of this low-cost strategy were astounding. Nissan hoped to sell 100,000 in its first year; it sold over 140,000. Although the profit margin on each car was lower than for the Honda or the Camry, the extra sales volume brought Nissan a huge profit. Its pursuit of a low-cost, low-price strategy in the midsize car segment has been very successful and has hurt its competitors. For example, for the first time in its history, Honda was forced to offer discounts on its Accord, and sales of the Camry and Mazda 626 were below projections. Clearly, a low-cost strategy can pay big dividends.

ful buyers, substitute products, and new entrants. The cost leader is protected from **industry competitors** by its cost advantage. Its lower costs also mean that it will be less affected than its competitors by increases in the price of inputs if there are **powerful suppliers** and less affected by a fall in the price it can charge for its products if there are **powerful buyers**. Moreover, since cost leadership usually requires a big market share, the cost leader purchases in relatively large quantities, increasing bargaining power vis-à-vis suppliers. If **substitute products** start to come into the market, the cost leader can reduce its price to compete with them and retain its market share. Finally, the leader's cost advantage constitutes a **barrier to entry**, since other companies are unable to enter the industry and match the leader's costs or prices. The cost leader is therefore relatively safe as long as it can maintain its cost advantage—and price is the key for a significant number of buyers.

The principal dangers of the cost-leadership approach lurk in competitors' ability to find ways of producing at lower cost and beat the cost leader at its own game. For instance, if technological change makes experience-curve economies obsolete, new companies may apply lower-cost technologies that give them a cost advantage over the cost leader. The steel minimills discussed in Chapter 5 gained this advantage. Competitors may also draw a cost advantage from labor-cost savings. Foreign competitors in Third World countries have very low labor costs; for example, wage costs in the United States are on the order of 600 or so percent more than in Malaysia, China, or Mexico. Many American companies now assemble their products abroad as part of their low-cost strategy; many are forced to do so simply to compete.

Competitors' ability to easily imitate the cost leader's methods is another threat to the cost-leadership strategy. For example, the ability of IBM-clone manufacturers to produce IBM-compatible products at costs similar to IBM's (but, of course, sell them at a much lower price) was a major factor in contributing to IBM's troubles. Finally, the cost-leadership strategy carries a risk that the cost leader, in the single-minded desire to reduce costs, may lose sight of changes in customer tastes. Thus a company might make decisions that decrease costs but drastically affect demand for the product. For example, the Joseph Schlitz Brewing Co. lowered the quality of its beer's ingredients, substituting inferior grains to reduce costs. Consumers immediately caught on; demand for the product dropped dramatically. As mentioned earlier, the cost leader cannot abandon product differentiation, and even low-priced products, such as Timex watches, cannot be too inferior to the more expensive Seikos if the low-cost, low-price policy is to succeed.

Differentiation Strategy

The objective of the generic strategy of differentiation is to achieve a competitive advantage by creating a product—good or service—that is **perceived** by customers to be unique in some important way. The differentiated company's ability to satisfy a customer need in a way that its competitors cannot means that it can charge a **premium price**—a price considerably above the industry average. The ability to increase revenues by charging premium prices (rather than by reducing costs like the cost leader) allows the differentiator to outperform its competitors and gain above-average profits. The premium price is usually substantially above the price charged by the cost leader, and customers pay it because they believe the product's differentiated qualities to be worth the difference. Consequently, the product is priced on the basis of what the market will bear.[15] Thus Mercedes-Benz cars are much more expensive in the United States than in Europe because they confer more status here. Similarly, a BMW is not a lot more expensive to produce than a Honda, but its price is determined by customers who perceive that the prestige of owning a BMW is something worth paying for. Similarly, Rolex watches do not cost much to produce; their design has not changed very much for years; and their gold content is only a fraction of the watch price. Customers, however, buy the Rolex because of the unique quality they perceive in it: its ability to confer status on its wearer. In stereos, the name Bang & Olufsen of Denmark stands out; in jewelry, Tiffany & Co.; in airplanes, Learjets. All these products command premium prices because of their differentiated qualities.

Strategic Choices As Table 6.1 shows, a differentiator chooses a high level of product differentiation to gain a competitive advantage. Product differentiation can be achieved in three principal ways discussed in detail in Chapter 4: quality, innovation, and customer responsiveness. For example, Procter & Gamble claims that its product quality is high and that Ivory soap is 99.44 percent pure. Maytag Corporation stresses reliability and the best repair record of any washer on the market. IBM promotes the quality service provided by its well-trained sales force. Innovation is very important for technologically complex products, where new features are the source of differentiation, and many people pay a premium price for new and innovative products, such as a state-of-the-art computer, stereo, or car. When differentiation is based on customer responsiveness, a company offers comprehensive after-sales service and product repair. This is an especially important consideration for complex products such as cars and domestic appliances, which are likely to break down periodically. Companies like Maytag, Dell Computer, and Federal Express all excel in customer responsiveness. In service organizations, quality of service attributes are also very important. Why can Neiman-Marcus and Nordstrom charge premium prices? They offer an exceptionally high level of service. Similarly, firms of lawyers or accountants stress the service aspects of their operations to clients: their knowledge, professionalism, and reputation.

Finally, a product's appeal to customers' psychological desires can become a source of differentiation. The appeal can be to prestige or status, as it is with BMWs and Rolex watches; to patriotism, as with buying a Chevrolet; to safety of home and family, as with Prudential Insurance; or to value for money, as with Sears and JC Penney. Differentiation can also be tailored to age groups and to socioeconomic groups. Indeed, the bases of differentiation are endless.

A company that pursues a differentiation strategy strives to differentiate itself along as many dimensions as possible. The less it resembles its rivals, the more it is protected from competition and the wider is its market appeal. Thus BMWs are not just prestige cars; they also offer technological sophistication, luxury, and reliability, as well as good, although very expensive, repair service. All these bases of differentiation help increase sales.

Generally, a differentiator chooses to segment its market into many niches. Now and then a company offers a product designed for each market niche and decides to be a **broad differentiator**, but a company might choose to serve just those niches where it has a specific differentiation advantage. For example, Sony produces twenty-four models of television, filling all the niches from midpriced to high-priced sets. However, its lowest-priced model is always priced about $100 above that of its competitors, bringing into play the premium price factor. You have to pay extra for a Sony. Similarly, although Mercedes-Benz has filled niches below its old high-priced models with its S and C series, nobody would claim that Mercedes is going for every market segment. As mentioned earlier, General Motors was the first company that tried to fill most of the niches, from the cheapest Chevrolet to the highest-priced Cadillac and Corvette.

Finally, in choosing which distinctive competency to pursue, a differentiated company concentrates on the organizational function that provides the sources of its differentiation advantage. Differentiation on the basis of innovation and technological competency depends on the R&D function, as you saw in Chapter 5. Efforts to improve customer service depend on the quality of the sales function. A focus on a specific function does not mean, however, that the control of

costs is not important for a differentiator. A differentiator does not want to increase costs unnecessarily and tries to keep them somewhere near those of the cost leader. But, since developing the distinctive competency needed to provide a differentiation advantage is often expensive, a differentiator usually has higher costs than the cost leader. Still, it must control all costs that do not contribute to its differentiation advantage so that the price of the product does not exceed what customers are willing to pay. Since bigger profits are earned by controlling costs, as well as by maximizing revenues, it pays to control costs, though not to minimize them to the point of losing the source of differentiation.[16]

Advantages and Disadvantages The advantages of the differentiation strategy can now be discussed in the context of the five forces model. Differentiation safeguards a company against competitors to the degree that customers develop **brand loyalty** for its products. Brand loyalty is a very valuable asset because it protects the company on all fronts. For example, *powerful suppliers* are rarely a problem because the differentiated company's strategy is geared more toward the price it can charge than toward the costs of production. Thus a differentiator can tolerate moderate increases in the prices of its inputs better than the cost leader can. Differentiators are unlikely to experience problems with *powerful buyers* because the differentiator offers the buyer a unique product. Only it can supply the product, and it commands brand loyalty. Differentiators can pass on price increases to customers because customers are willing to pay the premium price. Differentiation and brand loyalty also create an *entry barrier* for other companies seeking to enter the industry. New companies are forced to develop their own distinctive competency to be able to compete, and doing so is very expensive. Finally, the threat of *substitute products* depends on the ability of competitors' products to meet the same customer needs as the differentiator's products and to break customers' brand loyalty. This can happen, as when IBM-clone manufacturers captured a large share of the home computer market, but many people still want an IBM, even though there are many IBM clones about. The issue is how much of a premium price a company can charge for uniqueness before customers switch products. In 1993 Philip Morris found out that it could increase the price of its Marlboro cigarettes only by so much before customers would switch to generic brands. When it announced price decreases to attract customers back, the price of its stock plummeted after investors realized that even a differentiator can only charge so much of a premium price before customers will desert its product.

The main problems with the differentiation strategy center on the company's long-term ability to maintain its perceived uniqueness in customers' eyes. We have seen in the last ten years how quickly competitors move to **imitate** and **copy** successful differentiators. This has happened in many industries, such as computers, autos, and home electronics. Patents and first-mover advantages—the advantages of being the first to market a product or service—last only so long, and as the overall quality of products produced by all companies goes up, brand loyalty declines. The story of the way American Express lost its competitive advantage, told in Strategy in Action 6.2, highlights many of the threats that face a differentiator.

A strategy of differentiation, then, requires the firm to develop a competitive advantage by making product/market/distinctive-competency choices that reinforce each another and together increase the value of a good or service in the

STRATEGY IN ACTION 6.2

Who Wants an American Express Card?

American Express Company's green, gold, and platinum credit cards used to be closely linked with high status and prestige. Obtaining an American Express (AmEx) card required a high income, and obtaining a gold and platinum card required an even higher one. AmEx carefully differentiated its product by using advertising that always featured famous people touting the virtues of possessing its card to emphasize its exclusivity and uniqueness. Consumers were willing to pay the high yearly fee to possess the card even though every month they were required to pay off the debit balance they had accumulated. AmEx's cards were a premium product that allowed the company to charge both customers and merchants more because it offered quality service and conferred status on the user. For many years its credit card operation was the money spinner of AmEx's Travel Related Services (TRS) Division, and the company's stock price soared as its profits reached over $200 million by 1990.

AmEx's differentiated strategy has been suffering in the 1990s, however. Rival companies like MasterCard and Visa have demonstrated how their cards can be used at locations where AmEx's cannot. Moreover, as they make clear, anybody can own a MasterCard or a Visa gold card; it is not just for the fortunate elite. In addition, various companies and banks have banded together to offer the consumer many other benefits of using their particular credit cards. For example, banks and airlines have been forming alliances that allow consumers to use a bank's credit card to accumulate miles toward purchase of an airline's tickets. Moreover, large companies like AT&T and General Motors have issued their own credit cards that offer customers savings on their products, often without a yearly fee.

The emergence of all these new credit cards has broken the loyalty of AmEx customers and shattered the card's unique image. It has now become one more credit card in an overcrowded market that has lost its differentiated appeal. By 1992 over two million of its users had deserted AmEx, and it took a loss of over $100 million.

AmEx is trying to fight back and restore profitability to its division. To reduce costs, it announced a layoff of over 5,000 employees in the TRS division; it started its own airline mileage program to try to attract its users back; and it has made its card more available to potential users. It has also tried to increase the number of outlets that accept the card by lowering the fees it makes merchants pay; for example, the card can now be used at Kmart. Finally, it hired a new advertising agency to try to restore its differentiated appeal.[17] However, analysts fear that these moves may do little to stem the tide and stop customer losses and that making the card more accessible may even further reduce its differentiated appeal. If anybody can use the card and use it anywhere, why choose AmEx?

eyes of consumers. When a product has uniqueness in customers' eyes, differentiators can charge a premium price. However, the disadvantages of a differentiation strategy are the ease with which competitors can imitate a differentiator's product and the difficulty of maintaining a premium price. When differentiation stems from the design or physical features of the product, differentiators are at great risk because imitation is easy. The risk is that over time products like cigarettes, VCRs, or stereos become *commodity-like* products, for which the importance of differentiation diminishes as customers become more price sensitive. When differentiation stems from service quality or reliability or from any *intangible source*, like the Federal Express guarantee or the prestige of a Rolex, a company is much more secure. It is difficult to imitate intangibles, and the

differentiator can reap the benefits of this strategy for a long time. Nevertheless, all differentiators must watch out for imitators and be careful that they do not charge a price higher than the market will bear.

Both Cost Leadership and Differentiation

Recently, changes in production techniques—in particular, the development of flexible manufacturing technologies (discussed in Chapter 5)—have made the choice between cost-leadership and differentiation strategies less clear-cut. Because of technological developments, companies have found it easier to obtain the benefits of both strategies. The reason is that the new flexible technologies allow firms to pursue a differentiation strategy at a low cost.

Traditionally, differentiation was obtainable only at high cost because the necessity of producing different models for different market segments meant that firms had to have short production runs, which raised manufacturing costs. In addition, the differentiated firm had to bear higher marketing costs than the cost leader because it was servicing many market segments. As a result, differentiators had higher costs than cost leaders that produced large batches of standardized products. However, flexible manufacturing may enable a firm pursuing differentiation to manufacture a range of products at a cost comparable to that of the cost leader. The use of robots and flexible manufacturing cells reduces the costs of retooling the production line and the costs associated with small production runs. Indeed, a factor promoting the current trend toward market fragmentation and niche marketing in many consumer goods industries is the substantial reduction of the costs of differentiation by flexible manufacturing.

Another way that a differentiated producer may be able to realize significant scale economies is by standardizing many of the component parts used in its end products. For example, in the mid 1980s Chrysler began to offer twelve different models of cars to different segments of the auto market. However, despite different appearances, all twelve models were based on a common platform, known as the K-car platform. Very different models of K-cars used many of the same components, including axles, drive units, suspensions, and gear boxes. As a result, Chrysler was able to realize significant scale economies in the manufacture and bulk purchase of standardized component parts.

A firm can also reduce both production and marketing costs if it limits the number of models in the product line by offering packages of options rather than letting consumers decide exactly what options they require. It is increasingly common for auto manufacturers, for example, to offer an economy auto package, a luxury package, and a sports package to appeal to the principal market segments. Package offerings substantially lower manufacturing costs because long production runs of the various packages are possible. At the same time, the firm is able to focus its advertising and marketing efforts on particular market segments so that these costs are also decreased. Once again the firm is getting gains from differentiation and from low cost at the same time.

Just-in-time inventory systems can also help reduce costs and improve the quality and reliability of a company's products. This is important to differentiated firms, where quality and reliability are essential ingredients of the product's appeal. Rolls-Royces, for example, are never supposed to break down. Improved quality control enhances a company's reputation and thus allows it to charge a premium price, which is one object of TQM programs.

Taking advantage of the new production and marketing developments, some firms are managing to reap the gains from cost-leadership and differentiation strategies simultaneously. Since they can charge a premium price for their products compared with the price charged by the pure cost leader, and since they have lower costs than the pure differentiator, they are obtaining at least an equal, and probably a higher, level of profit than firms pursuing only one of the generic strategies. Hence the combined strategy is the most profitable to pursue, and companies are quickly moving to take advantage of the new production, materials-management, and marketing techniques. Indeed, American companies must take advantage of them if they are to regain a competitive advantage, for the Japanese pioneered many of these new developments. This explains why firms like Toyota and Sony are currently much more profitable than their U.S. counterparts, General Motors and Zenith. However, American firms like McDonald's, Apple Computer, Intel, and Motorola are pursuing both strategies simultaneously.

Focus Strategy

The third pure generic competitive strategy, the focus strategy, differs from the other two chiefly because it is directed toward serving the needs of a **limited customer group** or **segment**. A focused company concentrates on serving a particular market niche, which may be defined geographically, by type of customer, or by segment of the product line.[18] For example, a geographic niche may be defined by region or even by locality. Selecting a niche by type of customer might mean serving only the very rich or the very young or the very adventurous. Concentrating only on a segment of the product line means focusing only on vegetarian foods or on very fast motor cars or on designer clothes. In following a focus strategy, a company is specializing in some way.

Once it has chosen its market segment, a company may pursue a focus strategy through either a differentiation or a low-cost approach. In essence, a focused company is a specialized differentiator *or* cost leader. Because of their small size, few focus firms are able to pursue cost leadership and differentiation simultaneously. If a focus firm uses a low-cost approach, it competes against the cost leader in the market segments where it has no cost disadvantage. For example, in local lumber or cement markets, the focuser has lower transportation costs than the low-cost national company. The focuser may also have a cost advantage because it is producing complex or custom-built products that do not lend themselves easily to economies of scale in production and therefore offer few experience-curve advantages. With a focus strategy, a company concentrates on small-volume custom products, where it has a cost advantage, and leaves the large-volume standardized market to the cost leader.

If a focuser pursues a differentiation approach, then all the means of differentiation that are open to the differentiator are available to the focused company. The point is that the focused company competes with the differentiator in only one or in just a few segments. For example, Porsche, a focused company, competes against General Motors in the sports car segment of the car market but not in other market segments. Focused companies are likely to develop differentiated product qualities successfully because of their knowledge of a small customer set (such as sports car buyers) or knowledge of a region. Furthermore, concentration on a small range of products sometimes allows a focuser to develop innovations

faster than a large differentiator can. However, the focuser does not attempt to serve all market segments because doing so would bring it into direct competition with the differentiator. Instead, a focused company concentrates on building market share in one market segment and, if successful, may begin to serve more and more market segments and chip away at the differentiator's competitive advantage. The way in which small software companies have emerged to take advantage of specialized niches in the outsourcing market, discussed in Strategy in Action 6.3, illustrates how focused companies can obtain a competitive advantage.

Strategic Choices Table 6.1 shows the specific product/market/distinctive-competency choices made by a focused company. Differentiation can be high or low because the company can pursue a low-cost or a differentiation approach. As for customer groups, a focused company chooses specific niches in which to compete, rather than going for whole market, like the cost leader, or filling a large number of niches, like a broad differentiator. A focuser may pursue any distinctive competency because it can pursue any kind of differentiation or low-cost advantage. Thus it might seek a cost advantage and develop a superior efficiency in low-cost manufacturing within a region. Or it could develop superior skills in customer responsiveness, based on its ability to serve the needs of regional customers in ways that a national differentiator would find very expensive.

The many avenues that a focused company can take to develop a competitive advantage explain why there are so many small companies in relation to large ones. A focused company has enormous opportunity to develop its own niche and compete against low-cost and differentiated enterprises, which tend to be larger. A focus strategy provides an opportunity for an entrepreneur to find and then exploit a gap in the market by developing an innovative product that customers cannot do without.[20] The steel minimills discussed in Chapter 5 are a good example of how focused companies specializing in one market can grow so efficient that they become the cost leaders. Many large companies started with a focus strategy; and, of course, one means by which companies can expand is to take over other focused companies. For example, Saatchi & Saatchi DFS Compton Inc., a specialist marketing company, grew by taking over several companies that were also specialists in their own market, such as Hay Associates, Inc., the management consultants.

Advantages and Disadvantages A focused company's competitive advantages stem from the source of its distinctive competency—efficiency, quality, innovation, or customer responsiveness. It is protected from **rivals** to the extent that it can provide a product or service that they cannot provide. This ability also gives the focuser power over its buyers because they cannot get the same thing from anyone else. With regard to powerful suppliers, however, a focused company is at a disadvantage, because it buys in small volumes and thus is in the suppliers' power. But as long as it can pass on price increases to loyal customers, this disadvantage may not be a significant problem. **Potential entrants** have to overcome the customer loyalty that the focuser has generated, and the development of customer loyalty also lessens the threat from substitute products. This protection from the five forces allows the focuser to earn above-average returns on its investment. Another advantage of the focus strategy is that it permits a company to stay close to its customers and to respond to their changing needs.

STRATEGY IN ACTION 6.3

Finding a Niche in the Outsourcing Market

Outsourcing occurs when one company contracts with another company to perform one of the value-creation functions on its behalf. Increasingly, many companies are finding it very difficult to keep up with the pace of technological change in the computer software industry and are outsourcing their data-processing needs to specialized software companies. For example, Electronic Data Systems Corp. (EDS), founded by Ross Perot and now owned by General Motors, has grown into a $9 billion computer services giant, which manages other companies' data processing operations using its own proprietary software. IBM is another large company trying to exploit this developing market.

As can be imagined, however, different kinds of organizations, such as universities, banks, insurance agencies, local governments, and utilities, have different kinds of data processing needs and problems. Consequently, each kind of company requires a specialized kind of software system, which can be customized to the specific needs. As a result, it is difficult for any one software company to service the needs of a wide range of different companies, and the outsourcing market in data processing is very fragmented. Large companies like EDS have only a small market share; for example, EDS had just 13 percent market share in 1992. Consequently, opportunities abound for small companies to enter the market and focus on the needs of particular kinds of companies.

Increasingly, small, specialized software companies are springing up to manage the needs of particular kinds of clients. An example is Systems & Computer Technology Corp., based in Malvern, Pennsylvania, which recently went head-to-head with EDS to secure a seven-year, $35 million outsourcing contract to service the data-processing needs of Dallas County. The company has yearly revenues of only $100 million, as against EDS's $ 9 billion, but it won the contract. It won because it specializes in servicing only the needs of customers like local government or higher education. It could show Dallas County its twelve ongoing contracts with municipal clients, whereas EDS could offer only its experience with one, a hospital.[19] Dallas County believed that Systems & Technology Corp. could better service its needs than a giant like EDS, and so the focused company won out over the differentiator.

Other focused companies are also springing up—for instance, the Bisys Group and Systematics Company, which serves the needs of banks and universities. It appears that in the data-processing industry, small, focused companies will be strong competitors because of their ability to provide specialized, personal service to specific clients in a way that large differentiators cannot do.

The difficulty of managing a large number of market segments that a large differentiator sometimes experiences is not an issue for a focuser.

Since a focuser produces at a small volume, its production costs often exceed those of a low-cost company. Higher costs can also reduce profitability if a focuser is forced to invest heavily in developing a distinctive competency—such as expensive product innovation—in order to compete with a differentiated firm. However, once again flexible manufacturing systems are opening up new opportunities for focused firms: small production runs become possible at a lower cost. Increasingly, small specialized firms are competing with large companies in specific market segments where their cost disadvantage is much reduced.

A second problem is that the focuser's niche can suddenly disappear because of technological change or changes in consumer tastes. Unlike the more generalist

differentiator, a focuser cannot move easily to new niches, given its concentration of resources and competency in one or a few niches. For example, a clothing manufacturer focusing on heavy metal enthusiasts will find it difficult to shift to other segments if heavy metal loses its appeal. The disappearance of niches is one reason that so many small companies fail.

Finally, there is the prospect that differentiators will compete for a focuser's niche by offering a product that can satisfy the demands of the focuser's customers; for example, GM's new top-of-the-line models are aimed at Lexus, BMW and Mercedes-Benz. A focuser is vulnerable to attack and therefore has to constantly defend its niche.

Being Stuck in the Middle

Each generic strategy requires a company to make consistent product/market/distinctive-competency choices to establish a competitive advantage. In other words, a company must achieve a fit among the three components of business-level strategy. Thus, for example, a low-cost company cannot go for a high level of market segmentation, like a differentiator, and provide a wide range of products because doing so would raise production costs too much and the company would lose its low-cost advantage. Similarly, a differentiator with a competency in innovation that tries to reduce its expenditures on research and development or one with a competency in customer responsiveness through after-sales service that seeks to economize on its sales force to decrease costs is asking for trouble because it will lose its competitive advantage as its distinctive competency disappears.

Successful business-level strategy choice involves serious attention to all elements of the competitive plan. There are many examples of companies that, through ignorance or through mistakes, did not do the planning necessary for success in their chosen strategy. Such companies are said to be **stuck in the middle** because they have made product/market choices in such a way that they have been unable to obtain or sustain a competitive advantage.[21] As a result, they have below-average performance and suffer when industry competition intensifies.

Some stuck-in-the-middle companies started out pursuing one of the three generic strategies but made wrong decisions or were subject to environmental changes. Losing control of a generic strategy is very easy unless management keeps close track of the business and its environment, constantly adjusting product/market choices to suit changing industry conditions. The Holiday Inn's experience in the 1980s, described in Strategy in Action 6.4, shows how a company can become stuck in the middle because the environment changes.

As the experience of Holiday Inns suggests, there are many paths to being stuck in the middle. Quite commonly, a focuser can get stuck in the middle when it becomes overconfident and starts to act like a broad differentiator. People Express, the defunct airline, exemplifies a company in this situation. It started out as a specialized air carrier serving a narrow market niche: low-priced travel on the eastern seaboard. In pursuing this focus strategy based on cost leadership, it was very successful; but when it tried to expand to other geographic regions and began taking over other airlines to gain a larger number of planes, it lost its niche. People Express became one more carrier in an increasingly competitive market, where it had no special competitive advantage against the other national carriers. The result was financial troubles. People Express was swallowed up by Texas Air and incorporated into Continental Airlines.

STRATEGY IN ACTION 6.4

Holiday Inns Makes a Comeback

The history of the Holiday Inns, Inc., motel chain is one of the great success stories in American business. Its founder, Kemmons Wilson, vacationing in the early 1950s, found existing motels to be small, expensive, and of unpredictable quality. This discovery, along with the prospect of unprecedented highway travel that would come with the new interstate highway program, triggered a realization: There was an unmet customer need, a gap in the market for quality accommodations. Holiday Inns was to meet that need.

From the beginning, Holiday Inns set the standard for motel features like air conditioning and icemakers, while keeping room rates reasonable. These amenities enhanced the motels' popularity, and a Wilson invention, motel franchising, made rapid expansion possible. By 1960 Holiday Inns motels dotted America's landscape; they could be found in virtually every city and on every major highway. Before the 1960s ended, more than 1,000 of them were in full operation, and occupancy rates averaged 80 percent. The concept of mass accommodation had arrived.[22]

By the 1970s, however, the motel chain was in trouble. The service offered by Holiday Inns appealed to the average traveler, who wanted a standardized product (a room) at an average price. In essence, Holiday Inns had been targeting the middle of the hotel-room market. But travelers were beginning to make different demands on hotels and motels. Some wanted luxury and were willing to pay higher prices for better accommodations and service. Others sought low prices and accepted rock-bottom quality and service in exchange. Although the market had fragmented into different groups of customers with different needs, Holiday Inns was still offering an undifferentiated, average-cost, average-quality product.[23]

Holiday Inns missed the change in the market and thus failed to respond appropriately to it, but the competition did not. Companies like Hyatt Corp. siphoned off the top end of the market, where quality and service sold rooms. Chains like Motel 6 and Days Inns captured the basic-quality, low-price end of the market. In between were many specialty chains that appealed to business travelers, families, or self-caterers—people who want to be able to cook in their hotel rooms. Holiday Inns' position was attacked from all sides. The company's earnings declined as occupancy rates dropped drastically, and marginal Holiday Inns motels began to close as competition increased.

Wounded but not dead, Holiday Inns began counterattacking in the 1980s. The original chain was upgraded to suit quality-oriented travelers. At the same time, to meet the needs of different kinds of travelers, the company created new hotel and motel chains, including the luxury Holiday Inn Crowne Plazas; the Hampton Inns, which serve the low-price end of the market; and the all-suite Embassy Suites. Holiday Inns attempted to meet the demands of the many niches, or segments of the hotel market that had emerged in the 1980s.[24]

Differentiators, too, can fail in the market and end up stuck in the middle if competitors attack their markets with more specialized or low-cost products that blunt their competitive edge. This happened to IBM in the large-frame computer market as personal computers became more powerful and able to do the job of the much more expensive mainframes. The increasing movement toward flexible manufacturing systems will aggravate the problems faced by cost leaders and differentiators. Many large firms will become stuck in the middle unless they make the investment needed to pursue both strategies simultaneously. No company is safe in the jungle of competition, and each must be constantly on the

lookout to exploit competitive advantages as they arise and to defend the advantages it already has.

To sum up, successful management of a generic competitive strategy requires strategic managers to attend to two main matters. First, they need to ensure that the product/market/distinctive-competency decisions they make are oriented toward one specific competitive strategy. Second, they need to monitor the environment so that they can keep the firm's sources of competitive advantage in tune with changing opportunities and threats.

6.5 CHOOSING AN INVESTMENT STRATEGY AT THE BUSINESS LEVEL

We have been discussing business-level strategy in terms of making product/market/distinctive-competency choices to gain a competitive advantage. However, there is a second major choice to be made at the business level: the choice of which type of investment strategy to pursue in support of the competitive strategy.[25] An *investment strategy* refers to the amount and type of resources—both human and financial—that must be invested to gain a competitive advantage. Generic competitive strategies provide competitive advantages, but they are expensive to develop and maintain. Differentiation is the most expensive of the three because it requires that a company invest resources in many functions, such as research and development and sales and marketing, to develop distinctive competencies. Cost leadership is less expensive to maintain once the initial investment in a manufacturing plant and equipment has been made. It does not require such sophisticated research and development or marketing efforts. The focus strategy is cheapest because fewer resources are needed to serve one market segment than to serve the whole market.

In deciding on an investment strategy, a company must evaluate the potential returns from investing in a generic competitive strategy against the cost of developing the strategy. In this way, it can determine whether a strategy is likely to be profitable to pursue and how profitability will change as industry competition changes. Two factors are crucial in choosing an investment strategy: the strength of a company's position in an industry relative to its competitors and the stage of the industry life cycle in which the company is competing.[26]

Competitive Position

Two attributes can be used to determine the strength of a company's relative competitive position. First, the larger a company's *market share*, the stronger is its competitive position and the greater are the potential returns from future investment. This is because a large market share provides experience-curve economies and suggests that the company has developed brand loyalty. The strength and uniqueness of a company's *distinctive competencies* are the second measure of competitive position. If it is difficult to imitate a company's research and development expertise, its manufacturing or marketing skills, its knowledge of particular customer segments, or its unique reputation or brand name capital, the company's relative competitive position is strong and its returns from the generic strategy increase. In general, the companies with the largest market share and strongest distinctive competencies are in the best position.

These two attributes obviously reinforce one another and explain why some companies get stronger and stronger over time. A unique competency leads to increased demand for the company's products, and then, as a result of larger market share, the company has more resources to invest in developing its distinctive competency. Companies with a smaller market share and little potential for developing a distinctive competency are in a weaker competitive position.[27] Thus they are less attractive sources for investment.

Life Cycle Effects

The second main factor influencing the investment attractiveness of a generic strategy is the *stage of the industry life cycle*. Each life cycle stage is accompanied by a particular industry environment, presenting different opportunities and threats. Each stage, therefore, has different implications for the investment of resources needed to obtain a competitive advantage. For example, competition is strongest in the shakeout stage of the life cycle and least important in the embryonic stage, so the risks of pursuing a strategy change over time. The difference in risk explains why the potential returns from investing in a competitive strategy depend on the life cycle stage.

Choosing an Investment Strategy

Table 6.2 summarizes the relationship among the stage of the life cycle, competitive position, and investment strategy at the business level.

Embryonic Strategy

In the embryonic stage, all companies, weak and strong, emphasize the development of a distinctive competency and a product/market policy. During this stage, investment needs are great because a company has to establish a competitive advantage. Many fledgling companies in the industry are seeking resources to develop a distinctive competency. Thus the appropriate business-level investment strategy is a **share-building strategy**. The aim is to build market share by developing a stable and unique competitive advantage to attract customers who have no knowledge of the company's products.

Table 6.2
Choosing An Investment Strategy at the Business Level

Stage of industry life cycle	Strong competitive position	Weak competitive position
Embryonic	Share building	Share building
Growth	Growth	Market concentration
Shakeout	Share increasing	Market concentration or harvest/liquidation
Maturity	Hold-and-maintain or profit	Harvest or liquidation/ divestiture
Decline	Market concentration, harvest, or asset reduction	Turnaround, liquidation, or divestiture

Companies require large amounts of capital to build research and development competencies or sales and service competencies. They cannot generate much of this capital internally. Thus a company's success depends on its ability to demonstrate a unique competency to attract outside investors, or venture capitalists. If a company gains the resources to develop a distinctive competency, it will be in a relatively stronger competitive position. If it fails, its only option may be to exit the industry. In fact, companies in weak competitive positions at all stages in the life cycle may choose to exit the industry to cut their losses.

Growth Strategies At the growth stage, the task facing a company is to consolidate its position and provide the base it needs to survive the coming shakeout. Thus the appropriate investment strategy is the **growth strategy**. The goal is to maintain a company's relative competitive position in a rapidly expanding market and, if possible, to increase it—in other words, to grow with the expanding market. However, other companies are entering the market and catching up with the industry innovators. As a result, companies require successive waves of capital infusion to maintain the momentum generated by their success in the embryonic stage. For example, differentiators are engaging in massive research and development, and cost leaders are investing in plant to obtain experience-curve economies. All this investment is very expensive.

The growth stage is also the time when companies attempt to consolidate existing market niches and enter new ones so that they can increase their market share. Increasing the level of market segmentation is expensive as well. A company has to invest resources to develop a new sales and marketing competency. Consequently, at the growth stage, companies fine-tune their competitive strategy and make business-level investment decisions about the relative advantages of a differentiation, low-cost, or focus strategy, given financial needs and relative competitive position. For example, if one company has emerged as the cost leader, the other companies in the industry may decide not to compete head-on with it. Instead, they pursue a growth strategy using a differentiation or focus approach and invest resources in developing unique competencies. Because companies spend a lot of money just to keep up with growth in the market, finding additional resources to develop new skills and competencies is a difficult task for strategic managers.

Companies in a weak competitive position at this stage engage in a **market concentration strategy** to consolidate their position. They seek to specialize in some way and adopt a focus strategy to reduce their investment needs. If very weak, they may also choose to exit the industry.

Shakeout Strategies By the shakeout stage, demand is increasing slowly and competition by price or product characteristics has become intense. Thus companies in strong competitive positions need resources to invest in a **share-increasing strategy** to attract customers from weak companies that are exiting the market. In other words, companies attempt to maintain and increase market share despite fierce competition. The way companies invest their resources depends on their generic strategy.

For cost leaders, because of the price wars that can occur, investment in cost control is crucial if they are to survive the shakeout stage. Differentiators in a strong competitive position choose to forge ahead and become broad differen-

tiators. Their investment is likely to be oriented toward marketing, and they are likely to develop a sophisticated after-sales service network. They also widen the product range to match the range of customer needs. Differentiators in a weak position reduce their investment burden by withdrawing to a focused strategy—the market concentration strategy—in order to specialize in a particular niche or product. Weak companies exiting the industry engage in a harvest or liquidation strategy, both of which are discussed later in this chapter.

Maturity Strategies By the maturity stage, a strategic group structure has emerged in the industry, and companies have learned how their competitors will react to their competitive moves. At this point companies want to reap the rewards of their previous investments in developing a generic strategy. Until now profits have been reinvested in the business, and dividends have been small. Investors in strong companies have obtained their rewards through capital appreciation because the company has reinvested most of its capital to maintain and increase market share. As market growth slows in the maturity stage, a company's investment strategy depends on the level of competition in the industry and the source of the company's competitive advantage.

In environments where competition is high because technological change is occurring or where barriers to entry are low, companies need to defend their competitive position. Strategic managers need to continue to invest heavily in maintaining the company's competitive advantage. Both low-cost companies and differentiators adopt a **hold-and-maintain strategy** to support their generic strategies. They expend resources to develop their distinctive competency so as to remain the market leaders. For example, differentiated companies may invest in improved after-sales service, and low-cost companies may invest in the latest production technologies, such as robotics. Doing so is expensive but is warranted by the revenues that will accrue from maintaining a strong competitive position.

Additionally, companies move to develop both a low-cost and a differentiation strategy simultaneously. Differentiators take advantage of their strong position to develop flexible manufacturing systems in order to reduce their production costs. Cost leaders move to start differentiating their products to expand their market share by serving more market segments. For example, Gallo moved into the premium wine and wine cooler market segments to take advantage of low production costs.

However, when a company is protected from industry competition, it may decide to exploit its competitive advantage to the full by engaging in a **profit strategy**. A company pursuing this strategy attempts to maximize the present returns from its previous investments. Typically, it reinvests proportionally less in its business and increases returns to shareholders. The strategy works well as long as competitive forces remain relatively constant, so that a company can maintain the profit margins developed by its competitive strategy. However, a company must be alert to threats from the environment and must take care not to become complacent and unresponsive to changes in the competitive environment.

All too often market leaders fail to exercise vigilance in managing the environment, imagining that they are impregnable to competition. For example, General Motors felt secure against foreign car manufacturers until changes in oil prices precipitated a crisis. Kodak, which had profited for so long from its strengths in film processing, was slow to respond to the threat of electronic imaging tech-

niques. Paradoxically, the most successful companies often fail to sense changes in the market. For example, Holiday Inn's failure to perceive changes in customer needs was to some extent the result of its single-minded focus on its original motel chain. Developing two chains side by side would have required more resources, but that was what the market demanded. As Strategy in Action 6.5 shows, Campbell Soup Co. is another example of a company that over time failed to pursue a hold-and-maintain strategy to manage the competitive environment.

Decline Strategies The decline stage of the industry life cycle begins when demand for the industry's product starts to fall. There are many possible reasons for decline, including foreign competition and product substitution. A company may lose its distinctive competency as its rivals enter with new or more efficient technologies. Thus it must decide what investment strategy to adopt in order to deal with new industry circumstances. Table 6.2 lists the strategies that companies can resort to when their competitive position is declining.[28]

The initial strategies that companies can adopt are market concentration and asset reduction.[29] With a market concentration strategy, a company attempts to consolidate its product and market choices. It narrows its product range and exits marginal niches in an attempt to redeploy its investments more efficiently and improve its competitive position. Reducing customer needs and the customer groups served may allow the company to pursue a focus strategy in order to survive the decline stage. (As noted earlier, weak companies in the growth stage tend to adopt this strategy.) That is what International Harvester did as the demand for farm machinery fell. It now produces only medium-sized trucks under the name Navistar.

An **asset reduction strategy** requires a company to limit or decrease its investment in a business and to extract, or milk, the investment as much as it can. This approach is sometimes called a **harvest strategy** because the company reduces to a minimum the assets it employs in the business and forgoes investment for the sake of immediate profits.[30] A market concentration strategy generally indicates that a company is trying to turn around its business so that it can survive in the long run. A harvest strategy implies that a company will exit the industry once it has harvested all the returns it can. Low-cost companies are more likely to pursue a harvest strategy simply because a smaller market share means higher costs and they are unable to move to a focus strategy. Differentiators, in contrast, have a competitive advantage in this stage if they can move to a focus strategy.

At any stage of the life cycle, companies that are in weak competitive positions may apply **turnaround strategies.**[31] The question that a company has to answer is whether there is a viable way to compete in the industry and how much will such competition cost. If a company is stuck in the middle, then it must assess the investment costs of developing a generic competitive strategy. Perhaps a company pursuing a low-cost strategy has not made the right product or market choices, or a differentiator has been missing niche opportunities. In such cases, the company can redeploy resources and change its competitive strategy.

Sometimes a company's loss of competitiveness may be due to poor strategy implementation. If so, the company must move to change its structure and control systems rather than its strategy. For example, Dan Schendel, a prominent management researcher, found that 74 percent of the turnaround situations that he and his colleagues studied were due to inefficient strategy implementation.

STRATEGY IN ACTION 6.5

Campbell Soup Cools

The name *Campbell Soup Co.* is closely linked with its well-known soups, and for many years they have been the source of the company's profitability. However, during the 1980s the company's fortunes declined as its top executives failed to manage the business and keep it abreast of changes in the environment. While competitors like Heinz and Nestlé were innovating products and introducing new cost-saving machinery, Campbell was content to do business the way it had always done, even though its costs were rising and its sales were stagnant. This state of affairs changed in 1990, when David W. Johnson arrived from Gerber Products Co. to revitalize the company.

Johnson moved immediately to reduce costs and to increase profits. He closed twenty inefficient plants, including Campbell's famous multistory Camden, New Jersey, factory where it had made soup in the traditional way in large copper pans. Moreover, he fired 16 percent of Campbell's work force and divested many of Campbell's unprofitable businesses. All these actions were part of his turnaround strategy to move Campbell back to a hold-and-maintain position in the food industry in order to redeploy its resources so that it could compete for market share against its more efficient rivals. His actions were successful, and the company's stock price doubled in one year as profits rebounded.

Although analysts have applauded his efforts, they have become concerned that Johnson may have been pursuing his cost-cutting strategy a little too vigorously and at the expense of new-product development. Normally, part of a hold-and-maintain strategy is investing resources to develop new products in order to build and maintain market share. However, Johnson killed many of the company's new product lines because they were unprofitable at the time, and has seemed reluctant to invest much in new-product development. Moreover, the company's advertising budget is stagnant.[32]

Since the company is not innovating and developing new products that would sustain its growth into the future, analysts fear that far from pursuing a hold-and-maintain strategy, Johnson may be milking existing brands to increase short-term profits at the expense of long-term profits. If Johnson is cutting back on investment to harvest the company, analysts wonder what the company will look like in the future. Will it still be a major food company or will it return to its origins as a soup maker?

The strategy-structure fit at the business level is thus very important in determining competitive strength.[33] We discuss it in detail in Chapter 13.

If a company decides that turnaround is not possible, either for competitive or for life cycle reasons, then the two remaining investment alternatives are **liquidation** and **divestiture.** As the terms imply, the company moves to exit the industry either by liquidating its assets or by selling the whole business. Both can be regarded as radical forms of harvesting strategy because the company is seeking to get back as much as it can from its investment in the business. Often, however, it can only exit at a loss and take a tax write-off. Timing is important, because the earlier a company senses that divestiture is necessary, the more it can get for its assets. There are many stories about companies that buy weak or declining companies, thinking that they can turn them around and then realize their mistake as the new acquisitions become a drain on their resources. Often the acquired companies have lost their competitive advantage, and the cost of

regaining it is too great. However, there have also been spectacular successes, like that achieved by Lee Iacocca, who engaged in a low-cost strategy involving the firing of more than 45 percent of Chrysler's work force.

6.6 SUMMARY OF CHAPTER

The purpose of this chapter is to discuss the factors that must be considered if a company is to develop a business-level strategy that allows it to compete effectively in the marketplace. The formulation of business-level strategy involves matching the opportunities and threats in the environment to the company's strengths and weaknesses by making choices about products, markets, technologies, and the investments necessary to pursue the choices. All companies, from one-person operations to the strategic business units of large corporations, must develop a business strategy if they are to compete effectively and maximize their long-term profitability. The chapter makes the following main points:

1. Selecting a business-level strategy involves choosing a generic competitive strategy.
2. At the heart of generic competitive strategy are choices concerning product differentiation, market segmentation, and distinctive competency.
3. The combination of those three choices results in the specific form of generic competitive strategy employed by a company.
4. The three generic competitive strategies are cost-leadership, differentiation, and focus. Each has advantages and disadvantages. A company must constantly manage its strategy; otherwise, it risks being stuck in the middle.
5. Increasingly, developments in manufacturing technology are allowing firms to pursue both a cost-leadership and a differentiation strategy and thus obtain the economic benefits of both strategies simultaneously. Technical developments also allow small firms to compete with large firms on equal footing in particular market segments and hence increase the number of firms pursuing a focus strategy.
6. The second choice facing a company is an investment strategy for supporting the competitive strategy. The choice of investment strategy depends on two main factors: (a) the strength of a company's competitive position in the industry and (b) the stage of the industry life cycle.
7. The main types of investment strategy are share building, growth, share increasing, hold-and-maintain, profit, market concentration, asset reduction, harvest, turnaround, liquidation, and divestiture.

Discussion Questions

1. Why does each generic competitive strategy require a different set of product/market/distinctive-competency choices? Give examples of pairs of companies in (a) the computer industry and (b) the auto industry that pursue different competitive strategies.

2. How can companies pursuing a cost-leadership, differentiation, or focus strategy become stuck in the middle? In what ways can they regain their competitive advantage?
3. Over the industry life cycle, what investment strategy choices should be made by (a) differentiators in a strong competitive position and (b) differentiators in a weak competitive position?
4. How do technical developments affect the generic strategies pursued by firms in an industry? How might they do so in the future?

Article File 6

Find an example (or several examples) of a company pursuing one or more of the three generic business-level strategies. What strategy is it? What product/market/distinctive-competency choices is it based on? What are its advantages and disadvantages?

Strategic Management Project: Module 6

This part of the project focuses on the nature of your company's business-level strategy. If your company operates in more than one business, you should concentrate here either on its core or most central business, or on its most important businesses. Using all the information you have collected on your company, answer the following questions:

1. How differentiated are the products/services of your company? What is the basis of their differentiated appeal?
2. What is your company's strategy toward market segmentation? If it segments its market, on what basis does it do so?
3. What distinctive competencies does your company have? (Use the information from the module in the last chapter, on functional-level strategy, to answer this question). Is efficiency, quality, innovation, customer responsiveness, or a combination of these factors the main driving force in your company?
4. Based on these product/market/distinctive-competency choices, what generic business-level strategy is your company pursuing?
5. What are the advantages and disadvantages associated with your company's choice of business-level strategy?
6. How could you improve its business-level strategy to strengthen its competitive advantage?
7. Is your company a member of a strategic group in an industry? If so, which one?
8. What investment strategy is your company pursuing to support its generic strategy? How does this match with the strength of its competitive position and the stage of its industry life cycle?

Endnotes

1. N. Darnton, "The Joy of Polyester," *Newsweek*, August 3, 1992, p. 61.
2. Derek F. Abell, *Defining the Business: The Starting Point of Strategic Planning* (Englewood Cliffs, N.J.: Prentice–Hall, 1980), p. 169.
3. R. Kotler, *Marketing Management*, 5th ed. (Englewood Cliffs, N.J.: Prentice-Hall, 1984). M. R. Darby and E. Karni, "Free Competition and the Optimal Amount of Fraud," *Journal of Law and Economics*, 16 (1973), 67–86.
4. Abell, *Defining the Business*, p. 8.
5. Michael E. Porter, *Competitive Advantage: Creating and Sustaining Superior Performance* (New York: Free Press, 1985).
6. R. D. Buzzell and F. D. Wiersema, "Successful Share Building Strategies," *Harvard Business Review* January–February (1981), 135–144. L. W. Phillips, D. R. Chang, and R. D. Buzzell, "Product Quality, Cost Position, and Business Performance: A Test of Some Key Hypotheses," *Journal of Marketing*, 47 (1983), 26–43.
7. Michael E. Porter, *Competitive Strategy: Techniques for Analyzing Industries and Competitors* (New York: Free Press, 1980), p. 45.
8. Abell, *Defining the Business*, p. 15.
9. Although many other authors have discussed cost leadership and differentiation as basic competitive approaches (e.g., F. Sherer, *Industrial Market Structure and Economic Performance*, 2nd. ed. (Boston: Houghton Mifflin, 1980), Porter's model (Porter, *Competitive Strategy*) has become the dominant approach. Consequently, this model is the one developed below, and the discussion draws heavily on his definitions. The basic cost-leadership/differentiation dimension has received substantial empirical support (e.g., D. C. Hambrick, "High Profit Strategies in Mature Capital Goods Industries: A Contingency Approach," *Academy of Management Journal*, 26 (1983), 687–707.
10. Porter, *Competitive Advantage*, p. 37.
11. Ibid., pp. 13–14.
12. D. Miller, "Configurations of Strategy and Structure: Towards a Synthesis," *Strategic Management Journal*, 7 (1986), 217–231.
13. L. Armstrong, "Altima's Secret: The Right Kind of Sticker Shock," *Business Week*, January 18, 1993, p. 37.
14. Porter, *Competitive Advantage*, pp. 44–46.
15. Charles W. Hofer and D. Schendel, *Strategy Formulation: Analytical Concepts* (St. Paul, Minn.: West, 1978).
16. W. K. Hall, "Survival Strategies in a Hostile Environment," *Harvard Business Review,* 58 (1980), 75–85. Hambrick, "High Profit Strategies," pp. 687–707.
17. L. Nathans Spiro and M. Landler, "Less-Than-Fantastic Plastic," *Business Week,* November 9, 1992, pp. 100–101.
18. Porter, *Competitive Strategy,* p. 46.
19. J. W. Verity, "They Make a Killing Minding Other People's Business," *Business Week,* November 30, 1992, p. 96.
20. Peter F. Drucker, *The Practice of Management* (New York: Harper, 1954).
21. Porter, *Competitive Strategy,* p. 43.
22. "The Holiday Inn Trip: A Breeze for Decades, Bumpy Ride in the '80s," *Wall Street Journal,* February 11, 1987, p. 1.
23. Holiday Inn, *Annual Report,* 1985.
24. Bureau of Labor Statistics, *U.S. Industrial Outlook* (Washington, D.C., 1986).
25. Hofer and Schendel, *Strategy Formulation,* pp. 102–104.
26. Our discussion of the investment, or posturing, component of business-level strategy draws heavily on Hofer and Schendel's discussion in *Strategy Formulation,* especially Chapter 6.
27. Hofer and Schendel, *Strategy Formulation,* pp. 75–77.
28. K. R. Harrigan, "Strategy Formulation in Declining Industries," *Academy of Management Review,* 5 (1980), 599–604.
29. Hofer and Schendel, *Strategy Formulation,* pp. 169–172.
30. L. R. Feldman and A. L. Page, "Harvesting: The Misunderstood Market Exit Strategy," *Journal of Business Strategy,* 4 (1985), 79–85.
31. C. W. Hofer, "Turnaround Strategies," *Journal of Business Strategy,* 1 (1980), 19–31.
32. J. Weber, "Campbell is Bubbling, But for How Long?" *Business Week,* June 17, 1991, pp. 56–58.
33. Hofer and Schendel, *Strategy Formulation,* p. 172.

7 Business-Level Strategy and the Industry Environment

7.1 OPENING CASE: THE GOODYEAR TIRE & RUBBER COMPANY

By the end of 1992 The Goodyear Tire & Rubber Company, the largest tire manufacturer in the United States, posted a profit of over $340 million on record sales of over $11 billion. This was a far cry from the situation in 1991, when the company had a record loss. For a while it looked as if the company, languishing under a debt of over $3.7 billion, might go bankrupt. What altered its fortunes was a combination of a new CEO, who restored the company's competitive advantage, and a change in the nature of industry competition.

Throughout the 1980s Goodyear sales had fallen as the company lost market share to its two main competitors, Michelin of France and Bridgestone of Japan. As you saw in Chapter 3, these companies had expanded rapidly into the United States, launching an aggressive strategy to build market share and penetrate the market. Their entry started a price war in the U.S. tire market, which especially hurt Goodyear because of the company's high costs. Goodyear also had a poor record in product innovation and had been slow to bring out new products that would attract its customers back. After the company's huge losses in 1991, its board of directors forced out the CEO, Tom Barrett, and replaced him with Stanley Gault, who had been the CEO of Rubbermaid. Gault immediately began to change the way Goodyear operated to restore its competitive advantage.

First, he embarked on a strategy of massively reducing operating costs. Gault's predecessor, Barrett, had started this process by investing over $4 billion in the 1980s in new, more efficient plant and equipment and by decreasing the size of the work force by over 20 percent. By 1991 output per man-hour had climbed 51 percent.[1] However, Gault took this process much further and began to slash costs everywhere. By example, he showed managers how to reduce costs. He began by eliminating company limousines for top executives and replacing them with family sedans. He sold off three of the five corporate jets and eliminated the Goodyear blimp, based in Houston, Texas. He even removed most of the light bulbs from his office to demonstrate his commitment to lower costs. The other Goodyear managers followed his lead and systematically began their cost-cutting efforts, with the spectacular results noted above.

To increase market share, Gault also worked on increasing innovation, quality, and the speed at which the company introduced new products. Goodyear had had many tires in development for years, including one named the Aquatread, a tire that performed very well on wet road surfaces. However, it had been slow to bring them to the market. In 1991 Gault decided on a bold strategy: Goodyear would introduce four new tires at once, including the Aquatread. Each tire was directed at a different market segment. For example, the Aquatread was aimed at the safety-conscious consumer, whereas another tire was constructed to lower gas costs. These moves were very successful. Its new tires, which had higher profit margins than Goodyear's older tires, restored customers' perceptions that Goodyear was a premium tire manufacturer, and sales of the new tires, particularly the Aquatread, surged. Indeed, Goodyear sold over 1 million Aquatreads in one year, 20 percent higher than its forecast. Gault's combined strategy of reducing costs and raising the differentiated appeal of the

company's products had paid off in the form of the huge increase in profits noted at the beginning of this case.

By 1991 U.S. tire manufacturers had grown weary of the rounds of price cutting and price wars that had plagued the industry and diminished their profits. Tire manufacturers started supporting each other's attempts to keep prices up and avoid price cutting and also began searching for new ways to compete that did not reduce industry profitability. One strategy they adopted was to develop new kinds of tires and aggressively market them to customers. Gault's strategy of developing innovative products coincided with this change in the industry from price to nonprice competition and helped promote Goodyear's turnaround and increased sales. From 1992 on Goodyear and its competitors were all benefiting from their new strategy of nonprice competition. By 1993 Goodyear was posting record profits, and its share price had climbed to over three times its 1990 value.

Discussion Questions

1. How did the nature of competition in the tire industry cause problems for Goodyear?
2. What strategies did Gault develop to turn the company around?

7.2 OVERVIEW

Even when companies have developed successful generic business-level strategies, they still face a crucial problem: how to respond to the actions of industry competitors, each of which is seeking to maximize its own competitive advantage and profitability. We turn now to this critical aspect of business-level strategy and examine the ways of maintaining a competitive advantage over time in different kinds of industry environments.

First, we focus on how companies in *fragmented industries* try to develop competitive strategies that support their generic strategies. Second, we consider the challenges of developing a competitive advantage in *embryonic and growth industries*. Third, we probe the nature of competitive relations in *mature industries*. Here we concentrate on how a set of companies that have been pursuing successful generic competitive strategies can use a variety of competitive techniques to manage the high level of competitive interdependence found in such industries. Finally, we assess the problems of managing a company's generic competitive strategy in *declining industries*, where rivalry between competitors is high because market demand is slowing or falling. By the end of the chapter, you will understand how the successful pursuit of a generic strategy depends on the selection of the right competitive tactics to manage the industry environment.

7.3 STRATEGY IN FRAGMENTED INDUSTRIES

A fragmented industry is one composed of a large number of small and medium-sized companies. For example, the video rental industry is still very fragmented, as is the restaurant industry, the health club industry, and the legal services industry. There are several reasons why an industry may consist of many small companies rather than a few large ones.[2] In some industries there are few scale economies, and so large companies do not have an advantage over smaller enterprises. Indeed, in some industries there are diseconomies of scale. Many home-

buyers, for example, have a preference for dealing with local real estate agents, whom they perceive as having better local knowledge than national chains. Similarly, in the restaurant business, many individuals have an aversion to national chains and prefer the unique style of a local restaurant. In addition, because of the lack of scale economies, many fragmented industries are characterized by low barriers to entry—and new entry keeps the industry fragmented. The video rental industry exemplifies this situation: the costs of opening up a video rental store are very moderate and can be borne by a single entrepreneur. High transportation costs, too, can keep an industry fragmented, for regional production may be the only efficient way to satisfy customer needs, as in the cement business. Finally, an industry may be fragmented because customer needs are so specialized that only small job lots of products are required, and thus there is no room for a large mass production operation to satisfy the market.

For some fragmented industries, these factors dictate the competitive strategy to pursue, and the focus strategy stands out as a principal choice. Companies may specialize by customer group, customer need, or geographical region, so that many small specialty companies operate in local or regional market segments. All kinds of custom-made products—furniture, clothing, rifles, and so on—fall into this category, as do all small service operations that cater to particular customer needs, such as laundries, restaurants, health clubs, and rental stores. Indeed, service companies make up a large proportion of the enterprises in fragmented industries because they provide personalized service to clients and therefore need to be close to clients.

However, entrepreneurs are eager to gain the cost advantages of pursuing a low-cost strategy or the sales-revenue-enhancing advantages of differentiation by circumventing the problems of a fragmented industry. The returns from consolidating a fragmented industry are often huge. During the last thirty years many companies have overcome industry structure problems and have begun consolidating fragmented industries. These companies include large retailers like Wal-Mart Stores, Sears, and JC Penney, fast-food chains like McDonald's and Burger King, and video rental chains such as Blockbuster Entertainment Corp. with its Blockbuster Video stores, as well as chains of health clubs, repair shops, and even lawyers and consultants. To grow, consolidate their industries, and become the industry leaders, they are utilizing three main strategies: (1) chaining, (2) franchising, and (3) horizontal merger.

Chaining

Companies like Wal-Mart Stores and Midas International Corporation are pursuing a **chaining** strategy in order to obtain the advantages of a cost-leadership strategy. They establish networks of linked merchandising outlets that are so interconnected that they function as one large business entity. The amazing buying power that these companies possess through their nationwide store chains allows them to negotiate large price reductions with their suppliers and promotes their competitive advantage. They overcome the barrier of high transportation costs by establishing sophisticated regional distribution centers, which can economize on inventory costs and maximize responsiveness to the needs of stores and customers (this is Wal-Mart's specialty). Last but not least, they realize economies of scale from sharing managerial skills across the chain and from nationwide, rather than local, advertising.

Franchising

For differentiated companies in fragmented industries, such as McDonald's or Century 21 Real Estate Corporation, the competitive advantage comes from the business strategy of **franchising.** With franchising, a local store operation is both owned and managed by the same person. When the owner is also the manager, he or she is strongly motivated to control the business closely and make sure that quality and standards are consistently high so that customer needs are always satisfied. Such motivation is particularly critical in a strategy of differentiation, where it is important for a company to maintain its uniqueness. One reason that industries fragment is the difficulty of maintaining control over, and the uniqueness of, the many small outlets that must be operated. Franchising avoids this problem. In addition, franchising lessens the financial burden of swift expansion, and so permits rapid growth of the company. Finally, a differentiator can reap the advantages of large-scale advertising, as well as the purchasing, managerial, and distribution economies of a large company, as McDonald's does very efficiently. Indeed, McDonald's is able to pursue cost leadership and differentiation simultaneously only because franchising allows costs to be controlled locally and differentiation can be achieved by marketing on a national level.

Horizontal Merger

Companies like Dillard's and Blockbuster Entertainment have been choosing a business-level strategy of **horizontal merger** to consolidate their respective industries. Such companies have arranged mergers of small companies in an industry in order to create a few large companies. For example, Dillard's arranged the merger of regional store chains in order to form a national company. By pursuing horizontal merger, companies are able to obtain economies of scale or secure a national market for their product. As a result, they are able to pursue a cost-leadership or a differentiation strategy.

The challenge in a fragmented industry is to choose the most appropriate means—franchising, chaining, or horizontal merger—of overcoming a fragmented market so that the advantages of the generic strategy can be realized. It is difficult to think of any major service activities—from consulting and accounting firms to businesses satisfying the smallest consumer need, such as beauty parlors and car repair shops—that have not been merged and consolidated by chaining or franchising.

7.4 STRATEGY IN EMBRYONIC AND GROWTH INDUSTRIES

Embryonic industries are typically created by the innovations of pioneering companies. Thus, Apple single-handedly created the market for personal computers, Xerox created the market for photocopiers, and McDonald's created the market for fast food. In most cases, the pioneering company can initially earn enormous profits from its innovation because it may be the only company in the industry. For example, before the entry of IBM into the personal computer market in 1981, Apple enjoyed a virtual monopoly in this market. Similarly, during the seventeen years before its patents expired, Xerox enjoyed a monopoly in the market for photocopiers, earning enormous profits as a result.[3]

But high profits that innovating companies often reap in an embryonic industry also attract potential imitators, spurring them to enter the market. Typically, such entry is most rapid in the growth stage of an industry and may cause the innovator to lose its commanding competitive position. Figure 7.1 shows how the profit rate enjoyed by the innovator in an embryonic industry can decline as imitators crowd into the market during its growth stage. Thus Apple's onetime monopoly position was competed away as hordes of other personal computer makers entered into the market in the early and mid 1980s, trying to share in Apple's success. Once its patents expired, Xerox, too, faced many imitators, and some of them, such as Canon and Ricoh were ultimately very successful in the photocopier market. In the fast-food market, the early success of McDonald's drew imitators, including Burger King, Wendy's, and Foodmaker, with its Jack-in-the-Box restaurants.

Although their market share has declined since their early days, companies such as Apple, Xerox, and McDonald's are still major competitors. Other early innovators were not so lucky. For example, in the mid 1970s EMI pioneered the development of the CAT scanner. Widely regarded as the most important advance in radiology since the x-ray, the CAT scanner takes three-dimensional x-ray pictures of the body. Despite its being the pioneer, however, EMI soon saw imitators such as General Electric capture the market. EMI itself withdrew from the CAT market in the early 1980s. Similarly, Bowman invented the pocket calculator, only to see Texas Instruments reap the long-run rewards of the innovation, and RC Cola pioneered the introduction of diet colas, but it was Coca-Cola and Pepsico that made enormous profits from the concept.

Given the inevitability of imitation, the key issue for an innovating company in an embryonic industry is how to exploit its innovation and build an enduring long-run competitive advantage based on low cost or differentiation. Three strategies are available to the company: (1) to develop and market the innovation itself; (2) to develop and market the innovation jointly with other companies through a strategic alliance or joint venture; and (3) to license the innovation to others and let them develop the market.

The optimal choice of strategy depends on three factors. First, does the innovating company have the **complementary assets** to exploit its innovation and obtain a competitive advantage? Second, how difficult is it for imitators to copy the company's innovation—in other words, what is the **height of barriers to imitation**? And third, are there **capable competitors** that could rapidly imitate the innovation? Before we discuss the optimal choice of innovation strategy, we need to examine these factors.

Complementary Assets

Complementary assets are the assets required to successfully exploit a new innovation and gain a competitive advantage.[4] Among the most important complementary assets are competitive manufacturing facilities capable of handling rapid growth while maintaining high product quality. Such facilities enable the innovator to move quickly down the experience curve without encountering production bottlenecks and/or product quality problems. An inability to satisfy demand because of these problems can create an opportunity for imitators to enter the marketplace. For example, Compaq Computer was able to grow rapidly in the market for MS-DOS personal computers during the mid 1980s at the expense of the product's pioneer, IBM, largely because IBM lacked the

Figure 7.1
How an Innovator's Profits Can Be Competed Away

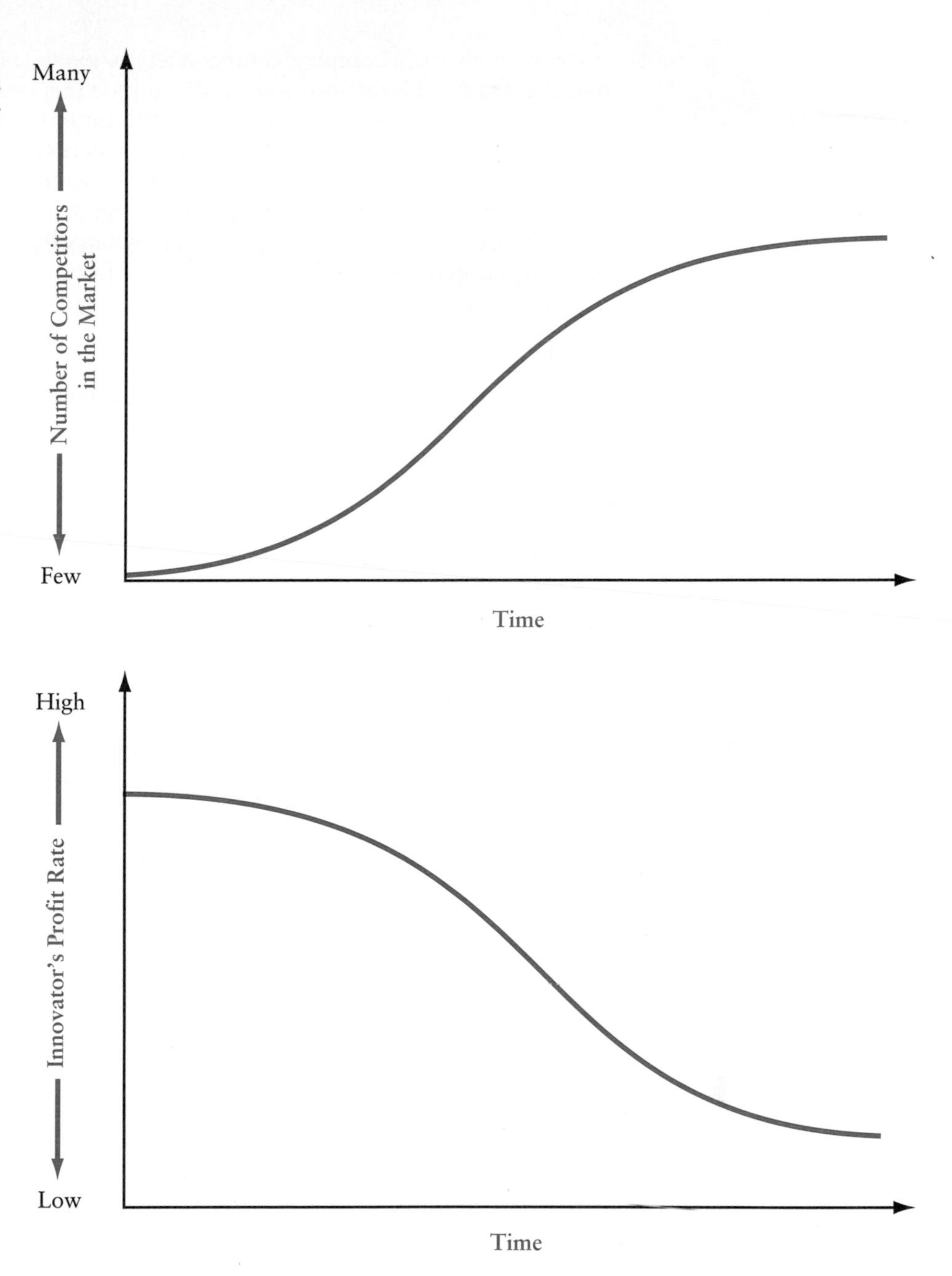

manufacturing facilities to satisfy the demand it had created for MS-DOS personal computers.

Complementary assets also include marketing know-how, an adequate sales force, access to distribution systems, and an after-sales service and support network. All of these assets can help an innovator build brand loyalty. They also help the innovator achieve market penetration more rapidly. In turn, the resulting increases in volume facilitate more rapid movement down the experience curve.

Developing such complementary assets is expensive, and embryonic companies often need large infusions of capital for this purpose. That is the reason first movers (the companies that are first in an industry) often lose out to late movers (companies that enter later)—large, successful companies, often established in other industries, that have the resources to quickly develop a presence in the new industry. A company like 3M exemplifies firms that can move quickly to capitalize on the opportunities arising when other companies open up new product markets, such as compact disks or floppy disks. Indeed, 3M is a late mover to be feared.

Barriers to Imitation

We first consider barriers to imitation in Chapter 4, in discussing the durability of competitive advantage. As you may recall, barriers to imitation are factors that prevent rivals from imitating a company's distinctive competencies. They can also be viewed as factors that prevent rivals, particularly late movers, from imitating a company's innovation. Although ultimately any innovation can be copied, the higher the barriers to imitation, the longer it takes for rivals to imitate the innovation.

Barriers to imitation give an innovator time to establish a competitive advantage and build more enduring entry barriers in the newly created market. For example, patents are among the most widely used barriers to imitation. By protecting its photocopier technology with a thicket of patents, Xerox was able to delay any significant imitation of its product for seventeen years. However, patents are often easy to invent around. For example, one study found that 60 percent of patented innovations were invented around within four years.[5] If patent protection is weak, a company might try to slow imitation by developing new products and processes in secret. The most famous example of this approach is Coca-Cola, which has kept the formulas for Coke a secret for generations. But Coca-Cola's success in this regard is an exception. A study of 100 companies has estimated that proprietary information about a company's decision to develop a major new product or process is known to its rivals within about twelve to eighteen months of the original development decision.[6]

Capable Competitors

Competitors' capability to imitate a pioneer's innovation depends primarily on two factors: (1) R&D skills and (2) access to complementary assets. Other things being equal, the greater the number of capable competitors with access to the R&D skills and complementary assets needed to imitate an innovation, the more rapid is imitation likely to be.

R&D skills are the ability of rivals to reverse-engineer an innovation in order to find out how it works and quickly develop a comparable product. Again consider the CAT scanner. GE bought one of the first CAT scanners produced by EMI, and GE's technical experts reverse-engineered it. Despite the product's technological complexity, they developed their own version of it, which allowed GE to quickly imitate EMI and to replace EMI as the major supplier of CAT scanners.

With regard to complementary assets, the access that rivals have to complementary assets such as marketing, sales know-how, or manufacturing capabilities is one of the key determinants of the rate of imitation. If would-be imitators

lack critical complementary assets, not only do they have to imitate the innovation; they may also have to imitate the innovator's complementary assets. This is expensive, as AT&T discovered when it tried to enter the personal computer business in 1984. AT&T lacked the marketing assets (sales force and distribution systems) necessary to support personal computer products. The lack of these assets and the time it takes to build them partly explain why four years after it originally entered the market AT&T had lost $2.5 billion and still had not emerged as a viable contender.

Three Innovation Strategies

The way in which these three factors—complementary assets, barriers to imitation, and the capability of competitors—influence the choice of innovation strategy is summarized in Table 7.1. The strategy of **developing and marketing the innovation alone** makes most sense when the barriers to imitating a new innovation are high, when the innovator has the complementary assets necessary to develop the innovation, and when the number of capable competitors is limited. High barriers to imitation buy the innovator time to establish a competitive advantage and build enduring barriers to entry through brand loyalty and/or experience-based cost advantages. Complementary assets allow rapid development and promotion of the innovation. The fewer the number of capable competitors, the less likely it is that any one of them will succeed in circumventing barriers to imitation and quickly imitating the innovation.

The strategy of **developing and marketing the innovation jointly with other companies through a strategic alliance or joint venture** makes most sense when barriers to imitation are high, there are several capable competitors, and the innovator lacks complementary assets. In such circumstances, it makes sense to enter into an alliance with a company that already has the complementary assets, in other words, with a capable competitor. Theoretically, such an alliance should prove to be mutually beneficial, and each partner can share in high profits that neither could earn on its own. The attempt by Body Shop International, described in Strategy in Action 7.1, to go it alone in the effort to enter the U.S. market rather than to form an alliance with U.S. partners illustrates the benefit of alliances in quickly exploiting an innovation.

The third strategy, **licensing**, makes most sense when barriers to imitation are low, the innovating company lacks the complementary assets, and there are many

Table 7.1
Strategies for Profiting from Innovation

Strategy	Does Innovator Have All Required Complementary Assets?	Likely Height of Barriers to Imitation	Number of Capable Competitors
Go It Alone	Yes	High	Few
Enter into Alliance	No	High	Limited
License Innovation	No	Low	Many

STRATEGY IN ACTION 7.1

Body Shop Opens Too Late

In 1976, Anita Roddick, a former flower child and the owner of a small hotel in southern England, had an idea. The rising sentiment against the use of animals in testing cosmetics and a wave of environmentalism, which focused on "natural" products, gave her the idea for a range of skin creams, shampoos, and lotions made from fruit and vegetable oils rather than animal products. Her products, moreover, would not be tested on animals. Roddick began to sell her line of new products from a small shop in Brighton, a seaside town, and the results surpassed her wildest expectations. Her line of cosmetics was an instant success, and to capitalize on it, she began to franchise the right to open stores called The Body Shop to sell her products. By 1993 there were over 700 of these stores around the world, with combined sales of over $250 million.

In Britain and Europe, to speed the growth of the company, Roddick mainly franchised her stores through alliances with other individuals and companies. In her push to enter the U.S. market in 1988, however, she decided to own her own stores and forgo the rapid expansion that franchising would have made possible. This was a costly mistake. Large U.S. cosmetic companies like Estée Lauder and entrepreneurs like Leslie Wexner of The Limited, were quick to see the opportunities that Roddick had opened up in this rapidly growing market segment. They moved fast to imitate her product lines, which was not technically difficult to do, and began to market their own natural cosmetics. For example, Estée Lauder brought out its Origins line of cosmetics, and Wexner opened the Bath and Body Works to sell his own line of natural cosmetics. Both these ventures have been very successful and have gained a large share of the market.

Realizing the competitive threat from imitators, in 1990 Roddick began to move quickly to franchise The Body Shop in the United States and by 1993 more than 150 stores had opened. Although the stores have been successful, the delay in opening them gave Roddick's competitors the opportunity to establish their own brand names and robbed her enterprise of the uniqueness that its products enjoy throughout Europe. Given that the United States is by far the world's biggest cosmetics market and natural cosmetics are its fastest-growing segment, this mistake will cost Body Shop billions of dollars in lost revenues in the years to come. When an innovation is easy to imitate and there are many capable competitors, entering into an alliance with others can speed the development of a new product.[7]

capable competitors. The combination of low barriers to imitation and many capable competitors makes rapid imitation almost certain. The innovator's lack of complementary assets further suggests that an imitator will soon capture the innovator's competitive advantage. Given these factors, since rapid diffusion of the innovator's technology through imitation is inevitable, by licensing out its technology the innovator can at least share in some of the benefits of this diffusion.[8]

7.5 STRATEGY IN MATURE INDUSTRIES

As a result of fierce competition in the shakeout stage, an industry becomes consolidated, and so a mature industry is often dominated by a small number of large companies. Although it may also contain medium-sized companies and a host of small specialized ones, the large companies determine the nature of industry competition because they can influence the five competitive forces.

Indeed, these are the companies that developed the most successful generic competitive strategies to manage the industry environment.

By the end of the shakeout stage, strategic groups of companies pursuing similar generic competitive strategies have emerged in the industry. For example, all the companies pursuing a low-cost strategy can be viewed as composing one strategic group. All those pursuing differentiation constitute another, and the focusers form a third. Companies have learned to analyze each other's strategies, and they know that their competitive actions will stimulate a competitive response from rivals in their strategic group and from companies in other groups that may be threatened by these actions. For example, a differentiator that starts to lower prices because it has adopted a more efficient technology not only threatens other differentiators in its group, but also threatens low-cost companies, which see their competitive edge being eroded. Hence, by the mature stage of the industry life cycle, *companies have learned the meaning of competitive interdependence.*

In mature industries, companies choose competitive moves to maximize their competitive advantage *within the structure of industry competition.* Indeed, to understand business-level strategy in mature industries, one must understand how large companies try to collectively stabilize industry competition to prevent entry, industry overcapacity, or cutthroat price competition, which would hurt all companies. (These efforts are indirect since explicit collusion among companies violates antitrust law.) The generic strategy pursued by one company directly affects other companies because companies are competing against one another in the same industry. How, then, can companies manage industry competition so as to *simultaneously* protect their individual competitive advantage *and* maintain industry rules that preserve industry profitability? (Remember that no generic strategy will generate above-average profits if competitive forces are so strong that companies are at the mercy of each other, powerful suppliers, and powerful customers.)

They can do so by using competitive moves and techniques to reduce the threat of each competitive force. In the next section, we examine the various price and nonprice methods that companies use—first, to deter entry into an industry, and second, to reduce the level of industry rivalry. We then discuss methods that companies employ to gain more control over suppliers and buyers.

7.6 STRATEGIES TO DETER ENTRY IN MATURE INDUSTRIES

Industry companies can utilize three main methods to deter entry by potential rivals and hence maintain and increase industry profitability. As Figure 7.2 shows, these methods are product proliferation, price cutting, and maintaining excess capacity.

Product Proliferation

Companies seldom produce just one product. Most commonly, they produce a range of products aimed at different market segments so that they have broad product lines. Sometimes, to reduce the threat of entry, companies tailor their range of products to fill a wide range of niches, thus creating a barrier to entry

Figure 7.2
Strategies for Deterring Entry

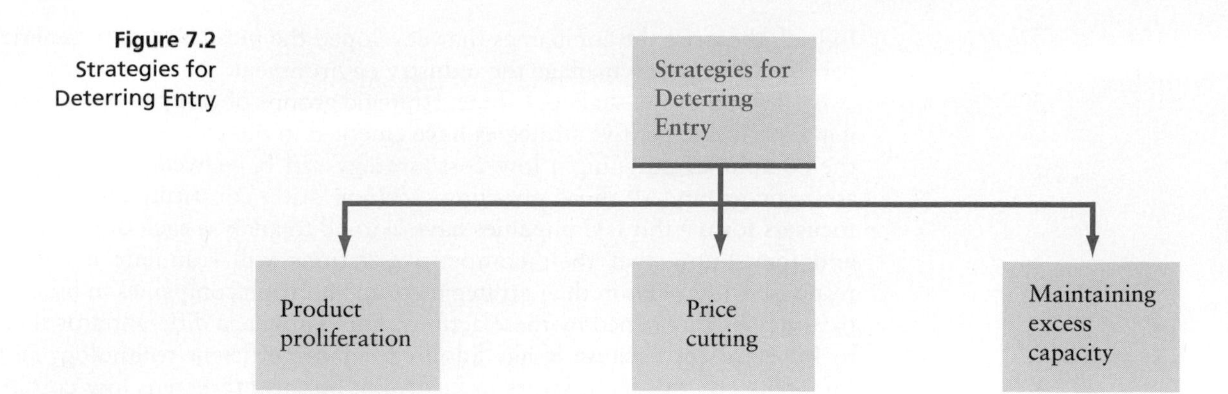

by potential competitors.[9] This strategy of pursuing a broad product line to deter entry is known as **product proliferation**.

Because the large U.S. carmakers were so slow to fill the small-car niches, they were vulnerable to the entry of the Japanese into these market segments in the United States. They really had no excuse for this situation, for in their European operations they had a long history of small-car manufacturing. They should have seen the opening and filled it ten years earlier, but their view was that small cars meant small profits. In the breakfast cereal industry, on the other hand, competition is based on the production of new kinds of cereal to satisfy or create new consumer desires. Thus the number of breakfast cereals proliferates, making it very difficult for prospective entrants to attack a new market segment.

Figure 7.3 indicates how product proliferation can deter entry. It depicts product space in the restaurant industry along two dimensions: (1) atmosphere, which ranges from fast food to candlelight dining, and (2) quality of food, which ranges from average to gourmet. The circles represent product spaces filled by restaurants located along the two dimensions. Thus McDonald's is situated in the average quality/fast-food area. A gap in the product space gives a potential entrant or an existing rival an opportunity to enter the market and make inroads. The shaded unoccupied product space represents areas where new restaurants can enter the market. However, filling all the product spaces creates a barrier to entry and makes it much more difficult for an entrant to gain a foothold in the market and differentiate itself.

Price Cutting

In some situations, pricing strategies involving price cutting can be used to deter entry by other companies, thus protecting the profit margins of companies already in an industry. For example, one price-cutting strategy is to initially charge a high price for a product and seize short-term profits, but then to aggressively cut prices in order to simultaneously build market share *and* deter potential entrants.[10] The incumbent companies signal to potential entrants that if they do enter the industry, the incumbents will use their competitive advantage to drive down prices to a level where new companies will be unable to cover their costs.[11] This pricing strategy also allows a company to ride down the experience

Figure 7.3
Product Proliferation in the Restaurant Industry

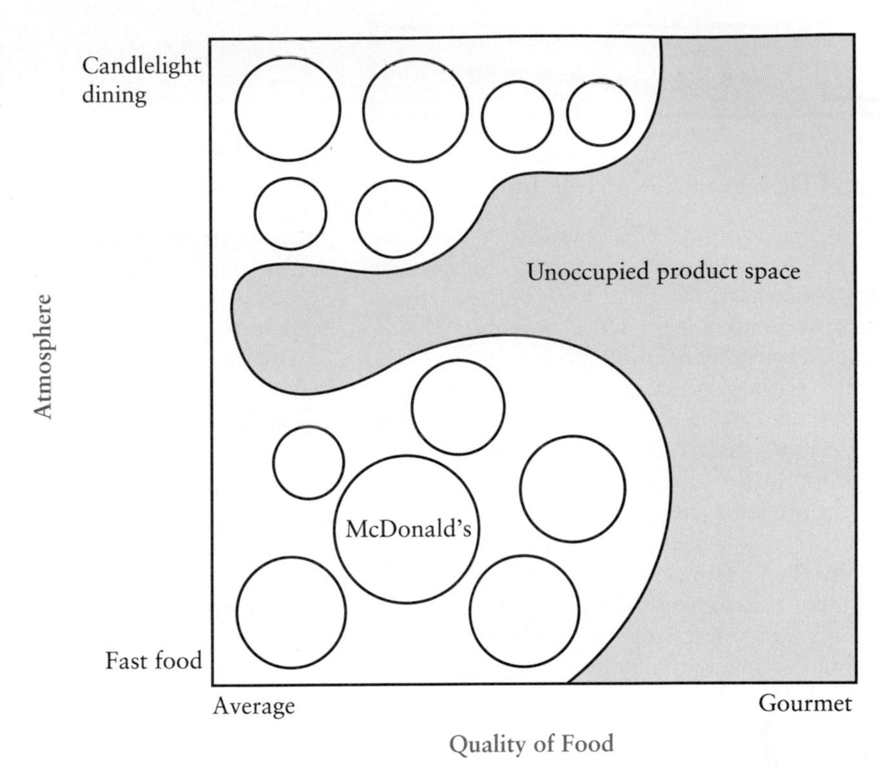

curve and obtain substantial economies of scale. Since costs would be falling along with prices, profit margins could still be maintained.

Still, this strategy is unlikely to deter a strong potential competitor—an established company that is trying to find profitable investment opportunities in other industries. For example, it is difficult to imagine a 3M being afraid to enter an industry because companies there threaten to drive down prices. A company like 3M has the resources to withstand any short-term losses. Hence, it may be in the interests of incumbent companies to accept new entry gracefully, giving up market share gradually to the new entrants to prevent price wars from developing.

Most evidence suggests that companies first skim the market and charge high prices during the growth stage, maximizing short-run profits.[12] Then they move to increase their market share and charge a lower price to rapidly expand the market, develop a reputation, and obtain economies of scale, driving down costs and barring entry. As competitors do enter, the incumbent companies reduce prices to retard entry and give up market share to create a stable industry context, where they can use nonprice competitive methods to maximize long-run profits. At that point, nonprice competition becomes the main basis of industry competition, and prices are quite likely to rise as competition stabilizes. Thus decisions on competitive pricing and product differentiation are linked; they are determined by the way a company manages its generic strategy to maximize profits when companies are highly interdependent. The airline industry, discussed in Strategy in Action 7.2, offers an illustration of how and when companies use these techniques both to build entry barriers to stave off new entrants and reduce rivalry.

STRATEGY IN ACTION 7.2

Ups and Downs in the Airline Industry

Before deregulation in 1978, competition over fares and ticket prices was not permitted in the airline industry, and the airlines had to find other ways to compete for customers. Their response was to attract customers by offering more frequent flights and better service. However, since they all imitated one another, no airline was able to get a competitive advantage over its rivals, and each airline's costs rose dramatically because of the cost of extra flights, improved meals, and so on. To cover the higher costs, the airlines constantly applied for fare increases. As a result, customers paid higher and higher fares to compensate for the airlines' inefficiency. In an attempt to cure this problem, Congress decided to deregulate the industry, allowing competition over ticket prices and free entry into the industry. The airlines did not want deregulation. (Why should they? They were receiving a nice profit as a protected industry.) But deregulation did take place in 1979, and the result was chaos.

Deregulation destroyed the old competitive rules of the game. Before deregulation, the major airlines knew how they could compete and were able to signal their intentions to one another so that they understood each other's competitive moves. In the new world of price competition, entry into the industry was easy, and a host of small airlines entered to compete with the majors. During regulation no airline had had to develop a generic strategy. There had been no incentive to keep costs low because cost increases could be passed on to consumers. In addition, all firms had used the same means to differentiate themselves, so that no airline had a competitive advantage in being unique. With no rules to tell them how to compete and no experience of free competition, the airlines waged a price war as new, low-cost entrants like People Express and Southwest Air sought to gain market share from the majors.

For several years price competition remained the principal competitive behavior in the airline industry, and the result was a low level of industry profitability. Most airlines lost money. However, by 1988 the airline industry had gone through a shakeout. Many of the new entrants that had precipitated the crisis had either gone bankrupt because of the price wars or had been swallowed up by the majors. The majors had also developed sophisticated business-level strategies based on the development of hub-and-spoke networks, which allowed them to build national route structures at low cost. These networks made it difficult for new firms to enter the industry because the majors held all the available gates at large airports. Through all these means, the majors had created new barriers to entry and therefore reduced the threat of new entrants. They were thus in a position to develop new competitive rules of the game to stabilize industry competition and prevent price competition.

Inside the industry, the majors also adopted competitive techniques to reduce the level of competitive rivalry. Very quickly the airlines imitated one another's pricing policies. On most route segments the prices charged by the airlines diverged by less than 5 percent, and the airlines used market signaling to communicate their intention of making changes such as raising prices. By 1990 the airlines also jointly started a policy of issuing nonrefundable tickets to reduce their costs and transfer risk to the consumer.[13]

Although all these price and nonprice techniques have reduced the number of new entrants and the level of rivalry, the airline industry is still not profitable. There is still overcapacity in the industry, which is dragging down industry profits, and many airlines are suffering losses. Nevertheless, the airlines collectively would be in a much worse position if they had not developed these techniques for managing their environment.

Maintaining Excess Capacity

A further competitive technique that allows companies to deter entry is to maintain a certain amount of excess productive capacity. As you will see in the next section, excess capacity is a major factor affecting the level of competition in an industry because it may lead to price cutting and reduced industry profitability. However, existing companies may prefer to possess some limited amount of excess capacity because it serves to warn potential entrants that if they enter the industry, existing firms can retaliate by increasing output and forcing down prices until entry would become unprofitable. But the threat to increase output has to be *credible*; collectively, industry incumbents must be able to quickly raise the level of production if entry appears likely. Thus some level of excess capacity might be preferred by firms in the industry.

7.7 STRATEGIES TO MANAGE RIVALRY IN MATURE INDUSTRIES

Beyond seeking to deter entry, companies also wish to utilize strategies to manage their competitive interdependence and decrease rivalry because unrestricted competition over prices or output will reduce the level of company and industry profitability. Several strategies are available to companies to manage industry relations. The most important are price signaling, price leadership, nonprice competition, and capacity control.

Price Signaling

All industries start out fragmented, with small companies battling for market share. Then, over time, the leading players emerge, and companies start to interpret each other's competitive moves. **Price signaling** is the first means by which companies attempt to structure industry competition in order to control rivalry among competitors.[14] Price signaling is the process by which companies convey their intentions to other companies about pricing strategy and how they will compete in the future or how they will react to the competitive moves of their rivals. There are several ways in which price signaling can help companies defend their generic competitive strategies.

First, companies may use price signaling to announce that they will respond vigorously to hostile competitive moves that threaten them. For example, companies may signal that if one company starts to cut prices aggressively, they will respond in kind to maintain the status quo and prevent any company from gaining a competitive advantage. Similarly, as noted in the last section, companies may signal to potential entrants that if the latter do enter the market, they will fight back by reducing prices or by other aggressive competitive moves. Thus price signaling *protects the existing structure of competitive advantage* by deterring potential imitators that may attempt to copy other companies' generic strategies.

A second, and very important, purpose of price signaling is to indirectly allow companies to coordinate their actions and avoid costly competitive moves that lead to a breakdown in industry pricing policy. One company may signal that it intends to lower prices because it wishes to attract customers who are switching to the products of another industry, not because it wishes to stimulate a price war. On the other hand, signaling can be used to improve industry profitability. The airline industry is a good example of the power of price signaling. In the

1980s signals of lower prices set off price wars, but in the 1990s the airlines have used price signaling to obtain uniform price increases. Nonrefundable tickets, too, originated as a market signal by one company that was quickly copied by all other companies in the industry. In sum, price signaling allows companies to give information to one another which enables them to understand one another's competitive product/market strategy and make coordinated, competitive moves.

Price Leadership

Price leadership—the taking on by one company of the responsibility for setting industry prices—is another way of using price signaling to enhance the profitability of product/market policy among companies in a mature industry.[15] By setting prices, the industry leader implicitly creates the price standards that other companies will follow. The price leader is generally the strongest company in the industry, the one with the best ability to threaten other companies that might cut prices or increase their output to seize more market share. For example, vast oil reserves made Saudi Arabia the price leader in the oil industry. This position allowed it to threaten that if other countries raised their output, it would do likewise, even though the price of oil would decline. Similarly, De Beers controls the price of diamonds because it controls their worldwide distribution.

Formal price leadership, or price setting by companies jointly, is illegal under antitrust laws, so the process of price leadership is often very subtle. In the auto industry, for example, auto prices are set by imitation. The price set by the weakest company—that is, the one with the highest costs—is often used as the basis for competitors' pricing. Thus U.S. carmakers set their prices, and Japanese carmakers then set theirs with reference to the U.S. prices. The Japanese are happy to do this because they have lower costs than U.S. companies and are making higher profits than U.S. carmakers without competing with them by price. Pricing is done by market segment. The prices of different auto models in the model range indicate the customer segments that the companies are aiming for and the price range they believe the market segment can tolerate. Each manufacturer prices a model in the segment with reference to the prices charged by its competitors, not by reference to competitors' costs. Price leadership thus helps differentiators charge a premium price and helps low-cost companies by increasing their margins. Thus it makes a combined low-cost/differentiation strategy very profitable.

Price leadership can stabilize industry relations by preventing head-to-head competition, and it raises the level of industry profitability so that companies have funds for future investments and good returns to shareholders. Price leadership has its dangers, however. It helps companies with high costs, allowing them to survive without becoming more productive or more efficient. Thus it may foster complacency: companies may keep extracting profits without reinvesting any to improve their productivity. In the long term, such behavior will make them vulnerable to new entrants that have lower costs because they have developed new productive techniques. That is what happened in the U.S. auto and the electronics industries when the Japanese entered these markets. After years of tacit price fixing, with General Motors as the leader, the carmakers were subjected to growing low-cost Japanese competition, to which they were unable to respond. Indeed, many U.S. auto companies have survived in the new competitive environment only because the Japanese carmakers were foreign firms. If they had been new U.S. entrants, the government would probably not have taken steps to protect them and Chrysler, and Ford and General Motors would be much smaller companies.

Table 7.2
Four Non-Price Competitive Strategies

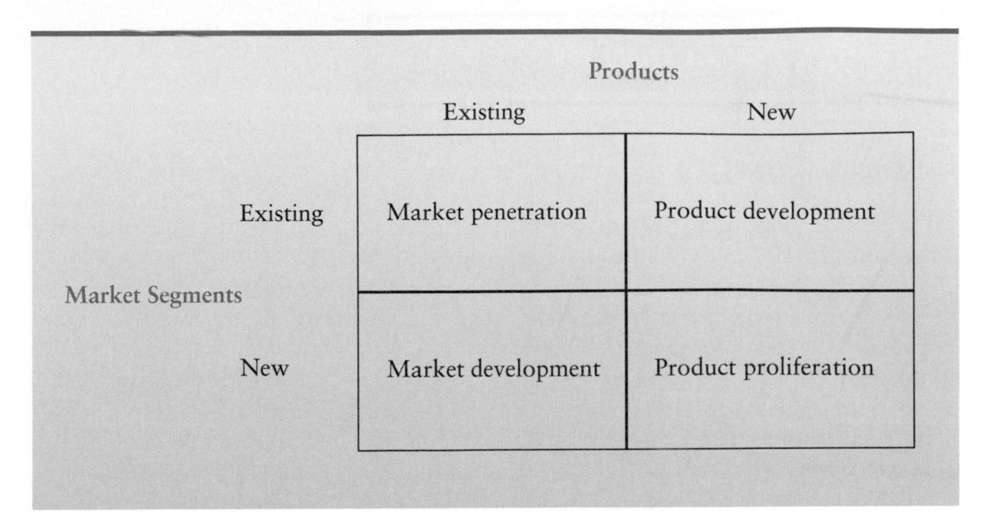

		Products	
		Existing	New
Market Segments	Existing	Market penetration	Product development
	New	Market development	Product proliferation

Nonprice Competition

A third very important aspect of product/market strategy in mature industries is the use of nonprice competition to manage industry rivalry. Applying various techniques to try to prevent costly price cutting and price wars does not preclude competition by product differentiation. In many industries, product differentiation is used as the principal competitive weapon to prevent competitors from obtaining access to a company's customers and attacking its market share. In other words, companies rely on product differentiation to deter potential entrants and manage industry rivalry. It allows them to compete for market share by offering products with different or superior features or by applying different marketing techniques. In Table 7.2, product and market segment dimensions are used to identify four nonprice competitive strategies based on product differentiation. (Notice that in this model we are considering new market segments, not new markets.)

Market Penetration When a company concentrates on expanding market share in its existing product markets, it is engaging in a strategy of market penetration.[16] Market penetration involves advertising to promote and build product differentiation. In a mature industry, the thrust of advertising is to influence consumer brand choice and create a brand name reputation for the company and its products. In this way, a company can increase its market share by attracting the customers of its rivals. Because brand name products often command premium prices, building market share in this situation is very profitable.

In some mature industries—for example, the soap and detergent, disposable diapers, and brewing industries—a market penetration strategy often becomes a way of life.[17] In these industries, all companies engage in intensive advertising and battle for market share. Each company fears that by not advertising it will lose market share to rivals. Consequently, in the soap and detergent industry, for instance, more than 10 percent of sales revenues go into advertising, with the aim of maintaining and perhaps building market share. These huge advertising outlays constitute a barrier to entry for prospective entrants. As Strategy in Action 7.3 details, Toys Я Us rose to prominence in the retail toy market by pursuing a market penetration strategy.

STRATEGY IN ACTION 7.3

Warfare in Toyland

Toys Я Us, based in Paramus, New Jersey, grew at an astonishing 25 percent annual rate throughout the 1980s and today holds a 20 percent share of the $15 billion toy retail market, which makes it the industry leader. To reach its dominant industry position, the company used a strategy of market penetration based on developing a nationwide chain of retail outlets and a cost-leadership strategy. To lower costs, Toys Я Us developed efficient materials management techniques for ordering and distributing toys to its stores. It also provided only a low level of customer service. Together, these moves allowed it to obtain a very low—17 percent—expense-to-sales ratio. Toys Я Us then used its low costs to promote an everyday low pricing philosophy. The company deliberately set out to undercut the prices of its rivals, and it succeeded, for its two largest competitors in the 1980s, Child World, Inc., and Lionel Corp., went bankrupt. Pursuing a market penetration strategy based on low cost thus brought spectacular results for Toys Я Us.

In the 1990s, however, the company's commanding position is being threatened by a new set of rivals, which are also pursuing market penetration strategies. Companies like Wal-Mart, Kmart, and Target are rapidly expanding the number of their stores and trying to beat Toys Я Us at its own game by selling toys at prices that are often below those of Toys Я Us. Indeed, Wal-Mart has more than doubled its share of the toy market—to over 13 percent—and both Kmart's and Target's sales are rapidly increasing. This new competition is squeezing profits for Toys Я Us, and the company is now turning to nonprice competition to attract customers. For example, Toys Я Us is promoting its wide range of products as a competitive advantage; it carries over 16,000 items as against 2,000 at a typical discount store. It has also decided to increase the level of customer service by offering customers more personalized attention. By emphasizing quality and customer responsiveness, as well as low price, the company seeks to fend off the new challenge from the discount stores and maintain its growth in the 1990s.[18]

Product Development Product development is the creation of new or improved products to replace existing ones.[19] The wet shaving industry exemplifies an industry that depends on product replacement to create successive waves of consumer demand, which then create new sources of revenue for industry companies. In 1989, for instance, Gillette came out with its new Sensor shaving system, giving a massive boost to its market share. In turn, Wilkinson Sword responded with its version of the product.

Product development is important for maintaining product differentiation and building market share. For instance, the laundry detergent Tide has gone through more than fifty different changes in formulation during the past forty years to improve its performance. The product is always advertised as Tide, but it is a different product each year. The battle over diet colas is another interesting example of competitive product differentiation by product development. Royal Crown Cola developed Diet Rite, the first diet cola. However, Coca-Cola and Pepsico responded quickly with their versions of the soft drink and, by massive advertising, soon took over the market. Refining and improving products is an important element in defending a company's generic competitive strategy in a mature industry, but this kind of competition can be as vicious as a price war.

Market signaling to competitors can also be an important part of a product development strategy. One company may let the others know that it is proceed-

ing with product innovations that will provide a competitive advantage that the others will be unable to imitate effectively because their entry into the market will be too late. For example, software companies like Microsoft often announce new operating systems years in advance. The purpose of such an announcement is to deter prospective competitors from making the huge investments needed to compete with the industry leaders and to let its customers know that the company still has the competitive edge so important to retaining customer loyalty. However, preemptive signaling can backfire, as IBM found out when it announced that its PS/2 operating system would not be compatible with the operating systems presently standard in the industry. Other companies in the industry collectively signaled to IBM and IBM's customers that they would band together to protect the existing operation systems, thus preserving industry standards and preventing IBM from obtaining a competitive advantage from its new technology. IBM subsequently backed down. If a preemptive move is to succeed, competitors must believe that a company will act according to its signals and stick to its position. If the threat is not credible, the signaling company weakens its position.

Market Development Market development involves finding new market segments for a company's products. A company pursuing this strategy wants to capitalize on the brand name it has developed in one market segment by locating new market segments in which to compete. In this way, it can exploit the product differentiation advantages of its brand name. The Japanese auto manufacturers offer an interesting example of the use of market development. When they first entered the market, each Japanese manufacturer offered cars aimed at the economy segments of the auto market. Thus both the Toyota Corolla and the Honda Accord were aimed at the small economy car segment. However, over time, the Japanese upgraded each car, and now each is directed at a more expensive market segment. The Accord is a leading contender in the midsize luxury sedan segment, while the Corolla fills the small-car segment that used to be occupied by the Celica, which is now aimed at a sportier market segment. By redefining their product offerings, Japanese manufacturers have profitably developed their market segments and successfully attacked their industry rivals, wresting market share from these companies. Although the Japanese used to compete primarily as low-cost producers, market development has allowed them to become differentiators as well.

Product Proliferation Product proliferation can be used to manage industry rivalry, as well as to deter entry. The strategy of product proliferation generally means that large companies in an industry all have a product in each market segment or niche and compete head-to-head for customers. If a new niche develops, like convertibles or oat bran cereals, then the leader gets a first-mover advantage, but soon all the other companies catch up, and once again competition is stabilized and industry rivalry is reduced. Product proliferation thus allows the development of stable industry competition based on product differentiation, not price—that is, nonprice competition based on the development of new products. The battle is over a product's perceived quality and uniqueness, not over its price.

Capacity Control Although nonprice competition helps mature industries avoid the cutthroat competing that reduces both company and industry levels of

profitability, in some industries price competition does periodically break out. This occurs most commonly when there is industry overcapacity, that is, when companies collectively produce too much output so that reducing price is the only way to dispose of it. If one company starts to cut prices, then the others quickly follow because they fear that the price cutter will be able to sell all its inventory and they will be left holding unwanted goods. Capacity control strategies can influence the level of industry output. They are the last set of strategies for managing industry rivalry that we discuss in this chapter.

Excess capacity may be caused by a shortfall in demand, as when a recession lowers the demand for automobiles and causes companies to give customers price incentives. In that situation, companies can do nothing except wait for better times. However, by and large excess capacity results from industry companies' simultaneous response to favorable conditions: they all invest in new plants to be able to take advantage of the predicted upsurge in demand. Paradoxically, each individual company's effort to outperform the others means that collectively the companies create industry overcapacity, which hurts them all. Figure 7.4 illustrates this situation. Although demand is rising, the consequence of each company's decision to increase capacity is a surge in industry capacity, which drives down prices.

To prevent the accumulation of costly excess capacity, companies must devise strategies that let them control—or at least benefit from—capacity expansion programs. Before we examine these strategies, however, we need to consider in greater detail the factors that cause excess capacity.[20]

Factors Causing Excess Capacity Capacity problems often derive from technological factors. Sometimes new, low-cost technology sometimes is the culprit because, to prevent being left behind, all companies introduce it simultaneously. A capacity problem occurs because the old technology is still being

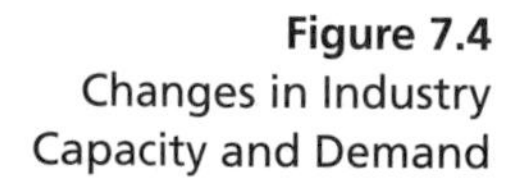
Figure 7.4
Changes in Industry Capacity and Demand

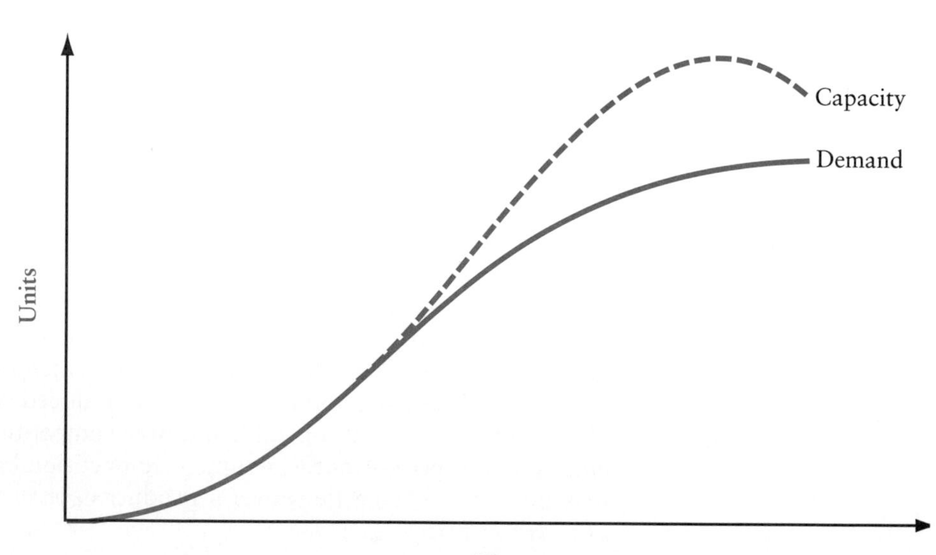

used to produce output. In addition, new technology is often introduced in large increments, which generate overcapacity. For instance, an airline that needs more seats on a route must add another plane, thereby adding hundreds of seats even though only fifty are needed. To take another example, a new chemical process may operate efficiently only at the rate of a 1,000 gallons a day, whereas the previous process was efficient at 500 gallons a day. If all industry companies change technologies, industry capacity doubles and enormous problems result.

Industry competitive factors also cause overcapacity. Obviously, entry into an industry is such a factor. Japan's entry into the semiconductor industry caused massive overcapacity and price declines in microchips. Similarly, the collapse of OPEC was due to the entry of new countries able to produce oil at competitive prices. Sometimes the age of a company's plant is the source of the problem. For example, in the hotel industry, given the rapidity with which the quality of hotel furnishings declines, customers are always attracted to new hotels. The building of new hotel chains alongside the old chains, however, can cause excess capacity. Often companies are simply making simultaneous competitive moves based on industry trends, but those moves eventually lead to head-to-head competition. Most fast-food chains, for instance, establish new outlets whenever demographic data show population increases. However, they seem to forget that all chains use such data. Thus a locality that has no fast-food outlets may suddenly see several being built at the same time. Whether they can all survive depends on the growth rate of demand relative to the growth rate of the fast-food chains.

Choosing a Capacity Control Strategy Given the various ways in which capacity can expand, clearly companies need to find some means of controlling it. If they are always plagued by price cutting and price wars, companies will be unable to recoup the investments in their generic strategies. Low industry profitability caused by overcapacity forces not just the weakest companies, but sometimes major players as well, to exit the industry. In general, companies have two strategic choices: (1) each company individually must try to preempt its rivals and seize the initiative, or (2) the companies collectively must find indirect means of coordinating with each other so that they are all aware of the mutual effects of their actions.

To *preempt* rivals, a company must forecast a large increase in demand in the product market and then move rapidly to establish large-scale operations that will be able to satisfy the predicted demand. By achieving a first-mover advantage, the company may deter other firms from entering the market since the preemptor will usually be able to move down the experience curve, reduce its costs and therefore its prices as well, and threaten a price war if necessary.

This strategy, however, is extremely risky, for it involves investing resources in a generic strategy before the extent and profitability of the future market are clear. Wal-Mart, with its strategy of locating in small rural towns to tap an underexploited market for discount goods, has preempted Sears and Kmart. Wal-Mart has been able to engage in market penetration and market expansion because of the secure base it established in its rural strongholds.

A preemptive strategy is also risky if it does not deter competitors, and they decide to enter the market. If they have a stronger generic strategy or more

resources, like AT&T or IBM, they can make the preemptor suffer. Thus, for the strategy to succeed, the preemptor must generally be a credible company with enough resources to withstand a possible price war.

As for *coordination* as a capacity control strategy, collusion on the timing of new investments is illegal under antitrust law, but tacit coordination is practiced in many industries as companies attempt to understand and forecast the competitive moves of their rivals. Generally, companies use market signaling to secure coordination. They make announcements about their future investment decisions in trade journals and newspapers. In addition, they share information about their production levels and their forecasts of industry demand so as to bring industry supply and demand into equilibrium. Thus a coordination strategy reduces the risks associated with investment in the industry.

7.8 SUPPLY AND DISTRIBUTION STRATEGY IN MATURE INDUSTRIES

As you saw in Chapter 3, when an industry becomes consolidated and comprises a few large companies, it gains strength vis-à-vis its suppliers and customers. Suppliers become dependent on the industry for buying their inputs, and customers for obtaining industry outputs. By the mature stage, in order to protect market share and improve product quality, many companies want to take over more of the distribution of their products and control the source of inputs crucial to the production process. When they seek ownership of supply or distribution operations, they are pursuing a strategy of vertical integration, which is considered in detail in Chapter 9. Here we discuss how the choice of a means of controlling the relationships between a company and its suppliers and distributors is an important determinant of the way in which a company supports its generic strategy and develops a competitive advantage.

By controlling supplier and distributor relationships, a company can ensure its ability to dispose of its outputs or acquire inputs in a timely, reliable manner, and therefore it can reduce costs and improve product quality. One way to analyze the issues involved in choosing a distribution/supplier strategy is to contrast the situation that exists between a company and its suppliers and distributors in Japan with the situation that exists in the United States. In this country, it is normal for a company and its suppliers to have an antagonistic relationship. Each tries to drive the best bargain to make the most profit. Moreover, the relationship between a company's buyers and suppliers tends to be superficial and anonymous because purchasing and distribution personnel are routinely rotated to prevent kickbacks. In contrast, in Japan, the relationship between a company and its suppliers and distributors is based on long-term personal relationships and trust. Suppliers in Japan are sensitive to the needs of the company, respond quickly to changes in the specification of inputs, and adjust supply to meet the requirements of a company's just-in-time inventory system. The results of this close relationship are lower costs and the ability to respond to unexpected changes in customers' demand. The close supplier/distributor relationship supports Japanese companies' generic strategy. Clearly, it pays a company to develop a long-term strategy toward its suppliers and distributors.

STRATEGY IN ACTION 7.4

Compaq and Dell Go Head-to-Head in Distribution

As new developments in technology alter the nature of competition in the personal computer industry, the distribution strategies of its major players are also changing. These changes are evident in the struggle between Dell Computer Corp. and Compaq Computer Corp. for the domination of the personal computer market. Founded by a team of engineers, Compaq has from the start emphasized the engineering and research side of the PC business. For example, it was the first company to bring out a computer using Intel's new 486 chip. Its differentiation strategy was to produce high-end PCs based on the newest technology, which would command a premium price. Compaq specialized in the business market and it developed a sophisticated dealer network to distribute, sell, and service its expensive PCs.

Dell, on the other hand, focused from the beginning on the marketing and distribution end of the PC business. Its low-cost strategy was to assemble a PC and then sell it through mail-order outlets directly to consumers, cutting out the dealer in order to offer the consumer a rock-bottom price. The company was viewed by its managers primarily as a distribution or mail-order company and not an engineering one.

As computers increasingly became commodity products and prices fell drastically, Compaq realized that its strategy of selling only through high-priced dealers would mean disaster. It changed its strategy to produce a low-cost computer and in 1993 began its own mail-order distribution, offering its machines directly to customers. Its new low-cost distribution strategy has been very successful, but as a result, Compaq is now battling Dell for the same customers. To compete, each company is advertising its ability to serve customers more quickly and efficiently than the other—for example, by offering next day delivery and installation of computers and by offering extended warranties. For these companies, their distribution and sales strategies have become a vital part of the competitive game.[21]

A company has many options to choose from in deciding on the appropriate way to distribute its products to gain a competitive advantage. It may distribute its products to an independent distributor, which in turn distributes them to retailers. Or a company might distribute directly to retailers or even to customers. As Strategy in Action 7.4 illustrates, companies may also need to change their distribution strategies as the industry changes.

In general, the complexity of a product and the amount of information needed about its operation and maintenance determine the distribution strategy chosen. For example, carmakers typically use franchisees rather than a general car dealership to control the distribution of their autos. The reason is the high level of after-sales service and support needed to satisfy customers. Carmakers are able to penalize franchisees by withholding cars from a dealership if customer complaints rise; thus they have effective control over franchisee behavior. Also by controlling the franchisees, they can tailor price and nonprice competition to industry conditions, and this allows the large carmakers to coordinate their actions by controlling effectively the thousands of separate dealerships across the country.

On the other hand, the large electronics manufacturers and the producers of consumer durables like appliances generally prefer to use a network of distribu-

tors to control distribution. To enhance market share and control the way products are sold and serviced, manufacturers choose five or six large distributors per state to control distribution. The distributors are required to carry the full line of a company's products and invest in after-sales service facilities. The result is that the manufacturer receives good feedback on how its products are selling, and the distributor becomes knowledgeable about a company's products and thus helps the company maintain and increase its control over the market. The company is able to discipline its distributors if they start to discount prices or otherwise threaten the company's reputation or generic strategy.

Large manufacturers like Johnson & Johnson, Procter & Gamble, and General Foods typically sell directly to a retailer and avoid giving profits to a distributor or wholesaler. They do so in part because they have lower profit margins than the makers of electronic equipment and consumer durables. However, this strategy also allows them to influence a retailer's behavior directly. For example, they can refuse to supply a particular product that a retailer wants unless the retailer stocks the entire range of the company's products. In addition, the companies are assured of shelf space for new products. Coca-Cola and Pepsico are two companies that are able to influence retailers to reduce the shelf space given to competing products or even to exclude them. They can do so because soft drinks have the highest profit margins of any product sold in supermarkets. Gallo is one of the few winemakers that controls the distribution and retailing of their own products. This is one reason Gallo is so consistently profitable.

In sum, devising the appropriate strategy for acquiring inputs and disposing of outputs is a crucial part of competitive strategy in mature industry environments. Companies can gain a competitive advantage through the way they choose to control their relationships with distributors and suppliers. By choosing the right strategy, they are able to control their costs, their price and nonprice strategies, and their reputation and product quality. These are crucial issues in mature industries.

7.9 STRATEGY IN DECLINING INDUSTRIES

Sooner or later many industries enter into a decline stage, in which the size of the total market starts to shrink. Examples include the railroad industry, the tobacco industry, and the steel industry. Industries start declining for a number of reasons, including technological change, social trends, and demographic shifts. The railroad and steel industries began to decline when technological changes brought viable substitutes for the products these industries manufactured. The advent of the internal combustion engine drove the railroad industry into decline, and the steel industry fell into decline with the rise of plastics and composite materials. As for the tobacco industry, changing social attitudes toward smoking, which are themselves a product of growing concerns about the health effects of smoking, have caused decline.

There are four main strategies that companies can adopt to deal with decline: (1) a **leadership strategy**, that is, seeking to become the dominant player in a declining industry; (2) a **niche strategy**, which focuses on pockets of demand that are declining more slowly than the industry as a whole; (3) a **harvest strategy**,

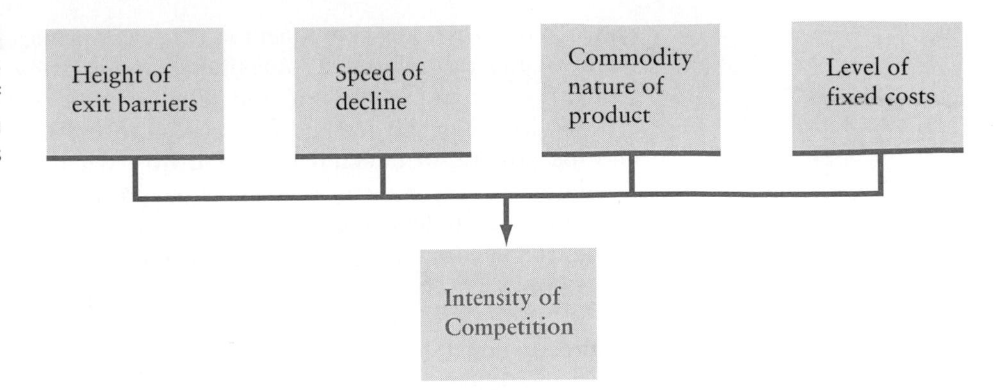

Figure 7.5
Factors That Determine the Intensity of Competition in Declining Industries

which optimizes cash flow; and (4) a **divestment strategy**, or selling off the business to others. We examine each of these strategies in detail later. For the time being, note that the choice of strategy depends in part on the severity of the increase in competitive intensity that comes about as a result of decline. We will look at this issue first before turning our attention to the choice of strategy.

The Severity of Decline

Because the size of the total market is shrinking, competition tends to intensify in a declining industry and profit rates tend to fall. The intensity of competition in a declining industry depends on four critical factors, indicated in Figure 7.5. First, the intensity of competition is greater in industries where decline is rapid as opposed to industries, such as tobacco, where decline is slow and gradual. Second, the intensity of competition is greater in declining industries where exit barriers are high. As you recall from Chapter 3, high exit barriers keep companies locked into an industry even when demand is falling. The result is the emergence of excess productive capacity, and hence an increased probability of fierce price competition. Third, and related to the previous point, the intensity of competition is greater in declining industries where fixed costs are high (as in the steel industry). The reason is that the need to cover fixed costs, such as the costs of maintaining productive capacity, can make companies try to utilize any excess capacity they have by slashing prices—an action that can trigger a price war. Finally, the intensity of competition is greater in declining industries where the product is perceived as a commodity—as it is in the steel industry—in contrast to industries where differentiation gives rise to significant brand loyalty, as was true until very recently of the declining tobacco industry.

Not all segments of an industry typically decline at the same rate. In some segments, demand may remain reasonably strong, despite decline elsewhere. The steel industry illustrates this situation. Although bulk steel products, such as sheet steel, have suffered a general decline, demand has actually risen for specialty steels, such as those used in high-speed machine tools. Vacuum tubes provide another example. Although demand for them collapsed when transistors

replaced them as a key component in many electronics products, for years afterward vacuum tubes still had some limited applications in radar equipment. Consequently, demand in this vacuum tube segment remained strong despite the general decline in the demand for vacuum tubes. The point, then, is that there may be **pockets of demand** in an industry where demand is declining more slowly than in the industry as a whole or not declining at all. Price competition thus may be far less intense among the companies serving such pockets of demand than within the industry as a whole.

Choosing a Strategy

As already noted, four main strategies are available to companies in a declining industry: a leadership strategy, a niche strategy, a harvest strategy, and a divestment strategy. Figure 7.6 provides a simple framework for guiding strategic choice. Note that intensity of competition in the declining industry is measured on the vertical axis, and company strengths *relative* to remaining pockets of demand on the horizontal axis.

Leadership Strategy

A leadership strategy involves growing in a declining industry by picking up the share of companies that are leaving the industry. This strategy makes most sense when the company has distinctive strengths that allow it to capture market share in a declining industry, and when the speed of decline and the intensity of competition in the declining industry are moderate.

Figure 7.6
Strategy Selection in a Declining Industry

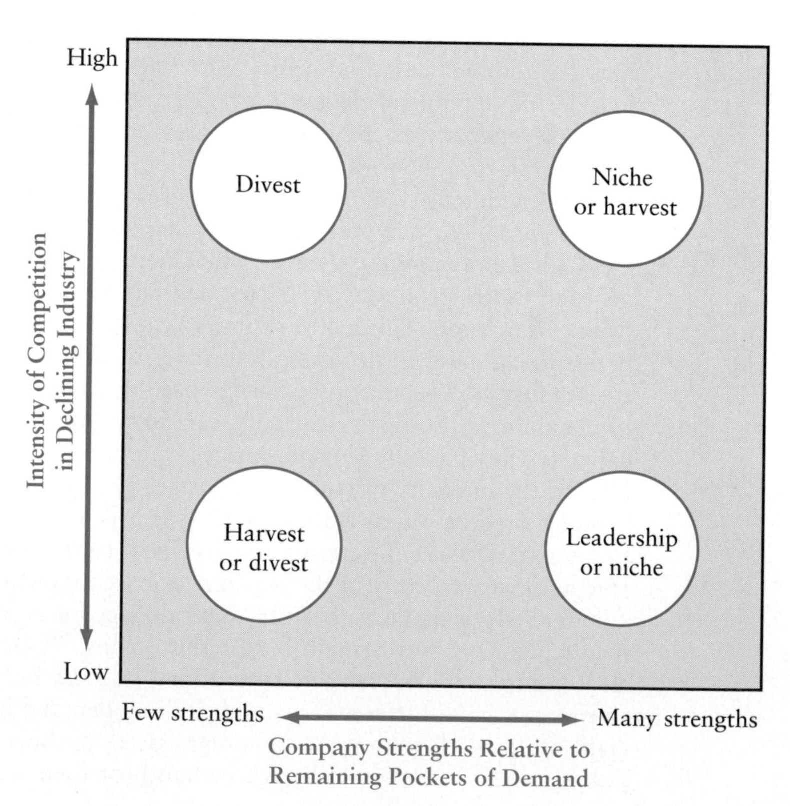

STRATEGY IN ACTION 7.5

How to Make Money in Vacuum Tubes

At its peak in the early 1950s the vacuum tube business was a major industry, in which companies such as Westinghouse, General Electric, RCA, and Western Electric had a large stake. Then along came the transistor, making most vacuum tubes obsolete, and one by one all the big companies exited the industry. One company, however, Richardson Electronics, not only stayed in the business, but also demonstrated that high returns are possible in a declining industry. Primarily a distributor, although it does have some manufacturing capabilities, Richardson Electronics bought the remains of a dozen companies in the United States and Europe as they exited the vacuum tube industry. Richardson now has a warehouse which stocks more than 10,000 different types of vacuum tubes. For many of them the company is now the world's only supplier, which helps explain why the company has a gross margin in the 35–40 percent range.

Richardson survives and prospers because vacuum tubes are vital parts of some older electronic equipment that would be costly to replace with solid state equipment. In addition, vacuum tubes still outperform semiconductors in some limited applications, including radar and welding machines. The U.S. government and General Motors are big customers of Richardson's.

Speed is the essence of Richardson's business. The company's Illinois warehouse offers overnight delivery to some 40,000 customers, processing 650 orders a day, with an average price of $550. Customers such as GM don't really care whether a vacuum tube costs $250 or $350; what they care about is the $40,000–$50,000 downtime loss that they face when a key piece of welding equipment isn't working. By responding quickly to the demands of such customers and by being the only major supplier of many types of vacuum tubes, Richardson has placed itself in a position that many companies in growing industries would envy—a monopoly position. As a result, its sales tripled to $101 million during the second half of the 1980s, while its profits quadrupled to $8.5 million and are still rising.[22]

Philip Morris Co. has pursued such a strategy in the tobacco industry. By aggressive marketing, Philip Morris has increased its market share in a declining industry and earned enormous profits in the process. The tactical steps that companies might use to achieve a leadership position include aggressive pricing and marketing to build market share, acquiring established competitors to consolidate the industry, and raising the stakes for other competitors—for example, by undertaking new investments in productive capacity. Such actions signal to other competitors that the company is willing and able to stay and compete in the declining industry. These signals may persuade other companies to exit the industry, which would further enhance the competitive position of the industry leader. Strategy in Action 7.5 offers an example of a company that has prospered by taking a leadership position in a declining industry—Richardson Electronics, the last company in the vacuum tube business.

Niche Strategy A niche strategy involves focusing on those pockets of demand in the industry where demand is stable or declining less slowly than the industry as a whole. The strategy makes sense when the company has some unique strengths relative to those niches where demand remains relatively strong. As an example, consider Naval Inc.; the company makes whaling

harpoons and small guns to fire them, and makes money at it. This might be considered rather odd, since whaling has been outlawed by the world community. However, Naval Inc. survived the terminal decline of the harpoon industry by focusing on the one group of people who are still allowed to hunt whales, although only in very limited numbers—North American Eskimos. Eskimos are permitted to hunt bowhead whales, provided that they do so only for food and not for commercial purposes. Naval is the sole supplier of small harpoon whaling guns to Eskimo communities, and its monopoly position allows it to earn a healthy return in this small market.[23]

Harvest Strategy As we note in Chapter 6, a harvest strategy is the best choice when a company wishes to get out of a declining industry and perhaps optimize cash flow in the process. This strategy makes the most sense when the company foresees a steep decline and a particularly intense competition or when it lacks strengths relative to remaining pockets of demand in the industry. A harvest strategy requires the company to cut all new investments in capital equipment, advertising, R&D, and the like. As illustrated in Figure 7.7, the inevitable result is that the company will lose market share, but because it is no longer investing in this business, initially its positive cash flow will increase. Essentially, the company is taking cash flow in exchange for market share. Ultimately, however, cash flows will start to decline, and at this stage it makes sense for the company to liquidate the business. Although this strategy is very appealing in theory, it can be somewhat difficult to put into practice. Employee morale in a business that is being run down may suffer. Furthermore, if customers catch on to what the company is doing, they may defect rapidly. Then market share may decline much faster than the company expected.

Figure 7.7
A Harvest Strategy

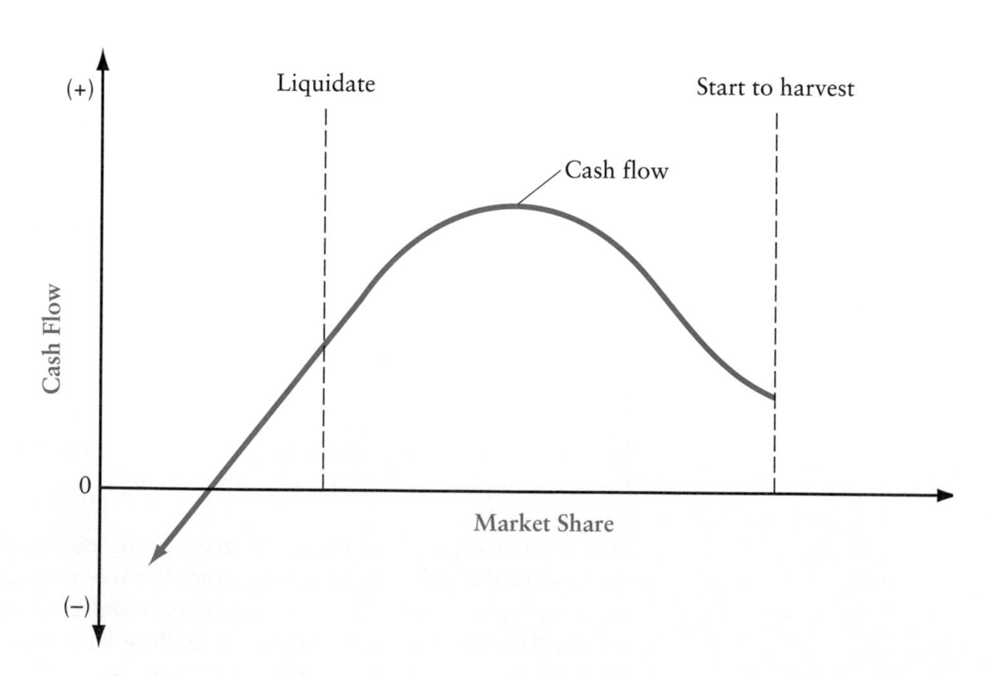

Divestment Strategy A divestment strategy rests on the idea that a company can maximize its net investment recovery from a business by selling it early, before the industry has entered into a steep decline. This strategy is appropriate when the company has few strengths relative to whatever pockets of demand are likely to remain in the industry and when the competition in the declining industry is likely to be intense. The best option may be to sell out to a company that is pursuing a leadership strategy in the industry. The drawback of the divestment strategy is that it depends for its success on the ability of the company to spot an industry decline before it becomes serious and to sell out while the company's assets are still valued by others.

7.10 SUMMARY OF CHAPTER

The purpose of this chapter is to discuss how the structure of the industry in which companies compete affects the level of company and industry profitability. Developing a generic competitive strategy and an investment strategy is only the first part, albeit a crucial one, of business-level strategy. Tailoring that generic strategy to the industry structure by choosing industry-appropriate competitive moves and product/market strategies is the second part of successful strategy formulation at the business level. Companies must always be on the alert for changes in industry conditions and in the competitive behavior of their rivals if they are to respond to these changes in a timely manner. The chapter makes the following main points:

1. In fragmented industries composed of a large number of small companies, the principal forms of competitive strategy are chaining, franchising, and horizontal merger.
2. In embryonic and growth industries, developing a strategy to profit from technical innovations is a crucial aspect of competitive strategy. The three strategies a company can choose from are (1) to develop and market the technology itself, (2) to do so jointly with another company, or (3) to license the technology to existing companies.
3. Mature industries are composed of a few large companies whose actions are so highly interdependent that the success of one company's strategy depends on the responses of its rivals.
4. The principal competitive moves and strategies used by companies in mature industries to deter entry are product proliferation, price cutting, and maintaining excess capacity.
5. The principal competitive moves and strategies used by companies in mature industries to manage rivalry are price signaling, price leadership, nonprice competition, and capacity control.
6. Companies in mature industries also need to develop a supply and distribution strategy to protect the source of their competitive advantage.
7. In declining industries where market demand has leveled off or is falling, companies must tailor their price and nonprice strategies to the new competitive environment. They also need to manage industry capacity to prevent the emergence of capacity expansion problems.

8. There are four main strategies that a company can pursue when demand is falling: leadership, niche, harvest, and divestment strategies. The choice of strategy is determined by the severity of industry decline and the company's strengths relative to the remaining pockets of demand.

Discussion Questions

1. Why are industries fragmented? What are the main ways in which companies can turn a fragmented industry into a consolidated one?
2. What are the key problems involved in maintaining a competitive advantage in a growth industry environment? What are the dangers associated with being the leader?
3. Discuss how companies can use (a) product differentiation and (b) capacity control strategies to manage rivalry and increase industry profitability.

Article File 7

Find examples of the way in which competition in an industry environment affects the business strategy pursued by a company or group of companies.

Strategic Management Project: Module 7

This part of the project continues the analysis of your company's business-level strategy and considers how conditions in the industry environment affect the company.

1. What kind of industry environment (for example, embryonic, mature) does your company operate in? (Use the information from Module #3 of the project to answer this question).
2. Discuss how your company has tailored its business-level strategy to its industry. For example, if your company is operating in an embryonic industry, discuss the ways it has attempted to increase its competitive advantage over time. If it operates in a mature industry, discuss how it has tried to manage the five forces of industry competition.
3. What new strategies would you advise your company to pursue to increase its competitive advantage? For example, what kinds of strategy toward buyers or suppliers should it adopt? How should its attempt to differentiate its products in the future?
4. Based on this analysis, do you think your company will be able to maintain its competitive advantage in the future? Why or why not?

Endnotes

1. P. Nulty, "The Bounce Is Back at Goodyear," *Fortune*, September 7, 1992, pp. 70–72.
2. M. Porter, *Competitive Strategy: Techniques for Analyzing Industries and Competitors* (New York: Free Press, 1980), pp. 191–200.
3. Much of this section is based on Charles W. L. Hill, Michael Heeley, and Jane Sakson, "Strategies for Profiting from Innovation," *Advances in Global High Technology Management*, (Greenwich, Conn.: JAI Press, 1993), III, 79–95.
4. The importance of complementary assets was first noted by D. J. Teece. See D. J. Teece, "Profiting from Technological Innovation," in *The Competitive Challenge*, ed. D. J. Teece (New York: Harper & Row, 1986), 26–54.
5. E. Mansfield, M. Schwartz, and S. Wagner, "Imitation Costs and Patents: An Empirical Study," *Economic Journal*, 91 (1981), 907–918.
6. E. Mansfield, "How Rapidly Does New Industrial Technology Leak Out?" *Journal of Industrial Economics*, 34 (1985), 217–223.
7. G. R. Jones, *Organizational Theory: Text and Cases* (Reading, Mass.: Addison-Wesley, 1995).
8. This argument has been made in the game theory literature. See R. Caves, H. Cookell, and P. J. Killing, "The Imperfect Market for Technology Licenses," *Oxford Bulletin of Economics and Statistics*, 45 (1983), 249–267; N. T. Gallini, "Deterrence by Market Sharing: A Strategic Incentive for Licensing," *American Economic Review*, 74 (1984), 931–941; and C. Shapiro, "Patent Licensing and R&D Rivalry," *American Economic Review*, 75 (1985), 25–30.
9. J. Brander and J. Eaton, "Product Line Rivalry," *American Economic Review*, 74 (1985), 323–334.
10. P. Milgrom and J. Roberts, "Predation, Reputation, and Entry Deterrence," *Journal of Economic Theory*, 27 (1982), 280–312.
11. Sharon M. Oster, *Modern Competitive Analysis* (New York: Oxford University Press, 1990), pp. 262–264.
12. Donald A. Hay and Derek J. Morris, *Industrial Economics: Theory and Evidence* (New York: Oxford University Press, 1979), pp. 192–193.
13. G. R. Jones and M. W. Pustay, "Interorganizational Coordination in the Airline Industry," *Journal of Management*, 14 (1989), 529–546.
14. Porter, *Competitive Strategy*, pp. 76–86.
15. Scherer, *Industrial Market Structure and Economic Performance*, Ch. 8.
16. H. Igor Ansoff, *Corporate Strategy* (London: Penguin Books, 1984), pp. 97–100.
17. Robert D. Buzzell, Bradley T. Gale, and Ralph G. M. Sultan, "Market Share—A Key to Profitability," *Harvard Business Review* (January–February 1975), 97–103. Robert Jacobson and David A. Aaker, "Is Market Share All That It's Cracked Up to Be?" *Journal of Marketing*, 49 (1985), 11–22.
18. M. Maremont and G. Bowens, "Brawls in Toyland," *Business Week*, December 21, 1992, pp. 36–37.
19. Ansoff, *Corporate Strategy*, pp. 98–99.
20. The next section draws heavily on Marvin B. Lieberman, "Strategies for Capacity Expansion," *Sloan Management Review*, 8 (1987), 19–27; and Porter, *Competitive Strategy*, pp. 324–338.
21. K. Pope, "Out for Blood, For Compaq and Dell Accent is on Personal in the Computer Wars," *Wall Street Journal*, February 13, 1993, pp. A1, A6.
22. C. W. L. Hill, *International Business: Competing in the Global Marketplace* (Homewood, Ill.: Irwin, 1994).
23. Jack Willoughby, "The Last Iceman," *Forbes*, July 13, 1987, pp. 183–202.

8 Strategy in the Global Environment

8.1 OPENING CASE: SWAN OPTICAL CORP.

When most people think of multinational enterprises, they think of large complex companies such as General Electric, General Motors, and Procter & Gamble. In reality, however, an increasing number of small and medium-sized companies have become multinational enterprises in recent decades. Take Swan Optical Corp. Started in the 1960s by Alan Glassman, the company manufactures and distributes eyewear. By the end of the 1980s this company was generating annual gross revenues in excess of $20 million. Thus the company is not exactly small, but it is no corporate giant either. However, Swan Optical is a multinational company, with production facilities on three continents and customers around the globe.

Swan began its move toward becoming a multinational in the 1970s. At that time the strong dollar made U.S.-based manufacturing very expensive. Low-priced imports were taking an ever larger share of the U.S. eyewear market. Swan realized that it could not survive unless it also began to import. Initially, the company purchased eyewear from independent overseas manufacturers, primarily in Hong Kong. However, Swan was not satisfied with the quality and delivery of those products, and as the volume of imports increased, Glassman decided that the best way to guarantee quality and delivery was to set up Swan's own foreign manufacturing operation. According to Glassman, taking an ownership interest in foreign factories gives Swan the control necessary to influence quality and delivery schedules. Consequently, in conjunction with a Chinese partner, Swan opened a manufacturing facility in Hong Kong, in which it took a majority shareholding.

The choice of Hong Kong as a location for manufacturing eyewear was influenced by the combination of low labor costs, a skilled work force, and tax breaks given by the Hong Kong government. By 1986, however, the increasing industrialization of Hong Kong and a growing labor shortage had pushed up wage rates to such an extent that Hong Kong could no longer be considered a low-cost location. In response, Glassman and his Chinese partner opened a manufacturing plant in mainland China to take advantage of the lower wage rates. The factory manufactures parts for eyewear frames. The parts are shipped to the Hong Kong factory for final assembly and then distributed to markets in both North and South America. The Hong Kong factory now employs 80 people, and the China plant between 300 and 400.

Around the same time Swan began to look at opportunities to invest in foreign eyewear companies that enjoyed a reputation for fashionable design and high-quality products. Its objective this time was not to lower costs, but to gain a differential advantage by launching a line of high-quality designer eyewear. Lacking in-house design capability to support such a line, Swan turned to foreign manufacturers that had such capability. It invested in factories in France and Italy, taking a minority shareholding in each case. These factories supply eyewear for Swan's Status Eye division, which markets high-priced designer eyewear.[1]

Discussion Questions

1. How has international expansion helped Swan Optical strengthen its competitive position?
2. What lessons does Swan Optical's experience hold for a company trying to establish a competitive advantage in the global marketplace?

8.2 OVERVIEW

In Chapters 5 through 7 we have been looking at the functional and business-level strategies that companies pursue in order to build and maintain a competitive advantage. In this chapter, we consider the contribution of global strategy to the process of building and maintaining a competitive advantage. The opening case offers an example of the link between global strategy and competitive advantage: a relatively small company's expansion abroad for the sake of a low-cost structure and a product line that is differentiated from that of its competitors by superior design. Swan Optical expanded globally in order to better attain the objectives of low cost and differentiation. In this sense, Swan's global expansion can be seen as a move to support its business-level strategy.

Keeping the connection between global strategy and competitive advantage firmly in mind, we begin this chapter by looking at ways in which companies can profit from global expansion. Then we consider the different strategies that companies use to compete in the global marketplace, and discuss the advantages and disadvantages of these strategies. Next we examine the different means that companies employ to enter foreign markets—including exporting, licensing, setting up a joint venture, and setting up a wholly owned subsidiary. The chapter closes with a discussion of the benefits and costs of entering into strategic alliances with global competitors.

8.3 PROFITING FROM GLOBAL EXPANSION

Expanding globally allows companies, large or small, to increase their profitability in ways not available to purely domestic enterprises. Companies that operate internationally can (1) earn a greater return from their distinctive competencies; (2) realize what we refer to as location economies by dispersing individual value creation activities to those locations where they can be performed most efficiently; and (3) ride down the experience curve ahead of competitors, thereby lowering the costs of value creation.

Transferring Distinctive Competencies

The concept of distinctive competencies is first considered in Chapter 4. Distinctive competencies are defined there as *unique strengths that allow a company to achieve superior efficiency, quality, innovation, or customer responsiveness*. Such strengths typically find their expression in product offerings that other companies find difficult to match or imitate. Thus distinctive competencies form the bedrock of a company's competitive advantage. They enable a company to lower the costs of value creation and/or to perform value-creation activities in ways that lead to differentiation and premium pricing.

Companies with valuable distinctive competencies can often realize enormous returns by applying those competencies, and the products they produce, to foreign markets where indigenous competitors lack similar competencies and products. For example, as described in Strategy in Action 8.1, McDonald's has

STRATEGY IN ACTION 8.1

McDonald's Goes International

In the mid 1970s McDonald's faced a problem: after three decades of rapid growth, the U.S. fast-food market had finally begun to show signs of maturity. McDonald's responded to the slowdown by rapidly expanding abroad. By 1980, 28 percent of all the company's new store openings were abroad; by 1986 the figure was 40 percent; and by 1990 it was closer to 60 percent. By the late 1980s McDonald's had operations in forty-five countries and was already generating almost one-fourth of its revenues outside the United States—and it had no plans to slow down.

The key to the company's strategy is its export of the management skills that spurred its growth in the United States. McDonald's built its U.S. success on a formula that included close relations with suppliers, nationwide marketing might, strict control over store-level operating procedures, and a franchising system that encourages individual franchisees to be entrepreneurial.

While this system worked flawlessly in the United States, some modifications have had to be made in other countries. One of the company's biggest challenges has been to infuse every store with the same gung-ho culture and standardized operating procedures that are the hallmark of its success in the United States. To aid in this task, in many countries McDonald's has enlisted the help of large partners through a joint venture arrangement. The partners play a key role in learning and transplanting the organization's values.

Foreign partners have also played a crucial role in helping McDonald's adapt its marketing methods and menu to local conditions. While U.S.-style fast-food remains staple fare on the menu, local products have also been added. In Brazil, for example, McDonald's sells a soft drink made from the guarana, an Amazonian berry. And patrons of McDonald's in Malaysia, Singapore, and Thailand have savored milk shakes flavored with durian, a foul-smelling fruit that is considered by the locals to be an aphrodisiac. Beyond local product additions, foreign partners can help steer the company away from potentially expensive pitfalls. Thus in Japan, Den Fujita, president of McDonald's Co. (Japan), avoided suburban locations, which are the typical choices in the United States and stressed urban sites that consumers could walk to without a car.

McDonald's biggest problem, however, has been to replicate its U.S. supply chain in foreign countries. In the United States, suppliers are fiercely loyal to McDonald's. They have to be: their fortunes are closely linked to those of McDonald's. McDonald's maintains rigorous specifications for all the raw material products it uses, which is the key to its consistency and quality control. Outside the United States, however, the company has found that suppliers are far less willing to make the investments needed to meet McDonald's specifications. In Britain, for instance, McDonald's had difficulties trying to get local bakeries to produce the hamburger bun. After quality problems at two local bakeries, McDonald's put up its own money to build a bakery in Britain that would supply its restaurants. In a more extreme case, when McDonald's decided to open its first restaurant in Russia, it found that local suppliers simply lacked the capability to produce goods of the quality it demanded. The company was forced to vertically integrate through the local food industry on a heroic scale, importing potato seeds and bull semen and indirectly managing dairy farms, cattle ranches, and vegetable plots. It has also had to construct the world's largest food-processing plant, at a cost of $40 million. The restaurant itself only cost $4.5 million.[2]

expanded rapidly overseas in recent years to exploit its distinctive competencies in managing fast-food operations. These competencies have proved to be just as valuable in countries as diverse as France, Russia, China, Germany, and Brazil as they have been in the United States. Before McDonald's entry, none of these

countries had American-style fast-food chains, so McDonald's was bringing in unique skills and a unique product. The lack of indigenous competitors with similar competencies and products, and consequently the lack of competition, have greatly enhanced the profitability of this strategy for McDonald's.

In an earlier era U.S. companies such as Kellogg, Coca-Cola, H. J. Heinz, and Procter & Gamble expanded overseas to exploit their distinctive competencies in developing and marketing branded consumer products. These competencies and the resulting products, which were developed in the U.S. market during the 1950s and 1960s, yielded enormous returns when applied to European markets, where most indigenous competitors lacked similar marketing skills and products. Their near monopoly on consumer marketing skills allowed these American companies to dominate many European consumer product markets during the 1960s and 1970s. Today many Japanese companies are expanding globally to exploit their distinctive competencies in production, materials management, and new product development—competencies that many of their indigenous North American and European competitors seem to lack.

Realizing Location Economies

Location economies are the economies that arise from performing a value-creation activity in the optimal location for that activity, wherever in the world that might be (transportation costs and trade barriers permitting). Locating a value-creation activity in the optimal location for that activity can have one of two effects: *lower the costs of value creation, helping the company achieve a low-cost position, or enable a company to differentiate its product offering and charge a premium price*. Thus efforts to realize location economies are consistent with the generic business-level strategies of low cost and differentiation. As shown in the Opening Case, both of these considerations spurred Swan Optical to seek opportunities abroad. It moved its manufacturing operations out of the United States, first to Hong Kong and then to mainland China, in order to take advantage of low labor costs, thereby lowering the costs of value creation. At the same time, Swan shifted some of its design operations from the United States to France and Italy, reasoning that skilled Italian and French designers could probably help the company better differentiate its product. In other words, Swan saw China as the optimal location for performing manufacturing operations and France and Italy as the optimal locations for performing design operations. The company has configured its value chain accordingly so that it can *simultaneously* pursue both a low-cost strategy and a differentiation strategy. To generalize from the Swan example, this kind of thinking helps spin a *global web* of value-creation activities, with different stages of the value chain being set up in those locations around the globe where value added is maximized or where the costs of value creation are minimized.

Moving Down the Experience Curve

As you recall from Chapter 5, the experience curve refers to the systematic decrease in production costs that have been observed to occur over the life of a product. In Chapter 5, we point out that learning effects and economies of scale underlie the experience curve and that moving down the experience curve allows a company to lower the costs of value creation. The company that moves down

the experience curve most rapidly will have a cost advantage over its competitors. Moving down the experience curve is therefore consistent with the business-level strategy of cost leadership.

Many of the underlying sources of experience-based cost economies are to be found in the plant. This is true of most learning effects and of the economies of scale derived from spreading the fixed costs of building productive capacity over a large output. It follows that the key to riding down the experience curve as rapidly as possible is to increase the accumulated volume *produced by a plant* as quickly as possible. Since global markets are larger than domestic markets, companies that serve a global market *from a single location* are likely to build up accumulated volume faster than companies that focus primarily on serving their home market or on serving multiple markets from multiple production locations. Thus serving a global market from a single location is consistent with moving down the experience curve and establishing a low-cost position. In addition, to get down the experience curve quickly, companies need to price and market very aggressively so that demand expands rapidly. They also need to build production capacity capable of serving a global market. Another point to bear in mind is that the cost advantages of serving the world market from a single location will be all the more significant if that location is also the optimal one for performing that value-creation activity; that is, if the company is *simultaneously* realizing cost economies from experience-curve effects *and* from location economies.

One company that has excelled in the pursuit of such a strategy has been Matsushita. Along with Sony and Philips NV, in the 1970s Matsushita was in the race to develop a commercially viable VCR. Although Matsushita initially lagged behind both Philips and Sony, it was ultimately able to get its VHS format accepted as the world standard and to reap enormous experience curve based cost economies in the process. This cost advantage subsequently constituted a formidable barrier to new competition. Matsushita's strategy involved building global volume as rapidly as possible. To ensure that it could accommodate worldwide demand, it increased production capacity 33-fold, from 205,000 units in 1977 to 6.8 million units by 1984. By serving the world market from a single location in Japan, Matsushita was able to realize significant learning effects and economies of scale. These allowed it to drop its prices by 50 percent within five years of selling its first VHS-formatted VCR. As a result, by 1983 Matsushita was the world's major VCR producer, accounting for approximately 45 percent of world production and enjoying a significant cost advantage over its major competitors. The next largest company, Hitachi, accounted for only 11.1 percent of world production in 1983.[3]

Summary

It is important to recognize that the different ways of profiting from global expansion are all linked to the generic *business-level strategies* of cost leadership and differentiation. Companies that transfer distinctive competencies to other countries are trying to realize greater gains from their low-cost or differentiation-based competitive advantage. Companies such as Swan Optical that attempt to realize location economies are trying to lower their costs and/or increase value added so that they can better differentiate themselves from their competitors. And companies that serve a global market in order to ride more quickly down the experience curve are trying to build a competitive advantage based on low cost, as Matsushita did with its VHS-formatted VCRs.

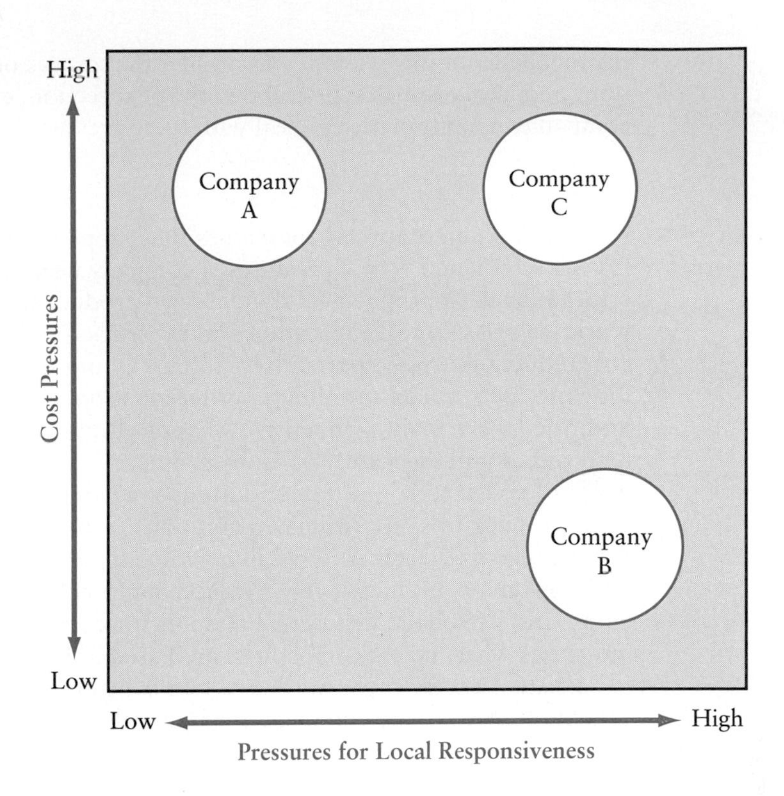

Figure 8.1 Pressures for Cost Reduction and Local Responsiveness

8.4 PRESSURES FOR COST REDUCTIONS AND LOCAL RESPONSIVENESS

Companies that compete in the global marketplace typically face two types of competitive pressures: *pressures for cost reductions* and *pressures to be locally responsive* (see Figure 8.1). These competitive pressures place conflicting demands on a company. Responding to pressures for cost reductions requires that a company try to minimize its unit costs. To attain this goal, a company may have to base its productive activities at the most favorable low-cost location, wherever in the world that might be. It may also have to offer a standardized product to the global marketplace in order to ride down the experience curve as quickly as possible. On the other hand, responding to pressures to be locally responsive requires that a company differentiate its product offering and marketing strategy from country to country in an effort to accommodate the diverse demands arising from national differences in consumer tastes and preferences, business practices, distribution channels, competitive conditions, and government policies. Because differentiation across countries can involve significant duplication and a lack of product standardization, it may raise costs.

While some companies, such as Company A in Figure 8.1, face high pressures for cost reductions and low pressures for local responsiveness, and others, such as Company B, face low pressures for cost reductions and high pressures for local responsiveness, many companies are in the position of Company C. They face high pressures for *both* cost reductions and local responsiveness. Dealing with these conflicting and contradictory pressures is a difficult strategic challenge for a company, primarily because being locally responsive tends to raise costs. In

the remainder of this section, we consider the sources of pressures for cost reductions and local responsiveness and in the next section, examine the strategies that companies adopt in order to deal with these pressures.

Pressures for Cost Reductions

Increasingly, international companies must cope with pressures for cost reductions. To respond to these pressures, a company needs to lower the costs of value creation by mass-producing a standardized product at the optimal location in the world, in order to realize location and experience-curve economies. Pressures for cost reductions can be particularly intense in industries producing commodity-type products, where meaningful differentiation on nonprice factors is difficult and price is the main competitive weapon. Products that serve universal needs tend to fall into this category. Universal needs exist when the tastes and preferences of consumers in different nations are similar, if not identical. This obviously applies to conventional commodity products such as bulk chemicals, petroleum, steel, sugar, and the like. It also tends to be true for many industrial and consumer products—for instance, hand-held calculators, semiconductor chips, and personal computers. Pressures for cost reductions are also intense in industries where major competitors are based in low-cost locations, where there is persistent excess capacity, and where consumers are powerful and face low switching costs. Many commentators have also argued that the liberalization of the world trade and investment environment in recent decades has generally increased cost pressures by facilitating greater international competition.[4]

Pressures for cost reductions have been intense in the global tire industry in recent years. Tires are essentially a commodity product where differentiation is difficult and price is the main competitive weapon. The major buyers of tires, automobile companies, are powerful and face low switching costs, so they have been playing tire companies off against each other in an attempt to get lower prices. And the decline in global demand for automobiles in the early 1990s has created a serious excess capacity situation in the tire industry, with as much as 25 percent of world capacity standing idle. The result has been a worldwide price war, with almost all tire companies suffering heavy losses in the early 1990s. In response to the cost pressures, most tire companies are now trying to rationalize their operations in a way consistent with the attainment of a low-cost position. They are moving production to low-cost facilities and offering globally standardized products in an attempt to realize experience-curve economies.[5]

Pressures for Local Responsiveness

Pressures for local responsiveness arise from differences in consumer tastes and preferences; differences in infrastructure and traditional practices; differences in distribution channels; and host government demands.

Differences in Consumer Tastes and Preferences

Strong pressures for local responsiveness emerge when consumer tastes and preferences differ significantly between countries, as they may for historic or cultural reasons. In such cases, product and/or marketing messages have to be customized to appeal to the tastes and preferences of local consumers. This typically creates pressures for the delegation of production and marketing functions to national subsidiaries.

In the automobile industry, for example, there is a strong demand among North American consumers for pickup trucks. This is particularly true in the

South and West, where many families have a pickup truck as a second or third car. In contrast, in European countries pickup trucks are seen purely as utility vehicles and are purchased primarily by companies rather than individuals. Consequently, the marketing message needs to be tailored to the different nature of demand in North America and Europe.

As a counterpoint, Professor Theodore Levitt of the Harvard Business School has argued that consumer demands for local customization are on the decline worldwide.[6] According to Levitt, modern communications and transport technologies have created the conditions for a convergence of the tastes and preferences of consumers from different nations. The result is the emergence of enormous global markets for standardized consumer products. Levitt cites worldwide acceptance of McDonald's hamburgers, Coca-Cola, Levi Strauss blue jeans, and Sony television sets, all of which are sold as standardized products, as evidence of the increasing homogeneity of the global marketplace.

Levitt's argument, however, has been characterized as extreme by many commentators. For example, Christopher Bartlett and Sumantra Ghoshal have observed that in the consumer electronics industry buyers reacted to an overdose of standardized global products by showing a renewed preference for products that are differentiated to local conditions.[7] They note that Amstrad, the fast-growing British computer and electronics company, got its start by recognizing and responding to local consumer needs. Amstrad captured a major share of the British audio player market by moving away from the standardized inexpensive music centers marketed by global companies such as Sony and Matsushita. Amstrad's product was encased in teak rather than metal cabinets, with a control panel tailor-made to appeal to British consumers' preferences. In response, Matsushita had to reverse its earlier bias toward standardized global design and place more emphasis on local customization.

Differences in Infrastructure and Traditional Practices Pressures for local responsiveness arise from differences in infrastructure and/or traditional practices among countries, creating a need to customize products accordingly. Fulfilling this need may require the delegation of manufacturing and production functions to foreign subsidiaries. For example, in North America consumer electrical systems are based on 110 volts, whereas in some European countries 240 volt systems are standard. Thus domestic electrical appliances have to be customized to take this difference in infrastructure into account. Traditional practices also often vary across nations. For example, in Britain people drive on the left-hand side of the road, thus creating a demand for right-hand drive cars, whereas in France people drive on the right-hand side of the road, and therefore want left-hand drive cars. Obviously, automobiles have to be customized to take this difference in traditional practices into account.

Differences in Distribution Channels A company's marketing strategies may have to be responsive to differences in distribution channels among countries. This may necessitate the delegation of marketing functions to national subsidiaries. In the pharmaceutical industry for example, the British and Japanese distribution system is radically different from the U.S. system. British and Japanese doctors will not accept or respond favorably to an American-style high-pressure sales force. Thus pharmaceutical companies have to adopt different marketing practices in Britain and Japan compared with the United States—soft sell versus hard sell.

Host Government Demands Economic and political demands imposed by host country governments may necessitate a degree of local responsiveness. For example, the politics of health care around the world requires that pharmaceutical companies manufacture in multiple locations. Pharmaceutical companies are subject to local clinical testing, registration procedures, and pricing restrictions, all of which make it necessary that the manufacturing and marketing of a drug should meet local requirements. Moreover, since governments and government agencies control a significant proportion of the health care budget in most countries, they are in a powerful position to demand a high level of local responsiveness. More generally, threats of protectionism, economic nationalism, and local content rules (which dictate that a certain percentage of a product should be manufactured locally) all dictate that international businesses manufacture locally. Part of the motivation for Japanese auto companies setting up U.S. production, for example, is to counter the threat of protectionism increasingly voiced by the U.S. Congress.

Implications Pressures for local responsiveness imply that it may not be possible for a company to realize the full benefits from experience-curve and location economies. For example, it may not be possible to serve the global marketplace from a single low-cost location, producing a globally standardized product and marketing it worldwide to achieve experience-curve cost economies. In practice, the need to customize the product offering to local conditions may work against the implementation of such a strategy. Automobile companies, for instance, have found that Japanese, American, and European consumers demand different kinds of cars, which means customizing products for local markets. In response, companies like Honda, Ford, and Toyota are pursuing a strategy of establishing top-to-bottom design and production facilities in each of these regions so that they can better serve local demands. Although such customization brings benefits, it also limits the ability of a company to realize significant experience-curve cost economies and location economies.

In addition, pressures for local responsiveness imply that it may not be possible to transfer wholesale from one nation to another the skills and products associated with a company's distinctive competencies. Concessions often have to be made to local conditions. For an example, take another look at Strategy in Action 8.1. It describes some of the concessions to local conditions that McDonald's has had to make in different national markets.

8.5 STRATEGIC CHOICE

There are four basic strategies that companies use to enter and compete in the international environment: an international strategy, a multidomestic strategy, a global strategy, and a transnational strategy.[8] Each of these strategies has its advantages and disadvantages. The appropriateness of each strategy varies with the extent of pressures for cost reductions and local responsiveness. Figure 8.2 illustrates when each of these strategies is most appropriate. In this section we describe each strategy, identify when it is appropriate, and discuss its pros and cons.

Figure 8.2
Four Basic Strategies

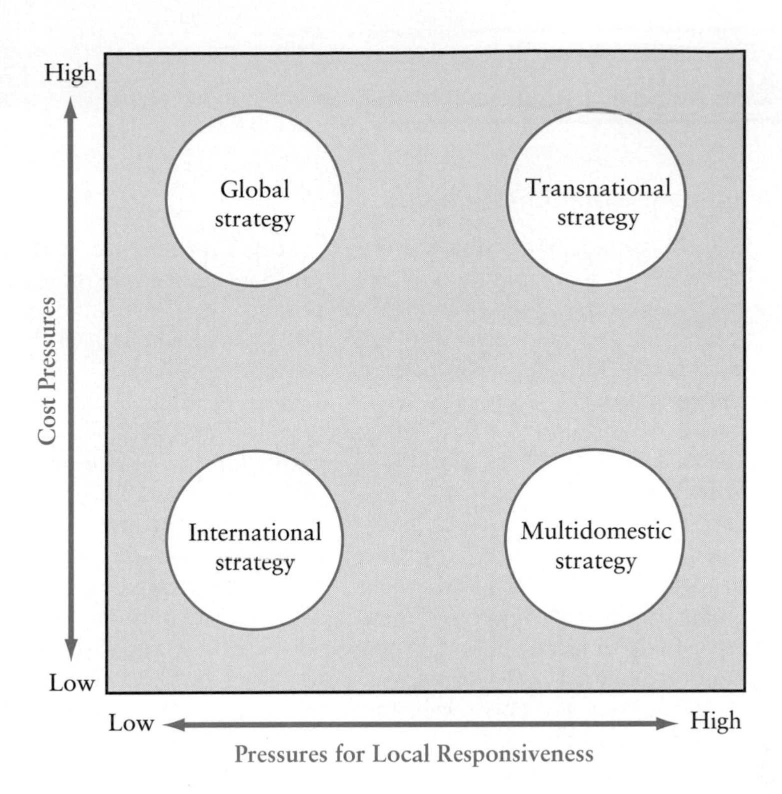

International Strategy

Companies that pursue an international strategy try to create value by transferring valuable skills and products to foreign markets where indigenous competitors lack those skills and products. Most international companies have created value by transferring differentiated product offerings developed at home to new markets overseas. Accordingly, they tend to centralize product development functions (for instance, R&D) at home. However, they also tend to establish manufacturing and marketing functions in each major country in which they do business. But although they may undertake some local customization of product offering and marketing strategy, this tends to be rather limited in scope. Ultimately, in most international companies the head office retains tight control over marketing and product strategy.

International companies include such enterprises as Toys Я Us, McDonald's, IBM, Kellogg, and Procter & Gamble. Indeed, the majority of U.S. companies that expanded abroad in the 1950s and 1960s fall into this category. As an example, consider Procter & Gamble, which is profiled in Strategy in Action 8.2. Traditionally, Procter & Gamble has had production facilities in all of its major markets outside of the United States, including Britain, Germany, and Japan. These facilities, however, manufactured differentiated products that had been developed by the U.S. parent company and that were often marketed using the marketing message developed in the United States. Historically at least, local responsiveness on the part of P&G has been quite limited, which is now causing problems for P&G, as Strategy in Action 8.2 explains.

STRATEGY IN ACTION 8.2

Procter & Gamble's International Strategy

Procter & Gamble, the large U.S. consumer products company, has a well-earned reputation as one of the world's best marketers. With over eighty major brands, P&G generates more than $20 billion in revenues worldwide. Together with Unilever, P&G is a dominant global force in laundry detergents, cleaning products, and personal care products. P&G expanded abroad in the post–World War II years by pursuing an international strategy—transferring brands and marketing policies developed in the United States to Western Europe, initially with considerable success. Over the next thirty years this policy resulted in the development of a classic international company, in which new product development and marketing strategies were pioneered in the home country and only then transferred abroad. Although the company did make some attempts to adapt marketing policies to accommodate differences among countries, by and large such adaptation was fairly minimal.

The first signs that this strategy was flawed began to emerge in the 1970s, when P&G suffered a number of major setbacks in Japan. By 1985, after thirteen years in Japan, P&G was still losing $40 million a year there. The company had introduced disposable diapers in Japan and at one time commanded an 80 percent share of the market, but by the early 1980s it had seen its share slip to 8 percent. In P&G's place, three major Japanese consumer products companies dominated the market. P&G's problem was that the Japanese found its diapers, developed in America, too bulky. Taking advantage of this fact, the Japanese consumer products company, Kao, developed a line of trim-fit diapers, which accorded better with Japanese consumers' preferences. Kao supported the introduction of its product with a marketing blitz and was quickly rewarded with a 30 percent share of the market. As for P&G, only belatedly did it realize that it had to modify its diapers to suit the needs and preferences of Japanese consumers. Now the company has increased its share of the Japanese market to 30 percent. Moreover, in an example of global learning, P&G's trim-fit diapers, originally developed for the Japanese market, have now become a bestseller in the United States.

P&G's experience with disposable diapers in Japan prompted the company to rethink its new product development and marketing philosophy. P&G has now admitted that its U.S.-centered way of doing business no longer works. Since the late 1980s P&G has been trying to delegate far more responsibility for new product development and marketing strategy to its major subsidiary companies in Japan and Europe. As a result it has become a company that is more responsive to local differences in consumer tastes and preferences, as well as more willing to admit that good new products can be developed outside the United States.

Despite the apparent changes at P&G, it is still not clear that P&G has achieved the revolution in thinking needed to alter its long-established practices. P&G's recent venture into the Polish shampoo market perhaps illustrates that the company still has some way to go. In the summer of 1991 P&G entered the Polish market with its Vidal Sasson Wash & Go, an all-in-one shampoo and conditioner, which is a bestseller in America and Europe. The launching of the product was supported by an American-style marketing blitz on a scale never before seen in Poland. At first the campaign seemed to be working as P&G captured more than 30 percent of the market for shampoos in Poland, but in early 1992 sales suddenly plummeted. Then came the rumors: Wash & Go caused dandruff and hair loss, allegations that P&G has strenuously denied. Next came the jokes. One making the rounds in Poland runs as follows: "I washed my car with Wash & Go and the tires went bald." And when President Lech Walesa proposed in 1993 that he also become prime minister, critics derided the idea as a "two in one solution, just like Wash & Go."

Where did P&G go wrong? The most common theory is that it promoted Wash & Go too hard in a country that has little enthusiasm for brash American-style advertising. A poll by Pentor, a private market research company in Warsaw, found that almost three times more Poles disliked P&G's commercials than liked them. Pentor suggested that the high-profile marketing campaign backfired because years of Communist party propaganda

have led Polish consumers to suspect that advertising is simply a way to shift goods that nobody wants. These criticisms all seem to imply that P&G was once again stumbling because it had transferred a product and marketing strategy wholesale from the United States to another country without modification to accommodate the needs and preferences of local consumers.[9]

An international strategy makes sense if a company has a valuable distinctive competency that indigenous competitors in foreign markets lack and if the company faces relatively weak pressures for local responsiveness and cost reductions. In such circumstances, an international strategy can be very profitable. However, when pressures for local responsiveness are high, companies pursuing this strategy lose out to companies that place a greater emphasis on customizing the product offering and market strategy to local conditions. Moreover, because of the duplication of manufacturing facilities, companies that pursue an international strategy tend to incur high operating costs. Hence this strategy is inappropriate in industries where cost pressures are high.

Multidomestic Strategy

Companies pursuing a multidomestic strategy orient themselves toward achieving maximum local responsiveness. Like companies pursuing an international strategy, they tend to transfer skills and products developed at home to foreign markets. However, unlike international companies, multidomestic ones extensively customize both their product offering and their marketing strategy to different national conditions. Consistent with this approach, they also tend to establish a complete set of value-creation activities—including production, marketing, and R&D—in each major national market in which they do business. As a result, they generally cannot realize value from experience-curve effects and location economies and therefore often have a high-cost structure.

A multidomestic strategy makes most sense when there are high pressures for local responsiveness and low pressures for cost reductions. The high-cost structure associated with the duplication of production facilities makes this strategy inappropriate in industries where cost pressures are intense. Another weakness of this strategy is due to the fact that many multidomestic companies have developed into decentralized federations in which each national subsidiary functions in a largely autonomous manner. Consequently, after a time they begin to lose the ability to transfer the skills and products derived from distinctive competencies to their various national subsidiaries around the world. In a famous case that illustrates the problems this can cause, the ability of Philips NV to establish its V2000 VCR format as the dominant design in the VCR industry during the late 1970s, as opposed to Matsushita's VHS format, was destroyed by the refusal of its U.S. subsidiary company to adopt the V2000 format. Instead, the subsidiary bought VCRs produced by Matsushita and put its own label on them.

Global Strategy

Companies that pursue a global strategy focus on increasing profitability by reaping the cost reductions that come from experience-curve effects and location economies. That is, they are pursuing a low-cost strategy. The production, marketing, and R&D activities of companies pursuing a global strategy are

concentrated in a few favorable locations. Global companies tend not to customize their product offering and marketing strategy to local conditions. This is because customization raises costs since it involves shorter production runs and the duplication of functions. Instead, global companies prefer to market a standardized product worldwide so that they can reap the maximum benefits from the economies of scale that underlie the experience curve. They also tend to use their cost advantage to support aggressive pricing in world markets.

This strategy makes most sense in those cases where there are strong pressures for cost reductions and where demands for local responsiveness are minimal. Increasingly, these conditions prevail in many industrial goods industries. In the semiconductor industry, for example, global standards have emerged, creating enormous demands for standardized global products. Accordingly, companies such as Intel, Texas Instruments, and Motorola all pursue a global strategy. However, as noted earlier, these conditions are not found in many consumer goods markets, where demands for local responsiveness remain high (as in the markets for audio players, automobiles, and processed food products). The strategy is inappropriate when demands for local responsiveness are high.

Transnational Strategy

Christopher Bartlett and Sumantra Ghoshal argue that in today's environment, competitive conditions are so intense that in order to survive in the global marketplace companies *must exploit experience-based cost economies and location economies, transfer distinctive competencies within the company, and at the same time pay attention to pressures for local responsiveness.*[10] Moreover, they note that in the modern multinational enterprise, distinctive competencies do not reside just in the home country but they can develop in any of the company's worldwide operations. Thus they maintain that the flow of skills and product offerings should not be all one way, from home company to foreign subsidiary, as in the case of companies pursuing an international strategy. Rather, the flow should also be from foreign subsidiary to home country, and from foreign subsidiary to foreign subsidiary—a process they refer to as **global learning**. Bartlett and Ghoshal term the strategy pursued by companies that are trying to achieve all of these objectives simultaneously a **transnational strategy**.[11]

A transnational strategy makes sense when a company faces high pressures for cost reductions and high pressures for local responsiveness. In essence, *companies that pursue a transnational strategy are trying to simultaneously achieve low-cost and differentiation advantages.* As attractive as this sounds, in practice the strategy is not an easy one to pursue. As mentioned earlier, pressures for local responsiveness and cost reductions place conflicting demands on a company. Being locally responsive raises costs, which obviously makes cost reductions difficult to achieve. How then, can a company effectively pursue a transnational strategy?

Some clues can be derived from the case of Caterpillar Inc. The need to compete with low-cost competitors such as Komatsu of Japan has forced Caterpillar to look for greater cost economies. However, variations in construction practices and government regulations across countries mean that Caterpillar also has to be responsive to local demands. Therefore, as illustrated in Figure 8.3, Caterpillar confronts significant pressures for cost reductions and for local responsiveness.

To deal with cost pressures, Caterpillar redesigned its products to use many identical components and invested in a few large-scale component manufactur-

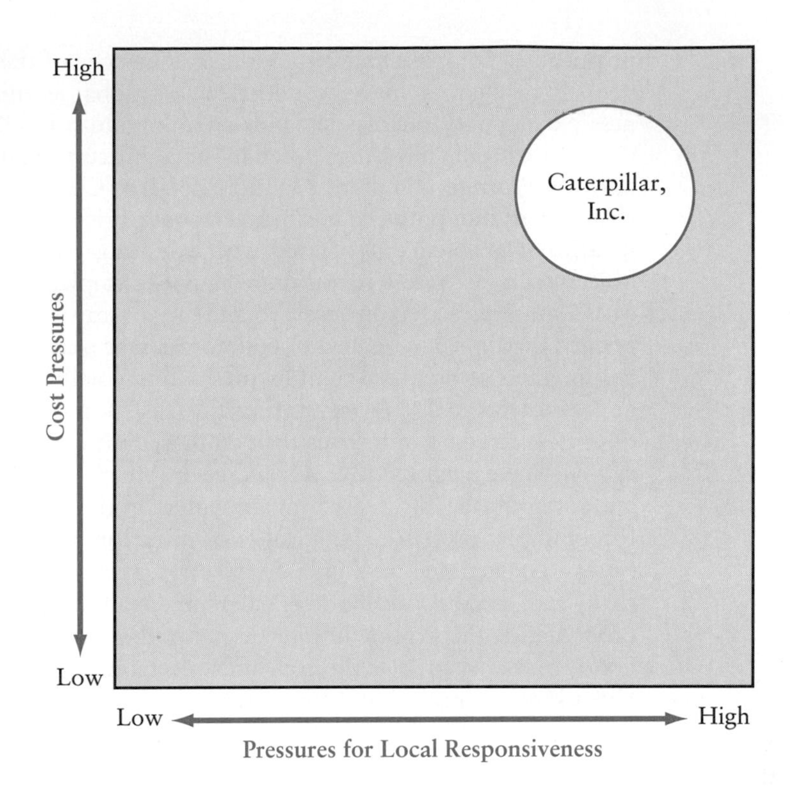

Figure 8.3
Cost Pressures and Pressures for Local Responsiveness Facing Caterpillar

ing facilities, sited at favorable locations, to fill global demand and realize scale economies. At the same time the company augments the centralized manufacturing of components with assembly plants in each of its major global markets. At these plants, Caterpillar adds local product features, tailoring the finished product to local needs. Thus Caterpillar is able to realize many of the benefits of global manufacturing while reacting to pressures for local responsiveness by differentiating its product among national markets.[12]

Unilever provides another example. Once a classic multidomestic company, in recent years Unilever has had to shift more toward a transnational strategy. A rise in low-cost competition, which increased cost pressures, has forced Unilever to look for ways of rationalizing its detergents business. During the 1980s Unilever had seventeen different and largely self-contained detergents operations in Europe alone—an enormous duplication in terms of assets and marketing. Moreover, because Unilever was so fragmented it could take as long as four years for the company to introduce a new product across Europe. Now Unilever is trying to weld its European operation into a single entity, with detergents being manufactured in a handful of cost-efficient plants, and standard packaging and advertising being used across Europe. According to company estimates, the result could be an annual cost saving of over $200 million. Unilever recognizes, however, that because of national differences in distribution channels and brand awareness, it must still remain locally responsive, even as it strives to realize economies from consolidating production and marketing at the optimal locations.[13]

Despite such examples as Caterpillar and Unilever, Bartlett and Ghoshal admit that building an organization capable of supporting a transnational strategic

posture is a complex and difficult task. The core of the problem is that simultaneously trying to achieve cost efficiencies, global learning, and local responsiveness places contradictory demands on an organization.[14] Exactly how a company can deal with the dilemmas posed by such difficult organizational issues is a topic that we return to and discuss in more detail in Chapter 13, when we examine the structure of international business. For now, it is important to note that the organizational problems associated with pursuing what are essentially conflicting objectives constitute a major impediment to implementing a transnational strategy. Companies that attempt to pursue a transnational strategy can become bogged down in an organizational morass that only leads to inefficiencies.

It might also be noted that, by presenting it as the only viable strategy, Bartlett and Ghoshal may be overstating the case for the transnational.[15] Although doubtless in some industries the company that can adopt a transnational strategy will have a competitive advantage, in other industries global, multidomestic, and international strategies remain viable. In the global semiconductor industry, for example, pressures for local customization are minimal and competition is purely a cost game, making a global strategy optimal. Indeed, this is the case in many industrial goods markets where the product serves universal needs. On the other hand, the argument can be made that to compete in certain consumer goods markets, such as the consumer electronics industry, a company has to try and adopt a transnational strategy.

Summary

The advantages and disadvantages of each of the four strategies discussed above are summarized in Table 8.1. Although a transnational strategy appears to offer the most advantages, it should not be forgotten that implementing it raises difficult organizational issues. More generally, as already shown in Figure 8.2, the appropriateness of each strategy depends on the relative strength of pressures for cost reductions and for local responsiveness.

8.6 THE CHOICE OF ENTRY MODE

Considering entry into a foreign market raises the question of the best mode of such entry. There are five main choices: exporting, licensing, franchising, entering into a joint venture with a host country company, and setting up a wholly owned subsidiary in the host country. Each entry mode has its advantages and disadvantages and managers must weigh these carefully when deciding which mode to use.[16]

Exporting

Most manufacturing companies begin their global expansion as exporters and only later switch to one of the other modes for serving a foreign market. Exporting has two distinct advantages: it avoids the costs of establishing manufacturing operations in the host country, which are often substantial; and it may be consistent with realizing experience-curve cost economies and location economies. By manufacturing the product in a centralized location and then exporting it to other national markets, the company may be able to realize substantial scale economies from its global sales volume. That is how Sony came to

Table 8.1
The Advantages and Disadvantages of the Four Traditional Strategies

Strategy	Advantages	Disadvantages
Global	• Ability to exploit experience-curve effects • Ability to exploit location economies	• Lack of local responsiveness
International	• Transfer of distinctive competencies to foreign markets	• Lack of local responsivenes • Inability to realize location economies • Failure to exploit experience-curve effects
Multidomestic	• Ability to customize product offerings and marketing in accordance with local responsiveness	• Inability to realize location economies • Failure to exploit experience-curve effects • Failure to transfer distinctive competencies to foreign markets
Transnational	• Ability to exploit experience-curve effects • Ability to exploit location economies • Ability to customize product offerings and marketing in accordance with local responsiveness • Reaping benefits of global learning	• Difficulties in implementation because of organizational problems

dominate the global television market, how Matsushita came to dominate the VCR market, and how many Japanese auto companies originally made inroads into the United States auto market.

On the other hand, there are a number of drawbacks to exporting. First, exporting from the company's *home* base may not be appropriate if there are lower-cost locations for manufacturing the product abroad (that is, if the company can realize location economies by moving production elsewhere). Thus, particularly in the case of a company pursuing a global or transnational strategy, it may pay to manufacture in a location where conditions are most favorable from a value-creation perspective and then export from that location to the rest of the globe. This, of course, is not so much an argument against exporting as an argument against exporting from the company's *home* country. For example, many United States electronics companies have moved some of their manufacturing to the Far East because low-cost but highly skilled labor is available there. They export from that location to the rest of the globe, including the United States.

Another drawback is that high transport costs can make exporting uneconomical, particularly in the case of bulk products. One way of getting around this

problem is to manufacture bulk products on a regional basis. Such a strategy enables the company to realize some economies from large-scale production while limiting transport costs. Thus many multinational chemical companies manufacture their products on a regional basis, serving several countries in a region from one facility.

Tariff barriers, too, can make exporting uneconomical, and the threat to impose tariff barriers by the government of a country the company is exporting to can make the strategy very risky. Indeed, the implicit threat from Congress to impose tariffs on Japanese cars imported into the United States led directly to the decision by many Japanese auto companies to set up manufacturing plants in the United States.

Finally, a common practice among companies that are just beginning to export also poses risks. A company may delegate marketing activities in each country in which it does business to a local agent, but there is no guarantee that the agent will act in the company's best interest. Often foreign agents carry the products of competing companies and thus have divided loyalties. Consequently, the foreign agent may not do as good a job as the company would if it managed marketing itself. One way to solve this problem is to set up a wholly owned subsidiary in the host country to handle local marketing. By so doing, the company can both reap the cost advantages that arise from manufacturing the product in a single location and exercise tight control over marketing strategy in the host country.

Licensing

International licensing is an arrangement whereby a foreign licensee buys the rights to manufacture a company's product in the licensee's country for a negotiated fee (normally, royalty payments on the number of units sold). The licensee then puts up most of the capital necessary to get the overseas operation going.[17]

The advantage of licensing is that the company does not have to bear the development costs and risks associated with opening up a foreign market. Licensing therefore can be a very attractive option for companies that lack the capital to develop operations overseas. It can also be an attractive option for companies that are unwilling to commit substantial financial resources to an unfamiliar or politically volatile foreign market where political risks are particularly high.

Licensing has three serious drawbacks, however. First, it does not give a company the tight control over manufacturing, marketing, and strategic functions in foreign countries that it needs to have in order to realize experience-curve cost economies and location economies—as companies pursuing both global and transnational strategies try to do. Licensing typically involves each licensee setting up its own manufacturing operations. Hence the company stands little chance of realizing experience-curve cost economies and location economies by manufacturing its product in a centralized location. When these economies are likely to be important, licensing may not be the best way of expanding overseas.

Second, competing in a global marketplace may make it necessary for a company to coordinate strategic moves across countries so that the profits earned in one country can be used to support competitive attacks in another. Licensing, by its very nature, severely limits a company's ability to do so. A licensee is unlikely to let a multinational company take its profits (beyond those due in the form of

royalty payments) and use them to support an entirely different licensee operating in another country.

A third problem with licensing is the risk associated with licensing technological know-how to foreign companies. For many multinational companies, technological know-how forms the basis of their competitive advantage, and they would want to maintain control over the use to which it is put. By licensing its technology, a company can quickly lose control over it. RCA, for instance, once licensed its color television technology to a number of Japanese companies. The Japanese companies quickly assimilated RCA's technology and then used it to enter the U.S. market. Now the Japanese have a bigger share of the U.S. market than the RCA brand. Similar concerns are now surfacing over the 1989 decision by Congress to allow Japanese companies to produce the advanced FSX fighter under license from McDonnell Douglas. Critics of this decision fear that the Japanese will use the FSX technology to support the development of a commercial airline industry that will compete with Boeing and McDonnell Douglas in the global marketplace.

Franchising

Whereas licensing is a strategy pursued primarily by manufacturing companies, franchising, which resembles it in some respects, is a strategy employed chiefly by service companies. For example, both McDonald's and Hilton Hotels Corp. have expanded internationally by franchising.[18] In the case of franchising, the company sells to franchisees limited rights to use its brand name in return for a lump-sum payment and a share of the franchisee's profits. However, unlike the parties to most licensing agreements, franchisees have to agree to abide by strict rules as to how they do business. When McDonald's enters into a franchising agreement with a foreign company, it expects that company to run its restaurants in the same way that McDonald's restaurants elsewhere in the world are run.

The advantages of franchising are similar to those of licensing. Specifically, the franchiser does not have to bear the development costs and risks of opening up a foreign market on its own, for the franchisee typically assumes those costs and risks. Thus, using a franchising strategy, a service company can build up a global presence quickly and at a low cost.

The disadvantages, however, are less pronounced than in the case of licensing. Since franchising is a strategy used by service companies, a franchiser does not have to consider the need to coordinate manufacturing in order to achieve experience-curve effects and location economies. Nevertheless, franchising may inhibit a company's ability to achieve global strategic coordination.

A more significant disadvantage of franchising concerns quality control. The foundation of franchising arrangements is the notion that the company's brand name conveys a message to consumers about the quality of the company's product. Thus a business traveler booking into a Hilton International hotel in Hong Kong can reasonably expect the same quality of room, food, and service, as she would receive in New York. The Hilton brand name is a guarantee of the consistency of product quality. However, foreign franchisees may not be as concerned about quality as they should be, and poor quality may mean not only lost sales in the foreign market, but also a decline in the company's worldwide reputation. For example, if the business traveler has a bad experience at the Hilton in Hong Kong, she may never go to another Hilton hotel and steer her

colleagues away as well. The geographic distance separating it from its foreign franchisees, and the sheer number of individual franchisees—tens of thousands in the case of McDonald's—can make it difficult for the franchiser to detect poor quality. Consequently, quality problems may persist.

To obviate this drawback, a company can set up a subsidiary in each country or region in which it is expanding. The subsidiary might be wholly owned by the company or a joint venture with a foreign company. The subsidiary then assumes the rights and obligations to establish franchisees throughout that particular country or region. The combination of proximity and the limited number of independent franchisees that have to be monitored reduces the quality control problem. Besides, since the subsidiary is at least partly owned by the company, the company can place its own managers in the subsidiary to ensure the kind of quality monitoring it wants. This organizational arrangement has proved very popular in practice. It has been used by McDonald's, KFC, and Hilton Hotels Corp. to expand their international operations, to name just three examples.

Joint Ventures

Establishing a joint venture with a foreign company has long been a favored mode for entering a new market. The most typical form of joint venture is a 50/50 venture, in which each party takes a 50 percent ownership stake and operating control is shared by a team of managers from both parent companies. Some companies, however, have sought joint ventures in which they have a majority shareholding (for example, a 51 percent to 49 percent ownership split). This permits tighter control by the dominant partner.[19]

Joint ventures have a number of advantages. First, a company may feel that it can benefit from a local partner's knowledge of a host country's competitive conditions, culture, language, political systems, and business systems. (See Strategy in Action 8.1 for an example of how McDonald's benefited from this.) Thus for many U.S. companies joint ventures have involved the American company providing technological know-how and products and the local partner contributing the marketing expertise and local knowledge needed to compete within that country. Second, when the development costs and risks of opening up a foreign market are high, a company might gain by sharing these costs and risks with a local partner. Third, in many countries political considerations make joint ventures the only feasible entry mode. For example, historically many U.S. companies found it much easier to get permission to set up operations in Japan if they went in with a Japanese partner than if they tried to enter on their own.[20]

Despite these advantages, joint ventures can be difficult to establish and run because of two main drawbacks. First, as in the case of licensing, a company that enters into a joint venture risks losing control over its technology to its venture partner. To minimize this risk, a company can seek a majority ownership stake in the joint venture, for as the dominant partner it would be able to exercise greater control over its technology. The trouble with this strategy is that it may be difficult to find a foreign partner willing to accept a minority ownership position.

The second disadvantage is that a joint venture does not give a company the tight control over its subsidiaries that it might need in order to realize experience-curve effects or location economies—as both global and transnational companies try to do—or to engage in coordinated global attacks against its global rivals. Consider the entry of Texas Instruments (TI) into the Japanese semicon-

ductor market. When TI established semiconductor facilities in Japan, its sole purpose was to limit Japanese manufacturers' market share and the amount of cash available to them to invade TI's global market. In other words, TI was engaging in global strategic coordination. To implement this strategy, TI's Japanese subsidiary had to be prepared to take instructions from the TI corporate headquarters regarding competitive strategy. The strategy also required that the Japanese subsidiary be run at a loss if necessary. Clearly, a Japanese joint venture partner would have been unlikely to accept such conditions since they would have meant a negative return on investment. Thus, in order to implement this strategy, TI set up a wholly owned subsidiary in Japan, instead of entering this market through a joint venture.

Wholly Owned Subsidiaries

A **wholly owned subsidiary** is one in which the parent company owns 100 percent of the stock. To establish a wholly owned subsidiary in a foreign market, a company can either set up a completely new operation in that country or acquire an established host country company and use it to promote its products in the host market.

Setting up a wholly owned subsidiary offers three advantages. First, when a company's competitive advantage is based on its control of a technological competency, a wholly owned subsidiary will normally be the preferred entry mode, since it reduces the company's risk of losing this control. Consequently, many high-tech companies prefer wholly owned subsidiaries to joint ventures or licensing arrangements. Wholly owned subsidiaries tend to be the favored entry mode in the semiconductor, electronics, and pharmaceutical industries. Second, a wholly owned subsidiary gives a company the kind of tight control over operations in different countries that it needs if it is going to engage in global strategic coordination—taking profits from one country to support competitive attacks in another. Third, a wholly owned subsidiary may be the best choice if a company wants to realize location economies and experience-curve effects. As you saw earlier, when cost pressures are intense, it may pay a company to configure its value chain in such a way that value added at each stage is maximized. Thus a national subsidiary may specialize in manufacturing only part of the product line or certain components of the end product, exchanging parts and products with other subsidiaries in the company's global system. Establishing such a global production system requires a high degree of control over the operations of national affiliates. Different national operations have to be prepared to accept centrally determined decisions as to how they should produce, how much they should produce, and how their output should be priced for transfer between operations. A wholly owned subsidiary would, of course, have to comply with these mandates, whereas licensees or joint venture partners would most likely shun such a subservient role.

On the other hand, establishing a wholly owned subsidiary is generally the most costly method of serving a foreign market. The parent company must bear all the costs and risks of setting up overseas operations—in contrast to joint ventures, where the costs and risks are shared, or licensing, where the licensee bears most of the costs and risks. But the risks of learning to do business in a new culture diminish if the company acquires an established host country enterprise. Acquisitions, though, raise a whole set of additional problems, such as trying to

marry divergent corporate cultures, and these problems may more than offset the benefits. (The problems associated with acquisitions are discussed in Chapter 10).

Choosing Among Entry Modes

The advantages and disadvantages of the various entry modes are summarized in Table 8.2. Inevitably, there are tradeoffs in choosing one entry mode over another. For example, when considering entry into an unfamiliar country with a track record of nationalizing foreign-owned enterprises, a company might favor a joint venture with a local enterprise. Its rationale might be that the local partner will help it establish operations in an unfamiliar environment and will speak out against nationalization should the possibility arise. But if the company's distinctive competency is based on proprietary technology, entering into a joint venture might mean risking loss of control over that technology to the joint venture partner, which would make this strategy unattractive. Despite such hazards, some generalizations can be offered about the optimal choice of entry mode.

Distinctive Competencies and Entry Mode When companies expand internationally to earn greater returns from their distinctive competencies, transferring the skills and products derived from their competencies to foreign markets

Table 8.2
The Advantages and Disadvantages of Different Entry Modes

Entry Mode	Advantages	Disadvantages
Exporting	Ability to realize location and experience-curve economies	High transport costs Trade barriers Problems with local marketing agents
Licensing	Low development costs and risks	Lack of control over technology Inability to realize location and experience curve economies Inability to engage in global strategic coordination
Franchising	Low development costs and risks	Lack of control over quality Inability to engage in global strategic coordination
Joint Ventures	Access to local partner's knowledge Sharing development costs and risks Political acceptability	Lack of control over technology Inability to engage in global strategic coordination Inability to realize location and experience economies
Wholly owned subsidiaries	Protection of technology Ability to engage in global strategic coordination Ability to realize location and experience economies	High costs and risks

where indigenous competitors lack those skills, the companies are pursuing an international strategy. The optimal entry mode for such companies depends to some degree on the nature of their distinctive competency. In particular, we need to distinguish between companies with a distinctive competency in technological know-how and those with a distinctive competency in management know-how.

If a company's competitive advantage—its distinctive competency—derives from its control of proprietary *technological know-how*, licensing and joint venture arrangements should be avoided, if possible, in order to minimize the risk of losing control of that technology. Thus, if a high-tech company is considering setting up operations in a foreign country in order to profit from a distinctive competency in technological know-how, it should probably do so through a wholly owned subsidiary.

However, this rule should not be viewed as a hard and fast one. For instance, a licensing or joint venture arrangement might be structured in such a way as to reduce the risks of a company's technological know-how being expropriated by licensees or joint venture partners. We consider this kind of arrangement later in the chapter when we discuss the issue of structuring strategic alliances. To take another exception to the rule, a company may perceive its technological advantage as being only transitory, and expect rapid imitation of its core technology by competitors. In such a case, the company might want to license its technology as quickly as possible to foreign companies in order to gain global acceptance of its technology before imitation occurs. Such a strategy has some advantages. By licensing its technology to competitors, the company may deter them from developing their own, possibly superior, technology. It also may be able to establish its technology as the dominant design in the industry (as Matsushita did with its VHS format for VCRs), ensuring a steady stream of royalty payments. Such situations apart, however, the attractions of licensing are probably outweighed by the risks of losing control of technology, and therefore licensing should be avoided.

The competitive advantage of many service companies, such as McDonald's or Hilton Hotels, is based on *management know-how*. For such companies, the risk of losing control of their management skills to franchisees or joint venture partners is not that great. The reason is that the valuable asset of such companies is their brand name, and brand names are generally well protected by international laws pertaining to trademarks. Given this fact, many of the issues that arise in the case of technological know-how do not arise in the case of management know-how. As a result, many service companies favor a combination of franchising and subsidiaries to control franchisees within a particular country or region. The subsidiary may be wholly owned or a joint venture. In most cases, however, service companies have found that entering into a joint venture with a local partner in order to set up a controlling subsidiary in a country or region works best because a joint venture is often politically more acceptable and brings a degree of local knowledge to the subsidiary.

Pressures for Cost Reduction and Entry Mode The greater the pressures for cost reductions, the more likely it is that a company will want to pursue some combination of exporting and wholly owned subsidiaries. By manufacturing in the locations where factor conditions are optimal and then exporting to the rest of the world, a company may be able to realize substantial location economies and experience-curve effects. The company might then want to

export the finished product to marketing subsidiaries based in various countries. Typically, these subsidiaries would be wholly owned and have the responsibility for overseeing distribution in a particular country. Setting up wholly owned marketing subsidiaries is preferable to a joint ventures arrangement or to using a foreign marketing agent because it gives the company the tight control over marketing that might be required to coordinate a globally dispersed value chain. In addition, tight control over a local operation enables the company to use the profits generated in one market to improve its competitive position in another market. Hence companies pursuing global or transnational strategies prefer to establish wholly owned subsidiaries.

8.7 GLOBAL STRATEGIC ALLIANCES

Strategic alliances are cooperative agreements between companies that may also be competitors. In this section, we deal specifically with strategic alliances between companies from different countries. Strategic alliances run the range from formal joint ventures, in which two or more companies have an equity stake, to short-term contractual agreements in which two companies may agree to cooperate on a particular problem (such as developing a new product). There is no doubt that collaboration between competitors is in fashion. The 1980s saw a virtual explosion in the number of strategic alliances. Examples include a cooperative arrangement between Boeing and a consortium of Japanese companies to produce the 767 wide-bodied commercial jet; an alliance between Eastman Kodak and Canon of Japan under which Canon manufactures a line of medium-volume copiers for sale under Kodak's name; an agreement between Texas Instruments and Kobe Steel Inc. of Japan to make logic semiconductors in Japan; and an agreement between Motorola and Toshiba to pool their technological know-how and manufacture microprocessors.

Advantages of Strategic Alliances

Companies enter into strategic alliances with actual or potential competitors in order to achieve a number of strategic objectives.[21] First, as noted earlier in this chapter, strategic alliances may be a way of facilitating entry into a foreign market. For example, Motorola initially found it very difficult to gain access to the Japanese cellular telephone market. In the mid 1980s the company complained loudly about formal and informal Japanese trade barriers. The turning point for Motorola came in 1987, when it formed its alliance with Toshiba to build microprocessors. As part of the deal, Toshiba provided Motorola with marketing help—including some of its best managers. This aided Motorola in the political game of winning government approval to enter the Japanese market and obtaining allocations of radio frequencies for its mobile communications systems. Since then Motorola has played down the importance of Japan's informal trade barriers. Although privately the company still admits they exist, with Toshiba's help Motorola has become skilled at getting around them.[22]

Second, many companies have entered into strategic alliances in order to share the fixed costs (and associated risks) that arise from the development of new products or processes. Motorola's alliance with Toshiba was partly motivated by a desire to share the high fixed costs associated with setting up an operation to manufacture microprocessors. The microprocessor business is so capital inten-

STRATEGY IN ACTION 8.3

The IBM, Toshiba, and Siemens Alliance

On July 18, 1992, three of the world's largest high-technology companies, IBM, Toshiba, and Siemens, announced a strategic alliance to build a new generation of semiconductor chips. These three companies are, respectively, the world's biggest computer company and chipmaker, Japan's second largest chipmaker, and Europe's third largest semiconductor producer. The goal of their alliance is the development of a new semiconductor chip on whose tiny silicon surface will be etched what amounts to a street map of the entire world. Those electronic streets will link some 600 transistors. Targeted to be introduced in 1998, the chips will store 256 million bits of data, or about two copies of the complete works of William Shakespeare. This technology will have the capability of creating microprocessors with the power of today's supercomputers.

The reasons for the alliance are clear: to share the enormous costs and risks involved in the venture. The cost of developing the chip is estimated at about $1 billion. Building factories to produce the chip in economical volumes will cost each company another $1 billion. In addition to sharing these costs, the companies also hope that jointly developing the chip will give it a greater chance of becoming an accepted standard in an industry where being the standard is everything.[23]

sive—it cost Motorola and Toshiba close to $1 billion to set up their facility—that few companies can afford the costs and risks of going it alone. Similarly, the alliance between IBM, Toshiba, and Siemens, highlighted in Strategy in Action 8.3, is partly based on the desire to share the fixed costs of developing new microprocessors.

Third, many alliances can be seen as a way of bringing together complementary skills and assets that neither company could easily develop on its own. This was a factor in the strategic alliance between France's Thompson and Japan's JVC to manufacture videocassette recorders. JVC and Thompson are trading competencies; Thompson needs product technology and manufacturing skills, whereas JVC needs to learn how to succeed in the fragmented European market. Both sides believe that there is an equitable chance for gain. Similarly, in 1990 AT&T struck a deal with NEC Corp. of Japan to trade technological skills. AT&T will give NEC some of its computer-aided design technology. In return, NEC will give AT&T access to the technology underlying NEC advanced logic computer chips. Such equitable trading of distinctive competencies seems to underlie many of the most successful strategic alliances.

Finally, it may make sense to enter into an alliance if it helps the company set technological standards for its industry and if those standards benefit the company. For example, in 1992 the Dutch electronics company, Philips, entered into an alliance with its global competitor, Matsushita, to manufacture and market the digital compact cassette (DDC) system pioneered by Philips. The motive for this action was that linking up with Matsushita would help Philips establish the DCC system as a new technological standard in the recording and consumer electronics industries. The issue is an important one because Sony has developed a competing minicompact disk technology, which Sony hopes to establish as a new technical standard. Since the two technologies do very similar things, there

is probably room for only one new standard. The technology that becomes the new standard will be the one to succeed. The loser in this race to establish a technical standard will in all probability have to write off an investment worth billions of dollars. Philips sees the alliance with Matsushita as a tactic for winning the race, for it ties a potential major competitor into its standard.

Disadvantages of Strategic Alliances

The various advantages discussed above can be very significant. Nevertheless, some commentators have criticized strategic alliances on the grounds that they give competitors a low-cost route to gain new technology and market access. For example, Robert Reich and Eric Mankin have argued that strategic alliances between U.S. and Japanese companies are part of an implicit Japanese strategy to keep higher-paying, higher-value-added jobs in Japan while gaining the project-engineering and production-process skills that underlie the competitive success of many U.S. companies.[24] They have viewed Japanese success in the machine tool and semiconductor industries as largely built on U.S. technology acquired through various strategic alliances. And they have asserted that increasingly, American managers are aiding the Japanese in achieving their goals by entering into alliances that channel new inventions to Japan and provide a U.S. sales and distribution network for the resulting products. Although such deals may generate short-term profits, in the long run, according to Reich and Mankin, the result is to "hollow out" U.S. companies, leaving them with no competitive advantage in the global marketplace.

Reich and Mankin have a point; alliances do have risks. Unless it is careful, a company can give away more than it gets in return. On the other hand, there are so many examples of apparently successful alliances between companies, including alliances between U.S. and Japanese companies, that Reich and Mankin's position seems more than a little extreme. It is difficult to see how the Motorola-Toshiba alliance, the Ford-Mazda alliance, or the twenty-five-year-old Fuji-Xerox alliance to build and market photocopiers in Asia, fit their thesis. In all of these cases, both partners seemed to have gained from the alliance. Since Reich and Mankin undoubtedly do have a point, the question becomes *why do some alliances benefit the company, whereas in others it can end up giving away technology and market access and get very little in return*? The next section provides an answer to this question.

8.8 MAKING STRATEGIC ALLIANCES WORK

The benefits that a company derives from a strategic alliance seem to be a function of three factors: partner selection, alliance structure, and the way in which the alliance is managed. We look at each of these issues in turn.

Partner Selection

One of the keys to making a strategic alliance work is to select the right kind of partner. The right kind of partner has three principal characteristics. First, it must be able to help the company achieve its strategic goals, whether they be market access, sharing the costs and risks of new product development, or gaining access to critical core competencies. In other words, the partner must have capabilities that the company values but lacks. Second, the partner must

share the company's vision of the alliance's purpose. If two companies approach an alliance with radically different agendas, the chances are that it will end in divorce.

Third, the partner must be one that is unlikely to try to opportunistically exploit the alliance for its own ends, expropriating the company's technological know-how, while giving little in return. In this respect, companies that have a reputation for fair play to maintain probably make the best alliance partners. For example, IBM is involved in so many strategic alliances that it would not pay the company to trample roughshod over individual alliance partners, expropriating their technological know-how and giving little in return. Such action would tarnish IBM's hard-won reputation of being a good company with which to enter into an alliance. In turn, this would make it more difficult for IBM to attract alliance partners in the future. Since IBM attaches great importance to establishing alliances with other enterprises, the company is unlikely to engage in the kind of opportunistic behavior that Reich and Mankin highlight. IBM has a reputation for fair play to maintain. Similarly, a need to safeguard their reputation makes it less likely (though not impossible) that Japanese companies such as Sony, Toshiba, or Fuji, which have a history of entering into alliances with non-Japanese companies, would opportunistically exploit an alliance partner.

In order to select a partner with the above characteristics, a company has to undertake a comprehensive search of potential alliance candidates before choosing a partner. It needs to collect as much pertinent publicly available information on potential alliance partners as possible. It also needs to collect data from informed third parties, such as companies that have been involved in alliances with potential partners, investment bankers who have had dealings with potential partners, and former employees of potential partners. In addition, the company must get to know its potential alliance partner as well as possible before making a commitment to enter an alliance. Face-to-face meetings between senior managers (and perhaps middle-level managers) are important in this regard, to ensure that the chemistry is right.

Alliance Structure

Having selected a partner, the company should try to structure the alliance in such a way that its risks of giving too much to the partner without getting anything in return are reduced to an acceptable level. There are at least four ways in which a company can protect itself against a partner's opportunism. (Opportunism includes the theft of technology and/or markets that Reich and Mankin describe.) First, alliances can be designed to make it difficult, if not impossible, to transfer technology that is not meant to be transferred. Specifically, the design, development, manufacture, and service of a product manufactured by an alliance may be structured so as to *wall off* the most sensitive technologies and prevent their leakage to the other participant. For example, in the alliance between General Electric and Snecma to build commercial aircraft engines, General Electric tried to reduce the risk of excess transfer by walling off certain sections of the production process. The modularization effectively cut off the transfer of what GE felt was key competitive technology, while permitting Snecma access to final assembly. Similarly, in the alliance between Boeing and the Japanese to build the 767, Boeing walled off research, design, and marketing functions, considered more central to Boeing's competitive position, while allowing the Japanese to share in production technology. Boeing also walled off new technologies not required for 767 production.[25]

Second, contractual safeguards can be written into an alliance agreement. For example, TRW Inc., has three strategic alliances with large Japanese auto component suppliers to produce seat belts, engine valves, and steering gears for sale to Japanese-owned auto assembly plants in the United states. TRW has clauses in each of its alliance contracts that bar the Japanese companies from competing with TRW to supply American-owned auto companies (GM, Ford, and Chrysler) with component parts. These clauses protect TRW against the possibility that the Japanese companies are entering into the alliances to gain access to TRW's home market and become its competitor there.

Third, both parties to an alliance can agree in advance to exchange skills and technologies that each wants from the other, thereby ensuring a chance for equitable gain. Cross-licensing agreements are one way of achieving this goal. For example, in the case of the alliance between Motorola and Toshiba, Motorola has licensed some of its microprocessor technology to Toshiba, and in return Toshiba has licensed some of its memory chip technology to Motorola.

Fourth, the risk of opportunism by an alliance partner can be decreased if the company extracts in advance a significant *credible commitment* from its partner, which would make it less likely that the alliance would end with the company giving away much and getting little in return. The long-term alliance between Xerox and Fuji to build photocopiers to supply the Asian market illustrates such a commitment. Rather than enter into an informal agreement or some kind of licensing arrangement (which Fuji initially wanted), Xerox insisted that Fuji invest in a 50/50 joint venture to serve Japan and East Asia. This venture constituted such a significant investment in people, equipment, and facilities that Fuji was from the outset committed to making the alliance work in order to earn a return on that investment. By agreeing to enter into a joint venture, Fuji made a credible commitment to the alliance, and Xerox felt secure in transferring its photocopier technology to Fuji.

Managing the Alliance

Once a partner has been selected and an appropriate alliance structure agreed on, the task facing the company is to maximize the benefits from the alliance. One important ingredient appears to be a sensitivity to cultural differences. Differences in management style can often be attributed to cultural differences. Managers need to make allowances for such differences when dealing with their partner. In addition, managing an alliance successfully involves building interpersonal relationships among managers from the different companies—a lesson that can be drawn from the successful strategic alliance between Ford and Mazda. This alliance has resulted in the development of such best-selling cars as the Ford Explorer and the Mazda Navajo. Ford and Mazda have set up a framework of meetings within which managers from Ford and Mazda not only discuss matters pertaining to the alliance, but also have sufficient nonwork time to allow them to get to know each other better. The resulting personal friendships can help build trust and facilitate harmonious relations between the two companies. Moreover, personal relationships can create an informal management network between the companies, and this network can then be used to help solve problems that arise in more formal contexts, such as joint committee meetings between personnel from both firms.

A major factor determining how much a company gains from an alliance is its ability to learn from alliance partners. Gary Hamel, Yves Doz, and C. K. Prahalad reached this conclusion after a five-year study of fifteen strategic alliances between major multinationals. They focused on a number of alliances between Japanese companies and Western (European or American) partners. In every case in which a Japanese company emerged from an alliance stronger than its Western partner, the Japanese company had made a greater effort to learn. Indeed, few Western companies seemed to want to learn from their Japanese partners. They tended to regard the alliance purely as a cost-sharing or risk-sharing device, rather than as an opportunity to learn how a potential competitor does business.[26]

For example, consider the alliance between General Motors and Toyota Motor Corp. to build the Chevrolet Nova. This alliance is structured as a formal joint venture, called New United Motor Manufacturing Inc., in which both parties have a 50 percent equity stake. The venture owns an auto plant in Fremont, California. According to one of the Japanese managers, Toyota achieved most of its objectives from the alliance: "We learned about U.S. supply and transportation. And we got the confidence to manage U.S. workers."[27] All that knowledge was then quickly transferred to Georgetown, Kentucky, where Toyota opened a plant of its own in 1988. By contrast, although General Motors got a new product, the Chevrolet Nova, some GM managers complained that their knowledge was never put to good use inside GM. They say that they should have been kept together as a team to educate GM's engineers and workers about the Japanese system. Instead they were dispersed to different GM subsidiaries.[28]

When entering an alliance, a company must take some measures to ensure that it learns from its alliance partner and then puts that knowledge to good use within its own organization. One suggested approach is to educate all operating employees about the partner's strengths and weaknesses and make clear to them how acquiring particular skills will bolster their company's competitive position. For such learning to be of value, the knowledge acquired from an alliance has to be diffused throughout the organization—as did not happen at GM. To spread this knowledge, the managers involved in an alliance should be used as a resource in familiarizing others within the company about the skills of an alliance partner.

8.9 SUMMARY OF CHAPTER

In this chapter we examine the various ways in which companies can profit from global expansion and review the strategies that companies engaged in global competition can adopt. We also discuss the optimal choice of entry mode to serve a foreign market and explore the issue of strategic alliances. The following points have been made in this chapter:

1. For some companies, international expansion represents a way of earning greater returns by transferring the skills and product offerings derived from their distinctive competencies to markets where indigenous competitors lack those skills.

2. Because of national differences, it pays a company to base each value-creation activity it performs at the location where factor conditions are most conducive to the performance of that activity. We refer to this strategy as focusing on the attainment of location economies.
3. By building sales volume more rapidly, international expansion can assist a company in the process of moving down the experience curve.
4. The best strategy for a company to pursue may depend on the kind of pressures it must cope with: pressures for cost reductions or for local responsiveness. Pressures for cost reductions are greatest in industries producing commodity-type products, where price is the main competitive weapon. Pressures for local responsiveness arise from differences in consumer tastes and preferences, as well as from national infrastructure and traditional practices, distribution channels, and host government demands.
5. Companies pursuing an international strategy transfer the skills and products derived from distinctive competencies to foreign markets, while undertaking some limited local customization.
6. Companies pursuing a multidomestic strategy customize their product offering, marketing strategy, and business strategy to national conditions.
7. Companies pursuing a global strategy focus on reaping the cost reductions that come from experience-curve effects and location economies.
8. Many industries are now so competitive that companies must adopt a transnational strategy. This involves a simultaneous focus on reducing costs, transferring skills and products, and local responsiveness. Implementing such a strategy, however, may not be easy.
9. There are five different ways of entering a foreign market—exporting, licensing, franchising, entering into a joint venture, and setting up a wholly owned subsidiary. The optimal choice among entry modes depends on the company's strategy.
10. Strategic alliances are cooperative agreements between actual or potential competitors. The advantages of alliances are that they facilitate entry into foreign markets, enable partners to share the fixed costs and risks associated with new products and processes, facilitate the transfer of complementary skills between companies, and help companies establish technical standards.
11. The drawbacks of a strategic alliance are that the company risks giving away technological know-how and market access to its alliance partner while getting very little in return.
12. The disadvantages associated with alliances can be reduced if the company selects partners carefully, paying close attention to reputation, and if it structures the alliance so as to avoid unintended transfers of know-how.

Discussion Questions

1. In a world of zero transportation costs, no trade barriers, and nontrivial differences between nations with regard to factor conditions, companies must expand internationally if they are to survive. Discuss.

2. Plot the position of the following companies on Figure 8.1: Procter & Gamble, IBM, Coca-Cola, Dow Chemicals, USX, and McDonald's. In each case, justify your answer.
3. Are the following global industries or multidomestic industries: bulk chemicals, pharmaceuticals, branded food products, moviemaking, television manufacture, personal computers, and airline travel?
4. Discuss how the need for control over foreign operations varies with the strategy and distinctive competencies of a company. What are the implications of this for the choice of entry mode?
5. A small Canadian company that has developed a set of valuable new medical products using its own unique biotechnology know-how is trying to decide how best to serve the European Union market. Its choices are as follows: (a) manufacture the product at home and let foreign sales agents handle marketing; (b) manufacture the products at home but set up a wholly owned subsidiary in Europe to handle marketing; and (c) enter into a strategic alliance with a large European pharmaceutical company. The product would be manufactured in Europe by a 50/50 joint venture, and then marketed by the European company. The cost of investment in manufacturing facilities is a major one for the Canadian company but not outside its reach. If these are the company's only options, what option would you advise it to choose? Why?

Article File 8

Find an example of a multinational company that in recent years has switched its strategy from a multidomestic, international, or global strategy to a transnational strategy. Identify why the company made the switch and any problems that the company may be encountering while it tries to change its strategic orientation.

Strategic Management Project: Module 8

This module requires you to identify how your company might profit from global expansion, the strategy that your company should pursue globally, and the entry mode that it might favor. With the information you have at your disposal, answer the questions regarding the following two situations:

A. Your company is already doing business in other countries

1. Is your company creating value or lowering the costs of value-creation by realizing location economies, transferring distinctive competencies abroad, or realizing cost economies from the experience curve? If not, does it have the potential to?
2. How responsive is your company to differences between nations? Does it vary its product and marketing message from country to country? Should it?
3. What are the cost pressures and pressures for local responsiveness in the industry in which your company is based?

4. What strategy is your company pursuing to compete globally? In your opinion, is this the correct strategy, given cost pressures and pressures for local responsiveness?
5. What major foreign market does your company serve and what mode has it used to enter this market? What are the advantages and disadvantages of using this mode? Might another mode be preferable?

B. Your company is not yet doing business in other countries

1. What potential does your company have to add value to its products or lower the costs of value creation by expanding internationally?
2. On the international level, what are the cost pressures and pressures for local responsiveness in the industry in which your company is based? What implications do these pressures have for the strategy that your company might pursue if it chose to expand globally?
3. What foreign market might your company enter and what entry mode should it use to enter this market? Justify your answer.

Endnotes

1. C. S. Trager, "Enter the Mini-Multinational," *Northeast International Business* (March 1989) 13–14.
2. Sources: Kathleen Deveny et al., "McWorld?" *Business Week*, October 13, 1986, pp. 78–86. "Slow Food," *Economist*, February 3, 1990, p. 64.
3. "Matsushita Electrical Industrial in 1987," in *Transnational Management*, ed. C. A. Bartlett and S. Ghoshal (Homewood, Ill.: Irwin, 1992).
4. C. K. Prahalad and Yves L. Doz, "The Multinational Mission: Balancing Local Demands and Global Vision" (New York: Free Press, 1987). Prahalad and Doz actually talk about local responsiveness rather than local customization.
5. "The Tire Industry's Costly Obsession with Size," *Economist*, June 8, 1993, p. 65–66.
6. T. Levitt, "The Globalization of Markets," *Harvard Business Review*, (May–June, 1983), 92–102.
7. C. A. Bartlett and S. Ghoshal, *Managing Across Borders*, (Boston, Mass.: Harvard Business School Press, 1989).
8. This section is based on Bartlett and Ghoshal, *Managing Across Borders.*
9. Sources: Guy de Jonquieres and C. Bobinski, "Wash and Get Into a Lather in Poland," *Financial Times*, May 28, 1992, p. 2. "Perestroika in Soapland," *Economist*, June 10, 1989, pp. 69–71. "After Early Stumbles P&G Is Making Inroads Overseas," *Wall Street Journal*, February 6, 1989, p. B1. Bartlett and Ghoshal, *Managing Across Borders.*
10. Bartlett and Ghoshal, *Managing Across Borders.*
11. Ibid.
12. T. Hout, M. E. Porter, and E. Rudden, "How Global Companies Win Out," *Harvard Business Review*, (September–October, 1982), 98–108.
13. Guy de Jonquieres, "Unilever Adopts a Clean Sheet Approach," *Financial Times*, October 21, 1991, p. 13.
14. Bartlett and Ghoshal, *Managing Across Borders*,.
15. Ibid.
16. This section draws on the following studies: C. W. L. Hill, P. Hwang, and W. C. Kim, "An Eclectic Theory of the Choice of International Entry Mode," *Strategic Management Journal*, 11 (1990), pp. 117–128. C. W. L. Hill and W. C. Kim, "Searching for a Dynamic Theory of the Multinational Enterprise: A Transaction Cost Model," *Strategic Management Journal*, 9 (1988), Special Issue on Strategy Content, pp. 93–104. See also E. Anderson and H. Gatignon, "Modes of Foreign Entry: A Transaction Cost Analysis and Propositions," *Journal of International Business Studies*, 17 (1986), 1–26; and F. R. Root, *Entry Strategies for International Markets* (Lexington, Mass.: Heath, 1980).
17. For a general discussion of licensing, see F. J. Contractor, "The Role of Licensing in International Strategy," *Columbia Journal of World Business*, (Winter 1982), 73–83.
18. J. H. Dunning and M. McQueen, "The Eclectic Theory of International Production: A Case Study of the International Hotel Industry," *Managerial and Decision Economics*, 2 (1981), 197–210.
19. For a review of the literature of joint ventures, see B. Kogut, "Joint Ventures: Theoretical and Empirical Perspectives," *Strategic Management Journal*, 9 (1988), 319–332.
20. D. G. Bradley, "Managing Against Expropriation" *Harvard Business Review* (July–August 1977), 78–90.
21. See K. Ohmae, "The Global Logic of Strategic Alliances," *Harvard Business Review*, (March–April 1989) 143–154; G. Hamel, Y. L. Doz, and C. K. Prahalad, "Collaborate with

Your Competitors and Win!" *Harvard Business Review* (January–February 1988) 133–139; W. Burgers, C. W. L. Hill, and W. C. Kim, "Alliances in the Global Auto Industry," *Strategic Management Journal*, in press.
22. "Asia Beckons," *Economist*, May 30, 1992, pp. 63–64.
23. Sources: "Chip Diplomacy," *Economist*, July 18, 1992, p. 65. O. Port, "Talk About Your Dream Team," *Business Week*, July 27, 1992, pp. 59–60.
24. R. B. Reich and E. D. Mankin, "Joint Ventures with Japan Give Away Our Future," *Harvard Business Review*, (March–April 1986), 78–90.
25. T. W. Roehl and J. F. Truitt, "Stormy Open Marriages Are Better," *Columbia Journal of World Business*, (Summer 1987), 87–95.
26. Hamel, Doz, and Prahalad, "Collaborate with Your Competitors and Win!" pp. 133–139.
27. B. Wysocki, "Cross Border Alliances Become Favorite Way to Crack New Markets," *Wall Street Journal*, March 4, 1990, p. A1.
28. Ibid.

9 Vertical Integration, Diversification, and Strategic Alliances

9.1 OPENING CASE: DIVERSIFICATION AT DAIMLER-BENZ

For years Germany's Daimler-Benz AG enjoyed a well-earned reputation as one of the world's premier makers of high-quality luxury cars. During the mid 1980s, however, under the leadership of a new CEO, Edzard Reuter, Daimler-Benz embarked on a dramatic strategic change. Reuter transformed Daimler-Benz from a focused company producing luxury cars and trucks under the Mercedes-Benz label into Germany's largest industrial conglomerate, with annual revenues in the $60 billion range. He achieved this by acquiring a number of major German companies, including electronics and consumer goods manufacturer AEG and the aerospace companies Dornier Aircraft and Messerschmitt-Boelkow-Blohm (MBB). Daimler-Benz subsequently combined Dornier and MBB into Deutsche Aerospace. Deutsche Aerospace is now the effective owner of Germany's 37.9 percent stake in the European Airbus Industrie consortium, which is competing head-to-head with Boeing in the world commercial jet aircraft market.

The logic underlying Reuter's diversification strategy was based on a number of factors. First, he believed that the intensity of rivalry in the global automobile industry would increase. Japanese competitors were beginning to move up market into Mercedes-Benz's territory, making it more difficult for Daimler-Benz to hold on to its differential advantage. Second, Reuter reasoned that in this new competitive environment the companies that would come out on top would be those that were able to incorporate leading-edge technology into their cars before rivals did. Third, he believed that by acquiring electronics and aerospace businesses Daimler-Benz could gain access to just such leading-edge technological know-how. In short, Reuter believed that technological developments were creating enormous opportunities for sharing know-how across the aerospace, automobile, and electronics businesses.

However, Reuter's ambitious plans have yet to bring the gains that he so boldly predicted for them. Since the mid 1980s the company's profits have stagnated. A prime reason has been the poor performance of Daimler-Benz's new businesses. AEG was losing money when Daimler-Benz bought it. According to analysts, AEG has yet to show a profit. Similarly, MBB has turned out to be a perennial money loser. As a result, by the early 1990s the Mercedes-Benz car business, even though it made up only 40 percent of Daimler-Benz's total revenues, accounted for 90 percent of profits. To make matters worse, there are signs that the car business may be running into trouble. In 1992, for the first time ever, Daimler-Benz's archrival, BMW, sold more cars than Daimler-Benz. BMW sold an estimated 590,000 cars around the world in 1992, well ahead of the 530,000 Mercedes-Benz cars that were sold.

Reuter claims that these problems are short-run ones and that in the long run the diversification strategy will pay off. Others are not so sure. Many analysts always thought that Reuter had an exaggerated view of the potential for sharing technology among the aerospace, auto, and electronic businesses. They were also puzzled as to why a diversified conglomerate had to be built to share such know-how, particularly at a time when many other companies were sharing know-how through strategic alliances. Critics of Reuter's policies also point to serious morale problems that have begun to emerge

within the enlarged group. Managers at AEG were apparently unhappy about being ordered to hand over their lucrative aerospace division to Deutsche Aerospace. The Dornier-MBB combination has also run into problems. The two aerospace companies had radically different cultures and were old rivals before their marriage enforced by Daimler-Benz. Now MBB's Munich-based managers apparently resent having to report to the Deutsche Aerospace head office in Stuttgart, which is staffed primarily by old Dornier personnel. Furthermore, managers at Mercedes-Benz resent having most of their company's profits used to finance money-losing business units such as AEG and MBB, and Mercedes-Benz's engineers dislike being lumped together with companies they perceive to be inferior. In addition, there is the perception that Reuter's focus on diversification has sapped capital and diverted top management's attention from the company's core car-making business; hence Mercedes-Benz's recent loss of leadership in the German automobile industry to BMW.[1]

Discussion Questions

1. Evaluate critically the logic underlying Daimler-Benz's diversification strategy. How might this strategy add value to Daimler-Benz's established automobile business?
2. Identify ways in which Daimler-Benz's diversification strategy might have destroyed rather than created value.
3. Do you think that Daimler-Benz needed to diversify in order to gain access to leading-edge technological know-how? What other approach than diversification might the company have used?

9.2 OVERVIEW

Corporate-level strategy is concerned with two main questions: (1) what business areas should a company participate in so as to maximize its long-run profitability? and (2) what strategies should it use to enter into and exit from business areas? The first question is the focus of this chapter, and the second of Chapter 10. In choosing business areas to compete in, a company has several options. The main ones are to vertically integrate into adjacent businesses or to diversify into a number of different business areas. In this chapter, we explore these options in depth and examine their pros and cons. We also look at strategic alliances as alternatives to vertical integration and diversification.

The Opening Case describes the corporate strategy of one company, Daimler-Benz. When in the mid 1980s Daimler-Benz reduced its dependence on its core car- and truck-making business by diversifying into new business areas—specifically aerospace and electronics—it chose to do so through acquisitions rather than new ventures. However, as the case shows, this strategy has not created value. Indeed, to judge by the recent performance of the company's Mercedes-Benz car operation, noted in the case, one could argue that the strategy has dissipated rather than created value for the company's customers and stockholders.

As you will see in this chapter and Chapter 10, the experience of Daimler Benz is not uncommon; many corporate-level strategies do seem to have dissipated rather than created value. Therefore, we repeatedly stress that to succeed, corporate level strategies should *add value* to the company. To understand what this means, we have to go back to the concept of the value chain, introduced in Chapter 5. *To add value, a corporate strategy should enable a company, or one or more of its business units, to perform one or more of the value-creation functions at a lower cost, or perform one or more of the value-creation functions in*

a way that allows for differentiation and a premium price. Thus a company's *corporate* strategy should help in the process of establishing a distinctive competency and competitive advantage *at the business level.* This does not seem to have occurred at Daimler-Benz; hence the company's current problems.

9.3 VERTICAL INTEGRATION

Vertical integration means that a company is producing its own inputs (backward or upstream integration) or is disposing of its own outputs (forward or downstream integration). A steel company that supplies its iron ore needs from company-owned iron ore mines exemplifies backward (upstream) integration. An auto manufacturer that sells its cars through company-owned distribution outlets illustrates forward (downstream) integration. Figure 9.1 illustrates four *main* stages in a typical raw-material-to-consumer production chain. For a company based in the assembly stage, backward integration involves moving into intermediate manufacturing and raw-material production. Forward integration involves movement into distribution. At each stage in the chain, *value is added* to the product. What this means is that a company at that stage takes the product produced in the previous stage, transforms it in some way, and then sells the output at a higher price to a company at the next stage in the chain. The difference between the price paid for inputs and the price at which the product is sold is a measure of the value added at that stage.

As an example of the value added concept, consider the production chain in the personal computer industry, illustrated in Figure 9.2. In the personal computer industry, the raw materials companies include the manufacturers of specialty ceramics, chemicals, and metals such as Dow Chemical and Union Carbide. These companies sell their output to the manufacturers of intermediate products. The intermediate manufacturers, which include companies such as Intel and Motorola, transform the ceramics, chemicals, and metals they purchase into computer components such as microprocessors, memory chips, and disk drives. In doing so they *add value* to the raw materials they purchase. These components are then sold to assembly companies such as Apple and Compaq, which take these components and transform them into personal computers—that is, *add value* to the components they purchase. Many of the completed personal computers are then sold to distributors such as Bizmart and Computer World, which in turn sell them to final customers. The distributors also *add value* to the product by making it accessible to customers, and by providing service and support. Thus value is added by companies at each stage in the raw-materials-to-consumer chain.

Figure 9.1 Stages in the Raw-Material-to-Consumer Production Chain

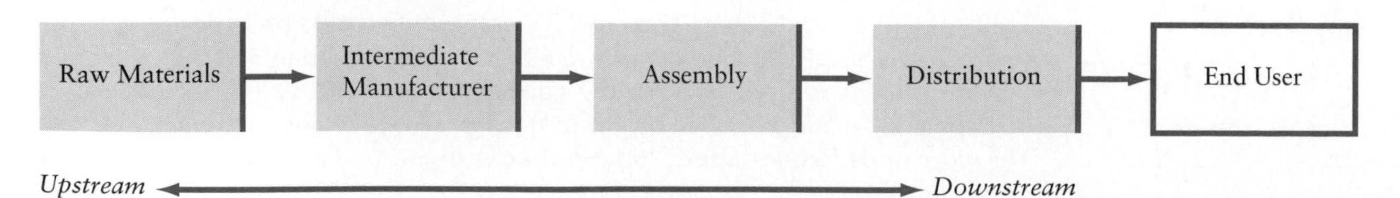

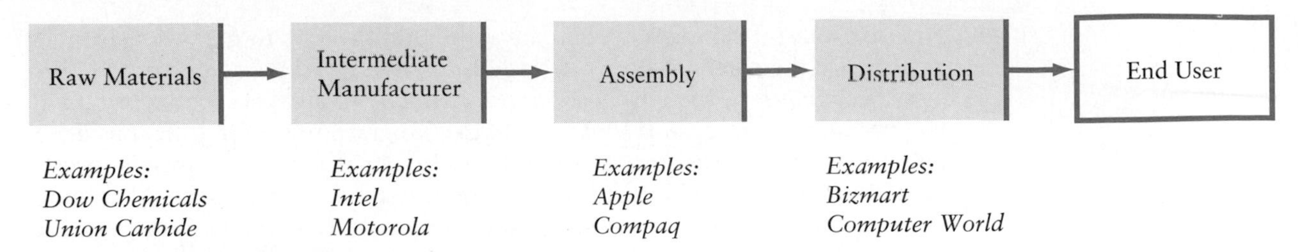

Figure 9.2
The Raw-Material-to-Consumer Production Chain in the Personal Computer Industry

Viewed this way, vertical integration involves a choice about which value added stages of the raw-material-to-consumer chain to compete in. In the personal computer industry, most companies have not integrated into adjacent stages. However, there are some major exceptions. For example, IBM and Digital Equipment are involved in both the intermediate manufacturer and assembly stage of the industry. They are vertically integrated enterprises. In contrast, many of their competitors in the end-user market, such as Compaq and Apple, are not vertically integrated.

Finally, note that besides forward and backward integration, it is also possible to distinguish between **full integration** and **taper integration** (see Figure 9.3).[2] A company achieves full integration when it produces all of a particular input needed for its processes or when it disposes of all of its output through its own operations. Taper integration occurs when a company buys from independent suppliers in addition to company-owned suppliers or when it disposes of its output through independent outlets in addition to company-owned outlets. The advantages of taper integration over full integration are discussed later in the chapter.

Creating Value Through Vertical Integration

A company pursuing vertical integration is normally motivated by a desire to strengthen the competitive position of its original, or core, business.[3] There are four main arguments for pursuing a vertical integration strategy. Vertical integration (1) enables the company to build barriers to new competition, (2) facilitates investments in efficiency-enhancing specialized assets, (3) protects product quality, and (4) results in improved scheduling.

Building Barriers to Entry By vertically integrating backward to gain control over the source of critical inputs or vertically integrating forward to gain control

Figure 9.3
Full and Taper Integration

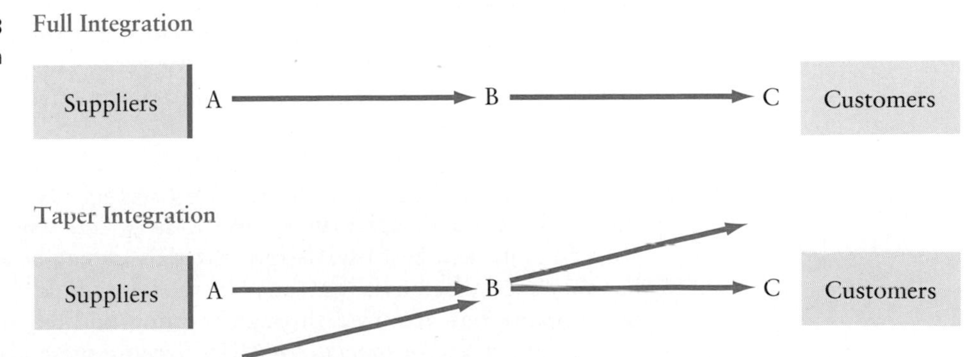

over distribution channels, a company can build barriers to new entry into its industry. To the extent that this strategy is effective, *it limits competition in the company's industry, thereby enabling the company to charge a higher price and make greater profits than it could otherwise.*[4] To grasp this argument, consider a famous example of this strategy from the 1930s. At that time commercial smelting of aluminum was pioneered by companies like Alcoa and Alcan. Aluminum is derived from smelting bauxite. Although bauxite is a common mineral, the percentage of aluminum in bauxite is usually so low that it is not economical to mine and smelt. During the 1930s only one large-scale deposit of bauxite had been discovered where the percentage of aluminum in the mineral made smelting economical. This deposit was on the Caribbean island of Jamaica. Alcoa and Alcan vertically integrated backward and acquired ownership over this deposit. This action created a barrier to entry into the aluminum industry. Potential competitors were deterred from entry because they could not get access to high-grade bauxite; it was all owned by Alcoa and Alcan. Because they had to use lower-grade bauxite, those that did enter the industry found themselves at a cost disadvantage vis-à-vis these two companies. This situation persisted until the 1950s, when new high-grade deposits were discovered in Australia and Indonesia.

More recently, a similar strategy has been pursued by vertically integrated companies in the computer industry like IBM and Digital Equipment. These companies manufacture the main components of computers such as microprocessors and memory chips, design and assemble the computers, produce the software that runs the computers, and sell the final product directly to end users. The original rationale behind this strategy was that many of the key components and software used in computers contained proprietary elements. These companies reasoned that by producing this proprietary technology in-house they could limit rivals' access to it, thereby building barriers to entry. Thus when IBM introduced its PS/2 personal computer system in the mid 1980s, it announced that certain component parts incorporating proprietary technology would be manufactured in-house by IBM. IBM's objective here was to limit rapid imitation of its PS/2 system by making it difficult for rivals, such as Compaq, to duplicate the functions performed by its proprietary components.

While this strategy worked well from the 1960s until the early 1980s, it has been failing since then. In the early 1990s the worst performers in the computer industry were precisely the companies that pursued the vertical integration strategy: IBM and Digital Equipment. What seems to have happened is that the shift to open standards in computer hardware and software has nullified the advantages for computer companies of being extensively vertically integrated. In addition, new personal computer companies such as Compaq found that they could quickly reverse-engineer and duplicate the proprietary components that companies such as IBM placed in their computers, effectively circumventing this barrier to entry.

Facilitating Investments in Specialized Assets A specialized asset is an asset that is designed to perform a specific task and whose value is significantly reduced in its next best use.[5] A specialized asset may be a piece of equipment that has very specialized uses, or it may be the know-how or skills that an individual or company has acquired through training and experience. *Companies (and individuals) invest in specialized assets because these assets allow them to lower the costs of value creation and/or to better differentiate their product offering*

from that of competitors, thereby facilitating premium pricing. A company might invest in specialized equipment because it enables it to lower its manufacturing costs and increase its quality, or it might invest in developing highly specialized technological knowledge because doing so lets it develop better products than their rivals. *Thus specialization can be the basis for achieving a competitive advantage at the business level.*

For reasons that we explore in the next paragraphs, a company may find it very difficult to persuade other companies in *adjacent* stages in the raw-material-to-consumer production chain to undertake investments in specialized assets. Consequently, to realize the economic gains associated with such investments, it may have to vertically integrate into such adjacent stages and make the investments itself. As an illustration, imagine that Ford has developed a new, high-performance, high-quality, and uniquely designed carburetor. The carburetor will increase fuel efficiency, which in turn will help differentiate Ford's cars from those of its rivals—that is, it will give Ford a competitive advantage. Ford has to decide whether to make the carburetor in-house (vertical integration), or contract out manufacturing to an independent supplier (outsourcing). Manufacturing these carburetors requires substantial investments in equipment *that can be used only for this purpose*. Because of its unique design, the equipment cannot be used to manufacture any other type of carburetor for Ford or any other auto firms. Thus the investment in this equipment constitutes an investment in specialized assets.

First consider this situation from the perspective of an independent supplier that has been asked by Ford to make this investment. The supplier might reason that once it has made the investment it will become dependent on Ford for business *since Ford is the only possible customer for the output of this equipment*. The supplier perceives this as putting Ford in a strong bargaining position and worries that once the specialized investment has been made Ford might use this position to squeeze down prices for the carburetors. Given this risk, the supplier declines to make the investment in specialized equipment.

Now consider Ford's position. Ford might reason that if it contracts out production of these carburetors to an independent supplier it might become too dependent on that supplier for a vital input. Since specialized equipment is required to produce the carburetors, Ford cannot easily switch its orders to other suppliers that lack the equipment. Ford perceives this as increasing the bargaining power of the supplier and worries that the supplier might use its bargaining strength to demand higher prices.

The situation of **mutual dependence** that would be created by the investment in specialized assets makes Ford hesitant to contract out and makes any potential suppliers hesitant to undertake the investments in specialized assets required to produce the carburetors. The real problem here is a lack of trust. Neither Ford nor the supplier completely trusts the other to play fair in this situation. The lack of trust arises from the **risk of holdup**, that is, of being taken advantage of by a trading partner after the investment in specialized assets has been made.[6] Because of this risk, Ford might reason that the only safe way to get the new carburetors is to manufacture them itself. Indeed, Ford may be unable to persuade any independent supplier to manufacture them. Therefore, Ford decides to make the carburetors rather than buy them from an independent source.

To generalize from this example, when achieving a competitive advantage requires one company to make investments in specialized assets in order to trade

STRATEGY IN ACTION 9.1

Specialized Assets and Vertical Integration in the Aluminum Industry

To see how an investment in a specialized asset can lead to vertical integration, consider the case of an aluminum refining company. Aluminum refineries are designed to refine bauxite ore and produce aluminum. The metal content and chemical composition of bauxite ore varies from deposit to deposit. Each type of ore requires a specialized refinery; that is, the refinery must be designed for a particular type of ore. Running one type of bauxite through a refinery designed for another type reportedly increases production costs by 20 to 100 percent.[7] Thus the value of an investment in a specialized aluminum refinery and the cost of the output produced by that refinery depend on it receiving the right kind of bauxite ore.

Imagine that an aluminum company has to decide whether to invest in an aluminum refinery designed to refine a certain type of ore. Assume further that this ore is produced only by a bauxite company at a single bauxite mine. Using a different type of ore would raise production costs by 50 percent. Therefore, the value of the aluminum company's investment depends on the price it must pay the bauxite company for this bauxite. Given this situation, once the aluminum company has made the investment in a new refinery, there is nothing to stop the bauxite company from raising bauxite prices; the aluminum company is locked into its relationship with its bauxite supplier. The bauxite company can increase bauxite prices secure in the knowledge that as long as the resulting increase in the total production costs of the aluminum company is less than 50 percent, the aluminum company will continue to buy from it. Thus once the aluminum company has made the investment, the bauxite company can hold up the aluminum company.

How can the aluminum company reduce the risk of holdup? The answer is, by purchasing the bauxite company. If the aluminum company can purchase the bauxite company, or that company's bauxite mine, it need no longer fear that bauxite prices will be increased after the investment in an aluminum refinery has been made. In other words, it makes economic sense for the aluminum company contemplating the investment to engage in vertical integration. By eliminating the risk of holdup, vertical integration makes the specialized investment worthwhile. It has been argued that these kinds of considerations have driven aluminum companies to pursue vertical integration to such a degree that, according to one study, 91 percent of the total volume of bauxite is transferred within vertically integrated aluminum companies.[8]

with another, the risk of holdup may serve as a deterrent, and the investment may not take place. Consequently, the potential for competitive gains from specialization would be lost. To prevent such loss, companies vertically integrate into adjacent stages in the value chain. This consideration has driven automobile companies to vertically integrate backward into the production of component parts, steel companies to vertically integrate backward into the production of iron, computer companies to vertically integrate backward into chip production, and aluminum companies to vertically integrate backward into bauxite mining. The rationale underlying vertical integration in the aluminum industry is explored in greater detail in Strategy in Action 9.1.

Protecting Product Quality By protecting product quality, vertical integration enables a company to become a differentiated player in its core business. The banana industry illustrates this situation. Historically, a problem facing food

companies that import bananas was the variable quality of delivered bananas, which often arrived on the shelves of American stores either too ripe or not ripe enough. To correct this problem, major American food companies, such as General Foods, have integrated backward to gain control over supply sources. Consequently, they have been able to distribute bananas of a standard quality at the optimal time for consumption to American consumers. Knowing that they can rely on the quality of these brands, consumers are willing to pay more for them. Thus by vertically integrating backward into plantation ownership, the banana companies have built consumer confidence, which enables them in turn to charge a premium price for their product. Similarly, when McDonald's decided to open up its first restaurant in Moscow, it found, much to its initial dismay, that in order to serve food and drink indistinguishable from that served in McDonald's restaurants elsewhere, it had to vertically integrate backward and supply its own needs. The quality of Russian-grown potatoes and meat was simply too poor. Thus, to protect the quality of its product, McDonald's set up its own dairy farms, cattle ranches, vegetable plots, and food-processing plant within the Soviet Union. (See Strategy in Action 8.1.)

The same kind of considerations can result in forward integration. Ownership of distribution outlets may be necessary if the required standards of after-sales service for complex products are to be maintained. For example, in the 1920s Kodak owned retail outlets for distributing photographic equipment. The company felt that few established retail outlets had the skills necessary to sell and service its photographic equipment. By the 1930s, however, Kodak decided that it no longer needed to own its retail outlets because other retailers had begun to provide satisfactory distribution and service for Kodak products. The company then withdrew from retailing.

Improved Scheduling It is sometimes argued that strategic advantages arise from the easier planning, coordination, and scheduling of adjacent processes made possible in vertically integrated organizations.[9] This can be particularly important in companies trying to realize the benefits of just-in-time inventory systems, discussed in detail in Chapter 5. For example, in the 1920s Ford profited from the tight coordination and scheduling that is possible with backward vertical integration. Ford integrated backward into steel foundries, iron ore shipping, and iron ore mining. Deliveries at Ford were coordinated to such an extent that iron ore unloaded at Ford's steel foundries on the Great Lakes was turned into engine blocks within twenty-four hours. Thus Ford substantially lowered its cost structure by eliminating the need to hold excessive inventories.

The enhanced scheduling that vertical integration makes feasible may also enable a company to respond better to sudden changes in demand conditions, or to get its product into the marketplace faster. A situation in the microprocessor industry of the early 1990s illustrates this point. Demand for microprocessors was running at an all-time high, and most microprocessor manufacturing plants were operating at full capacity. At that time several microprocessor companies that specialized in chip design but contracted out manufacturing found themselves at a strategic disadvantage. For example, in 1991 Chips & Technologies succeeded in designing a clone of Intel's 386 microprocessor. Chips & Technologies sent its clone design to Texas Instruments (TI) to be manufactured, only to find that it had to wait fourteen weeks until TI could schedule time to manufac-

ture Chips & Technologies's 386 clone. In that short span prices for 386 microprocessors fell from $112 to $50. By the time TI produced the 386 clone for Chips & Technologies, the company had missed the best part of the market. Had Chips & Technologies been vertically integrated into manufacturing, this would not have occurred.[10]

Arguments Against Vertical Integration

Vertical integration has its disadvantages. Most important among them are (1) cost disadvantages, (2) disadvantages that arise when technology is changing fast, and (3) disadvantages that arise when demand is unpredictable. These disadvantages imply that the benefits of vertical integration are not always as substantial as they might seem initially.

Cost Disadvantages Although often undertaken to gain a production cost advantage, vertical integration can raise costs if a company becomes committed to purchasing inputs from company-owned suppliers when low-cost external sources of supply exist. For example, General Motors makes 68 percent of the component parts for its vehicles in-house, more than any other major automaker (at Chrysler the figure is 30 percent, and at Toyota, 28 percent). That vertical integration has caused GM to be the highest-cost producer among the world's major car companies. In 1992 GM was paying $34.60 an hour in United Auto Workers wages and benefits to its employees at company-owned suppliers for work that rivals could get done at half these rates by independent nonunionized suppliers.[11] Thus, as General Motors exemplifies, vertical integration can be a disadvantage when a company's own sources of supply have higher operating costs than those of independent suppliers.

Company-owned suppliers might have high operating costs compared with independent suppliers because company-owned suppliers know that they can always sell their output to other parts of the company. Not having to compete for orders lessens the incentive to minimize operating costs. Indeed, the managers of the supply operation may be tempted to pass on any cost increases to other parts of the company in the form of higher transfer prices, rather than looking for ways to lower those costs. Thus the lack of incentive to reduce costs can raise operating costs. The problem may be less serious, however, when the company pursues taper, rather than full, integration, since the need to compete with independent suppliers can produce a downward pressure on the cost structure of company-owned suppliers.

Technological Change When technology is changing fast, vertical integration poses the hazard of tying a company to an obsolescent technology.[12] Consider a radio manufacturer that in the 1950s integrated backward and acquired a manufacturer of vacuum tubes. When in the 1960s transistors replaced vacuum tubes as a major component in radios, this company found itself tied to a technologically obsolescent business. Switching to transistors would have meant writing off its investment in vacuum tubes. Therefore, the company was reluctant to change and instead continued to use vacuum tubes in its radios while its non-integrated competitors were rapidly switching to the new technology. Since it kept making an outdated product, the company rapidly lost market share. Thus vertical integration can inhibit a company's ability to change its suppliers or its distribution systems to match the requirements of changing technology.

Demand Uncertainty Vertical integration can also be risky in unstable or unpredictable demand conditions. When demand is stable, higher degrees of vertical integration might be managed with relative ease. Stable demand allows better scheduling and coordination of production flows among different activities. When demand conditions are unstable or unpredictable, achieving close coordination among vertically integrated activities may be difficult. The resulting inefficiencies can give rise to significant bureaucratic costs.

The problem involves balancing capacity among different stages of a process. For example, an auto manufacturer might vertically integrate backward to acquire a supplier of carburetors that has a capacity exactly matching the auto manufacturer's needs. However, if demand for autos subsequently falls, the automaker will find itself locked into a business that is running below capacity. Clearly, this would be uneconomical. The auto manufacturer could avoid this situation by continuing to buy carburetors on the open market rather than making them itself.

If demand conditions are unpredictable, taper integration might be somewhat less risky than full integration. When a company obtains only part of its total input requirements from company-owned suppliers, in times of low demand it can keep its in-house suppliers running at full capacity by ordering exclusively from them.

Bureaucratic Costs and the Limits of Vertical Integration

As already noted, although vertical integration can create value, it may also result in substantial costs caused by a lack of incentive on the part of company-owned suppliers to reduce their operating costs, by a possible lack of strategic flexibility in times of changing technology, or by uncertain demand. Together, these costs form a major component of what we refer to as the **bureaucratic costs** of vertical integration. Bureaucratic costs are simply the costs of running an organization. They include the costs that stem from bureaucratic inefficiencies, such as those we have just discussed. The existence of bureaucratic costs places a limit on the amount of vertical integration that can be profitably pursued: it makes sense for a company to vertically integrate only if *the value created by such a strategy exceeds the bureaucratic costs associated with expanding the boundaries of the organization to incorporate additional upstream or downstream activities.*

Commonsense reasoning suggests that not all vertical integration opportunities have the same potential for value creation. Although vertical integration may initially have a favorable impact, the value created by additional vertical integration moves into areas more distant from a company's core business is likely to become increasingly marginal. The more marginal the value created by a vertical integration move, the more likely it is that the bureaucratic costs associated with expanding the boundaries of the organization into new activities will outweigh the value created. Once this occurs, a limit to profitable vertical integration will have been reached.[13]

However, it is worth bearing in mind that the pursuit of taper integration rather than full integration may decrease the bureaucratic costs of vertical integration. This occurs because taper integration creates an incentive for in-house suppliers to reduce their operating costs and increases the company's ability to respond to changing demand conditions. Hence it reduces some of the organizational inefficiencies that raise bureaucratic costs.

9.4 STRATEGIC ALLIANCES AS AN ALTERNATIVE TO VERTICAL INTEGRATION

The disadvantages associated with vertical integration raise the question of whether it is possible to reap the benefits of vertical integration without having to bear the same level of bureaucratic costs. Can the benefits associated with vertical integration be captured through outsourcing activities to other companies? The answer seems to be a qualified yes. Under certain circumstances, companies can realize the gains linked with vertical integration, without having to bear the bureaucratic costs, if they enter into **long-term cooperative relationships** with their trading partners. Such long term-relationships are typically referred to as **strategic alliances.** However, companies will generally be unable to realize the gains associated with vertical integration if they enter into **short-term contracts** with their trading partners. To see why this is so, we first discuss the problems associated with short-term contracts. Then we look at strategic alliances and long-term contracts as an alternative to vertical integration and discuss how companies can build enduring, long-term relationships with their trading partners.

Short-Term Contracts and Competitive Bidding

A short-term contract is one that lasts for a year or less. Many companies use short-term contracts to structure the purchasing of their inputs or the sale of their outputs. A classic example is the automobile company that uses a **competitive bidding strategy** to negotiate the price for a particular part produced by component suppliers. For example, General Motors often solicits bids from a number of different suppliers for producing a component part and awards a one-year contract to the supplier submitting the lowest bid. At the end of the year the contract is put out for competitive bid again. Thus there is no guarantee that the company that won the contract one year will hold on to it the next.

The benefit of this strategy is that it forces suppliers to keep down their prices, which has advantages for the cost structure of a company like GM. But GM's lack of long-term commitment to individual suppliers may make them very hesitant to undertake the type of investments in specialized assets that may be needed to improve the design or quality of component parts or to improve scheduling between GM and its suppliers. Indeed, with no guarantee that it would remain a GM supplier the following year, as the supplier may refuse to undertake investments in specialized assets. GM then may have to vertically integrate backward in order to realize the gains associated with specialization.

In other words, the strategy of short-term contracting and competitive bidding, *because it signals a lack of long-term commitment to its suppliers on the part of a company*, will make it very difficult for that company to realize the gains associated with vertical integration. This is not a problem when there is minimal need for close cooperation between the company and its suppliers to facilitate investments in specialized assets, improve scheduling, or improve product quality. In such cases competitive bidding may be optimal. However, when this need is significant, considerations do arise. A competitive bidding strategy can be a serious drawback.

Interestingly enough, there are signs that GM, by adopting a competitive bidding stance with regard to its suppliers, has placed itself at a competitive disad-

vantage. In 1992 the company instructed its part suppliers to cut their prices by 10 percent, regardless of prior pricing agreements. In effect, GM tore up existing contracts and tried to force through its policy by threatening to weed out suppliers that did not agree to the price reduction. Although such action may yield short-term benefits for GM, there is a long-term cost to be borne: the loss of trust and the hostility between the company and its suppliers. According to press reports, several suppliers have claimed that they are cutting back on research for future GM parts. They have also indicated that they will impart new ideas to Chrysler or Ford, both of which have recently taken a more cooperative approach to forging long-term relationships with suppliers.[14]

Strategic Alliances and Long-Term Contracting

Long-term contracts are long-term cooperative relationships between two companies. Such agreements are often referred to in the popular press as *strategic alliances*. Typically in these arrangements, one company agrees to supply the other, and the other company agrees to continue purchasing from that supplier; both make a commitment to jointly seek ways of lowering the costs or raising the quality of inputs into the downstream company's value-creation process. If it is achieved, such a stable long-term relationship lets the participating companies share the value that might be created by vertical integration while avoiding many of the bureaucratic costs linked with ownership of an adjacent stage in the raw-material-to-consumer production chain. Thus long-term contracts can substitute for vertical integration.

Consider the cooperative relationships that many of the Japanese auto companies have with their component-parts suppliers (the *keiretsu* system) which exemplify successful long-term contracting. These relationships often go back decades. Together, the auto companies and their suppliers work out ways to increase value-added—for instance, by implementing just-in-time inventory systems or by cooperating on component-part designs to improve quality and lower assembly costs. Part of this process involves the suppliers making substantial investments in specialized assets in order to better serve the needs of the auto companies. Thus the Japanese auto majors have been able to capture many of the benefits of vertical integration without having to bear the bureaucratic costs associated with formal vertical integration. The component-parts suppliers also benefit from these relationships, for they grow with the company they supply and share in its success.

In contrast to their Japanese counterparts, U.S. auto companies have historically tended to pursue formal vertical integration (General Motors manufactures 68 percent of its own component parts and Ford 47 percent, compared with less than 30 percent among most Japanese auto companies).[15] According to several studies, the increased bureaucratic costs of managing extensive vertical integration have helped place GM and Ford at a competitive disadvantage relative to their Japanese competition.[16] Moreover, when U.S. auto companies decide not to vertically integrate, they do not necessarily enter into cooperative long-term relationships with independent component suppliers. Instead, they have tended to use their powerful position to pursue an aggressive competitive bidding strategy, playing off component suppliers against each other. Although Ford and Chrysler are now backing away from such a policy, it remains in force at GM, as noted earlier.

Other industries yield similar examples of effective and ineffective strategies regarding suppliers. Strategy in Action 9.2 details the different approaches used by two companies in the computer industry.

Building Long-Term Cooperative Relationships

The interesting question raised by the preceding section is how can a company achieve a stable long-term strategic alliance with another, given the lack of trust and the fear of holdup that arises when one company has to invest in specialized asset in order to trade with another. How have companies like Toyota managed to develop such enduring relationships with their suppliers, and how has Quantum Corporation managed to build such a successful long-term relationship with MKE of Japan? (See Strategy in Action 9.2.)

Companies can take some specific steps to ensure that a long-term cooperative relationship can work and to lessen the chances of a partner reneging on an agreement. One of those steps is for the company making investments in specialized assets to demand a **hostage** from its partner. Another is to establish a **credible commitment** on both sides to build a trusting long-term relationship.[18]

Hostage Taking

Hostage taking is essentially a means of guaranteeing that a partner will keep its side of the bargain. The cooperative relationship between Boeing and Northrop illustrates this type of situation. Northrop is a major subcontractor for Boeing's commercial airline division, providing many component parts for the 747 and 767 aircraft. To serve Boeing's special needs, Northrop has had to make substantial investments in specialized assets. In theory, because of the sunk costs associated with such investments, Northrop is dependent on Boeing, and Boeing is in a position to renege on previous agreements and use the threat to switch orders to other suppliers as a way of driving down prices. However, in practice Boeing is unlikely to do so since the company is also a major supplier to Northrop's defense division, providing many parts for the Stealth bomber. Boeing has had to make substantial investments in specialized assets in order to serve Northrop's needs. Thus both companies are *mutually dependent*. Boeing, therefore, is unlikely to renege on any pricing agreements with Northrop, since it knows that Northrop could respond in kind. Each company holds a hostage that can be used as insurance against the other company's unilateral reneging on prior pricing agreements.

Credible Commitments

A credible commitment is a believable commitment to support the development of a long-term relationship between companies. To understand the concept of credibility in this context, consider the relationship between General Electric and IBM. GE is one of the major suppliers of advanced semiconductor chips to IBM, and many of the chips are customized to IBM's own requirements. To meet IBM's specific needs, GE has had to make substantial investments in specialized assets that have little other value. As a consequence, GE is dependent on IBM and faces a risk that IBM will take advantage of this dependence to demand lower prices. Theoretically, IBM could back up its demand with the threat to switch to another supplier. However, GE reduced this risk by having IBM enter into a contractual agreement that committed IBM to purchase chips from GE until the end of the 1990s. In addition, IBM agreed to share in the costs of developing the customized chips, thereby reducing GE's investments in specialized assets. Thus, by publicly committing itself to

STRATEGY IN ACTION 9.2

Vertical Integration Versus Outsourcing: Quantum Corporation and Seagate Technologies

Quantum Corporation and Seagate Technologies are both major producers of disk drives for personal computers and workstations. However, in recent years the two companies have pursued very different vertical integration strategies. Seagate is a vertically integrated manufacturer of disk drives that both designs and manufactures its own disk drives. Quantum, on the other hand, specializes in design and outsources most of its manufacturing to a number of independent suppliers, including, most importantly, Matsushita Kotobuki Electronics (MKE) of Japan. These different strategies have yielded different results for the two companies, with Quantum's sales growth far outstripping that of Seagate.

Quantum makes only its newest and most expensive products in-house. Once a new drive is perfected and ready for large-scale manufacturing, the company turns over manufacturing to MKE. MKE and Quantum have cemented their partnership over eight years. At each stage in the designing of a new product, Quantum's engineers send the latest drawings to a production team at MKE. MKE examines the drawings and proposes changes that make new disk drives easier to manufacture. When the product is ready for manufacture, eight to ten Quantum engineers travel to MKE's plant in Japan for at least a month to work on production ramp up.

By meshing their skills, Quantum and MKE have created a revolutionary new disk drive design that gives Quantum's latest drives two key advantages over those produced by competitors such as Seagate: lower prices and higher reliability. In most disk drives, the circuit board, which is the brain of the drive, holds about eighteen semiconductors inserted front and back. By working together, Quantum and MKE figured out a way to increase the power of these semiconductors. As a result, they were able to reduce the number of semiconductors to nine, and to place them all on one side of the board. The new practice has cut the number of component parts by 30 percent and halved production time, substantially reducing unit costs and prices. With fewer parts, the drives break down less often, and so reliability has increased as well.

In contrast, Seagate has been criticized for being slow to introduce new products and for a general lack of innovation in recent years. Seagate's problem, according to critics, is its being tied into obsolete production technologies, which its less integrated rivals such as Quantum have bypassed. Seagate has also found that the high fixed costs associated with being an integrated manufacturer cause its earnings to decline more rapidly than Quantum's in a slump, since Seagate has to deal with excess capacity, whereas Quantum does not. By the same token, though, when demand is strong and capacity is tight, Seagate does not have to pay high prices to independent suppliers, like companies that rely more on outsourcing—such as Quantum—may be forced to do. However, in a tacit admission that being fully integrated was not optimal, Seagate has begun to outsource more. Seagate now pursues a taper, rather than full, integration strategy, with about 40 percent of its disk drive production being outsourced through suppliers.[17]

a long-term contract and by putting some money into the development of the customized chips, IBM has essentially made a *credible commitment* to continue purchasing those chips from GE.

Maintaining Market Discipline A company that has entered into a long-term relationship also needs to have sanctions that can be applied to a partner if it fails to live up to its side of the bargain. Otherwise a company can become too dependent on an inefficient partner. Since it does not have to compete with other

organizations in the marketplace for the company's business, the partner may lack the incentive to be cost efficient. Consequently, a company entering into a cooperative long-term relationship must be able to apply some kind of market discipline to its partner.

It holds two strong cards. First, even long-term contracts are periodically renegotiated, generally every four to five years. Thus a partner knows that if it fails to live up to its commitments, the company may refuse to renew the contract. Second, some companies engaged in long-term relationships with suppliers use a **parallel sourcing policy**—that is, they enter into a long-term contract with two suppliers for the same part (as is the practice at Toyota, for example).[19] This arrangement gives the company a hedge against a defiant partner, for each supplier knows that if it fails to comply with the agreement, the company can switch all its business to the other. This threat is rarely made explicit, since that would be against the spirit of building a cooperative long-term relationship. But the mere awareness of parallel sourcing serves to inject an element of market discipline into the relationship as the arrangement signals to suppliers that if the need arises, they can be replaced at short notice.

Summary By establishing credible commitments or by taking hostages, companies may be able to use long-term contracts to realize much of the value associated with vertical integration yet not have to bear the bureaucratic costs of formal vertical integration. As a general point, it should be noted that the growing importance of just-in-time inventory systems as a way of reducing costs and enhancing quality is increasing the pressure on companies to enter into long-term agreements in a wide range of industries. These agreements thus might become much more popular in the future. However, when such agreements cannot be reached, formal vertical integration may be called for.

9.5 DIVERSIFICATION

Up until this point we have been dealing with vertical integration and its alternatives. It is now time to move on and consider diversification. There are two major types of diversification: related diversification and unrelated diversification. **Related diversification** is diversification into a new business activity that is linked to a company's existing business activity, or activities, by commonality between one or more components of each activity's value chain. Normally, these linkages are based on manufacturing, marketing, or technological commonalities. The diversification of Philip Morris into the brewing industry with the acquisition of Miller Brewing is an example of related diversification because there are marketing commonalities between the brewing and tobacco business (both are consumer product businesses in which competitive success depends on brand-positioning skills). **Unrelated diversification** is diversification into a new business area that has no obvious connection with any of the company's existing areas.

In this section, we first consider how diversification can create value for a company, and then we examine some reasons why so much diversification apparently dissipates rather than creates value. We also take into account the bureaucratic costs of diversification. Finally, we discuss some of the factors that determine the choice between the strategies of related and unrelated diversification.

Creating Value Through Diversification

Most companies first consider diversification when they are generating financial resources *in excess* of those necessary to maintain a competitive advantage in their original, or core, business.[20] The question they must tackle is how to invest the excess resources in order to create value. The diversified company can create value in three main ways: (1) by acquiring and restructuring poorly run enterprises, (2) by transferring competencies among businesses, and (3) by realizing economies of scope.

Acquiring and Restructuring A restructuring strategy rests on the presumption that an efficiently managed company can create value by acquiring inefficient and poorly managed enterprises and improving their efficiency.[21] This approach can be considered diversification because the acquired company does not have to be in the same industry as the acquiring company for the strategy to work. Improvements in the efficiency of an acquired company can come from a number of sources. First, the acquiring company usually replaces the top management team of the acquired company with a more aggressive top management team. Second, the new top management team is encouraged to sell off any unproductive assets, such as executive jets and elaborate corporate headquarters, and to reduce staffing levels. Third, the new top management team is also encouraged to intervene in the running of the acquired businesses to seek out ways of improving the unit's efficiency, quality, innovativeness, and customer responsiveness. Fourth, to motivate the new top management team and other employees of the acquired unit to undertake such actions, increases in their pay may be linked to increases in the performance of the acquired unit. In addition, the acquiring company often establishes performance goals for the acquired company that cannot be met without significant improvements in operating efficiency. It also makes the new top management aware that failure to achieve performance improvements consistent with these goals within a given amount of time will probably result in their losing their jobs. This system of rewards and punishments established by the acquiring company gives the new managers of the acquired enterprise every incentive to look for ways of improving the efficiency of the unit under their charge.

There are some good examples of how successful a restructuring strategy can be in terms of its impact upon a company's profitability—for instance, the British conglomerates BTR Inc and Hanson Trust Plc.[22] But the strategy has its critics. Some contend that constant pressures to meet challenging performance objectives within such companies can lead to short-run profit maximization and risk avoidance by business unit managers.[23] Moreover, the arms-length relationship between the corporate headquarters and business unit management, common in such enterprises, allows this type of behavior to go undetected until a good deal of damage has been done. The poor performance of portfolio diversifiers, such as Gulf & Western Industries, Consolidated Foods, and ITT, lends weight to these criticisms. More than anything else, the conflicting examples suggest that the strategy is difficult to implement.

Transferring Competencies Companies that base their diversification strategy on transferring competencies seek out new businesses related to their existing business by one or more value-creation functions—for example, manufacturing, marketing, materials management, and R&D. They may want to create value by drawing on the distinctive skills in one or more of their

existing value-creation functions in order to improve the competitive position of the new business. Alternatively, they may acquire a company in a different business area in the belief that some of the skills of the acquired company can improve the efficiency of their existing value-creation activities. If successful, such competency transfers can *lower the costs of value creation* in one or more of a company's diversified businesses or enable one or more of a company's diversified businesses to undertake their value-creation functions in a way that leads to *differentiation* and a *premium price.*

An example is Germany's Daimler-Benz, profiled in the Opening Case. The maker of Mercedes-Benz cars, in recent years Daimler has diversified into household goods, defense electronics, automation systems, and aerospace. This strategy is rooted in a belief that the transfer of state-of-the-art technological know-how between the different businesses of the company will enhance the competitive position of each, enabling all of Daimler-Benz's businesses to better differentiate themselves with regard to technology.

For such a strategy to work, the competencies being transferred must involve activities that are important for establishing a competitive advantage. All too often companies assume that any commonality is sufficient for creating value. General Motors' acquisition of Hughes Aircraft, made simply because autos and auto manufacturing were going electronic and Hughes was an electronics concern, demonstrates the folly of overestimating the commonalities among businesses. To date, the acquisition has failed to realize any of the anticipated gains for GM, whose competitive position has only worsened. Similarly, one may question the value that Daimler-Benz might create from transferring technological know-how between autos and aerospace (see Opening Case).

Philip Morris's transfer of marketing skills to Miller Brewing, discussed earlier, is perhaps one of the classic examples of how value *can* be created by competency transfers. Drawing on its marketing and brand-positioning skills, Philip Morris pioneered the introduction of Miller Lite, the product that redefined the brewing industry and moved Miller from number six to number two in the market. Rockwell International's diversification into factory automation with the company's 1985 acquisition of Allen-Bradley Canada Ltd. is another example of skill transfers. In this case, skill transfers were based on technological linkages between different activities. Rockwell gave Allen-Bradley strong research and development support and Rockwell's own electronics technology, and Allen-Bradley's factory automation expertise boosted efficiency in Rockwell's commercial and defense factories.[24]

Economies of Scope **Economies of scope** arise when two or more business units share resources such as manufacturing facilities, distribution channels, advertising campaigns, R&D costs, and so on. Each business unit that shares resources has to invest less in the shared functions.[25] For example, the costs of General Electric's advertising, sales, and service activities in major appliances are low because they are spread over a wide range of products. In addition, such a strategy can utilize the capacity of certain functions better. For example, by producing the components for the assembly operations of two distinct businesses, a component-manufacturing plant may be able to operate at greater capacity, thereby realizing *economies of scale* in addition to economies of scope. Thus a diversification strategy based on economies of scope can help a company attain a low-cost position in each of the businesses in which it operates. Diversification

to realize economies of scope can therefore be a valid way of supporting the generic business-level strategy of cost leadership.

However, like competency transfers, diversification to realize economies of scope is possible only when there are significant commonalities between one or more of the value-creation functions of a company's existing and new activities. Moreover, managers need to be aware that the bureaucratic costs of coordination necessary to achieve economies of scope within a company often outweigh the value that can be created by such a strategy.[26] Consequently, the strategy should be pursued only when sharing is likely to generate a *significant* competitive advantage in one or more of a company's business units.

Procter & Gamble's disposable diaper and paper towel businesses offer one of the best examples of the successful realization of economies of scope. These businesses share the costs of procuring certain raw materials (such as paper) and developing the technology for new products and processes. In addition, a joint sales force sells both products to supermarket buyers, and both products are shipped by means of the same distribution system. This resource sharing has given both business units a cost advantage that has enabled them to undercut their less diversified competitors.[27]

Bureaucratic Costs and the Limits of Diversification

While diversification can create value for a company, it often ends up doing just the opposite. For example, in a study that looked at the diversification of thirty-three major U.S. corporations between 1950 and 1986, Michael Porter observed that the track record of corporate diversification has been dismal.[28] Porter found that most of the companies had divested many more diversified acquisitions than they had kept. He concluded that the corporate diversification strategies of most companies have dissipated value instead of creating it. More generally, a large number of academic studies support the conclusion that *extensive* diversification tends to depress rather than improve company profitability.[29]

One reason for the failure of diversification to achieve its aims is that all too often the *bureaucratic costs* of diversification exceed the value created by the strategy. The level of bureaucratic costs in a diversified organization is a function of two factors: (1) the number of businesses in a company's portfolio and (2) the extent of coordination required between the different businesses of the company in order to realize value from a diversification strategy.

Number of Businesses The greater the number of businesses in a company's portfolio, the more difficult it is for corporate management to remain informed about the complexities of each business. Management simply does not have the time to process all the information needed to assess the strategic plan of each business unit objectively. This problem began to occur at General Electric in the 1970s. As then CEO Reg Jones commented,

> I tried to review each plan in great detail. This effort took untold hours and placed a tremendous burden on the corporate executive office. After a while I began to realize that no matter how hard we would work, we could not achieve the necessary in-depth understanding of the 40-odd business unit plans.[30]

The information overload in extensively diversified companies may lead corporate-level management to base important resource allocation decisions only on the most superficial analysis of each business unit's competitive position.

Thus, for example, a promising business unit may be starved of investment funds, while other business units receive far more cash than they can profitably reinvest in their operations. Furthermore, the lack of familiarity with operating affairs on the part of corporate-level management increases the chances that business-level managers might deceive corporate-level managers. For instance, business-unit managers might blame poor performance on difficult competitive conditions, even when it is the consequence of poor management. Thus information overload can result in substantial inefficiencies within extensively diversified companies that cancel out the value created by diversification. These inefficiencies include the suboptimal allocation of cash resources within the company and a failure by corporate management to successfully encourage and reward aggressive profit-seeking behavior by business-unit managers.

The inefficiencies arising from information overload can be viewed as one component of the bureaucratic costs of extensive diversification. Of course, these costs can be reduced to manageable proportions if a company limits the scope of its diversification. Indeed, a desire to decrease these costs lay behind the 1980s divestments and strategic concentration strategies of conglomerates of the 1960s and 1970s, such as Esmark Corporation, General Electric, ITT, Textron, Tenneco, and United Technologies. For example, under the leadership of Jack Welch, GE switched its emphasis from forty main business units to sixteen main business units contained within three clearly defined sectors.

Coordination Among Businesses The coordination required to realize value from a diversification strategy based on competency transfers or economies of scope can also be a source of bureaucratic costs. Both the transfer of distinctive competencies and the achievement of economies of scope demand close coordination among business units. The bureaucratic mechanisms needed for this coordination give rise to bureaucratic costs. (We discuss the mechanisms for achieving coordination in Chapter 12).

A more serious matter, however, is that substantial bureaucratic costs can result from an inability to identify the unique profit contribution of a business unit that is sharing resources with another unit in an attempt to realize economies of scope. Consider a company that has two business units—one producing household products (such as liquid soap and laundry detergent) and another producing packaged food products. The products of both units are sold through supermarkets. In order to lower the costs of value creation, the parent company decides to pool the marketing and sales functions of each business unit. Pooling allows the business units to share the costs of a sales force (one sales force can sell the products of both divisions) and gain cost economies from using the same physical distribution system. The organizational structure required to achieve this might be similar to that illustrated in Figure 9.4. The company is organized into three main divisions: a household products division, a food products division, and a marketing division.

Although such an arrangement may create value, it can also give rise to substantial control problems and hence bureaucratic costs. For example, if the performance of the household products business begins to slip, identifying who is to be held accountable—the management of the household products division or the management of the marketing division—may prove difficult. Indeed, each may blame the other for poor performance: The management of the household products division might blame the marketing policies of the marketing division, and the management of the marketing division might blame the poor quality and

high costs of products produced by the household products division. Although this kind of problem can be resolved if corporate management directly audits the affairs of both divisions, doing so is costly in terms of both the time and the effort that corporate management must expend.

Now imagine the situation within a company that is trying to create value by sharing marketing, manufacturing, and R&D resources across ten businesses rather than just two. Clearly, the accountability problem could become far more severe in such a company. Indeed, the problem might become so acute that the effort involved in trying to tie down accountability might create a serious information overload for corporate management. When this occurs, corporate management effectively loses control of the company. If accountability cannot be sorted out, the consequences may include an inability by corporate management to encourage and reward aggressive profit-seeking behavior by business-unit managers, poor resource allocation decisions, and a generally high level of organizational slack. All of these inefficiencies can be considered part of the bureaucratic costs of diversification to realize economies of scope.

Limits of Diversification Thus, although diversification can create value for a company, it inevitably involves bureaucratic costs. As with vertical integration, the existence of bureaucratic costs places a limit on the amount of diversification that can be profitably pursued. Given the existence of bureaucratic costs, it makes sense for a company to diversify only as long as *the value created by such a strategy exceeds the bureaucratic costs associated with expanding the boundaries of the organization to incorporate additional business activities.*

Remember that the greater the number of business units within a company and the greater the need for coordination among those business units, the larger the bureaucratic costs are likely to be. Hence a company that has twenty businesses, all of which are trying to share resources, incurs much larger bureaucratic costs than a company that has ten businesses, none of which are trying to share resources. The implications of this relationship are quite straightforward. Specifically, the greater the number of businesses already in a company's portfolio and the greater the need for coordination among those businesses, the more probable it will be that the value created by a diversification move will be

Figure 9.4
The Structure of a Company Sharing Marketing Between Two Business Units

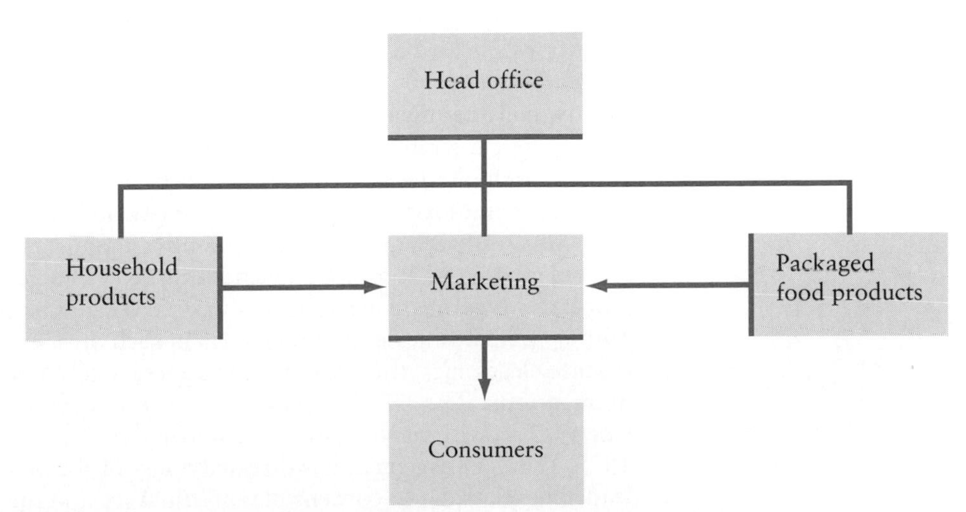

outweighed by the resulting increase in bureaucratic costs. Once this occurs, a profitable limit to the diversified scope of the enterprise will have been reached. However, many companies continue to diversify past this limit, and their performance declines. To solve this problem a company must reduce the scope of the enterprise through divestments. Strategy in Action 9.3 discusses a company—ICI—that overdiversified and subsequently had to divest itself of previously acquired businesses. In Chapter 10 we look at a number of other companies that have made the same mistake.

Diversification That Dissipates Value

Another reason that so much diversification fails to create value is that many companies diversify for the wrong reasons. As a consequence, they end up dissipating value rather than creating it. This is particularly true of diversification to pool risks or to achieve greater growth, both of which are often given by company managers as reasons for diversification.

Consider **diversification to pool risks**. The benefits of risk pooling are said to come from merging imperfectly correlated income streams to create a more stable income stream. An example of risk pooling might be USX's diversification into the oil and gas industry in an attempt to offset the adverse effects of cyclical downturns in the steel industry. According to the advocates of risk pooling, the more stable income stream reduces the risk of bankruptcy and is in the best interests of the company's stockholders.

However, this argument ignores two facts. First, stockholders can easily eliminate the risks inherent in holding an individual stock by diversifying their own portfolios, and they can do so at a much lower cost than the company can. Thus, far from being in the best interests of stockholders, attempts to pool risks through diversification represent an unproductive use of resources. Second, research on this topic suggests that corporate diversification is not a very effective way to pool risks.[32] The business cycles of different industries are not easy to predict and in any case tend to be less important than a general economic downturn, which hits all industries simultaneously. International Harvester illustrates the point. By 1979 International Harvester had diversified into three major businesses: agricultural equipment, construction equipment, and trucks. These businesses were supposed to follow different business cycles, cushioning the company against severe fluctuations. In the early 1980s, however, all these businesses suffered a downturn at the same time, cumulating a $2.9-billion loss for Harvester.

Now consider **diversification to achieve greater growth**. Such diversification is not a coherent strategy because growth on its own does not create value. Growth should be the *by-product*, not the objective, of a diversification strategy. However, companies sometimes diversify for reasons of growth alone, rather than to gain any well-thought-out strategic advantage. ITT under the leadership of Harold Geneen took this path. Geneen turned ITT from an international telecommunications company into a broadly based conglomerate consisting of more than 100 separate businesses, with interests in such diverse areas as baking, car rental, defense electronics, fire hydrants, insurance, hotels, paper products, and telecommunications. The strategy had more to do with Geneen's desire to build an empire than with maximizing the company's value.[33] Since Geneen's departure in 1979, ITT's management has divested many of the businesses acquired under his leadership in order to concentrate on insurance and financial services.

STRATEGY IN ACTION 9.3

ICI Diversifies, Then Declines, Then Breaks Itself in Two

Formed in 1926 by the merger between a number of chemical concerns, Britain's Imperial Chemical Industries Plc (ICI) has always been a diverse company, but in the 1980s ICI embarked on a new wave of diversified acquisitions aimed at expanding its presence in a broad range of high-value-added specialty chemicals operations. By the early 1980s ICI was already involved in activities such as bulk chemicals, explosives, fertilizers, paints, commodity plastics, and pharmaceuticals. It added to this portfolio in 1985 by purchasing the advanced plastics materials operations of the American firm Beatrice Company for $750 million. In 1986 it bought Glidden, another American company, for $580 million. This acquisition made ICI the world's biggest paint manufacturer. In 1987 it made still another purchase, acquiring American Stauffer Chemical for $1.7 billion. ICI retained American Stauffer's specialty agrochemical business, but sold off the rest. As a result, by the end of the 1980s ICI was Britain's largest manufacturing enterprise and the world's fourth largest chemical company.

Expanding the scope of ICI's business activities, however, did little for the company's bottom line. In 1990 ICI saw its pretax profits drop by 36 percent to $1.7 billion, on sales of $23 billion. Meanwhile, ICI's specialty chemicals operations did not do as well as the company had hoped. In 1990 ICI's paints and other specialty products enjoyed a profit margin of only 2.8 percent, compared with a margin of 5.7 percent in the company's more traditional bulk chemical operations.

In May 1991 these financial problems attracted the attention of Hanson P.l.c., one of Britain's best-known corporate raiders. Hanson has thrived by purchasing conglomerates like ICI and then breaking them up and selling off the parts to other companies, usually for a substantial profit. Hanson purchased a 4.1 percent stake in ICI and threatened to make a full takeover bid. Although the full bid never materialized and Hanson subsequently sold off its stake for a handsome profit, the threatened takeover started a debate in ICI about the rationale behind its diversification strategy.

After detailed consideration, ICI's top management reached two main conclusions. First, although many of ICI's businesses were linked in some way to the chemical industry, ICI's management recognized that there were far fewer synergies among the company's operations than it had initially thought. In the final analysis, ICI's top management concluded that there was little commonality between bulk chemicals and pharmaceuticals, between plastics and paint, and between explosives and advanced materials. Second, the company had become so diverse that top management found itself spread too thinly over too many different businesses. The company simply was not able to give the kind of top management attention and financial resources to many of its businesses that they required. In other words, the value created by the strategy of diversification was questionable, whereas the bureaucratic costs of managing a large and complex diversified entity were substantial. Thus diversification at ICI had dissipated rather than created value.

Accordingly, in 1992 ICI's top management decided to start breaking up the company into its constituent parts. The first stage in this process was completed in March 1993, when ICI was split in two. One part, which retains the name ICI, consists of the businesses dealing in industrial chemicals, paints, and explosives. According to the company, bits of this operation will probably be sold off in the future. The other part, now called Zeneca, has taken ICI's drug, pesticide, seed, and specialty chemical businesses. ICI believes that the two companies will do better on their own than they did as part of a larger enterprise.[31]

Related or Unrelated Diversification?

One issue that a company must resolve is whether to diversify into businesses related to its existing business by value-chain commonalities or into totally new businesses. The distinction here is between related diversification and unrelated diversification. By definition, a related company can create value by resource sharing and by transferring competencies between businesses. It can also carry

out some restructuring. By way of contrast, since there are no commonalities between the value chains of unrelated businesses, an unrelated company cannot create value by sharing resources or transferring competencies. Unrelated diversifiers can create value only by pursuing an acquisition and restructuring strategy.

Since related diversification can create value in more ways than unrelated diversification can, one might think that related diversification should be the preferred strategy. In addition, related diversification is normally perceived as involving fewer risks because the company is moving into business areas about which top management has some knowledge. Probably because of those considerations, most diversified companies display a preference for related diversification.[34] However, research suggests that the average related company is, at best, only marginally more profitable than the average unrelated company.[35] How can this be, if related diversification is associated with more benefits than unrelated diversification?

The answer to this question is quite simple. Bureaucratic costs arise from (1) the number of businesses in a company's portfolio and (2) the extent of coordination required among the different businesses in order to realize value from a diversification strategy. An unrelated company does not have to achieve coordination between business units and so it has to cope only with the bureaucratic costs that arise from the number of businesses in its portfolio. In contrast, a related diversified company has to achieve coordination between business units if it is to realize the value that comes from skill transfers and resource sharing. Consequently, it has to cope with the bureaucratic costs that arise *both* from the number of business units in its portfolio *and* from coordination among business units. Thus, although it is true that related diversified companies can create value in more ways than unrelated companies, they have to bear higher bureaucratic costs in order to do so. These higher costs may cancel out the higher benefits, making the strategy no more profitable than one of unrelated diversification. Table 9.1 lists the sources of value and costs for each strategy.

How then is a company to choose between these strategies? The choice depends on a comparison of the relative value-added and the bureaucratic costs associated with each strategy. In making this comparison, it is important to note that the opportunities for creating value from related diversification are a function of the extent of commonalities between the skills required to compete in the company's core business and the skills required to compete in other industrial and commercial areas. Some companies' skills are so specialized that they have few applications outside the core businesses. For example, since the commonalities between steelmaking and other industrial or commercial operations are few, most steel companies have diversified into unrelated industries (LTV into defense contracting, USX into oil and gas). When companies have less specialized skills, they can find many more related diversification opportunities outside the core business. Examples include chemical companies (such as Dow Chemical and Du Pont) and electrical engineering companies (such as General Electric). Consequently, the opportunities available to them to create value from related diversification are much greater.

Thus it pays a firm to concentrate on related diversification when (1) the company's core skills are applicable to a wide variety of industrial and commercial situations and (2) the bureaucratic costs of implementation do not exceed the value that can be created through resource sharing or skill transfers. The second condition is likely to hold only for companies that are moderately diversified. At

Table 9.1
Comparing Related and Unrelated Diversification

Strategy	Ways of Creating Value	Source of Bureaucratic Costs
Related diversification	• Restructuring • Transferring skills • Economies of scope	• Number of businesses • Coordination among businesses
Unrelated diversification	• Restructuring	• Number of businesses

high levels of related diversification, the bureaucratic costs of additional diversification are likely to outweigh the value created by that diversification, and the strategy may become unprofitable.

By the same logic, it may pay a company to concentrate on unrelated diversification when (1) the company's core functional skills are highly specialized and have few applications outside the company's core business; (2) the company's top management is skilled at acquiring and turning around poorly run businesses (and many are not); and (3) the bureaucratic costs of implementation do not exceed the value that can be created by pursuing a restructuring strategy. However, the third condition is *unlikely* to hold for companies that are highly diversified. Thus, no matter whether a company pursues a related or an unrelated diversification strategy, the existence of bureaucratic costs suggests that there are very real limits to the profitable diversification of the company.

9.6 STRATEGIC ALLIANCES AS AN ALTERNATIVE TO DIVERSIFICATION

Diversification can be unprofitable because of the bureaucratic costs associated with implementing the strategy. One way of trying to realize the value associated with diversification, without having to bear the same level of bureaucratic costs, is to enter into a strategic alliance with another company to start a new business venture.

In this context, strategic alliances are essentially agreements between two or more companies to share the costs, risks, and benefits associated with developing new business opportunities. Many strategic alliances are constituted as formal joint ventures in which each party has an equity stake. Other alliances take the form of a long-term contract between companies in which they agree to undertake some joint activity that benefits both. Agreements to work together on joint R&D projects often take this form.

Strategic alliances seem to be a particularly viable option when a company wishes to create value from transferring competencies or sharing resources between diversified businesses in order to realize economies of scope. Alliances offer companies a framework within which to share the resources required to establish a new business. Alternatively, alliances enable companies to swap complementary skills to produce a new range of products. For example, consider the alliance between United Technologies and Dow Chemical to build plastic-based composite parts for the aerospace industry. United Technologies was already involved in the aerospace industry (it built Sikorsky helicopters), and Dow

Chemical had skills in the development and manufacture of plastic-based composites. The alliance called for United Technologies to contribute its advanced aerospace skills and for Dow to contribute its skills in developing and manufacturing plastic-based composites to a joint venture in which each company would have a 50 percent equity stake. The joint venture was to undertake the task of developing, manufacturing, and marketing a new line of plastic-based composite parts for the aerospace industry. Through the alliance, both companies would become involved in new activities. They would, in short, be able to realize some of the benefits associated with related diversification without having to merge activities formally or bear the costs and risks of developing the new products on their own.

Bureaucratic costs have been reduced because neither Dow nor United Technologies actually expanded its own organization, nor did either company have to coordinate internal skill transfers. Rather, after incorporation, the joint venture has been operating as an independent company, and both Dow and United Technologies receive payment in the form of dividends.

Of course, there is a down side to such alliances. For one thing, profits must be split with an alliance partner, whereas with full diversification a company gets to keep all of the profits. Another problem is that when a company enters into an alliance, it always runs the risk that it might give away critical know-how to its alliance partner, who might then use that know-how to compete directly with the company in the future. For example, having gained access to Dow's expertise in plastic-based composites, United Technologies might dissolve the alliance and produce these materials on its own. However, such risk can be minimized if Dow gets a *credible commitment* from United Technologies. By entering into a formal joint venture, rather than a more loosely structured alliance, United Technologies has given such a commitment because it has had to invest substantial amounts of capital. Thus if United Technologies tried to produce plastic-based composites on its own, it would essentially be competing against itself.

9.7 SUMMARY OF CHAPTER

The purpose of this chapter is to examine the different corporate-level strategies that companies pursue in order to maximize their value.

1. Corporate strategies should *add value* to a corporation. To add value, a corporate strategy should enable the company, or one or more of its business units, to perform one or more of the value-creation functions at a lower cost or in a way that allows for differentiation and a premium price.
2. Vertical integration can enable a company to achieve a competitive advantage by helping build barriers to entry, facilitating investments in specialized assets, by protecting product quality, and helping improve scheduling between adjacent stages in the value chain.
3. The disadvantages of vertical integration include cost disadvantages if a company's internal source of supply is a high-cost one and a lack of flexibility when technology is changing fast or when demand is uncertain.

4. Entering into a long-term contract can enable a company to realize many of the benefits associated with vertical integration without having to bear the same level of bureaucratic costs. However, to avoid the risks associated with becoming too dependent on its partner, a company entering into a long-term contract needs to seek a credible commitment from its partner or establish a mutual hostage-taking situation.
5. Diversification can create value through the pursuit of a restructuring strategy, competency transfers, and the realization of economies of scope.
6. The bureaucratic costs of diversification are a function of the number of independent business units within the company and the extent of coordination between those business units.
7. Diversification motivated by a desire to pool risks or achieve greater growth is often associated with the dissipation of value.
8. Related diversification is preferred to unrelated diversification because it enables a company to engage in more value-creation activities and is less risky. If a company's skills are not transferable, the company may have no choice but to pursue unrelated diversification.
9. Strategic alliances can enable companies to realize many of the benefits of related diversification without having to bear the same level of bureaucratic costs. However, when entering into an alliance, a company does run the risk of giving away key technology to its partner. The risk of this occurring can be minimized if a company gets a credible commitment from its partner.

Discussion Questions

1. When is a company likely to choose related diversification and when unrelated diversification? Discuss with reference to an electronics manufacturer and an ocean shipping company.
2. Why was it profitable for General Motors and Ford to integrate backward into component-parts manufacturing in the past, and why are both companies now trying to buy more of their parts from outside?
3. Under what conditions might concentration on a single business be inconsistent with the goal of maximizing stockholder wealth? Why?
4. General Motors integrated vertically in the 1920s, diversified in the 1930s, and expanded overseas in the 1950s. Explain these developments with reference to the profitability of pursuing each strategy. Why do you think vertical integration is normally the first strategy to be pursued after concentration on a single business?

Article File 9

Find an example of a company whose vertical integration or diversification strategy appears to have dissipated rather than created value. Identify why this has been the case and what the company should do to rectify the situation.

Strategic Management Project: Module 9

This module requires you to assess the vertical integration and diversification strategy being pursued by your company. With the information you have at your disposal, answer the questions, and perform the tasks listed:

1. How vertically integrated is your company? If your company does have vertically integrated operations, is it pursuing a strategy of taper or full integration?
2. How diversified is your company? If your company is already diversified, is it pursuing a related diversification strategy, an unrelated diversification strategy, or some mix of the two?
3. Assess the potential for your company to create value through vertical integration. In reaching your assessment, also consider the bureaucratic costs of managing vertical integration.
4. On the basis of your assessment in question 3, do you think your company should (a) outsource some operations that are currently performed in-house, or (b) bring some operations in-house that are currently outsourced? Justify your recommendations.
5. Is your company currently involved in any long-term cooperative relationships with suppliers or buyers? If so, how are these relationships structured? Do you think that these relationships add value to the company? Why?
6. Is there any potential for your company to enter into (additional) long-term cooperative relationships with suppliers or buyers? If so, how might these relationships be structured?
7. Assess the potential for your company to create value through diversification. In reaching your assessment, also consider the bureaucratic costs of managing diversification.
8. On the basis of your assessment in question 7, do you think your company should (a) sell off some diversified operations, or (b) pursue additional diversification? Justify your recommendations.
9. Is your company currently trying to transfer skills or realize economies of scope by entering into strategic alliances with other companies? If so, how are these relationships structured? Do you think that these relationships add value to the company? Why?
10. Is there any potential for your company to transfer skills or realize economies of scope by entering into (additional) strategic alliances with other companies? If so, how might these relationships be structured?

Endnotes

1. Sources: "The Flawed Vision of Edzard Reuter," *Economist*, April 27, 1991, pp. 65–66. Krystal Miller, "BMW Zooms Ahead of Mercedes–Benz in Worldwide Sales for the First Time," *Wall Street Journal*, January 20, 1993, Section B1. John Templeman, "Daimler's Drive to Become a High-Tech Speedster," *Business Week*, February 12, 1990, pp. 55–58.
2. K. R. Harrigan, "Formulating Vertical Integration Strategies," *Academy of Management Review*, 9 (1984), pp. 638–652.
3. This is the essence of Chandler's argument. See Alfred D. Chandler, *Strategy and Structure* (Cambridge, Mass.: MIT

Press, 1962). The same argument is also made by Jeffrey Pfeffer and Gerald R. Salancik, *The External Control of Organizations*, (New York: Harper & Row, 1978). See also K. R. Harrigan, *Strategic Flexibility* (Lexington, Mass.: Lexington Books, 1985); K. R. Harrigan, "Vertical Integration and Corporate Strategy," *Academy of Management Journal*, 28 (1985), pp. 397–425; and F. M. Scherer, *Industrial Market Structure and Economic Performance* (Chicago: Rand McNally, 1981).

4. For details, see Martin K. Perry, "Vertical Integration: Determinants and Effects," *Handbook of Industrial Organization*, ed. R. Schmalensee and R. D. Willig, (Elsevier Science Publishers, 1989) I, Amsterdam, pp. 183–255.
5. This section is based on the transaction cost approach popularized by Oliver E. Williamson, *The Economic Institutions of Capitalism* (New York: Free Press, 1985).
6. Ibid.
7. J-F. Hennart, "Upstream Vertical Integration in the Aluminum and Tin Industries," *Journal of Economic Behavior and Organization*, 9 (1988), 281–299.
8. Ibid.
9. A. D. Chandler, *The Visible Hand* (Cambridge, Mass.: Harvard University Press, 1977).
10. Julia Pitta, "Score One for Vertical Integration," *Forbes*, January 18, 1993, pp. 88–89.
11. Joseph White and Neal Templin, "Harsh Regimen: A swollen GM Finds It Hard to Stick with Its Crash Diet," *Wall Street Journal*, (September 9, 1992), p. A1.
12. Harrigan, *Strategic Flexibility*, pp. 67–87.
13. For a detailed theoretical rationale for this argument see G. R. Jones and C. W. L. Hill, "A Transaction Cost Analysis of Strategy-Structure Choice," *Strategic Management Journal*, 9 (1988) 159–172.
14. Kevin Kelly, Zachary Schiller, and James Treece, "Cut Costs of Else," *Business Week*, March 22, 1993, pp. 28–29.
15. Standard & Poor's Industry Survey, *Autos—Auto Parts*, June 24, 1993.
16. See James Womack, Daniel Jones, and Daniel Roos, *The Machine That Changed the World* (New York: Rawson Associates, 1990); and James Richardson, "Parallel Sourcing and Supplier Performance in the Japanese Automobile Industry," *Strategic Management Journal*, 14 (1993), pp. 339–350.
17. Sources: G. Pascal Zachary, "High-Tech Firms Find It's Good to Line Up Outside Contractors," *Wall Street Journal*, July 7, 1992, p. A1; Shawn Tully, "The Modular Corporation," *Fortune*, February 8, 1993, pp. 106–114.
18. Williamson, *Economic Institutions*.
19. Richardson, "Parallel Sourcing," pp. 339–350.
20. This resource-based view of diversification can be traced to Edith Penrose's seminal book, *The Theory of the Growth of the Firm* (Oxford: Oxford University Press, 1959).
21. See, for example, Jones and Hill, "A Transaction Cost Analysis," pp. 159–172; and Williamson, *Markets and Hierarchies*, (New York: Free Press), pp. 132–175.
22. See C. W. L. Hill, "Profile of a Conglomerate Takeover: BTR and Thomas Tilling," *Journal of General Management*, 10 (1984), pp. 34–50.
23. See C. W. L. Hill, M. A. Hitt, and R. E. Hoskisson, "Declining U.S. Competitiveness: Reflections on a Crisis," *Academy of Management Executive*, 2 (February 1988), pp. 51–59; and R. E. Hoskisson, M. A. Hitt, and C. W. L. Hill, "Managerial Incentives and Investment in R&D in Large Multiproduct Firms," *Organization Science*, 4 (1993), pp. 325–341.
24. "Rockwell: Using Its Cash Hoard to Edge Away from Defense," *Business Week*, February 4, 1985, pp. 82–84.
25. D. J. Teece, "Economies of Scope and the Scope of the Enterprise," *Journal of Economic Behavior and Organization*, 3 (1980), pp. 223–247.
26. For a detailed discussion, see C. W. L. Hill and R. E. Hoskisson, "Strategy and Structure in the Multiproduct Firm," *Academy of Management Review*, 12 (1987), pp. 331–341.
27. Michael E. Porter, *Competitive Advantage: Creating and Sustaining Superior Performance* (New York: Free Press, 1985), p. 326.
28. Porter, "From Competitive Advantage to Corporate Strategy," *Harvard Business Review*, (May–June 1987), 43–59.
29. For a survey of the evidence, see V. Ramanujam and P. Varadarajan, "Research on Corporate Diversification: A Synthesis," *Strategic Management Journal*, 10 (1989), pp. 523–551.
30. C. R. Christensen et al., *Business Policy Text and Cases* (Homewood, Ill.: Irwin, 1987), p. 778.
31. Sources: Scott McMurray, "ICI Changes Tack and Splits Itself into Two Businesses," *Wall Street Journal*, March 5, 1993, p. B3; "Hanson Likes the Look of ICI," *Economist*, May 18, 1991, pp. 69–70.
32. For a survey of the evidence, see. C. W. L. Hill, "Conglomerate Performance over the Economic Cycle," *Journal of Industrial Economics*, 32 (1983), pp. 197–212; and D. T. C. Mueller, "The Effects of Conglomerate Mergers," *Journal of Banking and Finance*, 1 (1977) pp. 315–347.
33. Michael Brody, "Caught in the Cash Crunch at ITT," *Fortune*, February 18, 1985, pp. 63–72.
34. For example, see C. W. L. Hill, "Diversified Growth and Competition," *Applied Economics*, 17 (1985), pp. 827–847; and R. P. Rumelt, *Strategy, Structure and Economic Performance* (Boston: Harvard Business School Press, 1974). G. R. Jones and C. W. L. Hill, "A Transaction Cost Analysis of Strategy Structure Choice," *Strategic Management Journal*, 1988, pp. 159–172.
35. See H. K. Christensen and C. A. Montgomery, "Corporate Economic Performance: Diversification Strategy Versus Market Structure," *Strategic Management Journal*, 2 (1981), 327–343; and Jones and Hill, "A Transaction Cost Analysis," pp. 159–172.

10 Building and Restructuring the Corporation

10.1 OPENING CASE: XEROX RESTRUCTURES

In the early 1980s with its core photocopier business under attack from Japanese companies such as Canon and Ricoh, Xerox's top management took the decision to diversify into the financial service industry. The move was an attempt to counterbalance its troubled copier business and protect Xerox's income stream. The Wall Street investment community reacted with disapproval, arguing that Xerox was running away from problems in its core business. It also noted that the expansion of Xerox's portfolio would make it more difficult for the investment community to make sense of the company. Despite these criticisms, Xerox went ahead. In order to enter the financial services industry, an area in which it had no prior experience, Xerox decided to acquire established enterprises with sound management and a good track record. Over the course of several years Xerox acquired several companies, including Crum and Forster, Inc., an insurance company, Furman Selz, an investment banking concern, and Van Kampen Merritt, a mutual fund business.

By the mid 1980s this strategy seemed to be paying off. At that time the financial services arm was contributing almost half of Xerox's profits. However, this was also a boom period for the financial services industry in general. By the late 1980s the picture began to change. Strong management had revolutionized the performance of Xerox's photocopier business by focusing on superior product quality and tight cost controls. This enabled the company to capture market share back from Japanese competitors (see the Opening Case of Chapter 4 for details). At the same time, the performance of the financial service businesses began to deteriorate rapidly. Indeed, although Xerox's financial services operations contributed one-third of Xerox's 1991 revenues of $13.8 billion, they accounted for only 3 percent of profits. The root of the problem was that Xerox's financial services businesses had turned out to be high-cost providers in an industry that was becoming increasingly competitive. While they could make good returns in the easy years of the mid 1980s, they were struggling in the lean years at the end of the decade. To make matters worse, in 1992 the balance sheet of the Crum and Forster insurance business was hard hit by massive insurance losses from Hurricanes Andrew and Iniki, an event that led to Moody's Investors Service downgrading the bond rating of Crum and Forster and placing some $6 billion of Xerox debt under review.

Xerox began to reconsider the logic underlying its diversification strategy in May 1991, when Paul Allaire became chairman of the company. Allaire had been the major architect of the company's comeback in copiers. He had no tie to the diversification strategy, which was the brainchild of the former CEO, David Kearns. Under Allaire's leadership Xerox quickly fenced off financial services from the rest of the company, declining to prop up these faltering businesses with profits from copiers. After reviewing the company's diversification strategy, Allaire decided that Xerox's shareholders would be best served by a complete disengagement of the financial services operations from the rest of the company. Wall Street reacted positively to the news, but at the same time securities analysts noted that the restructuring could not be achieved without some financial pain for Xerox and its shareholders.

The process of divestment began in October 1992, when Xerox sold its Van Kampen Merritt mutual fund business to Clayton Dubilier & Rice for $360 million. To make its troubled Crum and Forster insurance business marketable, Xerox took a $470 million charge in the fourth quarter of 1992, primarily to strengthen the balance sheet of Crum and Forster, thereby making it more attractive to potential buyers. Xerox is also slicing Crum and Forster into pieces, which, the company reckons, can be sold more easily than the entire unit. Even so, Xerox's management admits that some time may pass before they can unload all of Crum and Forster. As for the Furman Selz investment banking concern, Xerox is currently negotiating with this unit's managers as to a possible management buyout.

Once all of the financial services businesses are sold, Xerox will be able to remove about $2.6 billion worth of debt from its books. But analysts point out that the debt is already being serviced by the financial service businesses themselves, so the sale would not free up any additional funds for the rest of Xerox's business. In a move to strengthen the company's equity base, Xerox stated that it intends to issue as much as $500 million of new equity in 1993, which will dilute the earnings value of Xerox shares by as much as 5 percent. Most securities analysts see this dilution as an inevitable result of a series of bad investment decisions made in the early 1980s. It is part of the price Xerox shareholders must pay for management's unsuccessful attempt to diversify into financial services.[1]

Discussion Questions

1. Is there any way in which Xerox might have been able to add value to the financial services operations it acquired in the early 1980s? If not, why do you think that the company pursued this strategy?
2. Do you think that the interests of Xerox's shareholders are best served by the divestment of Xerox's financial services businesses?

10.2 OVERVIEW

Chapter 9 discusses the corporate-level strategies that companies pursue in order to become multibusiness enterprises. This chapter builds on the material in Chapter 9 to address three issues. First, what are the relative merits of the different *vehicles* or *means* that companies can use to enter new business areas? The choice here is between acquisitions, internal new ventures, and joint ventures. **Acquisitions** involve buying an existing business; **internal new ventures** involve starting a new business from scratch; and **joint ventures** typically involve starting a new business from scratch with the assistance of a partner. As recounted in the Opening Case, Xerox chose acquisitions rather than internal new ventures or joint ventures to diversify into the financial services industry. This choice of vehicle for diversification made sense, given that Xerox lacked any knowledge of the financial services industry. By acquiring established financial services businesses, Xerox was also buying management know-how about the industry.

The second issue that we address in this chapter is restructuring. For reasons that we touch upon in Chapter 9 and discuss further in this chapter, during the 1970s and 1980s many companies became too diversified or too vertically integrated. In recent years there has been a fairly dramatic shift away from these two strategies, with companies selling off many of their diversified activities and refocusing on their core businesses. The Opening Case describes how this situation happened at Xerox, which undid during the early 1990s most of the diversification into financial services that it had undertaken in the early 1980s; it sold off most of its previously acquired units, often at a loss. In this chapter, we

explore why so many companies are now restructuring and examine the different strategic options open to companies pursuing a restructuring strategy.

The final issue that we deal with in this chapter is portfolio planning techniques. Portfolio planning techniques refer to a family of conceptual planning tools devised in the 1960s by management consultants to aid in deciding what type of business areas a company should be involved in. These techniques have recently fallen into disfavor. Indeed, critics argue that they have done a great disservice to the companies that utilized them. We consider why this might be the case.

10.3 ACQUISITIONS VERSUS INTERNAL NEW VENTURES AS ENTRY STRATEGIES

As noted above, there are three vehicles for pursuing corporate-level strategies such as diversification and vertical integration: acquisitions, internal new ventures, and joint ventures. In this section, we discuss the choice between acquisitions and internal new ventures as alternative vehicles for *entering* new business areas. In the next section, we consider why so many acquisitions apparently fail to deliver their promised benefits, and we discuss guidelines for undertaking successful acquisitions. Then we explore similar issues for internal new ventures and finally turn to joint ventures, which are something of a special case.

Entry into a new business area through acquisition involves purchasing an established company, complete with all its facilities, equipment, and personnel. Entry into a new business area through internal new venturing means starting a business from scratch: building facilities, purchasing equipment, recruiting personnel, opening up distribution outlets, and so on. The choice between acquisition and internal new venturing as the preferred entry strategy is influenced by several factors: (1) barriers to entry, (2) the relatedness of the new business to existing operations, (3) the comparative speed and development costs of the two entry modes, (4) the risks involved in the different entry modes, and (5) industry life cycle factors.[2]

Barriers to Entry

As you recall from Chapter 3, barriers to entry arise from factors associated with product differentiation (brand loyalty), absolute cost advantages, and economies of scale. When barriers are substantial, a company finds entering an industry through internal new venturing difficult. To enter, a company may have to construct an efficient-scale manufacturing plant, undertake massive advertising to break down established brand loyalties, and quickly build up distribution outlets—all hard-to-achieve goals likely to involve substantial expenditures. In contrast, by acquiring an established enterprise, a company can circumvent most entry barriers. It can purchase a market leader, which already benefits from substantial scale economies and brand loyalty. Thus the greater the barriers to entry, the more is acquisition the favored entry mode.

Relatedness

The more related a new business is to a company's established operations, the lower are the barriers to entry and the more likely it is that the company has accumulated experience with this type of business. These factors heighten the

attractiveness of new venturing. For example, IBM entered the personal computer market in 1981 by new venturing. The entry was very successful, enabling IBM to capture 35 percent of the market within two years. IBM was able to enter by this mode because of the high degree of relatedness between the personal computer market and IBM's established computer mainframe operations. IBM already had a well-established sales force and brand loyalty, and it had considerable expertise in the computer industry. Similarly, companies such as Du Pont and Dow Chemical Co. have successfully entered closely related chemical businesses through internal new venturing.

In contrast, the more unrelated a new business is, the more likely is entry to be through acquisition. By definition, unrelated diversifiers lack the specific expertise necessary to enter a new business area through greenfield development (i.e., starting a business from scratch). An unrelated diversifier choosing internal new venturing has to develop its own expertise for competing in an unfamiliar industry. The learning process can be lengthy and involve costly mistakes before the company fully understands its new industry. In the case of an acquisition, however, the acquired business already has a management team with accumulated experience in competing in that particular industry. When making an acquisition, a company is also buying knowledge and experience. Thus, as you saw in the Opening Case, when Xerox decided to diversify into the financial services industry (which was a case of unrelated diversification), it did so by acquiring established companies.

Speed and Development Costs

As a rule, internal new venturing takes years to generate substantial profits. Establishing a significant market presence can be both costly and time consuming. In a study of corporate new venturing, Ralph Biggadike of the University of Virginia found that on the average it takes eight years for a new venture to reach profitability and ten to twelve years before the profitability of the average venture equals that of a mature business. He also found that cash flow typically remains negative for at least the first eight years of a new venture.[3] In contrast, acquisition is a much quicker way to establish a significant market presence and generate profitability. A company can purchase a market leader in a strong cash position overnight, rather than spend years building up a market-leadership position through internal development. Thus, when speed is important, acquisition is the favored entry mode.

Risks of Entry

New venturing tends to be an uncertain process with a low probability of success. Studies by Edwin Mansfield of the University of Pennsylvania concluded that only between 12 and 20 percent of R&D-based new ventures actually succeed in earning an economic profit.[4] Indeed, business history is strewn with examples of large companies that lost money through internal new venturing. For example, in 1984 AT&T entered the computer market through an internal new venture. Company officials predicted that by 1990 AT&T would rank second in data processing, behind IBM, but that never occurred. In 1985 AT&T's computer division lost $500 million, and in 1986 it lost $1.2 billion.[5] AT&T subsequently decided that it would never build up a presence in data processing through internal new venturing. In 1991 the company changed its strategy and acquired for $7.5 billion NCR Corp. a company with substantial computer operations of its own.

When a company makes an acquisition, it is acquiring known profitability, known revenues, and known market share; thus it reduces uncertainty. Essentially, internal new venturing involves the establishment of a business venture with a very uncertain future, whereas acquisition allows a company to buy an established business with a track record. Thus many companies favor acquisitions.

Industry Life Cycle Factors

We discuss the general importance of the industry life cycle in Chapter 3. The industry life cycle has a major impact on many of the factors that influence the choice between acquisitions and internal new venturing. In embryonic and growth industries, barriers to entry are typically lower than in mature industries because established companies in the former are still going through a learning process. They do not have the same experience advantages as the established companies in a mature industry environment. Given these factors, entry by an internal new venture during the early stage of the industry life cycle means lower risks and development costs, as well as fewer penalties in terms of expansion speed, than entry into a mature industry environment. Thus internal new venturing tends to be the favored entry mode in embryonic and growth industries, whereas acquisition tends to be the favored mode in mature industries. Indeed, many of the most successful internal new ventures have been associated with entry into emerging industries—for instance, IBM's entry into the personal computer arena and John Deere Co.'s entry into the snowmobile business.

Summary

Internal new venturing seems to make most sense when the following conditions exist: the industry to be entered is in its embryonic or growth stage; barriers to entry are low; the industry is closely related to the company's existing operations (the company's strategy is one of related diversification); and the company is willing to accept the attendant time frame, development costs, and risks. On the other hand, acquisition makes most sense when the following conditions obtain: the industry to be entered is mature; the barriers to entry are high; the industry is not closely related to the company's existing operations (the company's strategy is one of unrelated diversification); and the company is unwilling to accept the time frame, development costs, and risks of internal new venturing.

10.4 ACQUISITIONS: PITFALLS AND GUIDELINES FOR SUCCESS

For the reasons just noted, acquisitions have long been a popular vehicle for expanding the scope of the organization into new business areas. However, despite this popularity, there is ample evidence that many acquisitions fail to add value for the acquiring company, and indeed, often end up dissipating value. For example, management consultants McKinsey & Company applied these two tests to fifty-eight major acquisitions undertaken between 1972 and 1983: (1) did the return on the total amount invested in the acquisitions exceed the cost of capital, and (2) did the acquisitions help their parent companies outperform the competition in the stock market? Twenty-eight out of the fifty-eight acquisitions clearly failed both tests, and six others failed one.[6] More generally, there is a

wealth of evidence from academic research suggesting that many acquisitions fail to realize their anticipated benefits. In a major study of the postacquisition performance of companies acquired during the 1960s and 1970s, David Ravenscraft and Mike Scherer concluded that many good companies were acquired during this period and, on average, their profits and market shares declined following acquisition.[7] They also noted that a smaller but substantial subset of those good companies experienced traumatic difficulties, which ultimately led to their being sold off by the acquiring company (as occurred in the case of Xerox's financial services acquisitions—see the Opening Case). In other words, Ravenscraft and Scherer's evidence, like that presented by McKinsey & Company, suggests that many acquisitions destroy rather than create value.[8]

Why Acquisitions Fail

Why do so many acquisitions apparently fail to create value? There appear to be four major reasons: (1) companies often experience difficulties when trying to integrate divergent corporate cultures; (2) companies overestimate the potential economic benefits from an acquisition; (3) acquisitions tend to be very expensive; and (4) companies often do not adequately screen their acquisition targets.

Integration Having made an acquisition, the acquiring company has to integrate the acquired business into its own organizational structure. Integration can entail the adoption of common management and financial control systems, the joining together of operations from the acquired and the acquiring company, or the establishment of linkages to share information and personnel. When integration is attempted, many unexpected problems can occur. Often they stem from differences in corporate cultures. After an acquisition, many acquired companies experience high management turnover, possibly because their employees do not like the acquiring company's way of doing things.[9] Recent research evidence suggests that the loss of management talent and expertise, to say nothing of the damage from constant tension between the businesses, can materially harm the performance of the acquired unit.[10]

For example, four years after Fluor bought St. Joe Minerals Corporation in one of the largest acquisitions of 1981, only seven of the twenty-two senior managers who had run St. Joe before the acquisition remained. Instead of reaping gains from an established winner, Fluor found itself struggling to transform a business that was fast becoming a loser. The crux of the problem was a clash in corporate cultures between Fluor, a centralized and autocratic organization, and St. Joe, a decentralized company. St. Joe's senior management resented the centralized management style at Fluor, and many managers left in protest.[11]

Overestimating Economic Benefits Even when companies achieve integration, they often overestimate the potential for creating value by joining together different businesses. They overestimate the strategic advantages that can be derived from the acquisition and thus pay more for the target company than it is probably worth. Richard Roll has attributed this tendency to hubris on the part of top management. According to Roll, top managers typically overestimate their ability to create value from an acquisition, primarily because rising to the top of a corporation has given them an exaggerated sense of their own capabilities.[12]

Coca-Cola's 1975 acquisition of a number of medium-sized winemaking companies illustrates the situation where a company overestimates the economic

benefits from an acquisition. Reasoning that a beverage is a beverage, Coca-Cola wanted to use its distinctive competency in marketing to dominate the U.S. wine industry. But after buying three wine companies and enduring seven years of marginal profits, Coca-Cola finally conceded that wine and soft drinks are very different products, with different kinds of appeal, pricing systems, and distribution networks. In 1983 it sold the wine operations to Joseph E. Seagram & Sons for $210 million—the price Coca-Cola had paid for the purchases and a substantial loss when adjusted for inflation.[13]

The Expense of Acquisitions Acquisitions of companies whose stock is publicly traded tend to be very expensive. When a company bids to acquire the stock of another enterprise, the stock price frequently gets bid up in the acquisition process. This is particularly likely to occur in the case of contested bids, where two or more companies simultaneously bid for control of a single target company. Thus the acquiring company must often pay a premium over the current market value of the target. In the early 1980s acquiring companies paid an average premium of 40 to 50 percent over current stock prices for an acquisition. Between 1985 and 1988, when takeover activity was at its peak, premiums of 80 percent were not uncommon. Indeed, in the giant contested takeover bid for RJR Nabisco during late 1988, the stock price of RJR was bid up from $45 per share prior to the takeover attempt to $110 per share by the time RJR was sold—a premium of over 200 percent!

The debt taken on to finance such expensive acquisitions can later become a noose around the acquiring company's neck, particularly if interest rates rise. Moreover, if the market value of the target company prior to an acquisition was a true reflection of that company's worth under its management at that time, a premium of 50 to 80 percent over this value means that the acquiring company has to improve the performance of the acquired unit by just as much if it is to reap a positive return on its investment. Such performance gains, however, can be very difficult to achieve.

Inadequate Preacquisition Screening After researching acquisitions made by twenty different companies, Philippe Haspeslagh of INSEAD (a French business school) and David Jemison of the University of Texas came to the conclusion that one reason for acquisitions failure is management's inadequate attention to preacquisition screening.[14] They found that many companies decide to acquire other firms without thoroughly analyzing the potential benefits and costs. After the acquisition is completed, many acquiring companies discover that instead of buying a well-run business, they have purchased a troubled organization. That was Xerox's experience when it purchased the Crum and Forster insurance business in the early 1980s. Only after the acquisition was completed did Xerox learn that Crum and Forster was a high-cost provider of insurance. Strategy in Action 10.1 offers another example of a lack of screening and its consequences: the acquisition of The Seven-Up Company by Philip Morris.

Guidelines for Successful Acquisition

To avoid pitfalls and make successful acquisitions, companies need to take a structured approach that involves three main components: (1) target identification and preacquisition screening, (2) bidding strategy, and (3) integration.[16]

STRATEGY IN ACTION 10.1

A Tale of Two Acquisitions: How Philip Morris Triumphed with Miller Brewing and Failed with The Seven-Up Company

One of the most successful acquisitions of the 1960s and 1970s was the Philip Morris 1969 purchase of the Miller Brewing Company. At the time Miller was a poorly performing company in a fragmented and rather sleepy brewing industry, while Philip Morris was widely regarded as one of the best marketing companies in the world. When Philip Morris purchased Miller, the company was the seventh-placed brewer in the U.S. market. Philip Morris believed that by applying its distinctive competency in marketing to Miller it could revitalize Miller's products and gain significant market share. This belief was reasonable, given the lack of strong marketing companies in the brewing industry at that time. After the acquisition, the first step by Philip Morris was to transfer many of its top marketing personnel to Miller. The new management team quickly repositioned Miller's product line and also began developing new products—the most successful of which was Miller Lite, a low-calorie beer introduced in 1975. Backed by an aggressive marketing campaign, Miller's market share surged from around 5 percent in 1970 to 21 percent in 1979, while operating income increased sixteenfold over the same period.

Fresh from what was a stunning example of how to create value through a diversified acquisition, Philip Morris tried to adopt the same strategy in the soft-drink industry. It acquired the number three soft-drink company, Seven-Up, and set about transferring marketing personnel to Seven-Up. As at Miller, the Philip Morris personnel tried to reposition Seven-Up's product line, but with singularly unimpressive results. After investing eight years of effort and hundreds of millions of dollars, all Philip Morris had to show was a two-point decline in Seven-Up's market share, from 9 percent to 7 percent. Ultimately, Philip Morris sold Seven-Up to another company.

What went wrong? Why had a strategy that worked so well at Miller fail so miserably at Seven-Up? The answer was that the soft-drink industry and the brewing industry were very different. While the brewing industry in 1971 had no strong marketing companies, the soft-drink industry of 1979 was dominated by two of the most efficient marketing companies in the world, Coca-Cola and Pepsico. Seven-Up had survived and prospered in this industry by focusing on the niche for lemon-lime soft drinks and by not challenging Coca-Cola and Pepsico. Moreover, unlike Miller, Seven-Up was a highly regarded marketing company in its own right. Under Philip Morris, Seven-Up directly challenged Coca-Cola and Pepsico, introducing a caffeine-free cola. Coca-Cola and Pepsico responded in kind by introducing their first lemon-lime soft drinks, and Seven-Up found itself involved in a bear knuckle price and marketing war with two very effective giants. As a result, the company lost market share.

Philip Morris made a mistake by not adequately examining the soft-drink industry. It assumed that the industry would be a pushover, just like the brewing industry, whereas even the most elementary comparison of the facts would have revealed that the two industries were very different, as were Miller and Seven-Up. Had Philip Morris adequately screened both Seven-Up and the soft-drink industry, it would have discovered that Seven-Up was already a very efficient marketing company and that the soft-drink industry was populated by very good marketing enterprises. In such a situation, there was very little value that Philip Morris could add to Seven-Up, and there was little potential for increasing Seven-Up's market share through marketing.[15]

Screening Thorough preacquisition screening increases a company's knowledge about potential takeover targets, leads to a more realistic assessment of the problems involved in executing an acquisition and integrating the new business

into the company's organizational structure, and lessens the risk of purchasing a potential problem business. The screening should begin with a detailed assessment of the strategic rationale for making the acquisition and identification of the kind of enterprise that would make an ideal acquisition candidate.

Next, the company should scan a target population of potential acquisition candidates, evaluating each according to a detailed set of criteria, focusing on (1) financial position, (2) product market position, (3) competitive environment, (4) management capabilities, and (5) corporate culture. Such an evaluation should enable the company to identify the strengths and weaknesses of each candidate, the extent of potential synergies between the acquiring and the acquired companies, potential integration problems, and the compatibility of the corporate cultures of the acquiring and the acquired companies.

The company should then reduce the list of candidates to the most favored ones and evaluate them further. At this stage, it should sound out third parties, such as investment bankers, whose opinions may be important and who may be able to give valuable insights about the efficiency of target companies. The company that leads the list after this process should be the acquisition target.

Bidding Strategy The objective of bidding strategy is to reduce the price that a company must pay for an acquisition candidate. The essential element of a good bidding strategy is timing. For example, Hanson PLC, one of the most successful takeover machines of the 1980s, always looks for essentially sound businesses that are suffering from short-term problems due to cyclical industry factors or from problems localized in one division. Such companies are typically undervalued by the stock market and thus can be picked up without payment of the standard 40 or 50 percent premium over current stock prices. With good timing, a company can make a bargain purchase. (For more information on bidding strategy, see Strategy in Action 10.2.)

Integration Despite good screening and bidding, an acquisition will fail unless positive steps are taken to integrate the acquired company into the organizational structure of the acquiring one. Integration should center on the source of the potential strategic advantages of the acquisition—for instance, marketing, manufacturing, procurement, R&D, financial, or management synergies. Integration should also be accompanied by steps to eliminate any duplication of facilities or functions. In addition, any unwanted activities of the acquired company should be sold. Finally, if the different business activities are closely related, they will require a high degree of integration. In the case of a company like Hanson PLC, the level of integration can be minimal, for the company's strategy is one of unrelated diversification. But a company such as Philip Morris requires greater integration because its strategy is one of related diversification.

10.5 INTERNAL NEW VENTURES: PITFALLS AND GUIDELINES FOR SUCCESS

Science-based companies that use their technology to create market opportunities in related areas tend to favor internal new venturing as an entry strategy. Du Pont, for example, has created whole new markets with products such as

STRATEGY IN ACTION 10.2

Anatomy of a Failed Takeover Bid

Just like an acquisition that subsequently fails, a failed takeover bid can be expensive and harm the company that initiated it. The attempted acquisition of the German tire maker Continental, by the Italian tire company Pirelli, offers an illustration. Pirelli decided to initiate the takeover bid in late 1990. The stated purpose behind the bid was to consolidate the operations of Continental and Pirelli into a larger, "pan-European" tire maker, which would be capable of going head-to-head with global companies like Goodyear and Michelin. The underlying rationale was a belief that larger size would bring with it economies of scale and transform the Pirelli-Continental combination into a formidable global competitor.

In preparation for the bid, Pirelli lined up a number of Continental's shareholders in its camp. These "allies" held approximately 30 percent of Continental's outstanding shares. Pirelli promised to compensate these shareholders for any drop in the value of their shareholding that might follow the bid. It also promised its allies that if the acquisition could not be completed by November 30, 1991, the bid would be dropped. Then Pirelli launched the takeover bid, purchasing 5 percent of Continental's stock and informing Continental's management that it was interested in acquiring majority control. At the same time Pirelli revealed its hand by disclosing details of its plans to compensate its allies should Continental's share price drop and the bid fail to be completed by November 30, 1991.

Continental's management responded in a tepid fashion to the bid. It agreed to enter into negotiations with Pirelli, since not doing so might result in a hostile takeover bid. At the same time, it pointed out that big is not always beautiful, particularly in the tire industry, where giants such as Michelin and Goodyear were losing money. Moreover, now aware of the November 30 deadline, Continental's management decided to drag out the negotiations, reasoning that if little progress was made Pirelli would start to lose allies.

This is exactly what occurred. To make matters worse, Pirelli had little meaningful response to Continental's jibe that big is not always best, which indicated to many observers that Pirelli had not adequately thought through the rationale for the bid. As the negotiations continued into the summer of 1991, several of Pirelli's top managers, suspecting that Continental was dragging its feet on purpose, urged Pirelli's CEO, Leopold Pirelli, to withdraw from negotiations and make a hostile takeover bid for Continental. However, he refused and instead signed an agreement with Continental, which stated Pirelli's intention not to acquire any more shares in Continental. A number of Pirelli's top managers then resigned in protest.

No agreement was reached by November 30. Continental had succeeded in drawing out the negotiations, and on December 1 Pirelli formally withdrew the bid. But in the thirteen months since the bid had been launched, the tire industry had slid into a serious price war and Continental's stock price had plunged by one-third. Under the terms of its agreement with its allies in the abortive takeover attempt, Pirelli now had to compensate them for their loss as a result of the fall in share price during this period, which amounted to 350 billion lire ($287 million) The failed bid cost Pirelli dearly indeed.

This example offers three important lessons in making a successful takeover bid. First, the bidding company should have a very clear strategic rationale for the takeover attempt and should be able to articulate how it is going to create value from the takeover. Pirelli failed on both counts. Second, the bidding company should not reveal its takeover strategy to the target. By revealing the deal it had struck with its allies in the takeover attempt, Pirelli gave Continental an incentive to drag out the takeover negotiations. Third, the bidding company should set out a clear timetable for completing the bid. Because it did not do so, Pirelli allowed the negotiations to drag on for thirteen months, at great cost to the company.[17]

cellophane, nylon, Freon, and Teflon—all internally generated innovations. Another company, 3M, has a near-legendary knack for shaping new markets from internally generated ideas. Internal new venturing, however, need not be based on radical innovations. Although IBM was an imitator rather than an innovator, it successfully entered the personal computer market in 1981 through a venture-based strategy rather than by acquisition. Similarly, Gillette Co. successfully diversified into the manufacture of felt-tip pens, and John Deere diversified into snowmobiles—both through internal new venturing.

Despite the popularity of the internal new venture strategy, however, the failure rate for internal new ventures is reportedly very high just as it is for acquisitions. Although there is less research evidence on the failure rate of internal new ventures, the evidence on the failure rate of new products indicates the scope of the problem, since most internal new ventures are associated with new product offerings. According to this evidence, somewhere between 33 and 60 percent of all new products that reach the marketplace fail to generate an adequate economic return.[18] Such statistics suggest that the failure rate for internal new ventures is indeed substantial.

Why Internal New Ventures Fail

Three reasons are often given to explain the relatively high failure rate of internal new ventures: (1) ventures fail because companies enter a new market on too small a scale, (2) ventures fail due to poor commercialization of the new venture product, and (3) ventures fail because of poor corporate management of the venture process.

Scale of Entry Research suggests that large-scale entry into a new business is the best way for an internal venture to succeed. Although in the short run large-scale entry means significant development costs and substantial losses, in the long run (that is, after eight to twelve years) it brings greater returns than small-scale entry.[19] Figure 10.1 plots the relationships among scale of entry, profitability, and cash flow over time for successful small-scale and large-scale ventures. The figure shows that successful small-scale entry involves lower losses, but that in the long run large-scale entry generates greater returns. However, perhaps because of the costs of large-scale entry and the potential losses if the venture fails, many companies prefer a small-scale entry strategy. Acting on this preference can be a major mistake, for the company fails to build up the market share necessary for long-term success.

Commercialization Many internal new ventures are high-technology operations. To be commercially successful, science-based innovations must be developed with market requirements in mind. Many internal new ventures fail when a company ignores the basic needs of the market. A company can become blinded by the technological possibilities of a new product and fail to analyze market opportunities properly. Thus a new venture may fail because of a lack of commercialization or because it is marketing a technology for which there is no demand. For example, consider the desktop computer marketed by NeXT, the company started by the founder of Apple, Steven Jobs. The NeXT system failed to gain market share because the computer incorporated an array of expensive technologies that consumers simply did not want—such as optical disk drives, and hi-fi sound. The optical disk drives, in particular, turned off customers because they

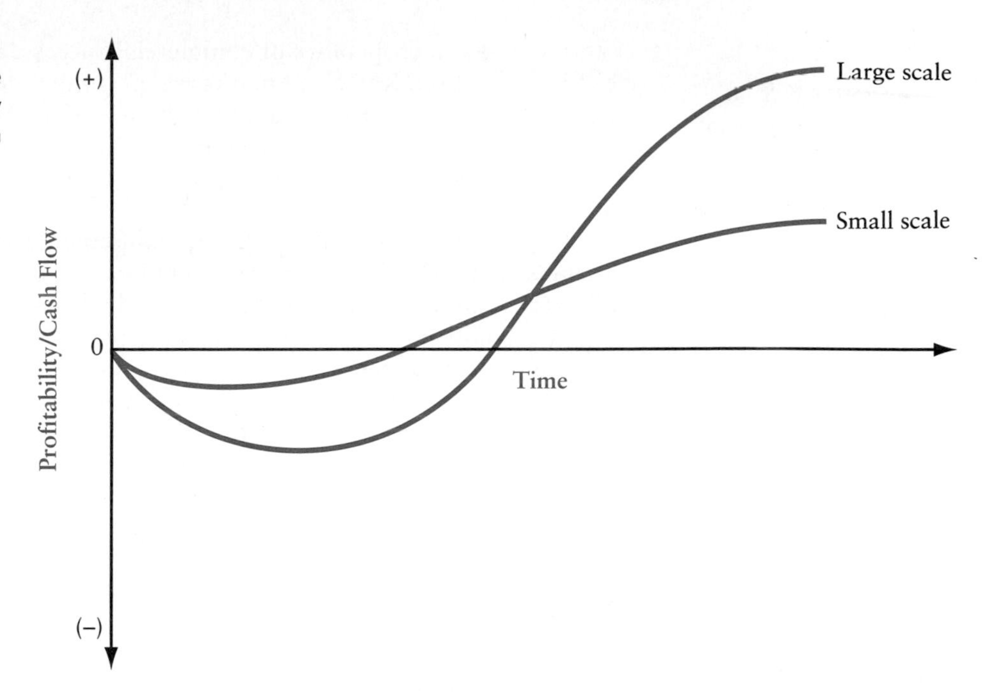

Figure 10.1
The Impact of Large-Scale versus Small-Scale Entry on Profitability and Cash

made it tough to switch work from a PC with a floppy drive to a NeXT machine with an optical drive. In other words, NeXT failed because its founder was so dazzled by leading-edge technology that he ignored customer needs.

Poor Implementation Managing the new venture process raises difficult organizational issues.[20] Although we deal with the specifics of implementation in later chapters, we must note some of the most common mistakes here. The shotgun approach of supporting many different internal new venture projects can be a major error, for it places great demands on a company's cash flow and can result in the best ventures being starved of the cash they need for success.

Another mistake involves a failure by corporate management to set the strategic context within which new venture projects should be developed. Simply taking a team of research scientists and allowing them to do research in their favorite field may produce novel results, but these results may have little strategic or commercial value.

Failure to anticipate the time and costs involved in the venture process constitutes a further mistake. Many companies have unrealistic expectations regarding the time frame involved. Reportedly, some companies operate with a philosophy of killing new businesses if they do not turn a profit by the end of the third year—clearly an unrealistic view, given the evidence that it can take eight to twelve years before a venture generates substantial profits.

Guidelines for Successful Internal New Venturing

To avoid the pitfalls just discussed, a company should adopt a structured approach to managing internal new venturing. New venturing typically begins with R&D. To make effective use of its R&D capacity, a company must first spell out its strategic objectives and then communicate them to its scientists and engineers. Research, after all, makes sense only when it is undertaken in areas relevant to strategic goals.[21]

To increase the probability of commercial success, a company should foster close links between R&D and marketing personnel, for this is the best way to ensure that research projects address the needs of the market. The company should also foster close links between R&D and manufacturing personnel, to ensure that the company has the capability to manufacture any proposed new products.

Many companies successfully integrate different functions by setting up project teams. Such teams comprise representatives of the various functional areas. The task of these teams is to oversee the development of new products. For example, Compaq's success in introducing new products in the personal computer industry has been linked to its use of project teams, which oversee the development of a new product from its inception to its market introduction.

Another advantage of such teams is that they can significantly reduce the time it takes to develop a new product. Thus, while R&D personnel are working on the design, manufacturing personnel can be setting up facilities, and marketing personnel can be developing its plans. Because of such integration, Compaq needed only six months to take the first portable personal computer from an idea on a drawing board to a marketable product.

To use resources to the best effect, a company must also devise a selection process for choosing only the ventures that demonstrate the greatest probability of commercial success. Picking future winners, however, is a tricky business, since by definition new ventures have an uncertain future. A study by G. Beardsley and Edwin Mansfield found the uncertainty surrounding new ventures to be so great that it usually took a company four to five years after launching the venture to reasonably estimate the venture's future profitability.[22] Nevertheless, some kind of selection process is necessary if a company is to avoid spreading its resources too thinly over too many projects.

Once a project is selected, management needs to monitor the progress of the venture closely. Evidence suggests that the most important criterion for evaluating a venture during its first four to five years is market share growth rather than cash flow or profitability. In the long run, the most successful ventures are those that increase their market share. A company should have clearly defined market share objectives for an internal new venture and decide to retain or kill it in its early years on the basis of its ability to achieve market share goals. Only in the medium term should profitability and cash flow begin to take on greater importance.

Finally, the association of large-scale entry with greater long-term profitability suggests that a company can increase the probability of success for an internal new venture by thinking big. Thinking big means the construction of efficient-scale manufacturing facilities ahead of demand, large marketing expenditures, and a commitment by corporate management to accept initial large losses as long as market share is expanding.

10.6 JOINT VENTURES AS AN ENTRY STRATEGY

In some situations, a company prefers internal new venturing to acquisition as an entry strategy into new business areas yet hesitates to commit itself to an internal new venture because of the risks and costs of building a new operation up from the ground floor. Such a situation is most likely to occur when a company sees the possibility of establishing a new business in an embryonic or

growth industry but the risks and costs associated with the project are more than it is willing to assume on its own. In these circumstances, the company may prefer to enter into a joint venture with another company and use the joint venture as a vehicle for entering the new business area. Such an arrangement enables the company to share the substantial risks and costs involved in a new project.

To illustrate, in 1990 IBM and Motorola set up a joint venture whose purpose is to provide a service that will allow computer users to communicate over radio waves. Customers buying the service will use hand-held computers, made by Motorola, to communicate by means of a private network of radio towers that IBM had built across the United States. The venture is aimed at the potentially enormous market of people who could benefit from using computers in the field—for instance, people who repair equipment in offices and insurance claims adjusters. Analysts estimate that the market for such a service is currently in the tens of millions of dollars but could reach the billions over the next decade.[23]

Because of the embryonic nature of the industry, the venture faces substantial risks. A number of competing technologies are on the horizon. For example, laptop computers are being fitted with modems that can communicate with host computers through cellular telephone networks. Although cellular networks are more crowded and less reliable than radio networks, that state of affairs could change. Thus there is no guarantee that communication between computers over radio waves is the technology of the future. Given this uncertainty, it makes sense for IBM and Motorola to combine in a joint venture and share the risks associated with building up this business.

In addition, a joint venture makes sense when a company can increase the probability of successfully establishing a new business by joining forces with another company. For a company that has some of the skills and assets necessary to establish a successful new venture, teaming up with another company that has complementary skills and assets may increase the probability of success.

Again, the joint venture between IBM and Motorola provides an example. Motorola dominates the market for mobile radios and already manufactures hand-held computers, but it lacks a nationwide radio network through which users of hand-held computers might communicate with each other. IBM lacks radio technology, but it does have a private network of radio towers (originally built for communicating with 20,000-plus IBM service people in the field), which covers more than 90 percent of the country. Combining Motorola's skills in radio technology with IBM's radio network in a single joint venture increases significantly the probability of establishing a successful new business.

However, there are three main drawbacks to such an arrangement. First, a joint venture allows a company to share the risks and costs of developing a new business, but it also requires the sharing of profits if the new business succeeds. Second, a company that enters into a joint venture always runs the risk of giving critical know-how away to its joint venture partner, which might use that know-how to compete directly with the company in the future. As we point out in discussing global strategic alliances in Chapter 8, however, joint ventures may be structured to minimize this risk. Third, the venture partners must share control. If the partners have different business philosophies, time horizons, or investment preferences, substantial problems can arise. Conflicts over how to run the joint venture can tear it apart and result in business failure.

In sum, although joint ventures often have a distinct advantage over internal new venturing as a means of establishing a new business operation, they also

have certain drawbacks. When deciding whether to go it alone or cooperate with another company in a joint venture, strategic managers need to assess carefully the pros and cons of the alternatives.

10.7 RESTRUCTURING

So far we have focused on strategies for expanding the scope of a company into new business areas. We turn now to their opposite: strategies for reducing the scope of the company by *exiting* from business areas. In recent years reducing the scope of a company through restructuring has become an increasingly popular strategy, particularly among the companies that diversified their activities during the 1960s, 1970s, and 1980s. In most cases, companies that are engaged in restructuring are divesting themselves of diversified activities in order to concentrate on their core businesses. The Opening Case, you recall, describes how Xerox has restructured itself—selling off most of the diversified financial services activities that it had acquired during the early 1980s—in order to focus top management attention on its core photocopier business. Other large, diversified, well-known companies have pursued similar strategies. They include General Electric, which began restructuring in 1981, when Jack Welch became its CEO, and Sears, which recently sold off its Allstate Insurance business, Coldwell Banker real estate business, and Dean Witter Reynolds stockbroker business, in order to focus more on its core retailing operations. (For details of restructuring at Sears see Strategy in Action 10.3.)

The first question that must be asked is why are so many companies restructuring at this particular time? After answering it, we examine the different strategies that companies adopt for exiting from business areas. Then, we discuss the various turnaround strategies that companies employ to revitalize their core business area.

Why Restructure?

One reason for so much restructuring in recent years has been earlier overdiversification. There is plenty of evidence that in the heyday of the corporate diversification movement, which began in the 1960s and lasted until the early 1980s, many companies over-diversified.[24] More precisely, the bureaucratic inefficiencies created by expanding the scope of the organization outweighed the additional value that could be created by such a move, and company performance declined. As performance declined, the stock price of many of these diversified companies fell, and they found themselves vulnerable to hostile takeover bids. Indeed, a number of diversified companies were acquired in the 1980s and subsequently broken up. This is what happened to US Industries and SCM Corporation, two diversified conglomerates that were acquired and then broken up by Hanson Industries. Similarly, after the diversified consumer products business RJR Nabisco was acquired by Kohlberg, Kravis & Roberts in a 1988 leveraged buyout, RJR sold off many of its diversified businesses to independent investors or to other companies.

A second factor driving the current restructuring trend is that in the 1980s many diversified companies found their core business areas under attack from new competition. Xerox's copier business was attacked by Canon and Ricoh.

And Sears still faces profound competitive challenges in the retailing industry, where demand is shifting from department stores such as Sears to low-cost discounters such as Costco, or niche stores like The Gap. (Again, see Strategy in Action 10.3 for details). The top management of these companies found that in order to devote the necessary attention to their troubled core business, it had to shed its diversified activities, which had become an unwelcome distraction.

A final factor of some importance is that innovations in management processes and strategy have diminished the advantages of vertical integration or diversification. In response, companies have reduced the scope of their activities through restructuring and divestments. For example, ten years ago there was little understanding of how long-term cooperative relationships between a company and its suppliers could be a viable alternative to vertical integration. Most companies considered only two alternatives for managing the supply chain: vertical integration or competitive bidding. As we note in Chapter 9, however, if the conditions are right, a third alternative for managing the supply chain, *long-term contracting*, can be a superior strategy to both vertical integration and competitive bidding. Like vertical integration, long-term contracting facilitates investments in specialization. But unlike vertical integration, it does not involve high bureaucratic costs, nor does it dispense with market discipline. As this strategic innovation has spread throughout the business world, the advantages of vertical integration have declined.

Exit Strategies

Companies can choose from three main strategies for exiting business areas: divestment, harvest, and liquidation (see Figure 10.2). You have already encountered all three in Chapter 7, where we discuss strategies for competing in declining industries. We review them briefly here.

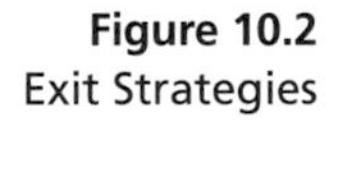

Figure 10.2
Exit Strategies

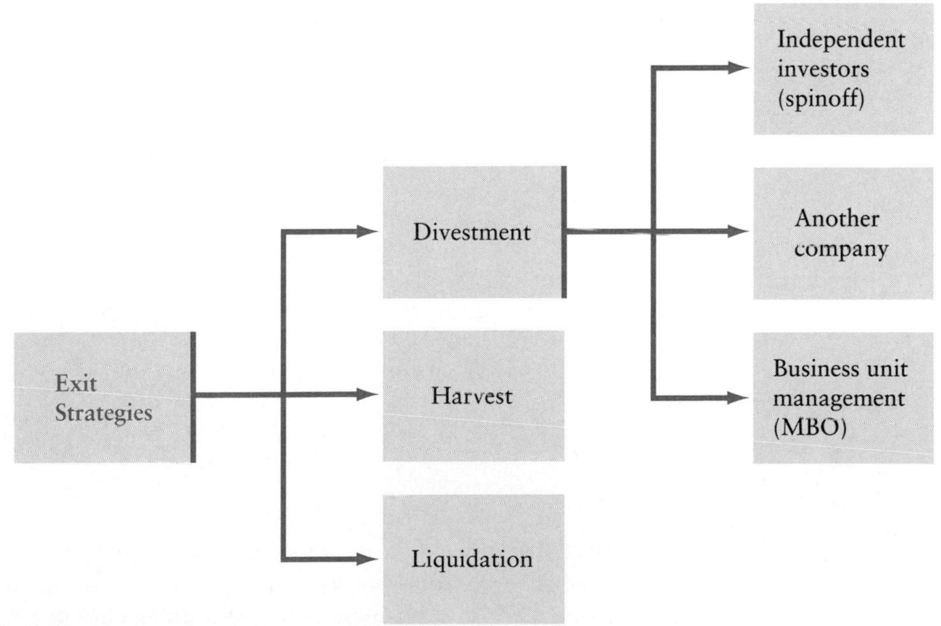

STRATEGY IN ACTION 10.3

Restructuring at Sears

Back in 1981 Sears, which was then the largest retailer in the United States, announced in a single week that it would acquire Dean Witter Reynolds Inc., the country's fifth largest stockbroker, and Coldwell, Banker & Co., the nation's biggest real estate broker, for a total of $800 million. The idea was to team these two financial services operations up with Allstate Insurance, which Sears had acquired back in 1934, and which was then the world's second largest personal property and casualty insurer. At the heart of Sears strategy was a desire to leverage its fabled "bond of trust" with the consumer into the fast-growing financial services industry. Its CEO, Edward Brennan, often referred to this strategy as "socks to stocks." Sears felt that its retail customers would be strongly attracted to financial services providers that were owned by Sears. Indeed, the company planned to locate offices for its financial services operations in Sears department stores, and to use its catalog mailing list as a channel for selling financial services.

However, the years since 1981 have not been kind to Sears. While the financial services operations of the company did well, its core retailing operation ran into serious problems. During most of the 1980s the earnings of the Sears retail group fell at an annual rate of 7 to 8 percent, and its market share slumped. The share of department store merchandise accounted for by Sears fell from 9 percent in 1982 to 6 percent in 1992. More significantly, Sears did little to keep up with the growth of discount and niche retailers such as Wal-Mart, Costco, The Home Depot, and Toys Я Us, all of which ate into Sears's blue-collar clientele. Critics charged that senior executives at Sears seemed more interested in new ventures and the potential for synergy than in the basic business of running Sears stores. As a result, Sears was slow to respond to new competition, and its sales stagnated.

The problems in the Sears retail operations attracted the scorn of Wall Street and at least one abortive takeover attempt in early 1988, when rumors of a $50.2 billion takeover bid by Revlon Group Chairman Ronald O. Perelman were making the rounds on Wall Street. Sears responded to the 1988 takeover threat by announcing a decision to sell its Chicago headquarters and introducing an "everyday low pricing" strategy at its stores. Both moves failed. After a year Sears abandoned its efforts to sell the Sears Tower, and it never managed to convince consumers that it had the lowest prices in town—probably because it did not.

Meanwhile, the stock continued to slump. To make matters worse, in 1992 the fabled Sears bond of trust with consumers was blown apart when it was revealed that the Sears automobile services operation had been systematically overcharging consumers for repairs. At the same time Moody's Investors Service, noting Sears's growing burden of debt, lowered its bond rating on the company. The stock slumped further and investors pushed the company to take drastic action. The company's response came in September 1992, when Sears announced plans to sell Dean Witter Reynolds and Coldwell, Banker & Co., and to spin off 20 percent of Allstate Insurance to independent investors. In effect, Sears was turning its back on thirteen years of diversification and an investment of billions of dollars so that top management could devote more time to revitalizing its troubled retailing arm. The change in strategy was a humiliating admission by the company's top managers, and particularly CEO Brennan, that they had mishandled the strategic direction of the company. The irony of the move is that Sears is getting out of its most profitable activities in order to concentrate on its least profitable, but core, operations—retailing.[25]

Divestment Of the three main strategies, divestment is usually the favored one. It represents the best way for a company to recoup as much of its initial investment in a business unit as possible. The idea is to sell the business unit to

the highest bidder. Three types of buyers are possible: independent investors, other companies, and the management of the unit to be divested. Selling off a business unit to independent investors is normally referred to as a **spinoff**. A spinoff makes good sense when the unit to be sold is profitable and when the stock market has an appetite for new stock issues (which is normal during market upswings, but *not* during market downswings). Thus, for example, in 1992 the timber products company Weyerhaeuser successfully spun off its Paragon Trade Brands to independent investors. Investors snapped up the stock of the new issue, which makes "own label" disposable diapers for supermarket chains and is highly profitable. However, spinoffs do not work if the unit to be spun off is unprofitable and unattractive to independent investors or if the stock market is slumping and unresponsive to new issues.

Selling off a unit to another company is a strategy frequently pursued when a unit can be sold to a company in the same line of business as the unit. In such cases, the purchaser is often prepared to pay a considerable amount of money for the opportunity to substantially increase the size of its business virtually overnight. For example, in 1987 Hanson Industries sold off its Glidden paint subsidiary, which it acquired six months earlier in the takeover of SCM Corporation, to Imperial Chemicals Industry (ICI). Glidden was the largest paint company in the United States, and ICI was the largest manufacturer of paint outside the United States, so the match made a good deal of sense from ICI's perspective, while Hanson was able to get a substantial price for the sale.

Selling off a unit to its management is normally referred to as a **management buyout** (**MBO**). MBOs are very similar to leveraged buyouts (LBOs), discussed in Chapter 2. In an MBO, the unit is sold to its management, which often finances the purchase through the sale of high-yield bonds to investors. The bond issue is normally arranged by a buyout specialist, such as Kohlberg, Kravis & Roberts, which, along with management, will typically hold a sizable proportion of the shares in the MBO. MBOs often take place when financially troubled units have only two other options: a harvest strategy or liquidation. An MBO can be very risky for the management team involved, since its members may have to sign personal guarantees to back up the bond issue and may lose everything if the MBO ultimately fails. On the other hand, if the management team succeeds in turning around the troubled unit, its reward can be a significant increase in personal wealth. Thus an MBO strategy can be characterized as a *high risk–high return* strategy for the management team involved. Faced with the possible liquidation of their business unit, many management teams are willing to take the risk. However, the viability of this option depends not only on a willing management team, but also on there being enough buyers of high yield–high risk bonds—so-called junk bonds—to be able to finance the MBO. In recent years, the general slump in the junk bond market has made the MBO strategy a more difficult one for companies to follow.

Harvest and Liquidation Since the pros and cons of harvest and liquidation strategies are discussed in detail in Chapter 6, we note just a few points here. First, a harvest or liquidation strategy is generally considered inferior to a divestment strategy since the company can probably best recoup its investment in a business unit by divestment. Second, a harvest strategy involves halting investment in a unit in order to maximize short-to-medium-term cash flow from that unit before liquidating it. Although this strategy seems fine in theory, it is

often a poor one to apply in practice. Once it becomes apparent that the unit is pursuing a harvest strategy, the morale of the unit's employees, as well as the confidence of the unit's customers and suppliers in its continuing operation, can sink very quickly. If this occurs, as it often does, then the rapid decline in the unit's revenues can make the strategy untenable. Finally, a liquidation strategy is the least attractive of all to pursue since it requires the company to write off its investment in a business unit, often at a considerable cost. However, for a poorly performing business unit where a selloff or spinoff is unlikely and where an MBO cannot be arranged, it may be the only viable alternative.

10.8 TURNAROUND STRATEGY

Many companies restructure their operations, divesting themselves of their diversified activities, because they wish to focus more on their core business area. As in the case of Sears and Xerox, this often occurs because the core business area is itself in trouble and needs top management attention. An integral part of restructuring, therefore, is the development of a strategy for turning around the company's core or remaining business areas. In this section, we review in some detail the various steps that companies take to turn around troubled business areas. We first look at the causes of corporate decline and then discuss the main elements of successful turnaround strategies.

The Causes of Corporate Decline

Seven main causes stand out in most cases of corporate decline: poor management, overexpansion, inadequate financial controls, high costs, the emergence of powerful new competition, unforeseen shifts in demand, and organizational inertia.[26] Normally, several, if not all, of these factors are present in a decline situation. For example, IBM's decline in the early 1990s was brought on by a high-cost structure, powerful new low-cost competition from personal computer makers, a shift in demand away from mainframe computers (IBM's main business), and IBM's slow response to these factors due to organizational inertia.

Poor Management Poor management covers a multitude of sins, ranging from sheer incompetence to neglect of core businesses and an insufficient number of good managers. Although not necessarily a bad thing, one-person rule often seems to be at the root of poor management. One study found that the presence of a dominant and autocratic chief executive with a passion for empire-building strategies often characterizes many failing companies.[27] Another study of eighty-one turnaround situations found that in thirty-six cases troubled companies suffered from an autocratic manager who tried to do it all and, in the face of complexity and change, could not.[28] Examples of autocratic CEOs include Bill Bricker, the former CEO of Diamond Shamrock; Harold Geneen, the former CEO of ITT; and Roy Mason, the former CEO of the onetime *Fortune* 500 and later bankrupt Charter Company. In a review of the empirical studies of turnaround situations, Richard Hoffman identified a number of other management defects commonly found in declining companies.[29] These included a lack of balanced expertise at the top (for example, too many engineers), a lack of strong middle

management, a failure to provide for orderly management succession by a departing CEO (which may result in an internal succession battle), and a failure by the board of directors to monitor adequately management's strategic decisions.

Overexpansion The empire-building strategies of autocratic CEOs such as Bricker, Geneen, and Mason often involve rapid expansion and extensive diversification. Much of this diversification tends to be poorly conceived and adds little value to a company. As already pointed out in this chapter and in Chapter 9, the consequences of too much diversification include loss of control and an inability to cope with recessionary conditions. Moreover, companies that expand rapidly tend to do so by taking on large amounts of debt financing. Adverse economic conditions can limit a company's ability to meet its debt requirements and can thus precipitate a financial crisis.

Inadequate Financial Controls The most common aspect of inadequate financial controls is a failure to assign profit responsibility to key decision makers within the organization. A lack of accountability for the financial consequences of their actions can encourage middle-level managers to employ excess staff and spend resources beyond what is necessary for maximum efficiency. In such cases, bureaucracy may balloon and costs spiral out of control. This is precisely what happened at Chrysler during the 1970s. As Lee Iacocca later noted, Jerry Greenwald, whom Iacocca brought in to head the finance function in 1980, "had a hell of a time finding anybody who could be identified as having specific responsibility for anything. They would tell him, 'Well, everyone is responsible for controlling costs.' Jerry knew very well what that meant—in the final analysis nobody was."[30]

High Costs Inadequate financial controls can lead to high costs. Beyond this, the most common cause of a high-cost structure is low labor productivity. It may stem from union-imposed restrictive working practices (as in the case of the auto and steel industries), management's failure to invest in new labor-saving technologies, or, more often, a combination of both. Other common causes include high wage rates (a particularly important factor for companies competing on costs in the global marketplace) and a failure to realize economies of scale because of low market share.

New Competition Competition in capitalist economies is a process characterized by the continual emergence of new companies championing new ways of doing business. In recent years few industries and few established companies have been spared the competitive challenge of powerful new competition. Indeed, many established businesses have failed or run into serious trouble because they did not respond quickly enough to such threats. Powerful new competition is a central cause of corporate decline. IBM has been hammered by powerful new competition from personal computer makers, Sears has been hard hit by powerful new competition from discount and niche stores (see Strategy in Action 10.3), and Xerox's photocopier business was confronted by powerful new competition from Japan, and particularly Canon and Ricoh (see Opening Case). In all of these cases, the established company failed to appreciate the strength of new competitors until it was in serious trouble.

Unforeseen Demand Shifts Unforeseen, and often unforeseeable, shifts in demand can be brought about by major changes in technology, economic or political conditions, and social and cultural norms. Although such changes can open up market opportunities for new products, they also threaten the existence of many established enterprises, necessitating restructuring. The classic example is clearly the 1974 OPEC oil price increase, which, among other things, hit the demand for autos, oil-fired central heating units, and many oil-based products, such as vinyl phonographic records. Similarly, the oil price collapse of 1983–1986 devastated many oil field drilling companies and forced them into undertaking drastic restructuring.

Organizational Inertia On their own, the emergence of powerful new competition and unforeseen shifts in demand might not be enough to cause corporate decline. What is also required is an organization that is slow to respond to such environmental changes. As you saw in Chapter 4, where we first touch on the issue of corporate decline, organizational inertia stands out as a major reason why companies are often so slow to respond to new competitive conditions. For more details see Chapter 4.

The Main Steps of Turnaround

There is no standard model of how a company should respond to a decline. Indeed, there can be no such model because every situation is unique. However, in most successful turnaround situations, a number of common features are present. They include changing the leadership, redefining the company's strategic focus, divesting or closing unwanted assets, taking steps to improve the profitability of remaining operations, and, occasionally, making acquisitions to rebuild core operations.

Changing the Leadership Since the old leadership bears the stigma of failure, new leadership is an essential element of most retrenchment and turnaround situations. For example, as the first step in implementing a turnaround, IBM replaced CEO John Akers with an outsider, Lou Gerstner. To resolve a crisis, the new leader should be someone who is able to make difficult decisions, motivate lower-level managers, listen to the views of others, and delegate power when appropriate.

Redefining Strategic Focus For a single-business enterprise, redefining strategic focus involves a reevaluation of the company's business-level strategy. A failed cost leader, for example, may reorient toward a more focused or differentiated strategy. For a diversified company, redefining strategic focus means identifying the businesses in the portfolio that have the best long-term profit and growth prospects and concentrating investment there.

Asset Sales and Closures Having redefined its strategic focus, a company should divest as many unwanted assets as it can find buyers for and liquidate whatever remains. It is important not to confuse unwanted assets with unprofitable assets. Assets that no longer fit in with the redefined strategic focus of the company may be very profitable. Their sale can bring the company much-needed cash, which it can invest in improving the operations that remain.

Improving Profitability Improving the profitability of the operations that remain after asset sales and closures involves a number of steps to improve efficiency, quality, innovation, and customer responsiveness. We discuss many of the functional-level strategies that companies can pursue to achieve these ends in Chapter 5, so you may want to review that chapter for details. Note, though, that improving profitability typically involves one or more of the following steps: (1) layoffs of white- and blue-collar employees; (2) investments in labor-saving equipment; (3) assignment of profit responsibility to individuals and subunits within the company, by a change of organizational structure if necessary; (4) tightening financial controls; (5) cutting back on marginal products; (6) reengineering business process to cut costs and boost productivity; and (7) introducing total quality management processes.

Acquisitions A somewhat surprising but quite common turnaround strategy involves making acquisitions, primarily to strengthen the competitive position of a company's remaining core operations. For example, Champion International Corporation used to be a very diversified company manufacturing a wide range of paper and wood products. After years of declining performance, in the mid 1980s Champion decided to focus on its profitable newsprint and magazine paper business. The company divested many of its other paper and wood products businesses, but at the same time it paid $1.8 billion for St. Regis Corp., one of the country's largest manufacturers of newsprint and magazine paper.

10.9 PORTFOLIO PLANNING: A FLAWED MANAGEMENT TOOL

During the 1960s and 1970s a number of management consulting companies developed a series of conceptual techniques whose stated purpose was to help the top officers of diversified corporations better manage their portfolio of businesses. These techniques, collectively referred to as portfolio planning techniques, were actively peddled by management consultants and eagerly applied at a number of diversified companies. The results often ranged from indifferent to disastrous. In this section, we examine one of the most famous of these techniques, the Boston Consulting Group's portfolio planning matrix. Then we consider why these techniques for managing a portfolio of businesses so often failed to work in practice.

The Boston Consulting Group Business Matrix

The main objective of the Boston Consulting Group (BCG) technique is to help senior managers identify the cash flow requirements of the different businesses in their portfolio. The BCG approach involves three main steps: (1) dividing a company into strategic business units (SBUs) and assessing the long-term prospects of each; (2) comparing SBUs against each other by means of a matrix that indicates the relative prospects of each; and (3) developing strategic objectives with respect to each SBU.

Defining and Evaluating Strategic Business Units According to the BCG, a company must create an SBU for each economically distinct business area that

it competes in. When top managers identify SBUs, their objective is to divide a company into strategic entities that are relevant for planning purposes. Normally, a company defines its SBUs in terms of the product markets they are competing in. Having defined SBUs, top managers then assess each according to two criteria: (1) the SBU's relative market share and (2) the growth rate of the SBU's industry.

The objective when identifying an SBU's relative market share is to establish whether that SBU's market position can be classified as a strength or a weakness. **Relative market share** is defined as the ratio of an SBU's market share to the market share held by the largest rival company in its industry. If SBU X has a market share of 10 percent and its largest rival has a market share of 30 percent, then SBU X's relative market share is 10/30, or 0.3. Only if an SBU is a market leader in its industry will it have a relative market share greater than 1.0. For example, if SBU Y has a market share of 40 percent and its largest rival has a market share of 10 percent, then SBU Y's relative market share is 40/10 = 4.0.

According to the Boston Consulting Group, market share gives a company cost advantages from economies of scale and learning effects. An SBU with a relative market share greater than 1.0 is assumed to be farthest down the experience curve and therefore to have a significant cost advantage over its rivals. By similar logic, an SBU with a relative market share smaller than 1.0 is assumed to be at a competitive disadvantage because it lacks the scale economies and low-cost position of the market leader. BCG characterizes SBUs with a relative market share greater than 1.0 as having a high relative market share and SBUs with a relative market share smaller than 1.0 as having a low relative market share.

The objective when assessing industry growth rates is to determine whether industry conditions offer opportunities for expansion or whether they threaten the SBU (as in a declining industry). The growth rate of an SBU's industry is assessed according to whether it is faster or slower than the growth rate of the economy as a whole. Industries with growth rates faster than the average are characterized as having high growth. Industries with growth rates slower than the average are characterized as having low growth. BCG's position is that high-growth industries offer a more favorable competitive environment and better long-term prospects than slow-growth industries.

Comparing Strategic Business Units The next step of the BCG approach is comparing SBUs against each other by means of a matrix based on two dimensions: relative market share and high growth. Figure 10.3 provides an example of such a matrix. The horizontal dimension measures relative market share; the vertical dimension measures industry growth rate. Each circle represents an SBU. The center of each circle corresponds to the position of that SBU on the two dimensions of the matrix. The size of each circle is proportional to the sales revenue generated by each business in the company's portfolio. The bigger the circle, the larger is the size of an SBU relative to total corporate revenues.

The matrix is divided into four cells. SBUs in cell 1 are defined as **stars**, in cell 2 as **question marks**, in cell 3 as **cash cows**, and in cell 4 as **dogs**. BCG argues that these different types of SBUs have different long-term prospects and different implications for cash flows.

- **Stars**. The leading SBUs in a company's portfolio are the stars. They have a high relative market share and are based in high-growth industries. They have

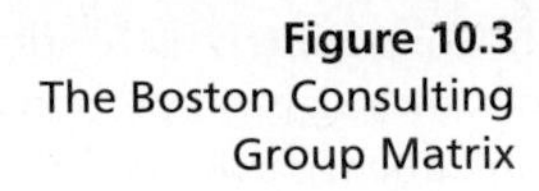
Figure 10.3
The Boston Consulting Group Matrix

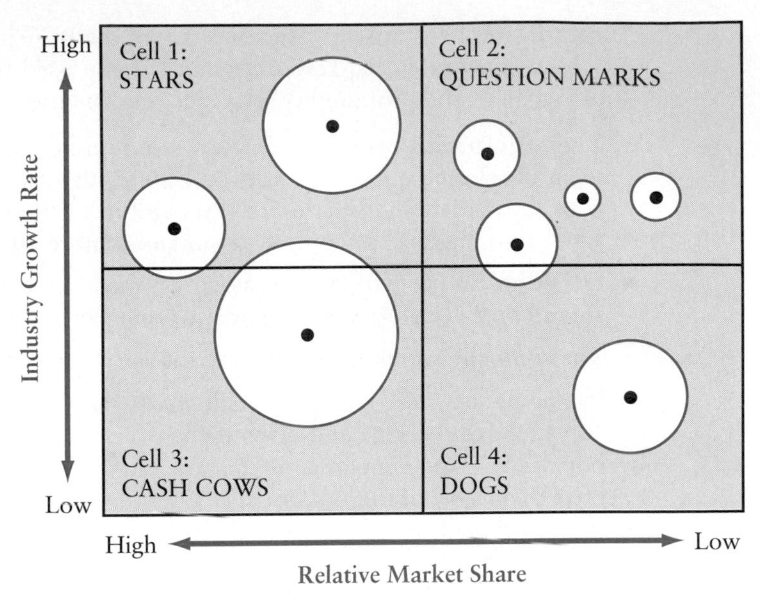

Source: Perspectives, No. 66, "The Product Portfolio." Adapted by permission from The Boston Consulting Group, Inc., 1970.

both competitive strengths and opportunities for expansion. Thus they offer long-term profit and growth opportunities.

- **Question marks.** SBUs that are relatively weak in competitive terms—that is, that have low relative market shares—are question marks. However, they are based in high-growth industries and thus may offer opportunities for long-term profit and growth. A question mark can become a star if nurtured properly. To become a market leader, a question mark requires substantial net injections of cash; it is cash hungry. The corporate head office has to decide whether a particular question mark has the potential to become a **star** and is therefore worth the capital investment necessary to achieve stardom.
- **Cash cows.** SBUs that have a high market share in low-growth industries and a strong competitive position in mature industries are cash cows. Their competitive strength comes from being farthest down the experience curve. They are the cost leaders in their industries. BCG argues that this position enables such SBUs to remain very profitable. However, low growth implies a lack of opportunities for future expansion. As a consequence, BCG argues that the capital investment requirements of cash cows are not substantial, and thus they are depicted as generating a strong positive cash flow.
- **Dogs.** SBUs that are in low-growth industries but have a low market share are dogs. They have a weak competitive position in unattractive industries and thus are viewed as offering few benefits to a company. BCG suggests that such SBUs are unlikely to generate much in the way of a positive cash flow and indeed may become cash hogs. Though offering few prospects for future growth in returns, dogs may require substantial capital investments just to maintain their low market share.

Strategic Implications The objective of the BCG portfolio matrix is to identify how corporate cash resources can best be used to maximize a company's future growth and profitability. BCG recommendations include the following:

- The cash surplus from any cash cows should be used to support the development of selected question marks and to nurture stars. The long-term objective is to consolidate the position of stars and to turn favored question marks into stars, thus making the company's portfolio more attractive.
- Question marks with the weakest or most uncertain long-term prospects should be divested to reduce demands on a company's cash resources.
- The company should exit from any industry where the SBU is a dog.
- If a company lacks sufficient cash cows, stars, or question marks, it should consider acquisitions and divestments to build a more balanced portfolio. A portfolio should contain enough stars and question marks to ensure a healthy growth and profit outlook for the company and enough cash cows to support the investment requirements of the stars and question marks.

The Problem with Portfolio Planning

Though portfolio planning techniques may sound reasonable, if we take the BCG matrix as an example, there at least four main flaws. First, the model is simplistic. An assessment of an SBU in terms of just two dimensions, market share and industry growth, is bound to be misleading, for a host of other relevant factors should be taken into account. Although market share is undoubtedly an important determinant of an SBU's competitive position, companies can also establish a strong competitive position by differentiating their product to serve the needs of a particular segment of the market. Thus a business having a low market share can be very profitable and have a strong competitive position in certain segments of a market. The auto manufacturer BMW is in this position, yet the BCG matrix would classify BMW as a dog because it is a low-market-share business in a low-growth industry. Similarly, industry growth is not the only factor determining industry attractiveness. Many factors besides growth determine competitive intensity in an industry and thus its attractiveness.

Second, the connection between relative market share and cost savings is not as straightforward as BCG suggests. Chapter 5 makes clear that a high market share does not always give a company a cost advantage. In some industries—for example, the U.S. steel industry—low-market-share companies using a low-share technology (minimills) can have lower production costs than high-market-share companies using high-share technologies (integrated mills). The BCG matrix would classify minimill operations as the dogs of the American steel industry, whereas in fact their performance over the last decade has characterized them as star businesses.

Third, a high market share in a low-growth industry does not necessarily result in the large positive cash flow characteristic of cash cow businesses. The BCG matrix would classify General Motors' auto operations as a cash cow. However, the capital investments needed to remain competitive are so substantial in the auto industry that the reverse is more likely to be true. Low-growth industries can be very competitive, and staying ahead in such an environment can require substantial cash investments.

STRATEGY IN ACTION 10.4

How Portfolio Planning Techniques Nearly Destroyed Cabot Corporation

In the 1970s Cabot Corporation was one of the eager adopters of the Boston Consulting Group's (BCG) portfolio planning matrix. By all accounts, applying these techniques nearly destroyed the company. Cabot is one of the world's leading industrial companies, with 1992 revenues of $1.5 billion. Its products are rarely seen by the public but are all around us. They include carbon black, which is primarily used in rubber products and inks, tantalum powders used by the electronics industry, and plastics concentrates.

After an analysis undertaken with the aid of the BCG, in the late 1970s the company decreed that its traditional chemical businesses were cash cows. The plan was to milk these divisions for cash that would then be reinvested in star divisions, which included diversification efforts in metal manufacturing, ceramics, semiconductors, and a gas transmission business. The result, however, was to throw good chemical earnings into businesses in which Cabot had no experience and to which it could add little value. In the meantime, Cabot's chemical operations were starved of the capital that they needed to keep them operating efficiently. Moreover, morale in the chemical operations began to slide as managers realized that funds were being siphoned off to support other operations. Consequently, throughout much of the 1980s Cabot's return on assets declined.

Ultimately, the Cabot family, which owns 30 percent of the stock, woke up to what was going on and brought in a new CEO, Sam Bodman, to run the business. Bodman spent his first few years restructuring Cabot, selling off many of those businesses that the BCG had designated as stars and redirecting funds toward the company's core chemical operations. He spent over $500 million on refurbishing and expanding the long-ignored chemical plants and building five new ones. At the same time research efforts were redirected toward Cabot's traditional areas of expertise, organic chemicals, where the emphasis was on adding value to Cabot's commodity products.

As a result, Cabot's operating costs have fallen dramatically, while a new generation of specialty chemicals has allowed the company to widen margins. After years of financial malaise, in 1992 Cabot's earnings surged 55 percent ahead of the 1991 figures despite zero revenue growth due to the effect of divestments.[31]

Fourth, in general *none* of the portfolio planning techniques pay attention to the source of value creation from diversification. They treat business units as independent, whereas in fact they may be linked by the need to transfer skills and competencies or to realize economies of scope. More importantly, they trivialize the process of managing a large diversified company. They suggest that success is simply a matter of putting together the right portfolio of businesses, whereas in reality it comes from managing a diversified portfolio to *create value*, whether by leveraging distinctive competencies across business units, by sharing resources to realize economies of scope, or by achieving superior governance. By diverting top management attention away from these vital tasks and by legitimizing underinvestment in core business areas designated as cash cows, portfolio management techniques may have done a great disservice to the corporations that adopted them. For instance, as Strategy in Action 10.4 recounts, the active application of portfolio planning techniques nearly destroyed Cabot Corporation.

10.10 SUMMARY OF CHAPTER

This chapter discusses the strategies that multibusiness corporations pursue to build and restructure their portfolio of businesses. We consider the pros and cons of entering new business areas via acquisitions, internal new ventures, and joint ventures. We also assess the rationale and methods companies use to exit from business areas and the means they employ to turn around troubled business units. More specifically, the following points have been made:

1. The choice of an appropriate entry strategy is influenced by barriers to entry, relatedness, speed and development costs of entry, risks of entry, and industry life cycle considerations.
2. Internal new venturing seems to make most sense when the industry to be entered is in its embryonic or growth stage; when barriers to entry are low; when the industry is closely related to the company's existing operations (the company's strategy is one of related diversification); and when the company is willing to accept the attendant time frame, development costs, and risks.
3. Acquisition makes most sense when the industry to be entered is mature; when the barriers to entry are high; when the industry is not closely related to the company's existing operations (the company's strategy is one of unrelated diversification); and when the company is unwilling to accept the time frame, development costs, and risks of internal new venturing.
4. Many acquisitions fail because of poor postacquisition integration, overestimation of the value that can be created from an acquisition, the high cost of acquisition, and poor preacquisition screening.
5. Guarding against acquisition failure involves structured screening, good bidding strategies, and positive attempts to integrate the acquired company into the organization of the acquiring one.
6. Many internal new ventures fail because of entry on too small a scale, poor commercialization, and poor corporate management of the internal venture process.
7. Guarding against failure involves a structured approach toward project selection and management, integration of R&D and marketing to improve commercialization of a venture idea, and entry on a significant scale.
8. Joint ventures may be the preferred entry strategy when (a) the risks and costs associated with setting up a new business unit are more than the company is willing to assume on its own and (b) the company can increase the probability of successfully establishing a new business by teaming up with another company that has skills and assets complementing its own.
9. The current popularity of restructuring is due to (a) overdiversification by many companies in the 1970s and 1980s, (b) the rise of competitive challenges to the core business units of many diversified enterprises, and (c) innovations in management process that have reduced the advantages of vertical integration and diversification.
10. Exit strategies include divestment, harvest, and liquidation. The choice of exit strategy is governed by the characteristics of the relevant business unit.

11. The causes of corporate decline include poor management, overexpansion, inadequate financial controls, high costs, the emergence of powerful new competition, unforeseen shifts in demand, and organizational inertia.
12. Responses to corporate decline include changing the leadership, redefining the company's strategic focus, divestment or closure of unwanted assets, taking steps to improve the profitability of the operations that remain, and occasionally, acquisitions to rebuild core operations.
13. Portfolio planning techniques are a set of conceptual tools whose stated purpose is to help the top officers of diversified companies better manage the portfolio of businesses that the company owns. The best-known of these techniques is the Boston Consulting Group's matrix.
14. The weaknesses of the BCG matrix include (a) the simplistic categorization of businesses, (b) untenable assumptions about relationships between market share, growth, and profitability, and (c) failure to focus on the source of value creation.

Discussion Questions

1. Under what circumstances might it be best to enter a new business area by acquisition, and under what circumstances might internal new venturing be the preferred entry mode?
2. Given the obvious difficulties of succeeding with acquisitions, why do so many companies continue to make them?
3. IBM has decided to diversify into the cellular telecommunication business. What entry strategy would you recommend that the company pursue? Why?
4. Review the change in the composition of GE's portfolio of businesses under the leadership of Jack Welch (1981 to the present). How has GE's portfolio been reorganized? From a value creation perspective, what is the logic underlying this reorganization?

Article File 10

Find an example of a company that has made an acquisition that apparently failed to create any value. Identify and critically evaluate the rationale used by top management to justify the acquisition at the time the acquisition was made. Explain why the acquisition subsequently failed.

Strategic Management Project: Module 10

This module requires you to assess your company's use of acquisitions, internal new ventures, and joint ventures as strategies for entering a new business area and/or as attempts to restructure its portfolio of businesses.

A. If your company has entered a new business area during the last decade

1. Pick one new business area that your company has entered into during the last ten years.
2. Identify the rationale for entering this business area.
3. Identify the strategy used to enter this business area.
4. Evaluate the rationale for using this particular entry strategy. Do you think that this was the best entry strategy to use? Justify your answer.
5. Do you think that the addition of this business area to the company has added or dissipated value? Again, justify your answer.

B. If your company has restructured its business during the last decade

1. Identify the rationale for pursuing a restructuring strategy.
2. Pick one business area that your company has exited from during the last ten years.
3. Identify the strategy used to exit from this particular business area. Do you think that this was the best exit strategy to use? Justify your answer.
4. In general, do you think that exiting from this business area has been in the company's best interest?

Endnotes

1. Sources: L. Hooper, "Xerox Plans to Withdraw Completely from the Financial Services Industry," *Wall Street Journal*, January 19, 1993, p. A3. T. Smart, "So Much for Diversification," *Business Week*, February 1, 1993, p. 31. T. Smart, "A Cloud Over Xerox," *Business Week*, November 9, 1992, p. 48.
2. For further details, see H. L. Ansoff, *Corporate Strategy* (New York: McGraw-Hill, 1965); E. R. Biggadike, *Corporate Diversification: Entry, Strategy and Performance* (Cambridge, Mass.: Division of Research, Harvard Business School, 1983); M. S. Salter and W. A. Weinhold, *Diversification Through Acquisition: Strategies for Creating Economic Value* (New York: Free Press, 1979); G. S. Yip, "Diversification Entry: Internal Development Versus Acquisition," *Strategic Management Journal*, 3 (1982), 331–345; and P. Haspeslagh and D. Jemison, *Managing Acquisitions* (New York: Free Press, 1991).
3. Biggadike, *Corporate Diversification.*
4. E. Mansfield, "How Economists See R&D," *Harvard Business Review* (November–December 1981) 98–106.
5. P. Petre, "AT&T's Epic Push into Computers," *Fortune*, May 25, 1987, pp. 42–50.
6. "Do Mergers Really Work? *Business Week*, June 3, 1985, pp. 88–100.
7. D. J. Ravenscraft and F. M. Scherer, *Mergers, Selloffs, and Economic Efficiency* (Washington, D.C.: Brookings Institution, 1987).
8. Ibid. For additional evidence on acquisitions and performance, see R. E. Caves, "Mergers, Takeovers, and Economic Efficiency," *International Journal of Industrial Organization*, 7 (1989), 151–174; M. C. Jensen and R. S. Ruback, "The Market for Corporate Control: The Scientific Evidence," *Journal of Financial Economics*, 11 (1983), 5–50; R. Roll, "Empirical Evidence on Takeover Activity and Shareholder Wealth," in *Knights, Raiders and Targets*, ed. J. C. Coffee, L. Lowenstein, and S. Rose (Oxford: Oxford University Press, 1989); and A. Schleifer and R. W. Vishny, "Takeovers in the 60s and 80s: Evidence and Implications," *Strategic Management Journal*, 12 (Winter 1991) Special Issue, 51–60.
9. See J. P. Walsh, "Top Management Turnover Following Mergers and Acquisitions," *Strategic Management Journal*, 9 (1988), 173–183.
10. See A. A. Cannella and D. C. Hambrick, "Executive Departure and Acquisition Performance," *Strategic Management Journal*, 14 (1993), 137–152.
11. "Fluor: Compounding Fractures from Leaping Before Looking," *Business Week*, June 3, 1985, pp. 92–93.
12. R. Roll, "The Hubris Hypothesis of Corporate Takeovers," *Journal of Business*, 59 (1986), 197–216.
13. "Coca-Cola: A Sobering Lesson from Its Journey into Wine," *Business Week*, June 3, 1985, pp. 96–98.
14. Haspeslagh and Jemison, *Managing Acquisitions.*
15. "The Seven-Up Co., Division of Philip Morris Incorporated. *Harvard Business School Case* 385–321.

16. For views on this issue, see L. L Fray, D. H. Gaylin, and J. W. Down, "Successful Acquisition Planning," **Journal of Business Strategy,** 5 (1984), 46–55; C. W. L. Hill, "Profile of a Conglomerate Takeover: BTR and Thomas Tilling," *Journal of General Management,* 10 (1984), 34–50; D. R. Willensky, "Making It Happen: How to Execute an Acquisition," *Business Horizons* (March–April 1985), 38–45; and Haspeslagh and Jemison, *Managing Acquisitions.*
17. "Pre-Merger Management," *Economist,* December 7, 1991, p. 81.
18. See Booz, Allen, & Hamilton, *New Products Management for the 1980's*, privately published research report, 1982; A. L. Page, PDMA's *New Product Development Practices Survey: Performance and Best Practices,* PDMA 15th Annual International Conference, Boston, October 16, 1991; and E. Mansfield, "How Economists See R&D," *Harvard Business Review,* (November–December 1981) 98–106.
19. Biggadike, "The Risky Business of Diversification," *Harvard Business Review,* (May–June 1979).
20. R. A. Burgelman, "A Process Model of Internal Corporate Venturing in the Diversified Major Firm," *Administrative Science Quarterly*, 28 (1983), 223–244.
21. I. C. MacMillan and R. George, "Corporate Venturing: Challenges for Senior Managers," *Journal of Business Strategy*, 5 (1985), 34–43.
22. G. Beardsley and E. Mansfield, "A Note on the Accuracy of Industrial Forecasts of the Profitability of New Products and Processes," *Journal of Business*, 23 (1978) 127–130.
23. P. B. Carroll, "IBM, Motorola Plan Radio Link for Computers," *Wall Street Journal*, January 29, 1990, pp. B1, B5.
24. For example, see Shleifer and Vishny, "Takeovers in the 60s and 80s," pp. 51–60.
25. See G. A. Patterson and F. Schwadel, "Back in Time," *Wall Street Journal*, September 30, 1992, p. 1; J. Flynn, "Smaller but Wiser," *Business Week*, October 12, 1992, pp. 28–29; and B. Bremner, "The Big Store's Trauma," *Business Week*, July 10, 1989, pp. 50–55.
26. See J. Argenti, *Corporate Collapse: Causes and Symptoms*, (New York: McGraw-Hill, 1976); R. C. Hoffman, "Strategies for Corporate Turnarounds: What Do We Know About Them?" *Journal of General Management*, 14 (1984), 46–66; D. Schendel, G. R. Patton, and J. Riggs, "Corporate Turnaround Strategies: A Study of Profit Decline and Recovery," *Journal of General Management*, 2 (1976), 1–22; and S. Siafter, *Corporate Recovery: Successful Turnaround Strategies and Their Implementation*, (Hammondsworth, England: Penguin Books, 1984), pp. 25–60.
27. D. B. Bibeault, *Corporate Turnaround*, (New York: McGraw-Hill, 1982).
28. See Siafter, *Corporate Recovery*, pp. 25–60.
29. Hoffman, "Strategies for Corporate Turnarounds," pp. 46–66.
30. Lee Iacocca, *Iacocca: An Autobiography* (New York: Bantam Books, 1984), p. 254.
31. N. Chakravarty, "White Slacks and Carbon Black," *Forbes*, October 26, 1992, pp. 122–124.

IV Implementing Strategy

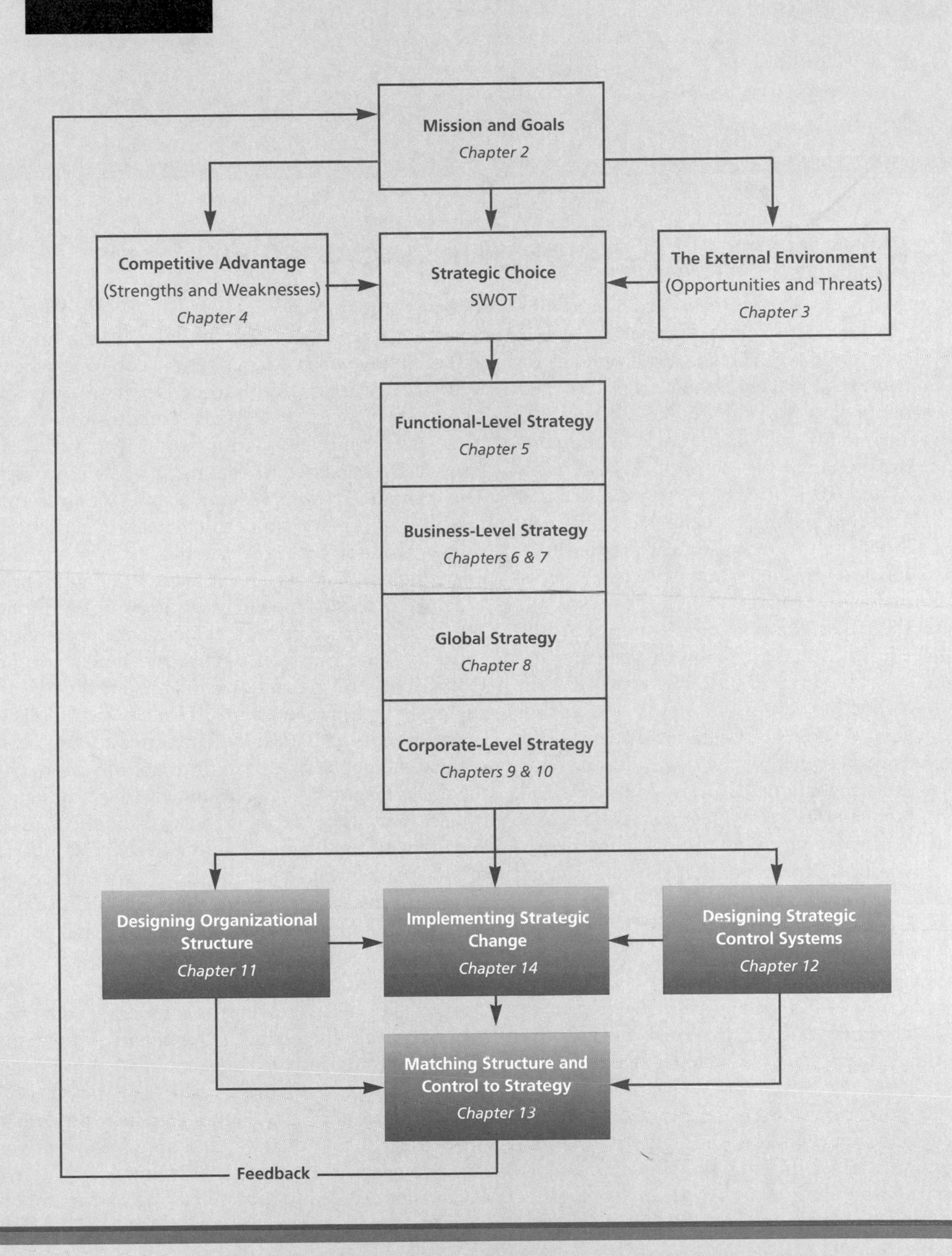

11 Designing Organizational Structure

11.1 OPENING CASE: CHRYSLER'S CROSS-FUNCTIONAL PRODUCT TEAMS

After many years of poor performance and mounting losses, Chrysler Corp., the number three U.S. carmaker, has been experiencing a turnaround in the 1990s. Its new car models like the Dodge Viper, the cab-forward LH cars, and the low-cost Neon have been attracting many customers back to the company and away from Japanese imports. The company's profits and stock price have surged upward as a result. How has Chrysler achieved this turnaround? Chrysler's top management attributes its success to its new product team structure, which uses cross-functional product teams.

As with the other U.S. car companies, Chrysler used to have a functional approach to designing and producing its cars. In a functional approach, the responsibility for the design of a new car would be allocated to many different design departments, each of which was responsible for the design of one component, such as the engine or body. Managers further up the hierarchy were responsible for coordinating the activities of the different design departments in order to ensure that the components were compatible with one another. Top managers were also responsible for coordinating the activities of support functions, such as purchasing, marketing, and accounting, with the design process as their contributions were needed. When the design process was finished the new car was then turned over to the manufacturing department, which decided how best to produce it.

Chrysler's functional approach slowed down the product development process and made cross-functional communication difficult and slow. Each function pursued its activities in isolation from other functions, and it was left to top management to provide the integration necessary to coordinate functional activities. As a result, it took Chrysler an average of five years to bring a new car to market, a figure that was well behind the Japanese, who took two to three years. Chrysler's structure was raising its costs, slowing innovation, and making the company less responsive to the needs of its customers. The company's top managers began to search for a new way of organizing its value-creation activities to turn it around. To begin this process, top management looked at the way Japanese companies were organized, and particularly at the way the Honda Motor Co. structured its value-creation activities. Chrysler sent fourteen of its managers to study Honda's system and to report back on its operation.[1]

Honda had pioneered the "Honda Way" concept to organize its activities. It created small teams, comprising members of different functions, and gave them the responsibility and authority to manage a project from its conception phase, through all design activities, to final manufacture and sale. Honda had found that when it used these cross-functional teams, product development time dropped dramatically because functional communication and coordination was much easier in teams. Moreover, design costs were much lower when different functions worked together to solve problems as they emerged because the need to change a design later—for example, to add a second air bag—could cost millions of dollars. Honda had also found that its policy of decentralizing authority to the team kept the organization flexible, innovative, and able to take advantage of emerging technical opportunities.

Chrysler decided to imitate Honda's structure and took the opportunity to do so when it chose to build

an expensive luxury car called the Viper. To manage the development of this new car, Chrysler created a cross-functional product team consisting of eighty-five people.[2] It established the team in the huge new research and development center that it had built in Auburn Hills, Michigan, and gave it the authority and responsibility to bring the car to market. The outcome was dramatic. Within one year top management could see that the team had achieved what would have taken three years under Chrysler's old system. In fact, the team brought the car to market in just thirty-six months at a development cost of $75 million—results that compared favorably with those obtained by Japanese companies.

With this success in hand, Chrysler's top management moved to restructure the whole company according to the product team concept. Top management divided up functional personnel and assigned them to work in product teams charged with developing new cars, such as the cab-forward designs. The number of levels in Chrysler's hierarchy decreased since authority was decentralized to managers in the product teams, who were responsible for all aspects of new car development. Instead of having to integrate the activities of different functions, top managers could concentrate on allocating resources among projects, deciding future product developments, and challenging the teams to continually improve their efforts. As noted earlier, Chrysler's efforts brought the reward of a dramatic drop in costs and an increase in quality and customer responsiveness. Chrysler's stock price doubled in 1993 as customers rushed to buy its cars.

Discussion Questions

1. Why was Chrysler's functional approach to new car development running into problems?
2. What are the advantages of Chrysler's new product team structure?

11.2 OVERVIEW

As the story of Chrysler's turnaround suggests, in this chapter we examine how a company should organize its activities to create the most value. In Chapter 1, we define strategy implementation as the way in which a company creates the organizational arrangements that allow it to pursue its strategy most effectively. Strategy is implemented through organizational design. **Organizational design** involves selecting the combination of organizational structure and control systems that lets a company pursue its strategy most effectively—that lets it *create and sustain a competitive advantage.*

The primary role of organizational structure and control is twofold: (1) to *coordinate* employees' activities so that they work together to most effectively implement a strategy that increases competitive advantage, and (2) to *motivate* employees and provide them with the incentives to achieve superior efficiency, quality, innovation, or customer responsiveness. Chrysler's strategy, for example, was to increase efficiency and quality by implementing a new product development process. This strategy required managers to adopt a structure allowing increased cross-functional coordination, so that people in different functions like manufacturing, materials management, and research and development could learn new ways of cooperating in order to reduce costs or improve quality. Manufacturing, for instance, had to adapt to a just-in-time inventory system to reduce inventory costs, and R&D had to learn how to work with manufacturing to design new products that could be produced reliably and inexpensively. However, top management had to provide the incentives for employees to learn new work methods. Chrysler's manufacturing employees received bonuses for learning to operate under the increased pressures that a just-in-time inventory system

puts on the production process; and engineers were rewarded with promotions and bonuses for coming up with innovative product designs.

Organizational structure and control shape the way people behave and determine how they will act in the organizational setting. If a new CEO wants to know why it takes a long time for people to make decisions in a company, or why there is a lack of cooperation between sales and manufacturing, or why product innovations are few and far between, he or she needs to look at the design of the organizational structure and control system and to analyze how it coordinates and motivates employee behavior. An analysis of how structure and control works makes it possible to change them to improve both coordination and motivation. Good organizational design allows an organization to improve its ability to create value and obtain a competitive advantage.

In this chapter, we examine the organizational structures available to strategic managers to coordinate and motivate employees. In Chapter 12, we consider the strategic control systems that managers use in conjunction with their organizational structures to monitor and reward corporate, divisional, and functional performance. Chapter 13 then traces the ways in which different strategy choices lead to the use of different kinds of structure and control systems. After reading this section of the book, you will be able to choose the right organizational design for implementing a company's strategy. You will understand the principles behind Chrysler's redesign of its organizational structure and control system.

11.3 THE ROLE OF ORGANIZATIONAL STRUCTURE

After formulating a company's strategy, management must make designing organizational structure its next priority, for strategy is implemented through organizational structure. The value-creation activities of organizational personnel are meaningless unless some type of structure is used to assign people to tasks and connect the activities of different people or functions.[3] As discussed in Chapter 4, each organizational function needs to develop a distinctive competency in a value-creation activity in order to increase efficiency, quality, innovation, or customer responsiveness. Thus each function needs a structure designed to allow it to develop its skills and become more specialized and productive. However, as functions become increasingly specialized, they often begin to pursue their own goals exclusively and forget about the need to communicate and coordinate with other functions. The goals of R&D, for example, center on innovation and product design, whereas the goals of manufacturing often revolve around increasing efficiency. Left to themselves, the functions have little to say to one another, and value-creation opportunities are lost.

The role of organizational structure is to provide the vehicle through which managers can coordinate the activities of the various functions or divisions to fully exploit their skills and capabilities. For example, to pursue a cost-leadership strategy, a company must design a structure that facilitates close coordination between the activities of manufacturing and R&D to ensure that innovative products can be produced both reliably and cost-effectively. To achieve gains from synergy between divisions, managers must design mechanisms for allowing divisions to communicate and share their skills and knowledge. In pursuing a global or multidomestic strategy, managers must create the right kind of organizational structure for managing the flow of resources and capabilities between

domestic and foreign divisions. In Chapter 13, we examine in detail how managers match their strategies to different kinds of structure and control systems. Our goal now is to examine the basic building blocks of organizational structure in order to understand how it shapes the behavior of people and functions.

Building Blocks of Organizational Structure

The basic building blocks of organizational structure are differentiation and integration. **Differentiation** is the way in which a company allocates people and resources to organizational tasks in order to create value.[4] Generally, the greater the number of different functions or divisions in an organization and the more skilled and specialized they are, the higher is the level of differentiation. For example, a company like General Motors, with its more than 300 different divisions and a multitude of different sales, research and development, and design departments, has a much greater level of differentiation than a local manufacturing company or restaurant. In deciding how to differentiate the organization in order to create value, management faces two choices.

First, management must choose how to distribute *decision-making authority* in the organization to best control value-creation activities; these are **vertical differentiation** choices.[5] For example, top management must decide how much authority to delegate to managers at the divisional or functional level. Second, management must choose how to divide up people and tasks into functions and divisions to increase their ability to create value; these are **horizontal differentiation** choices. For example, should there be separate sales and marketing departments or should the two be combined? Or what is the best way to divide up sales personnel to maximize their ability to serve customer needs—by type of customer or region in which they are located?

Integration is the means by which a company seeks to coordinate people and functions to accomplish organizational tasks.[6] As just noted, when separate and distinct value-creation functions are created, they tend to pursue their own goals and objectives. An organization has to create an organizational structure that lets the different functions and divisions coordinate their activities to pursue a strategy effectively. An organization uses integrating mechanisms, as well as the various types of control systems discussed in the next chapter, to promote coordination between functions and divisions. In the Chrysler case, for instance, to speed innovation and product development, the company established cross-functional teams so that employees from different functions could work together to exchange information and ideas. Similarly, establishing organizational norms, values, and a common culture that supports innovation promotes integration.

In short, differentiation refers to the way in which a company divides itself up into parts—functions and divisions—and integration refers to the way in which the parts are then combined. Together, the two processes determine how an organizational structure will operate and how successfully managers will be able to create value through their chosen strategies.

Differentiation, Integration, and Bureaucratic Costs

Implementing a structure to coordinate and motivate task activities is very expensive. The costs of operating an organizational structure and control system are called **bureaucratic costs**. The more complex the structure—that is, the higher the level of differentiation and integration—the higher are the bureaucratic costs of managing it. For example, the more differentiated the company, the more managers there are in specialized roles, and the more resources each

manager requires to perform that role effectively. Managers are expensive, and the more managers a company employs the higher are its bureaucratic costs. Similarly, the more integrated the company, the more managerial time is spent in face-to-face meetings to coordinate task activities. Managerial time also costs money, and thus the higher the level of integration, the more costly it is to operate the structure. A large company, like IBM or GM, spends billions of dollars a year to operate its structures: to pay its managers and employees and to provide them with the resources—offices, computers, equipment, laboratories, and so forth—that they need to create value.

The high bureaucratic costs associated with strategy implementation reduce a company's profits as fast or faster than poor strategy formulation and thus directly impact bottom-line organizational performance. This is why good organizational design is so important. You may recall from Chapter 4 that profit is the difference between revenues and costs. Bureaucratic costs are a large component of the cost side of the equation. Thus a poor organizational design—for instance, one that has too many levels in the hierarchy or a badly thought-out pattern of work relationships—results in high costs and can directly reduce profits. By contrast, good organizational design, which economizes on bureaucratic costs, can give a company a low-cost advantage which raises profits.

Organizational design also affects the revenue side of the equation. If strategic managers choose the right structure to coordinate value-creation activities, they enhance the company's ability to create value, charge a premium price, and thus increase revenues. Chrysler's new structure increased its ability to create value, as well as reduced its costs. Thus good design affects both the revenue and cost

Figure 11.1
How Organizational Design Increases Profitability

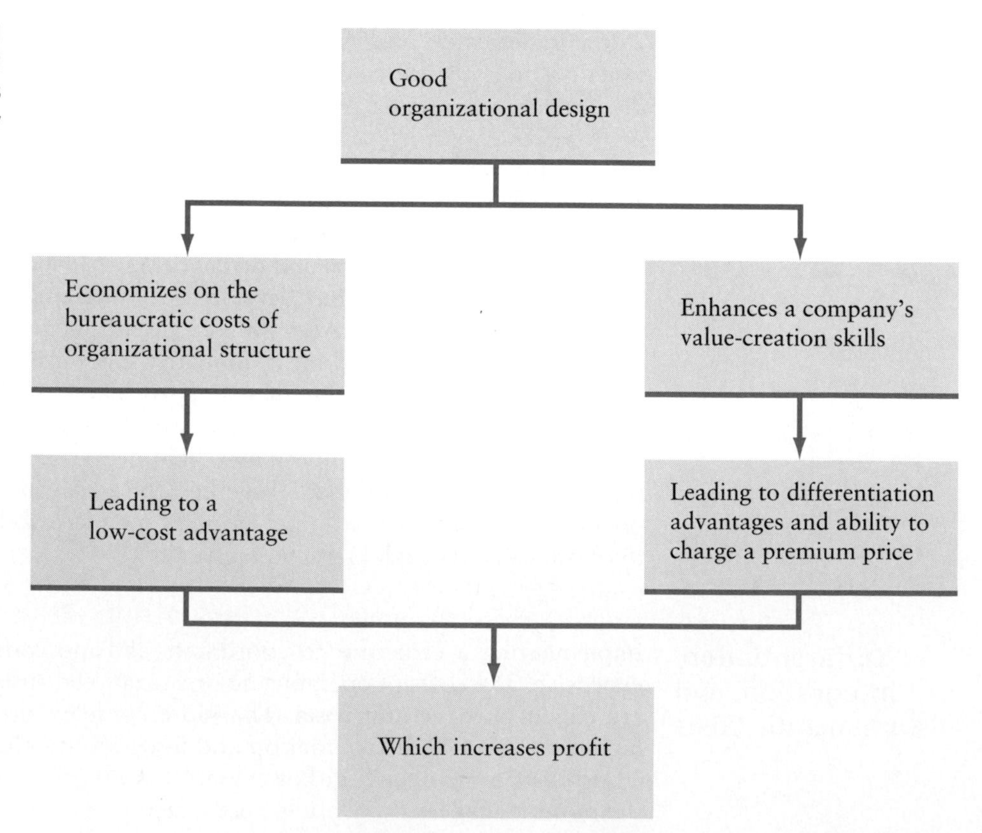

Figure 11.2
Tall and Flat Structures

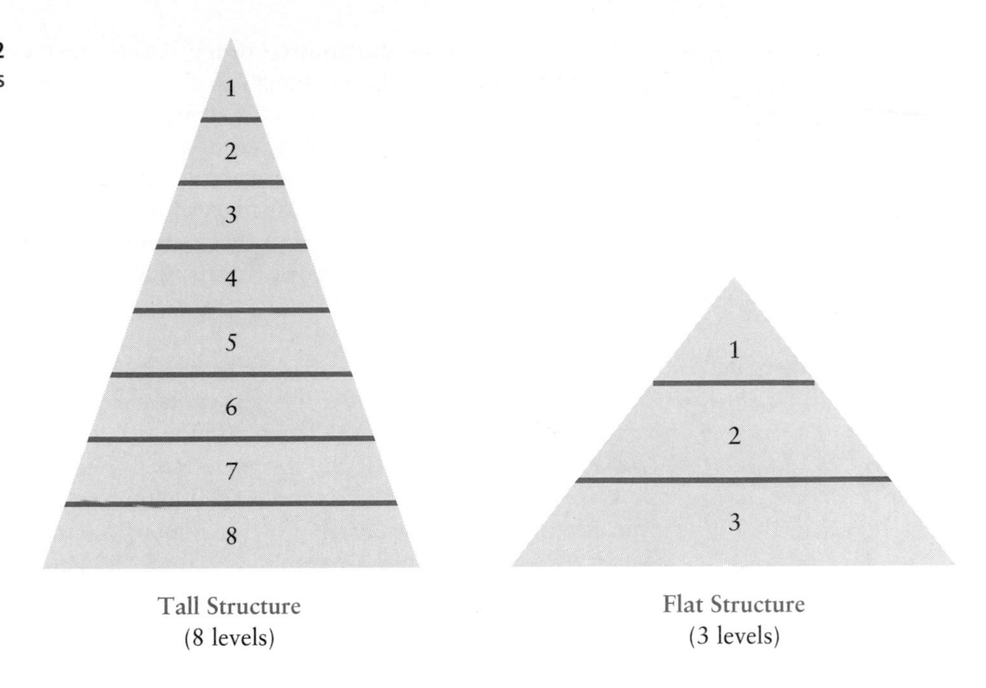

side of the profit equation, as Figure 11.1 illustrates. This is why strategy implementation is such a vital issue. In today's competitive environment, more and more companies are restructuring or reengineering their organizations to improve bottom-line performance by good organizational design. Consequently, it is necessary to understand the principles behind organizational design. We start by looking at differentiation.

11.4 VERTICAL DIFFERENTIATION

The aim of vertical differentiation is to specify the reporting relationships that link people, tasks, and functions at all levels of a company. Fundamentally, this means that management chooses the appropriate number of hierarchical levels and the correct span of control for implementing a company's strategy most effectively. The organizational hierarchy establishes the authority structure from the top to the bottom of the organization. The **span of control** is defined as the number of subordinates a manager directly manages.[7] The basic choice is whether to aim for a **flat structure**, with few hierarchical levels and thus a relatively wide span of control, or a **tall structure**, with many levels and thus a relatively narrow span of control (Figure 11.2). Tall structures have many hierarchical levels relative to size; flat structures have few levels relative to size.[8] For example, research suggests that the average number of hierarchical levels for a company employing 3,000 persons is seven. Thus an organization having nine levels would be called tall, whereas one having four would be called flat. With its 4,000 employees and four hierarchical levels, Liz Claiborne, for instance, has a relatively flat structure. On the other hand, before reorganization, Westinghouse, with its ten hierarchical levels, had a relatively tall structure. Now it has seven levels—the average for a large organization.

Companies choose the number of levels they need on the basis of their strategy and the functional tasks necessary to achieve this strategy.[9] For example, high-tech companies often pursue a strategy of differentiation based on service and quality. Consequently, these companies are usually flat, giving employees wide discretion to meet customers' demands without having to refer constantly to supervisors.[10] (We discuss this subject further in Chapter 12). The crux of the matter is that the allocation of authority and responsibility in the organization must match the needs of corporate-, business-, and functional-level strategy.

Problems with Tall Hierarchies

As a company grows and diversifies, the number of levels in its hierarchy of authority increases to allow it to efficiently monitor and coordinate employee activities. Research shows that the number of hierarchical levels relative to company size is predictable as the size increases.[11] (Figure 11.3.)

Companies with approximately 1,000 employees usually have four levels in the hierarchy: chief executive officer, departmental vice presidents, first-line supervisors, and shop-floor employees. By 3,000 employees, they have increased their level of vertical differentiation by raising the number of levels to eight. Beyond 3,000 employees, however, something interesting happens. Even when companies grow to 10,000 employees or more, the number of hierarchical levels rarely increases beyond nine or ten. As organizations grow, managers apparently try to limit the number of hierarchical levels.

Managers try to keep the organization as flat as possible and follow what is known as the **principle of the minimum chain of command,** which states that an organization should choose a hierarchy with the minimum number of levels of authority necessary to achieve its strategy. Managers try to keep the hierarchy as flat as possible because when companies become too tall problems occur, making strategy more difficult to implement and raising the level of bureaucratic costs.[12] Several factors that raise bureaucratic costs are illustrated in Figure 11.4 and discussed below.

Figure 11.3
Relationship Between Company Size and Number of Hierarchical Levels

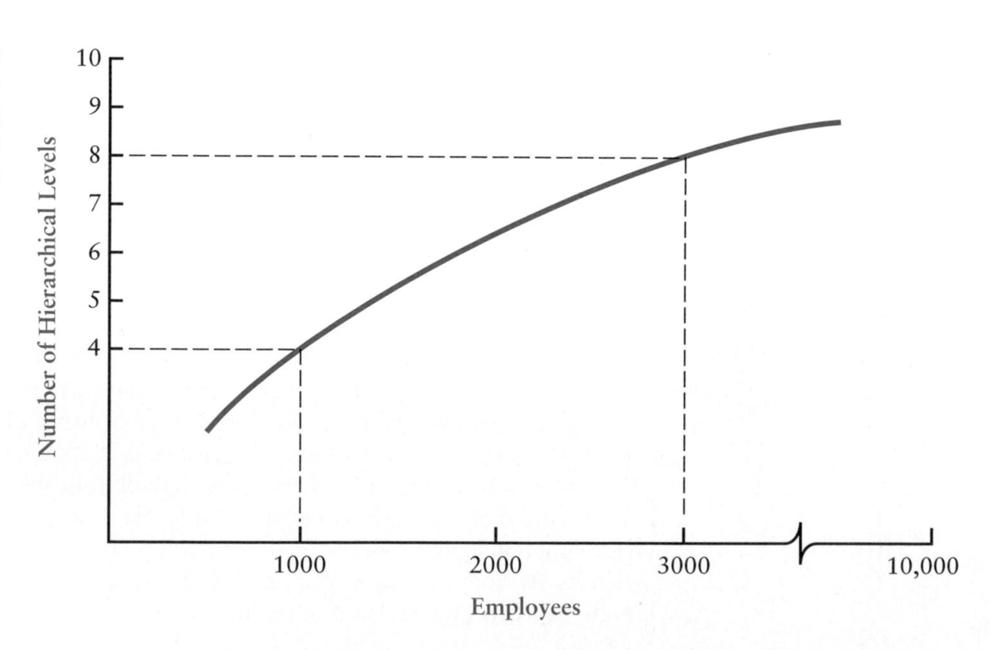

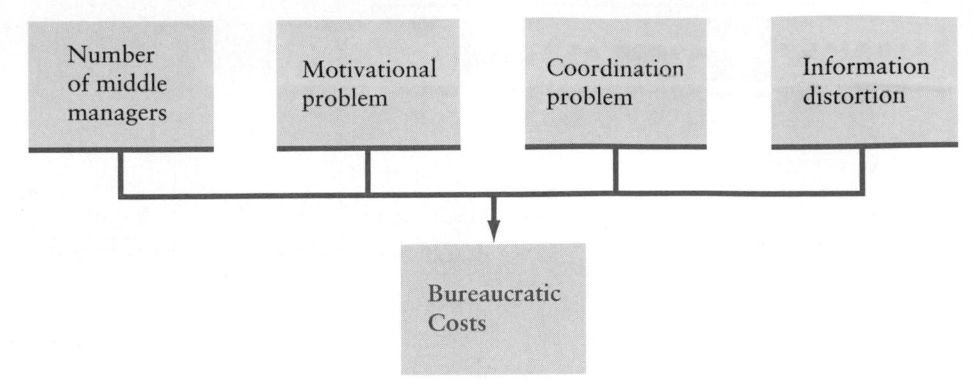

Figure 11.4 Sources of Bureaucratic Costs

Coordination Problems Too many hierarchical levels impede communication and coordination between employees and functions and raise bureaucratic costs. Communication between the top and the bottom of the hierarchy takes much longer as the chain of command lengthens. This leads to inflexibility, and valuable time is lost in bringing a new product to market or in keeping up with technological developments.[13] For Federal Express, communication and coordination are vital in its business; therefore, to avoid communication problems, the company allows a maximum of only five layers of management between the employee and the chief executive officer.[14] On the other hand, Procter & Gamble had a tall hierarchy. The company needed twice as much time as its competitors to introduce new products until it moved to streamline its structure and reduce its number of hierarchical levels to improve coordination and reduce costs.[15] Other companies have also taken measures to flatten their structures in order to speed communication and decision making. Strategy in Action 11.1 describes the changes made at General Electric and Alcoa.

Information Distortion More subtle but just as important are the problems of information distortion that accompany the transmission of information up and down the hierarchy. Going down the hierarchy, managers at different levels (for example, divisional or corporate managers) may misinterpret information, either through accidental garbling of messages or on purpose, to suit their own interests. In either case, information from the top may not reach its destination intact. For instance, a request to share divisional knowledge among divisions to achieve gains from synergy may be overlooked or ignored by divisional managers who perceive it as a threat to their autonomy and power. This attitude among managers was one of the problems that led Lee Iacocca to reorganize Chrysler so that cost-cutting measures could be coordinated across divisions.

Information transmitted upward in the hierarchy may also be distorted. Subordinates may transmit to their superiors only information that improves their own standing in the organization. The greater the number of hierarchical levels, the more scope subordinates have to distort facts, so that the bureaucratic costs of managing the hierarchy increase. Similarly, bureaucratic costs will increase if managers start to compete with each other. Furthermore, when they are free from close corporate supervision, they may hoard information to promote their own interests at the expense of the organization's. This also reduces coordination.

STRATEGY IN ACTION 11.1

How to Flatten Structure

Tall hierarchies cause such severe coordination and communications problems that many companies have been striving to shrink their hierarchies. At General Electric, CEO Jack Welch has flattened the hierarchy from nine levels to four to bring him closer to his divisional managers and shorten the time it takes them to make decisions. Similarly, in Alcoa, planning and decision making at the divisional level was scrutinized by five levels of corporate management before divisional managers were allowed to proceed with their plans. Alcoa's chairman, Paul O'Neill, wiped out these layers so that divisional managers would report directly to him. At both companies, these changes have brought top management closer to customers and provided divisional managers with the autonomy to be innovative and responsive to customer needs. Moreover, flattening the hierarchy has saved these companies billions of dollars in managerial salaries and significantly reduced bureaucratic costs. Flattening their structures has clearly paid off for them.

Motivational Problems A proliferation of levels reduces the scope of managerial authority. As the number of levels in the hierarchy increases, the amount of authority possessed by managers at each hierarchical level falls. For example, consider the situation of two identically sized organizations, one of which has three levels in the hierarchy and the other seven. Managers in the flat structure have much more authority, and greater authority increases their motivation to perform effectively and take responsibility for the organization's performance. Besides, when there are fewer managers, their performance is more visible, and therefore they can expect greater rewards when the business does well. By contrast, in the tall organization, managers' ability to exercise authority is limited, and their decisions are being constantly scrutinized by their superiors. As a result, managers tend to pass the buck and refuse to take the risks that are often necessary when new strategies are pursued. This increases the bureaucratic costs of managing the organization because more managerial time is spent coordinating task activities. Thus the shape of the organization's structure strongly affects the motivation of people within it and the way in which strategy is implemented.[16]

Number of Middle Managers Another drawback of tall structures is that many hierarchical levels imply many middle managers, and employing managers is expensive. As noted earlier, managerial salaries, benefits, offices, and secretaries are a huge expense for an organization and involve high bureaucratic costs. If the average middle manager costs a company a total of $200,000 a year, then employing 100 surplus managers will cost $20 million a year. U.S. oil companies recognized this fact when oil prices fell in 1986, and recently many companies like IBM, Compaq, and Procter & Gamble have moved to downsize their hierarchies, terminating thousands of managers. When these companies made billions of dollars in profits, they had little incentive to control the number of levels in the hierarchy and the number of managers. Once they grew aware of the cost of these managers, however, the companies ruthlessly purged the hierar-

chy, reducing the number of levels, and thus of managers, to lower bureaucratic costs and restore profitability.

To offer another example, when companies grow and are successful, they often hire personnel and create new positions without much regard for the effect of these actions on the organizational hierarchy. Later, when managers review that structure, it is quite common to see the number of levels reduced because of the disadvantages just discussed. Deregulation, too, prompts a reduction in levels and personnel. In a deregulated environment, companies must respond to increased competition. After deregulation, AT&T, as well as a number of airline companies, reduced costs and streamlined their structures so that they could respond more rapidly to opportunities and threats brought about by increased competition. For example, Delta Air Lines announced in 1993 that it would lay off over 600 pilots, or 7 percent of its work force, and retire fifteen jets for an annual saving of over $100 million.

In sum, many problems arise when companies become too tall and the chain of command becomes too long. Strategic managers tend to lose control over the hierarchy, which means that they lose control over their strategies. Disaster often follows as a tall organizational structure decreases, rather than promotes, motivation and coordination between employees and functions and as bureaucratic costs escalate. However, one way to partially overcome such problems, and lessen bureaucratic costs, is to decentralize authority—that is, vest authority in the hierarchy's lower levels, as well as at the top. Because this is one of the most important implementation decisions a company can make, we discuss it next in more detail.

Centralization or Decentralization?

Authority is centralized when managers at the upper levels of the organizational hierarchy retain the authority to make the most important decisions. When authority is decentralized, it is delegated to divisions, functional departments, and managers at lower levels in the organization. By delegating authority in this fashion, management can economize on bureaucratic costs and avoid communication and coordination problems because information does not have to be constantly sent to the top of the organization for decisions to be made.

First, when strategic managers delegate operational decision-making responsibility to middle managers, this reduces information overload, and strategic managers can spend more time on strategic decision making. Consequently, they can make more effective decisions and economize on their time, which reduces bureaucratic costs. Second, when managers in the bottom layers of the organization become responsible for adapting the organization to suit local conditions, their motivation and accountability increase. The result is that decentralization promotes organizational flexibility and reduces bureaucratic costs because lower-level managers are authorized to make on-the-spot decisions. As AT&T has demonstrated, this can be an enormous advantage for business strategy. AT&T has a tall structure, but it is well known for the amount of authority it delegates to lower levels. Operational personnel can respond quickly to customer needs and so ensure superior service, which is a major source of AT&T's competitive advantage. Similarly, to revitalize its product strategy, Westinghouse has massively decentralized its operations to give divisions more autonomy and encourage risk taking and quick response to customer needs.[17] The third advantage of decentralization is that when lower-level employees are given the right to

make important decisions, fewer managers are needed to oversee their activities and tell them what to do. Fewer managers mean lower bureaucratic costs.

If decentralization is so effective, why do not all companies decentralize decision making and avoid the problems of tall hierarchies? The answer is that centralization has its advantages, too. Centralized decision making allows easier coordination of the organizational activities needed to pursue a company's strategy. If managers at all levels can make their own decisions, planning becomes extremely difficult, and the company may lose control of its decision making. Centralization also means that decisions fit broad organization objectives. For example, when its branch operations were getting out of hand, Merrill Lynch & Co. increased centralization by installing more information systems to give corporate managers greater control over branch activities. Similarly, Hewlett-Packard centralized research and development responsibility at the corporate level to provide a more directed corporate strategy. Furthermore, in times of crisis, centralization of authority permits strong leadership because authority is focused on one person or group. This focus allows for speedy decision making and a concerted response by the whole organization. Perhaps Iacocca personifies the meaning of centralization in times of crisis. He provided the centralized control and vision needed for Chrysler's managers to respond creatively to the company's problems and move to the product team structure, which has helped restore its profitability. On the other hand, Honda's experience with recentralizing authority, detailed in Strategy in Action 11.2, warns against going too far with this strategy.

Summary: Vertical Differentiation

Managing the strategy-structure relationship when the number of hierarchical levels becomes too great is difficult and expensive. Depending on a company's situation, the bureaucratic costs of tall hierarchies can be reduced by decentralization. As company size increases, however, decentralization may become less effective. How then, as firms grow and diversify, can they economize on bureaucratic costs without becoming too tall or decentralized? How can a firm like Exxon control 300,000 employees without becoming too bureaucratic and inflexible? There must be alternative ways of creating organizational arrangements to achieve corporate objectives. The first of these ways is to choose the appropriate form of horizontal differentiation: to decide how best to group organizational activities and tasks in order to create value.

11.5 HORIZONTAL DIFFERENTIATION

Whereas vertical differentiation concerns the division of authority, horizontal differentiation focuses on the division and grouping of tasks to meet the objectives of the business.[18] Because, to a large degree, an organization's tasks are a function of its strategy, the dominant view is that companies choose a form of horizontal differentiation or structure to match their organizational strategy. Perhaps the first person to address this issue formally was the Harvard business historian Alfred D. Chandler.[19] After studying the organizational problems experienced in large U.S. corporations such as Du Pont and General Motors as they grew and diversified in the early decades of this century, Chandler reached two conclusions: (1) that in principle organizational structure follows the growth

STRATEGY IN ACTION 11.2

Honda's Change of Heart

In 1992 Honda Motor Co., like many other Japanese firms, found itself facing increased competition in a depressed global marketplace. It realized that its strategy of relying on product innovation to increase its sales growth had led it to neglect the cost and efficiency side of the equation. As a result, its profit margins were eroding. Under its founder, Shoichiro Honda, Honda had pioneered the concept of the "Honda Way," based on a decentralized, participative, consensus approach to management (see Opening Case). At Honda, teams led the decision-making process, and authority was decentralized throughout the company.

However, Honda's new president, Nobuhiko Kawamoto, concluded that this process had gone too far. He decided to recentralize authority in order to provide the control and direction needed to slash costs and increase efficiency. He began to give Honda's top managers more and more authority for corporate-wide strategy, and made them responsible for overseeing both the company's domestic and global strategy. The effect of this move was unexpected. Many of his top executives found it physically impossible to assume the extra responsibility that this new policy of centralization required. One key executive, Shoichiro Irimajiri, who was assigned responsibility for overseeing both Honda's global R&D *and* manufacturing operations, was forced to resign abruptly after his doctors told him that his extra workload had pushed him to the brink of a heart attack. As Kawamoto commented, maybe he had given Irimajiri too much responsibility.[20]

Since the new policy of centralization was not working, Kawamoto had to find a new solution to the centralization-decentralization problem. He decided to delegate more authority back down the hierarchy on a global basis. Managers in Honda's North American, European, and Japanese divisions would take over responsibility for managing strategy for their divisions. The role of Honda's corporate executives would be to provide coordination among divisions and facilitate the sharing of skills and resources to reduce costs. In this way, Honda hopes to strike a new balance between centralization and decentralization, so that it can remain innovative and responsive to customer needs in order to encourage sales growth, but at the same time become more efficient to reduce costs. The company has returned to the "Honda Way" it pioneered.

strategy of a company, or, in other words, the range and variety of tasks it chooses to pursue; and (2) that American enterprises go through stages of strategy and structure changes as they grow and diversify. In other words, a company's structure changes as its strategy changes in a predictable way.[21] The kinds of structure that companies adopt are discussed in this section.

Simple Structure

The simple structure is normally used by the small, entrepreneurial company involved in producing one or a few related products for a specific market segment. Often in this situation, one person, the entrepreneur, takes on most of the managerial tasks. No formal organization arrangements exist, and horizontal differentiation is low because employees perform multiple duties. A classic example of this structure is Apple Computer in its earliest stage, as a venture between two persons. Steven Jobs and Steven Wozniak worked together in a garage to perform all the necessary tasks to market their personal computer: they bought the component parts, assembled the first machines, and shipped them out to customers. The success of their product, however, made this simple

structure outdated almost as soon as it was adopted. To grow and perform all the tasks required by a rapidly expanding company, Apple needed a more complex form of horizontal differentiation. It needed to invest resources in creating an infrastructure to develop and enhance its distinctive competencies. Although developing a more complex structure raises bureaucratic costs, this is acceptable as long as the structure increases the amount of value a company can create.

Functional Structure

As companies grow, two things happen. First, the range of tasks that must be performed expands. For example, it suddenly becomes apparent that the services of a professional accountant or production manager or marketing expert are needed to take control of specialized tasks. Second, no one person can successfully perform more than one organizational task without becoming overloaded. The entrepreneur, for instance, can no longer simultaneously produce and sell the product. The issue arises, then, as to what grouping of activities, or what form of horizontal differentiation, can most efficiently handle the needs of the growing company at least cost. The answer for most companies is a **functional structure**. Functional structures group people on the basis of their common expertise and experience or because they use the same resources.[22] For example, engineers are grouped in a function because they perform the same tasks and use the same skills or equipment. Figure 11.5 shows a typical functional structure. Here, each of the rectangles represents a different functional specialization—research and development, sales and marketing, manufacturing, and so on—and each function concentrates on its own specialized task.

Advantages of a Functional Structure

Functional structures have several advantages. First, if people who perform similar tasks are grouped together, they can learn from one another and become better—more specialized and productive—at what they do. Second, they can monitor each other and make sure that all are performing their tasks effectively and not shirking their responsibilities. As a result, the work process becomes more efficient, reducing manufacturing costs and increasing operational flexibility.

A second important advantage of functional structures is that they give managers greater control of organizational activities. As already noted, many difficulties arise when the number of levels in the hierarchy increases. If you group people into different functions, however, each with its own managers, then several different hierarchies are created, and the company can avoid becoming too tall. For example, there will be one hierarchy in manufacturing and another in

Figure 11.5
Functional Structure

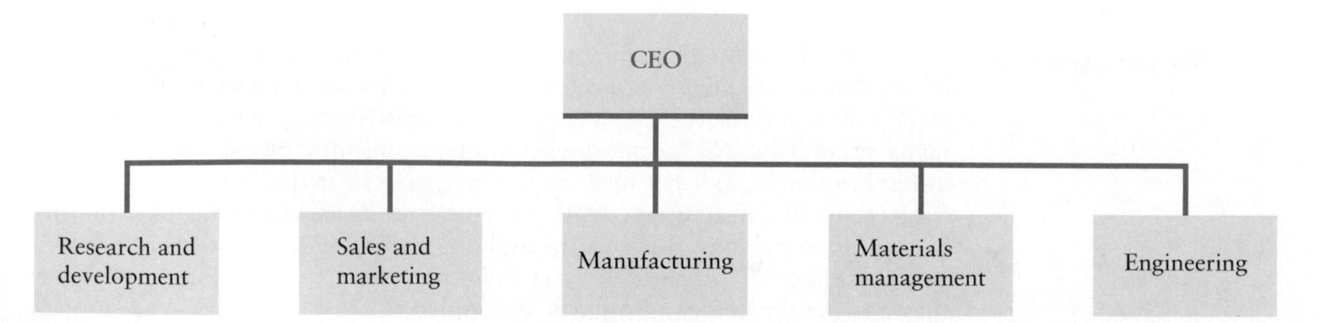

accounting and finance. Managing the business is much easier when different groups specialize in different organizational tasks and are managed separately.

Problems with a Functional Structure

In adopting a functional structure, a company increases its level of horizontal differentiation to handle more complex task requirements. The structure allows it to keep control of its activities as it grows. This structure serves the company well until it starts to grow and diversify. If the company becomes geographically diverse and begins operating in many locations or if it starts producing a wide range of products, control and coordination problems arise. Control becomes looser, lowering a company's ability to coordinate its activities and increasing bureaucratic costs.[23]

Communications Problems As separate functional hierarchies evolve, functions grow more remote from one another. As a result, it becomes increasingly difficult to communicate across functions and to coordinate their activities. This communication problem stems from **functional orientations**.[24] With greater differentiation, the various functions develop different orientations to the problems and issues facing the organization. Different functions have different time or goal orientations. Some functions, such as manufacturing, see things in a short time frame and concentrate on achieving short-run goals, such as reducing manufacturing costs. Others, like research and development, see things from a long-term point of view, and their goals (that is, innovation and product development) may have a time horizon of several years. These factors may cause each function to develop a different view of the strategic issues facing the company. For example, manufacturing may see a problem as the need to reduce costs, sales may see it as the need to increase customer responsiveness, and research and development may see it as the need to create new products. In such cases, the functions have trouble communicating and coordinating with one another, and bureaucratic costs increase.

Measurement Problems As the number of its products proliferates, a company may find it difficult to gauge the contribution of a product or a group of products to its overall profitability. Consequently, the company may be turning out some unprofitable products without realizing it and may also be making poor decisions on resource allocation. This means that the company's measurement systems are not complex enough to serve its needs. For example, Dell Computer's explosive growth caused it to lose control of its inventory management systems; hence it could not accurately project supply and demands for the components that go into its personal computers. Problems with its organizational structure have plagued the company, reducing efficiency and quality. As one manager commented, designing its structure to keep pace with its growth has been like "building a high performance car while going around the race track."[25]

Location Problems Location factors may also hamper coordination and control. If a company is producing or selling in many different regional areas, then the centralized system of control provided by the functional structure no longer suits it because managers in the various regions must be flexible enough to respond to the needs of these regions. Thus the functional structure is not complex enough to handle regional diversity.

Strategic Problems Sometimes the combined effect of all these factors is that long-term strategic considerations are ignored because management is preoccupied with solving communication and coordination problems. As a result, a company may lose direction and fail to take advantage of new opportunities while bureaucratic costs escalate.

Experiencing these problems is a sign that the company does not have an appropriate level of differentiation to achieve its objectives. It must change its mix of vertical and horizontal differentiation in order to allow it to perform the organizational tasks that will enhance its competitive advantage. Essentially, these problems indicate that the company has outgrown its structure. It needs to invest more resources in developing a more complex structure, which can meet the needs of its competitive strategy. Once again, this is expensive, but as long as the value a company can create is greater than the bureaucratic costs of operating the structure, it makes sense to adopt a more complex structure. Many companies choose a multidivisional structure.

Multidivisional Structure

The multidivisional structure possesses two main innovations over a functional structure, which let a company grow and diversify while overcoming control loss problems. First, each distinct product line or business unit is placed in its own self-contained unit or division, with all support functions. For example, Pepsico has three major divisions, soft drinks, snack foods, and restaurants, and each division has its own functions, such as marketing and research and development. The result is a higher level of horizontal differentiation. Second, the office of corporate headquarters staff is created to monitor divisional activities and to exercise financial control over each of the divisions.[26] This staff contains corporate managers who oversee all divisional and functional activities, and it constitutes

Figure 11.6
Multidivisional Structure

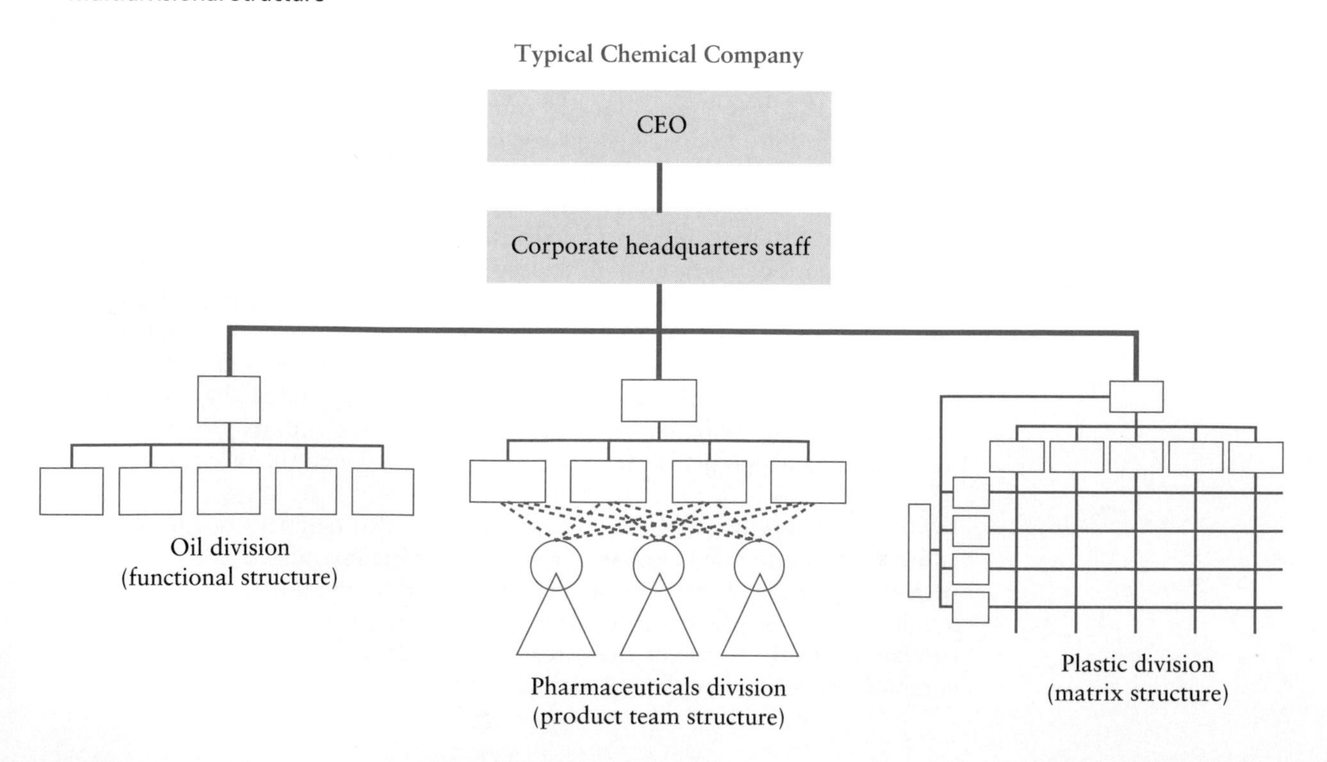

an additional level in the organizational hierarchy. Hence, there is a higher level of vertical differentiation in a multidivisional structure than in a functional structure. Figure 11.6 presents a typical divisional structure found in a large chemical company such as Du Pont. Although this company might easily have seventy operating divisions, only three—the oil, drugs, and plastics divisions—are represented here.

As a self-contained business unit, each division possesses a full array of support services. For example, each has self-contained accounting, sales, and personnel departments. Each division functions as a profit center, making it much easier for corporate headquarters staff to monitor and evaluate each division's activities.[27]

The bureaucratic costs of operating a multidivisional structure are very high compared with a functional structure. The size of the corporate staff is a major expense, and companies like GM and IBM have thousands of managers on their corporate staffs even after downsizing. Similarly, the use of product divisions, each with its own specialist support functions, is a major expense. However, once again, if higher bureaucratic costs are offset by a higher level of value creation, it makes sense to move to a more complex structure.

Each division is also able to adopt the structure that best suits its needs. Figure 11.6 shows that the oil division has a functional structure because its activities are standardized; the drug division has a product-team structure; and the plastics division has a matrix structure (both these structures are discussed in detail later in this chapter). Similarly, General Motors operates the whole corporation through a multidivisional structure, but each auto division organizes itself into different product groups, based on the type of auto made.

In the multidivisional structure, day-to-day operations of a division are the responsibility of divisional management; that is, divisional management has **operating responsibility**. However, corporate headquarters staff, which includes members of the board of directors, as well as top executives, is responsible for overseeing long-term plans and providing the guidance for interdivisional projects. This staff has **strategic responsibility**. Such a combination of self-contained divisions with a centralized corporate management represents a higher level of both vertical and horizontal differentiation, as noted earlier. These two innovations provide the extra control necessary to coordinate growth and diversification. Because this structure—despite its high bureaucratic costs—has now been adopted by over 90 percent of all large U.S. corporations, we need to consider its advantages and disadvantages in more detail.

Advantages of a Multidivisional Structure

When managed effectively at both the corporate and the divisional levels, a multidivisional structure offers several advantages. Together, they can raise corporate profitability to a new peak because they allow the organization to operate more complex kinds of corporate-level strategy.

Enhanced Corporate Financial Control The profitability of different business divisions is clearly visible in the multidivisional structure.[28] Because each division is its own profit center, financial controls can be applied to each business on the basis of profit criteria. Typically, these controls involve establishing targets, monitoring performance on a regular basis, and selectively intervening when problems arise. Corporate headquarters is also in a better position to allocate corporate financial resources among competing divisions. The visibility of divisional performance means that corporate headquarters can identify the

divisions in which investment of funds would yield the greatest long-term returns. In a sense, the corporate office is in a position to act as the investor or banker in an internal capital market, channeling funds to high-yield uses.

Enhanced Strategic Control The multidivisional structure frees corporate staff from operating responsibilities. The staff thus gains time for contemplating wider strategic issues and for developing responses to environmental changes. The multidivisional structure also enables headquarters to obtain the proper information to perform strategic planning functions. For example, separating individual businesses is a necessary prerequisite for the application of portfolio planning techniques.

Growth The multidivisional structure lets the company overcome an organizational limit to its growth. By reducing information overload at the center, headquarters personnel can handle a greater number of businesses. They can consider opportunities for further growth and diversification. Communication problems are reduced by applying accounting and financial control techniques as well as by implementing policies of "management by exception," meaning that corporate headquarters intervenes only when problems arise.

Stronger Pursuit of Internal Efficiency Within a functional structure, the interdependence of functional departments means that performance of functions within the company cannot be measured by objective criteria. For example, the profitability of the finance function, marketing function, or manufacturing function cannot be assessed in isolation, as they are only part of the whole. This often means that within the functional structure considerable degrees of organizational slack can go undetected. Resources might be absorbed in unproductive uses. For example, the head of the finance function might employ a larger staff than required for efficiency to reduce work pressures inside the department. Generally, a larger staff also brings a manager higher status. But because a divisional structure prescribes divisional operating autonomy, the divisions' efficiency can be directly observed and measured in terms of profit. Autonomy makes divisional managers accountable for their own performance; they can have no alibis. The general office is thus in a better position to identify inefficiencies.

A multidivisional structure then has a number of powerful advantages. That is why, no doubt, it seems to be the preferred choice of most large diversified enterprises today. Indeed, research suggests that large business companies that adopt this structure outperform those that retain the functional structure.[29]

Disadvantages of a Multidivisional Structure

A multidivisional structure has its disadvantages as well. Good management can eliminate some of them, but others are inherent in the way the structure operates and require constant attention. They are discussed next.

Establishing the Divisional-Corporate Authority Relationship The authority relationship between corporate headquarters and the divisions must be correctly established. The multidivisional structure introduces a new level in the hierarchy—the corporate level. The problem lies in deciding how much authority and control to assign to the operating divisions and how much authority to retain at corporate headquarters. This problem was first noted by Alfred Sloan, the

founder of General Motors. He introduced the multidivisional structure at General Motors, which became the first company to adopt it.[30] He created General Motors' familiar five-automobile divisions: Oldsmobile, Buick, Pontiac, Chevrolet, and Cadillac. What he found, however, was that when headquarters retained too much power and authority, the operating divisions lacked sufficient autonomy to develop the business strategy that might best meet the needs of the division. On the other hand, when too much power was delegated to the divisions, they pursued divisional objectives, with little heed to the needs of the whole corporation. For example, all the potential gains from synergy discussed earlier would not be achieved. Thus the central issue in managing the multidivisional structure is how much authority should be centralized at corporate headquarters and how much should be decentralized to the divisions. This issue must be decided by each company in reference to the nature of its business and its corporate-level strategies. There are no easy answers, and over time, as the environment changes or the company alters its strategies, the balance between corporate and divisional control will also change. Strategy in Action 11.3 illustrates this problem. It highlights the changes that Digital Equipment Corp. has made in its multidivisional structure so that it might respond to the environment.

Distortion of Information If corporate headquarters puts too much emphasis on divisional return on investment—for instance, by setting very high and stringent return on investment targets—divisional managers may choose to distort the information they supply top management and paint a rosy picture of the present situation at the expense of future profits. That is, divisions may maximize short-run profits—perhaps by cutting product development or new investments or marketing expenditures. This may cost the company dearly in the future. The problem stems from too tight financial control. General Motors has suffered from this problem in recent years, as declining performance has prompted managers to try to make their divisions look good to corporate headquarters. On the other hand, if the divisional level exerts too much control, powerful divisional managers may resist attempts to use their profits to strengthen other divisions and therefore disguise their performance. Thus managing the corporate-divisional interface involves coping with subtle power issues.

Competition for Resources The third problem of managing the divisional structure is that the divisions themselves may compete for resources, and this rivalry will prevent synergy gains from emerging. For example, the amount of money that corporate personnel has to distribute to the divisions is fixed. Generally, the divisions that can demonstrate the highest return on investment will get the lion's share of the money. But that large share strengthens them in the next time period, and so the strong divisions grow stronger. Consequently, divisions may actively compete for resources, and by doing so, reduce interdivisional coordination.

Transfer Pricing Divisional competition may also lead to battles over **transfer pricing**. As we discuss in Chapter 9, one of the problems with vertical integration or related diversification is setting transfer prices between divisions. Rivalry among divisions increases the problem of setting fair prices. Each supplying division tries to set the highest price for its outputs to maximize its own return on investment. Such competition can completely undermine the corporate

STRATEGY IN ACTION 11.3

About-Face at DEC

Digital Equipment Corp. (DEC), the computer maker, has had trouble finding a structure that would allow it to operate its businesses effectively in today's competitive environment. In 1992 the company suffered a $2.9 billion loss, largely attributable to problems caused by its organizational structure. Under its former chairman and founder, Kenneth Olsen, who was ousted in 1992, the company had developed a tall, centralized structure, in which all important business decisions were made at the top of the organization, by Olsen and his top management team. Managers of the divisions had little freedom to make pricing or product decisions in their individual markets, and R&D activities were also centralized at the top of the organization. As a result the organization could not respond to the changing needs of customers who were rapidly switching to the products of other manufacturers such as Adobe, Dell, and Sun Microsystems. In addition, under Olsen, the hierarchy had become very tall as the corporate staff and staff functions grew in size to manage the divisions' businesses. Consequently, it was very difficult to disentangle the individual profit contributions of the different divisions. DEC was functioning as one big, monolithic organization, and the advantages of the multidivisional structure were being lost.

DEC's new CEO, Robert Palmer, who took over in 1992, recognized these problems and moved swiftly to change the way the structure operated. In 1993 he announced that DEC would restructure itself into nine independent divisions, each focusing on a particular product, such as minicomputers, or industry sector, such as consumer or business. Moreover, each division was set up as a separate profit center, and divisional managers were given full responsibility for turning around their operations. It was their responsibility to increase profit by further reducing bureaucratic costs or by finding new ways to enhance their value-creation skills. Palmer also massively reduced the size of the corporate staff, laying off thousands of managers or assigning them to the divisions to move the business closer to the customer.

To change DEC, Palmer focused on decentralizing authority to the divisions and flattening the organization to improve its ability to be responsive to the customer. He hopes that the new operating structure will increase the speed of product development and allow each business unit to better compete with rivals. The role of the corporate center will be to facilitate resource transfers among business units and especially to transfer the results of company-wide R&D so that new-product development can be speeded up. If the new structure does not work and DEC cannot quickly produce new products to attract its customers back, the company is likely to face bankruptcy.

culture and make the corporation a battleground. Many companies have a history of competition among divisions. Some, of course, may encourage competition, if managers believe that it leads to maximum performance.

Short-Term Research and Development Focus If extremely high return on investment targets are set by corporate headquarters, there is a danger that the divisions will cut back on research and development expenditures to improve the financial performance of the division. Although this will inflate divisional performance in the short term, it will reduce a division's ability to innovate products and lead to a fall in the stream of long-term profits. Hence, corporate headquarters personnel must carefully control their interactions with the divisions to ensure that both the short- and long-term goals of the business are being achieved.

Bureaucratic Costs As noted earlier, because each division possesses its own specialized functions, such as finance or research and development, multidivisional structures are expensive to run and manage. Research and development is especially costly, and so some companies centralize such functions at the corporate level to serve all divisions. The duplication of specialist services, however, is not a problem if the gains from having separate specialist functions outweigh the costs. Again, management must decide if duplication is financially justified. Activities are often centralized in times of downturn or recession—particularly advisory services and planning functions. Divisions, however, are retained as profit centers.

The advantages of divisional structures must be balanced against their disadvantages, but, as already noted, the disadvantages can be managed by an observant, professional management team that is aware of the issues involved. The multidivisional structure is the dominant one today, which clearly suggests its usefulness as the means of managing the multibusiness corporation.

Matrix Structure

A matrix structure differs from the structures discussed so far in that the matrix is based on two forms of horizontal differentiation rather than on one, as in the functional structure.[31] In the product matrix design, activities on the vertical axis are grouped by *function,* so that there is a familiar differentiation of tasks into functions such as production, research and development, and engineering. In addition, superimposed on this vertical pattern is a horizontal pattern based on differentiation by *product or project.* The result is a complex network of reporting relationships among projects and functions, as depicted in Figure 11.7.

This structure also employs an unusual kind of vertical differentiation. Although matrix structures are flat, with few hierarchical levels, employees inside the matrix have two bosses: a **functional boss**, who is the head of a function, and a **project boss**, who is responsible for managing the individual projects. Employees work on a project team with specialists from other functions and report to the project boss on project matters and the functional boss on matters relating to functional issues. All employees who work in a project team are called **subproject managers** and are responsible for managing coordination and communication among the functions and projects.

Matrix structures were first developed by companies in high-technology industries such as aerospace and electronics—by companies like TRW Inc. and Hughes Aircraft. These companies were developing radically new products in uncertain, competitive environments, and speed of product development was the crucial consideration. They needed a structure that could respond to this strategy, but the functional structure was too inflexible to allow the complex role and task interactions necessary to meet new-product development requirements. Moreover, employees in these companies tend to be highly qualified and professional and perform best in autonomous, flexible working conditions. The matrix structure provides such conditions. For example, this structure requires a minimum of direct hierarchical control by supervisors. Team members control their own behavior, and participation in project teams allows them to monitor other team members and learn from each other. Furthermore, as the project goes through its different phases, different specialists from various functions are required. Thus, for example, at the first stage the services of research and development specialists may be called for, and then at the next stage engineers and

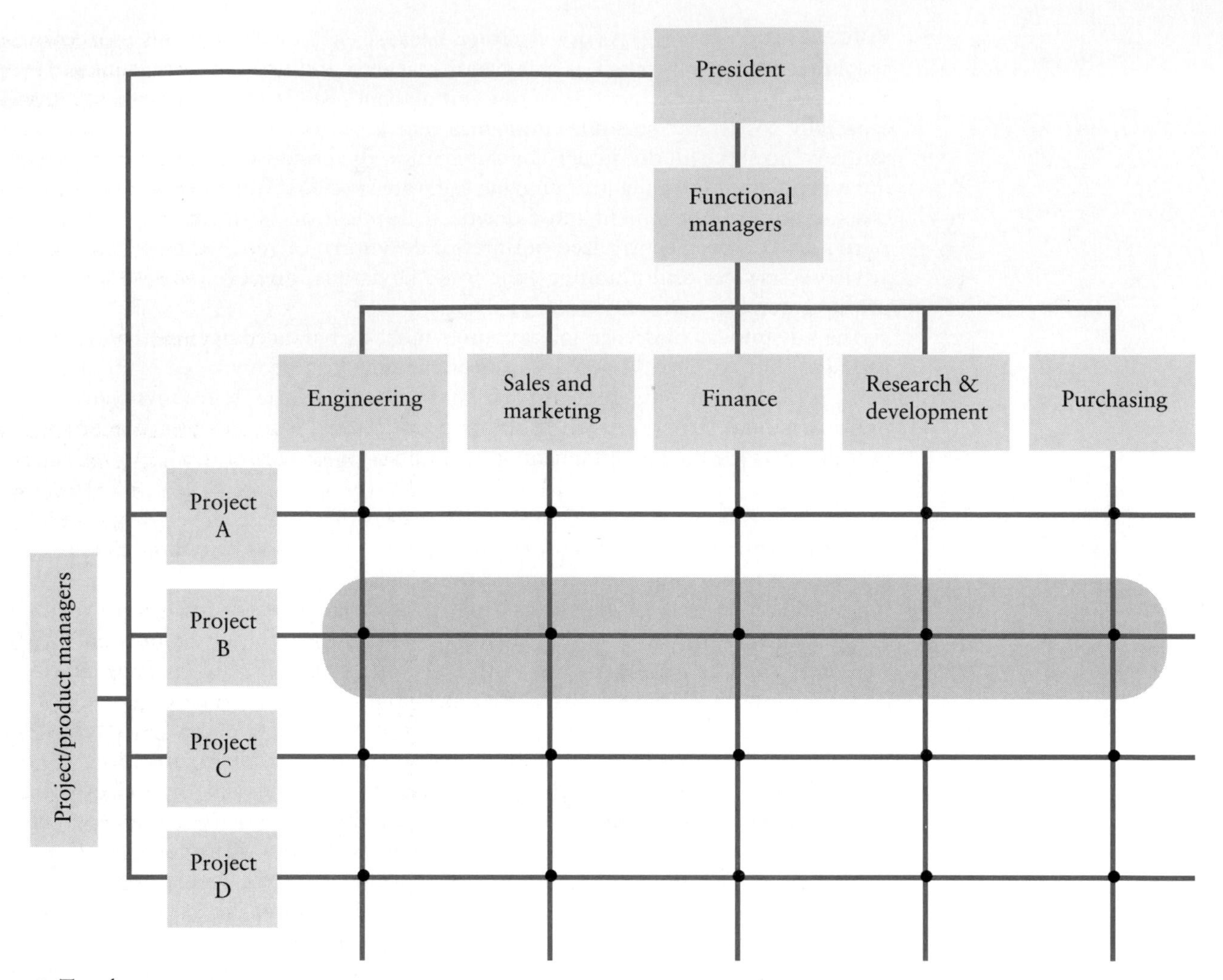

Figure 11.7
Matrix Structure

marketing specialists may be needed to make cost and marketing projections. As the demand for the type of specialist changes, team members can be moved to other projects that require their services. Thus the matrix structure can make maximum use of employee skills as existing projects are completed and new ones come into existence. Finally, the freedom given by the matrix not only provides the autonomy to motivate employees, but also leaves top management free to concentrate on strategic issues, since they do not have to become involved in operating matters. On all these counts, the matrix is an excellent tool for creating the flexibility necessary for quick reactions to competitive conditions.

There are disadvantages to the matrix structure, however.[32] First, the bureaucratic costs of operating this structure are very high compared with those of operating a functional structure. Employees tend to be highly skilled, and therefore both salaries and overheads are high. Second, the constant movement of employees around the matrix means that time and money are spent in establishing new team relationships and getting the project off the ground. Third, the subproject manager's role, balancing as it does the interests of the project with the function, is difficult to manage, and care must be taken to avoid conflict between

functions and projects over resources. Over time, it is possible that project managers will take the leading role in planning and goal setting, in which case the structure would work more like a product or divisional structure. If function and project relationships are left uncontrolled, they can lead to power struggles among managers, resulting in stagnation and decline rather than increased flexibility. Finally, the larger the organization, the more difficult it is to operate a matrix structure, because task and role relationships become complex. In such situations, the only option may be to change to a multidivisional structure.

Given these advantages and disadvantages, the matrix is generally used only when a company's strategy warrants it. There is no point in using a more complex structure than necessary because it will only cost more to manage. In dynamic product/market environments, the benefits of the matrix in terms of flexibility and innovation are likely to exceed the high bureaucratic costs of using it, and so it becomes an appropriate choice of structure. However, companies in the mature stage of the industry life cycle or those pursuing a low-cost strategy would rarely choose this structure because it is expensive to operate. We discuss it further in Chapter 13.

Product Team Structure

A major structural innovation in recent years has been the **product team structure**. It has similar advantages to a matrix structure but is much easier and far less costly to operate because of the way people are organized into permanent cross-functional teams, as Figure 11.8 illustrates.

In the product team structure, as in the matrix structure, task activities are divided along product or project lines to reduce bureaucratic costs and to increase management's ability to monitor and control the manufacturing

Figure 11.8
Product Team Structure

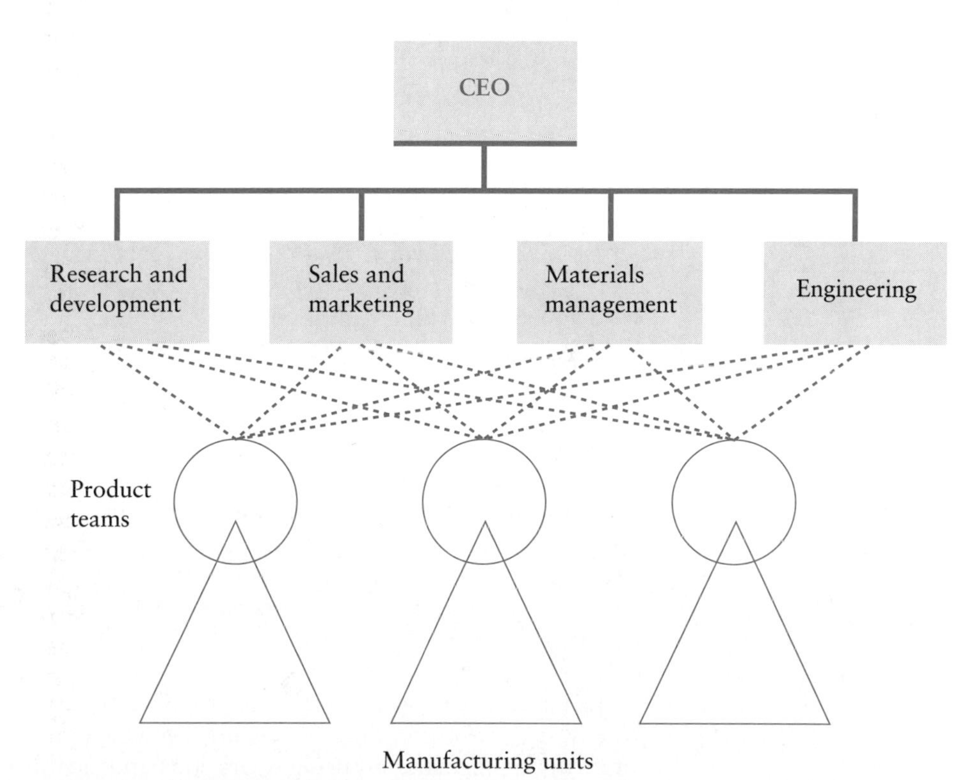

STRATEGY IN ACTION 11.4

Restructuring at Lexmark

Lexmark Corp., a printer and typewriter manufacturer, was a division of IBM until it was sold off by IBM in 1992 to a New York investment firm. As an IBM division, it had performed badly, and IBM sold it after years of losses brought on by high operating costs and an inability to produce new products that could compete with Hewlett-Packard and Japanese printer makers like Epson. Its new top-management team, led by Marvin Mann, an ex-IBM executive, had the task of reengineering its structure to turn the company around.

Mann first destroyed the organizational structure that the company had developed under its former IBM management. Like the rest of IBM, the division had a tall, centralized structure, where all important decisions were made high in the organization by top managers. This slowed down decision making and made it very difficult to communicate across functions because so many managers at different levels and in different functions had to sign off on new plans.

Moving quickly to change this system, Mann streamlined the company's hierarchy, which meant terminating 60 percent of its managers and eliminating all staff managers—that is, those with no direct-line responsibility. This action cut out three levels in the hierarchy. He then decentralized authority to the product managers of the company's four product groups and told them to develop their own plans and goals. In addition, to continue the process of decentralization, product managers were instructed to develop cross-functional teams comprising employees from all functions—with the goal of finding new and improved ways of organizing task activities to reduce costs. The teams were to use competitive benchmarking and evaluate their competitors' products in order to establish new performance standards to guide their activities. Finally, as an incentive for employees to work hard at increasing efficiency, innovation, and quality, Mann established a company stock ownership scheme to reward employees for their efforts.

The reengineering of the organizational structure to a product team structure has been very successful for Lexmark. The company made a profit of over $100 million on sales of $2 billion in 1993, and its rate of product development has increased dramatically. Lexmark's new structure is viewed by many as a benchmark that IBM should adopt in its continuing restructuring efforts.

process. However, instead of being assigned only *temporarily* to different projects, as in the matrix structure, functional specialists are placed in *permanent* cross-functional teams. As a result, the costs associated with coordinating their activities are much lower than in a matrix structure, where tasks and reporting relationships change rapidly. Cross-functional teams are formed right at the beginning of the product development process so that any difficulties that arise can be ironed out early on, before they lead to major redesign problems. When all functions have direct input from the beginning, design costs and subsequent manufacturing costs can be kept low. Moreover, the use of cross-functional teams speeds innovation and customer responsiveness because when authority is decentralized to the team, decisions can be made more quickly. You saw in the Opening Case how Chrysler moved to a product team structure. Strategy in Action 11.4 offers another example: Lexmark Corp.'s shift to a product team structure in order to reduce costs and speed product development.

Geographic Structure

When a company operates as a geographic structure, geographic regions become the basis for the grouping of organizational activities. For example, a company may divide its manufacturing operations and establish manufacturing plants in

different regions of the country. This allows it to be responsive to the needs of regional customers and reduces transportation costs. Similarly, service organizations like store chains or banks may organize their sales and marketing activities on a regional, rather than national, level to get closer to their customers. A geographic structure provides more control than a functional structure because there are several regional hierarchies carrying out the work previously performed by a single centralized hierarchy. A company like Federal Express clearly needs to operate a geographic structure to fulfill its corporate goal: next-day delivery. Large merchandising organizations, such as Neiman Marcus, Dillard, and Wal-Mart, also moved to a geographic structure soon after they started building stores across the country. With this type of structure, different regional clothing needs—sun wear in the West, down coats in the East—can be handled as required. At the same time, because the purchasing function remains centralized, one central organization can buy for all regions. Thus a company both achieves economies of scale in buying and distribution and reduces coordination and communication problems. For example, Neiman Marcus developed a geographic structure similar to the one shown in Figure 11.9 to manage its nationwide store chain.

In each region, it established a team of regional buyers to respond to the needs of customers in each geographic area, for example, the Western, Central, Eastern, and Southern regions. The regional buyers then fed their information to the central buyers at corporate headquarters, who coordinated their demands to obtain purchasing economies and to ensure that Neiman Marcus's high quality standards, on which its differentiation advantage depends, were maintained nationally.

However, the usefulness of the matrix, product team, or geographic structure depends on the size of the company and its range of products and regions. If a company starts to diversify into unrelated products or to integrate vertically into

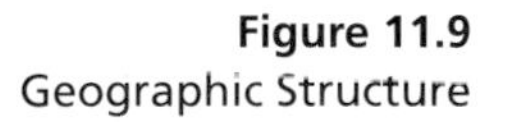
Figure 11.9
Geographic Structure

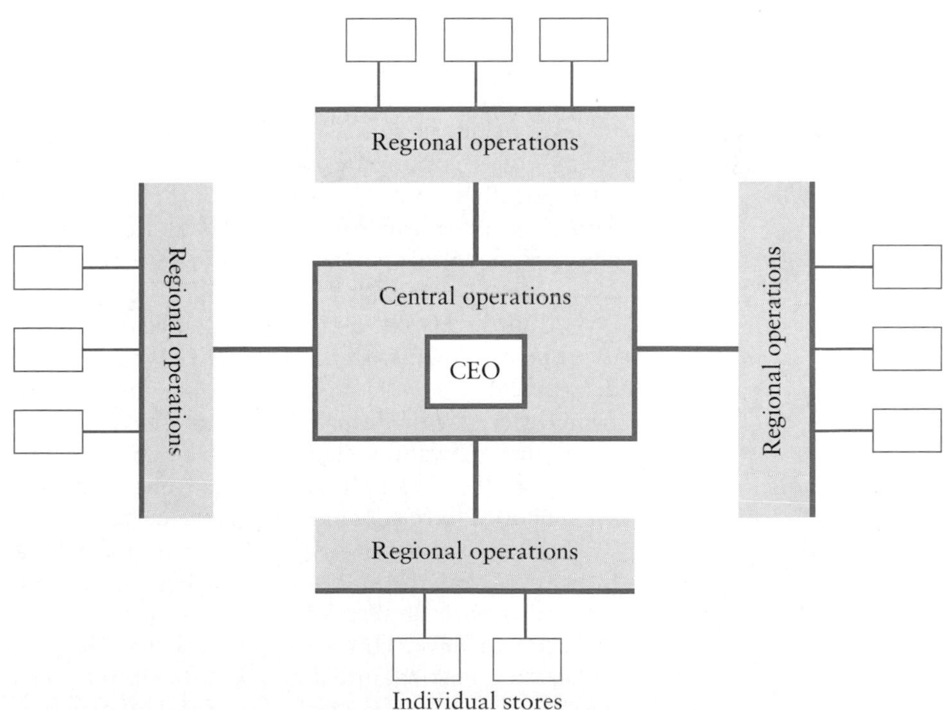

new industries, these structures cannot handle the increased diversity and a company must move to a multidivisional structure. Only the multidivisional structure is complex enough to deal with the needs of the large, multibusiness company.

11.6 INTEGRATION AND INTEGRATING MECHANISMS

As just discussed, an organization must choose the appropriate form of differentiation to match its strategy. For example, greater diversification requires that a company move from a functional structure to a divisional structure. Differentiation, however, is only the first organizational design decision to be made. The second concerns the level of integration necessary to make an organizational structure work effectively. As noted earlier, integration refers to the extent to which an organization seeks to coordinate its value-creation activities and make them interdependent. The design issue can be summed up simply: the higher a company's level of differentiation, the higher is the level of integration needed to make organizational structure work effectively.[33] Thus if a company adopts a more complex form of differentiation, it requires a more complex form of integration to accomplish its goals. Federal Express, for example, needs an enormous amount of integration and coordination to allow it to fulfill its promise of next-day package delivery. It is renowned for its innovative use of integrating mechanisms, such as customer-liaison personnel, to manage its transactions quickly and efficiently. As with increasing the level of differentiation, however, increasing the level of integration is expensive. There are high bureaucratic costs associated with using managers to coordinate value-creation activities. Hence a company only integrates its task activities to the extent necessary to implement its strategy effectively.

Forms of Integrating Mechanisms

There is a series of integrating mechanisms that a company can use to increase its level of integration as its level of differentiation increases.[34] These mechanisms—on a continuum from simplest to most complex—are listed in Table 11.1, together with the examples of the individuals or groups that might perform these integrating roles. Note that bureaucratic costs also increase as a company adopts more complex integrating mechanisms.

Direct Contact The aim behind establishing direct contact among managers is to set up a context within which managers from different divisions or functional departments can work together to solve mutual problems. However, managers from different functional departments have different subunit orientations but equal authority and so may tend to compete rather than cooperate when conflicts arise. For example, in a typical functional structure, the heads of each of the functions have equal authority; the nearest common point of authority is the CEO. Consequently, if disputes arise, no mechanism exists to resolve the conflicts apart from the authority of the boss. In fact, one sign of conflict in organizations is the number of problems sent up the hierarchy for upper-level managers to solve. This wastes management time and effort, slows down strategic decision making, and makes it difficult to create a cooperative culture in the

Table 11.1

Types and Examples of Integrating Mechanisms	
Direct contact	Sales and production managers
Liaison roles	Assistant sales and plant managers
Task forces	Representatives from sales, production, and research and development
Teams	Organizational executive committee
Integrating roles	Assistant vice president for strategic planning or vice president without portfolio
Integrating departments	Corporate headquarters staff
Matrix	All roles are integrating roles

company. For this reason, companies choose more complex integrating mechanisms to coordinate interfunctional and divisional activities.

Interdepartmental Liaison Roles A company can improve its interfunctional coordination through the interdepartmental liaison role. When the volume of contacts between two departments or functions increases, one of the ways of improving coordination is to give one person in *each* division or function the responsibility for coordinating with the other. These people may meet daily, weekly, monthly, or as needed. Figure 11.10a depicts the nature of the liaison role, the small circle representing the individual inside the functional department who has responsibility for coordinating with the other function. The responsibility for coordination is part of an individual's full-time job, but through these roles, a permanent relationship forms between the people involved, greatly easing strains between departments. Furthermore, liaison roles offer a way of transferring information across the organization, which is important in large, anonymous organizations whose employees may know no one outside their immediate department.

Temporary Task Forces When more than two functions or divisions share common problems, then direct contact and liaison roles are of limited value because they do not provide enough coordination. The solution is to adopt a more complex form of integrating mechanism called a task force. The nature of the task force is represented diagrammatically in Figure 11.10b. One member of each function or division is assigned to a task force created to solve a specific problem. Essentially, task forces are *ad hoc committees,* and members are responsible for reporting back to their departments on the issues addressed and solutions recommended. Task forces are temporary because, once the problem is solved, members return to their normal roles in their departments or are assigned to other task forces. Task force members also perform many of their normal duties while serving on the task force.

Permanent Teams In many cases, the issues addressed by a task force are recurring problems. To solve these problems effectively, an organization must establish a permanent integrating mechanism, such as a permanent team. An

Figure 11.10
Forms of Integrating Mechanisms

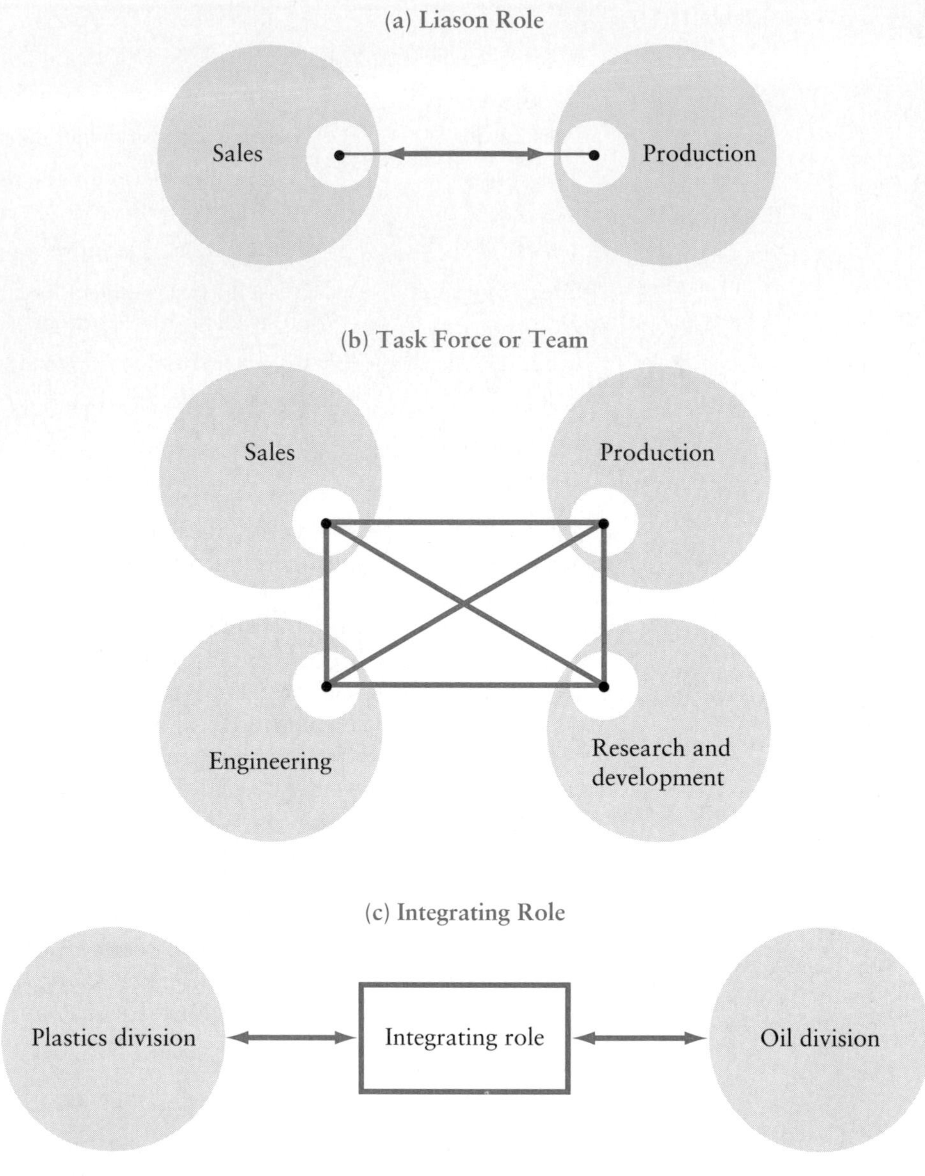

example of a permanent team is a new-product development committee, which is responsible for the choice, design, and marketing of new products. Such an activity obviously requires a great deal of integration among functions if new products are to be successfully introduced, and establishing a permanent integrating mechanism accomplishes this. Intel, for instance, emphasizes teamwork. It formed a council system based on approximately ninety cross-functional groups, which meet regularly to set functional strategy in areas such as engineering and marketing and to develop business-level strategy.

The importance of teams in the management of the organizational structure cannot be overemphasized. Essentially, permanent teams are the organization's

STRATEGY IN ACTION 11.5

Teamwork at AT&T

Like other large companies, AT&T had developed a very tall, centralized structure to manage its activities. While the telephone industry was regulated, it cared little about the way its massive bureaucracy slowed down decision making. However, after deregulation, a major problem facing the company was how to speed the development of new telephones and answering machines that could compete with those of Japanese companies like Panasonic and Sony. These companies led the market both in terms of the features and the low price of telephone products, and AT&T was a poor third in the competitive marketplace.

Its answer was to bypass the bureaucracy by creating cross-functional teams. Previously, AT&T had employed the usual functional approach to managing product development: the product started in engineering and then went to manufacturing, which in turn handed the product over to marketing. This was a slow and time-consuming process. In the new approach, John Hanley, the AT&T vice president of product development, decided to form teams of six to twelve people from all these functions to handle all aspects of the development process. Each team was given a time deadline for the various project phases and then left to get on with the job. The results were astonishing. Product development time was reduced by 50 percent, for example, AT&T's new 4200 phone was produced in one year, not the usual two, costs went down, and quality went up. Today AT&T's answering machines and cordless phones are the market leaders, and AT&T has extended the use of cross-functional teams throughout its business.

standing committees, and much of the strategic direction of the organization is formulated in these meetings. Henry Mintzberg, in a study of how the managers of corporations spend their time, discovered that they spend almost 60 percent of their time in these committees.[35] The reason is not bureaucracy but rather that integration is possible only in intensive, face-to-face sessions, in which managers can understand others' viewpoints and develop a cohesive organizational strategy. The more complex the company, the more important these teams become. Westinghouse, for example, has established a whole new task force and team system to promote integration among divisions and improve corporate performance.

As discussed earlier, the product team structure is based on the use of cross-functional teams to speed products to market. These teams assume the responsibility for all aspects of product development. The way in which AT&T made use of cross-functional teams to speed product development in its race to compete with Japanese manufacturers—described in Strategy in Action 11.5— illustrates how these teams can increase coordination and integration among functions.

Integrating Roles The integrating role is a role whose only function is to prompt integration among divisions or departments; it is a full-time job. As Figure 11.10c indicates, the role is independent of the subunits or divisions being integrated. It is staffed by an independent expert, who is normally a senior manager with a great deal of experience in the joint needs of the two departments. The job is to coordinate the decision process among departments or divisions so

that the synergetic gains from cooperation can be obtained. One study found that Du Pont had created 160 integrating roles to provide coordination among the different divisions of the company and improve corporate performance.[36] Once again, the more differentiated the company, the more common are these roles. Often people in these roles take the responsibility for chairing task forces and teams, and this provides additional integration.

Integrating Departments Sometimes the number of integrating roles becomes so high that a permanent integrating department is established at corporate headquarters. Normally, this occurs only in large, diversified corporations, which see the need for integration among divisions. This department consists mainly of strategic planners and may indeed be called the strategic planning department. Corporate headquarters staff in a divisional structure can also be viewed as an integrating department from the divisional perspective.

Matrix Structure Finally, when differentiation is very high and the company must be able to respond quickly to the environment, a matrix structure becomes the appropriate integrating device. The matrix contains many of the integrating mechanisms already discussed. The subproject managers integrate among functions and projects, and the matrix is built on the basis of temporary task forces.

Integration and Control

Clearly, firms have a large number of options open to them when they increase their level of differentiation as a result of increased growth or diversification. The implementation issue is for managers to match differentiation with the level of integration to meet organizational objectives. Note that while too much differentiation and not enough integration will lead to failure of implementation, the converse is also true. That is, the combination of low differentiation and high integration will lead to an overcontrolled, bureaucratized organization, where flexibility and speed of response are reduced rather than enhanced by the level of integration. Besides, too much integration is expensive for the company because it raises bureaucratic costs. For these reasons the goal is to decide on the optimum amount of integration necessary for meeting organizational goals and objectives. A company needs to operate the simplest structure consistent with implementing its strategy effectively.

In practice, integrating mechanisms are only the first means through which a company seeks to increase its ability to control and coordinate its activities. To facilitate the use of integrating mechanisms and to make organizational structure work, a company must create the control and incentive structure through which people are motivated to perform task activities in the organizational setting. In the next chapter, we discuss the various kinds of control systems that organizations can use to make their organizational structures work effectively.

11.7 SUMMARY OF CHAPTER

This chapter discusses the issues involved in designing a structure to meet the needs of a company's strategy. Companies can adopt a large number of structures to match changes in their size and strategy over time. The structure that a com-

pany selects will be the one whose logic of grouping activities (that is, its form of horizontal differentiation) best meets the needs of its business or businesses. The company must match its form of horizontal differentiation to vertical differentiation. That is, it must choose a structure and then make choices about levels in the hierarchy and degree of centralization or decentralization. It is the combination of both kinds of differentiation that produces internal organizational arrangements. However, once the company has divided itself into parts, it must then integrate itself. A company must choose the appropriate level of integration to match its level of differentiation if it is to successfully coordinate its value-creation activities. Since differentiation and integration are expensive, a company's goal is to economize on bureaucratic costs by adopting the simplest structure consistent with achieving its strategy. We stress the following points:

1. Implementing a strategy successfully depends on selecting the right structure and control system to match a company's strategy.
2. The basic tool of strategy implementation is organizational design. Good organizational design increases profits in two ways. First, good design economizes on bureaucratic costs and lowers the costs of value-creation activities. Second, good design enhances the ability of a company's value-creation functions to achieve superior efficiency, quality, innovativeness, and customer responsiveness and obtain a differentiation advantage.
3. Differentiation and integration are the two design concepts that decide how a structure will work. The higher the level of differentiation and integration, the higher are bureaucratic costs.
4. Differentiation has two aspects: (a) vertical differentiation, which refers to how a company chooses to allocate its decision-making authority; and (b) horizontal differentiation, which refers to the way that a company groups organizational activities into functions, departments, or divisions.
5. The basic choice in vertical differentiation is whether to have a flat or a tall structure. Tall hierarchies have a number of disadvantages, such as problems with communication and information transfer, motivation, and cost. Decentralization or delegation of authority, however, can solve some of these problems.
6. As a company grows and diversifies, it adopts a multidivisional structure. Although a multidivisional structure has higher bureaucratic costs than a functional structure, it overcomes the control problems associated with a functional structure and gives a company the capability to handle its value-creation activities effectively.
7. Other specialized kinds of structures include the matrix, product team, and geographic structures. Each has a specialized use, and to be chosen, must match the needs of the organization.
8. The more complex the company and the higher its level of differentiation, the higher is the level of integration needed to manage its structure.
9. The kinds of integrating mechanisms available to a company range from direct contact to matrix structure. The more complex the mechanism, the greater are the costs of using it. A company should take care to match these mechanisms to its strategic needs.

Discussion Questions

1. What is the difference between vertical and horizontal differentiation? Rank the various structures discussed in this chapter along these two dimensions.
2. What kind of structure best describes the way your (a) business school and (b) university operates? Why is the structure appropriate? Would another structure fit better?
3. When would a company decide to change from a functional to a multidivisional structure?
4. When would a company choose a matrix structure? What are the problems associated with managing this structure and why might a product team structure be preferable?

Article File 11

Find an example(s) of a company that has recently changed its organizational structure. What changes did it make? Why did it make these changes? What effect did these changes have on the behavior of people and subunits?

Strategic Management Project: Module 11

This module asks you to identify the type of organizational structure used by your organization and to explain why your company has selected this form of differentiation and integration. If you are studying a company in your area, you will probably have more information about the company's structure than if you are studying a company using published sources. However, you can make many inferences about the companies structure from the nature of its activities, and if you write to the company, it may provide you with an organizational chart and other information.

1. How large is the company, as measured by the number of its employees? How many levels in the hierarchy does it have from the top to the bottom?
2. Based on these two measures, and any other information that you may have, would you say your company operates with a relatively tall or flat structure? What effect does this have on people's behavior?
3. Does your company have a centralized or a decentralized approach to decision making? How do you know?
4. In what ways do the company's vertical differentiation choices affect the behavior of people and subunits? Do you think the company's choice of vertical differentiation is appropriate for its activities? Why or why not?
5. What changes (if any) would you make in the way the company operates in a vertical direction?

6. Draw an organizational chart showing the main way in which your company groups its activities. Based on this chart, what kind of structure (e.g., functional or divisional) does your company operate with?
7. Why did your company choose this structure? In what ways is it appropriate for its business? In what ways is it not?
8. What changes (if any) would you make in the way your company operates in a horizontal direction?
9. Given this analysis, does your company have a low or a high level of differentiation?
10. What kind of integration or integration mechanisms does your company use? Why? Does its level of integration match its level of differentiation?
11. Based on the analysis of your company's level of differentiation and integration, would you say your company is coordinating and motivating its people and subunits effectively? Why or why not?
12. What changes in the company's structure would you recommend to make it work more effectively? What changes has the company itself made to improve effectiveness? Why?

Endnotes

1. D. Woodruff and E. Lesly, "Surge at Chrysler," *Fortune,* November 9, 1992, pp. 88–96.
2. "Chrysler Reengineers Product Development Process," *Information Week,* September 7, 1992, p. 20.
3. J. R. Galbraith, *Designing Complex Organizations* (Reading, Mass.: Addison-Wesley, 1973).
4. J. Child, *Organization: A Guide for Managers and Administrators* (New York: Harper & Row, 1977), pp. 50–72.
5. R. H. Miles, *Macro Organizational Behavior* (Santa Monica, Calif.: Goodyear, 1980), pp. 19–20.
6. Galbraith, *Designing Complex Organizations.*
7. V. A. Graicunas, "Relationship in Organization," in *Papers on the Science of Administration,* ed. L. Gulick and L. Urwick, (New York: Institute of Public Administration, 1937), pp. 181–185. J. C. Worthy, "Organizational Structure and Company Morale," *American Sociological Review,* 15 (1950), 169–179.
8. Child, *Organization,* pp. 50–52.
9. G. R. Jones, "Organization-Client Transactions and Organizational Governance Structures," *Academy of Management Journal,* 30 (1987), 197–218.
10. H. Mintzberg, *The Structuring of Organizations* (Englewood Cliffs, N.J.: Prentice-Hall, 1979), p. 435.
11. Child, *Organization,* p. 51.
12. R. Carzo, Jr., and J. N. Yanousas, "Effects of Flat and Tall Organization-Structure," *Administrative Science Quarterly,* 14 (1969), 178–191.
13. A. Gupta and V. Govindardan, "Business Unit Strategy, Managerial Characteristics, and Business Unit Effectiveness at Strategy Implementation," *Academy of Management Journal,* 27 (1984), 25–41. R. T. Lenz, "Determinants of Organizational Performance: An Interdisciplinary Review," *Strategic Management Journal,* 2 (1981), 131–154.
14. W. H. Wagel, "Keeping the Organization Lean at Federal Express," *Personnel* (March 1984), 4.
15. J. Koter, "For P&G Rivals, the New Game Is to Beat the Leader, Not Copy It," *Wall Street Journal,* May 6, 1985, p. 35.
16. G. R. Jones, "Task Visibility, Free Riding and Shirking: Explaining the Effect of Organization Structure on Employee Behavior," *Academy of Management Review,* 4 (1984), 684–695.
17. "Operation Turnaround—How Westinghouse's New Chairman Plans to Fire Up an Old Line Company," *Business Week,* December 14, 1983, pp. 124–133.
18. R. L. Daft, *Organizational Theory and Design,* 3rd ed. (St. Paul, Minn.: West, 1986), p. 215.
19. Alfred D. Chandler, *Strategy and Structure* (Cambridge, Mass.: MIT Press, 1962).
20. C. Chandler and J. B. White, "Honda's Middle Managers Will Regain Authority in New Overhaul of Company," *Wall Street Journal,* May 16, 1992, p. A2.
21. The discussion draws heavily on Chandler, *Strategy and Structure;* and B. R. Scott, *"Stages of Corporate Development"* (Cambridge, Mass.: Intercollegiate Clearing House, Harvard Business School, 1971).
22. J. R. Galbraith and R. K. Kazanjian, *Strategy Implementation: Structure System and Process,* 2nd ed. (St. Paul, Minn.: West, 1986); Child, *Organization.* R. Duncan; "What Is the

Right Organization Structure?" *Organizational Dynamics* (Winter 1979), 59–80.

23. O. E. Williamson, *Markets and Hierarchies: Analysis and Antitrust Implications* (New York: Free Press, 1975).
24. P. R. Lawrence and J. Lorsch, *Organization and Environment* (Boston: Division of Research, Harvard Business School, 1967).
25. K. Pope, "Dell Refocuses on Groundwork to Cope with Rocketing Sales," *Wall Street Journal,* June 18, 1993, p. B5.
26. Chandler, *Strategy and Structure;* Williamson, *Markets and Hierarchies*; L. Wrigley, "Divisional Autonomy and Diversification" (Ph.D. diss., Harvard Business School, 1970).
27. R. P. Rumelt, *Strategy, Structure, and Economic Performance* (Boston: Division of Research, Harvard Business School, 1974); Scott, "Stages of Corporate Development"; Williamson, *Markets and Hierarchies.*
28. The discussion draws on each of the sources cited in endnotes 20–27, and also on G. R. Jones and C. W. L. Hill, "Transaction Cost Analysis of Strategy-Structure Choice," *Strategic Management Journal,* 9 (1988), 159–172.
29. H. O. Armour and D. J. Teece, "Organizational Structure and Economic Performance: A Test of the Multidivisional Hypothesis," *Bell Journal of Economics,* 9 (1978), pp. 106-122.
30. Alfred Sloan, *My Years at General Motors* (New York: Doubleday, 1983), Ch. 3.
31. S. M. Davis and R. R. Lawrence, *Matrix* (Reading, Mass.: Addison-Wesley, 1977); J. R. Galbraith, "Matrix Organization Designs: How to Combine Functional and Project Forms," *Business Horizons,* 14 (1971), 29–40.
32. Duncan, "What Is the Right Organizational Structure?" Davis and Lawrence, *Matrix.*
33. P. R. Lawrence and J. Lorsch, *Organization and Environment* pp. 50–55.
34. J. R. Galbraith, *Designing Complex Organizations,* Ch. 1; Galbraith and Kazanjian, *Strategy Implementation,* Ch. 7.
35. Henry Mintzberg, *The Nature of Managerial Work* (Englewood Cliffs, N.J.: Prentice-Hall, 1973), Ch. 10.
36. Lawrence and Lorsch, *Organization and Environment,* p. 55.

12 Designing Strategic Control Systems

12.1 OPENING CASE: GETTING IT RIGHT AT McDONALD'S

In the restaurant business, maintaining product quality is a major problem because the quality of food, service, and the restaurant premises varies with the chefs and waiters as they come and go. If a customer gets a bad meal or poor service or dirty silverware, not only that customer may be lost, but other potential customers, too, as negative comments travel by word of mouth. Consider then the problem Ray Kroc, the man who pioneered McDonald's growth, faced when McDonald's franchises began to open by the thousands throughout the United States. How could he maintain product quality to protect the company's reputation as it grew? Moreover, how could he try to increase efficiency and make the organization responsive to the needs of customers to promote its competitive advantage? Kroc's answer was to develop a sophisticated control system, which specified every detail of how each McDonald's restaurant was to be operated and managed.

Kroc's control system was based on several components. First, he developed a comprehensive system of rules and procedures for both franchise owners and employees to follow in running each restaurant. The most effective way to perform such tasks as cooking burgers, making fries, greeting customers, or cleaning tables was worked out in advance, written down in rule books, and then taught to each McDonald's manager and employee through a formal training process. For example, prospective franchise owners had to attend "Hamburger University," the company's training center in Chicago, where in an intensive, month-long program they learnt all aspects of a McDonald's operation. In turn, they were expected to train their work force and make sure that employees understood operating procedures thoroughly. Kroc's goal in establishing this system of rules and procedures was to standardize McDonald's activities so that whatever franchise customers walked into they would always find the same level of quality in food and service. If customers always get what they expect from a restaurant, the restaurant has developed superior customer responsiveness.

However, Kroc's attempt to control quality went well beyond written rules and procedures specifying task activities. He also developed McDonald's franchise system to help the company control its structure as it grew. Kroc believed that a manager who is also a franchise owner (and receives a large share of the profits) is more motivated to maintain higher efficiency and quality than a manager paid on a straight salary. Thus McDonald's reward and incentive system allowed it to keep control over its operating structure as it expanded. Moreover, McDonald's was very selective in selling its franchises; the franchisees had to be people with the skills and capabilities to manage the business, and a franchise could be revoked if the holder did not maintain quality standards.

McDonald's managers frequently visited restaurants to monitor franchisees, and franchisees were allowed to operate their restaurant only according to McDonald's rules. For instance, they could not put in a television or otherwise modify the restaurant. McDonald's was also able to monitor and control the performance of its franchisees through output control. Each franchisee provided McDon-

ald's with information on how many meals were sold, on operating costs, and so forth. So, using this mix of personal supervision and output control, managers at McDonald's corporate headquarters would quickly learn if sales in a franchise declined suddenly, and thus they could take corrective action.

Within each restaurant, franchise owners also paid particular attention to training their employees and instilling in them the norms and values of quality service. Having learned about McDonald's core cultural values at their training sessions, franchise owners were expected to transmit McDonald's concepts of efficiency, quality, and customer service to their employees. The development of shared norms, values, and an organizational culture also helped McDonald's standardize employee behavior so that customers would know how they would be treated in a McDonald's restaurant. Moreover, McDonald's tried to include customers in its culture. It had customers bus their own tables, but it also showed concern for customer needs, by building playgrounds, offering Happy Meals, and organizing birthday parties for customers' children. In creating its family-oriented culture, McDonald's was ensuring future customer loyalty because satisfied children are likely to remain loyal customers as adults.

Through all these means, McDonald's developed a control system that allowed it to expand its organization successfully and create an organizational structure that has led to superior efficiency, quality, and customer responsiveness. Its control system has played an important role in McDonald's becoming the largest and most successful fast-food company in the world, and many other fast-food companies have imitated it.

Discussion Questions

1. What were the main elements of the control system created by Ray Kroc?
2. In what ways would this control system facilitate McDonald's strategy of global expansion?

12.2 OVERVIEW

In Chapter 11, we discuss the various kinds of organizational structures available to companies when they implement their strategies. In this chapter, we consider the various kinds of strategic control systems that companies use to make these structures operate efficiently. Strategic control systems allow top managers to monitor and evaluate the performance of divisions, functions, and employees and to take corrective action to improve their performance. These systems provide information about how well a company's strategy and structure are working. **Strategic control** is the process of establishing the appropriate types of control system at the corporate, business, and functional levels in a company, which allow strategic managers to evaluate whether a company is *achieving superior efficiency, quality, innovation, and customer responsiveness and implementing its strategy successfully.*

First we outline the process and function of strategic control. We then discuss the relationship between types of control system and bureaucratic costs using an agency theory perspective. Next we examine the main types of control that companies can use: output control, bureaucratic control, and organizational culture. Finally, we discuss how the design of reward systems is an important part of the strategic control process. In Chapter 13, we consider in detail how to match organizational structure and control to corporate-, business-, and functional-level strategy.

12.3 STRATEGIC CONTROL SYSTEMS

As we note in Chapter 11, implementation involves selecting the right combination of structure and control for achieving a company's strategy. Structure assigns people to tasks and roles (differentiation) and specifies how these are to be coordinated (integration). Nevertheless, it does not of itself provide the mechanism through which people can be *motivated* to make the structure work. Hence the need for control. Put another way, management can develop *on paper* an elegant organizational structure with the right distribution of task responsibility and decision-making authority, but only the appropriate strategic control systems will make this structure work. To understand why strategic control is such a vital aspect of implementing strategy, we need to look at the function of strategic control.

The Function of Strategic Control

The primary function of strategic control systems is to provide management with the information it needs to control its strategy and structure. For example, if it is to achieve superior efficiency, a company pursuing a low-cost strategy needs information on the level of its costs relative to its competitors, on what its competitors are doing, on the way its production costs have changed over time, on the price of its inputs, and so forth. A company has to collect this information and then use it to plan future strategic moves—for instance, to introduce new laborsaving machinery or to expand globally. H. J. Heinz, a cost leader, found in 1993 that along with a record increase in sales its costs had risen so much that it needed to reduce its work force of 36,000 people by 8%. Heinz used the information provided by its control systems to make this strategic decision. A company has to collect the information that allows it to evaluate its performance and take corrective action. Similarly, a company has to collect information to evaluate the way its structure is working. Suppose that a company operating with a functional structure finds its costs rising and its quality falling and that managers trace this problem to a lack of cooperation among functions. Having this information, managers can decide that the company must change to a product structure and use cross-functional teams to increase cooperation and speed product development. Again, the information produced by an organization's control systems has provided managers with feedback on the operation of their structures so that they can take corrective action.

Strategic control systems are the formal target-setting, monitoring, evaluation, and feedback systems that provide management with information about whether the organization's strategy and structure are meeting strategic performance objectives. An effective control system should have three characteristics: it should be *flexible* enough to allow managers to respond as necessary to unexpected events; it should provide *accurate information,* giving a true picture of organizational performance; and it should supply managers with the information in a *timely manner* because making decisions on the basis of outdated information is a recipe for failure.[1] As Figure 12.1 shows, designing an effective strategic control system requires four steps.

1. *Establish the standards or targets against which performance is to be evaluated.* The standards or targets that managers select are the ways in which a company chooses to evaluate its performance. General performance stan-

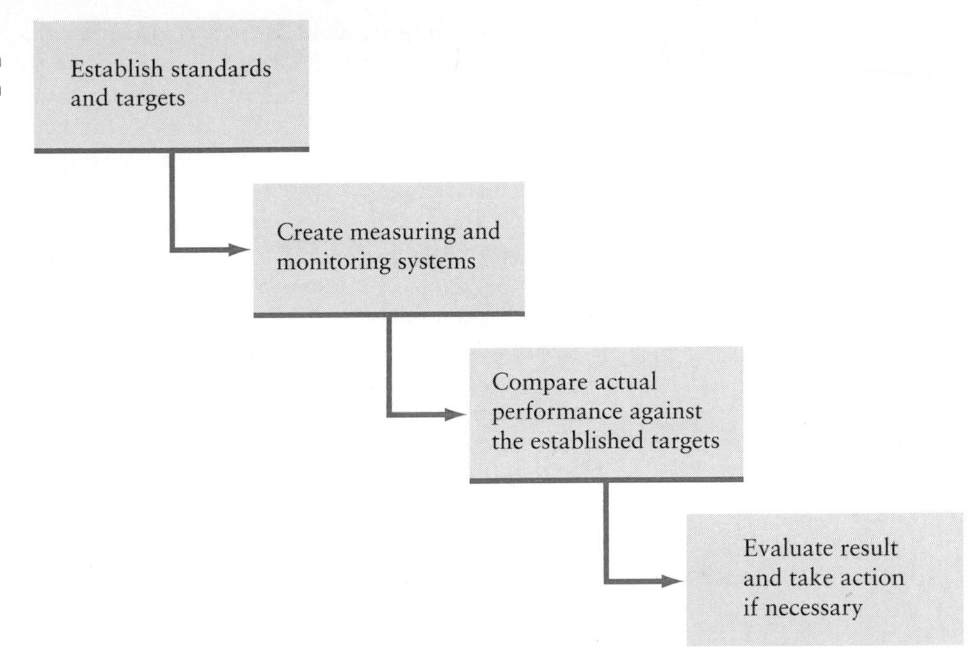

Figure 12.1
Steps in Designing An Effective Control System

dards often derive from the goal of achieving superior efficiency, quality, innovation or customer responsiveness. Specific performance targets are derived from the strategy pursued by the company. For example, if a company is pursuing a low-cost strategy, then "reducing costs by 7 percent a year" might be a target. If the company is a service organization like McDonald's, its standards might include time targets for serving customers or guidelines for food quality.

2. *Create the measuring or monitoring systems that indicate whether the targets are being reached.* The company establishes procedures for assessing whether work goals at all levels in the organization are being achieved. In many cases, measuring performance is a difficult task because the organization is engaged in many complex activities. For example, managers can measure quite easily how many customers their employees serve: they can count the number of receipts from the cash register. Yet how can they judge how well their research and development department is doing when it may take five years for products to be developed? Or how can they measure the company's performance when the company is entering new markets and serving new customers? Or how can they evaluate how well divisions are integrating? The answer is that they need to use various types of control, which we discuss later in this chapter.
3. *Compare actual performance against the established targets.* Managers evaluate whether—and to what extent—performance deviates from the targets developed in step 1. If performance is higher, management may decide that it had set the standards too low and may raise them from the next time period. The Japanese are renowned for the way they use targets on the production line to control costs. They are constantly trying to raise performance, and they constantly raise the standards to provide a goal for managers to work

toward. On the other hand, if performance is too low, managers must decide whether to take remedial action. This decision is easy when the reasons for poor performance can be identified—for instance, high labor costs. More often, however, the reasons for poor performance are hard to uncover. They may involve external factors, such as a recession. Or the cause may be internal. For instance, the research and development laboratory may have underestimated the problems it would encounter or the extra costs of doing unforeseen research. For any form of action, however, step 4 is necessary.

4. *Initiate corrective action when it is decided that the target is not being achieved.* The final stage in the control process is to take the corrective action that will allow the organization to meet its goals. Such corrective action may involve changing any aspect of strategy or structure discussed in this book. For example, managers may invest more resources in improving R&D, or decide to diversify, or even decide to change their organizational structure. The goal is to continually enhance an organization's competitive advantage.

Levels of Control

Generally, performance is measured at four levels in the organization: the corporate, divisional, functional, and individual levels. Managers at the corporate level are most concerned with overall and abstract measures of organizational performance such as profit, return on investment, or total labor force turnover. The aim is to choose performance standards that measure overall corporate performance. Similarly, managers at the other levels are most concerned with developing a set of standards to evaluate business- or functional-level performance. These measures should be tied as closely as possible to task activities needed to achieve superior efficiency, quality, innovativeness, and customer responsiveness at each level. Care must be taken, however, to ensure that the standards used at each level do not cause problems at the other levels—for example, that divisions' attempts to improve their performance do not conflict with corporate performance. Furthermore, controls at each level should provide the basis on which managers at the levels below can select their control systems. Figure 12.2 illustrates these links.

An Agency Theory Perspective on Organizational Control

Agency theory offers a useful way of understanding the complex control problems that arise when an organization allocates task responsibility and authority among people and subunits at different levels in the organization. An agency relation arises whenever one party delegates decision-making authority or control over resources to another. At the top of a company, for example, shareholders delegate authority to top management to utilize organizational resources effectively for the shareholder's benefit; thus managers become the agents of shareholders. Similarly, inside the organization, whenever managers delegate authority to managers below them in the hierarchy and give them the right to control resources, an agency relation is established.

Managers who control resources have the responsibility for using them to the best advantage to benefit the organization. For example, the corporate center expects the operating divisions to use their resources to enhance their divisions' competitive advantage, just as shareholders expect top managers to work to increase the value of their investments. However, delegating authority to managers

Figure 12.2
Levels of Organizational Control

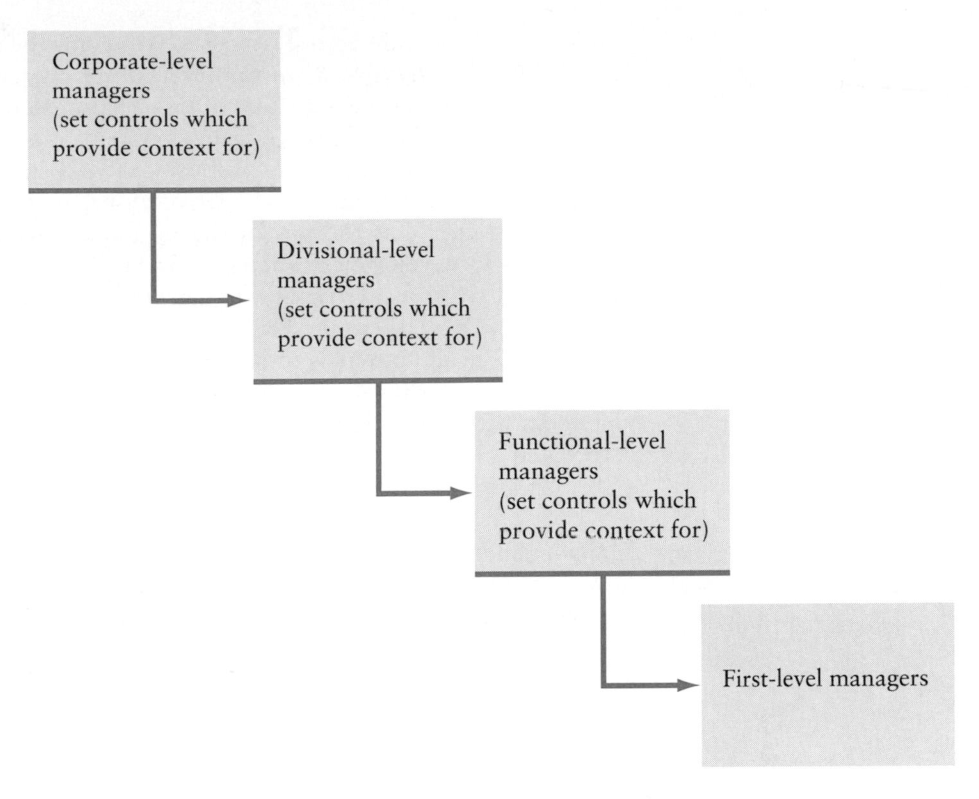

raises the issue of determining accountability for the use of resources. A manager often finds it very difficult to evaluate how well a subordinate has performed because the latter possesses an *information advantage*—that is, a manager higher up the organization has trouble obtaining the information needed to assess the quality of the performance of a manager further down the organization ladder.

As you saw in Chapter 2, sometimes managers have the incentive to pursue their own goals at the expense of stockholder goals. For instance, top managers might prefer to grow the company at the expense of profitability because salaries are closely correlated with company size. Managers at lower levels might also prefer to pursue their own goals, such as developing large staffs, expanding their expense accounts, or building their own empires instead of making the hard choices necessary to build competitive advantage. As noted in Chapter 11, one of the functions of corporate managers is to discipline divisional managers in order to increase efficiency.

When it is difficult to monitor and evaluate the performance of a subordinate *and* the subordinate has an incentive to pursue goals and objectives that are different from the superior's, an **agency problem** exists. An example of such a problem is the situation where divisional managers deliberately disguise poor divisional performance from corporate managers to further their own interests. Hence the challenge for shareholders and managers at all levels in the organization is (1) to overcome their information disadvantage and (2) to shape the behavior of those further down the organization so that they follow the goals set by those higher up.

In agency theory, the central issue is to overcome the agency problem by *developing control systems to align the interests of shareholders and managers at different levels* so that the structure of task relationships in an organization functions effectively. The purpose of control systems is to provide shareholders and managers with information they can use to review performance, identify problems, and allocate resources to improve an organization's competitive advantage. For example, at the top of the organization, the role of the board of directors is to develop performance standards they can use in evaluating top managers' activities and to create an incentive structure that would motivate top managers and align their interests with those of shareholders.[2] Likewise, the role of corporate headquarters is to develop control systems that allow top management to monitor and evaluate the performance of divisional managers and provide them with the incentives to work toward corporate objectives. This pattern is repeated all the way down the organization.

Bureaucratic Costs and Organizational Control Systems

Managers need to develop control systems that supply them with the information they require in order to monitor and evaluate subordinates' performance. However, gathering this information is expensive and gives rise to *bureaucratic costs*. For example, every hour a manager spends monitoring a subordinate to make sure the subordinate performs effectively costs money. Since organizational control, like organizational structure, is expensive, a company should design its control systems so that it can collect the information it needs to control its value-creation activities at as low a cost as possible.

The types of control system that organizations can use to overcome the agency problem range from those that measure organizational outputs or outcomes to those that measure and control organizational behaviors.[3] In general, outputs are much easier and cheaper to measure than behaviors because outputs are relatively tangible or objective. Hence, to collect information about performance, companies first turn to *output controls*. Then, to motivate managers, it is common to make managers' rewards contingent on the outputs or outcomes of their actions, that is, on the level of their performance. Thus shareholders may control the performance of a CEO by giving the CEO stock options that are related to the company's ROI, a form of outcome measurement. Corporate managers, in turn, may reward divisional managers based on the performance of the division.

In many situations, however, organizational outputs cannot be easily measured or evaluated. For example, measuring organizational innovation or customer responsiveness is much more difficult than measuring efficiency. In addition, the more complex the value-creation activities, the harder it is to use output control because evaluating the work of people such as research and development scientists or strategic planners is both difficult and expensive. Similarly, the higher the interdependence among functions or divisions—for instance, when a company is seeking to achieve gains from synergy—the tougher it is for a company to pinpoint *individual* divisional contributions to performance.

In these situations, shareholders and managers usually develop *bureaucratic control* systems which shape the behaviors necessary to reach output targets.[4] Bureaucratic controls such as rules and procedures are the principal ways of shaping or standardizing behavior. Another way to shape behavior and align interests between parties to encourage high performance is by developing a *cor-*

Table 12.1
Types of Control Systems

Market control	Output control	Bureaucratic control	Organizational culture
Stock price	Divisional goals	Rules and procedures	Norms
ROI	Functional goals		Values
Transfer pricing	Individual goals	Standardization	Socialization

porate culture that bonds managers and employees to an organization by making their membership in it valuable. For example, a culture might offer long-term benefits such as career paths that reward employees who specialize in an organization so that they develop the skills to increase its distinctive competencies.

Table 12.1 shows the various types of control systems an organization can use to monitor and coordinate its activities. We discuss each of these types in turn and also consider the use of different kinds of control mechanisms at the various organizational levels—corporate, divisional, functional, and individual. Agency problems will not be overcome and organizational structure will not function effectively unless corporate-level managers use these controls to monitor, evaluate, and reward divisions, functions, and employees. In the rest of this chapter, we discuss the various options open to companies in designing such a control system.

12.4 MARKET CONTROL

One of the principal ways in which shareholders try to influence managers is by using market control to monitor and evaluate company performance. **Market control** is the most objective kind of output control, for it is based on objective financial measures of performance. The performance of one company is compared with that of another in terms of stock market price or return on investment.

Stock Market Price

Stock price is a useful measure of a company's performance primarily because the price of the stock is determined competitively by the number of buyers and sellers in the market. Movements in the price of a stock provide shareholders with feedback on a company's performance. Stock market price acts as a powerful means of control because top managers' compensation is often linked to stock price; consequently, they tend to be sensitive to falls in the stock market prices. Falling stock price may also provoke shareholder unrest and takeover attempts, and this too serves to control managerial action. Finally, because stock price reflects the long-term future return from the stock, it can be regarded as an indicator of the company's long-run potential.

There are many large and well-known companies whose shareholders are complaining bitterly about the performance of the top management team, yet have been unable to influence top management. At Eastman Kodak, for example, CEO Kay R. Whitmore, who took over in 1990, has been unable to turn around

that company's performance. Many of the acquisitions that Kodak had embarked on to improve corporate performance proved a dismal failure and a waste of stockholder's money. Kodak has been slow to downsize its operations and respond to the realities of a new competitive market. Other examples of companies where captive boards have been unable for long periods to influence top management despite declining performance include Sears, American Express, Westinghouse, and Digital Equipment Corp. Moves are presently afoot to change the laws governing corporations so that shareholders and institutional investors might have more power to intervene quickly when corporate performance is declining and to effectively control top management.

Return on Investment

Return on investment (ROI), determined by dividing net income by invested capital, is another form of market control. At the corporate level, the performance of the whole company can be evaluated *against* other companies, and it is in this sense that ROI can be used as a market control by shareholders and by top managers. Top managers, for example, can assess how well their strategies have worked by comparing their performance against that of similar companies. In the personal computer industry, companies like Dell Computer, Compaq, and Apple Computer use ROI to gauge their performance relative to their competitors. A declining ROI signals a potential problem with a company's strategy or structure. Apple's ROI, for example, has been falling in relation to Dell's and Compaq's. The reason, according to analysts, is that Apple has been rather slow both in product innovation and in reacting to the price-cutting moves of its rivals.

ROI can also be used inside the company at the divisional level to judge the performance of an operating division by comparing it with a similar freestanding business or with other internal divisions. Indeed, one reason for selecting a multidivisional structure is that each division can be evaluated as a self-contained profit center. Consequently, management can directly measure the performance of one division against another, just as at the corporate level the performance of a company can be measured against other companies. General Motors' moved to a divisional structure partly because it could then use this standard. It gave GM's corporate managers information about the relative costs of the various divisions, allowing them to base capital allocations on relative performance. Similarly, manufacturing companies often establish production facilities at different locations, domestically and globally, so that they can measure the relative performance of one against the other. For example, Xerox was able to identify the relative inefficiency of its U.S. division by comparing its profitability with that of its Japanese counterpart. ROI is a powerful form of market control at the divisional level, especially if divisional managers are rewarded on the basis of their performance vis-à-vis other divisions. The most successful divisional managers become the next generation of corporate executives.

Issues with Market Control

As already indicated, market control is feasible only when some form of a comparison system exists. In comparisons with other companies, market controls such as ROI or stock market price function well. But whether market control can work at the divisional level depends on the skills of managers and their willingness to reach equitable solutions over transfer prices for products. Finally, failure to meet stock price or ROI targets also indicates that corrective action is

necessary. It signals the need for corporate reorganization in order to meet corporate objectives, and such reorganization could involve a change in structure or liquidation and divestiture of businesses. It can also signal the need for new strategic leadership. In recent years, the CEOs of American Express, Digital Equipment, Westinghouse, and GM have all been ousted by disgruntled boards of directors, dismayed at the declining performance of their companies relative to the competition.

12.5 OUTPUT CONTROL

When no market system can be devised to allocate and price organizational resources because no system of comparison (among companies or divisions) exists, managers must turn to alternative methods of control to shape the behavior of divisions, functions, and personnel. The easiest and cheapest kind of control available is output control. To apply output control, a company estimates or forecasts appropriate targets for its various divisions, departments, or personnel, and then monitors their performance relative to these targets. Often the company's reward system is then linked to performance on these targets so that output control also provides an incentive structure for motivating managers at all levels in the organization.

Divisional Goals

In creating divisional goals, corporate management sets the standards for judging divisional performance. Such standards include sales, productivity, growth, and market share goals. Divisional managers use the standards as the basis for designing the organizational structure to meet the objectives. Generally, corporate managers try to raise these standards over time to force divisions to adopt more effective strategies and structures. At General Electric, for example, CEO Jack Welch has set clear performance goals for GE's over three hundred divisions. He expects each division to be number one or two in its industry in terms of market share. Divisional managers are given considerable autonomy to formulate a strategy to meet this goal, and the divisions that fail are divested. For example, GE is currently trying to find a buyer for NBC, the network rated third.

Functional Goals

Output control at the functional level is achieved by setting goals for each function. As discussed earlier, the four building blocks of competitive advantage are efficiency, quality, customer responsiveness, and innovation. These four criteria can serve as goals against which functional performance can be evaluated so that output control can be applied directly to enhance a company's competitive advantage. We discuss in Chapter 4 how competitive benchmarking can be used to create a system of output controls for shaping the behavior of functions and for motivating functional personnel. As at the divisional level, functional goals are established to encourage development of functional competencies that provide the company with a competitive advantage at the business level.

For example, in the sales function, goals related to efficiency (such as cost of sales), quality (such as number of returns), and customer responsiveness (such as the time needed to respond to customer needs) can be established for the whole

STRATEGY IN ACTION 12.1

Output Control and Acquisitions

Informix Corp., based in Menlo Park, California, specializes in producing software that links networks of UNIX-based PCs and workstations. In 1988, to expand its product range and give it a fully developed distribution system, which would make it the leading competitor in its market niche, Informix decided to purchase Innovative Software of Kansas City. The acquisition was a disaster. Instead of an improvement in its value-creation capabilities, Informix saw a dramatic increase in its operating costs: its work force had swelled from 350 to 1,200 people, and it had to manage two sets of sales forces, manufacturing operations, and all the other value-creation functions. In 1990 the company registered a $46.3 million loss and its future was in jeopardy.

Informix's CEO, Philip White, realized that he had to regain control of the company's structure if he was to get costs back under control. He established a series of strict output controls for the various functions and forced them to carefully monitor and evaluate their activities in order to find new ways of organizing to reduce costs. For example, he established a target for cutting costs in manufacturing, which forced managers to streamline and combine the two manufacturing operations. Within four years, manufacturing costs dropped from 13 percent of revenue to 5 percent. In product development, he established stringent targets for profit returns from new products, which forced managers to carefully screen potential new products. The result was the launch of a large number of highly successful products which have greatly boosted revenues. Indeed, White's program of output control has been so successful that the company's stock, which was trading at $1.31 in January 1992, was over $35 by 1993, and the company has a commanding lead over its competitors.

function. Then sales personnel can be given specific goals—related to functional goals—which they in turn are required to achieve. Functions and individuals are then evaluated on the basis of achieving or not achieving their goals, and in sales compensation is commonly pegged to achievement. The achievement of these goals is a sign that the company's strategy is working and meeting organizational objectives. The way in which Informix Corp. used output controls to make its structure work after an acquisition illustrates many of the advantages of output control. Informix's approach is highlighted in Strategy in Action 12.1.

Individual Goals

Output control at the individual level is also common. You have already seen how sales compensation is normally based on individual performance. In general, whenever employee performance can be easily monitored and evaluated, output controls are usually appropriate. Thus piece-rate systems, in which individuals are paid according to exactly how much they produce, are characteristic output control systems. For many jobs, output control is more difficult because individuals' performance is harder to evaluate. For example, if individuals work in teams, it is impossible or very expensive to measure their individual outputs; hence often team-based reward systems are used. If the work is extremely complex, as in the case of research and development scientists or top managers, then the incentive system must be tied to more general measures, such as ROI or stock price. Accordingly, Microsoft's principal programmers are given stock

options tied to the company's stock price which have made many of them millionaires. Stock options also form an important part of the compensation package for most top managers.

Issues with Output Control

The inappropriate application of output control at any level of the organization can lead to unintended and unfortunate consequences. For instance, the wrong goals may be used to evaluate divisions, functions, or individuals. If short-term measures of performance, such as quantity produced, are relied on, they can conflict with quality goals. In a classic example of the unintended consequence of output control, an employment placement agency rewarded its workers on the basis of how many people they placed weekly in new jobs. The result was that they directed prospective applicants to job positions for which they were totally unsuited—for instance, they sent accountants to production-line jobs. Realizing its mistake, the agency changed the reward system to emphasize how long new employees stayed in their positions after placement. The moral of the story is clear: Monitoring, evaluating, and rewarding employee behavior requires the right set of controls. The problem of choosing the right set of output controls to motivate managers is also exemplified in Strategy in Action 12.2, which describes the way the former CEO of Giddings and Lewis, William J. Fife, used output control. As this incident suggests, the wrong control system can have the unintended effect of producing conflict among managers and departments.

The inappropriate use of output control can also promote conflict among divisions. As noted earlier, clashes over transfer prices may occur at the divisional level. In general, setting across-the-board output targets, such as ROI targets, for divisions can lead to destructive results if divisions single-mindedly try to maximize divisional profits at the expense of corporate objectives. Moreover, to reach output targets, divisions may start to distort the numbers and engage in strategic manipulation of the figures to make their divisions look good.[5] The way in which Sears's use of output control caused problems with customers is another example of how not to use output control.

In 1992, faced with deteriorating company performance, Sears decided to change to an incentive system that rewarded store employees according to how much they sold. In Sears's auto shops, for instance, an employee's sales commission was directly linked to the dollar value of the specific autoparts the employee had sold. The consequence of this approach, as consumer affairs officials in California discovered, was that employees sold customers millions of dollars of unnecessary repairs, such as new shock absorbers or tires. An undercover study by the state's Consumer Affairs Department claimed that on thirty-two out of thirty-eight undercover runs, Sears charged an average of $235 extra for unnecessary repairs.[7] When the company's top management found out about this unintended effect of output controls, it scrapped the system and removed the incentive for employees to oversell. However, these accusations have hurt customer relations, and the company has had to face the problem of rebuilding customer trust.

As the Sears example suggests, strategic managers need to design output controls that stimulate managers to pursue long-run profitability goals but not at the expense of other organizational stakeholders. In practice, output or market controls must be used in conjunction with bureaucratic control and culture if the right strategic behaviors are to be achieved.

STRATEGY IN ACTION 12.2

How Not to Use Output Control to Get Ahead

William J. Fife masterminded the turnaround of Giddings and Lewis, Inc., a manufacturer of automated factory equipment for companies like GM, Boeing, AMR, and Ford. In 1988 the company was losing money and had a declining customer base. By 1993 Fife had made it the largest company in the industry, with sales that for every quarter exceeded year-earlier results and a stock price that had quadrupled since Fife sold its stock on the open market in 1989. Nevertheless, in April 1993 the board of directors decided that Fife was no longer a suitable leader and asked him to resign because, as the board saw it, his use of output controls was damaging the future of the company.

Fife's turnaround strategy relied on broadening the company's product base by innovating products to suit new kinds of customers, for example, airlines and consumer manufacturing companies. Then his goal was to increase sales by promoting customer responsiveness. As an example to his managers and employees, Fife would fly anywhere in the United States to personally solve customer problems. To promote his strategy of increasing sales through innovation and customer responsiveness, Fife made extensive use of output controls as the main way of evaluating the performance of his product and financial managers. Periodically, he would sit down with his executives and review the financial, sales, and cost figures for a product or product range.

However, when the figures failed to please him, he would verbally attack and abuse the executive concerned in front of his peers, who sat through the assault in embarrassed silence. Any attempts to fight back would merely prolong the attack, and top managers began to complain to board members that Fife was destroying work relationships. Moreover, top managers claimed that Fife's preoccupation with the short-term bottom line was causing problems for the organization because his focus on sales and cost targets was forcing them to cut back on research and development or customer service to meet the stringent targets that he set. Eventually, they pointed out, this practice would hurt customer relations. Thus Fife's managers claimed that his exclusive focus on output control goal setting was reducing flexibility and integration and threatening the company's future performance.

Whatever the truth in these claims, the board of directors (which Fife had appointed) listened to the disgruntled managers and decided that for the good of the organization they should ask Fife to resign. As Clyde Folley, the acting chairman put it, the board wanted "Nice quiet, level leadership" and the reestablishment of good working relationships between managers at all levels.[6] However, the stock market reacted differently to the news of Fife's departure, and the company's stock price plunged by over 20% on the announcement. Clearly, shareholders liked the effect of Fife's output controls on company performance even if his managers did not.

12.6 BUREAUCRATIC CONTROL

Market and output controls require relatively objective, measurable standards for monitoring and evaluating performance. Often measurable standards are difficult or expensive to develop, and when they are not sufficient to fulfill corporate objectives, managers must turn to bureaucratic control. **Bureaucratic control** is control through the establishment of a comprehensive system of rules and procedures to direct the actions or behavior of divisions, functions, and individuals.[8] Rules standardize behavior and make outcomes predictable. If employees follow the rules, then actions are performed and decisions handled

the same way time and time again. The result is predictability and accuracy, which are the goals of all control systems. In using bureaucratic control, the intention is not to specify the goals, but to standardize the way of reaching them.

Standardization

Standardization refers to the degree to which a company specifies decision making and coordination processes so that employee behavior becomes predictable.[9] Standardization reduces the agency problem because it specifies the behaviors required of divisions, functions, or individuals. In practice, there are three things that an organization can standardize: *inputs, conversion activities,* and *outputs.*

1. *Standardization of inputs.* One way in which an organization can control the behavior of both people and resources is by standardizing the inputs into the organization. This means that the organization screens inputs and allows only those that meet specified standards to enter. For example, if employees are the input in question, then one way of standardizing them is to recruit and select only those people who possess the qualities or skills specified by the organization. Arthur Andersen & Company, the accounting firm, is a very selective recruiter, as are most prestigious organizations. If the inputs in question are raw materials or component parts, then the same considerations apply. The Japanese are renowned for high quality and precise tolerances they demand from component parts to minimize problems with the product at the manufacturing stage. Just-in-time inventory systems also help standardize the flow of inputs.
2. *Standardization of conversion activities.* The aim of standardizing conversion activities is to program work activities so that they are done the same way time and time again. The goal is predictability. Bureaucratic controls, such as rules and procedures, are among the chief means by which companies can standardize throughputs, as McDonald's has done. Another way is to organize production tasks so that semifinished goods move from one production stage to the next in a predictable way to reduce the time and resources needed to produce outputs. The goal is to improve the efficiency with which goods are produced and to find improved ways to control and standardize production. Output controls here can be used by management to monitor and evaluate the success of its standardization efforts.
3. *Standardization of outputs.* The goal of standardizing outputs is to specify what the performance characteristics of the final product or service should be—what the dimensions or tolerances of the product should conform to, for example. To ensure that their products are standardized, companies apply quality control and use various criteria to measure this standardization. One criterion might be the number of goods returned from customers or the number of customer complaints. On production lines, periodic sampling of products can indicate whether they are meeting performance characteristics. Given the intensity of foreign competition, companies are devoting extra resources to standardizing outputs, not just to reduce costs but to retain customers. If the product's performance satisfies customers, they will continue buying from that company. For example, if you purchase a Japanese car and have no problems with its performance, which car are you most likely to buy

next time? That is why companies such as U.S. carmakers have been emphasizing the quality dimension of their products. They know how important standardizing outputs is in a competitive market.

As you saw earlier, McDonald's uses bureaucratic control to standardize all its activities. First, the quality of its inputs are standardized through controlling food suppliers and franchise holders. Then, in the throughput phase, its food operations are totally standardized by mechanization and by the training given restaurant employees. Consequently, in the output phase, burgers are produced uniformly and efficiently, with quick customer responsiveness. In general, fast-food restaurants and all types of service-oriented chain stores use standardization as a principal means of control.

Issues with Bureaucratic Control

As with other kinds of controls, the use of bureaucratic control is accompanied by problems which must be managed if the organization is to avoid strategic problems. First, top management must be careful to monitor and evaluate the usefulness of bureaucratic controls over time. Rules constrain people and lead to standardized, predictable behavior. However, rules are always easier to establish than to get rid of, and over time the number of rules an organization uses tends to increase. As new developments lead to additional rules, often the old rules are not discarded, and the company becomes overly bureaucratized. Consequently, the organization and the people in it become inflexible and are slow to react to changing or unusual circumstances. Such inflexibility can reduce a company's competitive advantage by lowering the pace of innovation and by reducing customer responsiveness. Similarly, inside the organization integration and coordination may fall apart as rules impede communication between functions. Managers must therefore be continually on the alert for opportunities to reduce the number of rules and procedures necessary to manage the business and should always prefer to discard a rule rather than use a new one.

The second major problem is the cost of using bureaucratic controls. Just as structure is expensive, so is bureaucratic control. To give a dramatic example, according to a recent estimate, 20 percent of the cost of health care is spent on managing the paperwork necessary to satisfy organizational and government health care rules and procedures. This amount runs into billions of dollars a year. Hence reducing the number of rules and procedures to the essential minimum is important. Management frequently neglects this task, however, and often only a change in strategic leadership brings the company back on course.

Output control and bureaucratic control work together and are typically used together. For example, in a multidivisional structure, first market controls and output controls are set up by corporate headquarters to monitor and evaluate divisional performance. Then inside each division bureaucratic controls are used to standardize behaviors so that divisional employees work toward divisional goals. Moreover, to prevent short-term profit-seeking behaviors from emerging because of the sole emphasis on output control, it is necessary to apply bureaucratic controls to evaluate other aspects of a division's or function's performance. For example, to prevent divisional managers from reducing research and development expenditures in order to improve bottom-line performance, the corporate center may establish rules that specify how much divisional managers must spend on R&D. Likewise, it is dangerous to only use

output control in evaluating salespeople, because this may encourage the hard sell at the expense of long-term customer loyalty—as happened at Sears. Hence many companies use bureaucratic control and also try to develop common norms and values and build an organizational culture to promote customer responsiveness.

12.7 ORGANIZATIONAL CULTURE

Organizational culture may be defined as the specific collection of norms, standards, and values that are shared by members of an organization and affect the way an organization does business.[10] Employees are not controlled by some external system of constraint, such as direct supervision, outputs, or rules and procedures. Rather, they are said to *internalize* the norms and values of the organization and make them part of their own value system.[11] Thus the value of culture for an organization is its ability to specify norms and values that govern employee behavior and solve the agency problem.[12]

Socialization is the term used to describe how people learn organizational culture. Through socialization, people internalize the norms and values of the culture and learn to act like existing personnel.[13] Control through culture is so powerful because, once these values are internalized, they become a part of the individual's values, and the individual follows organizational values without thinking about them. Very often the culture of an organization is transmitted to its members through the stories, myths, and language that people in the organization use, as well as by other means. (Figure 12.3 summarizes the various ways of transmitting culture.)

For example, some organizations, like Apple Computer and Microsoft are characterized by very informal working relationships; people come in and out of work as they please, wear casual clothes, and address each other informally. In other organizations, strict dress codes and forms of address between managers and subordinates are enforced and communication is only allowed through formal channels. The way in which culture developed in an IBM-Apple joint venture, described in Strategy in Action 12.3, illustrates how organizational culture affects organizational members' behavior.

Since both an organization's structure—the design of its task and reporting relationships—and its culture shape employees' behavior, it is crucial to match

Figure 12.3
Ways of Transmitting Culture

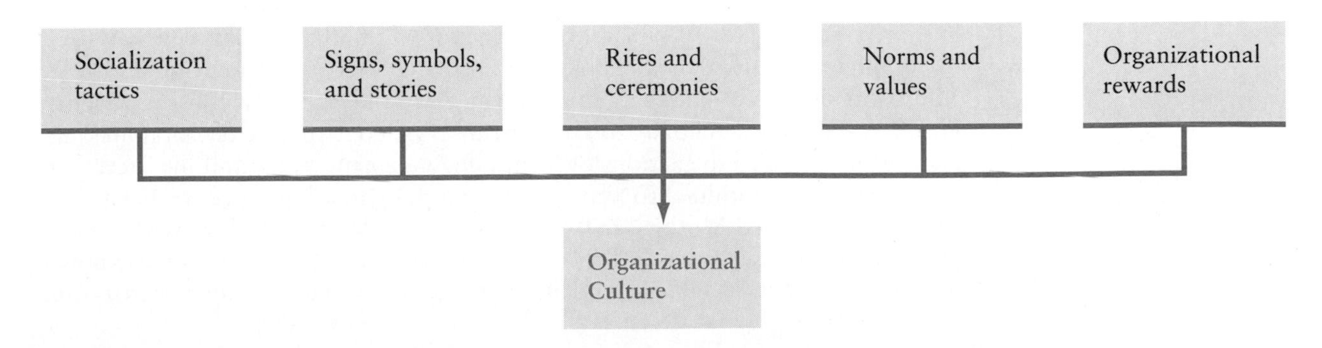

organizational structure and culture in order to implement strategy. The ways that organizations design and create their structures are discussed in Chapter 11. The question that remains is, how do they design and create their cultures? In general, organizational culture is the product of strategic leadership.

Culture and Strategic Leadership

First, organizational culture is created by the strategic leadership provided by an organization's founder and top managers. The organization's founder is particularly important in determining culture because the founder "imprints" his or her values and management style on the organization. For example, Walt Disney's conservative influence on the company he established continued until well after his death. Managers were afraid to experiment with new forms of entertainment because they were afraid "Walt Disney wouldn't like it." It took the installation of a new management team under Michael Eisner to turn around the company's fortunes and allow it to deal with the realities of the new entertainment industry. Similarly, Bill Gates has had a major influence on creating Microsoft's free-wheeling workaholic entrepreneurial culture, and at Hewlett-Packard, the founders established that company's norm that employees were expected to be innovative and self-reliant. For example, at Hewlett-Packard there is an informal norm that employees should experiment and use company resources to pursue independent projects as long as the projects are in the company's interests.

Over time, the leadership style established by the founder is transmitted to the company's managers, and as the company grows, it typically attracts new managers and employees who share the same values. Moreover, members of the organization typically recruit and select only those who do share their values. Thus over time a company's culture becomes more and more distinct as its members become more similar. The virtue of these shared values and common culture is that it *increases integration and improves coordination among organizational members*. For example, the common language that typically emerges in an organization because people share the same beliefs and values facilitates cooperation among managers. Similarly, rules and procedures and direct supervision are less important when shared norms and values control behavior and motivate employees. When organizational members buy into cultural norms and values, this bonds them to the organization and reduces the agency problem discussed earlier. That is, they are more likely to commit themselves to organizational goals and work actively toward achieving those goals.

Strategic leadership also affects organizational culture through the way managers design organizational structure—the way managers delegate authority and divide up task relationships. Microsoft chairman Bill Gates, for example, has always tried to keep his company as flat as possible, and has decentralized authority to small teams which are given control of all the resources they need to complete a project. As a result, he has created an entrepreneurial culture in Microsoft in which managers experiment and take risks. By contrast, Henry Ford I designed his company to give him absolute control over decision making. He even scrutinized the actions of his top management team, and his successor, Henry Ford II, continued to manage the company in a highly centralized way. The result for Ford Motor Car Co. was an organizational culture where managers became conservative and afraid to take risks, and the company was known for its slow pace of change and innovation. Thus the way an organization

STRATEGY IN ACTION 12.3

Taligent's New Culture

Taligent is a new company created through a joint venture by IBM and Apple to explore ways of developing a new operating system that would compete with Microsoft's Windows. The CEO, Joe Guglielmi, was charged with the mission of creating a corporate culture for Taligent that would enable it to blend the human and technological resources of both IBM and Apple to produce innovative products. Because the cultures of IBM and Apple are so different, Guglielmi faced a considerable challenge in creating a culture for the new company.

Apple has a freewheeling culture that encourages the company's scientists and programmers to experiment and to form informal task forces and teams to solve problems. To encourage creativity and quick decision making, norms and values emphasize employees' empowerment and their freedom to find their own solutions to problems. A manager's role is not to monitor or oversee employee activities, but to act as a facilitator and provide employees with the resources they need in order to solve problems. The use of formal decision-making procedures is kept to a minimum and face-to-face contact is the norm. By contrast, IBM has a very conservative, hierarchical culture, and decision making is a formal, centralized process. Both this process and the approach to problem solving are highly structured; managers at all levels of the hierarchy have to follow set procedures for approving a project. Norms and values emphasize the importance of consensus, and the company has specified procedures for monitoring and evaluating performance on an ongoing basis. As a result, decision making at IBM is very slow, since employees are used to following rules closely.

Guglielmi, brought up in the IBM culture, has had to tackle the problem of managing people who, used to Apple's much looser culture, resent having to report to IBM managers, who constantly want to know what's going on. For his part, Guglielmi has disliked not knowing what his Apple employees are doing and misses the security that IBM's hierarchical culture provides. To find a culture at Taligent that both Apple and IBM people can live with, he has accepted the informal Apple style, right down to an informal way of dressing, in order to speed decision making and enhance creativity. However, he has also created a system of output control to measure team performance periodically because he believes that no control means no direction and less creativity.

designs its structure affects the cultural norms and values that develop within the organization. Managers need to be aware of this fact when implementing their strategies.

Over time the culture that emerges in an organization can cause strategic problems. For example, if top managers all accept the same set of norms and values, the danger arises that they will be unable to steer the organization in a new strategic direction should the environment change and new competitors or technology demand such a change. Furthermore, having designed their structures, managers become used to the way they operate, and managers rarely recognize the important effect structure has on cultural norms and values. Thus organizational culture can promote *inertia*. At IBM, for instance, managers were unable to see—until it was too late—that the development of powerful personal computers and interactive, networking software would have long-term implications for IBM's cash cow, mainframe computers. Their blindness resulted from the tenets of IBM's culture that mainframes would always be the dominant product

design and personal computers would only be appendages to mainframes. Moreover, IBM's tall, centralized structure slowed decision making and encouraged the development of conservative norms and values, making managers averse to risk and reluctant to challenge the status quo. Digital Equipment Corp. (DEC) experienced problems similar to IBM's because its founder, Ken Olsen, told his managers for many years that "personal computers are just toys." Like Henry Ford, he developed a tall, centralized structure, which gave him total control over the organization—at least until the board of directors finally replaced him in a coup and put Robert Palmer in charge. (See Strategy in Action 11.3.)

As Chapter 1 points out, cognitive biases can distort the decision-making process. Over time the norms and values of an organization's culture can bias decision making and cause managers to misperceive the reality of the situation facing their company. To prevent these strategic leadership problems from arising, great care needs to be taken in composing the top management team.

The Composition of the Top Management Team

The composition of the top management team helps determine the company's strategic direction, and the personalities and vision of the team's members establish the norms and values that lower-level managers will follow. Researchers have found that when a company has a diverse top management team, with managers drawn from different functional backgrounds or from different organizations or national cultures, the threat of inertia and of faulty decision making is reduced. One of the reasons for IBM's failure to change was that almost all of its top managers came from inside IBM, and from the mainframe computer division. They had all been exposed to the same set of learning experiences and had developed similar norms and values. When Coca-Cola concluded that its top management team was becoming too inbred and homogeneous, it deliberately recruited a new top management team, including the CEO, composed of several foreign nationals, to manage its global strategy. Like Coco-Cola, many organizations are paying increasing attention to planning for executive succession in the top management team so that they can manage their cultures over time.

Traits of Strong Corporate Cultures

Several scholars in the field have tried to uncover the common traits that strong corporate cultures share and to find out whether there is a particular set of values that dominates strong cultures but is missing from the weak. Perhaps the best-known attempt is T. J. Peters and R. H. Waterman's account of the norms and values characteristic of successful organizations and their cultures.[14] They argue that successful organizations show three common value sets. First, successful companies have values promoting a *bias for action.* The emphasis is on autonomy and entrepreneurship, and employees are encouraged to take risks—for example, to create new products, even though there is no assurance that these products will be winners. Managers are closely involved in the day-to-day operations of the company and do not simply make strategic decisions isolated in some ivory tower, and employees have a "hands-on, value-driven approach."

The second set of values stems from the *nature of the organization's mission.* The company must stick with what it does best and maintain control over its core activities. A company can easily get sidetracked into pursuing activities outside its area of expertise just because they seem to promise a quick return. Man-

agement should cultivate values so that a company "sticks to the knitting," which means staying with the businesses it knows best. A company must also establish close relations with the customer as a way of improving its competitive position. After all, who knows more about a company's performance than those who use its products or services? By emphasizing customer-oriented values, organizations are able to learn customer needs and improve their ability to develop products and services customers desire. All these management values are strongly represented in companies such as IBM, Hewlett-Packard, and Toyota which are sure of their mission and take constant steps to maintain it.

The third set of values bears on *how to operate the organization*. A company should try to establish an organizational design that will motivate employees to do their best. Inherent in this set of values is the belief that productivity is obtained through people and that respect for the individual is the primary means by which a company can create the right atmosphere for productive behavior. As William Ouchi has noted, a similar philosophy pervades the culture of Japanese companies.[15] Many U.S. companies pay this kind of attention to their employees—for instance, Eastman Kodak, Procter & Gamble, and Levi Strauss. An emphasis on entrepreneurship and respect for the employee leads to the establishment of a structure that gives employees the latitude to make decisions and motivates them to succeed. Because a simple structure and a lean staff best fit this situation, the organization should be designed with only the number of managers and hierarchical levels that are necessary to get the job done. The organization should also be sufficiently decentralized to permit employee participation but centralized enough for management to make sure that the company pursues its strategic mission and that cultural values are followed.

These three main sets of values are at the heart of an organization's culture, and management transmits and maintains them through strategic leadership. Pursuing these values is not enough to ensure organizational success, however, and over time cultural values should change to suit the environment in which the company is operating. A company needs to establish the values that are good for it and base its organizational structure and control system on them. When that is accomplished, only those people who fit the values are recruited into the organization, and, through training, they become a part of the organization's culture. Thus the types of control systems chosen should reinforce and build on one another in a cohesive way. Organizational culture cannot by itself make structure work. It must be backed by output and bureaucratic controls and matched to a reward system so that employees will in fact cultivate organizational norms and values and modify their behavior to organizational objectives.

Summary: Types of Control Systems

Choosing a control system to match the firm's strategy and structure offers management a number of important challenges. Management must select controls that provide a framework to accurately monitor, measure, and evaluate whether or not they have achieved their goals and strategic objectives. Market and output controls must be backed up with bureaucratic control and organizational culture to ensure that the firm is achieving its goals in the most efficient way possible. In general, these controls should reinforce one another, and care must be taken to ensure that they do not result in unforeseen consequences, such as competition among functions, divisions, and individuals. It is the difficulty of

changing organizational culture that many top managers point to when they talk about reengineering their organization so that it can pursue new strategic goals. This is because culture is the product of the complex interaction of many factors such as top management, organizational structure and the organization's reward and incentive systems.

12.8 STRATEGIC REWARD SYSTEMS

Organizations also strive to control employee behavior by linking reward systems to their control systems.[16] An organization must decide which behaviors it wishes to reward, adopt a control system to measure these behaviors, and then link the reward structure to them. How to relate rewards to performance is a crucial strategic decision because it determines the incentive structure that affects the way managers and employees at all levels in the organization behave. You learned earlier how structure and control shape employee behavior. The design of the organization's incentive system is a vital element in the control process because it motivates and reinforces desired behaviors—that is, the behaviors desired by shareholders and managers. The incentive system can be used to overcome the agency problem and to align the interests of shareholders and managers, or of managers at different levels.

As Chapter 2 points out, top managers can be encouraged to work in the shareholders' interests by being rewarded with stock options linked to the company's long-term performance. Furthermore, as also noted earlier, companies such as Kodak and GM are requiring managers to buy company stock. When managers are made shareholders, the agency problem is greatly diminished, and managers are more motivated to pursue long-term rather than short-term goals. Similarly, in designing a pay system for salespeople, the choice would be whether to motivate salespeople through straight salary or salary plus a bonus based on how much is sold. Neiman Marcus, the luxury retailer, pays employees a straight salary because it wants to encourage high-quality service but discourage hard sell. Thus there are no incentives based on quantity sold. On the other hand, the pay system for rewarding car salespeople encourages high-pressure selling; it typically contains a large bonus for the number and price of cars sold.

Since the design of a company's reward system affects the kinds of behaviors found in an organizational setting, clearly it also affects the *kinds of norms, values, and culture that develop in an organization.* Thus top management teams rewarded solely by salary and those rewarded by stock options linked to performance are likely to have different norms and values. Specifically, top management teams rewarded with stock options may be more entrepreneurial and more concerned with increasing efficiency, quality, and innovation than those that lack this reward. Companies like Sears, GM, Kodak, and Westinghouse, which previously made little attempt to link performance to rewards, had slow-moving, bureaucratic cultures. All these companies now require managers to own company stock.

We now take a closer look at the types of reward systems available to strategic managers.[17] Generally, reward systems are found at the individual and group or total organizational levels. Often these systems are used in combination; for

example, merit raises at the individual level may be accompanied by a bonus based on divisional or corporate performance. Within each type, several forms of reward systems are available.

Individual Reward Systems

Piecework Plans Piecework plans are used when outputs can be objectively measured. Essentially, employees are paid on the basis of some set amount for each unit of output produced. Piecework plans are most commonly used for employees working on production lines, where individuals work alone and their performance can be directly measured. Because this system encourages quantity rather than quality, the company normally applies stringent quality controls to ensure that the quality is acceptable.

Commission Systems Commission systems resemble piecework systems, except that they are normally tied not to what is produced, but to how much is sold. Thus they are most commonly found in sales situations. Often the salaries of salespeople are based principally on commission to encourage superior performance. Thus first-rate salespeople can earn more than $1 million per year.

Bonus Plans Bonus plans at the individual level generally reward the performance of a company's key individuals, such as the CEO or senior vice presidents. The performance of these people is visible to the organization as a whole and to stakeholders such as shareholders. Consequently, there is a strong rationale for paying these individuals according to some measure of functional or divisional performance. A company must proceed carefully, however, if it is to avoid problems such as emphasis on short-run rather than long-term objectives. For example, paying bonuses based on quarterly or yearly ROI rather than on five-year growth can have a markedly different effect on the way strategic managers behave. As noted earlier, many companies are now insisting that members of their top management team own stock in their company. The aim is to motivate managers and tie their interests to those of the shareholders. As Strategy in Action 12.4 details, Campbell Soup Co. was one of the first companies to take this approach.

Group and Organizational Reward Systems

Group and organizational reward systems provide additional ways in which companies can relate pay to performance. In general, the problem with these systems is that the relationship is less direct and more difficult to measure than in the case of individually based systems. Consequently, they are viewed as less motivating. The most common reward systems at these levels involve group bonuses, profit sharing, employee stock options, and organization bonuses.

Group-based Bonus Systems Sometimes a company can establish project teams, or work groups, that perform all the operations needed to turn out a product or provide a service. This arrangement makes it possible to measure group performance and offer rewards on the basis of group productivity. The system can be highly motivating because employees are allowed to develop the best work procedures for doing the job and are responsible for improving their own productivity. For example, Wal-Mart supports a group bonus plan based on controlling shrinkage (that is, employee theft).

STRATEGY IN ACTION 12.4

How to Motivate a Top Manager

For years, Campbell Soup Co., based in Camden, New Jersey, has experienced deteriorating performance. Its operating costs are well above its archrival, Heinz Soup Co., which under the leadership of its CEO, Anthony J. F. O'Reilly, has been achieving record sales and profits. O'Reilly is paid a very high salary and bonus; in fact in 1992 he earned almost $37 million in salary and stock options. Heinz's other top managers are also given stock options. It was no surprise, therefore, when in 1993 Campbell Soup's board of directors, attributing Heinz's superior performance to its stock option plan for top managers, announced that it too was establishing a stock option plan for its CEO, David Johnson, and more than seventy other managers.

Under the terms of the plan, the CEO would be required to hold Campbell shares worth three times his 1992 salary of $757,000 by the end of 1994. Senior vice presidents would be expected to hold shares worth twice their salaries; vice presidents, shares worth one year's salary; and senior executives, shares worth one-half their salaries. Top managers would have to hold these shares for as long as they worked for the company. Clearly, Campbell's goal is to tie the fortunes of managers to the fortunes of the company. If the company reduces its costs by successfully reengineering its structure, the top managers will make millions of dollars in capital appreciation on their stock. But if their efforts fail to improve the company's performance, they will lose millions.

Profit-Sharing Systems Profit-sharing plans are designed to reward employees on the basis of the profit a company earns in any one time period. Such plans encourage employees to take a broad view of their activities and feel connected with the company as a whole. Wal-Mart uses this method as well to develop its organizational culture.

Employee Stock Option Systems Rather than reward employees on the basis of short-term profits, a company sometimes establishes an employee stock ownership system (ESOP) and allows employees to buy its shares at below-market prices, heightening employee motivation. As shareholders, the employees focus not only on short-term profits, but also on long-term capital appreciation, for they are now the company's owners. Over time, if enough employees participate, they can control a substantial stock holding, as do the employees of United Air Lines, and thus become vitally interested in the company's performance. ESOPs can be very important in developing corporate culture, as suggested by another IBM-Apple joint venture, described in Strategy in Action 12.5.

Organization Bonus Systems Profit is not the only basis on which a company can reward organization-wide performance. Rewards are also commonly based on cost savings, quality increases, or production increases obtained in the last time period. Because these systems usually require that outputs be measured accurately, they are most common in production-line organizations or in service companies, where it is possible to cost out the price of the services of personnel. The systems are mainly a backup to other forms of pay systems. In rare situa-

STRATEGY IN ACTION 12.5

Should Kaleida have an ESOP?

IBM and Apple Computer established a joint venture, named Kaleida Labs, Inc., to develop software for operating multimedia—a system where sound, text, vision, music, and so forth are simultaneously intertwined into programs for computers or television. To head the new venture, the companies recruited an entrepreneur, Nathaniel Goldhaber, who was given free rein to create a structure and culture that would speed product development. However, in 1993 Goldhaber was relieved of his duties as CEO; it was felt that he had not provided the strategic leadership that would bring the new company forward and mold the companies' 105 engineers into successful product teams. According to Goldhaber, creating a control and incentive structure to motivate these professional employees had been his hardest task, and he had proposed to IBM and Apple that he should be allowed to sell the company's stock to the public. Had they agreed, he would have been able to create an ESOP and reward engineers with stock options to motivate them. However, IBM and Apple rejected this strategy and decided to replace him and bring in a seasoned IBM veteran to manage the product development process. It remains to be seen what this new manager will do.

tions, however, they become the principal means of control. That is the case at Lincoln Electric Co., a company renowned for the success of its cost-savings group plan.

Control through organizational reward systems complements all the other forms of control we discuss in this chapter. Rewards act as the oil that makes a control system function effectively. To ensure that the right strategic behaviors are being rewarded, rewards should be closely linked to an organization's strategy. Moreover, they should be so designed that they do not lead to conflicts among divisions, functions, or individuals. Since organizational structure and organizational control and reward systems are not independent dimensions of organizational design, but are highly interrelated, they must be compatible if an organization is to implement its strategy successfully. Matching structure and control to strategy is the issue we focus on in Chapter 13.

12.9 SUMMARY OF CHAPTER

This chapter examines the types of control and reward systems available to strategic managers both to shape and to motivate behavior in order to enhance organizational performance. Companies must select the combination of controls that will make their organizational structure function effectively and meet the company's strategic objectives. Companies use market, output, and bureaucratic control, as well as culture, simultaneously because different types of controls fit different situations and different stakeholder groups.

The essential task for companies is to select controls that are consistent with one another and also match the organizational structure. Companies with a high

level of differentiation and integration require a more complex set of controls than those with a low degree of differentiation and integration. This chapter makes the following main points:

1. Organizational structure does not operate effectively unless the appropriate control and incentive systems are in place to shape and motivate employee behavior.
2. An agency problem exists when the interests of shareholders and managers, or managers at different levels in the organization, differ and one stakeholder group finds it difficult to monitor and control the behavior of the other. To solve the monitoring problem, companies develop control and incentive systems.
3. Strategic control is the process of setting targets, monitoring, evaluating, and rewarding organizational performance.
4. Control takes place at all levels in the organization: corporate, divisional, functional, and individual.
5. Effective control systems are flexible, accurate, and able to provide quick feedback to strategic planners.
6. Many kinds of performance standards are available to implement a company's strategy. The kinds of measures managers choose affect the way a company operates.
7. Control systems range from those directed at measuring outputs or productivity to those measuring behaviors or actions.
8. The two main forms of market control are stock market price and return on investment (ROI).
9. Output control establishes goals for divisions, functions, and individuals. It can be used only when outputs can be objectively measured.
10. Bureaucratic control through rules and standard operating procedures is used to control and standardize behavior when it is very difficult or expensive to measure outputs.
11. Organizational culture is the collection of norms and values that govern the way in which people act and behave inside the organization. Culture is control through a system of norms and values that individuals internalize as they are socialized into an organization.
12. An organization's culture is the product of a founder's or top management team's values and attitudes; of the way managers choose to design the organization's structure; and of the strategic reward systems managers use to shape and motivate employee behavior.
13. An organization's reward systems constitute the final form of control. A company designs its reward systems to provide employees with the incentives to make its structure work effectively and to align their interests with organizational goals and objectives.
14. Organizations use all these forms of control simultaneously. Management must select and combine those that are consistent with each other and with the strategy and structure of the organization.

Discussion Questions

1. What are the relationships among differentiation, integration, and strategic control systems? Why are these relationships important?
2. For each of the structures we discuss in Chapter 11, outline the control systems most suitable for managing them.
3. What kind of control and reward systems you would be likely to find in (a) a small manufacturing company, (b) a chain store, (c) a high-tech company, and (d) a big five accounting firm?

Article File 12

Find an example of a company that has recently changed one or more of its control and incentive systems. Which of its control systems did it change (for instance, output control or culture)? Why did it make the change? What does it hope to achieve by the change? How will changing the control system affect the way its structure operates?

Strategic Management Project: Module 12

For this part of your project you need to obtain information about your company's control and incentive systems. This information may be hard to obtain unless you are doing your project on a real company and can interview managers directly. However, some forms of information, such as top management compensation, are available in the company's annual reports or 10-K. If your company is well known, magazines like *Fortune* or *Business Week* frequently report on corporate culture or control issues. Nevertheless, you may be forced to make some bold assumptions to complete this part of the project.

1. What are the major kinds of control problems facing your company? How do these control problems relate to your organization's structure, which you identified in the last chapter?
2. With the information at your disposal, list the main kinds of control systems used by your organization to solve these problems. Specifically, what use does your company make of (a) market control, (b) output control, (c) bureaucratic control, and (d) organizational culture?
3. What kinds of behaviors is the organization trying to (a) shape and (b) motivate through the use of these control systems?
4. Where would an agency problem most likely arise in your company? How does your company use its control systems to resolve or manage agency problems?
5. What role does the top management team play in creating the culture of your organization? Can you identify the characteristic norms and values that

describe the way people behave in your organization? How does the design of the organization's structure affect its culture?

6. Collect the salary and compensation data for your company's top management from its annual reports. How does the organization use rewards to shape and motivate its managers? For example, how much of top managers' total compensation is based on bonuses and stock options and how much is based on straight salary?
7. Does the organization offer other kinds of employees any incentives based on performance? What kinds of incentives? For example, is there an employee stock ownership plan in operation?
8. Based on this analysis, do you think that your organization's control system is functioning effectively? For example, is your organization collecting the right kinds of information? Is it measuring the right kinds of behavior? How could the control system be improved?
9. To what degree is there a match between your company's structure and its control and incentive systems? That is, are its control systems allowing it to operate its structure effectively? How could they be improved?

Endnotes

1. W. G. Ouchi, "The Transmission of Control Through Organizational Hierarchy," *Academy of Management Journal,* 21 (1978), 173–192; W. H. Newman, *Constructive Control* (Englewood Cliffs, N.J.: Prentice-Hall, 1975).
2. H. L. Tosi, Jr., and L. R. Gomez-Mejia, "The Decoupling of CEO Pay and Performance: An Agency Theory Perspective," *Administrative Science Quarterly,* 34, (1989), 169–189. H. Milton and A. Raviv, "Optimal Incentive Contracts with Imperfect Information," *Journal of Economic Theory,* 20, (1979), 231–259.
3. W. G. Ouchi, "The Relationship Between Organizational Structure and Organizational Control," *Administrative Science Quarterly,* 22 (1977), 95–113.
4. J. D. Thompson, *Organizations in Action* (New York: McGraw-Hill, 1967), Ch. 10; W. G. Ouchi, "A Conceptual Framework for the Design of Organizational Control Systems," *Management Science,* 25 (1979), 833–848.
5. E. Flamholtz, "Organizational Control Systems as a Managerial Tool," *California Management Review* (Winter 1979), 50–58.
6. R. L. Rose, "After Turning Around Giddings and Lewis, Fife Is Turned Out Himself," *Wall Street Journal,* June 22, 1993, A1.
7. J. Flynn and C. Del Valle, "Did Sears Take Its Customers for a Ride?" *Business Week,* August 3, 1992, pp. 24–25.
8. O. E. Williamson, *Markets and Hierarchies* (New York: Free Press, 1975); W. G. Ouchi, "Markets, Bureaucracies, and Clans," *Administrative Science Quarterly,* 25 (1980), 129–141.
9. H. Mintzberg, *The Structuring of Organizations* (Englewood Cliffs, N.J.: Prentice-Hall, 1979), pp. 5–9.
10. L. Smircich, "Concepts of Culture and Organizational Analysis," *Administrative Science Quarterly,* 28 (1983), 339–358.
11. G. R. Jones, "Socialization Tactics, Self-Efficacy, and Newcomers' Adjustments to Organizations," *Academy of Management Journal,* 29 (1986), 262–279.
12. Ouchi, "Markets, Bureaucracies, and Clans," p. 130.
13. J. Van Maanen and E. H. Schein, "Towards a Theory of Organizational Socialization," in *Research in Organizational Behavior,* ed. B. M. Staw (Greenwich, Conn.: JAI Press, 1979), pp. 1, 209–264.
14. T. J. Peters and R. H. Waterman, *In Search of Excellence: Lessons from America's Best-Run Companies* (New York: Harper & Row, 1982).
15. W. G. Ouchi, *Theory Z. How American Business Can Meet the Japanese Challenge* (Reading, Mass.: Addison-Wesley, 1981).
16. E. E. Lawler III, *Motivation in Work Organizations* (Monterey, Calif.: Brooks/Cole, 1973); Galbraith and Kazanjian, *Strategy Implementation,* Ch. 6 (St. Paul, Minn.: West, 1992).
17. E. E. Lawler III, "The Design of Effective Reward Systems," in *Handbook of Organizational Behavior,* ed. J. W. Lorsch (Englewood Cliffs, N.J.: Prentice-Hall, 1987), 386–422; R. Mathis and J. Jackson, *Personnel,* 2nd ed. (St. Paul, Minn.: West, 1979), p. 456.

13 Matching Structure and Control to Strategy

13.1 OPENING CASE: HUGHES AIRCRAFT REENGINEERS ITS STRUCTURE

Hughes Aircraft Company, owned by General Motors, is one of the large U.S. defense companies that has been battered by the end of the cold war and the decline in the defense budget. Hughes had been accustomed to a protected environment in which lavish government revenues allowed it to develop advanced technology for military uses, such as missiles, satellites, and radar systems. However, by 1990, Hughes was confronted with a major strategic problem: how to compete in a new environment, where government revenues were scarce and where its skills and capabilities were directed at military uses. To survive, Hughes had to find a new strategy, based on developing new technology for nonmilitary uses—and find it fast.

As a first step in changing Hughes's direction, GM appointed C. Michael Armstrong, an ex-IBM top manager, as CEO of Hughes in 1991. In IBM's European division, Armstrong had developed a reputation as someone who could turn around a company and redeploy its resources quickly and effectively. GM hoped he could do so at Hughes. Armstrong began his task by analyzing the company's strategy and structure. What he found was a firm pursuing a differentiated strategy based on developing advanced technological products. To pursue its differentiated strategy, Hughes had developed a divisional structure to lead its development efforts. It had created seven separate technology divisions, each responsible for a different kind of product—missiles, radar, and so forth. Over time, the organization had become very tall and centralized, as each technology division developed its own empire to support its efforts. The primary coordination between divisions took place at the top of the organization where top divisional managers met regularly with corporate managers to report on and plan future product developments.

Armstrong recognized that this fit between strategy and structure might be appropriate for a company operating in a protected environment, where money was not a problem. But it was not appropriate for a company facing intense pressure to lower costs and develop products for nonmilitary applications, such as consumer electronics and home satellites. The divisional structure duplicated expensive R&D activities, and no mechanism was in place to promote the sharing of knowledge and expertise among the different divisions. Moreover, there were few incentives for managers to cut costs because scarce resources had not been a problem, and managers had been rewarded mainly for the success of their product development efforts. Armstrong realized that to make the company more competitive and improve the way it utilized its skills and resources he had to find a new operating strategy and structure.

Armstrong began the process of change by focusing the company's strategy on customers and markets, not on technology and products. Henceforth the needs of customers, not the needs of technology, would be the logic behind the organization of the company's activities. He changed the structure from a divisional one based on technology to a structure based on the needs of customers. The seven technology divisions were reengineered into five market groups according to the kinds of customer needs they were satisfying. Thus consumer electronics became one market group, while industrial and commercial applications became another. Then techno-

logical expertise was reorganized to serve the needs of each kind of customer. Continuing his reengineering program, Armstrong slashed the number of levels in the managerial hierarchy, eliminating two levels in order to bring managers closer to the customer. He continued this reengineering effort by decentralizing authority and pushing decision making down into the divisions, so that lower level managers could better respond to customer needs. In addition, he reorganized the company's international operations by transferring Hughes managers from the United States to foreign countries so that they would be closer to their customers.

To make this new customer-oriented structure work effectively, Armstrong also changed the organization's control systems. He created a system of output controls based on benchmarking competitors' costs to provide managers with standards against which to evaluate their performance, and to force them to pay attention to costs and quality. He then set up new incentive programs for managers and workers at all levels, linking the programs to achievement of the new targets for efficiency, quality, and customer responsiveness. Finally, he worked hard with his top management team to establish and promote the norms and values of a customer-oriented organizational culture across the new market divisions. Henceforth at Hughes technology would be made to fit the customer and not vice versa.

Armstrong's efforts to engineer a new fit between strategy and structure at Hughes have been spectacularly successful. His top management team has fully bought into the new corporate culture, and divisional managers are adopting new entrepreneurial values based on meeting customer needs. The company's costs have dropped by 30 percent, its profits have leaped up by over 50 percent, and its stock has shot up by over 40 percent since Armstrong took over.[1] Hughes is now organized to pursue a simultaneous differentiation/low-cost strategy, using its leading-edge technology to provide customers with quality products at competitive prices. It looks as if Hughes is one defense company that will do well in the new competitive environment.

Discussion Questions

1. What problems did Armstrong discover with Hughes Aircraft Company's strategy and structure?
2. What steps did he take to reengineer the company?

13.2 OVERVIEW

At Hughes, Michael Armstrong and his top management team moved to implement the right mix of structure and control systems so that the company could pursue a new strategy to manage the competitive environment. In this chapter, we discuss how strategic choice at the corporate, business, and functional levels affects the choice of structure and control systems—in other words, how to match different forms of structure and control to strategy. As we emphasize in Chapter 1, the issue facing strategic managers is to match strategy formulation with strategy implementation. All the tools of strategy formulation and implementation are discussed in previous chapters. Now we put the two sides of the equation together and examine the issues involved in greater detail.

First, we consider how functional-level strategy and the attempt to achieve superior efficiency, quality, innovation, and customer responsiveness affect structure and control. Second, we examine how a company's choice of generic business-level strategy influences the choice of structure and control for implementing the strategy. Third, we focus on the implementation of a global strategy and discuss how to match different global strategies with different global structures. Fourth, we take up the special problems that different kinds of corporate-level strategy pose for strategic managers in designing a structure

and note how changes in corporate-level strategy over time affect the form of structure and control systems adopted by a company. Finally, we examine the problems relating to the two entry strategies discussed in Chapter 10: managing mergers and acquisitions and providing the organizational setting that encourages internal venturing.

13.3 STRUCTURE AND CONTROL AT THE FUNCTIONAL LEVEL

In Chapter 5, in dealing with functional-level strategies, we discuss how a company's functions can help it achieve superior efficiency, quality, innovation, and customer responsiveness—the four building blocks of competitive advantage. We also discuss how distinctive competencies could be developed in each function. Then, in Chapter 6, we show that at the business level different generic competitive strategies require the development of different types of distinctive competencies. In this section, we consider how a company can create a structure and control system that permit the development of various distinctive functional competencies or skills.

Decisions at the functional level fall into two categories: choices about the level of vertical differentiation and choices about monitoring and evaluation systems. (Choices about horizontal differentiation are not relevant here because we are considering each function individually.) The choices made depend on the distinctive competency that a company is pursuing.

Manufacturing

In manufacturing, functional strategy usually centers on improving efficiency, quality, and customer responsiveness. A company must create an organizational setting in which managers can learn from experience curve effects how to economize on costs. Traditionally, to move down the experience-curve quickly, companies have exercised tight control over work activities and employees and developed tall, centralized hierarchies to squeeze out costs wherever possible. As part of their attempt to increase efficiency, companies have also made great use of bureaucratic and output controls to reduce costs. Activities are standardized—for example, human inputs are standardized through the recruitment and training of personnel, the work process is standardized or programmed to reduce costs, and quality control is used to make sure that outputs are being produced correctly. In addition, managers are closely monitored and controlled through output control.

Recently, however, following the lead of Japanese companies such as Toyota and Sony, which operate total quality management (TQM) and flexible manufacturing systems, many U.S. companies have been moving to change the way they design the manufacturing setting. As we have discussed in Chapter 5, successful TQM requires a different approach to organizational design. With TQM, the inputs and involvement of all employees in the decision-making process are necessary to improve production efficiency and quality. Thus it becomes necessary to decentralize authority in order to motivate workers to improve the production process. In TQM, work teams are created and workers are given the

responsibility and authority to discover and implement improved work procedures. Quality control circles are created to exchange information and suggestions about problems and work procedures. A bonus system or ESOP is frequently established to motivate workers and to allow them to share in the increased value that TQM often produces. No longer are managers employed purely to supervise workers and make sure they are doing the job. Each team assumes the supervisory burden and this results in a major savings of bureaucratic costs. Work teams are often given the responsibility for controlling and disciplining their own members and even the right to decide who should work in their team. Frequently, norms and values become an important means of control in these settings, and this type of control matches the new decentralized team approach.

However, while workers are given more freedom to control their activities, the extensive use of output control and the continuous measurement of efficiency and quality standards ensure that the work team's activities meet the goals set for the function by management. Standardization is still the principal form of control, and efficiency and quality increase as new and improved work rules and procedures are developed to raise the level of standardization. The aim is to find the match between structure and control and a TQM approach so that manufacturing develops the distinctive competency that leads to superior efficiency and quality.

Research and Development

The functional strategy for a research and development department is to develop a distinctive competency in innovation and, as in Hughes Aircraft, to develop technology that results in products that fit customer needs. Consequently, the department's structure and control systems should be designed to provide the coordination necessary for scientists and engineers to bring products quickly to market. Moreover, these systems should also motivate R&D scientists to develop innovative products or processes. In practice, R&D departments typically have flat, decentralized structures and group scientists into teams. Flatter structures give research and development personnel the freedom and autonomy to be innovative. Furthermore, because it is difficult to evaluate research and development scientists and the importance of their outputs can only be judged over the long term, adding layers of hierarchy would simply raise bureaucratic costs and waste resources.[2] By using teams, a company can exploit scientists' ability to work jointly in solving problems and to enhance each other's performance. In small teams, too, common norms and values that highly trained employees bring to the situation promote coordination. A culture for innovation frequently emerges to control employee behavior, as has occurred at Motorola and Intel, where the race to be first energizes the R&D teams. Strategy in Action 13.1 describes Intel's use of R&D teams to innovate and improve computer chips.

To spur teams to work effectively, the reward system should be linked to the performance of the team. If scientists, individually or in a team, do not share in the profits that a company obtains from its new products or processes, they may have little motivation to contribute greatly to the team. Moreover, scientists could leave a company to set up their own company in competition with their former employer. To prevent the departure of their key employees and to encourage high motivation, companies like Merck, Intel, and Microsoft give their

STRATEGY IN ACTION 13.1

Intel's R&D Department

Intel Corp. is the world leader in the development of chips, or the microprocessors that are the heart of all computers. It is very profitable, and in 1992 it earned record profits because it had a monopoly on the production of the 486 chip, which was then the industry standard. In the race to produce new and improved chips, Intel is constantly under attack from companies like Motorola, Digital Equipment, and Japan's NEC and has to protect its competitive advantage. Consequently, the need to develop new chips or improved versions of existing ones forms the basis of the company's differentiation strategy.

To speed product development, Intel has developed a team structure in its R&D department. To try to ensure that it will always have the leading-edge technology, the company has six different teams working on the next generation of chips so that each team's innovations can be put together to make the final product—for example, the Pentium chip that Intel unveiled in 1993. However, it also has six teams simultaneously working on the subsequent generation of chips and six teams working on the generation of chips to follow that one. In other words, to sustain its leading-edge technology and maintain its monopoly, the company has created a team structure where its scientists and engineers work on the frontiers of chip research so that they can control the technology of tomorrow. This approach has certainly paid off for Intel. The company's stock price doubled in 1992 and again in 1993. Indeed, it is expected to outperform the market for as long as Intel's teams succeed in making the company the innovation leader in the chip industry.

researchers stock options and rewards tied to their individual performance, as well as to the performance of their team and of the company.

Sales

Like research and development, the sales function usually has a flat structure. Most commonly, three hierarchical levels—sales director, regional or product sales managers, and individual salespeople—can accommodate even large sales forces. Flat structures are possible because the organization does not depend on direct supervision for control. Salespeople's activities are often complex; moreover, because they are dispersed in the field, these employees are difficult to monitor. Rather than depend on the hierarchy, the sales function usually employs output and bureaucratic controls. Output controls, such as specific sales goals or goals for increasing customer responsiveness, can be easily established and monitored by supervisors. Then output controls can be linked to a bonus reward system to motivate salespeople. Bureaucratic controls—for instance, detailed reports that salespeople file describing their interactions with customers—can also be used to standardize salespeople's behavior and make it easy for supervisors to review their performance.[3]

Similar design considerations apply to the other functions, such as accounting, finance, engineering, or human resource management. Managers must select the right combination of structure and control mechanisms to allow each function to contribute to achieving superior efficiency, quality, innovation, and customer responsiveness. In today's competitive environment, where reducing costs is often required for survival, more and more companies are flattening their functional hierarchies and decentralizing control to reduce bureaucratic costs.

However, to reduce the agency problem, companies have to develop control and incentive systems that align employee interests with those of the organization and that motivate the employees.

13.4 STRUCTURE AND CONTROL AT THE BUSINESS LEVEL

Building competitive advantage through organizational design starts at the functional level. But the key to successful strategy implementation is a structure that links and combines the skills and competencies of a company's value-creation functions, allowing it to pursue a business-level strategy. In this section, we consider the organizational design issues for a company seeking to implement one of the generic competitive business-level strategies in order to retain its competitive advantage.

Generic Business-Level Strategies

Designing the right mix of structure and control at the business level is a continuation of designing a company's functional departments. Having implemented the right structure and control system for each individual function, the company must then implement the organizational arrangements so that all the functions can be managed together to achieve business-level strategy objectives. Because the focus is on managing cross-functional relationships, the choice of *horizontal differentiation* (grouping of organizational activities) and *integration* for achieving business-level strategies becomes very important.[4] Control systems must also be selected with the monitoring and evaluating of cross-functional activities in mind. Table 13.1 summarizes the appropriate organizational structure and control systems that companies can use when following a low-cost, differentiation, or focused strategy.

Table 13.1
Generic Strategy, Structure, and Control

	Strategy		
	Cost Leadership	Differentiation	Focus
Appropriate structure	Functional	Product-team or matrix	Functional
Integrating mechanisms	Center on manufacturing	Center on R&D or marketing	Center on product or customer
Output control	Great use (e.g., cost control)	Some use (e.g., quality goals)	Some use (e.g., cost and quality)
Bureaucratic control	Some use (e.g., budgets, standardization)	Great use (e.g., rules, budgets)	Some use (e.g., budgets)
Organizational culture	Little use (e.g., quality control circles)	Great use (e.g., norms and values)	Great use (e.g., norms and values)

Cost-Leadership Strategy and Structure

The aim of the cost-leadership strategy is to make the company pursuing it the lowest-cost producer in the market.[5] At the business level, this means reducing costs not just in production, but across all functions in the organization—including research and development and sales and marketing.

If a company is pursuing a cost-leadership strategy, its research and development efforts probably focus on product and process development rather than on the more expensive product innovation, which carries no guarantee of success. In other words, the company stresses research that improves product characteristics or lowers the cost of making existing products. Similarly, a company tries to decrease the cost of sales and marketing by offering a standard product to a mass market rather than by offering different products aimed at different market segments, which is also more expensive.[6]

To implement such a strategy, the cost leader chooses a structure and control system that has a low level of bureaucratic costs. As we discuss in earlier chapters, bureaucratic costs are the costs of managing a company's strategy through structure and control. Structure and control are expensive, and the more complex the structure—the higher its level of differentiation and integration—the higher are bureaucratic costs. To economize on bureaucratic costs, a cost leader will therefore choose the simplest or least expensive structure compatible with the needs of the low-cost strategy.

In practice, the structure chosen is normally a functional structure. This structure is relatively inexpensive to operate because it is based on a low level of differentiation and integration. Even in a functional structure, cross-functional teams can be organized around the manufacturing function. For example, a TQM program implemented through task forces and teams can be developed to integrate the activities of manufacturing and the other functions. This allows for continuous improvements in the rules and procedures for standardizing task activities, which is a major source of cost saving.[7]

A cost-leadership company also tries to keep its structure as flat as possible to reduce bureaucratic costs, and functional structures have relatively flat structures. The cost leader continuously evaluates whether or not it needs that extra level in the hierarchy and whether or not it can decentralize authority—perhaps to the work group—to keep costs low. Seagate Technology, the producer of hard disks, is an example of a cost leader that continually streamlines its structure to maintain a competitive advantage. It periodically reduces levels in the hierarchy and institutes strict production controls to minimize costs. This process has kept it ahead of its Japanese competitors. Similarly, John Reed, the chairman of Citicorp recently flattened his organization's structure, wiping out two levels of management and terminating dozens of executives to reduce costs. His cost-cutting efforts helped turn a loss of $457 million in 1991 into a $722 million profit in 1992, and Citicorp's share price increased from $9 to $29.[8]

To further reduce costs, cost-leadership companies try to use the cheapest and easiest forms of control available—output controls. For each function, a company adopts output controls that allow it to closely monitor and evaluate functional performance. In the manufacturing function, for example, the company imposes tight controls and stresses meeting budgets based on production, cost, or quality targets.[9] In research and development, too, the emphasis falls on the bottom line. R&D personnel eager to demonstrate their contribution to saving costs may focus their efforts on improving process technology, where actual savings are calculable. H. J. Heinz clearly illustrates such efforts. In following a cost-

leadership strategy, it places enormous emphasis on production improvements that can reduce the cost of a can of beans. Like manufacturing and research and development, the sales function is closely monitored, and sales targets are usually challenging. Cost-leadership companies, however, are likely to reward employees through generous incentive and bonus plans to encourage high performance. Often their culture is based on values that emphasize the bottom line. H. J. Heinz, Lincoln Electric, and Pepsico are examples of such companies.

In short, pursuing a successful cost-leadership strategy requires close attention to the design of structure and control in order to limit bureaucratic costs. Managers, rules, and organizational control mechanisms cost money, and low-cost companies must try to economize when implementing their structures. When a company's competitive advantage depends on achieving and maintaining a low-cost advantage, adopting the right organizational arrangements is vital.

Differentiation Strategy and Structure

To pursue a differentiation strategy, a company must develop a distinctive competency in a function such as research and development or marketing and sales. As discussed earlier, doing so usually means that a company produces a wider range of products, serves more market niches, and generally has to customize its products to the needs of different customers. These factors make it difficult to standardize activities; they also increase the demands made on functional personnel. Hence the differentiated company usually employs a more complex structure—that is, a structure with a higher level of differentiation and integration—than the cost leader. Consequently, the bureaucratic costs of a differentiator are higher than those of a cost leader, but these costs are recouped through higher value it adds to its differentiated products.

For example, to make its product unique in the eyes of the customer, a differentiated company must design its structure and control system around the *particular source* of its competitive advantage.[10] Suppose that the differentiator's strength lies in technological competency; the company has the cutting-edge technology. In this case, the company's structure and control systems should be designed around the research and development function. Implementing a *matrix structure* like Texas Instruments and TRW Systems have done, promotes innovation and speeds product development, for this type of structure permits intensive cross-functional integration. Integrating mechanisms, such as task forces and teams, help transfer knowledge among functions and are designed around the research and development function. For example, sales, marketing, and production targets are geared to research and development goals; marketing devises advertising programs that focus on technological possibilities, and salespeople are evaluated on their understanding of new product characteristics and their ability to inform potential customers about them. Stringent sales targets are unlikely to be set in this situation because the goal is quality of service.

As you saw in Chapter 11, however, there are many problems associated with a matrix structure. The changing composition of product teams, the ambiguity arising from having two bosses, the use of more complex integration mechanisms, and the greater difficulty of monitoring and evaluating the work of teams greatly increase the bureaucratic costs necessary to coordinate and control task activities. Nevertheless, companies are willing to incur the higher bureaucratic costs of a matrix structure when it allows them to create more value from their differentiation strategy.

Sometimes the advantages of a differentiation strategy can be obtained from a less expensive structure. For example, when the source of the differentiator's competitive advantage is superior quality or customer responsiveness, companies design a structure around their products, and a *product-team* or *geographic* structure may fit best. In a product-team structure, each product group can focus on the needs of a particular product market. Support functions like research and development or sales are organized by product, and task forces and teams have a product, not a research orientation. If a company's differentiation strategy is based on serving the needs of a number of different market segments, a geographic structure becomes appropriate. Thus, if it focuses on types of customers, a differentiated company may use a geographic structure designed according to a regional logic, or even according to different types of customers, such as businesses, individual consumers, or the government. Both Compaq and Rockwell have recently reorganized their structures to concentrate on the needs of specific customers or regions. The new geographic structure allows them to become more responsive to the needs of specific groups of customers and to serve those needs better. For example, information about changing customer preferences can be quickly fed back to R&D and product design so that a company can protect its competitive advantage.

The control systems used to match the structure can also be geared to the company's distinctive competency. For the differentiator, it is important that the various functions do not pull in different directions; indeed, cooperation among the functions is vital for cross-functional integration. But when functions work together, output controls become much harder to use. In general, it is much more difficult to measure the performance of people in different functions when they are engaged in cooperative efforts. Consequently, a company must rely more on behavior controls and shared norms and values when pursuing a strategy of differentiation. That is why companies pursuing a differentiation strategy often have a markedly different kind of culture than those pursuing a low-cost strategy. Because the quality of human resources—good scientists, designers, or marketing people—is often the source of differentiation, these organizations have a culture based on professionalism or collegiality, a culture that emphasizes the distinctiveness of the human resource rather than the high pressure of the bottom line.[11] Hewlett-Packard, Motorola, and Coca-Cola, all of which emphasize some kind of distinctive competency, exemplify firms with professional cultures.

The bureaucratic costs of operating the structure and control system of the differentiator are higher than the cost leader's, but the benefits are also greater if companies can reap the rewards of a premium price. Companies are willing to accept a higher level of bureaucratic costs provided that their structure and control systems lead to superior efficiency, quality, innovation, or customer responsiveness.

Implementing a Combined Differentiation and Cost-Leadership Strategy

As we discuss in Chapter 6, pursuing a combined differentiation and low-cost strategy is the most difficult challenge facing a company at the business level. On the one hand, the company has to coordinate its activities around manufacturing and materials management to implement a cost-reduction strategy. On the other, it must also coordinate its activities around the source of its differentiation advantage, such as R&D or marketing, to protect its competency in innovation or customer responsiveness. For many companies in this situation, the

answer has been the product-team structure, discussed in Chapter 11. It is far less costly to operate than a matrix structure but provides a much higher level of cross-functional integration than the functional structure.

As you recall from Chapter 11, a product-team structure groups task activities by product, and each product line is managed by a cross-functional team, which provides all the support services necessary to bring the product to market. The role of the product team is to protect and enhance a company's differentiation advantage while coordinating with manufacturing to lower costs. Chrysler, Hallmark, and Xerox are among the companies that have recently reorganized from a functional to a product-team structure so that they can simultaneously speed product development and control their operating costs.

Moreover, companies have also been switching from a matrix structure to a product-team structure because their costs of using the matrix far exceeded the benefits. At Digital Equipment Corp., for example, bureaucratic costs were rising steeply because different project teams were duplicating each other's work, but the company lacked the centralized control needed to utilize resources well. After shifting to the product-team structure, it could control resource allocation between projects and product lines more effectively. It could also create output controls to motivate project management to both reduce costs *and* speed product development. John Fluke Mfg., a leader in electronic testing tools, is another example of a company that has made use of product teams to speed product development. The company assembles "Phoenix teams"—cross-functional groups that are given 100 days and $100,000 to identify a market need and a new product to fill it.[12] So far these teams have led to the development of two successful new products. Strategy in Action 13.2 describes how 3M uses cross-functional teams to promote a culture of innovation.

Focus Strategy and Structure

In Chapter 6, we define focus strategy as a strategy directed at a particular market or customer segment. A company focuses on a product or range of products aimed at one sort of customer or region. This strategy tends to have higher production costs than the other two strategies because output levels are lower, making it harder to obtain substantial economies of scale. As a result, a focused company must exercise cost control. On the other hand, because some attribute of its product usually gives the focused company its unique advantage—possibly its ability to provide customers with high-quality, personalized service—a focused company has to develop a unique competency. For both these reasons, the structure and control system adopted by the focused company has to be inexpensive to operate but flexible enough to allow a distinctive competency to emerge.

The focused company normally adopts a functional structure to meet these needs. This structure is appropriate because it is complex enough to manage the activities necessary to service the needs of the market segment or produce a narrow range of products. At the same time, the bureaucratic costs of operating a functional structure are relatively low, and there is less need for complex, expensive integrating mechanisms. This structure permits more personal control and flexibility than the other two, and so reduces bureaucratic costs while fostering the development of a distinctive competency.[13] Given its small size, a focused company can rely less on bureaucratic control and more on culture, which is vital to the development of a service competency. Although output controls need to be used in production and sales, this form of control is inexpensive in a small organization.

The combination of functional structure and low cost of control helps offset the higher costs of production while still allowing the firm to develop unique strengths. It is little wonder, then, that there are so many focused companies. Additionally, because a focused company's competitive advantage is often based on personalized service, the flexibility of this kind of structure lets the company respond quickly to customer needs and change its products in response to customer requests. The structure, then, backs up the strategy and helps the firm develop and maintain its distinctive competency.

Au Bon Pain Company Inc., a fast-food chain specializing in fancy coffees and baked goods such as croissants, is a good example of a company that recognized the need to design a structure and control system to match a focused strategy aimed at an upscale customer group. To encourage franchises to perform highly and satisfy customer needs, it decentralized control to each franchise, making each a self-contained functional unit. Then, through a profit-sharing plan that rewarded cost cutting and quality, it gave each franchise manager the incentive to create a set of control arrangements that minimized costs but maximized quality of service. The result was a strategy-structure fit that led to a massive increase in franchise profits.

Summary Companies pursuing a generic business-level strategy must adopt the appropriate form of structure and control if they are to use their resources effectively to develop superior efficiency, quality, innovation, and customer responsiveness. Companies are willing to bear the bureaucratic costs of operating organizational structure and control systems if these systems increase their ability to create value from lowering their costs or charging a premium price for their products. Hence, over time, companies must manage and change their structures to allow them to create value. However, many companies do *not* use the right forms of structure over time and fail to manage their strategies. These companies are not as successful and do not survive as long as those that do match their strategy, structure, and control systems.[14]

13.5 DESIGNING A GLOBAL STRUCTURE

In Chapter 8, we note that most large companies have a global dimension to their strategy because they produce and sell their products in international markets. For example, Procter & Gamble and food companies such as Heinz, Kellogg Co., and Nestlé Enterprises Inc., have production operations throughout the world, as do the large auto companies and computer makers. In this section, we examine how the four principal global strategies a company can adopt affect its choice of structure and control.

You may recall from Chapter 8 that (1) a *multidomestic strategy* is oriented toward local responsiveness, and a company establishes semiautonomous national units in each country in which it operates to produce and customize products to local markets; (2) an *international strategy* is based on R&D and marketing being centralized at home and all the other value-creation functions being decentralized to national units; (3) a *global strategy* is oriented toward cost reduction, with all the principal value-creation functions centralized at the

STRATEGY IN ACTION 13.2

How 3M Uses Teams to Build Culture

A company well known for product innovation, 3M aims to achieve at least 25 percent of its growth each year through new products developed within the last five years. To promote product development, 3M has always taken care to design its structure and culture so that they provide employees with the freedom and motivation to experiment and take risks. For example, 3M has an informal norm that researchers should use 15 percent of their time to develop projects of their own choosing. It was this norm that brought about the development of new products such as Post-it note pads. In addition, 3M has been careful to establish career ladders for its scientists in order to gain their long-term commitment, and it rewards successful product innovators with substantial bonuses. All these practices have gained the loyalty and support of its scientists and helped create a culture of innovation.

The company has also recognized the increasing importance of linking and coordinating the efforts of people in different functions to speed the product development effort. As we have noted, people in different functions tend to develop different subunit orientations and to focus their efforts on their own tasks to the exclusion of the needs of other functions. The danger of such tendencies is that each function will develop norms and values that suit its own needs but do little to promote organizational coordination and integration.

To avoid this problem, 3M has established a system of cross-functional teams composed of members of the product development, process development, marketing, manufacturing, packaging, and other functions to create organization-wide norms and values of innovation. So that all groups have a common focus, the teams work closely with customers; customers' needs become the platform on which the different functions can then apply their skills and capabilities. For example, one of 3M's cross-functional teams worked closely with diaper makers to develop the right kind of sticky tape for their needs.[15]

To promote integration in the team, and foster cooperative norms and values, each team is headed by a "product champion," who takes the responsibility for building cohesive team relationships and developing a team culture. In addition, one of 3M's top managers becomes a "management sponsor," whose job is to help the team get resources and to provide support when the going gets tough. After all, product development is a very risky process and many projects do not work out. Finally, 3M established the Golden Step Program to honor and reward cross-functional teams that introduce successful new products. Through all these means, 3M has used its cross-functional teams to create a culture where innovation is a valued activity and to develop norms and values that support and reward the sharing of information among scientists and among people in different functions. Clearly, all this attention to creating a culture of innovation has paid off for 3M.

optimal global location; and (4) a *transnational strategy* attempts to achieve both local responsiveness and global integration so that some functions are centralized at the optimal global location while others are decentralized, both to achieve local responsiveness and to facilitate global learning.

If a company is to operate each strategy successfully, the need to coordinate and integrate global task activities increases as the company moves from a multidomestic to an international to a global and then to a transnational strategy. For example, the bureaucratic costs of managing a transnational strategy are much higher than those of managing a multidomestic strategy. To achieve a transnational strategy, a company transfers its distinctive competencies to the global location where they can create the most value; then it establishes a

global network to coordinate the foreign and domestic divisions. This coordination involves managing global resource transfers to facilitate global learning. Compared with the other strategies, more managerial time has to be spent coordinating organizational resources and capabilities to achieve the global synergies that justify pursuing a transnational strategy. By contrast, pursuing a multidomestic strategy does not require coordination of activities on a global level because value-creation activities are handled locally, by country or world region. The international and global strategies fit in between the other two strategies: although products have to be sold and marketed globally, and hence global product transfers must be managed, there is less need to coordinate resource transfers than for a transnational strategy.

The implication, then, is that as companies change from a multidomestic to an international, global, or transnational strategy they require a more complex structure and control system to coordinate the value-creation activities associated with that strategy. Therefore, the bureaucratic costs increase at each stage: for a multidomestic strategy, they are low, for an international strategy, medium; for a global strategy, high; and for a transnational strategy, very high (see Table 13.2). In general, the choice of structure and control systems for managing a global business is a function of three factors:

1. The decision how to distribute and allocate responsibility and authority between domestic and foreign managers so that effective control over a company's foreign operations is maintained.
2. Selection of a level of horizontal differentiation that groups foreign operation tasks with domestic operations in a way that allows the best use of resources and serves the needs of foreign customers most effectively.
3. Selection of the right kinds of integration mechanism and organizational culture to make the structure function effectively.

Table 13.2
Global Strategy-Structure Relationships

	Multidomestic Strategy	International Strategy	Global Strategy	Transnational Strategy
	Low ◄—	Need for Coordination		—► High
	Low ◄—	Bureaucratic Costs		—► High
Centralization of Authority	Decentralized to National Unit	Core Competencies Centralized Others Decentralized to National Units	Centralized at Optimal Global Location	Simultaneously Centralized and Decentralized
Horizontal Differentiation	Global Area Structure	International Division Structure	Global Product Group Structure	Global Matrix Structure "Matrix in the Mind"
Need for Complex Integrating Mechanisms	Low	Medium	High	Very High
Organizational Culture	Not Important	Quite Important	Important	Very Important

Table 13.2 summarizes the appropriate design choices for companies pursuing each of these strategies.

Multidomestic Strategy and Structure

When a company pursues a multidomestic strategy, it generally operates with a global area structure (Figure 13.1). When using this structure, a company duplicates all value-creation activities and establishes a foreign division in every country or world area in which it operates. Authority is then decentralized to managers in each foreign division, and they devise the appropriate strategy for responding to the needs of the local environment. Because corporate headquarters managers are much farther away from the scene of operations, it makes sense to decentralize control and grant decision-making authority to managers in the foreign operations. Managers at global headquarters use market and output controls, such as rate of return, growth in market share, or operation costs to evaluate the performance of foreign divisions. On the basis of such global comparisons, they can make global capital allocation decisions and orchestrate the global transfer of new knowledge among divisions.

A company that makes and sells the same products in many different markets often groups its foreign subsidiaries into world regions to simplify the coordination of products across countries. Europe might be one region, the Pacific Rim another, and the Middle East a third. Such grouping allows the same set of market and bureaucratic controls to be applied across all divisions inside a region. Thus companies can obtain synergies from dealing with broadly similar cultures because information can be transmitted more easily. For example, consumer preferences regarding product design and marketing are likely to be more similar among countries in one world region than among countries in different world regions.

Because the foreign divisions themselves have little or no contact with each other, no integrating mechanisms are needed. Nor does a global organizational culture develop as there are no transfers of personnel or informal contacts among managers from the various world regions. Car companies like Chrysler, General Motors, and Ford all used to employ global area structures to manage their foreign operations. Ford of Europe, for example, had little or no contact with its U.S. parent, and capital was the principal resource exchanged.

One problem with a global area structure and a multidomestic strategy is that the duplication of specialist activities raises costs. Moreover, the company is not capitalizing on opportunities to trade information and knowledge on a global basis or to take advantage of low-cost manufacturing opportunities.

Figure 13.1
Global Area Structure

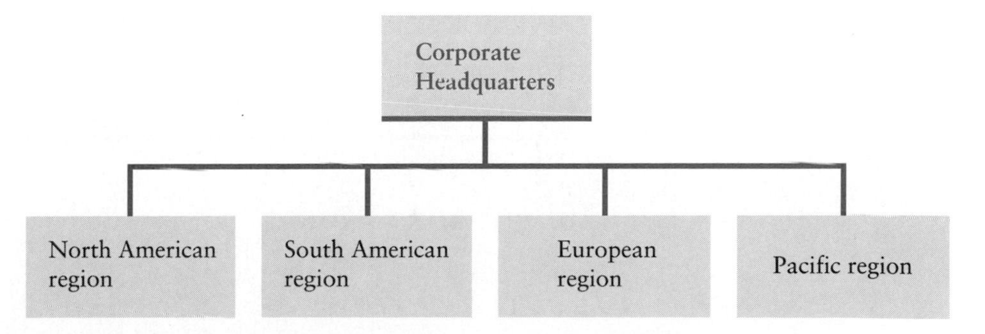

Multidomestic companies have chosen to keep bureaucratic costs low; however, they lose the many benefits of operating globally.

International Strategy and Structure

A company pursuing an international strategy adopts a different route to global expansion. Normally, the company shifts to this strategy when it begins selling its domestically made products in foreign markets. Until recently, companies like Mercedes-Benz or Jaguar made no attempt to produce in a foreign market; instead, they distributed and sold their domestically produced cars internationally. Such companies usually just add a **foreign operations department** to their existing structure and continue to use the same control system. If a company is using a functional structure, this department has to coordinate manufacturing, sales, and research and development activities with the needs of the foreign market. Efforts at customization are minimal, however.

In the foreign country, the company usually establishes a subsidiary to handle sales and distribution. For example, the Mercedes-Benz foreign subsidiaries allocate dealerships, organize supplies of spare parts, and, of course, sell cars. A system of bureaucratic controls is then established to keep the home office informed of changes in sales, spare parts requirements, and so on.

A company with many different products or businesses operating from a multidivisional structure has the challenging problem of coordinating the flow of different products across different countries. To manage these transfers, many companies create an international division, which they add to their existing divisional structure.[16] (See Figure 13.2.)

International operations are managed as a separate divisional business, whose managers are given the authority and responsibility for coordinating domestic product divisions and foreign markets. The international division also controls

Figure 13.2
International Division Structure

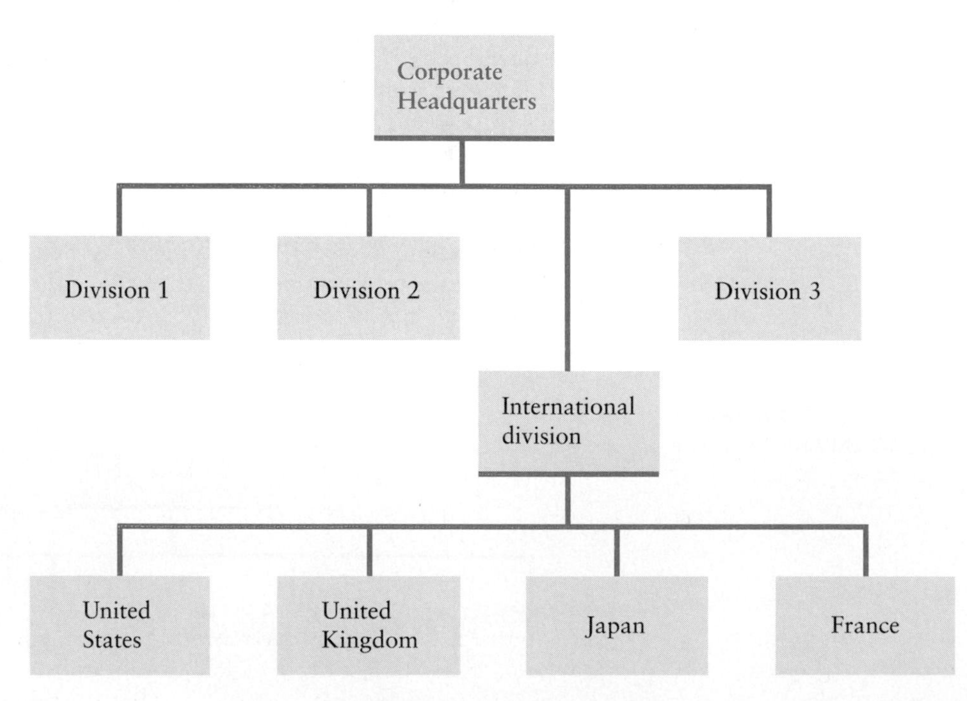

Figure 13.3
Global Product Group Structure

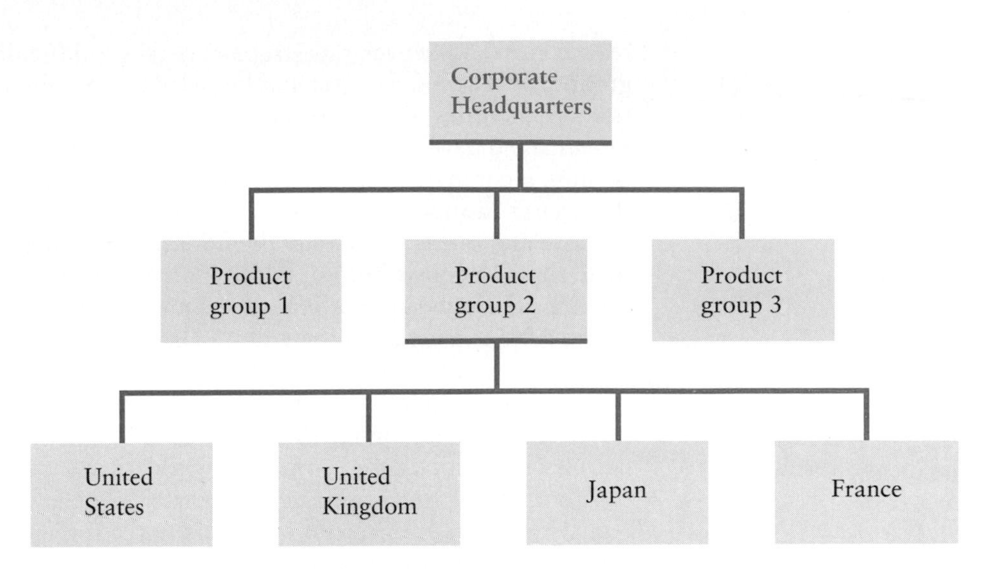

the foreign subsidiaries that market the products and decides how much authority to delegate to foreign management. This arrangement permits the company to engage in more complex foreign operations at relatively low bureaucratic costs. However, managers in the foreign countries are essentially under the control of managers in the international division, and if the domestic and foreign managers compete for control of operations in the foreign country, conflict and lack of cooperation can result.

Global Strategy and Structure

A company embarks on a global strategy when it starts to locate manufacturing and all the other value-creation activities in the lowest-cost global location to increase efficiency, quality, and innovation. In seeking to obtain the gains from global learning, a company must cope with greater coordination and integration problems. It has to find a structure that can coordinate resource transfers between corporate headquarters and foreign divisions while providing the centralized control that a global strategy requires. The answer for many companies is a **global product group structure** (Figure 13.3).

In this structure, a product group headquarters (similar to an SBU headquarters) is created to coordinate the activities of the domestic and foreign divisions within the product group. Product group managers in the home country are responsible for organizing all aspects of value creation on a global basis. The product group structure allows managers to decide how best to pursue a global strategy—for example, to decide which value-creation activities, such as manufacturing or product design, should be performed in which country to increase efficiency. Increasingly, U.S. and Japanese companies are moving manufacturing to low-cost countries like China but establishing product design centers in Europe or the United States to take advantage of foreign skills and capabilities.

Transnational Strategy and Structure

The main failing of the global product group structure is that while it allows a company to achieve superior efficiency and quality, it is weak when it comes to customer responsiveness because the focus is still on centralized control to

reduce costs. Moreover, this structure makes it difficult for the different product groups to trade information and knowledge, and obtain the benefits of cooperation. Sometimes the potential gains from sharing product, marketing, or research and development knowledge between product groups are very high, but because a company lacks a structure that can coordinate the groups' activities, these gains cannot be achieved.

More and more, companies are adopting **global matrix structures**, which let them simultaneously reduce costs by increasing efficiency *and* differentiate their activities through superior innovation and customer responsiveness. Figure 13.4 shows such a structure, adopted by a large chemical company like Du Pont.

On the vertical axis, instead of functions, are the company's *product groups*, which provide specialist services such as R&D, product design, and marketing information to the foreign divisions, or SBUs. For example, these might be the petroleum, plastics, drug, or fertilizer product groups. On the horizontal axis are the company's *foreign divisions, or SBUs*, in the various countries or world regions in which it operates. Managers in the foreign subsidiary control foreign operations and through a system of bureaucratic controls report to divisional personnel back in the United States. They are also responsible, together with U.S. divisional personnel, for developing control and reward systems that promote the sharing of marketing or research and development information to achieve gains from synergies.

This structure both provides a great deal of local flexibility and gives divisional personnel in the United States considerable access to information about local affairs. Additionally, the matrix form allows knowledge and experience to be transferred among geographic regions and among divisions and regions. Since it offers many opportunities for face-to-face contact between domestic and foreign managers, the matrix structure facilitates the transmission of company norms and values, and hence the development of a global corporate culture. This

Figure 13.4
Global Matrix Structure

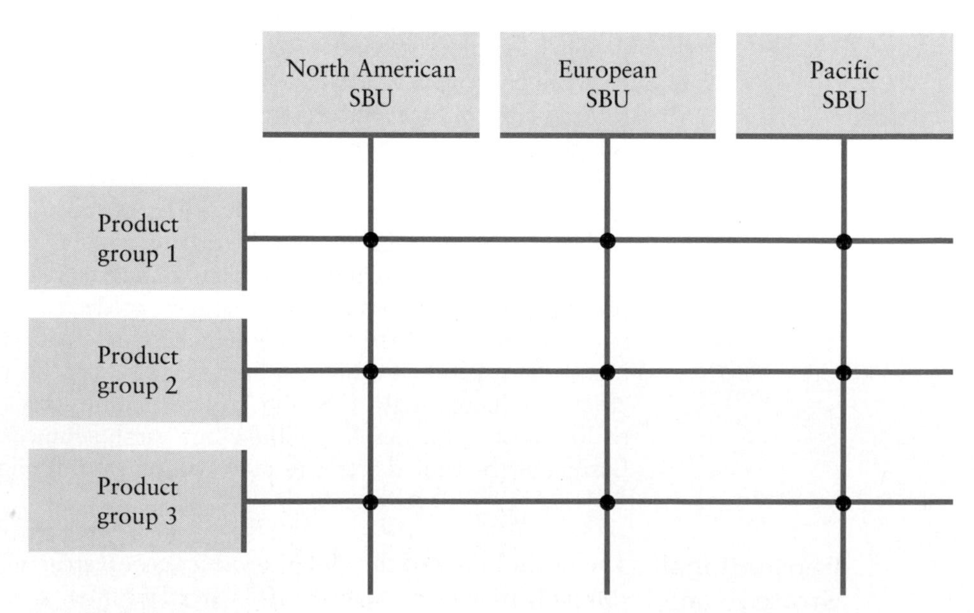

is especially important for an international company, where lines of communication are longer and information is subject to distortion. Club Med, Inc., for instance, fully exploits these synergies in the way it manages its holiday resorts. The matrix also lets each home division balance production so that, for example, a lack of demand in one world region can be compensated by increased demand in another. Philip Morris balances cigarette production: slumping demand in the United States is countered by supplying regions where cigarette sales are expanding. Similarly, Japanese car manufacturers plan their international strategy to compensate for import restrictions or currency changes in the world market.

To make these matrix structures work, many companies strive to develop a strong international organizational culture to facilitate communication and coordination among managers. For example, companies are increasingly transferring managers between foreign and domestic operations to give them foreign experience, so that they can develop a global view. Furthermore, to improve integration, companies are trying to form global networks of managers so that they can turn to each other for help on a global basis. The idea is to create a **matrix in the mind**—to develop the information networks that let a company capitalize on the skills and capabilities of its personnel globally.[17] To foster the development of the matrix-in-the-mind concept and promote cooperation, companies are also using electronic integrating devices such as on-line teleconferencing, and zap mail, between different parts of their operations, both globally and domestically. For example, Hitachi coordinates its nineteen Japanese laboratories by means of an on-line teleconferencing system, and both Microsoft and Hewlett-Packard make extensive use of electronic computer systems to integrate their activities.

These integration mechanisms provide the extra coordination that helps the global matrix structure work effectively. It is a very complex structure to operate and carries a high level of bureaucratic costs. However, the potential gains for a company in terms of superior efficiency, quality, innovation, *and* customer responsiveness make these costs worthwhile. More and more, in the complicated game of international competition, companies must adopt many of these elements of a global matrix to survive. Nestlé found itself in this situation, as Strategy in Action 13.3 details.

Summary Most large companies have an international component in their organizational structures. The issue for international companies, as for all others, is to adopt the structure and control system that best fits their strategy. The need to implement international strategy successfully has put increasing pressures on corporate managers to design the company's structure and controls so that the firm can respond to the challenges of the world market.

13.6 STRUCTURE AND CONTROL AT THE CORPORATE LEVEL

At the corporate level, a company needs to choose the organizational structure that will enable it to operate efficiently in a number of different businesses. The goal is always to use the structure and control system that is associated with the

STRATEGY IN ACTION 13.3

Reengineering Nestlé's Global Structure

Nestlé, based in Vevey, Switzerland, is the world's biggest food company. In 1992, its global sales passed $40 billion a year—a figure it wants to double by the year 2000. To achieve this goal, the company has been pursuing an ambitious program of global expansion by acquiring many famous companies—for instance Perrier, the French mineral water producer, and Rowntree Mackintosh, the British candy maker. In the United States, Nestlé bought the giant Carnation Company in 1985, and it also purchased Stouffer Foods Corp., and Contadina, among other large food companies.

Traditionally, Nestlé pursued a multidomestic strategy and managed its operating companies through a global area structure. In each country, each individual company—such as Carnation—was responsible for managing all aspects of its business-level strategy. Each Nestlé company throughout the world was free to control its own product development and marketing and to manage all local operations. Corporate resource decisions, such as capital investment, and acquisitions or expansion were decided at the Vevey headquarters by Nestle's corporate executives. Because all important corporate decisions were made centrally at headquarters, the size of the corporate staff needed to plan corporate strategy increased dramatically. By 1990 Nestlé's Chairman, Helmut Maucher, realized that the company had major problems.

Corporate managers had become very remote from the difficulties experienced by the operating companies, and the centralized operating structure slowed down decision making. Nestlé had trouble responding quickly to the changing environment. Moreover, the company was forfeiting all the gains from global learning and possible synergies from resource sharing between operating companies and world regions because each company was operated separately and corporate executives made no attempt to integrate across companies around the world. Maucher realized that the company could not increase its sales and profits through its existing operating structure. If it was to create more value, it had to find a new way of organizing its activities.

Maucher started the reengineering of Nestlé's structure from the top down. He massively reduced the power of corporate management by decentralizing authority to the managers of seven product groups, which he created to oversee the company's major product lines—for example, coffee, milk, and candy—on a global level. The role of each product group was to integrate the activities of operating companies in their area in order to obtain synergies and the gains from global learning. After the change, managers in the candy product group, for instance, began orchestrating the marketing and sale of Rowntree candy products, such as After Eight Mints and Smarties, throughout Europe, and sales climbed by 60 percent.

Maucher then turned his attention to how the operating companies worked in each country or world region. In the United States, for example, each Nestlé operating company, like Carnation, acted independently and separately. No attempt was made to share skills and resources even between businesses within the same country. Maucher changed this. He grouped all the operating companies within a country or region into one SBU and then created a team of SBU managers to link and coordinate the activities of the various companies in that country. When the different companies or divisions started to share joint purchasing, marketing, and sales activities, major cost savings resulted. In the United States, the SBU management team, headed by Timm Krull, reduced the number of sales officers nationwide from 115 to 22, and decreased the number of suppliers of packaging from 43 to 3.[18]

Finally, Maucher decided to use a matrix structure to integrate the activities of the seven global product groups with the operations of Nestlé's country- or region-based SBUs. The goal of this matrix structure is to have the company pursue a transnational strategy, allowing it to obtain the gains from global learning and cost reduction. For

example, Timm Krull now spends one week every month in Vevey with product group executives, discussing ways of exploiting and sharing the resources of the company on a global basis. So far, this new decentralized matrix structure has speeded decision making and product development and enabled the company to integrate the activities of its many new acquisitions. Maucher hopes it will help Nestlé reach its ambitious sales goal by the year 2000.

lowest level of bureaucratic costs. The structure normally chosen at the corporate level is the multidivisional structure. The larger and more diverse the businesses in the corporate portfolio, the more likely is the company to have a multidivisional structure. The reason is that each division requires the services of full-scale specialist support functions and that a headquarters corporate staff is needed to oversee and evaluate divisional operations. Once it selects a divisional structure, a company must make two more choices: the right mix of integrating mechanisms to match the particular divisional structure and the right control systems to make the divisional structure work. Below, we discuss how the corporate-level strategies of vertical integration, related diversification, and unrelated diversification affect the choice of structure and control systems.

As we discuss in Chapter 9, the main reason a company pursues vertical integration is to achieve *economies of integration* among divisions.[19] For example, the company can coordinate resource-scheduling decisions among divisions to reduce costs. For instance, locating a rolling mill next to a steel furnace saves the costs of reheating steel ingots. Similarly, the chief gains from related diversification come from obtaining *economies of scope* among divisions. Divisions benefit by the transfer of core competencies such as R&D or by sharing distribution and sales networks. With both of these strategies, the benefits to the company come from some transfer of resources among divisions. To secure these benefits, the company must coordinate activities among divisions. Consequently, structure and control must be designed to handle the transfer of resources among divisions.

In the case of unrelated diversification, however, the benefits to the company come from restructuring and the establishment of an *internal capital market,* which allows corporate personnel to make better allocations of capital than the external capital market. With this strategy, there are no transactions or exchanges among divisions; each operates separately. Structure and control must therefore be designed to allow each division to operate independently.

A company's choice of structure and control mechanisms depends on the degree to which a company must control the interactions among divisions. The more interdependent the divisions—that is, the more they depend on each other for resources—the more complex are the control and integration mechanisms required to integrate their activities and make the strategy work.[20] Consequently, as the need for integration increases, so too does the level of bureaucratic costs. However, once again, a company is willing to bear the increased bureaucratic costs associated with operating a more complex strategy if the strategy creates more value. This is illustrated in Table 13.3 which also indicates what forms of structure and control that companies should adopt to manage the three corporate strategies. We examine them in detail in the next sections.

Unrelated Diversification

Because there are *no linkages* among divisions, unrelated diversification is the easiest and cheapest strategy to manage; it is associated with the lowest level of bureaucratic costs. The main requirement of the structure and control system is that it lets corporate personnel easily and accurately evaluate divisional performance. Thus companies use a multidivisional structure, and each division is evaluated by strict return on investment criteria. A company also applies sophisticated accounting controls to obtain information quickly from the divisions so that corporate managers can readily compare divisions on several dimensions. Textron and Dover are good examples of companies that use sophisticated computer networks and accounting controls to manage their structures, which allow them almost daily access to divisional performance.

Divisions usually have considerable autonomy, unless they fail to reach their return on investment objectives. Generally, corporate headquarters is not interested in the types of business-level strategy pursued by each division unless there are problems. If problems arise, corporate headquarters may step in to take corrective action, perhaps replacing managers or providing additional financial resources, depending on the reason for the problem. If they see no possibility of a turnaround, however, corporate personnel may just as easily decide to divest the division. The multidivisional structure allows the unrelated company to operate its businesses as a portfolio of investments, which can be bought and sold as business conditions change. Usually, managers in the various divisions do not know one another, and they may not know what companies are in the corporate portfolio.

The use of market controls to manage a company means that no integration among divisions is necessary. This is why the bureaucratic costs of managing an unrelated company are low. The biggest problem facing corporate personnel is deciding on capital allocations to the various divisions so that the overall profitability of the portfolio is maximized. They also have to oversee divisional management and make sure that divisions are achieving return on investment targets.

Table 13.3
Corporate Strategy and Structure and Control

			Type of Control		
Corporate Strategy	Appropriate Structure	Need for Integration	Market Control	Bureaucratic Control	Organizational Culture
Unrelated diversification	Multidivisional	Low (no exchanges between divisions)	Great use (e.g., ROI)	Some use (e.g., budgets)	Little use
Vertical integration	Multidivisional	Medium (scheduling resource transfers)	Great use (e.g., ROI, transfer pricing)	Great use (e.g., standardization, budgets)	Some use (e.g., shared norms and values)
Related diversification	Multidivisional	High (achieve synergies between divisions by integrating roles)	Little use	Great use (e.g., rules, budgets)	Great use (e.g., norms, values, common language)

STRATEGY IN ACTION 13.4

Alco Standard Gets It Right

Alco Standard, based in Valley Forge, Pennsylvania, is one of the largest office supply companies in the United States, distributing office and paper supplies and materials through a nationwide network of wholly owned distribution companies. It pursues a highly successful strategy of unrelated diversification. Since 1965 the company has bought and sold over 300 different companies. It used to be involved in over 50 different industries, but now operates 50 businesses in only two main areas: office products and paper distribution. However, the corporate office makes no attempt to intervene in the activities of the different divisions.

The policy of Alco's top management is that authority and control should be completely decentralized to the managers in each of the company's businesses. Each business is left alone to make its own manufacturing or purchasing decisions even though some potential synergies, in the form of corporation-wide purchasing or marketing, are being lost. Top management pursues this nonintervention policy because it believes that the gains from allowing its managers to act as independent entrepreneurs exceed any potential economies of scope that might result from coordinating interdivisional activities. It believes that a decentralized operating system allows a big company to act like a small company, avoiding the problem of growing bureaucracy and organizational inertia.

At Alco, top management interprets its role as relieving the divisions of administrative chores, such as bookkeeping and accounting, and collecting market information on competitive pricing and products, which allows divisional managers to improve their business-level strategy. Centralizing these information activities reduces each division's bureaucratic costs and provides the standardization that lets top management make better resource allocation decisions. Alco's division heads are regarded as partners in the corporate enterprise and are rewarded through stock options linked to the performance of their divisions. So far, Alco has been very successful with its decentralized operating structure and has achieved a compound growth rate of 19 percent a year.[21]

Alco Standard's way of managing its businesses—described in Strategy in Action 13.4—demonstrates how to operate a strategy of unrelated diversification.

Vertical Integration

Vertical integration is a more expensive strategy to manage because *sequential resource flows* from one division to the next must be coordinated. The multidivisional structure effects such coordination. This structure provides the centralized control necessary for the vertically integrated company to achieve benefits from the control of resource transfers. Corporate personnel assume the responsibility for devising market and bureaucratic controls to promote the efficient transfer of resources among divisions. Complex rules and procedures are instituted to manage interdivisional relationships and specify how exchanges are to be made; consequently, bureaucratic costs rise. In addition, an internal transfer pricing system is created to allow one division to sell its products to the next. As previously noted, these complex links can lead to ill will among divisions, and so corporate personnel must try to minimize divisional conflicts.

Centralizing authority at corporate headquarters must be done with care in vertically related companies. It carries the risk of involving corporate personnel

in operating issues at the business level to the point where the divisions lose their autonomy and motivation. As we point out in Chapter 11, the company must strike the right balance of centralized control at corporate headquarters and decentralized control at the divisional level if it is to implement this strategy successfully.

Because their interests are at stake, divisions need to have input into scheduling and resource transfer decisions. For example, the plastics division in a chemical company has a vital interest in the activities of the oil division, for the quality of the products it gets from the oil division determines the quality of its own products. Divisional integrating mechanisms can bring about direct coordination and information transfers among divisions.[22] To handle communication among divisions, a company sets up task forces or teams for the purpose; it can also establish liaison roles. In high-tech and chemical companies, for example, integrating roles among divisions are common. These integrating mechanisms also increase bureaucratic costs.

Thus a strategy of vertical integration is managed through a combination of corporate and divisional controls. Although the organizational structure and control systems used for managing this strategy have higher bureaucratic costs than those used for unrelated diversification, the benefits derived from vertical integration often outweigh its extra costs.

Related Diversification

In the case of related diversification, divisions share research and development knowledge, information, customer bases, and goodwill to obtain gains from economies of scope. The process is difficult to manage, and so a multidivisional structure is used to facilitate the transfer of resources to obtain synergies. Even with this structure, however, high levels of resource sharing and joint production by divisions make it hard for corporate managers to measure the performance of each individual division. Besides, the divisions themselves may not want to exchange products or knowledge because transfer prices—inherently difficult to set—are perceived as unfair. If a related company is to obtain gains from synergy, it has to adopt complicated forms of integration and control at the divisional level to make the structure work efficiently.

First, market control is impossible because resources are shared. Therefore, the company needs to develop a corporate culture that stresses cooperation among divisions and to set corporate, rather than divisional, goals. Second, corporate managers must establish sophisticated integrating devices to ensure coordination among divisions. Integrating roles and teams are crucial because they provide the context in which managers from different divisions can meet and develop a common vision of corporate goals. Hewlett-Packard, for instance, created three new high-level integrating teams to make certain that the new products developed by its technology group made their way quickly to its product divisions. All this extra integration is very expensive, however, and must be carefully managed.

An organization with a multidivisional structure must have the right mix of incentives and rewards for cooperation if it is to achieve gains from sharing skills and resources among divisions. With unrelated diversification, divisions operate autonomously, and the company can quite easily reward managers on their division's individual performance. With related diversification, however, rewarding

divisions is more difficult because they are engaged in joint production, and strategic managers must be sensitive and alert to achieve equity in rewards among divisions. The aim always is to design the structure so that it can maximize the benefits from the strategy at the lowest bureaucratic cost.

Managing a strategy of related diversification also raises the issue of how much authority to centralize and how much to decentralize. Corporate managers need to take a close look at how their controls affect divisional performance and autonomy. If corporate managers get too involved in the day-to-day operations of the divisions, they can endanger divisional autonomy and undercut divisional managers' decision making. Corporate managers, after all, see everything from a corporate, rather than a divisional, perspective. For instance, in the Heinz example mentioned earlier, management tried to develop one form of competitive advantage, a low-cost advantage, in every division.[23] Although this approach may work well for Heinz, it may be markedly inappropriate for a company that is operating a totally diverse set of businesses, each of which needs to develop its own unique competency. Too much corporate control can put divisional managers in a straitjacket. When too many managers become involved in managing the business, performance suffers and bureaucratic costs escalate. Companies like IBM and General Motors experienced this problem; their corporate staffs became top-heavy, slowing decision making and draining company profits.

Managers must be sensitive to the need of readjusting their controls and form of divisional structure to achieve their objectives. Mixed structural forms, such as the strategic business unit (SBU) structure, are useful for this purpose because this structure can be designed so that companies can pursue different strategies together. For example, an SBU structure permits companies to manage the strategies of vertical integration, related diversification, and unrelated diversification simultaneously because divisions can be grouped into business units based on the similarities or differences among their businesses. When companies are grouped according to the types of benefit expected from the strategy, the costs of managing them are reduced and many of the problems just outlined are avoided. In the next sections, we look in more detail at the strategy implementation problems that emerge when companies acquire new businesses, develop new businesses through internal corporate venturing, or do both.

13.7 MERGERS, ACQUISITIONS, AND STRUCTURE

In Chapter 10, we note that mergers and acquisitions are principal vehicles by which companies enter new product markets and expand the size of their operations.[24] Earlier we discussed the strategic advantages and disadvantages of mergers. We now consider how to design structure and control systems to manage the new acquisitions. This issue is important because, as we note elsewhere, many acquisitions are unsuccessful, and one of the main reasons is that many companies do a very poor job of integrating the new divisions into their corporate structure.[25]

The first factor that makes managing new acquisitions difficult is the nature of the businesses that a company acquires. If a company acquires businesses related to its existing businesses, it should find it fairly easy to integrate them

STRATEGY IN ACTION 13.5

No Problems for ABP

One of the largest manufacturers of business forms in the United States, American Business Products (ABP) developed a multidivisional structure to manage its strategy of related diversification. The Atlanta-based company created three separate divisions to manufacture invoices, customized envelopes, and continuous forms for computer printers. However, in 1990, with the market for business products slowing down and profit margins shrinking, APB decided to break with the past and search for new business opportunities. It embarked on a strategy of unrelated diversification and bought Jen-Coat, a maker of plastic packaging for food and health care products, as well as Bookcrafters, a specialty printing company.[28] Because top management established distinct roles for corporate headquarters and for the operating divisions, ABP experienced no problems in managing the new businesses through its multidivisional structure. The role of the corporate center was to control finances, establish budgets, and manage executive compensation for the five divisions—that is, to focus on corporate-level strategy. The role of the division heads was to handle sales, marketing, and manufacturing—that is, to manage business-level strategy. This clear apportioning of responsibility has been good for the company, which has encountered no difficulties in managing both strategies simultaneously and is currently on the lookout for more acquisitions.

into its corporate structure. The controls already being used in the related company can be adapted to the new divisions. To achieve gains from synergies, the company can expand its task forces or increase the number of integrating roles, so that the new divisions are drawn into the existing divisional structure.

If managers do not understand how to develop connections among divisions to permit gains from economies of scope, the new businesses will perform poorly. Some authors have argued that that is why the quality of management is so important. A company must employ managers who have the ability to recognize synergies among apparently different businesses and so derive benefits from acquisitions and mergers.[26] For instance, Porter cites the example of Philip Morris, the tobacco maker, which took over Miller Brewing Company.[27] On the surface these seem to be very different businesses. But when their products are viewed as consumer products that are often bought and consumed together, the possibility of sales, distribution, and marketing synergies becomes clearer, and this merger was a great success.

If companies acquire businesses for the sake of capital market gains alone, however, strategy implementation is easier. If companies acquire unrelated businesses and seek to operate them only as a portfolio of investments, they should have no trouble managing the acquisitions. For example, consider the acquisition strategy of American Business Products, highlighted in Strategy in Action 13.5.

Implementation problems are likely to arise only when corporate managers try to interfere in businesses that they know little about or when they use inappropriate structure and controls to manage the new business and attempt to achieve the wrong kind of benefits from the acquisition. For example, if managers try to integrate unrelated companies with related ones, apply the wrong kinds of con-

trols at the divisional level, or interfere in business-level strategy, corporate performance suffers as bureaucratic costs skyrocket. These mistakes explain why related acquisitions are sometimes more successful than unrelated ones.[29]

Strategic managers therefore need to be very sensitive to the problems involved in taking over new businesses through mergers and acquisitions. Like other managers, they rarely appreciate the real issues inherent in managing the new business and the level of bureaucratic costs involved in managing a strategy until they have to deal with these issues personally. Even in the case of acquiring closely related businesses, new managers must realize that each business has a unique culture, or way of doing things. Such idiosyncrasies must be understood in order to manage the new organization properly. Over time new management can change the culture and alter the internal workings of the company, but this is a difficult implementation task. Besides, the bureaucratic costs of changing culture are often enormous because the top management team and the organizational structure have to be changed in order to change the way people behave. We discuss this in detail in Chapter 14, when politics and strategic change are considered.

13.8 INTERNAL NEW VENTURES AND STRUCTURE

The main alternative to growth through acquisition and merger is for a company to develop new businesses internally. In Chapter 10, we call this strategy the *new venturing process,* and we discuss its advantages for growth and diversification. Now we consider the design of the appropriate internal arrangements for encouraging the development of new ventures. At the heart of this design process must be the realization by corporate managers that internal new venturing is a form of entrepreneurship. The design should encourage creativity and give new venture managers the opportunity and resources to develop new products or markets. Hewlett-Packard, for example, gives managers a great deal of latitude in this respect. To encourage innovation, it allows them to work on informal projects while they carry out their assigned tasks.[30] More generally, management must choose the appropriate structure and controls for operating new ventures.[31]

One of the main design choices is the creation of **new venture divisions**. To provide new venture managers with the autonomy to experiment and take risks, the company sets up a new venture division separate from other divisions and makes it a center for new product or project development. Away from the day-to-day scrutiny of top management, divisional personnel pursue the creation of new business as though they were external entrepreneurs. The division is operated by controls that reinforce the entrepreneurial spirit. Thus market and output controls are inappropriate because they can inhibit risk taking. Instead, the company develops a culture for entrepreneurship in this division to provide a climate for innovation. Care must be taken, however, to institute bureaucratic controls that put some limits on freedom of action. Otherwise costly mistakes may be made and resources wasted on frivolous ideas.

In managing the new venture division, it is important to use integrating mechanisms such as task forces and teams to screen new ideas. Managers from research and development, sales and marketing, and product development are

heavily involved in this screening process. Generally, the champions of new products must defend their projects before a formal evaluation committee, consisting of proven entrepreneurs and experienced managers from the other divisions, to secure the resources for developing them. Companies such as 3M, IBM, and Texas Instruments are examples of successful companies that use this method for creating opportunities internally.

Care must be taken to preserve the autonomy of the new venture division. As mentioned earlier, the costs of research and development are high and the rewards uncertain. After spending millions of dollars, corporate managers often become concerned about the division's performance and introduce tight output controls or strong budgets to increase accountability. These measures hurt the entrepreneurial culture.

Sometimes, however, after creating a new invention, the new venture division wants to reap the benefits by producing and marketing it. If this happens, then the division becomes an ordinary operating division and entrepreneurship declines.[32] Strategic managers must take steps to provide a structure that can sustain the entrepreneurial spirit.[33] Hewlett-Packard has a novel way of dealing with new venturing. In the operating divisions, as soon as a new, self-supporting product is developed, a new division is formed to produce and market the product. By spinning off the product in this fashion, the company keeps all its divisions small and entrepreneurial. The arrangement also provides a good climate for innovation. In the last several years, however, Hewlett-Packard found that having many new venture divisions was too expensive and so has merged some of them. The company appears to be moving toward the creation of a single new venture division.

Internal new venturing is an important means by which large, established companies can maintain their momentum and grow from within.[34] The alternative is to acquire small businesses that have already developed some technological competency and to pump resources into them. This approach can also succeed, and it obviously lessens management's burden if the company operates the new business as an independent entity. In recent years Eastman Kodak has taken this path to diversification, buying a share in many small companies. By and large, companies are likely to operate in both ways, acquiring some new businesses and developing others internally. As increasing competition from abroad has threatened their dominance in existing businesses, companies have been forced to evaluate opportunities for maximizing long-term growth in new businesses, and many of them have made acquisitions.

13.9 SUMMARY OF CHAPTER

This chapter brings together strategy formulation and strategy implementation and examines how a company's choice of strategy affects the form of its structure and control systems. The reason that many companies like Hughes Aircraft, IBM, and General Motors experience problems with their structure should now be clear: they have lost control over their structures, and their bureaucratic costs are escalating. The issue for a company is to manage its structure and control system so that it can economize on bureaucratic costs and ensure that they

match the potential gains from its strategy. The following are the main points of the chapter:

1. Implementing strategy through organizational structure and control is expensive and companies need to constantly monitor and oversee their structures to economize on bureaucratic costs.
2. At the functional level, each function requires a different kind of structure and control system to achieve its functional objectives.
3. At the business level, the structure and control system must be designed to achieve business-level objectives, which involves managing the relationships among all the functions to permit the company to develop a distinctive competency.
4. Cost-leadership and differentiation strategies each require a structure and control system that matches the source of their competitive advantage. Implementing a simultaneous cost leadership and differentiation strategy is the problem facing many companies today.
5. As a company moves from a multidomestic to an international, global, and transnational strategy, it needs to switch to a more complex structure that allows it to coordinate increasingly complex resource transfers. Similarly, it needs to adopt more complex integration and control systems that facilitate global learning. When there are gains to be derived from synergy, companies frequently adopt an international matrix form to trade knowledge and expertise.
6. At the corporate level, a company must choose the structure and control system that will allow it to operate a collection of businesses.
7. Vertical integration, related diversification, and unrelated diversification require different forms of structure and control if the benefits of pursuing the strategy are to be realized.
8. As companies change their corporate strategies over time, they must change their structures because different strategies are managed in different ways.
9. The profitability of mergers and acquisitions depends on the structure and control systems that companies adopt to manage them and the way a company integrates them into its existing businesses.
10. To encourage internal new venturing, companies must design a structure that gives the new venture division the autonomy it needs in order to develop new products and protect it from excessive interference by corporate managers.

Discussion Questions

1. How should (a) a high-tech company, (b) a fast-food franchise, and (c) a small manufacturing company design their functional structures and control systems to implement a generic strategy?
2. If a related company begins to buy unrelated businesses, in what ways should it change its structure or control mechanisms to manage the acquisitions?

3. How would you design a structure and control system to encourage entrepreneurship in a large, established corporation?

Article File 13

Find an example (or examples) of a company that has changed its structure and control systems to better manage its strategy. What were the problems with its old structure? What changes did it make to its structure and control system? What effects does it expect these changes to have on performance?

Strategic Management Project: Module 13

This part of the strategic management project involves your taking the information you have collected in the last two chapters on organizational structure and control and linking it to the strategy pursued by your company, which you identified in earlier chapters.

1. What are the sources of your company's distinctive competencies? Which functions are most important to it? How does your company design its structure at the *functional level* to enhance its (a) efficiency, (b) quality, (c) innovativeness, (d) and customer responsiveness?
2. What is your company's business-level strategy? How does it design its structure and control system to enhance and support its business-level strategy? For example, what steps does it take to further cross-functional integration? Does it have a functional, product, or matrix structure?
3. How does your company's culture support its strategy? Can you determine any ways in which its top management team influences its culture?
4. What kind of international strategy does your company pursue? How does it control its global activities. What kind of structure does it use? Why?
5. At the corporate level, does your company use a multidivisional structure? Why or why not? What are the crucial implementation problems that your company must manage to effectively implement its strategy? For example, what kind of integration mechanisms does it employ?
6. Based on this analysis, does your company have high or low bureaucratic costs? Is this level of bureaucratic costs justified by the value it can create through its strategy?
7. Can you suggest ways of altering the company's structure to reduce the level of bureaucratic costs?
8. Can you suggest ways of altering the company's structure or control system to allow it to create more value? Would this change increase or decrease bureaucratic costs?
9. In sum, do you think your company has achieved a good fit between its strategy and structure?

Endnotes

1. J. Cole, "New CEO at Hughes Studied Its Managers, Got Them on His Side," *Wall Street Journal,* March 30, 1993, pp. A1, A8.
2. W. G. Ouchi, "The Relationship Between Organizational Structure and Organizational Control," *Administrative Science Quarterly,* 22 (1977), 95–113.
3. K. M. Eisenhardt, "Control: Organizational and Economic Approaches," *Management Science,* 16 (1985), 134–148.
4. J. R. Galbraith, *Designing Complex Organizations* (Reading, Mass.: Addison-Wesley, 1973); P. R. Lawrence and J. W. Lorsch, *Organization and Environment* (Cambridge, Mass.: Harvard University Press, 1967); D. Miller, "Strategy Making and Structure: Analysis and Implications for Performance," *Academy of Management Journal,* 30 (1987), 7–32.
5. Michael E. Porter, *Competitive Strategy: Techniques for Analyzing Industries and Competitors* (New York: Free Press, 1980); D. Miller, "Configurations of Strategy and Structure," *Strategic Management Journal,* 7 (1986), 233–249.
6. D. Miller and P. H. Freisen, *Organizations: A Quantum View* (Englewood Cliffs, N.J.: Prentice-Hall, 1984).
7. J. Woodward, *Industrial Organization: Theory and Practice* (London: Oxford University Press, 1965); Lawrence and Lorsch, *Organization and Environment.*
8. C. J. Loomis, "The Reed That Citicorp Leans On," *Fortune,* July 12, 1993, 90–93.
9. R. E. White, "Generic Business Strategies, Organizational Context and Performance: An Empirical Investigation," *Strategic Management Journal,* 7 (1986), 217–231.
10. Porter, *Competitive Strategy;* Miller, "Configurations of Strategy and Structure."
11. E. Deal and A. A. Kennedy, *Corporate Cultures* (Reading, Mass.: Addison-Wesley, 1985); "Corporate Culture," *Business Week,* October 27, 1980, pp. 148–160.
12. B. Saporito, "How to Revive a Fading Firm," *Fortune,* March 22, 1993, 80.
13. Miller, "Configurations of Strategy and Structure," R. E. Miles and C. C. Snow, *Organizational Strategy, Structure, and Process* (New York: McGraw-Hill, 1978).
14. Lawrence and Lorsch, *Organization and Environment.*
15. R. A. Mitsch, "Three Roads to Innovation," *Journal of Business Strategy,* 1990, September/October, pp. 18–21.
16. J. Stopford and L. Wells, *Managing the Multinational Enterprise* (London: Longman, 1972).
17. C. A. Bartlett and S. Ghoshal, *Managing Across Borders: The Transnational Solution* (Cambridge, Mass.: Harvard Business School, 1991).
18. A. Barrett and Z. Schiller, "At Carnation, Nestlé Makes the Very Best... Cutbacks," *Business Week,* March 22, 1993, 54.
19. G. R. Jones and C. W. L. Hill, "Transaction Cost Analysis of Strategy-Structure Choice," *Strategic Management Journal,* 9 (1988), 159–172.
20. Jones and Hill, "Transaction Cost Analysis."
21. S. Lubove, "How to Grow Big Yet Stay Small," *Forbes,* December 7, 1992, 64–66.
22. Lawrence and Lorsch, *Organization and Environment;* Galbraith, *Designing Complex Organizations;* Michael Porter, *Competitive Advantage: Creating and Sustaining Superior Performance* (New York: Free Press, 1985).
23. Porter, *Competitive Strategy.*
24. M. S. Salter and W. A. Weinhold, *Diversification Through Acquisition* (New York: Free Press, 1979).
25. F. T. Paine and D. J. Power, "Merger Strategy: An Examination of Drucker's Five Rules for Successful Acquisitions," *Strategic Management Journal,* 5 (1984), 99–110.
26. C. K. Prahalad and R. A. Bettis, "The Dominant Logic: A New Linkage Between Diversity and Performance," *Strategic Management Journal,* 7 (1986) 485–501; Porter, *Competitive Strategy.*
27. Porter, *Competitive Strategy.*
28. "ABP: Pushing the Envelope," *Financial World,* April 6, 1993, p. 20.
29. H. Singh and C. A. Montgomery, "Corporate Acquisitions and Economic Performance," unpublished manuscript, 1984.
30. T. J. Peters and R. H. Waterman, Jr., *In Search of Excellence* (New York: Harper & Row, 1982).
31. R. A. Burgelman, "Managing the New Venture Division: Research Findings and the Implications for Strategic Management," *Strategic Management Journal,* 6 (1985), 39–54.
32. N. D. Fast, "The Future of Industrial New Venture Departments," *Industrial Marketing Management,* 8 (1979), 264–279.
33. Burgelman, "Managing the New Venture Division."
34. R. A. Burgelman, "Corporate Entrepreneurship and Strategic Management: Insights from a Process Study," *Management Science,* 29 (1983), 1349–1364.

14 Implementing Strategic Change: Politics, Power, and Conflict

14.1 OPENING CASE: WHICH WAY FOR MERCK?

Merck & Co., Inc., the giant pharmaceutical company based in Whitehouse Station, New Jersey, is regarded as one of the best-managed companies in the United States. Over the years, the company's innovative research and development has created many blockbuster drugs, such as Mevacor, its new cholesterol-lowering drug, which is earning billions in revenues. Since 1986 Merck has been headed by Dr. P. Roy Vagelos, a famous researcher who pioneered the development of many of its new drugs, and the company has had dramatic success under his leadership. Like all the major pharmaceutical companies, however, Merck has been experiencing major problems recently. The increasing R&D costs of developing new drugs, combined with pressures from consumers and health maintenance organizations (HMOs) to reduce the price of drugs, have reduced the profits of the large pharmaceutical companies and Merck has been searching for a new strategy to prosper in this competitive new environment.[1]

As part of this strategy, Vagelos, who plans to retire when he reaches 65 in November 1994, decided to appoint Richard J. Markham as his successor as CEO, and in 1992 Markham was named president of Merck. Vagelos saw marketing as the key to future profitability in the industry. Therefore, he promoted Markham over four other top managers who were senior to Markham at Merck and who had been leading candidates to succeed Vagelos on his retirement. Vagelos believed that Markham, a brilliant marketing expert, not an R&D scientist, was best suited to tailor the company's strategy to its new competitive environment. Markham had risen quickly through the ranks of the company based on his success at promoting Merck's products and convincing powerful customers like HMOs to continue to prescribe Merck's expensive drugs. Describing him as an "agent of change," Vagelos believed that he could alter the company's focus and give it a new way to compete in the 1990s and beyond.[2] Imagine the surprise then when in July 1993, with no explanation, Merck suddenly announced that Markham had resigned. Why?

Markham's new strategy, with its emphasis on marketing rather than research, had caused a high level of conflict in Merck's top management team. First, Merck's success had been built on its R&D skills, and its scientists had been the acknowledged heroes of the corporation. Merck's scientists, and particularly the top managers in charge of research and development, resented Markham's new marketing-based strategy, which took both resources and prestige away from their activities. For example, Markham has decided that Merck would produce its own line of generic drugs, which it would sell side by side with its branded drugs. In this way Merck would be able to offer lower drug prices to HMOs while still keeping its share of the more expensive brand name market. However, many top managers thought that producing generic drugs cheapened the image of the company and was not in keeping with Merck's high-price differentiated image. They thought it might backfire and hurt their R&D reputation. Second, Markham had come into conflict with Merck's top managers over his proposed $5 billion purchase of Medco, a company that specialized in supplying generic drugs through mail order to the

customers of HMOs. In purchasing Medco, Merck would control a significant part of the distribution of generic drugs and have avenues for selling its own generic drugs. Markham's new marketing strategy was based on Merck taking control over both the production and the distribution of generic drugs. In the future Merck would be both a differentiator, still involved in the discovery of new drugs, and a cost leader in the production and distribution of generic drugs. Markham believed that this dual strategy would pay rich rewards.

However, such a radical change in strategy was apparently too much for Merck's top management team, and even for his mentor, Vagelos, to take. It called for a new vision of the company, one that would require new leadership from cost-conscious marketing- and production-oriented managers, who would directly threaten the power and status of Merck's R&D-oriented top management team.These top managers had already lost out when Vagelos had made Markham his successor, and they resented Markham's quick rise to power in the company. They would also lose further if Markham began to hire more production- and marketing-oriented managers, who would manage Merck's transition to a generic drug producer. Top managers began to resist the changes he was introducing and to lobby against his new strategy. They formed a coalition to convince Vagelos that Merck would only suffer from the changes Markham was proposing and that the company should retain its R&D focus. Using their power as the leaders of the function that gave Merck its chief distinctive competency—R&D—managers began to lobby for a change in strategic leadership. With dissent in its top management team and facing criticism from the board of directors, the company decided to end its experiment. Markham resigned, and the fight is on for who will now succeed Vagelos as head of the company.

Given the entrenched power of the top management team, the successor is likely to be one of its other members and probably someone from R&D. The question is whether Merck will still focus solely on R&D or gradually take up the strategy that Markham started, but proceed with it at its own pace and with one of the R&D managers at the helm? In July 1993 Merck announced that it was buying Medco for $6 billion, but there was still no word on who would lead the company after Vagelos retires.

Discussion Questions

1. What was the source of the conflict in Merck?
2. Why is the new head of Merck likely to come from R&D?

14.2 OVERVIEW

As we discuss in Chapter 4, one of the principal reasons that companies fail is their inability to change themselves and adapt to a new competitive environment because of *organizational inertia.* Once an organization is created and task and role relationships are defined, a set of forces is put into operation that makes an organization resistant to change and organizational inertia ensues. For example, in considering the Icarus Paradox in Chapter 4, we point out the tendency of organizations to continue relying on the skills and capabilities that made them successful even when those capabilities do not match the new competitive environment. We also note there is another cause of organizational inertia: the power struggles and political contests that take place at the top of an organization as managers strive to influence decision making to protect and enhance their positions.

In this chapter, we look at the way in which organizational politics and conflict affect the ability of an organization to overcome inertia, influence decision making, and change its strategy and structure. Until now in our study of strategic management, we have treated strategy formulation and implementation from

an impersonal, rational perspective, where decisions are made coldly and logically. In reality, this picture of how companies make decisions is incomplete because politics and conflict influence the decision-making process and the selection of organizational objectives. The power struggle at Merck for control of the corporation indicates the importance of politics in company decision making. Markham's failure to retain the support of Vagelos and Merck's top management team and his subsequent exit from the company is an example of the use of power in organizations to change organizational objectives. The problems between R&D-oriented managers and those who were marketing oriented underscores not only the issue of power, but also that of conflict between different interests—between those who wanted sales growth through higher-volume, lower-cost products and those who wanted growth to come from the development of new products. The difficulty Markham had in changing attitudes at Merck and the resistance of other managers to his innovations exemplify the problems of overcoming inertia and implementing strategic change.

This chapter considers each of these issues. We probe the sources of organizational politics and discuss how individuals, departments, and divisions seek to increase their power so that they can influence organizational decision making. Then we examine the nature of organizational conflict and note how managers must deal with conflict to make better strategy-structure choices. Finally, we consider why it is difficult to change organizations, and we outline ways in which managers can direct organizational change so that their company's strategy and structure match new competitive environments.

14.3 ORGANIZATIONAL POLITICS AND POWER

So far, we have assumed that in formulating the corporate mission and setting policies and goals strategic managers strive to maximize corporate wealth. This picture of strategic decision making is known as the **rational view**. It suggests that managers achieve corporate goals by following a calculated, rational plan, in which only shareholders' interests are considered. In reality, strategic decision making is quite different. Often strategic managers' decisions further their personal, functional, or divisional interests. In this **political view** of decision making, goals and objectives are set through compromise, bargaining, and negotiation.[3] Top-level managers constantly clash over what the correct policy decisions should be, and, as at Merck, power struggles and coalition building are a major part of strategic management. As in the public sphere, politics refers to the activities through which different individuals or groups in the organization try to influence the strategic management process to further their own interests.

In this section, we examine the nature of organizational politics and the process of political decision making. **Organizational politics** is defined as the tactics by which self-interested but interdependent individuals and groups seek to obtain and use power to influence the goals and objectives of the organization to further their own interests.[4] First, we consider the sources of politics and why politics is a necessary part of the strategic management process. Second, we look at how managers or divisions can increase their power so that they can influence the company's strategic direction. Third, we explore the ways in which the organization can manage politics to overcome inertia and bring about strategic change.

Sources of Organizational Politics

According to the political view of organizational decision making, several factors foster politics in corporate life. Figure 14.1 contrasts these factors with those underlying the rational view of organizational decision making.

The rational view assumes that complete information is available and no uncertainty exists about outcomes, but the political view suggests that strategic managers can never be sure that they are making the best decisions.[5] From a political perspective, decision making always takes place in uncertainty, where the outcomes of actions are difficult to predict. According to the rational view, moreover, managers always agree about appropriate organizational *goals* and the appropriate *means*, or strategies, for achieving these goals. According to the political view, on the other hand, the choice of goals and means is linked to each individual's, function's, or division's pursuit of self-interest. Disagreement over the best course of action is inevitable in the political view because the strategic decisions made by the organization necessarily help some individuals or divisions more than others. For example, if managers decide to invest in resources to promote and develop one product, other products will not be created. Some managers win, and others lose.

Given this point of view, strategy choices are never right or wrong; they are simply better or worse. As a result, managers have to promote their ideas and lobby for support from other managers so that they can build up backing for a course of action. Thus coalition building is vital in strategic decision making.[6] Managers join coalitions to lobby for their interests, because in doing so they increase their political muscle in relation to their organizational opponents.

Figure 14.1
Rational and Political Views of Decision Making

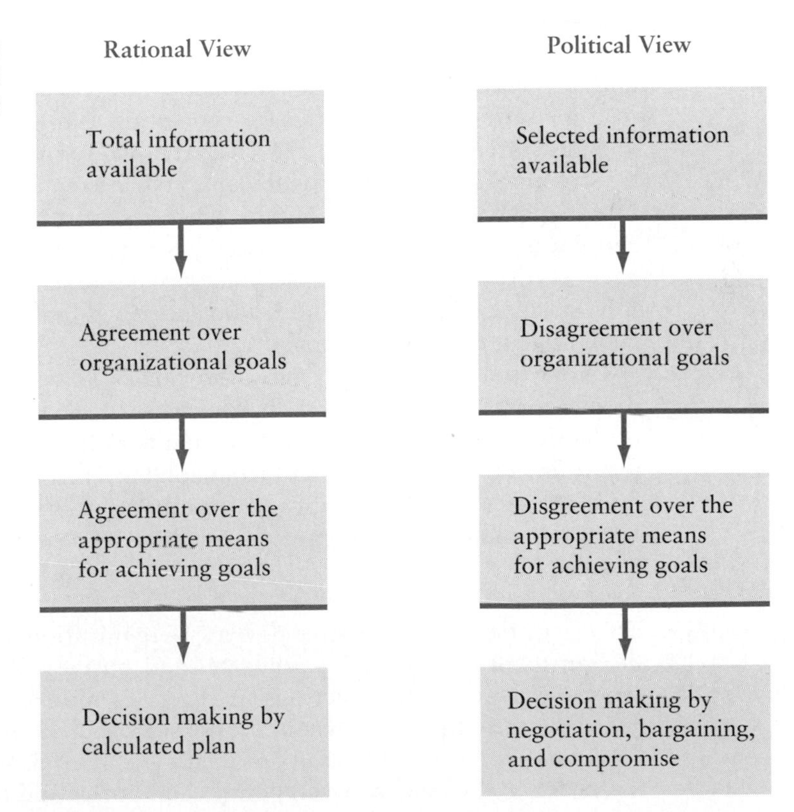

Managers also engage in politics for personal reasons. Because organizations are shaped like pyramids, individual managers realize that the higher they rise, the more difficult it is to climb to the next position.[7] If their views prevail and the organization follows their lead, however, *and* if their decisions bear results, they reap rewards and promotions. Thus by being successful at politics, they increase their visibility in the organization and make themselves contenders for high organizational office.

The assumption that personal, rather than shareholder or organizational, interest governs corporate actions is what gives the word *politics* bad connotations in many people's minds. But because no one knows for certain what decision is truly best, letting people pursue their own interest may in the long run mean that the organization's interests are being followed. Competition among managers stemming from self-interest may improve strategic decision making, with successful managers moving to the top of the organization over time. If a company can maintain checks and balances in its top management circles, politics can be a healthy influence, for it can prevent managers from becoming complacent about the status quo and thus avert organizational decline.

If politics grows rampant, however, and if powerful managers gain such dominance that they can suppress the views of managers who oppose their interests, then major problems may arise. Checks and balances fade, debate is restricted, and performance suffers. For example, at Gulf & Western, as soon as its founder died, the company sold off fifty businesses that the new top management considered pet projects (and therefore his political preferences) and not suited to the company's portfolio. Ultimately, companies that let politics get so out of hand that shareholder interests suffer are taken over by aggressive new management teams.

If kept in check, politics can be a useful management tool for overcoming inertia and bringing about strategic change. The best CEOs recognize this fact and create a strategic context in which managers can fight for their ideas and reap the rewards from successfully promoting change in organizational strategy and structure. For example, 3M is well known for its top management committee structure, in which divisional managers who request new funds and new venture managers who champion new products must present their projects to the entire top management team and lobby for support for their ideas. All top managers in 3M experienced this learning process, and presumably the ones in the top management team are those who succeeded best at mobilizing support and commitment for their concepts.

To play politics, managers must have power. **Power** can be defined as the ability of one individual, function, or division to cause another individual, function, or division to do something that it would not otherwise have done.[8] Power differs from authority, which stems from holding a formal position in the hierarchy. Power comes from the ability to informally influence the way other parties behave. Perhaps the simplest way to understand power is to look at its sources.

Sources of Power

To a large degree, the relative power of organizational functions and divisions derives from a company's corporate- and business-level strategies. Different strategies make some functions or divisions more important than others in achieving the corporate mission. We consider sources of power at the *functional or divisional level,* rather than at the individual level, because we are primarily interested in the links between politics and power and business- and corporate-level strategy. Figure 14.2 lists the sources of power that we discuss next.

Figure 14.2
Sources of Power

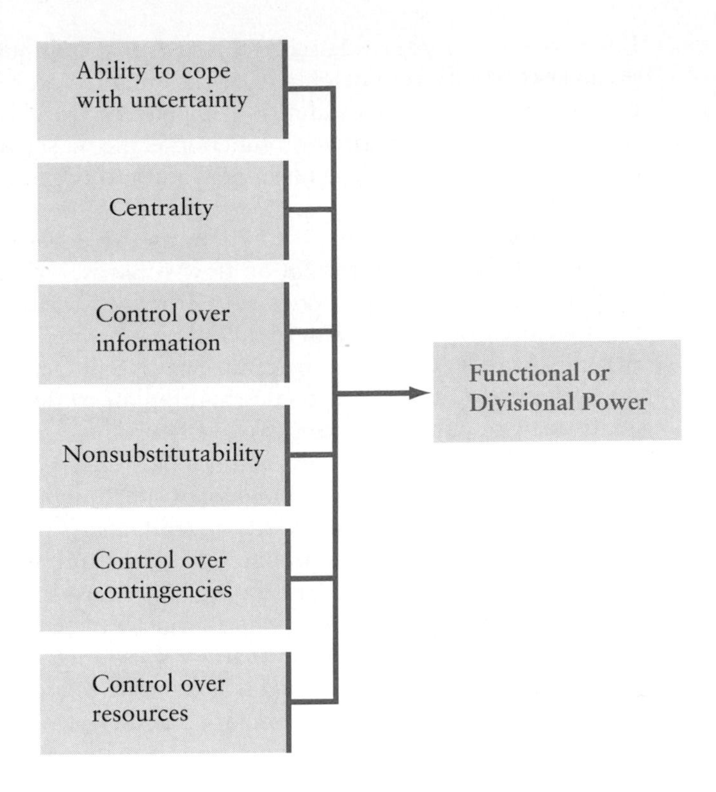

Ability to Cope with Uncertainty A function or division gains power if it can reduce uncertainty for another function or division.[9] Let us suppose that a company is pursuing a strategy of vertical integration. A division that controls the supply and quality of inputs to another division has power over it because it controls the uncertainty facing the second division. At the business level, in a company pursuing a low-cost strategy, sales has power over production because sales provide information about customer needs necessary to minimize production costs. In a company pursuing a differentiation strategy, research and development has power over marketing at the early stages in the product life cycle because it controls product innovations. But once innovation problems are solved, marketing is likely to be the most powerful function because it supplies research and development with information on customer needs. Thus a function's power depends on the degree to which other functions rely on it.

Centrality Power also derives from the **centrality** of a division or function.[10] Centrality refers to the extent to which a division or function is at the center of resource transfers among divisions. For example, in a chemical company, the division supplying specialized chemicals is likely to be central because its activities are critical to both the petroleum division, which supplies its inputs, and the end-using divisions such as plastics or pharmaceuticals, which depend on its outputs. Its activities are central to the production process of all the company's businesses. Therefore, it can exert pressure on corporate headquarters to pursue policies in its own interest.

At the functional level, the function that has the most centrality and therefore power is the one that provides the distinctive competency on which a company's

business-level strategy is based. Thus at Apple Computer the function with the greatest centrality is research and development because the company's competitive advantage rests on a technical competency. On the other hand, at Wal-Mart the purchasing and distribution function is the most central because Wal-Mart's competitive advantage depends on its ability to provide a low-cost product.

Control over Information Functions and divisions are also central if they are at the heart of the information flow—that is, if they can control the flow of information to other functions or divisions (or both).[11] Information is a power resource because, by giving or withholding information, one function or division can cause others to behave in certain ways. Sales, for instance, can control the way production operates. If sales manipulates information to satisfy its own goals—say, responsiveness to customers—production costs will rise, but production may be unaware that costs could be lowered with a different sales strategy. Similarly, research and development can shape managers' attitudes to the competitive prospects of different kinds of products by supplying favorable information on the attributes of the products it prefers and by downplaying others.

In a very real sense, managers in organizations are engaging in a subtle information game when they form policies and set objectives. We discuss in Chapter 11 how divisions can disguise their performance by providing only positive information to corporate managers. The more powerful a division, the easier it can do this. In both strategy formulation and implementation, by using information to develop a power base, divisions and functions can strongly influence policy in their own interests.

Nonsubstitutability A function or division can accrue power proportionately to the degree to which its activities are **nonsubstitutable** —that is, cannot be duplicated.[12] For example, if a company is vertically integrated, supplying divisions are nonsubstitutable to the extent that the company cannot buy in the marketplace what they produce. Thus the petroleum products division is not very powerful if large quantities of oil are available from other suppliers. In an oil crisis, the opposite would be true. On the other hand, the activities of a new venture division—a division in which new products are developed—are nonsubstitutable to the extent that a company cannot buy another company that possesses similar knowledge or expertise. If knowledge or information can be bought, the division is substitutable.

The same holds true at the functional level. A function and the managers within that function are powerful to the extent that no other function can perform their task. As in the case of centrality, which function is nonsubstitutable depends on the nature of a company's business-level strategy. If the company is pursuing a low-cost strategy, then production is likely to be the key function, and research and development or marketing has less power. But if the company is pursuing a strategy of differentiation, then the opposite is likely to be the case.

Thus the power that a function or division gains by virtue of its centrality or nonsubstitutability derives from the company's strategy. Eventually, as a company's strategy changes, the relative power of the functions and divisions also changes. This is the next source of power that we discuss.

Control over Contingencies Over time, the nature of the contingencies—that is, the opportunities and threats—facing a company from the competitive

environment will change as the environment changes.[13] The functions or divisions that can deal with the problems confronting the company and allow it to achieve its objectives gain power. Conversely, the functions that can no longer manage the contingency lose power. To give an example, if you look at which functional executives rose to top management positions during the last fifty years, you find that generally the executives who reached the highest posts did so from functions or divisions that were able to deal with the opportunities and threats facing the company.[14]

In the 1950s, for instance, the main contingency problem a company had to cope with was to produce goods and services. Pent-up demand from the years of World War II led to a huge increase in consumer spending for automobiles, homes, and durable goods. Goods needed to be produced quickly and cheaply to meet demand, and during this period the managers who rose to the top were from the *manufacturing* function or *consumer products* divisions. In the 1960s the problem changed. Most companies had increased their productive capacity, and the market was saturated. Producing goods was not as difficult as selling them. Hence *marketing and sales* functions rose to prominence. The rise of executives in companies reflected this critical contingency, for greater numbers of them emerged from the sales function and from *marketing-oriented* divisions than from any other groups. In the 1970s companies began to realize that competitive conditions were permanent. They had to streamline their strategies and structures to survive in an increasingly hostile environment. As a result, *accounting and finance* became the function that supplied most of the additions to the top management team. Today a company's business- and corporate-level strategy determines which group gains preeminence.

Control over Resources The final source of power that we examine is the ability to control and allocate scarce resources.[15] This source gives corporate-level managers their clout. Obviously, the power of corporate managers depends to a large extent on their ability to allocate capital to the operating divisions and to allot cash to or take it from a division on the basis of their expectations of its future success.

But power from this source is not just a function of the ability to allocate resources immediately; it also comes from the ability to *generate resources in the future*. Thus individual divisions that can generate resources will have power in the corporation. For example, divisions that can generate high revenues from sales to consumers have great power. At the functional level, the same kinds of consideration apply. The ability of sales and marketing to increase customer demand and generate revenues explains their power in the organization. In general, the function that can generate the most resources has the most power.

Summary The most powerful division or function in the organization, then, is the one that can reduce uncertainty for others, is most central and nonsubstitutable, has control over resources and can generate them, and is able to deal with the critical external strategic contingency facing the company. In practice, each function or division in the corporation has power from one or more of these sources, and so there is a distribution of power among functions and divisions. This condition gives rise to organizational politics, for managers form coalitions to try to get other power holders on their side and thus gain control over the balance of power in the organization.

Effects of Power and Politics on Strategic Change

Power and politics strongly influence a company's choice of strategy and structure, for the company has to maintain an organizational context that is responsive both to the aspirations of the various divisions, functions, and managers and to changes in the external environment. The problem companies face is that the internal structure of power always lags behind changes in the environment because, in general, the environment changes faster than companies can respond. Those in power never voluntarily give it up, but excessive politicking and power struggles reduce a company's flexibility, cause inertia, and erode competitive advantage.

For example, if power struggles proceed unchecked, change becomes impossible as divisions start to compete and to hoard information or knowledge to maximize their own returns. As we note in Chapter 13, this condition prevailed at TRW. It also occurred at Digital Equipment Corp. when its product groups became self-contained units that cared more about protecting their interests than about changing corporate strategy to survive in an increasingly hostile environment. In such situations, exchanging resources among divisions becomes expensive, and gains from synergy are difficult to obtain. These factors in turn lower a company's profitability and reduce organizational growth. Similar problems arise at the functional level. If one function starts to exercise its political muscle, the other functions are likely to retaliate by decreasing their cooperation with that function and not responding to its demands. Consider a company pursuing a low-cost strategy where the manufacturing function starts to exploit its position and ignores the need of sales to be responsive to customers. Over the long run, sales can hurt manufacturing by accepting bigger orders but at lower prices or even by seeking many small customer accounts to deliberately elevate production costs and so squeeze profits for the manufacturing function.

Managing Organizational Politics

To manage its politics, a company must devise organizational arrangements that create a **power balance** among the various divisions or functions so that no single one dominates the whole enterprise. In the divisional structure, the corporate headquarters staff play the balancing role because they can exert power even over strong divisions and force them to share resources for the good of the whole corporation. In a single-business company, a strong chief executive officer is important because he or she must replace the corporate center and balance the power of the strong functions against the weak. The forceful CEO takes the responsibility for giving the weak functions an opportunity to air their concerns and interests and tries to avoid being railroaded into decisions by the strong function pursuing its own interests. Laurence Tisch's restructuring of the CBS news division, detailed in Strategy in Action 14.1, illustrates many of the issues involved in managing organizational politics.

As the way Tisch managed CBS illustrates, the CEO of a large corporation has great potential for exercising power to bring about change. However, the CEO also plays another important role, that of arbiter of acceptable political decision making. Politics pervade all companies, but the CEO and top-level managers can shape its character. In some organizations, power plays are the norm because the CEOs themselves garnered power in that way. However, other companies—especially those founded by entrepreneurs who believed in democracy or in decentralized decision making—may not tolerate power struggles, and a different kind of political behavior becomes acceptable. It is based on a function or division manager's competency or expertise rather than on her or his ability to form

STRATEGY IN ACTION 14.1

Power Struggles at CBS

CBS, Inc. is a diversified entertainment and information company engaged in the principal businesses of broadcasting, recorded music, and publishing. One of America's most prestigious organizations, CBS experienced much turmoil in recent years. Its troubles began when outside investors, deciding that the company's profitability and return on assets were under par, led several takeover attempts against it. In successive attacks, Jesse Helms, a senator from North Carolina, Ivan Boesky, an arbitrageur, and finally Ted Turner, the founder of Turner Broadcasting System, Inc., announced takeover attempts.[16] CBS realized that it had to take these takeover attempts seriously if it wanted to remain independent.

First, Thomas Wyman, the chairman of CBS at the time, authorized a repurchase of CBS stock for $150 a share (Turner's offer was only $130). This increased CBS's debt from $510 million to $1.4 billion. Next, CBS searched for a white knight who would buy a major portion of CBS stock in the event that a hostile bid seemed likely to succeed. Laurence Tisch of Loews Companies Inc., agreed to play this role. By 1986, however, Tisch had purchased 25 percent of CBS stock, making him the largest stockholder, and board members, including Wyman, began to fear that he would take over CBS. Tisch did nothing to stop these rumors.[17]

Tisch began to take a more active role in CBS and to question or disagree with Wyman's policies. Wyman himself was now suffering on two fronts. Although he had been brought in by the legendary founder of CBS, William Paley, Paley had become increasingly disturbed that Wyman was not consulting him on CBS policy, particularly because CBS was going through bad times. Tensions increased, and at a board meeting at the end of 1986 Wyman revealed that he had been secretly negotiating with Coca-Cola for the sale of CBS to the soft drink company. Board members were shocked and withdrew their support. Wyman resigned, Paley became acting chairman, and Tisch became acting CEO.

After this power struggle, the pressing issue facing the company became changing CBS's strategy and structure to increase its ratings. The CBS news division posed a problem. It had been CBS's most prestigious operation since the golden days of Edward Murrow and Walter Cronkite, but the recruitment of a new president for the division, Van Gordon Sauter, had led to conflict between management and staff. Sauter believed that to earn the highest ratings the news should be entertaining, whereas the news staff believed that the news should remain free of entertainment value, as in the past. In the ensuing conflict, Dan Rather, Bill Moyers, and Don Hewitt, executive producer of *60 Minutes,* all offered to buy the news division and take it out of CBS. The offer was refused, but Tisch decided to remove Sauter to restore stability to the division.[18]

The next problem was changing CBS's structure and control system. The trend in the three main networks was to increase efficiency by downsizing and reducing staff and costs. Tisch, as the chief executive officer of CBS, began this change process by laying off staff. He eliminated more than 1,500 employees, about 9 percent of the CBS work force; this number included 150 people from the news division. He also severely cut expense accounts and reduced the slack that CBS personnel had previously enjoyed. Tisch's goal was to restructure CBS to attain a 12 percent return on his investment.[19]

powerful coalitions. At Pepsico, politics is of the cutthroat power-play variety, and there is a rapid turnover of managers who fail to meet organizational aspirations. At Coca-Cola, however, ideas and expertise are much more important in politics than power plays directed at maximizing functional or divisional self-interest. Similarly, Intel Corp. does not tolerate politicking or lobbying for personal gain; instead, it rewards risk taking and makes promotion contingent on performance, not seniority.

To design an organizational structure that creates a power balance, strategic managers can use the tools of implementation that we discuss in Chapters 11 and 12. First, they must create the right mix of integrating mechanisms so that functions or divisions can share information and ideas. A multidivisional structure offers one means of balancing power among divisions, and the matrix structure among functions. A company can then develop norms, values, and a common culture that emphasize corporate, rather than divisional, interests and that stress the company's mission. In companies such as Microsoft or 3M, for instance, culture serves to harmonize divisional interests with the achievement of corporate goals.

Finally, as we note earlier, strong hierarchical control by a gifted chief executive officer can also create the organizational context in which politics can facilitate the change process. When CEOs use their expert knowledge as their power, they provide the strong leadership that allows a company to overcome inertia and change its strategy and structure. Indeed, it should be part of the strategic manager's job to learn how to manage politics and power to further corporate interests because politics is an essential part of the process of strategic change.

14.4 ORGANIZATIONAL CONFLICT

Politics implies an attempt by one party to influence the goals and decision making of the organization to further its own interests. Sometimes, however, the attempt of one group to further its interests thwarts another group's ability to attain its goals. The result is conflict within the organization. **Conflict** can be defined as a situation that arises when the goal-directed behavior of one organizational group blocks the goal-directed behavior of another.[20] In the discussion that follows, we examine (1) the effect of conflict on organizational performance, (2) the sources of conflict, (3) the ways in which the conflict process operates in the organization, and (4) the ways in which strategic managers can regulate the conflict process using effective conflict resolution practices so that—just as in the case of politics—it yields benefits rather than costs.

Conflict: Good or Bad?

The effect of conflict on organizational performance is continually debated. In the past, conflict was viewed as always bad, or dysfunctional, because it leads to lower organizational performance.[21] According to that view, conflict occurs because managers have not implemented strategy correctly and have not designed the appropriate structure that would make functions or divisions cooperate to achieve corporate objectives. Without doubt, bad implementation can cause conflict and good design can prevent it. If carefully managed, however, conflict can increase organizational performance.[22] The graph in Figure 14.3 indicates the effect of organizational conflict on performance.

The graph shows that to a point conflict increases organizational performance. The reason is that conflict leads to *needed organizational change* because it exposes the sources of organizational inertia. Managers can then try to overcome inertia by changing structure and control systems, thus realigning the power structure of the organization and shifting the balance of power in favor of the group that can best bring about the changes the organization requires to

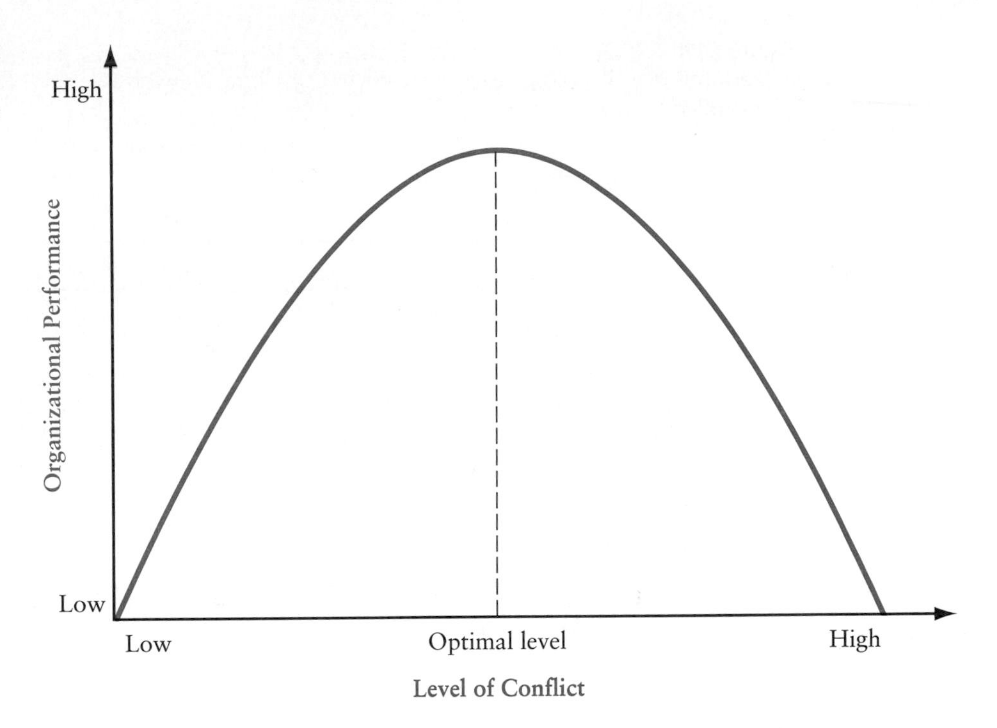

Figure 14.3
Effect of Conflict on Performance

prosper. Conflict signals the need for change. After the optimum point, however, a rise in conflict leads to a decline in performance, for conflict gets out of control and the organization fragments into competing interest groups. Astute managers prevent conflict from passing the optimum point and therefore can use it to promote strategic change. Managing conflict, then, like managing politics, is a means of improving organizational decision making and of allocating resources and responsibilities. Politics, however, does not necessarily cause conflict, and effective management of the political process is a way of avoiding destructive clashes among groups. Conflict in organizations has many sources, and strategic managers need to be aware of them, so that when conflict does occur it can be quickly controlled or resolved.

Sources of Conflict

As noted earlier, conflict arises when the goals of one organizational group thwart those of another. Many factors inherent in the way organizations operate can produce conflict among functions, divisions, and individuals.[23] We focus on three main sources of organizational conflict, and they are summarized in Figure 14.4.

Differentiation In Chapter 11, we define differentiation as the way in which a company divides authority and task responsibilities. The process of splitting the organization into hierarchical levels and functions or divisions may produce conflict because it brings to the surface the differences in the goals and interests of groups within the organization. This kind of conflict has two main causes.

Differences in subunit orientations As differentiation leads to the emergence of different functions or subunits in a company, each group develops a unique orientation toward the organization's major priorities, as well as its own view of

Figure 14.4
Sources of Organizational Conflict

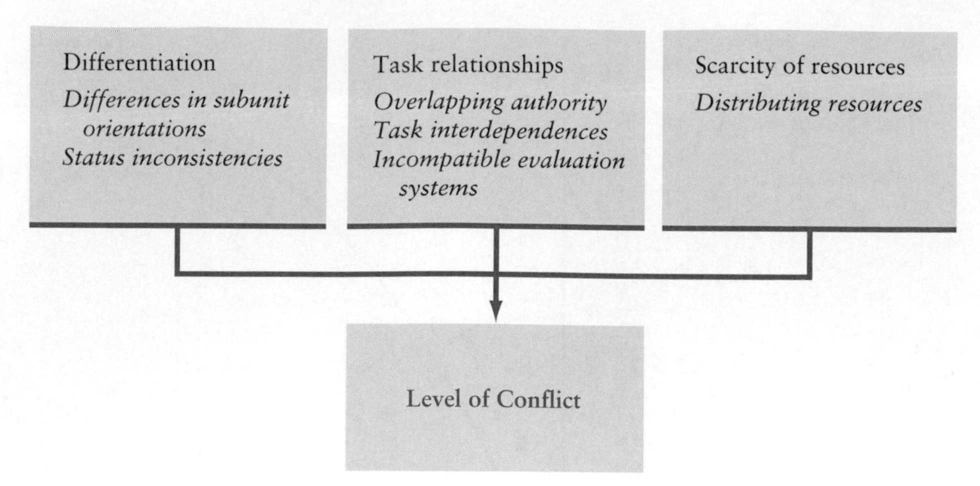

what needs to be done to increase organizational performance. Goals of the various functions naturally differ. For example, production generally has a short-term, cost-directed efficiency orientation. Research and development is oriented toward long-term, technical goals, and sales is oriented toward satisfying customer needs. Thus production may see the solution to a problem as one of reducing costs, sales as one of increasing demand, and research and development as product innovation. Differences in subunit orientation make strategy hard to formulate and implement because they slow a company's response to changes in the competitive environment and reduce its level of integration.

Differences in orientation are also a major problem at the divisional level. For example, cash cow divisions emphasize marketing goals, whereas stars promote technological possibilities. Consequently, it is extremely difficult for divisions such as these to find a common way of viewing the problem. In large corporations, such disagreements can do considerable harm because they reduce the level of cohesion and integration among divisions, hamper cooperation and synergy, and thus lower corporate performance. Many large companies, such as Digital Equipment, Westinghouse, and Procter & Gamble, have had to cope with this handicap; they responded by reorganizing their structure and improving integration. The struggle between managers in R&D and marketing at Merck is another illustration of the way in which differences in subunit orientations can cause organizational conflict.

Status inconsistencies In a differentiated company, over time some functions or divisions come to see themselves as more vital to its operations than others. As a result, they make little attempt to adapt their behaviors to the needs of other functions, thus blocking the goals of the latter. For example, at the functional level, production usually sees itself as the linchpin in the organization and the other functions as mere support services. This leads to line and staff conflict, where production, or line, personnel thwart the goals of staff, or support personnel.[24] The kind of business-level strategy that a company adopts may intensify line and staff conflict because it increases the status of some functions relative to others. In low-cost companies, production is particularly important, and in differentiators, marketing or research and development is most important.

At the divisional level, the divisions that are more central to the company's operations—for example, those that supply resources to the end-using divisions—may come to see themselves as the system's linchpins. They may also pay little attention to the end users' needs, such as development of new products. The end users may retaliate by buying in the marketplace or, more typically, by fighting over transfer prices, which, as we point out earlier, is a major sign of conflict among divisions. Thus the relationships among divisions must be handled carefully by corporate headquarters to prevent conflicts from flaring up and damaging interdivisional relationships.

Task Relationships As we discuss in Chapter 11, several features of task relationships may generate conflict among functions and divisions.[25]

Overlapping Authority If two different functions or divisions claim authority and responsibility for the same task, then conflict may develop in an organization. This often happens when an organization is growing, and thus functional or divisional relationships are not yet fully worked out. Likewise, when changes occur in task relationships—for instance, as when divisions start to share sales and distribution facilities to reduce costs—disputes over who controls what emerge. As a result, divisions may fight for control of the resource and thus spawn conflict. Strategy in Action 14.2 tells how a merger caused overlapping authority problems between two companies when BankAmerica took over Security Pacific.

Task interdependencies To develop or produce goods and services, the work of one function flows horizontally to the next so that each function can build on the contributions of the others.[26] If one function does not do its job well, then the function next in line is seriously hampered in its work, and this too, generates conflict. For example, the ability of manufacturing to reduce costs on the production line depends on how well research and development has designed the product for cheap manufacture and how well sales has attracted large, stable customer accounts. At the divisional level, when divisions are trading resources, the quality of the products supplied by one division to the next affects the quality of the next division's products.

The potential for conflict is great when functions or divisions are markedly interdependent. In fact, the higher the level of interdependence, the higher is the potential for conflict among functions or divisions.[27] Interdependence among functions, along with the consequent need to prevent conflict from arising, is the reason that managing a matrix structure is so expensive. Similarly, managing a strategy of related diversification is expensive because conflicts over resource transfers have to be continually dealt with. Conversely, with unrelated diversification, the potential for interdivisional conflict is minimal since divisions do not trade resources.

The merger between Burroughs Corporation and Sperry Corporation to form Unisys Corporation created the types of problems that must be managed to prevent conflict stemming from task interdependence. The CEO of Burroughs, W. M. Blumenthal, has taken enormous pains to manage new task interdependencies so that major conflicts among divisions can be avoided, and he has used a variety of integrating mechanisms to bring the two companies together. The problem is so severe because each company has the same set of functions, which must be merged in the long run.

STRATEGY IN ACTION 14.2

Who Controls What in a Merger?

When BankAmerica Corp. merged with Security Pacific in 1991, the merger was supposed to be a merger of equals, with the top managements of both banks jointly running the new company. For example, Richard Rosenberg, the chairman of BankAmerica, agreed to form an office of the chairman with Security Pacific's chairman Robert Smith; it was also agreed that Smith would succeed Rosenberg as the chairman of the new bank when Rosenberg retired. Similarly, there was supposed to be a fifty-fifty board split between the directors of both companies, and BankAmerica agreed to name four of Security Pacific's top managers to the new top management team.

After the merger, however, things did not work out as had been expected. BankAmerica had planned the merger hurriedly, without investigating the details of Security Pacific's financial condition thoroughly. After the merger, BankAmerica's managers began to find major flaws in the way Security Pacific's managers made loans and did business, for it had resulted in over $300 million of write-offs for the company, with equally large sums to follow. BankAmerica's top management team came to despise and ridicule the way Security Pacific did business. They blamed a large part of the problem on Security Pacific's culture, which was decentralized and freewheeling and where top managers lent large sums of money to clients on the basis of personal ties. By contrast, BankAmerica had developed a conservative, centralized decision-making style and curbed the autonomy of lower-level managers; loans were made according to company-wide criteria scrutinized by top management.

Believing that their culture was the one that had to be developed in the new organization, BankAmerica's managers began to use their power as the dominant party in the merger to strip authority from Security Pacific's managers and to take control of the reins of the new organization. Less than two weeks after the merger, Smith found himself relieved of all important decision-making authority, which was transferred to Rosenberg and his top management team.[28] Similarly, whenever BankAmerica's top managers were negotiating with Security Pacific's managers over future task and authority relationships, they used their power to cut the authority of Security Pacific's managers and to drive them from the organization. After a few months almost all Security Pacific's top managers had left the new organization, followed by thousands of middle-level managers, who, BankAmerica managers felt, could not be trusted to maintain the company's new cultural standards and way of doing business. Clearly, BankAmerica's top managers used their power to solve the problem of overlapping authority relationships and to destroy the decentralized culture of Security Pacific.

Incompatible evaluation systems We mention in Chapter 12 that a company has to design its evaluation and reward systems so that they do not interfere with task relationships among functions and divisions. Inequitable performance evaluation systems stir up conflict.[29] Typical problems include finding a way of jointly rewarding sales and production so that scheduling is harmonized and setßting budgets and transfer prices so that they do not lead to competition among divisions. Again, the more complex the task relationships, the harder it is to evaluate each function's or division's contribution to revenue, and the more likely is conflict to arise.

Scarcity of Resources Competition over scarce resources also generates conflict.[30] This kind of conflict most often occurs among divisions and between divisions and corporate management over the allocation of capital; however,

budget fights among functions can also be fierce when resources are scarce. As we discuss in other chapters, divisions resist attempts to transfer their profits to other divisions and may distort information to retain their resources. Other organizational stakeholders also have an interest in the way a company allocates scarce resources. For example, shareholders care about the size of the dividends, and unions and employees want to maximize their salaries and benefits.

Given so many potential sources of conflict in organizations, conflict of one kind or another is always present in strategic decision making. We need to consider how a typical conflict process works itself out in the organization and whether there are any guidelines that corporate managers can use to try to direct conflict and turn its destructive potential to good strategic use. A model developed by Lou R. Pondy helps show how the conflict process operates in organizations.[31] We discuss this in the next section.

The Organizational Conflict Process

Conflict is so hard to manage strategically because it is usually unexpected. The sources of conflict that we have just discussed are often inherent in a company's mode of operation. The first stage in the conflict process, then, is *latent conflict* —potential conflict that can flare up when the right conditions arise. (The stages in the conflict process appear in Figure 14.5.)

Latent conflicts are frequently activated by changes in an organization's strategy or structure that affect the relationship among functions or divisions. For example, if a company has been pursuing a dominant product strategy using a functional structure to implement the strategy, it might decide to widen its product range. To overcome problems of coordinating a range of specialist services over many products, the company may adopt a product structure. The new structure changes task relationships among product managers, and this in

Figure 14.5
Stages in the Conflict Process

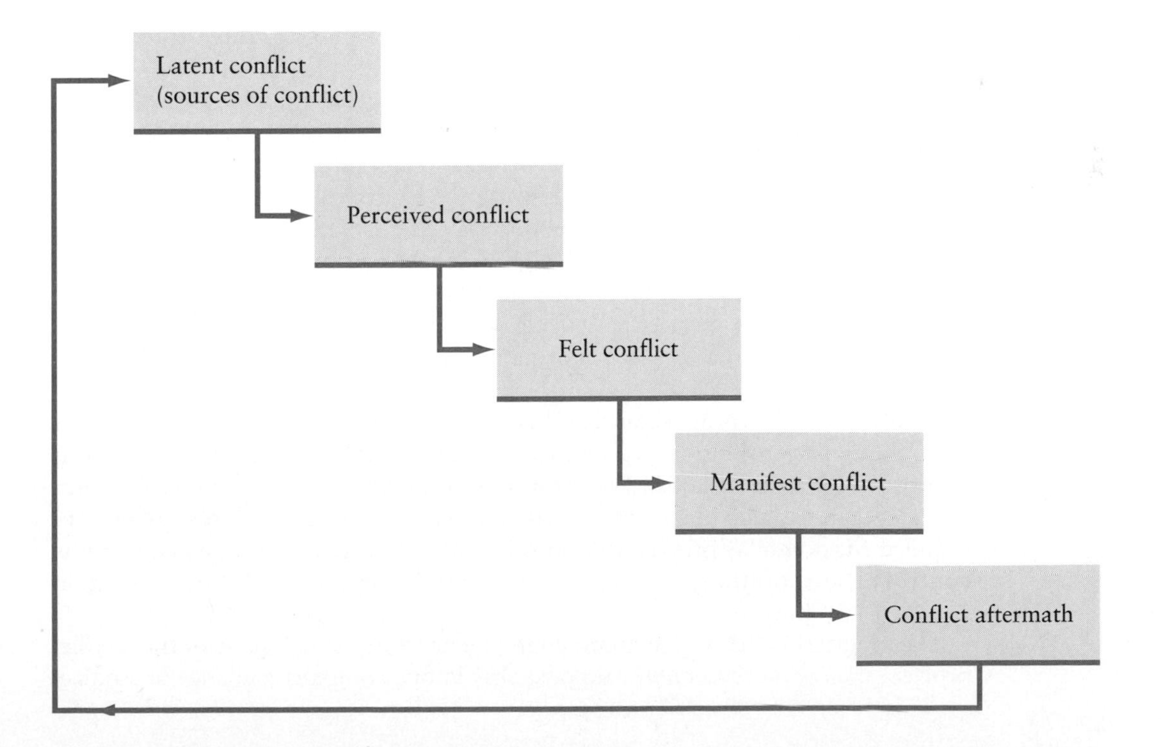

turn changes the relative status and areas of authority of the different functional and product managers. Conflict between functional and product managers or among product managers is likely to ensue.

Because every change in a company's strategy and structure alters the organizational context, conflict can easily arise unless the situation is carefully managed to avoid it. But avoidance is not always possible, and consequently the latent stage of the conflict process quickly leads to the next stage: *perceived conflict.*

Perceived conflict means that managers become aware of the clashes. After a change in strategy and structure, managers discover that the actions of another function or group are obstructing the operations of their group. Managers start to react to the situation, and from the perceived stage, they go quickly to the *felt conflict* stage. Here managers start to personalize the conflict. Opinions polarize, as one function or division starts to blame the others for causing the conflict. Production might blame the inefficiency of sales for a fall in orders, while sales might blame production for a fall in product quality. Typically, there is a marked lack of cooperation at this stage, and integration among functions or divisions breaks down as the groups start to polarize and develop an "us versus them" mentality. If not managed, this stage in the conflict process leads quickly to the next stage, *manifest conflict.*

At this point, the conflict among functions or divisions comes into the open, and each group strives to thwart the goals of the other. Groups compete to protect their own interests and block the interests of other groups. Manifest conflict can take many forms. The most obvious is open aggression among top managers as they start to blame other functions or divisions for causing the problem. Other forms of manifest conflict are transfer pricing battles and knowledge hoarding. Defamatory information about other divisions is also likely to be circulated at this stage in the conflict process. These actions are much worse than political maneuvering because divisions are trying not simply to promote their interests, but also to damage the performance of the other divisions. As a result, the company cannot achieve any gains from scheduling resource transfers or from developing synergy between divisions.

At the functional level, the effects of conflict can be equally devastating. A company cannot pursue a low-cost strategy if its functions are competing. If sales makes no attempt to keep manufacturing informed about customer demands, manufacturing cannot maximize the length of production runs. Similarly, a company cannot successfully differentiate if marketing does not inform research and development about changes in consumer preferences or if product engineering and research and development are competing over product specifications. Companies have experienced each of these conflicts at one time or another and suffered a loss in performance and competitive advantage because of them.

Manifest conflict is also common in top management teams, where managers are fighting for promotion to high office or for resources to enhance their status and prestige in the organization. You saw in the Opening Case how top managers at Merck, seeking to protect their own interests, conspired to remove Richard Markham as president. Manifest conflict is also common when a family controls a corporation, as a fight in the Dart Group, described in Strategy in Action 14.3, illustrates.

The long-term effects of manifest conflict emerge in the last stage of the conflict process, the *conflict aftermath.* Suppose that in one company a change in strategy

STRATEGY IN ACTION 14.3

Father and Son Go Head-to-Head

The $1.3 billion Dart Group, which owns large stakes in Crown, the nation's third largest book merchant, and Track Auto, a discount auto parts chain, is headed by Herbert Haft, now in his seventies. As chairman, Haft, who earned a reputation as a corporate raider from his attempts to take over Safeway and Eckerd Corp., keeps close control over his company and is known for his centralized management style.[32] In 1977 his son Robert Haft joined him as a manager in the Dart Group after leaving the Harvard Business School; he became chairman of Crown Books, a Dart division, and the heir apparent of his father as chairman of the Dart Group.

By 1993, however, tired of waiting for his father to retire as chairman and pass the reins of power to him, Robert Haft attempted a coup to oust his father as head of Dart. With the support of his mother and sister, he formed a plan to succeed his father. When his father discovered it, he took immediate steps to try to reduce the power his son had developed in the corporation and to consolidate his own position. He started by relieving Robert Haft of his duties as chairman of Crown Books, and then fired him after the details of his plot and the extent of the involvement of other family members became apparent.

Apparently Robert Haft would welcome a reconciliation, commenting that his "heart is always open to my father."[33] However, it appears that Herbert Haft has little desire to lose his power and give up control of the corporation he founded. The power of a king passes on at his death, and it appears that Herbert Haft wants to die in the saddle and feels that the place of a dutiful son should be at his knee.

led to conflict over transfer prices. Then divisional managers, with the help of corporate personnel, resolved the problem to everyone's satisfaction and reestablished good working relationships. In another company, however, the conflict between divisions over transfer prices was settled only by the intervention of corporate managers, who *imposed* a solution on divisional managers. A year later, a change in the environment occurred that made the transfer pricing system in both companies no longer equitable, and prices had to be renegotiated. How would the two companies react to this situation? The managers in the company in which the conflict was settled amicably will approach this new round of negotiations with a cooperative, and not an adversarial, attitude. However, in the company in which divisions never really established an agreement, a new round of intense clashes would be likely, with a resulting decline in organizational performance.

The conflict aftermath in each company was different because in one company conflict was resolved successfully but in the other it was not. The conflict aftermath sets the scene for the next round of conflict that will certainly occur because conflict is inherent in the ways companies operate and because the environment is constantly changing. The reason that some companies have a long history of bad relations among functions or divisions is that their conflict has never been managed successfully. In companies in which strategic managers have resolved the conflict, a cohesive organizational culture obtains. In those companies, managers adopt a cooperative, not a competitive, attitude when conflict occurs. The question that needs to be tackled, then, is how best to manage the conflict process strategically to avoid its bad effects and to make changes in strategy and structure as smooth as possible.

Managing Conflict Strategically

Given the way the conflict process operates, the goal of strategic managers should be to intervene as early as possible so that conflict does not reach the felt, and particularly the manifest, stage. At the manifest stage, conflict is difficult to resolve successfully and is much more likely to lead to a bad conflict aftermath. At what point, then, should managers intervene?

Ideally, managers should intervene at the latent stage and act on the sources of conflict.[34] Good strategic planning early on can prevent many of the problems that occur later, and it can facilitate the process of change. For example, when managers are changing a company's strategy, they should be considering the effects of these changes on future group relationships. Similarly, when changing organizational structure, strategic managers should anticipate the effects of the changes on functional and divisional relationships. Many large organizations do act in this way and require that the potential consequences of changes in strategy and structure on the organization be included in the strategic planning process to prevent conflict from arising later on.

Nevertheless, often it is impossible to foresee the ramifications of changes in strategy. Organizations are complex, and many unexpected things can happen as managers implement organizational change. Consequently, managers cannot always intervene at the latent stage to forestall conflict. Thus changes in strategy or structure may lead to failure, as when Apple Computer went to a divisional structure or when Eastman Kodak's instant camera proved a financial disaster.

Frequently, intervention is possible only between the felt and the manifest stage. It is at midpoint that managers may have the best chance of resolving the problem. Managers can adopt a number of different solutions, or conflict resolution strategies, and we consider them next.

Conflict Resolution Strategies

Using Authority As we discuss in Chapter 11, integration among functions and divisions is a major problem because they have equal authority and thus cannot control each other. When functions cannot solve their problems, these problems are often passed on to corporate managers or to the chief executive officer, who has the authority to impose a solution on parties. In general, there are two ways of using authority to manage conflict. First, the chief executive officer or corporate managers can play the role of arbiters and impose a solution on the parties in conflict. Second, they can act as mediators and try to open up the situation so that the parties in conflict can find their own solution. Research shows that the latter approach works better because it leads to a good conflict aftermath.

Changing Task Relationships In this approach, the aim is to change the interdependence among functions or divisions so that the source of the conflict is removed. Task relationships can be altered in two ways. First, strategic managers can *reduce* the degree of dependence among the parties. For example, they can develop a structure in which integration among groups is easier to accomplish. Thus a shift from a functional to a divisional structure can reduce the potential for conflict.

Alternatively, conflict may arise because the correct integrating mechanisms for managing task interdependence have not been adopted. In this case, managing the conflict means *increasing* integration among divisions and functions. In high-tech companies, in which functions are very highly task interdependent, managers

can use a matrix structure to provide the integration necessary to resolve conflict. In a divisional structure, managers can use integrating roles and establish integrating departments to allow divisions to price and transfer resources. At Hewlett-Packard, corporate staff created three integrating committees to allow divisions to share resources and thus minimize conflict over product development. Increased integration prevents conflicts from emerging. Managers also use structure through the process of strategy implementation to solve conflicts.

Changing Controls Conflict can also be managed by altering the organization's control and evaluation systems. For example, in some organizations it may be possible to develop joint goals among functions and divisions and to create a reward system based on the achievement of these joint goals, as when sales and production are jointly rewarded on the basis of how much revenue they generate. Similarly, corporate evaluation systems can be created to measure the degree to which divisions cooperate with one another. We discuss in Chapter 13 how TRW attempted to develop such evaluation systems so that divisions could share information and knowledge while being appropriately rewarded for it. Finally, to some degree, conflict is the result of managers in one function not appreciating the position of those in another. To give managers a broader perspective and to overcome differences in subunit orientations, managers can be rotated among divisions and given assignments at the corporate level to show them the problems faced by managers elsewhere in the company.

Summary: Organizational Conflict

Conflict is an ever present organizational phenomenon, which must be managed if the firm is to achieve its objectives. The whole process of strategy-structure choice creates the potential for conflict, and in a rapidly changing environment conflict is increasingly likely. It is part of the strategic manager's job to develop the personal skills needed to solve conflict problems. These skills involve the ability to analyze the organizational context, pinpoint the source of the problem, and handle managers who are in conflict so that organizational change can be successfully implemented.

14.5 IMPLEMENTING STRATEGIC CHANGE: STEPS IN THE CHANGE PROCESS

In the modern corporation, change rather than stability is the order of the day. Rapid changes in technology, the competitive environment, and customer demands have increased the rate at which companies have to alter their strategies to survive in the marketplace.[35] Consequently, companies have to go through rapid structural reorganizations as they outgrow their structures. E. F. Hutton, for example, estimates that more than half of the top 800 major corporations have undergone major restructuring in recent years.[36] In this section, we discuss the problems associated with managing such changes in strategy and structure.

The management of strategic change involves a series of distinct steps that managers must follow if the change process is to succeed. These steps are listed in Figure 14.6.

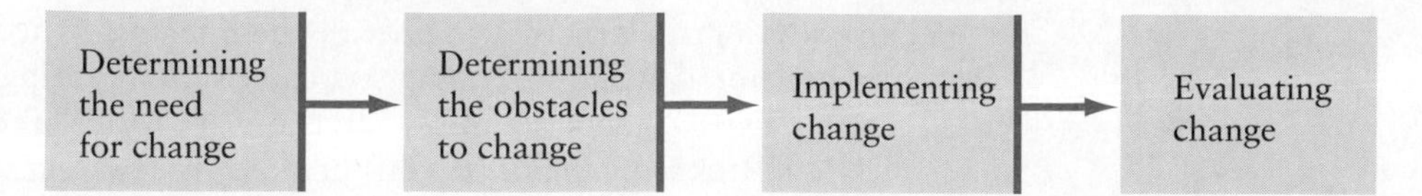

Figure 14.6
Stages in the Change Process

Determining the Need for Change

The first step in the change process involves strategic managers determining the need for change. Sometimes this change is obvious, as when divisions are fighting or competitors introduce a product that is clearly superior to anything that the company has in production. More often, however, managers have trouble determining that something is going wrong in the organization. Problems may develop gradually, and organizational performance may be slipping for a number of years before it becomes obvious. At CBS, for example, profitability fell, but because it was a reputable stock, the fall caused little stir. After a lapse of time, however, investors realized that the stock had been undervalued and that CBS could be made to perform better. In other words, outside investors realized sooner than inside management did that there was a need for change.

Thus the first step in the change process occurs when the company's strategic managers or others in a position to take action recognize that there is a gap between desired company performance and actual performance.[37] Using measures such as a decline in stock price or market share as indicators that change is needed, managers can start looking for the source of the problem. To discover it, they conduct a SWOT analysis. First, they examine the company's strengths and weaknesses. For example, management conducts a strategic audit of the functions and divisions and looks at their contribution to profitability over time. Perhaps some divisions have become relatively unprofitable as innovation has slowed without management's realizing it. Management also analyzes the company's level of differentiation and integration to make sure that it is appropriate for its strategy. Perhaps a company does not have the integrating mechanisms in place to achieve gains from synergy. Management then examines environmental opportunities and threats that might explain the problem. For instance, the company may have had intense competition from substitute products without being aware of it, or a shift in consumer tastes or technology may have caught it unawares.

Once the source of the problem has been identified, management must determine the ideal future state of the company—that is, how it should change its strategy and structure. A company may decide, like CBS, to lower its costs by streamlining its operation. Or, like Merck or General Motors, it may increase its research and development budget or diversify into new products to increase its future profitability. Essentially, strategic managers apply the conceptual tools that this book has described to work out the best strategy and structure for maximizing profitability. The choices they make are specific to each individual com-

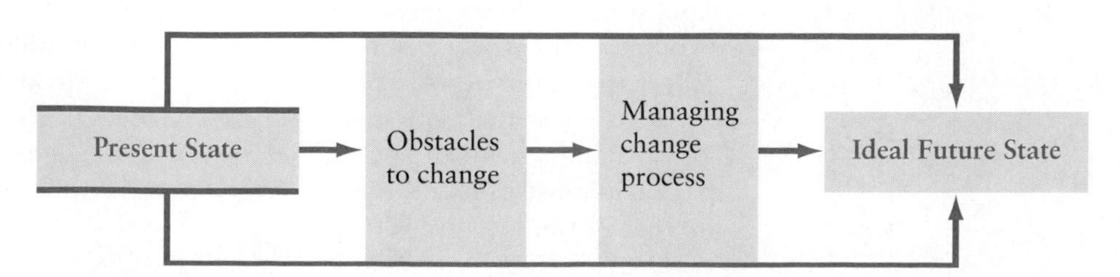

Figure 14.7
A Model of Change

STRATEGY IN ACTION 14.4

Turnaround at Sunbeam-Oster

In 1990 Sunbeam-Oster Company, Inc., the well-known small-appliance maker had a $40 million loss; in 1991 it made a $47 million profit. This turnaround in the company's fortunes was achieved by the actions of one man, Paul Kazarian, a former investment banker who identified the cause of Sunbeam's problems and knew what to do to solve them.

In 1990 Kazarian led a group of investors in the hostile takeover of Sunbeam and paid $660 million for the company. He had convinced these investors that Sunbeam's recent poor showing was due to a mismanagement of its resources and capabilities, and he laid out a plan for changing the company if they were successful. He had identified three main problems at the company: that it was in far too many different businesses and business segments, many of which were losing money; that its structure was inefficient and leading to high costs; and that it was not investing its money in the businesses with the biggest payoff.

In a presentation to investors, Kazarian outlined the way to change the company and offered his vision of the Sunbeam of the future. His first proposed change was to sell off Sunbeam's money-losing businesses and invest the proceeds in the company's core businesses to build their competitive advantage. For example, he outlined a plan for investing capital to develop new products in the company's core businesses, such as small appliances. Second, he proposed to streamline the company's remaining businesses and to rationalize their operating structures, reducing the levels in the hierarchy and downsizing the corporate staff to decrease costs.

After the takeover, he implemented this new strategy and transformed the company. By 1992 Sunbeam-Oster was worth over $1.5 billion; thus Kazarian had created over $1 billion of value. However, his success in identifying the company's problems and devising a new strategy was not matched by his skills in managing the restructured organization. Despite the amazing operating results, in January 1993 Kazarian was informed that Sunbeam's board of directors had voted him out of office. Whereas no one doubted his analytical skills, apparently Kazarian lacked interpersonal skills, and it was claimed that he went out of his way to abuse and humiliate managers, employees, and suppliers.[38] His confrontational management style was impeding the top management team's ability to restructure the company and to prepare it for future growth. Despite his firing, Kazarian did not lose all, however. Under the terms of his contract, he got to keep his $1.75 million salary for the next four years. In addition, he has the stock options he received as part of the takeover.

pany, and, as noted earlier, there is no way that managers can determine their correctness in advance. Strategy in Action 14.4 describes the choices Paul Kazarian made to turn around Sunbeam-Oster and determine its future course.

As the planning of Sunbeam's turnaround suggests, the first step in the change process involves determining the need for change, analyzing the organization's current position, and determining the ideal future state that strategic managers would like it to attain. This process is diagrammed in Figure 14.7.

Determining the Obstacles to Change

The second step in the change process is determining the obstacles to change.[39] Strategic managers must analyze the factors that are causing organizational inertia and preventing the company from reaching its ideal future state. Obstacles to change can be found at four levels in the organization: corporate, divisional, functional, and individual.

At the corporate level, several potential obstacles must be considered. First, changing strategy or structure even in seemingly trivial ways may significantly affect a company's behavior. For example, suppose that to reduce costs the company decides to centralize all divisional purchasing and sales activities at the corporate level. Such consolidation could severely damage each division's ability to develop a unique strategy for its own individual markets. Or suppose that in response to low-cost foreign competition the company decides to pursue a policy of differentiation. This action would change the balance of power among functions and lead to politicking and even conflict as functions start fighting to retain their status in the organization. A *company's present structure and strategy* are powerful obstacles to change. They produce a massive amount of inertia, which has to be overcome before change can take place. This is why change is usually such a slow process.

The *type of structure* a company uses can also impede change. For example, it is much easier to change strategy if a company is using a matrix rather than a functional structure, or if it is decentralized rather than centralized, or if it has a high rather than a low level of integration. Decentralized, matrix structures are more flexible than highly controlled functional structures. It is easier to change subunit orientations, and thus there is a lower potential for conflict.

Some *corporate cultures* are easier to change than others. For example, change is notoriously difficult in the military because everything is sacred to obedience and the following of orders. Some cultures, however, such as Hewlett-Packard's, are based on values that emphasize flexibility or change itself; they are much easier to change when change becomes necessary. Similar factors operate at the divisional level. Change is difficult at the divisional level if divisions are *highly interrelated and trade resources*, because a shift in one division's operations will affect other divisions. Consequently, it is more difficult to manage change if a company is pursuing a strategy of related, rather than unrelated, diversification. Furthermore, changes in strategy affect divisions in different ways because change generally favors the interests of some divisions over those of others. Divisions may thus have different attitudes to change, and some will not support the changes in strategy that the company makes. Existing divisions may resist establishing new product divisions because they will lose resources and their status in the organization will diminish.

The same obstacles to change exist at the functional level. Like divisions, different functions have different strategic orientations and react differently to the changes management proposes. For example, in a decline situation, sales will resist attempts to cut back on sales expenditures in order to reduce costs if it believes the problem stems from inefficiency in manufacturing. At the individual level, too, people are notoriously resistant to change because change implies uncertainty, which breeds insecurity and the fear of the unknown.[40] Because managers are people, this individual resistance reinforces the tendency of each function and division to oppose changes that may have uncertain effects on them.

All these obstacles make it difficult to change organizational strategy or structure quickly. That is why American car manufacturers took so long to respond to the Japanese challenge. They were accustomed to a situation of complete dominance and had developed inflexible, centralized structures, which inhibited risk taking and quick reaction. Paradoxically, companies that experience the greatest uncertainty may become best able to respond to it. When they have been forced to change often, they develop the ability to handle change easily.[41] Strategic managers must understand these potential obstacles to change as they design

a company's new strategy and structure. All these factors may spawn conflict, which can dramatically affect a company's ability to move quickly to exploit new strategic opportunities. Obstacles to change must be recognized, and the strategic plan must take them into account. The larger and more complex the organization, the harder it is to implement change because inertia is likely to be more pervasive. Strategy in Action 14.5, which tells how Michael Walsh overcame inertia at Tenneco, illustrates a way of overcoming obstacles to change in a large, complex organization.

Implementing Change

As Walsh's experiences at Tenneco suggest, implementing change—that is, introducing and managing change—raises several questions. For instance, who should actually carry out the change: internal managers or external consultants? Although internal managers may have the most experience or knowledge about a company's operations, they may lack perspective because they are too much a part of the organization's culture. They also run the risk of appearing to be politically motivated and of having a personal stake in the changes they recommend. Companies therefore often turn to external consultants, who can view a situation more objectively. Outside consultants, however, must spend a lot of time learning about the company and its problems before they can propose a plan of action. It is for this reason that many companies like Tenneco and IBM have brought in new CEOs from outside the company to spearhead their change efforts. In this way, companies can get the benefits of both inside information and external perspective.

Generally, a company can take two main approaches to change: top-down change or bottom-up change.[42] With **top-down change**, a strong CEO such as Walsh or a top management team analyzes how to alter strategy and structure, recommends a course of action, and then moves quickly to implement change in the organization. The emphasis is on speed of response and management of problems as they occur. **Bottom-up change** is much more gradual. Top management consults with managers at all levels in the organization. Then, over time, it develops a detailed plan for change, with a timetable of events and stages that the company will go through. The emphasis in bottom-up change is on participation and on keeping people informed about the situation, so that uncertainty is minimized.

The advantage of bottom-up change is that it removes some of the obstacles to change by including them in the strategic plan. Furthermore, the purpose of consulting with managers at all levels is to reveal potential problems. The disadvantage of bottom-up change is its slowness. On the other hand, in the case of the much speedier top-down change, the problems may emerge later and may be difficult to resolve. Lumbering giants like Tenneco and IBM often need top-down change because managers are so unaccustomed to and threatened by change that only a radical restructuring effort provides the momentum to overcome organizational inertia. Organizations that change the most find change easiest because inertia has not yet built up.

Evaluating Change

The last step in the change process is to evaluate the effects of the changes in strategy and structure on organizational performance. A company must compare the way it operates after implementing change with the way it operated before. Managers use indices such as changes in stock market price or market share to assess the effects of change in strategy. It is much more difficult,

STRATEGY IN ACTION 14.5

The Shakeout at Tenneco

A sprawling conglomerate, Tenneco, Inc., operates in such businesses as natural gas, shipbuilding, auto parts, chemicals, and farm equipment. In 1991 the company, which is based in Houston, Texas, was ranked 27th in the *Fortune* 500, with sales at over $14 billion. However, when Michael H. Walsh became president of Tenneco in 1991 he entered a company that had experienced falling earnings for years and was expected to post a net loss of $732 million in 1991. His mission was to turn around Tenneco and restructure its assets.

Walsh was used to the challenge of changing a large company. He had successfully turned around Union Pacific Corp., a large railroad company, and it was on the basis of his reputation as a change agent that Tenneco's board of directors had hired him. On taking over the restructuring effort, Walsh's first step was to analyze Tenneco's problems in order to see why it was having them. What he found were serious flaws in the company's structure and culture, which led to poor performance in the various operating divisions. For example, Case, the company's agricultural equipment maker, was in very poor financial shape and was a major contributor to poor corporate performance. To keep Case afloat, top management had continually siphoned off the profits of the chemicals and auto parts divisions, which were doing well. As a result, managers in these divisions had little incentive to improve divisional performance or to cooperate with one another and share resources or capabilities. Moreover, over the years, top management had failed to institute a rigorous system of market and output controls to monitor and control divisional performance. Divisional managers had been allowed to run their operations with little corporate oversight; consequently, they had made investments that supported their interests but not those of the corporation. Over time, with few checks on their activities, the divisions had become top heavy and uncompetitive. As already mentioned, they also lacked any incentive to cooperate and together improve corporate performance.

Walsh recognized that the way Tenneco's structure and culture were working had become a powerful obstacle to change. He realized that to change divisional managers' behavior and overcome the

however, to assess the effects of changes in structure on company performance because they are so much harder to measure. Whereas companies can easily measure the increased revenue from increased product differentiation, they do not have any sure means of evaluating how a shift from a product to a divisional structure has affected performance. Managers can be surveyed, however, and over time it may become obvious that organizational flexibility and the company's ability to manage its strategy have increased. Managers can also assess whether the change has decreased the level of politicking and conflict and strengthened cooperation among the divisions and functions.

Organizational change is a complex and difficult process for companies to manage successfully. The first hurdle is getting managers to realize that change is necessary and to admit that there is a problem. Once the need for change is recognized, managers can go about the process of recommending a course of action and analyze potential obstacles to change. Depending on the organization and the extent of the problem the company is dealing with, either bottom-up or top-down change is appropriate. However, in both cases it is best to use a mix of internal managers and external consultants to implement the change. After implementing change, managers assess its effects on organizational performance and then the whole process is repeated as companies strive to increase their level of performance. This is why companies in which change is a regular occurrence

inertia that had brought the company continual losses he would have to change the corporate-divisional relationship. He started from the top down by changing managers' attitudes and behavior. First, he instituted a set of output controls and made it clear that these goals would be monitored and enforced. Then he created a system of teams in which the managers from the different divisions met together to critique each other's performance. In addition, he flattened the corporate hierarchy, wiping out three layers of corporate managers in order to bring him closer to the divisions and to let the heads of the divisions function as the company's top management team. Previously, divisional managers had met one-on-one with the CEO; now they operated as a corporate team.

With this change in structure, Walsh decentralized more control to divisional managers. At the same time, however, he made them more accountable for their actions, since each manager's performance was now more visible to the CEO and to other top managers. As a result, top managers had more incentive to improve corporate performance. These changes effectively destroyed the inertia permeating Tenneco's old organizational structure and led to the evolution of a new culture, in which corporate, not divisional, goals and values guided divisional behavior. Walsh has continued these change efforts at all levels of the company. To change attitudes and behavior at the functional level, he has instituted a system of quality teams in every division in the company. In these cross-functional teams, employees are expected to search for solutions to improve quality and reduce costs, and Walsh regularly videotapes messages to Tenneco employees exhorting them to find new ways of improving performance. He also set an example from the top by wiping out top management perks like private dining rooms, luxury yachts, jets, and cars.

Throughout the company, Walsh has tried to destroy the old culture of apathy, where managers and employees were content to maintain the status quo and avoid confronting the company's problems. So far, Walsh's efforts to change the company have been spectacularly successful. Tenneco made a net profit of over $500 million in 1993, and analysts forecast steadily increasing gains over the years from his restructuring efforts. Overcoming obstacles to change in a company may be a very difficult process, but as Tenneco's experience suggests, managers, employees, and shareholders can reap big dividends from it.

find it much easier to manage than do companies in which complacent managers start a change effort only when the company is already in trouble.

14.6 SUMMARY OF CHAPTER

This chapter has examined the political side of strategy formulation and implementation and discussed the problems that can arise in managing changes in strategy and structure. It should now be apparent that organizations are not just rational decision-making systems in which managers coldly calculate the potential returns from their investments. Organizations are arenas of power, in which individuals and groups fight for prestige and possession of scarce resources. In the pursuit of their interests, managers compete and come into conflict. The very nature of the organization makes this inevitable. Managers have to deal with politics and conflict creatively to achieve organizational benefits from them. They also have to manage the process of organizational change so that the company can maximize its ability to exploit the environment. The most successful companies are those in which change is regarded as the norm and managers are constantly seeking to improve organizational strengths and eliminate weaknesses so that they can maximize future profitability. This chapter makes the following main points:

1. Organizational decision making is a combination of both rational and political processes. Formation of coalitions, compromise, and bargaining are integral parts of the strategic management process.
2. Organizational politics occurs because different groups have different interests and different perceptions of the appropriate means to further their interests.
3. To play politics, managers must have power. Power is the ability of one party to cause another party to act in the first party's interest.
4. The sources of power available to strategic managers include coping with uncertainty, centrality, control over information, nonsubstitutability, and control over contingencies and resources.
5. Politics must be managed if the company is to obtain benefits from the process, and one of the best ways of doing so is to create a power balance in the organization. A strong chief executive officer or a well-designed structure can create a power balance.
6. Organizational conflict exists when divisions, functions, or individuals go beyond competition and strive to thwart each other's goals. Conflict can be defined as a situation that occurs when the goal-directed behavior of one group blocks the goal-directed behavior of another.
7. Whether conflict is good or bad for the organization depends on the way it is managed. In general, conflict is useful in exposing organizational weaknesses, but it must be managed quickly, before it gets out of hand.
8. Conflict is inherent in the nature of an organization's design. The sources of conflict include differentiation, task relationships, and scarcity of resources.
9. Conflict can be regarded as a process with a series of stages. These stages are latent conflict, perceived conflict, felt conflict, manifest conflict, and conflict aftermath.
10. Organizational change is the process by which companies alter their strategy and structure to improve performance.
11. Organizational change is managed through a series of stages. First, the need for change must be recognized, and the company must decide on its ideal future state. Then the obstacles to change must be analyzed and included into the change plan, and change must be implemented. Finally, the change process must be evaluated to assess its effects on organizational performance.
12. Well-run organizations are constantly aware of the need to monitor their performance, and they institutionalize change so that they can realign their structures to suit the competitive environment.

Discussion Questions

1. How can managing (a) politics and (b) conflict in organizations lead to improved organizational decision making? How might a company create a system of checks and balances in the organization through the design of its structure and control systems?

2. How might conflict and politics affect the formulation and implementation of (a) generic competitive strategies and (b) corporate-level strategies?
3. What are some of the political problems a company might encounter if it takes over a related business and tries to integrate it into its organizational structure? (Hint: Use the sources of power to frame your answer.)
4. Discuss how you would set up a plan for change for an unrelated company that is starting to pursue a strategy of related diversification. What problems will the company encounter? How should it deal with them?

Article File 14

Find an example of a company that has been experiencing conflict or political infighting between managers or subunits. What is the source of the problem? What effect has this had on organizational performance? What steps is the organization taking to control or manage the problem?

Strategic Management Project: Module 14

For the final part of the strategic management project, your task is to examine how your organization has managed the process of conflict, politics, and strategic change.

1. To what extent are political contests between top managers or between divisions or functions common in your organization? Can you find any examples of power struggles or political contests in your organization?
2. Using the sources of power discussed in the chapter (for example, centrality, control over resources), draw a map of the power relationships among the various managers, divisions, or functions in your organization. On the basis of this analysis, which managers or subunits are the most powerful? Why? How do managers in the powerful subunits use power to influence decision making?
3. Given the nature of your organization's strategy and structure, what are the likely sources of conflict in your organization? Can you find any examples of conflicts that have occurred there?
4. How does the CEO or top management team try to manage conflict or politics? Is yours a very political or conflictual organization? Why?
5. Find some examples of recent changes in your company's strategy or structure. Why did your company make these changes? How well do you think top management managed the change process?
6. What do you think are the major obstacles to change in your organization?
7. What other changes do you think your company should make in its strategy or structure?

Endnotes

1. P. Annin and A. Underwood, "A Week of Woes Raises More Questions About Saint Merck," *Newsweek,* August 2, 1993, p. 35.
2. E. Tanouye, M. Waldholz, and G. Anders, "Stunning Departure of Merck Chief Signals Turmoil Inside and Out," *Wall Street Journal,* July 16, 1993, pp. A1, A4.
3. A. M. Pettigrew, *The Politics of Organizational Decision Making* (London: Tavistock, 1973).
4. R. H. Miles, *Macro Organizational Behavior* (Santa Monica, Calif.: Goodyear, 1980).
5. J. G. March and H. A. Simon, *Organizations* (New York: Wiley, 1958).
6. J. G. March, "The Business Firm as a Coalition," *The Journal of Politics,* 24 (1962), 662–678; D. J. Vredenburgh and J. G. Maurer, "A Process Framework of Organizational Politics," *Human Relations,* 37 (1984), 47–66.
7. T. Burns, "Micropolitics: Mechanism of Institutional Change," *Administrative Science Quarterly,* 6 (1961), 257–281.
8. R. A. Dahl, "The Concept of Power," *Behavioral Science,* 2 (1957), 201–215; G. A. Astley and P. S. Sachdeva, "Structural Sources of Intraorganizational Power," *Academy of Management Review,* 9 (1984), 104–113.
9. This section draws heavily on D. J. Hickson, C. R. Hinings, C. A. Lee, R. E. Schneck, and D. J. Pennings, "A Strategic Contingencies Theory of Intraorganizational Power," *Administrative Science Quarterly,* 16 (1971), 216–227; and C. R. Hinings, D. J. Hickson, J. M. Pennings, and R. E. Schneck, "Structural Conditions of Interorganizational Power," *Administrative Science Quarterly,* 19 (1974), 22–44.
10. Hickson et al., "A Strategic Contingencies Theory."
11. Pettigrew, *The Politics of Organizational Decision Making.*
12. Hickson et al., "A Strategic Contingencies Theory"; Pettigrew, *The Politics of Organizational Decision Making.*
13. Hickson et al., "A Strategic Contingencies Theory."
14. H. A. Landsberger, "The Horizontal Dimension in Bureaucracy," *Administrative Science Quarterly,* 6 (1961), 299–232.
15. G. R. Salancik and J. Pfeffer, "The Bases and Use of Power in Organizational Decision Making: The Case of a University," *Administrative Science Quarterly,* 19 (1974), 453–473.
16. "Corporate Shoot-Out at Black Rock," *Time,* September 22, 1986, 68–72.
17. "Civil War at CBS," *Newsweek,* September 15, 1986, 46–54.
18. P. W. Barnes, "Tisch Wins Praise for Fast Action at CBS," *Wall Street Journal,* October 28, 1986, p. A5.
19. P. J. Boyers, "Three New Bosses are Slashing Operations and Putting Nearly Everyone's Job on the Line," *New York Times,* November 2, 1986, p. 26.
20. J. A. Litterer, "Conflict in Organizations: A Reexamination," *Academy of Management Journal,* 9 (1966), 178–186; S. M. Schmidt and T. A. Kochan, "Conflict: Towards Conceptual Clarity," *Administrative Science Quarterly,* 13 (1972), 359–370; Miles, *Macro Organizational Behavior.*
21. *Miles, Macro Organizational Behavior.*
22. S. P. Robbins, *Managing Organizational Conflict: A Nontraditional Approach* (Englewood Cliffs, N.J.: Prentice-Hall, 1974); L. Coser, *The Functions of Social Conflict* (New York: Free Press, 1956).
23. This discussion owes much to the seminal work of the following authors: Lou R. Pondy, "Organizational Conflict: Concepts and Models," *Administrative Science Quarterly,* 2 (1967), 296–320; and R. E. Walton and J. M. Dutton, "The Management of Interdepartmental Conflict: A Model and Review," *Administrative Science Quarterly,* 14 (1969), 62–73.
24. M. Dalton, *Men Who Manage* (New York: Wiley, 1959); Walton and Dutton, "The Management of Interdepartmental Conflict."
25. R. T. King, Jr., "A Bad Buy? BankAmerica Finds It Got a Lot of Woe with Security Pacific," *Wall Street Journal,* July 22, 1993, A1, A4.
26. J. D. Thompson, *Organizations in Action* (New York: McGraw-Hill, 1967).
27. Walton and Dutton, "The Management of Interdepartmental Conflict," p. 65.
28. Walton and Dutton, "The Management of Interdepartmental Conflict"; J. McCann and J. R. Galbraith, "Interdepartmental Relationships," in *Handbook of Organizational Design,* ed. P. C. Nystrom and W. H. Starbuck (New York: Oxford University Press, 1981).
29. Ibid., p. 68.
30. Pondy, "Organizational Conflict," p. 300.
31. Ibid., p. 310.
32. M. Lewyn, "Behind the Bloody Battle of Dart's Boardroom," *Business Week,* June 28, 1993, pp. 96–97.
33. A. Miller, F. Chadeya, and B. Shenitz, "Dysfunctional Discounters," *Newsweek,* July 12, 1993, p. 47.
34. Ibid., p. 316.
35. T. J. Peters and R. H. Waterman, Jr., *In Search of Excellence* (New York: Harper & Row, 1982).
36. J. Thackray, "Restructuring Is the Name of the Hurricane," *Euromoney* (February 1987), 106–108.
37. R. Beckhard, *Organizational Development* (Reading, Mass.: Addison-Wesley, 1969). W. L. French and C. H. Bell, Jr., *Organization Development,* 2nd ed. (Englewood Cliffs, N.J.: Prentice-Hall, 1978).
38. G. Smith, M. Schroeder, and L. Therrien, "How to Lose Friends and Influence No One," *Business Week,* January 25, 1993, pp. 42–43.
39. L. C. Coch and R. P. French, Jr., "Overcoming Resistance to Change," *Human Relations* (August 1948), 512–532; P. R. Lawrence, "How to Deal with Resistance to Change," *Harvard Business Review* (January–February 1969), 4–12.
40. P. Kotter and L. A. Schlesinger, "Choosing Strategies for Change," *Harvard Business Review* (March–April 1979), 106–114.
41. J. R. Galbraith, "Designing the Innovative Organization," *Organization Dynamics* (Winter 1982), 5–25.
42. M. Beer, *Organizational Change and Development* (Santa Monica, Calif.: Goodyear, 1980); L. E. Greiner, "Patterns of Organizational Change," *Harvard Business Review* (May–June 1967), 3–5.

V Cases in Strategic Management

Introduction

Analyzing and Writing a Case Study

Section A

Small Business and Entrepreneurship Cases

Section B

Business Level: Domestic and Global Cases

Section C

Corporate Level: Domestic and Global Cases

Introduction: Analyzing and Writing a Case Study

WHAT IS CASE STUDY ANALYSIS?

Case study analysis is an integral part of a course in strategic management. The purpose of a case study is to provide students with experience of the strategic management problems faced by actual organizations. A case study presents an account of what happened to a business or industry over a number of years. It chronicles the events that managers had to deal with, such as changes in the competitive environment, and charts the managers' response, which usually involved changing the business- or corporate-level strategy. The cases in Part V of this book cover a wide range of issues and problems that managers have had to confront. Some cases are about finding the right business-level strategy to compete in changing conditions. Some are about companies that grew by acquisition, with little concern for the rationale behind their growth, and how growth by acquisition affected their future profitability. Each case is different because each organization is different. The underlying thread in all the cases, however, is the use of strategic management techniques to solve business problems.

Cases prove valuable in a strategic management course for several reasons. First, cases provide you, the student, with experience of organizational problems that you probably have not had the opportunity to experience firsthand. In a relatively short period of time, you will have the chance to appreciate and analyze the problems faced by many different companies and to understand how managers tried to deal with them.

Second, cases illustrate the theory and content of strategic management—that is, all the information presented to you in the previous chapters of this book. This information has been collected, discovered, and distilled from the observations, research, and experience of managers and academics. The meaning and implication of this information are made clearer when they are applied to case studies. The theory and concepts help reveal what is going on in the companies studied and allow you to evaluate the solutions that specific companies adopted to deal with their problems. Consequently, when you analyze cases, you will be like a detective who, with a set of conceptual tools, probes what happened and what or who was responsible, and then marshals the evidence that provides the solution. Top managers enjoy the thrill of testing their problem-solving abilities in the real world. It is important to remember, after all, that no one knows what the right answer is. All that managers can do is to make the best guess. In fact, managers say repeatedly that they are happy if they are right only half the time in solving strategic problems. Strategic management is an uncertain game, and using cases to see how theory can be put into practice is one way of improving your skills of diagnostic investigation.

Third, case studies provide you with the opportunity to participate in class and to gain experience in presenting your ideas to others. Instructors sometimes

will call on students as a group to identify what is going on in a case, and through classroom discussion the issues in and solutions to the case problem will reveal themselves. In such a situation, you will have to organize your views and conclusions so that you can present them to the class. Your classmates may have analyzed the issues differently from you, and they will want you to argue your points before they will accept your conclusions; so be prepared for debate. This mode of discussion is an example of the dialectical approach to decision making that you may recall from Chapter 1. This is how decisions are made in the actual business world.

Instructors also may assign an individual, or more commonly a group, to analyze the case before the whole class. The individual or group probably will be responsible for a thirty- to forty-minute presentation of the case to the class. That presentation must cover the issues involved, the problems facing the company, and a series of recommendations for resolving the problems. The discussion then will be thrown open to the class, and you will have to defend your ideas. Through such discussions and presentations, you will experience how to convey your ideas effectively to others. Remember that a great deal of managers' time is spent in these kinds of situations, presenting their ideas and engaging in discussion with other managers, who have their own views about what is going on. Thus you will experience in the classroom the actual process of strategic management, and this will serve you well in your future career.

If you work in groups to analyze case studies, you also will learn about the group process involved in joint work. When people work in groups, it is often difficult to schedule time and allocate responsibility for the case analysis. You will always find group members who shirk their responsibilities or group members who are so sure of their own ideas that they try to dominate the group's analysis. Most of the strategic management takes place in groups, however, and it is best if you learn about these problems now.

ANALYZING A CASE STUDY

As just mentioned, the purpose of the case study is to let you apply the concepts of strategic management when you analyze the issues facing a specific company. To analyze a case study, therefore, you must examine closely the issues with which the company is confronted. Most often you will need to read the case several times: once to grasp the overall picture of what is happening to the company and then several times more to discover and grasp the specific problems.

Generally, detailed analysis of a case study should include eight areas:

1. The history, development, and growth of the company over time
2. The identification of the company's internal strengths and weaknesses
3. The nature of the external environment surrounding the company
4. A SWOT analysis
5. The kind of corporate-level strategy pursued by the company
6. The nature of the company's business-level strategy
7. The company's structure and control systems and how they match its strategy
8. Recommendations

To analyze a case, you need to apply the course concepts to each of these areas. Which concepts to use is obvious from the chapter titles. For example, to analyze the company's environment, you would use Chapter 3, on environmental analysis.

To help you further, we next offer a brief guide to some of the main strategic management concepts that can be used to analyze the case material for each of the points we have just noted.

1. *Analyzing the company's history, development, and growth* A convenient way to investigate how a company's past strategy and structure affect it in the present is to chart the critical incidents in its history—that is, the events that were the most unusual or the most essential for its development into the company it is today. Some of the events have to do with its founding, its initial products, how it made new product market decisions, and how it developed and chose functional competencies to pursue. Its entry into new businesses and shifts in its main lines of business are also important milestones to consider.

2. *Identifying the company's internal strengths and weaknesses* Once the historical profile is completed, you can begin the SWOT analysis. Take all the incidents you have charted and use them to develop an account of the company's strengths and weaknesses as they have emerged historically. Examine each of the value creation functions of the company, and identify the functions in which the company is currently strong and currently weak. Some companies might be weak in marketing; some might be strong in research and development. Make lists of these strengths and weaknesses. The table on page C6 gives examples of what might go in these lists.

3. *Analyzing the external environment* The next step is to identify environmental opportunities and threats. Here you should apply all the concepts from Chapter 3, on industry and macroenvironments, to analyze the environment the company is confronting. Of particular importance at the industry level is Porter's five forces model and the stage of the life cycle model. Which factors in the macroenvironment will appear salient depends on the specific company being analyzed. However, use each concept in turn—for instance, demographic factors—to see if it is relevant for the company in question.

Having done this analysis, you will have generated both an analysis of the company's environment and a list of opportunities and threats. The table also lists some common environmental opportunities and threats that you might look for, but the list you generate will be specific to your company.

4. *Evaluating the SWOT analysis* Having identified the company's external opportunities and threats, as well as its internal strengths and weaknesses, you need to consider what your findings mean. That is, you need to balance strengths and weaknesses against opportunities and threats. Is the company in an overall strong competitive position? Can it continue to pursue its current business- or corporate-level strategy profitably? What can the company do to turn weaknesses into strengths and threats into opportunities? Can it develop new functional, business, or corporate strategies to accomplish this change? *Never merely generate the SWOT analysis and then put it aside*. Because it provides a succinct summary of the company's condition, a good SWOT analysis is the key to all the analyses that follow.

5. *Analyzing corporate-level strategy* To analyze a company's corporate-level strategy, you first need to define the company's mission and goals. Sometimes the

Table 1
A SWOT Checklist

Potential internal strengths	Potential internal weaknesses
Many product lines?	Obsolete, narrow product lines?
Broad market coverage?	Rising manufacturing costs?
Manufacturing competence?	Decline in R&D innovations?
Good marketing skills?	Poor marketing plan?
Good materials management systems?	Poor materials management systems?
R&D skills and leadership?	Loss of customer good will?
Information system competencies?	Inadequate information systems?
Human resource competencies?	Inadequate human resources?
Brand name reputation?	Loss of brand name capital?
Portfolio management skills?	Growth without direction?
Cost of differentiation advantage?	Bad portfolio management?
New-venture management expertise?	Loss of corporate direction?
Appropriate management style?	Infighting among divisions?
Appropriate organizational structure?	Loss of corporate control?
Appropriate control systems?	Inappropriate organizational structure and control systems?
Ability to manage strategic change?	High conflict and politics?
Well-developed corporate strategy?	Poor financial management?
Good financial management?	Others?
Others?	
Potential environmental opportunities	**Potential environmental threats**
Expand core business(es)?	Attacks on core business(es)?
Exploit new market segments?	Increases in domestic competition?
Widen product range?	Increase in foreign competition?
Extend cost or differentiation advantage?	Change in consumer tastes?
Diversify into new growth businesses?	Fall in barriers to entry?
Expand into foreign markets?	Rise in new or substitute products?
Apply R&D skills in new areas?	Increase in industry rivalry?
Enter new related businesses?	New forms of industry competition?
Vertically integrate forward?	Potential for takeover?
Vertically integrate backward?	Existence of corporate raiders?
Enlarge corporate portfolio?	Increase in regional competition?
Overcome barriers to entry?	Changes in demographic factors?
Reduce rivalry among competitors?	Changes in economic factors?
Make profitable new acquisitions?	Downturn in economy?
Apply brand name capital in new areas?	Rising labor costs?
Seek fast market growth?	Slower market growth?
Others?	Others?

mission and goals will be stated explicitly in the case; at other times you will have to infer them from available information. The information you need to collect to find out the company's corporate strategy includes such factors as its line(s) of business and the nature of its subsidiaries and acquisitions. It is important to analyze the relationship among the company's businesses. Do they trade or exchange

resources? Are there gains to be achieved from synergy? Or is the company just running a portfolio of investments? This analysis should enable you to define the corporate strategy that the company is pursuing (for example, related or unrelated diversification, or a combination of both) and to conclude whether the company operates in just one core business. Then take your SWOT analysis and debate the merits of this strategy. Is it appropriate, given the environment the company is in? Could a change in corporate strategy provide the company with new opportunities or transform a weakness into a strength? For example, should the company diversify from its core business into new businesses?

Other issues should be considered as well. How and why has the company's strategy changed over time? What is the claimed rationale for any changes? Often it is a good idea to analyze the company's businesses or products to assess its situation and identify which divisions contribute most to or detract from its competitive advantage. It is also useful to explore how the company has built its portfolio over time. Did it acquire new businesses or did it internally venture its own? All these factors provide clues about the company and indicate ways of improving its future performance.

6. *Analyzing business-level strategy* Once you know the company's corporate-level strategy and have done the SWOT analysis, the next step is to identify the company's business-level strategy. If the company is a single-business company, then its business-level strategy is identical to its corporate-level strategy. If the company is in many businesses, then each business will have its own business-level strategy. You will need to identify the company's generic competitive strategy—differentiation, low cost, or focus—and its investment strategy, given the company's relative competitive position and the stage of the life cycle. The company also may market different products using different business-level strategies. For example, it may offer a low-cost product range and a line of differentiated products. You should be sure to give a full account of a company's business-level strategy to show how it competes.

Identifying the functional strategies that a company pursues to build competitive advantage through superior efficiency, quality, customer responsiveness, and innovation and to achieve its business-level strategy is very important. The SWOT analysis will have provided you with information on the company's functional competencies. You should further investigate production, marketing, or research and development strategy to gain a picture of where the company is going. For example, pursuing a low-cost or a differentiation strategy successfully requires a very different set of competencies. Has the company developed the right ones? If it has, how can it exploit them further? Can it pursue both a low-cost and a differentiation strategy simultaneously?

The SWOT analysis is especially important at this point if the industry analysis, particularly Porter's model, has revealed the threats to the company from the environment. Can the company deal with these threats? How should it change its business-level strategy to counter them? To evaluate the potential of a company's business-level strategy, you must first perform a thorough SWOT analysis that captures the essence of its problems.

Once you complete this analysis, you will have a full picture of the way the company is operating and be in a position to evaluate the potential of its strategy. Thus you will be able to make recommendations concerning the pattern of its future actions. But first you need to consider strategy implementation, or the way the company tries to achieve its strategy.

7. *Analyzing structure and control systems* The aim of the analysis here is to identify what structure and control systems the company is using to implement its strategy and to evaluate whether that structure is the appropriate one for the company. As we discuss in Chapter 13, different corporate and business strategies require different structures. Chapter 13 provides you with the conceptual tools to determine *the degree of fit between the company's strategy and structure*. For example, does the company have the right level of vertical differentiation (for instance, does it have the appropriate number of levels in the hierarchy or decentralized control?) or horizontal differentiation (does it use a functional structure when it should be using a product structure?)? Similarly, is the company using the right integration or control systems to manage its operations? Are managers being appropriately rewarded? Are the right rewards in place for encouraging cooperation among divisions? These are all issues that should be considered.

In some cases, there will be little information on these issues, whereas in others there will be a lot. Obviously, in writing each case, you should gear the analysis toward its most salient issues. For example, organizational conflict, power, and politics will be important issues for some companies. Try to analyze why problems in these areas are occurring. Do they occur because of bad strategy formulation or because of bad strategy implementation?

Organizational change is an issue in most of the cases because the companies are attempting to alter their strategies or structures to solve strategic problems. Thus as a part of the analysis, you might suggest an action plan that the company in question could use to achieve its goals. For example, you might list in a logical sequence the steps the company would need to follow to alter its business-level strategy from differentiation to focus.

8. *Making recommendations* The last part of the case analysis process involves making recommendations based on your analysis of the case. Obviously, the quality of your recommendations is a direct result of the thoroughness with which you prepared the case analysis. The work you put into the case analysis will be obvious to the professor from the nature of your recommendations. Recommendations are directed at solving whatever strategic problem the company is facing and at increasing its future profitability. Your recommendations should be in line with your analysis—that is, should follow logically from the previous discussion. For example, your recommendations generally will center on the specific ways of changing functional, business, and corporate strategy and organizational structure and control to improve business performance. The set of recommendations will be specific to each case, and so it is difficult to discuss these recommendations here. Such recommendations might include an increase in spending on specific research and development projects, the divesting of certain businesses, a change from a strategy of unrelated to related diversification, an increase in the level of integration among divisions by using task forces and teams, or a move to a different kind of structure to implement a new business-level strategy. Again, make sure your recommendations are mutually consistent and are written in the form of an action plan. The plan might contain a timetable that sequences the actions for changing the company's strategy and a description of how changes at the corporate level will necessitate changes at the business level and subsequently at the functional level.

After following all these stages, you will have performed a thorough analysis of the case and will be in a position to join in class discussion or present your

ideas to the class, depending on the format used by your professor. Remember that you must tailor your analysis to suit the specific issue discussed in your case. In some cases, you might omit completely one of the stages of the analysis because it is not relevant to the situation you are considering. You must be sensitive to the needs of the case and not apply the framework we have discussed in this section blindly. The framework is meant only as a guide and not as an outline that you must use to do a successful analysis.

WRITING A CASE STUDY

Often, as part of your course requirements, you will need to write up one or more of the cases and present your instructor with a written case analysis. This may be an individual or a group report. Whatever the situation, there are certain guidelines to follow in writing a case that will improve the evaluation that your analysis will receive from your teacher. Before we discuss these guidelines, and before you use them, make sure that they do not conflict with any instructions your teacher has given you.

The structure of your written report is critical. Generally, if you follow the stages of analysis discussed in the previous section, *you already will have a good structure for your written discussion.* All reports begin with an *introduction* to the case. In it, you outline briefly what the company does, how it developed historically, what problems it is experiencing, and how you are going to approach the issues in the case write-up. Do this sequentially, saying, "First, we discuss the environment of Company X. . . . Third, we discuss Company X's business-level strategy. . . . Last, we provide recommendations for turning around Company X's business."

In the second part of the case write-up, the strategic analysis section, do the SWOT analysis, analyze and discuss the nature and problems of the company's business-level and corporate strategy, and then analyze its structure and control systems. Make sure you use plenty of headings and subheadings to structure your analysis. For example, have separate sections on any important conceptual tool you use. Thus you might have a section on Porter's five forces model as part of your analysis of the environment. Or you might offer a separate section on portfolio techniques when analyzing a company's corporate strategy. Tailor the sections and subsections to the specific issue of importance in the case.

In the third part of the case write-up, present your solutions and recommendations. Be comprehensive, do this in line with the previous analysis so that the recommendations fit together, and move logically from one to the next. The recommendations section is very revealing because, as mentioned earlier, your teacher will have a good idea of how much work you put into the case from the quality of your recommendations.

Following this framework will provide a good structure for most written reports, though obviously it must be shaped to fit the individual case being considered. Some cases are about excellent companies experiencing no problems. In such instances, it is hard to write recommendations. Instead, you can focus on analyzing why the company is doing so well and using that analysis to structure the discussion. There are some minor points to note that also can affect the evaluation you receive.

1. Do not repeat in summary form large pieces of factual information from the case and feed them back to the instructor in the report. The instructor has read the case and knows what is going on. Rather, use the information in the case to illustrate your statements, to defend your arguments, or to make salient points. Beyond the brief introduction to the company, you must avoid being *descriptive;* instead, you must be *analytical.*

2. Make sure the sections and subsections of your discussion flow logically and smoothly from one to the next. That is, try to build on what has gone before so that the case study builds to a climax. This is particularly important for group cases. With group cases there is a tendency for people to split up the work and say, "I'll do the beginning, you take the middle, and I'll do the end." The result is bad because the parts of the analysis do not flow from one to the next, and it is obvious to the instructor that no real group work has been done.

3. Avoid grammatical and spelling errors. They make the paper seem sloppy.

4. Some cases dealing with well-known companies end in 1993 or 1994 because no later information was available when the case was written. If possible, do a library search for more information on what has happened to the company since then. Following are sources of information for performing this search:

Compact disc sources like Lotus One Source and InfoTrac provide an amazing amount of good information including summaries of recent articles written on specific companies that you can then access in the library.

F&S Predicasts provide a listing on a yearly basis of all the articles written about a particular company. Simply reading the titles gives an indication of what has been happening in the company.

10K annual reports often provide an organization chart.

Write to the company for information.

Fortune, *Business Week*, and *Forbes* have many articles on companies featured in the cases in this book.

Standard & Poor's industry reports provide detailed information about the competitive conditions facing the company's industry. Be sure to look at this journal.

5. Sometimes the instructor will hand out questions for each case to help you in your analysis. Use these as a guide for analyzing and writing the case because they often illuminate the important issues that have to be covered in the discussion.

If you follow the guidelines in this section, you should be able to write a thorough and effective evaluation.

GUIDELINES FOR THE STRATEGIC MANAGEMENT PROJECT

The case study guidelines just discussed also can be followed to help you research and write up the analysis for the strategic management project modules that are at the end of every chapter in this book. In order to answer the questions contained in each strategic management module, for example, it will be necessary to locate and access articles on the company you choose to study in

the same way that you will update the information on companies in the cases in this book. Obviously, you will need to collect more information on the company you choose because it is *your case*.

The guidelines also can be used to help you to write up your strategic management project. The experience you develop from analyzing one or more of the companies in the cases in this book, and writing up the analysis, should allow you to improve your analytical skills and help to improve the strategic management project. Essentially, in your strategic management project you are writing about and analyzing a company at the same time to show how that company creates value through its strategy and structure.

THE ROLE OF FINANCIAL ANALYSIS IN CASE STUDY ANALYSIS

Another important aspect of analyzing and writing a case study is the role and use of financial information. A careful analysis of the company's financial condition immensely improves a case write-up. After all, financial data represent the concrete results of the company's strategy and structure. Although analyzing financial statements can be quite complex, a general idea of a company's financial position can be determined through the use of ratio analysis. Financial performance ratios can be calculated from the balance sheet and income statement. These ratios can be classified into five different subgroups: profit ratios, liquidity ratios, activity ratios, leverage ratios, and shareholder-return ratios. These ratios should be compared to the industry average or the company's prior years of performance. It should be noted, however, that deviation from the average is not necessarily bad; it simply warrants further investigation. For example, younger companies will have purchased assets at a different price and will likely have a different capital structure than older companies. In addition to ratio analysis, a company's cash flow position is of critical importance and should be assessed. Cash flow shows how much actual cash a company possesses.

Profit Ratios

Profit ratios measure the efficiency with which the company uses its resources. The more efficient the company, the greater is its profitability. It is useful to compare a company's profitability against that of its major competitors in its industry. Such a comparison will tell you whether the company is operating more or less efficiently than its rivals. In addition, the change in a company's profit ratios over time will tell you whether its performance is improving or declining.

A number of different profit ratios can be used, and each of them measures a different aspect of a company's performance. The most commonly used profit ratios are as follows:

1. *Gross profit margin* The gross profit margin simply gives the percentage of sales available to cover general and administrative expenses and other operating costs. It is defined as follows:

$$\text{Gross Profit Margin} = \frac{\text{Sales Revenue} - \text{Cost of Goods Sold}}{\text{Sales Revenue}}$$

2. *Net profit margin* Net profit margin is the percentage of profit earned on sales. This ratio is important because businesses need to make a profit to survive in the long run. It is defined as follows:

$$\text{Net Profit Margin} = \frac{\text{Net Income}}{\text{Sales Revenue}}$$

3. *Return on total assets* This ratio measures the profit earned on the employment of assets. It is defined as follows:

$$\text{Return on Total Assets} = \frac{\text{Net Income Available to Common Stockholders}}{\text{Total Assets}}$$

Net income is the profit after preferred dividends have been paid. Preferred dividends are set by contract. Total assets include both current and non-current assets.

4. *Return on stockholders' equity* This ratio measures the percentage of profit earned on common stockholders' investment in the company. In theory, a company attempting to maximize the wealth of it stockholders should be trying to maximize this ratio. It is defined as follows:

$$\text{Return on Stockholders' Equity} = \frac{\text{Net Income Available to Common Stockholders}}{\text{Stockholders' Equity}}$$

Liquidity Ratios

A company's liquidity is a measure of its ability to meet short-term obligations. An asset is deemed liquid if it can be readily converted into cash. Liquid assets are current assets such as cash, marketable securities, accounts receivable, and so on. Two commonly used liquidity ratios are as follows:

1. *Current ratio* The current ratio measures the extent to which the claims of short-term creditors are covered by assets that can be quickly converted into cash. Most companies should have a ratio of at least 1 because failure to meet these commitment can lead to bankruptcy. The ratio is defined as follows:

$$\text{Current Ratio} = \frac{\text{Current Assets}}{\text{Current Liabilities}}$$

2. *Quick ratio* The quick ratio measures a company's ability to pay off the claims of short-term creditors without relying on the sale of its inventories. This is a valuable measure since in practice the sale of inventories is often difficult. It is defined as follows:

$$\text{Quick Ratio} = \frac{\text{Current Assets} - \text{Inventory}}{\text{Current Liabilities}}$$

Activity Ratios

Activity ratios indicate how effectively a company is managing its assets. Two ratios are particularly useful here.

1. *Inventory turnover* This measures the number of times inventory is turned over. It is useful in determining whether a firm is carrying excess stock in inventory. It is defined as follows:

$$\text{Inventory turnover} = \frac{\text{Cost of Goods Sold}}{\text{Inventory}}$$

Cost of goods sold is a better measure of turnover than sales, since it is the cost of the inventory items. Inventory is taken at the balance sheet date. Some companies choose to compute an average inventory

$$\left(\frac{\text{beginning inventory plus ending inventory}}{2}\right)$$

but for simplicity use the inventory at the balance sheet date.

2. *Days sales outstanding (DSO) or average collection period* This ratio is the average time a company has to wait to receive its cash after making a sale. It measures how effective the company's credit, billing, and collection procedures are. It is defined as follows:

$$\text{DSO} = \frac{\text{Accounts Receivable}}{\text{Total Sales/360}}$$

Accounts receivable is divided by average daily sales. 360 is the standard number of days used for most financial analysis.

Leverage Ratios

A company is said to be highly leveraged if it uses more debt than equity, including stock and retained earnings. The balance between debt and equity is called the *capital structure*. The optimal capital structure will be determined by the individual company. Debt has a lower cost because creditors take less risk; they know they will get their interest and principal. However, debt can be risky to the firm because if enough profit is not made to cover the interest and principal payments, bankruptcy can occur.

Three commonly used leverage ratios are as follows:

1. *Debt-to-assets ratio* The debt-to-asset ratio is the most direct measure of the extent to which borrowed funds have been used to finance a company's investments. It is defined as follows:

$$\text{Debt-to-Assets} = \frac{\text{Total Debt}}{\text{Total Assets}}$$

Total debt is the sum of a company's current liabilities and its long-term debt, and total assets are the sum of fixed assets and current assets.

2. *Debt-to-equity ratio* The debt-to-equity measure indicates the balance between debt and equity in a company's capital structure. This is perhaps the most widely used measure of a company's leverage. It is defined as follows:

$$\text{Debt-to-Equity} = \frac{\text{Total Debt}}{\text{Total Equity}}$$

3. *Times-covered ratio* The times-covered ratio measures the extent to which a company's gross profit covers its annual interest payments. If the times-covered ratio declines to less than 1, then the company is unable to meet its interest costs and is technically insolvent. The ratio is defined as follows:

$$\text{Times-covered Ratio} = \frac{\text{Profit Before Interest and Tax}}{\text{Total Interest Charges}}$$

Shareholder-Return Ratios

Shareholder-return ratios measure the return earned by shareholders from holding stock in the company. Given the goal of maximizing stockholder wealth, providing shareholders with an adequate rate of return is a primary objective of most companies. As with profit ratios, it can be helpful to compare a company's shareholder returns against those of similar companies. This will give you a yardstick for determining how well the company is satisfying the demands of this particularly important group of organizational constituents. Four commonly used ratios are given below.

1. *Total shareholder returns* Total shareholder returns measure the returns earned by time $t + 1$ on an investment in a company's stock made at time t. (*Time t* is the time at which the initial investment is made.) Total shareholder returns include both dividend payments and appreciation in the value of the stock (adjusted for stock splits) and are defined as follows:

$$\text{Total Shareholder Returns} = \frac{\text{Stock Price (t + 1) – Stock Price (t) + Sum of Annual Dividends per Share}}{\text{Stock Price (t)}}$$

Thus if a shareholder invests $2 at time t, and at time $t + 1$ the share is worth $3, while the sum of annual dividends for the period t to $t + 1$ has amounted to $0.2, total shareholder returns are equal to (3 – 2 + 0.2)/2=0.6, that is, a 60-percent return on an initial investment of $2 made at time t.

2. *Price-earnings ratio* The price-earnings ratio measures the amount investors are willing to pay per dollar of profit. It is defined as follows:

$$\text{Price-Earnings Ratio} = \frac{\text{Market Price per Share}}{\text{Earnings per Share}}$$

3. *Market to book value* Another useful ratio is market to book value. This measures a company's expected future growth prospects. It is defined as follows:

$$\text{Market to Book Value} = \frac{\text{Market Price per Share}}{\text{Earnings per Share}}$$

4. *Dividend yield* The dividend yield measures the return to shareholders received in the form of dividends. It is defined as follows:

$$\text{Dividend Yield} = \frac{\text{Dividend per Share}}{\text{Market Price per Share}}$$

Market price per share can be calculated for the first of the year, in which case the dividend yield refers to the return on an investment made at the beginning of the year. Alternatively, the average share price over the year may be used. A company must decide how much of its profits to pay to stockholders and how much to reinvest in the company. Companies with high growth prospects should

have a lower dividend payout ratio than mature companies. The rationale is that shareholders can invest the money elsewhere if the company is not growing. The optimal ratio depends on the individual firm, but the key decider is whether the company can produce better returns than the investor can earn elsewhere.

Cash Flow

Cash flow position is simply cash received minus cash distributed. The net cash flow can be taken from a company's Statement of Cash Flows. Cash flow is important for what it tells us about a company's financing needs. A strong positive cash flow enables a company to fund future investments without having to borrow money from bankers or investors. This is desirable because the company avoids the need to pay out interest or dividends. A weak or negative cash flow means that a company has to turn to external sources to fund future investments. Generally, companies in high-growth industries often find themselves in a poor cash flow position (because their investment needs are substantial), whereas successful companies based in mature industries generally find themselves in a strong cash flow position.

A company's internally generated cash flow is calculated by adding back its depreciation provision to profits after interest, taxes, and dividend payments. If this figure is insufficient to cover proposed new investment expenditures, the company has little choice but to borrow funds to make up the shortfall—or curtail investments. If this figure exceeds proposed new investments, the company can use the excess to build up its liquidity (that is, through investments in financial assets) or to repay existing loans ahead of schedule.

CONCLUSION

When evaluating a case, it is important to be *systematic*. Analyze the case in a logical fashion, beginning with the identification of operating and financial strengths and weaknesses and environmental opportunities and threats. Move on to assess the value of a company's current strategies only when you are fully conversant with the SWOT of the company. Ask yourself whether the company's current strategies make sense, given its SWOT. If they do not, what changes need to be made? What are your recommendations? Above all, link any strategic recommendations you may make to the SWOT analysis. State explicitly how the strategies you identify take advantage of company strengths to exploit environmental opportunities, how they rectify company weaknesses, and how they counter environmental threats. And do not forget to outline what needs to be done to implement your recommendations.

SECTION

A

SMALL BUSINESS AND ENTREPRENEURSHIP CASES

1. Starbucks: Taking the Espresso Lane to Profits
2. Ale-8-One Bottling Company
3. Magee Enterprises, Inc.
4. Northern Dairy Cooperative
5. The Scaffold Plank Incident
6. Ryka, Inc.: The Athletic Shoe with a "Soul"

CASE

1

Starbucks: Taking the Espresso Lane to Profits

Starbucks Coffee Corporation is a Seattle, Washington-based coffee company. It roasts and sells whole-bean coffees and coffee drinks through a national chain of retail outlets/restaurants. Though the sizes of the stores and their formats vary from small, street-corner espresso carts to full-size restaurants, most are modeled after the Italian coffee bars where regulars sit and drink espresso with their friends. The retail outlets/restaurants offer coffee by-the-pound, specialty mugs, and home espresso-making machines in addition to prepared Italian beverages such as lattes, mochas, and cappuccinos. They tend to be located in high-traffic locations such as malls, busy street corners, and even grocery stores (*Ledger Star*, March 29, 1993). Although the company's revenues originally were derived only from the sale of packaged, premium, roasted coffees, the bulk of the company's revenues now come from its coffee bars where people can purchase beverages and pastries in addition to coffee by the pound. Starbucks is credited with changing the way Americans view coffee, and its success has attracted the attention of investors nationwide.

THE HISTORY OF STARBUCKS

In 1971, three Seattle entrepreneurs, Jerry Baldwin, Zev Siegl, and Gordon Bowher, started selling whole-bean coffee in Seattle's Pike Place Market. They named their store Starbucks, after the first mate in *Moby Dick*. By 1982, the business had grown to a bustling business of five stores, a small roasting facility, and a wholesale business selling coffee to local restaurants. At the same time, Howard Schulze had been working as vice president of U.S. operations for Hammarplast, a Swedish housewares company in New York, marketing coffee makers to a number of retailers, including Starbucks (*Success*, 1993). Through selling to Starbucks, Schulze was introduced to the three founders who recruited him to bring marketing savvy to the loosely run company (*Inc.*, January 1993). Schulze, 29 and recently married, was anxious to leave New York, so he moved to Seattle and joined Starbucks as manager of retail sales and marketing.

One year later, Schulze visited Italy for the first time on a buying trip. As he strolled through the piazzas of Milan one evening, he was inspired by a vision. Coffee is an integral part of the romantic culture in Italy; Italians start their day at an espresso bar and return with their friends later on. There are 200,000 coffee bars in Italy, and 1,500 in Milan alone. Schulze believed that, given the chance, Americans would pay good money for a premium cup of coffee and a

This case was prepared by Melissa A. Schilling, University of Washington. This case was prepared as a basis for class discussion rather than to illustrate either effective or ineffective handling of administrative situations.

stylish, romantic place to enjoy it. Enthusiastic about his idea, Schulze rushed back to tell the Starbucks owners of his plan for a national chain of Starbucks cafes stylized on the Italian coffee bar. But the owners were less enthusiastic and said that they did not want to be in the restaurant business. Undaunted, Schulze wrote a business plan, videotaped dozens of Italian coffee bars, and began to look for investors. By April 1986 he had opened his first coffee bar, Il Giornale (named after the Italian newspaper), where he served Starbucks coffee. Following Il Giornale's immediate success, Schulze opened a second coffee bar in Seattle and then a third in Vancouver. In 1987 the owners of Starbucks finally agreed to sell Starbucks to Schulze for $4 million. The Il Giornale coffee bars took on the name of Starbucks, and a star was born (*Success*, 1993).

Convinced that Starbucks would one day be in every neighborhood in America, Schulze was intent on growing the company slowly with a very solid foundation. He hired top executives away from corporations such as PepsiCo and was determined that future profits would be well worth early losses. At first, the company's losses almost doubled, to $1.2 million from fiscal 1989 to 1990, as overhead and expenses ballooned with the expansion (*Inc.*, January 1993). Starbucks lost money for three years running, and the stress was hard on Schulze, but he stuck to his conviction not to "sacrifice long-term integrity and values for short-term profit" (*Success*, 1993). In 1991 sales shot up 84 percent, and the company broke into the black.

In 1988 Starbucks had 26 stores; by January 1993 Starbucks had grown to 165 stores with plans to open 78 more in 1993 and 90 in 1994. Everywhere Starbucks opened, people flocked to pay upwards of $1.85 for a cup of coffee. In June 1992 Starbucks went public at $17 a share and was up to $40 a share in April 1993. Enthusiastic analysts predicted that Starbucks could top $1 billion by the end of the decade, but Schulze plays down the company's early successes, asserting that it is better to "underpromise and overdeliver."

STARBUCKS' ENVIRONMENT

The History of the Coffeehouse

Coffee made its way up the Arabian peninsula from Yemen 500 years ago. At that time, coffeehouses were regularly denounced as "gathering places for men, women and boys of questionable morals, hubs of secular thought, centers of sedition and focal points for such dubious activities as the reading aloud of one's own poetry," (*Chicago Tribune*, February 28, 1993).

In Turkey and Egypt, coffeehouses were meeting places for "plotters and other fomenters of insurrection." In Arabian countries, it was considered improper for a Muslim gentleman to sit in a coffeehouse—it was deemed a waste of time and somewhat indecent to gather and discuss secular literature, though these activities later became the rage in European coffeehouses (*Chicago Tribune*, February 28, 1993).

In seventeenth-century London, coffeehouses were suggested as an alternative to the growing use of alcohol. Coffeehouses were a very popular place for the masses to gather since in a coffeehouse a poor person could keep his seat and not be "bumped" if a wealthier person entered. Coffeehouses became known as "penny institutions" where novel ideas were circulated (*Chicago Tribune*, February 28, 1993).

Around the turn of the twentieth century, espresso was invented in Italy. The name refers to the method of forcing high-pressure water through the coffee grounds, rather than the standard percolation techniques (*Los Angeles Times*, December 6, 1992). Espresso and cappuccino rapidly became the preferred beverage of the coffeehouse, and today most Italians and many other Europeans spurn the canned coffee that has been so popular in the United States.

The U.S. Coffee Industry

Americans have a long-standing reputation for buying the cheapest coffee beans available. Most American coffee buyers have to fight growers to keep them from just showing them the culls. Most of the canned coffee on American supermarket shelves is made from the robusta bean—considered to be the lowest quality bean and the highest in caffeine content. Japan, Germany, and Italy, on the other hand, are known for buying the best beans—primarily arabica. There are many different types and grades of arabica and robusta beans, though for years Americans have treated them as a generic commodity (a commodity, incidentally, second only to oil in world production) (*Chicago Tribune*, July 1, 1993).

U.S. coffee consumption peaked in 1962. At that time Americans were drinking an average of 3.1 cups per day. However, from the 1960s to the 1980s coffee consumption suffered a long, steady decline, bottoming out at an average consumption of 1.8 cups per day, or $6.5 billion annually. Whereas three-fourths of all Americans were regular coffee drinkers in the 1960s, today only half of Americans indulge. Since the early 1980s, coffee demand has been stagnant, with growth occurring only in some of the specialty coffees (*Wall Street Journal*, February 25, 1993).

Much of the decline in coffee consumption has been attributed to a growing enthusiasm for more healthful consumption habits in the United States. But though people are cutting down on caffeine, consumption of decaffeinated coffees has not been increasing. According to marketing consultants for the coffee industry, taste is even more important to consumers than health, so many coffee drinkers are cutting down their consumption or giving up coffee altogether rather than switching to decaffeinated brands. People's demand for better-tasting coffees also has hurt the instant coffee market. Sales for instant coffee plummeted 12 percent in the fourth quarter of 1992. While the instant coffee technology impressed consumers following its introduction in 1939, younger consumers appear to be spurning instants.

The more faithful coffee drinkers have turned to the gourmet decaffeinated coffees, specialty flavors, and whole-bean coffees. Even espresso, despite its potent flavor, is lower in caffeine than the canned coffees offered in supermarkets. It is made with arabica beans which are lower in caffeine, and the brewing method yields less caffeine per cup.

Brothers Gourmet Products, a leading marketer of whole-bean coffees to grocery retailers, reports that its sales have been increasing by about 25 percent a year, and the hottest sellers are its hazelnut and French vanilla flavored coffees. Sales of premium coffees have been slowly building since 1985, with an average annual increase of 13 percent. This has prompted many companies to begin offering more exclusive coffee bean blends, coffees with added artificial flavors, and espresso coffees. Today about 19 percent of all retail coffee sold is gourmet, adding up to a $780 million market.

In 1989 there were 1,000 gourmet coffee retailers nationwide; by 1999, that number is expected to reach 2,500. Every month, 75 new shops join the Specialty Coffee Association of America (SCAA). According to the SCAA, sales of gourmet coffee beans and drinks exploded in 1992 to more than $1 billion—a fivefold increase from 1983 (*Los Angeles Times*, April 14, 1993). The espresso craze is spreading around the country—by 1991, it had hit Minneapolis; in 1993, Manhattan. Espresso is even being offered in drive-throughs that offer a quick one-stop shop for cigarettes, newspapers, breakfast foods, and, of course, gourmet coffee for suburbanites facing a long morning commute (*Boston Globe*, June 19, 1993).

Coffee processors predict that by 1999 Americans will spend up to $3 billion a year on gourmet coffee beans or drinks, accounting for one-third of all coffee consumed. A large portion of that growth will come at the expense of Maxwell House, Folgers, and other commercial brands as consumers go upscale. General Foods (Maxwell House) has responded by producing an instant cappuccino and a packaged iced cappuccino in liquid form, aimed at customers who do not like a bitter coffee taste (*Houston Chronicle*, September 23, 1992). Nestlé also has developed a chilled coffee drink, and like General Foods' products, it will be marketed in grocery stores (*Los Angeles Times*, April 14, 1993). Grocery stores also want a piece of the action; many major grocery store chains (including Vons and Safeway) are expanding their selection of gourmet beans that customers can grind and pack themselves.

Some analysts are attributing the explosive growth in gourmet coffee to the poor economy: people are scaling back, but they still need their "minor indulgences." While they cannot afford a luxury car, they can still afford a luxury coffee (*Los Angeles Times*, April 14, 1993). Some people, however, are anticipating trouble on the horizon for the gourmet coffee business, citing several indicators as evidence:

- In California some coffeehouses already have closed due to excessive competition.
- Los Angeles is preparing to regulate coffeehouses (in response to complaints about rowdy late-night patrons)—a sign that the business is maturing. The city council is considering an ordinance that would require coffeehouses open past midnight to obtain a license.
- Coffee bean prices, while currently at an all-time low, are expected to rise in the near future, tightening margins for coffee merchants. Coffee farmers are switching to more profitable fruit and vegetable crops, reducing the world's supply of coffee beans (*Los Angeles Times*, April 14, 1993).

Competitors in the Premium Coffee and Coffee-Bar Market

Starbucks has not been the only company to benefit from the trend toward premium coffees; a swarm of other premium coffee producers and coffee bars have entered the market including Peet's Coffee and Tea in Emeryville, California; Barney's Coffee and Tea in Orlando, Florida; and Gloria Jean's Coffee Bean in Chicago, Illinois.

Peet's Coffee and Tea is a 27-year-old company based in San Francisco, an area Starbucks attacked with vigor due to its large number of sophisticated coffee consumers. Peet's opened three new stores in 1992, including one three blocks away from a Starbucks. But according to Terry Watson, a spokesperson

for Peet's Coffee and Tea, "The more stores specializing in good coffee, the better it is for business. I think competition has helped educate consumers to specialty coffee and better coffee" (*SFBT*, May 14, 1993).

Barney's Coffee & Tea Co. was founded in 1980 in Orlando, Florida. It now has 86 stores in 17 states, mostly in regional malls. While most of its stores are in Florida, it also has a strong presence in Atlanta, stores as far north as Buffalo, New York, and stores as far west as San Antonio, Texas (*Ledger Star*, March 29, 1993).

Gloria Jean's Coffee Bean is considered to be Starbucks' closest rival. Started by former beautician Gloria Jean Kvetko and her former homebuilder husband, Gloria Jean's currently has 124 stores in over 100 cities and will open 58 more (mostly franchises) by the end of 1993. Revenues at Gloria Jean's rose from $18 million in 1989 to $50 million in 1991 (*Business Week*, November 18, 1991). Gloria Jean's targets malls and usually does not provide restaurant seating. Instead customers may drink at a stand-up coffee bar or take their beverages with them. Many analysts are worried that Gloria Jean's will preempt Starbucks' attempt to capture the East Coast market, particularly as Howard Schulze holds tenuously to a slow-growth policy. Gloria Jean's has even infiltrated Starbucks' stronghold in Seattle, having opened a store in Seattle's downtown Westlake Mall.

Though both Barney's and Gloria Jean's sell coffee by the cup, their primary emphasis is on selling coffee beans. Neither tends to have seating in their stores, though a few outlets do. "For a long time the focus was on retailing coffee beans," says Ted Lingle, executive director of the Specialty Coffee Association of America, "then Starbucks figured out the real money is in beverage retailing" (*Ledger Star*, March 29, 1993).

Washington, D.C.-based First Colony Coffee and Tea Co. hopes to be Starbucks' newest rival. Originally an importer and roaster of gourmet coffees, it plans to start opening coffeehouses across the country. It has plans to open more than 50 stores within the next five years. Noting that Starbucks does not offer a wide variety of foods, First Colony president Gill Brockenbrough comments that First Colony will attract more customers by providing light lunch fare (*Ledger Star*, March 18, 1993; *Ledger Star*, March 29, 1993).

Then there are the current chains doing gourmet conversions: Baskin Robbins is transforming a chain of 38 sandwich shops into stylish cafes, and Winchell's executives say they are seriously considering putting cappuccino machines in some of the company's 200 shops (*Los Angeles Times*, April 14, 1993).

Turf wars already have begun in some markets; in fact, Starbucks currently is involved in a trade dress suit against the Second Cup, a chain of coffee stores/cafes based out of Toronto. Starbucks is suing the franchisor and franchisee of two Vancouver stores claiming that its distinctive look and operating style is being copied. The two stores named in the suit were recently remodeled, and Starbucks officials believe that customers might mistake the stores for Starbucks. Michael Bregman, chairman of MM/Muffins, the parent company of Second Cup, states that he thinks the litigation is really related to Starbucks' recent move into Second Cup's home market in Toronto. As of August 1993, the case was not resolved (*Nation's Restaurant News*, October 19, 1992).

Most competitors, however, do not see competition as a bad thing yet. According to Jim Minica, owner of a Houston-based coffee shop, "It's good for the coffee business as a whole to have more shops. It creates more interest and spreads the appreciation of quality coffee" (*Houston Chronicle*, March 15, 1993).

Seattle: The Cradle of the American Espresso Craze

Seattle's enthusiasm for coffee and espresso has been attributed to everything from Seattle's large Scandinavian population to its dreary weather. Some people believe it may be due to Seattle's sizable arts community which gave an immediate popularity to coffeehouses (*The Plain Dealer*, December 20, 1992). Whatever the source of Seattle's coffeemania, Seattle is the recognized capital of U.S. espresso consumption. Espresso is offered everywhere: in office towers, national fast-food chains, even gas stations. The Seattle *Yellow Pages* lists 100 separate entries under "Coffee—Retail." In August 1992 the *Seattle Times* estimated there were 232 espresso stands in the area. The downtown Woolworth's lunch counter even installed an espresso machine next to its corn dogs (*The Plain Dealer*, December 20, 1992). One Seattle espresso cart even boasts a six-figure income (*Chicago Tribune*, July 1, 1993).

While Seattle does not grow beans, its roasters sell to 50 states, and it is the country's leading supplier of espresso machine carts. For an $8,000–$15,000 investment, you can set up an espresso cart and be your own boss. The espresso craze has spawned an exploding business in making carts. Bob Burgess, of Burgess Enterprises in Seattle, notes, "In 1991, we got 15 calls a week for espresso carts. In 1992, that number had grown to 40–70 a week" (*Los Angeles Times*, December 6, 1992).

Two of Seattle's biggest roasters, Torrefazione Italia and Caffe Mauro (soon to be Cafe D'arte) have Italian origins, but Starbucks usually gets credit for first educating consumers about espresso. David Baron, marketing director for Torrefazione Italia, Inc., thinks that Seattle may have "peaked": espresso is showing up in as unlikely places as parking garages, furniture stores, car washes, and dental offices. Seattle even produces its own national coffee magazine, *Cafe Ole* (*Chicago Tribune*, July 1, 1993).

Visitors to Seattle cannot help but be amazed at the plethora of coffee bars and the Seattlelite's mastery of espresso lingo. Tourists to the city are often perplexed when they cannot just order "a cup of coffee." Stores not only provide many different varieties of coffee beans, but the preparation techniques available require substantially more coffee-vocabulary finesse than that possessed by the average American. The coffee craze in Seattle has inspired many people to wonder if the entire city could be addicted to caffeine. A local Seattle columnist has even dubbed the city "Latteland."

THE STRATEGY AT STARBUCKS

While many coffeehouses or espresso bars are franchised, Starbucks owns all of its stores outright. Despite the 300 or so calls a day from willing investors, Schulze feels it is important to the company's integrity to keep all stores company owned.

In designing Starbucks' strategy, Schulze had four companies in mind as role models: Nordstrom's provided a role model for service and is part of the reason that each employee must receive at least 24 hours of training. Home Depot, the home improvement chain, was Schulze's guideline for managing high growth. Microsoft gave Schulze the inspiration for employee ownership, resulting in Starbucks' innovative Bean Stock Plan. And Ben & Jerry's was Schulze's role model for philanthropy; Starbucks sponsors community festivals, donates

money to CARE for health and literacy programs in coffee-growing countries, and donates to charity any packages of beans that have been open for a week (*Money*, September 8, 1992).

Redefining "A Cup of Joe"

In order to make the coffee bar successful in the United States, Starbucks had to create coffee connoisseurs. Starbucks' employees spend a good portion of their time instructing customers on Starbucks' global selection of coffee. While many Americans were raised on commodity-like coffee composed of arabica beans mixed with less-expensive filler beans, Starbucks' coffee is strictly arabica. Dave Olsen, the company's chief coffee procurer, scours mountain trails in Indonesia, Kenya, Guatemala, and elsewhere in search of Starbucks' premium bean.

Olsen's standards are demanding. For example, to develop the summer blends, Olsen conducts exacting experiments with varying percentages of African beans in order to get the proper balance of flavor, body, and acidity. For 1993 he chose "Zambia for brightness, Burundi for great body and full flavor, and a complement of others to capture the floral aroma and taste intensity unique to African continents" (*PR Newswire*, June 2, 1993).

Olsen tests the coffees by "cupping" them—a process similar to wine tasting that involves inhaling the steam ("the strike" and "breaking the crust"), tasting the coffee, and spitting it out ("aspirating" and "expectorating") (*Sacramento Bee*, April 28, 1993).

He has had to convince coffee growers that it is worth growing premium coffees—an especially hard task since American coffee buyers are notorious purchasers of the "dregs" of the coffee beans. Traditionally most of the premium coffee beans were bought by Europeans and the Japanese. Starbucks recently outbid European buyers for the exclusive Narino Supremo bean crop. This Columbian coffee bean crop is very small and grows only in the high regions of the Cordillera mountain range. For years, the Narino beans were guarded zealously by Western Europeans who prized its colorful and complex flavor. It was usually used for upgrading blends. Starbucks was determined to make them available for the first time as a pure varietal. This required breaking Western Europe's monopoly over the beans by convincing the Columbian growers that it intended to use "the best beans for a higher purpose." Starbucks collaborated with a mill in the tiny town of Pasto, located on the side of the Volcano Galero. There they set up a special operation to single out the particular Narino Supremo bean, and Starbucks guaranteed to purchase the entire yield. Today Starbucks is the exclusive purveyor of Narino Supremo, purportedly one of the best coffees in the world (*Canada Newswire*, March 1, 1993).

Procurement is not the only area where extreme care differentiates Starbucks' product: roasting is close to an art form at Starbucks. Roasters are promoted from within the company and trained for over a year, and it is considered quite an honor to be chosen. The coffee is roasted in a powerful gas oven for 12 to 15 minutes while roasters use their sight, smell, and hearing to judge when beans are perfectly done. The color of the beans is even tested in an Agtron blood-cell analyzer, with the whole batch being discarded if the sample is not deemed perfect.

Though *Consumer Reports* deemed Starbucks' coffee as burnt and bitter, Starbucks' customers believe otherwise, and most of Starbucks' early growth can be attributed to enthusiastic word-of-mouth advertising. The typical Starbucks customer is highly proficient in the science of coffee beans and brewing

techniques. The coffee bars even have their own dialect; executives from downtown Seattle's businesses line up in force to order "tall-skinny-double mochas" and 2% short no-foam lattes."

Making Coffee Bars a Social Destination

In order to create American coffee enthusiasts with the dedication of their Italian counterparts, Starbucks needed to provide a seductive atmosphere in which to imbibe. The stores are sleek yet comfortable. Coffee preparers are referred to as "baristas," Italian for bartender, and *biscotti* is available in glass jars on the counter. The stores are well-lighted, they feature plenty of burnished wood and brass, and sophisticated artwork hangs on the walls. Jazz or opera music plays softly in the background. According to Schulze, "We're not just selling a cup of coffee, we are providing an experience" (*Business Week*, November 18, 1991).

As Americans cut down on their alcohol consumption, Schulze hopes to make coffee bars the new social destination. Coffee bars provide a "politically correct" alternative to traditional bars, and baby-boomers are joining the "black turtleneck crowd" in the numerous cafes sprouting up all over America. Stefan Bell, a young actor in San Francisco, comments, "Everyone is quitting alcohol and drugs. You see people coming in [to coffee bars] after AA meetings" (*Times*, May 24, 1993).

Decaffeinated latte also has provided a tastier solution for those people wishing to cut down on caffeine. There has been a marked consumer trend toward more healthful fare, causing overall coffee consumption to decline, and decaffeinated brands are not picking up the slack. Many consumers seem disappointed with the flavor of decaffeinated coffees and have opted to give up coffee entirely. Decaf sales in the grocery stores have been steadily dropping, making decaffeinated coffee one of the fastest-declining categories in the supermarket (*Wall Street Journal*, February 25, 1993). Gourmet coffee stores such as Starbucks are able to provide decaffeinated coffee drinks with all the pungent flavor of regular coffee, prompting many supermarket coffee shoppers to convert to the espresso habit.

Pampering Employees

Schulze believes that employee benefits are the key to competitiveness and growth. He states, "We can't achieve our strategic objectives without a work force of people who are immersed in the same commitment as management. Our only sustainable advantage is the quality of our work force. We're building a national retail company by creating pride in—and stake in—the outcome of our labor" *Inc.*, January 1993).

Starbucks' generous and comprehensive employee benefits package encompasses health care, stock options, training programs, career counseling, and product discounts for all workers, full-time and part-time alike. He has added heavy emphasis on preventative health care by providing a special deductible-exempt $300 allowance for annual physicals, and he also offers dental and vision care coverage. While many companies scrimp on these essentials, Schulze believes that without these benefits people do not feel financially or spiritually tied to their jobs. The stock options and the complete benefits package increase employee loyalty and encourage attentive service to the customer (*Inc.*, January 1993).

It was difficult to get insurers to sign Starbucks up since they did not understand why Starbucks would want to cover part-timers. The increase in premiums,

however, were offset by lower training costs due to the lower attrition rate (employee attrition for Starbucks is less than 50 percent, compared to a triple digit national average for retailers). This strategy has been successful for Starbucks in part because its employees are relatively young. Half of the management at Starbucks is under 50, and retail employees tend to be much younger. According to Orin Smith, chief financial officer of Starbucks, "I'd be surprised if we had 40-year-olds behind the counter 10 years from now" (*Inc.*, January 1993).

Despite the increased coverage, Starbucks' health care costs are well within the national average, running around $150 per employee per month. Its claims are lower, a fact reflected in the rates Starbucks pays. However, as workers age and have children, and as the company spreads eastward (health care costs are higher in the East), coverage costs are bound to rise.

Employee turnover is also discouraged by Starbucks' stock option plan (known as the Bean Stock Plan). Implemented in August 1991, the plan made Starbucks the only private company to offer stock options unilaterally to all employees. After one year, employees may join a 401(k) plan. There is a vesting period of five years; it starts one year after the option is granted, and then the employee is vested at 20 percent every year. In addition, every employee receives a new stock-option award each year, and a new vesting period begins. This plan required getting an exemption from the Securities and Exchange Commission, since any company with more than 500 shareholders has to report its financial performance publicly—a costly process which reveals valuable information to competitors.

The option plan did not go uncontested by the venture capitalists and shareholders on the board. Craig Foley, a director and managing partner of Chancellor Capital Management, Inc. (and the largest shareholder before the public offering), says, "Increasing the shareholders substantially dilutes our interest. We take that very seriously." In the end they were won over by a study conducted by Orin Smith, which revealed the positive relationship between employee ownership and productivity rates, and a scenario analysis of how many employees would be vested. Foley conceded that the company's culture was a major component of its profitability. "The grants are tied to overachieving. If you just come to work and do your job, that isn't as attractive as if you beat the numbers" (*Inc.*, January 1993).

Since the Bean Stock Plan was put into place, enthusiastic employees have been suggesting ways to save money and increase productivity. The strong company culture also has served as a levy against pilferage; Starbucks' inventory shrinkage is less than half of 1 percent.

Training programs are extensive at Starbucks. Each employee takes at least 25 hours worth of classes. Classes cover everything from coffee history to a seven-hour workshop called Brewing the Perfect Cup at Home (*Success*, 1993). Employee knowledge is critical since store employees frequently will have to educate consumers about espresso and its derivative beverages.

Schulze is also known for his sensitivity to the well-being of employees. Recently when an employee told Schulze that he had AIDS, Schulze reassured him that he could work as long as he wanted to, and that when he left, Starbucks would continue to cover his insurance. After the employee left the room, Schulze sat down and wept. Schulze attributes his concern for his employees to his memories of his father. According to Schulze his father "struggled a great deal and never made more than $20,000 a year, and his work was never valued, emotionally or physically, by his employer. . . . This was an injustice. . . . I want our employees to know we value them."

Growth

Howard Schulze has a strict slow-growth policy. Rather than trying to capture all the potential markets as soon as possible, Starbucks goes into a market and completely dominates it before setting its sights further abroad. Right now Schulze's goal is to conquer the East Coast market, with an initial push into Chicago and Washington, D.C. Starbucks already has 38 stores in Chicago and opened its first store in Washington in March 1993. By December 1993 there will be 10 of the company's outlets in the nation's capital (*Ledger Star*, March 29, 1993).

Some analysts fear that Schulze's relative slow-growth policy may stunt Starbucks' long-term potential. The espresso and coffee-bar craze is spreading heatedly nationwide, and analysts fear that Starbucks may be losing valuable markets to competitors. Though Starbucks has chosen a slow-growth policy relative to its potential, it made *Fortune's* 1993 list of the 50 fastest-growing companies. Starbucks has had an annual compounded growth rate of 80 percent over the past three years. This growth has exceeded the company's expectations, prompting the building of a new $11 million roasting and distribution plant in Kent, Washington. The new 300,000-square foot-plant will roast beans for Starbucks' retail stores nationwide and will serve as a storage place for merchandized products such as mugs and coffee makers. The plant is expected to roast and ship 25 million pounds of coffee beans yearly (*Seattle Times*, April 21, 1993). The Kent site was chosen for its proximity to freeways and ports (most of Starbucks' products are trucked to retail stores) and because Schulze felt a commitment to the Pacific Northwest (*PR Newswire*, April 20, 1993).

Choosing a Location

Currently Starbucks operates stores in the metropolitan areas surrounding Seattle; Chicago; Vancouver, B.C.; Portland, Oregon; Denver; Los Angeles; San Diego; San Francisco; and Washington, D.C. Its direct mail business serves customers in every state. Location choices have been easy; Starbucks opens its cafes in those cities where their direct mail business is strong (*Chicago Tribune*, February 28, 1993). By tracking addresses of mail-order customers to find the highest concentration in a city, Starbucks can ensure that its new stores have a ready audience. And though this normally would imply cannibalizing their mail-order sales, mail-order revenues doubled in 1992 (*Inc.*, January 1993). The two newest major target markets are Chicago and Washington, D.C.

On its eastbound trek, Starbucks made a big impression in Chicago. According to Schulze, "Before we came to Chicago in 1988, we noticed we had an unusually large number of mail-order customers. Specialty coffee simply wasn't available in Chicago." As of the summer of 1993, Starbucks already had 38 stores in Chicago, serving some 200,000 customers a week. And the coup de grâce of Starbucks' success in Chicago is that most of its customers there believe that Starbucks is a Chicago-based company. Schulze even recounts a story of a regular Chicago customer visiting a Starbucks while on a trip to Seattle and remarking, "We didn't know you had opened here as well!" (*Chicago Tribune*, May 17, 1993). Schulze intends to make the Chicago area a 75-store operation. Reportedly, much of this expansion will be in the suburbs, which currently account for only 10 of the 38 locations.

On March 26, 1993, Starbucks opened its flagship store in Washington, D.C. Located at DuPont Circle, the store celebrated its opening with live jazz music and extensive press coverage (*PR Newswire*, March 26, 1993). Schulze sees Washing-

ton, D.C. as the critical entry point for bringing espresso to the East. "Washington has a sophisticated palate," Schulze notes, and he has immediate plans for 10 stores. From D.C. the company will spread into Baltimore and New York.

Starbucks' newest market, and perhaps the most exciting, is its recent venture into Japan. In 1992 Heron Construction & Millwork Ltd. built a Starbucks Coffee Co. outlet in Richmond, B.C., and shipped it to Japan. The kiosk, located in the New Tokyo International Airport at Narita, was the company's first overseas store. The store is a flagship for Asia; fifteen more are planned for Asia's international airports if the Narita store is successful (*Vancouver Sun*, December 17, 1992).

New Approaches to Marketing Coffee

Starbucks has developed very creative marketing strategies for its products; for instance, in its "passport" promotion, customers received a frequent buyer bonus stamp in their "passport" every time they purchased a half-pound of coffee. And each time a customer bought a different coffee, Starbucks validated their "World Coffee Tour." Once a customer collected 10 stamps, they received a free half-pound of coffee. The passport also contained explanations of each type of coffee bean and its country of origin (*Washington Post*, June 30, 1993).

According to George Reynolds, senior vice president of marketing, Starbucks' goal is "to make a powerful aesthetic statement about the quality and integrity of our products, reaffirming through our visual identity the commitment we feel to providing the very best product and service for our customers." In May 1993 Starbucks was one of three recipients for the first annual Fortune/American Center for Design Beacon Award for Outstanding Integrated Communications and Design (*PR Newswire*, May 14, 1993).

Starbucks' creativity in marketing has turned to offering coffee in unusual outlets. Besides its stand-alone stores, Starbucks has set up cafes and carts in hospitals, banks, office buildings, supermarkets, and shopping centers. Recently it has begun putting Starbucks in bookstores. Barnes & Noble has reached an agreement with Starbucks to begin its "cafe-in-a-bookshop" plan. "Coffee and books go hand-in-hand," explained Starbucks' spokesperson Lisa McCrummen (*Orlando Sentinel*, July 6, 1993).

Starbucks also has signed a deal with Nordstrom's, a national chain of upscale department stores based in Seattle. By June 1992 Nordstrom's was serving Starbucks' coffee exclusively in all of its stores (*Seattle Times*, September 29, 1992). By September 1992 Nordstrom's had named Starbucks as the exclusive coffee supplier for its restaurants, employee lunchrooms, and catering operations. At that time Nordstrom's was operating 62 restaurants and 48 espresso bars. The agreement calls for Nordstrom's to serve a special "Nordstrom's blend" of Latin American and Indonesian coffees (*Nation's Restaurant News*, September 28, 1992).

Starbucks also has reached an agreement with Associated Services, an office coffee supplier for northern California. Associated Services will exclusively provide Starbucks coffee to the 5,000 northern California businesses it services. Associated Services also will furnish brewing equipment, condiments, and training to the offices (*PR Newswire*, July 6, 1993). Office coffee is a large segment of the coffee market and may be a growing area for Starbucks.

Perhaps the most creative outlet for its coffee is Starbucks' deal with Smith Brothers, one of the Northwest's oldest dairies. Smith Brothers now sells Starbucks' coffee on its home delivery routes. The idea for the alliance actually came

from the dairy, a longtime supplier for Starbucks. Management at Smith Brothers began to wonder if Starbucks' rapid growth might prompt them to look for other dairies to supply its milk. Earl Keller, sales manager for Smith Brothers, got the idea that "maybe if we were a good customer of theirs, it would be more difficult for them to leave us." The alliance made sense since both companies emphasize freshness in their products, and Starbucks had been looking for a way to make it more convenient for its customers to get bulk coffee. In 1992, Smith delivered 1,000 pounds of coffee beans a week. The coffee is sold at the same price as in Starbucks' retail stores, and the only complaint has been that Smith does not carry all 30 varieties (*Seattle Times*, November 6, 1992).

Starbucks Today

Today Starbucks has 220 stores and profits are "percolating." In 1992, Starbucks was voted one of *Inc.* magazine's five Entrepreneurs of the Year, out of 2,619 nominations. In 1993, *Fortune* named Starbucks as the thirty-ninth fastest-growing company.

For the 1992 fiscal year, Starbucks' net income surged 71 percent to $4.1 million, or 33 cents a share. Sales jumped 61 percent to $93.1 million. Since 1988, annual sales have risen ninefold. Analysts expect the company to earn approximately 50 cents per share in fiscal year 1993, on a sales growth of about 60 percent. This indicates sales for fiscal 1993 of about $149 million. Christopher E. Vroom, a retail analyst with Alex. Brown & Sons projects that Starbucks' sales could top $1 billion by the end of the decade (*Wall Street Journal*, January 8, 1993).

Since its initial public offering in July 1992, Starbucks' stock price has risen from $17 a share to $49 a share. Some investors have speculated that the stock may be overpriced and headed for a fall, but most investors remain enthusiastic, and according to Vroom, "Investors sense that Starbucks has phenomenal growth potential, good management and a strong concept" (*Wall Street Journal*, January 8, 1993).

Exhibit 1

Starbucks' Mission Statement

Establish Starbucks as the premier purveyor of the finest coffee in the world while maintaining our uncompromising principles as we grow. The following five guiding principles will help us measure the appropriateness of our decisions:

Provide a great work environment and treat each other with respect and dignity.

Apply the highest standards of excellence to the purchasing, roasting, and fresh delivery of our coffee.

Develop enthusiastically satisfied customers all of the time.

Contribute positively to our communities and our environment.

Recognize that profitability is essential to our future success.

Exhibit 2
Summary of Financial and Operating Data (in thousands, except per share and operating data)

	1988	1989	1990	1991	1992
Results of Operations Data:					
Net sales	$10,215	$19,218	$35,392	$57,650	$93,078
Operating income (loss)	(629)	(836)	806	2,909	6,371
Earnings (loss) before income taxes	(764)	(1,177)	812	2,409	4,104
Net earnings (loss)	(764)	(1,177)	812	2,409	4,104
Net earnings (loss) per share				$0.24	$0.33
Weighted average shares outstanding				10,156	12,438
Operating Data:					
Percentage change in comparable stores' sales	n/m	19.8%	26.4%	19.3%	20.8%
Sales per square foot for stores open for full year	$451	$437	$507	$596	$702
Average customer transactions per week	47,918	98,416	205,488	343,716	543,009
Number of stores open at end of year	26	46	75	107	154
Balance Sheet Data:					
Working capital	$ 2,166	$ 644	$ 4,470	$ 3,226	$40,591
Total assets	11,623	14,684	27,879	38,188	87,866
Long-term debt (including current portion)	2,154	5,525	3,900	8,100	—
Shareholders' equity	7,367	6,226	6,258	7,304	75,288

Exhibit 3
Balance Sheet
(in thousands, except share data)

	September 27, 1992	September 29, 1991
Assets		
Current Assets:		
Cash and cash equivalents	$20,778	$ 1,120
Short-term investments, at cost	$16,962	—
Accounts receivable (net allowance for doubtful accounts of $48 and $34)	1,571	853
Inventories	11,720	8,120
Prepaid expenses and other current assets	2,138	1,722
Total current assets	53,169	11,815
Property and equipment, net	33,568	22,338
Industrial revenue bond proceeds escrow account	—	2,895
Deposits and other assets	1,129	1,140
Total	$87,866	$38,188
Liabilities and Shareholders' Equity		
Current Liabilities:		
Accounts payable	$ 4,012	$ 3,430
Checks drawn in excess of bank balances	4,580	2,058
Accrued compensation and related costs	1,975	1,411
Other accrued expenses	2,011	1,040
Current portion of long-term debt	—	650
Total current liabilities	12,578	8,589
Long-term debt, less current portion	—	7,450
Redeemable preferred stock	—	14,845
Shareholders' Equity:		
Common stock—Authorized, 50,000,000 shares; issued and outstanding, 13,100,235 and 4,203,464 shares	77,605	7,012
Less stock subscription and notes receivable	(3,671)	(79)
	73,934	6,933
Series A preferred stock	—	248
Retained earnings including cumulative translation adjustment of $(166) and $142	1,354	123
Total shareholders' equity	75,288	7,304
Total	$87,866	$38,188

Exhibit 4
Statement of Earnings (in thousands, except earnings per share)

	September 27, 1992	September 29, 1991	September 30, 1990
Net sales	$93,078	$57,650	$35,392
Cost of sales and related occupancy costs	41,523	26,422	17,299
Store operating expenses	31,234	19,380	10,518
Other operating expenses	2,246	1,480	1,133
Depreciation and amortization	3,644	2,537	1,512
General and administrative expenses	8,060	4,922	4,124
Operating income	6,371	2,909	806
Interest, net	209	(23)	6
Earnings before income taxes	6,580	2,886	812
Income taxes	2,476	477	—
Net earnings	4,104	2,409	812
Preferred stock dividends accrued	(2,565)	(1,503)	(795)
Net earnings available to common shareholders	**$1,539**	**$906**	**$17**
Net earnings per share	**$0.33**	**$0.24**	
Weighted average shares outstanding	12,438	10,516	

Figure 1
U.S. per Capita Coffee Consumption

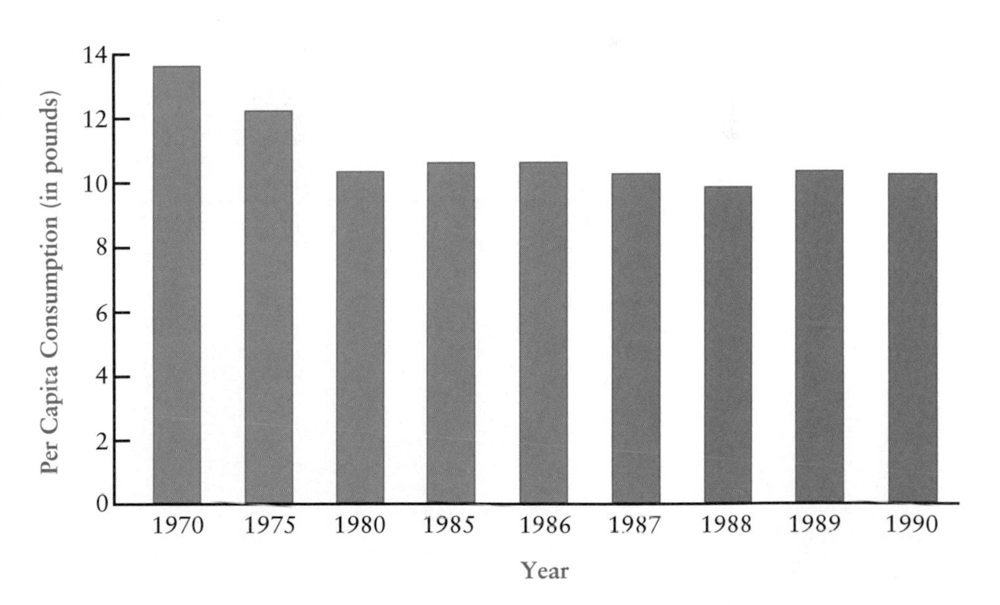

Figure 2
Net Sales

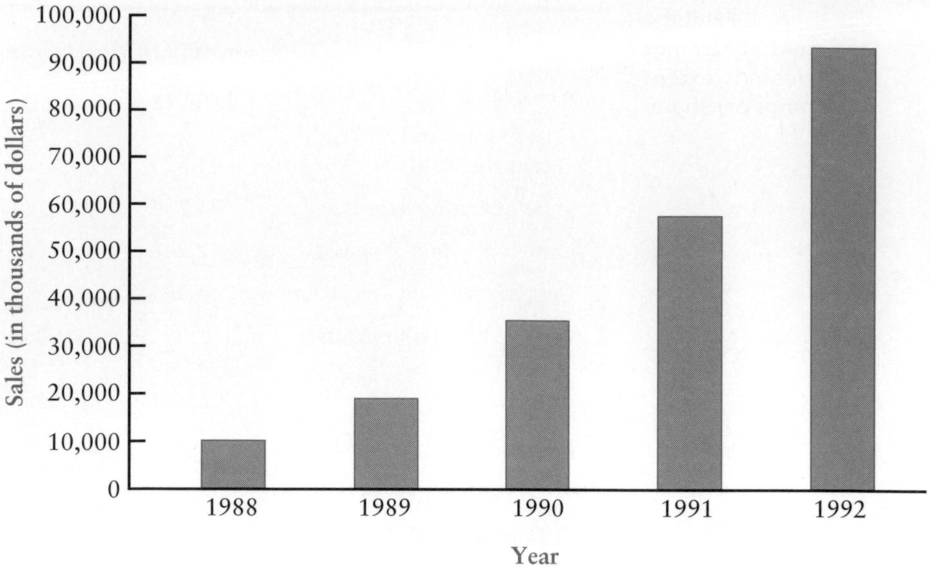

100,000
90,000
80,000
70,000
60,000
50,000
40,000
30,000
20,000
10,000
0
Sales (in thousands of dollars)
1988
1989
1990
1991
1992
Year

Figure 3
Net Income, 1988–1992

5000
4000
3000
2000
1000
0
–1000
–2000
Net Income (in thousands of dollars)
1988
1989
1990
1991
1992
Year

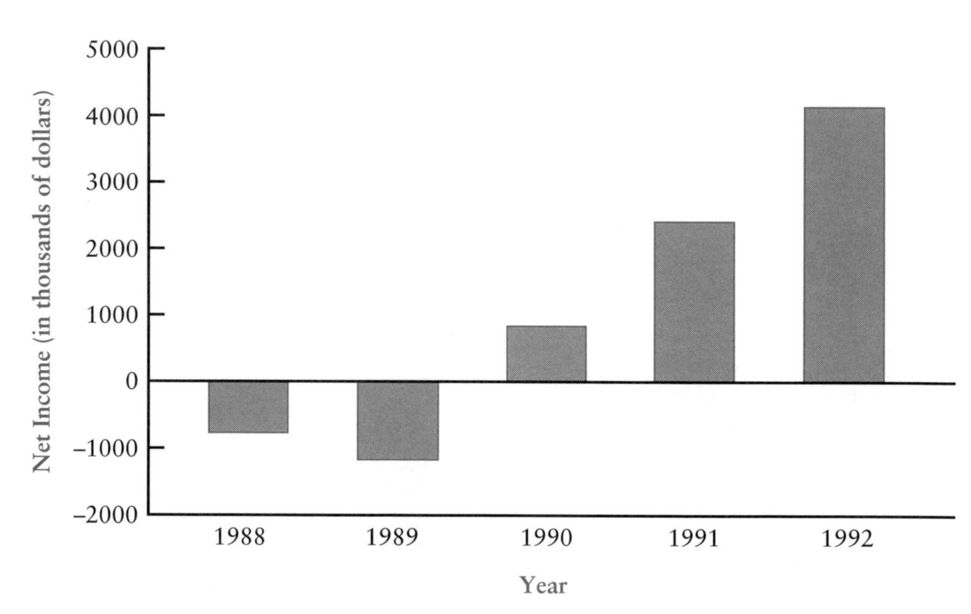

Figure 4
Retail Store Count

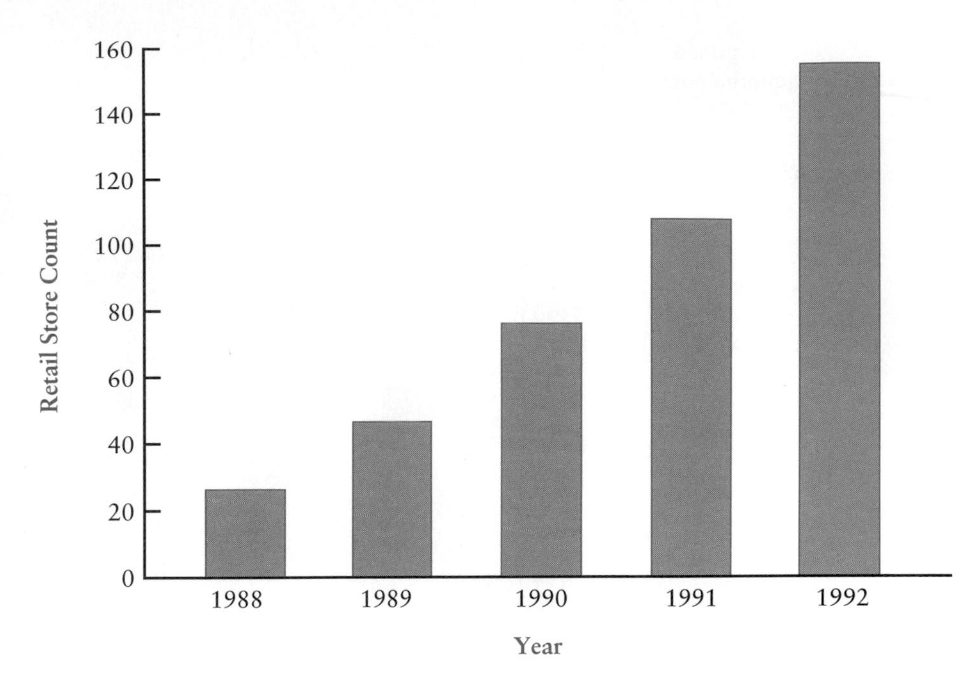

Figure 5
Comparable Store Sales Growth

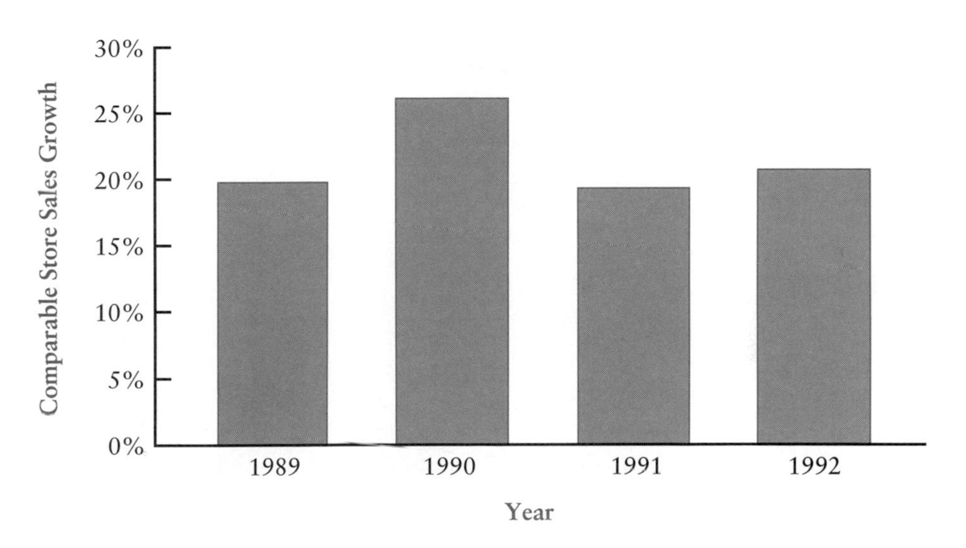

Figure 6
Sales per Square Foot

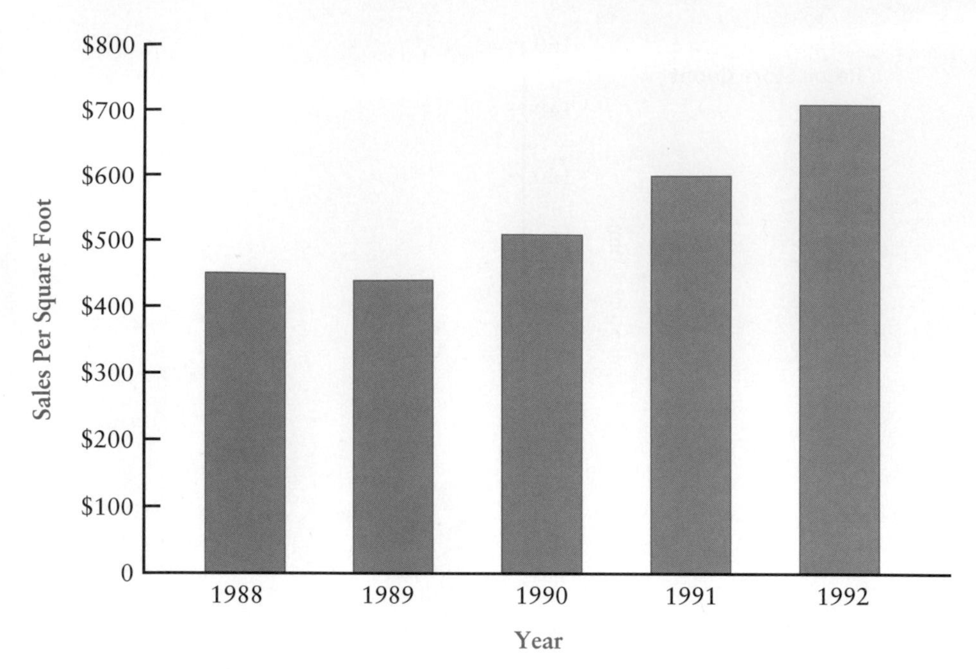

Figure 7
Average Customer Transactions

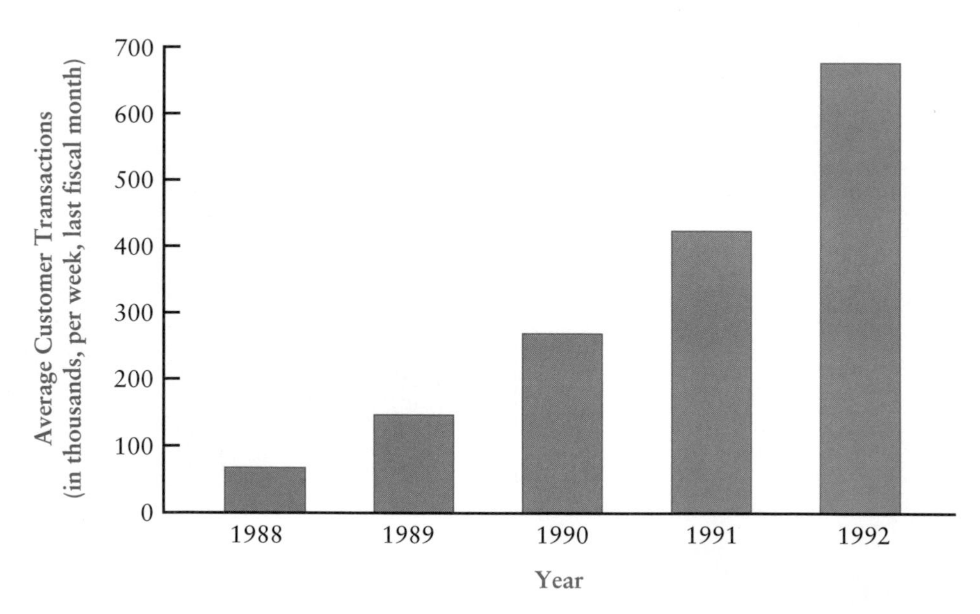

References

Abramovitch, Ingrid. "Miracles of Marketing: How to Reinvent Your Product." *Success*, April 1993.

Anderson Jon. "Something's Brewing. Tired of the Same Old Social Grind, Folks Are Flocking to Coffeehouses." *Chicago Tribune*, February 28, 1993.

Boston Globe. "Premium Fuel in the Morning," June 19, 1993.

Burr, Barry B. "Starbucks' Investors to Win in IPO." *Pensions & Investments*, June 22, 1992.

Canada Newswire. "Starbucks Secured Exclusive Columbia Narino Supremo Crop for Third Consecutive Year," March 1, 1993.

Clark, Jayne. "Good Route to Java Runs through Seattle." *The Plain Dealer*, December 20, 1992.

Criswell, Ann. "New Brew; Specialty Coffee Blends Aren't Just for Breakfast Anymore." *Houston Chronicle*, September 23, 1992.

Dinsmore, Christopher. "Coffeehouse Owners Set Sights on a Chain to Compete Nationally." *Ledger Star*, March 18, 1993.

———. "Hoping Cafes Are Its Cup of Tea." *Ledger Star*, March 29, 1993.

Gellene, Denise. "Designer Coffee Is Hot Stuff; Sales of Gourmet Varieties, as well as Beans and Drinks, Soared in 1992 to More Than $1 Billion, a Fivefold Increase from 1983." *Los Angeles Times*, April 14, 1993.

Geranios, Nicholas. "Specialty Coffee Emerges as Hot-selling Product." *Los Angeles Times*, December 6, 1992.

Goerne, Carrie. "Coffee Consumption Down, but Sales of Exotic Blends Perk Up." *Marketing News*, July 20, 1992.

Gunsch, Dawn. "Benefits Leverage Hiring and Retention Efforts." *Personnel Journal*, November 1992.

Hassell, Greg. "City to Perk Up; Drink's Popularity Prompts Slew of New Coffee Shops." *Houston Chronicle*, March 15, 1993.

Jung, Helen E. "Dining with Design—Nordstrom Finds Recipe for Success in Box Lunches." *Seattle Times*, September 29, 1992.

Kaye, Barry. "There's a Lot of (Star)bucks in Coffee Business: Upscale Java Joints Are Places to Socialize." *Times* (Burlingame, California), May 24, 1993.

Lazarus, George. "Starbucks Brews Plans for Chicago." *Chicago Tribune*, May 17, 1993.

Liddle, Alan. "Starbucks Slaps Second Cup with Trade Dress Suit." *Nation's Restaurant New Newspaper*, October 19, 1992.

Mangelsdorf, Martha E. "The Entrepreneur of the Year." *Inc.*, December 1992.

McCoy, Charles. "Entrepreneur Smells Aroma of Success in Coffee Bars." *Wall Street Journal*, January 8, 1993.

Nation's Restaurant News Newspaper. "Nordstrom Names Starbucks Supplier; Department Store Chain Makes Starbucks Corp. Exclusive Coffee Supplier," September 28, 1992.

Orlando Sentinel, July 6, 1993.

PR Newswire. "Starbucks Coffee Co. Enters First East Coast Market This Morning in Washington, D.C.," March 26, 1993.

———. "Starbucks Coffee Company Expands Roots in Pacific Northwest with New Kent Roasting Plant," April 20, 1993.

———. "Starbucks Coffee Co. Awarded Fortune's First Annual Beacon Award," May 14, 1993.

———. "Brewing the Quintessential Brunch: Summer, Sunday, and Starbucks," June 2, 1993.

———. "Starbucks Coffee Co. Opens Fifth East Coast Store in D.C.'s Dupont Circle," June 8, 1993.

———. July 6, 1993.

Rothman, Matt. "Into the Black." *Inc.*, January 1993.

Sacramento Bee. "Cupping Coffee," April 28, 1993.

Smith, David. "Richmond Firm on Ground Floor as Starbucks Pours Coffee in Japan." *Vancouver Sun*, December 17, 1992.

Stevens, John H. "Coffee Blends Nicely with Milk Deliveries." *Seattle Times*, November 6, 1992.

———. "Starbucks to Build in Kent." *Seattle Times*, April 21, 1993.

Stripling, Sherry. "Seattle Is Abuzz." *Chicago Tribune*, July 1, 1993.

Yang, Dori J. "Coffee: Fewer Cups, but a Much Richer Brew." *Business Week*, November 18, 1991.

Washington Post. "On the Fridge," June 30, 1993.

Williams, Scott. "Starbucks' Growth Is an Open Book." *Seattle Times*, June 29, 1993.

CASE

2

Ale-8-One Bottling Company

INTRODUCTION

Coca-Cola and PepsiCo dominate the U.S. soft drink industry, controlling a combined 74 percent of national market share as of 1991. It was not always this way: in the early part of this century, several thousand local and regional soft drink bottlers operated throughout the United States, and no national brands existed. But, with the rise of national and global brands, especially following World War II, fewer than 100 independent soft drink bottlers remain. U.S. Census data show the steep decline in the number of bottlers since 1947, though these counts do not distinguish independent bottlers from franchise bottlers producing and distributing national brands such as Coke and Pepsi (see Exhibit 1).

One survivor of this industry shakeout is the Ale-8-One Bottling Company of Winchester, Kentucky. Founded in 1902, originally as G. L. Wainscott Partners, "Ale-8" has been family owned and controlled for nearly a century. The company produces only one product, Ale-8-One, a semi-clear, ginger-flavored soft drink. At one level, the company clearly fails to keep pace in a competitive environment characterized by billion-dollar advertising and promotion budgets, intense competition for retail shelf space, constant discounting, and saturated distribution

Exhibit 1
U.S. Census of Manufacturers: Number of U.S. Soft Drink Bottlers

Year	Number
1947	5,618
1954	4,643
1963	3,905
1967	3,057
1972	2,273
1977	1,757
1982	1,236
1987	818

Note: Count includes both independent bottlers and franchises of national brands. Most are franchise bottlers.

This case was prepared by Brian Shaffer and Teri Shanander, University of Kentucky. This case was prepared as a basis for class discussion rather than to illustrate either effective or ineffective handling of administrative situations.

Illustration 1
Ale-8-One Sales Territory

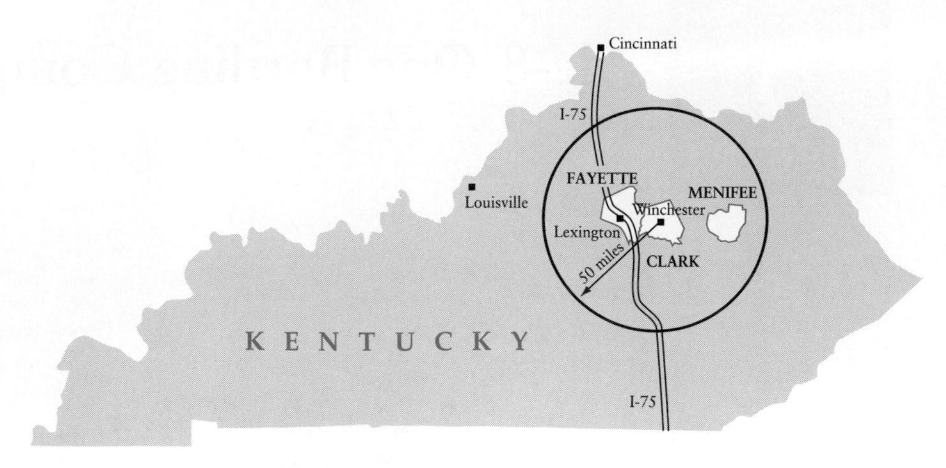

20 percent of sales are in Winchester and Clark County.
95 percent of sales are within a 50-mile radius of Winchester.

channels. Yet Ale-8-One serves a stable and growing customer base. Indeed, the company has doubled case shipments in every decade since World War II.

ALE-8-ONE DESCRIPTION AND HISTORY

In the small, rural town of Winchester, a unique ginger-flavored soft drink called Ale-8-One has been manufactured by the same family since 1927. The "Winchester Champagne" in the returnable emerald green bottle has developed a loyal, almost cult-like following. It is a beverage thought by Kentuckians to be highly addictive, and it is associated with local tradition and folklore. The people of Winchester possess a particularly unique loyalty to their native soft drink, unrivaled by any national soft drink brand sold in the local area. Some convenience stores devote more shelf space to Ale-8 than to Coke and Pepsi products.

With fifty employees and around $6.5 million in gross sales, Ale-8 ships one million cases per year. Ninety-five percent is sold within fifty miles of Winchester; a small amount goes to Cincinnati, Louisville, and other regional markets. (See Illustration 1.) Depending on the outlet, Ale-8's price is substantially higher

Exhibit 2
Income, Employment, and Educational Data for Selected Kentucky Counties

	U.S. Nat. Avg.	Fayette Co.	Clark Co.	Menifee Co.
Location		Lexington	Winchester	Rural area east of Winchester
Personal Income per Capita	$18,639.00	$19,320.00	$14,739.00	$8,206.00
Unemployment Rate	6.70%	3.80%	7.50%	12.50%
% of High School Graduates or Higher	78.40%	80.20%	65.10%	46.00%

than other soft drinks, even though its core customer base has comparatively low income.

Winchester is the county seat of Clark County, population 29,496. Clark County, and especially the counties east of Clark County, are primarily rural and characterized by light industry, agriculture, logging, and mining. The Appalachian Mountain region of eastern Kentucky is beset by poverty, illiteracy, chronic unemployment, and a lack of economic development (see Exhibit 2). Interstate 75 serves as a symbolic division between the rural areas of eastern Kentucky and the relatively prosperous areas of central Kentucky.

In contrast to the economic hardship of eastern Kentucky, the culture is characterized by tradition, loyalty, and commitment to family and community. Local people take pride in local things, such as their county football team. Ale-8's product and brand image fit nicely in this mountain culture. Riley Rogers Walton, an Ale-8 vice president and part-owner, attributes much of the strong loyalty to "Kentucky chauvinism." Kentuckians believe Ale-8 is special. Like horses or basketball, it's Kentucky.

In Winchester, Ale-8 is everywhere. One local intersection has an Ale-8 vending machine on all four corners. "I bet you wouldn't go in a house in Winchester that doesn't have an Ale-8 in it," proclaims Winchester Mayor Clyde Heflin. "The kids especially, they love it."

Clark County High School students frequently carry the green-bottled drink into school in the mornings. The school janitor supplements his income by redeeming empty bottles at the Ale-8 plant in Winchester at 20 cents each.

This devoted clan of Ale-8 drinkers has even found a way to compensate for the beverage's limited distribution. Parents mail cases of the soft drink to sons or daughters away at college. Military personnel from Kentucky had cases of Ale-8 shipped to Vietnam and, more recently, to the Middle East during Operation Desert Storm.

History has shown that competitors who try to tap into Ale-8's market with imitations of the Kentucky ale do not stand much chance of succeeding. Coca-Cola learned that lesson about 15 years ago. The Lexington, Kentucky, Coca-Cola Bottling Company introduced a new drink called "Mountain Ale" for marketing only in Kentucky. Mountain Ale was created to compete directly with Ale-8-One. It too was bottled in a green bottle and looked very similar to Ale-8. The taste of the drink was completely unsatisfactory to Ale-8 drinkers and, despite its lower price, Mountain Ale failed miserably. Coca-Cola made only one batch of "Mountain Ale" because there were no reorders. Even a giant in the soft drink industry could not capture the interest of Ale-8 loyalists.

The recipe for Ale-8-One is a closely guarded family secret created by G. L. Wainscott in 1926 and kept today in a Winchester bank safe-deposit box. Wainscott had been bottling several flavored soft drinks in Winchester since 1902. In 1906, he introduced Roxa-Kola that successfully competed with other colas then available.

During the 1920s, Coca-Cola systematically sued Ale-8, and other soft drink companies across America, over trademark infringement for using the word "cola." Ale-8 was taken to court by Coca-Cola on numerous occasions, and although each time it successfully defended its right to the Roxa-Kola name, Wainscott ultimately decided to focus on a non-cola product to avoid further litigation.

G. L. Wainscott developed a taste for ginger-based drinks during a trip to northern Europe and thought folks back home would like the flavor too. After

experimentation with the recipes he had acquired from his travels, Wainscott developed the formula for Ale-8-One.

The logo "Ale-8-One" was the result of the nation's first name-that-brand contest. The winning entry, "A Late One," was turned in by a fifteen-year-old girl, and it is thought to be a description of the beverage as the latest thing in soft drinks. Ale-8-One was adopted as a pun on her entry.

After Wainscott's death in 1944, the bottling stock was divided equally between his wife and his employees. Jane Rogers Wainscott inherited 50 percent of the stock, and the other half was divided among the company's employees. Upon her death in 1954, Wainscott's brother, Frank A. Rogers, received her portion of the stock.

In 1962, Rogers bought out the other shareholders and incorporated the Ale-8-One Bottling Company. The company has been under the complete guidance of the Rogers family ever since, and Ale-8-One has experienced tremendous growth and success under its leadership. Frank A. Rogers, Jr., came aboard the business as a manager in the 1960s, was later named president, and is now the company's chairman.

Production of Roxa-Kola was discontinued in 1964, and by 1974 the remaining "Wainscott" brands of fruit-flavored drinks were dropped in order to concentrate on Ale-8. The "flagship" product already accounted for over 98 percent of sales and cost less to produce than the fruit flavors. At the same time, Frank A. Rogers III (Buddy) joined the company's management.

Today, at age 78, Frank Rogers, Jr., remains active in the company as chairman of the board, and he still puts in some time on the bottling line as well. Buddy Rogers now serves as president and holds the majority interest of stock. Another son, David Rogers, and a daughter, Riley Rogers Walton, are also actively involved in the family business.

STRUCTURE OF MANAGEMENT ACTIVITIES

Management and Administration

Buddy Rogers and his sister, Riley Rogers Walton (vice president of personnel) carry out most of the managerial and administrative activities of the company including finance, personnel, and external relations. Because it is a family business, the organizational structure of Ale-8-One lacks formality, and the duties of Riley and Buddy often overlap. As vice president of personnel, Walton's responsibilities are varied and many. She is officially in charge of overseeing the profit-sharing plan and the investment advisers. She also helps to foster strong external relations by responding to all mail.

Exhibit 3
Growth in Case Shipments

1930s	50,000–75,000
1950s	150,000–200,000
1960s	300,000–350,000
1970s	500,000–750,000
1980s	950,000
1991	1,000,000

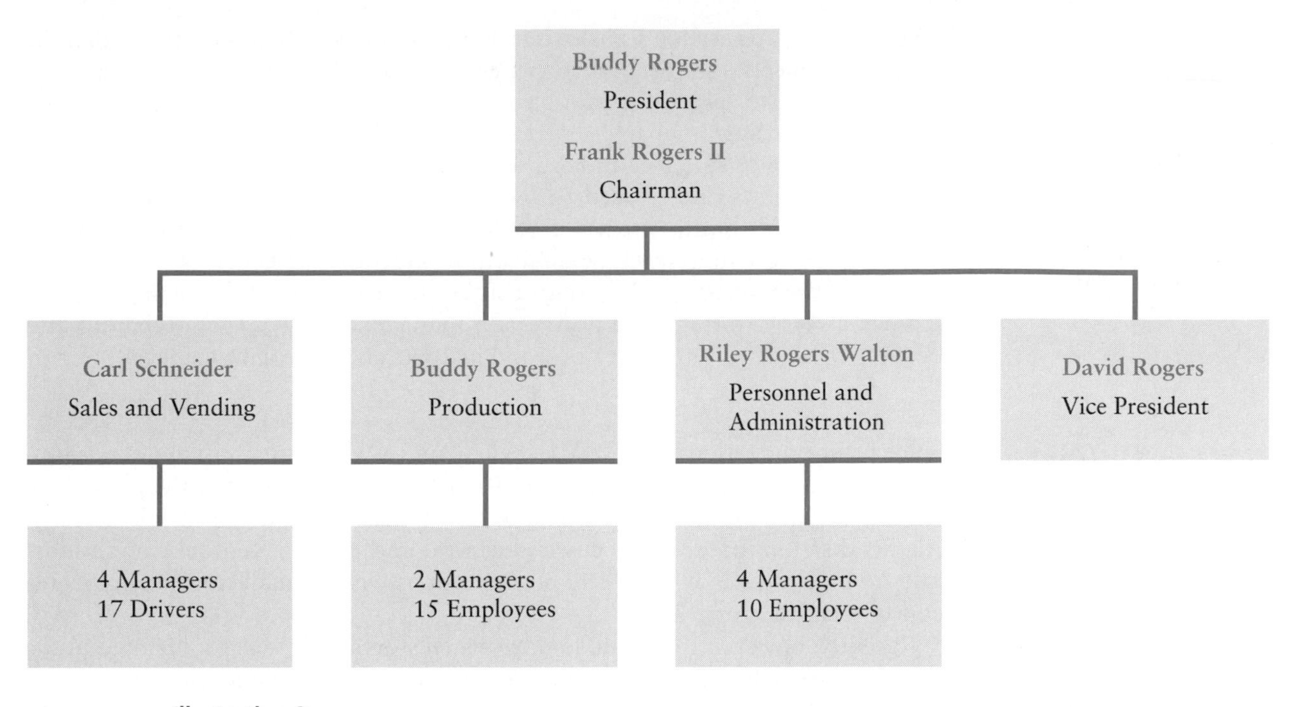

Illustration 2
Ale-8-One Organizational Chart

Rogers and Walton are assisted by an office manager, a manager of the Ale-8-One boutique, and an executive secretary. In an effort to operate in a more defined corporate manner, a comptroller was recently hired and reports to both Rogers and Walton.

David Rogers is also a vice president: however, he is not as involved with the business. Like the rest of the family members, he is a member of the Board of Directors and assists in setting company policy and planning overall strategy. See Illustration 2 for Ale-8-One's organization chart.

Production and Sourcing Operations

Based on cost and production criteria, the most crucial raw materials are sugar and glass. Sucrose purchases usually are done through long-term purchase contracts, while corn sugar is bought on spot markets unless weather threatens to disrupt prices and availability.

Glass bottles, both returnable and non-returnable, come from Mexico. The initial cost of returnables is substantially higher (see Exhibit 6), as are variable costs for sorting, cleaning, and sanitizing. Cost effectiveness with returnable bottles depends on a high redemption rate, though Ale-8 management is unsure about which bottle type is less expensive.

The Winchester plant uses two 3,000-gallon stainless steel tanks to mix syrup. Once the syrup is ready, one tank feeds the bottling line for three days, while the other tank is used to mix the next batch. Using a continuous flow process, seven parts water are blended with one part syrup, carbonated, and delivered to a filling machine. In turn, the filling machine services the bottling line, filling bottles which are then capped, inspected, and packed for shipment.

Seventeen employees run the bottling line on a four-day, forty-hour-per-week basis (three days in the winter, when demand is lower), filling an average of 5,000 bottles a day. At one million cases shipped in 1991, the plant is operating at about

70 percent of capacity for a single shift. However, Buddy Rogers estimates that the existing plant could ship 2.5 million cases per year if they went to two shifts.

The Winchester plant does not have canning facilities. Ale-8 is canned by the Coca-Cola Bottling company of Elizabethtown, Kentucky, along with 16-ounce non-returnable bottles (see Exhibit 4). This source accounts for about 12 percent of shipments and is used to service accounts outside the core territory, where returnable bottles are not practical. The arrangement with the Elizabethtown plant offers substantial flexibility in production and capacity.

Buddy Rogers is ultimately responsible for production. The plant manager reports directly to him. The production manager oversees the mechanics and bottlers working on the plant floor, and he reports to the plant manager.

Distribution

Since most production is in Ale-8's single plant in Winchester, distribution is limited. Seventeen truck drivers work a 50-mile radius surrounding the plant. The Ale-8 truck drivers have a dual responsibility: sales and delivery. Historically, Ale-8's distribution area has covered central and eastern Kentucky, with most sales to locally owned "mom and pop" stores as well as small convenience stores east of Clark County.

Recently, however, the small, family-owned stores that once proliferated in the area have been disappearing, and there has been a shift to large, chain supermarkets. This change within the retail environment has caused Ale-8 to reevaluate its distribution strategy. Though concentrating somewhat more on supermarkets, where soft drink sales growth has been significant, Ale-8 management is wary of the entry barriers to competing for grocery shelf space. Ale-8 still puts most of its emphasis on single unit sales through vending and convenience stores.

Ale-8 has long contemplated the potential for increased sales through expanded distribution. However, expanding beyond 200 miles causes shipping costs to be a big problem, and finding a means of distribution has been difficult in some areas. For example, Ale-8 brought in Brown Food Service, an independent distributor, to help increase the availability of their product in eastern Kentucky. The truck on which Ale-8 was delivered was an 18-wheeler, and each time the truck stopped to make a delivery it cost $20. The truck would not stop unless weekly Ale-8 sales generated at least a $20 profit at the retail outlet. In the mountains of eastern Kentucky, most of the retail stores are very small family-owned stores that do not generate enough sales to warrant a stop by the truck. Thus Brown Food Service was not an effective solution to the problem.

Despite such distribution woes, Ale-8-One continues the effort to expand sales beyond its core area through the use of independent distributors. They are slowly expanding into Indiana, southwestern Ohio, and all of Kentucky. Crown

Exhibit 4
Ale-8-One: Percent of Sales by Container Type

	Cases Shipped	Percent of Sales	Case Price	Production
12-oz. returnable	695,000	69.5	$7.80+$4.80 dep.	Winchester
12-oz. non-returnable	187,000	18.7	$11.60	Winchester
12-oz. can	75,000	7.5	$11.60	Elizabethtown
16-oz. non-returnable	43,000	4.3	$13.50	Elizabethtown

Distributing Co. now supplies Louisville and western Kentucky stores with Winchester's soft drink. Ale-8 also has enlisted the services of independent distributors in Indianapolis and Cincinnati.

While such arrangements have enabled Ale-8 to increase geographic coverage, the traditional market region still generates 95 percent of Ale-8 sales. The distribution agreements hold no provision for joint marketing efforts or any other resources for aggressive market development.

Carl Schneider, vice president of sales and vending (the only "non-family" vice president within the organization), is responsible for market development, sales, and vending operations. Led by Schneider, Ale-8 recently reformed its vending business practices. Typically, the company would sell, rent, or lend a vending machine to the merchant and sell the Ale-8 product to the merchant as well. The merchant would then be responsible for loading the machine and collecting the money. With Ale-8's new "Full Service Vending" program, Ale-8 retains ownership of the vending machine, places the machine in front of the merchant's store, stocks the machine, and collects the money. For providing the square footage, the merchant is paid 7 cents per container on sale. Full-service vending is more profitable for the merchant, who incurs less investment and inventory cost. Full-service vending allows Ale-8 to more accurately track sales and provides it with a direct, measurable return on its marketing dollars.

Schneider oversees all the distribution activities of the company. He has three sales managers to help him supervise the truck drivers: one is responsible for the territory east of Winchester; another works with the central Kentucky area, particularly Lexington; and the third sales manager is responsible for working with supermarket management to arrange for shelf space and promotions. The vending manager has three people assisting with vending activities.

Marketing

Several people play a role in Ale-8's marketing activities. As previously mentioned, Carl Schneider oversees sales-related activities and is responsible for the truck drivers who also act as sales representatives. Walton assists with Ale-8 promotions and directs merchandising in the Ale-8 shop. The shop sells clothing and other promotional merchandise featuring the Ale-8 logo. In 1990 Ale-8 retained Malone Marketing in Lexington to provide marketing services, mainly to develop and place radio and television advertising for its brand.

Research shows that typical Ale-8 drinkers are 18–34-year-old males from rural areas of Kentucky. In addition, the majority of Ale-8 consumers live within the 50-mile radius of the Winchester plant. As shown in Exhibit 5, the demographics of the profiled Ale-8 customer vary significantly from those of the general soft drink user. In contrast to colas, Ale-8 seems to be markedly more favored by males than females. While Coke is popular with 35–49-year-olds, there is a clear youth skew for Ale-8.

ALE-8'S PRODUCT MARKET STRATEGY

The dominant business strategy in the soft drink industry is characterized by brand name promotion, advertising, market research, and aggressive distribution. In contrast, Ale-8 caters only to a small pocket of the soft drink market and fails to keep up with industry norms of marketing and distribution, even within its own

Exhibit 5
Demographics of Lexington, Kentucky, Soft Drink Consumers

	Soft Drink Users	Ale-8 Users	Coke Users
Age of Respondent			
18–34 years	44%	56%	32%
35–49 years	35%	28%	42%
50 and over	20%	16%	24%
	Soft Drink Users	Ale-8 Users	Coke Users
Gender			
Male	37%	58%	46%
Female	58%	40%	50%
Refused	5%	2%	4%

sales region. Partly this is due to resource constraints, but Ale-8 management views its product as unique and believes that its product has no direct competition.

Ale-8-One produces only one product, sold in four types of containers. There is no such thing as Diet Ale-8 (although it is currently in the works), nor is there caffeine-free Ale-8. This strategy contrasts sharply with those of Coke and Pepsi, which both produce a wide array of soft drink products in several different types of containers.

Ale-8 has not changed its look in over 65 years. Ale-8's 12-ounce returnable green bottle, logo, and formula are unchanged since their inception in 1927. This link to the past fits and enhances the image of a family-owned, traditional, local product.

Ale-8-One has a very distinct taste. It is not a cola, nor does it taste like Sprite or 7-Up. It is similar to ginger ale, but heavier and sweeter. Buddy Rogers believes that the drink itself—not advertising and promotion—provides the explanation for Ale-8's popularity. Buddy calls it the best-tasting soft drink in the world, and he really means it.

Another distinctive aspect of the Ale-8 product is packaging. Coke and Pepsi abandoned returnable bottles in favor of cans and 2-liter plastic bottles in the early 1980s. Ale-8, with nearly 70 percent of unit sales in the traditional 12-ounce returnable bottle, is the only firm in Kentucky producing soft drinks in returnable bottles. With Ale-8's sales dominance in Winchester, merchants are cooperative about bottle redemption. Chain grocers outside the core area, however, are less than enthusiastic about handling returnables, which tends to retard sales growth. As the point of sale moves farther away from Winchester, sales are dominated by non-returnable bottles and cans, which carry much higher prices.

The traditional 12-ounce returnable is an important dimension of Ale-8's brand identity. A young man at work in Winchester, observed drinking a can of Coke, revealed that he drinks about 12 bottles of Ale-8 each day, but he refuses to purchase the "fake" (i.e., non-returnable) bottles sold in the workplace vending machine.

A major concern for Ale-8 management is the bottle return rate. Returnables cost 30 cents each, and the deposit was 10 cents until 1991. Facing a return rate of only 92.5 percent, Ale-8 raised the deposit to 20 cents. Despite widespread complaints from loyal consumers, the return rate quickly rose to 97 percent.

Buddy Rogers observes that the roads in Clark County were remarkably litter free in 1992.

The 20-cent deposit does, however, create some problems in pricing, as some purchasers view the deposit as part of the purchase price. For example, a 12-ounce can of Coke costs 62 cents in area convenience stores. A 12-ounce bottle of Ale-8 is only 45 cents, but with the 20 cent deposit, some consumers perceive Ale-8 as the higher-priced product. Even when comparing shelf prices of Ale-8 in different containers, the price of non-returnables is similar to that of returnables with the deposit cost included. Thus, for customers who wish to avoid the inconvenience of saving their bottles, there is no cost penalty for purchasing Ale-8 in the returnable bottle and no incentive to buy non-returnables if the packaging is less appealing.

The company notes that redemption rates rise significantly toward the end of the month. This may be seen as the Ale-8 savings plan. Cash-strapped Kentuckians are able to come up with $10 or $20 between paychecks by rounding up and cashing in their empty bottles. At $4.80 per case, the deposit value is substantial.

Despite questions about cost and efficiency, Buddy Rogers defends the returnable bottle as a classic case of serving the customer: "Coke and Pepsi may tell their customers that the aluminum can is convenient for them, but mostly it is convenient for Coke and Pepsi's production needs." However, other factors contribute to the company's reliance on the returnable bottle.

The inertia created by family business traditions is difficult to reverse. For one thing, plant operations revolve around the returnable bottle. Both bottle washing equipment and the existing bottling line are bought and paid for. The company has never determined which packaging type is least expensive, once all fixed and variable costs are considered. (See Exhibit 6.) Moreover, all the bottles scattered across eastern Kentucky and not yet redeemed represent a huge contingent liability. Much like airline frequent flier accounts, if all consumers cashed in their credits at once, a serious drain on cash flow would arise. Thus Ale-8 management is reluctant to even consider eliminating the returnable bottle.

Kentucky, like 40 other states, has no mandatory bottle deposit law. Ale-8's competitive position would benefit from the enactment of a bottle law, because all soft drink producers would be obligated to factor deposits into their pricing. Buddy Rogers finds it ironic that bottler trade associations contact him to solicit funds for lobbying against political initiatives for state-mandated bottle deposits.

While Ale-8 provides a unique taste, it also commands a premium price when purchased in volume at supermarkets. As shown in Exhibit 7, a case of Ale-8 cans costs $7–$8, compared to about $5–$6 for a case of Coke or Pepsi. Moreover, Ale-8 rarely offers promotional discounts, while Coke and Pepsi continuously engage in price wars. However, Exhibit 8 shows that the price of a single

Exhibit 6
Ale-8 Container Cost per Unit

	Cost per Unit
Ale-8 12-oz. returnable	$0.30
Ale-8 12-oz. non-returnable	$0.16
Ale-8 12-oz. can	$0.14
Ale-8 16-oz. non-returnable	$0.19

Exhibit 7
Grocery Sales: Ale-8 versus National Brands

Winchester	Shelf Space	Case Price	Delivery
Ale-8	10–15%	$7.60+$4.80	every other day
All Coca-Cola	25%	$6.00	daily
All PepsiCo	25%	$6.20	daily
Private label	25%	$4.00–$5.00	?
Lexington	**Shelf Space**	**Case Price**	**Delivery**
Ale-8	1–3%	$7.60+$4.80	weekly
All Coca-Cola	25%	$6.10	daily
All PepsiCo	25%	$5.78	daily
Private label	25%	$4.00–$5.00	?

unit of Ale-8 purchased in a convenience store is competitive with the prices of Coke and Pepsi. Thus Ale-8's pricing reflects the company's emphasis on single unit purchases.

As a local company, Ale-8 relies heavily on local connections and word of mouth to promote its product. It emphasizes public relations work in central Kentucky such as working with area schools and sponsoring community events. So, while Coke and Pepsi have such superstars as Michael Jordan, Shaquille O'Neill, and Cindy Crawford endorsing and promoting their products, Ale-8 attempts to reach its young market by putting ads in local high school football programs and by sponsoring county fairs.

In 1990 the Coca-Cola Classic brand alone was supported by $70 million in direct media dollars and Pepsi $73 million, which represents only a small frac-

Exhibit 8
Convenience Stores: Single Unit Sales

Winchester	Shelf Space	Unit Price
Ale-8 12-oz. returnable	15–40%	.45+.20
Ale-8 non-returnable (12 oz./16 oz.)		.62/.75
All Coca-Cola (12 oz./16 oz.)	20–25%	.62/.75
All PepsiCo (12 oz./16 oz.)	20–25%	.62/.75
Lexington	**Shelf Space**	**Unit Price**
Ale-8 12-oz. returnable	5%	.52+.20
Ale-8 non-returnable (12 oz./16 oz.)		.62/.75
All Coca-Cola (12 oz./16 oz.)	31%	.62/.75
All PepsiCo (12 oz./16 oz.)	36%	.62/.75

Exhibit 9
Price Comparisons: Side-by-Side Vending Machines

	Winchester	Lexington
Ale-8 12-oz. non-returnable	$0.60	$0.50
Can of Coca-Cola	$0.35	$0.35
Can of Pepsi	$0.35	$0.35

tion of Coke and Pepsi's corporate advertising budgets. In comparison, Ale-8's total advertising budget is $200,000 (roughly 3 percent of gross sales). Ale-8 does, however, have several catchy new radio jingles and television commercials encouraging consumers to "Pop a top on an Ale-8-One." A marketing consultant has worked to upgrade the quality and sophistication of Ale-8's ads so that they are more comparable to the ads of other soft drink brands. Coke and Pepsi advertise the most during June, July, and August which is the peak season for soft drink consumption. To avoid competing with the onslaught of new Coke and Pepsi ads, Ale-8 runs radio ads heavily in March, April, and May when rates are lower, but soft drink demand is also lower.

Ale-8's marketing agency not only advises working to improve the quality of the Ale-8 ads but suggests changing the brand image to appeal to a more universal market. More specifically, the agency wants to increase product acceptance by making Ale-8 more appealing to women, who do the majority of grocery shopping. Recent television commercials emphasize family values by showing the "all-American family" drinking Ale-8. Ultimately, the marketing agency suggests striving to spruce up Ale-8's image as strictly a rural soft drink consumed by people in the lower socioeconomic classes. This image is viewed as problematic for broader market expansion.

As previously mentioned, most Ale-8 sales are individual purchases from small convenience-type stores or vending machines. Ale-8 has 17 trucks that make deliveries to each retail outlet within 50 miles of the Winchester plant once a week. The Ale-8 truck drivers have grown accustomed to serving the traditional Ale-8 retailer (the small, family-owned store). There is certainly sufficient demand for Ale-8 in these stores. Thus the truck drivers merely have to deliver the product to the store each week, and the manager makes certain that the Ale-8 is put on the shelf.

Recently, Ale-8 has sought to increase distribution and sales to large supermarket chains. But Ale-8's truck drivers/salespersons have been slow to develop the necessary relationships with the supermarket personnel to ensure the proper distribution of the product within the store. They simply have continued their practice of delivering the product to the loading area, assuming that the product would make it safely to the shelf. As a consequence, Ale-8 has a reputation for not effectively servicing its supermarket accounts. The company is trying to counteract this problem by hiring a former Kroger employee to push the product through the supermarkets.

Coke and Pepsi, on the other hand, have representatives that visit the supermarkets daily to arrange for shelf space and promotional displays and to nurture their working relationship with store personnel. They service their accounts on a regular basis and offer incentives to store managers to boost sales. Ale-8 management believes that Coke and Pepsi have near complete control over grocery shelf space and that there is little that they can do about it.

Exhibits 7 and 8 illustrate the stark contrast between the shelf space allotted to Coke and Pepsi and that to Ale-8. Coke, Pepsi, and other private labels dominate the shelf space in supermarkets and in Lexington convenience stores. In the supermarkets, and out in front of the convenience stores, Coke and Pepsi have extremely large and prominent promotional displays. In Winchester, however, Ale-8 is awarded a significantly large portion of the shelf space in both convenience stores and supermarkets. In some convenience stores in Winchester, Ale-8 controls as much as 40 percent of shelf space, more than any national brand. Ale-8 vending machines, despite a price premium of 25 cents, outsell all competitors in the region (see Exhibit 9).

ALTERNATIVES FOR THE FUTURE

Some outside observers and consultants see Ale-8 as a sleeping giant—a marketer's dream. The product itself is good, the tradition and logo lend themselves to promotion, and the plant is capable of more than doubling production.

To this way of thinking, key challenges include redefining the brand's image to widen its appeal and solving a host of distribution problems, including packaging. The company might also need to increase the formalization of management structures and hire more managers with "professional" training in business. Some suggest that the Rogers family is content with its current level of success and is slow to respond to new opportunities. Buddy Rogers responds to this dilemma by underscoring the conservative values of the family company:

> [On expansion:] We could spend a million dollars or more just getting established in Cincinnati or Louisville, We don't have that kind of money and, even if we did, I wouldn't risk a ninety-two-year-old company and our fifty employees on a roll of the dice like that. . . . One of my favorite sayings is "You don't mess with success."
>
> [On Ale-8's marketing approach:] We have never won customers by advertising and promotion. People learn about our product from their friends or their family members. . . . We could put $20,000 into an ad campaign and never know what came of it. But if we spend $20,000 on ten or twelve vending machines, we'll know exactly how much we sell, at what price, and what is the return on that investment.
>
> [On Ale-8's brand image:] Our brand image and logo are hokey, but our loyal customers like it that way. And for those that wouldn't try our product, you don't change their minds by advertising anyway.

Reference

Booe, Martin. "A Bubbly Soft Drink Is the Toast of Kentucky: Move Over Bourbon and Moonshine. Locally-Made Soda Pop Becomes the Favorite Whistle-Water." *Los Angeles Times,* December 14, 1992.

CASE

3 Magee Enterprises, Inc.

With no investment capital, computer hacker and university student Marshall Magee successfully entered the computer software industry utilizing the unique shareware channel of distribution. Magee Enterprises, Inc., has grown rapidly, reaching sales of $2 million in only six years. Although Magee Enterprises remains a small company, the firm is interested in continuing a rapid pace of growth by building on existing products, as well as moving into new products and business ventures. In order to implement its growth strategy, Magee Enterprises is challenged with a transition to a more mature, professionally managed company while maintaining its entrepreneurial tradition.

Marshall Magee was once described in a magazine article as "an underachieving, antisocial computer nerd, flunking out of Auburn University."[1] Now the likable Magee is an acknowledged and respected member of the computer industry, having helped found the shareware channel of distribution where customers are allowed to try a software product *before* they buy it. His company, Magee Enterprises, has grown from $20 in sales in 1983 to over $2 million in sales for 1989.

Self-characterizing himself as a "hacker," Marshall Magee chronicles his academic career as an industrial engineering student at Auburn University. Unable to enroll in computer courses as a freshman in 1978, Magee explained that he had to find creative ways to gain access to the university's computer system. During his freshman year Magee estimates that he spent about 50 hours per week in the computer room. He did not date in those days and instead watched the sun rise after working all night in the computer room.

He would go to the computer center where a lot of business students were using the computer. Trading his computer expertise by doing other students' assignments, Magee then used their computer I.D.'s to gain time on the system. Later, he learned that by watching systems operators he could get their I.D.'s and password, thus getting to virtually whatever he needed.

Since the complete set of system manuals were in the computer room, Magee was able to study them to the point that he had a complete and thorough knowledge of the system. Referring to his hacking days, Magee described himself as a terror to the university, such that they hired him during his sophomore year.

Computer projects consumed most of his time. He wrote programs to analyze automobile accidents for the School of Industrial Engineering and did other odd consulting jobs. In the fall of 1982, he helped design three personal computer games—PC Man, Paratrooper, and J-Bird. PC Man was highly successful, earning approximately $750,000. Magee was persuaded by the owners to reinvest his

This case was prepared by Patricia P. McDougall, Georgia Institute of Technology and Karen D. Loch, Georgia State University. This case was prepared as a basis for class discussion rather than to illustrate either effective or ineffective handling of administrative situations.

1. Andrew Jaffe, "Revenge of the Nerd," *Atlanta Magazine* (August 1988), p. 33(4).

earning in their company. One day, he came to work and the company was gone. Having devoted all his time to designing the games, Magee had stopped accepting other consulting jobs; he was now broke and still struggling in school.

AUTOMENU

Early Development of Automenu

Magee sought the help of an attorney to collect his money from the game company. (Ultimately, Magee received about $1,500 total for his services.) The attorney offered to pay him for training his staff to work on PCs. Magee quickly realized that it would be easier for the workers if they had some sort of menu system that would allow them to select the different applications off the menu, rather than having to remember DOS commands.

Magee wrote a program in Basic which eventually became Automenu. He then rewrote it in Assembler to give the Automenu program speed, functionality, and reduced size. He took the Automenu program to a user group in Montgomery, Alabama. The user group offered him the opportunity to talk with other people about computers and to share programs. Magee describes the user group's response as "they thought the program was trash." In response to the group's feedback, Magee redesigned the program.

At another user group's meeting in the fall of 1983, someone handed him a $20 bill because he had used and liked the program. Magee asked the gentleman to instead make out a check to Magee Enterprises and mail it to his father's address. Magee jokingly states that he chose Magee Enterprises instead of Magee Software, mindful that with a generic name he could diversify someday and sell real estate or oil.

Early Efforts to Market and Distribute Automenu

In early 1984, Magee was introduced to electronic bulletin boards. Bulletin boards are an on-line information system offering a wealth of software programs, forums for discussions, and questions and answers on computer topics.*

Magee put Automenu on a few bulletin boards, hoping someone would like the program and offer him a job. He received a letter from an individual who liked the program and would send $20 if certain changes were made. Magee went to work, made the changes, and sent the program back to the individual only to find he was no longer interested. Another letter requested the program be put on CompuServe, one of the largest professional bulletin boards. Magee responded by placing Version 2.0 of the program on CompuServe and raised the price to $25.

That same fall he received a check for Version 2.0 from the Canadian office of Deloitte, Haskins, and Sells. Magee opened a bank account for Magee Enterprises and deposited the check. The check bounced. Some weeks later, Magee related the story to a fellow student. She explained that Deloitte, Haskins, and Sells was one of the Big Eight accounting firms, prompting Magee to revisit his banker. The problem had been that the check was drawn on a Canadian

*Electronic bulletin boards have become pervasive across the United States. The majority of the boards are owned by either private individuals or clubs, do not charge for on-line time, may or may not have a fixed annual fee, and have controls on uploading and downloading files. In contrast, commercial on-line sources such as CompuServe, The Source, and Genie, charge a fee for access time.

account, and when properly processed, the check cleared. Scattered checks from other corporations were received, two of which were around $500 each. By this time, the program had 78 registered users, primarily corporations.

In the first month (July 1985) that 3.0 was released (priced at $30), the company received $2,000, the total revenue for the past two years combined. Magee decided that if he wanted to really get the product out, it needed to be on bulletin boards around the country. With a population map, Magee targeted each U.S. population center of more than 500,000 people. Using the telephone in his father's office, he placed the program on a minimum of two bulletin boards in each of these areas.

THE SHAREWARE CONCEPT

Shareware is a "try before you buy" form of marketing in which software products are freely distributed through PC user groups and are placed on electronic bulletin boards accessible to computer users across the country. The programs can be downloaded or copied to PCs allowing any computer user an opportunity to experiment with a multitude of programs before buying. PC-File and PC-Talk III were two of the pioneer programs using shareware as their major means of distribution.

The concept of shareware was born in 1982 by a New York programmer, Andrew Fluegelman, who designed PC-Talk. He believed that people should pay only for programs that suited their needs. He encouraged free distribution, allowing potential buyers to "try-it-on for size." Shareware differs from public-domain software in that public-domain software is free. Shareware programs, originally called freeware, could not be altered or renamed, and authors retained the copyrights to their programs. Those who used the program regularly or found that it met their needs were expected to purchase the program by sending the author a registration fee. This concept remains true today; customers' consciences are expected to serve as an unofficial sales force. Even so, industry experts estimate that only 10 percent of the people using a shareware product actually pay the registration fee.[2]

For programmers, shareware provides an economical method of distributing their product without incurring the high costs of traditional advertising and marketing campaigns. Corporate America has become a big user of shareware products because of its low-cost, free evaluation, and typically strong support by individual users. Utilities, vertical applications, and telecommunication software developers have been the principal users of the shareware concept of marketing. Shareware also serves as a low-cost software source for users with relatively straightforward needs for word processing and spreadsheets.

In contrast to shareware, some programs do not offer the user the total package. For example, a word processing program may allow the user to do everything, but it will limit printing to only two pages. These programs which give the full-featured version only upon registration are often called "crippleware" or "hostage ware," since the true shareware concept offers the total and complete product.

2. Mike Hogan, "Try It, You'll Like It," *Forbes* (November 28, 1988), p. 227(2).

MAGEE ENTERPRISES AS A FULL-TIME VENTURE

Wanting to work on version 4.0 and develop a professional manual and package for his Automenu product, Magee decided to leave school in early 1986. Although he promised his father he would return to school in two or three quarters, Magee still lacks about three quarters to graduate.

He installed a telephone in his father's office and, using call forwarding, his mother agreed to answer the forwarded calls at home. To his surprise, the telephone rang the first day and was soon ringing about twice an hour thereafter. People first called for information and then ordered the product. Looking back, Magee attributes the sales takeoff after the telephone installation to corporations desiring to purchase the product, but first calling to ascertain that the company existed.

Although he completed writing version 4.0 by April of that year, it took six months to bring the product to market. Magee hired a technical writer to write the manual and then typeset it himself on a Macintosh. The lack of a manual had been a big customer complaint. The product finally was shipped in October 1986. Magee professes that at that time he knew nothing about diskettes, manuals, or packaging. He learned by talking with people and joined numerous PC user groups and actively attended meetings. He served as program director for the Atlanta PC Users' Group. He also became heavily involved in the Southeastern Software Association, a group that two years later named him Software Entrepreneur of the Year.

That fall, Magee Enterprises exhibited at Comdex for the first time. Comdex is the computer industry's leading mega-trade show, is held semi-annually, and is heavily attended by vendors, as well as users of systems. Vendors rent booths and exhibit their new products to dealers, and users are treated to elaborate demos and gimmicks to entice them to buy. Considerable press speculation takes place prior to Comdex as to who and what will make its debut. Comdex is regarded as a barometer for the direction of the industry.

ASSOCIATION OF SHAREWARE PROFESSIONALS

A collection of about 150 prominent shareware authors, including Magee, formed the Association of Shareware Professionals (ASP) in the spring of 1987. Magee has served as founding president and as press liaison and currently serves as vice president.

All of the association's meetings are conducted through CompuServe. The association has a forum in which to exchange business ideas, help individual authors, and set standards that will boost shareware's quality and credibility with the corporate buyer. Shareware distributors who display the ASP logo agree to distribute only the most current versions of shareware, to respect shareware authors' copyright requirements, and to follow an honesty-in-advertising rule. Ads must attempt to educate users about shareware and must include the statement "Shareware programs require separate payment to the authors if found useful."

ASP members also are expected to follow a code of conduct and representation that gives users consistency in terminology and business practices. In addition, ASP offers a list of all ASP-member products, complete with full

descriptions and current version numbers. ASP members are available on numerous bulletin boards. Consumers with complaints may go to ASP's ombudsman who manages the dispute-resolution service.

PRODUCTS

Automenu, Magee's first product, is a menu utility program for DOS, geared to corporate PC users who run multiple applications. It allows the user to create custom-designed menus to organize, control, and automate access to application programs and to execute DOS commands and batch files. The menu system reduces the need for training personnel in DOS and the finer points of PC-DOS computer systems.

Treeview, Magee's second product, is a hard disk and file management utility program for IBM and compatible PCs. Treeview, named for the branchlike graphic that displays files, was described by one reviewer as follows:

> The program is rich in file management functions with the ability to display a menu tree, view a file, change file attributes, edit (by calling your favorite editor from within Treeview), copy, and/or erase any file.[3]

Another reviewer criticized what he termed "an inadequate user's manual" but concluded that "Treeview is a great buy" and is well-supported.[4] Directree, QDOS, and XTree are competitive products to Treeview.

Treeview was found on a bulletin board by a member of Magee's R&D team in May 1988. The author agreed to sell total rights of the product. The product was enhanced, and its name was changed because of a trademark conflict. In the product's first three months of sales, its sales were two and a half times the price paid for the product. When Treeview appeared on the market, one reviewer commented that "now we know what Magee Enterprises has been doing, they have been working on a new product—Treeview—another great product from Magee Enterprises."

Led by Magee, the R&D team continues to look for similar opportunities while developing future in-house products. The R&D team is comprised of three members: Randal DePriest, Jim Everingham, and Don Bryant. Beginning in 1990 and with the institution of the company's first budgeting process, a percentage of total sales was allocated to R&D.

Product Support

Customers can call Magee Enterprises' bulletin board, The Big Peach, for technical support. It operates 24 hours a day, seven days a week for electronic information. About 150 calls per day are handled in this manner. The company also has one direct technical support telephone line available for customers to call with technical questions about products. There are also two incoming 800 numbers, one designated for sales information and the other for orders.

To become a registered user, the customer returns the warranty registration card included in the package. Magee Enterprises maintains a database of all

3. Executive Tools with Dr. Robert Frank," *Andrew Seybold's Outlook on Professional Computing*, September 1989.
4. *PC Resource*, September 1989, p. 106.

registered users, and they are notified of product upgrades as they become available. In the early days of the company, records of users were not systematically kept and updated, and, consequently, the database of early registrants is incomplete. All registered users received a copy of Magee's newsletter, *The Echo*.

Marketing

Automenu and Treeview are now distributed through a combination of dealers, distributors, direct sales, and the shareware concept. Originally, Automenu was distributed only through shareware. When corporations requested Automenu, dealers called Magee Enterprises, first having to locate the company. Consequently, Magee developed appropriate pricing and moved into traditional software distribution channels. A comparison of Magee Enterprises market distribution between 1989 and 1990 is presented in Exhibit 1. The company will continue to increase its emphasis on more traditional marketing channels. The advertising budget for 1989 was 5 percent of sales, and plans are to increase the dollar amount of the 1990 advertising budget by 100 percent.

The large majority of Magee Enterprises' registered users are corporations. Only honesty requires the user to send in the registration fee, although vendors, including Magee Enterprises, try to make it easier for managers to spot unregistered shareware. At one time, registered Automenu disks were blue and had a registration number, while shareware disks were gray with an "SW" serial number. Registered Treeview diskettes were green, and shareware diskettes were yellow. In return for the registration fee, Magee Enterprises sends the customer a manual, notice of updates and new product availability, and access to free technical support. A minimal charge is made for upgrades as they become available.

Magee views shareware as an important marketing concept for the company to get people to evaluate the product. Magee estimates that he gives away from 20,000 to 30,000 diskettes a year. He explains that if he gives away 3,000 diskettes at a trade show and if 2 percent of the people pay for the product, then that pays for all the disks. If 7 percent pay, that pays for his participation in the entire show.

Exhibit 1
Product Distribution Profile, 1989 versus 1990 (in percentages)

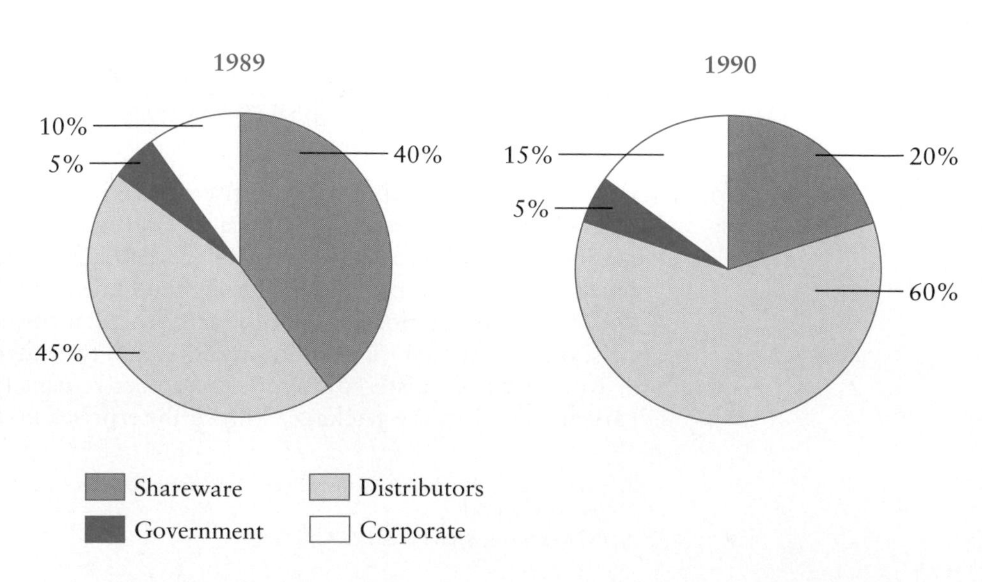

Exhibit 2
Product Pricing History

	Date Price Effective	Price
Automenu	March 1983	$20.00
	March, 1984	30.00
	March 1986	50.00
	July 1989	69.95
Treeview	November 1988	$39.95
	June 1989	50.00
	June 1990	25.00

The company changed its policy for handing out shareware copies of its programs beginning with the fall 1989 Comdex trade show. In the past, shareware was handed out to anyone who approached the booth. Now employees explain the product (the shareware concept) and impress upon the customer that the shareware diskette is an evaluation copy and if they are going to use it, they should send their registration fee. Since the institution of the policy, the number of diskettes given away at shows has decreased enormously.

Magee has used a one-to-one swap with other customers as a last resort, a practice that he says makes competitors furious. Magee tells the story of a purchasing agent who once called him about purchasing 500 copies of Automenu. The purchasing agent's boss was furious because rather than purchasing Automenu, he had purchased a competitor's product. The boss had heard that Automenu was the best product on the market. The purchasing agent was afraid he would lose his job over the incident and hoped that Magee might offer him a special price on 500 copies. Instead of charging him, Magee gave a one-to-one swap of Automenu for the competitor's product in return for the customer's promise to purchase all future copies from Magee.

Pricing

When questioned about how he set the price of Automenu, Magee related that someone had once told him to add up all his product costs and multiply by five. He did this and still not thinking it looked right, decided to double the price. The product's price history is presented in Exhibit 2.

By early 1989, Magee considered raising the price again because major competitor products were over $40. As shareware products have attained traditional commercial-level acceptance, price increases typically follow in order to better position themselves with their competitors. Magee believed that a price too low in comparison to his commercial competitors can sometimes be interpreted as a product of lesser value by the customer. This time, a market research effort was used to study the pricing issue.

Magee Enterprises offers site licensing as well as volume discounts for larger customers. When Tom Dickerson joined the company as head of sales, he proposed the idea of giving cash credit for previously purchased individual copies upon the purchase of a site license. This idea subsequently was adopted by customers of Magee products.

PUBLIC RELATIONS

Magee accepts frequent speaking engagements and attends numerous trade events. Employees feel that Magee's public exposure has been a contributing factor to the company's success.

LOGO

The company's logo has been in use since 1985 when Magee purchased it for $50 from an art student who was a little sister in his fraternity at Auburn. Since then, Magee has made good on his promise to her that if his company ever made any money he would take her to Las Vegas.

PRODUCTION AND PACKAGING

Originally Magee Enterprises subcontracted another company to mass copy the programs at the cost of about 75 cents per diskette. In 1988, two in-house diskette duplicators, one 3½ inch and one 5¼ inch, were purchased. The company uses the duplicators to mass copy programs from a master diskette. Over the first year, the savings Magee Enterprises realized was more than three times the cost of the equipment.

Different labels are used for registered and shareware software. The shareware label says shareware and gives a number to call to register. UPS picks up daily, with 4,000–5,000 programs shipped per month.

In May 1989, while Magee was away on business, an employee failed to reorder manuals when the supply dwindled below 5,000. The order was finally placed with only 1,800 remaining in inventory. This resulted in no product being shipped for about six weeks, throwing the company 3,500 orders behind. Numerous distributor, overseas, and hundreds of one time end-user orders accumulated. Customers were notified by mail and told of the problem. Follow-up letters were sent. In addition to letters, telephone calls were made to distributors throughout the crisis. Only one cancellation for three packages was received.

Compounding the problem was a switch of printers at the same time. Having used the same printer from the company's inception, Magee recently had gotten bids from several printing companies. The old printer had charged about $25,000 for 10,000 manuals, while the new printer charged about $16,000 for 10,000 manuals. After switching printers, the new printer did not have printing plates and was unable to do a rush job. This also delayed production.

Upon receipt of the manuals, the distributors' orders were shipped first. The remaining orders were shipped in the order they were received, with no preference given to large orders. All employees pitched in, working both days and evenings to ship the orders. It took approximately three weeks to catch up on the backlog.

Since the crisis, the company changed from a manual count system to a computerized inventory system based on orders shipped. The shipping room was reorganized. Pallets containing the minimum number of boxes, trays, sleeves,

diskettes, and manuals are placed in one area with back-up inventory placed in another area to allow for visual checks. Pink paper is wrapped around pallets at the reorder point. Magee described the changes: "We're doing very redundant checks because the people that caused the problem didn't realize the devastation it caused."

At the time of the crisis it was rumored that a major distributor was saying that Magee Enterprises could not fill its orders and suggested that customers try a different product. For the first time in its history, the company was forced to borrow money to cover the cash flow shortage. Fortunately, a year prior to the incident, Magee had set up a $25,000 line of credit which the company drew upon.

Production problems have plagued the company numerous times in the past. Magee expressed that whenever the company seemed to run out of something, it was always at a time when orders were high.

Early on, packaging was done by part-timers with about eight hours a week needed to fill routine orders. As volume grew, employees contributed one to two hours each week to support the packaging operation. Packaging parties, in which most of the employees worked three to four hours in the evening, were held every few weeks to fill large distributor orders.

Magee considers the product's packaging as critical, because in many instances the package may be all the customer sees of the company. Magee explains that the product is shipped in a bigger box to give the customer more perceived value, noting that if the diskette was merely shipped in the manual, customers wouldn't feel they were getting very much for their money. Both Automenu and Treeview are similarly packaged. A plastic tray holds the materials and gives the package support. The tray contains both 5¼ and 3½ inch diskettes, manual, color-coded warranty card, generic postage-paid comment card, and a technical support brochure.

COMPETITION IN THE SOFTWARE INDUSTRY

The software market can be defined in a variety of ways. International Data Corp. (IDC), a market research firm, divides the market by type of software: systems and utilities, application tools, and application solutions. Magee Enterprises' two products, Automenu and Treeview, fit the systems and utilities category and are limited to a PC-DOS environment.

The microcomputer software market started as a cottage industry with a mixture of computer aficionados designing programs out of their homes. Today the industry is highly competitive with a distinct consolidation trend, dominated by a few large companies.

The micro-software market has been compared to the music and book industries, where companies compete to make the "best-sellers" list. Several companies have become visible and are successful based on one or two major programs. An industry expert estimates that only about 10 percent of the thousands of software companies, mainstream and shareware alike, ever break a million dollars in sales. Magee Enterprises is among the 10 percent, primarily thanks to Automenu.[5] Magee estimates there are about 65 products in Automenu's utility category—an easily customized menu system—and estimates

5. Ibid.

the market size at 28 million personal computers, about 15–20 million of which probably have hard disks.

Magee considers Automenu's major competitor to be Direct Access. In 1986, Direct Access received editor's choice in a software review. Because magazines typically review products sold only through dealers, Automenu was not even mentioned in the article. At the time of the review, Direct Access was much smaller than Magee Enterprises, but the article catapulted Direct Access to the top.

Although Magee claims that Automenu has more users than does Direct Access, he notes that Direct Access's sales revenues are higher due to higher pricing. In comparing products, Magee considers Direct Access easier for the customer to use but lacks the flexibility that corporate America likes. Numerous software reviews list flexibility as one of the strengths of Automenu.

In the year following Direct Access's selection as editor's choice, Automenu made its mark in the shareware arena. Automenu was named as one of the "best-selling shareware programs for IBM PCs and compatibles" in February 1987 in *PC Week*.[6] In May 1989 it was listed by *Changing Times* magazine as the "best of the almost-free software" for menu utilities.[7]

The manager of departmental computing for Coca-Cola Foods in Houston discovered Automenu on a bulletin board a few years ago. She found it worth sharing with her colleagues and recounts, "It caught on like wildfire. It saved our company a tremendous amount of time."[8]

The line between commercial software and shareware began to blur in 1989. In turn, Automenu enjoyed more frequent reviews by mainstream software journals. Automenu was called "The Right Recipe for Customer Menu Control" by a mainstream software evaluation specialist in August 1989. He graded it a 2+, on a scale of 1–5 with 1 being the highest value, for its overall efficiency, quality, reliability, and benefit to the user.[9] In October 1989, *PC Magazine* identified the top-ten sellers of utility programs on the market, as shown in Exhibit 3. The ranking was based on the number of packages sold in a five-week period. The reviewers recognized Automenu as "the program that has grown from shareware roots to become the cornerstone of a software house with over a million dollars in annual sales that targets corporate needs."[10]

Utility programs represent a large category of software whose objective is to make the computer easier to operate for the user. Often each utility package will specialize in one or several related functions, such as menuing or disk and file maintenance. While all the ranked packages are utility programs, none perform the same function as does Automenu. Sixth-ranked X-Tree Professional is considered a direct competitor of Magee's other product, Treeview.

An in-house competitive information sheet was developed for Magee Enterprises' employees to use at trade shows. It lists the different competitors and their programs' capabilities, as shown in Exhibits 4 and 5.

6. Amy Bermar, "For Shareware Authors, Honesty's Still Best Policy, But It Won't Make Them Rich," *PC Week* 4 (February 10, 1987), p. 49(3).
7. Kristen Davis, "Best of the Almost-Free Software," *Changing Times* 43 (May 1989), p. 41(4).
8. Charles Bermant, "In Search of Utilities Software," *Personal Computing* 12 (May 1988), p. 139(5).
9. Gary King, "Automenu System the Right Recipe for Custom Menu Control," *Atlanta Computer Spectrum* (August 1989), p. 22(1).
10. Gus Venditto, "Pipeline: A Look at the Trends Shaping the Personal Computer Market-Utility Makers Team up for the Battles Ahead," *PC Magazine* (October 31, 1989), p. 63(2).

Exhibit 3
Top-Ten Sellers of Utility Programs

1. Fastback Plus 2.01, Fifth Generation Systems, Inc.
2. The Norton Utilities Advanced Edition 4.5, Peter Norton Computing
3. Automenu, Magee Enterprises Inc.
4. LapLink III, Traveling Software, Inc.
5. PC Tools Deluxe 5.5, Central Point Software
6. X-Tree Professional, X-Tree, Inc.
7. Above Disc 3.0, Above Software
8. Sideways 3.2, Funk Software
9. Battery Watch, Traveling Software, Inc.
10. DESQview 2.2, Quarterdeck Office Systems

Source: *PC Magazine*, October 31, 1989, p. 63.

Input, a market research firm, found that software vendors who provide good support to customers enjoy a distinct advantage in the highly competitive market. IDC reports that $5.7 billion was spent on U.S.-based microcomputer services in 1987. That number continues to grow by over 10 percent annually and is projected to reach over $10 billion in 1990. Estimated revenues of systems and utilities software worldwide is projected to reach upwards of $18 billion (not distinguished by hardware level).[11] Magee views his customer responsiveness as essential to the success of his company and a key to his entry into the corporate world. He stresses this fact, stating that many of his corporate customers indicated that he was one of the few shareware authors responding to their checks.

Prior to 1990, no formal market research data were gathered by the company. Employees Dana Jordan and Karin Rogers, the force behind the developing marketing program, emphasize that market research is included in the 1990 budget. The marketing research function will work closely with the R&D team in order to be responsive to the competitive marketplace.

FACILITY

Until 1988, the company was housed in Magee's father's office. Magee, Sr., is a manufacturer's representative for electronic components. Magee paid a straight 10 percent commission on all sales to his father for rent. Figuring that he was paying the equivalent of about $80 a square foot by this time, Magee rented new space a few miles away for $6 a square foot. The company is located in a light industrial park in Norcross, a suburb of Atlanta, Georgia.

Drawing upon his industrial engineering background, Magee spent three months designing a 9,000-square foot office and purchasing about $90,000 in equipment, which depleted the company's cash reserves. The move occurred over one weekend and went very smoothly.

11. "Computers & Office Equipment," *Standard & Poor's Industry Surveys* (April 1989), pp. C93–C107.

Menu System Comparison

Magee

	Auto menu 4.5	Direct Access	Direct Net	Perfect Menu	Menu Blocks	Menu Works	Hot 3.0
Mouse support	●			●		●	●
Required memory (kb)	32	256	256*	512	128**	258	256
Minimum resident memory to execute application (kb)	0	0	0	0	62**	3	128
Network compatible	●		●				
Screen blanker	●	●	●	●	●	●	●
Screen blanked message	●				●	●	
Password protection for menu items	●	●	●	●	●	●	
Multiple password protection for menu items	●		●				
On-line help	●			●	●	●	●
Timed execution	●					●	
Usage tracking		●	●	●	●		
Menu building facility	●	●	●	●	●	●	●
Knowledge of DOS required to set up menu	●	●	●	●	●	●	●
Maximum number of items per screen	8	20	20	20	8	9	15
Maximum number of screens per menu file	8	1	1	N/A	1	9	1
Linkable menus	●			●	●	●	●
Multiple menus on-screen							●
Encrypt menu data files	●						
Total number of possible menu selections	Unlimited	400	400	640	Unlimited	Unlimited	Unlimited
Ability to pass parameters to application	●	●	●	●	●	●	●
Ability to prompt user for input	●	●	●			●	●
Descriptions for each menu item	●			●	●		●
Available memory displayed on menu	●				●		
Time/date displayed on menu	●	●	●	●	●	●	
Customize colors	●	●	●	●		●	●
Price	69.95	89.95	245.00		79.95	24.95	179.95

*Direct Net requires an additional 128kb with usage tracking enabled.

**Menu Blocks requires an additional 145kb with the help system enabled and another 5kb with password protection enabled.

Exhibit 4
Automenu Competitive Information Sheets

Within a year Magee outgrew its quarters. The landlord was able to persuade the tenant next door to Magee to relocate to another suite, allowing Magee to expand. A schematic drawing of the expanded facility is presented as Exhibit 6.

File Manager Comparison

Magee

	Treeview 1.1	XTree Pro	Tree86 ver. 2.0	Q Dos II	Norton Commander 2.0	Pathminder	Lotus Magellan
Mouse support	●		●		●		
Multiple directory windows	6				2		
User defined keys	30						10
Prototyping (Point & Go)	●						●
EMS support	●	●	●			●	●
Show all files on one drive	●	●	●				●
Show all files on all drives		●	●				●
Show all files in subdirectories	●						●
EGA 43/VGA 50 line support	●		●		●		
Macros	●						●
Tag files by range of dates/times	●						(1)
Tag files by filename mask	●	(1)	(1)	●	●		(1)
Modify file date/time	●						
Modify file attributes	●	●	●	●		●	
Update target directory	●						
Graphical directory tree	●	●	●	●	●	●	●
Move files across directories	●	●	●	●	●	●	●
Move files across drives		●			●		●
Built-in file viewer	●	●	●	●	●		●
Ability to hook in external viewer	●						●
Built-in editor		●		●	●	●	●
Ability to hook in external editor	●		●		●		●
Execute program	●	●	●	●	●	●	●
Fuzzy search							●
Customize colors	●	●	●	●	(2)	●	(2)
Print file and/or directory tree		●	●			●	●
Maximum files per window	2515	16000	N/A	700	N/A	N/A	N/A
Required memory (kb)	256	256	256	256	256	256	512
Minimum resident memory to execute application (kb)	158	85	89	123	18	4	4
Price	50.00	129.00	89.95	79.95	89.95	89.95	199.00

(1) - Indirectly accomplished (2) - Limited customization

Exhibit 5
Treeview Competitive Information Sheets

Before the expansion, the facility was primarily an open area, with a private office for Magee. Partitions offered little privacy, and one employee described

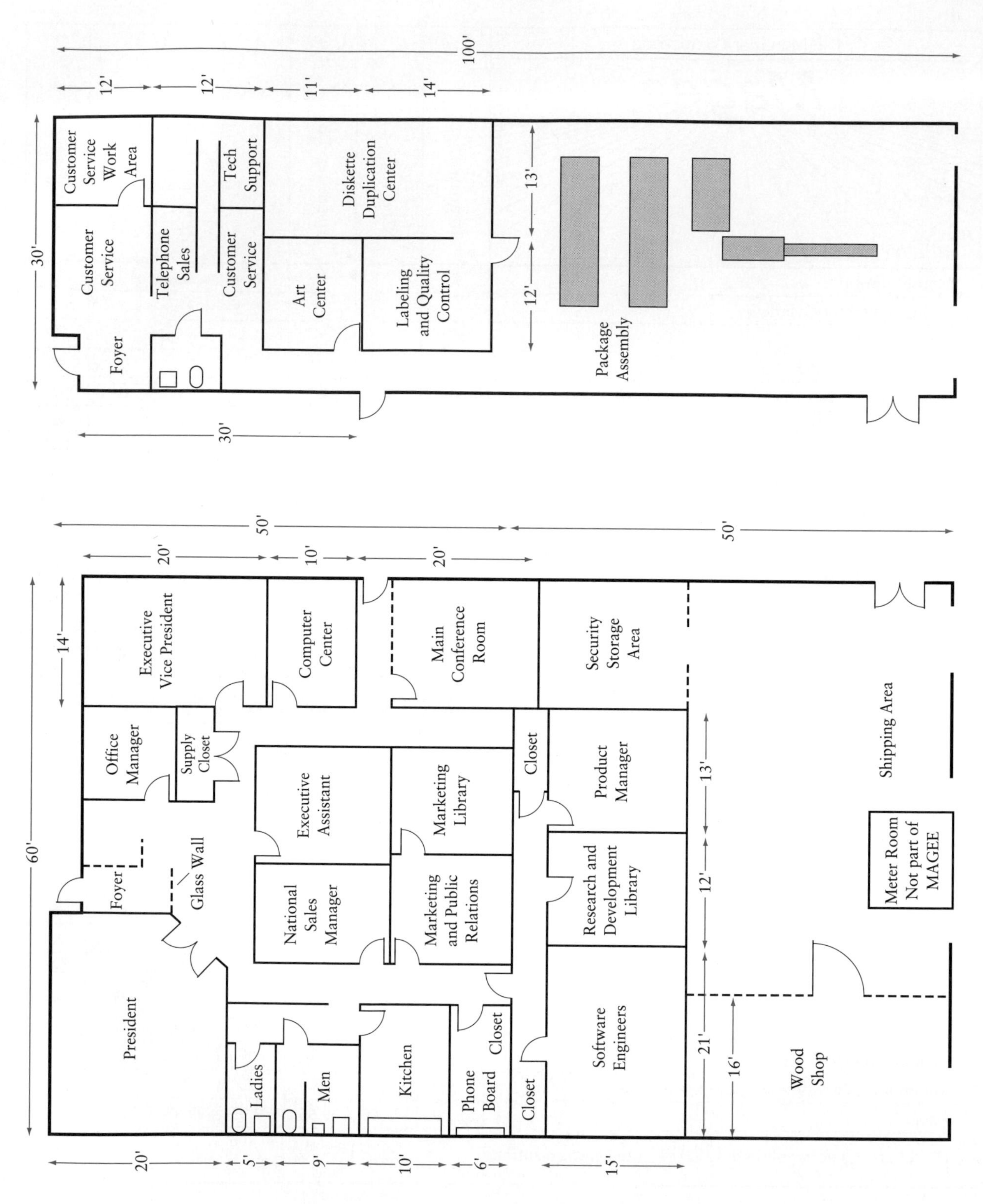

Exhibit 6
Facility Floor Plan

the office environment as "a jungle." The installation of numerous walls to create private offices, the grouping of functional area offices, a private, security-controlled programming area, and a computer room were some of the physical changes that occurred with the expansion.

Concurrent with the expansion, Magee started in motion the process of separating the packaging, customer service, and technical support functions of the company into a separate entity. Magee has not named the as yet unofficial company but indicated his intentions to sponsor a company-wide contest to choose a name. He envisions that the company will invoice Magee Enterprises for its services. R&D, marketing, and sales would be done out of Magee Enterprises.

The new company will package and prepare advertising graphic designs for other software dealers, as well as for Magee Enterprises. Magee Enterprises is already experimenting with small jobs of 100–150 packages per month for a limited number of customers in an attempt to learn the business. The customers are friends of Magee. No active customer recruitment has been undertaken, as management considers itself currently too busy with Automenu and Treeview. Tom Jones, executive vice president, expressed that within the next few months the company will have a plan to become actively involved in the packaging business. Magee feels that this additional source of income will provide greater stability for the corporation.

As reflected in Exhibit 6, the proposed new company is housed adjacent to Magee Enterprises. A card-key access security door connects the two facilities. Magee foresees the packaging company eventually occupying a separate facility.

Prior to the expansion, Magee Enterprises had only perimeter security. Magee appears to genuinely enjoy showing visitors the security controls that have been implemented. Magee feels that he is not paranoid about security, but as the company adds more people, limiting access is important. He also feels that it will be very important to show future packaging customers that the company can offer security for their product.

After 5:00 P.M. the security door between Magee Enterprises and the packaging company will open for only specific cardholders, and the programming area will be the most tightly controlled area. Only Magee, Jones, and the programmers will have access to these rooms.

HUMAN RESOURCES

The first employees were hired in the fall of 1986. Magee hired a friend and his younger brother part-time to assemble packages. Both were in school and held other part-time jobs in addition to working for Magee. The first non-family or friend employee was hired in August 1987. By 1990, the company had 14 employees. An organizational chart is presented in Exhibit 7.

Tom Jones joined the company at the time of the major production crisis. At that time, Jones agreed to work for the company for four months to straighten out the problems. Both Magee and Jones refer to their business relationship as one of fate. Jones' background includes ten years as president and CEO of Wells Fargo Armored Corporation, a division of Wells Fargo. After retiring from Wells Fargo, Jones did various consulting jobs. He then managed a long-distance

Exhibit 7 Magee Enterprises, Inc.

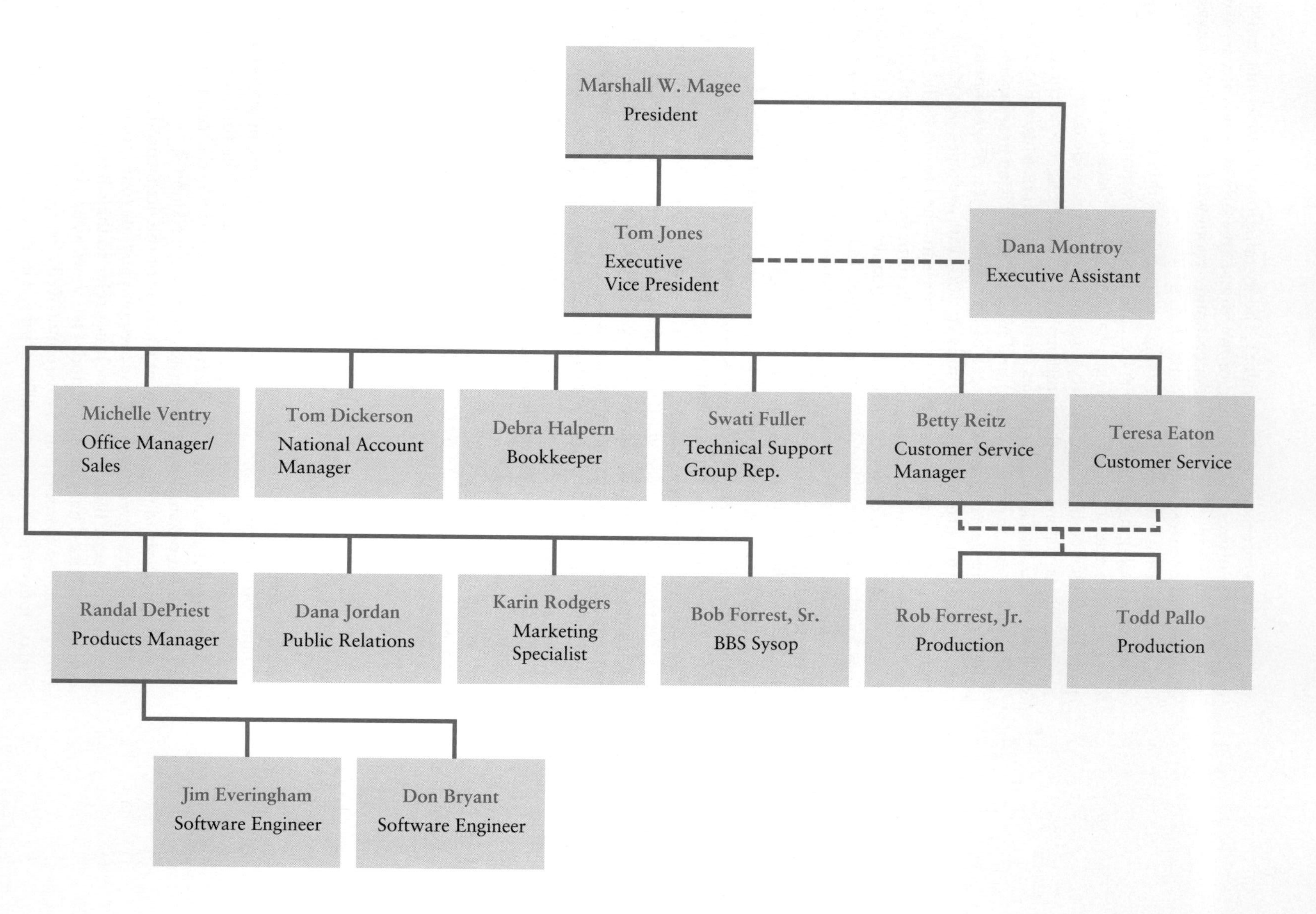

telecommunications business in Macon, Georgia. While Jones indicates that he thoroughly enjoyed working with "a great group of young people," all of whom he hired, he tired of the four nights a week away from home. He saw the business as having a good niche but limited growth prospects. Jones feels the experience gave him a good learning base for a high-tech industry. After resigning from the telecommunications business, Jones once again considered the consulting arena. At age 56, Jones is the most senior Magee employee. Only two other employees are over 30 years of age. Jones states that he enjoys being around young people and having an impact on their personal and professional development.

When asked to describe the company and its employees at the time he joined the organization, Jones relates: "I walked in during the production crisis. There was confusion. Marshall was beside himself. He's kind and doesn't say others had failed him, but that's what happened." Jones goes on to describe Magee as a genius in software, but who, by his own admission, does not really enjoy day-to-day management. Jones describes the employees at the time he joined the organization as having basic talents, tremendous brain power, but little job experience.

Jones introduced such practices as project sheets, which defined projects and due dates for specific projects. Employees first had to define what they did on a daily and occasional basis. Tasks done occasionally had to be placed on a project sheet. Each step and the time frame to accomplish it was listed on the sheet. The project sheets lessened the natural tendency to ignore daily tasks when also working on major projects. Jones refers to the project sheets as a method for teaching employees to prioritize and to inject self-discipline into the organization. Project sheets have been abandoned as Jones feels they are no longer necessary.

Following the major production crisis, Jones had all employees working on Friday night to fill back orders. Magee explained in an interview that he could never have gotten employees to work on a weekend. Describing himself as "too easy" and "unable to say no" to employees' requests, Magee indicates that he intends to distance himself more and more from the management of employees, leaving the daily operational management of the company to Jones.

Jones stresses cross-training within the organization. Magee taught basic computing classes. There are also classes in Automenu and Treeview, as well as customer service.

The company does not have a personnel manual, although one is currently being prepared. In addition to basic personnel practices, the manual will have salary grades and ranges and details of an individual bonus program which management plans to present. At the time Jones arrived, Magee had some basic written policies related to such items as vacation and sick leave, but they were never distributed. Magee refrained from distributing the policies since an attorney had warned him to be careful in what he distributed to employees—with distribution came obligation to the policy.

Benefits provided by the company include medical, dental, and life insurance. On occasion, Magee has helped an employee with school expenses and has given bonuses for especially good work. Christmas, 1989, the company issued thank-you checks to each employee. The amount of each employee's check was a little more than their normal bi-weekly check.

Before coming to Magee Enterprises, Jones related that people told him programmers are impossible to manage. Jones contends that he has found little

Exhibit 8
Sales of Magee Enterprises, Inc.

1983	$20
1984	$200
1985	$15,000
1986	$175,000
1987	$800,000
1988	$1,200,000
1989	$2,000,000

difference in managing programmers as opposed to other employees, if he just pays attention to the needs of each employee. He describes true programmers as thinking of themselves as mavericks, with their computers as an extension of themselves. He began involving programmers in brainstorming sessions with marketing. Their compensation is handled in the same manner as that of other employees, although Jones said it is actually easier to place them at a specific range based on their background.

In assessing his human resources situation, Magee states that in some instances in the past, he probably should have paid higher salaries to purchase certain levels of experience. He relates: "My philosophy had been to take very young employees who I could pay a lot less and then train them, but I didn't realize I wouldn't have the time to train them." Magee feels that he is consistently hiring better and better employees. Newly hired employees are sometimes moving ahead of more tenured employees, with reporting relationships reversing themselves in some cases. Many of the recent hires fill management roles in the organization which previously did not exist.

COMPANY OWNERSHIP

Marshall Magee owns 100 percent of Magee Enterprises, Inc. He has stated that he is "a strict believer in 100 percent ownership and will not ever give anyone a piece of my pie." Originally the company was structured as a sole proprietorship. When it was incorporated in October 1988, Magee injected a cash infusion of $40,000 from his personal savings.

Evidently, Jones foresees Magee Enterprises as possibly a corporate umbrella for numerous companies Magee may create—Magee Software, a packaging company, Magee Europe, and other companies.

SALES INFORMATION

Sales figures for the company are presented in Exhibit 8. Automenu has in excess of 250,000 registered users, and Treeview has over 1,500 registered users.

VISION

In 10 years Magee wants to be the largest software company in the Southeast. Another goal is to have Microsoft and IBM as his company's major competitors in five years. In the meantime, Magee plans to add new products and to improve old ones, keeping Automenu a moving target.

Jones states that in the next few months he and Magee will resolve how the company will compete in Europe. Internationally, Magee Enterprises has two dealers in England, two in Germany, and one in Australia.

In assessing his role in the company, Magee judges himself to be a good programmer and software designer and has a good feel for what people want. He also considers himself as a capable spokesman for the company, with the ability to talk on different technical levels. Reflecting on his personal goal within the company, Magee states:

> I want to build the company to the point that I don't do much programming. I'd rather come up with ideas for the product, work out the details and hire people to make the product a reality. The biggest problem is coming up with ideas. Implementing them is pretty much like building a house—dream up what the house should be like and you can build it. I'm looking for my builders and construction crew right now.

CASE

4

Northern Dairy Cooperative

In August 1993, James Green, the 56-year-old director of Northern Dairy Cooperative (NDC), sat looking at the discouraging preliminary annual statements for the cooperative. He realized that some changes were needed to reverse the poor performance of the company. While sales had increased, the farmers were being paid only for their milk and not receiving the handsome dividends that other cooperatives were paying. The members were getting restless and threatening to transfer to another co-op. Green anticipated rebellion when the current figures were presented to the farmers. Going out of business was a definite possibility, a likelihood he had avoided considering for the past twelve years since carefully putting together this organization.

NDC'S HISTORY

NDC was actually a combination of two, separately incorporated cooperatives. The larger of these two co-ops, Holstein Cooperative (HC), included about 100 farmers exclusively milking Holstein cows; Holstein milk is high in protein and water content and low in fat. The smaller Jersey Farmers Cooperative (JFC) comprised of about 10 farmers milking only Jersey cows; Jersey milk is rich in fat and lower in water content than Holstein milk. The two milk-producing groups are normally mutually exclusive because of the content formula for pricing milk. It is easier for Holstein dairy owners to receive premiums because of the higher values placed on protein content. Normally, the owners of a milk cooperative are the farmers; however, NDC was owned by the two separate cooperatives, HC and JFC. Benefits, such as earnings for milk delivered, are paid in lump sums by NDC to the two owner cooperatives, which then pass the benefits on to each of their member farmers.

More than 16 years ago, Green, then a middle-sized (200 Holstein cows) dairy farmer, and Humperdinck, a large (1,000 cows, mostly Holstein) dairy farmer, had talked 140 farmers into joining together to market their milk. They argued that the larger organization would have more clout in a market made up of about three very large processors and about four small ones. One of the stipulations of most cooperatives is that the co-op buy the entire amount produced by each farmer. The milk is picked up daily at the farms and transported to the cooperative's plant. The co-op pays the farmers a price that is controlled by the govern-

This case was prepared by Robert A. Blumenthal, University of Washington, and Javad Kargar, North Carolina Central University. This case was prepared as a basis for class discussion rather than to illustrate either effective or ineffective handling of administrative situations.

ment but that is set by the average price paid for milk in the Midwest. This is called the MW, or "order," price. The price goes up and down at different times of the year and more or less follows a seasonal pattern. Usually, the price paid for milk goes up in the spring and summer and down in the late fall and winter.

The arrangement worked for a while, and NDC was successful in acting as the wholesale distributor of the raw milk. But, as the oversupply of milk grew, it became harder to peddle all of the milk. Green, Humperdinck, and the other members of the NDC board of directors decided that if NDC became the processor, their problems would be solved. So in 1975 the board got the memberships of the two co-ops to agree to build a new cheese plant, which converted their surplus milk into bulk cheddar cheese. The cheese was then sold to Kraft and other processed-cheese manufacturers. Eventually, other kinds of cheeses were produced and sold by NDC to local retailers: Colby, Monterey Jack, Pepper Jack, and mozzarella. The bulk cheddar cheese was packaged in 500-pound barrels that were shipped weekly to Kraft and other processors, who converted this bulk cheese into such products as Velveeta™ and presliced "American" specialties. Not all of NDC's output was packed in barrels. Some was made into 20-pound blocks for further processing into smaller weights, such as 2-pound loaves and "random weights" (these are the small packages bought in grocery stores by retail customers). NDC makes money on cheese when the price paid for milk goes down. The dairy farmer makes money when the price for milk goes up.

Even with the government's dairy-herd reduction program, milk surpluses continued to grow. Dairy farmers still believe that in order to increase income, you must buy more cows and produce more milk. As inflation rates rose and milk prices fell, farmers expanded their herds and milk production, thinking that their cash-flow problems would be solved. All this did was to aggravate the surplus situation, and it became harder and harder to market raw milk. In 1985 NDC had an opportunity to lease/option a very small liquid-milk and ice cream processor located across the street from the cheese plant. The co-op's directors saw this as a chance to protect the distribution of their milk and, against the wishes of their bank, entered into an agreement to lease the plant with an option to purchase in 5 years. The board then contracted with a local milk salesman to distribute the products of their combined operations. They provided this distributor with office and warehouse space on-site at the fluid plant. The products sold through this on-site distributor were various classes of bottled milk, various forms of cream, sour cream, cottage cheese, butter, and ice cream. Since NDC's plants produced only pasteurized cheese, liquid milk, cream, and ice cream, the other products were purchased wholesale from competitors.

Actually, the best solution to the surpluses of raw milk is to convert liquid surpluses into powdered milk and whey, which can be sold very profitably on both national and international markets. There is a large national market for whey, which is used as an additive to many high-volume food products, while the market for powdered milk is larger overseas. This solution, however, was not available to small co-op processors because of the installation costs for powder plants, which required about $15 million for an efficient operation.

One of the requirements for cooperative members is that they buy their own products for personal use. Consequently, a small, 1,000-square-foot retail store was opened when the cheese plant was built in 1975. The store was run by Dan Ushihara, a former Safeway manager. The store originally stocked just the milk and cheese products of NDC. The most popular products were NDC's ice cream

and "squeaky cheese." Squeaky cheese is made from cheese curds which, when eaten within 48 hours after production, give off a squeaking sound when chewed. Gradually, Ushihara added other specialty food items made in the state and deli-type sandwiches for lunch. As time went on, a few novelty hard and soft items, such as aprons, containers, and gifts, were added. At the time of this writing, Ushihara had added several mail-order Christmas gift items that he marketed to local customers and registered visitors from bus tours. The tours stopped at the cheese plant to watch the cheese-manufacturing process through observation windows on the second floor over the retail store and to buy ice cream cones. The morning newspaper of the largest nearby city had rated the plant's ice cream the best but least-known ice cream in the state in an editorial. Because of the store's limited space, Ushihara was constrained to stock small volumes. He was creative, however. Adding the mailed-flyer increased his dollar volume beyond that garnered from the normal in-store traffic. The store was staffed by women who had been associated with the local dairy community for years. They were willing, but Ushihara's management style made them somewhat grumpy and intransigent.

After building the cheese plant, the company soon found that it had not incorporated enough warehouse space for the cheese. Consequently, it leased a refrigerated warehouse about two miles from the plant site. The lower floor was devoted to packaged cheese in retail sizes, while the upper floor was used to store packing materials. The 20-pound boxes were shipped to the warehouse from the cheese plant, and the cheese was then cut into 2-pound loaves and random weights. These loaves were wrapped, sorted, and repacked semiautomatically into cases of like products, which were then moved into cold storage to await distribution to retailers. This part of the organization was headed by Sam Rusoff and carried out by six female packagers and a male warehouseman. Rusoff was loyal to the company, but he was highly introverted, conservative with money, words, and time, and had a poor reputation for working with people in the company. Unfortunately, the packagers were unhappy under his supervision.

DAIRY INDUSTRY

Consumption of Fluid Milk

Per capita milk consumption in the United States dropped from 26.7 gallons annually in 1970 to 21.2 gallons in 1985, and the health-fitness craze almost bypassed milk producers. Milk marketers finally have realized that they must become more aggressive and innovative. New product lines range from high-calcium and fermented varieties of milk to carbonated versions, but large-scale marketing is difficult in an industry where there are virtually no national brands. Some local dairies and area dairy associations, such as the California Milk Advisory Board, recently developed substantial advertising campaigns to promote milk. The United Dairy Industry Association, the National Dairy Board, and the Dairy Promotion Federated Association run national and local television ads. The industry's generic dairy advertising budget increased from about $66 million in 1983 to about $126 million in 1987. Intensified marketing may have contributed to a 1.5 percent increase in per capita milk consumption from 1985 to 1986.

The consumption of fluid milk has increased 12 percent over the past six years. Low-fat milk outsells whole milk and is expected to compose 70 percent of sales

by the late 1990s. Calcium-enriched milk is being produced in response to studies that have found an increased need for calcium among women.

Government Attempt to Control Surpluses In about 1982, the government, seeing that the milk supply significantly exceeded demand, offered to buy out dairy herds with the stipulation that the farmers who benefited from the buy-out could not reenter the market for five years. This action temporarily reduced the supply, but those farmers who had not entered the buy-out program saw an advantage in increasing their herds. In addition, new technology in breeding and automatic feeding methods allowed them to significantly increase their rates of production, thus further exacerbating the surplus problem. Another phenomenon that was occurring at the time of this writing was the rise in wheat and feed costs and the decline in milk prices, a combination that put the farmers in a cash bind. The farmer's solution to this situation was the same old formula: more cows plus more milk equals more money. (Note: there is a difference between the farmers' plight and NDC's situation.)

Consumption of Cheese

Cheese is the second-biggest seller in the dairy departments of supermarkets. Cheese manufacturers are delivering variety, healthy options, and convenience for today's consumer. Sales of specialty cheese foods are increasing, which in turn is helping to increase the sales of premium natural cheeses.

Overall, cheese sales have more than doubled during the past 20 years. Per capita consumption of cheese in 1977 stood at 16 pounds, according to the U.S. Department of Agriculture. Per capita consumption by 1988 totaled 24 pounds, which represents a 50 percent increase in only 11 years. During the past decade, sales of American-type cheeses rose 35 percent, while sales of other cheese varieties increased more than 70 percent.

According to a recent study by Frost and Sullivan, an international market research firm, mozzarella sales have increased 225 percent during the past 10 years, rising almost 20 percent per year. Frost and Sullivan also predict that mozzarella sales will grow about 10.5 percent a year through 1992.

According to a special report for *Dairy* magazine, during 1986 a total of 251 new products used cheese as an ingredient. In 1987, 370 new items contained cheese. Cheese scored its biggest gain as an ingredient in entrées—frozen dinners and sandwiches, pizzas, and other Italian items and Mexican meals.

Total cheese sales are expected to continue to grow. In a recent study, the United Dairy Industry Association predicted that per capita cheese sales would top the 28-pound mark by 1993. Find/SVP, a market research group based in New York, is forecasting an annual growth rate of at least 4 percent through 1993.

Consumption of Ice Cream

During World War II, the reduced supplies of sugar and milk curtailed the production of ice cream, but production later rebounded sharply, and by 1950 consumption had grown to 16 quarts per capita. The period between 1955 and 1985 saw a leveling off of the growth in ice cream consumption. National production of ice cream rose from 500,000 gallons in 1950 to over 1.2 million gallons annually in 1975, after which it leveled off, barely reaching 1.3 million gallons by 1984. Drugstores began replacing their soda fountains with more profitable drug and cosmetic lines, and the bulk of ice cream sales shifted to

custard stands, mom-and-pop stores, fast-food outlets, and supermarkets. By 1960, the majority of ice cream sales occurred in supermarkets. Supermarket chains began introducing their own store brands of ice cream, which were lower in butterfat, artificially flavored, higher in air content, and cheaper.

The new markets evolving in the 1980s were a result of the revolution in the marketing and manufacturing of ice cream and ice cream–type desserts. Superpremium ice cream brands began to flourish in the 1980s, and their sales have outperformed traditional ice cream. Superpremium ice creams are much richer and denser than other ice creams, with a butterfat content of 16 percent and a low air content. Advertising, not traditionally done by ice cream manufacturers, is now the key to increasing sales and opening new markets. The new trend is toward ice cream on a stick as well as other novelties aimed at the adult market first and at children only secondarily. The net result has been the introduction of gourmet frozen novelties, especially in new packaging and smaller sizes that target adults and single householders.

Growth in the ice cream market has remained steady for the past two decades. Industry analysts predicted that in 1988 the superpremium segment would continue to grow annually at 15 percent. A decline of 8 percent in sales of the regular style and 22 percent in economy styles occurred through 1988. Premium ice cream sales during 1987 and 1988 accounted for 58 percent of the market versus 24 percent for superpremium and 18 percent for economy. In 1987, analysts estimated superpremium ice cream sales to be $1.8 billion. Ice cream sales in the United States were expected to reach $4.3 billion by 1991 (*Advertising Age*, September 7, 1987). At this time, upscale ice cream novelties marketed to adult consumers were also increasing in popularity. Sales of ice cream novelties in 1988 topped $1 billion. Gourmet, light and diet, "healthy," and nondairy novelties had started to be produced. These innovative desserts were designed to take advantage of the baby-boomers' taste for the new and novel. During the 1987–1988 period this segment of the industry was experiencing the most growth.

Ice Cream Industry Structure The ice cream industry has been comprised mainly of regional and local dairies and small specialty producers. Improved refrigeration and transportation of frozen foods has opened the door to national distribution of ice cream products. Major national distributors, such as Kraft and Pillsbury, have entered the ice cream market through acquisition of profitable family-owned ice cream outlets, expansion of existing facilities, or construction of new factories and facilities. According to industry analysts, 80 percent of the ice cream bought today is for home consumption (as opposed to on-the-spot snacking), only 58 percent of which is purchased at supermarkets (*Quick Frozen Foods*, July 1988), an indication that these chains are apparently missing a chance to sell more ice cream.

Overall, the number of plants producing ice cream declined from a high of 1,628 in 1970 to 884 in 1982. Large manufacturers were able to build facilities that could produce thousands of gallons of ice cream daily and then, through their distribution networks, to transport the ice cream to warehouses and ultimately to supermarkets and other retail outlets. Smaller manufacturers still operate regionally on a small scale and have geographically scattered plants. They rely heavily on independent distributors but often handle their own transportation to ensure freshness and prompt delivery.

Traditionally, the ice cream industry did not purchase media advertising. The introduction of national distributors changed that attitude, however, as the large

Table 1
Types of Ice Cream

Ice Cream Type	Butterfat	Overrun	Additives	Calories
Ordinary	10–20%	80–100%	Yes	<150
Premium	12–16%	40–60%	No	180
Superpremium	16–20%	<40%	No	260
Ice milk	2–7% milkfat			
Sherbet	1–2% milkfat			
Frozen yogurt	6% fat			

national chains expanded their markets through such advertising. Media advertising is credited with helping Frusen Gladje successfully compete with Häagen Dazs. The entrance of national food chains into the ice cream market increased industry advertising by as much as 600 percent (*Quick Frozen Foods*, July 1988).

Quality and Price The quality standards for ice cream are based on butterfat percentage and overrun used in production. Superpremium ice creams are typically low in overrun and high in butterfat (see Table 1 for types of ice cream).

Price is based on the quality of the ice cream (see Table 2 for price estimates by class during the 1992–1993 period). The estimated average composition costs for ice cream are shown in Table 3.

Ice Cream Economics The market, according to some analysts, is nearing the saturation point for superpremium products, declining for economy and standard products, and still growing for upscale novelties. The competition is intense, especially in the superpremium and novelty markets.

Farm Credit Conditions

The dairy industry is in ferment. Processors are getting larger through investment and mergers in order to stay in business. Small, poorly capitalized firms are going out of business. The profits seem to be in retail and specialized products, which carry higher mark-ups than the commodities. Some firms have profited by entering the retail field, such as Stew Leonard in Norwalk, Connecticut. Banks, previously having encouraged heavy borrowing by the farmers, have now

Table 2
Ice Cream Price Estimates by Class 1992–1993

Class	Producers	Price
Luxury	Specialty brands (Godiva, Gelare)	\$2.49–\$3.75 per pint
Superpremium	Homemade specialty (Häagen Dazs, Frusen Gladje)	\$1.69–\$2.19 per pint
Premium	Best-selling brands (Ben & Jerry's, Breyers, Dreyers)	\$2.59–\$3.49 per gallon
Standard	Local dairy brands	\$1.99–\$2.59 per half-gallon
Economy	Store brands and inexpensive local dairy brands	\$0.99–\$1.00 per half gallon

Table 3
Cost Composition for Half-Gallons

Composition	Private Labels %	Premium %
Raw materials	32.4	24.0
Processing and packaging	19.2	14.2
Administrative expense	1.4	1.4
Distribution expense	5.9	4.2
Manufacturing operating profit	2.7	2.0
Distributors' mark-up	16.0	32.7
Retail mark-up	22.4	21.5

retrenched and are making credit scarce. The history of dairy farm debt coincides with most agricultural farm debt in the United States. In 1971, U.S. farm debt amounted to about $54 billion. By 1976, it had nearly doubled to $91 billion. By 1985 farm debt had reached crisis proportions, with the total U.S. farm debt peaking at more than $212 billion. This was higher than the combined foreign debt of Argentina, Brazil, and Mexico. The agriculture industry tends to ride a roller-coaster. In the 1970s the industry looked invincible; in fact, in 1973–1974 many, including the bankers, believed that farmland would not depreciate. Bankers were basing their lending rates on inflated land values and increased collateral percentages on cattle life spans of 3–4 years. Between 1972 and 1979 the boom in farm products created $447 billion in new wealth and new credit (Ben Gisin, *Farmers and Ranchers*, 1988). Milk subsidies continued to rise rapidly through the late 1970s; however, after the 1981 peak, the bottom fell out of the market, and prices continued to drop through June 1988. Support prices for 3.6 percent butterfat milk went from $9 per hundredweight (cwt.) in 1978 to a peak of over $13 in 1981, then fell to about $10.67 per cwt. in January 1988. According to Mark Drabenscott, senior economist with the Federal Reserve in Kansas City, "American agriculture is under its greatest financial stress since the Great Depression" (Needles, Anderson, Caldwell, *Principles of Accounting*, 1984).

Banks were hard hit. The major lenders in the agriculture industry include the Farmers Home Administration, commercial banks, FLBs (Federal Land Banks—part of the Farm Credit System [FCS]), insurance firms, and others, such as the Commodity Credit Corporation. In 1985, 62 commercial farm banks failed; in 1986, 59 failed, and in the first six weeks of 1987, 8 farm banks failed. Half of the $51 billion in agriculture loans were considered uncollectable by the commercial banks. The Farm Credit System was the hardest hit creditor by far, owning one-third of the total farm debt (over $200 billion). The FCS is the biggest bank in America, is not a private bank, and is not part of the federal government. It is a farmer-owned cooperative, and in late 1975 it asked Congress for a "bailout" and proceeded to post the largest financial loss of any institution in the history of our country—totaling $2.7 billion.

These conditions forced the banks to institute new requirements for farmers. The farmers, formerly the banks' best customers, had to pay for the losses by making double payments at nearly intolerable terms: more collateral, the maintenance of impossible ratios, significantly higher interest rates, and more stringent reporting. Banks were insisting on current ratios from 1.5 to 2 to 1, 0.9 to 0.3 to 1 debt to net worth ratios, and 1.4 to 2 to 2 debt coverage ratios. With

feed prices rising, borrowing to increase herds and facilities becoming nearly impossible, and milk prices declining, the farmers' backs were to the wall.

COMPETITION

NDC's main local competitors in 1993 were Golden Dairy, Carnation, Life Milk, Cache Valley Cheese, Mozzarella, Mountain Cheese, and Sun Valley Cheese.

Golden Dairy was the largest local competitor in 1993. The company has the largest group of farmers and provides excellent benefits for them; must buy all of the farmers' output, and therefore the farmers are very loyal to the company. Golden Dairy has superior distribution channels, both in state and out of state. NDC is known for the quality of its cheeses and ice cream but is not well distributed in the retail market. It is very difficult to get the major distributors of cheese, Associated Grocers (AG) and two others, to market NDC's products. AG is controlled by Golden Dairy, whose president is a director of AG as well as a director of one of the two major local banks. This president sees to it that no other company in the milk-processing industry gets credit from his bank. It is an "old boys'" industry with established structure, pricing, and relationships. Everyone knows everyone else, and there are no secrets. There are established turfs. Golden Dairy is known as the second-best cheese and ice cream quality producer in the state. But Golden Dairy has little variety among products and poor coverage among independent retailers. Sales for Golden Dairy totaled $600 million in 1993, and the company expected strong growth in the future.

The second-largest ice cream and fluid milk producer in 1993 was Carnation. The company has built a new ice cream plant, and overall it has reasonably current equipment. It has strong but rigid management. The company has annual contracts with farmers, but its distribution equipment is old. Total sales for Carnation were $200 million in 1993.

The third-largest competitor in 1993 was Life Milk. This company has excellent capitalization and superior institutional distribution systems for milk and soft/fluid products. But it has poor-quality ice cream with poor distribution. Total sales for Life Milk were $100 million in 1993. Life Milk buys milk as needed and does not have any vision or innovation. Life Milk does not produce cheese.

The fourth-largest competitor in 1993 was Cache Valley Cheese. This company produces only average and poor-quality cheese at low prices. Cache Valley Cheese is strong financially and has a multistate distribution system. Total sales for Cache Valley Cheese in 1988 were about $75 million, and it is looking for a merger.

Another large local competitor, Pride, is the biggest producer of milk and milk products in the state. It also makes and sells a small amount of cheddar at retail but derives virtually all of its profit by producing powdered milk and selling it overseas.

Mozzarella is another competitor, although it makes only mozzarella and sells to pizza parlors and restaurants. Total sales for Mozzarella were $25 million in 1993, with excellent profitability, and the company plans to expand its operations, having $25 million in financing committed. The owner of the company is over 74 years old and has no clear successor.

Mountain Cheese is another competitor in the state capital producing a line of specialty cheeses, such as Pepper Jack and other flavored cheeses. The com-

pany has a good reputation with customers and is very innovative with its products. Mountain's production plant is very old, however, and has a limited capacity. Total sales for Mountain in 1993 were $15 million.

Sun Valley Cheese makes mostly cheddar, which it sells to Mexican restaurants along with other condiments used in the preparation of Mexican food. The company has a strong specialty distribution to restaurants. Sun Valley's management is very rigid, and its plant has old production equipment. Total sales for Sun Valley Cheese in 1993 were about $2 million.

Another competitor in California produces 200,000 pounds of cheddar a day in a completely automated plant costing over $150 million and owned by six international companies. Other competitors are primarily out-of-state producers from Idaho and Utah.

Much of the data given above applies to the fluid and soft milk products division of NDC. Fluid milk is so competitive that it is often wholesaled below cost. The only bright spot is its ice cream. The company sells its premium-grade ice cream in its own state but also markets half-gallon bricks of a medium grade under other labels. NDC also manufactures ice cream for the state's Dairy Queen chain. During the summer, this is a major contributor to sales. The equipment in the fluid plant is decrepit and out-of-date, which has an impact on the quality of the fluid milk but does not seem to affect the quality of the ice cream.

NORTHERN DAIRY COOPERATIVE

Production at NDC

The milk, after being delivered to the fluid plant from the farmers, is first pasteurized, then separated according to whether it is intended for use in fluid milk and soft products, such as ice cream and cottage cheese, or in cheese. Milk intended for fluid consumption is classified as "Class A," which has a higher wholesale price and more stringent quality requirements than classes B and C, which are known as "commercial" classes. The prices for all these products are determined by the regional orders or commodity markets for them and do not leave a lot of room for profit. The best of all worlds for cheese wholesale prices is when the price of cheese is rising and milk costs are either not rising as fast or are declining. The worst of all worlds is when cheese wholesale prices are declining while milk costs are still going up. What is meant by cost is what the NDC pays the farmers. The government supported Class A prices by paying the difference between the order price and a support-price level.

The greatest amount of cheese is sold for further processing to such companies as Kraft. The price of cheese is affected not only by the auction price in the commodity markets but also by the amount of cheese held in storage by the government. In 1992 this storage amount was being slowly reduced. Cheese in 500-pound barrels is sold at usually no more than a cent or two per hundredweight over cost. NDC produces the largest amount of cheese (cheddar and Monterey Jack) in the state with simple technology and reasonably reliable equipment. NDC's production capacity was considerably greater than its market could consume, so most of its production was sold to Kraft.

Production figures for the 1992 and 1993 fiscal years are shown in Table 4, with production costs shown in Table 5.

Table 4
Production Figures for 1992 and 1993 (Year Ended July 31)

	1993	1992
Fluid milk products (in pounds)		
Cheese products	125,319,520	136,967,570
Fluid milk products	45,625,356	32,624,682
Direct labor cost/lb.	.0090	.0092
Operating costs/lb.	.0335	.0374
Cheese plant production		
Milk pounds processed	140,078,610	138,436,099
Cheese produced		
Barrels	9,120,341	9,334,157
Blocks (20-lb.)	4,783,178	5,135,113
Cheese yields per pound		
Milk processed	10.49%	10.45%
Direct labor cost/lb.	.0326	.0328
Operating cost/lb.	.1018	.1001
Warehouse development		
Pounds sold		
Random weights	802,005	589,303
2 pounders	1,831,090	1,838,788
5 & 10 pounders	379,436	442,196
20-lb. blocks	1,212,688	1,003,245
Direct labor cost/lb.	.0360	.0316
Operating costs/lb.	.1843	.1522

NDC's Organizational Structure

Paul Canoli was the general manager hired by the board and given overall responsibility for running the whole company. Canoli was near retirement age and had previously worked for a major distributor in the food industry, but not in the dairy industry. He did not understand the financial aspects of the business and was preoccupied with sales goals and strategies. As a consequence, he addressed only profitability when reporting to the board. He was not considered competent to deal with the bank, so that duty was left to the controller.

NDC has three divisions: cheese, milk, and packaging. In addition, there is an administrative department, which handles invoicing, payroll, payables, and so on.

The cheese division, managed by Jim Cook, aged 45, is staffed by about 60 people, is well organized, and operates efficiently under Cook's strong, authoritarian management style. Cook, who is married with seven children, is not only very reliable but plans and organizes his work carefully. He had some education in the dairy business and worked for Kraft before coming to NDC. (One of his personal goals was to earn an MBA.) He maintained carefully researched graphs of the cheese and milk operations and was fond of giving long-winded explanations of what was going on in the industry. His greatest skill was planning and organizing, while his greatest weakness was his inability to make organizational decisions. Cook could be cooperative with senior management but also could be obstreperous unless persuaded by hard evidence. When asked to follow through

Description	Kraft Barrels	USDA Barrels	Market Raw Milk	2-lb. Loaves Cheese	Random Weights Cheese	2% Milk/ Gallon	Dairy Queen Ice Cream Mix
Milk price	$1.977	$1.2540	$0.3300	$1.7000	$1.7250	$1.4290	$2.6090
Less:							
Distribution discount							.2870
Trade allowances				.1000	.1000	.0107	.0261
Bill backs for transportation				.0750	.0750		.0600
Net sales price	$1.977	$1.2540	$0.3300	$1.5250	$1.5500	$1.4183	$2.2359
Total variable costs	$1.2511	$1.2818	$0.2550	$1.4020	$1.4777	$1.3358	$2.1015

Table 5
Production Costs
(as of July 31, 1993)

on some recommendations by the board, he did so unenthusiastically. The cheese division depends on the fluid plant for the milk it makes into cheese, so cooperation between the plants is crucial. Once the milk is received by the cheese plant, there is no further interaction with the fluid plant, except for occasional labor sharing when the cheese plant needs extra help. Technology for producing cheese is the responsibility of "the shift cheese maker," whose control over production depends on his personal skill and intuition. While the process is predictable, variations must be made on the basis of the interpretations of the "cheese maker." The cheese division, which is organized by the Teamsters, often works two shifts. Its morale is good, its productivity high, and its procedures extremely well-organized and carefully planned. Quality is high.

The milk division is organized by the United Food & Commercial Workers union and typically operates from about 2 A.M. until about 3 P.M. It has a permissive manager, Jack Mahin, who never gets anything accomplished and tries to work both sides of the street. Mahin is about 59, recently widowed, and devoted to his work. He has been with NDC for about three years, having previously worked for Carnation as a milk plant manager. He has only a high school diploma and no formal training, but he has had years of experience. His reputation at Carnation was that of a nice guy who could never get anything done. His best quality is his ability to win the trust of his employees. Mahin has an assistant, Allen Smith, who has been with the company for about a year and is the son of a former employee. Smith is very smart, but constant frustrations have made him depressed and somewhat less than reliable. His main responsibility is handling the distributors and their product needs.

The milk division is always in an uproar and produces poor-quality liquid milk products. In addition, the attitude of the workers is very negative, turnover is extremely high, and the pay is at rock-bottom of scale. Milk and soft-goods production technology is clearly understood and unchanging, with the "filling" operations mechanized. Ice cream production is fragmented, but it works. Slight changes in the production process are made by the chief ice cream technician, who is responsible for flavor decisions. While the ice cream processing is done by employees who have been with the company for many years, the milk operation is carried out by large numbers of new personnel who turn over

constantly. Within this plant is an assembly area where orders are assembled for pickup by distributors and where there is a lot of contact with wholesale customers. Orders for fluid milk, cottage cheese, ice cream, and sour cream are assembled here and loaded into distributors' trucks. Billing for these products is also done in this area. While the processing of orders is well understood and not complicated, there is not enough planning here, and the temperature of the cooler is not properly regulated (it is usually too high), which causes spoilage. Fixing the cooler has been a priority for more than a year, but while it has worked on, it has never been fixed.

The packaging division is managed by Sam Rusoff, who is efficient, uncooperative, and operates on extremely authoritarian principles. This division receives cheese in bulk from the cheese plant and packages it as smaller units which can be marketed to retail stores. Production in this division is semiautomated so that a production line can be formed. Individual orders are assembled here and picked up by customers or shipped out to them. This division therefore has a lot of contact with customers. Order completion forms are sent to the cheese plant where the orders are billed by the administrative office. Sam Rusoff has to coordinate with Jim Cook at the cheese plant to run his division efficiently.

All three divisions are in different buildings, separated by distances from a quarter mile to about two miles. The administrative department is in the cheese plant, upstairs over the retail store. It is ruled by controller Mike Shephard, a CPA with what is described as an extremely negative attitude and not a lot of previous experience. He is sensible, but because the board of directors does not pay much attention to his recommendations, he has become contentious and difficult to reason with. (Green, Mahin, Shephard, Rusoff, and Cook all belong to the same social club and have formed an impenetrable clique.) The administrative department has old computer equipment which often loses its load to electrical outages caused by overloads from the cheese plant. Collections are very slow, taking on average about 60 days, while terms are ten days. Accounts payable records are in such bad shape that no accurate figures can be obtained through the system. Collections from the distributors lag, with many well over 120 days past due. Some NDC payables are being paid out twice or three times, others not at all. Some customers are not invoiced due to lost paperwork. The company has certified audits at every year end, but the CPA firm used does not seem to pick up on the problems. There are three clerks handling all of the work in this department. The people in this office are continually harassed by the treasurer's wife and by farmers who pass through the office, so morale is not good. Receivable and payable ageing is produced, but means nothing.

NDC's Marketing

Marketing at NDC is simple. Houman Gere, the general manager, is in charge, making all major contacts in the industry. A road salesman, Ernie Moon, has been employed to check displays, make emergency deliveries, return damaged goods, and keep customers happy. The company sold its products to an Alaskan chain of grocery stores and one trip a year was made by the general manager to contract for those sales. Sales promotions, which include special price reductions compensated for by overshipping products, are planned on a quarterly basis. No record is kept of these overshipments. No media advertising is done. Moon is suspected of overzealously distributing these overshipments, but no one has tried to do a quantitative analysis. The farmers are very proud of the quality of the

	Fiscal Year Ended July 31				
Proceeds	1993	1992	1991	1990	1989
Net sales	24,638	32,686	31,840	29,151	24,947
Inventory at end of year	1,617	1,880	2,039	2,044	2,001
Less prior year's inventory	(1,910)	(2,039)	(2,044)	(2,001)	(2,186)
Gross income from products	24,345	32,527	31,835	29,194	24,762
Fees from marketing members' milk	70	71	87	254	475
Gross proceeds	24,415	32,598	31,922	29,448	25,237
Operating expenses					
Manufacturing and processing	5,231	6,441	5,779	5,698	5,280
Distribution, including purchased products	1,649	1,958	2,172	1,734	1,362
General & administrative	624	626	487	491	504
Total operating expenses	7,504	9,025	8,438	7,923	7,146
Other income (expense)					
Interest expense—nonmember debt	(304)	(288)	(291)	(277)	(587)
Corporate restructuring expense (Note 1)	(108)	0	0	0	0
Hauling income from members	44	68	0	0	0
Miscellaneous income	6	6	0	0	0
Miscellaneous expenses	0	0	14	4	5
Interest income	0	6	2	15	5
Net other expense	(362)	(208)	(275)	(258)	(577)
Net proceeds	16,549	23,365	23,209	21,267	17,514
Milk settlements with members	(16,591)	(24,258)	(23,682)	(21,305)	(17,739)
Net undistributed proceeds (deficit)	(42)	(893)	(473)	(38)	(225)
Accumulated undistributed net proceeds (Beginning of year)			31	69	28
Accumulated undistributed net proceeds (End of year)	(42)	(893)	(442)	31	(197)

Table 6
Northern Dairy Cooperative Financial Statements: Consolidated Comparative Income Statements (in thousands)

cheese and ice cream their co-op produces and do as much as they can individually to encourage the purchase of their products by local stores. The fluid milk products are another story. Farmers, distributors, and retailers constantly complain of sour and curdled milk, late deliveries, and partially filled containers.

NDC's Finances

NDC has just enough working capital, with a $2 million line of credit from the bank, to continue operations without embellishing its equipment, staff, or strategies. It has gotten more difficult to make a profit, however, and in the last couple of years NDC has lost money. Its current ratio is about 1.2 to 1. Its debt to equity ratio is about 2 to 1. It has sufficient equity to continue operations but not to make a lot of changes (see Tables 6 and 7 for the company's financial statements as well as the Notes to Financial Statements). NDC owns the 9 acres on which its cheese plant is located, but it leases the other sites. NDC's bank, the

July 31	1993	1992	1991	1990	1989
Assets					
Current assets					
Cash	16	4	39	9	14
Receivables	2,513	2,371	2,705	2,249	1,821
Notes receivable	21	21	26	20	0
Inventory (Note 2)	1,617	1,910	2,039	2,044	2,001
Prepaid expenses	12	24	9	34	16
Total current assets	4,179	4,330	4,818	4,356	3,852
Property & equipment (Note 3)					
Land	406	406	148	148	148
Buildings & leaseholds	1,315	1,305	998	995	943
Equipment	2,926	2,765	2,146	1,953	1,508
Less accumulated depreciation	(2,313)	(1,989)	(1,643)	(1,302)	(1,007)
Net property & equipment	2,337	2,487	1,649	1,794	1,592
Total Assets	6,516	6,817	6,467	6,150	5,444
Liabilities & Members' Equity					
Current liabilities					
Bank overdraft	258	67	56	157	101
Notes payable	1,278	1,395	1,848	1,535	1,037
Current portion long-term debt	285	362	338	137	109
Payables to members	1,039	1,193	1,214	1,220	1,165
Other trade payables	489	557	280	303	432
Accrued expenses	186	164	139	100	93
Callable term notes	0	144	234	322	342
Total current debt	3,535	3,882	4,109	3,774	3,279
Long-term debt					
Senior notes payable	795	1,062	668	771	755
Subordinate notes payable			1,563	1,567	1,334
Total long-term debt	795	1,062	2,231	2,338	2,089
Members' equity					
Members' certificate equity	7	7	7	7	7
Accumulated undistributed net proceeds (Note 4)	60	120	120	31	69
Per unit retains (Note 5)	2,119	1,746			
Total members' equity	2,186	1,873	127	38	76
Total Liabilities & Members' Equity	6,516	6,817	6,467	6,150	5,444

Table 7
NDC's Comparative Balance Sheets (dollars in thousands)

largest in the state, recently gave notice that it was withdrawing the credit line and wished the company to bank elsewhere. This decision was not motivated by any default on terms. The bank's decision was based on its perception that the

Notes to Financial Statements

Inventory Details	Years			
	1993	1992	1991	1990
Finished products	1,453,589	1,611,235	1,586,414	1,565,991
Packaging materials	230,869	258,920	282,900	280,548
Ingredients & supplies	128,061	86,379	87,448	84,301
Raw milk	88,756	73,784	82,646	66,652
Other finished goods	8,973	8,885	4,488	3,673
Totals	1,910,248	2,039,203	2,043,896	2,001,164

Note 1. During 1992 the company incurred nonrecurring costs to restructure the co-op as a for-profit corporation from a nonexempt federal agricultural cooperative. Much of the cost involved legal options, research, special accounting advice, and additional administrative expenses.

Note 2. Inventories of cheese and other dairy products are stated as estimated net realizable value, which often approximates average cost. This is a normal practice for agricultural cooperatives. Inventories of retail merchandise, packaging, and supplies are stated as the lower of cost or market, FIFO.

Note 3. Amounts included for 1991 and 1992 due to purchase of land and buildings.

Note 4. Accumulated undistributed net proceeds are funds due retired members which were disputed liabilities.

Note 5. Pre-unit retains were certificates of debt held by the members which they converted to equity to improve the company's capitalization and cover losses. The difference between 1991 and 1992 is due to delayed agreement by some of the farmer members.

dairy industry was now becoming high risk. The fact that NDC's board refused to follow the bank's advice not to purchase the fluid plant, of course, did not improve the relationship. Since there were only four other banks in the state capable of floating a $2 million credit line, and one of those was unavailable because of an interlocking directorship related to NDC's largest competitor, the job of locating a willing bank was incredibly difficult. To date, all losses have been financed by the dairy farmers, but until now that did not require any cash from the farmers. All of the losses were handled by creative bookkeeping, but by now all legitimate arguments for these accounting manipulations have worn thin. It has gotten to the point where either the farmers put up the cash, some outside source makes an investment, or the company has to be liquidated. Financing a co-op from external sources is a very complex operation and is extremely rare. In addition, the tax ramifications of doing so pose many constraints. Green and Humperdinck are worried and looking for a way out. The situation is even more threatening to them because the firm's debts have been guaranteed by the largest producers and any losses incurred from liquidation would be devastating to their own operations.

CASE

5 The Scaffold Plank Incident

What had started as a typically slow February day in the lumber business had turned into a moral dilemma. With 12 inches of snow covering the ground, construction (and lumber shipments) had ground to a halt and on the 26th of the month, the company was still $5,000 below break-even point. In the three years since he had been in the business, Bob Hopkins knew that a losing February was nothing unusual, but the country seemed to be headed for a recession, and as usual, housing starts were leading the way into the abyss.

Bob had gone to work for a commercial bank immediately after college but soon found the bureaucracy to be overwhelming and his career progress appeared to be written in stone. At the same time he was considering changing jobs, one of his customers, John White, offered him a job at White Lumber Company. The job was as a "trader," a position that involved both buying and selling lumber. The compensation was incentive-based and there was no cap on how much a trader could earn. White Lumber, although small in size, was one of the bank's best accounts. John White was not only a director of the bank but one of the community's leading citizens.

It was a little after 8:00 A.M. when Bob received a call from Stan Parrish, the lumber buyer at Quality Lumber. Quality was one of White Lumber's best retail dealer accounts, and Bob and Stan had established a good relationship.

"Bob, I need a price and availability on 600 pieces of 3 × 12 Doug fir-rough-sawn—2 & better grade—16-feet long," said Stan, after exchanging the usual pleasantries.

"No problem, Stan. We could have those ready for pickup tomorrow and the price would be $470 per thousand board feet."

"The price sounds good, Bob. I'll probably be getting back to you this afternoon with a firm order," Stan replied.

Bob poured a third cup of coffee and mentally congratulated himself. Not bad, he thought—a two-truck order and a price that guaranteed full margin. It was only a half-hour later that Mike Fayerweather, his partner, asked Bob if he had gotten any inquiries on a truck of 16-foot scaffold plank. As Bob said he hadn't, alarm bells began to go off in his brain. While Stan had not said anything about scaffold plank, the similarities between the inquiries seemed to be more than coincidence.

While almost all lumber undergoes some sort of grading, the grading rules on scaffold plank were unusually restrictive. Scaffold planks are the wooden planks that are suspended between metal supports, often many stories above the ground. When you see painters and window-washers six stories in the air, they

This case was prepared by Stewart C. Malone and Brad Brown, University of Virginia. This case was prepared as a basis for class discussion rather than to illustrate either effective or ineffective handling of administrative situations.

generally are standing on scaffold plank. The lumber had to be free of most of the natural defects found in ordinary construction lumber and had to have unusually high strength in flexing. Most people would not be able to tell certified scaffold plank from ordinary lumber, but it was covered by its own rules in the grading book, and if you were working ten stories above the ground, you definitely wanted to have certified scaffold plank underneath you. White Lumber did not carry scaffold plank, but its rough 3 × 12s certainly would fool all but the expertly trained eye.

At lunch, Bob discussed his concerns about the inquiry with Mike.

"Look, Bob, I just don't see where we have a problem. Stan didn't specify scaffold plank, and you didn't quote him on scaffold plank," observed Mike. "We aren't even certain that the order is for the same material."

"I know all that, Mike," said Bob, "but we both know that four inquiries with the same tally is just too big a coincidence, and three of those inquiries were for Paragraph 171 scaffold plank. It seems reasonable to assume that Stan's quotation is for the same stuff."

"Well, it's obvious that our construction lumber is a good deal cheaper than the certified plank. If Stan is quoting based on our 2 & better grade and the rest of his competition is quoting on scaffold plank, then he will certainly win the job," Mike said.

"Maybe I should call Stan back and get more information on the specifications of the job. It may turn out that this isn't a scaffold plank job, and all of these problems will just disappear."

The waitress slipped the check between the two lumbermen. "Well, that might not be such a great idea, Bob. First, Stan may be a little ticked off if you were suggesting he might be doing something unethical. It could blow the relations between our companies. Second, suppose he does say that the material is going to be used for scaffolding. We would no longer be able to say we didn't know what it was going to be used for, and our best legal defense is out the window. I'd advise against calling him."

Bob thought about discussing the situation with John White, but White was out of town. Also, White prided himself on giving his traders a great deal of autonomy. Going to White too often for answers to questions was perceived as showing a lack of initiative and responsibility.

Against Mike's earlier warnings, Bob called Stan after lunch and discovered to his dismay that the material was going to be used as scaffold plank.

"Listen, Bob, I've been trying to sell this account for three months and this is the first inquiry that I've had a chance on. This is really important to me personally and to my superiors here at Quality. With this sale, we could land this account."

"But, Stan, we both know that our material doesn't meet the specs for scaffold plank."

"I know, I know," said Stan, "but I'm not selling it to the customer as scaffold plank. It's just regular construction lumber as far as we are both concerned. That's how I've sold it, and that's what will show on the invoices. We're completely protected. Now just between you and me, the foreman on the job kinda winked at me and told me it was going to be scaffolding, but they're interested in keeping their costs down too. Also, they need this lumber by Friday, and there just isn't any scaffold plank in the local market."

"It just doesn't seem right to me," replied Bob.

"Look, I don't particularly like it, either. The actual specifications call for 2-inch thick material, but since it isn't actually scaffold plank, I'm going to order 3-inch planks. That is an extra inch of strength, and we both know that the load factors given in the engineering tables are too conservative to begin with. There's no chance that the material could fail in use. I happen to know that Haney Lumber is quoting a non-scaffold grade in a 2-inch material. If we don't grab this, someone else will and the material will be a lot worse than what we are going to supply."

When Bob continued to express hesitation, Stan said "I won't hear about the status of the order until tomorrow, but we both know that your material will do this job OK—scaffold plank or not. The next year or two in this business are going to be lean for everyone, and our job—yours and mine—is putting lumber on job sites, not debating how many angels can dance on the head of a pin. Now if Quality can't count on you doing your job as a supplier, there are plenty of other wholesalers calling here every day who want our business. You better decide if you are going to be one of the survivors or not! I'll talk to you in the morning, Bob."

The next morning, Bob found a note on his desk telling him to see John White ASAP. Bob entered John's oak-paneled office and described the conversation with Stan yesterday. John slid a company sales order across the desk, and Bob saw it was a sales order for the 3 × 12s to Quality Lumber. In the space for the salesman's name, Bob saw that John had filled in "Bob Hopkins." Barely able to control his anger, Bob said, "I don't want anything to do with this order. I though White Lumber was an ethical company, and here we are doing the same thing that all the fly-by-nighters do," sputtered Bob in concluding his argument.

John White looked at Bob and calmly puffed on his pipe. "The first thing you better do, Bob, is to calm down and put away your righteous superiority for a moment. You can't make or understand a good decision when you are as lathered up as you are. You are beginning to sound like a religious nut. What makes you think that you have the monopoly on ethical behavior? You've been out of college for four or five years, while I've been making these decisions for forty years. If you go into the industry or the community and compare your reputation with mine, you'll find out that you aren't even in the same league."

Bob knew John White was right. He had, perhaps, overstated his case, and in doing so, sounded like a zealot. When he relaxed and felt as though he was once again capable of rational thought, he said, "We both know that this lumber is going to be used for a purpose for which it is probably not suitable. Granted, there is only a very small chance that it will fail, but I don't see how we can take that chance."

"Look, Bob, I've been in this business for a long time, and I've seen practices that would curl your hair. Undershipping (shipping 290 pieces when the order calls for 300), shipping material a grade below what was ordered, bribing building inspectors and receiving clerks, and so on. We don't do those things at my company."

"Don't we have a responsibility to our customers, though?" asked Bob.

"Of course we do, Bob, but we aren't policemen, either. Our job is to sell lumber that is up to specification. I can't and won't be responsible for how the lumber is used after it leaves our yard. Between the forest and the final user, lumber may pass through a dozen transactions before it reaches the ultimate user. If we are to assume responsibility for every one of those transactions, we would probably have time to sell about four boards a year. We have to assume,

just like every other business, that our suppliers and our customers are knowledgeable and will also act ethically. But whether they do or don't, it is not possible for us to be their keepers."

Bob interjected, "But we have reason to believe that this material will be used as scaffolding. I think we have an obligation to follow up on that information.

"Hold on, just a second, Bob. I told you once we are not the police. We don't even know who the final user is, so how are we going to follow up on this? If Stan is jerking us around, he certainly won't tell us. And even if we did know, what would we do? If we are going to do this consistently, that means we would have to ask every customer who the final end user is. Most of our customers would interpret that as us trying to bypass them in the distribution channel. They won't tell us, and I can't blame them. If we carry your argument to its final conclusion, we'll have to start taking depositions on every invoice we sell.

"In the Quality Lumber instance, we are selling material to the customer as specified by the customer, Stan at Quality Lumber. The invoice will be marked, 'This material is not suitable for use as scaffold plank.' Although I'm not a lawyer, I believe that we have fulfilled our legal obligation. We have a signed purchase order and are supplying lumber that meets the specifications. I know we have followed the practices that are customary in the industry. Finally, I believe that our material will be better than anything else that could conceivably go on the job. Right now, there is no 2-inch dense 171 scaffold plank in this market, so it is not as though a better grade could be supplied in the time allotted. I would argue that we are ethically obligated to supply this lumber. If anyone is ethically at fault, it is probably the purchasing agent who specified a material that is not available."

When Bob still appeared to be unconvinced, John White asked him, "What about the other people here at the company? You're acting as though you are the only person who has a stake in this. It may be easy for you to turn this order down—you've got a college degree and a lot of career options. But I have to worry about all of the people at this company. Steve out there on the forklift never finished high school. He's worked here thirty years and if he loses this job, he'll probably never find another one. Janet over in bookkeeping has a disabled husband. While I can't afford to pay her very much, our health insurance plan keeps their family together. With the bills her husband accumulates in a year, she could never get him on another group insurance plan if she lost this job.

"Bob, I'm not saying that we should do anything and then try to justify it, but business ethics in the real world is not the same thing you studied in the classroom. There it is easy to say, 'Oh, there is an ethical problem here. We better not do that.' In the classroom, you have nothing to lose by taking the morally superior ground. Out here, companies close, people lose their jobs, lives can be destroyed. To always say, 'No, we won't do that' is no better than having no ethics at all. Ethics involves making tough choices, weighing costs and benefits. There are no hard-and-fast answers in these cases. We just have to approach each situation individually."

As Bob left John's office, he was more confused than ever. When he first entered his office, he had every intention of quitting in moral indignation, but John's arguments had made a lot of sense to him, and he both trusted and respected John. After all, John White had a great deal more experience than he did and was highly respected in both the community and the lumber industry. Yet he was still uncomfortable with the decision. Was selling lumber to Quality merely a necessary adjustment of his ivory tower ethics to the real world of business? Or was it the first fork in the road to a destination he did not want to reach?

CASE

6 Ryka, Inc.: The Athletic Shoe with a "Soul"

> Ryka has a great story to tell. We are the only athletic footwear company that is exclusively for women, by women, and now supporting women.—Sheri Poe

It was the day after Christmas 1990, and Sheri Poe, president and chief executive officer of Ryka, Inc., knew she was on the verge of the marketing break she had been waiting for. During the past year, Poe had sent several free pairs of Ryka athletic shoes to Oprah Winfrey. Now Poe was going to be featured as a successful female entrepreneur on Winfrey's popular talk-show, with a television viewing audience numbering in the tens of millions—almost entirely women. Ryka's new line of Ultra-Lite aerobic shoes had just begun to penetrate the retail market. Poe could not have planned for a better advertising spot than Winfrey tossing pairs of Ryka shoes into the studio audience exclaiming, "Can you believe how light these are?"

After the "Oprah" broadcast, the Ultra-Lite line became an overnight success. Lady Foot Locker immediately put the Ultra-Lite shoe line in 200 stores, up from the 50 that had been carrying Ryka's regular line of athletic shoes. Retailers were swamped by consumer requests for Ryka products, and the sharp upturn in consumer demand quickly exhausted their inventories. It took Poe over three months to catch up with the orders. Many industry analysts believe that the shot in the arm provided by the Ultra-Lite sales literally saved the company.

Ryka, Inc., designs, develops, and markets athletic footwear for women, including aerobic, aerobic/step, cross-training, walk-run, and walking shoes. The company's products are sold all over the world in sporting goods, athletic footwear specialty, and department stores.

As a new entrant in the highly competitive athletic footwear industry, an industry with very deep pockets, the fledgling Ryka, Inc., had no choice but to rely on low-budget, "guerrilla marketing" tactics such as the "Oprah" show appearance. Since that time, however, Ryka has turned to more traditional marketing techniques such as radio and glossy magazine advertising. Ryka print ads (see Figure 1) appear regularly in *City Sports, Shape, American Fitness, Elle,* and *IDEA Today,* magazines that target women aged 21–35, who care not just about how they look but who are serious about physical fitness.

COMPANY BACKGROUND

Ryka was first organized in 1986 as ABE Corporation but changed its name to Ryka in February 1987 when it commenced operations. The company was

This case was prepared by Valerie J. Porciello, Alan N. Hoffman, and Barbara Gottfried, Bentley College. The authors would like to thank Jeffrey Shuman, Holly Fowler, Maura Riley, Liliana Prado, Christine Forkus, Sally Strawn, and Mary Fandel for their valuable contributions to this case.

Figure 1
Ryka Print Ad

co-founded by Martin P. Birrittella and his wife, Sheri Poe. Prior to founding Ryka, Birrittella had worked at Matrix International Industries as a vice president of sales and marketing from 1980 to 1986. At Matrix, he was responsible for developing and marketing footwear and health and fitness products; he has two patents pending for shoe designs that have been assigned to Matrix. From 1982 to 1985, Sheri Poe was national sales manager for Matrix. She then moved to TMC Group, a $15 million giftware maker based in New Hampshire, where she was national accounts manager from May 1986 to June 1987.

Sheri Poe, Ryka's current president and chief executive officer, is one of only two women CEOs in the state of Massachusetts. Poe admits being an exercise fanatic who really knew nothing about making athletic shoes when she co-founded Ryka. In 1986 Poe had injured her back in an aerobics class and was convinced that the injury had been caused by her shoes, which had never fit properly. After an exhaustive search for footwear that would not stress her body, Poe realized that many other women probably were having the same trouble as she was finding a shoe that really fit, and decided to start her own women's athletic footwear company. As she conceived it, what would make Ryka distinctive was that rather than adapting men's athletic shoes for women, Ryka would design athletic shoes especially suited for women's feet and bodies. Despite heavy odds, Poe was able to realize her goal: Ryka introduced its first two styles of athletic shoes in September 1987 and began shipping the shoes in March 1988.

In 1987 Poe had considerable difficulty obtaining venture capital to start a women's athletic shoe company. Potential investors questioned her ability to compete with industry leaders such as Nike and Reebok, given that she had no money and no retail experience. They turned down her requests for loans. Ironically, some of those same venture capitalists now call Poe to ask how they can get in on her $8 million business.

Since she could not get anything out of the venture capitalists, Poe leveraged her own house, then turned to family and friends to help finance the company. She also continued to search for more open-minded commercial investors and eventually discovered a Denver investment banker who was willing to do an initial public offering. Poe got a $250,000 bridge loan before the initial public offering—which happened to be about the time the stock market crashed in October 1987. Nevertheless, Ryka went public on April 15, 1988, and despite the unstable market, 4 million shares in the company were sold at one dollar each in less than a week. The Denver firm completed a second offering before failing. Poe then turned to Paulson Capital Corporation in Oregon for a third offering in mid-1990.

SHERI POE

Sheri Poe believes that the fact that Ryka's president is a woman inspires other women to buy the company's products. As she points out, "We're the only company that can tell women that the person running the company is a woman who works out every day." Even Nike doesn't have a woman making all its product decisions.

In fact, Poe's image and profile is the most critical component in Ryka's marketing strategy. Rather than using professional models, Ryka's print advertisements feature Poe working out; in the company's recent venture into television

advertising spots, Poe is the company spokesperson. The caption on a 1992 ad for Ryka's 900-series aerobic shoes reads, "Our president knows that if you huff and puff, jump up and down, and throw your weight around you eventually get what you want," cleverly referring to Poe's own determination to succeed, and including her audience as co-conspirators who know how hard it is for a woman to make it in the business world because they have "been there" themselves.

As part of Ryka's unique marketing strategy, Poe appears on regional television and radio shows throughout the country and has been interviewed by numerous magazines and newspapers. Feature articles on Poe and Ryka have appeared in *Entrepreneurial Woman, Executive Female,* and *Working Woman.* Poe has successfully worked the woman angle: she particularly appeals to today's working women because although she has become something of a celebrity, she considers herself a down-to-earth woman who also happens to be a successful executive, and a [divorced and now remarried] mother. A *Boston Business Journal* article describes her as a CEO whose title "does not cramp [her] style . . . she eschews power suits for miniskirts and jeans, drives herself to work, and lets calls from her kids interrupt her meetings."

THE ATHLETIC FOOTWEAR INDUSTRY

The $11 billion athletic footwear industry is highly competitive. Three major firms control the market: Nike, Reebok, and L.A. Gear. Second-string competitors include Adidas, Avia, Asics, and Converse. All of these companies have greater financial strength and more resources than Ryka. While Ryka's sales were $12.1 million in 1992, Nike's were $3.4 billion, Reebok's $3.0 billion, and L.A. Gear's $430 million.

In 1987, the industry as a whole grew at a rate of 20 percent; but by 1991 its annual growth rate had shrunk to approximately 4 percent. The athletic footwear market is now considered a mature market. Despite the subdued growth characteristics of the overall industry, however, a number of its submarkets are expanding via high specialization, technological innovation, and image and fashion appeal.

Product Specialization

The athletic footwear industry is divided into various sub-markets by specialization. Product use categories include basketball, tennis, running, aerobic, cross-training, and walking. Ryka competes only in the latter three markets: aerobics, cross-training, and walking shoes.

Aerobic Segment The aerobic segment of the athletic shoe industry accounts for approximately $500 million in annual sales. Reebok pioneered the segment and continues to be the industry leader. The market is primarily made up of women and has grown rapidly in recent years. Ryka's number-one market is aerobics; in 1991, 80 percent of Ryka's sales resulted from the Ultra-Lite and step aerobic lines.

Walking Segment The second major market Ryka competes in is the walking segment. This high-growth market is now the fourth-largest product cate-

gory in the athletic shoe industry. In 1991, 70 million people walked for exercise and sales reached $1.7 billion. Reebok leads this market and is concentrating its marketing efforts on young women. Nevertheless, while the male and younger female walking markets have experienced some growth, the walking segment is primarily focused on women 45–55 years old. Ten percent of Ryka's sales are derived from its Series 500 walking shoe, and the company expects the walking shoe segment to be its greatest growth category.

Cross-Training Segment Ryka also competes in the cross-training segment of the athletic shoe market. Cross-training shoes are popular because they can be used for a variety of activities. Nike created this segment, and maintains the lead in market share. Overall sales for the segment are at $1.2 billion, and growth is strong. Ryka earns 10 percent of its revenues from its cross-training shoes.

Technological Innovation

Reebok and Nike are fast moving toward the goal of identifying themselves as the most technologically advanced producers of performance shoes. Ryka understands that it must keep up with research and development to survive. In October 1988 Ryka introduced its nitrogen footwear system, "Nitrogen/ES"—the "ES" stands for Energy Spheres. The system was developed over a two-year period by a design team with over 35 patents in shoe design and state-of-the-art composite plastics. The idea is that the ES ambient air compression spheres contain nitrogen microballoons that provide significantly more energy return than the systems of any of Ryka's major competitors. Consumer response to the Nitrogen/ES shoe was overwhelming, and in 1989 Ryka discontinued sales of a number of models that did not include this special feature.

Two patents were filed for the Nitrogen/ES system. One has been granted; the other is pending. Although patents are intended to provide legal protection, the cost of defending patents can be quite high. With the vast resources available to Ryka's competition, it would be easy for Reebok or Nike to adopt Ryka's technology at little or no risk of an infringement suit. Ryka's limited financial resources would disable it from enforcing its rights in an infringement action.

Fashion

Ryka has focused on performance rather than fashion because Poe believes that fashion-athletic footwear is susceptible to trends and the economy, but performance shoes will not be affected because women always need to protect their bodies. Nevertheless, a large segment of athletic footwear consumers purchase products based on looks rather than function. In fact, the fashion market is a mainstay of Ryka's major competitors, especially Reebok, the originators of the fashion aerobic shoe market: 80 to 90 percent of fashion aerobic shoe buyers do not participate in the sport.

Although Ryka shoes are as technologically advanced as Reebok, Nike, or L.A. Gear's, they are often overlooked by fashion-conscious consumers unfamiliar with the Ryka name. Despite the fact that Ryka's sales have grown even during these recessionary times, retailers have not always carried Ryka shoes because they prefer to stock only those brands that are easily recognizable. The lack of a nationally recognized name is a serious concern for any company; thus for Ryka, as for its competitors, expensive, leading edge advertising campaigns have played an essential part in its marketing initiatives.

A ROCKY START

Given the saturation of the athletic footwear market, athletic shoe companies need more than a good product to stay alive; they need powerful marketing and advertising. Ryka concentrates much of its energies on marketing. As a new manufacturer in an already crowded industry, Poe understands the possibility of being marketed right out of business by big competitors with deep pockets like Nike and Reebok. Ryka's approach is to offer similar products but to focus on the most cost-effective ways to reach a target market, thus carving out a niche that the industry giants have overlooked.

To protect a niche, it is critical to stay one step ahead of the competition. Unfortunately for Ryka, Poe had to learn this lesson the hard way. When the company was first founded, it tried unsuccessfully to challenge the brand name manufacturers in all product categories, including running, tennis, aerobics, walking, and cross-training shoes. However, given its limited capital and the huge advertising budgets of Reebok, Nike, and L.A. Gear, Ryka could not compete in all of these different markets at once. Instead, Ryka cut back and chose to focus on aerobic shoes, and secondarily on their walking-shoe line. Thus, in addition to limiting product line breadth, Ryka has designed its marketing approach to attract a specific set of customers rather than a broad audience. Poe does not believe that Ryka has to be a giant to succeed. Rather, she contends that Ryka needs to maximize its ability to perform in a particular niche within a large industry.

A NEW DIRECTION

In the already crowded athletic footwear industry, the various competitors are continually jockeying for a better market position and competitive edge. Currently, women are, and probably will continue to be, the fastest-growing segment of the athletic footwear market. Women's athletic footwear accounts for 55 percent of Reebok's sales, 60 percent of Avia's, 45 percent of L.A. Gear's, and 17 percent of Nike's $2.2 billion in domestic sales. In recent years, Reebok and Nike have fought for the number-one spot in the women's market, and Reebok initially prevailed; but in each of the past two years, Nike has posted a 30 percent growth in the market. This unparalleled growth in the women's athletic footwear market is the most important trend in the sporting goods industry today, and it is in this niche that Ryka is staking its future.

An important part of the Ryka mission stems from the fact that its shoes are made specifically for women. While the big-name shoe companies were merely making smaller sizes of men's shoes made on men's lasts, Ryka developed a fitness shoe built specifically for women with a patented design for better shock absorption and durability. Ryka had a first mover advantage in this segment and has a sustained competitive advantage in that none of the other companies in the athletic shoe industry can boast having a business strategy focused on women. All other contenders have other lines or are concentrated in other niches. Ultimately, however, it is the Ultra-Lite mid-sole, Ryka's most significant and successful product advancement, that keeps Ryka up with its competition in its market. The Ryka Ultra-Lite aerobics shoe weighs 7.7 ounces, or roughly 30 percent of the weight of a regular aerobic shoe. Within two months of its intro-

duction in December 1990, the company had sold all of its Ultra-Lites at a unit price of $70 a pair (retail). It took three months before additional shoe orders could be filled. Some investment firms were concerned that Ryka might not be able to capitalize on the success of its new line given its difficulty keeping retailers supplied with sufficient quantities. Eventually, Ryka did lose some ground to Nike and Reebok—both of which quickly jumped into the lightweight aerobic shoe market. Despite the competition, however, Ryka's Ultra-Lite lines are a success, accounting for close to 90 percent of its total sales for 1991.

After establishing a solid foundation in the aerobics category, Ryka again turned its attention to product differentiation. Its current product line includes the Series 900 aerobic/step shoes, the Series 700 aerobic shoes, the Series 800/ cross-training shoes, and the Series 500 walking shoes. To make sure its shoes were not perceived as "too specialized," Ryka designed the Aerobic Step 50/50 and a lightweight version of it, the Step-Lite 50/50, each of which can be worn for both high-impact and step aerobics. Ryka also designed a dual purpose walk/run shoe, the 570, for women who complement their walking routine with running but who do not want to own shoes for every activity. Ryka is now considering entering the medical footwear market because an increasing number of podiatrists and chiropractors are recommending Ryka walking shoes to their patients.

THE RYKA ROSE FOUNDATION

The Ryka ROSE (Regaining One's Self Esteem) Foundation is a not-for-profit organization created by Sheri Poe to help women who have been the victims of violent crimes. The foundation was launched in September 1992, and Poe herself personally pledged $250,000. Poe founded the ROSE Foundation because she was raped at age 19. The trauma resulting from the rape led to further suffering from bulimia. She sees herself as a survivor who needed to do something to help fellow victims: "For me, having a company that just made a product was not enough. I wanted to do something more."

Ryka has made a commitment to donate 7 percent of its pre-tax profits to the foundation and to sponsor special fundraising events to help strengthen community prevention and treatment programs for women who are the victims of violent crimes. Ryka includes information on the foundation on brochures that are packaged with each box of shoes in the hope that its social conscience may favorably influence some consumers. But for Poe, it is more than a marketing ploy. She considers Ryka's financial commitment to the ROSE Foundation a natural extension of the company's commitment to women.

The foundation has created alliances with health clubs, non-profit organizations, and corporations in an effort to reach women directly with educational materials and programs. In addition, the ROSE Foundation funds a $25,000 grants program to encourage organizations to develop creative solutions to the widespread problem of violence against women. One of the foundation's beneficiaries, the National Victim Center, received an award of $10,000 to set up a toll-free (800) telephone number for victims and their families through which they can obtain immediate information, referrals, and other types of assistance.

Poe hopes that the foundation will act as a catalyst for coalition-building to help stop violence against women. But she also envisions the foundation as a

means of involving retailers in marketing socially responsible programs directly to women. Lady Foot Locker has taken advantage of this opportunity and became the first retailer to join forces with the ROSE Foundation. In October, Lady Foot Locker conducted a two-week promotional campaign in their 550 U.S. stores in conjunction with the ROSE Foundation. The retailer distributed free education brochures and held a special sweepstakes contest to raise awareness about the issue of violence against women. Customer response was overwhelmingly positive, and Lady Foot Locker is considering a future partnership with the ROSE Foundation. Foot Locker, Champs, and Athletic X-press also have expressed interest in the foundation.

MVP Sports, a New England retailer, also has participated in Ryka's activities to stop violence against women. The company, which operates eight stores in the New England area, sponsored a two-week information-based campaign featuring Sheri Poe that included radio, television, and newspaper advertisements. In addition, Doug Barron, president of MVP Sports, was so impressed with the concept and progressive thinking of the Ryka ROSE Foundation that he decided that his company would donate $2 to the foundation for each pair of Ryka athletic shoes sold during the 1992 holiday season. Poe sees MVP Sports' support as an important first step toward actively involving retailers in Ryka's efforts to help prevent violence against women and is reaching out to other retailers who she hopes will follow suit.

Poe considers Ryka and its foundation unique. As she sees it, the company has a great story to tell. It is the only athletic footwear company that is exclusively for women, by women, and now supporting women, "the first athletic shoe with a 'soul.'" And Poe is banking on her hunch that the foundation will appeal to Ryka customers who appreciate the idea that their buying power is helping women less fortunate than they are.

Nevertheless, Poe's choice to make Ryka a socially responsible company right from the beginning, rather than waiting until the company is fully established, has had consequences for its financial status. Some industry analysts have suggested that Ryka would be better off funneling any extra cash back into the company until it is completely solvent and its product lines and name recognition automatic. But others argue that the reputation Ryka has garnered as an ethical company, as concerned about social issues as about the "bottom line," effectively appeals to kind-hearted women consumers. For them, the ROSE Foundation is worth in "good press" whatever it has cost the company in terms of actual investment dollars, because the company has effectively carved out a niche that speaks on many different levels to women's ethical and consumer concerns.

MARKETING

Ryka's promotional strategy is aimed at creating both brand awareness and sales at the retail level. By garnering the support of professional sports organizations early on, Ryka acquired instant name recognition in a variety of key audiences. In 1988 Ryka entered into a six-figure, 8-year licensing agreement with the U.S. Ski Team which permitted Ryka to market its products as the official training shoes of the Team. Also in 1988, the American Aerobics Association International boosted Ryka's brand name recognition when it replaced Avia with Ryka

as the association's preferred aerobics shoes. The next year, *Shape* magazine labeled Ryka number one in its aerobic shoe category.

Ryka also has begun sponsoring both aerobics teams and aerobics competitions. In July 1992, 25 countries competed in the World Aerobic Championships in Las Vegas, Nevada. The Canadian team was sponsored by Ryka Athletic Footwear. In September 1992 Ryka was the premier sponsor and the official shoe of the Canadian National Aerobic Championship held in Vancouver, B.C. To ensure the success of the event and build awareness for the sport of competitive aerobics, Ryka successfully promoted the nationals through retailers, athletic clubs, and individuals. Given that virtually every previous aerobics competition worldwide had been sponsored by Reebok, Canada's selection of Ryka as its official sponsor marked a significant milestone for Ryka, as well as marking Ryka's international recognition as a core brand in the women's athletic market.

The Ryka Training Body

Early on, Sheri Poe determined that the most effective way to reach Ryka's female aerobic niche would be through marketing to aerobics instructors and targeted Ryka's advertising accordingly. In fact, Ryka spends almost as much as industry leaders on print advertisements in aerobics instructors' magazines and very little on print advertising elsewhere. On the other hand, unlike its big competitors, Ryka does not use celebrity endorsements to sell its products, because the company markets on the theory that women will care more about what feels good on their feet than about what any particular celebrity has to say.

Beyond advertising in aerobics magazines, Ryka has successfully used direct mail marketing techniques to target aerobics instructors. The Ryka Training Body is comprised of more than 40,000 women employed as fitness instructors and personal trainers throughout the country. They receive product information four to six times per year, as well as discounts on shoes. Ryka also has a group of its instructors tied to specific local retailers. The instructors direct their students to those retailers, who then offer discounts to the students. Finally, Ryka-affiliated instructors offer demonstrations to educate consumers about what to look for in an aerobics shoe.

In addition to increasing sales, the relationship between Ryka and the aerobics profession has led to significant product design innovations. Aerobic instructors' suggestions, based on their own experience, as well as on feedback from students in their classes, has led to improvements such as more effective cushioning and better arch support in the shoes. Poe considers these teachers as the link to Ryka's customers. In fact, as a direct result of instructor feedback, Ryka was the first manufacturer to respond to the new step aerobics trend by developing and marketing lightweight shoes specifically designed to support up and down step motions.

Salespeople

Ryka's marketing efforts are also aimed at the people who sell Ryka products. In Ryka's early days, Poe and her advertising manager, Laurie Ruddy, personally visited retail stores to meet salespeople and "sell" them on Ryka products. Now the vice president of sales and marketing maintains contact with retailers using incentive programs, give-aways, and small monetary bonuses to keep salespeople excited. The company also provides premiums, such as fanny packs or water bottles for customers.

Advertising Budget

Given the highly competitive nature of the athletic footwear industry, effective advertising is crucial in distinguishing among brands and creating brand preference. As a 2-year-old company in 1989, Ryka was particularly capital-intensive, given that it was trying to penetrate the athletic shoe market. Its $3.5 million loss that year is largely attributable to advertising spending of approximately $2.5 million, but that amount was nothing compared to Nike, Reebok, and L.A. Gear which, combined, spent more than $100 million on advertising during the same period.

At that time, Ryka advertised only in trade publications; therefore, recognition among consumers was lagging. Since then, Ryka ads have appeared in *Shape, City Sports, American Fitness, Elle,* and *Idea Today* magazines. By 1992 Poe could claim that Ryka's brand recognition had grown dramatically, even though Ryka's advertising and marketing budget was only about 9 percent of sales. Poe attributes Ryka's marketing success to its direct marketing techniques, especially its targeting of certified aerobic instructors to wear Ryka shoes.

In October 1992, after three successive quarters of record sales and little profitability, Poe announced that Ryka was going to expand its direct marketing to consumers, even if it required increased spending to penetrate the marketplace beyond aerobics instructors. But Ryka is still in another league compared to industry giants when it comes to budgets. Ryka's total advertising budget is estimated at approximately $1.5 million, while Nike could afford to spend $20 million on a 1991 pan-European campaign to launch a single product, and Reebok is currently spending $28 million on its "I Believe . . ." ad campaign which specifically targets women.

OPERATIONS

As is common in the athletic footwear industry, Ryka shoes are made by independent manufacturers in Europe and the Far East, including South Korea and Taiwan, according to Ryka product specifications. Ryka's first three years were rough, in large part because of the poor quality of the products provided by its manufacturer in Taiwan. Now, however, the shoes are made in Korea with strict quality control measures in effect. The company relies on a Far Eastern buying agent, under Ryka's direction, for the selection of suppliers, inspection of goods prior to shipment, and shipment of finished goods.

Ryka's management believes that this sourcing of footwear products minimizes company investment in fixed assets as well as reducing cost and risk. Given the extent of the underutilized factory manufacturing capacity in countries outside of South Korea and Taiwan, Ryka's management believes that alternative sources of product manufacturing are readily available, should the company have need of them. Because of the volatility of international and economic relations in today's global marketplace, and in order to protect itself from complete dependence on one supplier, Ryka has resolved to keep itself free of any long-term contract with manufacturers beyond the terms of purchase orders issued. Orders are placed on a volume basis through its agent and Ryka receives finished products within 120 days of an order. If necessary, Ryka may pay a premium to reduce the time required to deliver finished goods from the factory to meet customer demand.

The principal raw materials in Ryka shoes are leather, rubber, ethylvinyl acetate, polyurethane, cambrelle, and pigskin, all of which are readily available both in the United States and abroad. Nevertheless, even though Ryka could locate new sources of raw materials within a relatively short period of time if it needed to for its overseas operations, its business could be devastated by any interruptions in operations, whereas Reebok and Nike have large stockpiles of inventory and would be less affected by any difficulties with suppliers.

Distribution

Ryka products are sold in sporting goods stores, athletic footwear stores, selected high-end department stores, and sport specialty retailers including Foot Locker, Lady Foot Locker, Athlete's Foot Store, Foot Action, US Athletics, Oshman's, and Nordstrom's.

Ryka's major distribution relationship is with the 476 Lady Foot Locker stores in the United States and 250 Lady Foot Locker stores in Canada. In November 1992 Ryka announced that in early 1993, 400 Lady Foot Locker stores would display permanent Ryka signage, identifying Ryka as a brand especially promoted by Foot Locker. Both Sheri Poe and Amy Schecter, vice president of retail marketing for Lady Foot Locker, agree that Ryka shoes have seen solid sales in Lady Foot Locker stores, and the Lady Foot Locker's display of permanent Ryka signage expresses the confidence Lady Foot Locker has in Ryka's future success.

During the spring of 1992 FOOTACTION USA, a division of the Melville Corporation, and the second largest specialty footwear retailer in the country, began selling Ryka athletic shoes on a trial basis in 40 stores. The trial was so successful that FOOTACTION agreed to purchase five styles of Ryka shoes for its stores, and in September 1992 Ryka announced that 150 FOOTACTION stores would begin to carry its products nationally.

On November 3, 1992, Ryka announced that it received orders from three large retail sporting goods chains, adding well over 200 store outlets to its distribution network. The twelfth largest sporting goods retailer in the country, MC Sporting Goods, based in Grand Rapids, Michigan, now carries five styles of Ryka athletic shoes in each of its 73 stores. In addition, Ryka has received orders from the Tampa, Florida–based Sports and Recreation, which will sell four styles of Ryka athletic shoes in all of its 23 sporting goods stores. Charlie Burks, head footwear buyer for sports and recreation, based his decision to stock Ryka shoes on his sense that the chain's customers are looking for new, exciting styles of athletic shoes at affordable prices, and that Ryka delivers on performance, fashion, and value. Ryka shoes are also carried in more than 135 Athletic Express stores.

In the competitive athletic footwear industry, distributors and retailers have considerable clout. In 1989 Lady Foot Locker and Foot Locker retailers accounted for 13 percent of Ryka's net sales. But the company realized it needed a broader pool of retailers. More recently, Ryka has managed to control its customer base such that no single customer or group under common control accounts for more than 10 percent of its total revenue.

Human Resources

When Ryka was in its early stages, Poe set out to gain credibility through human resources. The company offered industry-standard salaries, stock options, and the opportunity for significant input into the day-to-day operations of the

company. In addition, Poe attracted four top executives from Reebok for positions in sales, advertising, and public relations. This high-powered team performed so effectively that sales doubled between Ryka's first and second years. But total executive compensation was too much for the young company. Poe realized that a change in strategy was necessary, and three of the four Reebok veterans have since left.

Early on, in 1988, Ryka had only four employees. Ryka now employs 22 people at its Norwood headquarters, as well as 35 sales representatives across the country. Ryka's small size gives it a certain flexibility, enabling the company to concentrate on continual streamlining and improvement, so that new ideas and adjustments can be implemented and in the stores within 120 days.

In November 1992 Ryka appointed Roy S. Kelvin as vice president and chief financial officer to reinforce its commitment to the financial community. Poe sees Kelvin, a former New York investment banker, as instrumental to helping the company grow. But Poe's appointment of Kelvin is also seen as acknowledgment of the fact that she is competing for funds in an "old-boy's" network, so it is extremely valuable to have an "old boy" to help build her list of contacts. Kelvin's main priorities are helping to secure domestic financing, reduce operating expenses, and improve profit margins.

FINANCIALS

Ryka originally financed its operations principally through public stock offerings, warrant exercises, and other private sales of its common stock, netting an aggregate of approximately $7.2 million. In July 1990 Ryka completed its public stock offering, which raised net proceeds of $3.5 million, allowing the company to market its products aggressively during the fall of 1990 and beyond. So far, Ryka has sold shares to private investors who control 65 percent of the shares.

In September 1992 Ryka extended the date for redemption of its outstanding common stock purchase warrant issues in the company's 1990 public offering another two weeks in response to requests made from warrant holders. Poe was very pleased with the response to the warrant solicitation and agreed to the extension to allow the maximum number of holders to exercise their warrants. If all public and underwriter warrants are exercised, the company will receive approximately $6.3 million in gross proceeds.

In 1991 Ryka signed an agreement with its Korean trading company to increase its line of credit from $2.5 million to $3.5 million. In addition, working capital resources come from a letter of credit financing agreement, coupled with an accounts receivable line of credit.

Ryka's product costs are higher than those of the industry leaders for several reasons. First, because Ryka is significantly smaller than the industry leaders, it cannot take advantage of volume production discounts. Second, the company has opted to pay somewhat higher prices for its products than would be charged by alternate suppliers in order to achieve and maintain higher quality. Finally, higher production costs have resulted from Ryka's inventory financing arrangement with its Korean trading company, which includes financing costs, commissions, and fees as part of cost of sales.

Exhibit 1
Ryka, Inc.
Summary of 1992 Results

	Year Ended December 31		
	1992	1991[1]	Percent Change
Gross sales	$13,329,777	$8,838,911	50.8%
Discounts, returns and allowances	1,136,134	860,986	32.0%
Net Sales	12,193,643	7,977,925	52.8%
Cost of goods sold	8,867,375	5,231,346	69.5%
Gross profit	3,326,268	2,746,579	21.1%
Operating expenses			
General and administrative	1,239,245[2]	1,287,925	-3.8%
Marketing	1,722,618	1,396,769	23.3%
Research and development	148,958	155,576	-4.3%
Total operating expenses	3,110,821	2,840,270	9.5%
Operating income (loss)	215,447	(93,691)	
Other (income) expense			
Interest expense	516,455	418,469	23.4%
Interest income	(4,196)	(12,648)	- 66.8%
Total other (income) expense	512,259	405,821	26.2%
Net loss	(296,812)	(499,512)	- 40.6%
Net loss per share	($0.01)	($0.03)	
Weighted average shares outstanding	19,847,283	18,110,923	
Cash and cash equivalents	$1,029,161	$166,030	519.9%
Current assets	$8,199,411	$4,367,255	87.7%
Total assets	$8,306,262	$4,498,021	84.7%
Current liabilities	$4,134,974	$3,623,668	14.1%
Stockholder's equity	$4,153,410	$834,902	397.5%

1. To provide comparability with the current year presentation, $410,000 of 1991 product financing expenses have been classified from Cost of goods sold to Interest expense.

2. General & administrative expense includes a charge of $138,000 to reserve a receivable relating to the liquidation of the Company's licensed distributor in the U.K.

Ryka has taken on some formidable competition in the form of Nike and Reebok. For Ryka to prosper, Sheri Poe must successfully carve out a niche in the women's athletic shoe market before Ryka runs out of money. Time is becoming increasingly scarce.

Exhibit 2
Ryka, Inc.
Financial Data, 1988–1992

	Year Ended December 31				
	1992	1991	1990	1989	1988
Statement of Operations Data:					
Net sales	$12,193,643	$7,977,925	$4,701,538	$4,916,542	$991,684
Gross profit before inventory write-down	3,326,268	2,746,579	1,013,445	1,364,340	308,901
Inventory write-down to lower of cost or market			906,657		
Gross profit	3,326,268	2,746,579	106,888	1,364,340	308,901
Costs and expenses	3,110,821	2,840,270	3,598,728	4,368,774	1,687,806
Operating income (loss)	215,447	(93,691)	(3,491,840)	(3,004,434)	(1,378,905)
Interest expense, net	512,260	405,821	218,817	548,149	148,485
Expenses incurred in connection with termination of merger agreement			377,855		
Net loss	$(296,813)	$(499,512)	$(4,088,512)	$(3,552,583)	$(1,527,390)
Net loss per share	$(0.01)	$(0.03)	$(0.27)	$(0.31)	$(0.16)
Weighted average shares outstanding	19,847,283	18,110,923	15,336,074	11,616,088	9,397,360
Number of common shares outstanding	23,101,948	18,136,142	18,005,142	13,242,500	10,252,500
Balance Sheet Data:					
Total assets	$8,319,229	$4,498,021	$2,711,713	$3,553,000	$2,073,058
Total debt	410,673	68,256	86,149	974,521	247,340
Net working capital	4,077,404	743,587	1,097,827	1,643,352	1,140,173
Stockholders' equity	4,166,377	834,902	1,299,264	1,848,059	1,341,858

Exhibit 3
Ryka's Stock Price
1992/1991

	1992		1991	
Calendar period	High	Low	High	Low
First quarter	$2.31	$0.53	$1.06	$0.22
Second quarter	$2.44	$1.19	$0.87	$0.50
Third quarter	$1.69	$1.19	$0.90	$0.56
Fourth quarter	$1.89	$0.97	$0.78	$0.56

Ryka's common stock is traded on NASDAQ.

The company does not pay dividends to its stockholders and does not plan to pay dividends in the foreseeable future.

Works Consulted

Colter, Gene. "On Target: Athletics Shoes Just for Women; Womens' Awareness of Athletic Shoes; Special Super Show Athletics Issue," *Footwear News*, February 18, 1991.

Dutter, Greg. "Making Strides," *Sporting Goods Business,* March 1992, v25 n3 p34(1).

Fucini, Suzy. "A Women's Game: Women Have Become the Hottest Focus of Today's Marketing," *Sporting Goods Dealer,* August 1992, p34(3).

Goodman, Doug. "Reebok Chief Looks Beyond Nike," *Advertising Age,* January 29, 1990, v61 n5 p57(1).

Grimm, Matthew. "Nike Targets Women with Print Campaign," *Adweek's Marketing Week,* December 10, 1990, v33 n12 p12(1).

Hower, Wendy. "Gender Gap: The Executive Suite Is Still Wilderness for Women," *Boston Business Journal,* July 27, 1992, v12 n23 sec2 p5(2).

Kelly, Craig T. "Fashion Sells Aerobics Shoes," January 1990, v23 n1 p39(1).

Lee, Sharon; McAllister, Robert; Rooney, Ellen; Tedeschi, Mark. "Community Ties Nourish Growth of Aerobic Sales; Aerobic Programs Boost Sales of Aerobic Shoes," *Footwear News,* October 7, 1991, v31 n33 p17(1).

Magiera, Marcy. "Nike Again Registers No. 1 Performance," *Advertising Age,* May 7, 1990, v61 n19 p4(1).

———. "Nike Again Registers No. 1 Performance," *Advertising Age,* January 29, 1990, v61 n5 p16(1).

"New England Retailer Joins Ryka in Fight Against Domestic Violence," *Business Wire,* November 13.

"Nike Takes Reebok's Edge; Advertising Expenditures of Top Sports Shoes Manufacturers," Nexis "mrktng," April 16, 1992, p10(1).

Poe, Sheri. "To Compete with Giants, Choose your Niche," *Nation's Business,* July 1992, v80 n7 p6(1).

Powell, Robert J. "Ryka Is Off and Running," *Boston Business Journal,* February 29, 1988, v8 n1 p3.

"Ryka Adds 100 Stores to Distribution Network," *Business Wire,* November 3, 1992.

"Ryka Announces Extension for Warrant Redemption," *Business Wire,* September 11, 1992.

"Ryka Announces Record First Quarter 1991 Results," *Business Wire,* April 24, 1991.

"Ryka Completes $4.7 Million Offering," *Business Wire,* July 24, 1990.

"Ryka Introduces New Nitrogen System," *Business Wire,* October 20, 1988.

"Ryka Launches ROSE Foundation to Help Stop Violence Against Women," Ryka, Inc., News Release, September 28, 1992.

Ryka 1991 in Review, Annual Report, Ryka, Inc.

"A Ryka Rose: Sheri Poe on Career, Family and Purpose," *Sporting Goods Dealer,* September 1992.

"Ryka to Expand Its Presence in Foot Locker Stores," *Business Wire,* June 4, 1992.

"Ryka Vaults to $8M in Its Lightweight Sneaks," *Boston Business Journal,* March 30, 1992, v12 n6 p9.

Simon, Ruth. "The No-P/E Stocks, *Forbes,* October 2, 1989, p40.

Touby, Laurel Allison. "Creativity vs. Cash," *Working Woman,* November 1991, v16 n11 p73(4).

Witt, Louise. "Ryka Turns to Aerobics for Toehold in Market," *Boston Business Journal,* April 1, 1991, v11 n6 p6.

Wolfensberger, Beth. "Shoe Markers Have Itch to Enter Niche Markets," *Boston Business Journal,* March 19, 1990, v10 n4 p7.

SECTION

B

Business Level: Domestic and Global Cases

7. Coca-Cola versus Pepsi-Cola and the Soft Drink Industry
8. The Computer Industry: The New Industry of Industries?
9. Compaq Computer Corporation in 1994
10. The Rise of IBM
11. The Fall of IBM
12. The Japanese Beer Industry
13. Asahi Breweries, Ltd.
14. The Global Auto Industry: Toward the Year 2000
15. The Toyota Corporation in 1994
16. Big Changes at General Motors
17. The Boeing Corporation: Commercial Aircraft Operations
18. BE Aerospace: 1992
19. Blockbuster Entertainment Corporation
20. Video Concepts, Inc.
21. Cineplex Odeon
22. Circle K Corporation
23. Electrimex
24. R. H. Macy & Co.: Another Miracle on 34th Street?

CASE 7

Coca-Cola versus Pepsi-Cola and the Soft Drink Industry

With retail revenues estimated to exceed $46 billion in 1991, the U.S. soft drink industry was considered an integral part of the American way of life. The two leading competitors, Coca-Cola and Pepsi-Cola, had engaged in an ever increasing rivalry that had been labeled "The Cola Wars." The wars had continued into the 1990s, and the landscape of the soft drink industry had been vastly altered.

INDUSTRY STRUCTURE

Soft drinks consisted of a flavor base, a sweetener, and carbonated water. In 1990, cola-flavored drinks accounted for approximately 70% of the market, and lemon-lime products accounted for 12% (see Exhibit 1). Diet and caffeine-free products were sold across all flavor categories and composed 30% and 6%, respectively, of the market in 1990.

In the United States, soft drink consumption grew from 0.6 gallons per person per year in 1899 to 22.7 gallons in 1970, 34.5 gallons in 1980, and 47.4 gallons in 1990. Soft drinks accounted for a remarkable 26% share of U.S. beverage consumption, up from 12.4% in 1970. Growth had historically occurred primarily in the 15–24 and 25–34 age groups and had slowed to 3% per year in 1990.

The prospects for the future growth in U.S. soft drink consumption were actively debated. Some industry observers had argued for years that U.S. soft drink consumption was approaching its limits and that the industry would not regain the 5% annual growth common in the late 1970s and mid-1980s. Others believed that innovations in product development, advertising, and distribution channels would fuel continued industry growth.

Three major participants were involved in the production and distribution of soft drinks: concentrate and syrup producers, bottlers, and retail channels.

Concentrate Producers

Concentrate producers manufactured basic soft drink flavors and sold them to bottlers. Although there were many concentrate producers in the United States at the end of 1991, the bulk of industry sales was accounted for by a few firms, notably Coca-Cola and Pepsi-Cola (Exhibit 2).

There were several other national producers, including Seven-Up, Dr Pepper, Royal Crown, Canada Dry, and A&W. There were also several dozen regional and private label producers who held modest shares of their regional markets such as Polar and White Rock. Regional producers typically sold a wide line of soft drink flavors—such as cola, grape, orange, cream soda, and ginger ale—which were distributed through major food chains. Financial results for leading soft drink producers are given in Exhibit 3.

Early in their history, Coca-Cola and Pepsi-Cola granted franchises for the right to bottle their soft drinks. This practice spread to other leading concentrate producers. Under the agreements, franchisees were granted the exclusive right to bottle and distribute a concentrate company's line of branded soft drinks within a defined territory in perpetuity. Franchisees were not allowed to market a directly competitive brand; for example, a Coca-Cola bottler could not sell Royal Crown (RC) Cola. However, franchisees could sell noncompetitive brands and decline to market a concentrate producer's secondary lines. A Coca-Cola bottler could thus turn down Coca-Cola's lemon-lime drink, Sprite, in order to bottle Seven-Up.

The manufacturing process for concentrate was simple and required little capital investment. For regular soft drinks, concentrate producers typically sold only flavor concentrate, and bottlers purchased the sweetener themselves. Coca-Cola was an exception, and had traditionally sold syrup that already contained sweetener, charging its bottlers the list price of sweetener. In 1980, Coca-Cola began to sell concentrate without sweetener to its largest bottlers. For diet drinks, all producers sold their bottlers both concentrate and artificial sweetener. The cost of concentrate represented approximately 20% of a concentrate producer's selling price to bottlers.

A concentrate producer's most significant costs were for advertising, promotion, market research, and bottler relations (see Exhibit 4 for data on advertising spending in the United States). Marketing programs were jointly implemented and financed by concentrate producers and bottlers. The concen-

Exhibit 1
U.S. Market Share by Soft Drink Flavor and Category, Percent

	1971	1975	1981	1985	1986	1987	1988	1989	1990
Cola	57.6	58.0	64.0	67.5	68.8	69.0	69.0	69.5	69.9
Lemon-lime	12.0	12.7	12.6	12.2	11.3	10.6	10.4	12.0	11.7
Pepper	4.1	6.6	5.7	4.9	4.6	4.7	5.1	5.3	5.6
Root Beer	4.4	4.1	3.0	2.7	2.2	2.4	2.4	2.6	2.7
Orange	4.8	3.9	5.7	0.8	1.4	1.0	0.8	2.4	2.3
Others	17.1	14.7	9.0	11.9	11.7	12.3	12.3	8.2	7.8
	100.0	100.0	100.0	100.0	100.0	100.0	100.0	100.0	100.0
Caffeine-Free						4.1	4.6	5.2	6.0
Diet				23.1	24.0	24.8	25.9	27.7	30.0

Source: John C. Maxwell, Jr., and *Beverage Industry*.

Exhibit 2 U.S. Soft Drink Market Shares by Case Volume (percent)

	1966	1970	1975	1980	1982	1984	1985	1986	1987	1988	1989	1990
Coca-Cola Co.												
Classic							5.8	19.1	19.8	19.9	19.5	19.4
Coca-Cola	27.7	28.4	26.2	25.3	24.6	22.5	14.4	2.4	1.7	1.3	0.9	0.7
Cherry Coke							1.6	1.7	1.2	0.9	0.7	0.6
Diet Coke					0.3	5.2	6.3	7.2	7.7	8.1	8.8	9.1
Diet Cherry Coke								0.2	0.4	0.3	0.3	0.2
Tab	1.4	1.3	2.6	3.3	4.0	1.6	1.1	0.6	0.4	0.3	0.2	0.2
Caffeine-Free Coke, Diet Coke and Tab						1.8	1.8	1.7	1.7	1.9	2.2	3.1
Sprite and diet Sprite	1.5	1.8	2.6	3.0	3.3	3.8	4.2	4.3	4.3	4.3	4.4	4.4
Others	2.8	3.2	3.9	4.3	2.5	2.6	1.9	2.6	2.7	2.8	3.0	2.7
Total	33.4	34.7	35.3	35.9	34.7	37.5	37.1	39.8	39.9	39.8	40.0	40.4
PepsiCo, Inc.												
Pepsi-Cola	16.1	17.0	17.4	20.4	20.3	19.1	18.2	18.6	18.6	18.4	17.8	17.3
Diet Pepsi	1.9	1.1	1.7	3.0	3.3	3.2	3.7	4.4	4.8	5.2	5.7	6.2
Caffeine-Free Pepsi and Diet Pepsi					0.4	2.7	2.3	2.0	1.8	2.0	2.1	2.3
Mountain Dew	1.4	0.9	1.3	3.3	3.2	3.0	2.9	3.0	3.3	3.4	3.6	3.8
Diet Mountain Dew										0.4	0.5	0.5
Slice							0.7	1.5	1.3	1.1	1.0	0.9
Diet Slice							0.6	1.0	1.0	0.7	0.6	0.4
Others	1.0	0.8	0.7	1.1	0.9	0.7	0.2	0.1	0.0	0.1	0.4	0.4
Total	20.4	19.8	21.1	27.8	28.1	28.7	28.6	30.6	30.8	31.3	31.7	31.8
Seven-Up	6.9	7.2	7.6	6.3	6.7	6.8	5.7	5.0	5.1	4.7	4.3	4.0
Dr Pepper	2.6	3.8	5.5	6.0	5.2	5.0	4.7	4.8	5.0	5.3	5.6	5.8
Royal Crown Co.	6.9	6.0	5.4	4.7	3.9	3.1	2.9	3.0	2.9	2.8	2.7	2.6
Cadbury-Schweppes	NA	NA	NA	NA	NA	NA	4.5	4.2	3.7	3.5	3.1	3.2
Other Companies	29.8	28.5	25.1	19.3	21.4	18.9	16.5	12.6	12.6	12.6	12.6	12.2
Total (million cases)	2,927	3,670	4,155	5,180	5,510	6,130	6,500	6,770	7,155	7,530	7,680	7,914

Source: John C. Maxwell, Jr., and *Beverage Industry*.

structures of a typical concentrate producer and bottler as of 1986 are shown in Exhibit 5.

There were four types of soft drink bottlers. The first were independent, privately owned bottlers. Many of these were small and marketed only Coca-Cola or Pepsi-Cola products, although others achieved substantial growth by buying up franchises in contiguous areas and by taking on secondary brands such as Dr Pepper or Seven-Up. A second group of bottlers consisted of large, publicly owned, multibrand franchise firms, based in major metropolitan areas. The third category of bottlers were Coca-Cola and Pepsi-Cola franchises that were owned and operated by diversified companies. The fourth category of bottlers included the operations of concentrate producers themselves. The types of bottlers used varied among concentrate producers and changed over time.

Retail Outlets

Industry analysts divided the retail channels for soft drinks into four types: food stores, fountain, vending, and other. Distribution of sales by channel is shown in Exhibit 6.

In food stores, rival bottler sales forces fought fiercely for shelf space to ensure maximum visibility, accessibility, and support for the product line. Carbonated soft drinks were among the five largest-selling product lines sold by food stores, traditionally yielding a 20% gross margin (about average for food products) and accounting for 3.5% of food store revenues in 1990.

Fountain sales involved the sales of syrup to restaurants or convenience stores, which mixed the syrup with carbonated water for immediate consumption. Soft drink sales were extremely profitable for fountain outlets, with gross margins in

Exhibit 5
Comparative Cost Structure and Financial Structure of a Typical Concentrate Producer and Bottler (per standard 8-oz./24-bottle case), 1986

	Concentrate Producer		Bottler	
	Dollars per Case	Percent Total	Dollars per Case	Percent Total
Profit and Loss Data				
Net Sales	.55	100%	3.80	100%
Cost of sales	.15	27	2.30	60
Gross profit	.40	73	1.50	40
Selling and delivery	.01	2	.95	25
Advertising and marketing	.24	42	.10	3
General and administration	.05	11	.12	3
Pretax Profit	.10	18	.35	9
Balance Sheet Data				
Cash, investments	.14		.05	
Receivables	.01		.18	
Inventories	.05		.10	
Net property, plant and equipment	.05		.62[a]	
Total assets	.25		.95	
Pretax profit as % of assets	.40		.37	

[a] 80% = equipment

structures of a typical concentrate producer and bottler as of 1986 are shown in Exhibit 5.

There were four types of soft drink bottlers. The first were independent, privately owned bottlers. Many of these were small and marketed only Coca-Cola or Pepsi-Cola products, although others achieved substantial growth by buying up franchises in contiguous areas and by taking on secondary brands such as Dr Pepper or Seven-Up. A second group of bottlers consisted of large, publicly owned, multibrand franchise firms, based in major metropolitan areas. The third category of bottlers were Coca-Cola and Pepsi-Cola franchises that were owned and operated by diversified companies. The fourth category of bottlers included the operations of concentrate producers themselves. The types of bottlers used varied among concentrate producers and changed over time.

Retail Outlets

Industry analysts divided the retail channels for soft drinks into four types: food stores, fountain, vending, and other. Distribution of sales by channel is shown in Exhibit 6.

In food stores, rival bottler sales forces fought fiercely for shelf space to ensure maximum visibility, accessibility, and support for the product line. Carbonated soft drinks were among the five largest-selling product lines sold by food stores, traditionally yielding a 20% gross margin (about average for food products) and accounting for 3.5% of food store revenues in 1990.

Fountain sales involved the sales of syrup to restaurants or convenience stores, which mixed the syrup with carbonated water for immediate consumption. Soft drink sales were extremely profitable for fountain outlets, with gross margins in

Exhibit 5
Comparative Cost Structure and Financial Structure of a Typical Concentrate Producer and Bottler (per standard 8-oz./24-bottle case), 1986

	Concentrate Producer		Bottler	
	Dollars per Case	Percent Total	Dollars per Case	Percent Total
Profit and Loss Data				
Net Sales	.55	100%	3.80	100%
Cost of sales	.15	27	2.30	60
Gross profit	.40	73	1.50	40
Selling and delivery	.01	2	.95	25
Advertising and marketing	.24	42	.10	3
General and administration	.05	11	.12	3
Pretax Profit	.10	18	.35	9
Balance Sheet Data				
Cash, investments	.14		.05	
Receivables	.01		.18	
Inventories	.05		.10	
Net property, plant and equipment	.05		.62[a]	
Total assets	.25		.95	
Pretax profit as % of assets	.40		.37	

[a] 80% = equipment

trate producers usually took the lead in developing the programs, particularly in product planning, market research, and advertising. Bottlers assumed a larger role in developing trade and consumer promotions. Bottlers usually paid for two-thirds of promotional costs, while advertising costs were typically split 50/50.

Concentrate producers employed extensive sales and marketing support staff to work with and help improve the performance of their franchised bottlers. They set standards for their bottlers and suggested operating procedures. Concentrate producers also negotiated directly with their bottlers' major suppliers—particularly sweetener and packaging suppliers—to encourage reliable supply, faster delivery, and lower prices.

Bottlers

Bottlers purchased concentrate, added carbonated water and sometimes sweetener, bottled or canned the soft drink, and delivered it to customer accounts. Major concentrate producers used "store door" delivery, whereby soft drinks were delivered directly to individual retail outlets, bypassing retailers' warehouses. Bottler route salespeople stocked and maintained food store shelves. Small national brands, such as Shasta and Faygo, distributed through food store warehouses. Although retailers earned higher gross margins on warehouse-delivered soft drinks, store door delivery yielded higher profit per square foot due to lower in-store handling costs and faster turnover of inventory.

The bottling process was extremely capital-intensive and involved specialized, high-speed lines. Lines were interchangeable only for packages of similar size and construction, thus each major package type required separate bottling equipment. Bottling and canning lines cost from $100,000 to several million dollars, depending on volume and packaging type.

The total number of bottling plants in the United States fell from 2,613 (1974) to 1,522 (1984) and 780 (1990). "Megaplants" produced as many as 2,000 cans per minute. In 1989, the seven largest bottlers operated 176 plants and produced 46.5% of industry volume.

Bottlers packaged soft drinks in various types of containers. In 1960, returnable glass bottles accounted for 94% of soft-drink volume, nonreturnable glass bottles accounted for 2% and steel and aluminum cans for 4%. Throughout the 1960s, 1970s, and 1980s, a host of new packages was introduced. By 1990, cans accounted for 52% of the market, plastic bottles 30%, nonreturnable glass bottles 12%, and returnable glass bottles 6%.

Forty-one percent of total can production was sold to the carbonated soft drink industry, with five can companies accounting for 98% of sales to the soft drink industry. Plastic containers were supplied primarily by six firms that sold 20% of their plastic container production to the soft drink industry. Bottlers purchased their own packages; however, each of the concentrate producers negotiated with can and plastic container suppliers about package price, availability, and design.

In addition to packaging, bottlers purchased nutritive (or caloric) sweeteners such as sugar and high fructose corn syrup (HFCS) for use in regular soft drinks. The soft drink industry accounted for a large portion of total U.S. consumption of nutritive sweeteners.

Concentrate accounted for approximately 20% of bottlers' cost of goods sold, packaging approximately 35%, and nutritive sweeteners approximately 10%. Labor and fuel accounted for most of the remaining variable costs. The cost

Exhibit 4 (continued) U.S. Advertising Spending by Brand ($ millions)

	1975	1980	1981	1982	1983	1984	1985	1986	1987	1988	1989	1990
Seven-Up Company (continued)												
Cherry 7-Up									8.7	14.5	4.4	0.2
Like				3.7	9.0	9.1	1.5	*	*	*	*	*
Others					1.1	2.6		NA	NA	NA	NA	NA
Total	$13.5	$33.4	$30.5	$32.2	$44.7	$54.3	$55.5	$41.5	$46.8	$49.4	$36.8	$40.1
Royal Crown Cola												
Royal Crown	$10.5	$6.5	$3.0	$6.2	$4.0	$6.5	$5.1	$6.4	$6.4	$5.9	$6.2	$1.4
Diet Rite Cola	3.5	3.4	5.1	4.2	5.4	5.7	3.5	2.9	3.5	2.3	1.9	3.2
Others	0.4	0.1	0.1	6.0	5.6	2.2	NA	NA	NA	NA	NA	NA
Total	$14.4	$10.0	$8.2	$16.4	$15.0	$14.4	$8.6	$9.3	$9.9	$8.2	$8.1	$4.6
Canada Dry	$5.2	$10.1	$7.9	$8.9	$0.8	$15.5	$12.4	$11.6	$8.0	$7.1	$4.6	$4.5
Shasta	$2.8	$4.4	$4.1	$6.1	$6.1	$6.3	$4.6	*	*	$1.4	*	*
All Others	$10.5	$26.3	$29.5	$38.4	$24.0	$75.3	$30.4	NA	NA	NA	NA	NA
Industry Total	$114	$241	$235	$317	$307	$490	$385	$389	$392	$458	$428	$498

Source: *Advertising Age*, *Beverage Industry*, *Leading National Advertisers*, company annual reports.

Exhibit 4 U.S. Advertising Spending by Brand ($ millions)

	1975	1980	1981	1982	1983	1984	1985	1986	1987	1988	1989	1990
Coca-Cola Company												
Coca-Cola[a]	$20.3	$35.6	$38.3	$44.9	$41.7	$64.1	$71.6	$57.4	$57.8	$85.2	$77.4	$90.4
Diet Coke				38.0	20.9	48.3	40.6	40.3	40.0	56.8	59.2	69.1
Cherry Coke							6.6	10.0	7.2	1.0	0.5	0.1
Sprite	2.6	10.7	11.5	16.2	21.2	35.3	22.2	24.6	22.2	22.4	22.5	23.4
Diet Sprite							6.7	5.0	3.3	7.5	2.2	7.6
Tab	6.5	12.6	15.2	22.0	25.2	31.8	15.6	5.1	0.5	*[b]	*	*
Others	5.0	12.2	8.5	3.9	10.7	1.7	NA	NA	NA	NA	NA	NA
Total	$34.4	$71.1	$73.5	$125.0	$119.7	$181.2	$163.3	$142.4	$131.0	$172.9	$161.8	$190.6
Pepsi-Cola Company												
Pepsi-Cola	$15.0	$39.7	$31.2	$39.1	$22.8	$47.8	$56.9	$54.9	$60.2	$70.9	$71.9	$79.4
Diet Pepsi	3.7	11.6	13.8	15.0	20.6	44.7	32.9	33.8	35.5	48.5	57.2	76.5
Pepsi Free (Regular and sugar-free)			4.2	23.0	20.6	14.6	9.1	*	*	*	*	
Mountain Dew	2.8	10.2	13.0	8.4	8.4	11.2	9.0	8.3	8.0	5.7	9.1	11.7
Diet Mountain Dew										4.2	1.6	1.6
Pepsi Light	0.9	5.2	5.1	5.4	6.2	0.3	0.4	*	*	*	*	*
Others	2.9	0.5	2.6	3.2	3.2	0.0	NA	NA	NA	NA	NA	NA
Total	$25.4	$67.3	$65.7	$75.3	$84.2	$124.6	$108.3	$97	$103.7	$129.3	$139.8	$169.2
Dr Pepper Company												
Dr Pepper	$4.9	$11.0	$9.7	$10.0	$6.0	$11.7	$9.6	$9.6	$11.3	$14.5	$17.8	$24.1
Pepper Free					2.6	1.3	0.5	0.3	*	*	*	*
Diet Dr Pepper	1.6	2.9	3.1	4.5	3.5	5.6	5.7	6.8	9.2	9.7	9.4	6.6
Others	1.3	4.1	2.4	0.4	0.2	0.2	0.0	NA	NA	NA	NA	NA
Total	$7.8	$18.0	$15.2	$14.9	$12.3	$18.8	$14.9	$16.7	$20.5	$24.2	$27.2	$30.7
Seven-Up Company												
7-Up	$10.2	$25.5	$23.4	$19.6	$21.2	$29.7	$22.3	$33.3	$27.1	$27.6	$27.2	$31.4
Diet 7-Up	3.3	7.9	7.1	7.8	11.9	15.5	15.6	8.2	11.0	7.3	5.2	8.5

[a] After 1985, includes advertising for both new Coke and Coca-Cola Classic.

[b] Advertising support under $250,000 where indicated with an asterisk (*).

Exhibit 3 (continued) Financial Data for the Leading Soft Drink Competitors, 1972–1990 ($ millions)[a]

	1972	1975	1980	1981	1982	1983	1984	1985	1986	1987	1988	1989	1990
Dr Pepper Company (continued)													
Net income/sales	10.5%	8.6%	7.8%	8.1%	2.4%	3.9%	–13.4%	2.3%	2.5%	–0.1%	–4.5%	3.0%	5.7%
Net income/equity	26%	24%	24%	24%	8%	14%	NA	30%	NA	–1%	–31%	18%	43%
Long-term debt/assets	0%	0%	7%	8%	45%	42%	NA	67%	80%	78%	80%	79%	75%
ROYAL CROWN COMPANY													
Corporate sales[a]	191	258	438	450	470	490	524	986	1,102	1,109	1,122	1,175	1,231
Net income/sales	6.3%	5.2%	2.3%	3.4%	3.4%	3.1%	0.6%	0.6%	–0.8%	1.6%	3.2%	–0.1%	–0.9%
Net income/equity	22%	17%	10%	14%	14%	12%	3%	5%	–9%	15%	23%	–1%	–11%
Long-term debt/assets	NA	NA	38%	34%	24%	22%	37%	47%	50%	38%	46%	46%	46%
Worldwide Soft Drink Operations													
Sales	NA	NA	221	230	243	242	NA	72	111	105	112	120	133
Operating income	NA	NA	14	23	27	22	NA	12	20	17	15	23	24
Operating income/sales	NA	NA	6.3%	9.9%	11.1%	9.1%	NA	16.7%	18.0%	16.2%	13.4%	19.2%	18.0%
CADBURY-SCHWEPPES (million pounds)													
Corporate sales[b]	NA	NA	NA	NA	NA	NA	NA	NA	1,839	2,031	2,382	2,843	
Net income/sales	NA	NA	NA	NA	NA	NA	NA	NA	5.5%	5.5%	7.1%	9.8%	
Net income/equity	NA	NA	NA	NA	NA	NA	NA	NA	43%	43%	67%	84%	
Long-term debt/assets	NA	NA	NA	NA	NA	NA	NA	NA	26%	17%	18%	33%	
Worldwide Soft Drink Operations													
Sales	NA	NA	NA	NA	NA	NA	NA	NA	NA	1,154	1,365	1,699	
Operating income	NA	NA	NA	NA	NA	NA	NA	NA	NA	89	109	147	
Operating income/sales	NA	NA	NA	NA	NA	NA	NA	NA	NA	7.7%	8.0%	8.7%	
Assets	NA	NA	NA	NA	NA	NA	NA	NA	NA	362	354	413	
Operating income/assets	NA	NA	NA	NA	NA	NA	NA	NA	NA	25%	31%	36%	
Non-U.S. Soft Drink Operations													
Sales	NA	NA	NA	NA	NA	NA	NA	NA	NA	926	1,070	1,343	
Operating income	NA	NA	NA	NA	NA	NA	NA	NA	NA	73	89	117	
Operating income/sales	NA	NA	NA	NA	NA	NA	NA	NA	NA	7.9%	8.3%	8.7%	

Source: Company annual reports

[a] Cadbury-Schweppes purchased the Canada Dry brands in 1986 and acquired Crush International in 1989.

[b] The soft drink operations of Royal Crown were purchased by DWG Corporation in late 1984.

Exhibit 3 (continued) Financial Data for the Leading Soft Drink Competitors, 1972–1990 ($ millions)[a]

	1972	1975	1980	1981	1982	1983	1984	1985	1986	1987	1988	1989	1990
Worldwide Soft Drink Operations (continued)													
Assets	NA	NA	1,266	1,355	1,389	1,249	1,039	1,319	2,616	2,780	3,994	6,198	6,465
Operating income assets	NA	NA	19.3%	18.6%	15.7%	10.1%	23.8%	20.0%	13.3%	15.2%	11.4%	10.9%	11.9%
Capital expenditures	NA	NA	140	127	111	94	84	161	194	202	198	268	334
Non-U.S. Soft Drink Operations													
Sales	NA	NA	NA	NA	NA	NA	NA	NA	NA	NA	971	1,153	1,489
Operating income	NA	NA	NA	NA	NA	NA	NA	NA	NA	NA	50	99	94
Operating income/sales	NA	NA	NA	NA	NA	NA	NA	NA	NA	NA	5.1%	8.6%	6.3%
COCA-COLA ENTERPRISES													
Sales									1,951	3,329	3,874	3,882	4,034
Net income/sales									1.4%	2.7%	3.9%	1.8%	2.3%
Operating income/sales									8.6%	10.1%	9.1%	8.0%	8.1%
Net income/equity									2%	6%	8%	4%	6%
Assets									3,811	4,250	4,669	4,732	5,021
Long-term debts/assets									47%	49%	44%	37%	39%
Seven-Up Company													
Corporate sales[a]	133	214	9,650	10,722	11,586	12,976	13,814	15,964	271	297	266	247	230
Net income/sales	9.0%	9.5%	5.7%	6.2%	6.7%	7.0%	6.4%	7.9%	−2.4%	2.5%	−8.9%	0.7%	2.1%
Net income/equity[b]	24%	23.6%	19%	20%	21%	22%	22%	26%	−2.5%	14.8%	−34.4%	−2.5%	−11.7%
Long-term debt/assets	4%	2%	36%	38%	39%	26%	22%	42%	66%	62%	107%	109%	99%
Worldwide Soft Drink Operations[c]													
Sales	*	*	NA	NA	NA	NA	NA	NA	*	*	*	*	*
Operating income	*	*	NA	NA	NA	NA	NA	NA	*	*	*	*	*
Operating income/sales	*	*	NA	NA	NA	NA	NA	NA	*	*	*	*	*
DR PEPPER COMPANY													
Corporate sales[d]	77	138	339	370	516	560	142	174	181	207	244	267	311

[a] Seven-Up was purchased by Philip Morris in 1978. In 1986, Seven-Up was acquired by Hicks and Haas, but it operated as an independent company.

[b] Seven-Up had negative stockholders' equity in 1988, 1989, and 1990.

[c] Corporate activities were based solely in the soft drink industry where indicated with an asterisk (*).

[d] Dr Pepper was purchased by Hicks and Haas in 1986 but continued to operate as an independent company.

Exhibit 3 Financial Data for the Leading Soft Drink Competitors, 1972–1990 ($ millions)[a]

	1972	1975	1980	1981	1982	1983	1984	1985	1986	1987	1988	1989	1990
THE COCA-COLA COMPANY													
Corporate Sales	1,876	2,773	5,475	5,699	6,021	6,829	7,364	7,904	6,977	7,658	8,065	8,622	10,236
Net income/sales	10.1%	9.0%	7.7%	8.5%	8.5%	8.2%	8.5%	9.1%	13.4%	12.0%	13.0%	20.0%	13.5%
Net income/equity	22%	21%	20%	21%	18%	19%	23%	24%	27%	29%	31%	49%	36%
Long-term debt/assets	5%	3%	10%	9%	17%	18%	18%	23%	19%	15%	14%	10%	8%
Worldwide Soft Drink Operations													
Sales	NA	NA	4,522	4,683	4,516	4,695	5,015	5,510	5,645	6,229	6,516	6,981	8,587
Operating income	NA	NA	732	804	873	859	880	881	1,001	1,433	1,691	1,908	2,160
Operating income/sales	NA	NA	16.2%	17.2%	19.3%	18.3%	17.5%	16.0%	17.7%	23.0%	25.9%	27.3%	25.1%
Assets	NA	NA	2,436	2,472	2,521	2,671	3,010	3,680	3,287	4,174	3,809	4,620	5,363
Operating income/assets	NA	NA	30%	33%	65%	62%	29%	24%	30%	34%	44%	41%	40%
Capital expenditures	NA	NA	224	251	249	238	295	326	176	170	239	352	460
Non-U.S. Soft Drink Operations													
Sales	NA	NA	NA	NA	NA	NA	NA	2,677	3,629	4,109	4,503	4,759	6,125
Operating income	NA	NA	NA	NA	NA	NA	NA	613	843	1,109	1,339	1,517	1,801
Operating income/assets	NA	NA	NA	NA	NA	NA	NA	22.9%	23.2%	27.0%	29.7%	31.9%	29.4%
Capital expenditures	NA	NA	NA	NA	NA	NA	NA	101	102	92	159	216	321
PEPSICO, INC.													
Corporate sales[b]	1,560	2,709	5,975	7,027	6,811	7,166	7,699	8,057	9,110	11,485	12,533	15,242	17,803
Net income/sales	5.1%	4.6%	4.4%	4.2%	3.3%	4.0%	2.8%	6.8%	5.0%	5.2%	6.1%	5.9%	6.0%
Net income/equity	16%	18%	20%	20%	14%	17%	12%	30%	22%	24%	24%	23%	22%
Long-term debt/assets	34%	35%	31%	27%	28%	24%	23%	36%	33%	25%	21%	38%	33%
Worldwide Soft Drink Operations													
Sales	661	1,065	2,768	2,772	2,908	2,940	2,908	3,129	3,450	4,099	4,638	5,777	6,523
Operating income	85	111	244	252	218	126	247	264	349	423	455	676	768
Operating income/sales	12.9%	10.4%	8.8%	9.1%	7.5%	4.3%	8.5%	8.4%	10.1%	10.3%	9.8%	11.7%	11.8%

[a] Financial data for soft drink operations includes both concentrate activities and company-owned bottlers. Although direct comparisons are not possible due to differences in ownership of bottling activities (e.g., Coca-Cola owned no bottling activities in 1990, Pepsi's company-owned bottlers represented 51% of total 1990 volume), data are separately listed for Coca-Cola Enterprises (Coca-Cola bottlers that were spun off into a separate company in 1986).

[b] Pepsi-Cola purchased the international operations of Seven-Up in 1986.

Exhibit 2 U.S. Soft Drink Market Shares by Case Volume (percent)

	1966	1970	1975	1980	1982	1984	1985	1986	1987	1988	1989	1990
Coca-Cola Co.												
Classic							5.8	19.1	19.8	19.9	19.5	19.4
Coca-Cola	27.7	28.4	26.2	25.3	24.6	22.5	14.4	2.4	1.7	1.3	0.9	0.7
Cherry Coke							1.6	1.7	1.2	0.9	0.7	0.6
Diet Coke					0.3	5.2	6.3	7.2	7.7	8.1	8.8	9.1
Diet Cherry Coke								0.2	0.4	0.3	0.3	0.2
Tab	1.4	1.3	2.6	3.3	4.0	1.6	1.1	0.6	0.4	0.3	0.2	0.2
Caffeine-Free Coke, Diet Coke and Tab						1.8	1.8	1.7	1.7	1.9	2.2	3.1
Sprite and diet Sprite	1.5	1.8	2.6	3.0	3.3	3.8	4.2	4.3	4.3	4.3	4.4	4.4
Others	2.8	3.2	3.9	4.3	2.5	2.6	1.9	2.6	2.7	2.8	3.0	2.7
Total	33.4	34.7	35.3	35.9	34.7	37.5	37.1	39.8	39.9	39.8	40.0	40.4
PepsiCo, Inc.												
Pepsi-Cola	16.1	17.0	17.4	20.4	20.3	19.1	18.2	18.6	18.6	18.4	17.8	17.3
Diet Pepsi	1.9	1.1	1.7	3.0	3.3	3.2	3.7	4.4	4.8	5.2	5.7	6.2
Caffeine-Free Pepsi and Diet Pepsi					0.4	2.7	2.3	2.0	1.8	2.0	2.1	2.3
Mountain Dew	1.4	0.9	1.3	3.3	3.2	3.0	2.9	3.0	3.3	3.4	3.6	3.8
Diet Mountain Dew										0.4	0.5	0.5
Slice							0.7	1.5	1.3	1.1	1.0	0.9
Diet Slice							0.6	1.0	1.0	0.7	0.6	0.4
Others	1.0	0.8	0.7	1.1	0.9	0.7	0.2	0.1	0.0	0.1	0.4	0.4
Total	20.4	19.8	21.1	27.8	28.1	28.7	28.6	30.6	30.8	31.3	31.7	31.8
Seven-Up	6.9	7.2	7.6	6.3	6.7	6.8	5.7	5.0	5.1	4.7	4.3	4.0
Dr Pepper	2.6	3.8	5.5	6.0	5.2	5.0	4.7	4.8	5.0	5.3	5.6	5.8
Royal Crown Co.	6.9	6.0	5.4	4.7	3.9	3.1	2.9	3.0	2.9	2.8	2.7	2.6
Cadbury-Schweppes	NA	NA	NA	NA	NA	NA	4.5	4.2	3.7	3.5	3.1	3.2
Other Companies	29.8	28.5	25.1	19.3	21.4	18.9	16.5	12.6	12.6	12.6	12.6	12.2
Total (million cases)	2,927	3,670	4,155	5,180	5,510	6,130	6,500	6,770	7,155	7,530	7,680	7,914

Source: John C. Maxwell, Jr., and *Beverage Industry*.

Exhibit 6
Retail Outlets for Soft Drinks

	Food Stores	Fountain	Vending	Other[a]
Percent of Industry Volume by Channel				
1987	41%	22%	12%	25%
1982	42	20	12	26
Brand Share by Channel, 1991				
Coca-Cola brands	34%	63%	45% est.	27% est.
Pepsi-Cola brands	32	25	34 est.	24 est.
Other brands	34	12	21 est.	49 est.

Source: *Jesse Myer's Beverage Digest, Beverage World, Business Week.*

[a] Includes bottles and cans sold through restaurants and convenience stores.

the range of 75%. Coca-Cola served its fountain outlets with a dedicated sales force, by-passing the local bottler. Local Pepsi-Cola bottlers handled the fountain accounts in their territories and sold syrup to the local outlets of companies carrying Pepsi products.

In the vending channel, bottlers purchased, installed, and supplied machines. Concentrate producers often offered rebates to encourage their bottlers to invest in vending machines and allocate all or most of the vending slots (usually four to six per machine) to their products. One source estimated that Coca-Cola bottlers owned 50% more vending machines in the United States than Pepsi bottlers. On average, bottlers obtained significantly higher margins through vending machines than from other channels. Coca-Cola bottlers, for example, often earned over half of their total profits from vending operations.

There was also a host of smaller channels for soft drinks. Restaurants, caterers, and institutional buyers such as airlines often served soft drinks in bottles and cans rather than from a fountain. Convenience stores accounted for an increasing volume, particularly through "single serve" cold cases. Some mass merchandisers also allocated shelf space to soft drinks. Sales to these diverse outlets were handled by local bottlers.

THE DEVELOPMENT OF THE U.S. SOFT DRINK INDUSTRY

Soft drinks had existed since the early 1800s, when many U.S. druggists had concocted blends of fruit syrups and carbonated soda water that they sold at their soda fountains.

Coca-Cola

Coca-Cola was formulated in 1886 by Dr. John Pemberton, a pharmacist in Atlanta, Georgia. The drink was sold as a refreshing elixir at the fountain counter of Jacobs' Pharmacy, of which Dr. Pemberton was part owner. Eventually, Asa Candler became sole owner of the pharmacy and thus the rights to the

soft drink. Candler began selling the syrup used to make the drink to other pharmacies, established a sales force, and began advertising the drink on signs placed in train stations and town squares. The advertising budget reached $100,000 in 1901. Candler granted the first bottling franchise for the drink in 1899 for $1, believing that the future of the drink rested with fountain sales.

Coca-Cola's bottler network grew quickly, and in 1916, a standard 6½-ounce "skirt" bottle was designed for use by all franchisees. This bottle eventually became one of the best-known images in the world. In 1920, U.S. Supreme Court Justice Oliver Wendell Holmes ruled that the nickname "Coke" could only mean Coca-Cola, because "it means a single thing coming from a single source, and well known to the community. Coca-Cola probably means to most persons the plaintiff's familiar product to be had everywhere."

In 1919, Ernest Woodruff purchased the Coca-Cola Company from Asa Candler's heirs for $25 million. In 1923, his son, Robert W. Woodruff, who was to become the most dominant figure in Coca-Cola's history, was made CEO. Woodruff began working with the company's franchised bottlers to make Coca-Cola available wherever and whenever a consumer might want it. He pushed the bottlers to place the beverage "in arm's reach of desire" and argued that if Coke were not conveniently available when the consumer was thirsty, the sale would be lost forever.

In 1929, Coca-Cola and its bottlers began to offer an open top cooler for bottled Coca-Cola to store keepers and gas station operators at extremely low prices. In 1937, the company introduced the first coin vending machine. Woodruff also initiated "lifestyle" advertising for Coca-Cola, which emphasized the product's role in a consumer's life rather than the product's attributes. The product's famous motto during the 1920s and 1930s was "The Pause That Refreshes." The company continued to own its original bottling operations around Atlanta and began to buy back a few franchises that were underperforming.

Woodruff also began to develop Coca-Cola's international business, principally through export. His most memorable action may have been the decision, made at the request of General Dwight Eisenhower at the beginning of World War II, to see "that every man in uniform gets a bottle of Coca-Cola for 5¢ wherever he is and whatever it costs." Coca-Cola bottling plants followed the march of American troops around the world. This action established a dominant market share for Coca-Cola in most European and Asian countries, a lead which the company still held in 1991.

In the years immediately following World War II, Coca-Cola substantially outsold its closest rival, Pepsi-Cola, and held 70% of the cola segment of the market. Hundreds of small, regional soft drink companies continued to produce a wide assortment of flavors that comprised the remaining 30% of the market.

Pepsi-Cola

Pepsi-Cola was invented in 1893 in New Bern, North Carolina, by pharmacist Caleb Bradham. Like Coca-Cola, Pepsi-Cola expanded through franchised bottlers. Its growth in the early 1900s was not as strong, however, and the company was on the brink of bankruptcy several times.

Pepsi-Cola used a standard 12 ounce bottle, which its bottlers sold at a retail price of 10¢ compared to Coca-Cola's 5¢ for its 6½-ounce unit. In 1933, Pepsi-Cola lowered the price to 5¢, and in 1939, it launched its radio advertising jingle, "Twice as much for a nickel, too. Pepsi-Cola is the one for you." In 1940,

the jingle was rated by the radio industry as the second best-known song in America, behind the Star Spangled Banner.

Seven-Up

Seven-Up was introduced in 1929 and specialized in lemon-lime drinks packaged in a distinctive green bottle. Seven-Up managers took pride in the close, cooperative relations that they established with their bottlers, who were referred to as "developers." The vast majority of Seven-Up developers also bottled Coca-Cola, Pepsi-Cola, or RC Cola. By the 1950s, Seven-Up achieved national distribution through its franchise network and owned a small number of bottling operations.

Dr Pepper

Dr Pepper was formulated in 1885 by a fountain clerk in Waco, Texas. Dr Pepper produced a uniquely flavored drink, based on a combination of juices. Dr Pepper enjoyed strong consumer loyalty, although it was said that a consumer had to try Dr Pepper several times to become accustomed to it. The formula allowed the bottlers to add less sugar than the leading brands.

Dr Pepper historically had been a regional producer in the Southwest, where it maintained a network of franchised bottlers for which it was the primary brand. In 1962, a U.S. court ruled that Dr Pepper was not a cola, thus Coca-Cola or Pepsi-Cola bottlers were able to carry it. Dr Pepper began moving aggressively to expand from its Southwest base by granting franchises to Coca-Cola and Pepsi-Cola bottlers across the country.

Royal Crown Cola

Royal Crown Cola, a specialist in cola drinks, introduced its first cola in 1935. The company was considered by many analysts to be the most innovative concentrate producer due to its introduction of the first diet soft drink and the first decaffeinated diet cola. It employed independent franchise bottlers, who often marketed Seven-Up, Dr Pepper, and other smaller brands. Royal Crown was the strongest in the midwestern United States where its bottlers were most numerous.

THE COLA WARS COMMENCE

After World War II, important changes occurred in both the U.S. soft drink industry and the nation itself. Although these changes had the greatest effect on the two industry leaders, Coca-Cola and Pepsi-Cola, they also affected the smaller concentrate producers, as described in the Appendix.

Alfred Steele

In 1950, Alfred Steele accepted an offer to become CEO at Pepsi-Cola. A former Coca-Cola marketing executive, he had apparently irritated Robert Woodruff with his style. At the time, Pepsi-Cola was nearly bankrupt and had lost much of the market position that it gained in the 1930s. Steele later stated, "When I arrived at Pepsi, the vice-presidents figured that I had come to liquidate the company."[1]

1. J. C. Louis and Harvey Z. Yazijian, *The Cola Wars* (New York: Everest House, 1980).

Steele made "Beat Coke" his theme and claimed that he saw the day when Pepsi would outsell Coke. Pepsi-Cola executives encouraged bottlers to focus on sales through supermarkets, which were springing up in the growing suburbs. Pepsi introduced several new bottle sizes, including the first 24-ounce bottle, which was intended for family consumption. New advertising campaigns were developed, and in 1955 Steele married actress Joan Crawford, who toured as guest speaker at regional bottler meetings.

Between 1950 and 1958, Pepsi-Cola revenues increased over 300%. The Pepsi-Cola Company also began to expand its international operations in earnest during this period.

Donald Kendall

Donald Kendall became CEO of Pepsi-Cola in 1963. Kendall had gained fame in 1959 when he convinced Vice President Richard Nixon to bring Soviet Premier Nikita Khruschev by the Pepsi booth at the American Exhibition in Moscow.

PepsiCo expanded its product line in the 1960s and 1970s, introducing Diet Pepsi; Mountain Dew, a lemon-lime drink; and Pepsi Light, a semi-diet drink. PepsiCo also launched its "Pepsi Generation" advertising theme, which positioned the product as the choice of the young and "young at heart." Bottlers were praised at meetings as "veterans in the war against Coca-Cola," who "invaded" Coke markets with new "sales weapons."[2]

Under the leadership of President and Chief Operating Officer Andrall E. Pearson, PepsiCo established stringent standards for its bottlers' "store door" deliveries, with the goal of gaining and maintaining retail shelf space for PepsiCo products. As Pepsi and its competitors raised their standards for store delivery during the 1970s, the soft drink and snack food sections of food stores were no longer viewed as in permanent disarray due to high product turnover, but became recognized as the best-maintained parts of the stores.

Throughout the 1950s and 1960s, Pepsi-Cola had sold its concentrate to bottlers at a price 20% lower than Coca-Cola. In the early 1970s, Pepsi increased its concentrate price to equal that of Coca-Cola. The increase was permitted under the Pepsi-Cola franchise agreement, and PepsiCo avoided fierce bottler opposition by promising to use the extra margin to increase advertising and promotion. In 1975, the Pepsi-Cola brand first overtook Coca-Cola in terms of market share in food stores, as measured by Nielsen audits.

Under Kendall's leadership, the Pepsi-Cola Company was renamed PepsiCo, and diversified into snack foods, (Frito-Lay), restaurants (Pizza Hut and Taco Bell), trucking, and sporting goods. Kendall reportedly purchased Frito-Lay in 1965 partly because chips go well with cola, and Pizza Hut in 1977 in part to obtain a new fountain outlet.

Robert Woodruff

At Coca-Cola, Robert Woodruff remained an influential figure. In 1954, Coca-Cola's sales and profits declined for the first time since before World War II. In 1955, the company changed the bottle that it had used since 1916, increasing its size to 12 ounces. In the late 1950s, Coca-Cola introduced even larger bottle sizes that could be sold through food stores, and in 1961, Coca-Cola began to sell its soft drinks in cans as well as bottles.

2. Pat Watters, *Coca-Cola: An Illustrated History* (New York: Doubleday, 1978).

In 1955, the company changed its advertising motto to "Be Really Refreshed," and in 1960, to "No Wonder Coke Refreshes Best." Throughout the 1960s and 1970s, commercials portrayed Coke as part of American life. In meetings with Coca-Cola bottlers, executives discussed only the growth of their own brand and never voiced the name Pepsi-Cola. Industry observers often referred to Coca-Cola as "Mother Coke."

In the 1960s and 1970s, Coca-Cola introduced several new products, including the lemon-lime drink Sprite (1961); the diet drinks Tab (1963), Fresca (1966), and diet Sprite (1974); and Mr. Pibb (1972). The company stated that it would not extend the Coca-Cola or Coke names to any of its new products. Advertising expenditures were steadily increased, and Coca-Cola commercials in the United States were designed to portray a positive image of Coke as part of American life. Coca-Cola began diversifying into other beverages in 1960 when it purchased the Minute Maid orange juice company. In following years, it diversified into several other beverage areas, including coffee, wine, and spring water.

In 1976, Paul Austin, then CEO of Coca-Cola, stated in an article that U.S. soft drink consumption had matured and Coca-Cola's largest growth would come from the international market. International sales by 1980 accounted for 62% of Coca-Cola's soft drink volume, in contrast to 20% of PepsiCo's.

THE PEPSI CHALLENGE

In 1974, a Pepsi-Cola sales manager in Dallas, Texas, initiated blind taste tests of Pepsi-Cola and Coca-Cola to improve his product's third-place market position, behind both Coca-Cola and Dr Pepper. The taste tests were conducted in "Challenge Booths" located in food stores and were based on Pepsi market research that indicated that 58% of consumers preferred Pepsi-Cola to Coca-Cola in blind taste tests. Pepsi's market share began to increase immediately, and Pepsi eventually became the number-two brand in Dallas.

In 1975, the challenge was extended to other markets in which Pepsi-Cola was weak and the bottlers were company-owned. The Challenge, which covered 20% of Pepsi-Cola's sales, was highlighted in advertising, store displays, trade communications, and in-store Challenge Booths. In 1977, the Pepsi Challenge was launched nationwide and by 1980, the Pepsi-Cola brand gained an additional market share lead of 1.3% over Coca-Cola in food stores.

John Sculley, who became president of Pepsi U.S.A. in 1980, urged Pepsi bottlers to expand sales through vending and fountain outlets. Sculley was quoted in 1980 as saying, "I want our bottlers to defend their competitive position in food stores but also to go for the competitors' jugular by attacking its high margin vending business." Sculley also increased the price of the concentrate for Diet Pepsi and used the greater margin to increase advertising in the growing diet segment.

Coca-Cola responded to the nationwide Pepsi Challenge by initiating major retail price discounts in selected markets where Pepsi-Cola was weak, the Pepsi bottler was an independent franchisee, and the Coca-Cola bottler was company owned. Coca-Cola initially used price selectively as a competitive weapon, with the cost of price promotions still split approximately two-thirds to the bottler and one-third to the concentrate producer. By the late 1970s, price discounting was widespread.

NEW LEADERSHIP AT COKE

Industry observers were surprised in 1981 when Roberto Goizueta, a Cuban-born chemical engineer, was selected as the chief executive officer of The Coca-Cola Company. As one of his first acts, Goizueta issued a 1,200 word strategy statement that called for dramatic changes at Coca-Cola and a focus on growth in the U.S. soft drink market.

Goizueta stated that the company would use the Coca-Cola brand name as competitive "equity" and would no longer treat it as sacrosanct. Price discounting would be used when necessary to maintain Coca-Cola's dominant position. In 1981, industry price discounting reached a new level of intensity, and by the end of the year, approximately 50% of the food store volume of both Coca-Cola and Pepsi-Cola was sold at a discount. Nielsen audits in that year indicated that a 192-ounce case of Coca-Cola cost less than Pepsi-Cola.

Goizueta also stated that Coca-Cola would fund increased advertising and promotions by raising the price of Coca-Cola syrup. The franchise agreement that had been in place for 60 years was amended to eliminate the fixed price of syrup. In exchange for the amended agreement, Coca-Cola agreed to sell concentrate (without sweetener) rather than syrup to some of its largest bottlers.

In 1982, Coca-Cola changed its advertising theme. Goizueta stated "With our new slogan, 'Coke is it,' we're saying that we're number one and not ashamed of it. Our former slogan, 'Have a Coke and Smile,' was wonderful, but we were in a fight and our slogan was a ballad. The momentum has now shifted from Purchase, New York (headquarters of PepsiCo) to Atlanta."[3]

Goizueta's strategic plan also extended Coca-Cola's corporate strategy. The corporation's private label coffee and tea businesses were sold, as were a plastic-manufacturing company and a wine business. In 1982, Coca-Cola acquired Columbia Pictures, perceiving growth potential and marketing synergies with beverages. Goizueta stated that Coca-Cola would become a "beverage and entertainment enterprise, strong in both businesses."

Coca-Cola also made changes in its bottling network. Coke encouraged poorly performing bottlers to sell their operations and sold most of its own bottlers through leveraged buyouts. Between 1980 and 1984, ownership changes occurred in franchises representing 50% of Coca-Cola volume. Coca-Cola executives indicated that the company had played some role in each purchase and had offered to raise capital for potential buyers in several cases. The company sometimes took a partial equity position in the refranchised bottlers, but remained committed to maintaining an independent bottling network. By 1985, only 11% of Coca-Cola's volume was produced by company-owned bottlers.

One of the most dramatic examples of Coca-Cola's franchise management was its 1982 decision to take Coca-Cola Bottling of New York private. The bottler was a $700 million corporation listed on the New York Stock Exchange. The company had diversified outside soft drink bottling and had an average return on equity of 10% in the five years prior to 1982. The Coca-Cola Company acquired 35% of the bottler and arranged for private investors to acquire the remaining 65%. Charles Millard, chief executive officer of Coca-Cola of

3. *Industry Week,* November 1982.

New York later said, "We became a born-again bottler, as we again focused on our mainline business of selling soft drinks."[4]

PRODUCT LINE AND PACKAGING DEVELOPMENTS

Growing health concerns and the development of the artificial sweetener aspartame contributed to the development of new soft drink products in the 1980s. Changes also occurred in product packaging and advertising.

The Diet Segment

In July 1982, Coca-Cola announced the nationwide introduction of a new diet cola, diet Coke. Consumer surveys indicated that diet Coke was considered far superior to Tab, the company's existing diet product. While some bottlers voiced strong resistance to the use of the Coke brand name, diet Coke exceeded even the company's expectations. By early 1983, diet Coke gained national distribution and was supported by annual advertising expenditures of $50 million. By the end of 1983, diet Coke had become the largest selling diet soft drink in the United States.

In the early 1980s, aspartame, marketed under the NutraSweet brand, was hailed as the new standard in artificial sweeteners. It raised fewer health concerns than earlier artificial sweeteners, but was far more expensive (costing almost twice as much as the equivalent amount of sugar). NutraSweet was patented and licensed to other producers by G.D. Searle. The patent was to expire in 1992.

In 1984, PepsiCo became the first soft drink company to use 100% aspartame in its diet beverages. All major concentrate producers followed within months; however, Pepsi-Cola was able to obtain delivery of aspartame before Coca-Cola, and used its six-week lead to promote Diet Pepsi against diet Coke. Industry sources indicated that the growth of Diet Pepsi exceeded that of diet Coke during this period. Coca-Cola launched a national advertising campaign stating that diet Coke had 100% aspartame, even though it was available only in certain areas. Pepsi-Cola immediately responded by emphasizing at the point of purchase that its products carried the label "100% NutraSweet," while the Coca-Cola labels could not make this claim.

The Caffeine-Free Segment

Royal Crown announced a diet caffeine-free cola, RC/100, in 1980. In 1983, PepsiCo introduced two caffeine-free colas, Pepsi Free and Sugar Free Pepsi Free, supported by an annual advertising budget of $100 million heavily weighted toward television. By the end of the year, Pepsi's new products held a combined share of the caffeine-free market segment of almost 50%. Soon after Pepsi introduced its new products, Coca-Cola introduced Caffeine-Free Coke, diet Coke, and Tab, each of which was supported by television advertising. By 1984, surveys indicated that 15% to 20% of American consumers expressed serious concern about caffeine consumption.

4. *Beverage World*, July 1984.

Other Flavor Segments

In late 1984, Pepsi-Cola introduced two lemon-lime drinks, Slice and diet Slice, which contained 10% fruit juice (neither Seven-Up nor Sprite contained fruit juice). Cherry Coke, a blend of Coca-Cola and cherry flavoring, was introduced in early 1985. Cherry Coke was supported with a substantial advertising campaign and began to gain share rapidly.

In mid-1985, Coca-Cola introduced Minute Maid Orange and diet Minute Maid Orange, sodas that contained 10% juice. Coke's entry into the juice category precipitated a proliferation of offerings by the two companies. PepsiCo expanded its Slice product line to include mandarin orange and introduced Cherry Pepsi in Canada and the United Kingdom. Coca-Cola added a lemon lime flavor to its Minute-Maid Group. Pepsi countered with apple and cherry cola Slice.

The Three-Liter Bottle

In 1984, Pepsi became the first concentrate producer to introduce the three-liter plastic bottle, which had been spurred by an innovation of one of its bottlers, and gained a four month window before Coca-Cola could secure supplies for its own bottlers. Products packaged in three-liter bottles sold for significantly less per ounce at retail than those in two-liter bottles, although the packaging cost per ounce was slightly higher.

Advertising

Pepsi-Cola began a new marketing campaign in 1984, with the slogan "Choice of a New Generation." The company secured endorsements from singers Michael Jackson and Lionel Richie in 1984, former Democratic vice presidential candidate Geraldine Ferraro in 1985, and actor Michael J. Fox in 1986, which were widely covered in the media and were used to generate excitement during conventions of Pepsi-Cola bottlers. Many advertising executives believed that the new campaign was particularly successful in building loyalty for Pepsi among teenagers.

In late 1984, Coca-Cola launched a series of commercials that featured Bill Cosby emphasizing Coca-Cola's "lightness." Cosby explained that Coca-Cola was lighter than Pepsi-Cola (because it contained less sugar), and hence was more refreshing. Coca-Cola's advertising recall increased, and Coke's market share relative to Pepsi's increased in some regions.

THE COCA-COLA REFORMULATION

In April 1985, Coca-Cola announced that it would change the formula of its 99-year-old Coca-Cola brand. While Coke's total 1984 soft drink sales had grown rapidly with the introduction of diet Coke, sales of regular Coca-Cola had suffered.

On the day of Coca-Cola's announcement, the reformulation was the lead story on all three network evening news programs. Surveys indicated that over 90% of Americans heard about the change within 24 hours, and that 70% tried the new drink within a month of its introduction. The new Coke contained more sweetener, and consumers indicated that they believed that it tasted more like Pepsi. Groups of consumers organized to resist the change. Bottlers also contributed to the clamor: to them, the traditional formula was synonymous with motherhood and apple pie.

On the day that Coke announced its reformulation, Pepsi held a press conference and declared a holiday for its employees. To make Coke drinkers aware that new Coke was more like Pepsi, the company ran national advertisements that invited disgruntled Coca-Cola drinkers to Pepsi-Cola, saying: "For 87 years Coke and Pepsi have been eyeball to eyeball. It looks like they just blinked . . . we welcome the new Pepsi drinkers to the new Pepsi generation."

In July 1985, Coca-Cola announced that it would bring back its original formula under the name Coca-Cola Classic, while retaining the new formula under the name Coke. Coke would be the company's flagship brand and the cola product sold to fountain outlets. The company also stated that new Coke would be introduced in all international markets.

In August 1985, Coca-Cola adopted a "Megabrand" strategy for Coca-Cola Classic and new Coke under the advertising slogan, "We've Got a Taste for You." Nielsen audits indicated that in the third quarter of 1985, Classic outsold Coke approximately three-to-one in food stores. Across all brands, however, both Coca-Cola and Pepsi held a 31% share in the take-home market.

In January 1986, the Coca-Cola Company announced that Coca-Cola Classic would henceforth be considered its flagship brand. Separate advertising agencies were hired for Coca-Cola Classic, which was promoted with the slogan, "Red, White, and You," and for new Coke, which was promoted with the theme, "Catch the Wave." In early 1986, some Coca-Cola franchised bottlers said publicly that the Coca-Cola company should drop the word "Classic" from the Coca-Cola name, and industry analysts were questioning whether new Coke would survive.

Reflecting on the introduction of new Coke, a former Coke marketer recalled "all the signs were that [the "lightness" campaign] was working, but 'lightness' got steamrollered by New Coke." Some insiders said that the reformulation would have been dropped if Coke had not been intent on finding new ways to attack Pepsi. Similarly, Pepsi's early introduction of three-liter bottles in 1984 was continued despite lukewarm reception by consumers. A Pepsi marketer explained, "Even if it wasn't working, we had to stay out front on this. . . . Basically, we wanted to jump off the cliff before Coke."[5]

NEW LEADERSHIP AT PEPSI-COLA

Wayne Calloway became the chairman and chief executive officer of PepsiCo in 1986. Calloway was the former president of Frito-Lay, the corporation's snack food subsidiary, which contributed 33% of total 1986 sales. He pointed out, "PepsiCo doesn't have one flagship, it has three flagships [soft drinks, snack foods and restaurants]. And people would kill to have just one of them."

Calloway planned to instill focus on profitability to develop a consumer products company with "the best possible return on equity."[6] This focus was later expressed by the president and CEO of Pepsi-Cola Worldwide Beverages, who decried the "mindless pursuit of market share to the exclusion of all else," and stated that by 1992, Pepsi-Cola would be number one in share of industry profit.[7]

5. *Forbes,* November 27, 1989.
6. *The Wall Street Journal,* June 13, 1991.
7. *Beverage World,* April 1990.

THE TRANSFORMATION OF THE BOTTLING NETWORKS

Several developments of the 1980s brought important changes to the bottling industry. Advertising by concentrate producers increased substantially, raising bottlers' costs (advertising expenses were split evenly between the concentrate producer and its bottlers). Although margins historically had been consistent across brands, the ingredients included in new aspartame and juice drinks made those products 10% to 15% more expensive for bottlers than regular soft drink brands. Broader product lines also increased bottler manufacturing and distribution costs. Shelf space limitations forced choices among the multiple brands, line extensions, and package types, yet food stores faced an extremely competitive environment and fought any retail price increase.

Throughout the 1970s, the bottling networks of Coca-Cola and Pepsi-Cola had been owned by independent bottlers, multibrand franchise firms, diversified companies, and the concentrate producers themselves. During the 1980s, however, large portions of the various bottling networks were purchased by multiple franchise owners and concentrate producers. By 1990, the major diversified companies, including Beatrice and General Cinema, had sold their bottling operations, and independently owned franchisees (who owned 45% of all bottling plants) accounted for only 17% of industry volume.

Coca-Cola

In the Coca-Cola network, the changes begun by Robert Goizueta in the early 1980s continued. One hundred to 150 of Coca-Cola's 350 franchises came up for sale in the mid-1980s. In 1986, the company acquired two of its biggest franchises, those owned by Beatrice and by J.T. Lupton, a private Coca-Cola bottler that accounted for 15% of Coca-Cola's U.S. volume and 40% of Dr Pepper's volume. The acquisitions increased Coca-Cola's bottler ownership from 11% to 38% of its total volume.

The acquisitions culminated in the creation and November 1986 sale of 51% of Coca-Cola Enterprises, Inc. (CCE) to the public. After its creation, Coca-Cola Enterprises renegotiated deals with suppliers and food outlets, consolidated territories in prime markets, cut its work force by 20%, and cut costs by merging distribution and raw materials purchasing. CCE's net selling price fell 2.5% per case in 1987 and 1988. In 1989, CCE shipped 20% more soda than it had shipped in 1986. CCE's profits were volatile throughout the late 1980s.

In late 1986, Coca-Cola proposed that its franchise agreement be replaced with the Master Bottler Contract, which eliminated both fixed syrup prices and franchisees' right to the Coca-Cola trademark. By 1989, nearly 70% of Coca-Cola's U.S. volume was covered by the new Master Bottler Contract. Between 1978 and 1989, bottlers under the new contract experienced a 60% increase in the price of Coca-Cola syrup.

PepsiCo

In 1986, PepsiCo acquired independent bottler MEI for $600 million and Allegheny Beverages for $168 million. The acquisitions increased PepsiCo's company-owned bottlers to 32% of total volume. After 1986, PepsiCo spent $3.7 billion to purchase additional bottlers so that by 1990, 51% of PepsiCo's volume was distributed by company-owned bottlers, and joint venture agreements covered an additional 16% of volume.

In the years following PepsiCo's acquisitions, its company-owned bottling operations (COBO) focused on gaining production and distribution efficiencies, efforts that appeared to be more successful than those of Coca-Cola Enterprises. Between 1987 and 1990, Pepsi's company-owned bottlers in the South reduced their cost structure by 30¢ per case.

The purchases ultimately led to significant changes in the organization of PepsiCo's soft drink operations. In February 1988, the Pepsi Bottling Group was combined with Pepsi-Cola USA and the fountain operations to create the Pepsi-Cola Company. Four regional divisions were established, each with responsibilities for manufacturing, distribution, retail and on-premise sales, employee relations, finance, and field marketing. Within each division, area offices had responsibilities for both franchised and company-owned bottlers. Roger Enrico, president and CEO of Pepsi Cola Worldwide Beverages, planned to transform the U.S. Beverage Division from a "razzmatazz marketing company with an operations hobby . . . to a great marketing company with a world-class operating capability."[8]

THE COLA WARS WIDEN

The Battle for Fountain Accounts

In 1990, Wendy's International, Inc., and Burger King switched their fountain accounts from Pepsi to Coca-Cola. Industry experts attributed PepsiCo's loss to the competitive strength of its restaurant business. As part of the new Burger King contract, Coca-Cola provided a team of marketing executives to assist the company with discounts and promotions. Burger King's switch reduced Pepsi's total fountain sales by 13%, and increased Coca-Cola's sales by 6.5%. Fountain outlets comprised 25% of the market in 1990. Growth had been strongest in gasoline/convenience stores and grocery stores, but sales to the fast food industry, which was overbuilt by an estimated 30%, had declined.

In 1991, Pepsi-Cola ran an advertisement in a restaurant trade journal that alleged that Coca-Cola gave preferential pricing to McDonald's. Coca-Cola denied the claim and in an internal memo that was leaked to the press, suggested that Marriott Corporation's recent switch to Pepsi-Cola may have been preceded by a loan from Pepsi. Neither Pepsi nor Marriott commented on the accusation. By the end of 1991, multiple accounts had switched from Coca-Cola to Pepsi-Cola and vice-versa.

New Product Introductions

Coca-Cola created a new products group in 1989. The group reformulated grapefruit-flavored soda Fresca and introduced the sports drink PowerAde and Caffeine Free Coca-Cola Classic. In 1991, Coca-Cola launched a reformulated version of its cherry Coke and diet cherry Coke. The company planned a 1992 introduction for Mocha Cooler, a flavored coffee, and test marketed a reintroduction of new Coke under the name Coke II in Spokane, Washington, and Chicago, Illinois.

Pepsi responded to Coca-Cola's 1990 test marketing of Coke II in Spokane, Washington, through its regional structure, including $1 million barrage of television advertisements, coupons, and appeals to retailers.

8. *The Harbus News*, October 15, 1990.

PepsiCo tested a new sports drink, All Sport, in 1990, and planned to distribute it nationally in four flavors. In 1991, PepsiCo announced that it would distribute single-servings of Ocean Spray juices in stores and vending machines nationwide. The company was also reported to be developing a clear, colorless Pepsi by taking advantage of the fact that colas were naturally clear. Industry experts believed that the new Pepsi could lure consumers of "new age" drinks that were marketed as wholesome refreshment. PepsiCo was expected to join with Thomas J. Lipton, Inc., to distribute brewed tea and coffee products.

Price and Promotion

In the first nine months of 1989, soft drink prices increased 3.3%. It was the first time since 1981 that prices had risen more than 2.6%.

Coca-Cola restructured the promotions side of its U.S. marketing department in 1989 to accommodate an increasing number of promotional joint ventures with companies in the entertainment and sports industries and with "prestige accounts" such as Walt Disney World. Like most of Coca-Cola's marketing efforts, promotion efforts would be run from the corporation's centralized operations in Atlanta.

Advertising

According to Video Storyboard, the annual television advertising campaigns of both Coca-Cola and Pepsi-Cola were among the top 10 most memorable throughout the 1980s. Pepsi-Cola's annual campaigns were more memorable than Coca-Cola's in seven of the eight years between 1983 and 1990.

After the disappointing results of new Coke, which held a market share of 1% by 1991, Coca-Cola insiders noted a "reluctance on the part of the marketing people to be too creative, too avant-garde."[9] The head of Coke's marketing department reportedly did not want to pursue trendy ideas so as not to resemble Pepsi.

In the early 1990s, Pepsi-Cola's innovative advertisements ranged from Ray Charles singing, "You've Got the Right One Baby, Uh-Huh," the most popular ad in the nation according to one survey, to spots that portrayed Coca-Cola drinkers as lifeless and "uncool." Advertisements in the "uncool" campaign, such as the one that showed rap singer M.C. Hammer turning into a lounge singer after one sip of Coke, were labeled a new Pepsi Challenge by some Coca-Cola employees.

PENETRATING INTERNATIONAL MARKETS

The soft drink industry was not as well developed internationally as in the United States. Concentrate producers, local bottlers, and retail outlets were found in most areas, yet in many countries product lines were narrower and channels were relatively undeveloped.

In the late 1980s, international per capita consumption, excluding the Soviet Union and China, was 15% of the U.S. levels. The outlook for international soft

9. *The Wall Street Journal,* October 1, 1991.

drink sales was strong for the 1990s, with expected growth between 8% and 12% per year.

Coca-Cola

Coca-Cola estimated that its worldwide market share of soft drinks was 47% in 1990. Coke's lead was particularly strong in Europe, where its market share was 50%, and in Japan, where it held an 80% share of cola sales. Earnings from Japanese operations accounted for 21% of the company's total earnings in 1990, with Europe comprising 33%, and other international markets totaling 26%.

Coca-Cola used several tactics to develop its international markets. In Taiwan, for example, Coca-Cola took a 49% stake in its Taiwan bottler, a family-owned concern which lacked capital, and expanded its management and facilities. Coca-Cola improved point-of-sale marketing, increased advertising, and introduced new packaging sizes. Promotions included baseball and basketball seminars led by American coaches, concert sponsorships for pop artists such as Stevie Wonder, and an invitation to the chef of the Taipei Hilton to create 10 Chinese dishes using Coke. Coke increased its market share in Taiwan from 6% to 40% between 1985 and 1990, while limiting Seven-Up and Pepsi to a combined share of 4%.[10] In France, Coca-Cola bought out the contract of a poorly performing franchisee in 1989. By 1990, sales volume in France had increased 23%. Just days after the Berlin wall fell, Coca-Cola shipped soda to East Germany from a new plant in Dunkirk.

PepsiCo

In 1990, PepsiCo's worldwide soft drink market share was less than half of Coca-Cola's. At its first ever international convention in 1990, Pepsi Cola announced plans to spend $1 billion in five years to upgrade overseas plants, improve distribution and bolster international marketing programs. The company estimated that its overseas volume would increase from its current level of 2 billion cases to 5 billion cases by 1995 and set the goal of closing the international sales gap between Coke and Pepsi. Coca-Cola international executives stated that Pepsi was "dreaming."

Although Pepsi-Cola operated in at least 150 countries, executives conceded that the company had not made much money outside Canada and the Middle East, where it held the leadership position in a number of countries. In those markets in which PepsiCo was a distant number two to Coca-Cola, its profit margin averaged 6% compared with a 14% margin in the United States and 12% in international sales of snack foods.[11] Pepsi-Cola planned to focus on the most lucrative international markets and to increase its share of markets such as Europe (where it held a 10% share) and Japan (where it held a 9% share) by emphasizing diet colas, vending machines, and fountain sales. In 1990, 11 times as many vending machines per capita were installed in the United States as in Europe.

In 1990, Wayne Calloway stated that Pepsi would use "guerrilla warfare" to attack Coke in selected international markets, noting that "as big as [Coca-Cola is], you certainly don't want a shootout at high noon."[12]

10. *Business Week,* November 26, 1990.
11. *The Wall Street Journal,* June 13, 1991.
12. Ibid.

CORPORATE DIRECTIONS

In 1989, Coca-Cola sold its 49% stake in Columbia Pictures to Sony Corporation and reinvested the money in its overseas soft drink operations. The chief operating officer of Coca-Cola stated that the company's "business in the 1990s will be to grow the world." Coca-Cola targeted an 8% to 10% growth rate in its international sales and planned to accelerate its practice of taking minority interests in joint ventures with key overseas bottlers.

Pepsi executives defined the company's critical challenges in the 1990s as penetrating new distribution channels and focusing on low cost production. In 1991, Pepsi-Cola executives stated that they would target one million "distribution opportunities—ranging from a hot dog stand to large accounts—where you can buy a Coke but you can't buy a Pepsi."

In the two years ending in 1990, PepsiCo invested over $2 billion, 40% of its domestic capital spending, in its restaurant chains, Taco Bell, Pizza Hut, and Kentucky Fried Chicken. During the same two year period, over $1.5 billion, the bulk of international spending, was invested in the international snack food group, whose operating profit margins averaged 15%.

APPENDIX

Smaller Concentrate Producers

Although the two largest concentrate producers have led many of the changes in the soft drink industry that have occurred since the 1950s, smaller concentrate producers have also played an important role in the industry's evolution.

Seven-Up

After World War II, Seven-Up emphasized its product's medicinal benefits for both children and adults, with slogans such as "Tune Tiny Tummies" and "Cure for Seven Hangovers." The product was also widely used as a mixer with alcoholic beverages. Seven-Up and Seagram's Seven Crown whiskey became a particularly popular drink. The cost to bottlers of Seven-Up concentrate was approximately 15% higher than Coca-Cola, because it required less sugar and thus saved its bottlers some sweetener cost. At retail, Seven-Up sold at prices that were comparable to Coca-Cola.

In the 1960s, Seven-Up found that its sales were significantly skewed toward older buyers and that its product was viewed as an aid for indigestion or as a mixer, but not as a soft drink. In 1968, Seven-Up launched its "Uncola" advertising campaign, which was designed to position Seven-Up to the 16- to 24-year age group as the soft drink alternative to colas. In 1970, Seven-Up introduced a diet version of its product, which contained saccharin. Consumer taste surveys indicated that Diet Seven-Up had less aftertaste than other diet colas containing saccharin. As a result of its changes, Seven-Up became the dominant soft drink in the lemon-lime category, which comprised approximately 12% of the total soft drink market during the 1960s and 1970s.

In 1978, Seven-Up was acquired by Philip Morris, a leading cigarette and beer producer, for $520 million, or 20 times earnings. To arrest the decline in market share that had begun in 1974, Philip Morris embarked on a restructuring and

upgrading program and placed experienced executives from the cigarette and beer industries in key Seven-Up positions. Promotional support to bottlers and chain stores was reduced, marketing expenditures were increased substantially, and a new ad campaign, "America's Turning Seven-Up," was designed to boost consumer awareness. Although sales improved, the soft drink company recorded losses in the first four years of the 1980s. In 1981, Philip Morris decided to exploit the fact that Seven-Up had never contained caffeine by adopting the advertising slogan, "Never had it, never will." Advertisements showed other soft drink brands that contained caffeine and implied that caffeine was unhealthy.

By the mid-1980s, Seven-Up's declining share and minimal profits fed rumors that Philip Morris would sell its soft drink operations. After Philip Morris purchased General Foods for $5.7 billion in October 1985, expectations that it would sell Seven-Up grew. Shortly thereafter, PepsiCo announced that it would purchase Seven-Up without its company-owned bottlers, for $380 million. In February 1986, the Coca-Cola Company announced that it would purchase Dr Pepper Company from Forstmann Little & Company for $470 million.

PepsiCo's purchase of Seven-Up's domestic operations was blocked by the Federal Trade Commission. Pepsi eventually purchased Seven-Up's Canadian and international operations for $246 million. Once PepsiCo lost its bid for Seven-Up's domestic operations, Coca-Cola dropped its pursuit of Dr Pepper.

The Dr Pepper/Seven-Up Company

Philip Morris sold its interests in Seven-Up's domestic soft drink operations to an investment firm led by the partners Hicks & Haas. By October 1986, Hicks & Haas completed leveraged buyouts of A&W Brands, Inc., a specialty concentrate producer operating in niche markets, for $75 million; Dr Pepper's concentrate business for $416 million; and Seven-Up's domestic soft drink operations for $240 million. At the end of 1986, Hicks & Haas held a 13.5% share of the U.S. soft drink market and was the third largest concentrate producer.

In 1986, the management (but not the operations) of Dr Pepper and Seven-Up were merged, and in 1988, ownership was transferred to management and investment bankers (75%) and employees (25%). Between 1986 and 1990, Dr Pepper experienced strong sales growth in the South and West, where its operations were focused, and from the introduction of Diet Dr Pepper. Seven-Up maintained its nationwide distribution but experienced sales decline in 1988, 1989, and 1990. The company diverted marketing funds from Seven-Up and Diet Seven-Up for two disappointing product introductions and reduced its total marketing budget in 1989 and 1990.

Consolidation of Small Producers

In 1984, the Royal Crown Company was acquired by financier Victor Posner. In the same year, the Canada Dry brand was sold to R.J. Reynolds, which also purchased the Sunkist brand from General Cinema in 1984, combining it with earlier purchases of Del Monte Division's Hawaiian Punch and Cott Beverages. By 1985, R.J. Reynolds controlled 4.6% of the U.S. soft drink market.

In June 1986, R.J. Reynolds abandoned its aspirations of becoming a noncola soft drink power and sold its Canada Dry and Sunkist soft drink operations to Cadbury-Schweppes. The sale included the brands Canada Dry, the nation's top-selling ginger ale; Schweppes, the leading tonic water; Canada Dry Seltzers,

leaders in the club soda/seltzer category; and Sunkist orange soda, which had experienced a severe sales decline. In 1989, Cadbury-Schweppes Beverages acquired Crush International from Procter & Gamble, including the Crush and Hire's brands. In the same year, the company also relocated its beverage headquarters from London, England, to Stamford, Connecticut. In 1990, Cadbury-Schweppes refranchised its Canada Dry, Hire's, and Crush products, with the goal of making the brands national.

CASE

8

The Computer Industry: The New Industry of Industries?

INTRODUCTION

Peter Drucker once referred to the automobile industry as the "industry of industries," not only because of the size and complexity of the industry but also because the rise of the automobile has revolutionized the way people live and work in the twentieth century. Many believe that the computer industry is now in the process of surpassing the automobile industry as the "industry of industries." According to the U.S. Commerce Department, the combined computer and electronics sector of the U.S. economy is now 40 percent larger than the automobile industry and represents the largest single industry in the United States.[1] Worldwide, the computer industry is still smaller than the automobile industry, but it is catching up fast. More important than any comparison of size, however, is the impact that the computer revolution is now having, and will continue to have, on the way people live and work. The transformation in society ushered in by the microprocessor promises to be every bit as profound as that wrought by the internal combustion engine. For companies competing in this industry, this represents an enormous opportunity. But at the same time, driven by relentless technological innovation, changes in the structure of the industry that have occurred over the past decade have altered dramatically the nature of competition, forcing prices and profit margins down and driving some long-established competitors, such as IBM and Digital Equipment, deep into the red. This case looks in detail at the changes that have taken place in the structure of the computer industry over the past two decades and at the changes that might take place in the future.

THE INDUSTRY PRIOR TO 1980

Until the late 1970s nearly all computers were complex machines used to perform mind-numbing calculations and routine bookkeeping chores. They were used mostly at medium-sized and large companies, universities, and government bureaucracies. They came in two basic sizes—mainframes and minicomputers. Mainframes managed the major data processing needs of large organizations. Smaller and less expensive minicomputers were used in smaller organizations or the divisions of large organizations. All of these systems were multi-user systems

This case was prepared by Charles W. L. Hill, University of Washington. This case was prepared as a basis for class discussion rather than to illustrate either effective or ineffective handling of administrative situations.

1. Standard & Poor's Industry Surveys, *Computers*, December 31, 1992.

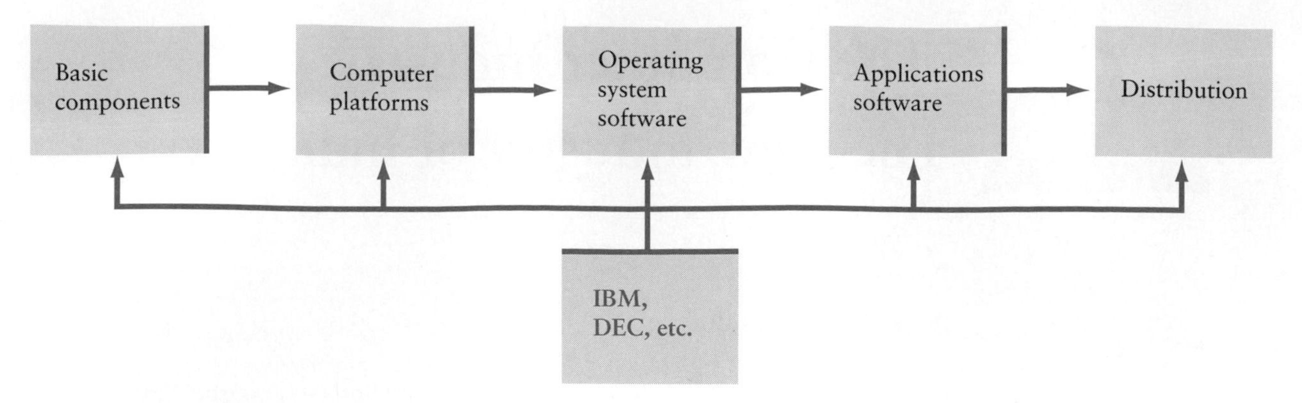

Figure 1
The Vertical Structure of the Computer Industry–Pre-1980

that could be accessed by several individuals at once through remote terminals. They usually required their own specialist support staff to maintain them. They were also, by modern standards, slow and expensive—by the late 1970s a typical mainframe could cost $1 million to purchase and $100,000 per year to operate.[2] Given such costs, demand was limited. In 1980, for example, worldwide demand amounted to 10,000 mainframes and 105,000 minicomputers.[3] This compares with worldwide demand for personal computers and workstations in 1990 of 25 million units.[4]

IBM was the dominant force in this industry. In 1980 IBM accounted for 38 percent of the industry's revenues, 60 percent of its profits, and 75 percent of worldwide mainframe sales.[5] Other industry players included mainframe manufacturers such as Amdahl, Burroughs, Control Data, Fujitsu, ICL, and Sperry and a handful of minicomputer manufacturers including, most notably, Digital Equipment Corporation (DEC), Hewlett-Packard, and Wang. Most of these companies pursued a very similar strategy: they were all vertically integrated enterprises that sold systems based upon their own proprietary standards for hardware and software. Thus, for example, software written for an IBM machine could not be run on a DEC machine.

The vertical structure of the industry is illustrated in Figure 1. As can be seen, there were five main stages in the process of creating a computer. The first was manufacturing basic components such as the central processing unit (CPU), disk drives, and memory devices. The second stage involved assembling these components into computer platforms. The third stage was the development of an operating system to run the computer's hardware. The design of an operating system depended upon the type of hardware used. The fourth stage was developing applications software for activities such as data base management, word processing, payroll processing, inventory control, and general ledger accounting systems. Applications software had to be compatible with the operating system of a machine. The fifth and final stage of the industry was distribution. Most computer companies at this time were involved in all five stages of the industry. This was certainly true for the two largest computer companies, IBM and DEC.

2. "Personal Best," *The Economist, The Computer Industry,* February 27, 1993, p. 5.
3. Ibid.
4. Stratford Sherman, "The New Computer Revolution," *Fortune* , June 14, 1993, pp. 56–84.
5. "Personal Best," *The Economist, The Computer Industry*, February 27, 1993, p. 5.

THE MIGHTY MICROPROCESSOR

No one factor has done more to change the structure of the computer industry over the last two decades than the emergence of high-powered, low-cost microprocessors. In 1971 Intel developed the first microprocessor. Prior to this period the brains of a computer—the central processing unit, or CPU—was not a single computer chip. No single chip could contain enough switches to handle all of a computer's needs, so designers had to use a number of processor chips to construct a CPU, perhaps as many as six. In addition, mainframes produced during the 1960s utilized another 20 or so processor chips to handle specialized tasks, such as routing data to and from the magnetic tapes where data was stored. Using a new technology, referred to as complimentary metal oxide semiconductor (CMOS), Intel managed to cram most of the switches necessary to run a computer on a single chip.

In a statement that was to prove prophetic, Intel claimed that its new programmable "microcomputer on a chip" had "ushered in a new era of integrated electronics." However, Intel first had to increase the power of the microprocessor. The power of a microprocessor is measured by the millions of instructions per second (MIPS) it can carry. (An instruction is one line of software code.) The first Intel microprocessor, the 4004 series, had 2,300 transistors and a rating of 0.06 MIPS (it could carry 60,000 instructions a second.)[6] By comparison, a typical modern mainframe carries a rating of 100 MIPS. With such a power gap, the microprocessor initially was not taken very seriously. However, in 1978 Intel produced the first generation of the microprocessor that was to make it rich, the 8086 chip. The 8086 chip had 29,000 transistors and a rating of 0.6 MIPS, making it ten times faster than its predecessor.

A variant of the 8086, the 8088, caught the eye of IBM in 1980 when it was looking for a microprocessor to power its first personal computer. Introduced in 1981, the IBM machine sold in the millions, rapidly becoming the industry standard. However, since the main components of IBM's PC, the Intel 8088 CPU and the MS-DOS operating system, could be bought "off-the-shelf," there was nothing to stop would-be imitators from making their own "clones" of IBM's machine. To maintain IBM compatibility, all of these clones used the MS-DOS operating system. DOS in turn ran only on microprocessors that used chips designed according to Intel's standard—a standard tightly controlled by Intel.

With revenues and earnings growing at a compound rate of 65 percent, Intel invested heavily to develop new, more powerful generations of its microprocessor. Known as the "X86" series, these have included the 286, 386, 486, and Pentium chip. The 486 chip has 1.2 million transistors and a rating of 54 MIPS. The Pentium chip, introduced in 1993, contains a staggering 3.2 million transistors and has a rating of 100 MIPS—as much as a modern mainframe. Despite its power, the cost of an individual chip is surprisingly low. Most of the costs are up front in the form of huge R&D and capital costs. Intel spent $900 million on R&D in 1992, nearly three times what it spent in 1989. Further, Intel estimates that building a plant to produce the 386 chip cost $200 million, the 486 chip cost $1 billion, and full-scale production of the Pentium will require an investment of $5 billion.[7] However, the operating costs of these plants are low. A 486 chip, which was sell-

6. "The Coming Clash of Logic," *The Economist*, July 3, 1993, pp. 21–23.
7. Ibid.

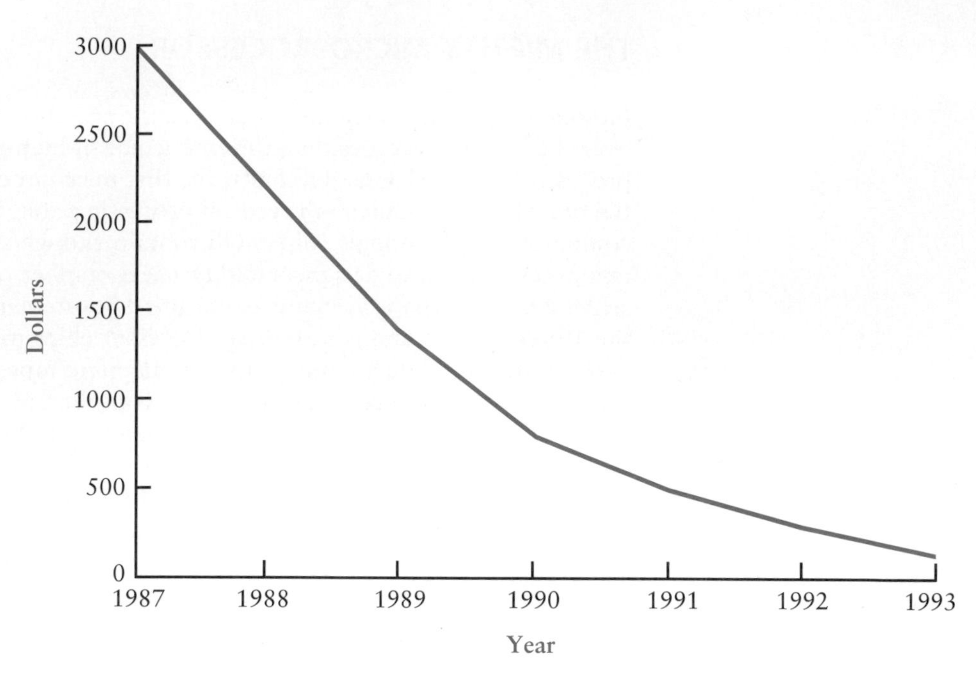

Figure 2
Cost of Computing Power per MIPS for Personal Computers (in Dollars)

ing for a $300 a unit in mid 1993, costs Intel only $20 to produce. In other words, once Intel recoups the fixed costs associated with developing a new chip and setting up a plant, it can make enormous returns. With over 40 million personal computers forecast to be shipped in 1993, 90 percent of which will be equipped with Intel microprocessors, the volume is certainly there to make this possible.

One tangible consequence of the economics and the science of making microprocessors has been the rapid fall in the price of computing power, as measured in MIPS, that has occurred in recent years. Figure 2 illustrates the rapid fall in the cost of computing power between 1987 and 1993. As can be seen, the cost of computing power per MIPS fell from $3,000 in 1987 to under $200 by 1993, and it will continue to fall in the future as new microprocessors such as the Pentium come on-stream. As a result of advances in microprocessor technology, on average, personal computers doubled in power and halved in price every 18 months.

Intel's Competition

Until recently, Intel faced little direct competition. Although Motorola also produced microprocessors for Apple computers, Apple's relatively small market share similarly limited Motorola's share of total microprocessor sales. In recent years, however, Intel has faced increasing competitive threats from two sources: manufacturers of Intel clones and manufacturers of microprocessors that utilize the so-called RISC technology.

Intel Clones

Under the terms of its original agreement with IBM, Intel had to allow a second supplier to produce its chips under license. Since 1982 Advanced Micro Devices (AMD) has been making chips for Intel under license, exchanging the right to produce Intel's chips for AMD-designed products. This arrangement broke down in 1985 when Intel launched its 386 microprocessor. Intel claimed that AMD had not delivered any worthwhile products and withdrew AMD's license. The dispute went to court and has been bouncing from judge to judge ever since.

In 1991 AMD felt confident enough of winning its case to launch its own version of Intel's 386 chip. It was soon joined by Cyrix, a privately owned Texas chipmaker. By early 1993 AMD had managed to capture half of the 386 market with chips that were both cheaper and more powerful than those produced by Intel. Intel was forced into a price war, which cut the price of 386 microprocessors 40 percent in less than a year. Intel also continued to fight both AMD and Cyrix in the courts. In June 1993 the California appeals court threw out AMD's rights to Intel's technology. AMD promptly appealed to California's supreme court and continued to sell the 386 chip. Moreover, in early 1993 both AMD and Cyrix entered the 486 market with copied chips that Intel claims they have no right to sell. Nonetheless, at best, AMD and Cyrix had the capacity to serve only 15 percent of the demand for 486 chips.

RISC Technology While Intel continues to dominate the microprocessor market despite the presence of AMD, Cyrix, and Motorola, the company may not always have things its own way. Intel's microprocessors use a technology known as Complex Instruction Set Computing (CISC). An alternative microprocessor technology, known as Reduced Instruction Set Computing (RISC), was pioneered by IBM in the 1970s. RISC technology recently has begun to emerge as a possible threat to Intel's hegemony in the microprocessor market. RISC technology cuts the number of instructions that a microprocessor has to handle to complete a task, thereby increasing the speed of the chip. RISC microprocessors have long been able to deliver more speed per dollar than CISC microprocessors but have remained in the personal computing wilderness because they have been unable to take instructions from popular personal computer software, which was written for Intel's CISC chips. What may be changing the equation is the emergence of Microsoft's new Windows NT software.

Microsoft's MS-DOS operating system and Windows graphical interface, which run on Intel microprocessors, have emerged as standards in the industry. Windows NT, which was due to be introduced in mid 1993, is an operating system aimed at the fast-growing market for software that can link networks of personal computers together (the NT stands for "new technology"). Windows NT should be able to run software written for previous versions of Windows. Unlike Windows, however, Windows NT will work not only with Intel's chips, but with a number of RISC-based microprocessors, all of which are reportedly as fast as Intel's Pentium. These include microprocessors made by Digital Equipment (the Alpha Chip), Silicon Graphic's MIPS subsidiary, and the Power PC microprocessor, which is the product of an alliance among IBM, Apple, and Motorola. The Power PC reportedly is as fast as Intel's Pentium chip, while DEC's Alpha chip is faster. Motorola began shipping the first Power PC chips in June 1993 for $450 per unit. This compares to the $975 per unit Intel is charging for its Pentium.[8]

RISC chips still face many obstacles. Perhaps the key issue is whether the RISC chips will be able to run popular software designed for Microsoft's MS-DOS and Windows operating systems. Although the Windows NT operating system should run on a number of RISC chips, it can do so only through a technological trick called emulation, which slows down the operation of the software, thereby nullifying the most powerful advantage of RISC microprocessors—their speed. The manufacturers of RISC chips also have to pursue manufacturers of personal computers to use their chip rather than Intel's. Most are holding off on this issue until it has

8. P. Burrows, "Challenging the King of Chips," *Business Week*, July 26, 1993, pp. 76–77.

been shown that RISC chips can run popular Windows software. So far, only Apple and IBM have committed themselves to incorporating a RISC chip in their PCs, the Power PC, and they are part of the alliance that developed the chip.

THE PERSONAL COMPUTER REVOLUTION

The personal computer market was born in the late 1970s when a number of companies, including Apple, Commodore, and Tandy, began marketing PCs. What made the PC possible was the development of the microprocessor. The most successful of the early personal computer companies was Apple, which utilized a Motorola microprocessor and its own proprietary operating system. Alone among its rivals. Apple saw itself as "changing the world."[9] The Apple II, introduced in 1979, was the machine that promised to do just that. By 1980 Apple had grown into a $117 million company while the microcomputer market itself was generating revenues of about $1 billion—large enough to attract the attention of IBM.

IBM Jumps into the Fray

Alarmed by the rapid growth of this new market segment, in July 1980 IBM established a team in its Entry Systems Division and gave it the task of developing a personal computer. The time frame was an unheard-of one for IBM: one year! Bill Lowe, head of the IBM team, which was code-named Project Chess, knew that it was impossible to build a PC from scratch in one year. The best that they could do was gather hardware and software from other companies, get these components to work together as a system, and then stick an IBM label on the machine. That is what they did. In the process they broke with the IBM tradition of keeping software and hardware development in-house. For the brains of the system—the central processing unit—they chose the 8088 microprocessor, manufactured by Intel. To control the Intel 8088, IBM chose MS-DOS, an operating system sold by Microsoft, then an obscure Seattle software company. IBM did not demand any kind of exclusive deal with these two companies. Lowe and his team further broke with IBM tradition by publishing full technical details of the system, including software codes. The intention here was to make it easy for independent software companies to write software applications for the IBM machine—such as word processing and spreadsheet software. Lowe and his team recognized that it was not technical wizardry that sold computers, it was software applications. By breaking with IBM practice and adopting an open standard, they hoped to encourage the rapid development of software applications.

In theory, establishing an open standard made imitation easy. IBM believed, however, that it could maintain control over the technology. Its rationale was the IBM PC's ROM-BIOS chip. ROM stands for "read only memory," and BIOS for "basic input/output system." The BIOS of a computer is a special computer code that links the operating system of the computer to its hardware. The BIOS of the

9. For an entertaining history of the early days of the computer industry, see R. X. Cringely, *Accidental Empires,* New York: HarperBusiness, 1992. Much of this section is drawn from this source.

IBM PC was stored in the ROM chip installed on the main computer circuit board of the machine. To be completely compatible with the IBM PC, an imitator would have to either use IBM's ROM-BIOS chip, which was not for sale, or devise a chip just like IBM's. But here was the catch: the lines of the computer code stored in the ROM chip were copyrighted by IBM, so copying the code in IBM's BIOS chip would violate copyright laws. Since operating system and application software written for IBM's ROM-BIOS would not function on any other ROM-BIOS system, IBM thought that it had a way of curtailing imitation. It was wrong.

Enter the Clones

Introduced on schedule in mid 1981, the IBM PC was an instant success. Backed by the legendary IBM brand name, business users turned in droves to the machine. By 1983 IBM had 40 percent of the market for personal computers and demand was outstripping IBM's ability to supply the market. But from that point on it was all downhill. IBM had badly miscalculated. A small start-up company in Houston called Compaq Computer succeeded in doing what IBM thought highly unlikely: it produced a copy of IBM's ROM-BIOS chip without violating IBM's copyright. It did this by writing its own software code that enabled Compaq's chip to perform the same functions as the IBM chip, without using the same code. Compaq introduced its first personal computer—a misnamed 28-pound portable—in September 1982.

What Compaq could do other companies could, and did. Soon another company, Phoenix Technologies, succeeded in reverse engineering the IBM chip. Unlike Compaq, however, Phoenix did not make personal computers. Instead it sold its IBM-compatible ROM-BIOS chips to anyone who wanted one, in effect opening the doors to a flood of imitators—the so-called clone manufacturers. Soon start-up companies were springing up all over the globe manufacturing IBM-compatible PCs. Like Compaq, many of these clone makers sold to dealers who could not get enough machines from IBM. Like Compaq, they also found that without IBM's overhead they were able to underprice IBM's PC by about $800.

IBM responded in 1984 by lowering its price on the PC and introducing the PC-AT, a completely new personal computer that was powered by Intel's 80286 microprocessor. Compared to the IBM PC, the AT was very fast. It was also innovative, with a 20 megabyte hard disk drive in addition to the standard floppy disk drives. At $4,000 per unit, it was also rather expensive. More problematic than the high price, however, was the fact that the early ATs were flawed. The hard disk drives incorporated in the early AT models had a tendency to crash because of a faulty drive controller card. The problem had arisen because the AT had been rushed to market without adequately testing the hard disk drive. IBM had to halt production while it developed a new controller card. This created an opening for the clone manufacturers, which were able to imitate the AT and step into the breach. Again, Compaq was first. The company was shipping its own 286 Deskpro machines only six months after IBM had introduced the AT and months before IBM resolved the disk drive problem and resumed shipments of the AT.

Again, others followed, and IBM's market share began to slide. By 1986 IBM's share had slipped to 17.3 percent, followed by Apple with 11.4 percent. In 1986 IBM took another knock when Compaq beat it to the market by six months

Figure 3
Worldwide Revenues from Personal Computers and Other Computer Hardware (in Billions of Dollars)

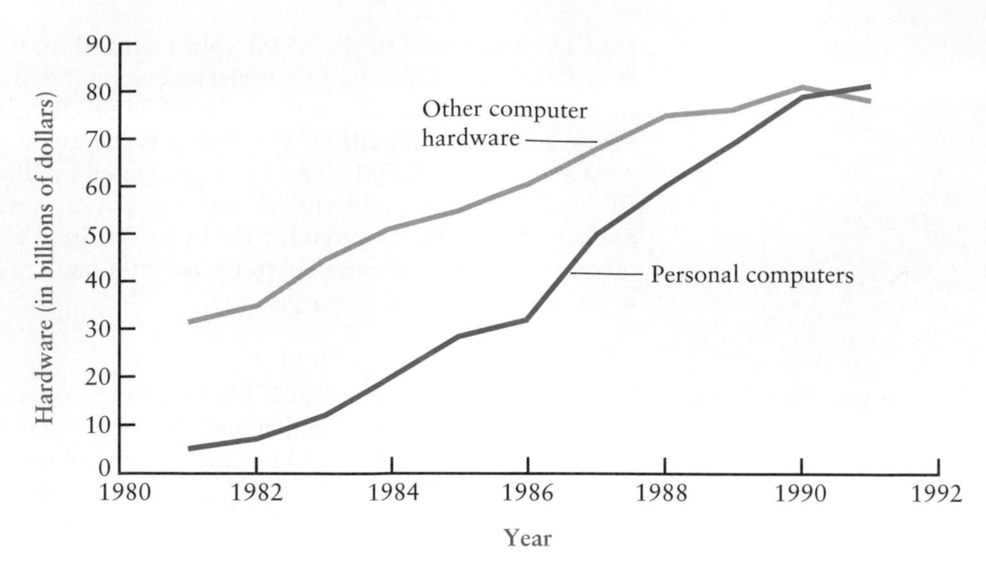

with a new personal computer based on Intel's 386 microprocessor. At the same time, a flood of new companies continued to enter the PC market. These included Dell Computer, AST, and Gateway 2000, all of which specialized in the provision of low-priced IBM-compatible clones. Dell, in particular, changed the rules of the game in the industry by selling directly to customers via mail order, rather than through computer dealers.

The Early 1990s

Fueled by the flood of low-priced clones, continual improvements in computing power and software applications, and repeated waves of new product introductions, growth in personal computer shipments exploded. In 1983 less than 5 million personal computers were shipped. In 1987 the figure was 16 million, in 1990 it was 24 million, and by 1993 the number was closer to 30 million.[10] Forecasts suggest that shipments of PCs may close in on 45 million units per year by 1996.[11] In 1991 worldwide revenues from personal computer sales, at $80 billion, surpassed for the first time revenues from all other computer hardware, which was valued at $78 billion (see Figure 3 for details).[12] In 1992 U.S. sales of personal computers were around $34 billion, dwarfing all other segments of the computer industry. By comparison, revenues from mainframe sales in the United States were only $13 billion.[13]

The leaders in this market were IBM, Apple, Compaq, NEC, and Dell (see Figure 4 for market share figures).[14] Apple and NEC both manufacture proprietary systems utilizing their own operating systems. As such, their share of the market is likely to remain limited to no more than the 15 percent to 17 percent they cur-

10. Standard & Poor's Industry Surveys, *Computers*, December 31, 1992.
11. Stratford Sherman, "The New Computer Revolution,"*Fortune*, June 14, 1993, pp. 56–84.
12. J. W. Verity, "Deconstructing the Computer Industry," *Business Week*, November 23, 1993, pp. 90–100.
13. Standard & Poor's Industry Surveys, *Computers*, December 31, 1992.
14. "Duel," *The Economist*, January 30, 1993, pp. 57–58.

Figure 4
Worldwide Market Share in Personal Computers, 1992 (by Value)

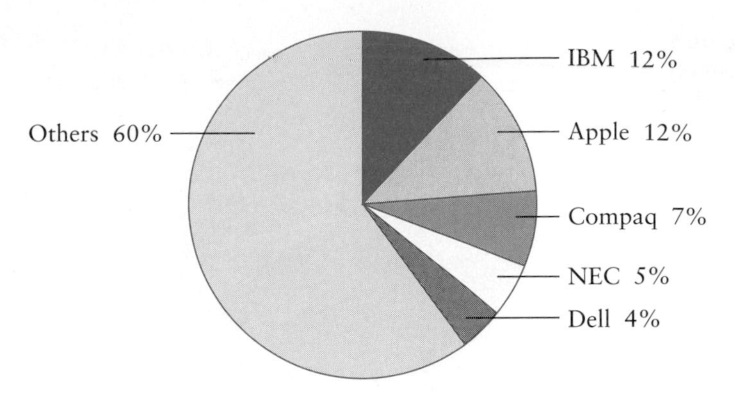

rently account for. IBM, Compaq, and Dell all manufacture IBM-compatible systems. At 12 percent, IBM's share of the market had declined from 40 percent in 1983 and 17 percent in 1986. Among them, IBM, Compaq, and Dell accounted for 22.5 percent of the world market for personal computers in 1992. The remaining 60 percent was taken up by a myriad of IBM-compatible clone manufacturers including, most notably, AST, Packard Bell, Gateway 2000, and Zeos.

Several notable changes in the nature of the industry also took place in the early 1990s. The first was the growth in demand for home computers. In the mid 1980s only about 8 percent of personal computers were sold for use in the home, while 80 percent were sold for use in businesses. By 1992, however, 27 percent of all personal computers were sold for use at home, while 64 percent were sold for use in businesses.[15] The shift toward home use is perhaps not surprising given that virtually all large and medium-sized businesses had personal computers by 1992. In contrast, only 25 percent of U.S. households had a personal computer in 1992.[16] Industry analysts predict that by 1996, 42 percent of all personal computers will be sold for home use, 36 percent for use in small and medium-sized businesses, and only 16 percent for use in large businesses—down from 30 percent in 1992.[17] The predicted decline in the proportion of sales accounted for by large businesses reflects saturation in this particular market segment.

A related change was in the channels of distribution used. As of 1989, 63 percent of all personal computers, by value, were shipped through traditional computer dealers. By 1992 this figure had slumped to 50 percent. Part of the reason for the slump was the trend to sell personal computers via mail order which had been pioneered by Dell Computer and Zeos. Also responsible was the increasing number of personal computers sold through discount retailers such as Costco and Wal-Mart. For further details of distribution channels, see Figure 5.[18]

Perhaps the most significant change to take place in the early 1990s, however, was the emergence of wide-scale price discounting. The price cutting was started by trouble at Compaq. In 1991 Compaq's sales fell by 9 percent to \$3.3 billion and its net profit by 71 percent to \$131 million. Compaq reacted to these problems by ousting its CEO and founder, Rod Canion, in early 1992 and replacing

15. P. Burrows, "There's No Place Like Home," *Business Week*, September 6, 1993, p. 80.
16. Standard & Poor's Industry Surveys, *Computers*, December 31, 1992.
17. P. Burrows, "There's No Place Like Home," *Business Week*, September 6, 1993, p. 80.
18. Standard & Poor's Industry Surveys, *Computers*, December 31, 1992.

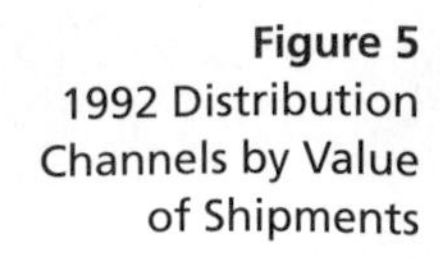

Figure 5
1992 Distribution Channels by Value of Shipments

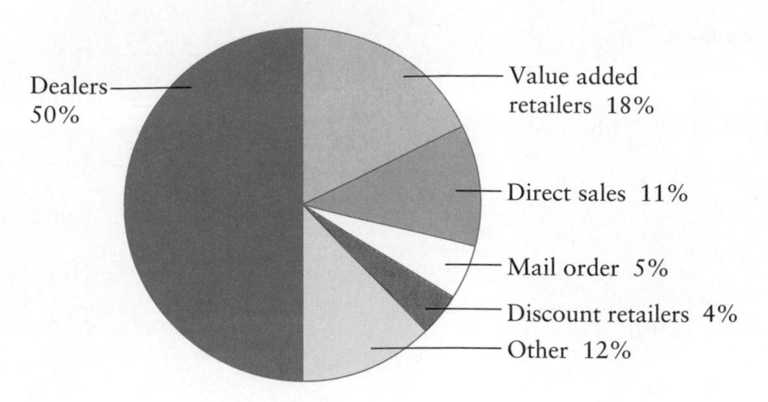

him with Eckhard Pfieffer. Under Pfieffer's leadership, the company bought out a new range of low-priced computers in June 1992 aimed primarily at the home and small business markets. Prior to 1992 Compaq had targeted major corporate customers—in 1991 they bought 80 percent of all Compaq machines. The new machines were priced at one-third of Compaq's old range of machines and less than the prices charged by many clone makers. The clone makers responded by cutting their prices, and Compaq responded in October 1992 by cutting its prices by another third. This was followed in January by further cuts of around 16 percent on some models. Compaq's price cutting did not just elicit responses from the clone makers—IBM and Apple also cut their prices. The price cutting at Apple was particularly dramatic, since the company had long had a policy of premium pricing for its proprietary Macintosh system.

As a result of repeated rounds of price cutting, between mid 1991 and mid 1993, the price of a typical high-end personal computer—such as one utilizing an Intel 486 DX/33—fell from around $3,200 to just under $2,000.[19] The price cutting helped demand surge during 1992 and 1993—worldwide unit shipments of PCs increased by 15 percent in 1992. However, the price cutting also put pressure on margins. Industry average net profit margins for 1993 were predicted to run it at around 2 percent, down from 8 percent in 1990.[20]

A shortening of product life cycles has been another response to competitive pressures in the industry. With prices being continually cut, companies are trying to get ahead of their competitors by introducing new products more frequently. They believe that the company that is first to market with a leading edge technology can charge higher prices than its rivals, thereby escaping the quagmire of a price war. In 1990 the average computer spent about a year in the catalogue before being replaced. Now machines are being replaced by more advanced and powerful models every six months. To a large degree, the shortening of product life cycles has been helped along by the rapid growth in the laptop and notebook segment of the personal computer market. During the 1990s there was a profusion of new product offerings in this segment.

Apple Stands Alone

Ever since IBM introduced its PC in 1981, and was quickly followed by a clutch of imitators that adhered to IBM's de facto standard, industry pioneer Apple Computer has been the odd man out. In contrast to the IBM standard based upon

19. "That Shrinking Feeling," *The Economist*, July 24, 1993, pp. 63–64.
20. Ibid.

Intel's family of microprocessors and Microsoft's MS-DOS operating system, Apple has used Motorola microprocessors and its own proprietary operating system. Apple has always viewed its object-oriented operating system software, which made its computers easy to use, as a source of competitive advantage.

Apple's success dates back to 1979 with the introduction of the Apple II computer. But the company was hit hard by the introduction of the IBM PC. Its response was the Macintosh. Introduced in January 1984, the Macintosh incorporated several innovative features including a screen that could be divided into windows and a "desktop metaphor" that let users launch programs by pointing with a "mouse" at familiar-looking graphics symbols. Reasoning that its innovative features allowed Apple to differentiate itself from the IBM PC and clones, Apple decided to charge a premium price for the Macintosh and then plow some of that back into advertising to gain market share. The strategy did not work. Although an almost fanatical group of "Mac" users did emerge, the Macintosh failed to establish itself as the machine of choice in the corporate world, and Apple's market share continued to decline. From over 13 percent in 1984, Apple saw its share of worldwide PC unit shipments plunge to 7.2 percent in 1987.[21]

In 1987 Apple introduced the Macintosh II range of computers with color screens and superfast Motorola microprocessors. While the machine proved popular with Apple's established customer base, it failed to win converts away from the IBM-compatible standard. By 1990 Apple's market share of worldwide PC unit shipments stood at 6.9 percent—near the point of no return. With such a low market share, Apple was finding it increasingly difficult to pursuade software companies to write applications software for the Mac. Most of them preferred to focus their attention on IBM-compatible machines, which by this time accounted for 90 percent of the installed base of personal computers. The result was that major new software applications and upgrades almost invariably appeared for IBM-compatible machines first. To make matters worse, in 1990 Microsoft introduced Windows 3.0. Windows 3.0, which ran on MS-DOS, incorporated many of the features that made Apple's operating system software so attractive, including a mouse-pointing device, pull-down menus, and an ability to divide the screen into windows.

With the rationale for maintaining a premium price fast disappearing, in 1990 Apple slashed prices in an attempt to build market share. Lower prices did generate extra demand for the Mac. Unit sales in the first half of 1991 ran 85 percent above those in the same time period of 1990. In 1991 Apple's share of units shipped rose to 8.3 percent, while its share of worldwide PC sales by value rose to around 12 percent—a figure it maintained in 1992 and 1993.[22] Apple's ability to hold on to 12 percent of the market was helped by its 1991 introduction of the Powerbook, the first Mac portable, which at the time led the field for innovative notebook computers. The 7.1-pound Powerbook became the first notebook computer to top $1 billion in annual sales. However, the innovative features incorporated in the Powerbook, such as the built-in mouse, were soon imitated by a host of rivals. Moreover, Apple has had to pay for its more aggressive pricing strategy with lower margins. The company's gross margin, which stood at 53 percent in fiscal 1990, declined to 38 percent in the quarter that ended in March 1993, and looks set to fall to the 20–30 percent range that most manufacturers of IBM-compatible machines earn.

21. "What Price Glory," *The Economist*, August 24, 1991, pp. 61–62.
22. Alan Deutschman, "Odd Man Out," *Fortune*, July 26, 1993, pp. 42–56.

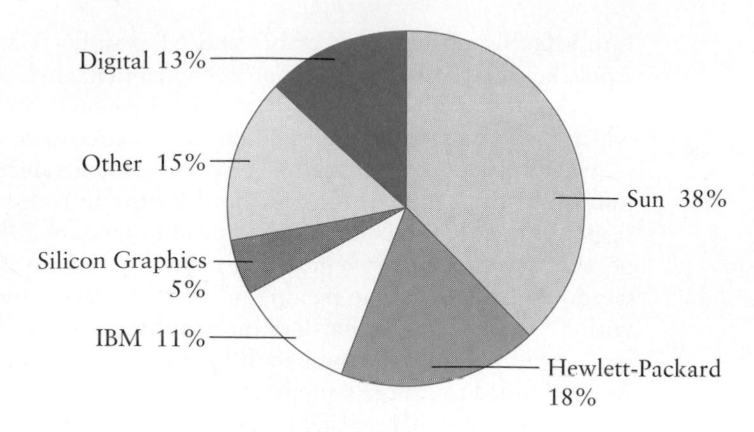

Figure 6
Share of Worldwide Workstation Market, 1992 (Units Shipped)

WORKSTATIONS, MINICOMPUTERS, AND MAINFRAMES

In addition to personal computers, the computer market also contains three other segments: the workstation, minicomputer, and mainframe computer segments. In 1991 while worldwide sales of computers were valued at $80 billion, workstations were $10 billion, minicomputers were $40 billion, and mainframes were about $28 billion.[23] Of the three segments, the workstation segment is currently growing fastest. While demand for both mainframes and minis slipped during the early 1990s, and may continue to fall for the rest of the decade, demand for workstations has grown at a healthy pace.

Workstations

Workstations are high-powered desktop computers with advanced graphics capabilities. Most use RISC-based microprocessors and the UNIX operating system, which originally was developed by AT&T. They have found their biggest market in the engineering and scientific communities, where they are used for applications such as computer-aided design.

The workstation market was created by Apollo Computer in 1982, although the market did not take off until Sun Microsystems introduced its first workstation in 1983. The market grew rapidly in the mid 1980s, reaching $4.5 billion in 1988. By 1991 the worldwide market was valued at $10 billion and it was predicted to grow to $12.5 billion by 1993—making it roughly 15 percent of the size of the personal computer market.[24] As with personal computers, the price of workstations has been falling as their power has increased. Most low-end workstations now sell for only marginally more than high-end personal computers. The current market leader is Sun Microsystems, which in 1992 accounted for about 38 percent of all workstations shipped (see Figure 6 for details).[25] Sun is followed by Hewlett-Packard (which acquired Apollo) with 18 percent of the market, Digital Equipment Corporation, with around 13 percent of the market, and IBM with 11 percent of the market.

23. Standard & Poor's Industry Surveys, *Computers*, December 31, 1992.
24. Ibid.
25. Ibid.

The strategy of market leader Sun has been to try and establish its Sparc RISC microprocessor and its SunOS version of the UNIX operating system as industry standards. However, Sun faces formidable competition. In 1992 and 1993 Digital Equipment unveiled new systems based upon its Alpha chip. The advantage of DEC's Alpha chip is that it can run on both UNIX and Windows NT operating systems, which may allow the company to bridge the gap between workstations and personal computers. Hewlett-Packard and IBM have also emerged as formidable competitors and are marketing workstations based upon their own RISC chips and versions of UNIX. In addition, Silicon Graphics has emerged as a strong force in the market for workstations with advanced three-dimensional graphic capabilities.

The growth in demand for workstations is now starting to be fueled by increasing demand for client/server systems. A typical client/server system consists of a powerful workstation configured as a file server. Users, typically equipped with either personal computers or low-end workstations, are linked to the server via a local area network(LAN). Users apply their own tools and software applications to manipulate the data stored on a server. Alternatively, they may access the server to use specialized applications that require high power and that are stored on the server. Client/server systems linked together by LANs are now making rapid inroads into the corporate community, where they are taking over many of the functions previously performed by mainframes and minicomputers.

One factor holding back the growth of the workstation market has been a failure to standardize different versions of the UNIX operating system. Each major workstation company has written its own version of UNIX. The result is a series of incompatible operating systems. The lack of a standardized UNIX operating system has limited the availability of applications software. Since an application written for one version of UNIX may not run on another version of UNIX, software companies have found themselves faced with the unattractive prospect of writing applications for a series of fragmented market niches. Rather than devote valuable programming resources to such a task, they have focused upon larger markets—such as the personal computer market.

Minicomputers

Minicomputers encompass both small-scale and medium-scale systems. Small-scale systems range in price from $10,000 to $100,000. They are used in automation, control, and communications processing environments. They are also increasingly used as local area network servers where they compete with high-end workstations. Small-scale systems typically support between 2 and 32 users. Medium-scale systems support 33 to 130 users in a commercial environment. The price of an average mid-range system ranges from $100,000 to $1 million. Worldwide sales of mid-range systems were in the $45 billion range in 1992, making them the biggest market segment after personal computers.

During the early 1980s demand in this segment of the industry was growing at 30 percent per year. However, the general maturation of this segment, as well as the loss of market share to high-end workstations and personal computers, slowed growth rates into the low single digits during the early 1990s. This trend is expected to continue as high-end workstations and personal computers become ever more powerful. The inevitable consequence has been the emergence of excess capacity and pricing pressure.

The minicomputer segment is still dominated by vertically integrated companies that use their own proprietary hardware and software. The market leader is IBM, which in 1991 had 18 percent of the worldwide market, followed by Digital Equipment with 11 percent, NEC with 6 percent, Fujitsu with 5 percent, and Hewlett-Packard with 3 percent.[26] In recent years a number of companies that once did well in this segment have exited. These include Wang, Prime Computer, and Control Data. Others, such as Digital Equipment, are in deep financial trouble. In 1992 DEC lost $2.8 billion and ended up firing its CEO and founder, Kenneth Olsen.

Despite such problems, however, both IBM and Hewlett-Packard continue to do well in this segment. IBM, which is beset with troubles elsewhere, has done well with its AS/400 series minicomputer. Although the AS/400 still has proprietary architecture, it is succeeding in part because many users are downsizing from IBM mainframes to the AS/400. They are choosing the AS/400 because of its reliability and power and because of the ease of transition from an IBM mainframe for those downsizing. Moreover, with an installed base of 200,000 AS/400 machines by 1992, there are more software applications available for this platform than perhaps any other in the minicomputer market.

Hewlett-Packard (HP) has done well with a new line of minicomputers based upon its own proprietary RISC technology, PA-RISC (the same technology used in its workstations). In an attempt to increase the installed base of machines utilizing PA-RISC technology, HP has selectively licensed this technology to a small group of companies. HP's minicomputer line is divided between commercial and technical. The technical line uses the UNIX operating system, while the commercial line uses HP's own proprietary MPE operating system. However, HP is quick to point out the ease of communication between UNIX and its MPE system due to the common central processing units, data communications facilities, databases, and compiler tools.

Mainframes

The mainframe segment of the computer industry has been the most troubled in recent years. Once the mainstay of the computer industry, the mainframe market is now in decline. Worldwide revenues from mainframe sales were $28 billion in 1991, down from $31 billion in 1990. In 1992 they slumped to $25 billion. The decline in the mainframe market is a reflection of the dramatic growth in the personal computer and workstation markets and the trend toward linking these machines together via local area networks. LANs are now taking over many of the functions that were at one time performed by a mainframe—hence the decline in mainframe revenues.

IBM continues to dominate the mainframe market, accounting for about 47 percent of the market in 1991. IBM's total installed base in mainframes now numbers about 50,000. While this might sound large, it is nothing compared to the installed base for personal computers, which is predicted to hit 135 million in 1993. IBM is followed by Fujitsu with 10 percent of the 1991 market, Hitachi with 8 percent, Unisys with 6 percent, and Amdahl with 4 percent.[27] With demand in decline and excess capacity emerging, there has been an outbreak of intense price competition in this segment. Between early 1992 and early 1993 IBM's mainframe prices dropped by 30 percent, according to one estimate.

26. Ibid.
27. Ibid.

Reflecting this, with the exception of Unisys, which has staged a turnaround, most mainframe manufacturers now appear to be losing money. Indeed, the return on assets for U.S. mainframe companies fell from an average of 12.8 percent in 1988 to minus 7.6 percent in 1992.[28]

There are, however, signs of growth in a new breed of mainframe computer that utilizes massively parallel processing (MPP) architecture. The idea behind MPP architecture is to join together hundreds, thousands, or even tens of thousands of cheap but powerful microprocessors, such as Intel's 486 chip. When coupled with the appropriate software, a hundred small processors can often execute large programs in a fraction of the time that it would take even the largest mainframes—the so-called supercomputers. Furthermore, MPP machines can do the work of mainframes and traditional supercomputers for a tenth or twentieth of the cost. Although MPP technology has yet to be perfected, companies currently focusing on developing MPP machines include Intel, Silicon Graphics, Thinking Machines, and Sequent Computer.

SOFTWARE

As noted earlier, prior to the 1980s the computer industry was characterized by companies that produced computer platforms that were based upon proprietary hardware and that ran on proprietary operating systems. Many of the software applications used on these systems were also proprietary and many more were customized to the needs of a particular organization. There was, in short, no retail mass market in computer software. The growth of the personal computer market and the near hegemony of the IBM standard based upon the Intel microprocessor architecture and Microsoft's MS-DOS operating system has changed all of this. Today the personal computer market is the largest and fastest-growing segment of the computer industry. Moreover, 80–90 percent of the 135 million PCs installed by 1993 utilized an Intel microprocessor and a Microsoft MS-DOS operating system. One consequence of this transformation in the industry has been the creation of an enormous mass retail market for software applications where none existed before.

In 1993 the worldwide software market was estimated to be worth between $60 billion and $65 billion. Of this, approximately $25 billion comes from personal computer software, $18 billion from minicomputer software, and $20 billion from mainframe software. Demand for software is expected to continue growing at around 16 percent per annum throughout the mid 1990s, with the most rapid growth coming in the personal computer segment.[29]

Operating Systems

The manufacturers of mainframes and minicomputers continue to be vertically integrated companies that utilize their own proprietary operating system software. As a result, sales of this software is closely linked to sales of their hardware—which are growing only slowly in the case of minicomputers and are declining in the case of mainframes. In personal computers the situation is very different. As a result of IBM's 1981 decision to base its first PC on the MS-DOS

28. Stratford Sherman, "The New Computer Revolution," *Fortune*, June 14, 1993, pp. 56–84.
29. Standard & Poor's Industry Surveys, *Computers*, December 31, 1992.

operating system, and not to bar Microsoft from selling to other computer manufacturers, Microsoft has become the dominant supplier of operating system software for manufacturers of personal computers based on the IBM standard. To date Microsoft has sold over 100 million copies of MS-DOS, making it the best-selling software program of all time.

In 1990 Microsoft introduced its Windows 3.0 software. Windows 3.0 was not an operating system itself. Rather, it was a graphical user interface that made MS-DOS easy to use. Windows 3.0 incorporated many of the features that had made the Apple Macintosh computer so attractive to users, including pull-down menus, icons, windows, and a mouse-pointing device. By early 1993 Microsoft had sold approximately 25 million copies of Windows, and sales were growing at a very rapid rate, increasing by over 150 percent between fiscal 1992 and 1993. The next version of Windows for personal computers, which will be based on Windows NT, is scheduled for release in mid 1994. Code-named Chicago, the next generation of Windows will not require the MS-DOS operating system. It will in effect be an operating system rather than a graphical user interface. It will run all applications software written for Windows 3.0 and beyond. Like Windows NT, Chicago will be able to utilize the full power of 32-bit microprocessors such as Intel's 386 and 486 chips. Currently this is not possible due to limitations inherent in the MS-DOS system, which was written for less-powerful 16-bit microprocessors.

In order to ensure the rapid penetration of MS-DOS and Windows, Microsoft has been offering large discounts to computer manufacturers to pre-install MS-DOS and Windows on their personal computers. As a result, in 1992 more than half of all PCs sold worldwide came with Windows pre-installed, and the percentage is growing.[30]

The biggest uncertainty in the operating system software market concerns the future shape of operating system software to manage computer networks. Network operating system software is aimed at the market for software that links together client/server systems into local area networks and, increasingly, organizationwide networks (wide area networks—WANs). As noted earlier in the case, LANs are one of the fastest-growing areas of the computer industry. Increasing numbers of organizations are now using LANs to take over many of the functions previously performed by mainframes and minicomputers. Currently, the market leader in network software is Novell, whose Netware holds something like 67 percent of the installed base of all network operating systems, which amounts to about 10 million linked PCs and workstations.[31]

Windows NT, introduced in mid 1993, is Microsoft's attempt to capture share in the network market. With over 4.1 million lines of code (instructions), Windows NT is four times as big as any other Microsoft computer program and is probably the most complex computer program ever written. Developed by a team of 200 programmers who have been working around the clock for three years, Windows NT looks just like regular Windows to the user, but it is far more powerful. Microsoft will sell two versions of Windows NT, a desktop version which will retail for $495 ($295 for current owners of Windows) and an advanced server edition which will sell for $2,995.[32] Whether Microsoft will be able to capture share from Novell, which has the advantage of a dominant installed base in the network market, remains an open question.

30. Stratford Sherman, "The New Computer Industry," *Fortune*, June 14, 1993, pp. 56–84.
31. Standard & Poor's Industry Surveys, *Computers*, December 31, 1992.
32. K. Rebello, "Big Game Hunter Bill Gates," *Business Week*, May 31, 1993, pp. 84–85.

Applications

Applications software falls into two main segments: (1) mainframe and minicomputer applications and (2) personal computer applications. Many mainframe and minicomputer applications are customized for individual users—such as a large corporation—or a particular type of user—such as health care providers. They are used to perform a multitude of functions such as payroll and accounts management, financial management, control of manufacturing processes, inventory management, and so on. Many of the vertically integrated computer companies still have an enormous stake in this area, including IBM, which is still the largest software company in the world with annual software revenues of $10 billion (by comparison, Microsoft's revenues are under $4 billion). In addition, several independent software companies including, most notably, Computer Associates, have been gaining share in this market.

In the market for applications for personal computers, Microsoft has emerged as a leader in recent years. In 1991 Microsoft's share of PC applications, such as word processing, spreadsheets, and data-base management programs, was 29 percent. In 1992 it jumped to 44 percent in a segment of the industry where U.S. sales grew from $5.9 billion to $7.6 billion.[33] In second place was Lotus with a share of 11.7 percent, down from 13 percent in 1991. Number three in applications was WordPerfect with an 8 percent share. Microsoft's dominance in applications is relatively recent. Prior to 1990 the dominant companies in application software were WordPerfect in word processing applications, Lotus in spreadsheets, and Borland in the data-base market. What changed things was the introduction of Windows 3.0 in 1990. Microsoft quickly followed this with the introduction of a series of applications programs written for the Windows operating environment. By gaining a jump on its rivals in applications software, Microsoft was able to build momentum on which it has capitalized. While Microsoft still trails its three main rivals in sales of applications written for MS-DOS, it is the clear leader in sales of applications written for Windows—and Windows is where the growth is.

There are, however, signs that price competition is beginning to develop in the personal computer applications market. In early 1992 most applications for PCs sold at around $500, but that was in the days when a personal computer sold for $3,000. As the price of personal computers has fallen, consumers have become increasingly reluctant to pay large amounts for software. In addition, the market for major applications, such as word processing and spreadsheets, may be getting saturated. In this environment, introductory deals and cut-price offers to lure users into "upgrading" into rival applications have cut the price of some software to as low as $100.[34]

THE COMPUTER INDUSTRY IN THE MID 1990s AND BEYOND

The computer industry of the 1970s was dominated by a handful of large, vertically integrated companies. By the mid 1990s the industry had fragmented. Estimates suggest that the computer industry of 1965 had at most 2,500 companies;

33. "Microsoft's Market Share Increased to 44% in 1992," *The Wall Street Journal*, January 20, 1993, p. B6.
34. "Today Windows, Tomorrow the World," *The Economist*, May 22, 1993, p. 25.

today it may have more than 50,000.[35] As recently as 1980 the industry was dominated by vertically integrated manufacturers such as IBM, DEC, and Wang. In 1992 IBM lost $4.9 billion, DEC lost $2.8 billion, and Wang filed for Chapter 11 bankruptcy. Meanwhile, Intel and Microsoft have emerged as the most profitable companies in the industry.

The value chain of the "new" computer industry is illustrated in Figure 7. While the industry is still divided into five main stages, there are several segments within each stage. Vertically integrated giants, such as IBM, which are active in each stage of the industry, can still be found in the new computer industry, but increasingly they are an anachronism. More typical are companies such as Intel, which focuses on just one part of the basic component stage of the industry—microprocessors. Similarly, in the basic components stage there are companies that specialize in disk drives, flat top displays (such as those used in laptop computers), memory chips, and so on. At the computer platform stage of the industry are found successful companies that focus on just one aspect of this stage. Compaq focuses on personal computers, Sun on workstations, and Hewlett-Packard and DEC on workstations and minicomputers. IBM currently is the only company with a presence in all four main segments of the computer platform stage of the industry.

Moving on to operating systems, Microsoft is found; it produces not only MS-DOS and Windows but also a network operating system, Windows NT. There are also companies such as Novell, which currently focuses just on network operating systems. In addition, there are a number of companies that produce UNIX-based operating systems. Most of these companies, however, are active in the computer platform stage of the industry and produce their own "proprietary" variants of UNIX to run their machines (e.g., Sun Microsystems, Hewlett-Packard). Finally, there are companies such as IBM, which still produces its own non-UNIX proprietary operating systems in-house.

The applications software stage of the industry is also populated by a number of focused companies. These include Lotus and WordPerfect, which produce applications software for MS-DOS and Windows-based machines, and Computer Associates, which produces software for UNIX and proprietary systems. As noted earlier, Microsoft also has a strong presence in MS-DOS and Windows application software.

Finally, there is the distribution stage. Here a number of different ways of delivering computer platforms and software to end users has emerged. Direct sales forces and mail order represent two ways of delivering systems to consumers that are used by computer platform companies. For example, Dell Computer sells via mail order, while DEC makes use of a direct sales force. On the other hand, computer dealers, mass market retailers, and value added retailers are all independent entities with no operations elsewhere in the industry. In addition, a lot of software is sold by independent mail order houses.

The Future

Looking to the future, a number of issues are arising that may continue to promote dramatic change in the industry. First, the power of the micro-processor seems set to increase, as does the trend toward miniaturization that has long characterized the industry. The development of new technologies, such as flash

35. "Harsh New World," *The Economist, The Computer Industry*, February 27, 1993, pp. 7–8.

Figure 7
The Value Chain of the "New" Computer Industry

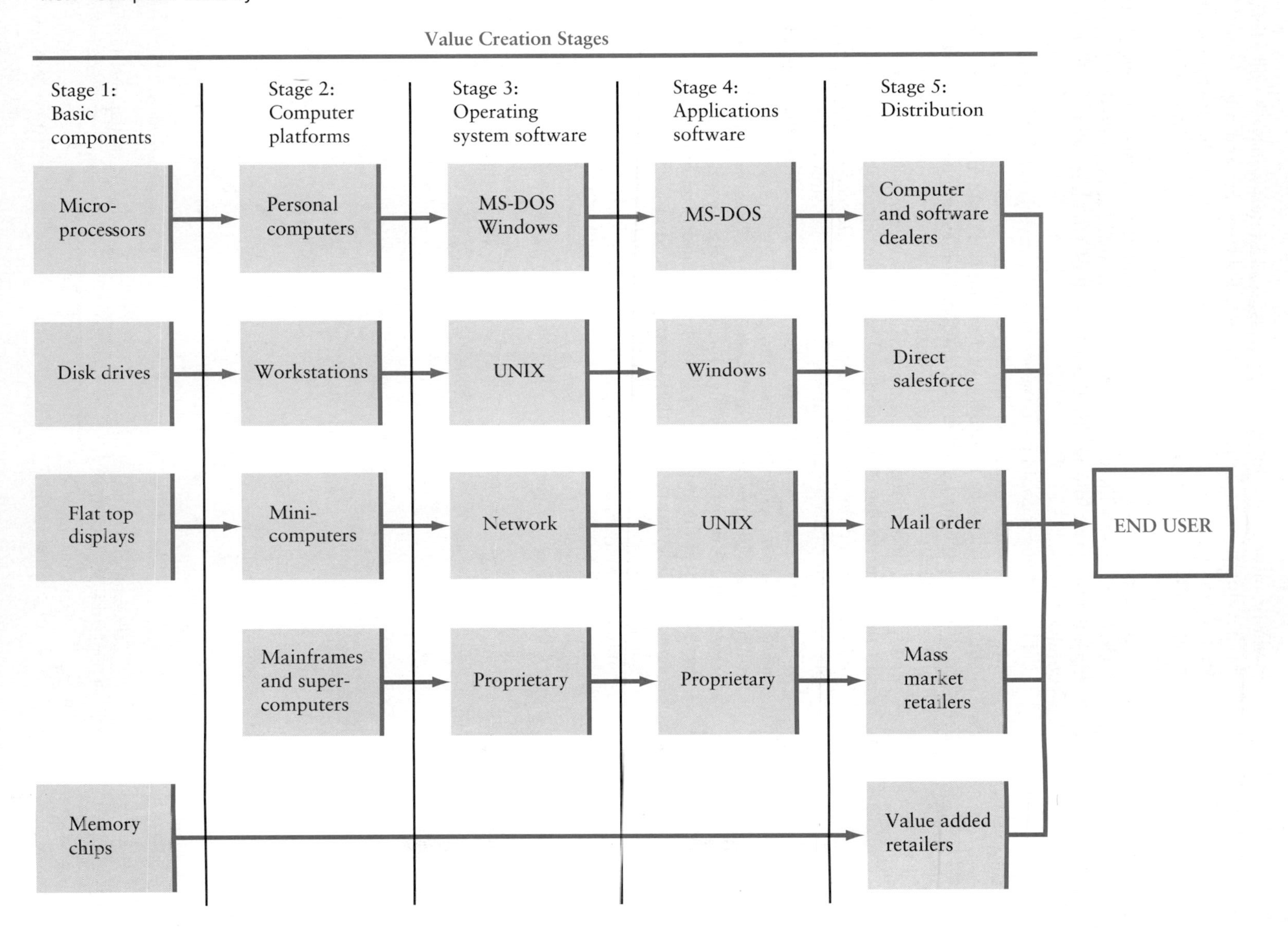

memory, more powerful micro-processors, and new software will all facilitate the development of extremely compact, lightweight, and high-powered computers. Second, continuing technological advances, coupled with the development of more efficient manufacturing processes, will result in a decline in the cost of computing power. Third, over the next decade most information is expected to assume the same digital format that is used in computers. This includes not just television and telephone transmissions, but also music recordings, newspapers, journals, and books—all of which may make their way onto compact disks.

These changes could pave the way for a convergence between the computer industry, telecommunications industry, and the media, entertainment, and publishing industries (see Figure 8). Vast amounts of information in our society are produced by the media, entertainment, and publishing industries. Once stored in digital format, the computer industry has the technology required to store, manipulate, and analyze this information. However, it lacks the means to transmit this information. This is controlled by the telephone companies, both wire and cellular, and the cable television companies. It seems highly likely, therefore, that computer, telecommunications, and cable television will join forces to transmit information to whoever wants it in whatever form that they choose. Furthermore, the media, entertainment, and publishing industries, as the source of so much of this information, inevitably will be drawn into the web of linkages between these various industries. Just how these events will play out, and how they will affect the structure of the computer industry, remains to be seen. What seems possible, however, is that we are witnessing the birth of a new information age that will be dominated by those companies that can best create, transmit, store, analyze, and manipulate information.

Figure 8
The Emerging Information Industry

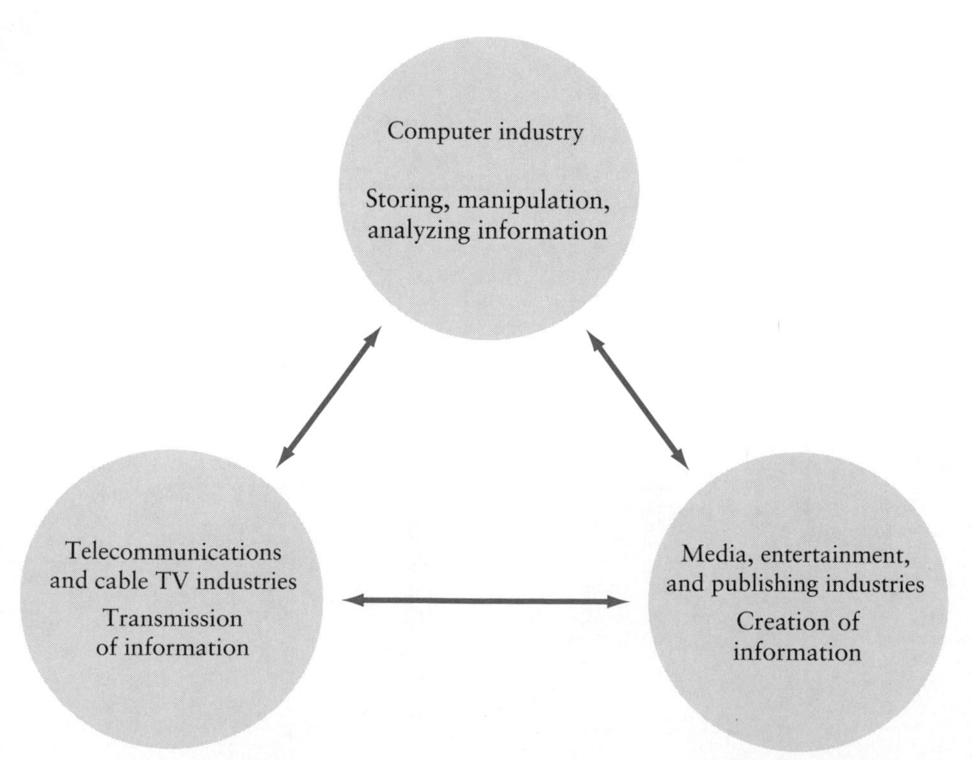

CASE 9

Compaq Computer Corporation in 1994

INTRODUCTION

This case traces the strategic development of Compaq Computer Corporation from its establishment in 1981 through to 1994. The case should be read in conjunction with Case 10, "The Computer Industry: The New Industry of Industries?" Compaq went from infancy to being the fastest-growing new venture in American business history in under two years. It subsequently established itself as a premium manufacturer of IBM-compatible personal computers. By the early 1990s, however, Compaq's margins were under severe pressure from competitors such as Dell and Gateway 2000 which were selling machines that were comparable to Compaq's for prices that were 30 percent to 40 percent lower. Compaq responded by radically overhauling its strategy during 1992 in order to compete head-to-head with the likes of Dell and Gateway 2000. The result seems to be a leaner and more efficient company.

COMPAQ IN THE 1980s

In the Beginning

Compaq Computer Corporation was established in 1981 by three ex-Texas Instruments executives, Bill Murto, Jim Harris, and Rod Canion. The three men had left Texas Instruments in early 1981 after deciding to set up a company of their own. Initially, they had no clear idea of what they wanted to do. Their first idea was to build plug-in hard disks for IBM PCs. This idea was vetoed by prospective investors, because too many companies already were competing in that market. A month later, Rod Canion and Jim Harris were eating dinner in a Houston restaurant when suddenly they got a better idea: why not build a portable version of IBM's personal computer?

This time investors were more interested. In January 1982 Canion persuaded Sevin Rosen Management Company, the venture capital company headed by Benjamin Rosen that had financed premier software company Lotus, to put up $20,000 to develop a prototype. The management team had six months to get a working model ready to show prospective dealers. If the reaction was favorable, Rosen promised further funding. A five-man engineering team began working day and night to complete the design. The prototype was finally finished only hours before its demonstration to dealers.

This case was prepared by Charles W. L. Hill, University of Washington. This case was prepared as a basis for class discussion rather than to illustrate either effective or ineffective handling of administrative situations.

Initial dealer reaction was strong. Unlike most so-called IBM compatibles at the time, Compaq's machine could run most IBM PC software straight out of the package. Just as important from the dealer's perspective, IBM was proving unable to meet the huge demand that it had created for the PC following its 1981 introduction. In 1983 IBM produced 600,000 PCs, twice its original plan. Even so, most of IBM's dealers were on allocation. Unless the dealers could find a machine to fill the gap, many of them stood to lose money. Compaq's portable looked as if it would do the job.

On the basis of the favorable dealer reaction, Sevin Rosen raised a further $30 million for Compaq. Benjamin Rosen became chairman of the new company while Canion was appointed CEO. The company saw a window of opportunity in the personal computer market created by IBM's short-run inability to meet demand. Compaq's original business plan was aggressive. The plan called for the recruitment of experienced executives from large corporations and the construction of a manufacturing plant capable of producing 5,000 machines per month. The hope was that by reaching high-volume production quickly, Compaq would be able to penetrate major retail stores before other PC-compatible manufacturers had a chance.

Among the first executives recruited was John Gribi, another former Texas Instruments man, who as Compaq's chief financial officer set up an accounting system that would not be overwhelmed by the company's projected growth. John Walker, who was senior vice president of Datapoint Corp., was recruited to establish a manufacturing system that could maintain quality control at mass production rates. And to make sure that the new Compaq computers reached the retail market, Canion hired H. L. "Sparky" Sparks, a 20-year IBM veteran who had managed sales and service of IBM's personal computer.

Thanks to the "open architecture" of IBM's PC, Compaq was able to buy most components of the IBM machine off the shelf, including Microsoft's operating system and the Intel 8088 microprocessor chip that was the PC's brain. However, special instructions copyrighted by IBM were built into a microchip to make the operating system run (the ROM-BIOS chip). Compaq's software engineers had to mimic this program without violating the terms of the copyright. A team of 15 programmers worked for nine months and spent $1 million to get the job done.

Following urging by Sparks, Compaq pursued an aggressive dealership strategy that guaranteed high margins for dealers. Compaq planned to price its product so that dealers could gross 38 percent on sales made at the suggested retail price, rather than the 32 percent on sales of IBM's computers. Compaq also planned to sell its machine exclusively through dealers, rather than setting up its own direct sales force that would skim off business with large corporations.

With extensive dealer support, Compaq's 28-pound portable computer sold well following its introduction in early 1983. The machine retailed at $2,995, about $400 less than IBM's PC system. In its first year of sales, Compaq sold over 50,000 units and reported sales of $111 million, an all-time record for a new start-up. By comparison, Apple Computer took four years to reach the $100 million mark. IBM responded by introducing a portable of its own in early 1984, but to no avail. IBM's portable actually ran fewer IBM PC programs than Compaq's and was two pounds heavier. By the end of 1984 Compaq was outselling IBM's portable 5 to 1. In mid 1984 the company moved to new manufacturing facilities capable of turning out 10,000 machines a month, while 1984 sales tripled to $325.

The Deskpro and the Deskpro 286

Compaq realized that the niche it had created would not be sufficient for future growth. Following the instant success of the portable machine, Compaq set to work on a non-portable IBM-compatible machine. The result was the Deskpro, a family of four machines based on Intel's 8086 microprocessor, introduced in mid 1984. The Intel chip used in the Deskpro range was more than twice as fast as the chip used in the Compaq portable and IBM PC. Compaq's research had revealed that many PC programs, such as spreadsheets, took a long time to run on the older machines and that users were hungry for more power.

Toward the end of 1984 IBM introduced the AT personal computer. The AT ran on Intel's 80286 microprocessor, which was significantly faster than the 8086 chip used in the original Deskpros. The AT was highly demanded by scientists and engineers who require quick processing speeds to run complicated programs. The AT was also a multiuser machine that allowed several people to operate remote terminals at the same time. Significantly, though, the AT was incompatible with some of the best-selling software running on the IBM PC and Compaq machines at the same time.

Compaq's response to IBM's move was to design an upgrade of the Deskpro range that could utilize the 80286 microprocessor. The task of developing a response to the AT fell to Kevin Ellington, a 21-year veteran of Texas Instruments. Ellington created a multidepartment team whose members worked in parallel. As engineers were designing the new product, manufacturing managers were setting up a new factory to produce the computer, a marketing executive was busy positioning it, and an assistant treasurer was arranging to pay for it.

Within six months Compaq had begun shipping its upgraded version of the Deskpro, the Deskpro 286 range. Meanwhile, IBM's AT was plagued with production problems and lapses in quality control. Once again, Compaq was able to take advantage of a market that IBM had created but was unable to satisfy. Compaq shipped 10,000 units of the new 286 range in its first 90 days.

The Deskpro 386

In 1986 Intel introduced another microprocessor, the 80386, that promised personal computer speeds far exceeding those of the IBM AT and Compaq's Deskpro 286 range. Rumors abounded that IBM was working on a new line of personal computers, to be introduced in early 1987, that would use the 80386 chip and replace the original IBM PC line. Against this background, on September 9, 1986, Compaq unveiled the Deskpro 386, the first computer based on Intel's 80386 chip. Compaq had beat IBM to the market by six months in what many characterized as a gutsy bid to seize the technological lead.

The Deskpro 386 quickly emerged as the most powerful personal computer on the market. The machine ran IBM PC software two to three times faster than the IBM AT and had 10 times the internal memory. With this capacity, the machine was capable of handling jobs previously run on minicomputers. For example, the power of the Deskpro 386 made it possible to perform sophisticated scientific and engineering design tasks on a personal computer. Although at $6,499 and $8,799 the two models of the Deskpro 386 initially retailed for two to three times the price of most personal computers, they were half the price of the smallest minicomputers.

Despite fears that many buyers might wait to see IBM's new system before purchasing an 80386 machine, early sales of the Deskpro 386 were better than expected. The company sold 75,000 Deskpro 386s in its first full year. More important, the 386 established Compaq as the technological leader and opened

up the door to many large corporations and new applications. According to Compaq, 40 percent of the Deskpro 386s it sold in 1986 were being used for non-traditional PC jobs such as computer-aided design, and 15 percent took work from minicomputers or mainframes.

Organization and Management During the 1980s

The themes of team work and consensus management were central to Compaq's culture during the 1980s. To promote team work the company was divided into product teams, each of which had its own marketing, manufacturing, engineering and accounting staff. A team took a product through from start to finish. The team approach at Compaq assumed that accountants and engineers, for example, had something valuable to contribute to decisions about manufacturing and marketing. At the same time, Compaq recognized the need for coordination between the different product areas of the firm. To achieve this, superimposed on the product teams were four main functional groups: marketing, engineering, sales, and manufacturing. By centralizing marketing, for example, the company could make sure a new model did not prematurely kill off any of Compaq's current PCs.

Team work was reinforced at Compaq by an open management style and an emphasis on consensus management that encouraged individuals at all levels in the company to express their opinions. Early in 1983 the commitment to consensus management at Compaq was put to the test. Compaq's CEO, Rod Canion, had become keen on the idea of producing a lap-top computer, small enough to fit in a briefcase. Although there was general support for the idea, a researcher named Mary Dudley was assigned to survey the market. She concluded that there was little demand for a lap-top computer. After Dudley presented and re-presented her negative assessment, Canion felt compelled to drop the project.

A further feature of Compaq that was unusual for a new start-up was the experience of its management team. Compaq made a point of hiring people with big company experience. Each manager in the start-up team already had years of relevant experience with major corporations. Of Compaq's 21 officers in 1987, 17 were Texas Instruments alumni who had as much as 21 years of experience. Similarly, programmers had an average of 15 years outside experience before joining Compaq.

All of Compaq's employees received stock options when they joined the company. As CEO Rod Canion once explained: "When we left Texas Instruments we were determined to start a company with people who could work in a Fortune 500 company. We wanted to combine the discipline of a big company with an environment where people felt they could participate in success. We wanted the best of both worlds. And we wanted to do it right."

Distribution Strategy During the 1980s

By 1987 Compaq had built up a network of dealers that stretched around the globe. With nearly 3,000 stores on its books, Compaq had a larger dealer network than IBM. Unlike IBM and Apple, however, Compaq had no direct sales force and did not compete with its retailers. Many dealers had criticized IBM and Apple for allowing their factory sales teams to compete with authorized dealers. Even though they were approached by customers wanting to buy direct, throughout the 1980s Compaq continued to sell only through authorized dealers. In turn, this dedication to retailers produced a level of dealer loyalty that was perhaps unequaled in the industry.

COMPAQ IN THE 1990S

By 1990 Compaq had built up an enviable position in the personal computer industry. The company was known for building high-powered and reliable personal computers that commanded a premium price. It also had a reputation for being among the most innovative companies in the industry, as witnessed by its success in producing the first IBM-compatible machine and the first personal computer based on Intel's 386 microprocessor. The company manufactured its PCs in three locations: Houston, Texas; Erksin, Scotland; and Singapore. Over half of its revenues were generated from foreign operations. The primary customers were large corporations. Its market share in the United States was 7.8 percent—making it number three in the industry after IBM and Apple. In 1990 Compaq earned record gross profits of $784 million on record revenues of $3.6 billion, up from profits of $5 million and revenues of $111 million in 1983, the company's first year of operation. Meanwhile, the company's stock price hit an all-time high of $75 a share in late 1990 ($150 per share when adjusted for stock splits), up from less than $15 a share in 1987. However, things were about to take a dramatic turn for the worse at Compaq.

Compaq's Slump

The late 1980s saw rapid growth in the business of a number of low-priced manufacturers of IBM-compatible personal computers including, most notably, AST, Dell Computer, and Gateway 2000. In addition, it was estimated that there were about 300 small "no-name" companies producing low-priced PCs for sale in the U.S. market. These companies were all pursuing a very different strategy from Compaq. While Compaq continued to sell premium-priced machines through its dealer network, Dell and Gateway 2000 began selling directly to customers via mail order—a strategy that enabled them to keep prices down. In addition, unlike Compaq which always had a large R&D budget, these companies operated with low R&D budgets. In 1990 Compaq's R&D spending was equivalent to about 7 percent of revenues, compared to around 3 percent at AST and Dell. AST, Dell, and Gateway also contracted out far more manufacturing than Compaq. While Compaq made many of the key components to its PCs in-house—a strategy that helped Compaq ensure high quality control—AST, Dell, and Gateway were primarily assembly operations, purchasing most of their components from independent vendors. These factors allowed AST, Dell, and Gateway to undercut Compaq's prices by as much as 30 percent to 40 percent. A further factor working in Dell's and Gateway's favor was that both companies offered 24-hour telephone assistance to buyers, whereas Compaq actively discouraged phone calls to the company, preferring inquiries to be handled by its dealers.

Despite record sales and earnings, the first signs of trouble arose in 1990 when Compaq's share of the U.S. PC market slipped to 7.8 percent, down from 8.7 percent in 1989. Indeed, Compaq's record revenues and profits in 1990 were largely due to the rapid growth of its European operations, then under the direction of a German executive, Eckhard Pfeiffer. Pfeiffer had built up the European operation from nothing into a $1.8 billion business in six years.

Things started to come to a head in April 1991 when AST, Dell, and IBM all beat Compaq to the market by announcing the impending introduction of personal computers based on Intel's new 486 microprocessor. Compaq, which had long prided itself on being the industry leader in innovation, was still months off a similar announcement. At the same time, Compaq found itself facing a sharp

slump in sales growth and market share. With inventories piling up, Compaq cut prices by as much as 34 percent. The result was slimmer margins, but sales and market share continued to slump. Compaq's prices were still significantly above those of its rivals. For example, in May 1991 Compaq was asking $4,799 for a notebook computer based on Intel's 386SX microprocessor. While this was down from $6,999 before the cuts, it was still substantially more than the $3,795 that AST was asking for a similar machine.

In June 1991 the picture worsened still further. The growth in personal computer sales had slowed significantly as a result of the global recession. Against this background, Compaq reported second-quarter results that showed that sales had fallen 17 percent and net profits 81 percent compared to the same period a year earlier. At this point CEO Rod Canion started to rethink the strategy of the company. Canion decided to begin developing a direct sales force to sell computers to corporate customers. He also planned to split the company into two largely autonomous units—one to develop and handle high-end systems such as workstations and network servers and the other to handle mainstream PCs. At the same time, Canion resisted pressure from within the company—particularly from Eckhard Pfeiffer who had been appointed chief operating officer in 1991—to cut Compaq's overhead. Rather, Canion reaffirmed Compaq's commitment to producing innovative PCs and argued that this required heavy R&D spending. Canion remained convinced that the market for PCs would rebound and that Compaq would soon be able to once more command a premium price for its personal computers. He did, however, begin to look for workforce reductions. Despite the development of a direct sales force, Canion also reaffirmed the company's commitment to its dealer network.

These moves did little to stem the slump at Compaq. On October 23, 1991, Compaq reported third-quarter revenues of $709 million, 18 percent lower than the previous year, and a net loss of $70 million. This was Compaq's first loss ever. In part the loss reflected the company's decision to take a $135 million charge to reduce its work force by 12 percent (1,400 employees) and restructure operations. But even without the one-time charge, Compaq's earnings would have been $65 million, down from $124 million in the same quarter of 1990.

On October 24 Compaq's board met to discuss the situation. By this point chairman Benjamin Rosen was convinced that Compaq had to move more rapidly to change its strategy. As Compaq's earnings slumped, Rosen had seen the value of his shareholding in Compaq fall from close to $50 million in 1990 to $25 million by October 1991. After a ten-hour board meeting, Rosen and the company's six other directors asked company officers to leave the room. In the closed meeting that followed, the board took the decision to replace Canion as CEO with Eckhard Pfeiffer. Canion was offered a seat on the board, but he declined and resigned from the company. Many in the company felt that replacing Canion, who was an engineer, with Pfeiffer, a life-long marketing man, signaled a change in the culture of the company.

Pfeiffer Takes Over

Pfeiffer moved quickly. On November 5 he met with stock analysts and announced a major change in Compaq's strategy. Pfeiffer stated that Compaq must slash costs, introduce more new products, introduce them more quickly, and make use of a wider variety of distribution outlets. He also indicated that the company would pursue some markets that it previously had shunned, includ-

ing the home, education and small-business markets. To achieve these changes, Compaq officials indicated that the company would lean on suppliers for better deals, shut facilities, consolidate operations, and send production overseas. Pfeiffer made it clear that Compaq had left behind Canion's strategy of selling premium-priced machines to the largest companies. While he stated that Compaq would continue to offer top-of-the-line hardware to corporate users, he stressed that Compaq would develop low-priced machines to compete directly with those offered by discount computer makers such as Dell and AST.

In the meantime, Pfeiffer had outlined already his plans to the company's top management. He decided that Compaq's production costs, and therefore its prices, probably could be cut by as much as 50 percent. June 1992 was selected as the target date for introduction of a new line of low-cost PCs. These PCs would be aimed at the broad market and would be sold through multiple distribution channels. Pfeiffer believed that with aggressive cost-cutting Compaq could achieve much lower prices and still earn profit margins in the 30 percent to 35 percent range.

Cutting Costs

To compete in a more price competitive environment, Pfeiffer realized that he had to get Compaq's unit costs down by as much as 50 percent. His first step was to communicate this goal to all managers. Prior to this period, Compaq's senior management had never articulated cost control as a major goal of the company. Compaq's engineering culture had placed a higher value on being able to develop and produce new products quickly than on making them inexpensive. While each part of the company had a priority list, cost minimization was not near the top of anyone's list. For example, in manufacturing, cost containment was the fifth objective; under Pfeiffer it became the number-two objective, second only to quality. In purchasing, cost minimization had been the number-seven objective; under Pfeiffer it became the number-one objective.

To lower costs, Compaq decided that it would no longer pursue peak performance at any price. Prior to 1992 Compaq packed its machines with plenty of extra features. Many of these were to be excluded or replaced by less-expensive features in its new models (see Table 1). Compaq machines also were deliberately

Table 1
How Compaq Cut Features and Costs in its New Models

Deskpro 386/25—1991 machine	ProLine 3/25—1992 machine
Modular design for easy upgrades, including microprocessor	Simpler, lower cost motherboard for reliability but limited upgrade capacity
Five 32-bit expansion slots to handle high performance add-ons	Only two 16-bit expansion slots, limiting hardware options
More durable, heavy-duty, mechanical keyboard	Light membrane keyboard with fewer mechanical parts
240 watts of power for add-ons	Standard 70-watt power supply
Audio board for sound	No audio board
Intel 386DX-25 chip, 60 megabyte Quantum disk drive	Slightly slower Intel 386SX-25 chip, 40 megabyte Quantum disk drive
List price: $2,744	List price: $1,152

overbuilt. For example, it built casings that were designed to withstand a fall down three flights of stairs. Pfeiffer deemed this unnecessary. It also had included eight layers of radio-emissions shields in its machines when four would do the job. In addition, all Compaq machines had been tested for 96 hours, a practice known as burn-in. By studying actual failures, tracing them back to the source, and then rectifying the problem, Compaq found that it could reduce the burn-in time on its basic models to only two hours. Cutting the number of burn-in racks and other space-saving steps freed up so much floor space in the Houston factory that Compaq no longer needed 270,000 square feet of rented space nearby. Along the same lines, Compaq stopped individual testing of the subassemblies in its PCs. It now tests only the finished machines and a sample of the subassemblies.

Compaq also moved to outsource more key components. The company had been one of the few PC manufacturers to make its own power supplies; they are now made by an independent supplier. Compaq also introduced competitive bidding practices with suppliers. According to company officers, competitive bidding alone saved the company $165 million in the first nine months of 1992. When longtime partner Conner Peripherals, Inc.'s prices were found to be significantly higher than those of Quantum Corp.'s, Compaq made Quantum its main supplier of disk drives, even though Compaq had a 20 percent stake in Conner (Compaq subsequently sold its stake for $86 million). As a result of such moves, the cost of most components dropped by about 30 percent between 1991 and 1992.

Further cost savings came from reorganizations and related staff cuts. Four separate PC engineering organizations were consolidated into two: one for product development and one for production. In the past, engineers were encouraged to redesign parts whenever they got a better idea. They typically redesigned processor boards, the heart of a PC, 14 times before production started. Now the design team has a goal of just two redesigns. As of 1993 they had succeeded in reducing the number of redesigns to just three. Such changes have enabled Compaq to cut its engineering staff by 20 percent.

Further cost savings have come from the economies of scale that result from high-volume production. In October 1991 all three Compaq factories—in Houston, Singapore, and Scotland— were running only a single shift. With volume demand stimulated by its new line of low-priced personal computers, by December 1992 Houston and Singapore were operating three shifts, while Scotland was operating two. This increase in capacity utilization helped Compaq to bring its unit costs down by 52 percent between October 1991 and October 1992.

Product Positioning

Pfeiffer set up a new business unit to handle the development of the new line of low-cost machines that were to be introduced in mid 1992. By December 1991 he was being briefed on a machine that looked nothing like a Compaq and did not even bear the Compaq label. The issue being actively debated in the company at this time was whether attaching the Compaq label to a low-priced machine might not devalue the Compaq brand. Although the majority of managers were in favor of not attaching the Compaq label to the new machines, Pfeiffer took the opposite tack. He decided that brand name was still important, and that while the Compaq brand may no longer enable the company to charge a premium price, it would help the company to gain volume. So Compaq's new low-priced machines were sold under the Compaq brand name.

The first fruits of Compaq's strategic shift appeared on schedule in June 1992 when the company introduced 45 new models—mostly low-priced ProLine desktop PCs and Contura notebooks. This boosted Compaq's total product range to 76 models. At the same time, in a move that rocked the industry, the company announced a 32 percent across-the-board price cut on all of its existing models. Suddenly the price differential between Compaq's high-quality machines and low-priced clones fell from 35 percent to 15 percent, while Compaq's ProLine, with prices beginning at under $900, undercut many of the clone makers. The initial low prices were followed by a further round of price cuts in October 1992 when it announced price reductions of up to 32 percent. Some of its main competitors, such as Dell, followed suit in an attempt to maintain a price advantage. Compaq retaliated in January 1993 by cutting prices once more, this time by up to 16 percent. Predictably, Dell retaliated in kind, cutting its prices by about 9 percent in February 1993. Compaq responded in March 1993 when prices on some desktop models were cut by up to 15 percent.

As an aid to increasing market penetration and creating a greater share of non-corporate business, Compaq changed its advertising strategy and broadened its distribution channels. While Compaq's R&D budget was being squeezed and the company was cutting back on its engineering staff, the advertising budget was increased. Pfeiffer personally reviewed every advertisements before it went out. His influence was reflected in a marked shift in the orientation of advertising. While most traditional Compaq advertisements emphasized computer terminology such as RAM and ROM, the new advertisements were more reader-friendly and stressed the benefits of its products to the user in straightforward language.

Compaq also expanded its dealer network. In Canion's day Compaq had emphasized selling through its computer dealers; in 1992 Compaq rapidly began to add discount superstores like Office Depot, Bizmart, and Service Merchandise to its list of distributors. By the end of 1992 the company had more than doubled its worldwide dealer network from a year earlier to 9,000 outlets. In March 1993 Compaq announced that it would follow its Texas rival, Dell Computer, and start to sell its PCs directly to customers via mail order. The company set up a phone bank capable of receiving 10,000 calls per week and expected to hire as many as 150 people to staff the operation. Compaq predicts that mail order sales will amount to $170 million in 1993. The company also expects computer dealers, which accounted for about half of the industry's sales in 1991, to generate only 27 percent of total personal computer sales by 1995.

The expansion in distribution outlets and the opening of new distribution channels has not been achieved without cost. Some of Compaq's long-established dealers have been alienated by this process. Dealers have complained about unreasonably long order backlogs. One dealer noted that he lost a major order for 32 Compaq machines in April 1993 because Compaq had told the dealer that they couldn't be delivered until June. In the event, it transpired that the customer simply ordered the 32 machines directly from Compaq's mail order operation and received them within a week. Compaq acknowledges that many traditional dealers have had to wait for new machines, but denies that it has intentionally diverted inventory to new sales channels. Nevertheless, in early 1993 the company admitted that it was able to fill only about half of the orders that it received from traditional dealers.

Income Data (Million $)

Year Ended Dec. 31	Revs.	Oper. Inc.	% Oper. Inc. of Revs.	Cap. Exp.	Depr.	Int. Exp.	Net Bef. Taxes	Eff. Tax Rate	[3]Net Inc.	% Net Inc. of Revs.	Cash Flow
1992	4,100	482	11.8	159	159	47.5	[2]311	31.4%	213	5.2	372
1991	3,271	469	14.3	[1]160	164	43.9	[2]174	24.7%	131	4.0	295
1990	3,599	784	21.8	[1]325	135	54.9	[2]671	32.2%	455	12.6	590
1989	2,876	573	19.9	362	84	46.8	[2]498	33.1%	333	11.6	417
1988	2,066	408	19.8	286	48	27.7	[2]375	31.9%	255	12.4	304
1987	1,224	255	20.8	113	22	14.2	[2]229	40.5%	136	11.1	158
1986	625	100	16.0	50	14	11.2	[2]75	42.7%	43	6.9	57
1985	504	61	12.1	36	9	10.1	44	39.3%	27	5.3	35
1984	329	24	7.3	30	4	5.4	16	21.5%	13	3.9	17
1983	111	5	4.2	13	1	1.4	5	46.9%	3	2.3	4

Balance Sheet Data (Million $)

Dec. 31	Cash	Curr. Assets	Curr. Liab.	Curr. Ratio	Total Assets	% Ret. on Assets	Long-Term Debt	Common Equity	Total Cap.	% LT Debt of Cap.	% Ret. on Equity
1992	357	2,319	960	2.4	3,142	7.3	Nil	2,007	2,183	Nil	11.1
1991	452	1,783	639	2.8	2,826	4.8	73	1,931	2,188	3.3	7.0
1990	435	1,688	644	2.6	2,718	18.2	73	1,859	2,074	3.5	28.9
1989	161	1,312	564	2.3	2,090	18.0	274	1,172	1,526	17.9	33.3
1988	281	1,115	480	2.3	1,590	19.6	275	815	1,110	24.8	40.3
1987	132	681	343	2.0	901	19.8	149	400	558	26.7	43.2
1986	57	260	119	2.2	378	12.3	73	183	259	28.1	26.6
1985	77	240	99	2.4	312	9.8	75	137	213	35.3	21.5
1984	28	189	122	1.6	231	7.2	Nil	109	110	Nil	12.7
1983	52	105	30	4.0	121	NM	Nil	48	91	Nil	NM

Data as orig. reptd.; data prior to 1983 as reptd. in prospectus dated 12/9/83. 1. Net of curr. yr. retirement and disposals. 2. Incl. equity in earns. of nonconsol. subs. 3. Bef. spec. items. NM–Not Meaningful

Exhibit 1
Income and Balance Sheet Data

THE EARLY RESULTS

Boosted by strong demand for its low-priced computers, shipments surged and 1992 revenues at Compaq rose 25 percent from a year earlier to top $4.1 billion. The company's operating income also increased, but only by 3 percent to $482 million. Throughout the first half of 1993 Compaq's shipments continued to grow. In the first quarter of 1993 revenues were up 106 percent from $783 million in the same quarter of 1992. However, profit margins were lower. Compaq's profit margin fell to 23 percent at the end of the first quarter, down from 26.9 percent at the end of the year and 33.5 percent during the same period in 1992. Wall Street reacted positively to the performance improvement at Compaq. By

September 1993 Compaq's stock was trading in the mid $50s, up from $22 per share two years earlier. However, not all were happy. One analyst noted that "the margin thing is getting ugly, absolutely abysmal. . . . Compaq's market share gains are becoming an increasingly Pyrrhic victory." In September 1993 Compaq announced that it expected personal computer shipments in the United States to be relatively flat for the second half of 1993 after having grown by 40 percent during the first half of 1992. Compaq's stock rose $3 per share to $56¼ on the news.

Bibliography

Arnst, Catherine and Stephanie Anderson Forest. "Compaq: How It Made Its Impressive Move out of the Doldrums," *Business Week*. November 2, 1992, pp. 146–151.

Bartimo, Jim. "Compaq Chief Maps Numerous Major Changes," *The Wall Street Journal*, November 6, 1991, p. A3.

Bartimo, Jim and Karen Blumenthal. "Compaq's Canion is Unexpected Casualty of the Brutal Personal Computer Wars," *The Wall Street Journal,* October 28, 1991, p. B1.

Canion, Rod. "Creating a Strong Management Team." Keynote Address by Rod Canion, CEO, Compaq Computer Corporation. Annual Meeting, Houston, Texas, May 15, 1985.

Davis, Jo Ellen. "Will Compaq be Dethroned as the King of the Compatibles?" *Business Week,* July 28, 1986, p. 67.

Davis, Jo Ellen and Geoff Lewis. "Who's Afraid of IBM?" *Business Week*, June 29, 1987, pp. 68–74.

Duke, Paul. "Compaq's Two New Models Help Lift Stock," *The Wall Street Journal,* October 8, 1987, p. 62.

———. "Powerful 386 Personal Computers Show Promise, but Software Lags," *The Wall Street Journal,* January 19, 1988, p. 20.

Hayes, Thomas. "Compaq's Explosive Growth," *The New York Times,* February 22, 1986, p. 31.

Ivey, Mark. "Can Rod Canion Stop Compaq's Erosion?" *Business Week,* November 4, 1991, pp. 134–140.

Kirkpatri, David. "The Revolution at Compaq Computer," *Fortune,* December 14, 1992, pp. 80–88.

Kotkin, Joel. "The Smart Team at Compaq Computer," *Inc.*, February 1986, pp. 48–56.

Lancaster, Hal and Michael Allen, "Compaq Computer Finds Itself Where It Once Put IBM," *The Wall Street Journal,* January 13, 1992, p. B4.

Lewis, Geoff. "The Verdict on IBM's System/2: Clonemakers Are Still in the Game," *Business Week,* May 4, 1987, pp. 118–121.

Lewis, Pete. "Whether or When to Buy OS/2," *The New York Times,* December 27, 1987, p. 8.

O'Reilly, Brian. "Compaq's Grip on IBM's Slippery Tail," *Fortune,* February 18, 1985, pp. 74–83.

Pope, Kyle. "Margin Worry," *The Wall Street Journal,* April 22, 1993, p. B7.

———. "Computer Dealers Accuse Compaq of Jilting Them," *The Wall Street Journal,* April 7, 1993, p. B1.

———. "Compaq Plans a Mail-Order Operation," *The Wall Street Journal,* March 12, 1993, p. B6.

———. "Compaq is Hoping to Get Bigger by Thinking Smaller," *The Wall Street Journal,* January 7, 1993, p. B4.

Sanger, David. "One Computer Maker IS Hot: Compaq Scores in a Weak Field," *The New York Times*, August 13, 1985, p. 29.

Standard & Poor's, "Computers and Office Equipment: Basic Analysis," *Industry Surveys,* October 1, 1987.

CASE

10 The Rise of IBM

In 1900 Charles Flint, a financier and arms merchant, owned among many other businesses two business machine manufacturers: the International Time Recording Co. (ITR), a clock manufacturer, and Computing Scale Co. of America, a weighing scale and food slicing machine manufacturer. In the search for new markets for its products, ITR began to produce new kinds of time-measuring machines that, among other things, permitted the rapidly expanding Bell telephone company to time its customers' long-distance calls. By 1910 ITR had become the leader in the time-recording industry with sales over $1 million. Computing Scale's main product was a scale that weighed items and calculated the cost per unit; the company also sold meat and cheese slicers to retail stores.

Toward the end of the nineteenth century, engineer Herman Hollerith invented a tabulating machine that sorted cards by punching holes. Any kind of data could be recorded by punching holes in cards according to a standard procedure and then the data could be analyzed statistically to provide a picture of the overall results. Potential customers for this device were organizations that needed a way of managing and manipulating large amounts of information, such as government agencies, railroads, and retail establishments. The U.S. Census Bureau, for example, saw the potential of this device for handling its national data collection efforts and Hollerith was awarded a contract for managing the data processing of the 1890 census. Holes were punched in cards to represent different census attributes like age, sex, and national origin. The cards were then sorted by these punched holes and Hollerith's tabulating machine would then supply the requested data such as the statistics for the percentage of people in a certain age group in a certain state.

The punch card machine required a huge number of punched cards—in the census, one for every family unit—that could be used only once, so each machine sale provided card revenue. Nevertheless, the potential uses of the machine were limitless since any kind of data could be recorded on these cards. James Powers, an employee of the U.S. Census Bureau, immediately saw the potential of the tabulating machine and from his experience with Hollerith's machines at the Census Bureau he understood its strengths and weaknesses. Using this information, Powers invented an improved tabulating machine. Using his contacts at the Census Bureau, he managed to secure the contract for the 1910 census beating out Hollerith.

Hollerith was now in a difficult position because he had lost his principal customer and lacked the resources to improve his machine and to find new customers. He approached Flint to get Flint to invest in the business. Flint,

seeing the opportunity to broaden his company's line of business machines, decided instead to acquire Hollerith's Tabulating Machine Company. In 1911 Flint merged it with ITR and Computing Scale to form the Computing Tabulating & Recording Company (CTR).

In operating his business, Hollerith had developed the practice of leasing, rather than selling, his machines to customers. He had opted for leasing because his machines were prone to breaking down, and they needed frequent repair as their mechanical components tended to break down with repeated use. By leasing his machines and backing them with an efficient repair service, Hollerith kept his customers happy. Moreover, customers liked the arrangement because it lowered their costs. Using CTR's resources, the Hollerith tabulating machines were continually improved over time, and as new machines were developed, they were leased to customers and replaced the old machines. These leases provided CTR with a continuing source of revenue, but more important, each of CTR's customers was required to buy punch cards from CTR. Seventy-five percent of tabulating revenues and most of the profit came from the sale of the punched cards, while only 25 percent came from the lease of the actual machine itself. In 1912 CTR's profits were $541,000 with 66 percent of this total coming from ITR, its time machine division. By 1913, however, profits rose to $613,000 with most of the increase traceable to revenues from punch cards and tabulators. The revenue produced by its new tabulator business proved very important to CTR because the next year, 1914, profits plunged to $490,000 due to a decline in the time clock sector. Only the tabulating business kept the company afloat.

THE IMPACT OF THOMAS WATSON

In 1914, to build CTR's business, Flint agreed to hire Thomas Watson as the general manager of CTR. Watson was a former employee of National Cash Register (NCR), another major business machine company, which he had joined in 1895 when he was 21 years old. Watson had a passion for selling and began selling pianos, sewing machines, and organs when he was 18. The opportunity to earn large commissions eventually led him to NCR where a mentor took an interest in his career and helped him develop his selling skills to the point where he became the star salesman at NCR within three years. Watson became an NCR branch manager in 1899.

To exploit Watson's talents, NCR assigned him to create an independent company using NCR funds. It was called Watson's Cash Register and Second Hand Exchange and was designed to beat NCR's competitors in the used cash register market. Just as NCR had a virtual monopoly over the sale of new cash registers, so Watson set out to monopolize the used cash register market by deliberately undercutting competitors' prices. With their businesses failing, NCR would then acquire its competitors. This practice was blatantly illegal, and in 1912, Watson along with 29 other NCR managers were indicted for violation of antitrust laws. Watson was fined and sentenced to one year in jail; however, he won on appeal, and having quarreled with the head of NCR he decided to leave the company. Watson had other offers in the boat, auto, and retail industries, but because he wanted to use his knowledge of business machines, he accepted Flint's offer at CTR.

Watson's experience at NCR was significant for CTR because he implemented many of NCR's sales practices at CTR. Although NCR's competitors had higher-quality cash registers than NCR, NCR consistently beat the competition because of the way it organized and rewarded its sales force. NCR had developed the practice of granting salespeople exclusive rights to a territory and then paying them on commission. Salespeople would pursue all sales opportunities in their territories aggressively and they would call continually on customers in order to build strong, personal relationships with them. This sales strategy had been developed by the leader of NCR, John Patterson, who believed that a product was worthless until it was sold and that salespeople were the key to selling the product. Patterson insisted that NCR salespeople answer repair calls immediately and instilled in them the notion that they were selling a service, not just a product. NCR created a training school in 1894 to train its salespeople; it also established the NCR "Hundred Point Club" which recognized and rewarded salespeople who exceeded their quotas. Members of the club received bonuses and trips to conventions in big cities, coverage in the company newspaper, and personal congratulations from Patterson. Watson took full advantage of his knowledge of NCR's sales practices and transferred them to CTR. He also took full advantage of his entrepreneurial ability to sense unmet customer needs; he was fascinated by the potential of the punch card tabulating machine.

In 1904 Watson saw a friend at Eastman Kodak using a Hollerith punch card tabulating machine to monitor salespeople. Each time a sale was completed, all the data were stored onto a card, which was sorted and tabulated monthly to generate reports indicating what each person sold, which products were selling best in which regions, and so on. The cards were permanent records that could be filed, accumulated, and printed automatically. The punch card system eliminated boring jobs such as copying ledger entries and writing bills. Furthermore, the machines were relatively inexpensive (compared to employing clerks to keep records), dependable, and fast. Thus, as head of CTR, Watson became most interested in the tabulating machine side of the business even though ITR's time measurement business generated the highest sales and profits at the time.

When Watson became president of CTR in 1915 he convinced Flint that CTR should devote most of its resources to developing the tabulator side of the business. Watson implemented a plan to develop new tabulators, recorders, and printers to print the output of the tabulating machine. To achieve this new plan, the company funded the development of a research laboratory to improve the tabulating machines and established a facility to train salespeople. His goal was to create a sales force like NCR's sales force and to make better tabulating machines than CTR's competitors. To help provide the revenue to achieve this, Watson licensed foreign companies to produce and sell the tabulators in foreign markets. The licensees paid a royalty to CTR based on sales. This was the beginning of CTR's international strategy. Within two years, CTR's research laboratory created a new line of tabulators that were easier to use than competitors' models and that were priced below its competitors and offered for lease on favorable terms.

Powers was still CTR's major competitor at this time. To compete with Powers, which had tabulators as good as CTR's, Watson used the strategy that NCR had developed in the cash register business: sell a service, not just a product. Watson, like Patterson, emphasized that the salesperson's role was to provide good quality customer service, not merely to lease and install a machine.

What CTR was selling was a way to handle information. This new philosophy was to guide the company's future mission.

Watson established the "100 Percent Club" to reward his best salespeople, and employees were paid generous commissions for meeting and exceeding their quotas. Those who met quotas and joined the 100 Percent Club were honored at conventions and received special status in the organization; 80 percent of employees made the club. In addition, employees received a premium salary and good benefits. The company's policy of internal promotion made it possible for hard-working employees to advance quickly in the organization. These employment practices made it easy for CTR to attract and retain good salespeople and to gain the commitment of its work force which was famous for championing the company's products.

By 1917 CTR's sales had increased to $8.3 million from $4.2 million in 1914. All three of its divisions were doing well. Computing Scale's products were now used throughout the United States in places such as shipyards and factories to measure the quantity of products such as nuts and bolts. CTR had record sales during World War I. CTR had 1,400 tabulators on lease by the end of the war.

Virtually all big insurance companies, railroads, and government agencies used CTR's tabulators. In addition to the leased machines, the sales of punch cards were increasing and contributing to company revenues. In 1919, CTR launched a new printer that displayed the data collected and analyzed in the Hollerith tabulators and card sorters. The printer was priced below the machine made by Powers and was so successful that CTR had a backorder for the printers and Watson planned to build a new production plant to meet the high demand.

The large expenditures on research and development and on developing and training a skilled national sales force put a severe strain on CTR's resources. The strain was so severe that when sales revenues dropped from a record of $16 million in 1920 to $10.6 million in 1921, due to a slump in the national economy, CTR had to seek outside funds to survive. Fortunately for the company, Guaranty Trust Bank lent CTR the money it needed to meet current liabilities, and in 1922 sales revenues rebounded and the company made a profit. However, the company had to cut costs in every area, including sales and R&D, and CTR learned not to let cash balances go too low and implemented policies of low dividends, high revenues, and careful cost controls. In addition, the company intentionally refrained from introducing its new products until a mass market had developed for its new range of tabulating machines.

Watson became chairman of CTR in 1924 and renamed the company International Business Machines (IBM). This new name not only presented an integrated image of the company's three main product lines but also indicated the direction Watson planned for the company—the company's business was to provide advanced business machines for both the domestic and foreign markets.

IBM's strategy from the 1920s on was to produce and lease business machines that collect, process, and present large amounts of data. From 1924 to 1941, IBM's primary business was the production and lease of punched card tabulating machines and the sale of punch cards; punched cards still contributed most to the revenues of the company. As the technology of punch card tabulators became more advanced, they were able to sort 400 cards a minute and could print paychecks and address labels. Tabulating machines were used increasingly by large companies to keep records on their employees and suppliers and to keep track of their customer accounts. Companies usually leased IBM's machines and IBM would develop a specific punch card system to meet the needs of each indi-

vidual customer. For example, IBM would help the customer design a coding system appropriate to each client's information processing needs.

The potential of punch card tabulating machines had been recognized by other companies as well. While the Powers Accounting Machine Corp. had long been IBM's competitor, new computers included Burroughs, National Cash Register, Remington Rand, and Underwood Elliot Fisher. Underwood, which was created in 1927, ruled the typewriter industry with its Model 5 and had a sales force as good as IBM's, while Burroughs was the leader in adding machines. At this time, IBM was not interested in mass producing machines like typewriters and adding machines unless such machines could be made part of the tabulating system. Its strategy was to lease its machines and then support the machines with trained service representatives who were available to handle a customer's problems and to make suggestions for improving a customer's information processing as the individual business changed.

Leasing gave IBM several competitive advantages over Burroughs, NCR, and Remington Rand, which all sold their machines to customers. First, it allowed the company to retain control over outdated technology which could not be resold in the used market (a problem NCR had encountered which reduced its profits). Second, leasing made it easier for the customer because they were not committed to a large capital outlay or the threat of purchasing a machine that would be outmoded quickly by technological change. Third, leasing provided IBM with a steady cash flow. Fourth, and very important, by leasing its machine IBM was also able to force customers to purchase the thousands of punch cards they used each month from IBM.

IBM's practice of requiring customers to buy its cards led to an antitrust suit in 1936, and the Supreme Court ruled that IBM should discontinue requiring customers to buy cards from it alone. This ruling had little impact on IBM because IBM was the most convenient supplier of cards and its sales force serviced the machines and made sure that customers were kept happy.

During the 1920s and 1930s IBM also began to develop specialized tabulators to handle specific types of information processing needs for customers. For example, IBM developed a proofing machine to be used by banks that could sort and add checks, a very labor-intensive process. This proof machine, called the IBM 405, was launched in 1932 and became IBM's most profitable product at the time. The 405 consisted of a punch, sorter, and accounting machine. Operators punched holes in cards to represent data; the sorter then put the cards in the appropriate bins; the cards were then taken out of the bins and run through the accounting machines, which generated printouts of the data and which also could print checks. Some customers rented verifiers which attached to the punch to ensure the cards were prepared properly. IBM trained its customers' employees on how to use the 405 machines at no cost to promote customer loyalty and to ensure a demand for its products.

By 1939 IBM was the biggest and most powerful business machine company in the United States. IBM owned about 80 percent of the keypunches, sorters, and accounting machines used for tabulating purposes. By this time Remington Rand and Burroughs were minor competitors and the Powers company had disappeared, unable to match IBM's strengths in sales and research and development.

Also by 1939 Watson had reorganized the company's business divisions to meet the needs of IBM's new focus on tabulating machines. The punch card tabulating division became the center of the company business, and the company's other products were now oriented around this division. For example, Watson

decided to keep ITR, which sold time clocks among other things, because customers purchased many time cards that were similar to punch cards. He sold off the largest part of the scale division because it no longer fit the company's new direction. He bought Electromatic Typewriter Co. because it was working on keypunch consoles. This purchase proved very significant; by 1945 IBM had developed this company into the U.S. leader in electric typewriters, which were sold by IBM's large, well-trained sales force.

In 1939 total revenues were $34.8 million and profits were $9.1 million. Sales of punch cards were about $5 million of this and had higher profit margins than any other product. The start of World War II accelerated the demand for IBM's tabulating machines and sales rose to $143.3 million by 1943. However, profits were only $9.7 million due to the wartime excess profits tax. IBM achieved higher sales with mobile punch card units that followed supply controllers across war zones so that bookkeeping could be done on the battlefield. For example, a mobile unit would go to a Pacific Island and compute the soldiers' payroll. The tabulators also recorded bombing results, casualties, prisoners, displaced persons, and supplies. A punch card record was maintained on every man drafted and followed him until he was discharged from the military.

By 1945 IBM had begun aggressively to pursue the idea that just producing business machines was not enough; supplying customers with a way to manage their information processing needs was even more important. This change in focus was very significant; IBM now saw its role as developing new and different kinds of products to suit its customers' needs, rather than in finding new ways to use and improve existing machines. This change in operating philosophy proved very important with the development of the first working computer.

THE COMPUTER AGE

Toward the end of World War II, a research team at the University of Pennsylvania constructed a computer to solve math problems for the Army; the machine, called the ENIAC, could compute ballistic tables to accurately aim and fire the big guns of World War II. In 1946 the ENIAC was the only working computer in the world. This computer was the size of a small house and had 18,000 vacuum tubes, which were apt to burn out. The machine cost $3 million to build, took a long time to set up, and was very difficult to use. The inventors of the computer, J. Presper Eckert and John Mauchley, realized that computers could perform the same function as punch card tabulating machines only much more quickly because they processed information electronically rather than mechanically. They realized that their computer eventually could replace tabulating machines in business, so they created a company to develop and manufacture their computer for commercial use. Their machine and company was called Univac. In 1948 they received an order from the U.S. Census Bureau for their computer, just as Hollerith 60 years before had received an order for his tabulating machine. In the same year Prudential Insurance also ordered a Univac. These organizations were two of IBM's largest customers and so IBM took notice of the new technology and became interested in the Univac computer. In 1950 Remington Rand, which also sold typewriters, tabulators, filing cabinets, and electric shavers, forestalled IBM and bought Eckert and Mauchley's company to gain entry into the new computer market. Just as Watson had realized the potential of the punch card

machine, so Remington Rand realized the potential of the computer. The race was on between IBM and Remington Rand to become the company that would dominate the next generation of business machines: computers.

IBM'S RACE TO CATCH UP

IBM had not ignored technical developments in the tabulating industry. By 1948 it had developed an electromechanical machine called the MARK I that was 51 feet long by 8 feet high and cost $1 million. This machine was more advanced than a punch card machine, but it was still not a true computer because it did not use vacuum tubes, and it was slower than the Univac. The company was still not committed to the new technology, however, and it took the arrival of Tom Watson, Sr.'s two sons, Tom Jr. and Arthur ("Dick") who joined IBM at the end of the war to bring IBM up to speed.

Tom Watson, Jr., convinced his father that IBM would lose everything if it did not embrace the new technology and enter the computer age. He pointed out that large IBM customers such as the Prudential and Metropolitan Life insurance companies had been complaining for a long time that the punch card system required too much storage space and was becoming too slow and cumbersome to handle the volume of information these companies were generating. Under Tom Jr.'s leadership IBM began to check into new kinds of storage systems, such as magnetic tapes, and to look at the machine that used the new electronic circuits to sort data and handle calculations: the computer. After studying the ENIAC computer, Tom Jr. encouraged IBM's research laboratory managers to recruit more electronic specialists. He prodded IBM to incorporate electronic circuits in punch card machines because a primitive electronic circuit could perform 5,000 additions per second compared to 4 per second for the fastest mechanism in a punch card machine.

Working quickly, and with access to the company's large resource base, in 1946 IBM developed a new machine, the 603 Electronic Multiplier, that could compute payroll in one-tenth the time a mechanical punch card machine could do it. The machine was upgraded to the 604 which had electronic circuits that also allowed the machine to divide. The 604 was not a true computer because numbers were still processed from punch cards rather than from signals recorded in the machine's memory circuits. Nevertheless, when it was introduced in mid 1948 it sold by the thousands. Both machines matched IBM's existing punch card equipment which made it easy for IBM customers to upgrade to the new machines. The machine's success convinced Tom Jr. and Sr. that electronics would grow even faster; from this time on, the company committed its resources to the new technology and to the development of an advanced new computer system.

IBM began working on its first family of electronic computers, called the 701 series, in 1949. Tom Jr. became president of domestic IBM in 1952, the same year the 701 was launched. The 701 was a scientific computer for use in laboratories, but it was not as advanced as the Univac. However, although Remington Rand was ahead in technology, the company lacked IBM's vision and Rand would not permit punch card salespeople to sell Univacs. Tom Jr., however, placed IBM's sales force behind its computer and required both senior executives and engineers to help its sales force in operating the new machine. By 1953 IBM had installed 32 701 computers and had 164 on order compared to Remington Rand's 33 installations and 24 orders.

The 702, a commercial computer for general accounting applications, was launched in 1954. This machine was faster than the Univac and with this machine IBM took the technological lead. By 1956 IBM had 87 computers installed at various businesses and 190 on order, compared to all other competitors' combined installations of 41 and combined orders of 40 computers.

Because all its machines were leased, it was easy for IBM to upgrade its customers to its new advanced machines. When the 705 was developed to replace the 702, and the 704 to replace the 701, IBM retained and increased its market share. Between 1950 and 1956, IBM's revenues tripled from $214.9 million to $743.3 million. The average growth rate of the company from 1946 to 1955 was 22 percent. Watson decided to expand IBM's product line as fast as the market would allow.

IBM's technological success was due to the way Tom Watson, Jr., had totally changed the company's research and development thrust. IBM's research laboratory had been dominated by mechanical engineers because its punch card machines operated on mechanical principles. None of its engineers really understood electronics. So Tom Jr. hired a new laboratory director and increased the size of the R&D staff from 500 mechanical engineers and technicians in 1950 to over 4,000 electrical engineers by 1956. Tom Jr. also created a smaller lab in California to specialize in developing advanced information storage devices; in less than three years the laboratory developed a computer disk that stored data on magnetic tape rather than punch cards, a storage system that became the backbone of IBM's future computer systems and a major source of its competitive advantage.

Tom Watson, Jr., also led the development of the IBM 650 in 1956. It provided enough data processing power for most general commercial applications. The 650 was less powerful than the 700 series but it was much cheaper. The 650 introduced thousands of punch card customers to computers. It was designed to work with ordinary punch card equipment but to make the punch card system much more powerful and versatile. For example, life insurance companies compute insurance premiums from actuarial tables based on age, sex, and other customer factors. Using a 650, these actuarial tables could be loaded into the computer memory, and when the punch card containing information of a particular customer was loaded into the machine the computer did the calculations and furnished the total premium. Previously a clerk had to figure the totals and record the information on a punch card for recording purposes.

IBM put its huge sales force behind the 650 machine; as a result of its efforts, within a year almost 1,000 machines were sold. Most computers were used in administrative offices and in factories where the computer was used to control the manufacturing process. By the end of the 1950s, IBM had a 75 percent market share. The remaining market was divided among Remington Rand, Honeywell Electronics, NCR, and a few others. Although Underwood Typewriter and NCR attempted to launch small computers, they were unable to produce as good a performer as the 650.

THE TRANSISTOR

In 1956 the transistor, which weighed 100 times less than the vacuum tube, was developed by William Shockley at Bell Labs. Compared to a vacuum tube, the transistor required less electrical power, had the potential to miniaturize computing systems, and, most important, could perform calculations at a much

faster rate. The transistor made the design of a more complex and powerful computer feasible; it also made it possible to sell the computer at a price that most large companies could afford.

IBM's electronic researchers had been successfully using the vacuum tube, and as the mechanical engineers before them, they were reluctant to change to new technology: a transistor-based computer technology. So Tom Watson, Jr., sent a memo to R&D personnel stating that no more IBM machines would be designed using vacuum tubes. This memo started a whole new thrust in IBM's research efforts that led to the 7000 computer series, IBM's first computer based on transistors rather than vacuum tubes. However, IBM's scientists had a major problem in wiring transistors together to produce the new advanced computer until the integrated circuit was invented in 1959 by a Fairchild Semiconductor engineer. With the arrival of the integrated circuit, thousands of transistors could be joined together on a circuit board the size of a fingernail. In turn, thousands of integrated circuits could be joined together to make the first modern computer. By the early 1960s, IBM computers guided Polaris missiles and Air Force jets. When integrated circuits were mass produced, their cost fell from $1,000 per circuit in 1960 to a few cents per circuit by 1970, and IBM developed successive generations of more powerful machines to exploit the new technology.

REDEFINING THE INDUSTRY

As a result of this succession of technological developments, by 1960 IBM's computer division was disorganized and had a product line consisting of eight newer transistor-based computers and several older vacuum tube machines. This mixed product line caused several problems for IBM's customers and its sales force because the computers were not compatible and could not work together. For example, if a customer expanded and wanted to upgrade to a larger or newer computer, the customer had to lease a whole new range of equipment and rewrite all the programs to make the computer work. The disjointed product line also caused problems for IBM's personnel.

Because IBM's product line had grown so large, Watson decided to split the Data Processing Division into two units: one for the newer machines that rented for over the average price of $10,000 a month and one for older, less-powerful machines that rented for less than $10,000 a month. This decision caused competition between managers of the different product lines, each of whom fought to obtain resources to develop and improve their particular product line. It also led to a duplication of research and development efforts.

The diverse range of computers IBM now leased also made it more difficult for IBM's sales force to learn the characteristics of the different systems associated with each computer and to inform customers about the suitability of a given system for the particular business involved. IBM's technological thrust had outpaced the ability of the company to service its products adequately. Its attempt to dominate the industry by being the first mover in technology had resulted in the development of a fragmented product line that was confusing its customers and its employees. The company needed a new strategy to grow.

Watson's answer was that IBM needed to build a new line of computers that would cover the needs of the whole computer market. The project was called the System/360, representing the 360 degrees in a circle, because IBM wanted to

meet the needs of every user in both the scientific and business community. The 360 was intended to make all other computers, both IBM's and its competitors, obsolete. All the 360 computers would be compatible with one another. Moreover, they would all use the same operating language, software, disk drives, printers, and so on. The goal of the new design was to lock in customers to IBM's computer systems and to make it very difficult for customers to change to competitors' products—both because of superior product quality and because their incentive would be to upgrade to a more powerful machine that was compatible with their old machines. The other goal of the system was to make better use of IBM's research and development resources and to make it easier for its sales force to sell an integrated package of products to customers.

The project was challenging because hardware and software had to be developed and coordinated across the whole of its product line. This meant that all of the different parts of the mainframe system—storage devices, central processors, terminals, and printers—had to be compatible, as did the components used in the various parts of the system. To ensure the compatibility of the new system, and the supply and quality of the component parts, IBM began producing many of its own electronic components itself. From this point on IBM became involved in all aspects of the mainframe computer business—it would design and manufacture almost all of the components that would be used in its mainframe computers, it would manufacture its mainframes in its own factories, and it would distribute and sell its mainframes itself. IBM opened six new plants around the world to manufacture the System/360 computers. Over a four-year period, $5 billion was invested and 50,000 new employees were hired as part of IBM's ambitious expansion plan.

The System/360 mainframe computer was launched in 1964 and captured 70 percent of the market. The project was an immense success and put IBM way ahead of its competitors. Although before the 360, competitors such as RCA, Burroughs, Honeywell, Univac, and GE sold machines that performed much better than IBM computers for the same price, the compatible design and the power of the System/360 beat all competitors. Moreover, marketing played as large a role in the success of the project as technology. While all its competitors had access to integrated circuits and could produce an advanced computer, only IBM had the capacity to provide a customer a complete information processing service—the machine itself, installation and maintenance, and the quality personalized service that allowed it to retain and tie up its customers.

Due to the technical superiority of the System/360 mainframes and the reputation for quality service established by IBM's sales force, IBM dominated the computer industry. The 360 spurred growth in the whole industry. In 1963 there were only 11,700 computers in the United States; this figure doubled in 1965 and redoubled in 1969. By 1969 IBM leased over 50,000 computer systems which generated sales revenues of $7.196 billion and earnings of $934 million, a staggering figure for the time. A large part of these revenues was generated from IBM's international operations.

GLOBAL DEVELOPMENT

IBM's movement into global markets began in 1908 when Herman Hollerith made a licensing agreement with the British Tabulating Company (BTC) to pro-

duce and sell Hollerith tabulators throughout the British Empire. Tom Watson, Sr., continued with Hollerith's vision of IBM as an international company and established IBM's foreign department. After World War I, he began to build small manufacturing plants in Germany, France, and Great Britain to evade the tariffs these countries levied on foreign imports. Sales and marketing agencies were created throughout Europe, Latin America, and parts of Asia. The branches were called Watson Business Machines and their function, as in the United States, was to provide the high level of customer service that supported IBM's business machines. In 1935 foreign revenue was $1.6 million, with punch cards once again being the biggest contributor. By 1939 over 12 percent of IBM's revenues came from foreign operations.

During World War II, IBM's plants in Europe and Japan were seized. However, even though IBM's German plant, which contributed 50 percent of the foreign department's revenue, was in ruins, by 1945 foreign revenues were almost $2 million. After the war, IBM's British plant became the largest facility outside North America, and in 1949 IBM renegotiated the 1908 agreement with the BTC whereby BTC would receive a free, nonexclusive license on all current IBM products in exchange for letting IBM sell its new products through its own sales organization. This agreement resulted in the creation of a new subsidiary called IBM U.K. which, selling IBM's new advanced computers, soon came to dominate the British and European markets.

In 1949 Dick Watson, who spoke German, French, Italian, and Spanish, was put in charge of IBM's international operations, and in 1950 the foreign department was renamed IBM World Trade Division and became an independent subsidiary that would receive product and financial support from IBM's Domestic Division but would operate on its own. By 1950 the World Trade Division had 10 factories producing machines and over 20 facilities making cards throughout the world. World Trade operated in 58 countries through subsidiaries such as IBM Deutschland, IBM France, and many smaller units in Latin America and Africa.

Of World Trade's 16,000 employees in 1954, only 200 were Americans, because Dick Watson believed that most success would be achieved if each subsidiary was responsive to the needs of its own region or country. Dick Watson set high standards for World Trade, hired good people as country managers, and was responsive to local customs.

By 1967 foreign revenues were $1.6 billion and net earnings were $209 million. World Trade sales were equal to IBM's Domestic Division sales. Although IBM operated in 130 countries, Europe accounted for two-thirds of foreign revenue. In 1970 Dick Watson resigned from IBM to become the U.S. ambassador to France. With his departure, the World Trade Division was further divided into world regions: Europe, the Middle East, Africa, the Americas, and the Far East. By 1970 foreign revenues had increased to $3.5 billion and once again accounted for almost 50 percent of IBM's total revenues.

IBM'S STRUCTURE

IBM's Domestic Division, which was led by Tom Watson, Jr., was responsible for research and development and for financing the operations of the entire global company. By 1950 not only was IBM Domestic designing and manufacturing a large number of different models of computer, it was also designing and

manufacturing many of the component and peripheral parts used in the computers such as disk drives, transistors, printers, and file storage and servers. Many of these products were produced throughout the world and distributed by IBM's international division. The increase in the range of IBM's activities, both domestically and internationally, put considerable strain on IBM's organizational structure, which began to cause it many problems.

IBM was run largely by Tom Watson, Sr., until he retired in 1955. Watson oversaw all of IBM's operations, and a line of top managers was always waiting to see him. No formal organizational chart existed in IBM because Watson believed that people should be interested in all aspects of IBM's activities rather than focusing on specific jobs. The company had no clear chain of command, no policy of decentralization which gave lower-level managers the right to make independent decisions, and no formal planning process or business policies. Knowledge was simply in employees' heads and strategy emerged gradually over time from discussion and negotiations between Watson and his top management team.

After Tom Watson, Sr.'s retirement, Tom Watson, Jr., and Al Williams, IBM's president at this time, decided to construct an organizational chart to see who had reported to Watson and found that 38 to 40 top managers reported directly to him. It was obvious that this highly centralized management style could not continue if the rapidly growing company was to stay on top of the computer industry. Already unmade decisions were accumulating because managers lacked the authority to make decisions, and now they looked to Tom Watson, Jr., to take the lead.

Tom Jr. wanted to break with his father's centralized, autocratic style of management in order to speed communication and decision making, so he and Al Williams reorganized IBM's operating structure to decentralize control to managers who were given the responsibility of managing the different functional areas of the company. The organizational chart they devised put Red Lamotte in charge of sales and R&D and Al Williams in charge of finance, while Tom Jr. would take control of the company's strategy. Unfortunately, this reorganization simply divided the chaos among three people instead of one. There were still far too many managers reporting to the three top managers, and they were unable to control IBM's operations adequately. So in 1956 IBM was reorganized along divisional lines.

IBM Domestic was broken up into five separate divisions: the Field Engineering Division, which primarily served commercial customers; the Federal Systems Division, which primarily served government customers; the Systems Manufacturing Division, which manufactured the computers; the Component Manufacturing Division, which manufactured the components; and the Research Division, which performed the basic research and design activities. In each division a general manager was given the responsibility of making decisions for the division and developing its strategy. The World Trade Division would continue to operate separately from IBM Domestic.

This multidivisional structure ensured that each general manager had a clearly defined task. At the top of the organization, Tom Jr. created a top management team of six people, consisting of himself and the heads of the five divisions, to oversee the company's strategy. Each of the five general managers was responsible for a major part of IBM, and Tom Jr. was to oversee the entire company. He claimed that his ability to choose and retain an intelligent top management team was his greatest contribution to IBM.

Watson also created a corporate staff of experts in sales and marketing, finance, manufacturing, personnel, and communications to advise him and to oversee the activities of the divisions. The corporate staff was seen as staff or advisory managers to the general managers of the division who were the line managers with responsibility for bottom-line operating results. It was the line manager's job (the general manager and other divisional managers) to meet production targets, beat sales quotas, and increase market share. The staff manager's job was to give advice to line managers—the heads of the divisions who were their superiors, to convey policy from corporate headquarters to the operating divisions, and to ensure that the proper objectives were in place and being met. Each line manager would be evaluated solely on his or her unit's results, and each staff manager would be rated on his or her effort in making IBM a world leader.

IBM's divisional structure produced many tensions between corporate (staff) and divisional (line) personnel. For example, as a part of their role, staff managers often would identify problems that needed to be addressed in the divisions and would write memos to line managers suggesting how to solve them. Line managers, however, viewed these moves as interference and an intrusion into their area of operations. They began to guard their territories from corporate personnel who had no direct authority over general managers in IBM's structure.

To resolve these tensions, Williams created a check and balance system in IBM called *contention management.* This system forced both staff and line managers to meet and encouraged them to debate the merits of an idea. However, no operating plan became final without staff approval. When line and staff managers could not agree, the problem would be sent to the corporate management committee—the top six executives—to resolve the problem. Over time, an increasing number of issues were sent to the top of the organization to resolve because line and staff managers could not agree on priorities and future policy. This slowed communication and decision making; eventually, it became accepted that the top management committee would resolve important strategic issues.

Thus, despite Watson's claimed policy of decentralizing authority to divisional managers and their subordinates, much of IBM's decision making remained centralized at the top of the organization, and managers from IBM's mainframe division—its chief revenue earner—had the most power in shaping corporate decision making.

THE IBM CULTURE

The centralized approach that was developing at IBM had important implications for IBM's culture and the values that guided the company. Because IBM's managers began to rely on their superiors to make important policy decisions, they became very conservative in their approach and became increasingly afraid to take risks and to go out on their own. IBM developed many bureaucratic rules and operating procedures that specified how decisions were to be made and how to resolve disputes. Slowly but surely the entrepreneurial values that had allowed the company to capitalize quickly on new technologies changed to emphasize values of conforming to the IBM way: commitment and loyalty to the company and respect and obedience to superiors.

IBM's conservative culture was reinforced by its policy of long-term employment. The company became known throughout the industry for its job security and good pay. With IBM's high rate of growth, internal promotion was easy to come by, and employees rose rapidly through the corporate ranks. In 1955 employee stock options were offered for the first time. In 1966 managers were required to attend an in-house IBM manager school, where they were trained in IBM's philosophy on communications, sales and service efforts, meetings, and employee treatment such as visiting workers with sick spouses. This policy taught employees the IBM way and helped to cement IBM's corporate culture and its style of doing business.

NEW MANAGEMENT AND NEW CHALLENGES

In 1970 Dick Watson resigned to become the U.S. ambassador to France and Tom Watson, Jr., suffered a heart attack which resulted in his retirement in 1971. When Tom Watson, Jr., appointed T. V. Learson as CEO in 1971 the period of the Watson family's control over IBM came to an end. IBM was the largest, most successful computer company in the world and had complete domination over the global mainframe computer industry. Each year, its revenues and profit reached record levels; the company plowed back over 10 percent of its revenue to fund future research and development to allow it to maintain its dominance in the mainframe market.

Despite its impressive performance, however, all was not well with the company. Although the situation was masked by increasing revenues from World Trade, by 1970 IBM was starting to slow down. While the company had grown at an annual rate of 22 percent from 1946 to 1955, its growth was only 16 percent per year from 1955 to 1970. Indeed, its stock price actually declined in 1970 despite record sales. Why? IBM was beginning to face increased competition from other companies in the mainframe computer market and from companies that began to produce computers for other segments of the computer market. The challenge for Learson was to use IBM's vast resources to exploit a computer market that was growing by leaps and bounds. How could the company exploit its privileged position to dominate the computer market of the future? The answers were not long in coming.

References

Mercer, David. *The Global IBM*. New York: Dodd, Mead, 1988.

Sober, Robert. IBM: *Colossus in Transition*. New York: Times Books, 1981.

Watson, Thomas, Jr., and Peter Petre. *Father and Son & Co.: My Life at IBM and Beyond*. New York: Bantam Books, 1990.

"The Intimate Tale of IBM's First Family." *Fortune*, June 14, 1990, pp. 92–131.

CASE

11 The Fall of IBM

T. V. Learson took over as CEO of IBM from Tom Watson, Jr., in 1971 and became the head of a company that had a 75 percent share of the world market for mainframe computers—computers powerful enough to manage the information processing needs of an entire company. Learson had made a major personal contribution to IBM's emergence as the dominant global mainframe manufacturer when he led the development of IBM's highly successful 360 mainframe series, the series that led to the rapid rise in the company's fortunes. IBM's 360 mainframes fully automated a company's manual information processing systems, such as payroll and accounting or customer recordkeeping, and made the punch card obsolete. As the former head of the 360 program, Learson understood the critical importance of research and development in maintaining and defending IBM's preeminent position in the mainframe market, and so he initiated and oversaw the development of IBM's new, more powerful System/370 computer series.[1]

Technical advances lowered the System/370's price per calculation to 60 percent below that of the System/360s, and the 370 had a larger information storage system as well. The 370s still used the software of the 360s, however, so they were primarily an upgrade rather than a replacement of the 360. Nevertheless, the 370 machines became the backbone of IBM's mainframe product line from the early 1970s on. Most of the advances that IBM made to its mainframe computers from this time on were designed primarily to improve the 370 machines' processing power or the performance of the various components of the 370 series, such as its software, printers, and especially its storage capacity. The 370 series became the industry standard that IBM's competitors tried to match and outperform.

Under Learson's control and then under the control of Frank Cary, who became CEO when Learson retired in 1973, IBM continued to enjoy its domination of the mainframe market. By 1980 IBM had a market value of $26 billion, four times its size in 1971.

INCREASING COMPETITION

Although IBM's continued domination of the mainframe market produced record increases in revenues and profits every year, its performance masked some major problems that were developing during the 1970s and 1980s. The first

This case was prepared by Gareth R. Jones and Susan L. Peters, Texas A&M University. This case was prepared as a basis for class discussion rather than to illustrate either effective or ineffective handling of administrative situations.

1. D. Mercer, *The Global IBM* (New York: Dodd, Mead, 1988), p. 58.

major problem, which Cary had recognized as early as 1970, was that the mainframe computer market was starting to mature. Almost every large U.S. business company possessed a mainframe computer, as had most scientific and higher education institutions. IBM also had saturated the international market. As a result, IBM's rate of growth was falling; even though its revenues were increasing, they were increasing at a decreasing rate. In the mature mainframe market, competition was increasing from companies that were trying to find ways to attract IBM's customers and share in the huge revenues in the mainframe computer market. Its major competitors at the time were Amdahl, Honeywell, Burroughs, Univac, NCR, and Control Data.

Many of these companies began offering IBM's customers mainframe systems at a lower cost than the expensive IBM systems. Initially, IBM faced competition only from companies selling IBM-compatible peripheral equipment such as disk drives, storage devices, and printers at lower prices than IBM's products. Its sales force had been able to ward off such threats. Now, however, the nature of competition was changing. IBM's competitors began selling cheaper, higher performing, and IBM-compatible central processing units (CPUs), the brain of the computer and the source of its processing power. For the first time they were offering a low-price alternative to the IBM mainframe while IBM was still pursuing its high-priced leased strategy backed by excellent customer service. Another emerging low-price threat came from leasing companies that would buy old 360s from IBM and lease them on better terms than IBM offered, attracting price-conscious IBM customers. While these competitive threats were small, they nevertheless gave IBM cause for concern.

From 1970 on IBM became concerned about the threat of low-cost foreign competition in the mainframe computer market after witnessing the decline in several U.S. industries, including automobiles, due to the entry of low-cost Japanese competitors. The price of integrated circuits, the heart of a mainframe computer, was plummeting at this time, and Japanese companies had the technical capability to build a powerful computer that could match or exceed the IBM 370. The existence of a low-cost global competitor was a major threat to IBM's domination both of the U.S. market and the global market.

To respond to the threat of low-cost competition, Cary announced that IBM would spend $10 billion to build new automated plants to produce low-cost computers over a six-year period. In this way IBM would be able to meet the challenge of low-priced computers should the threat materialize and its customers start to switch to low-cost competitors. John Opel, who became IBM's CEO in 1981, also was concerned about competition from Japan and he carried on with Cary's low-cost producer strategy. Under his control IBM spent $32 billion from 1980 to 1985 to find ways to reduce manufacturing costs.

IBM's push to reduce manufacturing costs did not fit well with its strategy of offering excellent-quality customer service using its very expensive sales force to sell and service its machines. It was unlikely that IBM would ever be able to compete on price with its competitors because its customer service and support activities raised its costs so much. Moreover, competing on price had never been a part of its strategy; IBM always had competed on its unique ability to provide customers with an integrated full-line computer service. Analysts wondered whether Opel was spending too much to lower manufacturing costs and whether the $32 billion could not be better spent in some other way.

CHANGES IN TECHNOLOGY

Changes in mainframe technology also caused a change in IBM's strategy during the 1970s. As a result of technological innovations, particularly the plunging costs of integrated circuits, the life span of a mainframe computer—the time it could be used until it was technologically outdated—was shortening rapidly and development costs were increasing. Formerly, customers would use the same IBM mainframe for several years, but now IBM was forced to replace its leased computers every two or three years, making it difficult to recoup development costs and obtain the premium price on its machines that it was accustomed to.

Because a computer's life span was getting shorter, and because of the growth of low-cost competition, IBM under Cary and then Opel decided to phase out IBM's system of leasing its machines to customers and instead to begin selling them—a major change in IBM's strategy. Although this move increased revenue in the short term, it had major repercussions for the company in the long term. First, the leasing system had tied IBM to its customers and ensured that when customers upgraded and expanded their computer systems they would look first at IBM machines. Moreover, leasing facilitated IBM's strategy of providing customers with excellent customer service and guaranteed the company a steady cash flow and control of the used machine market. With the end of leasing, IBM would be more susceptible to fluctuations in the demand for its products because its customers would be able to shop around.

From 1980 on, IBM began to face major competition from 370 clone manufacturers, large companies like Amdahl (which had a faster 370 processor than IBM), and Hitachi Data Systems (whose low-price machine generated record sales throughout the 1980s). IBM's customers began to feel more comfortable about buying 370 clones from companies that also promised quality support and service at low cost.[2] IBM's sales growth for its biggest mainframe dropped from 12 percent annually in 1984 to 5 percent annually in 1990 as a result of the increased competition. Increased mainframe competition with Amdahl and Hitachi Data Systems also led to price discounting despite the fact that IBM attempted to offer its customers a unique package that included software and services in addition to hardware. The days when IBM could demand whatever price it wanted for its machines were over.

The end of its leasing program also led to increased competition from independent computer leasing companies which would buy older mainframes and then sell the older processors at a price that was frequently only 10 percent of IBM's newest machine. These companies also disassembled mainframes in order to make smaller computers; for example, they could make two smaller machines out of one larger machine. In response to this price competition, IBM was forced to reduce the price of its machines.

The end of leasing, combined with a growth in low-cost competition, changed the nature of industry competition in ways that the company did not expect. IBM's strategy was now to protect its mainframe market from competitors and to hang on to its customers at all costs. IBM devoted most of its huge resources to developing technically superior mainframe products, to lowering their cost of production, and to supporting its very expensive but very successful sales force.

2. John Verity, "A Slimmer IBM May Still Be Overweight," *Business Week,* December 18, 1989, pp. 197–208.

IBM's focus on protecting its mainframe market blinded it to threats from the emergence of new kinds of computers. Even when it did recognize the competitive threat, IBM's operating structure and culture, shaped by its preeminent position as the world's leading mainframe computer company, made it difficult for IBM's managers to see emerging problems in its environment and to react quickly to the changes that technology was bringing about in the computer industry. The way IBM handled the emerging threat from new kinds of computers such as minicomputers, personal computers, and workstations illustrates many of the problems it experienced as a result of a corporate mindset that "mainframes were king."

THE MINICOMPUTER MARKET

One of the new computer markets that emerged in the 1970s was the minicomputer market. Minicomputers are smaller and significantly cheaper than mainframe computers and are priced anywhere from $12,000 to $700,000. The readily falling price of integrated circuits during the 1960s and 1970s made it feasible to build a minicomputer that could be afforded by small businesses or used in specialized technical or scientific applications. IBM had ignored this new market segment, preferring to focus its resources on developing and improving its profitable 360 and 370 series of computers.

It was left to two MIT researchers to pioneer the development of a smaller, powerful computer, and they founded the Digital Equipment Corporation (DEC) which in 1965 launched the PDP-8, a computer that could handle the smaller information processing needs and tasks of companies like small businesses, offices, factories, and laboratories. The venture was very successful, and by 1968 DEC's sales reached $57 million and earnings were $6.8 million. DEC's computer competed with the lower end of the 360 range. The computer sold well in research facilities, but it did not do as well in business because IBM dominated this market with its powerful sales force. DEC had plans to develop a more powerful machine, however, and as it grew it was quickly expanding its own national service network, imitating IBM's.

To meet DEC's challenge, which was still seen as a minor issue, Cary formed the General Systems Division in 1969 to produce the System/3 which was to be IBM's small, powerful minicomputer. IBM did not, however, rethink its technology or invest resources to develop a new minicomputer technology to make a product to suit this new market segment. Rather, IBM tried to adapt its existing mainframe technology to the minicomputer market.

IBM's top managers had risen up the ranks of IBM from the mainframe division, and they were conditioned by the idea that the level of computing power was everything. "The bigger the better" was the philosophy of these managers. Moreover, big machines meant big revenues. IBM's mainframe managers saw the potential earning power of the minicomputer as insignificant when compared to the huge revenues generated by its mainframes. More fundamentally, however, IBM's top managers did not want competition from a new computer division inside the company which would absorb large amounts of the company's resources and might change the company's future direction and strategy.

The result was that when the System/3s were developed they were too big and expensive to compete with DEC's machine and too small to compete with IBM's own mainframes, so they failed to make much inroad into what was becoming a very big market segment. As the minicomputer segment of the market continued to grow rapidly in the 1970s, Cary tried to increase the importance of the minicomputer group inside IBM's corporate hierarchy by reorganizing IBM's Data Processing Division and splitting it into two units: General Systems to make small minicomputers and Data Systems to make the mainframes. He hoped that this change would force IBM managers to change their mindset and support the company's move into the new markets.

So strong was the entrenched position of mainframe managers that Cary's change of structure created huge divisional rivalry between mainframe and minicomputer managers. The mainframe division saw itself as in direct competition for resources with the minicomputer division, and managers in both units failed to cooperate and to share technological resources to develop the new range of machines. When General Systems finally produced a smaller minicomputer called the 8100, it did not have a technological edge over the DEC machine. Nevertheless, it was successful, as many IBM customers had large sums of money tied up in IBM mainframes and were reluctant to switch suppliers. Moreover, IBM's powerful sales force (although at first reluctant to push minicomputers for fear of reducing their commissions) could service the needs of the minicomputer users. By the end of 1980, over 100,000 minicomputers had been sold. IBM and DEC were the industry leaders, the new companies that had sprung up, such as Hewlett-Packard and Wang, were also increasing their market share.

In 1986 DEC introduced its new VAX 9000 minicomputer which shocked IBM's mainframe managers because it had the same speed and capacity as IBM's largest 370 mainframe, the 3090, but cost only 25 percent as much. For the first time, mainframe managers were forced to accept the fact that minicomputers might be feasible substitutes for mainframes in many applications. Although DEC gained the business of some large financial service companies and corporate data processing centers with its new machine, market segments previously dominated solely by IBM, it still could not seize many of IBM's loyal customers who were locked into IBM systems. Nevertheless, DEC's share of the minicomputer market grew from 19 percent in 1984 to 25 percent in 1988, while IBM's share dropped from 24 percent to 16 percent in the same period.

Finally, in 1988 IBM brought out a minicomputer, the AS/400 series, that was superior to DEC's VAX. The AS/400 series was based on RISC (reduced instruction set computing) technology and fast RISC chips that could equal and exceed the speed of large mainframes, including IBM's own mainframes.[3] Many large companies that had a great deal of money invested in IBM mainframes now moved to adopt the IBM minicomputer system because it was compatible with their IBM mainframe systems. As a result of the success of its new minicomputers, IBM increased its market share from about 16 percent in 1988 to 28 percent in 1992 while DEC's fell.[4] DEC now plans to produce machines based on RISC, but in the interim, it has introduced new machines to compete with IBM's

3. John Verity, "The New IBM," *Business Week*, December 16, 1991, pp. 112–118.
4. John Verity, "IBM's Major Triumph in Minis," *Business Week*, March 16, 1992, p. 111.

AS/400s on price.[5] IBM now has a $14 billion business in minicomputers, which have gross margins of 56 percent.

THE PERSONAL COMPUTER

Another technological breakthrough, the microprocessor or "computer on a chip," sparked the development of the personal computer. The personal computer was developed in 1977 by Steven Jobs and Stephen Wozniak who founded Apple Computer. By 1980 Apple's sales had grown to $117 million.[6] Once again, IBM stood by and watched as a new market segment was created. This time, recognizing the mistakes it had made in the microcomputer market by not moving quickly enough to develop a machine to compete with the industry leader, it decided to move quickly to create its own machine to compete with Apple's.

In the mainframe market, IBM made its own chips, circuit boards, disk drives, terminals, tape drives, and printers; wrote its own proprietary software for its machines; and helped to develop software to meet the needs of its customers. As a result, its machines were not compatible with those of its rivals which used their own proprietary hardware and software. The machines of different manufacturers would not work together. In 1981, however, in an effort to enter the PC market quickly, IBM outsourced and bought the inputs it needed to make its personal computer from other companies. For example, Intel supplied the 8088 microchip that was the heart of the IBM machine and Microsoft delivered MS-DOS, its programming language and software applications for the new machine. Finally, computer stores, not the IBM sales force, were used to sell the new IBM PCs to get the machines to individual customers quickly.

IBM's first PC was introduced at a price of $1,565 in 1981 and was more powerful than the first Apple computer. Intel's 8088 chip had more main memory and was more powerful than the chip used in the Apple II computer, and Microsoft's operating system, MS-DOS, was better than the current industry standard. These features, combined with the power of the IBM brand name, made the IBM PC an immediate success, and it quickly became the industry standard for all other PCs.[7] Backed by IBM's legendary service, business users turned to the machines in the thousands. By 1984 IBM had seized 40 percent of the personal computer market, but the IBM PC still could not be produced or distributed fast enough to meet the enormous customer demand.[8]

Even the runaway success of the IBM PC became a threat to the company because its competitors rapidly imitated the IBM PC; soon clone manufacturers were selling IBM-compatible personal computers as powerful or more powerful than IBM's own machines. For example, Compaq, founded in 1981, began to clone IBMs and produced a high-powered machine that seized a large share of the high-price business market. In 1986 Compaq beat IBM to the market with a machine using Intel's new powerful 386 chip. At the same time, other clone makers like Zenith and Packard Bell attacked the low-price segment of the computer market and began producing PCs that undercut IBM's.

5. Gary McWilliams, "Can DEC Squeeze One Last Blast from VAX?" *Business Week,* October 28, 1991, p. 134.
6. Deidre Depke and Richard Brandt, "PCs: What the Future Holds," *Business Week,* August 12, 1991, pp. 58–64.
7. Ibid.
8. Mercer, pp. 106–111.

IBM, threatened both in the high-price and the low-price end of the PC market, fought back with the PS/2 which had a proprietary hardware channel that IBM made sure could not be imitated, as its first personal computer had been. However, customers resisted buying the new PS/2 because they did not want to become locked into a new IBM system that was not compatible with IBM's old system and that was not compatible with their other software or hardware investments. In the face of hostility from its customers, and losing market share, IBM was forced to back down and in 1988 began producing PS/2s that were compatible with the existing industry standard—its own older standard.

It was suddenly clear to IBM that it no longer controlled the rules of the competitive game in the personal computer industry. Nonetheless, it was still slow to change its strategy. Despite the fact that its cheaper rivals had machines that were as powerful as its own, IBM still attempted to charge a premium price for its product and so its customers went elsewhere. IBM's share of U.S. PC sales dropped from about 37 percent in 1985 to 24 percent in 1988. Clone makers continued to improve IBM's older standard, and IBM's market share declined to 16.5 percent in 1990.[9]

In 1991 a major price war broke out in the PC market, brought on in large part because of the steadily dropping price of computer hardware such as Intel's microprocessors. IBM reduced prices three times to compete, and prices of the PS/2 were cut as much as 25 percent.[10] Partly due to price competition, a typical 386 PC which had cost $3,500 in early 1991 cost $1,600 in late 1991 and only $1,200 in early 1992. Also in 1992 IBM introduced new low-priced lines of computers like the PS/Value Point targeted at the fastest-growing segment of the computer market, the home market, and to business customers who do not need all the features of the high-end PS/2. These new models have been very successful and are in great demand. Nonetheless, IBM does not hold a dominant position in the PC market; in 1992 its market share was 12 percent, the same as its rival Apple and about twice that of rivals like Dell, Compaq, and NEC.

The PC price wars continued into 1993. In February 1993, Dell Computer, a rapidly growing clone maker, introduced price cuts of 5 percent to 22 percent across its entire product line. In response, IBM cut prices as much as 16 percent on some models including PS/Value Point.[11] Apple cut prices five times in 1993 for a reduction of up to 33 percent on its three highest-priced computers in an effort to increase U.S. sales.[12] PC makers also battled over distribution and the offering of extras such as warranties. PCs currently range from $500 clones to $2,000 laptops to $25,000 network hubs.[13] PCs dominate the computer industry with world sales of $93 billion in 1993 compared to mainframe sales of $50 billion.[14] The laptop segment of the PC market alone reached $5.67 billion in 1990. IBM, however, did not have a product for this market segment until 1991 and it faces tough competition from the market leader Toshiba and from Apple.[15]

9. Depke and Brandt.
10. Ibid.
11. Richard Hudson and Laurence Hooper, "IBM Slashes PC Prices in the U.S., Europe, Moving Swiftly to Counter Rivals' Cuts," *The Wall Street Journal*, February 12, 1993, p. B6.
12. Bill Richards, "Apple Computer Cuts Its PC Prices Fifth Time in 1993," *The Wall Street Journal*, August 12, 1993, p. B1.
13. Depke and Brandt.
14. Ibid.
15. John Bryne, Deidre Depke, and John Verity, "IBM: As Markets and Technology Change, Can Big Blue Remake Its Culture?" *Business Week*, June 17, 1991, pp. 24–32.

By 1992 it was clear to IBM and to industry analysts that IBM was just one more competitor in a very competitive market. Since 1990 IBM's PC division has yet to show a profit because of the intense price competition and because IBM's costs are above its competitors like Compaq, which moved quickly to slash costs in 1990 when the price of PCs began tumbling.

IBM's response to competition in the personal computer industry throughout the 1980s clearly was affected by its "mainframe mindset." Even though it was clear that new segments of the computer market were developing and that new uses for computers were being found, IBM managers still discounted the potential threat to mainframes from either the minicomputer or the personal computer. IBM was not alone in being unable to sense the significance of changes in the environment. Kenneth Olsen, one of the founders of DEC, the minicomputer maker, went on record saying that "personal computers are just toys" in discounting the challenge of PCs to minicomputers, just as IBM had discounted the threat of minicomputers to mainframes ten years before. The Olsen philosophy blinded IBM's top management to the prospect that powerful PCs could become a threat to IBM's main line of business, mainframes. This predicament was somewhat surprising given that the computer industry always had been dominated by technological change, and IBM's success was itself the result of it moving quickly and decisively to exploit the opportunities of new technology—the punch card machine, the transistor, and the integrated circuit.

Throughout the 1980s, IBM's personal computer division (which is the biggest personal computer operation in the world) could not respond quickly to the price-cutting moves of its rivals and could not introduce new kinds of personal computers as a result of its centralized decision-making style. Whenever a competitor reduced prices, managers of the personal computer division had to get approval from the corporate management committee to cut prices, a process that sometimes took months. As a result, the PC division was never able to forestall its rivals. Moreover, just as in the case of minicomputers, rivalry between PC and mainframe managers hampered efforts to exploit quickly the potential of the powerful new microprocessors.

IBM's competitors moved quickly to increase the power of their PCs by exploiting the power of the new generation of microprocessors. They also encouraged the development of powerful new netware software that could link PCs together and to a more powerful computer, such as a minicomputer or a workstation, so that a network of PCs could work as effectively as a mainframe—but more conveniently and at only a fraction of the cost.

WORKSTATIONS

Workstations are the fourth wave of computers following mainframes, minicomputers, and PCs. While PCs are designed for individual jobs like word processing and financial analysis, workstations essentially are very powerful PCs designed to be connected to each other and to a mainframe through software. Workstations can analyze financial results and track inventories much faster than PCs and much more cheaply than minicomputers or mainframes. A network of workstations can also be linked to an even more powerful workstation (or minicomputer) called a file server, which contains a company's files and databases or which can retrieve them from a company's mainframe computer. Workstations,

usually priced from $5,000 to $100,000, were first developed for scientists and engineers but increasingly are utilized by business professionals. New network software links workstations so that many people can work together simultaneously on the same project. These desktop machines have "user-friendly" graphic displays and allow people at different machines to share data and software. By 1988, the workstation market was $4.7 billion.[16] Workstations have a 45 percent profit margin compared to 58 percent for minicomputers.[17]

Prior to 1989 IBM was a small player in this segment. Underestimating the potential power of personal computers and slow to develop powerful minicomputers (its AS/400 series was introduced only in 1988), IBM managers once again failed to see the potential of an emerging market. IBM had only a 3.9 percent market share in 1987 compared to Sun Microsystems's 29 percent and Apollo's 21 percent, the two upstart companies that innovated the workstation. Once they realized the importance of this market segment, both IBM and DEC introduced workstations based on RISC (reduced instruction set computing) processors which make machines two to three times faster by eliminating all insignificant instructions. IBM introduced the IBM RT PC workstation in 1986, but the machine failed due to an underpowered microprocessor. Notwithstanding its problems, IBM launched the RS/6000 workstation in 1989 and captured 18 percent of the market by the end of 1991.[18]

Competition in the workstation market is increasing as a result of market growth. This segment was growing 27 percent annually by 1992, compared to 5 percent for the whole computer industry. As the price of workstations falls, more and more small businesses, which could not afford to use mainframe or minicomputers, can afford workstations. The workstation market also is very important to large computer makers because workstations can be used in networks with larger mainframe computers. Thus controlling the workstation market protects a company's mainframe market. By the end of 1991, the workstation market was $11.3 billion, and IBM was facing severe competition from DEC, Sun, Apollo, and Hewlett-Packard, all of which sell RISC workstations.

SOFTWARE AND SERVICES

Designing software, the instructions that allow computers to perform tasks, and providing customer service, particularly assistance in the design of programs to manage company-specific databases and systems, have been a rapidly expanding segment of the computer industry for the past 20 years. IBM always has realized the importance of developing proprietary software that can link and join its mainframes, minicomputers, workstations, and personal computers to provide customers with a totally integrated computer package. It failed, however, to recognize the developing market for more general operating language and software applications.

16. Stuart Gannes, "IBM and DEC Take on the Little Guys," *Fortune,* October 10, 1988, pp. 108–114.
17. Leslie Helm, "DEC Discovers It Can't Live by VAX Alone," *Business Week,* November 21, 1988, pp. 104–105.
18. Carol Loomis and David Kirkpatrick, "The Hunt for Mr. X: Who Can Run IBM?" *Fortune,* February 22, 1993, pp. 68–72.

By 1981, 33 percent of total computer industry revenue came from software and services, a figure which had risen to an estimated 50 percent in 1993. Although software and services accounted for 33 percent of IBM's total revenues by 1990, 68 percent of this revenue came from supporting customers' IBM mainframe computer systems, which represent a declining share of the computer market. Thus IBM, tied to software that supports mainframes, is not in a strong position to compete in the new software and services market.

IBM's failure to realize the potential for software seems surprising given that it had outsourced the operating language for its personal computer to Microsoft and saw the success of the MS-DOS operating system. IBM's focus on mainframes and its continuing belief that its own proprietary hardware and software would become the industry standard seems to have been the source of its reluctance to enlarge and expand its software operations. In 1980, when IBM had the opportunity to indirectly control the software market by purchasing a large chunk of Microsoft stock at a low price, it declined to do so.

IBM soon found that developing new applications software was a difficult business to be in. First, IBM had a hard time recruiting talented programmers who were not attracted to IBM's bureaucratic and conservative corporate culture in which centralized decision making limited their opportunities to be creative and to take risks. Second, talented software programmers found they could make more money if they were in business for themselves; any programmer who could develop a new system generally started his or her own company. Microsoft recognized this problem early on; consequently, Bill Gates, Microsoft's chairman, gives his top programmers large stock options to encourage their best performance. Many of them have become millionaires as a result.

In today's computer market developing better and more advanced software is crucial to selling more hardware, or computers of all kinds. So, late as usual, IBM embarked on a program to forge alliances with many small independent software companies to develop software for IBM machines quickly—mainframes, minis, workstations, and PCs. One of IBM's goals is to rejuvenate sales of its mainframe by encouraging software companies to write programs that make mainframes the key part of a computer network that links personal computers and workstations.[19] IBM spent $100 million in 1989 to acquire equity stakes in twelve software developers, including Interactive Images for Graphics, Inc., Polygen Corporation for scientific software, and American Management Systems, Inc., for mainframe software. Marketing agreements were made with several other firms. IBM loans software developers up to $50,000 for start-up costs and takes a seat on the developer's board.[20] For example, IBM is working on a project called Systems Application Architecture (SAA), which is a set of rules for links between programs and computers. SAA will facilitate the creation of networks with all types of machines, including mainframes and PCs.[21]

In 1988 IBM created a new unit to launch applications software and established a position called "complementary resource marketing manager," with responsibility for connecting software "business partners" with IBM customers.

19. Walecia Konrad, "Information Processing: Survival of the Biggest," *Business Week,* April 2, 1990, pp. 66, 68.
20. Deidre Depke, "Suddenly, Software Houses Have a Big Blue Buddy," *Business Week,* August 7, 1989, pp. 68–69.
21. Ibid.

Salespeople are expected to sell the products of these software partners as well as IBM products.[22] Although most of the programs are for mainframes, many can be adapted to work with networks based on PCs.[23] Software and services accounted for 40 percent of IBM's revenue in 1992, and IBM wants to get 50 percent of revenues from software and services by the year 2000.[24]

SYSTEMS INTEGRATION AND OUTSOURCING

Traditionally, IBM limited its service activities to providing support for its own proprietary software and hardware. It did not use its skills to analyze various aspects of a customer's business, such as its inventory control or warehousing operations, and then custom design and install an appropriate mix of hardware and software to meet the customer's needs, a service known as systems integration.[25] Moreover, it had not recognized the developing market for outsourcing data processing whereby one company agrees to take over and manage all aspects of the data processing function for another company in return for a fee. By 1992, however, the systems integration and outsourcing market generated more revenues than the mainframe market.

IBM's failure to see the developing market segment for systems integration and outsourcing had not been lost on one of IBM's star salesmen, Ross Perot. When IBM capped the amount of money that Perot could earn from commissions in selling computers, and when it ignored his plan to start an IBM division whose function would be to provide data management services to customers to advise them on ways to manage their data files and systems, Perot left IBM and started Electronic Data Services (EDS).

The systems integration market and outsourcing market is now growing at 19 percent annually. IBM's failure to enter this market segment early allowed its competitors—principally EDS and Andersen Consulting, the accounting firm which early established a computer consulting division—to gain a first mover advantage and to dominate the market. Currently, EDS has 50 percent of the outsourcing business of managing a company's data storage and management needs, compared to IBM's 6 percent, while Andersen dominates the market for advising companies on their software and hardware needs. IBM leads primarily in the market for government contracts.

To develop a presence in this lucrative market quickly, IBM began developing alliances with various organizations. It formed a joint venture with Coopers & Lybrand to provide management consulting in selected industries. IBM also teamed with AT&T to make IBM's mainframes work better with AT&T's network management systems.[26] IBM established the Integrated Systems Solutions Corporation subsidiary in 1991 to provide a platform for IBM to enter the data processing outsourcing market. Its business is increasing; for example, in 1992 it received a 10-year $3 billion agreement to run computer systems for

22. Ibid.
23. Loomis and Kirkpatrick.
24. IBM 1992 Annual Report, p. 40.
25. Lewis, *Business Week*, February 14, 1988, pp. 92–98.
26. John Verity, *Business Week*, April 8, 1991, pp. 83–84.

McDonnell Douglas Corporation. The subsidiary does outsourcing for 30 companies, including Continental Bank. IBM will run all of a client company's systems from mainframes and workstations to voice and data telecommunications.[27] It is aggressively advertising its strengths and services in this area.

THE NEW COMPUTER INDUSTRY

By 1990 IBM received about 50 percent of its gross profit from mainframe hardware, software, peripherals, and maintenance; 6 percent from minicomputers; 18.5 percent from PCs and workstations; and 12.4 percent from non-maintenance software and services.[28] However, the future revenue-generating potential of each of these market segments is uncertain as the boundaries between the segments grow less clear. Will workstations replace minicomputers? Will workstations and minicomputers replace mainframes? Will a network of PCs linked by advanced software to a mainframe eliminate the need for minicomputers or workstations? Obviously, IBM has the most to gain from making mainframes the center of a computer network, but its competitors have as much to gain from making minicomputers and powerful workstations the way of the future.

By 1990 IBM was facing stiff competition in all the developing segments of the computer market from companies that were mainly specialized in one market niche, like Microsoft in the software segment or Sun Computer in the workstation niche. IBM was fighting to increase its market share in each market segment but was suffering because of tough competition from strong competitors that had developed their own loyal customer following.

Moreover, the market for mainframe computers, its principal source of revenue, was declining as machines such as PCs and workstations were able to perform mainframe tasks at a lower cost. It had been estimated that, while 80 percent of 1986 computer industry profits were attributable to mainframe computer sales, by 1991 sales of mainframe computer systems accounted for only 20 percent of industry profits. The PC revolution had reduced costs and allowed customers to buy much cheaper computer systems to do the work previously performed by expensive mainframes and minicomputers.

As a result of this shift, suppliers of computer components such as chips and software have been the winners as their share of industry profits rose from 20 percent in 1986 to 31 percent in 1991. Thus, for example, the share prices of Microsoft and Intel, which control the software and microprocessor markets, respectively, have soared, as have the share prices of Conner, Quantum, and Seagate which dominate disk drives and Andersen Consulting and EDS which are the leaders in system integration. IBM's, however, has fallen dramatically from a high of $160 in 1987 to less than $50 in 1992.

To fight the trend toward PCs and workstations, IBM attempted to make its 370 computer the central component of a network of computers that link individual users to the mainframe. However, it did not succeed, as sales growth for its biggest mainframe, the 370, dropped from 4 percent a year in 1990 to less than 2 percent a year in 1992. Even many of IBM's 370 users began switching

27. James Hyatt, "IBM Signs Pact to Offer Service to McDonnell," *The Wall Street Journal,* December 30, 1992, p. A3.
28. Byrne, Depke, and Verity.

to IBM AS/400 minicomputers because they can perform the same task more easily and cheaply. The mainframe market is now the third largest market behind PCs and minicomputers.

IBM FIGHTS BACK: RESTRUCTURING

In 1985 John Akers became CEO and was charged with the task of using IBM's vast resources to make it the market leader in the new lucrative market segments of the computer industry and to reduce IBM's dependence on mainframes. He took over a company where managers were still arrogant and complacent and believed completely in IBM's preeminence despite all the warning signs that it had lost its competitive edge. Its top management committee, staffed primarily of managers from its mainframe division, seemed unable to make the kind of innovative decisions that would allow IBM to respond quickly to the rapidly changing computer environment. The result was the failure to develop products fast enough and a mistaken commitment to the mainframe computer. Even its renowned salespeople had become a problem for the company. Committed to the IBM product, they had become oriented to selling and servicing the mainframe; they were not oriented toward satisfying customer needs, which might be for a minicomputer or a workstation.

Akers launched a year of the customer in 1987 to refocus the sales force on meeting the needs of the customer rather than on the needs of the mainframe. Most important, Akers realized the need to restructure the company and to change IBM's highly centralized style of decision making if IBM was to be able to innovate the next generation of products and emerge as a market leader in the new market segments. Akers recognized that the biggest problem for IBM was its highly bureaucratic organizational structure which slowed decision making and continually frustrated attempts to be innovative and entrepreneurial.

The 1998 Restructuring

To speed decision making, in January 1998 Akers reorganized IBM into seven divisions based on the main product market segments in which the company was competing: personal computer systems, mid-range systems, mainframes, information systems and communications, technology development (such as microchips), programming, and software. The idea behind the reorganization was to demolish the mainframe mindset by giving the managers of each division the autonomy and responsibility for developing new products for their respective markets. No longer would mainframe managers be able to stifle the pace of change and discourage the development of products that threatened the dominance of the mainframe. The sales force, however, was to remain a separate entity whose job would still be to sell the whole line of IBM products. The logic for this was that the sales force could sell customers an integrated IBM computer system—a network of PCs, file servers, and mainframe—and provide the computer software, service, and systems consulting to tailor the system to the customers' individual needs.

The disadvantage of the single sales force was that each division would not be able to devise a sales strategy specific to its own competitive environment and salespeople would not be able to focus on a single product line. IBM felt that the economies of scale and scope provided by a unified sales force outweighed these disadvantages. Twenty-thousand employees were transferred from staff and lab

positions to the sales force and the commission system was revamped so that salespeople were now evaluated on total revenue, not on the number of units rented or sold.[29]

IBM's Contention System

If the first purpose of the reorganization was to focus IBM's activities more closely on the main segments of the computer market, the second purpose was to shorten the product development cycle and to speed products to market. Since the early 1970s, IBM had taken advantage of its dominance in the market to use a "contention" system to control new product development. In this system, two or more project teams designed competing product prototypes and a series of committees at both the divisional level and the corporate level met over a period of months to debate the merits of each project. A project would be approved after six committee members rated the two processes, which could take months or years; then the committee met to finalize the product plan. During this process if any committee member said, "I non-concur," meaning that he or she disagreed with the project, it would be sent back for further review or scrapped.

The result of the contention system was that the projects that were approved were generally successful. However, the time frame associated with making the decision was generally so long that products were late to market, putting IBM at a competitive disadvantage. For example, the small, independent team charged with the development of the first IBM PC launched the product in one year. However, once the PC group was put into the Information Systems & Communications Division and decision making became constrained by IBM's contention system, the speed of the development process slowed significantly. For example, the PS/2 was not introduced until 1987 instead of the 1985 target. This delay allowed clone makers of the older PCs to gain 33 percent of the market share in PCs. Other symptoms of IBM's overly bureaucratic approach to decision making included its failure to enter new market segments quickly. For example, IBM entered the PC market four years late; it was also a laggard in workstations. Similarly, IBM's top managers refused to recognize the importance of the growth of minicomputers and was hesitant to launch products that would compete with the mainframes.

The reorganization was designed to shorten the time it took to get a product to market and to overcome the hurdles to product development.[30] In the 1980s IBM no longer had the luxury of taking a long time to make competitive decisions, as smaller and more agile competitors were forging ahead and the product life cycle of computers was shortening.

In an attempt to cut costs, increase profitability, get close to the customer, and reduce bureaucracy, Akers embarked on a major campaign to downsize the organization. The 1985 work force of 405,000 was reduced to 389,300 in 1988 through early retirement and attrition. In addition, overtime and temporary employees, equivalent to 12,500 full-time employees, were cut.[31] Despite the facts that IBM closed plants, cut spending, and reduced capital outlays, costs grew faster than revenues during most of the reorganization. Moreover, analysts could not discern any noticeable change in IBM's strategy or the way it made decisions. Products were still late to market.

29. John Verity, *Business Week,* May 29, 1989, pp. 72–78.
30. Lewis.
31. Aaron Bernstein, "How IBM Cut 16,200 Employees without an Ax," *Business Week,* February 15, 1988, p. 98.

The 1988 reorganization was a failure. Although each division was supposed to become more autonomous, in reality most decisions still required approval by IBM's corporate headquarters managers—managers who had risen through the ranks from the powerful mainframe computer division. Products that might have cannibalized the sale of mainframes were still discouraged by corporate managers, who having achieved their success during the mainframe era were hesitant to introduce products to compete with mainframes. One example of the mainframe mindset involved the PC unit's push to get into the laptop market in 1989 by pricing the laptop competitively at $4,995. Corporate headquarters insisted on a price of $5,995 to meet corporate profit margin targets. As a result, many competitors were able to price their products lower than IBM's machines. Even though IBM later priced the machine lower, it never regained lost market share.[32]

To allow the personal computer division to respond faster to the quickly changing PC market, Akers decided to place the PC business in a separate operating unit. In 1991 Akers formed the IBM Personal Computer Co. and gave it control over the design, production, distribution, and marketing of IBM PCs. Prior to this change, distribution was performed by IBM's large sales and marketing division, but 1,200 former marketing and sales employees were transferred to the new PC unit, which also was to handle telephone sales. The corporate sales force was to continue to sell to big corporate customers.[33] In decentralizing authority to managers in the PC division, Akers was showing managers his plans for the IBM of the future.

The 1991 Restructuring

IBM announced another restructuring at the end of 1991 to try to decentralize decision-making authority to the divisions and to reduce the role of IBM corporate headquarters in setting divisional strategy.[34] Akers divided IBM into thirteen separate divisions: nine divisions were based on the company's main product lines and four divisions were to be marketing and service operations organized geographically. The nine manufacturing divisions were to supply the four marketing divisions. The goal of the restructuring effort was to make the divisions independent units operating under a broad IBM umbrella to free the divisions from corporate control.

Aker's plan was that each division would be an autonomous operating unit that could freely negotiate transfer prices of inputs with other divisions and, if a division wanted to, could buy from and sell to outside companies. The divisions were to treat each other the same as they would outside companies, and no favorable prices were to be granted to IBM divisions. Moreover, the performance of each division would be reported separately and each division would be accountable for its individual profits and losses. The heads of the divisions were responsible for developing annual business plans and were to guarantee IBM a certain return on money invested in their division. In the past, most managers did not know the details of an individual division's financial performance such as profit and loss statements.[35] Each divisional manager signed a contract to meet objectives in revenue growth, profit, ROA (return on assets), cash flow, customer

32. Verity, "The New IBM."
33. Laurence Hooper, "IBM Set to Unveil Restyled PC Business That Could Operate as a Separate Unit," *The Wall Street Journal*, September 3, 1992, p. A3.
34. Verity, "The New IBM."
35. Ibid.

satisfaction, quality, and morale.[36] If the divisional heads were successful, they would get a share of the profits; however, if they failed, their jobs were on the line. Financial results for all thirteen units were to be made public by 1994.[37]

The goal of this restructuring was to free up IBM's powerful resources and to make it more competitive. Division heads will have control over long-term development and business-level strategy. For example, the Personal Systems Division's manager can decide how PCs and workstations are produced and designed, and the PC division's research and development function will not compete directly with the mainframe division for resources. The hope is that the divisions will be able to compete with their smaller, more entrepreneurial rivals once they are freed from corporate bureaucracy.

The sales divisions will still be responsible for selling the whole range of IBM products, however, and control over sales will be centralized at corporate headquarters. The logic, once again, is that customers want a sales force that can handle their entire computer needs and that there are synergies from having one sales force provide a full set of products and services. IBM's traditional focus on service is still a strong competitive advantage. Analysts are, however, skeptical of having only one sales force, especially one in which representatives are still biased toward mainframes.[38] Many analysts feel that one sales force is a mistake and that giving each division its own sales force would be a better source of competitive advantage. Moreover, the huge costs of operating the sales force could be hard to allocate between divisions, causing rivalry among them.[39]

To demonstrate to IBM's thirteen operating divisions top management's commitment to IBM's more autonomous and more entrepreneurial approach to doing business, IBM's PC division was given total control over its own sales and named an independent unit in 1992. James Cannavino, the head of the PC unit, took total control over the PC division's strategy and organized the PC division around products instead of functions. The five product groups of the PC division are the low-cost Value-Points; PS/2; PS/1, aimed at home and small business users; portable products; and Ambra, a line of PCs built by an Asian contractor and sold in Europe. Each product group is in charge of its own brand development, manufacturing, pricing, and marketing.[40] This change was designed to allow the product groups to respond much more quickly to changes in the PC market, where products may have a life span of only six months to a year. In addition, Cannavino met with thirty-two CEOs of Silicon Valley start-ups and told them that he wanted to form alliances with them to speed the development of new hardware and software products such as multimedia and CD-ROM products. The IBM PC division is the world's largest PC company.

NEW MANAGEMENT AND NEW PLANS

Despite the 1991 organization, IBM's profits and revenues continued to decline; 1991 revenues fell 5 percent from 1990, the first decline since 1946. The com-

36. David Kirkpatrick, "Breaking up IBM," *Fortune,* July 27, 1992, pp. 44–58.
37. Ibid.
38. Verity, "The New IBM."
39. John Verity and Arnst, December 21, 1992, p. 32.
40. Catherine Arnst and Bart Ziegler, "A Freewheeling Youngster Named IBM," *Business Week,* May 3, 1993, pp. 134–138.

pany's 1991 loss of $2.8 billion was the first loss in IBM's history. In 1992 IBM's losses increased to $5 billion on $65 billion in revenues. In January 1993 the stock went below $46, the lowest price in 17 years, and pressure for change at the top was increasing.

Under pressure from investors and the public, John Akers resigned in January 1993. Although Akers reorganized and restructured, critics claimed that he never went far enough in implementing the reforms that would really turn around IBM. For example, despite the facts that between 1986 to 1992 a total of 100,000 IBM workers were cut mainly through early retirement and that Akers had removed the whole of IBM's former top management team to try to rid IBM of the "mainframe mindset," critics claimed that Akers had avoided initiating the major layoffs that were needed to restore profitability.[41]

In 1993 the board of directors searched for a replacement for Akers and shunning an insider, for fear that he could not bring a fresh perspective to IBM's problems, chose an outsider to be CEO of IBM, the first time an outsider had occupied the top job. Louis Gerstner, former CEO of RJR Nabisco, was recruited in March 1993. Gerstner had no experience in the computer industry, and IBM's stock price dropped $3 to a new low when Gerstner took over.[42]

Gerstner immediately hired outsiders to form a new top management team to run the company. Jerry York, former chief financial officer (CFO) at Chrysler was recruited as IBM's CFO, Gerry Czarnecki, who was in charge of cutbacks at Honolulu's Honfed Bank, became a vice president. These outsiders are tough cost-cutters, experienced at restructuring large companies.[43] Gerstner hired another outsider, Abby Kohnstamm, a former senior vice president of card-member marketing at American Express, to be vice president of corporate marketing.[44]

Gerstner and his top management team spent the whole of 1993 analyzing the IBM works as a prelude to "Reengineering the Corporation." Reengineering refers to a two-step process whereby an organization first identifies and analyzes each of the core business processes—manufacturing, marketing, research and development, and so on—that make a business work and then changes or reengineers them from the bottom up to improve the way they function. Gerstner formed an eleven-person "corporate executive committee" of IBM's top managers to spearhead the reengineering effort. Gerstner then gave each manager responsibility for heading a task force. Eleven task forces were formed to analyze IBM's main processes which were modeled on the reengineering effort that Cannavino had performed in the PC division. As discussed above, the result of that effort had led to the move to a product group structure where each group took control over its own manufacturing and marketing—a change that had been very successful. Gerstner hoped that a corporatewide effort would also prove successful.

Despite the fact that most analysts felt that Gerstner would continue with Akers' approach of decentralizing decision making to the divisions, and even spinning off IBM's businesses into independent companies, Gerstner has shown no sign of following this strategy. Gerstner has preferred to restructure the relationship between the corporate center and the divisions. Moreover, Gerstner

41. Catherine Arnst and Weber, *Fortune*, February 8, 1993, pp. 22–24.
42. Patricia Sellers and David Kirkpatrick, "Can This Man Save IBM?" *Fortune*, April 19, 1993, pp. 63–67.
43. Michael Miller, "IBM Is Planning a $2 Billion Charge to Slash Jobs," *The Wall Street Journal*, pp. A1, A8.
44. "Business Briefs: IBM 1993." *The Wall Street Journal*, May 25, 1993, p. B8.

(Dollars in millions except per share amounts)	1992	1991*	1990*	1989*	1988*
For the Year:					
Revenue	$64,523	$64,766	$68,931	$62,654	$59,598
Net earnings before effect of accounting changes	(6,865)	(598)	5,967	3,722	5,451
Per share	(12.03)	(1.05)	10.42	6.41	9.20
Effect of accounting changes†	1,900	(2,263)	—	—	290
Per share	3.33	(3.96)	—	—	.49
Net earnings	(4,965)	(2,861)	5,967	3,722	5,741
Per Share	(8.70)	(5.01)	10.42	6.41	9.69
Cash dividends paid	2,765	2,771	2,774	2,752	2,609
Per share	4.84	4.84	4.84	4.73	4.40
Investment in plant, rental machines and other property	4,698	6,502	6,548	6,410	5,431
Return on stockholders' equity	—	—	14.8%	9.6%	14.8%
At End of Year:					
Total assets	$86,705	$92,473	$87,568	$77,734	$73,037
Net investment in plant, rental machines and other property	21,595	27,578	27,241	24,943	23,426
Working capital	2,955	7,018	13,313	13,875	17,740
Total debt	29,320	26,947	19,545	16,717	13,380
Stockholders' equity	27,624	36,679	42,553	38,252	39,293

*Restated for AICPA Statement of Position, "Software Revenue Recognition."
†1992, income taxes; 1991, nonpension postretirement benefits; 1988, income taxes.

Exhibit 1
Five-Year Comparison of Selected Financial Data

announced that he believed that IBM should continue to follow its traditional strategy of providing customers with a full line of hardware and software products and services and announced his support for the mainframe division.

As a part of this full-line strategy, and despite expectations that he would decentralize IBM's sales force and give each division responsibility for its own sales, Gerstner announced in 1993 that he would not change the current companywide sales force structure. The current sales force of 40,000 salespeople would still pursue the strategy of one face to a customer because customers "do not want to be bothered by several salespeople." Apparently, Gerstner and his top management team believe that IBM's core strategy of being a full-service company is appropriate. They believe the company's main problem is that it is too big. To reduce size in 1992, Gerstner announced plans to shed 115,000 more jobs in 1993 and 1994, reducing the work force to 250,000 from a peak of 405,000 in 1985. Announcing in 1993 that "the last thing that IBM needs now is a corporate vision," Gerstner nevertheless identified four goals he has for IBM: (1) to get the company to the right size, (2) to spend more time with customers, (3) to determine the strategic issues by process reengineering, and (4) to build employee morale in the face of the huge layoffs.

Analysts wonder how Gerstner's strategy will work. They wonder whether Gerstner understands the divisional rivalries that have led to IBM's problems and why he expects his new strategy to result in faster product development and

(Dollars in millions except per share and stock prices)		Revenue	Gross Profit	Net Earnings	Per Share		Stock Prices	
					Earnings	Dividends	High	Low
1992	First quarter	$14,037	$7,133	$2,542*	$4.45*	$1.21	$98.13	$83.13
	Second quarter	16,224	7,863	734	1.29	1.21	98.63	81.63
	Third quarter	14,702	6,779	(2,778)	(4.87)	1.21	100.38	80.00
	Fourth quarter	19,560	7,679	(5,463)	(9.57)	1.21	81.13	48.75
Total		$64,523	$29,454	$(4,965)	$(8.70)	$4.84		
1991†	First quarter	$13,587	$7,248	$(1,707)††	$(2.99)††	$1.21	$139.75	$105.50
	Second quarter	14,764	7,581	126	.22	1.21	114.75	96.63
	Third quarter	14,447	7,174	177	.31	1.21	106.38	92.00
	Fourth quarter	21,968	10,690**	(1,457)	(2.55)	1.21	104.75	83.50
Total		$64,766	$32,693	$(2,861)	$(5.01)	$4.84		

*Includes benefit of $1,900 million, or $3.33 per share, cumulative effect of change in accounting for income taxes.

†Restated for AICPA Statement of Position, "Software Revenue Recognition."

††Includes charge of $2,263 million, or $3.96 per share, transition effect of change in accounting for nonpension postretirement benefits.

**Reclassified to conform with 1992 presentation.

There were 764,630 stockholders of record at December 31, 1992. During 1992, stockholders received $2,765 million in cash dividends. The regular quarterly cash dividend payable March 10, 1993, will be at the rate of $.54 per share. This dividend will be IBM's 312th consecutive quarterly cash dividend. The stock prices reflect the high and low prices for IBM's capital stock on the New York Stock Exchange composite tape for the last two years.

Exhibit 2
Selected Quarterly Data

the greater sharing of ideas and resources between divisions. Some critics argue that Gerstner should have aggressively pursued the strategy of breaking up IBM into fully independent operating units and that his new policy of encouraging the sharing of skills and resources between divisions will not work and is no break from the past. Moreover, they claim he has been slow to reduce IBM's operating costs and to reduce the lavish way in which it spends its resources. For example, IBM operates one of the largest fleets of private jets in the corporate world, maintains three country clubs for its employees, and has its own management school complete with skeet shooting and tennis courts.

Has Gerstner, in the first six months of his reign as IBM's CEO, bought into IBM's culture in which the mainframe mindset still controls the corporation? Gerstner replies that no amount of cost cutting will solve IBM's problem unless IBM can change from the inside out. IBM still spends 10 percent of its revenues on R&D and has many good ideas continually pouring from its development labs. According to Gerstner, the problem for the company is to use those ideas effectively, and the start of this is to reengineer the company to make better use of its resources. IBM also needs to increase integration among divisions so that they can share skills and resources more effectively. Gerstner believes that continuing Aker's strategy of breaking up IBM into thirteen separate companies would do nothing to ensure the survival of the company in the long run.

On September 26, 1993, IBM announced a loss of $46 million for the third quarter, compared to a $40 million loss in 1992, bringing its total loss in 1993 to $8.37 billion. Was Gerstner's strategy working, and when can IBM's investors and employees expect to see the results?

(Dollars in millions) For the year ended December 31:	1992	1991*†	1990*†
Cash Flow from Operating Activities:			
Net earnings	$(4,965)	$(2,861)	$5,967
Adjustments to reconcile net earnings to cash provided from operating activities:			
Effect of changes in accounting principles	(1,900)	2,263	—
Effect of restructuring charges	8,312	2,793	(843)
Depreciation	4,793	4,772	4,217
Amortization of software	1,466	1,564	1,086
(Gain) loss on disposition of investment assets	54	(94)	32
Other changes that provided (used) cash—			
Receivables	1,052	(886)	(2,077)
Inventories	704	(36)	17
Other assets	(3,396)	5	(3,136)
Accounts payable	(311)	384	293
Other liabilities	465	(1,179)	1,916
Net cash provided from operating activities	6,274	6,725	7,472
Cash flow from Investing Activities:			
Payments for plant, rental machines and other property	(4,751)	(6,497)	(6,509)
Proceeds from disposition of plant, rental machines and other property	633	645	804
Investment in software	(1,752)	(2,014)	(1,892)
Purchases of marketable securities and other investments	(3,284)	(4,848)	(1,234)
Proceeds from marketable securities and other investments	3,276	5,028	1,687
Net cash used in investing activities	(5,878)	(7,686)	(7,144)
Cash Flow from Financing Activities			
Proceeds from new debt	10,045	5,776	4,676
Payments to settle debt	(10,735)	(4,184)	(3,683)
Short-term borrowings less than 90 days—net	4,199	2,676	1,966
Proceeds from (payments to) employee stock plans-net	(90)	67	(76)
Payments to purchase and retire capital stock	—	(196)	(415)
Cash dividends paid	(2,765)	(2,771)	(2,774)
Net cash provided from (used in) financing activities	654	1,368	(306)
Effect of Exchange Rate Changes on Cash and Cash Equivalents	(549)	(315)	131
Net Change in Cash and Cash Equivalents	501	92	153
Cash and Cash Equivalents at January 1	3,945	3,853	3,700
Cash and Cash Equivalents at December 31	$4,446	$3,945	$3,853
Supplemental Data:			
Cash paid during the year for:			
Income taxes	$1,297	$2,292	$3,315
Interest	$3,132	$2,617	$2,165

*Restated for the American Institute of Certified Public Accountants Statements of Position, "Software Revenue Recognition."
†Reclassified to conform with 1992 presentation.

Exhibit 3
Consolidated Statement of Cash Flows

Exhibit 4
Consolidated Statement of Earnings

(Dollars in millions except per share amounts) For the year ended December 31:	1992	1991	1990
Revenue:			
Sales	$33,755	$37,093	$43,959
Software	11,103	10,498	9,865
Maintenance	7,635	7,414	7,198
Services	7,352	5,582	4,124
Rentals and financing	4,678	4,179	3,785
	64,523	64,766	68,931
Cost:			
Sales	19,698	18,571	19,401
Software	3,924	3,865	3,118
Maintenance	3,430	3,379	3,302
Services	6,051	4,531	3,315
Rentals and financing	1,966	1,727	1,579
	35,069	32,073	30,715
Gross Profit	29,454	32,693	38,216
Operating Expenses:			
Selling, general and administrative	19,526	21,375	20,709
Research, development and engineering	6,522	6,644	6,554
Restructuring charges	11,645	3,735	—
	37,693	31,754	27,263
Operating income	(8,239)	939	10,953
Other Income, principally interest	573	602	495
Interest Expense	1,360	1,423	1,324
Earnings before Income Taxes	(9,026)	118	10,124
Provision for Income Taxes	(2,161)	716	4,157
Net Earnings before Changes in Accounting Principles	$(4,965)	(598)	5,967
Effect of Changes in Accounting Principles	1,900	(2,263)	—
Net Earnings	$(6,865)	$(2,861)	$5,967
Per Share Amounts:			
Before Changes in Accounting Principles	$(12.03)	$(1.05)	$10.42
Effect of Changes in Accounting Principles	3.33	(3.96)	—
Net Earnings	$(8.70)	$(5.01)	$10.42

Average Number of Shares Outstanding:
1992—570,896,489; 1991—572,003,382; 1990—572,647,906

Exhibit 5
Consolidated Statement of Financial Position

(Dollars in millions) At December 31:	1992	1991
Assets		
Current Assets:		
Cash	$1,090	$1,171
Cash equivalents	3,356	2,774
Marketable securities, at cost, which approximates market	1,203	1,206
Notes and accounts receivable—trade, net of allowances	12,829	15,391
Sales-type leases receivable	7,405	7,435
Other accounts receivable	1,370	1,491
Inventories	8,385	9,844
Prepaid expenses and other current assets	4,054	1,657
	39,692	40,969
Plant, Rental Machines and Other Property	52,786	55,678
Less: Accumulated depreciation	31,191	28,100
	21,595	27,578
Investments and Other Assets:		
Software, less accumulated amortization (1992, $8,531; 1991, $6,950)	4,119	4,483
Investments and sundry assets	21,299	19,443
	25,418	23,926
	$86,705	$92,473
Liabilities and Stockholders' Equity		
Current Liabilities:		
Taxes	$979	$2,449
Short-term debt	16,467	13,716
Accounts payable	3,147	3,507
Compensation and benefits	3,476	3,241
Deferred income	3,316	3,472
Other accrued expenses and liabilities	9,352	7,566
	36,737	33,951
Long-Term Debt	12,853	13,231
Other Liabilities	7,461	6,685
Deferred Income Taxes	2,030	1,927
Total Liabilities	59,081	55,794
Stockholders' Equity:		
Capital stock, par value $1.25 per share— shares authorized: 750,000,000 Issued: 1992—571,791,950; 1991—571,349,324	6,563	6,531
Retained earnings	19,124	26,983
Translation adjustments	1,962	3,196
Treasury stock, at cost (shares: 1992—356,222; 1991—331,665)	(25)	(31)
	27,624	36,679
	$86,705	$92,473

CASE 12

The Japanese Beer Industry

INTRODUCTION

In 1980, after two decades of phenomenal growth during Japan's "economic miracle" years, the Japanese beer industry appeared to have changed from a growth to a mature industry. Beer consumption had leveled off; after increasing fivefold from 1955 to 1965, and then doubling between 1965 and 1975, it grew by only 15 percent from 1975 to 1980. And with Japan's population growing at a rate of only 0.4 percent a year, demand was not expected to increase significantly in the foreseeable future.

Virtually all the beer consumed by Japanese drinkers was produced by Japan's four brewers: Kirin, Asahi, Sapporo, and Suntory. These companies formed a profitable oligopoly protected by high entry barriers in distribution, advertising costs, and government regulation. In 1980 Kirin dominated the industry with a 60-plus market share. The company also acted as price leader, setting prices at a level high enough to allow the weakest two competitors, Asahi and Suntory, to survive. This arrangement was tacitly supported by the Japanese government because of the huge tax revenues that profitable beer companies brought in.

The Japanese brewers competed with each other mainly through development and control of distribution channels and advertising. While there had been a certain amount of product innovation, Asahi, Sapporo, and Suntory had learned from experience that when one of them came out with a new product that threatened to take market share away from Kirin, the industry leader would imitate the innovation and use its advantage in reputation, distribution, and financial clout to overwhelm the originator. Thus was a certain balance maintained; the three smaller brewers avoided directly attacking Kirin for fear of retaliation, while Kirin, for its part fearful that further share gains would put the company in violation of Japan's anti-monopoly law, restrained itself from doing anything that would further weaken its rivals.

Ten years later, however, the industry presented quite a different picture. In the mid-1980s, beer consumption picked up again, jumping 37 percent from 1985 to 1990. Demand was expected to continue to grow at a rate of 5 percent a year during the first half of the 1990s. Sales growth had not translated into higher profits, though, as an expensive new product war had broken out in the mid-1980s and taken firm root. The new product war had attracted great public interest and helped stimulate demand. It also had dramatically reversed Asahi's fortunes and produced the biggest market share shake-up in industry history. By 1991, however, the new product sweepstakes appeared to have become a negative-sum game, and the high costs of developing and advertising new beers had many in the industry longing for a return to the more stable and profitable competitive arrangements of the pre-1980s.

This case was prepared by Tim Craig, University of Victoria. This case was prepared as a basis for class discussion rather than to illustrate either effective or ineffective handling of administrative situations.

INDUSTRY HISTORY

About the time Samuel Taylor Coleridge (1772–1834) was penning the line "Water, water everywhere, nor any drop to drink," British and Dutch trading ships were off-loading kegs of beer in Japan. In 1870 Japan's first brewery, Spring Valley Brewery, was established by an American in Yokohama, and by the early twentieth century the popularity of beer had grown to the point where as many as 100 independent breweries were operating.

World War I proved to be a boon for Japanese brewers. Fueled by a consumer market in Southeast Asia that European producers were unable to supply because of the war, local breweries began exporting and expanding. The building of new plants was facilitated by the availability at bargain prices of brewing and bottling equipment from America, where prohibition had shut down scores of companies. Brands such as Sakura, Kabuto, Fuji, Union, and Cascade Beer flourished, along with today's familiar Kirin, Sapporo, and Asahi.

All was not a bed of hops, however. With the stock market crash and worldwide depression of the late 1920s and 1930s, demand plummeted, resulting in a period of brewery failures and consolidations. As Japan went to war in the late 1930s and 1940s, barley and hops became harder to obtain, there were shortages of needed electricity and coal, and beer taxes were raised continuously to provide war funds. By the end of the war only three brewers remained in Japan, and one of these went out of business in 1948. The two that remained were Kirin Beer, a descendant of Spring Valley, and Dai Nippon Breweries, which had evolved over a 40-year period through the merging of numerous independent brewers, among them the original Sapporo and Asahi.

In 1949 Dai Nippon Breweries, which controlled nearly three-quarters of the beer market, was declared to be in violation of Japan's anti-monopoly law, which had been imposed by the United States in its postwar occupation of Japan for the purpose of dissolving Japan's zaibatsu (financial cliques). Dai Nippon was split into two parts along geographical lines: its breweries and distribution network in western Japan became present-day Asahi Beer, while its breweries and distribution network in eastern Japan (including Tokyo) became Sapporo.

At the time of the breakup, Sapporo held 38.6 percent of the market, Asahi 36.1 percent, and Kirin 25.3 percent. The next 30 years were a Kirin success story, as Kirin steadily increased its share of the market at the expense of its rivals and came to dominate the industry (see Exhibit 1). Kirin's success is attributed to several factors:

1. The breakup of Dai Nippon into Sapporo and Asahi left Kirin with the only nationally recognized brand name and nationwide sales network, giving Kirin a scale advantage in advertising and, until the others could expand their distribution networks, a larger target market.
2. Kirin anticipated growing demand and, in order to meet it, built new production capacity aggressively, at the rate of one brewery every two years.
3. Kirin concentrated on the home consumption market, which was growing rapidly as refrigerator use became widespread during the 1950s and 1960s; Asahi and Sapporo, by contrast, focused on the shrinking commercial market, in which they traditionally had been strong.
4. The strong, bitter taste of Kirin's lager beer was right for the times. The diet in postwar Japan was poor and bland, and people craved strong tastes.

Exhibit 1
Comparative Market Share by Year, 1949–1990

Year	Kirin	Asahi	Sapporo	Suntory	Takara
1949	25.3%	36.1%	38.6%	—	—
1950	29.5	33.5	37.0	—	—
1951	29.5	34.5	36.0	—	—
1952	33.0	32.5	34.5	—	—
1953	33.2	33.3	33.4	—	—
1954	37.1	31.5	31.4	—	—
1955	36.9	31.7	31.4	—	—
1956	41.7	31.1	27.2	—	—
1957	42.1	30.7	26.2	—	1.0%
1958	39.9	30.9	27.5	—	1.7
1959	42.4	29.3	26.5	—	1.8
1960	44.7	27.2	26.0	—	2.1
1961	41.6	28.0	27.8	—	2.6
1962	45.0	26.4	26.4	—	2.2
1963	46.5	24.3	26.2	1.0%	2.0
1964	46.2	25.5	25.2	1.2	1.9
1965	47.7	23.2	25.3	1.9	1.9
1966	50.9	22.1	23.8	1.7	1.5
1967	49.4	22.0	25.0	3.2	0.4
1968	51.3	20.1	24.4	4.2	—
1969	53.3	18.9	23.3	4.5	—
1970	55.4	17.2	23.0	4.4	—
1971	58.9	14.9	22.1	4.1	—
1972	60.1	14.1	21.3	4.5	—
1973	61.3	13.6	20.3	4.8	—
1974	62.5	13.1	19.6	4.8	—
1975	60.8	13.5	20.2	5.5	—
1976	63.8	11.8	18.4	6.0	—
1977	61.9	12.0	19.6	6.5	—
1978	62.1	11.6	19.6	6.7	—
1979	63.0	11.0	19.2	6.8	—
1980	62.3	11.0	19.6	7.1	—
1981	62.8	10.3	20.0	6.9	—
1982	62.3	9.9	19.9	7.9	—
1983	61.3	10.2	19.9	8.6	—
1984	61.6	9.8	19.6	9.0	—
1985	61.4	9.5	19.8	9.3	—
1986	59.6	10.3	20.8	9.3	—
1987	56.9	12.9	20.7	9.5	—
1988	50.7	20.7	19.8	8.8	—
1989	48.4	24.8	18.4	8.4	—
1990	49.2	24.7	18.0	8.1	—

Through skillful advertising, Kirin succeeded in teaching the public that strong, bitter beer equals delicious beer.

Only two other firms have entered Japan's postwar beer industry. One is Takara, a distillery, which entered the beer market in 1957 and withdrew 11 years later after failing to achieve a viable position. The other is whiskey maker Suntory, which entered in 1963 and has survived, despite making a profit in beer in one year only, 1984. (There is also Orion, an Okinawa brewer whose beer was sold only in Okinawa until 1990, when it began appearing on "mainland" shelves in small quantities.)

DEMAND

For the first 10 years after the war, beer was a luxury product in Japan; in 1950 a single 633 milliliter bottle cost 132 yen, or about 2 percent of the average monthly salary for a university graduate. With economic recovery and rising incomes, however, beer gradually came to be affordable by the average Japanese. By the 1960s beer was drunk regularly by a wide variety of people of all income levels in Japan.

Overall demand for beer in Japan grew steadily during the first 30 years of the postwar period. From the 1970s through the mid 1980s, demand leveled off and the industry was viewed by many as mature, with limited potential for further growth. However, a boom in new products combined with other environmental changes (see below) revived growth, and the outlook for the 1990s was for continued market growth. In 1990 Nikko Research Center expected beer consumption to increase by 5 percent annually over the next few years. Exhibit 2 and Figure 1 show Japanese beer shipments for the postwar period. Exhibit 3 shows per capita beer consumption in Japan and other countries.

Figure 1
Beer Sales Growth, 1950–1990

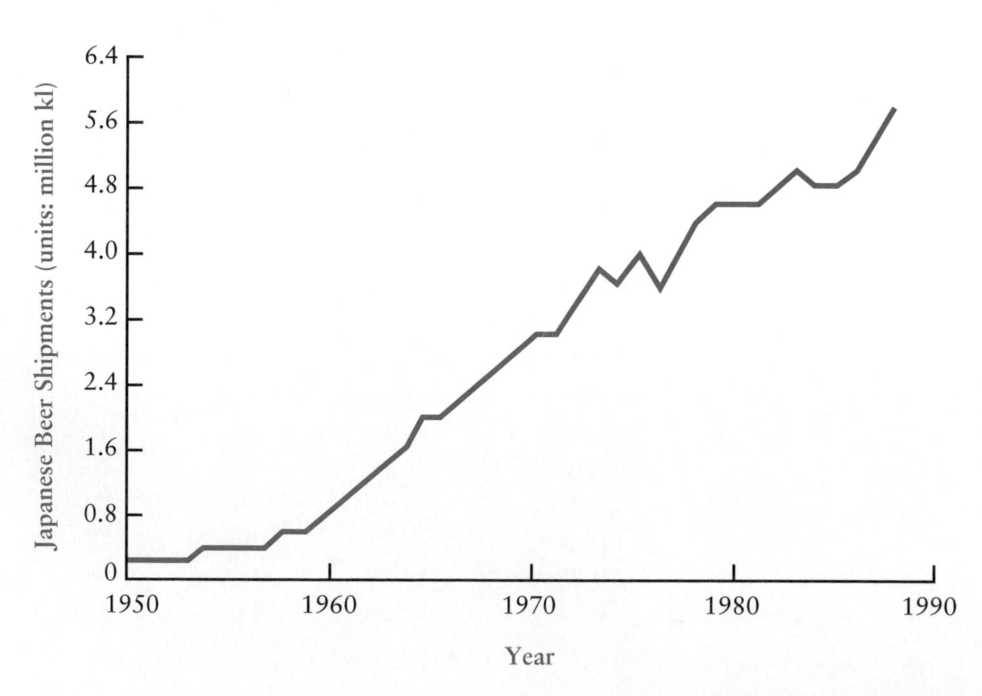

Exhibit 2
Japanese Beer Shipments, 1946–1990 (in Kiloliters)

Year	Domestic	Exports	Total
1947	91,270	—	91,270
1948	91,372	—	91,372
1949	140,495	731	141,226
1950	165,434	4,298	169,732
1951	261,007	9,699	270,706
1952	275,479	16,705	292,184
1953	372,054	15,757	387,811
1954	390,280	10,278	400,558
1955	403,413	7,371	410,784
1956	452,163	6,120	458,283
1957	551,536	6,815	558,351
1958	615,552	6,970	622,522
1959	744,947	6,843	751,790
1960	919,313	6,104	925,417
1961	1,232,663	7,064	1,239,727
1962	1,478,102	7,069	1,485,171
1963	1,685,916	6,596	1,692,512
1964	1,991,648	5,630	1,997,278
1965	1,989,147	6,013	1,995,160
1966	2,116,910	6,368	2,123,278
1967	2,410,602	11,547	2,422,149
1968	2,525,975	13,809	2,539,784
1969	2,730,637	12,569	2,743,206
1970	2,972,253	15,481	2,987,734
1971	3,052,746	15,380	3,068,126
1972	3,433,426	13,674	3,447,100
1973	3,811,156	13,930	3,825,086
1974	3,612,043	14,056	3,626,099
1975	3,955,519	13,978	3,969,497
1976	3,665,370	14,182	3,679,552
1977	4,131,678	15,728	4,147,406
1978	4,431,141	18,592	4,449,733
1979	4,499,156	18,408	4,517,564
1980	4,539,799	18,084	4,557,883
1981	4,638,889	18,796	4,657,685
1982	4,763,444	18,507	4,781,951
1983	4,942,317	23,670	4,965,987
1984	4,680,770	26,251	4,707,021
1985	4,785,328	27,435	4,812,763
1986	4,970,028	27,972	4,998,000
1987	5,340,047	29,330	5,369,377
1988	5,749,828	30,267	5,780,095
1989	6,054,120	n.a	n.a
1990	6,550,914	n.a	n.a

Exhibit 3
Per Capita Beer Consumption for Selected Countries, 1987 (in Liters per year)

Country	Per Capita Consumption
West Germany	144.3 liters
Czechoslovakia	130.0
Denmark	125.2
New Zealand	120.8
Austria	116.2
Australia	111.3
United States	90.1
Netherlands	84.3
Venezuela	72.4
Spain	64.5
Sweden	51.5
Japan	43.8

Demand varied by season, with more beer drunk in summer than in winter (see Exhibit 4). In recent years the seasonality of demand has weakened, however. Beer increasingly is seen as a year-round beverage, thanks to promotional efforts by the brewers and the development of some beers "especially created for drinking in cold weather."

TAXATION AND GOVERNMENT REGULATION

Beer was the richest source of liquor tax in Japan, in 1989 providing 2.5 percent of total Japanese government tax revenues. Tax by volume was 208.4 yen per liter, which amounted to 44 percent of the retail price. Including sales tax, a total

Exhibit 4
Percent of Yearly Sales by Month, 1979–1986

Month	Percent of sales
January	3.7
February	5.0
March	7.5
April	9.8
May	8.6
June	11.4
July	13.4
August	10.6
September	8.1
October	6.8
November	5.8
December	9.3

of 46.9 percent of the retail price of a bottle of beer was taxes. This compared with 36.6 percent for Great Britain, 18.3 percent for West Germany, 16.9 percent for France, and 12.7% for the United States.

Beer taxes traditionally were raised about once every four years, but they had not increased since 1984. With Japan entering an economic slowdown in 1991 and government tax receipts falling accordingly, a tax increase was seen as likely within the next two or three years.

Because of the importance of beer taxes as a source of government revenue, the Japanese beer industry was strictly regulated by the government through licensing requirements. Licenses were issued to producers, wholesalers, and retailers with the aim of avoiding "excess competition" which, it was feared, might drive weaker operations out of business.

Permits to produce beer were especially difficult to obtain; they were issued only for a specific piece of land, and in order to get one, a producer had to make at least 2,000 kiloliters of beer annually. The purpose of this regulation was to keep the number of beer companies to a handful, as it was easier to collect tax from a few large brewers than from many small ones scattered throughout the country. Because of the minimum production requirement, there were virtually no independent microbreweries or brew pubs in Japan. In the United States, by contrast, there were over 200 microbreweries, many putting out just 90 kiloliters a year. A consultant specializing in Japan's beer market calculated that reducing the minimum production requirement to 200 kiloliters would boost Japanese beer sales by around 2 percent, but there were no signs in 1990 that the government was considering changing its regulation.

The government also had traditionally limited the number of retail liquor licenses issued, again on the theory that this offered the best way to fully collect liquor taxes at minimal expense. In June 1989, however, the National Tax Administration Agency announced that 6,000 new regular licenses and 250 new licenses to large retailers (such as supermarkets and convenience store chains) would be issued to new entrants between 1990 and 1994 in an effort to promote greater competition in the alcoholic beverage market. The priority given to large-scale retailers was in part a response to foreign pressure, as the larger stores generally carry a higher proportion of imported products.

These changes were seen by many as the beginning of a major restructuring of the retailing of alcoholic beverages in Japan. In 1988 Japan had 122,000 mom-and-pop retail liquor outlets, most of which were tiny stores with an average turnover of 30 million yen and gross profits of 6 million yen annually. An analyst for Morgan Stanley International estimated that by 1998 the number of liquor stores would drop to around 60,000, while the number of large retailers would rise from 6,000 (in 1991) to about 30,000.

PRODUCTION AND DISTRIBUTION

Beer was defined under Japanese law as a beverage brewed by fermentation of malt, hops, and water. Other grains such as rice or corn could also be added to produce a smoother taste. The production process involved using yeast to ferment sugar present in the primary materials. Most of the raw materials were imported from Europe, North America, and Australia.

While all the Japanese brewers used the same basic ingredients and German production process, within these parameters lay a number of technical complexities and variations that produced tangible taste differences from beer to beer. The most important determinant of taste was said to be the particular yeast used, with different strains producing slightly different flavor and bouquet. The brewers all maintained yeast banks containing hundreds of strains and were constantly developing and testing new ones. Other brewing variations included the choice, quality, and combination of ingredients, the use of hulled versus unhulled malt, and temperature and degree of fermentation. It generally took from one to four years to develop and put on the market a new beer.

The number and geographic distribution of brewing plants was shaped by scale and transportation considerations. There were considerable economies of scale in beer production, thanks to large outdoor tanks which were invented in the late 1960s. Beer is heavy and transportation costs considerable, so the companies had located their breweries fairly evenly around the country near major population centers. In 1991 Kirin had 14 breweries; Sapporo, 10; Asahi 7; and Suntory, 3.

Beer was sold in bottles, cans, and kegs of various sizes (See Exhibit 5). The most common bottle was the returnable 633 milliliter bottle. Twenty 633 milliliter bottles made up one case, the standard measuring unit for beer sales. The most common cans were the 350 and 500 milliliter sizes. The smaller kegs were take-home containers sold directly to consumers, while the larger kegs went to commercial operations such as bars and restaurants.

In 1988, 67 percent of the beer sold in Japan came in bottles, 26 percent in cans, and 7 percent in kegs. A trend toward canned beer, and away from bottles, had been under way for some time. In 1983 canned beer had accounted for only 13 percent of total sales.

There were two basic beer markets in Japan: the home-use market and the commercial market. The home-use market included home delivery sales (typically, a consumer would have a retail shop deliver a case of beer to his home periodically); the gift market (smartly packaged gift sets of beer were sold through department stores during Japan's two major gift-giving seasons in July and December); and sales through liquor shops, food stores, and vending machines. The commercial market included sales through restaurants, bars, and hotels. In 1990 the home-use market accounted for around 75 percent of sales, the commercial market for 25 percent. The home-use market had grown steadily in size relative to the commercial market over the postwar period (see Exhibit 6).

Exhibit 5
Main Types and Sizes of Beer Containers

Bottles	Cans	Kegs
1,957 ml	1,000 ml	25,000 ml
633 ml	700 ml	15,000 ml
500 ml	500 ml	10,000 ml
334 ml	350 ml	3,000 ml
	250 ml	2,000 ml
	200 ml	1,200 ml
	135 ml	

Exhibit 6
Relative Size of Home-use and Commercial Markets (Percent of Total Consumption)

Year	Home Market	Commercial Market
1950	25%	75%
1962	53%	47%
1978	70%	30%
1987	71.3%	28.7%

Figure 2 shows Japan's beer distribution system. There were two kinds of distributors, the exclusive distributor, which handled only one or a limited number of brands, and the general distributor, which handled all four brands. Exclusive distributors were more common. The distribution system worked as an important barrier to entry. The inability to establish strong distribution channels is often cited as the main reason for the failure in beer of Takara, a distillery that entered the beer market in 1957 but withdrew 10 years later without ever gaining more than a 2 percent share. Suntory's 1963 entry into the beer market was facilitated by an agreement reached with Asahi which allowed Suntory to share Asahi's distribution network.

There were approximately 173,000 retail outlets for beer in Japan in 1988, most of which were liquor stores that sold to both consumers and commercial establishments. Retailers independently chose which brands to sell.

COST STRUCTURE

Production costs were roughly the same for all the brewers, accounting for about 58 percent of the producers' share of the retail cost of a bottle of beer. Fixed costs made up a significant portion of the brewers' spending, which meant that the smaller the firm, the lower profit margins tended to be. In particular, the costs for sales force, advertising, and promotion were mostly fixed, varying little with volume. This gave market share leader Kirin a clear scale advantage. For example, because Kirin could spread its advertising costs over a larger volume,

Figure 2
Beer Distribution System

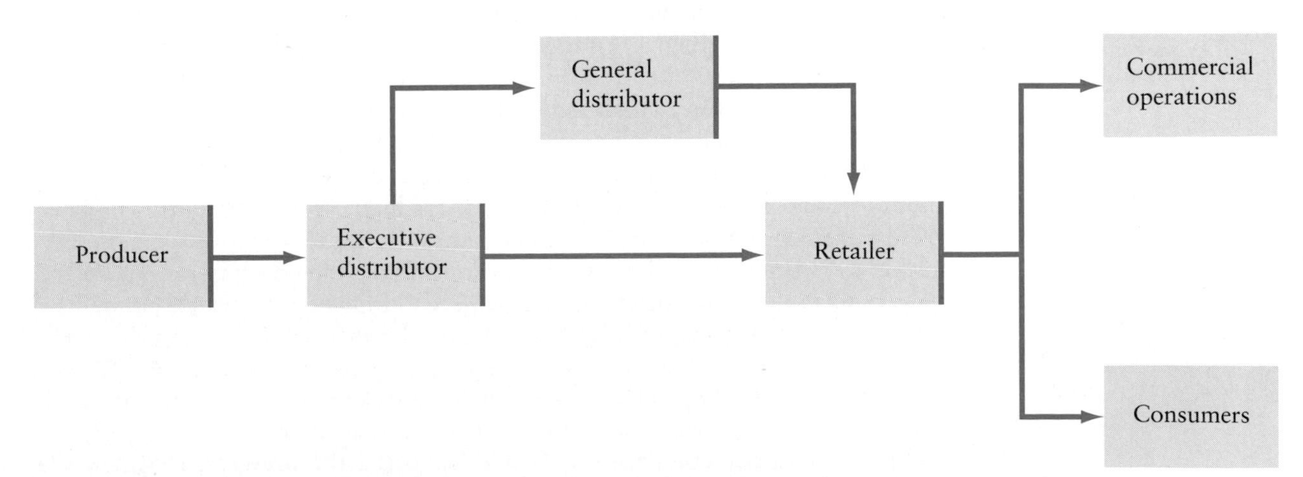

Exhibit 7
Cost Analysis per Average 633 Milliliter Bottle of Beer for Kirin, Sapporo, and Asahi, 1991

	Kirin	Sapporo	Asahi
Retail price	¥320	¥320	¥320
Liquor tax	131.9	131.9	131.9
Retailer and wholesaler margin	63.5	63.5	63.5
Cost of sales			
Materials cost	49.3	45.9	47.6
Labor	8.7	7.7	5.7
Other manufacturing	14.8	18.2	17.1
	72.8	71.8	70.5
Other costs			
Sales promotion	7.6	9.9	9.3
Transportation	7.3	7.6	8.3
Salaries and wages	5.7	8.1	7.1
Advertising expenses	5.5	13.4	11.9
Other administrative expenses	14.7	15.6	15.7
	40.9	54.5	52.4
Operating income	10.9	(1.8)	1.7

its advertising cost per bottle was only about 5.5 yen, compared to more than double that for its competitors. Exhibit 7 shows the cost makeup of the retail price of a bottle of beer.

PRICING

The retail price of beer was set directly by the government (the National Tax Board) until 1964, after which "free pricing" was introduced. In practice, however, there was little price competition. The four producers strictly maintained a standard producer price, a standard wholesale price, and a standard retail price for beer, with Kirin, due to its dominant market share, acting as price leader. In April 1988, for example, Kirin suddenly announced a 10 yen price cut in its 500 milliliter cans for the stated reason of passing on to consumers gains from the appreciation of the yen (which reduced the cost of imported barley and hops), and the other three companies immediately followed suit. Similarly, in March 1990 all four companies raised prices in concert, citing increasing material and labor costs and distribution sector demands for higher profit margins. This provoked public disapproval and an investigation by Japan's Fair Trade Commission. No evidence of a price cartel was found, but the commission asked the brewers to take action to liberalize prices. The four companies responded by running a joint newspaper advertisement in October 1990, stating that "the price of beer is supposed to be set independently by each store." A Sapporo spokesman noted that producers were inclined to keep prices in line with each other because many consumers view cheaper goods as inferior.

The lack of price competition, besides favoring the brewers, reflected the interests of the Japanese government, which depended on a financially healthy

brewing industry for important tax revenues. A Kirin spokesman stated, "The government has been giving preference to stability in the beer market, eliminating excess competition, to avoid a state of panic that might lead to a decrease in tax income."

At the end of 1990, a small amount of discounting could be seen at the retail level. A Tokyo survey found that Japanese beer brands were being sold at uniform prices in 99 percent of 668 convenience stores, department stores, and liquor shops and in 91 percent of 111 supermarkets. Foreign brands, including those produced in Japan under license, were sold at varying prices at different stores (from 178 yen to 240 yen for a 350 milliliter can). Kirin and Suntory spokespersons stated that a gradual trend toward price differentiation was probably starting, due in part to the increasing number of large-scale retail outlets, which did more discounting.

IMPORTS, EXPORTS, AND LICENSED PRODUCTION

Foreign beers, including both imports and licensed production in Japan of foreign brands, accounted for just 2 percent of the beer consumed in Japan. The geographic distance separating Japan from foreign markets, the heavy weight of beer, and the fact that beer has a limited shelf life—the taste of canned or bottled beer begins to deteriorate three or four months after production—meant that beer was not a particularly suitable product for large-scale import to and export from Japan. Many pointed also to country differences in climate, diet, and tastes as factors that limited international trade in beer. Barriers that inhibited exports to Japan included a small customs duty charged on imported beer and, more important, the complex and multitiered distribution system which required relatively small and frequent shipments due to limited warehouse space.

In 1988 Japan's brewers exported 30,000 kiloliters of beer, or 0.5 percent of total shipments. In the same year, around 20,000 kiloliters of foreign beer were imported, accounting for about 0.35 percent of domestic consumption.

Because of the limitations to trade in beer, licensing agreements increasingly had come to be used by Japanese and foreign brewers to make their products available in each other's markets. In Japan, under licensing agreements, Kirin brewed Heineken, Asahi brewed Coors and Lowenbrau, Sapporo brewed Miller, and Suntory brewed Budweiser and Carlsberg. Abroad, Molson produced Kirin in Canada and San Miguel brewed Asahi in Indonesia.

NATURE OF COMPETITION

Through the Early 1980s: Prior to the "New Product Boom"

In the absence of price competition, the brewers competed with each other in other ways. Prior to the mid-1980s, competition through advertising, quality (i.e., keeping fresh beer on the shelves), and development and control of distribution channels was the rule.

In addition, two types of product differentiation had been tried by Kirin's competitors, but without much success in terms of market share gain. The first was the introduction of canned and bottled "draft" beer, which generally has a smoother taste than traditional lager. In order to bottle or can freshly brewed

beer, either heat pasteurization or filtering is required to remove microorganisms which shorten shelf life. In Japan, beer that is heat pasteurized is known as "lager," while beer that is filtered is called "draft." (Outside Japan, "lager" has a different meaning: it is the name for beer produced by "bottom fermenting," in which the yeast sinks to the bottom of the brewing vat during fermentation; beer produced by "top fermenting" is called "ale.")

Until 1964 all the canned and bottled beer produced in Japan was heat-pasteurized lager. Suntory introduced Japan's first bottled draft beer in 1967, using a microfilter developed by NASA. Asahi brought out its own draft in 1968, followed by Sapporo in 1977, and, finally, Kirin in 1985. Although draft beer's share of the market grew steadily during this period, reaching 41 percent in 1985 and 62 percent in 1989, no company was able to increase its market share significantly via draft beer.

More short-lived than the "draft war" was an outbreak of packaging-based product differentiation in the late 1970s and early 1980s known as the "container war." Led by Asahi and Suntory, the brewers began packaging beer in unique containers of various sizes, shapes, and designs; there were take-home mini-barrels for parties, rocket-shaped containers called space shuttles, and cans and beer ads featuring cartoon penguins and raccoons. As with the introduction of draft beer, however, this differentiation strategy had little effect on market share. By the mid-1980s it had been largely abandoned.

Mid-1980s to Early 1990s: The "New Product Boom"

By the mid-1980s, a number of environmental trends had developed in Japan that set the stage for an era of intensified competition dominated by a powerful new weapon, new product development.

One key trend was demographic. The generation of beer drinkers that provided the backbone of support for Kirin's lager beer, the industry's dominant brand, was the generation born before World War II. By 1983, however, only 35 percent of Japan's population had been born before the war, and it was the post-war generation that was consuming the most beer. A new generation of "main users," the 10 percent of beer drinkers that consume 50 percent of the beer in Japan, was in place, ripe for new beers that matched their modern tastes. The younger generation still drank Kirin lager but were not necessarily devoted to it; many chose it because they had been taught by their elders that Kirin was the real beer drinker's beer.

Another change was that more women were drinking beer, particularly the young, working women who play a major role as trend setters. Women were widely believed in Japan to prefer a lighter, smoother-tasting beer.

One result of economic prosperity and rising incomes was that by the 1980s an "era of consumer choice" had arrived in Japan. "Keeping up with the Joneses" was being replaced by self-expression, and many products, including beer, were no longer commodities but ways to satisfy and express one's individual taste. Skyrocketing land prices, which pushed the dream of building one's own home beyond the reach of the average salaried worker, served to block one avenue of expressive consumption and funneled people's purchasing toward non-housing consumer goods. For many beer drinkers, this translated into an eagerness to try new beers and to the feeling that drinking the old standard, Kirin lager, was passé. This trend caused Kirin president Hideyo Motoyama to admit, "Unfortunately, the young in Tokyo have an impression that Kirin is not fashionable."

Change was also under way in the way beer was bought and sold. Fast disappearing were the days when Grandpa would call the local liquor shop and simply say, "Send over a case of beer." With more singles and young couples living in urban apartments and fewer traditional homes with three generations under one roof, there was often no space for a case of beer. Instead, more and more people were buying a few cans at a time from convenience stores, supermarkets, and vending machines. This led to more active choice making on the part of the consumer. Standing in front of a vending machine or reach-in display case in a store, the buyer had an array of labels spread before him or her, which encouraged experimenting with different brands.

There was also new variety in the marketplace. By 1985 foreign beers such as Budweiser and Heineken had worked their way into Japanese stores and vending machines and, although not capturing significant market share, were being widely advertised. More telling was the *chu-hai* boom of 1985. Chu-hai, a light cocktail made from *shochu* (a potato-based wine similar to vodka), soda, and fruit flavoring was invented that year and became an instant hit. It was easy to drink, which made it particularly popular among inexperienced drinkers such as students and women. The success of the chu-hai and the accompanying rise in shochu sales came at the direct expense of the beer companies and drove home the point that demand existed for greater novelty and variety in alcoholic beverages.

The four brewers responded similarly to these changes, interpreting them as a call for increased development and marketing of newer products to meet consumers' growing desire for different beers and greater variety. The result was a new product boom which began in the early and mid-1980s and then took off in earnest in 1987 with the unprecedented success of Asahi's "Super Dry."

The new product boom falls into two distinct phases. The first was the pre–Super Dry period, roughly from 1983 to 1987. Because no single new product had ever had a dramatic effect on market share in the industry, the aim of most new product development at this time was to create and fill a new niche. "Many varieties, small volume" was the watchword, and the accepted industry definition of a "hit" new product was one that sold 1 million cases in a year. Kirin, Sapporo, and Suntory all developed and marketed "light" and all-malt beers, and Asahi reformulated its main product, Asahi draft. Among the success stories were Suntory's "Malt's" (an all-malt introduced in 1986, which sold 2 million cases its first year, and Asahi's new draft in 1986, which helped the company gain market share for the first time in several years.

While the level of new product competition in the pre–Super Dry period was greater than that at any previous time, it was still relatively moderate in terms of new product introduction frequency, sales targets, and perceived stakes. This was in sharp contrast to the more ambitious goals and perceived higher stakes that were created in 1987 by the appearance and unprecedented success of Asahi Super Dry.

In March 1987 Asahi put on the market a new beer, Asahi Super Dry, characterized by a higher alcohol content (5 percent compared to the usual 4.5 percent), less sugar, and a smooth but sharp taste. Although originally designed not to head the Asahi lineup but to complement the previous year's new draft beer, the product surpassed all expectations and became the biggest hit in industry history. Asahi's initial sales target of 1 million cases had to be revised upward five times within six months, and by the end of the year, 13.5 million cases of Super Dry had been sold. Super Dry created a new beer category, "dry" beer, which was to be imitated by brewers all over the world.

The effect of Super Dry on Asahi's position in the industry was far greater than anyone could have anticipated. The company more than doubled its market share: from 10.3 percent in 1986 to 12.9 percent in 1987, 20.7 percent in 1988, and 24.8 percent in 1989. Super Dry allowed Asahi to establish important new distribution channels and sales outlets, and for the first time in 28 years, Asahi passed Sapporo to reach second place in market share. By 1989 Super Dry accounted for more than 20 percent of all beer consumed in Japan.

As the popularity of Super Dry became evident, Kirin, Sapporo, and Suntory all came out with their own versions of "dry" beer. None of these proved successful, however. Thanks to its first-mover advantage, creative and continual promotion, and, in the opinion of many, simply better taste, Super Dry became firmly rooted in beer drinkers' minds as *the* dry beer.

The scale of Super Dry's success revolutionized thinking in the Japanese brewing industry. At the very least, it confirmed the belief that Japanese drinkers were open to new and "modern" beers with fresh images and tastes that matched the times. Equally important, Super Dry demonstrated that what was at stake was not just the loyalty of any particular niche, such as the fashion-conscious young, but a mass market, including Japan's "main users"; Super Dry had succeeded at the expense of the standard beer drinker's beer, Kirin lager. Super Dry was called a "home run," and it further boosted the level of new product competition as each company sought to be the next to hit a home run. The aim of new product development changed from "many varieties, small volume" to "many varieties, medium or large volume," and the accepted definition of a hit product jumped from 1 million to 10 million cases.

The success of Super Dry also changed consumer expectations about beer. The Super Dry story was widely told in the media, generating high public interest in the "beer wars" (as the competition was called) and further increasing consumers' expectations for new products.

After Super Dry, the number of new beers introduced per year jumped again, as it was considered impossible for a brewer to compete in the industry without participating aggressively in the new product race. Each year, one or two new products proved extremely popular among consumers, and a company that did not put new products on the market seemed assured of losing market share.

Kirin, which generally had taken a passive approach to marketing new beers for fear of cannibalizing sales of its top-selling lager, jumped into the new product game in earnest after suffering a 10 percent plus market share loss to Super Dry. The company announced a "full-line" strategy in 1989 and by 1990 had no less than 15 brands in its product lineup. Kirin's biggest hit was Ichiban Shibori (literally "first extract"; the name sounds much better in Japanese), brought out in 1990. Starting with a first-year sales target of 10 million cases, Ichiban Shibori ended up selling 35 million cases in 1990, and by mid-year 1991 second-year sales were expected to hit 70 million. Combined with still-strong Kirin lager, Ichiban Shibori gave Kirin two solid pillars around which to anchor its broad lineup and helped the company gain in 1990 for the first time in six years.

Sapporo brought out a large number of new beers, both before and after Super Dry, but not many of them sold well. One of those that did was Japan's first "seasonal" beer, Fuyu Monogatari ("Winter Tale"), a 5.5 percent alcohol beer made to be drunk with the kinds of foods eaten in winter, sold only from October through February each year, and featuring a wintry quote from Shake-

speare on the label. (The seasonal concept would later be used by Suntory with its Summer Beer Nouveau and Kirin with Aki Aji, or Autumn Taste.) After a period of slipping market share and uncertainty with regard to its product lineup and positioning, Sapporo's product strategy in 1991 had settled around four main and a few niche beers. The four main beers were: (1) Sapporo's mainstay draft Black Label; (2) Ebisu (a rich-tasting, all-malt with a strong following among beer "connoisseurs"); (3) Fuyu Monogatari (still a strong seller in its fourth year); and (4) the smooth-tasting Ginjikomi (made using hulled malt), 1991's most successful new beer. In early 1991 Sapporo's president stated, "Even if the economy turns bad, we will continue developing and marketing new products; that's what the market wants."

With the exception of Malt's, which in 1991 was the top brand in the all-malt segment of the market, Suntory had not had much luck in the new product race. A number of new Suntory beers had enjoyed good first-year sales but had then fallen off. In 1991 the company discontinued four recent brands and concentrated on Malt's, the 1991 draft Beer Ginjo, and the seasonal Beer Nouveau, which came in both a summer and an autumn version. A Suntory light beer—no light beer had yet sold well in Japan—was due out in early 1992. In 1990 Suntory's vice president said that Suntory considered the new product market not yet mature and that the company would continue to aggressively create and market new beers.

Figure 3 and Exhibit 8 show the number and names of new beers introduced per year. Figure 4 shows the changes in market share that occurred before and during the new product boom, including the dramatic shift that occurred when Asahi Super Dry was introduced.

By 1991 not everyone was happy with the continuing new product boom and the competitive dynamics it created. The head of R&D in Sapporo's Production Division said:

Figure 3
Number of New Product Introductions in the Japanese Beer Industry by Year, 1964–1991

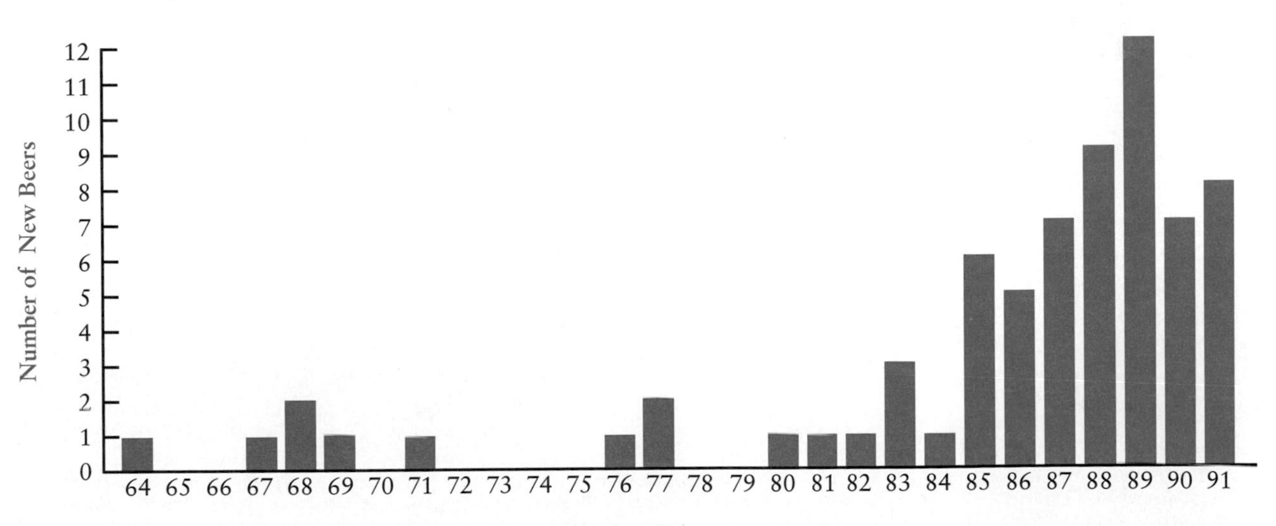

Exhibit 8 New Product Introductions, 1964–1991

Year	No.	Asahi	Kirin	Sapporo	Suntory
1964	1				Bin Nama
1965	0				
1966	0				
1967	1				Jun Nama
1968	2	Hon Nama Black			
1969	1			Sapporo Light	
1970	0				
1971	1			Ebisu	
1972	0				
1973	0				
1974	0				
1975	0				
1976	1		Mainburoi		
1977	2			Bin Nama	Merutsuen
1978	0				
1979	0				
1980	1		Kirin Light Beer		
1981	1		Kirin Nama		
1982	1	Kuro Nama			
1983	3	(Lowenbrau)		Kuro Nama Ebisu Draft	Nama Merutsuen
1984	1		(Heineken)		Penguin's Bar (Budweiser)
1985	6	Rasuta Mild	News Beer Kirin Beer Light	Next One Classic Weizen	
1986	5	Nama Koku-kire	Export	Quality Our's	Malt's (Carlsberg)
1987	7	100% Malt Super Dry (Coors)	Heartland Kirin Classic Heartland Alt	Edelpils (Miller)	New Sun. Nama
1988	9	(Coors Light)	Kirin Dry Fine Malt Half & Half	Extra Dry Malt 100 On The Rocks Fuyu Monogatari	Suntory Dry Dry 5.5
1989	12	Super Yeast (Der Lowenbrau)	Fine Draft Fine Pilsner Malt Dry Cool 1497	Sapporo Draft Hardy Cool Dry Black Label	Sae Malt's S. Prem
1990	7		Ichiban Shibori Mild Lager	Hokkaido Byakuya Monoga.	Jun Nama The Earth Beer Nouveau
1991	8	Z Horoniga	Premium Aki Aji	Ginjikomi	Ginjo Beer Nouv, Sum. Sum. Sento

Note: The definition of a "new product" is as follows. A new product is one in which the beer itself is new or different—in ingredients and/or brewing method, and therefore in taste—from products previously offered by the producer. It must be announced and advertised to the consumer as a new or improved beer. (Thus unpublicized adjustments in the taste of existing products are not considered new products.) A previously marketed beer offered in a new type or size of container is not considered a new product. Product names in parentheses are foreign brands produced under license in Japan; these are not considered new product introductions.

Figure 4
Market Share Shifts in the Japanese Beer Industry, 1970–1990

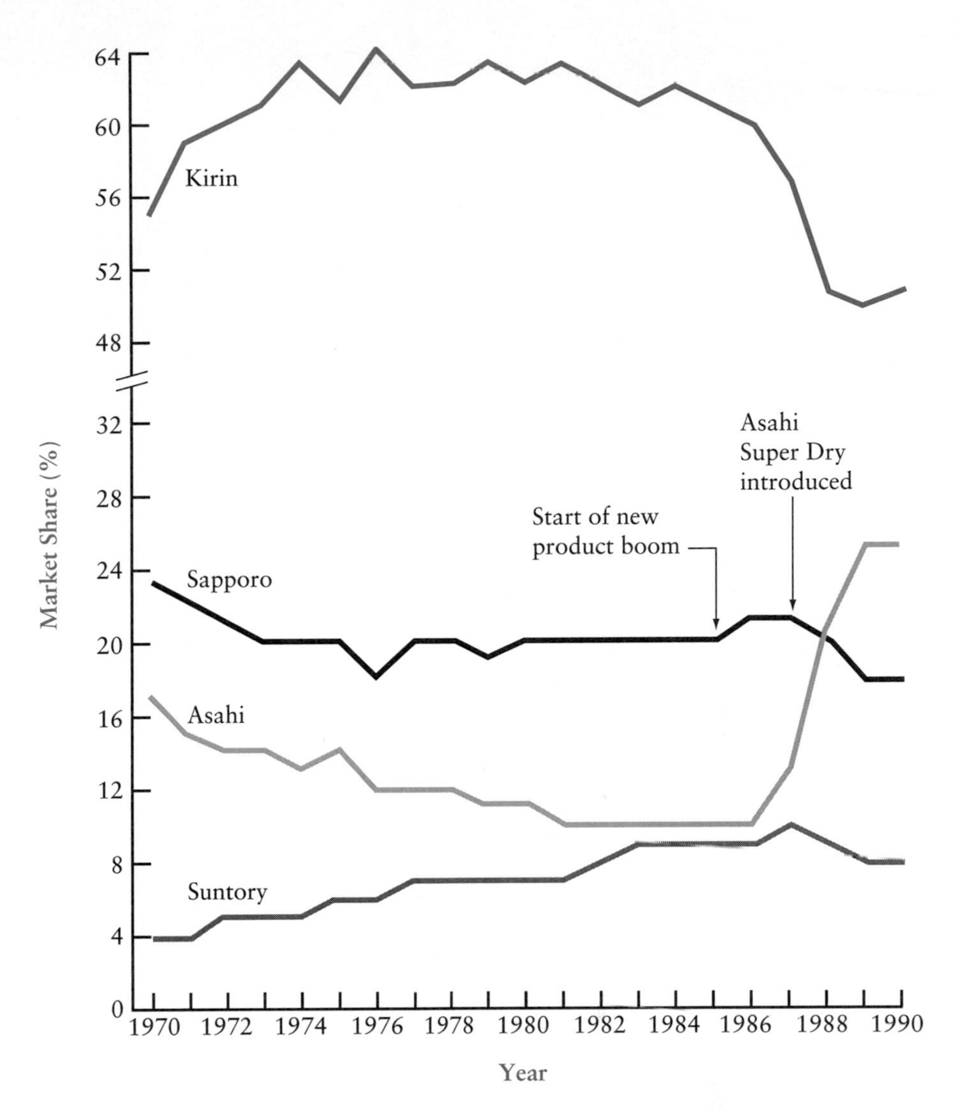

The current level of new product development is quite expensive. It takes a lot of money to develop an original new beer, and on top of that many of the recent new brands require materials or production methods that are more costly than those used to brew the old standards. Plus, to give a new product a chance to become a hit, you need to advertise it heavily, and that costs money. We seem to be caught in this cycle where if one company tries to differentiate itself, say by developing a certain type of mini-keg spout, then the three others also have to do it. The originator gets a temporary advantage, but it's copied quickly, and the industry as a whole ends up hurting itself by having to do all these extra things that cost more but give no advantage over the competition. The result is that consumers end up drinking expensive beer.

CASE 13

Asahi Breweries, Ltd.

INTRODUCTION

In a noisy Tokyo pub in late 1991, Yasuo Matsui, head of Asahi Beer's Marketing Department, took a long, slow drink from his mug of Asahi "Z" draft beer and pondered his company's product strategy. The previous five years had been the most successful in company history. A revamped product development system had produced in 1987 the most successful new beer in industry history, Asahi Super Dry, whose record-breaking sales had more than doubled Asahi's market share and lifted the brewer past rival Sapporo into second place in the industry for the first time in over two decades. Success had created its own problems, however, as by 1991 Super Dry accounted for 95 percent of Asahi beer sales. Subsequent new product introductions, Super Yeast (1989) and "Z" (1991), had not met sales expectations, and with Asahi's rivals responding with upgraded product development efforts and some new hit beers of their own, the question for Matsui was how to maintain and further build on the success his company had gained with Super Dry.

COMPANY HISTORY: POSTWAR TO EARLY 1980s

Today's Asahi Beer was created in 1949 when the occupation forces, headed by General Douglas MacArthur, introduced Japan's anti-monopoly law to break up dominant companies in excessively concentrated industries. Dai Nippon Breweries, which at the time controlled 75 percent of the beer market, was split in half, with its breweries and distributors in western Japan becoming Asahi Beer and those in eastern Japan becoming Sapporo.

The story of Asahi Beer from its postwar origin until the early 1980s was essentially one of steady decline, from a market share of 36.1 percent at the time of the breakup of Dai Nippon Breweries to a low of 9.5 percent (barely above the 9.3 percent of last-place Suntory) by 1985. Four reasons are commonly given for the company's poor performance:

1. Asahi developed the complacency that often characterizes large, established companies.
2. Because of the way Dai Nippon Breweries was broken up, Asahi was strong in western Japan but weak in the higher-growth eastern Japan (which includes Tokyo).

This case was prepared by Tim Craig, University of Victoria. This case was prepared as a basis for class discussion rather than to illustrate either effective or ineffective handling of administrative situations.

3. Asahi was strong in the commercial market but weak in the growing home-consumption market.
4. Asahi allowed whiskey maker Suntory to share its distribution network when Suntory entered the beer market, thereby losing sales to the financially more powerful distiller.

Asahi hit bottom in 1981, when poor performance forced the company to implement an early retirement program for 550 employees and a stock repurchase rescue by Sumitomo Bank and a friendly chemical company were needed to save Asahi from a "greenmail" attempt. Sumitomo was Asahi's main bank, and since 1971 all Asahi presidents had come from Sumitomo. In 1982, continuing this tradition, Tsutomu Murai was sent from Sumitomo Bank to become Asahi's new president. Murai had a reputation as a turnaround manager, previously having been dispatched by Sumitomo to save car maker Mazda from bankruptcy following the 1973 oil crisis.

The organization that Murai found when he arrived at Asahi was rigid, risk-averse, and dominated by the accounting department and a cost-cutting mindset. Employee morale was low and there was a high degree of "sectionalism," or mistrust between the different functional areas. Relations were especially bad between the production and sales divisions, with each blaming the other for the company's poor performance. Production people felt: "No matter how good the beer we make is, it doesn't sell because the sales force does such a poor job that it sits in the distribution channels and the taste deteriorates." Salespeople felt: "If the production people were less egocentric and more in touch with consumer tastes, our beer would taste and sell better."

To revitalize the company, Murai initiated a corporate identity (CI) program which produced a new corporate philosophy trademark. He also sought to improve cross-functional relations within the company by forcing managers from different areas to work together. Cross-functional task forces, made up of seven to eight managers from different departments, were put in charge of designing and carrying out the corporate identity activities and given responsibility for dealing with issues such as data use, employee suggestions, and customer complaints.

Company retreats were also used to break down functional walls. Asahi's 600 managers of section chief or higher rank were split into six groups of 100 and sent on four-day, three-night outings of business (discussion about Asahi and what was needed to revive company fortunes) mixed with pleasure (eating, drinking, hot spring soaking). Participants reported that production and salespeople, thrown together, were at odds the first day or two but by the end had come to understand each other better and to feel closer, more like fellow Asahi employees and less like mistrustful adversaries.

NEW PRODUCT DEVELOPMENT AT ASAHI

By industry standards, Asahi had been relatively active in product innovation prior to the 1980s. Industry "firsts" by Asahi included Japan's first canned beer in 1958 and the mini-barrel that touched off the "container war" in 1977. Due to strong brand loyalties and rapid imitation by competitors, however, these

innovations tended to cannibalize Asahi's own products rather than boosting Asahi's market share. Looking back at this type of innovation, Asahi product development manager Makoto Sugiura said, "It's significant that this was niche marketing, competing around the edges, not a frontal attack at the center of beer taste range."

The taste of Asahi beer prior to the 1980s was the exclusive domain of the "production side," that is, the brewmasters in charge of R&D and brewing at the beer plants. This was territory that was off limits to marketing, as Makoto Sugiura explained:

> When it came to the matter of our beer's taste, production was in charge and we marketing people couldn't say anything. The production people were the specialists, the pros, and they used a lot of technical terms for analyzing beer that we didn't know. When we did ask them something concerning taste, they would pull the wool over our eyes, speaking in a technical language that we couldn't understand. They had a monopoly on the matter of what good taste was; they'd say "This is good taste, this is Asahi beer." The system was they'd make it and we'd try our hardest to sell it. The measure, or criterion, for how Asahi beer should taste was the personal preference of a certain high-level manager on the production side. Everyone adjusted to him; if he said a certain kind of beer was delicious, then that became, for Asahi, what delicious beer was.

While such a system may have been adequate for "niche marketing" or packaging-based innovation, it completely stymied the kind of consumer needs–driven product development that Asahi's marketers, sensitive to changing consumer tastes and behavior, felt was called for in the marketplace of the 1980s.

The door to marketing's participation in new product development at Asahi was opened by the CI campaign and new corporate philosophy that president Murai established in 1982. The basis of the new philosophy was to "consider the wants and needs of our customers." Sugiura explained:

> The CI concept itself was to give the consumer what he wants most, so from this point on making delicious beer was something both the production and marketing sides were deeply involved in. For the first time, we had a voice; we were the consumer.

In order to implement marketing's involvement in the development of new beers, a new product development system was established, which remained in use in 1991. Managing director Hisashi Usuba explained how it was set up:

> There are two ways we could have changed the organization. One was to create three separate departments, one in charge of brewing beer, one in charge of selling it, and one in charge of product development [see Figure 1B]. But if you do this, and I've experienced this a number of times, this sort of thing happens. The product development people, for example, would get completely involved only in new product development and wouldn't think much about production or sales. They would end up creating their own world. Sales and production people would feel that the product development people know nothing about what's going on in the marketplace or at the plants and are just following their own whims in product development. As a result, the product development department would get no cooperation from sales or production.
>
> So instead we created a larger Production Division and Sales Division and within each set up an independent section in charge of product development: the Production Project Section within the Production Division, and the Marketing Department's Product Planning Section within the Sales Division [see Figure 1C]. New product development is carried out by these two sections "playing catch with each other." This way the Production Division is one sphere, and the feeling among production people is that

Figure 1
Change in Asahi's Product Development Organization

(A) Pre-1992

Production division
- Brewmasters in charge of product development

Sales division
- Marketing shut out of product development

(B)

Production division

Sales division

Product development division

(C)

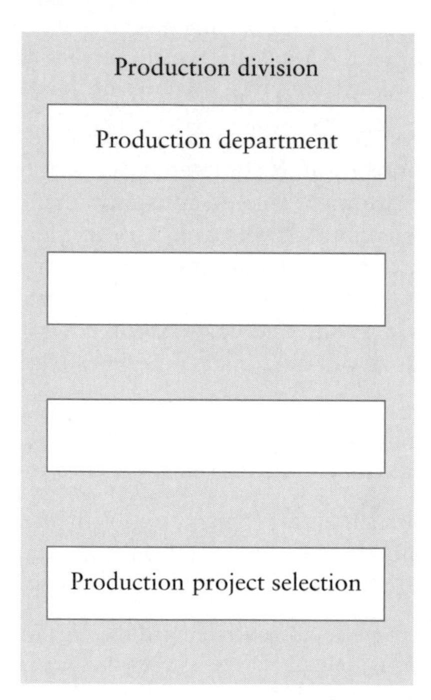

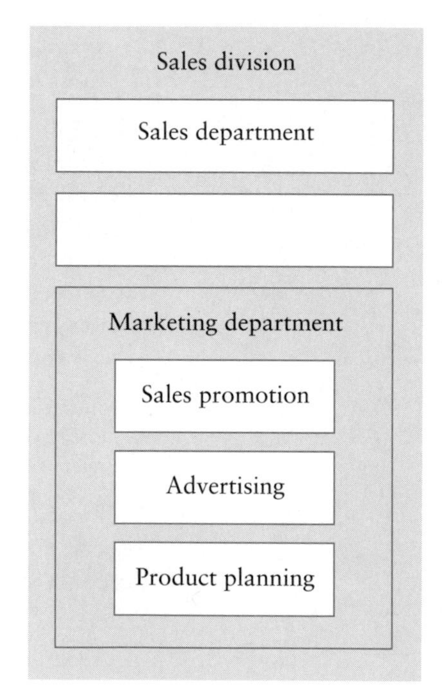

Production Project Section people are "part of us"; likewise, the Sales Division is one sphere, whose workers feel that Product Planning Section people are "part of us." This makes the cooperation of production and salespeople much easier to get.

The biggest change that this brought about was that market and taste surveys were now done not just by the production people but by the Production Project Section and the Product Planning Section in concert. This is important. When you do a taste survey, the data is not always clear, not easy to interpret, so different people read it quite differently. So if, as before, production does the surveying, they read the results in a way that is most convenient for them, that matches their beliefs and thinking. The change was made to prevent this; having marketing and production carry out surveys together resulted in a change from a "what suits production" to a "what do consumers want" approach to product development.

The core product development team was made up of about a dozen players, five from the marketing side (Product Planning Section) and seven from the production side (Production Project Section). Sugiura commented:

> It's no good to get a larger number of people involved; with more than this it would be too messy and cumbersome. As for creating the product concept, the decision to make "this kind of beer'; 95 percent of this is done by the marketing side. The idea was, if we got it wrong, if the new product flopped, we would be replaced.

One feature of the new system was that much of the hierarchy that once stood between those working on new products and top management was removed. Sugiura explained:

> Now, we dozen or so people of the Product Planning Section and the Production Project Section can go almost directly to the top with our ideas. Before, we needed a lot of "hankos" [seals, the equivalent of a superior's signature of approval] before our ideas got a hearing at the top. This speeds things up. Timing is extremely important in putting out new products, so the quicker you can go from proposal to action the better.

Re-drawing the lines in an organizational chart was an important first step toward creating a better product development system, but that alone did not guarantee that product development would work smoothly. A more difficult challenge was to build effective communication between the marketing and production personnel who now found themselves working together on the development of new beers. Hisashi Usuba talked about the importance of good marketing-production communication for product development and some of the barriers that must be overcome to achieve it:

> Good new product development depends very much on effective communication between the marketing and production people involved. The characteristics of a beer are hard to measure and state clearly, unlike, for example, the specs of an automobile. Some people are good at describing a beer; some aren't. To create a "product plan" for a new beer, words are needed that capture and convey acutely the product concept. Marketing people are not especially good at this; production people have the technical vocabulary to express a beer's characteristics much more precisely.
>
> Marketing people generally have a broad view of the world and are tuned in to the customers, to opinions out in the street. Production people, by contrast, spend more time shut up inside the plant and are more conservative. They're often called "technology crazy," meaning they're locked up in their own world, and don't know what's going on in the real world. The two groups even drink differently after work; technical people stick to one or two bars they know while marketing people drink around, try a lot of new places, and are therefore quick to pick up trends and information.
>
> To create successful new products, the input of both sides is needed, and so good communication between the two is essential. They need to build a common vocabulary for describing and creating beers, and the production people need to be made aware of trends in the marketplace. One thing we do a lot of to achieve this is "nomi-nication" [drinking communication; "nomi" is Japanese for drinking]. People from the Product Planning Section and the Production Project Section get together in the same room to drink beer and analyze data. In Japanese companies, there's a wall between marketing and production, but with this organizational set-up and our efforts to build communi cation and understanding, we've been very successful in tearing down this wall.

Beginning in 1984 Asahi product developers from the marketing and production sides met together every Monday evening to taste and talk about beer. The difficulty of bridging the language and orientation gap between the two groups

was attested to by a product planner who said in 1990, "We've been having these Monday meetings for four or five years now, and only recently have we come to be able to communicate effectively."

ASAHI SUPER DRY

The payoff from Asahi's revamped product development system came in 1987 when Asahi Super Dry hit the market, breaking all records for sales of a new beer in Japan. The development of Super Dry illustrates how the new product development process worked.

The product concept that resulted in Super Dry originated in a decision by Asahi's marketing-side product planners to compete not around the edges but at "the dead center of the consumer taste range." Sugiura talked about this decision:

> In 1984–85, when we were considering giving up competing around the edges and instead going for the dead center of the taste range, this was a big risk. The case of Coca-Cola changing the taste of Coke shows what can happen when a food or beverage maker changes the taste of its main product. Since this would be a big frontal attack, if we failed it would be all over for Asahi. But our market share had dropped to under 10 percent, so if we did nothing there would be a good chance of Asahi disappearing from the market anyway. So for this very reason, we were able to do the bold marketing we did, changing the taste of our beer and shooting for what we hypothesized was a new taste center.

Asahi marketers hypothesized that the center of the taste preference range had shifted away from where it was generally said to be—that is, away from the bitter, strong flavor that characterized Kirin's lager beer. The hypothesis was based on a change that had occurred in the Japanese diet. In the first two decades of the postwar period, the Japanese diet was relatively bland, and this produced in the people a craving for strong tastes to supplement their diet; in beer, this meant that Kirin's strong, bitter taste was considered delicious. But in the 20 years from 1966 to 1985, the Japanese overall diet had become richer (the amount of oil and fats purchased per household approximately doubled), while there was a trend in drinks and side dishes toward a lighter, plainer taste (the amount of sugar and salt used by Japanese dropped by about 50 percent).

To try to determine where the dead center of the taste range was, Asahi in 1984 conducted the first of what became an annual 5,000-person taste preference survey. (Previous to this, the only surveying of consumers carried out at Asahi consisted of giving out questionnaires to people going on tours of Asahi breweries.) The survey confirmed that consumer preference was in fact shifting away from Kirin's bitter and rich flavor to a more refreshing, sharper taste. The survey also produced a product blueprint that would lead to the reformulation of Asahi's standard draft and the eventual creation of Super Dry. As part of the taste survey, beer drinkers were asked what makes a delicious beer, and their answers (excluding "bitterness," which Asahi believed consumers had been educated by Kirin to equate with good taste) fell mainly into two groups. One was *koku*, which means rich taste, and the other was *kire*, which means refreshing, sharp, stimulating to the throat when swallowed. Koku and kire were generally

considered to be incompatible—a beer could have a rich taste or a sharp, refreshing taste, but not both. Asahi's marketing side Product Planning Section challenged the conventional wisdom and asked its production side counterparts to try to create a beer that was a little more koku than the most koku beer on the market, which was Kirin's lager, and at the same time a little more kire than the most kire beer on the market, Sapporo's Black Label draft. Such a beer, they reasoned, would be close to the center of the taste range. The Production Project Section took the product concept, translated it into a "product plan" written in the technical language that was meaningful to brewers and R&D people, and asked the company's R&D laboratory to create a test beer according to the plan.

Test beers were made and sent back to the Product Planning and Production Project sections where they were evaluated. R&D was then requested to "try making it more this way, can you give it more of this characteristic, and less of that?" This continued, with R&D experimenting with various ingredients and brewing method variations. Product Planning Section and Production Project Section members met together frequently to discuss the product, and it was during these meetings, which were sometimes amiable, sometimes quite heated, that the two sides reached a common understanding of what "koku" and "kire" meant. Repeatedly, the R&D people would make a beer and the two groups would sample it together, asking, "Is this more 'koku' than Kirin, is it more 'kire' than Black Label?" When they had what they thought filled the bill, that beer became Asahi's new draft. Put on the market in place of Asahi's existing draft in 1986 (and advertised with the slogan "rich in taste, yet also sharp and refreshing"), it sold well and helped produce a 12 percent growth in Asahi sales for that year.

Encouraged by the success of the new Asahi draft and feeling it was moving in the right direction taste-wise, the Product Planning Section next hypothesized, again based on taste preference surveys, that consumer tastes in beer were moving further away from koku and more toward kire. Accordingly, the taste concept for Super Dry was created: similar to the new draft but with an even sharper, clearer, more refined taste.

Super Dry was put on the market in March 1987, originally envisioned as a "support" product for mainstay Asahi draft, which had been successfully reformulated the year before. The new brand proved such a hit, however, that it quickly overtook Asahi draft as the company's best seller. Production could not keep up with demand, and at one point Asahi prohibited its employees from buying Super Dry in order to save it for customers. Kirin, Sapporo, and Suntory, hoping that Super Dry was a fad that would fade when winter came, were slow to respond with their own versions of dry beer. Then, when they finally had their dry beers ready to launch in early 1988, Asahi further delayed their market entry, forcing them to make last-minute labeling and advertising changes by threatening to take legal action for copyright infringement. By the time Asahi's rivals got their dry beers in stores, Super Dry had become synonymous with dry beer in the minds of consumers, and it continued to far outsell its imitators.

In 1987, 13.5 million cases of Super Dry were sold, causing the industry definition of a hit new product—up to that time it was one that sold a million cases in its first year—to be rewritten. Asahi sales for 1987 jumped 33 percent, and by 1989, thanks almost entirely to Super Dry, Asahi's market share had risen to 24.8 percent from just 10.3 percent three years earlier.

THE CONTRIBUTION OF LEADERSHIP AND CORPORATE CHANGE TO NEW PRODUCT SUCCESS

While the taste of Asahi's new draft and Super Dry, carefully developed to match changing consumer taste preferences, was a central reason for the new beer's success, an important role was also played by top management leadership and corporate change that had been carried out at Asahi. In 1986, Hirotaro Higuchi (like Murai from Sumitomo Bank) took over as president, bringing to Asahi an active hands-on management style that was well suited for leading a company that had been put back on track by Murai's efforts to improve employee morale, activate middle-level managers, and create a customer focus. Personnel section chief Ninomiya spoke about the contribution that Murai and Higuchi made to product development:

> The biggest thing in my opinion was the leadership of top management. They emphasized quality and originality and demanded these of workers. For the new product development people, a tremendous motivator was top management's willingness to use the fruits of their labor, to market the products they developed. Under the old system, the young people developing new products were stymied; their proposals had to be evaluated and decided on by a series of upper managers, who made judgments based on their own established values. The new things that younger people tried, as they rose toward the top, were rejected in favor of the old and traditional. What Higuchi did when he came in was to start actively and directly using ideas and proposals originating in lower levels of the organization. The distance between the people actually doing new product development and top management became shorter.

It was Higuchi who made the decision to launch Super Dry, over his initial concern that putting out another new brand so soon after the new Asahi draft would only cannibalize the draft. The product development team had kept pushing, and after drinking the new beer and finding it tasted good, Higuchi gave Super Dry the go-ahead. Higuchi also increased R&D spending and strongly supported Asahi's new products with enlarged budgets for advertising and promotion.

The customer focus and improved marketing-production relations that Murai had worked to achieve also paid off, as explained by Marketing Department head Matsui:

> At the time that we in marketing created the product concept for our new draft and asked the production/R&D people to produce this beer, a top production-side manager said to me: "In order to brew the kind of beer you are asking us to make, it will be necessary not just to change ingredients, but to re-do the entire production process from start to finish. We'll even have to develop a new yeast. That will be very tough." At that point I thought there was no way he would agree to what we were proposing. But to my surprise he continued: "But, let's give it a try." At this moment I strongly felt the effect of our CI campaign, a main theme of which was to throw out certain old ways and values and to respond to consumers by making products that meet their needs.

COMPETITORS' RESPONSE: AN INTENSIFIED NEW PRODUCT WAR

With Super Dry demonstrating the potential effect of a single new beer on a company's performance, Asahi's competitors geared up their own product development efforts. Like Asahi, the other Japanese brewers modified their

product development processes, creating systems with features such as joint leadership by marketing and production/R&D at the core; increased gathering and use of consumer information; a shorter route to top management approval; and earlier involvement in the process of all the various functions (design, packaging, legal affairs, advertising, sales, engineering, the brewing plants), whose cooperation would be required at some point before a new beer could be marketed. They stepped up their frequency of new product introduction and increasingly aimed for "home runs" like Super Dry as opposed to niche products.

The biggest change took place at Kirin, whose sales had been most hurt by Super Dry. Traditionally, the industry leader had followed a conservative approach to introducing new products, in order to defend its dominant brand, Kirin lager. Kirin president Hideyo Motoyama explained: "It's definitely true that we responded slowly to the trends toward canned and draft beer. But you must remember that Kirin's red label bottled Lager accounted for over half the beer drunk in Japan. Our number one priority was to avoid hurting sales of our main, dominant product."

After experiencing significant market share loss to Super Dry and other new offerings, however, Kirin did an about-face and launched a "full-line" strategy. Three new Kirin beers were introduced in 1988, followed by five in 1989. Then in 1990 Kirin brought out Ichiban Shibori (sold as "Ichiban" outside Japan), which began with a first-year sales target of 10 million cases but ended up selling 35 million cases, breaking the record that Super Dry had set. Not resting on its laurels, nor on a first-time-in-six-years market share gain, Kirin introduced two more new brands in 1991, including the seasonal Aki Aji (Autumn Taste), a 6 percent brew sold only during the fall. Aki Aji sold well in its first months on the market.

Neither Sapporo nor Suntory, by 1991, had hit a home run to match Super Dry or Ichiban Shibori, but Sapporo had the top-selling new launch of 1991 in its Ginjikomi, and Suntory had created a hit with its Beer Nouveau series (a takeoff on Beaujolais Nouveau, the French wine made from just-harvested grapes that was popular in Japan.) Indications were that all four companies had plans for further new product launchings in 1992. (See Exhibits 1, 2, 3, and 4 for profiles of the four beer companies.)

ASAHI'S FUTURE PRODUCT STRATEGY

While Super Dry had improved Asahi's fortunes tremendously, its dominance of the Asahi lineup had Matsui and the company's other product planners worried: With Asahi so dependent on sales of Super Dry, what if "dry" beer lost its popularity? Watching arch-rival Kirin, now with two sturdy "pillars" (Lager and Ichiban Shibori) around which to anchor its lineup, Matsui strongly felt the need for another Asahi bestseller to back up Super dry. Asahi's major new product intros for 1989 and 1991, Super Yeast and "Z," had been attempts to balance the Asahi lineup with one major brand that could carry the load should a "post-dry" era arrive. But those two brands, though supported by major promotional and advertising campaigns, had not sold as well as hoped.

An important but unanswered question was how long these new product wars would last. Asahi had more new beers in the pipeline, but was it wise to launch them? Did the potential still exist for a monster new hit, or were

Exhibit 1
Asahi Beer Profile, 1990

Income (¥ mil)	Sales	Operating Profit	Current Profit	Net Profit	Earnings per Share	Dividend per Share
December 1987	345,112	3,507	9,388	2,509	¥ 9.3	¥5.0
December 1988	544,866	14,547	14,962	4,750	¥15.6	¥8.0
December 1989	655,073	11,124	18,705	6,034	¥16.9	¥8.0
December 1990	730,800	15,059	17,246	6,119	¥14.8	¥8.0

Financial Data (¥ mil, December 1990)

Capital stock	125,669
Total assets	1,167,200
Shareholders' equity	270,967
Bank borrowings	249,126
Number of shareholders	29,845

Sales Breakdown (1990)

Beer	82% (79% in 1987)
Soft drinks and other	18% (21% in 1987)
Export ratio	0% (0% in 1987)

Areas of diversification: non-alcoholic beverages, wine, medicine, restaurants, Nikka whiskey (subsidiary)

Employees: 4,260 (Average age: 36.2)

Exhibit 2
Kirin Beer Profile, 1990

Income (¥ mil)	Sales	Operating Profit	Current Profit	Net Profit	Earnings per Share	Dividend per Share
January 1988	1,266,349	69,574	80,824	34,059	¥37.7	¥7.5
December 1988	1,178,849	41,077	64,691	29,013	¥32.1	¥7.5
December 1989	1,199,804	39,345	64,616	28,270	¥28.2	¥7.5
December 1990	1,355,787	63,133	84,919	35,841	¥35.8	¥8.0

Financial Data (¥ mil, December 1990)

Capital stock	102,004
Total assets	1,205,260
Shareholders' equity	493,064
Bank borrowings	18,091
Number of shareholders	111,975

Sales Breakdown (1990)

Beer	89% (93% in 1987)
Soft drinks	9% (6% in 1987)
Other	1% (1% in 1987)
Export ratio	0% (0% in 1987)

Areas of diversification: non-alcoholic beverages, whiskey (Seagram's), wine, restaurants, dairy products (Koiwai farms), medicine, biotechnology (plant genetic engineering)

Employees: 7,686 (Average age 39.5)

Exhibit 3
Sapporo Beer Profile, 1990

Income (¥ mil)	Sales	Operating Profit	Current Profit	Net Profit	Earnings per Share	Dividend per Share
December 1987	467,046	14,514	13,050	5,250	¥15.8	¥6.5
December 1988	489,655	5,011	13,503	6,137	¥18.4	¥5.0
December 1989	463,591	–(3,710)	7,454	8,448	¥25.3	¥5.0
December 1990	492,628	5,367	8,432	4,006	¥12.0	¥5.0
Financial Data (¥ mil, December 1990)						
Capital stock		41,167				
Total assets		562,849				
Shareholders' equity		124,315				
Bank borrowings		95,143				
Number of shareholders		28,168				
Sales Breakdown (1990)						
Beer		92% (94% in 1987)				
Soft drinks		5% (4% in 1987)				
Other		4% (2% in 1987)				
Export ratio		0% (0% in 1987)				

Areas of diversification: non-alcoholic beverages, wine, imported liquor, real estate

Employees: 4,035 (Average age: 41)

Exhibit 4
Suntory Profile, 1990

Income (¥ mil)	Sales	Net Profit	Dividend per Share	Reported per Share
December 1988	630,962	6,795	¥1.5	7,596
December 1989	777,008	6,159	¥2.5	16,055
December 1990	796,445	4,865	¥1.5	15,009
Financial Data (¥ mil, December 1990)				
Capital stock		30,000		
Total assets		1,006,224		
Net assets		220,507		
Bank borrowings		426,393		
Number of shareholders		50		
Sales Breakdown (1990)				
Liquor, wine		56.3%		
Beer		26.2%		
Foods		17.5%		

Areas of diversification: liquor and wine, non-alcoholic beverages, food processing, restaurants, publishing (TBS Britannica), entertainment, medicine

Employees: 5,089

consumers getting tired of the constant parade of new beers showing up in outlets and on television? Perhaps the company's resources should be focused on supporting Super Dry, instead of on creating and promoting more new beers for a market already flooded with them.

Some of Matsui's thoughts may have been echoed in the comments of Product Planning Section chief Makoto Sugiura concerning the new product boom:

> This new product competition has only been going on for a few years, it could be a temporary phenomenon. There's no history in this industry of new products being long-run stars. Super Dry is the first new beer to top 100 million cases. All the others that have started out well have faded after 3 or 4 years. Most of Kirin's new beers aren't selling well, even its draft, which looked like it would be a big hit. Now Ichiban Shibori's doing great, but it could disappear in five years. It could be that in 5 or 10 years, the only surviving beers will be our Super Dry, Kirin's Lager, Sapporo's Black Label, Suntory's Malt's. Then, after another 10 years, people will get bored or there might be a shift in taste preferences, and another new product war will start. Looking over the long term, people and beer don't change that much; stability is sought. Right now people are enjoying all the new products, but if it gets to the point where the new beers don't taste better or different, and the only thing new is the name and the package, then people will get sick of it all. I see that coming sooner or later. So it's your main product, the one or two that are going to survive, that count.

CASE 14

The Global Auto Industry: Toward the Year 2000

INTRODUCTION

The global auto industry of the mid 1990s looked very different from the auto industry of the 1960s. In the 1960s the industry was fragmented into a series of self-contained national markets with relatively little in the way of trade or contact between them. Even though companies such as Ford and General Motors had long had international subsidiaries, those subsidiaries operated on a fully autonomous basis with regard to design, production, and marketing. Typically, the structure of most national markets was consolidated, with a handful of companies dominating the local industry. There was a tendency for each national market to be dominated by "national champions." In the United States the national champions were General Motors, Ford, and Chrysler; in Japan they were Toyota and Nissan; in Germany they were Volkswagen, BMW, and Mercedes-Benz; in France they were Renault and Peugeot; in Italy the national champion was Fiat; while in Britain the national champion was British Leyland. The result, in most nations, was an absence of strong competition.

By the mid 1990s the picture was changing rapidly. The industry was becoming more global in scope. In particular, the volume of trade in automobiles and automobile components between the three main global markets, North America, Western Europe, and Japan, had increased rapidly. In addition, more and more companies were seeking to establish production facilities overseas as a protection against trade barriers and currency fluctuations. One consequence of these trends was the fragmentation of previously consolidated national markets and a commensurate increase in the intensity of competition around the globe.

THE INTERNATIONAL TRADE AND INVESTMENT ENVIRONMENT

One of the main factors that has helped to transform the world auto industry into more of a global industry has been the liberalization of the world trade and investment environment that has occurred over the past 50 years. The transformation was initiated in 1947 when 19 industrial nations signed an international treaty known as the General Agreement on Tariffs and Trade (GATT). The GATT committed member countries to lowering barriers to the free flow of goods between countries. By any measure, the GATT has been very successful.

This case was prepared by Charles W. L. Hill, University of Washington. This case was prepared as a basis for class discussion rather than to illustrate either effective or ineffective handling of administrative situations.

Between 1947 and 1979 the GATT, which now has over 100 members, succeeded in lowering the average tariffs on imports of goods into member countries by over 90 percent.[1]

By lowering barriers to the free flow of goods, the GATT made it possible for companies based in one country to export products to other countries. In the automobile industry, the main beneficiaries of this policy were Japan and Germany. During the 1960s companies based in both countries began to export passenger cars to the world's largest automobile market, the United States. By the early 1970s this flow of imports was helping to break up the cozy oligopoly that had existed in the United States. As a direct result of foreign competition, between 1960 and 1990 the share of the U.S. passenger car market accounted for by General Motors, Chrysler, and Ford fell from over 90 percent to around 64 percent. Japanese-owned companies increased their share from nothing to 31 percent, with German companies accounting for much of the remainder.

By the early 1980s the increasing inroads made by Japanese and German companies into the United States were beginning to raise concerns among certain segments of the American public about U.S. job losses. In response, the U.S. government negotiated a deal with the Japanese government under which the Japanese agreed to limit their exports of cars to the United States. Known as a voluntary export restraint (VER), under the deal Japanese companies limited exports to the United States to no more than 1.68 million vehicles per year. The agreement was revised in 1984 to allow Japanese producers to export 1.85 million vehicles, but the total was subsequently lowered again, and in 1992 it stood at 1.65 million vehicles per year.[2] Faced with limits on their exports from Japan, Japanese auto companies decided to invest heavily in U.S.-based productive capacity. This decision was reinforced by the rise in the value of the yen against the U.S. dollar during the mid 1980s, which eliminated much of Japan's cost advantage. As a result of inward investment by Japanese auto companies, by 1992 close to 20 percent of productive capacity in the United States was Japanese owned.[3]

Although events moved more slowly in western Europe, by the early 1990s it seemed likely that a similar transformation would occur there. Despite the GATT, a number of European auto markets, most notably those of France and Italy, had remained protected from foreign (and particularly Japanese) competition by high tariff barriers. This had limited the overall share of the European market accounted for by Japanese companies to around 11 percent by 1992. In addition, in 1991 the European Community (EC) negotiated a VER agreement with Japan which limited Japan's exports of autos to the EC to under 1.2 million vehicles a year until 1999. However, under the auspices of the European Community there had also been a concerted attempt to lower barriers to the free flow of goods *between* EC countries. This culminated in the Single European Act, which went into effect on December 31, 1992. The aim of the act was to lower a multitude of barriers to the free flow of goods and services between EC countries, including barriers to the free flow of automobiles. In advance of the act, Japanese companies had begun to invest heavily in production facilities in Britain. The Japanese plan was to serve the EC market from these facilities. As a result of this investment, by 1995 Japanese companies could be producing

1. J. Bhagwati, *Protectionism* (Cambridge, Mass.: MIT Press, 1988).
2. Larry Armstrong and Karen Miller, "Japan's Sudden Deceleration," *Business Week*, June 8, 1992, pp. 26–27.
3. Standard & Poor's Industry Surveys, *Autos–Auto Parts*, June 24, 1993.

around 800,000 vehicles a year in Europe, and by 2000 the figure could be as high as 2 million.[4]

LEAN PRODUCTION AND THE JAPANESE CHALLENGE

As noted above, one of the main beneficiaries of the more liberal trade and investment environment that has existed in the second half of the twentieth century has been Japanese auto companies. Lower trade barriers alone, however, are hardly enough to explain Japanese gains in both the North American and Western European market. The Japanese presence in both of these regions has grown because of the ability of Japanese companies to deliver a broad range of high-quality, well-designed automobiles at a reasonable cost to consumers. In turn, this ability was based on a series of process innovations pioneered primarily at Toyota and Nissan in the years following World War II. Until the early 1990s most U.S. and European automakers still utilized the "mass production" technology originally pioneered by Henry Ford in the 1920s. In contrast, most Japanese producers have been utilizing a technology that has been termed "lean production" for some years now. The differences between the two technologies are striking.[5]

The underlying philosophy of mass production technology is to mass produce each car model in order to spread the fixed costs of production over as many units as possible. To achieve this, the typical mass producer utilizes unskilled or semiskilled workers to mind expensive single purpose machines that churn out large volumes of the same product. The mass producer also adds many buffers—extra suppliers, extra workers, and extra space—to assure smooth production and to bypass any bottlenecks that might occur in the system (such as when a machine breaks down). In theory, this system gives the consumer lower-cost automobiles—at the expense of some variety. In practice, the extra workers, supplies, and space raise costs above those of the typical Japanese lean producer, while the boring and dispiriting method of work leads to an alienated work force that is prone to making mistakes. Consequently, relative to lean producers, mass producers tend to turn out high-cost, poor-quality cars.

In contrast, lean producers utilize flexible manufacturing technologies to produce limited amounts of a car at a cost that at one time could be achieved only through mass production. They utilize just-in-time inventory systems to eliminate buffer stocks of inventory. They utilize cross-functional teams comprised of engineering, manufacturing, and marketing personnel in an attempt to shorten new product development times. And they form the work force into multiskilled teams, eliminating the need for many of the "specialists" and "supervisors" found in mass production plants, thereby reducing the total work force. Moreover, the team organization seems to result in a more satisfying work environment, reducing both worker alienation and the mistakes born of boredom or frustration that seem to plague mass producers.

As a result of these features, relative to a mass producer, the typical lean producer can manufacture a wider range of higher-quality automobiles at a lower cost. They are also able to introduce new models more rapidly, thereby adapting

4. "The Enemy Within," *The Economist*, June 12, 1993, pp. 67–68.
5. See J. P. Womack, D. T. Jones, and D. Roos, *The Machine That Changed the World*, (New York: Rawson Associates, 1990).

Table 1
Assembly Plant Characteristics for Volume Producers (Averages for Plants in Each Region)

	Producers		
	Japanese in Japan	American in America	European
Productivity (Worker hours to build a vehicle)	16.8	25.1	36.2
Quality (Defects per 100 vehicles)	60.0	82.3	97.0
Inventories (days' supply for 8 sample parts)	0.2	2.9	2.0
Percent of work force in teams	69.3	17.3	0.6

Source: Adapted from J. P. Womack, D. T. Jones, and D. Roos, *The Machine That Changed the World* (New York: Rawson Associates, 1990), Figure 4.7, p. 92.

themselves more quickly to trends in the marketplace. Given these advantages, it is hardly surprising that the Japanese companies that pioneered lean production techniques, and particularly Toyota, Nissan, and Honda, are among the strongest automobile companies in the world. Proof of this can be found in Table 1, which summarizes assembly plant characteristics for a number of volume producers of different nationalities in 1989. As can be seen, relative to American and European producers, the typical Japanese producer took fewer worker hours to assemble a vehicle, achieved superior quality, held less inventories, and had a higher percentage of its work force in teams. The challenge facing many American and European companies is to replicate this performance.

What has to be remembered, however, is that the data given in Table 1 are averages. There is considerable variation in the efficiency of plants within the different national groupings. For example, the Japanese plants of Toyota, Nissan, and Honda are notably more efficient than those of some of the smaller Japanese companies (e.g., Isuzu, Suzuki, and Daihatsu). Moreover, by the early 1990s some of the best-managed plants owned by North American Companies were achieving productivity and quality levels close to those achieved at well-run Japanese plants. This was particularly true of a number of Ford and Chrysler plants and of GM's Saturn plant.

Diffusion of Lean Production

Since the late 1980s the productivity gap between Japanese and non-Japanese plants has closed somewhat as American and European producers have adopted Japanese lean production techniques. All three U.S. auto majors have entered into joint venture arrangements with Japanese partners in an attempt to learn more about Japanese production techniques, as have a number of European auto companies. Thus, for example, in the early 1980s GM entered into a joint venture with Toyota to build cars in Fremont, California. This joint venture has proved to be very successful, with the Fremont plant attaining productivity and quality levels comparable to those of Toyota's Japanese plants. So far, however, there are only limited signs that GM has been able to apply the lessons learned at the Fremont joint venture to its other U.S. plants, primarily due to the problems involved in making a huge bureaucracy like GM change direction. In recognition of the enormous inertia problems it faces in trying to change its own

Figure 1
Projected Sales by Region, 1992–2002

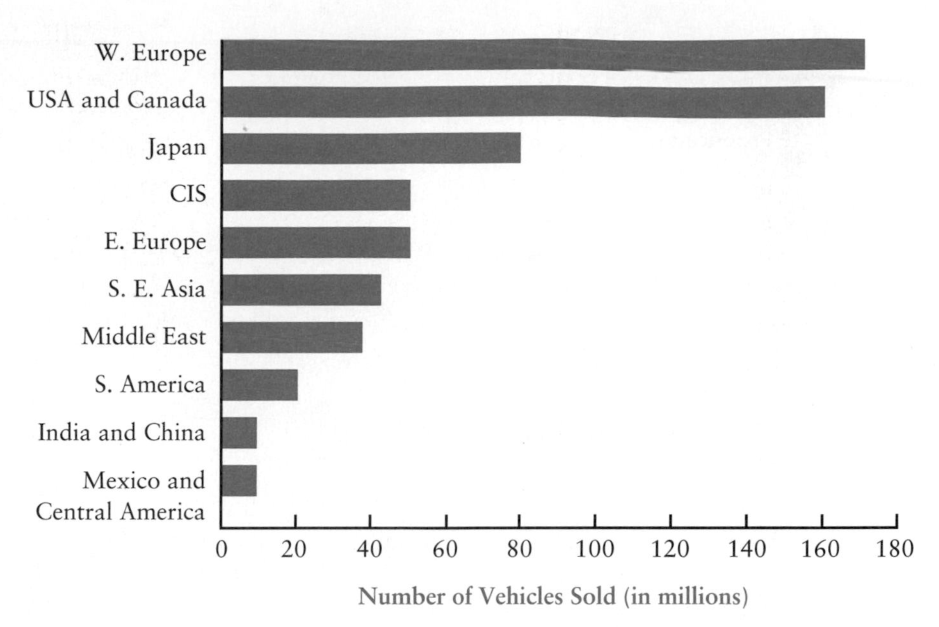

organization, GM set up a separate company, Saturn, to build cars utilizing "Japanese" lean production techniques. By 1994 Saturn had become one of the most successful of all GM operations.

THE GLOBAL INDUSTRY

There were 46 million automobiles produced worldwide in 1992.[6] The vast bulk of this production took place in three main regions: Japan, North America, and Western Europe. Each region accounted for approximately 30 percent of global production. The biggest single national car market is the United States, which in 1992 accounted for 12.8 million passenger cars and light trucks (light trucks include minivans, four-wheel-drive vehicles, and pick-up trucks that many Americans use as cars). However, if the European Community is viewed as a single car market, which in theory it has been since the Single European Act went into force in 1992, it becomes the world's largest car market with 12.9 million cars sold in 1992. Japan is the third largest car market, with 4.4 million new registrations in 1992.[7]

According to a University of Michigan study, between 1992 and 2002 Western Europe will be the largest single market, with 170 million vehicles being sold over this time period (see Figure 1).[8] The United States and Canada will constitute the second largest market, with total sales of 160 million vehicles predicted over the 1992–2002 period. Third will be Japan, with total sales of around 80 million being predicted for the 1992–2002 period. The fourth and fifth largest markets are predicted to be the Commonwealth of Independent States (the core of the former USSR), with total sales of about 50 million vehicles, and Eastern

6. Standard & Poor's Industry Surveys, *Autos–Auto Parts*, June 24, 1993.
7. Kevin Done, "Juggernaut Veers out of Fast Lane," *Financial Times*, October 21, 1993, p. 15.
8. "Survey of the Car Industry," *The Economist*, October 17, 1992, p. 4.

Table 2
Global Market Share and Production of World's Top 12 Producers

Company	Country of Origin	Global Production (millions of vehicles)	Global Market Share
General Motors	United States	7.0	15.2%
Ford	United States	5.4	11.7%
Toyota	Japan	4.7	10.2%
Volkswagen	Germany	3.1	6.7%
Nissan	Japan	3.1	6.7%
Fiat	Italy	2.5	5.4%
Peugeot-Citroen	France	2.1	4.6%
Honda	Japan	2.0	4.3%
Mitsubishi Motors	Japan	1.9	4.1%
Renault	France	1.8	3.9%
Mazda	Japan	1.6	3.5%
Chrysler	United States	1.5	3.3%

Europe, again with sales of 50 million vehicles. Both of these markets are completely new ones for Western businesses.

Viewed on a global basis, the industry looks increasingly fragmented. The global market share for the world's 12 largest automakers in 1992 is given in Table 2. As can be seen, GM still leads the pack with 15.2 percent of worldwide production, followed by Ford (11.7 percent), Toyota (10.2 percent), Volkswagen (6.7 percent), and Nissan (6.7 percent). In recent years, however, GM's share has declined, particularly in the United States, while that of Toyota, Nissan, and Honda has increased with Volkswagen holding steady.

The U.S. Market

As the world's largest single national market, what occurs in the U.S. auto market typically has repercussions for the whole global industry. Demand for passenger cars and light trucks in the United States has long followed a cyclical pattern, and the 1988–1992 period proved to be the low point in the cycle. As Figure 2 shows, between 1988 and 1991 sales of passenger cars and light trucks in the United States fell from just under 16 million to 12.4 million (light trucks include minivans, four-wheel-drive vehicles, pick-ups). Demand revived somewhat in 1992 and, spurred on by record-low interest rates, increased still further in 1993. For 1993 as a whole, demand is estimated to be slightly over 15 million vehicles. The arrow in Figure 2 indicates the long-term demand trend. This suggests that in 1993 demand returned to the trend line, after being below trend for a number of years.

The 1988–1992 Slump The 1988–1992 slump in U.S. demand contributed to large losses at the Big Three U.S. manufacturers. In 1991 Chrysler lost $538 million, Ford $2,258 million, and GM a staggering $4,992 million. This was followed by 1992 losses of $2,620 million at GM and $501.8 million at Ford. Chrysler, however, staged an impressive turnaround, as surging sales of its new minivan and Jeep models helped the company earn $505 million in 1992. For 1993 both Chrysler and Ford are predicted to make healthy profits, while GM's losses should narrow considerably.

Figure 2
Motor Vehicle Sales in the U.S. Market, 1975–1993 (in Millions of Units)

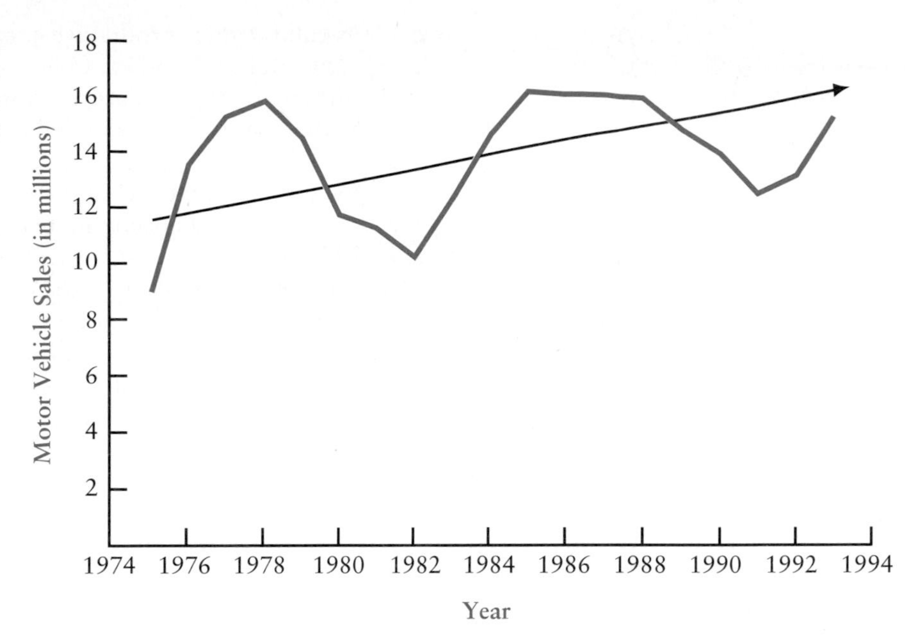

Source: Ward's *Automotive Reports* (various issues). The 1993 figures are estimates as of October 1993. The arrow indicates the trend line for demand growth.

In addition to slumping demand, two other factors helped contribute to the early 1990s profit slump at the U.S. Big Three. First, during the 1980s there was a surge of investment in U.S.-based productive capacity by Japanese companies, which increased the overall capacity dedicated to serving the U.S. market. Second, GM failed to reduce its capacity in line with its market share losses, which contributed to a serious excess capacity problem. Indeed, in December 1992 Ford estimated that the whole world was suffering from a serious excess capacity situation. In 1992, when approximately 46 million cars, trucks, and buses were produced worldwide, Ford estimated that worldwide excess capacity was equivalent to 33 assembly plants, enough capacity to produce an additional 8.2 million cars.[9]

The surge of Japanese investment in auto production capacity in the United States was driven largely by growing trade tensions and the rise in the value of the yen on world currency markets. The rise in the value of the yen has transformed Japan into a high-cost production location. In 1992 Japanese-owned "transplant" facilities manufactured 17.8 percent of all new cars sold in the United States, up from 2.7 in 1985.[10] Japanese transplants probably will be responsible for the production of 18 percent of all new car registrations in 1993. In the future this figure is likely to increase as Japanese and other foreign producers invest in U.S.-based production facilities. Indeed, in July 1992, BMW, the German luxury car maker, announced that it too would build a production plant in the United States. The BMW factory, which is to be built in Spartanburg, South Carolina, will come on stream in 1995. By 2000 plans call for it to be producing 70,000 cars per year.[11]

9. Krystal Miller, "In a Skid: Auto Industry Hit by Global Shakeout," *The Wall Street Journal,* December 29, 1992, p. A1.
10. Standard & Poor's Industry Surveys, *Autos–Auto Parts,* February 25, 1993.
11. John Templeman and David Woodruff, "The Beemer Spotlight Falls on Spartanburg, USA," *Business Week,* July 6, 1992, p. 38.

As for the Japanese, plans call for their productive capacity in the United States to increase from the present level of 2 million vehicles per year to about 3 million vehicles per year by the end of 1995.[12] Future additions in Japanese capacity are likely to be focused on the light truck market, which is still largely controlled by the Big Three.

If Japanese inward investment helped create excess capacity in the early 1990s, it was GM's slow response to its declining market share that helped perpetuate that excess. In 1978 GM accounted for 47.7 percent of the U.S. automobile market. By 1992 its share had slipped to 34.6 percent. However, this steep decline was not reflected in a commensurate cut in productive capacity. In 1991 GM had the capacity to assemble 6.7 million cars and light trucks in North America, but it produced only 4.5 million, suggesting that 32 percent of GM's capacity was excess to requirements. GM plans to reduce its productive capacity in North America to 5.4 million units by the end of 1995.[13]

The 1993 Recovery The 1993 recovery in U.S. demand for autos was unexpectedly robust. There seems to be two main reasons for the surge: historically low interest rates and pent-up demand for autos after four years of weak demand. Indeed, in 1993 some 37 percent of cars and light trucks in the United States were 10 years old or older, compared with 23 percent in 1981.[14] One interesting feature of the 1992–1993 demand revival was the extent to which it was weighted toward the light truck segment of the overall auto market. For example, between 1991 and 1992 sales of passenger cars in the United States increased from 8.17 million to 8.21 million units, an increase of only 0.5 percent. During the same period, sales of light trucks—which include minivans, four-wheel-drive vehicles, and pickup trucks—rose from 4.14 million to 4.66 million, an increase of 12.6 percent. This trend continued during the first half of 1993, with sales of passenger cars increasing by 0.5 percent against the same period in 1992, compared with an increase in light truck sales of 17.9 percent.[15]

This skew in demand growth worked to the favor of the U.S. companies, which had a much stronger presence in this market niche than their Japanese competitors. Imports of Japanese light trucks were handicapped by a 25 percent tariff on such imports (which was originally levied in 1989 by the Bush administration), and U.S.-based production facilities of the Japanese companies were geared toward producing cars, not light trucks.

In addition to this demand skew, the 1992–1993 recovery was notable for the fact that it was the first time in a generation that the U.S. Big Three took market share back from their foreign competitors. In the first half of 1993 the aggregate share of the U.S. auto market captured by the Big Three rose to 67.6 percent, up from 65.1 percent in the same period of 1992, and from 64.5 percent for the whole of 1992. Tables 3 and 4 give more detail. They reveal a strong performance by Chrysler and Ford in the passenger car segment and by Chrysler in the light truck segment. General Motors stood still, although its Saturn car division recorded impressive market share gains (from 0.9 percent in 1991 to 2.72 per-

12. Standard & Poor's Industry Surveys, *Autos–Auto Parts,* June 24, 1993.
13. Standard & Poor's Industry Surveys, *Autos–Auto Parts,* February 25, 1993.
14. D. P. Levin, "Auto Industry Has Time on Its Side," *The New York Times*, June 29, 1993, pp. C1, C17.
15. Standard & Poor's Industry Surveys, *Autos–Auto Parts,* June 24, 1993.

Table 3
Market Share of U.S. Dealer New Passenger Car Sales

Company	1991	1992	1993 (First Half)
General Motors	35.59%	34.62%	34.82%
Ford	20.01%	21.64	22.44
Chrysler	8.59	8.27	10.34
Honda	9.83	9.36	7.65
Toyota	9.08	9.25	8.78
Nissan	5.06	5.10	5.32
Mazda	2.71	3.02	2.87

Table 4
Market Share of U.S. Dealer Light Truck Sales

Company	1991	1992	1993 (First Half)
General Motors	34.04%	33.32%	32.83%
Ford	29.20	30.07	29.99
Chrysler	19.47	22.24	23.79
Toyota	6.49	5.67	5.29
Nissan	4.09	3.58	3.55
Mazda	2.95	1.95	1.35

cent in the first half of 1993). Among Japanese competitors, Honda saw the steepest fall in its sales, with Toyota and Mazda also suffering losses. Nissan, however, managed to increase its share of the passenger car market, although its share of the light truck market fell.[16] The fall in the share taken by Japanese companies was due partly to the high value of the Japanese yen, which by late 1993 was trading at 105 yen to the dollar, up in value from 125 yen to the dollar a year earlier. The increase in the value of the yen had raised the price of Japanese exports to the United States, effectively giving U.S.-based producers a price advantage. By late 1993 vehicles imported into the United States by Japanese producers cost, on average, $3,300 more than comparably equipped counterparts built by the Big Three.[17] Since Japanese producers did not have enough U.S. capacity to substitute for high-cost imports, they saw their market share decline. In addition, there are clear indications that the U.S. Big Three are closing the quality and productivity gap between them and the Japanese. According to J. D. Power's annual quality survey, 1993 model American cars averaged 1.13 defects per car, down from 1.36 defects per car in 1992. This compares with a 1993 figure of 0.94 defects per car for Asian manufacturers, and 1.28 defects per car for European manufacturers.[18]

16. Ibid.
17. James Bennet, "A Stronger Yen is Hurting Sales of Japan's Cars," *The New York Times*, November 5, 1993, pp. A1, C2.
18. N. Templin, "Toyota is Standout Once Again in J. D. Power Quality Survey," *The Wall Street Journal*, May 28, 1993, p. B1.

Future Trends By the mid 1990s a number of trends were apparent that might well shape the evolution of the U.S. auto market for the rest of the decade. The first of these was the increasing proliferation of competitors and models in the United States. By the early 1990s there were 23 automobile companies selling cars in the United States. Among them, these companies were selling 550 different auto models. Many of these companies, including most Japanese and German companies, were also either building cars in the United States or had plans to build them there in the future. The result would be an increase in productive capacity dedicated to serving the North American market.

The proliferation of models on offer in the United States was making it increasingly difficult for manufacturers to distinguish their products in a crowded field. Moreover, the proliferation of models, without a commensurate increase in demand, had been reflected in a decline in the sales volume for individual models over time. While the best-selling car models had once accounted for 1 million or more in annual unit sales, and had provided commensurate economies of scale, by the mid 1990s leading models accounted for less than 500,000 in sales. When taken together with more frequent model changes, the effect of model proliferation has been to increase the unit costs of developing, producing, and manufacturing automobiles. Furthermore, the inability to distinguish products from those of competitors in such a crowded field diminishes the effectiveness of costly advertising campaigns.

Another trend of some significance is that in recent years the price of new cars has risen at a faster rate than the increase in real income. In 1993 the average new car cost $17,692, up from $10,640 in 1983. With real incomes in the U.S. hardly growing at all, the net result has been to increase the number of weeks of work that is required to pay for a new car. In 1980 it took 18 weeks of pay for the average American to buy the average new car. By 1993 this figure had risen, almost without interruption, to 25.5 weeks.[19] While manufacturers rightly point out that the average 1993 car is characterized by better quality, better design, and more options than the average 1980 car, the decreasing affordability of autos could have a negative long-run impact.

A final trend in the United States of some significance is the start of a move toward cars powered by alternative fuels. In September 1990 the California Air Resources Board adopted tough new rules to reduce air pollution above Los Angeles. It requires that by 1998, 2 percent of the cars sold by each manufacturer in the state be zero-emission vehicles (ZEVs). The proportion increases to 10 percent in 2003. (Producers selling less than 30,000 cars per year in California are excluded from this regulation.) With over 2 million cars sold each year in California, this move is opening up the world's first market for environmentally friendly vehicles. With present technology, the only way to make a ZEV is to build an electric car. Against this background, most of the world's large car makers are now actively developing electric vehicles.[20]

Western Europe

January 1, 1993, saw the creation of a single unified market in the 12-member European Community. Analysts suggested that this would usher in a new era of competition in the Western European auto industry, particularly in markets such

19. "The Price Is High," *The Economist*, August 14, 1993, p. 63.
20. "Survey of the Car Industry," *The Economist*, October 17, 1992, pp. 13–15.

Table 5
Demand Changes in Western Europe's Big Six Auto Markets

Markets	Volume (Units), January–October 1993	Volume Change (%)	Share (%), January–October 1993	Share (%), January–October 1992
Germany	2,727,000	−18.6%	27.8	29.0
Italy	1,610,000	−22.1%	16.4	17.9
Britain	1,577,000	+12.1%	16.1	12.2
France	1,413,000	−17.3%	14.4	14.8
Spain	620,000	−25.1%	6.3	7.2

Source: Kevin Done, "U.K. Bucks Trend of Plunging Sales of New Cars," *Financial Times,* November 12, 1993, p. 2.

as Italy and France that had previously been protected by high trade barriers. Whatever the eventual outcome, the unification could not have come at a worse time for Europe's car makers. The early 1990s were a very tough time for the Western European auto industry. After sales of over 13.5 million vehicles in 1989, sales fell in each of the next four years to a projected 11.3 million in 1993.[21] The worst hit markets were France, Germany, Italy, and Spain, where demand was predicted to shrink by as much as 20 percent in 1993 (see Table 5 for details). The German industry, in particular, has been hit by a combination of high labor costs, an increase in the value of the deutschemark, and outdated production techniques.

The reverberations of this slump have been felt across the Continent, with some of Europe's best-known automakers, including Fiat, Mercedes-Benz, and Volkswagen, reporting heavy losses in 1993. At the same time, Japanese companies, following their practice in North America, continued to undertake substantial investments in European productive capacity, thereby exacerbating an already serious excess capacity situation. By the year 2000 Japanese automobile companies will have the capacity to build 2 million vehicles per year in Western Europe.

Table 6 gives details of recent market share figures and the 1993 sales slump for the 14 largest auto companies competing in the EC.[22] As can be seen, the EC market is quite fragmented. The largest company, Volkswagen, accounted for 16.1 percent of the market in the first nine months of 1993, but its sales had slumped 22 percent when compared with a year earlier. Volkswagen was followed by General Motors, Peugeot-Citroen, Ford, Fiat, and Renault, all of which saw their sales drop sharply when compared with a year earlier. Indeed, the only European operator to increase sales was Britain's Rover group, which posted a 12.5 percent increase in sales. This reflects not only the relative strength of the British economy, which accounts for most of Rover's sales, but also the increasing efficiency of this company, which has benefited from a close alliance with Honda (Honda owns 20 percent of Rover).

The European slump has had three main effects. First, many European companies are trying to trim their capacity and reduce their headcount. In hard-hit Germany, for example, Mercedes-Benz has announced plans to cut 14,000 jobs in

21. "Is There Room for Volkswagen?" *The Economist,* August 28, 1993, pp. 59–60.
22. "Back to the Way We Were," *The Economist,* November 6, 1993, p. 83.

Table 6
European Community Car Sales and Market Share, January–September 1993

Company	Unit Sales (000s)	Percent Change from a Year Earlier	Market Share (%)
Volkswagen	1,327	−22.0%	16.1%
General Motors	1,052	−11.4%	12.8%
Peugeot-Citroen	1,022	−16.2%	12.4%
Ford	985	−15.3%	12.0%
Fiat	962	−21.6%	11.7%
Renault	896	−15.5%	10.9%
Nissan	285	−4.7%	3.5%
Rover	277	+12.5%	3.4%
BMW	272	−16.4%	3.3%
Mercedes-Benz	243	−19.9%	2.9%
Toyota	200	−0.4%	2.4%
Mazda	125	−24.5%	1.5%
Honda	113	−8.1%	1.4%
Volvo	98	−16.4%	1.2%
All	8,245	−15.7%	100.0%

1994, and this is on top of cuts of 20,000 over the 1992–1993 period. Similarly, Volkswagen has announced that it needs to cut its employment from 103,000 in 1993 to only 72,000 in 1995. Since Volkswagen has an agreement with the government of Lower Saxony, its largest shareholder, to maintain its total head-count at 100,000 employees, it has been forced to look for creative ways of achieving this cut. As of November 1993 it was negotiating with its unions to see if they would accept a four-day workweek, which would have the same impact on Volkswagen's labor costs as a 30 percent reduction in employment.[23]

A second effect has been to raise talk of merger between some of Europe's sick car makers. Most notably, in October 1993 Renault and Volvo announced a plan to merge into a single company. The plan calls for the merger to be completed in January 1994. However, the plan is facing stiff resistance from Volvo's Swedish shareholders, who do not seem to relish the prospect of Volvo linking up with a French enterprise, particularly one in which the French government has a major shareholding.[24]

A third effect of the European slump has been to raise fresh calls for limits on Japanese competition. This time the calls are not just limited to Japanese imports into Europe, which are already restricted under a voluntary export restraint; they are also aimed at limiting Japanese production in Europe. The British government, where most of Japan's European production facilities are based, has not surprisingly vigorously rejected any such proposals, so it seems unlikely that the EC as a whole will adopt such a policy. However, a "fudge" is possible, in

23. Christopher Parkes, "VW Wants Four-Day Week or 30% Cut in Staff," *Financial Times*, October 30, 1993, p. 1, 24.
24. H. Carnegy and J. Ridding, "Time-out Called as Strains Start to Show," *Financial Times*, November 3, 1993, p. 2.

which the Japanese agree to limit the growth of their European production as a way of fending off more serious trade sanctions.[25]

Japan

For three decades Japanese production rose steadily, with no significant pullback, from 500,000 vehicles in 1960 to 13.5 million in 1990. However, in the early 1990s the picture changed rapidly. Sales fell 3 percent in 1991, 7.5 percent in 1992, and a further 5.8 percent in the first five months of 1993, for a total drop of 16 percent since sales peaked in 1990.[26] By mid 1993 the sales decline had left Japan's 11 auto companies with likely production for 1993 of under 11 million units, but with the capacity to produce 14.5 million units—signifying excess capacity equivalent to 3.5 million vehicles.[27]

Not surprisingly, these figures translated into slumping profits and even losses among Japan's automobile companies. From their peak in 1989–1990, pretax profits for the 11 Japanese auto companies fell 34 percent in fiscal 1990–1991, 48 percent in fiscal 1991–1992, and a further 35 percent in fiscal 1992–1993. Moreover, forecasts suggest that they will fall an additional 63 percent in fiscal 1993–1994.[28] Many companies, including Nissan and Mazda, registered their first ever losses. Industry leader Toyota, widely regarded as the most productive automobile company in the world, predicted that it would lose money in fiscal 1993–1994.

The imbalance between supply and demand is predicted to persist for some time, in part because of the difficulty that Japanese companies have in cutting employment. The lifetime employment system, which for years was depicted as a source of Japanese strength, has turned into something of a curse. Nevertheless, cuts are being made. Nissan announced that it would be forced to close one of its most famous plants, the Zama plant near Tokyo, in 1995. The company also has plans to cut its work force by 5,000 employees between 1993 and 1995, bringing its total down to 48,000. Honda has plans to cut 10 percent of its assembly line workers over the next 10 years. And Isuzu, which reported a loss of $102 million for fiscal 1991–1992, announced in November of 1992 that it would pull out of the passenger car market altogether and concentrate on truck and recreational vehicle production.

The reasons for this slump are not hard to find. The value of the yen has soared against that of other currencies, making Japanese cars ever more expensive. In the first nine months of 1993, the yen increased in value by about 20 percent against the U.S. dollar. Exports have been hit further by the closing of the perceived design and quality gaps between Japanese and U.S. autos. Together, these two factors have conspired to produce market share losses in the United States, Japan's largest export market. At the same time, the 1991 collapse of the Japanese property and stock markets ushered in Japan's most serious postwar recession and a slump in domestic demand for autos.

To make matters worse, the stock market slump appears to have brought to an end a period where Japanese auto companies benefited from an extremely low cost of capital. During their boom years, many auto companies issued

25. "The Enemy Within," *The Economist,* June 12, 1993, pp. 67–68.
26. Kevin Done, "Juggernaut Veers out of Fast Lane," *Financial Times,* October 21, 1993, p. 15.
27. Hideneka Kato, "Automakers Set to Boost Global Output," *Nikkei Weekly,* June 21, 1993, p. 7.
28. Kevin Done, "Juggernaut Veers out of Fast Lane."

convertible debentures (bonds that could be converted into stock at maturity). However, the crash in the Japanese stock market means that the holders of these bonds will in all probability redeem them for cash, not equity. Moreover, Japanese corporations will have to issue straight bonds in the future if they wish to raise capital. This trend will dramatically increase corporate borrowing costs, thereby eliminating a major competitive advantage that Japanese companies have enjoyed for decades.[29]

In response to these problems, as noted above, the Japanese auto companies have attempted to trim their domestic capacity, although their ability to achieve this quickly is limited by the lifetime employment system. At the same time, there are signs that despite the increase in the cost of capital, Japanese companies are accelerating their transfer of production facilities overseas. Table 7 summarizes the plans that major Japanese automakers have for changing their production capacity between 1993 and 1997.[30] As can be seen, a net reduction in Japanese capacity is predicted, but this is likely to be more than offset by net increases in North America, Europe, and Asia Pacific capacity. Indeed, it is questionable whether the planned reduction in capacity based in Japan will be sufficient given the loss of export markets and the predicted slow growth in Japanese domestic demand. At the same time, the planned expansions in European and, to a lesser extent, North American capacity must be a cause for concern given the current overcapacity in those markets. The planned increase in Asia Pacific capacity is also notable. This apparently reflects a belief that this will be a major economic growth area in the future.

Table 7
Planned Capacity Changes by Japan's Major Auto Companies, 1993–1997 (Projected 1997 Figures are in Thousands of Units; Changes from 1993 Given in Parentheses)

Company	Japan	North America	Europe	Asia Pacific	Overseas Total
Toyota	4,774 (+200)	820 (+215)	322 (+100)	584 (+205)	1,757 (+520)
Nissan	2,662 (–470)	450 (No change)	435 (+35)	433 (+245)	1,568 (+280)
Honda	1,428 (No change)	610 (No change)	100 (+10)	107 (+15)	817 (+25)
Mitsubishi	1,412 (No change)	240 (No change)	210 (+200)	400 (+50)	850 (+250)
Mazda	1,240 (No change)	240 (No change)	0 (No change)	24 (No change)	284 (No change)
Suzuki	720 (No change)	200 (No change)	125 (+40)	350 (+120)	675 (+160)
Others	1,941 (No change)	160 (No change)	185 (+30)	404 (+151)	749 (+181)
Total	14,147 (–270)	2,720 (+215)	1,377 (+415)	2,302 (+786)	6,700 (+1,416)

29. George Melloan, "Japanese Firms Are Losing One Key Advantage," *The Wall Street Journal*, March 29, 1993, p. A13.
30. Data from Hideneka Kato, "Automakers Set to Boost Global Capacity."

In addition to planned changes in capacity, Japanese auto companies are all currently reexamining their manufacturing and product development process to find ways to cut costs. Toyota, for example, cut its manufacturing costs by 100 billion yen ($625 million) in 1992 and is aiming for a similar reduction in 1993. These cost savings have come from a multitude of small cost-saving measures. Thus, by reducing the curve in the windscreen of its best-selling Corolla model, Toyota found that it could save 600 yen per car. Further cost savings have come from pressuring suppliers to reduce their costs.[31]

The Rest of the World

Although the global automobile market is currently dominated by North America, Western Europe, and Japan, there is a growing realization that demand in these areas is limited to replacement demand and that any dramatic surge in future growth is unlikely. Indeed, flat or even declining demand is possible. In contrast, rapid growth in other areas of the world is probable. In a recent study, a University of Michigan team suggested that the most rapid growth in the next decade would occur in the countries of Eastern Europe and the states of the former Soviet Union where auto ownership is at very low levels. In total, the Michigan team predicted that this area would create demand for 100 million new vehicles between 1992 and 2002 (see Figure 1 for details). Others question these figures. They point to the poor economic growth of this region and the high level of political and economic turbulence and suggest that Southeast Asia is likely to be the new growth area, not Eastern Europe. This certainly seems to be the view taken by Japan's major auto companies, if their planned expansions in foreign automaking capacity are any guide (see Table 5).

In any event, it is worth noting that not only do these regions promise to emerge as new markets but they may also be the home of new global competitors. Indeed, South Korea has already given rise to Hyundai, which has established a small but stable presence in both North America and Western Europe. Take Malaysia as another example; the country has one of the fastest sustained economic growth rates in the world. Between 1986 and 1992 Malaysia's economy expanded at 8–9 percent every single year. A great market opportunity perhaps, and yet Malaysia also has an indigenous car industry. Proton, Malaysia's national car company, commands a 70 percent share of the domestic market and is now making an aggressive sales push abroad, with exports to Britain and planned production facilities in Vietnam and, possibly, Chile.[32]

31. Michiyo Nakamoto, "Trimmed to the Bone," *Financial Times,* October 21, 1993, p. 15.
32. John Griffiths and Kieran Cooke, "Proton Sets up European Venture," *Financial Times,* November 3, 1993, p. 8.

CASE

15

The Toyota Corporation in 1994

INTRODUCTION

Toyota is Japan's largest car maker, largest exporter, and the third largest manufacturer of automobiles in the world. In 1993 Toyota held 33 percent of the Japanese auto market, well ahead of second-placed Nissan which held approximately 19 percent. It also held 9.4 percent of the global auto market. Only General Motors with 17.7 percent of the world market, and Ford, with 14.6 percent of the world market, held a larger share.[1] Toyota's rise to these heights has been dramatic and swift. In 1990 the company sold 4.12 million vehicles worldwide. This represented an increase from 3.3 million vehicles in 1980, 1.6 million vehicles in 1970, 149,694 vehicles in 1960, and only 11,706 vehicles in 1950.[2]

This case details the rise of Toyota from an obscure Japanese auto manufacturer into the giant of today. The central focus of the case is on explaining how the revolutionary production system developed at Toyota in the 1950s and 1960s came into being. More than anything else, it is this production system that explains the rise of Toyota to global dominance.

THE ORIGINS OF TOYOTA

The original idea behind the founding of the Toyota Motor Company came from the fertile mind of Toyoda Sakichi.[3] The son of a carpenter, Sakichi was an entrepreneur and inventor whose primary interest lay in the textile industry, but he had been intrigued by automobiles since a visit to the United States in 1910. Sakichi's principal achievement was the invention of an automatic loom that held out the promise of being able to lower the costs of weaving high-quality cloth. In 1926 Sakichi set up Toyoda Automatic Loom to manufacture this product. Sakichi then sold the patent rights to a British textile concern, Platt Brothers, in 1930 for about 1 million yen, a considerable sum in those days.

This case was prepared by Charles W. L. Hill, University of Washington. This case was prepared as a basis for class discussion rather than to illustrate either effective or ineffective handling of administrative situations.

1. Figures are from P. Ingrassia, and K. Graven, "Japan's Auto Industry May Soon Consolidate as Competition Grows," *The Wall Street Journal*, April 24, 1990, pp. 1, 10; and A. Borrus, "Will Japan Do to Europe What It Did to Detroit?" *Business Week*, May 7, 1990, pp. 52–54.
2. Figures are from A. Borrus. "Will Japan Do to Europe What It Did to Detroit?"; and M. A. Cusumano, *The Japanese Automobile Industry*, (Cambridge, Mass.: Harvard University Press, 1989), Appendix F.
3. This section is based primarily on the account given in M. A. Cusumano, *The Japanese Automobile Industry*.

Sakichi urged his son, Toyoda Kiichiro, to use this money to study the possibility of manufacturing automobiles in Japan. A mechanical engineer with a degree from the University of Tokyo, in 1930 Kiichiro became managing director of loom production at Toyoda Automatic Loom.

Kiichiro was at first reluctant to invest in automobile production. The Japanese market was at that time dominated by Ford and General Motors, both of which imported knock-down car kits from the United States and assembled them in Japan. Given this, the board of Toyoda Automatic Loom, including Kiichiro's brother-in-law and the company's president, Kodama Risaburo, opposed the investment on the grounds that it was too risky. Kiichiro probably would not have pursued the issue further had not his father made a deathbed request in 1930 that Kiichiro explore the possibilities for automobile production. Kiichiro had to push, but in 1933 he was able to get permission to set up an automobile department within Toyoda Automatic Loom.

Kiichiro's belief was that he would be able to figure out how to manufacture automobiles by taking apart U.S.-made vehicles and examining them piece by piece. He also felt that it should be possible to adapt U.S. mass production technology to manufacture cost efficiently at lower volumes. His confidence was based in large part upon the already considerable engineering skills and capabilities at his disposal through Toyoda Automatic Loom. Many of the precision engineering and manufacturing skills needed in automobile production were similar to the skills required to manufacture looms.

Kiichiro produced his first 20 vehicles in 1935 and in 1936 the automobile department produced 1,142 vehicles—910 trucks, 100 cars, and 132 buses. At this time, however, the production system was essentially craft-based rather than a modern assembly line. Despite some progress, the struggle might still have been uphill had not fate intervened in the form of the Japanese military. Japan had invaded Manchuria in 1931 and quickly found American-made trucks useful for moving men and equipment. As a result, the military felt that it was strategically important for Japan to have its own automobile industry. The result was the passage of an automobile manufacturing law in 1936 which required companies producing more than 3,000 vehicles per year in Japan to get a license from the government. Moreover, to get a license over 50 percent of the stock had to be owned by Japanese investors. The law also placed a duty on imported cars, including the knock-down kits that Ford and GM brought into Japan. As a direct result of this legislation, both GM and Ford exited from the Japanese market in 1939.

Once the Japanese government passed this law, Kodama Risaburo decided that the automobile venture could be profitable and switched from opposing to proactively supporting Kiichiro (in fact, Risaburo's wife, who was Kiichiro's elder sister, had been urging him to take this step for some time). The first priority was to attract the funds necessary to build a mass production facility. In 1937 Risaburo and Kiichiro decided to incorporate the automobile department as a separate company in order to attract outside investors—which they were successful in doing. Kiichiro Toyoda was appointed president of the new company. The company was named the Toyota Motor Company. (The founding family's name, "Toyoda," means "abundant rice field" in Japanese. The new name had no meaning in Japanese.)

Upon incorporation, Risaburo and Kiichiro's vision was that Toyota should expand its passenger car production as quickly as possible. However, once again fate intervened in the form of the Japanese military. Toyota had barely begun

passenger car production when war broke out; in 1939 the Japanese government, on advice from the military, prohibited passenger car production and demanded that the company specialize in the production of military trucks.

THE EVOLUTION OF THE TOYOTA PRODUCTION SYSTEM

After the end of World War II, Kiichiro was determined that Toyota should reestablish itself as a manufacturer of automobiles.[4] Toyota, however, faced a number of problems in doing this:

1. The Japanese domestic market was too small to support efficient scale mass production facilities such as those common in America by that time.
2. The Japanese economy was starved of capital, which made it difficult to raise funds to finance new investments.
3. New labor laws introduced by the American occupiers increased the bargaining power of labor and made it difficult for companies to lay off workers.
4. North America and Western Europe were full of large auto manufacturers eager to establish operations in Japan.

In response to the last point, in 1950 the new Japanese government prohibited direct foreign investment in the automobile industry and imposed high tariffs on the importation of foreign cars. This protection, however, did little to solve the other problems facing the company at this time.

From Mass Production to Flexible Production

At this juncture a remarkable mechanical engineer entered the scene: Ohno Taiichi. More than anyone else, it was Ohno who was to work out a response to the above problems. Ohno had joined Toyoda Spinning and Weaving in 1932 as a production engineer in cotton thread manufacture and entered Toyota when the former company was absorbed into the latter in 1943. Ohno worked in auto production for two years, was promoted and managed auto assembly and machine shops between 1945 and 1953, and in 1954 was appointed a company director.

When Ohno Taiichi joined Toyota the mass production methods pioneered by Ford had become the accepted method of manufacturing automobiles. The basic philosophy behind mass production was to produce a limited product line in massive quantities to gain maximum economies of scale. The economies came from spreading the fixed costs involved in setting up the specialized equipment required to stamp body parts and manufacture components over as large a production run as possible. Since setting up much of the equipment could take a full day or more, the economies involved in long production runs were reckoned to be considerable. Thus, for example, Ford would stamp 500,000 righthand door panels in a single production run and then store the parts in warehouses until

4. The material in this section is drawn from three main sources: M. A. Cusumano, *The Japanese Automobile Industry*; Ohno Taiichi, *Toyota Production System* (Cambridge, Mass.: Productivity Press, 1990; Japanese Edition, 1978); J. P. Womack, D. T. Jones, and D. Roos, *The Machine That Changed The World* (New York: Macmillan, 1990).

they were needed in the assembly plant, rather than stamp just those door panels that were needed immediately and then change the settings and stamp out left-hand door panels, or other body parts.

A second feature of mass production was that each assembly worker should perform only a single task, rather than a variety of tasks. The idea here was that as the worker became completely familiar with a single task, he could perform it much faster, thereby increasing labor productivity. Assembly line workers were overseen by a foreman who did not perform any assembly tasks himself, but instead ensured that the workers followed orders. In addition, a number of specialists were employed to perform nonassembly operations such as tool repair, die changes, quality inspection, and general "housecleaning."

After working in Toyota for five years and visiting Ford's U.S. plants, Ohno became convinced that the basic mass production philosophy was flawed. He saw five problems with the mass production system:

1. Long production runs created massive inventories that had to be stored in large warehouses. This was expensive both because of the cost of warehousing and because inventories tied up capital in unproductive uses.
2. If the initial machine settings were wrong, long production runs resulted in the production of a large number of defects.
3. The sheer monotony of assigning assembly line workers to a single task generated defects, since workers became lax about quality control. In addition, since assembly line workers were not responsible for quality control, they had little incentive to minimize defects.
4. The extreme division of labor resulted in the employment of specialists such as foremen, quality inspectors, and tooling specialists, whose jobs logically could be performed by assembly line workers.
5. The mass production system was unable to accommodate consumer preferences for product diversity.

In addition to these flaws, Ohno knew that the small domestic market in Japan and the lack of capital for investing in mass production facilities made the American model unsuitable for Toyota.

Reducing Set-up Times Given these flaws and the constraints that Toyota faced, Ohno decided to take a fresh look at the techniques used for automobile production. His first goal was to try and make it economical to manufacture autobody parts in small batches. To do this, he needed to reduce the time it took to set up the machines for stamping out body parts. Ohno and his engineers began to experiment with a number of techniques to speed up the time it took to change the dies in stamping equipment. This included using rollers to move dies in and out of position along with a number of simple mechanized adjustment mechanisms to fine tune the settings. These techniques were relatively simple to master, so Ohno directed production workers to perform the die changes themselves. This in itself reduced the need for specialists and eliminated the idle time that workers previously had enjoyed while waiting for the dies to be changed.

Through a process of trial and error, Ohno succeeded in reducing the time required to change dies on stamping equipment from a full day to 15 minutes by 1962, and as little as 3 minutes by 1971. By comparison, even in the early 1980s

many American and European plants required anywhere between 2 and 6 hours to change dies on stamping equipment. As a consequence, American and European plants found it economical to manufacture in lots equivalent to 10 to 30 days' supply and to reset equipment only every other day. In contrast, since Toyota could change the dies on stamping equipment in a matter of minutes, it manufactured in lots equivalent to just one day's supply, while resetting equipment three times per day.

Not only did these innovations make small production runs economical, they also had the added benefit of reducing inventories and improving product quality. Making small batches eliminated the need to hold large inventories, thereby reducing warehousing costs and freeing up scarce capital for investment elsewhere. Small production runs and the lack of inventory also meant that defective parts were produced only in small numbers and entered the assembly process almost immediately. This had the added effect of making those in the stamping shops far more concerned about quality. In addition, once it became economical to manufacture small batches of components, much greater variety could be included into the final product at little or no cost penalty.

Organization of the Workplace One of Ohno's first innovations was to group the work force into teams. Each team was given a set of assembly tasks to perform and team members were trained to perform each task that the team was responsible for. Each team had a leader who was himself an assembly line worker. In addition to coordinating the team, the team leader was expected to perform basic assembly line tasks and to fill in for any absent worker. The teams were given the job of housecleaning, minor tool repair, and quality inspection (along with the training required to perform these tasks). Time was also set aside for team members to discuss ways to improve the production process (the practice now referred to as "quality circles"). The immediate effect of this approach was to reduce the need for specialists in the work place and to create a more flexible work force in which individual assembly line workers were not treated simply as human machines. All of this resulted in increased worker productivity.

None of this would have been possible, however, had it not been for an agreement reached between management and labor after a 1950 strike. The strike was brought on by management's attempt to cut the work force by 25 percent (in response to a recession in Japan). After lengthy negotiations, Toyota and the union worked out a compromise. The work force was cut by 25 percent as originally proposed, but the remaining employees were given two guarantees, one for lifetime employment and the other for pay graded by seniority and tied to company profitability through bonus payments. In exchange for these guarantees, the employees agreed to be flexible in work assignments. In turn, this allowed for the introduction of the team concept.

Improving Quality One of the standard practices in the mass production automobile assembly plants was to fix any errors that occurred during assembly in a rework area at the end of the assembly line. Errors routinely occurred in most assembly plants either because bad parts were installed or because good parts were installed incorrectly. The belief was that stopping an assembly line to fix such errors would cause enormous bottlenecks in the production system. Thus it was thought to be more efficient to correct errors at the end of the line.

Ohno viewed this system as wasteful for three reasons: (1) since workers understood that any errors would be fixed at the end of the line, they had little incentive to correct errors themselves; (2) once a defective part had been embedded in a complex vehicle, an enormous amount of rework might be required to fix it; and (3) since defective parts were often not discovered until the end of the line when the finished cars were tested, a large number of cars containing the same defect may have been built before the problem was found.

In an attempt to get away from this practice, Ohno decided to look for ways to reduce the amount of rework at the end of the line. His approach involved two elements. First, he placed a cord above every work station and instructed workers to stop the assembly line if a problem emerged that could not be fixed. It then became the responsibility of the whole team to come over and work on the problem. Second, team members were taught to trace every defect back to its ultimate cause and then to ensure that the problem was fixed so that it would not reoccur.

Initially, this system produced enormous disruption. The production line was stopping all the time and workers became discouraged. However, as team members began to gain experience in identifying problems and tracing them back to their root cause, the number of errors began to drop dramatically and stops in the line became much rarer, so that today in most Toyota plants the line virtually never stops.

Developing the Kanban system

Once reduced set-up times had made small production runs economical, Ohno began to look for ways to coordinate the flow of production within the Toyota manufacturing system so that the amount of inventory in the system could be reduced to a minimum. Toyota produced about 25 percent of its major components in-house (the rest were contracted out to independent suppliers). Ohno's initial goal was to arrange for components and/or subassemblies manufactured in-house to be delivered to the assembly floor only when they were needed, and not before (this goal was later extended to include independent suppliers).

To achieve this, in 1953 Ohno began experimenting with what came to be known as the *kanban* system. At its most simple, under the *kanban* system, component parts are delivered to the assembly line in containers. As each container is emptied, it is sent back to the previous step in the manufacturing process. This then becomes the signal to make more parts. The system minimizes work in progress by increasing inventory turnover. The elimination of buffer inventories also means that defective components show up immediately in the next process. This speeds up the processes of tracing defects back to their source and facilitates correction of the problem before too many defects are made. Moreover, the elimination of buffer stocks, by removing all safety nets, makes it imperative that problems be solved before they became serious enough to jam up the production process, thereby creating a strong incentive for workers to ensure that errors are corrected as quickly as possible. In addition, by decentralizing responsibility for coordinating the manufacturing process to lower-level employees, the *kanban* system does away with the need for extensive centralized management to coordinate the flow of parts between the various stages of production.

After perfecting the kanban system in one of Toyota's machine shops, Ohno had a chance to apply the system broadly in 1960 when he was made general manager of the Motomachi assembly plant. Ohno already had converted the

machining, body stamping, and body shops to the *kanban* system, but since many parts came from shops that had yet to adopt the system, or from outside suppliers, the impact on inventories was initially minimal. However, by 1962 he had extended the *kanban* to forging and casting, and between 1962 and 1965 he began to bring independent suppliers into the system.

Organizing Suppliers

Assembly of components into a final vehicle accounts for only about 15 percent of the total manufacturing process in automobile manufacture. The remaining 85 percent of the process involves manufacturing more than 10,000 individual parts and assembling them into about 100 major components such as engines, suspension systems, transaxles, and so on. Coordinating this process so that everything comes together at the right time has always been a problem for auto manufacturers. The response at Ford and GM to this problem was massive vertical integration. The belief was that control over the supply chain would allow management to coordinate the flow of component parts into the final assembly plant. In addition, American firms held the view that vertical integration made them more efficient by reducing their dependence on other firms for materials and components and by limiting their vulnerability to opportunistic overcharging.

As a consequence of this philosophy, even today General Motors makes 68 percent of its own components in-house, while Ford makes 50 percent. When they haven't vertically integrated, U.S. auto companies historically have tried to reduce the procurement costs that remain through competitive bidding—asking a number of companies to submit contracts and giving orders to suppliers offering the lowest price.

Under the leadership of Kiichiro Toyoda during the 1930s and 1940s, Toyota essentially followed the American model and pursued extensive vertical integration into the manufacture of component parts. In fact, Toyota had little choice in this matter, since only a handful of Japanese companies were able to make the necessary components. However, the low volume of production during this period meant that the scale of integration was relatively small. In the 1950s, however, the volume of auto production began to increase dramatically. This presented Toyota with a dilemma: should the company increase its capacity to manufacture components in-house in line with the growth in production of autos, or should the company contract out?

In contrast to American practice, the company decided that while it should increase in-house capacity for essential subassemblies and bodies, it would do better to contract out for most components. Four reasons seem to bolster this decision:

1. Toyota wanted to avoid the capital expenditures required to expand capacity to manufacture a wide variety of components.
2. Toyota wanted to reduce risk by maintaining a low factory capacity in case factory sales slumped.
3. Toyota wanted to take advantage of the lower wage scales in smaller firms.
4. Toyota managers realized that in-house manufacturing offered few benefits if it was possible to find stable, high-quality, and low-cost external sources of component supply.

At the same time, Toyota managers felt that the American practice of inviting competitive bids from suppliers was self-defeating. While competitive bidding might achieve the lowest short-run costs, the practice of playing suppliers off against each other did not guarantee stable supplies, high quality, or cooperation beyond existing contracts to solve design or engineering problems. Ohno and other Toyota managers believed that real efficiencies could be achieved if the company entered into long-term relationships with major suppliers. This would allow them to introduce the *kanban* system, thereby further reducing inventory holding costs and realizing the same kind of quality benefits that Toyota was already beginning to encounter with its in-house supply operations. In addition, Ohno wanted to bring suppliers into the design process since he believed that suppliers might be able to suggest ways of improving the design of component parts based upon their own manufacturing experience.

As it evolved during the 1950s and 1960s, Toyota's strategy toward its suppliers had several elements. First, the company spun off some of its own in-house supply operations into quasi-independent entities in which it took a minority stake, typically holding between 20 percent and 40 percent of the stock. It then recruited a number of independent companies with a view to establishing a long-term relationship with them for the supply of critical components. Sometimes, but not always, Toyota took a minority stake in these companies as well. All of these companies were designated as "first-tier suppliers." First-tier suppliers were responsible for working with Toyota as an integral part of the new product development team. Each first tier was responsible for the formation of a "second tier" of suppliers under its direction. Companies in the second tier were given the job of fabricating individual parts.

Both first- and second-tier suppliers were formed into supplier associations. Thus by 1986 Toyota had three regional supply organizations in Japan with 62, 135, and 25 first-tier suppliers, respectively. A major function of the supplier associations was to share information regarding new manufacturing, design, or materials management techniques among themselves. Concepts such as statistical process control, total quality control, and computer-aided design were rapidly diffused among suppliers by this means.

Toyota also worked closely with its suppliers, providing them with management expertise, engineering expertise, and sometimes capital to finance new investments. A critical feature of this relationship was the incentives that Toyota established to encourage its suppliers to focus on realizing continuous process improvements. The basic contract for a component would be for four to five years, with the price being agreed in advance. If by joint efforts the supplier and Toyota succeeded in reducing the costs of manufacturing the components, then the additional profit would be shared between the two. If the supplier by its own efforts came up with an innovation that reduced costs, the suppliers would keep the additional profit that the innovation generated for the lifetime of the contract.

As a consequence of this strategy, today Toyota outsources more than almost any other major auto manufacturer. By the late 1980s Toyota was responsible for only about 27 percent of the value going into a finished automobile, with the remainder coming from outside suppliers. In contrast, General Motors is responsible for about 70 percent of the value going into a finished automobile. Other consequences include long-term improvements in productivity and quality among Toyota's suppliers that are comparable to the improvements achieved by Toyota itself. In particular, the extension of the kanban system to include sup-

Table 1
Vehicles Produced per Worker (Adjusted for Vertical Integration), 1965–1983

Year	General Motors	Ford	Nissan	Toyota
1965	5.0	4.4	4.3	8.0
1970	3.7	4.3	8.8	13.4
1975	4.4	4.0	9.0	15.1
1979	4.5	4.2	11.1	18.4
1980	4.1	3.7	12.2	17.8
1983	4.8	4.7	11.0	15.0

Source: M. A. Cusumano, *The Japanese Automobile Industry*, (Cambridge, Mass.: Harvard University Press, 1989), Table 48, p. 197.

pliers, by eliminating buffer inventory stocks, in essence forced suppliers to focus more explicitly on the quality of their product.

Consequences

The consequences of Toyota's production system included a surge in labor productivity and a decline in the number of defects per car. Table 1 compares the number of vehicles produced per worker at General Motors, Ford, Nissan, and Toyota between 1965 and 1983.

These figures are adjusted for the degree of vertical integration pursued by each company. As can be seen, in 1960 productivity at Toyota already outstripped that of Ford, General Motors, and its main Japanese competitor, Nissan. As Toyota refined its production system over the next 18 years, productivity doubled. In comparison, productivity essentially stood still at General Motors and Ford during the same period.

Table 2 provides another way to assess the superiority of Toyota's production system. Here the performance of Toyota's Takaoka plant is compared with that of General Motors' Framingham plant in 1987. As can be seen, the Toyota plant was more productive, produced far fewer defects per 100 cars, and kept far less inventory on hand.

A further aspect of Toyota's production system is that the short set-up times made it economical to manufacture a much wider range of models than is feasible at a traditional mass production assembly plant. In essence, Toyota soon found that it could supply much greater product variety than its competitors with little in the way of a cost penalty. This continues today; in 1990 Toyota was offering consumers around the world roughly as many products as General Motors (about 150), even though Toyota was still only half GM's size. Moreover, it could do this at a lower cost than GM.

Table 2
General Motors' Framingham Plant versus Toyota's Takaoka Plant, 1987

	GM Framingham	Toyota Takaoka
Assembly hours per car	31	16
Assembly defects per 100 cars	135	45
Inventories of parts (average)	2 weeks	2 hours

Source: J. P. Womack, D. T. Jones, and D. Roos, *The Machine That Changed the World*, (New York: Macmillan, 1990), Figure 4.2, p. 83.

DISTRIBUTION AND CUSTOMER RELATIONS

Toyota's approach to its distributors and customers as it evolved during the 1950s and 1960s was in many ways just as radical as its approach toward suppliers. In 1950 Toyota formed a subsidiary, Toyota Motor Sales, to handle distribution and sales. The new subsidiary was headed by Kaymiya Shotaro from its inception until 1975. Kaymiya's philosophy was that dealers should be treated as "equal partners" in the Toyota family. To back this up, he had Toyota Motor Sales provide a wide range of sales training and service training for dealership personnel.

Kaymiya then used the dealers to build long-term ties with Toyota's customers. The ultimate aim was to bring customers into the Toyota design and production process. To this end, through its dealers, Toyota Motor Sales assembled a huge database on customer preferences. Much of this data came from monthly or semiannual surveys conducted by dealers. These asked Toyota customers their preferences for styling, model types, colors, prices, and other features. Toyota also used these surveys to estimate the potential demand for new models. This information was then fed directly into the design process.

Kaymiya began this process in 1952 when the company was redesigning its Toyopet model. The Toyopet was primarily used by urban taxi drivers. Toyota Motor Sales surveyed taxi drivers to try and find out what type of vehicle they preferred. They wanted something reliable, inexpensive, and with good city fuel mileage—which Toyota engineers then set about designing. In 1956 Kaymiya formalized this process when he created a unified department for planning and market research whose function was to coordinate the marketing strategies developed by researchers at Toyota Motor Sales with product planning by Toyota's design engineers. From this time on marketing information played a critical role in the design of Toyota's cars and, indeed, in the company's strategy. In particular, it was the research department at Toyota Motor Sales that provided the initial stimulus for Toyota to start exporting during the late 1960s after predicting, correctly, that growth in domestic sales would slow down considerably during the 1970s.

OVERSEAS EXPANSION

Large-scale overseas expansion did not become feasible at Toyota until the late 1960s for one principal reason: despite the rapid improvement in productivity, Japanese cars were still not competitive.[5] In 1957, for example, the Toyota Corona sold in Japan for the equivalent of $1,694. At the same time the Volkswagen Beetle sold for $1,111 in West Germany, while Britain's Austin company was selling its basic model for the equivalent of $1,389 in Britain. Foreign companies were effectively kept out of the Japanese market, however, by a 40 percent value added tax and shipping costs.

Despite these disadvantages, Toyota tried to enter the United States market in the late 1950s. The company set up a U.S. subsidiary in California in October

5. The material in this section is based on M. A. Cusumano, *The Japanese Automobile Industry*.

1957 and began to sell cars in early 1958, hoping to capture the American small car market (which at that time was poorly served by the U.S. automobile companies). The result was a disaster. Toyota's cars performed poorly in road tests on U.S. highways. The basic problem was that the engines of Toyota's cars were too small for prolonged high-speed driving and tended to overheat and burn oil, while poorly designed chassis resulted in excessive vibration. As a result, sales were slow and in 1964 Toyota closed down its U.S. subsidiary and withdrew from the market.

The company was determined to learn from its U.S. experience and quickly redesigned several of its models based on feedback from American consumer surveys and U.S. road tests. As a result, by 1967 the picture had changed considerably. The quality of Toyota's cars were now sufficient to make an impact in the U.S. market, while production costs and retail prices had continued to fall and were now comparable with international competitors in the small car market.

In the late 1960s Toyota reentered the U.S. market. Although sales were initially slow, they increased steadily. Then the OPEC-engineered fourfold increase in oil prices that followed the 1973 Israeli/Arab conflict gave Toyota an unexpected boost. U.S. consumers began to turn to small fuel-efficient cars in droves, and Toyota was one of the main beneficiaries. Driven primarily by a surge in U.S. demand, worldwide exports of Toyota cars increased from 157,882 units in 1967 to 856,352 units by 1974 and 1,800,923 units by 1984. Put another way, in 1967 exports accounted for 19 percent of Toyota's total output. By 1984 they accounted for 52.5 percent.

Success brought its own problems. By the early 1980s political pressures and talk of local content regulations in the United States and Europe were forcing an initially reluctant Toyota to rethink its exporting strategy. Toyota already had agreed to "voluntary" import quotas with the United States in 1981. The consequence for Toyota was stagnant export growth between 1981 and 1984. Against this background, in the early 1980s Toyota began to think seriously about setting up manufacturing operations overseas.

TRANSPLANT OPERATIONS

Toyota's first overseas operation was a 50/50 joint venture with General Motors established in February 1983 under the name New United Motor Manufacturing, Inc. (NUMMI). NUMMI, which is based in Fremont, California, began producing Chevrolet Nova cars for GM in December 1984.[6] The maximum capacity of the Fremont plant is about 250,000 cars per year.

For Toyota, the joint venture provided a chance to find out whether it could build quality cars in the United States using American workers and American suppliers. It also provided Toyota with experience dealing with an American union (the United Auto Workers Union) and with a means of circumventing "voluntary" import restrictions. For General Motors, the venture provided an opportunity to observe in full detail the Japanese approach to manufacturing. While General

6. Niland Powell, "U.S.-Japanese Joint Venture: New United Motor Manufacturing, Inc.," *Planning Review*, January–February 1989, pp. 40–45.

Motors' role is marketing and distributing the plant's output, Toyota designs the product and designs, equips, and operates the plant. At the venture's start, 34 executives were loaned to NUMMI by Toyota and 16 by General Motors. The chief executive and chief operating officer are both Toyota personnel.

By the fall of 1986 the NUMMI plant was running at full capacity and the early indications were that the NUMMI plant was achieving productivity and quality levels close to those achieved at Toyota's major Takaoka plant in Japan. For example, in 1987 it took the NUMMI plant 19 assembly hours to build a car, compared to 16 hours at Takaoka, while the number of defects per 100 cars was the same at NUMMI as at Takaoka—45.[7]

Encouraged by its success at NUMMI, in December 1985 Toyota announced that it would build an automobile manufacturing plant in Georgetown, Kentucky. The plant, which came on stream in May 1988, officially had the capacity to produce 200,000 Toyota Camrys a year. Such was the success of this plant, however, that by early 1990 it was producing the equivalent of 220,000 cars per year. This success was followed by an announcement in December 1990 that Toyota would build a second plant in Georgetown with a capacity to produce a further 200,000 vehicles per year.[8] All told, when this plant comes on stream in 1995 Toyota will have the capacity to build 660,000 vehicles per year in North America.

In addition to its North American transplant operations, Toyota moved to set up production in Europe in anticipation of the 1992 lowering of trade barriers among the 12 members of the European Economic Community. In 1989 the company announced that it would build a plant in England with the capacity to manufacture 200,000 cars per year by 1997.

Despite Toyota's apparent commitment to expand U.S.- and European-based assembly operations, it has not all been smooth sailing. A major problem has been building an overseas supplier network that is comparable to Toyota's Japanese network. For example, in a 1990 meeting of Toyota's North American suppliers' association, Toyota executives informed their North American suppliers that the defect ratio for parts produced by 75 North American and European suppliers was 100 times greater than the defect ratio for parts supplied by 147 Japanese suppliers—1,000 defects per million parts versus 10 defects per million among Toyota's Japanese suppliers. Moreover, Toyota executives pointed out that parts manufactured by North American and European suppliers tend to be significantly more expensive than comparable parts manufactured in Japan.[9]

Due to these problems, Toyota has had to import many parts from Japan for its U.S. assembly operations. However, for political reasons Toyota is being pushed to increase the local content of cars assembled in North America. The company's plan was for 50 percent of the value of Toyota cars assembled in the United States to be locally produced by January 1991. To achieve this, Toyota has embarked upon an aggressive supplier education drive in the United States. This is aimed at familiarizing its U.S. suppliers with Japanese production methods.

7. From J. P. Womack, D. T. Jones, and D. Roos, *The Machine That Changed The World*.
8. J. B. Treece, "Just What Detroit Needs: 200,000 More Toyotas a Year," *Business Week*, December 10, 1990, p. 29.
9. M. A. Maskery, "Toyota Talks Tough to U.S. Suppliers," *Automotive News*, November 5, 1990, p. 2.

PRODUCT STRATEGY

Toyota's initial production was aimed at the small car/basic transportation end of the automobile market. This was true both in Japan and of its export sales to North America and Europe. During the 1980s, however, Toyota progressively moved up market and abandoned much of the lower end of the market to new entrants such as the South Koreans. Thus, the company's Camry and Corolla models, which initially were positioned toward the bottom of the market, have been constantly upgraded and now are aimed at the middle-income segments of the market. This upgrading reflects two factors: (1) the rising level of incomes in Japan and the commensurate increase in the ability of Japanese consumers to purchase mid-range and luxury cars and (2) a desire to hold onto its U.S. consumers, many of whom initially purchased inexpensive Toyotas in their early 20s and who have since traded up to more expensive models.

The constant upgrading of Toyota's models reached its logical conclusion in September 1989 when the company's Lexus division began marketing luxury cars to compete with Jaguars, BMWs, and the like. The Lexus range of cars includes the ES 250, which was initially priced at $22,000, and the LS 400, which comes fully loaded with a $43,000 price tag (for comparison, a Jaguar XJ6 costs $40,000). The initial purpose of Lexus was to go after America's luxury car market, which amounted to about 850,000 unit sales in 1989. The car is also being sold in Japan and Europe.

Encouraged by car testers who rated the Lexus LS 400 the best in its class, Toyota initially projected worldwide sales around 75,000 units for the Lexus models in 1990. The early results for Lexus fell short of expectations. Although the fully loaded LS 400 model appears to be selling well, the ES 250 model is not, primarily because it is not enough of a luxury car to appeal to luxury buyers. Moreover, a slowdown in the U.S. auto market and the increasing specter of recession during 1990 cut into Lexus's potential sales. As a result, Toyota scaled back its projections for first-year sales from 75,000 to 60,000.[10] In the event, Toyota sold 57,162 Lexus models in North America during the 1990 model year and has expectations for selling 100,000 cars a year by the mid 1990s.[11]

Another addition to Toyota's product range in recent years has been a minivan. As with the Lexus range, this vehicle was aimed at the North American market where the minivan segment has grown most rapidly. Toyota first introduced a minivan in 1986, but it flopped. In typical Toyota fashion, the company dispatched product planners and design engineers to showrooms to find out why. Among the problems they identified were that the minivans lacked an aisle down the center, the short wheelbase gave them a pitchy ride, and the engine was not easy to service. Based on this feedback, Toyota designers completely redesigned the vehicle and reintroduced it in April 1990 as the Previa minivan. The early result exceeded expectations. Toyota sold 50,000 Previas in the first year and believes that it could easily sell 100,000 per year in the future.[12]

10. "The Next Samurai," *The Economist*, December 23, 1989, pp. 69–72; M. Landler and W. Zellner, "No Joyride for Japan," *Business Week*, January 15, 1990, pp. 20–21.
11. "Elegant Nippon," *The Economist*, December 8, 1990, p. 73.
12. J. Flint, "The New Number Three?" *Forbes*, June 11, 1990, pp. 136–140.

TOYOTA IN 1994

In 1990 Toyota was widely regarded as the most efficient automobile company in the world. By 1994 it was still held in high regard, but the company's luster had been tarnished by a series of poor financial results and by a growing realization that Toyota might have problems making the transition from a Japanese company to a truly international operation. Toyota's financial troubles were the product of the confluence of a number of unfavorable factors. Following the collapse of Japan's bubble economy in 1991, the Japanese economy had entered into a recession that turned out to be far deeper than anyone had foreseen. With domestic demand for cars plummeting, Toyota relied more than ever on foreign sales to pick-up the slack. During 1992 and 1993 the yen also increased sharply in value against most major currencies, and particularly the U.S. dollar. This made Toyota's exports increasingly expensive, a fact that was reflected in falling export volume. To make matters worse, both the U.S. and European economies entered into a recession in the early 1990s, so overseas demand dropped. In 1993 the U.S. economy staged a recovery and demand for automobiles surged, but Toyota did not benefit. While the U.S. Big Three increased their share of the U.S. auto market by 4 percent during 1993, Toyota saw its share of passenger car sales fall to 8.5 percent from 9.25 percent in 1992. Part of Toyota's problem was that although the company was now building a large number of cars in the United States, many of the parts were still being imported from Japan. The increase in the price of parts that resulted from the yen's rise boosted Toyota's costs in the United States. Another factor working against Toyota was the widespread perception in the United States that the quality gap between U.S. and Japanese cars had closed considerably, while U.S. manufacturers now had a price advantage. (This perception was not actually borne out in J. D. Power's 1993 quality survey, which suggested that Toyota, which captured 7 out of 10 places on the list, was still by far the highest-quality manufacturer.)[13]

The sum total of these factors was that Toyota's profits had fallen for three straight years, and the company warned that it might actually lose money for the fiscal year ending June 1994 if the yen remained at historic highs against the dollar. For the fiscal year ending June 1993, Toyota reported a 17 percent fall in operating profits, while pretax profits fell 23.8 percent. This profit fall occurred despite the fact that Toyota had cut 160 billion yen from its operating costs in 1992–1993. In late 1993, however, the company forecast that pretax profits would return to the 1991–1992 level of 427 billion yen by 1995–1996. Toyota expects this profit rebound to be fueled by strong growth in emerging markets such as Southeast Asia, where the group sold more than 300,000 cars and trucks in 1992–1993, claiming a 20 percent market share, and by a revival in Japanese domestic demand.[14]

Given the possibility of a demand and profit rebound, Toyota does not plan any redundancies in Japan. To streamline production and reduce operating costs it has cut the number of its model specifications by 20 percent and component

13. N. Templin, "Toyota Is Standout Once Again on J. D. Power Quality Survey," *The Wall Street Journal*, May 28, 1993, p. B1.
14. H. Kato, "Toyota Projects Fourth Year of Falling Profits," *Nikki Weekly*, August 30, 1993, p. 8.

variations by 30 percent while it is also fine tuning its production system to try and find ways of driving down operating costs. The company's overall financial position remains strong. In 1993 Toyota's liquid assets had a book value of 2,100 billion yen, or more than $19 billion at 1993 exchange rates.[15]

Despite Toyota's rather optimistic long-run outlook, many industry observers, along with certain segments within Toyota itself, see a number of significant and deep structural problems beginning to emerge within the company. One problem is that the company is clearly struggling with what it means to be global, not just as a sales strategy but also as a fundamental grounding principle. While many truly global companies have an international management cadre, Toyota's management, both in Japan and overseas, remains dominated by Japanese executives. Moreover, observers note that Toyota's overseas operations have an umbilical link with the head office in Toyota City. Even relatively small decisions must be cleared with the head office before an overseas operation can move forward.[16]

Another problem at Toyota exists on the factory floor. Toyota's blue collar workers are among the most productive in the world. However, the work routines are grueling, with 8- to 10-hour days and work at an exhausting pace. This did not matter much when labor was in abundant supply and when few people were willing to question the Toyota way of operating, but there are signs that things are beginning to change. Like many other Japanese companies, due to an aging population Toyota is facing a shortage of young male factory workers. Moreover, the young factory workers that it does manage to recruit are starting to buck at a system that demands absolute loyalty to the company and a deadening work pace. How this will play itself out in the future is unclear, but it does seem as if Japan's younger generation does not share the sacrifice mentality of its parents and grandparents and may not be willing to work as hard without a substantial reward.

At the same time as it faces a blue-collar shortage, Toyota has found itself with a surplus of white-collar workers which, because of lifetime employment commitments, it cannot lay off. One result has been the emergence of a bloated middle management bureaucracy and a tall management hierarchy. This stands in contrast to the factory floor, where the situation is characterized by an absence of hierarchy. Since Toyota has recently committed itself to a policy of no redundancies, it is not clear how this situation will be resolved.

A final problem that Toyota has to deal with is that of growing trade tensions. Toyota's very success has created resistance in both the United States and Europe. Moreover, Toyota's aggressive pursuit of global market share has led other Japanese car companies to blame Toyota for some of their current problems. If only Toyota were a little less aggressive, they claim, trade tensions would not be so high and all Japanese car producers would benefit. In short, Toyota is being pressured by its domestic competitors, particularly Nissan, to rein back its global ambitions somewhat in the interests of the Japanese industry as a whole.

15. K. Done, "Toyota Warns of Continuing Decline," *Financial Times*, November 23, 1993, p. 23.
16. M. Keller, *Collision: GM, Toyota, Volkswagen and the Race to Own the 21st Century* (New York: Doubleday, 1993).

CASE

16

Big Changes at General Motors

General Motors (GM) is the largest industrial corporation in the world. 1992 net revenues were $132.4 billion and 750,000 people worked for the company.[1] The company was founded on September 16, 1908, when William C. Durant formed the General Motors Company. Into it he brought about 25 independent car companies, only four of which—Buick, Olds (now Oldsmobile), Oakland (now Pontiac), and Cadillac—survive as operating divisions today. Originally, each car company retained its own individual identity, and the GM Company was simply a holding company, a central office surrounded by 25 satellites that produced hundreds of models of cars principally targeted at wealthy customers—the costs of manufacturing cars had been so high up to this time that only the wealthy could afford them.

GM's principal competitor at this time was the Ford Motor Car Company. In 1908 Henry Ford announced the development of the Model T motor car which was to be produced by the revolutionary method of mass production. Ford's new mass production technology was based on moving conveyor belts, where the belt brought the car to be assembled to unskilled workers rather than having skilled workers work in small teams to make a car. Ford also pioneered the use of standardized auto parts that easily could be fitted together to make assembly easier and less costly. As a result of Ford's efforts, the costs of manufacturing cars plummeted and Ford created a mass market for the Model T car. Ford became the industry leader and GM was suddenly in a losing situation of producing a wide variety of expensive cars for a very small upscale market compared to Ford's single, inexpensive product targeted at the middle of the market. The Ford Motor Company grew rich during the period 1910–1920, while GM struggled to keep its head above water.

In 1920 Alfred P. Sloan took control of GM as CEO. He saw that major changes were necessary if GM was to be able to compete effectively with Ford. It was clear to Sloan that operating 25 different car companies producing hundreds of different models was very inefficient. Moreover, GM's high-cost–high-priced cars were competing against one another for the same set of wealthy customers. In addition, GM's car companies were not learning anything from one another, and they were all buying or making their own sets of auto components so that economies of scale in parts manufacturing or auto assembly were not being obtained. Sloan saw that GM's very survival was at stake and that the company needed to develop a new strategy and structure.

This case was prepared by Gareth R. Jones and Susan L. Peters, Texas A&M University. This case was prepared as a basis for class discussion rather than to illustrate either effective or ineffective handling of administrative situations.

1. GM 1992 Annual Report, p. 41.

GM'S NEW ORGANIZATION

Sloan searched for a new way to organize and manage GM's various car companies to increase their competitive advantage. While he saw the need to reduce costs and increase efficiency, he also saw that Ford's strategy of producing only one model of car for the whole market meant that Ford was ignoring the needs of other market segments, such as the luxury end which GM served. Moreover, he realized that customers in the middle of the market might want a superior product to the standard Ford Model T and that there was a lot of room to produce cars for market segments between those served by the standardized Model T and the expensive GM Models.

The problem Sloan faced was how to organize GM's 25 different car divisions to achieve both superior efficiency and customer responsiveness. The solution he hit upon was to group the 25 different companies into five major self-contained operating divisions that still exist today: Chevrolet, Pontiac, Oldsmobile, Buick, and Cadillac.

Each of the different divisions was given its own support functions like sales, manufacturing, engineering, and finance and became responsible for producing a range of cars aimed at a specific socioeconomic market segment. Chevrolet, for example, was to produce inexpensive cars for customers at the cheap end of the market; Pontiac, Oldsmobile, and Buick would produce more upscale cars for progressively more prosperous market segments, while Cadillac would specialize in the high-price, luxury end of the market. Sloan hoped that customers would move up to the next most expensive line of GM car as they prospered. GM carefully priced the cars of the different divisions to entice customers to move up, say from an Oldsmobile to a Buick, or a Buick to a Cadillac, as their fortunes rose. Realizing that customers might be confused about the number of GM models they would be choosing from, he was insistent that each division should develop a range of cars that had a unique image so that the cars of the different divisions would be clearly differentiated. Thus, for example, Cadillac customers should believe that the Cadillac they were buying was a product that was clearly superior to a Buick, not just a more expensive car with a different name.[2]

Sloan also hoped that reorganizing GM into five different car divisions would increase operating efficiency. Under Sloan's plan, each division became an independent profit center and was to be evaluated on its return on investment. Each division would be in control of its own strategy, and decision making was decentralized to the divisions where divisional managers became responsible for bottom line results. Sloan's idea was that this new way of organizing activities would create competition between divisions that would lead them to improve their efficiency in order to increase their share of organizational resources. As Sloan wrote in his autobiography, he thought the creation of independent operating divisions would increase the morale of the organization by placing each operation on its own foundation, assuming its own responsibility and contributing its share to the final result; develop statistics correctly reflecting the true measure of efficiency; and enable the corporation to direct the placing of additional capital where it will result in the greatest benefit to the corporation as a whole.[3]

2. A. P. Sloan, *My Years at General Motors* (Garden City, N. Y.: Doubleday, 1964).
3. Ibid., p. 50.

Sloan also recommended that interdivisional transactions of auto parts, technology, and so on should be set by a transfer pricing scheme based on cost plus some predetermined rate of return. To avoid protecting a high-cost internal supplier, however, he recommended a number of steps involving analysis of the parts and assembly operations of outside competitors to determine the fair price. In this way he hoped to keep down the cost of GM's inputs.

Sloan established a strong, professional, centralized headquarters staff to determine the fair price of inputs and to establish transfer prices between divisions. This staff's primary role would be to audit divisional performance and to plan strategy for the total organization. The divisions were to be responsible for all product-related decisions.

The results of this change in organizing GM's value creation activities were dramatic. By 1925 GM had become the dominant U.S. car company and had seized a large share of the market from Ford, which saw the demand for its Model T plummet as customers switched to GM's upscale cars. Ford was soon forced to close down his factory for seven months in order to retool the production line to produce different kinds of cars for different kinds of customers. Fewer and fewer customers wanted a Model T Ford—which only came in the color black—when they could get a better equipped, more prestigious, and more luxurious car at a price they could also afford.

With its new strategy and structure in place, GM took the lead in the U.S. car market, obtained the largest market share of any car manufacturer, and became the largest and most profitable car company in the world. From 1925–1975 it embarked in a continuous program to expand its product range to include all kinds of models of cars, full-size trucks, light-weight trucks, and various forms of specialized vehicles such as vans and ambulances.

As time went on, GM began to take over its suppliers and became very vertically integrated—owning over 50 percent of its suppliers. It took over Fisher Body which made the car bodies for GM cars, for example. GM also internally developed many of its own auto parts operations, such as its Delco division which still supplies GM with most of its electrical and electronic components.

From 1925–1975 GM dominated the U.S. car market controlling over 60 percent of domestic sales. Until 1975, GM, Ford, and Chrysler (known collectively as the Big Three) controlled over 90 percent of the U.S. car market and expanded globally to become major producers in Europe and the rest of the world. Given its glorious history, GM was not prepared for what was to come next.

CHANGES IN GM'S ENVIRONMENT

GM's preeminent position in the U.S. car market was broken in the 1970s by a combination of two factors that altered the nature of competition in the car industry forever: the oil crisis and the emergence of low-cost Japanese competition. The oil embargo of 1973 revealed the inefficiency of the Big Three's "gas guzzler" cars which frequently were able to achieve only 6–9 miles per gallon. U.S. consumers began to demand smaller, fuel-efficient vehicles which the Big Three were not equipped to build. The Japanese, however, had developed a competence in the production of small, fuel-efficient cars and U.S. consumers began to switch to their products. Moreover, as U.S. consumers began buying inexpensive

Japanese cars, such as the Honda Accord and the Toyota Celica they began to realize that these cars were not only inexpensive but reliable; for example, while Japanese cars averaged only 1.3 flaws per vehicle, Ford averaged 2, GM 2.5, and Chrysler almost 3.

The combination of the switch in consumer demand and the capability of the Japanese to dominate the small car niche precipitated a crisis for GM. Demand for its large sedans plummeted, and divisions like Buick and Cadillac began to lay off thousands of employees because of their inability to meet the change in consumer demand. Moreover, growing consumer awareness of quality problems in many GM models helped contribute to its declining market share.[4]

GM's operating philosophy that large cars mean large profits was revealed to be false, as the Japanese, who had been developing lean production techniques to reduce manufacturing costs, began to make large profits from selling small cars to U.S. consumers. Consumers flocked to the rapidly expanding Japanese car dealerships that were spreading over the United States during the 1970s. Within the space of five years, 1973–1978, GM (and the Big Three) was revealed to be not only a high-cost car maker but also a low-quality car maker. GM's extensive range of large, luxurious, boxy car models began to compare unfavorably to the inexpensive (and boxy) Japanese models and to the sleek European luxury sedans of Jaguar, Mercedes-Benz, and BMW, which also began to steal away GM's share of the luxury car market toward the end of the 1970s. GM was being attacked on both the inexpensive and the luxury ends of the market, and its profits fell drastically as the sales of its cars fell.

GM FIGHTS BACK

Reeling from the onslaught of the new competition, GM began to use its huge resources (in 1978, for example, despite its problems GM still earned $3.5 billion on $63 billion in sales) to try to restore its competitive advantage. Under the control of a new CEO, Roger Smith, who took over the company in 1980, GM began several major programs to reduce costs and improve quality. By 1990 the cost of these programs had exceeded $100 billion—enough money, analysts pointed out, to have bought both Toyota and Honda on the stock market, given their value at the time.

New Technology

To enhance its competitive position in automobiles and trucks, GM invested over $50 billion to improve and update its technology and to gain expertise in Japanese lean manufacturing techniques. Beginning in the early 1980s, Roger Smith championed the development of automated factories and robots as a way of reducing costs and raising productivity. Under his leadership, plants such as GM's Saginaw Vanguard plant in Michigan became heavily automated. In these automated factories, lasers inspect components and examine machine tools to determine if they are worn out. Automated equipment molds parts, and robots assemble the components. Automated vehicles pick up and distribute parts to the robots on the assembly line. Only 42 hourly employees work two shifts, and engineers and technicians operate the factory via computers. A computer

4. Jeremy Main, "Detroit's Cars Really Are Getting Better," *Fortune*, February 2, 1987, pp. 90–98.

network connects the production machines, enabling the facility to change product lines in 10 minutes compared to traditional factory changeover times of 10 hours.

While these automated factories were impressive, they proved very expensive to operate. For example, axles made in the new factories cost twice as much as ones produced conventionally. Moreover, they were subject to frequent down time as robots broke down and stopped the production line. To gain union support of automated technology, union workers went through extensive training in areas such as problem solving, team building, computers, and electronics; however, this move did little to reduce costs. Moreover, some robots remain unused because GM never trained workers to use the technology.[5] By some estimates, Gm's new automated factories were no more productive than those operated conventionally; GM seemed to lack the Japanese know-how to operate automated factories successfully.

The Saturn Project

In1982 GM started the Saturn Project, a major experiment to learn and develop the skills and competencies to manufacture low-cost quality cars. Roger Smith created a new division called Saturn which was given the task of creating a Japanese-like lean manufacturing unit that could produce a small car at the same cost as Japanese car companies. The Saturn division was deliberately kept separate from GM's other divisions so that new skills could be developed from scratch. GM chose Spring Hill, Tennessee, as the location for the new plant. In 1987 the board approved $1.9 billion for the new factory, equipment, and tooling. Saturn has become the biggest construction undertaking in GM's history. In addition to the traditional paint shop, body plant, and assembly plant, Saturn has a power train plant that produces engines and transmissions, a plastic molding plant, and a shop for consolidating the instrument panel and dashboard. Materials and parts move directly from one plant to the next. This integration differs from the normal GM assembly plant with major parts factories located far away from assembly operations. When parts are shipped to Saturn, they arrive at multiple docks close to where the parts are used, facilitating quick defect detections by line workers, instead of going to a central loading dock.[6]

The power train plant is Saturn's most advanced operation. A new technology called lost-foam casting was developed to manufacture the engine block and heads; the process produces complex parts with great accuracy, reducing costs on tools and machinery by 30 percent. Saturn can also assemble both manual and automatic transmissions on the same production line in any sequence, which results in zero inventory and lower costs. Production costs on power train lines should also be 20 percent to 40 percent lower than a traditional engine plant's production costs. The assembly line is made of wood instead of concrete, which is easier on people's feet. Workers can also ride with the car instead of walking along the assembly line.[7]

In 1988 Saturn began recruiting the first 3,000 workers from existing GM plants. In 1990 the plant moved into full production.[8] Saturn's mission is to sell 80 percent of its cars to people who would not have bought another GM car.

5. Alex Taylor III, "Can GM Remodel Itself?" *Fortune*, January 13, 1992, pp. 26–34.
6. James Treece, "Here Comes GM's Saturn," *Business Week*, April 9, 1990, pp. 56–62.
7. Ibid.
8. Ibid.

Seventy percent of Saturn buyers would not have bought a GM car. Saturn's first 70 dealers chosen were on the East and West Coasts to target the import buyer. Saturn went on sale in January 1991 and was priced from $10,000 to $12,000 to compete with the Honda Civic and Toyota Corolla. Production delays permitted only 4,245 cars to be shipped to dealers and early cars had a shaky start. In February 1991, 1,210 cars had to be recalled for faulty back seats; another 1,836 cars were recalled in May 1991 for bad engine coolant.[9] By 1991 Saturn built just 50,000 cars, which is short of its 240,000 capacity, and it lost $800 million.[10]

By 1992, however, Saturn was selling well and its cars were ranked in the top ten of customer satisfaction. It had a 17-day inventory of cars compared to a 62-day industry average.[11] However, Saturn still lost $700 million in 1992 and the skills that GM developed in lean manufacturing through its Saturn Project did not spread widely through the GM organization.[12] Moreover, GM realized that Saturn never could match the low costs of Japanese manufacturers. The division has built a high-quality product that is in great demand, however, and GM claimed the division broke even in 1993 and that Saturn should show a profit in 1994 and beyond. Currently, GM has to decide whether or not to invest $2 billion more in the division to allow it to develop the new models that will be necessary for it to compete in the future.

Strategic Alliances

In 1983, in another venture to learn Japanese techniques in lean manufacturing, GM created a joint venture with Toyota called New United Motor Manufacturing, Inc. (NUMMI) to produce Chevrolet Novas and Geo Prizms in GM's Fremont, California, plant, which GM had closed in 1982 because of poor quality and bad labor-management relations. Through the venture, Toyota would get the chance to see if it could make high-quality cars in the United States with American workers and suppliers, while GM would gain access to Toyota's lean manufacturing approach.[13] Each partner initially contributed $100 million; Toyota provided $100 million in cash, but GM's $100 million consisted primarily of assets including the Fremont plant. Toyota selected both the CEO and the president.[14] GM sent about 17 managers to NUMMI and Toyota sent 35. Toyota designed the assembly plant and runs daily operations.[15] GM markets and distributes the plant's output.

In 1984 NUMMI reopened under the control of Japanese management. By 1986 its productivity was higher than any other GM factory, and it was operating at twice the level it had operated at under GM management. One of the primary reasons for its success was the use of flexible work teams. At the NUMMI factory, Toyota divided the work force into 350 flexible work teams consisting

9. David Woodruff, "May We Help You Kick the Tires," *Business Week*, August 3, 1992, pp. 49–50.
10. Ibid.
11. Ibid.
12. David Woodruff, "Saturn: Labor's Love Lost?" *Business Week*, February 8, 1993, pp. 122–123.
13. Powell Niland, "Case Study: U.S.-Japanese Joint Venture: New United Motor Manufacturing, Inc. (NUMMI)," *Planning Review* 17 (January–February 1989): 40–45.
14. Maryann Keller, *Rude Awakening: The Rise, Fall, and Struggle for Recovery of General Motors* (New York: William Morrow, 1989), pp. 90–91, 129–144.
15. Richard Kauffman, "Working Partner," *Diablo Business* (California), April 1, 1992, Newsbank, Transportation Fiche 17, grids G7–G9.

of five to seven people plus a team leader. Each worker can do the jobs of the other workers, and workers regularly rotate jobs. In addition, all workers were taught procedures for analyzing jobs to improve the employee-task relationship. Team members designed all the team's jobs, timed each other using stopwatches, and continually attempted to find better ways of performing tasks. GM had employed 80 managers to perform this analysis; now not only do flexible work teams perform this analysis, they also take responsibility for monitoring product quality. The role of managers in the new factory is to provide shop floor workers with support, not to monitor or supervise their activities. From this venture GM learned how Toyota developed its lean production system; it also learned that work relationships are at least as important as automated factories in increasing productivity and reducing costs. It is getting the combination of the two working together that is the most important.[16]

GM'S RETURN FROM ITS INVESTMENT IN NEW TECHNOLOGY

By 1990, as a result of its investment in new automated technology, its Saturn Project, and its learning Japanese lean manufacturing techniques, GM was able to reduce significantly the number of defects per car, raise car quality, and reduce manufacturing costs. In 1990 GM's Cadillac division won the 1990 Malcolm Baldrige Quality Award, and *Motor Trend* magazine chose the Chevy Caprice as Car of the Year.[17] As a result of improvements in quality and styling, and the rising value of the yen, the Big Three's market share increased from 70 percent in 1991 to 72 percent in 1992. In 1992 GM introduced 16 new vehicles, including the very successful Cadillac Seville STS which was successfully marketed against Toyota's Lexus and Germany's Mercedes.[18]

Even after all these improvements throughout the 1980s, however, GM lags behind competitors in efficiency. It takes GM workers 40 percent longer to assemble a car than it does Ford employees.[19] On average it takes GM 4.55 workers per car per day compared to Ford's 3.01 workers, which translates into a $441 cost advantage on the factory floor for Ford.[20] GM also spends 20 percent to 25 percent more money to open a new factory than Ford does. GM still takes 42 to 48 months to redesign a car, which is 9 to 12 months slower than Japanese companies.[21] It takes 40 hours to assemble a Saturn compared to 20 hours to assemble a Toyota Camry.[22] GM's Corvette plant in Bowling Green, Kentucky, is the least efficient Big Three plant in North America; it takes 11.37

16. Julia Flynn and Aaron Bernstein, "GM Is Spreading the Gospel According to Toyota," *Business Week*, May 25, 1987, p. 120.
17. James Treece, "War, Recession, Gas Hikes...GM's Turnaround Will Have to Wait," *Business Week*, February 4, 1991, pp. 94–96.
18. Taylor, "Can GM Remodel Itself?"
19. William Hampton and James Norman, "General Motors: What Went Wrong," *Business Week*, March 16, 1987, pp. 102–110.
20. Jolie Solomon et al., "Can GM Fix Itself?" *Newsweek*, November 9, 1992, pp. 54–59.
21. Taylor, "Can GM Remodel Itself?"
22. Joseph White and Neal Templin, "Harsh Regimen: Swollen GM Finds a Crash Diet Means Uncomfortable Labor," *The Wall Street Journal*, September 9, 1992, pp. A1, A11.

workers to assemble a car, which is twice what Honda uses for the Acura NSX sports car. In addition, quality is below the industry average.[23] Furthermore, plants are not operating at capacity. GM plants average a 73 percent capacity rate compared to Ford's 95 percent.[24] The plant that produces the Cadillac Seville STS still only ran at 50 percent capacity in 1993.[25] GM's breakeven point—the number of cars needed to be sold to make zero profit—rose 30 percent from 1981 to 1986.[26]

Even though GM has raised its efficiency and quality, its competitors have increased theirs more. Other U.S. car companies, for example, had been learning the new manufacturing methods at least as well as GM, and the Japanese continued to refine theirs. From 1980 to 1987, for example, Ford's market share rose from 17 percent to 20 percent, while GM's dropped from 46 percent to 37 percent. In 1987 Ford earned higher profits than GM for the first time since 1924 when demand for the Model T peaked. Ford attributed this success to a $3 billion investment in a new line of cars, cost cutting, a quality emphasis, and employee participation.[27] Moreover, Ford is highly centralized, which made it easier for top management to pursue new quality policies quickly and to transfer new skills and techniques across the organization. GM, with its several divisions, found it much more difficult to transfer new information and knowledge between divisions, and top management orders were often lost in the bureaucracy.[28] By 1989 Ford sold 410,077 Tauruses and Sables through two divisions compared to GM's 537,080 GM10 cars marketed through four divisions.[29] In 1993, the Ford Taurus became the best-selling car in the United States, supplanting the Honda Accord.

Like GM, Chrysler struggled for survival in the early 1980s. Under the leadership of Lee Iacocca, Chrysler simplified its product line and concentrated on K-body cars like the Dodge Aries and Plymouth Reliant. A smaller product line made reducing costs and improving quality easier. Unlike GM, Chrysler focused on market niches like the minivan market, where competition was low, and became the leading seller of minivans. By 1993 Chrysler made a comeback by cutting operating costs and by redesigning new products in record time with cross-functional teams. Chrysler has now become the most efficient American developer of new vehicles with models such as the Eagle Vision, the Dodge Intrepid, and the Viper.

Moreover, after experimenting with NUMMI, Toyota decided to open its own plants in the United States following Honda's example. These Japanese companies now have the lowest cost–highest quality car manufacturing system in the United States.

23. David Woodruff, "End of the Line for the 'Home of the Corvette?'" *Business Week*, December 14, 1992, p. 35.
24. Alex Taylor III, "Why U.S. Carmakers?" *Fortune*, October 23, 1989, pp. 96–116.
25. Taylor, "Can GM Remodel Itself?"
26. Hampton and Norman, "General Motors: What Went Wrong."
27. Brian Dumaine, "Donald Petersen: A Humble Hero Drives Ford to the Top," *Fortune*, January 4, 1988, pp. 22–24.
28. Jeremy Main, "Detroit's Cars Really Are Getting Better," *Fortune*, February 2, 1987, pp. 90–100.
29. Alex Taylor III, "U.S. Cars Come Back," *Fortune*, November 16, 1992, pp. 52–94.

CHANGING ITS STRUCTURE

In the early 1980s, as a result of fierce competition from the Japanese, GM took a hard look at why it had run into its enormous problems. For example, why had it failed to develop new small cars and why had it not pioneered its own lean manufacturing techniques? GM's top managers began to realize that the way GM's multidivisional structure operated had negatively impacted the company's competitive advantage. Corporate managers found that Ford, Chrysler, and Japanese car companies operated with relatively flat, streamlined structures. GM, on the other hand, had five sprawling and independent operating divisions and a corporate headquarters staff of over 30,000 corporate managers. It had become a huge, lumbering bureaucracy. Roger Smith and his top management team, prompted by outside critics worried at GM's deteriorating performance, began to realize that GM's structure had reduced its competitive advantage in several ways.

First, each division performed its own research and development and engineering, and the duplication of activities across divisions was costing the company billions of dollars. Each division also purchased its inputs independently of other divisions so that economies of purchasing and distribution were being lost. Moreover, the different divisions were not sharing their knowledge about new, more efficient methods of manufacturing so that quality was slow to increase.

Second, each division produced cars in its own traditional way using its own platform—the basic design behind which cars are assembled and made. Each division also used several different platforms to make its range of cars, a practice that was very expensive because each platform required a different set of inputs as well as its own specific method of manufacturing. Moreover, a specific platform could not be used to produce other models of cars should patterns of consumer demand for a division's cars change. By contrast, Chrysler decided before 1980 to develop only one platform, the K-Platform, to build all its cars because this would lead to substantial economies of scale and savings in manufacturing costs.

Third, the sheer cost of GM's huge staff of corporate executives, a cost that many analysts calculated ran into the many billions of dollars, raised costs and slowed decision making.

Beyond reduced efficiency, GM's tall, overly bureaucratic structure slowed innovation as it took GM a long time to adopt new technological advances, such as radial tires and air bags. The corporate bureaucracy also slowed GM's ability to respond to customer demands and to recognize that customers' needs were changing. As mentioned earlier, GM was slow to see the move toward smaller, fuel-efficient, high-reliability cars from the long, boxy, chrome-laden, heavyweight vehicles that had become the main offering of the Big Three. Finally, GM and the Big Three had never made increased quality a focus of their attention because their corporate philosophy was that consumers wanted a new car every two or three years so that poor quality and car breakdowns were always the next owner's problem.

On all competitive fronts, GM's organizational structure had done little to enhance its competitive advantage, and its structure had become a positive liability compared to those of competitors. For example, whereas Toyota only had seven levels in its hierarchy in the early 1980s, there were 21 levels in GM's hierarchy. One consequence was that while it took GM 5 to 6 years to bring a new car to market; it took Toyota only 36 months.

THE 1984 REORGANIZATION

To try to solve many of these problems and increase its competitiveness, in 1984 GM consolidated its five powerful, autonomous divisions into two business groups. The operations of Chevy and Pontiac (CPC) divisions would be managed together, and this new group would concentrate on manufacturing and marketing small cars. The Buick, Oldsmobile, and Cadillac (BOC) divisions would be managed together, and the BOC group would focus on bigger, luxury cars.[30] The goal behind the change was to reduce costs by centralizing R&D, engineering, and purchasing activities at the level of the business group. GM hoped that this reorganization would speed product development and reduce overlap between the products of the different divisions which were competing for the same customers.

The 1984 reorganization added yet another layer of GM bureaucracy: in addition to corporate management and individual divisional managers there was now the level of group manager (e.g., BOC group manager). Divisions inside a group would produce car models from a limited number of platforms, and each model would be assembled from a limited number of inputs to reduce costs. Each division would then customize its models for specific groups of customers.

While this reorganization looked good on paper, in practice it proved to be disastrous. The result of centralizing decision making at the group level and standardizing the activities of the divisions inside a group was that by 1987 all the cars produced by a group began to look alike. Cars were basically similar and divisions had become merely marketing organizations. Consumers grew wary of GM's products because they had lost their differentiated appeal—something that had been central to Sloan's original strategy for GM. For example, Cadillac buyers did not know why they were paying more for a car that looked like other less expensive GM models such as Buicks, and sales of Cadillacs plummeted. After the reorganization, 80 percent of Buicks, Oldsmobiles, and Pontiacs differed only slightly in price and engineering; due to the lack of a unique image, sales for those three divisions fell sharply by 1989.

The basic problem was that key design decisions were made by central engineering and manufacturing staffs instead of by managers in the five divisions. Moreover, the central engineering design staff reported to top management only two layers away from the chairman and not to any automobile executive at the divisional level. Division managers had to bargain with the design staff to get their desired car styling because it raised the design staff's costs. This new structure solved few of the problems facing GM and prevented it from launching a real winner like Ford's Taurus. Moreover, costs had still not fallen as had been hoped because potential gains from standardizing production and inputs were not being obtained. While design time had been reduced, the result was poorer, not better customer responsiveness.

As Roger Smith recognized, GM needed to centralize many of its activities to achieve economies of scale and reduce costs, but it also needed to decentralize many activities to provide the flexibility needed to react to changes quickly and to allow divisions to design and develop products to meet the needs of their customers.

Realizing its mistake, GM's top management made some moves to reorganize the company to give control of engineering and design back to the divisions. However, the benefits of centralizing R&D and purchasing were realized and these activities became increasingly controlled at the group and corporate level.

30. Hampton and Norman, "General Motors: What Went Wrong."

Effects of the Reorganization

The Cadillac division benefited the most from the new policy of decentralization. Due to centralized engineering at the group level, Cadillac's image had become tainted and its sales had fallen. Due to an anticipated energy crisis in 1986, for example, GM had decided that the Cadillac Eldorado and Seville should be made smaller but should cost more. GM tried to target these cars at import buyers as well as traditional buyers, buyers in the over-50 age group. However, traditional customers did not like these models because they looked similar to cheaper cars; for example, the new Cadillacs looked like Buicks. As a result, 1986 sales were 51 percent less than 1985 sales.

To turn the division around, Cadillac was granted its own engineering team in 1988 and it moved quickly to forge a new identity for the division. Once again in control of its decision making, Cadillac managers lengthened the cars two inches, restyled them, increased advertising, and promoted test drives of the cars through direct mail. By 1990 Cadillac had gross margins of 40 percent to 50 percent, compared to 30 percent for the rest of GM's divisions. The Cadillac division has become very successful, launching redesigned models in 1991, 1992, and 1993. Their sales have been steadily rising, especially as the rising value of the yen has made Japanese luxury cars like the Lexus and the Infiniti relatively expensive.

Robert Stempel, who took over as CEO in 1990, refused to give the same level of autonomy and control of decision making to GM's other six divisions: Buick, Oldsmobile, Chevrolet, Pontiac, GMC Truck, and Saturn. Viewing the confusion of the 1984 reorganization, he believed that "one reorganization is enough for anyone's lifetime."[31] As a result, GM's other car divisions experienced mixed fortunes during the early 1990s.

In its small car CPC business group, GM implemented a major plan to reduce the number of car platforms and to centralize purchasing of inputs to costs through its GM10 program. The GM10 program was created to replace all of GM's mid-sized cars such as the Chevy Celebrity, the Pontiac 6000, the Buick Century, and the Olds Cutlass Supreme. Each of these four divisions would get a coupe and a sedan. At a cost of $7 billion, GM10 was the largest new model program ever created, indicating GM's interest in obtaining economies of scale from its reorganized car operations.

Because the company could not afford to introduce all eight GM10 models at the same time, it decided to launch the two-doors first and the four-doors later.[32] The Cutlass Supreme, Buick Regal, and Pontiac Grand Prix, all two-door models, were introduced in the 1988 model year and flopped because buyers preferred four-door sedans. The decision was a major error and four models were not introduced until 1989 with the last one launched in 1990—eight years after the beginning of the project. None of the cars has become a major seller of the order of a Ford Taurus or Honda Accord, and GM has yet to recoup its investment.

Buick sales declined from 1984 to 1988. Edward Mertz, who took over the division in 1986, sought the independence that Cadillac had achieved, and he established a major program to increase quality. Mertz began to listen to dealers, customers, and employees, and he created a team of engineers to handle dealer and customer complaints. This team communicated directly to plant engineers so changes could be continually made and quality improved. For example, the team found out which Buick characteristics customers still wanted and conveyed this information to the engineers who were instructed to work with manufacturing to

31. Alex Taylor III, *Fortune*, April 9, 1990, pp. 52–61.
32. Taylor, "U.S. Cars Come Back."

build quality into its cars. Buick decided to focus on core vehicles such as the Roadmaster, Park Avenue, and Regal, which were aimed at traditional Buick buyers—60-year-old, well-paid blue-collar workers. With its revised lineup of cars, Buick began doing fairly well in the mid-sized car segment. By 1991 sales of Buick's 1991 models increased 6.6 percent at a time when total U.S. car sales decreased 8.2 percent, and its cars were recognized as among the most reliable.

The upturn in Buick's fortunes came at the expense of Oldsmobile, however.[33] As a result of the reorganization, Oldsmobile's cars had come to look very similar to Buick's and were targeted at the same customer segment. But Buick had the reputation for quality; consequently, Olds' sales declined from 1.1 million cars in 1986 to about 560,000 cars in 1990. In 1993, with falling sales continuing, the future of the Oldsmobile division was called into question. So far, however, no plans have been announced to close the division.

The Chevrolet division has products ranging from $6,999 subcompacts to $18,155 trucks to $33,635 Corvettes and accounts for almost half of GM's annual vehicle sales. As with the other divisions, it suffered from poor design throughout the 1980s and by 1990 was desperately in need of new models to compete with the Japanese. For example, Chevy's sales of cars and light trucks dropped 4.7 percent in 1991 while Ford's increased 15 percent and Chrysler's rose 9.6 percent. By 1993 a new Monte Carlo, a revamped Chevy Camaro Z28, and the Pontiac Firebird helped the division regain sales.[34]

Despite these changes to its product line, however, throughout the 1980s Japanese carmakers continuously gained market share, mainly by stealing sales from GM. In 1978 American automakers had an 84 percent market share compared to 68 percent in 1989.[35] From 1985 to 1989, GM's market share declined from about 44 percent to about 33 percent while Japan's share increased from 19 percent to 26 percent. By 1990 Toyota and Honda both sold more cars in the United States than Chrysler.[36] Japan sold 3.3 million cars and trucks in the United States in 1990, while the United States exported less than 100,000 cars to Japan. In 1989 Toyota introduced the Lexus, and Nissan launched the Infiniti to compete with Cadillac for luxury sales. Other manufacturers upscaled their mid-sized cars to compete with GM's upper-end models. For example, Mitsubishi revamped the Diamante sedan and Mazda redesigned its 929 to compete with GM's Cadillac and Ford's Lincoln. Japan also decided to enter the profitable large truck segment dominated by Chevrolet. In 1993 Toyota introduced Japan's first full-sized pick-up truck to compete in the large truck segment which accounted for 41.6 percent of vehicles produced in the United States in 1992.

From 1992 on, however, GM and the Big Three steadily introduced a large number of new car models which have steadily helped them recapture market share from the Japanese and increase profits. Strong sales in the second half of 1993 and the first quarter of 1994 by GM and all the Big Three increased their market share to about 73 percent and contributed to increased profits for all. GM expects to be profitable in 1994. While new models and increased quality have helped GM and the Big Three, some analysts believe that the rising value of the yen that has made Japanese cars considerably more expensive than comparative U.S. models has contributed the most to this turnaround.

33. Alex Taylor III, "How Buick is Bouncing Back," *Fortune*, May 6, 1991, pp. 83–88.
34. Greg Bowens, "A Couple of Hunks on the Road," *Business Week*, May 10, 1993, p. 88.
35. Taylor, "Why U.S. Carmakers?"
36. Taylor, "U.S. Cars Come Back."

DIVERSIFICATION AT GM

During the 1980s, in an attempt to help it reduce costs and improve quality and customer responsiveness, GM began a program of diversification and acquisition. To improve the distinctive competencies of its core automotive business, GM made two large acquisitions: Electronic Data Systems (EDS) and the Hughes Aircraft Corporation.

Electronic Data Systems (EDS)

In 1984 GM was the largest user of computers in the world. Each of its divisions used different computer systems or programs, however, so that the corporation lacked an integrated computer network, making it difficult to communicate and share information between functions and divisions. Moreover, GM realized that many of the problems it had experienced with its advanced factories, and particularly with implementing robotically controlled manufacturing, were due to its lack of programming ability in computer-aided manufacturing (CAM). In order to develop competencies in CAM that would allow it to operate its new manufacturing systems effectively, in 1984 GM acquired EDS for $2.5 billion from Ross Perot. GM's goal was that EDS would program its manufacturing operations and integrate its computers into one network.

As it turned out, however, EDS had little experience in CAM; its strengths were in data processing.[37] EDS helps customers develop and customize computer hardware and software systems to match their needs, an activity called systems integration in which EDS is the leader. EDS also outsources its services, which entails running a client company's computer operations in return for a fee.[38] In 1989, for example, EDS received a 10-year, $1 billion contract to manage the computer and telecommunications facilities of Enron, a large natural gas company.[39] Thus, while EDS was able to help GM integrate its incompatible system of computers and automated machines, it could not help it to improve its CAM skills.[40]

Many analysts wondered why GM bought EDS, rather than simply buying its skills like other client companies had. They thought the money could have been spent better in developing GM's core skills in auto manufacturing. Fortuitous for GM, however, EDS was a rising star that has achieved record earnings consecutively from 1986 to 1993 and has proved to be a very valuable investment for the company. In 1993 GM announced that it would use EDS's profits to fund its massively underfunded corporate pension plan. EDS, however, has created few economies of scope for GM's core auto business.[41]

Hughes Aircraft

In 1985 GM acquired the Hughes Aircraft Corporation, a large defense contractor, for $5.2 billion. GM-Hughes operates in four business segments: 32 percent automotive, 18 percent telecommunications, 44 percent defense, and 6 percent commercial. GM's announced intention in buying Hughes was to create

37. Thomas Moore and Ross Perot, "Make-or-Break Time for General Motors; 'How I Would Turn Around GM.'" *Business Week*, February 15, 1988, pp. 32–50.
38. Wendy Zellner, "H. Ross Who? EDS Is Doing Just Fine on Its Own," *Business Week*, December 23, 1991, pp. 89–93.
39. Kevin Kelly, "EDS: How Sweet It Is to Have a Sugar Daddy," *Business Week*, September 18, 1989, pp. 110–111.
40. Brian O'Reilly, "EDS after Perot: How Tough Is It?" *Fortune*, October 24, 1988, pp. 72–76.
41. Taylor, "Can GM Remodel Itself?"

synergies with its car business by using Hughes's radar and satellite technology to develop advanced electronic systems, such as a guidance system, for future cars.[42] Once again, however, analysts wondered why GM would spend so much money on such a risky venture, one in which the returns were far into the future. As it happened, GM bought Hughes just as Hughes was facing the combined problems of production difficulties, high costs, reduced Pentagon spending, and federal investigations. For example, Hughes paid $200 million in penalties on a troubled Hughes program to connect U.S. Navy radar operations by satellite.

Progress has been slow in implementing aerospace technologies into GM automobiles, leaving Hughes Aircraft overly dependent on the Pentagon for business. By 1991, with the huge reductions in defense expenditures that occurred with the end of the Cold War, some analysts valued Hughes at only $3 billion. It remains to be seen what kind of return GM will receive for its investment in the future, but clearly it will have little return for its core auto business.

RESTRUCTURING

Throughout the 1980s General Motors was plagued by losses, declining market share, and poor management.[43] GM's top management was very slow to change company strategy. Roger Smith, CEO from 1981 to 1990, would not give GM's board of directors important financial data until the day before a meeting and was intolerant of criticism. Of 15 board members, three owed their positions to Smith, four had little or no business experience, two were retired businessmen, and one ran GM's bank. Outside directors were paid $45,000 and were given a new car quarterly for personal use.

In 1990 the board chose Robert Stempel, Roger Smith's hand-picked successor, to succeed Smith on his retirement. Stempel, who had been head of the BOC group, focused his activities on manufacturing and engineering and spearheaded GM's efforts to introduce new car models and to lower costs. Stempel was very slow to downsize the corporation or to reduce the size of both the white- and blue-collar work force, which analysts thought imperative to turn the company around. Even though GM's market share had declined rapidly (in 1978 GM had a 50 percent market share, by 1984 its share was 44.6 percent, and by 1992 market share was 35 percent), under both Smith and Stempel GM had not reduced the number of its manufacturing plants or downsized its work force in any significant way. Although GM announced in 1988 that it would close at least four of its 26 U.S. assembly plants and would cut 100,000 jobs, the downsizing process had been slow because Roger Smith insisted, unrealistically, that GM would reach a 50 percent market share again. Similarly, although it was generally recognized that GM was burdened by an overhead of 100,000 white-collar workers, resulting in excess management layers and redundant functions, top management could not bring itself to make drastic cuts.

In 1991 GM experienced record losses of over $4.5 billion and John Smale, a GM outside director and former CEO of Procter & Gamble, began looking for

42. Eric Schine, "GM and Hughes: Is the Marriage Fizzling?" *Business Week*, February 12, 1990, pp. 54–55.
43. "The Board Revolt: Business as Usual Won't Cut It Anymore at a Humbled GM," *Business Week*, April 20, 1992, pp. 31–36.

ways to stop the bleeding.[44] Prompted by Smale, in April 1992 the board finally took action. Robert Stempel was removed from the position as chairman of the GM board's executive committee and was replaced by Smale. Stempel remained CEO and a board member. Lloyd Reuss, Stempel's righthand man, was demoted from president to vice president of new car development and removed from the board. Jack Smith, former head of GM's successful European operations took over the president's position. Now the pace of change quickened.

At the end of 1991 GM announced that it would lay off 60,000 workers and close six more U.S. assembly plants by 1995 on top of the four assembly plant closings announced in February 1991. Four engine factories and 11 parts plants were to be closed. About 54,000 of GM's 304,000 blue-collar workers would be cut through attrition, early retirement, and layoffs. A total of 26,000 white-collar workers would also be cut, and the corporate staff was to be reduced from 13,500 people to around 2,300 people.[45]

For Stempel, these changes came too late, and under pressure from GM's board he resigned in October 1992. The board felt that Stempel was too hesitant to cut workers.[46] In November 1992 the board conferred major positions on younger GM executives, defying the tradition of top executives being in their mid-50s and 60s. Jack Smith, 54, was promoted to CEO; he is the youngest GM CEO since Alfred Sloan. Richard Wagoner, Jr., 39, became CFO and an executive vice president. Louis Hughes, 43, was to oversee international operations, and General Counsel Harry Pearce, 50, was given the extra duties of executive vice president and chairman of GM's Hughes Electronic Unit. John Smale remained as chairman to oversee this new management team, which the board believes has the expertise to turn around the company and bring it back to profitability. Smith quickly announced that he would cut 8,000 more white-collar workers by 1993 by offering attractive severance packages.

THE FUTURE

GM has learned many lessons as a result of its experience in the past 10 years. First, GM has learned the need to drop unsuccessful products and to trim its product line in order to cut costs. In 1985 GM had 85 car models, compared to 65 by the end of 1992. GM plans to introduce 22 new cars and trucks from 1990 to 1995 while phasing out older models.[47] Moreover, while GM used 14 platforms in 1993 to build its cars, it plans to produce all its new range of cars using only six basic platforms by the end of the 1990s: small, medium, and large front-wheel drives, Saturn, Corvette, and rear-wheel drives.[48]

Second, GM has learned the need to standardize components across models and to reduce the number of parts needed to produce a car. For example, GM engineers are working to reduce the number of parts used to make a car's basic metal frame by one-third.

44. Alex Taylor III, "What's Ahead for GM's New Team," *Fortune*, November 30, 1992, pp. 58–61.
45. GM 1992 Annual Report, pp. 1–2.
46. Kathleen Kerwin et al., "Crisis at GM," *Business Week*, November 9, 1992, pp. 84–86.
47. Treece, "War, Recession, Gas Hikes."
48. Alex Taylor III, "GM's Leaders Go on the Record," *Fortune*, March 9, 1992, pp. 50–60.

Third, GM has learned the need to streamline its operations and to decentralize decision making and integrate its design and manufacturing activities. Starting in 1990, GM consolidated its nine engine groups into five and brought together its divisional engineering and manufacturing units to eliminate redundancy. In 1992 five technical staffs at the GM Technical Center were combined into three. Restructuring has helped GM to be more flexible at decision making, to use resources more effectively, to increase management accountability, and to serve the customer better.[49]

Fourth, GM has learned the importance of managing its relationships with suppliers. GM currently buys 57 percent of its parts from its own divisions which have higher costs than outside suppliers.[50] Theoretically, car divisions are free to outsource, but in practice they are locked into GM's "allied plant" suppliers such as Central Foundry for casting and Delco for brakes.[51] GM has stated that its in-house parts operations will no longer be protected from efficient outside suppliers. GM has prodded suppliers to reduce costs by 20 percent; to help suppliers reduce costs, following the lead of Toyota, GM has implemented a "purchased input concept optimization with suppliers" (PICOS) strategy, where teams of GM engineers visit supplier plants and work with suppliers to reduce costs. The average productivity gain for 40 plants is 50 percent, floor space needs have been reduced 46 percent, and inventories have been cut 48 percent. GM also has been giving one supplier's plans to other suppliers in an attempt to get lower prices.[52] Plan sharing coupled with demands for suppliers to rebid on contracts that they had already won for 1993 has angered many suppliers, who insist that GM will destroy its partnership with suppliers in the long run if they buy parts primarily on the basis of price.[53] Nevertheless, GM is aggressively pursuing opportunities to reduce the cost of its inputs and has plans under way to spin off many of its supply companies and to let them sell to other car manufacturers to encourage increased efficiency and customer responsiveness.

GM's current strategy centers on the need to restore profitability to its core North American operations, a strategy that involves aggressive marketing, redesigned products, a more decentralized management style, and a profit rather than a market share goal.[54] CEO Jack Smith has defined GM's future objectives as to become profitable, satisfy consumers with better products, and to grow the business in future years. Smith has outlined five key strategies to regain profitability:

1. Focus resources on core products, cars and trucks. GM hopes to do well with the 1993 new cars such as the Cadillac Fleetwood, Chevy Camaro, Geo Prizm, and Pontiac Firebird and to build on cars introduced within the last

49. GM 1992 Annual Report, pp. 1–2.
50. David Woodruff and Zachary Schiller, "Smart Step for a Wobbly Giant," *Business Week*, December 7, 1992, p. 38.
51. Hampton and Norman, "General Motors: What Went Wrong."
52. James Treece, "The Lessons GM Could Learn for Its Supplier Shakeup," *Business Week*, August 31, 1992, p. 29.
53. Zachary Schiller, "GM Tightens the Screws—Only the Fittest of Its Suppliers Will Survive," *Business Week*, June 22, 1992, pp. 30–31.
54. Taylor, "GM's Leaders Go on the Record."

two years such as the Pontiac Grand Am, Buick Skylark, and Oldsmobile Achieva. Each car and truck division including Saturn and GMC Truck will have a separate marketing strategy.

2. Realign the organizational structure to support core products and meet cost and quality goals. The Cadillac Motor Car Division merged with Flint Automotive and has been given increased autonomy. Employees are also being transferred to work in creativity teams, which are self-managed teams responsible for speeding product development and for improving the efficiency of manufacturing activities.
3. Aggressively pursue cost and quality improvements. A great deal of costs are being cut in parts operations.
4. Implement common systems and processes and use the best industry practices throughout North American Operations. GM has created a centralized Vehicle Launch Center. Engineers from the car and truck divisions will work with engineers from the Engineering Center and Manufacturing in product development teams in an effort to introduce one vehicle program every 90 days.
5. Balance the needs of employees and unions with the needs of the company.[55]

Under its new top management team, GM reduced losses by $5.9 billion in 1991 and 1992 primarily because of increasing domestic sales and the rising value of the yen; GM is projected to earn a profit in 1994. The question concerns how GM can develop a strategy and structure that will support its efforts to lower costs and increase quality and that will provide it with a sustainable competitive advantage in its battle with Chrysler, Ford, and Japanese manufacturers in the years ahead. How small a company will GM become, and what will be the size of its market share in the years to come?

55. GM 1992 Annual Report, pp. 4–8.

Exhibit 1 General Motors Selected Financial Data

(Dollars in millions except per-share amounts)	1992	1991	1990	1989	1988	1987
Net sales and revenues	$132,429.4	$123,056.0	$124,705.1	$126,931.9	$123,641.6	$114,870.4
Net income (loss)	($23,498.3)	($4,452.8)	($1,985.7)	$4,224.3	$4,856.3	$3,550.9
Earnings (Loss) attributable to $1^2/_3$ par value common stock	($23,940.7)	($4,851.4)	($2,378.3)	$3,831.0	$4,413.1	$3,178.9
Cash dividends	945.4	983.4	1,804.7	1,813.2	1,540.5	1,579.6
Net income retained (loss accumulated) in the year	($24,886.1)	($5,834.8)	($4,183.0)	$2,017.8	$2,872.6	$1,599.3
Earnings (Loss) per share attributable to $1^2/_3$ par value common stock	($38.28)	($7.97)	($4.09)	$6.33	$7.17	$5.03
Cash dividends per share	1.40	1.60	3.00	3.00	2.50	2.50
Net income retained (loss accumulated) per share in the year	($39.68)	($9.57)	($7.09)	$3.33	$4.67	$2.53
Earnings attributable to Class E common stock	$278.4	$223.6	$194.4	$171.0	$160.3	$139.1
Cash dividends	76.1	62.5	52.4	45.6	34.8	27.4
Net income retained in the year	$202.3	$161.1	$142.0	$125.4	$125.5	$111.7
Earnings per share attributable to Class E common stock	$1.33	$1.14	$1.04	$0.90	$0.79	$0.66
Cash dividends per share	0.36	0.32	0.28	0.24	0.17	0.13
Net income per share retained in the year	$0.97	$0.82	$0.76	$0.66	$0.62	$0.53
Earnings (Loss) attributable to Class H common stock	($142.3)	$104.6	$160.0	$188.1	$256.9	$219.2
Cash dividends	53.3	54.3	63.4	71.1	56.2	47.2
Net income retained (loss accumulated) in the year	($195.6)	50.3	$96.6	$117.0	$200.7	$172.0
Earnings (Loss) per share attributable to Class H common stock	($2.29)	$1.39	$1.82	$1.94	$2.01	$1.67
Cash dividends per share	0.72	0.72	0.72	0.72	0.44	0.36
Net income retained (loss accumulated) per share in the year	($3.01)	$0.67	$1.10	$1.22	$1.57	$1.31
Average number of shares of common stocks outstanding (in millions)						
$1^2/_3$ par value	670.5	614.6	601.5	604.3	615.7	631.5
Class E	209.1	195.3	187.1	189.1	203.5	210.4
Class H	75.3	73.7	88.1	95.7	127.9	130.8
Cash dividends on capital stocks as a percent of net income	N/A	N/A	N/A	46.5%	34.1%	47.0%
Expenditures for real estate, plants, and equipment	$4,336.7	$4,255.1	$4,249.9	$4,416.1	$3,405.4	$4,800.5
Expenditures for special tools	$2,252.9	$2,956.8	$3,155.5	$2,927.8	$2,194.4	$2,346.2
Cash and marketable securities	$15,275.2	$10,192.4	$7,821.4	$10,213.3	$10,181.4	$7,819.3
Working capital (with GMAC on an equity basis)	$10,938.6	$10,807.1	$10,915.1	$17,404.8	$17,728.9	$13,049.7
Total assets	$191,012.8	$184,325.5	$180,236.5	$173,297.1	$164,063.1	$162,343.2
Long-term debt and capitalized leases (with GMAC on an equity basis)	$7,055.4	$6,699.1	$4,923.8	$4,565.7	$4,535.7	$4,313.4

Exhibit 2 General Motors Statement of Consolidated Cash Flows

	Years Ended December 31,		
(Dollars in millions)	1992	1991	1990
Cash Flows from Operating Activities			
Loss before cumulative effect of accounting changes	($2,620.6)	($4,992.0)	($1,985.7)
Adjustments to reconcile loss before cumulative effect of accounting changes to net cash provided by operating activities			
Depreciation of real estate, plants, and equipment	3,646.3	3,719.8	3,662.9
Depreciation of equipment on operating leases	2,498.5	1,965.1	1,441.2
Amortization of special tools	2,504.0	1,819.5	1,805.8
Amortization of intangible assets	310.2	411.4	451.7
Amortization of discount and issuance costs on debt issues	118.1	194.4	291.7
Provision for financing losses	144.5	947.1	814.5
Special provision for scheduled plant closings and other restructurings	1,237.0	2,820.8	2,848.0
Provision for inventory allowances	28.5	40.1	92.2
Pension expense, net of cash contributions	273.4	1,167.7	364.9
Gain on the sale of Daewoo Motor Co.	(162.8)	—	—
Net gain on sale of GM New York building	—	(610.3)	—
Write-down of investment in National Car Rental System Inc.	813.2	—	—
Provision for ongoing postretirement benefits other than pensions, net of cash payments	2,198.8	—	—
Change in other investments, miscellaneous assets, deferred credits, etc.	(298.7)	(1,034.8)	246.5
Proceeds from sale of trade receivables	—	349.3	—
Change in other operating assets and liabilities			
Accounts receivable	34.7	(1,067.6)	(285.2)
Inventories	886.4	(310.4)	(1,431.8)
Prepaid expenses and other deferred charges	(399.3)	129.0	(516.5)
Deferred taxes and income taxes payable	(1,956.6)	(3,874.9)	(1,711.8)
Other liabilities	1,560.8	3,390.4	1,701.9
Other	(469.8)	1,192.4	(1,008.7)
Net Cash Provided by Operating Activities	10,346.6	6,257.0	6,781.6
Cash Flows from Investing Activities			
Investment in companies, net of cash acquired	(134.7)	(779.1)	(906.9)
Expenditures for real estate, plants, and equipment	(4,336.7)	(4,255.1)	(4,249.9)
Expenditures for special tools	(2,252.9)	(2,956.8)	(3,155.5)
Proceeds from disposals of real estate, plants, and equipment	229.0	517.9	415.0
Proceeds from sale of GM New York building	—	254.9	—
Proceeds from sale and leaseback of capital assets	654.9	954.1	—
Proceeds from the sale of Daewoo Motor Co.	162.8	—	—
Change in other investing assets			
Investment in other marketable securities—acquisitions	(16,993.3)	(14,639.0)	(14,869.2)
Investment in other marketable securities—liquidations	16,634.5	14,995.6	15,241.2
Short-term liquid investments—GMAC	(1,216.0)	(2,134.2)	83.0

continued on page C284

Exhibit 2 General Motors Statement of Consolidated Cash Flows (continued)

	Years Ended December 31,		
(Dollars in millions)	1992	1991	1990
Change in other investing assets (continued)			
Finance receivables—acquisitions	(120,829.8)	(108,268.4)	(104,609.8)
Finance receivables—liquidations (net)	119,558.2	112,643.1	102,429.0
Finance receivables—other	2,749.8	493.7	2,548.6
Proceeds from sales of finance receivables	11,201.8	2,926.9	1,056.1
Notes receivable	2.0	(48.8)	1.3
Operating leases—net	(4,183.8)	(4,314.1)	(2,337.3)
Net Cash Provided by (Used in) Investing Activities	1,245.8	(4,609.3)	(8,354.4)
Cash Flows from Financing Activities			
Net decrease in short-term loans payable	(12,072.2)	(4,670.7)	(2,133.7)
Increase in long-term debt	18,884.8	15,830.4	14,406.5
Decrease in long-term debt	(18,588.0)	(12,665.1)	(10,355.8)
Redemption of Series H preference stocks	(243.9)	(225.1)	(207.2)
Redemption of Howard Hughes Medical Institute put options	(300.0)	(600.0)	—
Repurchases of common stocks	(7.2)	(10.4)	(362.3)
Proceeds from issuing common and preference stocks	5,555.7	2,506.6	375.7
Cash dividends paid to stockholders	(1,376.8)	(1,162.3)	(1,956.5)
Net Cash Used in Financing Activities	(8,147.6)	(996.6)	(233.3)
Effect of Exchange Rate Changes on Cash and Cash Equivalents	63.2	(57.7)	(130.8)
Net increase (decrease) in cash and cash equivalents	3,508.0	593.4	(1,936.9)
Cash and cash equivalents at beginning of the year	4,281.9	3,688.5	5,625.4
Cash and cash equivalents at end of the year	$7,789.9	$4,281.9	$3,688.5

Exhibit 3 General Motors Consolidated Balance Sheet

(Dollars in millions except per-share amounts)	December 31, 1992	1991
Assets		
Cash and cash equivalents	$7,789.9	$4,281.9
Other marketable securities	7,485.3	5,910.5
Total cash and marketable securities (Note 12)	15,275.2	10,192.4
Finance receivables—net (Note 13)	67,032.7	81,373.8
Accounts and notes receivable (less allowances)	6,476.7	6,498.5
Inventories (less allowances) (Note 1)	9,343.6	10,066.0
Contracts in process (less advances and progress payments of $4,026.4 and $2,500.9) (Note 1)	2,456.4	2,283.1
Net equipment on operating leases (less accumulated depreciation of $3,987.6 and $3,439.5)	11,427.1	8,653.0
Deferred income taxes (Note 10)	18,394.6	4,265.2
Prepaid expenses and other deferred charges	5,686.2	5,027.7
Other investments and miscellaneous assets (less allowances)	10,055.1	9,425.3
Property (Note 1)		
Real estate, plants, and equipment—at cost (Note 15)	68,833.6	67,772.4
Less accumulated depreciation (Note 15)	41,462.5	39,832.6
Net real estate, plants, and equipment	27,371.1	27,939.8
Special tools—at cost (less amortization)	7,979.1	8,419.5
Total property	35,350.2	36,359.3
Intangible assets—at cost (less amortization) (Notes 1 and 6)	9,515.0	10,181.2
Total Assets	$191,012.8	$184,325.5
Liabilities and Stockholders' Equity		
Liabilities		
Accounts payable (principally trade)	$9,678.4	$10,061.3
Notes and loans payable (Note 16)	82,592.3	94,022.1
United States, foreign, and other income taxes—deferred and payable (Note 10)	3,140.1	4,491.2
Postretirement benefits other than pensions (Note 7)	35,550.7	—
Other liabilities (Note 17)	51,506.1	45,602.2
Deferred credits (including investment tax credits—$509.2 and $644.5)	1,554.6	1,531.5
Total Liabilities	184,022.2	155,708.3
Stocks Subject to Repurchase (Notes 1 and 18)	765.0	1,289.6
Stockholders' Equity (Notes 3, 4, 5, and 18)		
Preferred stocks ($5.00 series, $153.0; $3.75 series, $81.4)	234.4	234.4
Preference stocks (E $0.10 series, $0.3 in 1992 and $1.0 in 1991; Series A Conversion, $1.8, and Series B 9⅛% Depositary Shares, $1.1, in 1992 and 1991; and Series C Depositary Shares, $0.3, Series D 7.92% Depositary Shares, $0.4, and Series G 9.12% Depositary Shares, $0.6, in 1992)	4.5	3.9

Exhibit 3 General Motors Consolidated Balance Sheet (continued)

(Dollars in millions except per-share amounts)	December 31, 1992	1991
Common stocks		
$1-2/3 par value (issued, 706,831,567 and 620,967,021 shares)	1,178.1	1,034.9
Class E (issued, 242,168,653 and 103,833,719 shares)	24.2	10.4
Class H (issued, 70,240,927 and 37,691,027 shares)	7.0	3.8
Capital surplus (principally additional paid-in capital)	10,971.2	4,710.4
Net income retained for use in the business (accumulated deficit)	(3,354.2)	(21,525.2)
Subtotal	9,065.2	27,523.0
Minimum pension liability adjustment (Note 6)	(2,925.3)	(936.8)
Accumulated foreign currency translation adjustments and net unrealized gains (losses) on marketable equity securities	85.7	741.4
Total Stockholders' Equity	6,225.6	27,327.6
Total Liabilities and Stockholders' Equity	$191,012.8	$184,325.5

Exhibit 4 General Motors Consolidated Financial Statements, Statement of Consolidated Income

(Dollars in millions except per-share amounts)	Year Ended December 31, 1992	1991	1990
Net Sales and Revenues (Note 1)			
Manufactured products	$113,323.9	$105,025.9	$107,477.0
Financial services	10,402.1	11,144.2	11,785.0
Computer systems services	4,806.7	3,666.3	2,787.5
Other income (Note 2)	3,896.7	3,219.6	2,655.6
Total Net Sales and Revenues	132,429.4	123,056.0	124,705.1
Costs and Expenses			
Cost of sales and other operating charges, exclusive of items listed below	105,063.9	97,550.7	96,155.7
Selling, general, and administrative expenses	11,621.8	10,817.4	10,030.9
Interest expense (Note 16)	7,305.4	8,296.6	8,771.7
Depreciation of real estate, plants, and equipment (Note 1)	6,144.8	5,684.9	5,104.1
Amortization of special tools (Note 1)	2,504.0	1,819.5	1,805.8
Amortization of intangible assets (Note 1)	310.2	411.4	451.7
Other deductions (Note 2)	1,575.4	1,547.0	1,288.3
Special provision for scheduled plant closings and other restructurings (Note 8)	1,237.0	2,820.8	3,314.0
Total Costs and Expenses	135,762.5	128,948.3	126,922.2

Exhibit 4 General Motors Consolidated Financial Statements, Statement of Consolidated Income (continued)

(Dollars in millions except per-share amounts)	Year Ended December 31, 1992	1991	1990
Loss before Income Taxes	(3,333.1)	(5,892.3)	(2,217.1)
United States, foreign, and other income tax credit (Note 10)	(712.5)	(900.3)	(231.4)
Loss before cumulative effect of accounting changes	(2,620.6)	(4,992.0)	(1,985.7)
Cumulative effect of accounting changes (Note 1)	(20,877.7)	539.2	—
Net Loss	(23,498.3)	(4,452.8)	(1,985.7)
Dividends and accumulation of redemption value on preferred and preference stocks (Note 18)	306.3	70.4	38.2
Loss on Common Stocks	($23,804.6)	($4,523.2)	($2,203.9)
Earnings (Loss) Attributable to Common Stocks			
$1⅔ par value before cumulative effect of accounting changes	($3,220.6)	($5,384.6)	($2,378.3)
Cumulative effect of accounting changes	(20,720.1)	533.2	—
Net loss attributable to $1⅔ par value	($23,940.7)	($4,851.4)	($2,378.3)
Class E before cumulative effect of accounting change	$278.4	$229.7	$194.4
Cumulative effect of accounting change	—	(6.1)	—
Net earnings attributable to Class E	$278.4	$223.6	$194.4
Class H before cumulative effect of accounting changes	$15.3	$92.5	$160.0
Cumulative effect of accounting changes	(157.6)	12.1	—
Net earnings (loss) attributable to Class H	($142.3)	$104.6	$160.0
Average number of shares of common stocks outstanding (in millions)			
$1⅔ par value	670.5	614.6	601.5
Class E	209.1	195.3	187.1
Class H	75.3	73.7	88.1
Earnings (Loss) Per Share Attributable to Common Stocks (Note 11)			
$1⅔ par value before cumulative effect of accounting changes	($4.85)	($8.85)	($4.09)
Cumulative effect of accounting changes	(33.43)	0.88	—
Net loss attributable to $1⅔ par value	($38.28	($7.97)	($4.09)
Class E before cumulative effect of accounting change	$1.33	$1.17	$1.04
Cumulative effect of accounting change	—	(0.03)	—
Net earnings attributable to Class E	$1.33	$1.14	$1.04
Class H before cumulative effect of accounting changes	($0.11)	$1.26	$1.82
Cumulative effect of accounting changes	(2.18)	0.13	—
Net earnings (loss) attributable to Class H	($2.29)	$1.39	$1.82

CASE

17

The Boeing Corporation: Commercial Aircraft Operations

INTRODUCTION

In 1990 the Boeing Co.'s commercial aircraft operations were flying high. The company was America's largest exporter. Boeing accounted for 54 percent of all new commercial aircraft orders in 1990. It had a record order book, with a backlog of 1,563 aircraft scheduled for delivery between 1990 and 2000. Valued at $100 billion, this backlog was more than enough to keep the company's factories humming until the end of the century. The company earned a net profit of $1.3 billion on revenues of $27.6 billion, and both of these figures were expected to grow over the next two years. And Boeing's factories were operating at full capacity, churning out 35 commercial jet aircraft a month.

At the same time, however, there were concerns. Boeing was facing increasing competition from Airbus Industrie. Airbus is a consortium of four European aircraft manufacturers—one British, one French, one German, and one Spanish. Founded in 1970, Airbus was initially regarded as being a marginal competitor that was unlikely to challenge Boeing's dominance. However, in recent years Airbus has confounded its critics, emerging as the world's second largest aircraft manufacturer. By 1990 Airbus accounted for 24 percent of all new orders for commercial aircraft, up from 14 percent in 1981. To make matters worse, there were clear signs that the world airline market was entering one of its periodic downturns. After making a combined profit of nearly $3 billion in 1989, the world's airlines reported a combined loss of $3 billion in 1990. A combination of weak demand and excess carrying capacity had triggered a price war in the airline industry. While airline travelers benefited, the bottom line of the airlines suffered. Boeing knew that the inevitable result would be the cancellation or postponement of aircraft orders, and a shrinking of its order backlog.

By late 1993 these developments had led to a deterioration in Boeing's position. The price war in the airline industry had continued unabated throughout the early 1990s, resulting in a combined loss among U.S.-based carriers of $7.1 billion between 1990 and 1992, more than the industry had made in its entire previous fifty-year history. A similar scenario was playing itself out in the international airline industry. In 1992, of the world's ten largest airline companies, only British Airways made a profit. As a major supplier to the airline industry, Boeing saw its order book backlog shrink from 1,563 in 1990 to 1,210 aircraft by 1992 as several major carriers canceled orders. Moreover, many of the orders that remained on Boeing's books no longer looked as secure as they once did. Several airlines transformed firm orders into options, while others pushed back delivery dates by several years. In response, Boeing was forced to cut back on

This case was prepared by Charles W. L. Hill, University of Washington. This case was prepared as a basis for class discussion rather than to illustrate either effective or ineffective handling of administrative situations.

both employment and its production schedule. Employment was down from its 1991 peak of 132,695 to 116,000 by the end of 1993. Production had been cut from its 1992 peak of 40 aircraft per month to 29 aircraft per month, and was projected to fall to 21 aircraft per month by mid 1994. This was reflected in a decline in Boeing's deliveries of aircraft, down from 446 aircraft in 1992 to 350 in 1993, and a probable 258 in 1994.

Nor had the threat from Airbus diminished. By 1992 Airbus had increased its share of the commercial aircraft market, measured by total order backlog, to 33 percent, largely at the expense of McDonnell Douglas Corporation. While Boeing's market share, at 56 percent of the total order backlog, looked healthy, there was no doubt that the rise of Airbus was of concern to Boeing, particularly because Airbus's operations were to some extent subsidized by the governments of Germany, France, Great Britain, and Spain. In fact, the allegation that Airbus benefited from government subsidies was at the center of a trade dispute between the United States and the European Community. Although a provisional deal between the United States and the EC was reached in mid 1992, under which the four European governments involved in the Airbus consortium agreed to phase out future subsidies, by late 1993 the trade dispute flared up again as the United States and the EC tried to reach an agreement on a wider global trade agreement, the General Agreement on Tariffs and Trade (GATT).

THE COMPETITIVE ENVIRONMENT

As of 1993 there were only three major producers in the commercial jet aircraft industry (see Exhibit 1). Boeing dominated, followed by Airbus, with McDonnell Douglas coming in a distant third. Both Boeing and Airbus produce a family of commercial aircraft (see Exhibit 2) while McDonnell Douglas currently offers just three planes: the MD-80, the MD-90 (a stretched version of the MD-80) and the MD-11. Both Boeing and Airbus are profitable; in 1992 Boeing made profits of $1.6 billion on sales of $30.1 billion. Although Airbus does not publish accounts, estimates suggest that in 1991 it made $250 million on sales of $8.5 billion. McDonnell Douglas is currently losing money on its commercial aircraft operations. McDonnell Douglas laid off 21,000 employees between 1990 and 1992 and has plans to cut 5,000 more in 1993. The company also cut back its projections of future production for the MD-80, MD-90 and the MD-11. Moreover, without outside financing it is unlikely that McDonnell Douglas will be able to go ahead and build the MD-12—its planned competitor for Boeing's 747. The company's future in the industry is clearly in jeopardy.

Exhibit 1
Order Backlog by Manufacturer as of December 1993

	Backlog	Percent	Value (in billions)	Percent
Boeing	1,259	54.5	$87.5	56.9
Airbus	701	30.4	50.8	33.0
McDonnell Douglas	217	9.4	12.8	8.3
Others	127	4.6	2.9	1.8
Total	2,304	100	154	100

Exhibit 2
Competing Product Lines

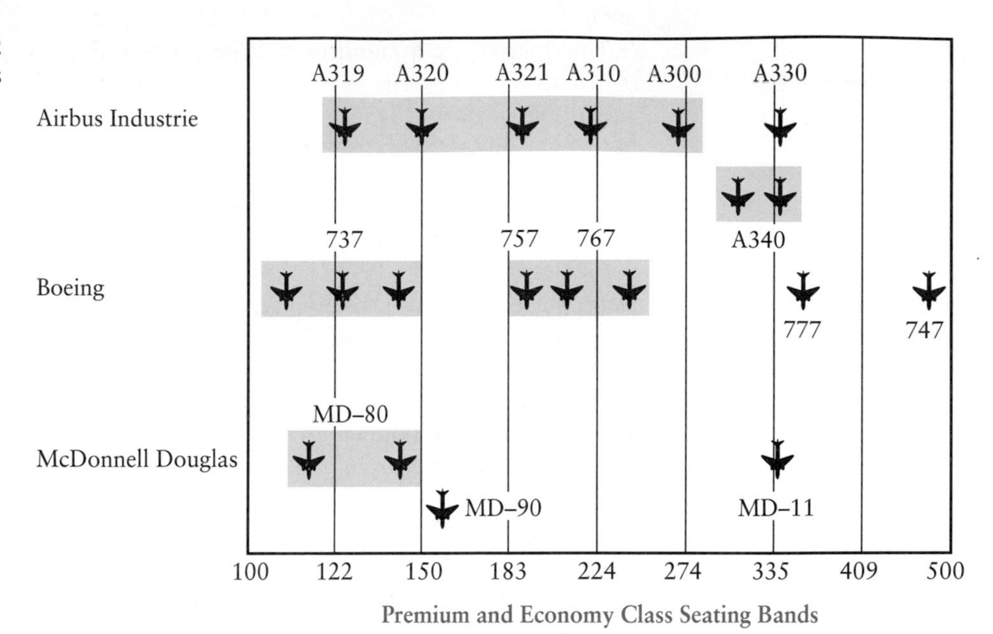

Airbus has recently made some notable inroads into Boeing's customer base. Almost 45 percent of all commercial aircraft are sold to U.S. carriers and Boeing has long had the inside track with most of them. In July of 1992, however, United Airlines, one of Boeing's most loyal customers, announced that it had signed a $3-billion deal to lease 50 A320s from Airbus and to take options on 50 more. In making this decision, United cited the range, speed, comfort, technology, and fuel efficiency of the A320. In addition, the deal guaranteed that Airbus would train United's pilots to fly the A320 and would allow United to get out of the lease on just eleven months' notice, reducing United's financial liability.

The Economics of Aircraft Production

The economics of production in the world commercial jet aircraft industry are characterized by a number of stylized facts. First, the capital costs of developing a new airliner are enormous. For example, McDonnell Douglas spent $1.5 billion on development and tooling for its MD-11 wide-bodied jetliner, introduced in the late 1980s, and it has calculated that the development costs for the proposed MD-12 airliner, which will compete with Boeing's 747, will cost about $5 billion. Similarly, Boeing has estimated that the company will spend $5 billion to develop its new 400-seat long-haul jet, the 777.

Second, given such enormous development costs, in order to break even a company has to capture a significant share of world demand. In the case of the MD-11, for example, McDonnell Douglas will have to sell more than 200 aircraft to break even, a figure that represents 13 percent of predicted industry sales for that aircraft category between 1990 and 2000. For an aircraft such as the MD-12 or Boeing's 777, it may take from 400 to 500 units to break even. Given this, it can take ten to fourteen years of production before an aircraft reaches its break-even point—and this on top of the five to six years of negative cash flows that occur during development.

Third, there is a significant experience curve in aircraft production. Due to learning effects, on average unit costs fall by about 20 percent every time accumulated output is doubled. One implication of this is that companies that fail to get down the experience curve face a significant unit-cost disadvantage. Companies that achieve only half of the market share required to break even will face a 20 percent unit-cost disadvantage.

Demand Conditions and Trends

Demand for aircraft is highly volatile, a fact that makes long-run planning difficult and that raises the risks involved in aircraft production. The commercial airline business is prone to boom and bust cycles. During the early 1990s the world's commercial airline industry was deep in a price war. Many major airlines were experiencing financial trouble. Pan Am, Continental, Eastern, Braniff and TWA were all either in bankruptcy or had recently folded. Many other airlines were losing money. The reasons included a worldwide recession—which had slowed down the growth in demand for air travel—and substantial excess carrying capacity—a result of the rapid additions to carrying capacity made by most major airlines during the 1980s. These additions to capacity were made on the basis of growth projections in airline travel that failed to materialize. Indeed, by 1993 close to 1,000 surplus jet aircraft, many of which had never flown a commercial flight, had been parked in the Arizona desert by U.S. airlines to await a pickup in demand.

The airlines' responses to this situation included canceling orders, slowing down their ordering of new aircraft, pushing back the delivery dates for aircraft already on firm order, and deciding not to convert into firm orders options that they had taken out on future aircraft deliveries. For example, in 1992 American Airlines canceled a number of options for new aircraft and extended the delivery dates of most planes it had on order. Taken together, American cut to only $3.3 billion what would have amounted to $15 billion in new aircraft over the 1993–96 period. Over the same period, United Airlines reduced its planned spending on aircraft from $6.6 billion to $3.2 billion. Worse still, in mid 1993 GPA Group, a huge aircraft leasing company, canceled orders for aircraft worth $7 billion. Thus, while both Boeing and Airbus entered the 1990s with record order books, the troubles in the airline business during the early 1990s cast a shadow over this once rosy picture. Indeed, in 1993 the number of cancellations exceeded the number of orders (see Exhibit 3).

On the positive side, the long-term outlook for demand is encouraging. In 1993 Boeing projected worldwide demand for 12,000 aircraft valued at $815 billion for the period between 1993 and 2010. Boeing projects that 5,500 commercial jet aircraft valued at $328 billion will be delivered by 2001. Airbus has similar expectations, projecting delivery of 11,600 new aircraft by the end of 2011. McDonnell Douglas is somewhat more optimistic, anticipating a market for 14,000 new planes over the next twenty years.

These forecasts are based upon several assumptions, one being that the global market for airline travel will double by 2005, and will expand more than two-and-a-half times by 2010. Much of the expansion is expected to be focused upon the Asian-Pacific region. Another assumption is that replacement demand will grow as a growing roster of older planes have to be taken out of service over the next twenty years. As of early 1993 the world's air fleets contained more than 2,100 planes that were over twenty years old. Most of these aircraft will prob-

Exhibit 3
Orders, Cancellations, and Deliveries

	1988	1989	1990	1991	1992	1993*
Orders	1,058	1,833	1,236	482	458	209
Canceled	9	36	58	143	138	262
Net Intake	1,049	1,797	1,178	339	320	–53
Deliveries	511	506	570	822	789	490
Changes	+538	+1,291	+608	–483	–469	–543

* First nine months of 1993.

ably be retired during the 1990s. Boeing expects 3,600 aircraft to be retired by 2010. A third assumption is that new telecommunications technologies and the development of alternative transport technologies will not impede air-travel growth. Contrary to the frequent assertion that technological advances such as videoconferencing will reduce the need for face-to-face contact—and hence air travel—Boeing maintains that modern technology will open up far-flung markets that otherwise would have been ignored, and that this will increase the demand for air travel.

In addition to a growth in overall demand during the next twenty years, aircraft manufacturers also foresee a gradual shift in demand towards larger aircraft. Reasons for this anticipated demand shift include more airline travel in the Asian-Pacific region (which typically involves longer flights than North American or European traffic), airport overcrowding, and a desire on the part of airlines to reduce costs. According to projections made by Boeing, single-aisle planes will account for 74 percent of deliveries during the 1990s, but will decrease to 60 percent by 2010. Boeing also predicts that the gain in market share will be largest among those planes with more than 350 seats. This category includes the Boeing 747 and 777, the Airbus A330 and A340, and the McDonnell Douglas MD-11. The share of total aircraft sales accounted for by this category is predicted to increase from 8 percent before 1993 to 24 percent in the first decade of the next century.

Pricing Pressures

For the entire history of the jet age, the cost of acquiring a new jet airliner has moved in one direction: up. There are now clear signs that this situation may be changing. In the 1970s and 1980s the price of acquiring a new jet airliner typically represented less than 40 percent of the cost of owning and operating the aircraft for, say, twenty years. Other expenses included fuel, maintenance, crew, pay, insurance, and airport gate fees. Today, the increased technology of jet aircraft has raised their price to such a level that purchase costs can account for as much as 80 percent of the total ownership cost over the lifetime of an aircraft. At this level, it is becoming increasingly difficult for cash-poor airlines to justify the purchase of new jet aircraft (see Exhibit 4 for pricing data).

In response, airlines are putting more pressure than ever before upon aircraft manufacturers to reduce their prices. Airline executives predict a reduction in commercial jet aircraft prices of 20 to 30 percent by the year 2000. A sign of things to come may be a December 1993 agreement between Boeing and Southwest Airlines Co. for the sale of 63 new Boeing 737-X jet airliners. Although this

Exhibit 4
1993 Estimated Prices

Aircraft	Number of Seats	Max. Range (in nautical miles)	Price Range (in millions)
Boeing 747	42–583	7,200	$140–165
Boeing 777	305–440	6,600	115–143
Boeing 767	218–290	6,165	80–88
Boeing 757	201	4,000	54–60
Boeing 737-300	108–146	2,500	34–40
Boeing 737-X	150	3,000	34–40
McDonnell Douglas MD-80	110–150	3,000	28
McDonnell Douglas MD-90	150	2,750	33
McDonnell Douglas MD-11	335	7,980	100
Airbus A320	150	3,000	47
Airbus A340	263–295	7,750	112–118

order represented a major shot in the arm for Boeing at a time when order cancellations and postponements have been running at a high level, the deal called for the 737-X to be priced at the same level as Boeing's existing 737-300 model—despite the fact that the 737-X will fly farther, faster, and more economically than the 737-300. In effect, Boeing gave Southwest Airlines a major discount on a next-generation product. Moreover, the small print of the deal specified that if market forces drive the price of the 737-X down below what Southwestern agreed to pay, Boeing will lower the price accordingly.

Trade Disputes

Both Boeing and McDonnell Douglas have argued that Airbus has an unfair competitive advantage due to the level of subsidy it receives from the governments of Great Britain, France, Germany, and Spain. They argue that the subsidies allow Airbus to set unrealistically low prices, to offer concessions and attractive financing terms to airlines, to write off development costs and to use state-owned airlines to obtain orders. In making such claims, Boeing and McDonnell Douglas have been supported by the U.S. government. According to a study by the Department of Commerce, Airbus received more than $13.5 billion in government subsidies between 1970 and 1990 ($25.9 billion if commercial interest rates are applied). Most of these subsidies took the form of loans at below-market interest rates and tax breaks. These subsidies were used to finance research and development, and to provide attractive financing terms for Airbus's customers. Thus for most customers Airbus was believed to have financed 80 percent of the cost of aircraft for a term of eight to ten years at an annual interest rate of approximately 7 percent. In comparison, the Export-Import Bank of the United States required a 20 percent down payment from Boeing and McDonnell Douglas customers, only financed 40 percent of the cost of an aircraft directly, and guaranteed the financing of the remaining 40 percent by private banks at an average interest rate of 8.4 to 8.5 percent for a period of ten years.

Airbus's response to these charges has been to point out that much of its success is not due to subsidies at all, but to a good product and a good strategy. Most observers do agree that Airbus's aircraft incorporate state-of-the-art tech-

nology, particularly in materials applications, systems for flight control and safety, and aerodynamics. Airbus also gained ground by initially emphasizing market segments not served by new aircraft, or not served at all. Thus Airbus took the initiative in targeting two segments of the market with wide-bodied, twin-engine aircraft, then in developing a next-generation aircraft for the 150-seat market, and most recently in going after the market below the 747 for a long thin airliner.

Airbus has also argued that both Boeing and McDonnell Douglas have for a long time benefited from U.S. government aid, and that the aid that it has received merely leveled the playing field. In the United States during World War I planes were built under government contract. The construction of mail planes was subsidized during the inter-war period. Almost all production was subsidized during World War II and continued at a high level after the war. The Boeing 707, for example, was a derivative of a military transport program that was subsidized by the U.S. government. Boeing's list of subsidized programs includes the B-17, B-29, B-47, B-52, and K-135, just to mention a few. Non-airline programs included the Minuteman missile, Apollo-Saturn, and space station programs.

More recently, a 1991 European Commission study tried to put a figure on the amount of subsidies currently received by the U.S. industry. The study contends that Boeing and McDonnell Douglas received between $18 billion and $22 billion in indirect government aid between 1976 and 1990. The report claimed that commercial aircraft operations benefited through Defense Department contracts by as much as $6.34 billion during the 1976 to 1990 period. In addition, the report claims that NASA has pumped at least $8 billion into commercial aircraft production over the same period, and that tax exemptions have been worth a further $1.7 billion to Boeing and $1.4 billion to McDonnell Douglas.

Boeing has rejected the claims made in the European Commission report. The company points out that the European report assumes that Boeing received direct grants from the U.S. government in the form of 5 percent being obtained for commercial work on top of every government military or space contract it receives. According to Boeing, this assumption is simply false. The company also claims that during the last ten years only 3 percent of Boeing's R&D spending has originated from Defense Department funding, and only 4 percent from NASA funding. Boeing also argues that the four companies in the Airbus consortium do twice as much military and space work as Boeing, and thus Airbus must receive a much larger indirect subsidy.

In mid 1992 the United States and Airbus reached an agreement that might have ended the long-standing dispute. The tentative agreement limits direct European subsidies to 33 percent of new development costs. Future subsidies must be paid back with interest. The agreement also limits indirect subsidies—such as military research that has applications to commercial aircraft—to 5 percent of development costs for commercial aircraft. Although Airbus officials now say that the controversy is over, Boeing officials say that they will be competing for years against subsidized products.

Although the July 1992 deal initially seemed to settle the long-standing trade dispute, the Clinton administration reopened the issue in mid 1993. According to U.S. trade representative Mickey Kantor, Airbus is still benefiting from government subsidies and the deal struck with the Bush administration needs to be reviewed. At the same time, Senator John Danforth introduced a bill in the U.S. Senate that could lead to the imposition of dumping duties on Airbus planes

(dumping is the practice of selling below the costs of production). Boeing, however, opposes Senator Danforth's bill, fearing that the European governments involved would match any U.S. measure with their own trade sanctions, and that the result would not be in Boeing's best interests. In explaining Boeing's position, observers note that between 1988 and 1992 Boeing sold 707 planes in Europe, compared to 296 for Airbus.

BOEING

The Early Years

The Boeing company was founded by William Edward Boeing, a Yale University engineering dropout who came to the Pacific Northwest in 1903 to make his fortune in the lumber industry. William Boeing's move into aircraft production started with a chance meeting at the University Club in Seattle with Conrad Westervelt, a young Navy lieutenant commander stationed in Seattle. The men became friends, and in 1915 both took their first airplane flight. Their interest in flying grew, and soon Boeing suggested to Westervelt that they could build a better aircraft than the rickety Curtiss seaplane they had both been practicing in. The result was Boeing's first plane, the Bluebill, a clumsy seaplane which Westervelt had designed.

Soon after, Westervelt was transferred to the East Coast, and his association with Boeing came to an end. Boeing tried to sell the Bluebill design to the Navy, but was quickly rebuffed. Undeterred, he hired a young MIT engineer, Tsu Wong, to improve upon the Bluebill's design. Shortly afterward, on July 15, 1916, Boeing incorporated his fledgling enterprise as the Pacific Aero Products Company (the name was soon changed to the Boeing Airplane Company). Boeing, whose lumber industry ventures had already made him a wealthy man, bankrolled what for years was to be a very marginal enterprise.

Wong's improved design of the Bluebill was designated the Model C. Boeing built five in hopes of persuading the Navy to purchase the plane. The Navy was initially lukewarm, but in 1917 the United States entered World War I, and the Navy suddenly needed more pilots and planes. In 1917 the Navy tested two Model Cs and then ordered 50 as trainers for a total price of $575,000—Boeing was in business. A contract to build 50 Curtiss flying boats under license soon followed, but then the war came to an end and orders dried up. For a time Boeing kept his business going by manufacturing furniture and speedboats. Then in 1925 the U.S. Post Office announced its interest in the development of a new mail plane. However, the Post Office insisted that the plane be powered by a heavy, slow, water-cooled Liberty engine. Boeing built a plane, the Model 40, that was powered by the Liberty. The Post Office purchased one but was unimpressed and ordered no more. Boeing then modified the Model 40, replacing the heavy Liberty engine with a revolutionary air-cooled Pratt & Whitney Wasp engine (which was lighter and more powerful than the Liberty) and installing two passenger seats in the fuselage; the Model 40A was born, Boeing's first commercial airplane.

Boeing's timing could not have been better. On February 2, 1925, Congress passed the Contract Air Mail Act, which turned over the job of flying the mail from the Post Office to private contractors who would bid for mail routes. With the new Model 40A plane, Boeing found that it could carry 1,200 pounds of

mail for $1.50 a pound and still make good money. The company used this rate to bid for the San Francisco–Chicago route. The closest competing bid was for $2.24 a pound, and Boeing was awarded the contract.

To operate the San Francisco–Chicago mail route, Boeing created a subsidiary company: Boeing Air Transport (BAT). BAT soon gained more mail routes, either by outbidding rivals for routes, or by acquiring companies that had mail routes. By 1928 BAT was carrying 30 percent of the nation's mail and passenger traffic, using the Boeing Model 40A plane. In the fall of 1928 Fred Rentschler, the president of Pratt & Whitney, suggested merging Boeing and BAT together with Pratt & Whitney to create a vertically integrated enterprise. William Boeing was quickly sold on the idea, and in early 1929 the companies were merged together under a new holding company, United Aircraft & Transport Corporation. In quick succession, the holding company then purchased three other aircraft companies, Stearman Aircraft of Wichita, Northrop Aircraft, and Sikorsky, along with two airline operations, Varney Stout Airlines and National Air Transport. All of the airlines were combined into a new subsidiary called United Air Lines, Inc.

With a guaranteed customer in United, Boeing quickly set to work to build a larger mail and passenger plane. The result was the twin-engine 247. Powered by Pratt & Whitney Wasp engines, the plane could carry ten passengers and had a top cruising speed of 160 miles per hour. United purchased 60 planes for a total of $4 million, the first of which was delivered in 1933. Another fifteen 247s were sold to independent airlines. TWA also wanted to purchase the plane. Boeing agreed to sell to United's competitor, but told them they would have to wait until after the United order was completed. Unwilling to wait, TWA turned to a small California aircraft manufacturer, Donald Douglas, and asked them to build a plane. The result was the DC-2, a fourteen-seat passenger plane which went into service only one year after the 247 and which was clearly so superior that even United soon switched to the plane.

At this point the U.S. government intervened in the industry. A move to break up many of the big business conglomerates that had been formed in the 1920s was gathering momentum in Congress. In late 1934 the Air Mail Act was passed. This act forbade any connection between aircraft manufacturers, engine manufacturers, and airlines, and effectively mandated the breakup of United Aircraft and Transport Corporation. Boeing Airplane Company was once more an independent enterprise. The only subsidiary that stayed linked to Boeing was the Wichita, Kansas–based Stearman Aircraft.

The War Years and its Aftermath

The mid 1930s was a tough period for Boeing. Donald Douglas had seized the initiative in commercial transport from Boeing's Model 247 with its DC-2 and later DC-3 plane. The company's employment fell from 1,700 to 700, and in 1934 it lost $266,000. What saved Boeing was the U.S. Army Air Corps, which was looking for a heavy bomber. The Army's specifications called for a multiengine bomber that could carry a ton of bombs 2,000 miles at more than 200 miles per hour. Boeing's board of directors allocated $275,000 to the project, effectively betting the company on the new plane's success.

The result was the four-engine Model 299, later named the B-17 and popularly referred to as the "flying fortress" on account of its numerous gun turrets. Along with its cousin, Boeing's B-29 "superfortress," the plane was to become the workhorse of the U.S. military in World War II. Initially, however, the Air

Corps favored Douglas's two-engine B-18 bomber, which cost considerably less, ordering 133 of them and throwing an order for thirteen B-17s Boeing's way as a consolation prize. For several years Boeing's B-17 program limped along on additional handouts of small B-17 orders from the military. By 1939 the future of Boeing, which lost over $2.5 million that year, looked grim, but the outbreak of World War II in September 1939 saved the company. Alarmed by events in Europe and by an increasingly belligerent Japan, in 1940 President Roosevelt announced that the United States would build 50,000 warplanes. In reality, by the day Japan surrendered, the United States had produced more than 137,000 combat aircraft, of which 7,000 were Boeing-built B-17s and 2,900 were B-29s.

While the war rescued Boeing from almost certain financial ruin, the end of the war meant a return to old problems. The Air Force canceled a large B-29 contract, and the resulting layoffs reduced the Seattle work force from 35,000 to 6,000, while Wichita went down from 16,000 to 1,500. Boeing knew it had to gain commercial business in order to survive. The company set about to produce a civilian version of its C-97 military transport and aerial tanker, which itself was a partial derivative of the B-29. The civilian version was designated Model 377; its more popular name was the Stratocruiser. The Stratocruiser was a four-engine plane with a pressurized cabin that could carry up to 100 passengers. It competed head-to-head with Douglas's DC-6 and Lockheed's Constellation for a share of the rapidly growing commercial airline market, and it basically failed due to underpowered engines. The airlines purchased nearly 600 Douglas DC-6s, 200 Lockheed planes, but only 55 Stratocruisers. Had it not been for the C-97 tanker version, the program would have been a complete disaster. Still, the program did have one tangible benefit that was to prove useful later: for the first time Boeing actually had a commercial sales department. This department, mostly staffed by engineers, began to develop long-term relationships with the few customers that did purchase the Stratocruiser, particularly Pan Am and United.

The Early Jet Age

With its commercial arm still floundering, Boeing had to capture military orders in order to stay in business. With the war over, the Air Force was looking to build a fleet of medium-weight bombers and had awarded study contracts to five U.S. companies, of which Boeing was one. A team of U.S. scientists, including three Boeing engineers, had been sent to Germany at the end of the war to review German work on jet aircraft. They found German wind-tunnel data on the advantages of sweptback wings. The data showed that sweptback wings would increase the speed of a plane, but it also showed that only a jet engine would deliver enough power to take advantage of this wing configuration. Although this data was made available to all U.S. manufacturers, only Boeing incorporated it into its new bomber design. The result was a radically new aircraft, the B-47. Powered by six jet engines, and with a 35-degree sweptback wing, the B-47 could cruise at 650 miles per hour. Among U.S. manufacturers, only Boeing had the advantage of a wind tunnel that was capable of simulating aircraft speeds of close to the speed of sound. The wind tunnel, funded out of profits from the B-29 program, provided the data that convinced Boeing of the virtues of a 35-degree sweptback wing (German data only went to a 29-degree sweptback wing). The wind-tunnel data also helped Boeing identify the best placement for the jet engines.

The first B-47 flew in 1947, and full production began in 1948. The Air Force insisted that the plane be built in Wichita, since it viewed Seattle as within the range of Russian bombers. It also insisted that Lockheed and Douglas be allowed to build some B-47s under license; this decision forced Boeing to transfer its newly gained technological expertise to two capable competitors. In the end Boeing produced some 1,400 B-47s, while Lockheed and Douglas together made another 700. At $3 million a plane, the program generated some badly needed cash for Boeing. All three manufacturers also learned an enormous amount about production efficiency from the program; by the end of the program in 1954 the time required to build a B-47 had been reduced to 7 percent of the time required to build the first production aircraft.

The B-47 program helped fund the development of Boeing's next jet bomber, the B-52. First rolled out in November 1951, the B-52 was a technological tour de force that showed just how much Boeing had learned from the B-47 program. Aerodynamically the B-52 was a larger version of the B-47, with much more powerful jet engines. The B-52 had a take-off weight of 480,000 pounds, twice that of the B-47, yet it could cruise at 600 miles per hour at 50,000 feet, 10,000 feet above the B-47's service ceiling, and could carry a bomb load of 54,000 pounds. The original price tag for the B-52 was $6 million. Eventually, a total of 744 B-52s were built, and the aircraft proved so durable that it served in 1991 in the Gulf War.

The 707 to the 747

Soon Boeing began to contemplate the obvious step: applying the B-47 and B-52 technology to a commercial jetliner. The catalyst was a trip by several Boeing executives to the 1950 Farnborough Air Show in England. The star attraction of the show was the new Comet, the world's first operational jet airliner, which had been built by Britain's de Havilland. The Comet was scheduled to go into service in the spring of 1952. Although Boeing's CEO Bill Allen, who had been at Farnborough, was cautious and somewhat skeptical about the opportunities for a jet airliner—particularly given the fiasco of the Stratocruiser—in April 1952 Boeing committed the company to developing a jetliner, the Model 707. This was due in large part to intense lobbying by Boeing's small commercial aircraft sales force, which at that time had no planes to sell. Although the original cost of developing and testing a prototype was high—estimated at about $15 million—Boeing was able to fund this from its successful B-47 and B-52 programs.

The 707 drew heavily upon the technology embodied in the B-47 and B-52. The prototype, which was called the Dash-80, adopted the same 35-degree sweptback wing as the B-47 as well as the same engine pod concept. Almost from the start Boeing went for a big aircraft, with a capacity of almost 100 passengers, in contrast to the Comet, which originally could take only 36 passengers. The Comet's chances of establishing itself were effectively wrecked in January 1954 when a Comet exploded in midair. All Comets were grounded, and a subsequent investigation revealed the cause of the crash: a small but rapidly expanding metal-fatigue crack had created nearly instant decompression of the cabin giving the effect of a bomb exploding. Boeing's prototype was by this time almost complete, but the company had already anticipated the problem that destroyed the de Havilland Comet by designing the fuselage so that a small crack would not propagate.

The first 707 prototype was rolled out on May 15, 1954. Still, the 707 was not an instant success. Although its nearest rival, Douglas's DC-8, was still on the drawing board, Boeing initially had trouble persuading airlines to adopt the 707. Most questioned Boeing's commitment to the commercial airline business. They also were attracted to the DC-8, whose width—three inches wider than the first 707 (the 707-120)—could accommodate six seats across instead of five, as in the 707-120. Moreover, the DC-8 promised a longer range than the initial 707, which could not complete the transatlantic route without a refueling stop in Newfoundland. The first 707 order was placed by Pan Am in October 1955—for twenty 707s. But at the same time the company also placed an order for twenty-five DC-8s, putting Boeing five orders behind a jetliner that had yet to be built. Boeing's moderate success selling a military version of the 707, the KC-135 tanker actually worked against Boeing, raising fears that the company was not really committed to commercial aircraft.

What turned the 707 program around was Boeing's decision to redesign the aircraft. The 707-320, or 707 Intercontinental, as the new version was called, was four inches wider than the 707-120, had bigger wings, more powerful engines, and a longer fuselage, all of which allowed for more passenger seats and a longer range. This decision to redesign was made, however, only after a bitter argument between Boeing's manufacturing and engineering people—who were opposed to any change on the grounds that it implied a considerable retooling cost—and the commercial sales force—which knew that the company had to be more responsive to its customers' needs. Ultimately, Boeing CEO Bill Allen intervened to push the redesign through. It proved to be a wise decision. Sales of the 707 improved, and by the fall of 1957 Boeing had finally pulled ahead of Douglas, with orders for 145 707s versus 124 DC-8s. This was a lead that Boeing was never to relinquish.

The first 707 entered service in 1958, and by the time the program ended in May 1991 more than a thousand 707s had been produced. It took eight years for 707 sales to amortize all development, tooling, and modification costs. The redesign of the 707 had significantly raised costs, yet these very changes helped solidify Boeing's reputation for engineering and product integrity.

The 707 was followed by the 727. A slightly smaller aircraft than the 707, the 727 was specifically designed for shorter runways that the 707 could not serve. The 727 represented another big bet for Boeing. The three-engine plane was rolled out on November 27, 1962, with costs of design and tooling for the 727 program of $150 million. Boeing estimated that it would sell approximately 300 727s, but by the time the last plane rolled off the production line in 1984 a total of 1,831 had been sold and delivered. The plane's success was simple to explain: it was an excellently engineered product that delivered all it promised and more.

Boeing's next jet airliner was the 737. The 737 was smaller than the 707 and 727. Designed primarily for short-haul routes, the 737 faced intense competition from Douglas's DC-9 and Britain's BAC-111. When the 737 program got the go-ahead in February 1965, orders had already been taken for more than 200 DC-9s and 100 BAC-111s. To make matters worse, the 737 had to compete for resources within Boeing against the 747 program and the supersonic transport project. Had it not been for the support of two outside directors, Crawford Greenewalt and George Weyerhaeuser, both of whom were strong supporters of the short aircraft concept, the 737 program might never have begun. Boeing's CEO, Bill Allen, was lukewarm at best. As it was, the 737 program was constantly short of skilled manpower.

The 737 was a short, stubby, two-engine aircraft that utilized the same cabin diameter as the 707 and 727. With a wider cabin than either the DC-9 or BAC-111, the 737 could seat six across, thus accommodating more passengers than its competitors could. Using the same cabin diameter as the 707 and 727 also allowed for some shared tooling, thereby lowering costs. Given the 737's late entry into the market (it was two years behind the DC-9 and BAC-111), sales were not expected to be dramatic. However, Boeing was able to build up a market base for the 737 by focusing upon many small airlines, both in the United States and overseas. The company was not against selling only two or three planes at a time to these "midgets"; by doing so it laid the groundwork for future sales growth when these midgets grew with increased air traffic. Southwest Airlines, for example, started out with just three 737s. By 1993, however, it was responsible for one of Boeing's biggest orders, 63 737-X aircraft.

Ultimately, the 737 turned out to be Boeing's best-selling jetliner ever. Between its 1967 introduction and the end of 1991, over three thousand 737s had been sold, a figure representing nearly half of all Boeing jetliners delivered worldwide since the first 707. The triumph of the 737 was the result of far more than a superior seating configuration. Like other Boeing aircraft, it was superbly engineered, reliable, efficient, and economical.

Boeing's next plane, the 747, arose out of Pan Am's desire for an aircraft bigger than either the 707 Intercontinental or the stretched version of the DC-8. Pan Am first raised the possibility of a 400-seat jet airliner in May of 1965. By December 1965 Pan Am had signed a letter of intent with Boeing calling for a 400-passenger airliner with a range of slightly over 5,000 miles; the ability to take off on a hot day, fully loaded, on not more than 8,000 feet of runway; and a cruising altitude of 35,000 feet. Pan Am committed itself to purchasing 25 planes for a price of $550 million, and the 747 program was born. It was the most ambitious aircraft project ever undertaken. Boeing spent $200 million just on the construction plant for the 747. Product development and tooling were to cost a further $200 million. Some 50,000 people were involved in the 747 program, including construction workers and subcontractors in just about every state and seventeen foreign countries. The 747 contained 4.5 million individual parts designed from 75,000 engineering drawings. With a full fuel load the plane would weigh 350 tons. To top it off, the company had agreed to provide Pan Am with the first production plane in December of 1969.

With Pan Am on board, Boeing found that other airlines were willing to place orders for the 747. Many of them had doubts about the usefulness of a 400-seat plane, but they were driven by the fear that their not having the 747 could give Pan Am a competitive advantage. Slowly Boeing began to build sales toward the estimated breakeven point for the 747 program, 400 planes.

The first 747 went into service on January 21, 1970. It was not an auspicious beginning. The plane suffered from the twin problems of excessive weight and weak engines. The first scheduled 747 flight was delayed for seven hours before departure, due to engine overheating. It was to be several months before Pratt & Whitney could deliver more powerful versions of the JT-90 engine that powered the 747. During that time Boeing had to suffer the ignominy of having up to thirty "hangar queens" sitting outside of its Everett facility waiting for delivery of the more powerful engine. Even with the new engine, however, sales were sluggish. There was a recession on, the plane was too big for the needs of many airlines, and its range—at just over 5,000 miles—was too limited for really long

hauls. Moreover, Boeing faced competition from two other smaller wide-bodied jets, the McDonnell Douglas DC-10 and the Lockheed L-1011, each of which carried about 250 passengers.

Boeing's solution was to offer a variation on the 747, the 747SP (for Special Performance). Almost fifty feet shorter and 30,000 pounds lighter than the 747, the 747SP carried 300 passengers and had a range of 7,000 miles, making it the world's longest-haul aircraft until the 1989 introduction of Boeing's 747-400. The 747-400 represented another engineering feat. It was a bigger plane than the original 747, with a range of 8,000 miles, a seating capacity of 550, and a two-person cockpit.

The original projections for the 747 estimated total demand of about 600 units. By the end of 1991, however, over a thousand 747s had either been sold or were on order and by the end of 1992 Boeing still had an order backlog for 214 747 aircraft. However, no new orders were coming in, prompting many industry analysts to suggest that the end of the 747 program might be in sight.

The Boeing Slump

In Seattle the Boeing slump of 1969–1971 is a legend. During the late 1960s Boeing had rapidly increased its work force in the Puget Sound region to over 100,000 as it served five major programs: the 707, 727, 737, 747, and supersonic transport (SST) program. The cash drains involved in developing the 737 and 747 were enormous. Although the SST program was largely government-funded, Boeing had spent $100 million (out of a total of $1 billion) on the program and had 1,500 engineers working full-time on the project.

Then in 1969 the economy went into a recession and the bottom dropped out of the airline market. Starting in 1970, there was a seventeen-month period when Boeing did not make a single sale to any U.S. airline; only an order backlog and a few foreign sales kept the production line going. To make matters worse, in May 1971 the government canceled the SST program.

The company had a negative cash flow for most of this period, forcing it to draw upon $1 billion of external credit. Boeing's Seattle-area employment shrank from 101,000 to 38,000 in twenty-four months. Unemployment soared, the local housing market slumped, and a famous sign placed on a billboard by the I-5 freeway leaving Seattle read, "Will the last person leaving SEATTLE—turn out the lights."

Two things pulled Boeing out of its tailspin: winning a government contract to build the Minuteman II missile system, and more significantly, the 727 program. By 1969 the 727 was viewed as a dying program, but the recession changed that. Boeing began to get feedback from airlines that wide-bodied jets such as the DC-10 and L-1011 were too big and uneconomical to operate on medium-haul routes between big cities, but that the 737 and DC-9s were too small. This created a market niche that the newly designed 727, the 727-200, was ideally suited to fill. Boeing upgraded the 727-200 to improve its range, power, and interior, and launched the Advanced 727-200 in 1971. For several years it was this program, along with the Minuteman, that provided Boeing with its only positive cash flow. By mid 1974 Boeing's Renton plant was turning out fourteen 727s per month and the worst of the Boeing slump was over. This was followed by a pickup in 737 and 747 orders after 1974 as the economy began to pull its way out of the recession.

The 757 and 767

By the mid 1970s Boeing was rebounding from the slump of the early 1970s. By 1978 Boeing had moved past the breakeven point on all four of its commercial jet aircraft models, the 707, 727, 737, and 747. With money in the bank for the first time in years, in 1978 Boeing embarked simultaneously upon two new commercial jet aircraft programs, the 757 and 767. The narrow-bodied 757—conceived originally as a replacement for the aging 727—had a range of 4,000 miles; the 767 was envisioned as a wide-bodied jet with 200 to 250 seats, that could fly transoceanic routes for which the 747 was considered too large. Both the 757 and 767 were to be twin-engine aircraft with an emphasis on fuel efficiency. Indeed, in terms of seat miles per gallon, the 757 ended up being 76 percent more fuel efficient than the 727-200 it replaced. Because the cockpits of the 757 and 767 were identical and both planes were designed for two-person crews, carriers operating both the 757 and 767 could move crews from one type of aircraft to the other with little or no additional training.

The 767 was also the first aircraft for which Boeing subcontracted out a significant amount of work to international partners. Boeing subcontracted the job of manufacturing the entire 767 fuselage except the cockpit—in all, about 90 percent of the total value of the aircraft—to a consortium of three Japanese manufacturers: Mitsubishi, Kawasaki, and Fuji. In explaining this decision, Boeing officials pointed out that 60 percent of the company's sales were to overseas customers, many of whom naturally wanted a piece of the action. Japanese carriers were among Boeing's best customers, so the decision made commercial sense. Moreover, Boeing felt that it might learn something about manufacturing efficiency from its Japanese partners. Nevertheless, the deal raised concerns among some that Boeing might be helping to create a future Japanese competitor.

The first flight of the 767 was in September of 1981, while the 757 had its maiden flight in February of 1982. By the late 1980s both aircraft had broken even and were making money for Boeing. As of January 1992 Boeing had 770 orders for the 757, of which 412 had been delivered. For the 767, orders totaled 598, of which 405 had been delivered. Both aircraft might have been even more successful had it not been for a change in the operating strategy of airlines toward "hub and spoke" systems. This shift in operating strategy was brought about by the increased competition in the U.S. airline industry that followed the deregulation of the industry in 1979. This shift in operating strategy increased demand for short-haul aircraft and, ironically, injected a new lease on life into the 737 program.

Organizational Problems

Despite having become the world's largest commercial jet aircraft manufacturer, by the late 1980s Boeing was experiencing some internal difficulties. The company had become known for a hierarchical, rigid, and semi-autocratic management style in which managers gave orders to their subordinates, rather than listened to their ideas. Reflecting the company's substantial military heritage, Boeing's management also tended to be very secretive and security-conscious, traits that led some customers to refer to the company's Seattle headquarters as "the Kremlin." Poor communication and turf problems appeared to be endemic within the organization. Individual divisions and departments seemed to be separated by invisible boundaries over which no one from another department or division was supposed to step. The consequences included a lack of effective interdepartmental and interdivisional cooperation. The company also lacked

vertical communication. Senior management was perceived as being out of touch with lower-level employees and unresponsive to their needs—a perception that translated into poor employee motivation.

The company's communications and motivational problems were compounded by two other factors. The first was the rapid hiring that took place during the 1980s, which resulted in the employment of a large number of relatively inexperienced people, both at the shop-floor level and at the middle-management level. Between 1984 and 1989 Boeing added 10,000 people annually to its payroll. As a result, by 1989 approximately half of the work force had been at Boeing less than five years. Many of the new hires were younger people who were not as receptive to Boeing's traditional hierarchical ways. Another problem was a by-product of the company's engineering strength. Like many engineering companies, many of Boeing's managers had engineering backgrounds. As a consequence, Boeing suffered from a lack of professional management skills, particularly the "soft" people skills associated with leadership, communication, and motivation. There was a sense at Boeing that the human element of the enterprise had been subordinated to engineering and technological considerations.

These deep-seated problems began to show in the company's 747-400 program. Boeing had missed promised delivery dates for the first time in decades, costs were way over budget, and quality problems were emerging. Japan Airlines and British Airways had complained about quality defects in their new $125 million 747-400s; Lufthansa and KLM were not getting their 747-400s on time. To make matters worse, quality inspections revealed several instances of miswiring in brand-new aircraft.

Related to this was the emergence of labor problems. By 1989 Boeing had accumulated a huge order backlog of close to $100 billion. To try and keep up with its delivery schedule the company was demanding that shop-floor employees work up to 200 hours of mandatory overtime per quarter. This had become a source of friction between the company and labor unions, particularly the International Association of Machinists (IAM). What is more, with one eye on the company's huge backlog, the IAM was demanding a double-digit wage increase in its 1989 contract negotiations with the company. Boeing argued that, given the enormous capital commitments required to start new aircraft programs, and the volatile nature of demand in the industry, such a wage increase was not realistic. Nonetheless, in October of 1989 the IAM members began what was to be a 48-day strike. In the end the union settled for the same pre-strike wage increase that the company had been offering: a 10 percent general wage increase spread over the three-year life of the contract, plus a 10.5 percent hike in annual lump-sum payments. However, mandatory overtime was reduced from 200 hours to 144 hours per quarter.

Boeing's shortcomings were also beginning to make themselves evident in the marketplace. The rapid rise of Airbus Industrie to the number-two spot in the commercial aerospace industry was as much a testament to Boeing's failure as it was to anything else. Airbus had gained market share by targeting segments poorly served by Boeing. The Airbus A330 and A340 filled a market gap for a 300 to 335-seat long-haul plane positioned between Boeing's 767 and 747 aircraft. Moreover, Airbus aircraft were viewed as being more technologically advanced than Boeing's. Airbus pioneered advanced avionics, such as the "fly-by-wire" nonmechanical navigation systems, the two-person cockpit, fuel tanks

in the tail, and the use of composite materials in major structural areas—all innovations that Boeing subsequently adopted. McDonnell Douglas also made a grab for this market segment with its 335-seat MD-11 jet while Boeing, as of mid 1990, still did not have a program announced.

Organizational Change

In response to the problems that were becoming evident at Boeing during the latter half of the 1980s, the company began to launch a program of organizational change. The change effort dated back to the appointment of Frank Shrontz as CEO in 1986 and then as chairman in 1988. Unlike his predecessors, Shrontz was neither an engineer nor a pilot. Rather, he was a lawyer with a Harvard MBA who made his name within Boeing running first the 737 program and later the commercial aircraft division while Boeing was developing the 757 and 767. Perhaps more than any previous Boeing chief, Shrontz was committed to improving Boeing's bottom line, by transforming the way the company operated. It was Shrontz who in 1987 initiated the cultural change process that is still ongoing today at Boeing. The mission, goals, objectives, and strategic initiatives for the commercial airplane operation generated by strategic thinking associated with the cultural change process at Boeing are summarized in Exhibit 5.

To start the process of change, Shrontz traveled around the company, arranging a series of face-to-face meetings with shop-floor workers. Other managers were excluded from these meetings. Among other things, Shrontz heard many complaints that first-line supervisors did not understand how to be receptive to ideas flowing up from the bottom of the organization—that supervisors were not people-oriented. He also found that many people felt "left out" of the company.

Another catalyst for change was the collaboration with the consortium of three Japanese manufacturers on the 767 program. Boeing's management had been impressed by the superior productivity and quality control achieved by their Japanese partners. Realizing that it was falling behind the curve on manufacturing excellence, the company planned a series of study missions to Japan in 1990 and 1991 for about a hundred of Boeing's top executives. The managers went in groups of eight and spent two weeks visiting a number of world-class manufacturing enterprises, including Toyota, NEC, Nippon Steel, and Komatsu. They generally came away impressed with the Japanese quest for continuous improvement in their manufacturing processes.

To share what they had learned in Japan, Boeing executives designed a course to train the next tier of managers within the organization. Called "Managing for World-Class Competitiveness," the four-day course is designed to encourage innovation and efficiency in every area of the company. In what is called a *cascade approach* to management training, each manager teaches his or her immediate subordinates. The plan is to have every employee go through the course by the end of 1993, including those on the factory floor. In addition, Boeing increasingly has been sending its supervisors and middle managers through management training programs, both in-house and at business schools, to train them in essential management skills.

In an attempt to become a world-class manufacturing company, in 1992 Boeing set two ambitious goals: to reduce costs by 25 percent to 30 percent and to halve aircraft production cycle time by 1998. For the 737 and 757 aircraft the company wants to cut cycle time from the current twelve months to six months.

Commercial Airplane Mission: *To be the industry leader in commercial airplanes and achieve a reasonable return on investment, by adhering to the Boeing principles: integrity, quality, technical excellence, and recognition of people as our key resource.*

Commercial Airplane Goals	Commercial Airplane Objectives	Commercial Airplane Strategic Initiatives
Our mission means:	Hence we must have:	And this is how:
Leadership		
• Products and services which best meet the needs of our customers. Outstanding quality, technical excellence, economic performance and after-sales support of our airplanes • A 60 percent market share	• The most competitive products • Leadership in customer satisfaction	• Introduce a new competitive airplane • Improve existing products • Ensure adequate capacity to respond to the market on a timely basis • Meet commitments • Deliver service-ready products • Improve our superior support network • Improve responsiveness to customer
Return		
• Ten-year average before-tax profit contribution of 10 percent of sales	• Superior productivity • Enhanced unit revenues • Continuous improvement as a way of life	• Reduce total costs • Maintain a healthy organization • Simplify processes • Reduce waste • Improve product cost visibility • Reduce price concessions
People		
• A working environment that is founded on integrity, open communication, trust, and individual growth	• Motivated and skilled people	• Ensure that all employees have the knowledge, tools, and skills to implement continuous improvement • Improve the work environment • Continuously improve individual capability • Improve evaluation and compensation systems • Improve communications
Citizenship		
• A responsible corporate citizen	• Leadership in the community	• Manage growth in the Puget Sound area • Participate in the community • Meet or exceed all environmental protection requirements

Source: The Boeing Corporation

Exhibit 5
Boeing's Mission, Goals, Objectives, and Strategic Initiatives

For the 747 and 767 aircraft, Boeing is aiming to reduce cycle time from eighteen months to nine months. Reducing cycle time and costs has involved various initiatives, including the introduction of a continuous quality improvement pro-

gram, the introduction of just-in-time inventory systems, and the re-engineering of work processes. The changes are most obvious at some of Boeing's new facilities; a recently completed $450 million factory to build wing structures in Frederickson, Washington, for example, shows the benefits of the new approach. The design of work processes in the factory was heavily influenced by ideas that Boeing executives had gathered on trips to Japan, as well as from suggestions from their own work force. By redesigning processes to eliminate production tasks, Boeing has managed to cut the time taken to build wing structures from 100 days to 15 days. A just-in-time inventory system has helped cut raw material inventories from six months to six weeks, while average lot size fell from sixteen to two.

Some notable improvements have also been made in the Renton, Washington, factory, which assembles the narrow-bodied 737 and 757 aircraft. In the first twelve months of the program, Boeing executives managed to cut five days out of the assembly time for the 737 and nine days out of the assembly time for the 757. Inventory was cut by $100 million in 1992, $15 million more than the initial target for that year. Similarly, at the 747 assembly facility in Everett, Washington, five days were cut out of the 45-day assembly cycle for the 747 in 1992, mostly by re-engineering work processes.

At the same time, not all of these changes have been accomplished easily or smoothly. There is still suspicion among the work force about the intentions of management, particularly during a period when Boeing is cutting back its total employment. While Boeing aims to "empower" shop floor employees so that they can suggest ways to do their jobs more efficiently, some note that the more efficient they make things, the more likely they are to render their own jobs unnecessary. Others complain that Boeing's approach to the 1992–1994 layoffs shows how little has really changed. Boeing has taken a "last in, first out" approach to its recent layoffs. One result, according to doubters, is that those most wedded to the old ways of doing things retain their jobs, while younger people, who were the most likely to buy into the cultural change process, are the ones getting laid off. This has led some employees to comment that although Boeing is currently "talking the talk" of change, senior management has yet to demonstrate that they can "walk the walk."

The 777 Program

More than anything else, the 777 program represents the shape of the new Boeing. The objective of the program, to which the company formally committed itself in October of 1990, is to build a two-engine, 350-seat, wide-bodied jet with a transoceanic range. Development costs are estimated to fall in the $5 billion range, and some 300 aircraft will have to be sold before the program breaks even. The plane is a response—some think a belated one—to the McDonnell Douglas MD-11 and Airbus A340 and A330 aircraft. When Boeing announced the launch of the 777, 32 airlines had already ordered 173 MD-11s, and 25 carriers had signed up for 217 Airbus A340s and A330s. Boeing was trailing by almost 400 aircraft. The first 777 plane is scheduled to go into service in mid 1995.

To build a plane that was designed with customer requirements in mind, Boeing invited eight U.S. and foreign airlines to help Boeing design the aircraft. The group included United (which launched the program with orders for 32 planes), American, Delta, British Airways, Japan Airlines, All Nippon Airways, Qantas, and Cathay Pacific. For almost a year, technical representatives from these airlines took up residence in Boeing's Everett, Washington, facility and met

with the engineering staff assigned to the 777 project. This was a dramatic shift for Boeing, which hitherto had always been very secretive about its design work.

Input from the eight carriers clearly determined the shape of the 777. They demanded a fuselage that was wider than the MD-11 and the two Airbus models so that they could pack another thirty or so seats onto the aircraft. The result is an aircraft that will be five inches wider than the MD-11 and twenty-five inches wider than the A-330. They wanted a plane in which the galleys and lavatories could be relocated almost anywhere within the plane's cabin within hours; Boeing has designed a plane whose interior can be completely rearranged in 3 to 4 hours, configuring it with one, two, or three classes to fit whatever a carrier's market of the moment demands. They wanted better overhead bins for carry-on baggage; Boeing designed new overhead bins to their requirements. American Airlines in particular wanted the 777 to have an option for folding wingtips, so that the plane could utilize the same airport space as American's narrower DC-10s and 767s. The 777 will have a 199-foot wingspan, only twelve feet shorter than the 747-400. Boeing devised a way of folding twenty-two feet of each wing, leaving a parked 777 with roughly the same wingspan as a DC-10 or 767.

In another departure with tradition, the 777 will be the first airliner that is designed entirely by computer. By using 3D CAD technology to engineer and test parts in virtual space, Boeing aims to dramatically reduce the need for expensive mockups and design changes, while cutting down on development time. Preassemblies are first created and put together in virtual space to make sure that everything fits. If things do not fit, they are redesigned on the computer until they do. Only then are real parts and subassemblies manufactured.

The design teams themselves are cross-functional, with engineering and production employees being put together so that they can design a plane that is easy to manufacture. Boeing also brought eighteen major suppliers into the 777 program, having them consult with project engineers and potential customers in order to rectify ahead of time any problems that might arise in production, thereby reducing the need for costly design changes late in the development cycle.

Building upon the 767 program, Boeing will also outsource a substantial proportion of the 777 to 3,500 external suppliers, with the Japanese trio that played a major part in the 767 also participating in the 777 program. It is estimated that 60 percent of the parts for the 777 will be outsourced to independent suppliers, compared with 30 percent of the parts for the two-decade-old 737 (see Exhibits 6 and 7). Twenty percent of the 777's structural work will be performed by the Japanese trio of Mitsubishi, Kawasaki, and Fuji Heavy Industries.

Boeing 2000

As Boeing approaches the year 2000, it faces a number of critical challenges. The first will be to make a profit on the 777 program in the face of intense competition from Airbus and McDonnell Douglas. As of December 31, 1992, Boeing had 122 firm orders for the 777, an encouraging start, but one that still leaves the company with a long way to go. Boeing is also considering two other major aircraft projects. The first is for a 600- to 800-passenger superjumbo jet. If Boeing does pursue this project, it may well be in conjunction with one or more of the partners in the Airbus consortium; this arrangement would help with development costs, which are projected to run into the $10-billion range, too much for one company to absorb given the enormous risks involved.

Another possibility is to build a supersonic transport (SST). Boeing is the senior member of the Supersonic Commercial Transport International Coopera-

Exhibit 6 Who Makes the 737

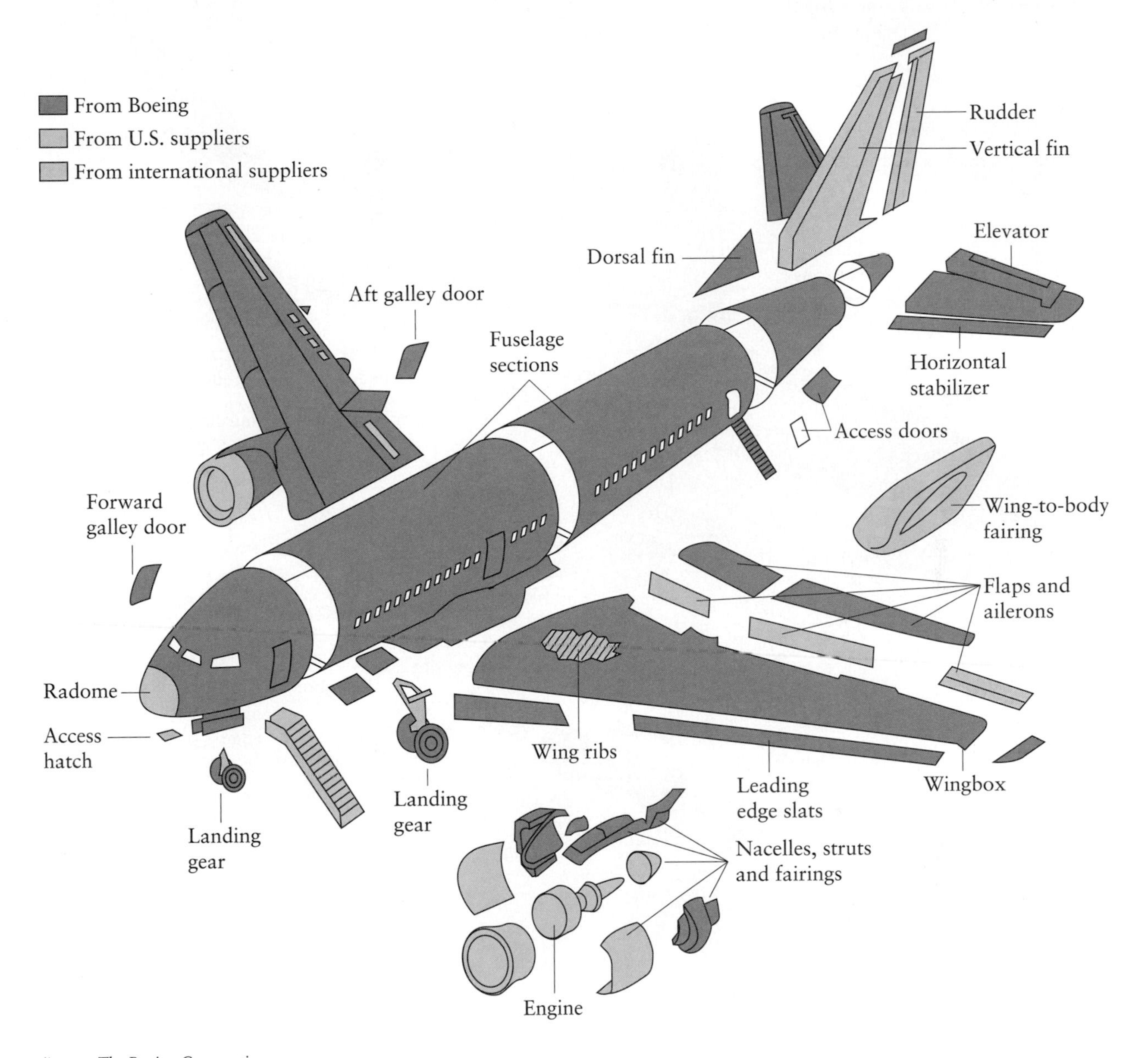

Source: The Boeing Corporation.

Exhibit 7 Who Will Make the 777

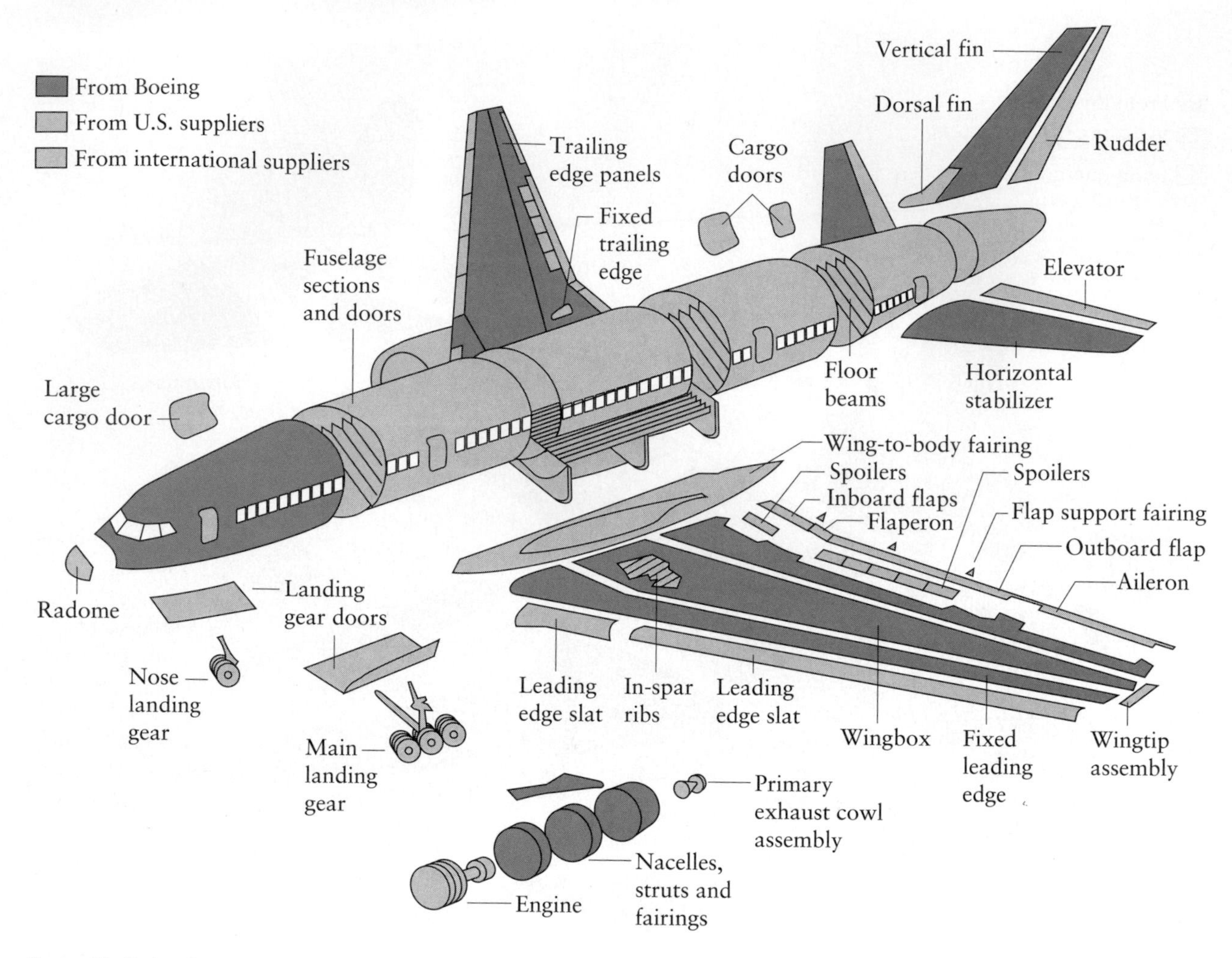

Source: The Boeing Corporation.

Income Data (Million $)

Year Ended Dec. 31	Revs.	Oper. Inc.	% Oper. Inc. of Revs.	Cap. Exp.	Depr.	Int. Exp.	[2]Net Bef. Taxes	Eff. Tax Rate	[3]Net Inc.	% Net Inc. of Revs.	Cash Flow
1992	30,184	3,001	9.9	2,212	961	133	2,256	31.1%	[4]1,554	5.1	2,515
1991	29,314	2,780	9.5	1,878	826	57	2,204	28.9%	1,567	5.3	2,393
[1]1990	27,595	2,208	8.0	1,609	678	28	1,972	29.8%	1,385	5.0	2,063
1989	20,276	1,208	6.0	1,372	627	24	922	26.8%	675	3.3	1,302
1988	16,962	1,015	6.0	709	567	26	820	25.1%	614	3.6	1,181
[1]1987	15,355	710	4.6	786	501	27	658	27.1%	[4]480	3.1	981
[1]1986	16,341	1,093	6.7	795	463	27	1,028	35.3%	665	4.1	1,128
1985	13,636	969	7.1	551	386	20	863	34.4%	566	4.2	952
1984	10,354	721	7.0	337	365	36	569	NM	787	7.6	1,152
1983	11,129	697	6.3	223	365	42	475	25.3%	355	3.2	720

Balance Sheet Data (Million $)

Dec. 31	Cash	Assets	Curr. Liab.	Ratio	Total Assets	% Ret. on Assets	Long-Term Debt	Com. Equity	Total Cap.	% LT Debt of Cap.	% Ret. on Equity
1992	3,614	8,087	6,140	1.3	18,147	9.2	1,772	8,056	10,003	17.7	19.3
1991	3,453	8,829	6,276	1.4	15,784	10.4	1,313	8,093	9,508	13.8	20.9
1990	3,326	8,770	7,132	1.2	14,591	10.0	311	6,973	7,459	4.2	21.2
1989	1,863	8,660	6,673	1.3	13,278	5.2	275	6,131	6,605	4.2	11.7
1988	3,963	8,561	6,705	1.3	12,608	4.9	251	5,404	5,903	4.3	11.8
1987	3,435	9,313	7,064	1.3	12,566	4.1	256	4,987	5,502	4.7	9.9
1986	4,172	8,478	5,659	1.5	11,068	6.5	263	4,826	5,409	4.9	14.5
1985	3,209	6,766	4,417	1.5	9,246	6.2	16	4,364	4,829	0.3	13.6
1984	1,595	6,170	4,040	1.5	8,485	9.9	284	3,695	4,445	6.4	23.3
1983	1,095	5,162	3,205	1.6	7,471	4.7	301	3,038	4,266	7.1	12.1

Data as orig. reptd. 1. Reflects merger or acquisition. 2. Incl. equity in earns. of nonconsol. subs. 3. Bef. spec. item(s). 4. Reflects accounting change. NM-Not Meaningful.

Source: Boeing Aviation Accounts

Exhibit 8
Financial Data

tion Study Group, which was established in 1990 to look into the feasibility of a new SST plane to replace the aging Concorde. Other members include McDonnell Douglas, Japanese Aircraft Industries, Alenia of Italy, Tupolev of Russia, and three of the four members of the Airbus consortium. At present Boeing sees the probability of developing an SST program as being around 50 percent; there are two big hurdles that must be overcome before Boeing can move forward. One is ecology: an SST must be able to fly through the ozone layer without damaging it to any significant extent, and its noise level—a factor that effectively killed any hope that Concorde had of being a commercial success—must be within acceptable limits. The other hurdle is economic: to be worthwhile the market must demand several hundred planes.

In addition to developing new planes, Boeing must also consider the possibility of new competition. The worry remains that the Japanese could move from being Boeing subcontractors to building their own commercial jet aircraft.

Aviastar of Russia has gained British financial backing and has announced its intention to replace McDonnell Douglas as the number-three builder of commercial aircraft in the world. Aviastar is no stranger to the aircraft business, having for years built cargo aircraft and jet engines for use in the former Soviet Union and the one-time communist countries of Eastern Europe. Taiwan is aggressively seeking partners that will give it airplane manufacturing expertise (a proposed deal with McDonnell Douglas fell through only after months of negotiations). And several of Boeing's smaller rivals are forming alliances to build planes designed to compete with Boeing products. One probable alliance, between several European companies, will result in a 100- to 120-seat jet commuter plane that could be used for short-haul hops.

Sources

Acohido, B. "Jet Sticker Shock," *Seattle Times,* December 5, 1993, pp. D1, D6.

Betts, P. "Boeing May Cut 747 Output as Industry Recession Bites," *Financial Times,* October 18, 1993, pp. 1, 14.

———. "Penalties for Excess Baggage," *Financial Times,* November 30, 1993, p. 13.

Coleman, B. "GATT to Rule Against German Aid to Airbus," *The Wall Street Journal,* January 16, 1992, p. 5.

Coleman, B. "Russia's Aviastar Intends to Challenge the West's Big Three Aircraft Makers," *The Wall Street Journal,* January 27, p. A12.

Core, O. C. "Airbus Arrives," *Seattle Times,* July 21, 1992, pp. C1-C3.

"Crash Landing," *The Economist,* January 30, 1993, pp. 29–30.

Dertouzos, M. L., Lester, R. K., and Solow, R. M. *Made in America.* Cambridge, Mass.: MIT Press, 1989.

"Dissecting Airbus," *The Economist,* February 16, 1991, pp. 51–52.

"The Jumbo War," *The Economist,* June 15, 1991, pp. 65–66.

Klepper, G. "Entry Into the Market for Large Transport Aircraft," *European Economic Review* 34: 775–803.

Lane, P. "Study Complains of Alleged Subsidies," *Seattle Times,* December 4, 1991, p. G2.

Rappleye, W. C. "Last of the Titans," *Financial World,* August 20, 1991, pp. 16–17.

Standard & Poor's Industry Surveys. *Aerospace Outlook,* July 1, 1993, pp. A15–A20.

Sterling, R. J. *Legend and Legacy.* New York: St. Martin's Press, 1992.

Stroud, M. "Worries Over a Technology Shift Follow McDonnell-Taiwan Accord," *Investor's Business Daily,* November 21, 1991, p. 36.

Toy, S., et al. "Zoom! Airbus Comes On Strong," *Business Week,* April 21, 1991, pp. 48–50.

West, K. "Boeing 2000," *Seattle Times,* October 21, 1992, pp. A1, A10, A11.

Yang, D. J. "How Boeing Does It," *Business Week,* July 9, 1990, pp. 46–50.

———. "Boeing Cuts Its Altitude as the Clouds Roll In," *Business Week,* February 8, 1993, p. 25.

———. "Reinventing Boeing," *Business Week,* March 1, 1993, pp. 60–67.

CASE

18 BE Aerospace: 1992

Travel is supposed to be exciting but the truth is that those long flights can be tedious. To pass the time some people try to sleep, some listen to the audio channels or read, others attempt to work. Many end up staring at the back of the seat immediately in front of them. For added excitement they "store the tray securely in the upright position." Now, some lucky passengers on British Airways, Cathay Pacific, and Singapore Airlines will now have an alternative: These three airlines have placed orders with BE Aerospace (BEA) for individual-seat videos that can be mounted either in seatbacks or on seat arms.[1] The initial function of these videos is to provide passenger entertainment, but they can be adapted for telephone service, fax, credit-card sales, games, and cabin management announcements. BE Aerospace has a prime-mover advantage with this new product that will undoubtedly appeal to most airlines as the competition for fare-paying passengers continues to increase. In addition to making individual-seat videos, BEA holds a dominant position in the broader $1.5 billion aircraft cabin interior products industry. A breakdown of industry revenues is shown in Table 1. Among other things, BEA manufactures and sells airplane seats, galley systems, coffeemakers, and passenger control units (such as the buttons in seat arms that call flight attendants and adjust overhead lights). Its customers include most of the world's airlines, plus Airbus Industrie, Boeing, and McDonnell Douglas. Airlines are the principal customers; airframe manufacturers are secondary.

This case is set in the fall of 1992 and provides information on BEA, its products, its industry and competitors, and its markets and customers. Details of BEA's growth since its inception in 1987 are provided along with information on the firm's management, its strategies and performance, and its operations. Your task is to consider future strategy options for the firm.

This case was prepared by Richard Reed and James W. Bronson, Washington State University. This case has been written for classroom use and discussion. The information that is presented is not intended to be indicative of either good or bad management practice. We would like to thank Jay Jacobson (Corporate and Financial Relations, New York) for providing us with the necessary information to compile this case study. We also wish to thank the firm of BEA and chairman Amin Khoury for granting permission to write the case. Any errors are ours and should not be attributed to Jay Jacobson or BEA's management.

1. This information and all other information used in the case has been obtained from BEA annual reports and accounts for 1990, 1991, and 1992, from SEC documents filed by BEA (Form 8, 8-K, 10-K), and from copies of overhead slides used in presentations prior to firm acquisitions. Where information has been obtained from other sources it is noted separately.

Table 1
Commercial Aircraft Interior Products Industry Sales (1992)

	1992 Sales (in millions)
Aircraft seating	$ 430
Ovens and coffeemakers	90
Galley systems	215
Other galley components	100
Lavatories	215
In-flight entertainment	200
Lighting	100
Other	150
	$1,500
Emerging Market	**Potential**
Individual-seat video	$300 per year

HISTORY AND BACKGROUND

BEA is a medium-sized firm with a market value of around $145 million.[2] The company was founded by a group of investors who had raised $3 million and were seeking to acquire a firm that (1) held a strong position in a niche market, and (2) would benefit from improved management. The group was led by the current chairman and CEO, Amin J. Khoury, whose background is in medical equipment, and included his brother, Robert J. Khoury (chief operating officer), and some professors from the Harvard Business School. While any firm in any industry was open for consideration, the target that the investor group identified as best fitting their acquisition criteria was Bach Engineering. Bach had a 15 percent share of the passenger control unit (PCU) market and competed primarily with the Avionics Division of EECO (50 percent share), but also competed with Matsushita and Hughes. Matsushita and Hughes produce PCUs mainly for their own aircraft systems that are sold to airframe manufacturers. With some leveraging of their capital, the group purchased Bach Engineering for $3.9 million in July 1987.[3]

The name of Bach Engineering was retained and, in the first year of operation under its new management, Bach's share of the PCU market rose to 20 percent. Sales increased from $2.7 million in 1987 to $4.1 million in 1989 but, while the sales figures looked good, operating income fell. Overhead doubled to almost $1 million and, after interest expense and the amortization of goodwill, the firm incurred a net loss of $0.6 million. In August 1989, EECO Avionics was purchased for $13.9 million and the firm's name was changed to BE Avionics. With this acquisition 1990 sales leapt to $22.9 million and operating income jumped to $4.9 million. BE Avionics went public in April 1990, with a stock offering on NASDAQ that raised $13.0 million, used to retire the firm's long-term debt. In 1991 sales increased to $24.3 million and operating income climbed to nearly $7.0 million. The bottom line was being improved by increasing market share

2. Calculated from a share value of $13.75, August 1992.
3. *Aviation Week,* May 25, 1992, pp. 66–67.

and reducing costs by closing some manufacturing facilities and moving production to other plants to boost efficiency. The firm was now firmly established on a growth path with improving profitability, and a second stock issue in October 1991 raised another $36 million. This new capital allowed further acquisitions. In February 1992 PTC Aerospace and APC were acquired for a total cost of $73.7 million. PTC is a leading U.S. manufacturer of aircraft seating and APC holds a similar position in aircraft galleys and appliances. In April 1992 Flight Equipment and Engineering Limited (FEEL), the largest British manufacturer of aircraft seating, was acquired for $14 million. In this busy year, the firm also changed its name to BE Aerospace and moved its accounting year-end from July to February. The new name better reflected the firm's expanded product range and the new accounting year made it easier to deal with its three latest acquisitions, which increased its total assets from $26 million to $180.7 million. In only five years BEA moved from being an investment wish list to being the largest integrated supplier of aircraft cabin interior products.

PRODUCT MARKETS

BEA operates in an industry that is expected to grow at 14 percent per annum over the next ten years.[4] It has three product divisions (seating, passenger entertainment and service, and galley systems) and two customer groups (airlines and aircraft manufacturers). Airlines are the dominant customers because they order parts directly from BEA for their existing fleets and specify their preferred supplier of aircraft interior products when ordering new airplanes from the aircraft manufacturers.

Seating

BEA is the largest producer of aircraft seating in the world and, in total, controls 25 percent of this $430 million market. Tourist-class seats cost approximately $1,000 each; the larger, heavier, and more complicated first- and business-class seats cost around $5,000 each. While BEA manufactures all classes of seat, its focus is on the much larger tourist-seating segment. The firm has improved designs for these seats with features such as footrests and improved PCUs. It has also developed seating that can be converted from tourist-class (three abreast) to business-class (two abreast). This creates flexibility for airlines by allowing them to tailor seating configurations to load requirements.

The seating market is not only segmented by class but also by type of plane. Commuter aircraft require lighter and more durable seats than longer-haul planes. These seats carry a higher profit margin than airliner seating and, over the next five years, demand is expected to increase by 50 percent. BEA is again the industry leader and controls a 55 percent share of this particular market.

By the end of 1992 BEA will have an "installed base" of 375,000 seats, worth some $475 million. Among others, the installed base is spread across thirteen of the world's twenty major airlines. The size of the installed base is important for two reasons. First, 46 percent of BEA's revenues arise from refurbishments, retrofits, and spare parts (the remaining 54 percent of revenues are generated

4. Morgan Stanley, 1991.

from new-aircraft equipment sales).[5] There is a seven- to eight-year refit cycle on airliners that makes BEA's revenues from this source comfortingly predictable. Airlines tend to get locked in to the original equipment manufacturer for the planes they fly because Federal Aviation Authority (FAA) safety requirements demand that aircraft be recertified and their maintenance manuals be rewritten if the components used in a refit vary from the original design. The second reason the size of the installed base is important comes from the add-on effect for new seat and equipment sales. Airlines can generate substantial savings by reducing maintenance costs and by not having to carry a large inventory of spare parts. All other things being equal, there are sizeable experience-curve effects in maintenance and economies in inventory control available for airlines by specifying that their new aircraft be produced with the same interior products as their existing fleets. Changing suppliers of seats, PCUs, galleys, and other equipment, or even increasing the number of suppliers, incurs a switching cost.

Passenger Entertainment and Service Systems

PCUs were at the heart of the original BEA and, arguably, this is where the firm is still its strongest. It controls 70 percent of new PCU sales and 70 percent of shipments for refits and repairs to the installed base. The firm manufactures PCUs that are compatible with every type of aircraft and multiplex distribution system (the system that carries audio signals to passengers' seats). Its customer base for PCUs includes nine out of every ten airlines throughout the world. Not surprisingly, BEA is also a manufacturer of multiplex distribution systems. These include hard-wired systems and a high-fidelity frequency-division multiplex system that is suited to narrow-bodied, long-haul aircraft. Rail and bus companies are fighting back against the airlines and are providing travelers with comparable entertainment facilities. BEA has adapted its audio distribution systems to gain entry to this new market and already has some systems installed and has firm orders for more. The size of the market is significant: there are over 3,000 passenger rail cars in the United States and Canada, and about 35,000 long-haul coaches.

BEA's introduction of the individual-seat video adds another dimension to airliner entertainment. These units can be installed in new or existing aircraft and are compatible with planes ranging from Boeing's 747 to executive jets. They allow the passenger (viewer) to select from a number of programs and are, in some respects, similar to cable TV. Like home entertainment systems of the near future, they have facilities for viewer interaction. It is already planned that the traveler will be able to make purchases of duty-free goods, make reservations and bookings, and be able to send faxes. The price of the individual-seat video is in the $2,000 to $5,000 range and currently carries a hefty 50 percent gross margin. British Airways, Cathay Pacific, and Singapore Airlines have ordered the units for some of their first- and business-class seats. BEA currently has backlog orders worth $29 million from these three airlines, and there is the potential for follow-up orders worth up to $250 million. The emerging market for individual-seat videos is an estimated $300 million per year and is driven by the need for airlines to offer passengers more amenities and improvements in service. Such substantial demand and profit potential has started attracting stiff competition. Matsushita, Hughes, and Sony, who already operate in the aircraft interior products industry, have the competencies necessary for competing with BEA; other firms outside the industry could also find the prospects attractive.

5. Figures based on fiscal year 1991, pro forma basis.

Galley Structures and Inserts

Galley structures, coffeemakers, ovens, water heaters, closets, and class dividers are not as exciting as individual-seat videos, but the fact that this portion of the industry is worth over $400 million per year certainly makes it interesting. BEA's acquisition of APC provided the firm with a 60 percent share of the coffeemaker market. These machines, which can brew a pot of coffee in as little as one-and-a-half minutes and have price tags of $5,000 and up, are an important source of revenues for the company. APC galley inserts have a good reputation with airlines because of their durability and low maintenance requirements. This reputation provides a platform for BEA's product development and market penetration strategies for galley ovens.

The company emphasizes higher-value-added galley structures for wide-bodied aircraft and is a supplier to the airlines for their airplanes manufactured by both Airbus Industrie and Boeing. BEA is the only domestic supplier of galley structures for Boeing's 747-400 airplane. Engineers at BEA have recently developed a new carbon-graphite panel for use in galley construction. Not only is it nearly twice as strong as existing panels but it is only three-fourths as heavy. In a wide-bodied jet the weight saving is five hundred pounds, which translates into a payoff for airlines in the form of less jet fuel, more passengers, and more cargo.

INDUSTRY

In 1992 most major economies in the world are experiencing recessions of various degrees. Japan and Germany remain relatively strong but are not as robust as they were. In the United States, occasional signs of a recovery keep economists optimistic, but a real economic upturn has failed to materialize. Interest rates in the United States have been pushed down to historically low levels and the value of the dollar keeps falling. Other countries, like Great Britain, are struggling with one of the worst recessions since the Great Depression of the 1930s.

The prospects for firms like BEA are forever tied to the fortunes of the airline industry which, in turn, are affected by economic prospects at the national and international levels. In 1991 the airline industry as a whole accumulated losses of $4 billion. Competition in the airline industry continues to become more cutthroat than ever as airlines competing for market share have initiated more and deeper cuts in fares (witness the very deep discounting during the summer of 1992).[6] Delta, for example, reduced its round-trip fares to Europe by as much as 40 percent. The fare from Atlanta to Madrid was cut from $818 to $498, and the fare from New York to Amsterdam fell to $448 from $600.[7] For some airlines, short-term survival has begun to take precedence over long-term profitability. This means more cuts in operating costs and reducing or cutting orders for new aircraft which, in turn, reduce income for companies like Boeing and their suppliers. While firms like American, Alaska, and Southwest Airlines have been able to rise to the continuing competitive challenge in the airline industry, others have not. Continental and TWA are operating in bankruptcy and Pan Am, Eastern, and Midway are now history. In short, the airline industry is in turmoil. Symptomatic of this is the 5 percent wage cut for Delta

6. *Aviation Week*, pp. 66–67.
7. *The Wall Street Journal* (Western Edition), August 5, 1992, p. B1.

employees[8] and the wave of takeover deals and consolidations. In the summer of 1992, Air Canada and Canadian Airlines International entered merger talks, but the idea was called off when the firms decided that they might be better allied with U.S. carriers than with each other. On August 18, 1992, Air Canada announced a deal with United Airlines, and Canadian Airlines began seeking links with American Airlines.[9] Air Canada may also become involved in a joint purchase of Continental.[10] British Airways bought a 49 percent stake in a German domestic carrier (renamed Deutsche BA), obtained a one-third stake in the Moscow-based joint venture Air Russia, and paid $750 million for a 44 percent stake in USAir.[11] While this last action by British Airways is strictly legal (foreign firms cannot own more than 25 percent voting stock in a U.S. airline and British Airways controls only 21 percent of USAir's voting stock), Robert Crandall of American Airlines and Stephen Wolf of United claim that it is unfair because British Airways will effectively control USAir. This argument gained validity when British Airways and USAir put in a joint bid for the assets of the bankrupt TWA—assets that would be of marginal value to USAir but would be very valuable to British Airways. In addition, the major airlines are having to deal with a flock of new entrants to the industry (Kiwi International Airlines, Reno Air, Destination Sun Airways, American Dreams Airways, Patriot Airlines, and more) that are capitalizing on the surplus of used airplanes, cheap fuel prices, falling labor costs, and the airport gates that have been left vacant by the demise of Pan Am and others.[12]

Despite the turmoil and gloom that has settled over the airlines and aircraft manufacturers, there is good news for the aircraft interior products industry: The installed base still requires refurbishment and retrofits. The downside for BEA is thus limited. In the longer term the outlook for all three industries is much brighter. Worldwide the trend is for more people to travel, and to travel more often. The number of revenue-passenger miles flown by airlines is expected to triple over the next twenty years. To meet this demand, the number of commercial aircraft in service is expected to grow from 9,000 to 16,500, with about 4,200 older and less efficient planes being retired from service. Because of the lower operating costs per revenue-passenger mile that are available from wide-bodied jets, the proportion of these airplanes is expected to increase from 28 percent of the current fleet to about 44 percent. The importance of this increase in wide-bodied jets for BEA can be seen in Table 2. Among other things, the net effect of more wide-bodied planes will be to double the number of seats. In addition to this source of increased demand for seats, new legislation is also lending a hand: The FAA has ruled that by 1997 any aircraft operating out of the United States must be fitted with seats that can withstand forces upon impact equal to sixteen times the force of gravity. Current seat designs are required to withstand only nine times the force of gravity. Over one million seats that are presently in service will be affected by the new ruling.

8. *CNN Business Report,* August 24, 1992.
9. *Business Week,* August 31, 1992, p. 34.
10. *The Wall Street Journal* (Western Edition), August 27, 1992, p. A3.
11. *Business Week,* August 24, 1992, pp. 54–61; *Fortune,* August 24, 1992, p. 137, and September 7, 1992, p. 8.
12. *Business Week,* August 31, 1992, p. 68–69.

Table 2
Product Revenues by Type of Aircraft Body

	Narrow-bodied (per plane, in thousands)	Wide-bodied (per plane, in thousands)
Seats	$180	$ 540
Galley structures	170	980
Galley inserts	70	480
In-flight entertainment	10	1,000
Total	$430	$3,000

The aircraft interior products industry is fragmented but is in the process of consolidation. BEA's acquisitions are speeding that process along. Like many other industries today, the market and the competition is global. BEA's principal competitors for seating include Weber Aircraft (a subsidiary of the U.K.-based multinational, Hanson PLC), Burns Aerospace (a subsidiary of Eagle Industries), SICMA, Koito, and Recaro. For passenger entertainment service systems, including PCUs, BEA's principal competitors are Matsushita Electronics and Hughes Avionics. For galley systems the list includes JAMCO, SELL (a subsidiary of Metallgesellschaft Gmbh) and Royal Inventum. For individual-seat videos, competitors will likely include Matsushita Electronics, Sony Transcom, Hughes, and industry newcomers Philips and GEC/Plessey. As shown in Table 3, not all of these firms compete in all product areas. Some competitors have a product range that is as wide as BEA's, but none currently has as large a presence in the

Table 3
Commercial Aircraft Cabin Interior Products Industry Competitor Analysis (1992)

Company	Revenues (in millions)	Share	Seats	Galley Products	In-Flight Entertainment	Lavatories	Lighting
BE Aerospace	$170	11%	X	X	X		
JAMCO	160	11		X		X	
Weber Aircraft	120	8	X	X		X	
SELL Gmbh	100	7		X		X	
Burns Aerospace	93	6	X				
Grimes Aerospace	80	5					X
Sony Transcom	70	5			X		
Matsushita	60	4			X		
Rumbold	50	3	X	X			
SICMA	45	3	X				
MAG	36	2				X	
Hughes Avionics	35	2			X		
Koito	30	2	X				
Inventum	30	2		X			
Nordskog	30	2		X			
Recaro	30	2	X				

marketplace or as much integration. Some, however, such as Weber Aircraft, Sony Transcom, Matsushita Electronics, and GEC/Plessey, are parts of much larger companies with very deep pockets; such firms may be willing to subsidize short-term losses to become dominant players in the industry in the longer run.

Rigorous testing and certification by the FAA (or similar foreign aviation authorities) create substantial barriers to entry into the aircraft interior products industry. In the United States the FAA grants licenses for the manufacture of aircraft assemblies and for aircraft repair. BEA holds certificates to manufacture aircraft components and to operate six licensed repair facilities. They also operate two repair facilities in Great Britain that are licensed by that country's Civil Aviation Authority. The stringent requirements of the customers also create barriers to entry. Aircraft manufacturers require on-time deliveries, zero defects, and involvement in new product development. The increasing rate of technological evolution may also be a barrier to entry. Aircraft interior products now use sophisticated electronics, flat-screen technology, carbon-fiber composites, and more. This, however, could be a double-edged sword. For example, firms in the defense industry, which have the skills necessary for working with these technologies, are being forced to look elsewhere for business as defense budgets continue to be reduced.

MANAGEMENT AND STRATEGY

Management

The investment group that started BEA has secured a return on its investment in the form of stocks, consultancy fees, and compensation packages for key officers in the company. Returns on the original equity were more than tenfold in the first three years. In addition, in 1992, Amin Khoury's wholly owned consulting firm received $1.25 million from BEA for investment banking services. Other consulting firms, in which some of BEA's directors have interests, have also received fees in the form of monetary payments, stocks, and stock options. The compensation packages for key officers include a guaranteed minimum annual salary plus retirement compensation worth several million dollars after any termination of employment. Personal financial security for senior management has, arguably, been achieved and it now appears that the focus of attention is on the firm's future strategy.

The substantial growth of BEA has meant some changes and necessary additions to the management structure. Marco Lanza, formerly a vice president with Sea Data (a firm specializing in oceanographic monitoring equipment), and who has been with BEA since its inception, was promoted to president of the In-Flight Entertainment Division in 1992. His previous job with BEA, vice president for Marketing and Product Development, has been expanded to group vice president and has been filled by Bud Jewell, formerly the president of Burns Aerospace and Air Maze Corporation. Duane Woodford, who was president of PTC Aerospace (the acquired aircraft seating company), is now president of the Seating Products Division. Similarly, Ernie Schwartz, who was president of APC (the acquired galley company), is now president of BEA's Galley Systems Division. Alex Hamid, BEA's director of finance and corporate controller, was brought on board with the acquisition of EECO Avionics in 1989. Amin Khoury

retains his position as chairman of the board, CEO, secretary and treasurer, and Robert Khoury remains as president and chief operating officer.

While BEA has grown mainly through acquisition, the makeup of its new management team suggests that there has been a change in philosophy and that senior management will not be content with conglomeration and a hands-off management style. They have put together a group of people with not only investment skills but also a breadth and depth of industry-specific knowledge that should permit sustained growth within the aircraft cabin interior products industry, will provide close operational control, and will allow the recognition of interdivisional synergies.

Strategies

BEA has used a broad combination of corporate strategies in its pursuit of growth and profits. Acquisition has been heavily featured and has been responsible for the majority of BEA's growth. Current guidelines for acquisitions require that the targets be leaders in their product line, be profitable in their own right, have good management, and be reasonably priced. This last requirement initially appears to be incompatible with the other three but the evidence from recent acquisitions suggests otherwise. The $73.7 million price tag for PTC and APC (both leaders, both profitable, and both with good management) bought over $100 million in sales, 35 percent of the U.S. aircraft-seat market, and a leading position in galley systems. The firms were acquired from Forstman-Little, a leveraged buyout firm that was trying to change the composition of its business portfolio. BEA also acquired FEEL, in Britain, at a good price because the owner and founder of the company was ready to retire. With the acquisition of FEEL, BEA has secured a position in the European refit and new-plane markets. In addition to the aggressive use of acquisition, BEA is starting to concentrate on product and market development as important components of the overall strategy. As mentioned, the firm has innovations with individual-seat videos, carbon-fiber panels in galleys, and new multiplex systems, and it has sought new customers in rail and bus transport. A market penetration strategy has also been adopted for galley ovens.

The business-level focus for BEA is on cost control through plant rationalizations and on differentiation through product design and service support. Price, while obviously still important, is not as critical as cost and differentiation in achieving and sustaining a competitive advantage. When an airline can lose $500,000 in revenues per day because one of its Boeing 747s is out of service, factors like parts availability take precedence over minor price differences between suppliers. Management at BEA believes that product dependability, close consultation in design and repair, and quick, dependable parts service are critical factors in attracting and retaining customers. These are things for which airlines are willing to pay a premium. It is becoming more and more difficult for small firms to survive in the industry as customers demand the engineering support and after-sales service that are necessary for maintaining the more technologically complex aircraft interiors in today's airliners. Only the larger firms, like BEA, have the ability to afford superior customer service and the capacity to amortize such costs over a large range of products and sales. Its acquisitions have guaranteed market penetration and allowed the firm to generate economies of scale in engineering, marketing, and after-sales service.

OPERATIONS AND FINANCE

Manufacturing

The firm has over 500,000 square feet of space in nine locations including California, Florida, Connecticut, and England (see Table 4). Some of the facilities are leased, some owned.[13] Most are multipurpose and include some combination of manufacturing, R&D, service, warehousing, and sales. The production of individual-seat videos will take place in the newly rented 55,000 square feet of space in Irvine, California. During this expansion, management is continuing to strive for improved efficiency. A manufacturing, service, and warehouse facility that was leased in Garden Grove, California, has been closed and the activities transferred to Litchfield, Connecticut. Plans for 1992 and 1993 also include improving FEEL's efficiency through the reorganization of its five operating facilities into two. While profitable and a leader in European airline-seat manufacture, FEEL currently requires twice as many employee-hours as the U.S. operations (PTC) to produce a seat and has only half the dollar sales per employee.

BEA has been able to increase its integration as acquisitions have continued. Manufacturing processes that were previously contracted out have been brought in-house and new production technologies have been introduced along with new materials for manufacture. Seats can be produced already furnished with PCUs and have in-flight entertainment systems installed in the factory. Similarly, entire galley systems can be designed and equipped with all the components made by BEA. In the areas of manufacturing where the firm is still not fully integrated it continues to buy materials and subassemblies from outside suppliers and subcontractors. The firm is moving towards contractual vertical integration where wholly owned integration is not feasible.

Table 4
BEA's Facilities by Location, Size, and Ownership

Location	Function	Facility Size (in square feet)	Owned or Leased
Litchfield, Connecticut	Manufacturing, service, research and development, sales, finance, and warehousing	147,652	Owned
Irvine, California	Corporate, manufacturing, service, research and development, sales, finance, and warehousing	55,000	Leased
Wellington, Florida	Corporate headquarters	3,000	Leased
Delray Beach, Florida	Manufacturing, service, research and development, sales, finance, and warehousing	52,000	Owned
Jacksonville, Florida	Manufacturing, service, warehousing, and finance	75,000	Owned
Altamonte Springs, Florida	Corporate, manufacturing, service, and warehousing	75,000	Leased
Leighton Buzzard, England	Corporate, manufacturing, service, research and development, sales, finance, and warehousing	64,350	Leased
Chesham, England	Manufacturing, service, and warehousing	65,600	Owned/Leased
Reading, England	Manufacturing	7,000	Leased

13. This excludes sales facilities located in Minneapolis, Seattle, France, Germany, Iran, Taiwan, and China (Beijing).

Product Development and Marketing

Over 1,400 people work for BEA and participate in the employee profit-sharing plan that was introduced in August 1988. Some 1,130 employees are engaged in manufacturing; 160 are engineers and product development personnel. BEA's research and development budget is being expanded. For the seven months ended February 1992, the firm spent $1.3 million on R&D, and in the following three months it spent just over $3 million.[14] It should, however, be noted that the real increase is not quite as large as it appears. The $3 million expenditure in the first quarter of BEA's 1993 year includes the R&D budgets for APC, PTC, and FEEL.

With its large installed-product base, BEA has most of the world's major airlines as its customers. Table 5 gives a list of BEA's customers. To improve its ability to serve its customers the company is merging the sales organizations from all its acquisitions. The intention is that the new marketing organization will provide an integrated, worldwide service to airlines and airplane manufacturers. In line with the management philosophy on product quality and performance, design capabilities, prompt delivery, and after-sales service, BEA has placed engineers on-site with a number of its major customers, in the belief that the presence of these people will help BEA to meet the unique needs of those customers. Such needs include providing a rapid response to requests for engineering services, flexibility with respect to special product features, on-time delivery, spare-parts availability, and personal attention to customer problems. At the end of May 1992, BEA had sixty-three people in sales and 10 on-site engineers that had, collectively, generated an order backlog worth $226 million.

Finance

Tables 6 and 7 show the income statement and balance sheet for BEA. The entry for 1992 reflects the change in the accounting year-end to February 29, thus showing income for seven months only. There are two other points worth noting for the interpretation of Tables 6 and 7: (1) the assets and business of PTC and APC were acquired on February 28, 1992, and (2) the seven-month period includes a substantial amortization of intangible assets.

Profitability in 1988 and 1989 were poor, but performance improved in 1990 and 1991. In 1992 sales were down, reflecting an industrywide deferral of spares purchases and refurbishment programs by airlines. BEA had a net loss of $1.7 million in 1992. This reflects a $5.1 million charge for intangible asset write-down and acquisition expenses. For the 1992–93 first quarter (the period ended May 30, 1992—not included in Table 6), BEA had sales of $45.1 million which, principally because of its acquisitions, have now grown to the point where they account for around 11 percent of the industry total. In the same period gross profit grew to $14.5 million, net earnings rose to $2.4 million, and earnings per share finished at $0.22 on 11.1 million shares. BEA has a policy of not paying dividends; instead, profits are plowed back into the firm and return on investment for stockholders comes wholly from capital appreciation of shares. In 1990, BEA's stock traded at a low of $4.75 and a high of $10.75; in 1991 the low was $7.50 with the high reaching $16.75; and for 1992 the low was $8.50 and the high $15.75 (up to August 26, 1992). The firm's stock is still receiving "buy" ratings from several brokerage firms.

Despite rapid growth, BEA has managed to maintain a relatively conservative capital structure. At the end of February 1992, long-term debt was $40.5 million

14. BEA Quarterly Report for the period ending May 30, 1992.

Table 5
BEA's Customer List, 1992

Aer Lingus	Balair
Aeroflot	Beech Aircraft
Aerocancun	Biman Bangladesh
Aeromexico	Boeing
Aerolineas Argentinas	Braathens S.A.F.E.
Aeroperu	Britannia Airways
Aerospatiale	British Aerospace
African Safari Airways	British Airways
Airbus Industrie	Business Express
Air Afrique	BWIA
Air Algerie	Caledonian Airlines
Air BC	Cameroon Airlines
Air Berlin	Canadair
Air Caledonie	Canadian Airlines International
Air Canada	Cargolux Airlines
Air China	Cathay Pacific
Air France	Catic/Harbin
Air Gabon	China Airlines
Air India	China Aviation
Air Jamaica	China Southern
Air Lanka	Comtrans
Air Mauritius	Commodore Aviation
Air New Zealand	Conair A/S
Air Niugini	Condor Enterprise
Air Ontario	Continental Airlines
Air Pacific	Cruzerio
Air Seychelles	CTA
Air 2000	Cyprus Airways
Air 3000	Dan Air
Air Tours International	de Havilland
Air Wisconsin	Delta Airlines
Air Zaire	Deutsche Airbus
Alaska Airlines	E-Systems
Aloha Airlines	Egyptair
Alitalia	El Al
All Nippon Airways	Emirates Airlines
American West Airlines	Ethiopian Airlines
American Eagle	EVA Airways
American Trans Air	Fairchild
Amtrak	Falcon Jet
Ansett Airlines	Federal Express
Ariana Afgan	Finnair
Aramco	Flight Support Int.
Aspen Airways	Garuda Indonesia
Austral	GATX
Australian Airlines	GEC Sensors
Austrian Airlines	German Cargo
Avensa	GPA/Air Tara
Avianca	GPA Expressair

Table 5
BEA's Customer List, 1992 (continued)

Gulf Air	Polaris
Hapag-Lloyd	Qantas Airways
Hawaiian Airlines	Qatar
Hensen Airlines	Rockwell International
Horizon Air	Royal Air Maroc
Iberia	Royal Brunei Airlines
Icelandair	Royal Jordanian
ILFC	Royal Thai Air Force
Indian Airlines	Saab
International Air Leases	Sabena
Iran Air	SAS
Japan Airlines	SATA
Japan Air System	Satair
JAT (Yugoslav Airlines)	Saudia Arabian Airlines
Kawasaki	Scanair
Kenya Airlines	Scenic Airlines
KLM	Shanghai Airlines
Korean Air	Singapore Airlines
Kuwait Airways	Solomon Airlines
LACSA	Southwest Airlines
Ladeco	Spanair
LAM	Spanish National Railroad
Lan Chile	States West Airlines
Lauda Air	Sterling Airways
Learjet	Surinam Airways
Lockheed Aircraft	Swissair
LOT	TAAG (Angola Airlines)
LTE	Taca International Airlines
LTU SUD	TAP Air Portugal
Lufthansa	Thai Airways International
Lufthansa Cityline	Tower Air
Malaysia Airlines	Tradewinds/Silk Air
Malev Hungarian Airlines	Transbrasil
MarkAir	Transwede
Martinair	Tunis Air
McDonnell Douglas	Turkish Airlines
Mexicana Airlines	TWA
Midwest Express	TW Express
MGM Grand Air	United Airlines
Middle East Airlines	USAir
Minerve S.A.	US Government
Nigeria Airways	UTA
Northwest Airlines	Varig
Olympic Airlines	VASP
Ontario Express	VIASA
Page Avjet Corp.	Virgin Atlantic
Pakistan Airlines	WestAir Commuter Airline
Paschall	World Airways
Patlon	Yemen Airways
Philippine Airlines	Zambia Airways

	Seven Months Ended	Year Ended				
	February 29, 1992	July 28, 1991	July 29, 1990	July 31, 1989	July 31, 1988	July 31, 1987
Statement of Operations (in millions)						
Net sales	$12,192	$24,278	$22,944	$4,127	$3,070	$2,732
Cost of sales	5,626	10,645	11,375	2,568	1,557	1,196
Gross profit	6,566	13,633	11,569	1,559	1,513	1,536
Operating expenses:						
Selling, general and administrative	4,871	3,609	3,425	974	832	668
Research and development	1,324	1,809	1,952	272	291	330
Operating earnings before amortization expense	371	8,215	6,192	313	390	538
Amortization expense	3,707	1,246	1,303	566	539	
Operating earnings (loss)	(3,336)	6,969	4,889	(253)	(149)	538
Interest (income) expense	(743)	(211)	1,564	354	287	13
Earnings (loss) from continuing operations before income taxes (benefit) and extraordinary item	(2,593)	7,180	3,325	(607)	(436)	525
Income taxes (benefit)	(860)	2,478	1,012			97
Earnings (loss) from continuing operations before extraordinary item	(1,733)	4,702	2,313	(607)	(436)	428
Discontinued operations						300
Earnings (loss) before extraordinary item	(1,733)	4,702	2,313	(607)	(436)	128
Extraordinary item, net of tax effect			723			
Net earnings (loss)	$(1.733)*	$4,702	$1,590	$(607)	$(436)	$128
Net earnings (loss) per common share	$(.18)	$.65	$.29	$(.12)	$(.09)	$.03
Common and Common Equivalent Shares	9,604	7,248	5,425	4,813	4,813	3,516

*Includes nonrecurring, non-cash charges of $3,055 resulting from the write-down of intangible assets and $2,090 in expenses related to the company's acquisition program.

Table 6
BE Aerospace, Inc., Income Statement

but by May 30, 1992, after the acquisition of FEEL, it had increased to $55.6 million (not shown in Table 7).[15] While BEA's aggregate credit line stands at $65 million, management does not believe that high leverage should be a permanent feature in the firm's capital structure and plans an aggressive reduction in long-term financial obligations. Between 1991 and 1992 intangible (and other) assets went from nearly $6.0 million to $52.1 million. These assets include production plans and drawings, product approvals, manuals, non-competition agreements, and the value of the installed base that comes with the acquired firms.

By the end of the 1992–93 first quarter, cash increased from $7.2 to $9.3 million, accounts receivable increased by $6.1 million, accounts payable were up by $5.6 million, and inventories jumped from $25.4 million to $36.8 million.

15. BEA Quarterly Report for the period ending May 30, 1992.

Table 7
BE Aerospace, Inc., Balance Sheets, February 29, 1992 and July 28, 1991

Assets (in millions)	1992	1991
Current Assets:		
Cash and cash equivalents	$7,155	$6,344
Accounts receivable—trade, less allowance for doubtful accounts of $879 (1992) and $138 (1991)	20,040	3,641
Inventories	25,421	6,072
Income tax refund receivable	797	
Deferred income taxes	3,420	604
Prepaid expenses and other current assets	573	193
Total current assets	57,406	16,854
Property and Equipment	25,794	3,215
Intangible and Other Assets	52,130	5,965
	$135,330	$26,034
Liabilities and Stockholders' Equity		
Current Liabilities:		
Accounts payable	$11,895	$647
Other current liabilities	13,644	2,459
Income taxes payable		248
Current portion of long-term debt	4,500	
Total current liabilities	30,039	3,354
Long-Term Debt	40,500	
Deferred Income Taxes	2,167	211
Other Liabilities	5,567	
Stockholders' Equity:		
Common stock, $.01 par value; 20,000,000 shares authorized, 10,535,132 shares issued and outstanding on February 29, 1992; 7,076,339 shares issued and outstanding on July 28, 1991	105	71
Additional paid-in capital	54,452	18,165
Retained earnings	2,500	4,233
Total stockholders' equity	57,057	22,469
	$135,330	$26,034

Current assets climbed to $77.4 million, current liabilities rose to $54.4 million, and total assets stood at $180.7 million.

THE FUTURE

There is no question that BEA is successful. Success, however, can be short-lived without a strategy for the future, ideally, one that capitalizes on the firm's previous successes. The issues that now face BEA's management include how to

capitalize on its previous success, how far to go (and in what direction), how fast, and by what means.

Through a blend of corporate- and business-level strategies, BEA's management has led the firm to a position where it has a dominant market share in a growth industry, has generated economies of scale, and has achieved a cost- and differentiation-based competitive advantage. To sustain that advantage, the firm has to keep investing and stay ahead of the competition. How should that investment be directed? If more growth is the answer, how should the firm grow: more acquisitions, market penetration, continued product and market development, or all three? How should the growth be financed? What are the risks of too much growth and overextension of debt and managerial control? Does BEA really need the security of larger size in an industry that is becoming more technologically complex and has the potential for attracting a whole new breed of competitors? How real is the threat of new competitors? Should BEA consider an alternative to more growth? Should it slow down and spend more time digesting its recent acquisitions, continue to focus on cost control and provide even more customer service? Should BEA continue to operate in just one industry? Is it time to consider a more defensive posture? Should it be looking to utilize its engineering competencies in new (diversified) areas? If BEA is at the point where diversification makes sense, should it be done through acquisition, internal development, or joint venture? Would this more conservative strategy make BEA a takeover target?

CASE

19 Blockbuster Entertainment Corporation

Blockbuster Entertainment Corporation (BEC) is one of the fastest-growing entertainment companies in the United States. Blockbuster started life in the video-rental industry in 1986 with nineteen stores; by 1993 it had over 2,400 stores in the United States and over 1,000 stores abroad, making it the biggest video-rental store chain in the world. In 1986 Blockbuster experienced a loss of $2.9 million on sales of $20 million. By 1992 sales and net income were $1.2 billion and $142 million respectively, and its after-tax profits in 1993 are expected to exceed $225 million (see Exhibit 1).[1] In the same period, the company's stock price has risen from an average of $.75 in 1986 to a high of $30 by October 1993 (despite four 2-for-1 stock splits) and in 1990 the stock was added to the S & P

Exhibit 1
Blockbuster's Net Income over Time (in Millions of Dollars)

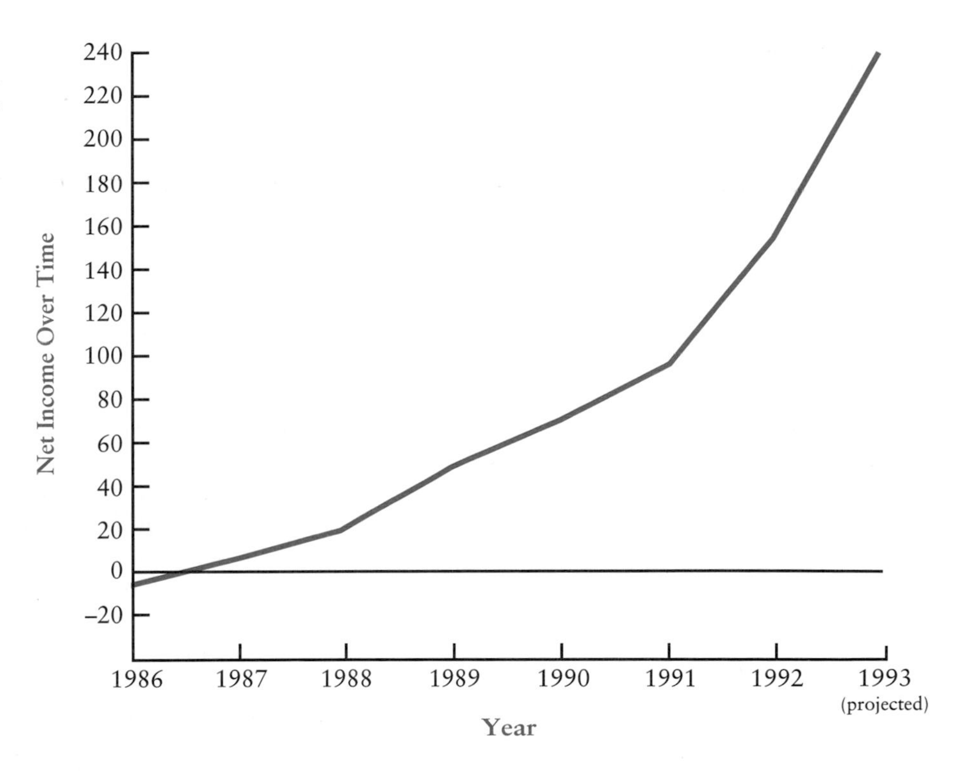

Source: Blockbuster Annual Reports.

This case was prepared by Gareth R. Jones and Susan L. Peters, Texas A & M University. This case was prepared as a basis for class discussion rather than to illustrate either effective or ineffective handling of administrative situations.

1. Blockbuster Entertainment Corp. Value Line, May 28, 1993.

Exhibit 2
VCR Penetration in U.S. Households 1980-1991

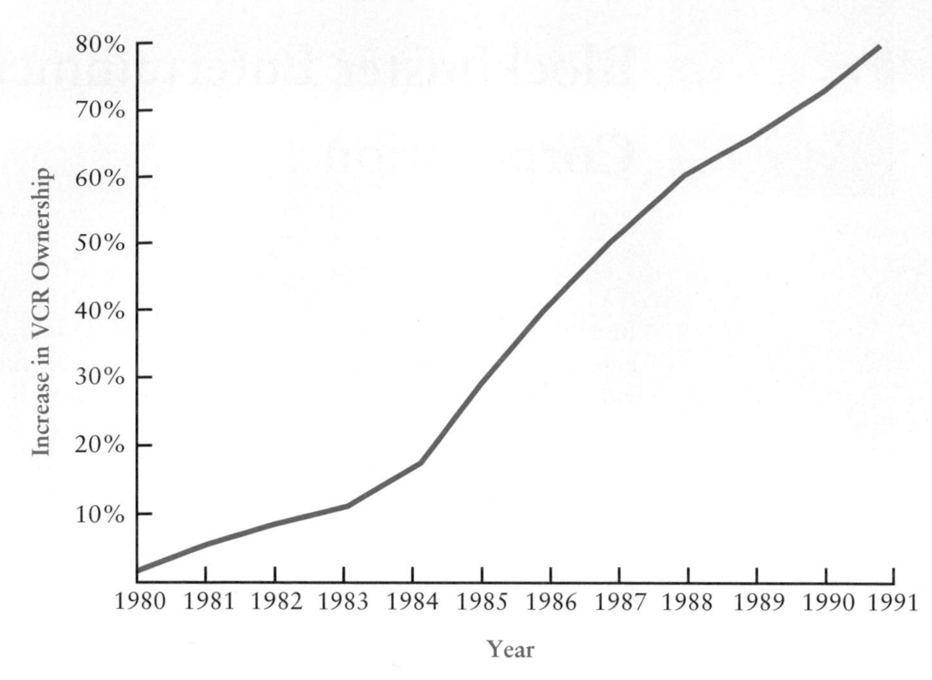

Source: Blockbuster 10-K Reports.

500 index.[2] How did the company achieve this remarkable performance, and how is it trying to stay on top in the highly competitive entertainment business?

BLOCKBUSTER'S HISTORY

David Cook, the founder of Blockbuster, formed David P. Cook & Associates, Inc., in 1978 to offer consulting and computer services to the petroleum and real-estate industries. He created programs to analyze and evaluate oil and gas properties and to compute oil and gas reserves.[3] When oil prices began to decline in 1983 due to the breakdown of the OPEC cartel, his business started to decline and Cook began evaluating alternative businesses in which he could apply his skills. He decided to exit his current business by selling his company and to enter the video-rental business based on a concept for a "video superstore." He opened his first superstore, called "Blockbuster Video" in October 1985 in Dallas, Texas.[4]

Cook developed his idea for a video superstore by analyzing the trends in the video industry that were occurring at that time. During the 1980s the number of households that owned VCRs was increasing rapidly (see Exhibit 2) and consequently, so were the number of video-rental stores set up to serve their needs.

In 1983 7,000 video-rental stores were in operation, by 1985 there were 19,000, and by 1986 there were over 25,000, of which 13,000 were individually

2. Blockbuster Entertainment Corporation 1990 Annual Report, p. 7.
3. Cook Data Services, Inc., 1984 10-K Report, pp. 2–3.
4. Cook Data Services, Inc., 1985 Annual Report, p. 1.

owned.[5] These "mom-and-pop" video stores generally operated for only a limited number of hours, offered customers only a limited selection of videos, and were often located in out-of-the-way strip shopping centers. These small stores often charged a membership fee in addition to the tape rental charge, and generally, customers brought an empty box to the video-store clerk who would exchange it for a tape if it was available—a procedure that was often time-consuming, particularly at peak times such as evenings and weekends.

Cook realized that as VCRs became more widespread and the number of film titles available steadily increased, customers would begin to demand a larger and more varied selection of titles from video stores. Moreover, they would demand more convenient store locations, and quicker in-store service than mom-and-pop stores could offer. He realized that the time was right for the development of the next generation of video stores, and he used this opportunity to implement his video superstore concept, which is still the center of Blockbuster's strategy.[6]

THE VIDEO SUPERSTORE CONCEPT

There are several components to Cook's superstore concept. First, Cook decided that in order to give his video superstores a unique identity that would appeal to customers, the stores should be highly visible stand-alone structures, rather than part of a shopping center. In addition, his superstores were to be large—between 3,800 and 10,000 square feet—well-lit, and brightly colored (for example, each store has a bright blue sign with "Blockbuster Video" displayed in huge yellow letters). Each store would have ample parking and would be located in the vicinity of a large urban population to maximize potential exposure to customers.

Second, each superstore was to offer a wide variety of tapes, such as adventure, children's, instructional, and video-game titles. Believing that movie preferences differ in different locations, Cook decided to have each store offer a different selection of between 7,000 and 13,000 film titles organized alphabetically in over thirty categories. New releases are arranged alphabetically against the back wall of each store to make it easier for customers to make their selections.

Third, believing that many customers, particularly those with children, wanted to keep tapes for longer than a one-day period, he created the concept of a three-day rental period for $3. (In 1991, a two-evening rental program was implemented, making new releases only $2.50 for two evenings during the first three weeks after release; after this period, the usual $3 for three evenings would apply.)[7] If the tape is available, it is behind the cover box. The customer takes the tape to the checkout line and hands the cassette and his or her membership card to the clerk, who scans the bar codes on both the tape and the card. The customer is then handed the tape and told that it is due back by midnight two days later. For example, if the tape is rented Thursday afternoon, it would be due back Saturday at midnight.

5. Blockbuster Entertainment Corporation 1986 Annual Report, p. 9.
6. S. Sandomir, *The New York Times,* June 19, 1991, pp. S22–S25.
7. Blockbuster Entertainment Corporation 1991 Annual Report, p. 24 (QData Corporation Microfiche: St. Petersburg, Florida).

Fourth, Cook's superstores targeted the largest market segments, adults in the 18- to 49-year-old group, and children in the 6- to 12-year-old group. Cook believed that if his stores could attract children, then the rest of the family would probably follow.[8] Blockbuster carries no X-rated moves and its goal is to be "America's Family Video Store."[9] New releases are carefully chosen based on reviews and box-office success to maximize their appeal to families.

Finally, believing that customers want to choose a movie and get out of the store quickly, Cook decided that his superstores would offer customers the convenience of long operating hours and quick service. Hours are generally from 10:00 A.M. to midnight seven days a week. Members pay no initial fee but must show a credit card or leave a check for a security deposit. Members receive a plastic identification card that is read by the point-of-sale equipment, which was developed by the company. This system uses a laser bar-code scanner to read important information from both the rental cassette and the ID card. The rental amount is computed by the system and due at the time of rental. Movie returns are scanned by laser and any late or rewind fees are recorded on the member's account and automatically recalled the next time the member rents a tape. This system reduces customer checkout time and increases convenience. In addition, this system provides data on demographics, cassette rental patterns, and the number of times each cassette has been rented.[10]

These five elements of Blockbuster's approach were successful, and customers responded well. Wherever Blockbuster opened, the local mom-and-pop stores usually closed down, unable to compete with the number of titles and the quality of service that a Blockbuster store could provide. By 1986, Blockbuster owned eight stores and had franchised eleven more to interested investors, who could see the potential of this new approach to video rental. Initially, the company opened stores in markets with a minimum population of 100,000. Franchises were located in Atlanta, Chicago, Detroit, Houston, San Antonio, and Phoenix (the franchise agreements will be discussed in greater detail later).[11] New stores, costing an estimated $500,000 to $700,000 to equip, gross an average of $70,000 to $80,000 a month.[12] The present name of Blockbuster Entertainment Corporation was officially adopted by Cook's company in May 1986.[13]

EARLY GROWTH AND EXPANSION

John Melk, an executive at Waste Management Corp. who had invested in a Blockbuster franchise in Chicago, was to change the history of the company. He contacted H. Wayne Huizenga, a former Waste Management colleague in February 1987 to tell him of the enormous revenue and profits his franchise was making.[14] Huizenga had experience in growing small companies in fragmented industries. In 1955, he had quit college to manage a three-truck trash-hauling

8. Greg Clarkin, "Fast Forward," *Marketing and Media Decisions,* March, 1990, pp. 57–59.
9. G. DeGeorge, *Business Week,* January 22, 1990, pp. 47–48.
10. Blockbuster Entertainment Corporation 1986 10-K Report, p. 7.
11. BEC 1986 10-K Report, pp. 7–9.
12. Sandomir, pp. S22–S25.
13. "Blockbuster Entertainment Corporation," *Moody's Industrial Manual,* pp. 2667–2668.
14. Sandomir, pp. S22–S25.

operation; in 1962 he bought his own operation, Southern Sanitation. In 1968, Southern Sanitation merged with Ace Partnership, Acme Disposal, and Atlas Refuse Service to form Waste Management. In succeeding years, Huizenga borrowed against Waste Management stock to buy over 100 small companies which provided such services as auto-parts cleaning, dry cleaning, lawn care and portable-toilet rentals. He used their cash flows to purchase yet more firms. By the time Huizenga, the vice chairman, resigned in 1984, Waste Management was a $6 billion Fortune 500 company and Huizenga was a very rich man.

Although Huizenga had a low opinion of video retailers, he agreed to visit a Blockbuster store. Expecting a dingy store renting X-rated films, he was pleasantly surprised to find a brightly lit family video supermarket. Detecting the opportunity to take Cook's superstore concept national, Huizenga, Melk, and Donald Flynn (another Waste Management executive) agreed to purchase 35 percent of Blockbuster Entertainment Corporation.[15] The three investors formed an agreement with Cook and BEC to purchase 2,526,696 shares of common stock for $18.6 million in 1986. The three men became directors of BEC at this time.

In 1987, CEO David Cook decided to take his money and leave Blockbuster to pursue another venture at Amtech Corporation. With the departure of the founder, Huizenga took over as CEO in April 1987 with the goal of making Blockbuster a national company and the industry leader in the video-rental market.[16]

Recognizing his inexperience in retailing and franchising, Huizenga hired top managers experienced in developing and growing a retail chain. First, he hired Luigi Salvaneschi, a former McDonald's executive who had gained considerable expertise in facility location during his involvement in the rapid expansion of McDonald's.[17] He also hired Thomas Gruber, a former McDonald's marketing executive, as the chief marketing officer.[18] Through their experience at McDonald's these men had the background to orchestrate Blockbuster's rapid growth.

BLOCKBUSTER'S EXPLOSIVE GROWTH

Together, Blockbuster's new top management team mapped out the company's growth strategy, the elements of which follow.

Location

Store location is a critical issue to a video rental store and Huizenga moved quickly with Salvaneschi to obtain the best store locations in each geographic area that Blockbuster expanded into.[19] They developed a "cluster strategy" whereby they targeted a particular geographic market, such as Dallas, Boston, or Los Angeles, and then opened up new stores one at a time until they had saturated the market. Thus, within a few years, the local mom-and-pop stores found themselves surrounded; many, unable to compete with Blockbuster, closed

15. Ibid., pp. S22–S25.
16. Blockbuster Entertainment Corporation 1987 Annual Report, pp. 4–5.
17. Sandomir, pp. S22–S25.
18. Ibid., pp. S22–S25.
19. Ibid., pp. S22–S25.

down. Video superstores were always located near busy, well-travelled routes to establish a broad customer base. The cluster strategy eventually brought Blockbuster into 133 television markets (the geographic area that a television station reaches), where it reached 75 percent to 85 percent of the U.S. population.[20]

Marketing

On the marketing side, Blockbuster's chief marketing officer, Tom Gruber, applied his knowledge of McDonald's family-oriented advertising strategy to strengthen Cook's original vision of the video retail business.[21] In 1988, he introduced "Blockbuster Kids" to strengthen the company's position as a family video store.[22] This promotion, aimed at the 6- to 12-year-old age group, introduced four characters and a dog to appeal to Blockbuster's young customers. The characters are Player, the leader of the gang; Stopper, who emphasizes safety; Rewind; Slo-Mo; and the dog, Pause. To further demonstrate its commitment to families, each store has forty titles recommended for children and a kids' clubhouse with televisions and toys; thus, children can amuse themselves while their parents browse for videos.[23] In addition, Blockbuster allows its members to specify what rating category of tapes (such as PG or R) may be rented through their account.[24] A policy called "Youth-Restricted Viewing" forbids R-rated tape rentals to children under seventeen without written permission from parents.

Blockbuster also implemented the free "Kidprint Program," through which a child's name, address, and height are recorded on a videotape that is given to parents and local police for identification purposes. In addition, Blockbuster has a program called "America's Most Important Videos Are Free," which offers free rental of public-service tapes about topics such as fire safety and parenting.[25] As another community service, BEC donated videocassettes to the U.S. Armed Forces in the Middle East during the Gulf War.[26] Finally, to attract customers and to build brand recognition, Gruber initiated joint promotions between Blockbuster and companies like Domino's Pizza, McDonald's, and Pepsi-Cola.

Operations

Blockbuster also made great progress on the operations side of the business. As discussed earlier, the operation of a Blockbuster superstore is designed to provide fast checkout and effective inventory management. The company designed its point-of-sale computer system to make rental and return transactions easy. A laser bar-code scanner reads important data from both the rental tape and the membership card to generate information on demographics and rental patterns as well as a summary report for financial control of each superstore. This system is available only to company-owned and franchised stores.[27]

20. Clarkin, pp. 57–59.
21. Ibid., pp. 57–59.
22. Blockbuster Entertainment Corporation 1988 Annual Report, p. 5 (QData Corporation Microfiche: St. Petersburg, Florida).
23. Clarkin, pp. 57–59.
24. Blockbuster Entertainment Corporation 1989 10-K Report, pp. 3–4 (QData Corporation Microfiche: St. Petersburg, Florida).
25. Clarkin, pp. 57–59.
26. BEC 1990 Annual Report, p. 7.
27. BEC 1989 10-K Report, p. 3.

Rapid expansion strains a company's operating systems. To support its stores, Blockbuster opened a 25,000 square foot distribution center in 1986 in Dallas, Texas, giving the company effective distribution and inventory management critical for long-term success. The distribution center has the capacity to store 200,000 cassettes and is used not only to receive tapes and ship them to the stores, but also to package cassettes in conformance with company standards. Each tape is removed from the original container and a label with a security device is affixed to the cassette. Each videotape is then bar coded and placed into a hard plastic rental case. The display carton is made by inserting foam and a security device into the original container and wrapping it. Initial inventory for a store is presorted by alphabet and by category. New releases are processed in the same way. The facility has the capacity to process the initial inventory requirement of about 10,000 tapes for up to three superstores per day. In addition, Blockbuster supplies the equipment and fixtures needed to operate a new store such as computer software and hardware, shelving, signs, and cash registers.[28] In 1987, the physical facilities of the distribution center were expanded to double capacity to 400,000 videocassettes.[29]

The buying power of the company also gives it another operations advantage. It is the largest single purchaser of prerecorded videotapes in the U.S. market and as a result is able to negotiate large discounts off retail price.[30] Cassettes are bought at an average of $40 per tape and rented three nights for $3. Thus, the cash investment on "hit" videotapes is recovered in forty-five to sixty days and the investment on non-hit titles is regained in two-and-a-half to three months. Blockbuster is also able to use its efficient distribution system to distribute extra copies of films declining in popularity to new stores where demand is increasing.[31] This ability to transfer tapes to where they are most demanded allows the company to use its inventory to the best advantage and to receive the maximum benefit from each videotape.

Management

For Blockbuster, as for any company, rapid growth poses the risk that control over daily operations will be lost. Recognizing this, Blockbuster established three divisions to manage the functional activities necessary to retain effective control over its operations as it grew. Blockbuster Distribution Corp. was created to handle the area licensing and franchising of new stores, and to service their start-up and operations. It offers both company-owned and franchised stores assistance with the selection, acquisition, assembling, packaging, inventorying, and distribution of videocassettes, supplies, and computer equipment. Blockbuster Management Corp. was established to assist with the training of new-store management, facility location and acquisition, and employee training. Finally, Blockbuster Computer Systems Inc. was formed to install, maintain, and support the software programs for the inventory and point-of-sale equipment.[32] Together these three divisions provide all the support services necessary to manage store expansion.

28. BEC 1986 10-K Report, p. 8.
29. Blockbuster Entertainment Corporation 1987 10-K Report, p. 11 (QData Corporation Microfiche: St. Petersburg, Florida).
30. BEC 1990 Annual Report, p. 15.
31. Eric Savitz, "An End to Fast Forward?" *Barron's,* December 11, 1989, pp. 13, 43–46.
32. Cook Data Services, Inc., 1985 Annual Report, p. 2.

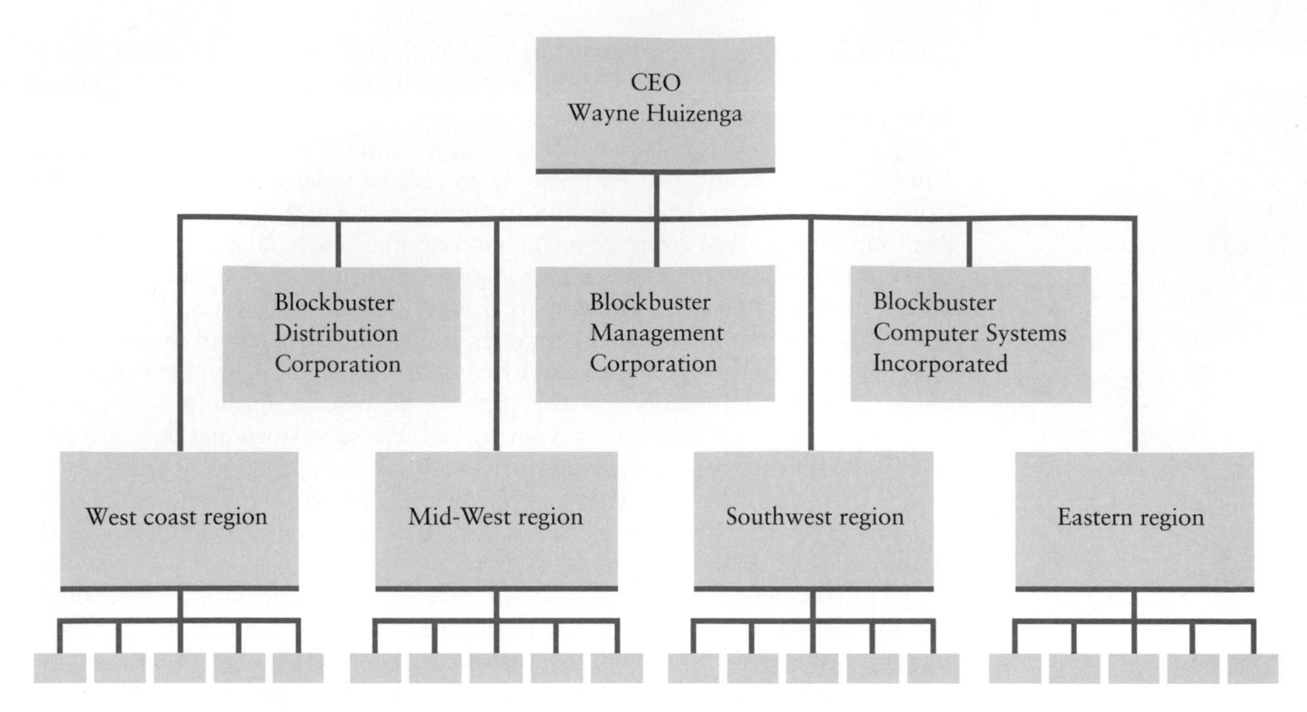

Exhibit 3
Blockbuster's Geographic Structure

Blockbuster also oversees store operations through a regional and district-level organizational structure.[33] In 1988 responsibility for store development and operations was decentralized to the regional level.[34] However, corporate headquarters is kept fully informed of developments in each regional area, and even in each store, through its computerized inventory and sales system. For example, Blockbuster's inventory and point-of-sale computer systems track sales and inventory in each store and each region.[35]

The organizational structure Blockbuster designed to manage its expansion is shown in Exhibit 3. As can be seen, these three functional divisions were set up so that they could quickly respond to the needs of new stores, facilitating Blockbuster's rapid growth and expansion. The role of regional management was to oversee the stores in their regions, providing advice and monitoring stores' performance to make sure that they kept up Blockbuster's high standards of operation as its chain of superstores grew.

NEW-STORE EXPANSION

With Blockbuster's functional-level skills established, the next step for Huizenga was to begin a rapid program of growth and expansion. Huizenga believed that expanding rapidly to increase revenue and market share was crucial for success in the videocassette rental industry. Under his control Blockbuster opened new

33. "Global Notes: Focus 1—Blockbuster Entertainment Corp. (BV)," *Research Highlights,* October 26, 1990, p. 9.
34. BEC 1988 Annual Report, pp. 4–5.
35. BEC 1987 Annual Report, p. 15.

Exhibit 4
Blockbuster Video Stores by Region

Year	Company-Owned	Franchises	Total
1985	1	0	1
1986	8	11	19
1987	71	62	133
1988	341	248	589
1989	561	518	1079
1990	787	795	1582
1991	1025	1003	2028
1992	2002	1125	3127

Source: Blockbuster Annual Reports.

stores quickly, developed a franchising program, and began to acquire competitors to increase the number of its stores.

Company-Owned Stores

To facilitate rapid expansion, Blockbuster began to use its skills in store location, distribution, and sales. At first Blockbuster focused on large markets, preferring to enter a market with a potential capacity for 500 stores—normally a large city. Later, Blockbuster decided to enter smaller market segments, like towns with a minimum of 20,000 people within driving distance.[36] All stores were built and operated using the superstore concept described earlier. Using the services of its three divisions, it steadily increased its number of new-store openings until by 1993 Blockbuster was opening one new store a day. By the end of 1993 it owned over 2,500 video stores. The growth in the number of company-owned stores over time is shown in Exhibit 4.

Acquisitions

Blockbuster's rapid growth is also attributable to Huizenga's skills in making acquisitions. Beginning in 1986 the company began to acquire many smaller video chains in order to gain a significant market presence in a city or region. In 1987, for example, the twenty-nine video stores of Movies To Go were acquired to expand Blockbuster's presence in the Midwest. Blockbuster then used this acquisition as a jumping-off point for opening many more stores in the region. Similarly, in 1989 it acquired 175 video stores from Major Video Corp. and Video Library to develop a presence in southern California. In 1991, it took over 209 Erol's Inc. stores to obtain the stronghold that Erol's previously held in the Mid-Atlantic states.

All acquired stores were made to conform to Blockbuster's standards and any store which could not was closed down. For example, forty substandard Erol's stores were closed down.[37] Most acquisitions were financed by existing cash flow or by issuing new shares of stock rather than taking on new debt. These deals reflect Huizenga's reluctance to borrow a great deal of money.[38]

36. M. McCarthy, *The Wall Street Journal,* March 22, 1991, pp. A1, A6.
37. BEC 1991 Annual Report, p. 40 (QData Corporation Microfiche: St. Petersburg, Florida).
38. Sandomir, pp. S22–S25.

Licensing and Franchising

Recognizing the need to build market share rapidly and develop a national brand name, Huizenga also recruited top management to put in place an ambitious franchise program. Franchising, in which the franchisee is solely responsible for all financial commitments connected with opening a new store, allowed Blockbuster to expand rapidly without incurring debt. The downside of franchising is that Blockbuster had to share profits with the franchise owners. When franchising, it is important to maintain consistency in stores. Thus, the franchisees were required to operate their stores in the same way as company-owned stores and to follow the same store format for rental selection and the use of proprietary point-of-sale equipment.

Blockbuster's current method of franchising was established in January 1988. Under this plan, a franchisee is granted the right to open a store for twenty years with renewal rights of an additional five years if the store is in compliance with agreements. All franchise owners pay an initial fee of up to $55,000 for the privilege of using the Blockbuster Video trademark. The capital investment required to open a store generally ranges from $425,000 to $650,000. All licensed and franchised stores must meet Blockbuster's design criteria and use its standardized operating systems so customers have no problems in identifying and using the company's stores.[39] A charge of up to $30,000 is assessed for software and the monthly software-maintenance fee varies from $500 to $650. Franchise owners pay royalty fees from 3 to 8 percent of gross revenue as determined by their agreement with Blockbuster, remit a certain percentage for marketing and promotions, and contribute 1 percent of gross receipts for national advertising. Contributions to national advertising began in 1989 when the 500th store was opened. All rental transactions must be recorded in the point-of-sale inventory control program and any inventory must be approved by BEC. Moreover, franchise owners are required to buy from Blockbuster at least 5,000 videotapes of the required initial inventory of 7,000.[40] In addition, the franchise owner must complete Blockbuster's training program or hire a manager who has completed Blockbuster's training program to run the store. Assistance with activities such as site selection and employee training are available for a fee.[41]

Franchising facilitated the rapid expansion of Blockbuster Video. By 1992 the company had over 1,000 franchised stores as compared to 2,000 company-owned stores (see Exhibit 4). However, recognizing the long-term profit advantages of owning its own stores Blockbuster began to repurchase attractive territories from franchisees.[42] In 1993, the company spent $248 million to buy the 400 stores of its two largest franchisees and, with a new store opening every day, by the end of 1993 it owned over 2,500 stores.

However, by the end of 1992, despite its rapid growth, Blockbuster still only controlled about 15 percent of the market—its 27,000 smaller rivals shared the rest (see Exhibit 5). Consequently, in 1993 Blockbuster announced plans for a new round of store openings and acquisitions that would give it a 25 to 30 percent market share within two or three years.

39. BEC 1989 10-K Report, p. 6.
40. Ibid., pp. 6–9.
41. Blockbuster Entertainment Corporation 1991 10-K Report, pp. 7–9 (QData Corporation Microfiche: St. Petersburg, Florida).
42. BEC 1990 Annual Report, p. 21.

Exhibit 5
Blockbuster's Market Share

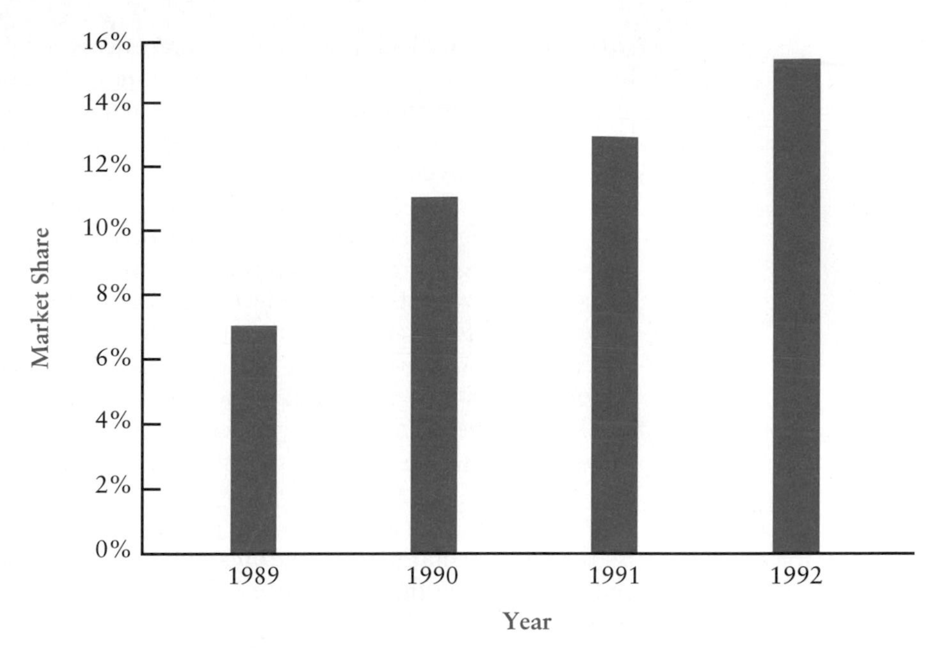

Source: Blockbuster Annual Reports.

THE HOME-VIDEO INDUSTRY

Revenues from video rentals now exceed the revenues obtained in movie theaters. For example, video-rental revenues rose to $11 billion in 1991 compared to movie theaters' $4.8 billion, cable movie channels like HBO's $5.2 billion, and pay-per-view's $133 million.[43] Domestic video revenue in 1992 was nearly $12 billion.[44] The huge growth in industry revenues has led to increased competition for customers, and, as noted above, 28,000 video stores operate in the United States.

Blockbuster Video does not face a direct national competitor, and it is the only company operating beyond a regional level. The next largest competitor, West Coast Video, had only $120 million in 1991 revenues.[45] In contrast, Blockbuster Video had 1991 rental revenues of $868 million.[46] Blockbuster does, however, face many competitors at the local and regional levels. For example, various supermarket chains across the United States, such as Kroger and Winn Dixie, had aggregate video-rental revenues of $1.35 billion in 1991.[47] Similarly, video stores in the Pacific and Mid-Atlantic states have six competitors within three miles and the competition between them has resulted in price wars in some areas. In the San Antonio market, for example, competition between video

43. BEC 1991 Annual Report, p. 10.
44. Blockbuster Entertainment Corporation 1992 Annual Report, p. 5.
45. Gail DeGeorge, Jonathan Levine, and Robert Neff, "They Don't Call It Blockbuster for Nothing," *Business Week,* October 19, 1992, pp. 113–114.
46. Value Line, May 28, 1993.
47. Scott Hume, "Blockbuster Means More than Video," *Advertising Age,* June 1, 1992, p. 4.

stores resulted in Blockbuster and its competitors reducing their prices to $2.00, but then HEB (a supermarket chain) responded by dropping its price to $1.50 and offering $.99 specials; this started a new price war. As a result, Blockbuster has been forced to give its stores some freedom in their pricing policies to meet local competitive conditions.

To handle increased competition from Blockbuster, some local competitors are emphasizing service. For example, salespeople at Video Factory in Buffalo, New York, wear tuxedos and use umbrellas to escort customers to their cars when it rains. Other competitors have introduced newer technology; California-based Tower Video, for example, rents 8-mm videos and laser disks, while Blockbuster concentrates on standard VHS videocassettes.[48] Stores can also compete by selling other products, such as pre-recorded videotapes, blank videotapes, candy, and video games. Blockbuster has begun selling these items and is testing the sale of laser disks, which it will carry if there is a demand.[49]

Mature Market

As the video-rental market matures, the level of competition in the industry is changing. During the 1980s, video rentals grew rapidly due to the proliferation of VCRs. By 1990, however, 70 percent of households had VCRs, compared to 2 percent in 1980; industry growth dropped from the previous double digits to 7 percent.[50] Exhibit 2 illustrates the changes in the percentage of people who owned VCRs for the period from 1980 to 1991. The slow growth in VCR ownership and rentals will make competition more severe and put increased pressures on the weaker companies in the industry. Blockbuster, however, with its strong national base, is in a good position to compete in the poorer environment.

To a large degree, competition in the video-rental industry is so fierce because it is relatively easy for new competitors to enter the market; the only purchase necessary is videotapes (which movie studios will supply to any potential purchaser). This ease of start-up accounts for the existence of so many video stores—more than 28,000 nationwide.[51] Blockbuster, however, unlike small video-rental companies, is able to negotiate discounts with tape suppliers because it buys new releases in such huge volumes.

Blockbuster's customers, who are principally individual families, do not pose a threat to the company. However, in an increasingly competitive situation, Blockbuster's three-day rental policy could be a disadvantage because of the "boomerang effect": all the highly demanded movies are checked out on Thursday so that they are not available until Sunday. Many of Blockbuster's customers come for the new releases; *Video Insider* magazine states that the twenty most popular movies at any one time account for 80 percent of tape rentals in the United States. Blockbuster, however, claims that the top fifty titles account for only 35 percent of its rental revenues, so its policy does not hurt sales; customers are not getting frustrated and going elsewhere when new releases are not available.[52]

48. McCarthy, pp. A1, A6.
49. Blockbuster Entertainment Corporation 1990 10-K Report, p. 6 (QData Corporation Microfiche: St. Petersburg, Florida).
50. McCarthy, pp. A1, A6.
51. Ibid., pp. A1, A6.
52. Savitz, pp. 43–46.

New Technology

One growing problem facing Blockbuster is the variety of new ways in which customers can view movies and other kinds of entertainment. Blockbuster has always felt competition both from other sources of movies—such as cable TV and movie theaters—and from other forms of entertainment—such as bowling, baseball games, and outdoor activities. Technology is now giving customers more ways to watch movies. New technological threats include pay-per-view or video-on-demand systems, digital compression, and direct broadcast satellites.

Pay-per-view movies could become a major competitive threat to video-rental stores. Currently, with pay-per-view systems, cable customers can call their local cable company and pay a fee to have a scheduled movie, concert, or sporting event aired on their television set.[53] Soon, a cable customer could call up their local "video company" and choose any movie to be aired on his or her television for a fee; the cable company would make the movies available when the customer wanted it. Increasingly, telephone companies are becoming interested in the potential for pay-for-view because the networks of fiber-optic cable they are installing in ordinary households can transmit movies as well. Huizenga claims Blockbuster is not overly concerned about pay-per-view systems because only one-third of U.S. households have access to pay-per-view, and fiber optics is expensive.[54] Moreover, it is claimed that home video rental is cheaper than pay-per-view and new releases are attained thirty to forty-five days before pay-per-view.

However, this threat may become much stronger as the technology improves and companies make moves to implement pay-per-view systems. Time Warner has already replaced coaxial cable with fiber optics to offer 150 cable channels in Queens, New York.[55] GTE Corporation is testing a system that transmits movies through fiber-optic cables. A bigger move comes from the largest U.S. cable operator, Tele-Communications, Inc. (TCI), which formed a strategic alliance with Carolco, a film producer, to release four movies for pay-per-view before they are released in the theater over the next 4 years. Pay-per-view will be the foundation of TCI's plan to install technology and fiber-optic transmission systems capable of providing homes with 500 cable channels.

Video-on-demand takes the pay-per-view concept further. Bellcore, the research branch of the regional Bell companies, invented video-on-demand. With this system (still in the trial stage), a customer will use an interactive box to select a movie from a list of thousands and the choice will be transmitted to an "information warehouse" that will store thousands of tapes in digital formats. The selected video will then be routed back to the customer's house through a series of switches, and a signal splitter will send the movie into the home through the phone lines. This essentially bypasses the local video-rental store because the movies are stored digitally on tape at the cable company's headquarters.

Movie companies or video stores like Blockbuster could function as the information warehouse from which the video selections are made; Blockbuster is interested in acting as the warehouse so that it can control the video-on-demand market, which could become a direct threat to video rental as the technology is refined. Blockbuster began discussions with Bell Atlantic Corporation, which is developing a video-on-demand system for customers in northern Virginia that will be tested in 1993. Bell Atlantic is developing a method of transmitting video

53. Shapiro, *The New York Times,* February 21, 1992, p. D6.
54. Sandomir, pp. S22–S25.
55. Ibid., pp. S22–S25.

over the "twisted-pair" or copper wire used in the phone lines; the method uses Asymmetric Digital Subscriber Lines (ADSL) to send 500,000 cycles of electric signals per second. A signal-processing chip located in the customer's home will pick up the signal, and the movie will be seen. Bell Atlantic will use its phone lines in the Washington, D.C., area to offer movies and other programs that customers can order and immediately watch at home; households can obtain the system by 1994. Bell hopes to offer between thirty and a hundred films, which would be instantly available to customers. Blockbuster, which would provide the movies for the video-on-demand system, views this move as an expansion of their business rather than cannibalization of video rentals.

U.S. West, one of the "Baby Bells," has also announced plans to build a video-on-demand network to serve 13 million homes in fourteen states; with its partner, Time Warner, it plans to eventually reach 25 percent of the viewing market. The linking of phone companies with other entertainment companies could become a direct threat to Blockbuster, but Huizenga believes he can make the local Blockbuster store the center of the video-on-demand network. He feels that phone companies will prefer to deal with Blockbuster than with companies like Time Warner or Paramount, which lack both Blockbuster's skills in video retailing and its established customer base—the 30 million customers who make 600 million trips per year to the local store. Note that if Blockbuster does become the information warehouse of video-on-demand systems, videotape rentals will decrease, hurting Blockbuster's own direct sales, but likely finishing off the local mom-and-pop stores; in the long run, Blockbuster will seize control of both the video-rental and video-on-demand market.

Other new technologies include digital compression and direct broadcast satellites. Digital compression allows up to five television channels to be sent on the same bandwidth that used to be able to carry only one channel. This provides more space for movies to be sent to customers.[56] Direct broadcast satellites (DBS) are also an emerging threat. Already, local cable service is becoming available throughout the United States by installing a small, two-foot diameter satellite dish. The dishes cost between $500 and $700 to purchase but as companies like Hughes Aircraft and Motorola gear up to mass-produce them, their cost is quickly falling. Existing cable companies are moving to gain control of the new satellite market; the number of channels available to transmit movies directly to people's homes could harm the video-rental industry because customers would no longer have to go to video-rental stores to get a movie.[57]

BLOCKBUSTER EXPANDS GLOBALLY

Blockbuster, under Wayne Huizenga, is attempting to exploit the skills and capabilities it has developed in the domestic video-rental market by expanding globally. Its great size and secure financial position provided by the large growth in its domestic revenues allows Blockbuster to diversify into global markets and to exploit the possibilities offered by the new technological developments discussed earlier. Satellite systems, for example, are gaining importance in the European market.

56. Ibid., pp. S22–S25.
57. "Global Notes," p. 9.

The Global Marketplace

Seventy percent of the world's VCRs are in countries outside the United States, and foreign countries account for half of total world video-rental revenues. The United States is the largest video market, with 1991 revenues of $11 billion. Japan is second, with $2.6 billion, followed by the United Kingdom with $1.4 billion and Canada with $1.2 billion.[58] Blockbuster has decided to seize this opportunity to increase its revenues by expanding abroad. Just as in the United States, Blockbuster has a program both to build new video superstores and to acquire foreign competitors abroad. Planning to be a leader in home entertainment around the world, Blockbuster's objective is to obtain a 25 percent share of international revenue by 1995 and to have 2,000 stores in international markets by 1996.[59]

Blockbuster began to expand into international markets in 1989 when it saw the opportunity to exploit its marketing expertise, superstore concept, operating knowledge, financial strength, and ability to attract franchisees abroad. In 1989 stores were opened in Canada and the United Kingdom.[60] In 1990, Blockbuster opened its first store in Puerto Rico. It continued its expansion into the United Kingdom, Canada, the Virgin Islands, Venezuela, and Spain. Franchise agreements were also signed in Japan, Australia, and Mexico.[61] For example, an Australian franchisee agreed to open 150 outlets over a five-year period.[62] A similar agreement was attained in Mexico.[63] By the end of 1990 there were forty-seven franchises or joint ventures in Canada, twenty-five in the United Kingdom (six were company-owned and nineteen were franchised, with one store each in Puerto Rico and Guam).[64]

In Japan, Blockbuster formed a joint venture in March 1991 with Den Fujita, who runs McDonald's Co. Japan and has a stake in Toys Я Us Japan Ltd. This venture opened fifteen stores in Japan in 1992 and will add thirty stores in 1993 and 1,000 stores within ten years. Due to fierce price competition, the Japan stores are meeting only 90 percent of sales projections.[65] Under the terms of this fifty-fifty joint venture agreement with Fujita & Co., Ltd., Blockbuster can franchise more stores in Japan.[66] Blockbuster is importing its video concepts to a market that is very interested in video rentals. By forming a joint venture, Blockbuster can benefit from the expertise of Japanese locals in running a business in Japan.

To expand in the United Kingdom, in February 1992 Blockbuster purchased Cityvision PLC, the United Kingdom's largest video retailer, for $81 million cash and 3.9 million shares of stock.[67] Under this arrangement, Blockbuster acquired around 97 percent of Cityvision's voting common stock and about 45 percent of its nonvoting preferred stock. At this time, Cityvision ran 875 stores in Britain and Austria under the name Ritz.[68] Blockbuster transformed the Ritz outlets into Blockbuster stores and used the chain as a start for further expansion into

58. BEC 1991 Annual Report, p. 18.
59. QRP Merrill Lynch Extended Company Comment, November 16, 1990.
60. Blockbuster Entertainment Corporation 1989 Annual Report, p. 27.
61. BEC 1990 Annual Report, p. 19.
62. "Stock Highlight: Blockbuster Ent. (NYSE-14)," *Value Line: Selection & Opinion,* March 8, 1991, pp. 168–169.
63. BEC 1990 Annual Report, p. 19.
64. QRP ML Extended Company Comment: Blockbuster ENTM(BV) (Merrill Lynch 1990), pp. 2–5.
65. DeGeorge, Levine, and Neff, pp. 113–114.
66. QRP ML Extended Company Comment: Blockbuster ENTM(BV) (Merrill Lynch 1990), pp. 2–5.
67. DeGeorge, Levine, and Neff, pp. 113–114.
68. BEC 1991 10-K Report, p. 4.

Europe, just as it had taken over large video chains in the United States on its way to becoming the national leader. Joint ventures are also being negotiated in France, Germany, and Italy. Blockbuster is increasing the number of franchised stores in Mexico, Chile, Venezuela, and Spain. By the end of 1992, the company had 952 stores in nine foreign countries with plans to establish at least 1,200 more by 1995.[69] Eighty-six percent of its international stores are company-owned and 14 percent are franchised.

Blockbuster created an international home-video division to oversee and manage its expansion into foreign markets. Besides having expertise in international operations, marketing, merchandising, product purchasing, distribution, franchising, real estate, and field support, this division is proficient at dealing with differences in entertainment, language, and business culture between different countries and is successfully implementing Blockbuster's domestic strategy in its foreign operations.[70]

Diversification

Blockbuster became a national video-rental chain because of the way it positioned itself in the market as a family-oriented store with a wide selection of videos, convenient hours and locations, and fast checkout. Recently, Blockbuster has begun expanding its entertainment concept into several new areas of business.[71] The major areas of diversification are into film entertainment programming and music retailing. In an effort to increase its revenue, Blockbuster is also making deals to broaden its range of product offerings.

Film Entertainment Programming To enter the programming aspect of the filmed entertainment business, Blockbuster has invested in both Spelling Entertainment Group, Inc. and Republic Pictures Corporation. Both of these companies have large film libraries—a source of inexpensive movies for Blockbuster's retail operations.[72] Blockbuster issued 7.6 million shares of common stock valued at $140 million to acquire a 48.2 percent interest in Spelling Entertainment from American Financial Corp., which is closely held by investor Carl Linder. Under the deal, Linder gains a 4 percent stake in Blockbuster; Blockbuster gains access to Spelling's library of 600 feature films and fifty-five television shows, including "Beverly Hills 90210." Spelling will sell its programs in Blockbuster's video stores. This deal also provides Blockbuster with access to the broadcast and cable television markets; and Spelling's proficiency in cable network programming could help Blockbuster, which might consider managing its own cable channel in the future.[73]

Blockbuster paid $25 million for a 35 percent stake in Republic Pictures, an independent film distributor and producer. Blockbuster has warrants to purchase an additional 810,000 shares.[74] Republic's programming library includes classics such as "High Noon," "The Quiet Man," and "The Bells of St.

69. DeGeorge, Levine, and Neff, pp. 113–114.
70. BEC 1992 Annual Report, p. 17.
71. DeGeorge, Levine, and Neff, pp. 113–114.
72. Value Line, May 28, 1993.
73. Laurie Grossman and Gabriella Stern, "Blockbuster to Buy Controlling Stake in Spelling in Swap," *The Wall Street Journal,* March 9, 1993, p. B9.
74. "Business Briefs: Blockbuster Entertainment Corporation," *The Wall Street Journal,* February 12, 1993, p. B6.

Mary's."[75] This investment also strengthens Blockbuster's hold in the programming side of the entertainment industry because Republic has ongoing deals with the television, home-video, and theatrical markets.

Music Blockbuster also chose the music business as an area into which it could expand its entertainment concept. As in the video-store industry, many music stores are mom-and-pop businesses or parts of small chains. Moreover, music stores are increasingly selling videos such as the Walt Disney collection, musicals, and family movies. Blockbuster saw a fit between selling records, cassettes, and compact discs and renting or selling videos. Thus it decided to employ the same strategy it had used in the video-rental market: opening new stores and acquiring chains of music stores using the revenues from its video superstores.

However, Blockbuster will not sell CDs and cassettes in its video stores. Instead, its music business will be operated independently, with separate stores that will use the same superstore concept that was so successful in the video-rental business. The stores will be very large (20,000 to 25,000 square feet) and will offer a wide selection of music products such as recorded music, computer software, games, and, possibly books. Blockbuster is developing a new design for its music stores that will attract customers of all ages and musical tastes. The stores will be clean and bright and will offer a large selection of all types of music. The tapes will be displayed by categories. The computer system used in the video stores will be tailored for the music stores; music customers will also get bar-coded membership cards.[76] The new music-store chain may be called "Chartbusters."

In addition, Blockbuster plans to build smaller outlets (10,000 to 15,000 square feet) and acquire existing chains. As part of its plan to diversify into the $8 billion record industry, Blockbuster agreed to buy Sound Warehouse and Music Plus, two record-store chains, for $185 million, including assumption of debt, from Shamrock Holdings Inc. At the time, Sound Warehouse was the seventh largest music retailer and Music Plus was the twelfth largest. These two retail chains had a total of 236 stores in thirty-five states, primarily in California and the South. This acquisition made Blockbuster the seventh largest music chain.

With 30 million video customers, Blockbuster can begin to introduce joint promotions and advertising between its music and video stores, such as giving a customer a 15 percent discount on a CD for renting two videos.[77] In this way it will encourage customers who visit one of its stores to visit the other as well. Its ability to attract families and young people gives it a great advantage here because in 1991, 64 percent of record sales were to people aged fifteen to thirty-four, Blockbuster's main customer group.[78] Blockbuster also hopes that it will be able to apply aspects of its video business to the music business as well, such as its computer software and store-management skills.

To strengthen its position in the music and video industries, Blockbuster agreed to develop a chain of "megastores" in the United States with Virgin

75. Grossman and Stern, p. B9.
76. BEC 1992 Annual Report, p. 23.
77. Johnnie Roberts, "Blockbuster Officials Envision Superstores for Music Business." *The Wall Street Journal,* October 28, 1992, pp. B10.
78. Ibid., p. B10.

Retail Group of London. Blockbuster will own 75 percent of the U.S. chain and Virgin will own 25 percent, but the two companies will share control equally. Virgin will manage the new stores, which will be named "Blockbuster Virgin Megastores." These stores will average 30,000 square feet and will sell videos, music products, and computer software.[79] The first store—a huge 30,000-square-foot, two-story store owned jointly by Blockbuster and Virgin—was opened in Los Angeles at the end of 1992. The store sells over 100,000 compact disk titles (about six times the average sold by a record store in a shopping mall) and has seventy-five listening headsets for customers to use. The second story has laser disks, videotapes, and computer games; Nintendo and Sega machines are available for customers to play games free. Virgin Atlantic Airways even has a ticket counter in the store![80] Ten additional megastores, which will be modeled after this store, will be opened in major U.S. cities in 1993 and 1994.

As part of its thrust for global expansion, Blockbuster has also acquired a 50 percent interest in the fifteen Virgin Megastores in France, Germany, Italy, Australia, and The Netherlands.[81] Under this agreement, the two companies will jointly develop more megastores (separate from the Chartbuster record stores) through continental Europe and Australia to become a dominant force in the European market.[82] Virgin's three-story, 40,000-square-foot Paris store earns $125 million in annual sales, 7 percent of the French music market.[83]

Although part of the entertainment business, music retailing is significantly different from video retailing. For instance, the target market for music is generally not families, whereas the video stores are built around families. However, Blockbuster has proven that it can manage its superstores efficiently, and its joint venture with Virgin should allow it to demonstrate its expertise.

Blockbuster faces strong competition in the U.S. music business. Because it is fifty years old, the record industry has more experienced competitors than the video industry. Some major competitors include the sixth largest retailer, Super Club, which owns Record Bar, Turtles, Tracks, Sam Goody's, and Tower Records. Tower, for example, plans to accelerate the development of its own 10,000- to 50,000-square-foot megastores.[84]

New Product Offerings In an effort to expand its product offerings, in November 1991 Blockbuster made an agreement with Philips Electronics N.V. whereby Philips will invest $66 million and take a 4 percent stake in Blockbuster. Under this agreement, Blockbuster will test renting to its video customers Philip's multimedia CD-interactive software, which combines video, audio, text, and graphics to create games and educational programs.[85] Blockbuster capitalized on cross-marketing opportunities by informing its video-game renters—potential

79. Helene Cooper, "Blockbuster and Virgin Retail Group Plan a Chain of 'Megastores' in the U.S.," *The Wall Street Journal,* November 17, 1992, p. B10.
80. "Blockbuster Entertainment Corporation," *Chain Store Age Executive Edition,* January 1993, p. 63.
81. Cooper, p. B10.
82. 1992 BEC Annual Report, p. 43.
83. "Blockbuster Entertainment Corporation," p. 63.
84. Cooper, p. B10.
85. Michael McCarthy and Bob Hagerty, "Philips to Put $66 Million in Blockbuster," *The Wall Street Journal,* November 19, 1991, p. B1.

CD-I customers—about the interactive software. In July 1992, Philips increased its stake to 13 million shares, or 7.9 percent, at a total cost of $149 million.[86] Philips also has a 51 percent stake in Super Club Holding which, as mentioned earlier, is a strong competitor of Blockbuster in the music business. Blockbuster would like to acquire some of the U.S. record stores owned by Super Club Holding & Finance S.A., including Turtles and Record Bar. In addition, Blockbuster is interested in Super Club's Video Towne and Alfalfa Video, which together are the third largest U.S. video chain.[87] Blockbuster, as noted earlier, wants to obtain a 25 percent share of the video-rental market over the next ten years.

In another new-product move, Blockbuster is working with IBM to develop a software program that would allow music-store customers to create a customized audio compact disk or cassette from a computerized inventory of thousands of different albums. The customer literally walks into a music store, creates a cassette or disk to order, and walks out with it. Another product is books on audiotape, the first major new product launched since video games were introduced in 1988.[88] In addition, film processing is being tested in some Florida stores.[89]

The company is also branching its entertainment concept. In 1990, it sponsored the first Blockbuster Bowl—Florida State University against Penn State—which sold out.[90] The company also sees opportunities in themed, family-oriented entertainment centers, which will have batting cages, miniature golf, a high-tech video arcade, virtual-reality computer simulators, play areas for children, food service, and merchandising. The first center will open in 1993.[91] In June 1990, Blockbuster formed a joint venture to develop and operate three amphitheaters, circular outdoor arenas for rock concerts and other entertainment events. The first amphitheater was opened in Phoenix, Arizona, in November 1990. Other entertainment deals include gaining exclusive rights to distribute the 1990 World Series and other major-league baseball video productions and exclusive retail rights to the 1992 Summer Olympics from NBC.[92] These events would be on video.

BLOCKBUSTER'S NEW STRUCTURE

In 1993, in an effort to manage the companies it acquired in its quest to become a full-service home entertainment retailer, Blockbuster reorganized and split into several divisions: domestic home video, international home video, music retailing, international music retailing, new-technology ventures, and other entertainment ventures (see Exhibit 6).[93]

86. DeGeorge, Levine, and Neff, pp. 113–114.
87. McCarthy and Hagerty, p. B1.
88. Hume, p. 4.
89. McCarthy, pp. A1, A6.
90. BEC 1990 Annual Report, p. 5.
91. BEC 1992 Annual Report, p. 31.
92. BEC 1990 Annual Report, p. 5.
93. Geraldine Fabrikant, "Blockbuster President Resigns: Video Chain Revamps to Adapt to New Units," *The New York Times*, January 5, 1993, p. D6.

Exhibit 6
Blockbuster's New Structure

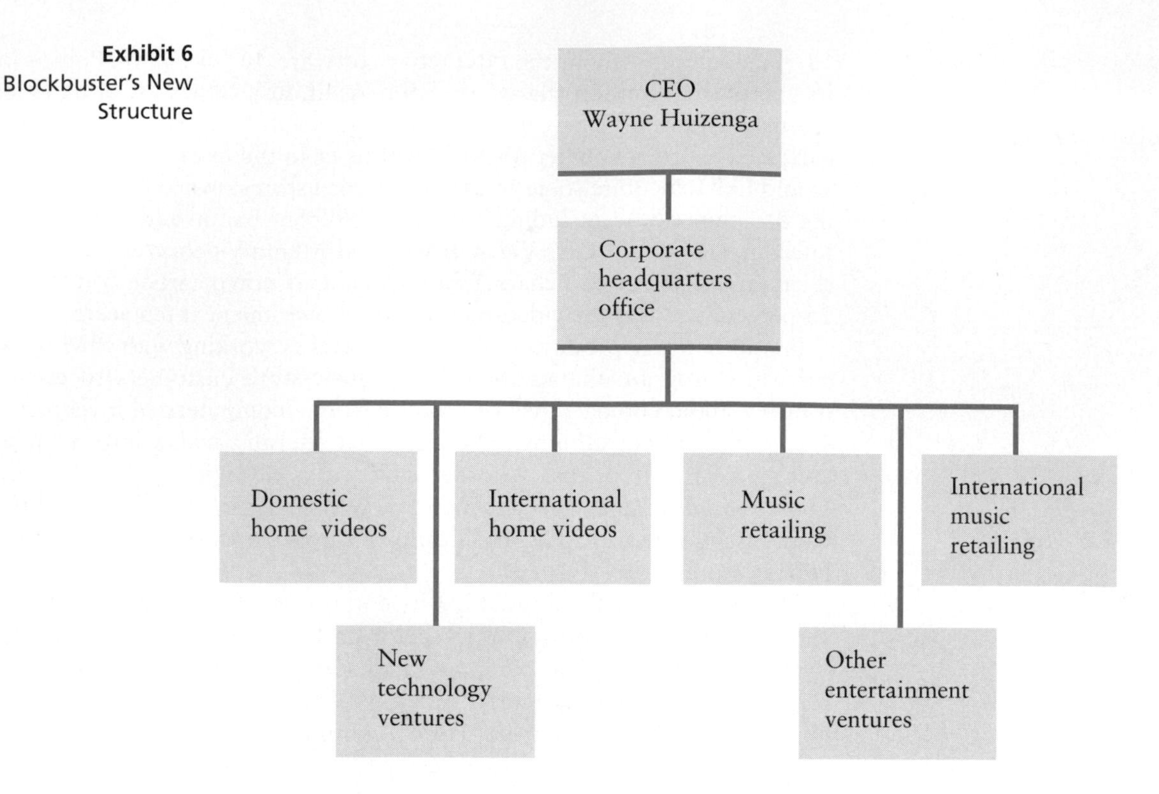

THE FUTURE

Expecting the video industry to continue growing, Blockbuster aims to increase net income by at least 20 percent a year over the next five years.[94] With a debt-to-capital ratio of only 17 percent and a healthy cash flow, Blockbuster's expansion plans are financially feasible.[95] In October 1992, Blockbuster Video opened its 3,000th store and its 1,000th international store.[96] In 1993, Blockbuster intends to expand locations in nine foreign countries: Australia, Austria, Canada, Chile, Japan, Mexico, Spain, the United Kingdom, and Venezuela. In addition, the company will continue to expand its music stores.[97] Blockbuster will also continue to allocate resources for the internal development of new entertainment-based technologies, resulting in more entertainment options for customers and allowing the company to protect its market position.

The question many analysts are asking is, Where will Blockbuster be in five years? Does it have the skills and capabilities to protect its position and develop its hold on the entertainment market to become the dominant company in the entertainment business, or given new technological developments will it lose its hold on the video-rental market, the ultimate source of the revenues it is using to diversify? Can the company maintain its amazing rate of growth?

94. BEC 1991 Annual Report, p. 6.
95. DeGeorge, Levine, and Neff, pp. 113–114.
96. BEC 1992 Annual Report, p. 3.
97. BEC 1992 Annual Report, p. 42.

Selected Financial Data
As of and for the Years Ended December 31 (in Thousands, Except per Share and Store Data)

	1992	1991	1990	1989	1988
Systemwide revenue	$1,985,839	$1,520,141	$1,133,150	$663,475	$283,691
Revenue	$1,200,494	$868,003	$632,670	$402,538	$179,779
Net income	142,034	93,681	68,654	44,152	17,526
Net income per common and common equivalent share—assuming full dilution	.76	.56	.42	.28	.12
Total assets	1,437,420	804,125	608,214	417,314	234,698
Long-term senior debt	173,000	24,000	67,927	24,218	39,488
Subordinated convertible debt	118,532	109,645	101,378	93,729	—
Total shareholders' equity	783,706	483,804	314,764	208,189	124,058
Cash dividends per share	.06	—	—	—	—
Number of stores at end of year:					
Video:					
Company-owned	2,002	1,025	787	561	341
Franchise-owned	1,125	1,003	795	518	248
Total video stores	3,127	2,028	1,582	1,079	589
Music:					
Company-owned	238	—	—	—	—
Joint venture	15	—	—	—	—
Total music stores	253	—	—	—	—

Blockbuster Entertainment Corporation and Subsidiaries
Consolidated Statements of Cash Flows for the Years Ended December 31 (In Thousands)

	1992	1991	1990
Cash Flows from Operating Activities:			
Net Income	$142,034	$93,681	$68,654
Adjustments to reconcile net income to cash flows provided by operating activities:			
Depreciation and amortization	265,211	189,215	124,106
Interest on subordinated convertible debt	8,945	8,267	7,649
Changes in operating assets and liabilities, net of effects from purchase transactions:			
Increase in accounts receivable	(9,593)	(14,602)	(6,848)
(Increase) decrease in merchandise inventories	3,786	(37,364)	(6,563)
(Increase) decrease in other current assets	(7,937)	366	989
Increase (decrease) in accounts payable and accrued liabilities	(38,349)	21,570	24,037
Increase in income taxes payable and related items	19,556	39,759	16,173
Other	(4,966)	(7,150)	(14,634)
	378,687	293,742	213,563
Cash Flows from Investing Activities:			
Purchases of videocassette rental inventory, net	(229,179)	(174,158)	(132,384)
Purchases of property and equipment, net	(79,425)	(60,629)	(79,796)
Cash used in acquisitions	(252,880)	(7,855)	(2,483)
Other	(22,893)	(15,603)	(15,390)
	(584,377)	(258,245)	(230,053)
Cash Flows from Financing Activities:			
Proceeds from the issuance of common stock, net	80,769	11,516	2,438
Proceeds from long-term senior debt	308,214	66,000	95,433
Repayments of long-term senior debt	(182,330)	(113,915)	(70,803)
Cash dividends paid	(7,154)	—	—
Other	(6,804)	—	(1,068)
	192,695	(36,399)	26,000
Increase (decrease) in Cash and Cash Equivalents	(12,995)	(902)	9,510
Cash and Cash Equivalents at Beginning of Year	48,398	49,300	39,790
Cash and Cash Equivalents at End of Year	$35,403	$48,398	$49,300

Blockbuster Entertainment Corporation and Subsidiaries
Consolidated Balance Sheets as of December 31 (In Thousands, Except Share Data)

	1992	1991
Assets		
Current Assets:		
Cash and cash equivalents	$ 35,403	$ 48,398
Accounts receivable, less allowance	43,995	31,770
Merchandise inventories	174,294	75,629
Other	22,523	6,797
Total Current Assets	276,215	162,594
Videocassette Rental Inventory, Net	305,277	232,171
Property and Equipment, Net	330,832	237,831
Intangible Assets, Net	404,412	103,314
Other Assets	120,684	68,215
	$1,437,420	$804,125
Liabilities and Shareholders' Equity		
Current Liabilities:		
Current portion of long-term senior debt	$ —	$ 501
Accounts payable	205,015	118,309
Accrued liabilities	94,062	30,025
Income taxes payable	12,827	15,303
Total Current Liabilities	311,904	164,138
Long-term Senior Debt, Less Current Portion	173,000	24,000
Subordinated Convertible Debt	118,532	109,645
Other Liabilities	50,278	22,538
Commitments and Contingencies	—	—
Shareholders' Equity:		
Preferred stock, $1 par value; authorized 500,000 shares; none outstanding	—	—
Common stock, $.10 par value; authorized 300,000,000 shares; issued and outstanding 190,730,493 and 162,100,554 shares, respectively	19,073	16,210
Capital in excess of par value	445,212	244,592
Cumulative foreign currency translation adjustment	(34,656)	—
Retained earnings	354,077	223,002
Total Shareholders' Equity	783,706	483,804
	$1,437,420	$804,125

Blockbuster Entertainment Corporation and Subsidiaries
Consolidated Statements of Operations for the Years Ended December 31 (In Thousands, Except per Share Data)

	1992	1991	1990
Revenue:			
Rental revenue	$856,171	$649,516	$468,287
Product sales	284,594	172,427	129,005
Royalties and other fees	59,729	46,060	35,378
	1,200,494	868,003	632,670
Operating Costs and Expenses:			
Cost of product sales	190,546	122,025	91,904
Operating expenses	679,440	494,615	344,394
Selling, general and administrative	105,877	96,983	77,062
Operating Income	224,631	154,380	119,310
Interest Expense	(13,047)	(14,179)	(14,212)
Interest Income	6,975	3,865	2,970
Other Income, Net	1,649	2,311	43
Income before Income Taxes	220,208	146,377	108,111
Provision for Income Taxes	78,174	52,696	39,457
Net Income	$142,034	$93,681	$68,654
Net Income per Common and Common Equivalent Share	$.77	$.56	$.43
Net Income per Common and Common Equivalent Share—assuming full dilution	$.76	$.56	$.42

CASE

20 Video Concepts, Inc.

As Chad Rowan, the owner of Video Concepts, Inc., looked over his monthly income statement, he could only shake his head over how it could have been so much different. In many ways he was a very successful entrepreneur, having started and grown a profitable business. In other ways, he felt trapped in a long-term no-win situation. The question now was what should he do given the current business environment. Basically, Chad had a profitable business but the profits were relatively small and had stopped growing since a strong competitor, Blockbuster Video, had moved into town. The profits, however, were not enough to pay off his long-term debts and provide him with any more than a subsistence living. In addition, the chances of selling his business for enough to pay off his debts, and then start another business, were not good.

In reflecting on what might have been, Chad commented:

> I had really hoped to expand Video Concepts into several similar sized towns within a couple of hours' driving distance from here. The financial projections, which had been fairly accurate until Blockbuster arrived, indicated expansion was possible. I thought I was growing fast and had put about as much capital into the business as I could afford. I had even hoped to get a partner to go into this business with me, and one was very interested. Right now, however, I do not feel that I'm getting a very good return on my time and capital.

Talking about the current situation, Chad said:

> I guess I'm getting a taste of my own medicine. As I grew, several local businesses went out of business, but the good news is that the total market has grown since Blockbuster opened its store. Their marketing clout has brought more people into the market.

To compete with Blockbuster, Chad has tried everything he can think of to get market share. He has said, "The only way to increase revenues seems to be to raise the rental price, but my lower price is the best marketing strategy I have. If I raise the price, I'm afraid I will lose a lot of market share."

BACKGROUND

Chad Rowan had been interested in having his own business since he had started and operated a lawn service business in high school. Chad had started in the ninth grade mowing lawns for his neighbors using his family's lawn mower. By

This case was prepared by John Dunkelberg and Tom Goho, Wake Forest University. This case was prepared as a basis for class discussion rather than to illustrate either effective or ineffective handling of administrative situations.

the time he had graduated from high school, his business had grown to a service that had purchased its own equipment: a riding mower, two smaller mowers, two blowers, a lawn aerator, an edger, and a trimmer. His business grew to the point that he employed three of his high school friends. The profits from this business were enough to pay his tuition to college, and he continued the business throughout his four college years.

Chad majored in business and took the only two courses that were available in entrepreneurship and small business management. During his senior year he did some research on the video rental business, which at that time was a relatively new industry. His research resulted in a research paper on the video rental business. The paper included a business plan for the start-up of a small video rental store with an inventory of about 500 videotapes. By the middle of his senior year, Chad knew he wanted to start in the videotape rental business, and he had already chosen the site, a vacant retail store in the downtown business district of his hometown.

Starting a Business

After graduation in 1987, Chad opened Video Concepts, a video rental store with 200 square feet of retail space and a 500 tape rental library in Lexington, North Carolina, a town of about 28,000 people. Video Concepts started slowly but was profitable within six months. Chad tried several innovative marketing techniques including home delivery, a free rental after ten rentals, and selling soft drinks and popcorn both at the store and with the delivered videos. To help reduce the expense of the start-up business, Chad lived at home with his parents and took only $500 a month for his own wages. Revenues that first year were $64,000 with all surplus cash flows being used to buy additional videotapes. At the end of the first year's operation, Chad decided to expand to a larger store.

A 1,000 square foot retail store was available in a small shopping center that served a major neighborhood area. Chad borrowed $80,000 from his banker to open this store using the value of some corporate stocks that he owned as collateral. The loan was a seven-year note with only interest due during the term of the loan and the entire principal due in seven years. The new store had 3,000 videotapes. Chad purchased all his new releases through Major Video, one of the top three wholesale distributors in the United States. To increase the size of his video library, he purchased over 2,000 used tapes from a firm that purchased tapes from bankrupt firms for resale. Over the next two years, Video Concepts continued to grow rapidly and remained profitable. Chad, however, continued to put all profits into the purchase of additional tapes. Revenues during the second year increased to $173,000, and $278,000 in the third year.

Growth Continues

The chance to open a third store became a reality when a furniture retail store located in Lexington's busiest shopping district decided to move to its own, larger building on the outskirts of town. The store contained 3,000 square feet of space, enough to hold over 12,000 tapes on display. Chad obtained a three-year lease on the store and opened his third video rental store in the fall of 1990. Video Concepts now had stores in the three main shopping areas of Lexington.

The new Video Concepts store used open display racks for the videotapes and customers could quickly and easily locate the type of movies they wanted by going to the section (i.e., new releases, horror, science fiction, action, classical,

etc.) and walking down the aisle. Checking out was quick and easy, thanks to a new computer software program that reduced checkout time to less than thirty seconds per customer. In addition, the software program provided a management information capability that allowed him to keep track of the number of times each tape was rented, how many tapes each customer rented, and who had past-due tapes. The system also allowed Chad to easily track sales on a daily, weekly, or monthly basis. The new store and the more efficient operation enabled Video Concepts to become a growing and fairly profitable business.

During the next year, growth at the three Video Concepts stores continued, with the majority of the growth coming from the new store. Chad continued the policy of a free rental after ten rentals, reduced the price per rental to $1.99 per night, and introduced some advertising centered primarily on local high school promotional events. The original two stores saw little growth in sales but remained profitable.

As his business had grown, the number of competitors had steadily decreased, and by the summer of 1991, only six of the original seventeen competitors were still operating. Chad thought his aggressive pricing strategy, high-quality service, and good selection of new releases were factors in the demise of some of his smaller competitors. His six competitors averaged a tape inventory of less than 1,000 videotapes and none had more than 1,600 tapes. Chad estimated that the present annual revenues from video rentals in Lexington was about $600,000.

The increase in video rental chain stores nationally had not gone unnoticed by Chad, and he had visited several competitors' stores in nearby cities. During his visits, Chad primarily had tried to see what the competition was doing and learn what he must do to be more efficient and stay competitive. Although he had visited Blockbuster Video stores in several nearby cities, Chad estimated that their stores would require annual revenues of at least $600,000 a store to be profitable. For this reason Chad believed that Lexington was too small to attract a major video rental chain store. He also believed that he had a store operation that was as well stocked and efficiently operated as a chain store operation.

With these thoughts in mind, he began paying himself a modest annual salary of $15,000. In addition, he was ready to start paying off the second loan of $200,000 that he had borrowed to open the new store. To obtain this last loan, Chad had used all the assets that he owned as collateral because he believed that these stores were an excellent investment. In the summer of 1991, with sales increasing in every month, Chad had reason to think that he had built a successful business.

SERIOUS COMPETITION ARRIVES

In August 1991 Blockbuster Entertainment announced that it would open a store in Lexington. Blockbuster, although a very young corporation, was the largest video rental chain store in the United States. Blockbuster had grown from 19 stores in 1986 to 2,028 (1,025 company-owned and 1,003 franchises) in 1991 with total revenues over $1.2 billion in 1992. The typical Blockbuster store carried 8,000 to 14,000 tapes, and the stores ranged in size from 4,000 to 10,000 square feet. In 1991 the 1,248 company-owned stores that had been in operation for more than a year were averaging monthly revenues of $74,984.

Although the growth in the United States in consumer spending on video rentals seemed to have slowed, Blockbuster Video believed it had the opportunity to take market share away from the smaller competitors through its strategy of building large stores with a greater selection of tapes than most of its competitors. As the largest video rental chain in the United States, Blockbuster also had advantages in marketing and in the purchase of inventory. Blockbuster Video's standard pricing was $3.50 per tape for two nights, but local stores had some pricing discretion.

In the fall of 1991, Blockbuster built a new store almost across the street from the main Video Concepts store. It purchased a vacant lot for $310,000 and then leased a 6,400 square foot building that was built to their specifications under a long-term lease agreement for $8.50 per square foot for the first three years. The cost of completely furnishing the building, including the videotapes, was about $375,000 and Blockbuster spent over $150,000 on the grand opening promotions. Thus Blockbuster spent about $835,000 to open its store compared to the just over $200,000 that Video Concepts had spent to open its similar-sized store. Blockbuster's operating costs were very similar to Video Concepts' since the computer checkout equipment was similar and both firms had approximately the same personnel costs. Both firms depreciated their tapes over twelve months.

BLOCKBUSTER'S IMPACT ON VIDEO CONCEPTS

Chad decided not to try to meet the grand opening blitz by Blockbuster with an advertising promotion of his own, but he did start including brochures on Video Concepts with each rental. The brochure noted that the rental fee at Video Concepts was lower than Blockbuster's, that Video Concepts had a new game section where Nintendo games were available, that Video Concepts was a family entertainment store (i.e., no X-rated videos), and that Video Concepts was a locally owned store that supported local school events. Chad felt his past reputation for low prices ($1.99 versus $3.50 at Blockbuster), his hometown ownership, and courteous service were the appropriate response to a well-financed competitor. He did not believe that he should even attempt to match Blockbuster's advertising budget and that he should not try to beat Blockbuster at its game. That is, he must continue to do what he did best and not try to match Blockbuster's marketing strategy. He did, however, increase the number of tapes purchased for each new release.

With the opening of the new Blockbuster store and its attendant grand opening marketing campaign, Video Concepts' revenues dropped about 25 percent for two months and then started slowly climbing back to its pre-opening levels. During this two-month period, Chad had worked even harder to provide excellent customer service through brief training sessions for his employees. He had always had employee training sessions, but these emphasized the competitive threat from Blockbuster and the need to provide the best customer service possible. The primary points of these sessions were directed toward informing customers, as they checked out, of how many rentals they had before they could obtain a free rental, the customer's ability to reserve videos, and Video Concepts' willingness to deliver videos to a customer's home at no extra charge. (These were all services that Blockbuster did not offer.)

Unfortunately, Video Concepts' revenues hit a plateau of just under $40,000 per month and stayed there, with the normal minor seasonal variations, for the next twelve months. During this time, Chad attempted several marketing promotions including rent one–get one free on the normally slow nights (Mondays, Tuesdays, and Wednesdays); mailed brochures to all Video Concepts customers, which included a brief highlighting of the advantages of shopping Video Concepts over Blockbuster (lower price and additional services); and a free rental coupon.

The promotions seemed to help Video Concepts maintain the current revenue level, but they also decreased the profitability of the operation. To try to improve the profitability, Chad examined his operation for ways of making it more efficient. By studying the hour-by-hour sales patterns, he was able to schedule his employees more efficiently. He also used the information provided by the software program to determine when the rentals of "hit" and/or new releases had peaked. Chad learned that there was a fairly good market for used tapes for a short period of time, but, if the tape was not sold during this time, he would end up with a tape that had very little rental demand and little resale value.

The problem with the "hit" videos was twofold. The first problem was the determination of how many tapes to purchase. There seemed to be little correlation between a hit at the box office and a hit from rentals. When the video was first released for rental, Chad would buy forty to fifty videotapes at a cost of about $60 each. The demand for these videos would be very high for about six weeks to three months, after which the demand would drop significantly. The second problem, therefore, was the determination of when and how many of the tapes to sell before the demand would drop to the level of non-hit videos. Chad believed that he had solved the second problem by carefully watching the sales figures for the tapes. Analysis of this information helped to minimize his investment in his inventory of tapes which marginally improved cash flow.

THE DILEMMA

Two years after Blockbuster had opened its store, Chad carefully analyzed the financial statements for Video Concepts. The company was profitable and had been able to maintain its market share. (See Exhibits 1 and 2.) What was evident was the fact that the arrival of Blockbuster had increased the demand for video rentals in Lexington to an estimated $1,300,000 a year. Blockbuster's share was estimated to be about $700,000 a year and the few remaining independents had around $100,000 a year in revenues.

To Chad the current situation was fairly straightforward. Video Concepts had a store that was comparable to Blockbuster's in tape selection, personnel costs, and efficiency of operation. Video Concepts had a cost advantage in having lower store leasing costs ($3.50 per square foot versus $8.50), but Blockbuster had a bigger advantage in being able to use its purchasing power to purchase videotapes at a much lower cost. Video Concepts' major marketing strength was its lower rental price ($1.99 versus $3.00), but Blockbuster utilized a much larger advertising budget to attract customers. (All of the Blockbuster stores in that region charged $3.50 rental except the one in Lexington.)

As had happened nationwide, the growth of video rental revenue leveled off in the Lexington area starting in 1992. (Nationwide in 1992, sales increased

only 4.7 percent for Blockbuster stores that had been in operation more than one year.) Future growth did not look bright as indications that advances in cable television technology could render video store rentals obsolete as fiber optics allow cable subscribers to order a wide variety of movies at home through pay-per-view services. This technology, however, is still in developmental stages, and its spread to small towns is certainly many years away.

Looking to the future, Chad felt that for all his efforts, the net income from the Video Concepts operation would not provide him as high a return on his time and his capital as he had expected. He was still paying only the interest on his long-term loans and paying off the debt seemed several years away. From Chad's viewpoint, he had several options. Chad considered raising the price of an overnight rental to $2.49 to make the business more profitable but was afraid of what the consequences of such a move might be. He also considered hiring someone to manage the business and find another job for himself. He had offers of corporate jobs in the past and was considering exploring this option again. Another alternative was to try to sell the business. As Chad pondered these alternatives, he tried to think of a solution that he may have overlooked. What he was sure of, however, was that he did not wish to keep working twelve-hour days at a business that did not seem to have a bright future.

Exhibit 1
Video Concepts, Inc.
Income Statement
One Year Ending
June 30, 1993

Revenues		$465,958
Cost of goods*		192,204
Gross profit		$273,754
Expenses		
Salaries**	$108,532	
Payroll taxes	11,544	
Utilities	20,443	
Rent	23,028	
Office expenses	26,717	
Maintenance	6,205	
Advertising expenses	4,290	
Interest expenses	27,395	
Total expenses		228,154
Income before taxes		45,600
Taxes		10,944
Net income		$34,656

* Cost of goods = purchase price minus market value of tapes. This method is used because most of the tapes purchased are depreciated over a twelve-month period.

** Salaries include Chad's salary of $15,000.

Cash	$15,274	Accounts payable	$15,429
Inventory	4,162	Sales taxes payable	2,415
Prepaid expenses	1,390	Withholding/FICA payable	3,270
Total current assets	$20,826	Total current liabilities	$21,114
Office equipment	$48,409	Bank term loan	$247,518
Furniture & fixtures	53,400	Common stock	20,800
Video cassette tapes	303,131	Retained earnings	24,153
Leasehold improvements	39,800		
Accumulated depreciation*	(151,981)		
Total assets	$313,585	Total liabilities & equity	$313,585

* Includes the depreciation of tapes.

Exhibit 2
Video Concepts, Inc.
Balance Sheet
June 30, 1993

References

"Blockbuster Goes after a Bigger, Tougher Rep." *Variety*, January 25, 1993, p. 151.

"Blockbuster, IBM Plans Set Retailers Spinning," *Variety*, May 17, 1993, p. 117.

"Blockbuster Idea Might Work for Computer Industry," *MacWeek*, May 24, 1993, p. 62.

"Blockbuster Sizes up PPV Potential: Talks Home Delivery with Bell Atlantic," *Billboard*, January 30, 1993, p. 11.

"Changes in Distribution Landscape Have Players Scouting Claims," *Billboard*, May 16, 1993, p. 52.

"Oscar Noms Mean Gold for Video Industry," *Variety*, February 24, 1992, p. 79.

"Play It Again and Again, Sam," *Newsweek*, December 16, 1991, p. 57.

"Recording Industry Hits Blockbuster," *Advertising Age*, May 17, 1993, p. 46.

"Record Store of Near Future: Computers Replace the Racks," *The New York Times*, May 12, 1993, p. A1.

"Stretching the Tape," *The New York Times*, April 22, 1993, p. B5.

"Video and Laser Hot Sheet," *Rolling Stone*, March 4, 1993, p. 72.

"VSDA Regaining Its Sense of Direction," *Variety*, June 8, 1992, p. 19.

CASE

21 Cineplex Odeon

Garth Drabinsky, Chairman and CEO of Cineplex Odeon, has never been known to shy away from a fight. On June 30, 1989, he was true to his reputation as he faced a group of uneasy shareholders at the company's annual meeting in a downtown Toronto theatre. Drabinsky had burly guards posted at the entrances and exits, instructed his public relations staff to keep their lips sealed and did not allow reporters to bring in any electronic equipment.

The firm stance reflected a hardball approach to business that had earned Drabinsky the nickname Darth, after the screen super-villain Darth Vader. But this reputation was based on more than just an aura of toughness and a knack for brilliant deals. It was founded on significant accomplishments in the movie industry. Through a combination of innovative theatre formats, bold acquisitions, and strong financial alliances, Drabinsky had developed Cineplex Odeon into the second largest theatre chain in North America (see Exhibit 1). In the process, Drabinsky had single-handedly changed the face of film exhibition, rejuvenating what had become a stagnant part of the industry.

As long as Drabinsky continued to pile success upon success his aggressive style and disregard for conventions were tolerated. His dominance over all aspects of Cineplex Odeon had been deemed necessary for the pursuit of his unique and ambitious vision. But now with doubts being raised about the financial health of Cineplex Odeon (see Exhibit 2, including footnotes), Drabinsky's reputation as a brilliant strategist was being subjected to increased scrutiny. Drabinsky was also facing strong resistance and had suffered serious setbacks in his recent attempts to gain a controlling interest in his company. All of these developments had created an unusually high level of anxiety and apprehension among the audience that had gathered for the company's annual meeting.

But the mounting pressure could hardly mute Drabinsky's forceful style. He ruled the meeting with an iron hand, disdainfully rejecting any attacks from the audience and defiantly reaffirming his faith in the future of Cineplex Odeon. "I am completely sanguine," he remarked, "that the company will continue to grow."[1] As far as Drabinsky was concerned, this was not the first time that he had found himself in a tight corner and once again, he was intent on confounding his critics.

This case was prepared by Joseph Lampel, New York University, and Jamal Shamsie, New York University, and is intended for use as the basis for class discussion. It is drawn entirely from published sources. The authors wish to acknowledge the assistance of Xavier Gonzalez-Sanfeliu.

1. "The Perils of Drabinsky," *Report on Business Magazine*, September 1989, pp. 46–50+.

Exhibit 1 Theatres in Operation

	1988		1987		1986		1985		1984	
	Screens	Locations	Screens	Locations	Screens	Locations	Screens	Locations	Screens	Locations
United Artists	2,677	686	2,048	485	1,595	437	1,124	329	1,063	344
Cineplex Odeon	1,832	502	1,644	492	1,510	495	1,117	394	439	170
American Multi-Cinema	1,614	278	1,528	277	1,336	263	956	182	800	156
General Cinema	1,400	321	1,358	332	1,275	342	1,163	333	1,083	331
Loews	822	221	310	87	300	85	232	66	215	66
Carmike	701	213	669	220	674	236	435	168	432	182
Hoyts	550	120	275	55	240	52	103	22	105	25
National Amusements	552	91	404	77	393	88	345	84	314	84
Mann	456	109	447	110	456	126	350	110	325	98
Famous Players	448	148	427	147	466	176	469	196	466	199

Source: *Variety*.

THE EARLY YEARS

A Consuming Passion

Garth Drabinsky's determination to beat the odds began early in life. Struck by polio at the age of three, he spent most of his childhood checking in and out of hospitals. After a long period of infirmity he was able to walk without a brace, although he has a pronounced limp to this day. The same willpower and concentration that Drabinsky used to confront his illness were later applied to other parts of his life. Although he excelled in a wide variety of activities, it was the silver screen that truly captured his passion.

But it was with his law studies at the University of Toronto in the early 1970s that Drabinsky began to make movies his life's work. He took a keen interest in the emerging field of entertainment law and later wrote a textbook on the subject that became a standard reference source. His studies, however, did not prevent him from producing a half-hour TV show starring William Shatner and launching a movie magazine that was given away free at cinemas.

In 1976, Drabinsky made a foray into movie production. His first film featured Donald Sutherland but was never completed. The following year, he teamed up with producer Joel Michaels to form a film production company that remained active for several years. Among the movies that the company produced were *The Silent Partner* with Christopher Plummer, *The Changeling* with George C. Scott, and *Tribute* with Jack Lemmon. Although acclaimed critically, none of these films brought in much money at the box office.

A Multiplex Strategy

In 1979, Garth Drabinsky joined forces with Nathan Taylor, an industry veteran who had long believed in the concept of theatres with multiple screens. Drabinsky found the idea appealing, and together the two formed Cineplex. Their first multiplex theatre was located in Toronto's Eaton Centre, a newly developed shopping centre. It contained as many as eighteen separate theaters, each with a seating capacity ranging between 60 to 150 people.

Exhibit 2
Income Statements

	In millions of U.S. dollars for the year ended December				
	1984	1985	1986	1987	1988
Revenues					
Admissions	$42.7	$85.0	$230.3	$322.4	$355.6
Concessions	12.3	24.9	71.4	101.6	114.6
Distribution and other	9.3	7.8	30.8	61.2	156.4*
Sales of properties#	2.8	6.6	24.4	35.0	69.2
	$67.1	$124.3	$356.9	$520.2	$695.8**
Expenses					
Operating expenses	48.7	89.5	258.3	371.9	464.3
Cost of concessions	3.7	6.0	13.7	18.8	21.6
Cost of sold properties	0.9	2.7	11.7	21.6	61.8
General and administrative	3.5	5.7	15.3	18.0	26.6
Depreciation & amortization†	2.1	3.7	14.3	24.0	38.1
	$58.9	$107.6	$313.3	$454.3	$612.4
Other income	0.1	0.3	—	—	3.6
Interest expenses@	2.5	4.0	16.2	27.0	42.9
Income taxes	2.2	5.0	6.3	4.3	3.7
Extraordinary items	5.6	2.3	1.4	—	—
Net income	$9.2	$10.3	$22.5	$34.6	$40.4

Shown as part of operating revenue
† Depreciation schedule changed from 1986 to lower this charge
@ Excludes interest costs that have been capitalized
* Includes proceeds from sale of 49% interest in Film House
** Later changed to $648.0 million to exclude proceeds from sale of Film House

Source: Cineplex Odeon Annual Reports.

Cineplex saw itself as a niche player. It countered the trend in the industry whereby exhibitors used their large theatres in order to get the potentially lucrative releases from the Hollywood distributors (see Appendix). Instead, the newly developed multiplex chain could use its small screens to show specialty movies, in particular foreign films and art films that could not be shown profitably in large theatres. As Taylor put it, Cineplex was not out to challenge the major chains, but to complement them:

> We are seeking to develop a market that to some extent doesn't exist. We are taking specialized markets and filling their needs. It's a latent market and a different niche than the major chains go after.[2]

But Cineplex could also try to get the successful U.S. films after they had completed their run with the larger theatre chains. It was commonly known that the share of the box office receipts passed to the distributor decreased with the run of the movie. Although this allowed exhibitors to keep more of the revenues, the inevitable decline in attendance ordinarily forced large theatres to discontinue

2. "Cineplex Getting in the Big Picture," *Financial Post*, June 14, 1980, p. 7.

exhibition once the number of empty seats exceeded a certain level. It was at this point that Cineplex could pick up the films, and by virtue of its small theaters keep most of the seats full.

The dominant advantages of the multiplex concept were primarily due to a carefully planned use of shared facilities. All the theatres in a location were served by a single box office and a single concession stand. The use of advanced projection technology made it possible for a handful of projectionists in a centralized projection booth to screen films in several theatres at once. Show times were staggered in order to avoid congestion. Even advertising costs were lowered by using a single ad for all the films playing at a particular location.

The success of the multiplex concept spurred Cineplex to expand its operations across Canada. The company also made an entry into the large U.S. market with the development of a fourteen-screen theatre complex in the Beverly Hills section of Los Angeles. By the end of 1982, the company had inaugurated almost 150 screens in as many as twenty different locations.

A Close Brush with Bankruptcy

The rapid rate of expansion brought Cineplex face to face with financial and market realities that its owners had not anticipated. During its expansion the company had amassed $21 million in debt, mostly in high and floating interest rates. This came in the midst of an economic recession that cut deeply into the company's earnings. To make matters worse, U.S. distributors were increasingly reluctant to supply Cineplex with the hit films for fear of alienating the two large Canadian exhibition chains, Famous Players and Canadian Odeon. Without the revenues of major U.S. releases the company's future was bleak.

Only drastic measures could avert imminent bankruptcy. Throughout 1983, Cineplex took steps to reduce its debt and improve its cash flow by selling off some of the company's assets, raising funds through the public offering of more shares, and persuading the banks to extend further credit. But these measures did not address the company's blocked access to major releases. To break through the barrier, Drabinsky sought government intervention. Using his legal training, Drabinsky marshalled the evidence and managed to convince the Canadian government that strong grounds existed for launching an investigation into the existence of a conspiracy aimed at depriving Cineplex of access to major releases.

In the face of government investigation, and possible sanctions, the U.S. distributors modified their stand and agreed to a system of competitive bidding that would ensure all had equal access to their films. With this hurdle surmounted Drabinsky was able to secure more firm financial backing, particularly from institutional investors. A large investment came from a holding company owned by the Bronfmans, one of Canada's most powerful business families.

To Drabinsky, the close brush with bankruptcy had also revealed a basic flaw in his company's position. He became acutely aware that his small theatres generated insufficient revenues to bid for early runs of the most lucrative U.S. films. So when the principal owner of Canadian Odeon passed away, Drabinsky saw an opportunity that was not to be missed. Canadian Odeon had been greatly weakened by the new bidding system that Drabinsky had helped to bring about. Alarmed by Odeon's poor performance, the heirs finally accepted Drabinsky's offer of little over $22 million dollars for the entire chain.

The acquisition of Canadian Odeon in the spring of 1984, at what many viewed as a bargain-basement price, ended a remarkable turnaround for a company which just two years earlier had faced bankruptcy. Now, with over 450 screens in as many as 170 different locations, Cineplex was a major player in the industry. Drabinsky relished his comeback, and was not above taking a passing shot at his detractors: "A lot of people who were waiting for me to go under were disappointed. Well, they didn't get their jollies."[3]

A BLOCKBUSTER STRATEGY

A Larger Than Life Experience

The formation of Cineplex Odeon crowned Drabinsky's comeback from the verge of bankruptcy, but he was not content to rest on his laurels. Now that he controlled one of North America's major theatre chains he set out to transform the moviegoing experience itself. With the advent of pay-television channels and prerecorded videocassettes, it was becoming increasingly difficult to lure moviegoers from the comfort of their homes.

Drabinsky aimed to change the public's perceptions by renovating the theatres, beginning with the physical format. Cineplex Odeon discarded the uniformly drab design common in most theatre chains in favor of artwork in the lobbies, lush woolen carpets spread over marble floors and coral-and-peach color-coordinated walls. The screening auditoriums featured scientifically contoured seats, digital background music and state-of-the-art projection systems. As a final touch, the company reintroduced real buttered popcorn in the concession stands and cafes that offered freshly made cappuccino.

But the metamorphosis could not be completed without a new company logo in the form of a curved bowl that was reminiscent of a Greek amphitheatre. Furthermore, in choosing colors for the logo, Drabinsky decided on a combination of imperial purple and fuschia. For him, the logo was no mere representation; it was intended to make people sit up and take notice. As Drabinsky put it: "I felt that this would be more of a bravado kind of statement. I don't think anyone was ready for this."[4]

Cineplex Odeon's new format differed sharply from the prevailing industry response to the threat posed by pay television and take-home videocassettes. Most theatre chains sought to cut their fixed costs by slicing old movie palaces into tiny cinemas, and eliminating many services that were deemed inessential. Drabinsky, on the other hand, believed that the moviegoing experience was not confined to what was shown on the screen. As the customer entered the theatre he was meant to leave behind mundane existence and gradually move into a different reality. In the words of Drabinsky:

> We are determined to give back to our patrons the rush and excitement and anticipation and curiosity that should be theirs when they leave the techno-regimented world of their daily lives for the fantasy world of escape that is the movies.[5]

3. David Olive, "Upwardly Mogul," *Report on Business Magazine,* December 1985, pp. 42–54.
4. Brian D. Johnson, "King of the Silver Screen," *Macleans,* September 28, 1987, p. 38.
5. David Toole, "Big Money at the Movies," *Macleans,* July 28, 1986, p. 22.

The transformation of reality is, however, very costly. Cineplex Odeon spends almost $3 million on a typical six-screen multiplex, a third more than the average for the industry. But as far as Drabinsky is concerned, the additional investment bears fruit not only at the box office, but at the concession counter as well. The classier upscale atmosphere is meant to entice customers into spending more time in the theatres before and after the movie, resulting in higher sales at the concession counter. Indeed, the concessions at Cineplex Odeon's theatres usually generated almost $2 per moviegoer, which is close to twice the industry average.

The additional revenues generated by higher concession sales covered only a small fraction of the fixed costs of a typical Cineplex Odeon theatre. In an effort to reduce costs, Drabinsky has imposed stringent cost controls throughout his organization. Odeon's management was Drabinsky's first target. Upon acquisition, Drabinsky dismissed about two-thirds of Odeon's head office staff and cut the pay of the remaining personnel by 10 percent. He also cancelled their company credit card as an incentive to frugality. As he put it at the time: "When you make people use their own money they think hard about the justification they'll have to provide when filing their expense claims."[6] The cost cutting campaign has not left any facet of the company's operations untouched. Even the traditional cardboard containers used to sell popcorn have been replaced with bags, a move that has saved Cineplex Odeon close to $1 million per year.

In spite of these measures, cost cutting alone has not been sufficient. Drabinsky has had to look for other sources of revenues to make up the difference. He raised admission fees well above the competition in most markets and began to show commercials before the screening of the main feature. Both moves were highly unpopular and irate patrons have expressed their anger in a number of cities, sometimes by protesting outside Cineplex Odeon's theatres. The most publicized of these protests occurred in New York City, where Mayor Ed Koch joined picketers in a call for a boycott of the chain because of its price increase.

The criticisms against Drabinsky were tempered by his use of promotional gimmicks. Most significant among these is the lower admission prices that are offered on Tuesdays, which are designed to make movies more accessible to the general public. Attendance at Cineplex theatres has climbed substantially for these Tuesdays, generating additional revenues as well as much needed goodwill among customers.

A Powerful Competitor

With Drabinsky at the helm, Cineplex Odeon launched a major expansion into North America's main movie markets. By and large, this expansion was based on a series of acquisitions in the United States (see Exhibit 3). In an industry known for tough negotiators and agile deal makers, Garth Drabinsky has gained a reputation as a tenacious and abrasive businessman. He uses his stamina and his adversarial style of bargaining to wear his interlocutors down, and then in a burst of energy he clinches the deal. His biggest acquisition involved the Plitt theatre chain, which had almost 600 screens in over 200 locations.

Drabinsky is implacable to his competitors. In every market he has entered he has used all the means at his disposal to gain market share and keep the competition on the defensive. He has pursued Famous Players, his long-standing rival in Canada, with special vengeance. In 1986, for example, Drabinsky seized an

6. Olive, p. 50.

Exhibit 3
U.S. Theatre Acquisitions

1985	Plitt Theatres Los Angeles, California 574 screens / 209 locations
1986	Septum Cinemas Atlanta, Georgia 48 screens / 12 locations
1986	Essaness Theatres Chicago, Illinois 41 screens / 13 locations
1986	RKO Century Warner Theatres New York, New York 97 screens / 42 locations
1986	Neighbourhood Theatres Richmond, Virginia 76 screens / 25 locations
1986	SRO Theatres Seattle, Washington 99 screens / 33 locations
1987	Walter Reade Organization New York, New York 11 screens / 8 locations
1987	Circle Theatres Washington, D.C. 80 screens / 22 locations

Source: Cineplex Odeon.

opportunity to lease part of a building in Toronto that housed the Imperial Theatre, a six-theatre complex operated by Famous Players. Since his part of the building contained the main entrance to all of the theatres in the complex, Drabinsky could now move to deny Famous Players public access. He used barbed wire and security guards with Doberman pinschers to enforce the blockade. Ultimately Famous Players was forced to close down and sell this key location to Cineplex Odeon, but not before it extracted a public apology from Drabinsky,[7] and a commitment that the facility will never be used to show motion pictures.

Drabinsky has also tried to use the size of his chain to obtain added clout with film studios and distributors. He has consistently used this clout to obtain potential hits on more favorable terms, but his insistence on having his way has created tensions in his relationships with his suppliers. The tensions erupted into the open in 1987 when Columbia Pictures rejected Drabinsky's demands that

7. Kathryn Harris, "Pushing It to the Limit; As Problems Arise for Cineplex Odeon," *LA Times*, June 19, 1988, p. 16.

Bernardo Bertolucci's oriental epic *The Last Emperor* be made available for wide release during the Christmas period. In retaliation Drabinsky refused to exhibit another of the studio's films that was slated for Christmas release. The episode created tensions in the existing relationship with Columbia, resulting in more of the studio's films being diverted to other chains, such as Famous Players, Drabinsky's major Canadian competitor.

Drabinsky's readiness to challenge industry conventions has upset many, who feel that he does not play by the rules. Walter Senior, the president of Famous Players, considers Drabinsky's tactics as ultimately destructive. As he put it in the aftermath of the Imperial Theatre affair: "We all learn in school that when you set out to destroy someone, it becomes a weakness."[8] Myron Gottlieb, Cineplex Odeon's Chief Administrative Officer, believes that much of the harsh treatment meted out to Drabinsky in the press reflects his impact on the industry, rather than simply his style:

> There's been a lot of press about Garth, and some of it's been negative up until now. Some of it has been because of his aggressiveness, but more of it is because of the antagonism to the waves he's created in the industry.[9]

Vertical Moves

In 1982, at a time when Cineplex was still a small company screening foreign and art films, Drabinsky moved to consolidate and expand the company's other film-related activities. These consisted mainly of a film making subsidiary originally started by Nathan Taylor, and a film distribution arm launched by Drabinsky in 1979.

The film making subsidiary was located just north of Toronto and was one of Canada's largest facilities that was rented out to various groups for film and television production. It included two sound stages, dressing and wardrobe rooms, a carpentry mill, a plaster shop, and editing and screening rooms. The distribution arm had been originally created by Drabinsky to provide foreign and art films to the newly developed Cineplex chain. It quickly developed into one of the largest distribution companies in Canada, acquiring the right to distribute films to theatres and on videocassettes, as well as for use on network and pay television.

In 1986, Drabinsky increased the involvement of his company in film making through the acquisition of the Film House. The Toronto-based facility consisted of a large film processing laboratory as well as a fully equipped post-production sound studio. Subsequent to its purchase, Cineplex Odeon increased the capacity of the film laboratory and constructed new upgraded sound facilities.

Meanwhile, Drabinsky expanded the film production and distribution activities of his company into the United States. With the move into this larger market, Cineplex Odeon was able to step up its level of participation in film making. It began to contribute toward the production of small-budget films such as Paul Newman's *The Glass Menagerie* and Prince's rock concert film *Sign 'O' the Times*.

Finally, Drabinsky entered into a collaborative venture with MCA, a large U.S. entertainment conglomerate. The two companies have agreed to jointly

8. Kevin Doyle, "A Man of Extremes," *Macleans*, September 28, 1987, p. 38.
9. "A Czar Is Born," *Canadian Business*, October 1984, pp. 38–40.

develop and operate a large film studio and theme park in Orlando, Florida, that would compete with Disney World. The move reflects Drabinsky's determination to make Cineplex Odeon into a corporation that straddles every part of the movie industry. As he had put it:

> It's an amalgamated company with revenue from theatres, distribution, production, the studio, and, down the road, live theatre. People aren't buying a share in this company just to have a share in a motion picture. They're getting a share in a vertically integrated entertainment corporation.[10]

A One Man Show

Cineplex Odeon is firmly under the control of Drabinsky, who has concentrated power in his hands over the years. He became president of the company in 1980, added the title of Chief Executive Officer in 1982 and was confirmed as Chairman of the Board in 1986. The titles reflect Drabinsky's total involvement with the company, and it is well known that no one else is allowed to speak on behalf of the company.

In both deed and word Drabinsky attempts to communicate to his employees the total commitment that is expected of them. The managers who work in close proximity to Drabinsky find his driving energy both exhilarating and exhausting. Lynda Friendly, Vice President of Marketing and Communications since 1982, who sits in on all of Drabinsky's interviews with the press, is inspired by his stamina and drive:

> Garth is so bloody energetic. I don't know how he does it. It's mind over matter. He stretches people to their absolute limit. He is a teacher, a mentor—a leader.[11]

Other officers, however, are finding Drabinsky's energy difficult to emulate. They do not appreciate the midnight phone calls they regularly receive from Drabinsky, nor do they agree that they must be ready to sacrifice all to their work. As a former Cineplex Odeon executive described it, the pressure that Drabinsky puts on managers is relentless:

> He works seven days a week and doesn't believe in holidays. Holidays are a disloyalty to the corporation and he *is* the corporation. He is tireless and he expects the same amount of dedication and effort from everyone else.[12]

Some of Drabinsky's immediate subordinates may have found his drive for total control unacceptable. His consolidation of power has been accompanied by a significant turnover among the top executives of the company. Several of the present executive officers have been appointed since 1986 (see Exhibit 4). Those who survived the transition are for the most part people with close personal ties to Drabinsky. Lynda Friendly, for example, has known Drabinsky since they attended synagogue together as teenagers. One of the most important loyalists is Myron Gottlieb, who has financially supported Drabinsky since the starting days of the company. Gottlieb's career in Cineplex Odeon closely dovetails that of Drabinsky. He became the Vice-Chairman of the Board in 1982 and was appointed to the position of Chief Administrative Officer in 1985.

10. "Movie Mogul," *Business Journal,* October 1982, pp. 36–38+.
11. Doyle, p. 38.
12. Michael Salter, "Canada's Toughest Bosses," *Report on Business Magazine,* December 1987, p. 91.

Operating Philosophy

By January 1, 1989, Cineplex Odeon was the second largest motion picture exhibitor in North America with just over 1,800 screens in 500 different locations (see Exhibit 1). Almost two-thirds of the company's screens were located in the U.S. and were spread out over twenty different states. The remaining one-third of these screens are situated in six different Canadian provinces. Cineplex Odeon theatres could be found in virtually all major population centers from New York to Los Angeles in the United States, and Toronto to Vancouver in Canada. Close to 90 percent of the chain's theatres, however, were located in leased premises, with rent calculated as a percentage of box office receipts subject to a minimum.

As of early 1989, the company also had close to 13,000 employees. These include film projectionists, cashiers, concession workers, ushers, and ticket takers. However, the bulk of these employees are hired on a part-time basis during seasons of high demand, and they are paid the minimum wage. Only about 15 percent of the employees are represented by unions. For each theatre, the information obtained from its computerized box office terminals is used to schedule the minimal amount of staff for any given show. In addition to staff employed to operate the theatre, Cineplex Odeon employs as many as 100 full-time architects, engineers, and draftsmen, all used for design and renovation of theatres.

The Cineplex Odeon chain of theatres is divided into districts, with each district under the control of a supervisor. The task of a district supervisor is to ensure that all theatres follow guidelines set by the head office. He also regularly inspects theatres and reports the results to the head office. His report is contrasted with information provided by an independent agency whose representatives visit each theatre on a random basis. In addition to this information, the head office relies on weekly reports supplied by the theatre's manager detailing market conditions, competitors' activities, and audience response to advanced screenings.

Exhibit 4
Management Profile

	G. I. Drabinsky	M. I. Gottlieb	J. M. Banks	A. Karp	L. Friendly	C. Bruner	E. Jacob
Title(s)	Chairman of Board; President; Chief Executive Officer	Vice-Chairman of Board; Chief Administrative Officer	Senior Executive Vice-President, Corporate Affairs	Senior Executive Vice-President	Executive Vice-President, Marketing & Communications	Senior Vice-President; Treasurer	Senior Vice-President; Chief Financial Officer
Age	40	45	57	48	39	31	35
Previous positions	Director since 1978	Director since 1980	Director 1983–1986	—	Senior V.P., Mktg & Comm.	Assistant Treasurer	V.P. and Corporate Controller
Year of entry	1980	1985	1987	1986	1982	1985	1987
Previous employment	Law firm	Investment firm	Law firm	Law firm	Not available	Public Accounting firm	Electronics firm

Source: Cineplex Odeon Form 10-K.

The centralization of information is matched by a consistent effort to centralize purchasing and accounting. All supplies and services are purchased centrally in order to maximize economies and reduce spoilage and waste. The computerized box office allows the company to monitor ticket sales, as well as exercise stringent controls on the handling of cash.

Cineplex Odeon puts a great deal of emphasis on a set of standards and practices which are set forth in staff orientation and training manuals. These standards are often drafted by Drabinsky, who goes to great length to ensure that they are followed to the letter. He visits theatres regularly, often dropping by unannounced to talk with cashiers or ushers. He also phones or sees twenty or twenty-five theatre managers a week.

All of this reflects Drabinsky's conviction that he must know everything that goes on in his theatres, and be always on the lookout for problems that need correcting. He has been known to deliver a silent but none-too-subtle reprimand to ushers by bending down in front of them to pick up a single piece of spilled popcorn. An employee who has observed Drabinsky in action observed: "Anything that is not absolutely perfect drives him crazy. He leaves people with a lasting impression when they screw up."[13]

Financial Structure

As of January 1, 1989, Cineplex Odeon had 23.9 million common shares and 23.6 subordinate restricted voting shares outstanding. The company made the transition from private to public financing in 1982 when it was listed on the Toronto Stock Exchange. The total value of its equity has been estimated at $375 million (see Exhibit 5).

A large block of shares, representing just over 30 percent of the company's total equity, have been in the hands of Claridge, a holding company. For the most part, Claridge handles the investments of the Bronfman family, who own the Seagram liquor business. The investment was made in 1983 to help Cineplex out of its early difficulties. Claridge had backed the development of the Eaton Centre, in the basement of which Cineplex had opened its first theatres.

In a subsequent deal Drabinsky sold a large block of shares to MCA, a U.S. entertainment conglomerate which owns Universal Studios. The deal allowed MCA to purchase up to 50 percent of the company's outstanding shares. However, MCA's control of Cineplex Odeon was restricted to 33% by Canadian law, which limits voting shares by foreign companies. MCA's total ownership is therefore represented by specially created subordinate restricted voting shares.

In 1987, Cineplex Odeon consummated its first offering of shares in the United States, and was listed on the New York Stock Exchange. In spite of this substantial enlargement of the company's equity base, most of the financing during 1987 and 1988 was through the use of debt. Not surprisingly, the price of Cineplex Odeon's shares has fluctuated. It reached a high of almost Cdn $25 a share around the time of the MCA purchase, but has dropped considerably since then. In spite of the decline, Drabinsky continues to defend his gross margins and insists that his chain boasts the highest return on equity among major exhibition chains. The fault, Drabinsky has claimed on one occasion, is to be found in the brokerage industry, and not in the performance of Cineplex Odeon:

13. "A New Hollywood Legend Called—Garth Drabinsky?" *Business Week*, September 23, 1985, p. 61+.

Exhibit 5
Balance Sheets

	In millions of U.S. dollars for the year ended December				
	1984	1985	1986	1987	1988
Current assets					
Cash & receivables	5.2	10.0	20.1	42.3	151.5
Distribution advances	3.8	5.3	9.0	21.3	36.9
Inventories and prepaid expenses	3.0	4.6	11.0	13.3	13.0
Property investments	—	—	16.6	22.7	25.6
Fixed assets					
Properties & equipment	49.2	53.3	208.9	261.5	296.7
Leaseholds	17.4	26.9	324.1	490.2	594.4
Accumulated depreciation*	4.3	7.2	19.6	40.2	66.3
Other assets					
Long-term investments	2.7	6.2	14.3	50.0	130.3
Goodwill#	0.6	0.6	40.9	52.6	54.0
Deferred charges	0.8	1.7	6.6	12.0	27.1
	$78.4	$101.4	$631.9	$925.7	$1263.2
Current liabilities					
Bank loans	—	4.8	0.1	20.7	21.7
Payables & accruals	10.0	13.5	47.7	74.9	129.5
Income taxes	—	0.4	1.9	4.6	5.7
Matured long-term debt	2.1	1.1	6.3	6.0	10.8
Long-term debt	36.1	40.7	317.6	449.7	663.8
Other liabilities					
Lease obligations	—	—	15.9	14.6	14.9
Deferred income taxes	0.8	4.2	11.1	13.3	10.4
Pension obligations	—	—	3.7	4.0	6.3
Minority interest	—	—	—	—	25.1
Shareholders' equity					
Capital stock	39.5	37.1	212.1	289.2	283.7
Translation adjustment	—	—	(3.6)	1.9	13.4
Retained earnings	(10.1)	(0.4)	19.1	46.8	77.9
	$78.4	$101.4	$631.9	$925.7	$1263.2

*As of 1986, depreciation rates were reduced to 2.5% from 5.0% straight-line for buildings and to 6.7% from 10.0% straight-line for equipment

#As of 1986, goodwill is being amortized over forty years instead of over twenty years

Source: Cineplex Odeon Annual Reports

The brokerage industry is just full of people who like to hear themselves speak, but there's not a lot of substance there. This company is complete substance from top to bottom.[14]

14. "Drabinsky's Movie Machine." *Financial Times of Canada*, August 26, 1985, p. 1+.

FUTURE HORIZONS

Relentless Growth

Cineplex Odeon has not slowed the pace of its expansion in spite of growing financial constraints. The company continues to construct new theatres, and to refurbish existing ones. At the present rate of expansion Cineplex Odeon will have twenty-one hundred screens in North America alone by 1992. For Drabinsky the expansion has a dual purpose. First, he would like to surge past his competitors and capture an increasing share of the North American market. Second, Drabinsky believes that only a larger Cineplex Odeon can force the major distributors to give the chain the big-budget movies at more favorable terms.

But several other large exhibition chains that compete with Cineplex Odeon are also on the move, building new multiscreen theatres and acquiring smaller chains (see Exhibit 1). Many in the industry fear that the proliferation of screens will not be matched by a corresponding increase in movie attendance. If anything, the strong likelihood of a major recession may aggravate the situation. It will also increase the reliance of exhibitors on the limited supply of major Hollywood releases.

In fact, Drabinsky's critics contend that costly acquisitions and expensive theatres are making Cineplex Odeon especially vulnerable to an industry slowdown. For his part, Drabinsky has sought to allay the fears of shareholders by insisting that the growth of Cineplex Odeon is neither haphazard nor reckless:

> I want you to appreciate that everything we do is part of a thoroughly studied, painstakingly thought-out game plan. We're not expanding for the sake of expanding.[15]

Plans for the expansion of theatres are not confined to the North American continent. Drabinsky has recently unveiled plans to spend around $100 million to develop over 100 screens in the United Kingdom by the end of 1990. He believes that better theatres and a faster release of major U.S. films can reverse the decline in attendance and reinvigorate the British market.

In addition to theatre expansion, Drabinsky has been getting his company increasingly involved in film production since it has the capacity to both distribute and exhibit movies. During 1988, Cineplex Odeon helped to finance and distribute movies by such noted directors as John Schlesinger and Oliver Stone. The company has also negotiated a joint production agreement with small production companies headed by Robert Redford and Taylor Hackford. But Drabinsky has frequently stated that Cineplex Odeon will restrict itself to a few low-budget films, and will not become involved in the risky business of producing big-budget movies.

Drabinsky has also extended his production activities to other entertainment areas. Cineplex Odeon had financed the run of some lavish Broadway musicals in Toronto during 1988. At present the company is converting the Toronto theatre it wrested from the Famous Players chain into a 2,100-seat centre for the performing arts. The theatre, which was a vaudeville palace in its previous incarnation, was to be restored to its former glory and then used to stage the Canadian Production of Andrew Lloyd Webber's *The Phantom of the Opera*. The musical was scheduled to open in the fall of 1989, and it was estimated that its initial production cost will total over $6.5 million.

15. "Market Apathy the Real Culprit, Drabinsky Says," *Toronto Globe and Mail*, May 13, 1988, p. B2.

A Performance Under Scrutiny

Drabinsky's continuous drive for growth has been putting pressure on the company's finances. During 1988, Cineplex Odeon asked the banks to boost its line of credit by another $175 million to $750 million. More recently, the company sold off 50 percent of the Film House, its film production operation in Toronto, as well as most of its share in the Florida theme park, to a British entertainment firm. The company has also been raising capital by selling off some of its theatres and then leasing them back.

In the opinion of a number of industry observers the true financial position of Cineplex Odeon is masked by the company's liberal accounting practices (see footnotes to Exhibit 2). In 1986, the company extended the period over which it would depreciate its properties and its goodwill, resulting in much higher values of its total assets. The company's operating profits are also believed to be overstated because of the inclusion of one-time sales of assets as part of operating revenue.

The financial uncertainty has created apprehension among the company's stockholders who can still recall his narrow escape from bankruptcy six years earlier. Drabinsky, however, denies that he is undermining Cineplex Odeon by involving the company in activities it can ill afford. He frequently reiterates his conviction that he must at all times be ready to take advantage of emerging opportunities and promising deals. When asked in a recent interview to predict the company's future development, he had this to say:

> If you asked me five years ago what Cineplex would look like today, I wouldn't have predicted what we have today. So when you ask me today what Cineplex will look like in five years, I can't tell you exactly.[16]

Publicly, Drabinsky has rebuffed his critics, and has sought to allay shareholders' fears. In private, however, he and his close associates recently made a move to gain control of Cineplex Odeon by making an offer to buy the 30 percent stake held by Bronfman's holding company. Taken together with the 8 percent stake that is already owned by Drabinsky and Gottlieb, they would have had enough shares to outvote and outflank MCA who was restricted to a 33 percent limit on voting rights.

But MCA moved swiftly to obtain an injunction preventing the deal from going through, even as Drabinsky and Gottlieb were putting on the finishing touches. A financial analyst attempted to explain the reasons for MCA's reaction:

> No one understands what Drabinsky and Gottlieb are up to. They pulled out of the Florida deal, they sold off Film House, they are taking bigger risks in film production, and now the Bronfmans are getting out. From MCA's point of view there are probably lots of reasons to stop Garth from getting control.[17]

MCA eventually managed to get the court to rule that the offer that had been made by Drabinsky and his associates should be extended to all of Cineplex Odeon's outstanding shareholders. This has forced Drabinsky to scramble for over $1 billion of financing in order to back such an offer. It is now widely speculated that if he is not able to raise this required amount, he could be forced out of the company that he has always considered to be his own.

16. " 'Darth' Plays Movie Hardball—and Wins," *Financial Times of Canada,* December 28, 1987.
17. "Clash of the Movie Titans," *Financial Post,* April 24, 1989, pp. 1, 6.

Appendix The Movie Industry

SUPPLY OF MOVIES

The number of movies available for exhibition has grown significantly over the past few years. Most of this growth in supply has resulted from the increased activities of smaller independent distribution companies. Exhibit 1 lists the numbers of feature-length films released over the last five years.

In spite of the growing number of suppliers, the bulk of the revenues still comes from the films that are distributed by the nine major companies that have dominated the industry for more than fifty years. Based in Hollywood, these include Paramount, Warner Brothers, Disney, Universal and Columbia. In 1988, the 159 films that were released by these firms accounted for more than 90 percent of the box office dollars in the U.S. and Canada.

The relative success of the major distributors stems in large part from their greater supply of capital. The typical Hollywood studio spent, on the average, almost $16 million for each of the films that they produced during 1988. Another $4 to $6 million was usually spent to market or advertise the movie and up to $2 million can be spent on making sufficient copies of the film so that it can be released to a wide number of theatres.

The movies of the smaller distributors are usually budgeted at under $5 million and frequently lack the major stars or production values that can increase their chances of striking it rich at the box office. In fact, an industry publication recently reported that more than half of the movies that are offered by the smaller distributors do not ever play in theatres, but are released directly into the videocassette market.

Although the major distributors continue to dominate the industry, they have long abandoned their practice of binding the most attractive movie directors and stars to long-term employment contracts. Most of the Hollywood movies are now typically made through contractual arrangements with thousands of smaller production outfits. The major distributor may either fund a movie from start to finish or provide a portion of the financing in return for a share of the proceeds.

In recent years, several of the significant firms among the smaller distributors have either folded their operations or merged with a major distributor as a result of lackluster financial results. Even some of the major distributors have merged together, such as the amalgamation of MGM with United Artists. These trends indicate that in the future, fewer major distributors will control the total number of movies that are available to theatres for exhibition.

Exhibit 1
Feature Length Films Released over the Last Five Years

	1984	1985	1986	1987	1988
Major distributors	169	149	142	133	159
Smaller distributors	210	271	296	354	330
Total	379	420	438	487	489

Source: *Variety*.

EXHIBITION OF MOVIES

Theatre chains that are responsible for exhibiting movies have increasingly adopted the use of a multiplex format. This is based upon the development of several screens in the same location, usually within or adjacent to a shopping centre. Such a format allows the theatres to offer a wide variety of films, while economizing on the use of facilities and employees.

Over the past decade, there has also been a growing emphasis upon improving the quality of theatres in order to entice more people to go out to movies. This has resulted in large-scale renovations of existing theatres as well as the construction of new ones. During this process, hundreds of smaller independent theatres have been forced to sell out to the larger chains that could more easily afford to make the necessary investments.

Industry estimates indicate that there were over 23,000 screens in the United States and Canada by the end of 1988. Almost fifty percent of these were collectively held by the top ten exhibition chains. In recent years, some of the major movie distributors have also begun to buy up theatre chains. These distribution companies have argued that by owning theatres, they can guarantee the public a higher quality presentation of their movies.

At the peak of the growth of the movie industry, the major distributors were forced to divest themselves of their theatres. In the late 1940s, the U.S. Justice Department had ruled that the same companies could not make as well as show movies. The legislation was a result of allegations that the movie distributors were restricting their movies to their own theatres and engaging in fixing prices. However, the attitudes toward restrictions on the ownership of movie theatres have become more relaxed in recent years. In part, this was made possible by clearer and more stringent laws that provide fairer access to movies by all exhibitors.

REVENUES FROM THEATRES

There is a widespread debate about the effects of recession on movie attendance. Some financial analysts have recently shown that box office receipts decreased during the early 1930s and during the early 1970s. In fact, ticket sales in 1971 dipped to 820 million before picking up again.

For the most part, however, annual ticket sales have been relatively stable at around one billion admissions per year for almost thirty years. The audience for movies in theatres has been heavily dominated by younger individuals, particularly below thirty years of age. But recent evidence has suggested that the traditional drop in attendance after the age of thirty has been lessening.

Box office receipts have risen considerably over the years, largely as a result of increases in the prices of tickets. There is considerable variation in ticket sales over the year, with almost half of the sales coming between late May and early September as well as between late November and early January. Exhibit 2 lists the box office totals for the U.S. over the past five years.

The average ticket price had risen to $4.11 in 1988, up from $3.36 in 1984. Theatre owners are generally reluctant to raise ticket prices more rapidly than inflation for fear of losing viewers. Increasingly, however, they have come to rely

Exhibit 2
Box Office Totals for the U.S. over the Past Five Years

1984	$4.0 billion
1985	$3.8 billion
1986	$3.7 billion
1987	$4.2 billion
1988	$4.4 billion

Source: *Variety.*

upon the lobby concession stand to make their profits. Once inside the theatres, moviegoers become a captive market for popcorn, soft drinks and candy that is sold at inflated prices. Recent surveys indicate that exhibition chains may derive as much as 20 percent of their revenues from high profit items that are sold at their concessions.

SPLITTING OF REVENUES

There has been considerable wrangling between the distributors and the exhibitors over the distribution of box office revenues. The distributors have tried to use their new sources of revenue from videocassettes and pay TV to reduce their dependence on the theatres.

In spite of the new sources of revenues for movies, distribution companies can usually reach more people through exhibiting their movies in theatres. More significantly, the values of their movies on videocassettes and pay TV are heavily dependent upon a respectable theatrical run. A successful movie will create more demand for pay TV as well as for videocassette rentals.

In recent years, the exhibitors have been able to use the increased supply of movies to negotiate a larger share of the box office receipts. But the observed increase in the total number of screens across the continent may allow the dis-

Exhibit 3
Distribution of Box Office Revenues

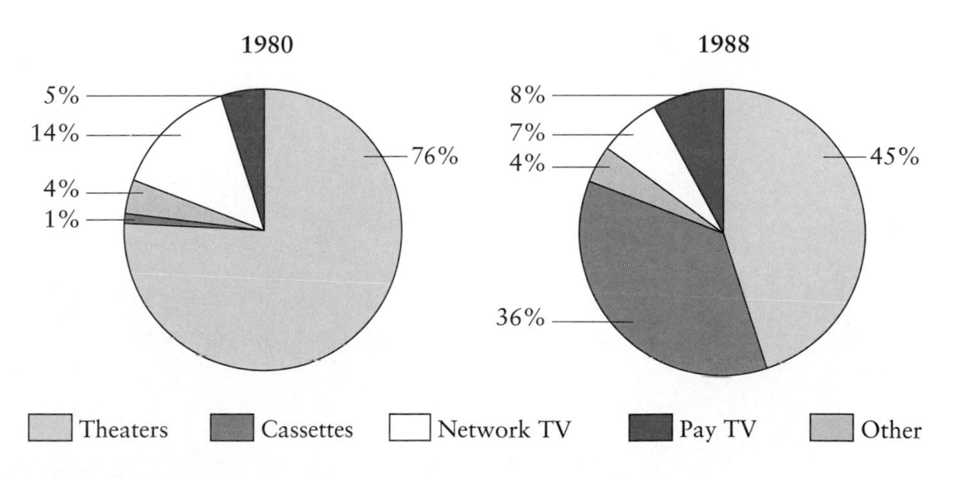

Source: *Variety.*

tributors to regain the advantage. Several growing exhibition chains may have to compete with each other to get the potential hit movies, which still tend to come from a few large Hollywood studios.

Typically, the distributor and the exhibitor split the box office revenue equally with each other. The distributor eventually passes on to the producers and investors about 20 percent of the revenues of a movie. The remainder is retained by the distributor to cover its own distribution and advertising costs.

CASE
22
Circle K Corporation

"Troubled Circle K Is Turning This Way and That"

Kathleen Kerwin, "Troubled Circle K is Turning This Way and That," *Business Week*, November 20, 1989, p. B4E.

"Circle K Posted $28.1 Million Loss for Its 3rd Quarter Ending FY 1990"

"Circle K Posted $28.1 Million Loss for Its 3rd Quarter Ending Fiscal Year 1990," *Wall Street Journal*, March 27, 1990, p. C9.

"Circle K: Eller Sued by Shareholders"

Barbara Grondin, "Circle K, Eller Sued by Shareholders," *Convenience Store News*, 25(14), November 13–December 15, 1989, p. 6.

"Karl Eller of Circle K, Always Pushing Deals, May Have Overdone It"

Roy Harris, Jr., "Karl Eller of Circle K, Always Pushing Deals, May Have Overdone It," *Wall Street Journal*, March 28, 1990, p. A1.

Who would have believed that Karl Eller's dream of having a Circle K convenience store on every corner would end in headlines such as these? What happened to that dream? Who's at fault? More importantly, what can Circle K do to turn itself around before they lose it all?

COMPANY BACKGROUND

As of May, 1990, Circle K was the second largest operator of convenience stores in the United States, operating under the orange, red and purple Circle K logo. The stores were located in 33 states, predominantly in the sunbelt region, with primary concentration in Florida (874 stores), Texas (750 stores), Arizona (679 stores) and California (578 stores). In total, the company operated approximately 4,685 stores in the U.S. and was involved in joint ventures or licensing agreements with companies that operated approximately 1,065 stores in eight foreign countries.[1] The foreign operations included stores in Japan, Hong Kong, Indonesia, Canada, United Kingdom, Finland and Australia. At the end of fiscal year 1989, Circle K employed over 29,000 people worldwide.[2]

This case was prepared by Helene Caudill, Toby Cordell, Jennifer Drury, Cheryl McGath, and Carol Pace under the supervision of Professor Sexton Adams, University of North Texas, and Professor Adelaide Griffin, Texas Woman's University. This case was prepared as a basis for class discussion rather than to illustrate either effective or ineffective handling of administrative situations.

The company was founded June 8, 1951, in El Paso, Texas, with headquarters now located in Phoenix, Arizona. Karl Eller, Circle K's Chairman and CEO, and American Financial Corporation owned 38 percent of the company.[3]

As a service company, Circle K's mission was to "satisfy our customers' immediate needs and wants by providing them with a wide variety of goods and services at multiple locations."[4] The company's principal line of business was convenience store operations. Retail sales consisted primarily of groceries, general merchandise and gasoline. Other sources of revenue included video game machine income, money order fees, commissions from the sale of lottery tickets, interest income and royalty income.[5] Substantially, all the stores were open seven days a week, 24 hours a day.

Acquisitions and Dispositions

By 1980, constant growth throughout the 1970s had boosted the Circle K convenience store number to 1,200.[6] The 1980s witnessed tremendous expansion of the Circle K chain under the direction of Chairman Karl Eller.

Eller became Chairman in 1983 with the support of 15 percent shareholder Carl Lindner. Shortly thereafter, Circle K acquired the 1,000-unit UtoteM convenience store chain from Lindner's American Financial Corporation. With this acquisition, Lindner increased his share of Circle K to 25 percent. This expansionary move provided Circle K with a means of using an efficient centralized commissary for preparing sandwiches and food for this combined group of stores.[7]

The UtoteM acquisition also began a buying spree that made Circle K, Inc., one of the largest convenience store companies, but one with a substantial debt burden for the future. Eller envisioned stores with many products and services available including movies, fast food, video games, and gasoline, one of the largest revenue and profit generators.[8] "Eller says he plans to focus on dominating the markets in which Circle K competes," reported Teresa Carson.[9] "Karl Eller just can't pass up a good deal," continued Carson.[10]

The number of Circle K stores nearly quadrupled between 1984 and 1989.[11] Circle K built 80 to 110 new stores annually from 1985 to 1989.[12] In 1987, 227 stores were added to the company by acquisition. Two very significant acquisitions occurred in 1988. In April of 1988, the Southland Corporation needed to raise cash for its leveraged buyout debt.[13] Southland assets of approximately 473 operating convenience stores, closed stores, store sites, stores under construction, administrative offices, and warehouses were acquired under Eller's direction. The purchase price was $147.5 million plus assumption of $3.9 million in obligations.[14]

In September of that same year, Circle K acquired Charter Marketing Group from an affiliate for a purchase price of $125 million. At the end of fiscal 1989, 4,685 stores were within the Circle K domain.[15] As Carson accurately stated, "Now the trick will be managing the company Eller has built."[16] The most significant increases in revenue for the 1989 year had their origins in these two acquisitions. Circle K felt that expansion into a 33-state area would provide a broader name recognition and give more appeal to its customer base. Furthermore, the increased store base would provide the company with greater purchasing power.[17]

A third 1988 purchase proved to be substantially less successful. On December 30, 1988, Circle K purchased assets of Stars to Go, Inc. (STG), to supply video movies to its stores. However, these assets were foreclosed upon and purchased by STG banks.[18]

Increasing difficulty in meeting the demands of a heavy debt burden led Circle K to make several dispositions. In 1987, Circle K sold 50 percent of their interest in their United Kingdom subsidiary, producing a pre-tax gain of $8.2 million.[19] The assets relating to the manufacture and distribution of ice were sold in October, 1988, producing a pre-tax gain of $10.5 million. In January, 1989, assets used in manufacturing and distributing sandwiches and fast-food items were sold for a pre-tax gain of $23.7 million. Supply agreements were made in both situations.[20] In the third quarter of the 1990 fiscal year (late 1989), Circle K sold the remaining 50 percent interest in the United Kingdom subsidiary, producing a $1 million after-tax loss.[21]

The November, 1989, annual meeting of Circle K was less than optimistic for all concerned. "Circle K won't build or buy any new stores in 1990," reported Chairman Eller. "Our overriding objective is to reduce our long-term debt position as rapidly and prudently as possible. Expansion has been achieved and consolidation is necessary."[22] At that point, however, Eller had relatively little left to unload. About 86 percent of the Circle K stores, and the land they were sitting on, had been sold and leased back to Circle K.[23]

The annual meeting brought influence from major stockholder Carl Lindner. Board member William Franke was appointed by the board to supervise the financial restructuring of Circle K. Among other plans, Franke intended to sell $200 million of Circle K's assets.[24]

By January, 1990, 25 stores in Hawaii had been sold to Hawaiian investors.[25] In addition, 350 stores in Washington, Oregon, Idaho, Montana, Utah, and Colorado were sold to PC Ventures, a Canadian concern. The stores continued to carry the Circle K name and to pay royalties to Circle K, Inc.[26] Another disposition set for early 1990 was the sale of 120 New England stores.[27] Circle K's Director of Public Relations commented, "We're really looking across the board at any areas where we don't have a strong market presence."[28] Even the company's skybox for Phoenix Cardinals football games would be offered for sale.[29] By the end of March, 1990, the Circle K store count had dropped to approximately 4,200 (see Exhibit 1).[30]

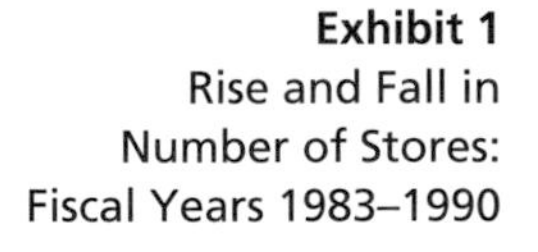
Exhibit 1
Rise and Fall in Number of Stores: Fiscal Years 1983–1990

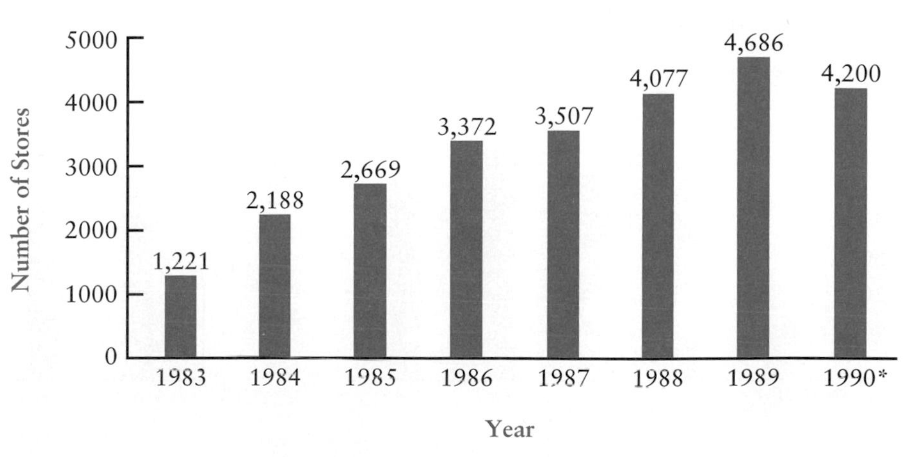

*Current number includes pending store sales.

Sources: Adapted from Circle K 1989 Financial Statements, *Wall Street Journal,* March 28, 1990, p. A5.

CONVENIENCE STORE INDUSTRY OVERVIEW

Definition of a Convenience Store

The fundamental definition of a convenience store (c-store) is a store which "charges higher prices than charged by mass marketers."[31] It sells fewer goods for more money—just the opposite of the mass marketer, which sells more goods for less money. John Thompson, son of Southland's founder, said, "My father's contribution to this business was that he invented high prices."[32]

Industry Growth

Both the total number of c-stores and those selling gasoline have more than doubled since 1981. According to industry analysts, there are "too many c-stores," just as once there were too many service stations.[33]

The explosive growth of c-stores during the last decade far outpaced population growth, thus decreasing the industry's potential customer base.[34] Comparison of c-stores' growth of 33 percent between 1984 and 1988, with the national population growth of 3.9 percent during that same period, made it clear that retailers were looking at a mature industry.[35] There were signs that this explosive growth was slowing. C-store ranks in 1988 grew at the relatively slow rate of 2.5 percent, following a 5.4 percent increase in 1987.[36] One consideration which stifled the industry's growth was the rapidly rising investment required. In 1987, the outlay for a new, urban c-store with inventory was $682,800; in 1982 it ballooned nearly 13 percent to $773,300.[37]

Lower Profits

Although the industry's sales had been increasing, profits were falling (see Exhibit 2). According to the National Association of Convenience Stores, annual pre-tax profits peaked in 1986 at $1.4 billion, falling 6.3 percent to $1.31 billion in 1987 and another 11.5 percent, to $1.16 billion in 1988.[38]

"Sales have become stale. The market is becoming saturated and it's getting tough to make a profit," said Dan Katz, Director of Marketing for Noble Communications, a research and marketing firm.[39] Kyle Krause, V.P. for Kraus Gentle Corporation, which owns the Kum & Go c-store chain, agreed: "As the market matures it won't be easy to make the dollars. Just because you grow doesn't mean you grow profitably."[40]

Exhibit 2
Convenience Store Industry

More stores, lower profits

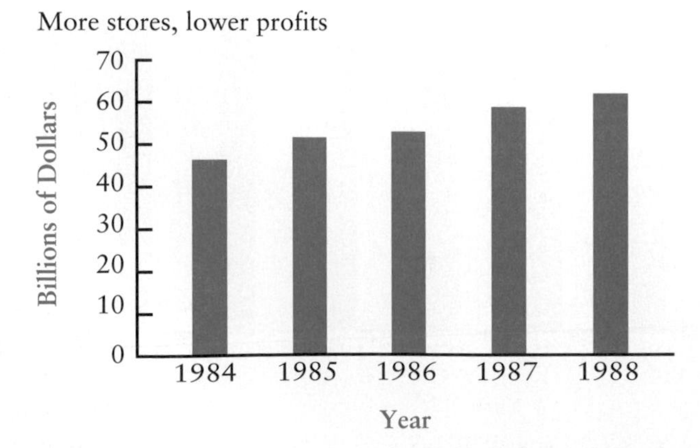

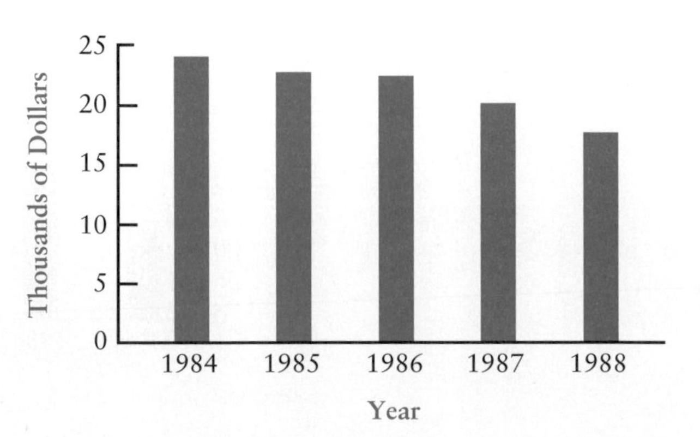

Source: National Association of Convenience Stores, *The New York Times,* October 8, 1989.

Lower profits were also experienced due to the rising costs of labor and capital, including the expense of complying with new Environmental Protection Agency rules on gasoline storage tanks and underground lines.[41] Furthermore, the convenience store industry was about to be hit with mandated minimum wage increases in successive years after nearly a decade of baseline rate stability.[42] Retailer reaction to the wage hike was mixed. "As far as labor goes, our problem will still be supply, not cost," said F. Higgins, president of Minit Mart Foods. "But when you factor in the cost of rising health insurance, higher wages do present a problem. As a result, marginal stores will come under even more pressure."[43]

According to Karl Eller, "Although the entire industry is under pressure at this time, I'm convinced that convenience stores in general will meet and eventually overcome the challenges of the marketplace."[44]

Location/Image

According to some 1985 surveys, consumers spent half their general merchandise dollars at stores in shopping centers. This implied that shopping centers were a prime vehicle for retail expansion, including convenience stores, requiring high volume locations. This appeared to be a trend that would continue into the future.[45] Another trend noted was that of locating c-stores on college campuses.[46] Some marketers also saw opportunities in small towns with populations of 10,000 or less, which were being abandoned by many of the large companies.[47]

Almost all large c-store chains, including those owned and operated by independent gasoline marketers, continued to spend heavily on modernization in 1987.[48] According to design consultants, proper design was particularly critical to convenience stores. Studies have demonstrated that without careful thought and planning, a store will not attain its full sales potential.[49]

Despite better locations and designs, c-stores still faced an image problem. Open around the clock, and always with a little cash in the register, the c-store, like the liquor store, attracted more than its share of violent crime. According to the FBI, c-store robberies increased 16 percent in 1988, while the overall business robbery rate increased only 4 percent.[50] This tended to frighten away some potential customers. Warranted or not, poor image was a major reason c-stores' customers were mostly male.[51]

Consumers

The population of young male blue-collar workers, the stores' most loyal customers, has been shrinking.[52] This left all the c-stores struggling to invigorate their marketing and broaden their appeal. "In the past if you ran a tight ship, kept your expenses to a minimum, kept shrinkage low, you were successful," said V. H. Van Horn, CEO of National Convenience Stores. "Today we find a culture that is customer-driven, not operations-driven."[53]

Many believed c-stores gained popularity due to an increasing number of two-income and single parent families trying to "cram" the most chores in the least amount of time.[54] "Years ago," said John Rosco, a former c-store operator, "the idea was that there were a lot of people who believe that their time was worth more than their money." These were the primary customers for c-stores. However, the vast majority of customers now "consider their money to be at least as important as their time, if not more so."[55]

Merchandise Mix

On the surface the c-store was an undifferentiated product. "We are the worst thieves around," said Ray Cox, a Circle K Sr. V.P. "As soon as one of us finds something that works, the copycats go to work."[56]

Many industry observers said the trick to maintaining a profitable c-store in the 1990s is tailoring to specific markets.[57] "You have to study your market and judge each c-store individually. Area and location play a significant role for the product mix in the c-store. You have to know your market and what your customers want," explained W. Englefield, President and CEO of Englefield Oil Company.[58]

In 1986, many c-stores added fast-food services, which in 1990 was the industry's third largest category behind gasoline and cigarettes.[59] "The movement into fast foods is obvious," said Kirby LeBof, President of the National Association of Convenience Stores. "Many started with beverages like soft drinks and coffee, then got into microwave foods. Now many are trying to differentiate themselves with delis and on-premise cooking."[60] Generally, the industry was divided into two fast-food camps: chains focusing on self-service and labor-saving equipment, versus those aiming to serve higher quality products by investing in the labor required to run a competitive food service program.[61]

Another avenue for c-stores to venture into was frozen yogurt. Virtually nonexistent a decade ago, the market for frozen yogurt was exploding.[62] Perceived as "chic" and better on the arteries than ice cream, soft-serve yogurt was touted as *the* dessert for the 1990s.[63] "The c-store industry is continually looking for ways to widen its customer base," said F. Button, a consultant specializing in yogurt programs for c-stores. "Frozen yogurt is the answer. Stores with soft-serve can attract steady customers they otherwise wouldn't get on a regular basis. We have people who now come in three to five times a week just to get their yogurt fix."[64] Besides association with a food that exudes an aura of earthiness, profit margins that could easily exceed 75 percent was an added attraction.[65]

These fast-food deals increased customer traffic and represented a chance to bring known products and food service expertise into outlets. It also was an attempt to improve the fast-food image among customers. These joint ventures benefited from the heavy advertising used by fast-food chains.[66]

After years of aggressive expansion, all the chains had to show for thousands of new stores were sharply declining profits. Convenience chains were desperately trying to woo customers back with a new generation of markets such as car washes and video rentals. However, in the rush to regain an edge, c-stores risked sacrificing convenience. "They are walking a fine line here," warned Barbara Grondin, editor in chief of *Convenience Store News*. "If the urge to satisfy everyone's needs means much bigger stores, it may wind up killing the convenient shopping that these stores are supposed to offer."[67]

This was a chance that the traditional c-stores had to take. "The gas stations simply have nicer stores at nicer locations," said C. Vroom, a food retailing analyst. "The only traditional c-stores that are going to do well are those with special product or geographic niches."[68]

Overseas Opportunities

In 1989, American convenience store operators were rushing to capitalize on new growth opportunities across the globe.[69] Traditional c-store operators and oil retailers agreed that abundant opportunities for overseas development of convenience stores existed. "Americans aren't the only people on earth willing

to pay a little extra in order to save time."[70] The American convenience store format enjoyed a prestigious reputation in many corners of the world, especially when compared to native retail segments.[71]

MANAGEMENT

Karl Eller

Circle K's Chairman of the Board, Karl Eller, was known to recognize a good opportunity and seize it. In the mid-1970s, Eller noticed a newspaper article about a Denver man who had choked to death on a piece of meat. The article stated that the deceased man owned two television stations. "I waited a few days," Eller stated. "Then I called and bought those stations."[72]

Eller's opportunistic nature was reflected in his career history. Starting as a salesman of billboard space, in ten years he built his small business into an outdoor-advertising and media company called Combined Communications Corporation. It was the country's largest billboard-advertising company, owning seven TV stations, fourteen radio stations, and two newspapers.[73] In 1979 he sold Combined Communications to Gannett Company for $367 million, and moved to Charter Company, a Florida oil company with some magazine and newspaper properties. After Charter Company started losing money, Eller moved to Columbia Pictures Industries, Inc., which he helped sell to Coca-Cola in the early 1980s. He left Columbia after Coca-Cola would not participate in a plan to erect a media empire around one of the three television networks.[74]

Following his departure from Columbia Pictures, Eller agreed to take over the Circle K convenience store chain from its founder Fred Hervey, a long-time friend of Eller.[75] After becoming Circle K's Chairman in 1983, Eller stated, "I think I see a tremendous opportunity to build Circle K into a national chain."[76]

Eller's Expansion

Former Gannett Company chairman Allen Neuharth, who purchased Combined Communications from Eller, brutally profiled the Circle K Chairman in his book, *Confessions of an S.O.B.* He stated, "At CCC, Eller had established himself as a first-class dealmaker. There's a big difference in being a dealmaker and a manager. He is interested primarily in going from deal to deal like a dog in heat. He doesn't care to manage what he gets."[77]

Indeed, Eller showed that he knew how to make deals as chairman for Circle K. After gaining control of the company in 1983, Eller conducted a campaign to expand what was then a 12-state convenience store chain into a nationwide giant that could take on Southland Corporation's 7-Eleven. While Southland scrambled to raise cash to help pay off debt, Eller tripled the number of Circle K stores by 1989 and established representation for the chain in the Northeast.[78] Industry analysts had declared that Eller had molded Circle K into the industry's most aggressive, fastest-growing player.[79]

The simple philosophy that Eller brought to Circle K was "offer one-stop shopping: groceries, fast food, gasoline, and bank services. Then just sit back and let the sales flow in while consumers, happy to save time, ignored high markups."[80] "We're a massive distribution system," explained Eller. "Whatever we can push through that store, we will."[81]

With the acquisitions, Eller tried to instill what has been called "a sense of urgency" in employees. Workers at acquired stores received newsletters on the mergers. Those employees with questions about the expansion were instructed to call a toll-free 800 number. Famous for his dawn to midnight work days, Eller tried to set a good example for his employees. In 1988, he got up at 5:00 A.M. on Christmas morning to visit 60 stores in Phoenix.[82]

Carl Lindner

Circle K's expansion was aided significantly by Eller's association with Carl Lindner, a Cincinnati financier. While building Combined Communications, Eller had purchased the Cincinnati *Enquirer* from Lindner. The sale left Lindner as the controlling shareholder in the company. This began the close relationship of Eller and Lindner.[83]

After Eller became the Chairman of Circle K, Lindner enabled him to purchase the UtoteM convenience store chain, which was owned by Lindner's American Financial.[84] Lindner also controlled Charter, the source of another block of stores purchased by the company. Furthermore, Lindner purchased many of the Circle K stores and then leased them back to the company.[85]

While Lindner doubled his stake in Circle K, which finally represented 38 percent of the stock, Lindner's American Financial helped Eller with his personal finances. American Financial sold Eller $10 million of Circle K stock and lent him $14.4 million to buy some shares from Fred Hervey, Circle K's founder.[86] As a result Eller owned 7.1 percent of the Circle K stock.[87]

Al Neuharth profiled Lindner in his book as well as Karl Eller. At one time Lindner was the second-largest stockholder in Neuharth's Gannett Company. His book contained the following description: "Lindner is straitlaced, soft-spoken, slow-talking. He buys his way into companies as a substantial shareholder, courts the management, then increases his holdings, maneuvers his way on the board, and ultimately takes control. He's done that at Penn Central, United Brands, Circle K, and others."[88]

Positive Choices

In 1988, Circle K received considerable media attention when the company announced some health plan exclusions in a January 1 letter to employees. The company stated that it would cut off the medical coverage of employees who became sick or injured as a result of AIDS, alcohol, drug abuse or self-inflicted wounds. The letter stated, "We believe that these personal life style decisions could seriously impact other participants' health care costs."[89] Civil libertarians protested the exclusion, stating that the policy was "an illegal and discriminatory practice."[90] In defense of its policy, Circle K said that it was permissible in a self-funded plan under ERISA, which exempted most self-insured health plans under state insurance laws. On a segment of NBC-TV's "Today" show, Eller stated, "We're trying to encourage our employees to make positive choices." However, in mid-August of 1988, after extensive newspaper and television coverage, Circle K suspended the plan.[91]

A Troubled Circle K

Eller was clearly counting on 1989 to be one of the best years ever for Circle K. On February 1, 1989, he proposed that the company hire Wasserstein, Perella & Company as consultants for "the second phase of the company's expansion." The three outside board members other than Lindner and his son were to over-

see the Wasserstein effort. These members were John Harbin and Dean Guerin, both Texas businessmen, and William Franke, a Phoenix investor.[92]

In May of 1989, Circle K was officially put on the block. Management was hoping that the investment bankers would find a buyer for the company or a joint-venture partner such as an oil company. Eller also announced that he might be interested in a leveraged buyout of the company.[93]

However, board members started receiving the independent appraisals from Wasserstein. "Wasserstein was giving a much more critical analysis of the operating side of Circle K than the board had heard before," said a director. After the expansion of previous years, Circle K was faced with fierce competition from oil companies who had opened their own convenience stores. Reports stated that Circle K had "grown too fast." Many of the recent acquisitions were not producing nearly enough to offset the additional debt burden, and Circle K was faced with a liquidity crisis.[94]

Another discovery which "dumbfounded" some board members was that Richard Smith, chairman of Steve's Homemade Ice Cream, was making critical marketing and operations decisions for Circle K as an unpaid consultant. "I don't think the chief executive officer can delegate responsibilities like that to a nonemployee," said director John Harbin.[95] Eller had given Smith broad powers to run Circle K marketing in the Spring of 1989.[96] He was consulting without pay, but some board members alleged that his products were getting assured shelf space. Eller described Smith as "probably one of the smartest merchandisers and buyers of products I've ever known," and insisted that he had been candid with the board about Smith's consulting.[97]

In September of 1989, Circle K ended its search for a buyer. During the four months that it was on the block, no one showed an interest in buying the company because of the weak junk-bond market and Circle K's troubled balance sheet. In addition, Eller also suspended his notion of a leveraged buyout. Wasserstein advisors stated that an LBO was unlikely to succeed given current market and operating conditions.[98]

Between the time that Circle K hired Wasserstein, Perella in February, 1989, and the announcement in September of 1989 that there would be neither a sale nor an LBO, some "fat trimming" changes were made in management. During that period, eleven members of management either left the company or were fired in cost-cutting moves. The positions vacated were mostly regional directors in the areas of marketing, advertising and promotions, operations, and beverages and food service.[99]

Management Redirection

At the annual meeting in late November of 1989, several changes occurred. First, to help Eller deal with the company's lenders, directors appointed fellow board member William A. Franke to supervise Circle K's financial restructuring. Next, the board ousted ice-cream magnate Richard Smith as marketing consultant. The board believed that as both a vendor to Circle K and an operations chief, he had a potential for conflicts of interest. Also, operating results had not been good under his leadership. Lindner was widely believed to have insisted on Smith's ouster in mid-November, but the directors contended it was instigated by the entire board.[100]

After Smith's departure, Franke had a big agenda at Circle K. He intended to cut back capital spending and inventory, sell $200 million in assets, and hire an operations executive.[101]

Combined with Franke's efforts, Lindner sent two of his executives to advise Circle K on the restructuring in late November of 1989. American Financial was also sending other managers to "help out" by reviewing the situation. "Lindner is trying to do a little bit of damage control and protect his investment," said Christopher E. Vroom, an analyst at Alex, Brown & Sons Inc.[102]

Another development that emerged at the annual meeting in November was the announcement from Robert M. Reade of his intention to resign as president, chief operating officer, and director of Circle K. No reason was given by Reade, but he continued to assist Circle K on a transitional basis in its restructuring effort.[103]

In January of 1990, Circle K announced that Robert A. Dearth would take over all three positions in Circle K management. Dearth possessed 21 years of experience in finance, management, and planning. He was formerly vice president and chief administrative officer of United Brands, of which Carl Lindner was chairman of the board.[104] Dearth's takeover is reflected in the organizational chart in Exhibit 3.

As for Eller, one director suggested that the board had been quietly reassigning many of his responsibilities, such as conducting crucial talks with lenders. Circle K's store operations basically were being run by the company's new president, Dearth. One board member said that a major condition of any reorganization plan may include an agreement for Eller to retire as chairman and chief executive officer.[105]

MARKETING

Centralized Operations

Major objectives of Circle K during 1989 were to take greater advantage of its purchasing power in dealing with its vendors, pass on price increases to its customers and reduce the magnitude of its promotions. To accomplish these objectives, the company centralized its marketing efforts, thus reducing the ability of its various regions to deviate from these objectives and fortifying its efforts by concentrating responsibilities into fewer, more focused marketing personnel.[106]

Other marketing objectives to be achieved by 1990 included:[107]

- Increase annual sales by 15 percent.
- Have 90 percent of the stores selling gasoline.
- Double per store sales.
- Sell 45,000 gallons of gasoline monthly per store.
- Increase fast-food sales to 15 percent of total sales (an increase from 12.5 percent in 1988).

Vendors

The company had done a good job of playing hardball with its suppliers. In 1989, Circle K established guidelines with its vendors requiring advance notice of price increases and developed systems to assist in monitoring these price controls.[108] In return for shelf space, co-op advertising, and promotional displays, it is getting better discounts.[109] These increases in discounts, in addition to allowances and rebates from its vendors due to increased merchandise volumes, made a positive impact on the corporation's fiscal year 1988 merchandise gross

Exhibit 3
Circle K Corporation
Organization Chart

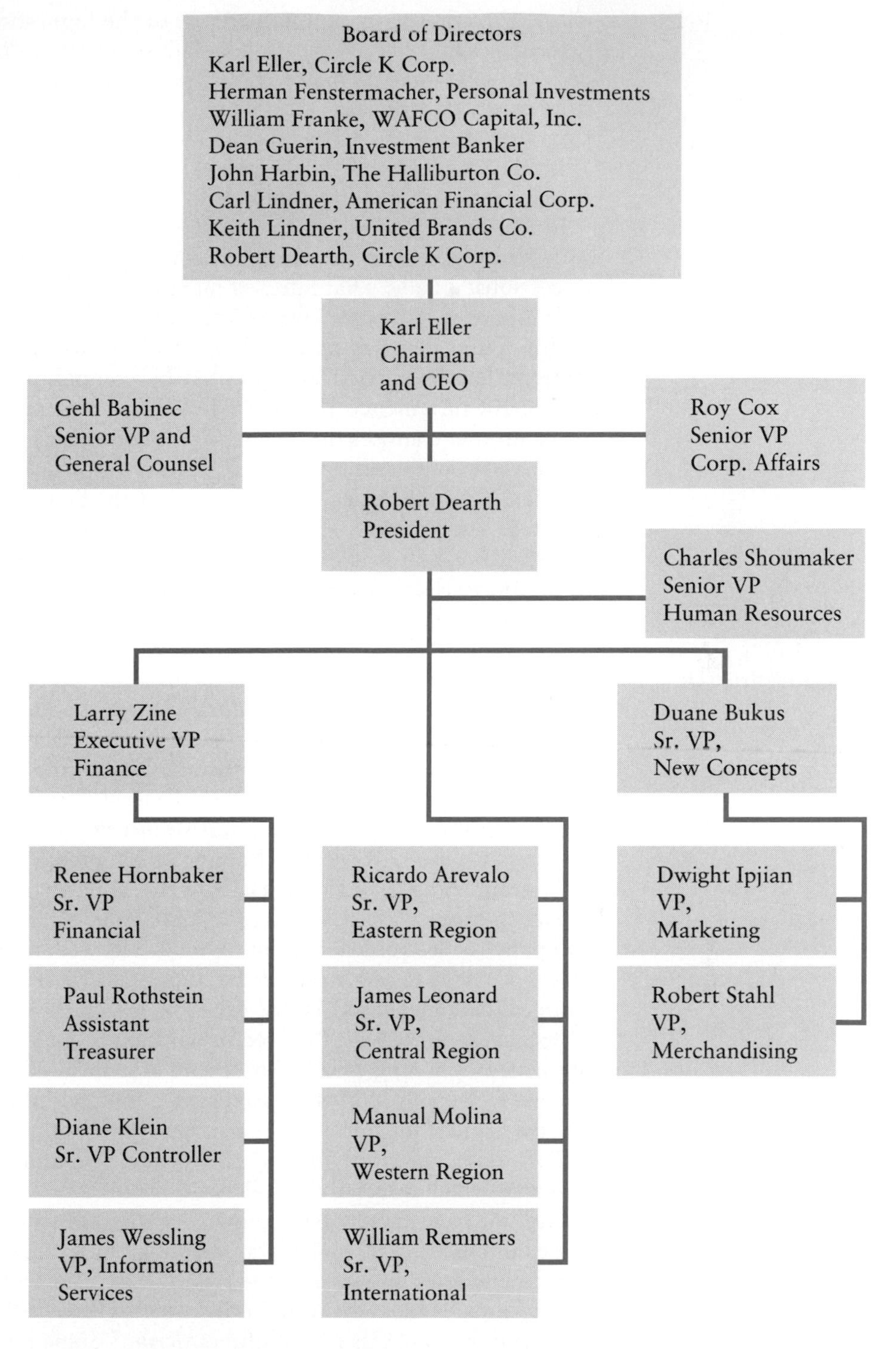

Source: Circle K Annual Report.

profit margin.[110] But vendors have complained about Circle K's unreasonable demands and their "it's my way or no way" attitude.[111]

Pricing

Circle K traditionally maintained one of the highest merchandise gross profit percentages in the convenience store industry, with profit margins of one to three percent higher than its main competitor, Southland.[112] In addition, the company's store prices exceed grocery store prices by about 10 percent to 15 percent, down from previous years.[113] However, in an effort to maintain market share, in fiscal 1989 the company relaxed its efforts in passing on its price increases to the customers and expanded its promotions.[114]

In April, 1989, Circle K determined that its pricing policies did not generate sufficient revenues to warrant their continuation so the company raised overall prices substantially. That fattened margins quickly, but hurt sales. The company then launched its "price busters" program, offering periodic deep discounts on such popular items as milk and beer to lure customers back into stores. That strategy has been tried and rejected by competitors such as Southland and National Convenience Stores.[115] Circle K's erratic pricing "is the kind of knee-jerk stuff that confuses the hell out of the consumer," said John F. Antico, Sr. V.P. for retail at Southland.[116]

Circle K said the price hikes were simply the first stage of a long-range plan to improve performance. The chain had been discounting too many high-volume items, such as soft drinks, that shaved storewide margins. They then tried to discount more selectively, but first had to raise margins overall.[117]

Merchandise Mix

Circle K continually enhanced the merchandise and services offered by its stores to increase traffic. One such product was the introduction into selected markets in 1989 of "Chiller," a new frozen carbonated beverage.[118] The company also had services such as video movie rentals, debit card programs, and sales of tickets for state-run lottery games. In 1987, Federal Express drops were scheduled to appear.[119] Every idea was not a hit. Also in 1987, Circle K bombed in its attempt to serve as a drop-off for dry cleaning and laundry.[120]

"We are going back to the basics of the convenience store industry, like milk, bread, and eggs," said R. Cox, a Circle K Sr. V.P. Computers will enable the company to electronically monitor what sells well, and to fine tune the product mix. "We have to move out of the bricks-and-mortar expansion phase into the store technology phase," stated Mr. Cox.[121]

Because management "is tired of working in the dark," the chain began testing a new scanning and point-of-sale system in January of 1990.[122] "I can't believe we've stayed in the business this long without knowing what we sold, what we sold it for, and if we're making a profit on it," said Eller.[123]

This move was partly due to a 1989 study conducted by Circle K's board of directors which revealed that Eller had concentrated so much on expansion that he did not have an adequate knowledge of what was being sold in his stores.[124] For example, Circle K had a large selection of hair nets, although studies showed that few women shopped at the stores. "We also had six brands of dog food, seven kinds of aspirin and nobody knows what else," said one director.[125] Mr. Eller said much of this is "rightful criticism." Some inventory practices still date to prior management and "we never got around to changing," he said.[126]

Fast Food

In 1986, Circle K signed an agreement to test market the sale of branded doughnuts, including Winchell's and Dunkin' Donuts, at selected test sites. It also signed an agreement with a hamburger restaurant to test market drive-through

hamburger units.[127] By July of 1988, Circle K had the Dunkin' Donuts program in 500 units and expected to expand it to at least 1,000 locations by 1990. The previous test with Winchell's was discontinued.[128]

In late 1987, Circle K's president declared that the ideal food service program would yield high gross profit dollars, higher margins with little labor involved, and major traffic building capabilities. But he indicated that the corporation was falling short of its goals.[129]

In January of 1990, Circle K and Oscar Mayer signed a three-year agreement under which Circle K would sell fresh deli sandwiches identified by stickers as being made with Oscar Mayer or Louis Rich luncheon meats.[130]

Gasoline Sales

As merchandise sales slowed, the profitability of Circle K increasingly depended on gasoline sales and its ability to maintain strong gross margins per gallon. Gasoline sales accounted for 42.3 percent of total sales during fiscal year 1989. Seventy-seven percent of all stores sold gasoline, with each store averaging almost 40,000 gallons per month.[131] However, Circle K was one of the few large chains that did not have an oil-company tie.[132]

Store Image/Location

"We are continually concerned about image and we are constantly developing ways to present a good image to customers. We want to be competitive and continue to attract new customers and keep the ones we've got," said Rick Dickerson, Circle K's Midwest division engineer and manager.[133] In 1989, the company began improving its image by remodeling stores, turning up the lighting, and lowering shelves, all in hopes of attracting more women.[134] "We're trying to get away from dependence on 18- to 34-year-old males with tool belts who pull up in a pickup truck," said R. Cox, Sr. V.P. for Corporate Affairs.[135]

Circle K also attempted to project a good image toward customers by making charitable contributions. In February of 1990, Circle K teamed up with Energy Fuels Development Corporation for a free "computers-for-school" promotion.[136] Circle K and the ethanol producer encouraged customers to visit the stores in the New Mexico area to purchase ethanol-blended gasoline in exchange for points that could be used to purchase computers. Furthermore, Circle K donated $1.1 million to United Cerebral Palsy affiliates across the country.[137]

In selecting store locations, the company looked for four-corner intersections with at least one street having a minimum 20,000-car daily volume of traffic.[138] In addition, "higher volumes must be generated to support the more expensive corner locations which we must obtain for maximum traffic," stressed Robert Reade, Circle K's past president.[139] Circle K took some creative approaches to increasing traffic by leasing space in a multiuse building, i.e., office space combined with retailing. "The company's aim was to get high traffic in a prime location," said Eller.[140]

COMPETITION

In May of 1990, Circle K ranked second in number of stores behind the convenience store leader, Southland. However, petroleum-owned companies have started closing in on their territory (see Exhibit 4).

Exhibit 4
Market Share by Number of Stores

Top 15 C-store chains, 1987–1989

Rank 1989	Rank 1988	Rank 1987	Company	No. of units—1989	% of total*
1	1	1	The Southland Corp.	7,205	8.7%
2	2	2	The Circle K Corp.	4,664	5.7%
3	14	+	Emro Marketing	1,673	2.0%
4	3	3	Conv. Food Mart	1,258	1.5%
5	7	6	Silcorp	1,168	1.4%
6	6	7	Nat. Conv. Stores	1,147	1.4%
7	5	4	Dairy Mart Conv. Stores	1,145	1.4%
8	4	5	Cumberland Farms	1,100	1.3%
9	15	14	Chevron Corp.	1,042	1.3%
10	8	+	Amoco	1,000	1.2%
11	11	9	Dilon Cos.	956	1.2%
12	8	8	Texaco Inc.	954	1.2%
13	+	+	Coastal Mart Inc.	850	1.0%
14	+	+	Majik Market Mgmt. Corp.	843	1.0%
15	12	10	Mobil	800	1.0%

*Based on 82,500 stores
+Not in Top 15 that year
Source: *Convenience Store News*, January 15–February 11, 1990, p. 46.

The Southland Corporation

The Southland Corporation went private in a $4.9 billion leveraged buyout in 1987 and actively sold assets to help pay down debt.[141] In January of 1990, Moody's Investors Service, Inc., downgraded the company's debt ratings based on declining operating performance and the increasingly competitive convenience store industry.[142] In February of 1990, Southland sold 50 percent of its interest in Citgo Petroleum in order to generate needed cash.[143] In March, 1990, after announcing a debt restructuring that included a $400 million, 75 percent buyout by its Japanese partners, Southland said it might file for bankruptcy if it couldn't close a deal.[144]

However, Southland had no plans to sell its distribution and food processing group. In 1989, this group increased sales to non-Southland c-stores and food service accounts by more than 17 percent.[145] Industry experts said that Southland's distribution centers could benefit by serving newcomers to the c-store industry that do not have knowledge of, or interest in, the distribution side. Oil companies constitute a prime possibility.[146]

The company's 1989 strategies included price cutting, which touched off an industry-wide price war, and more effective shelf stocking. Southland also started tailoring its offerings to specific neighborhoods—stocking more black health and beauty aids in some neighborhoods and more suntan oil near the beach. An additional tactic was increased advertising. The new campaign aimed

to persuade customers that 7-Eleven "is not just someplace you shop when you forgot to pick something up at the grocery store, but someplace that has everyday low prices." Television advertisements featured baby boomers straight out of "thirtysomething" with no sign of working-class men swinging by for six-packs of beer.[147]

In 1989, Southland started a public awareness campaign called "Read to Succeed." The campaign encouraged literacy through programs, grants, and advertising.[148]

In 1986, Southland received some controversial publicity when it upset some civil libertarians by pulling *Playboy* and *Penthouse* out of company-owned stores.[149]

National Convenience Stores

In 1989, National Convenience Stores owned and operated over 1,100 stores, mainly under the Stop N Go logo. The company ended fiscal year 1989 with a loss of nearly $8.9 million and scaled back operations from eleven states to just four.[150]

Strategies for 1989 included trying to climb upscale by featuring products for fitness buffs and gourmets. National had already been stocking over 600 items more than the average convenience store. It was also building stores triple the size of older ones, which already were more than 600 square feet larger than competitors'. To publicize its new look, which included more gas pumps and indoor table seating, National increased its 1989 advertising budget to $12 million, up from just $2 million five years earlier.[151]

Oil Companies

Convenience stores faced formidable competitors in the big oil companies, which turned thousands of repair garages into stores. Oil-based firms accounted for only three of the top fifteen companies in 1987, compared to six of the top fifteen in 1989.[152] "It's head-on collision of oil companies and convenience stores," said Eller.[153]

When oil companies faced their own crisis, with gasoline sales down and labor costs up, they responded by switching to self-service pumps and adding stores. The gas stations' prime corner locations and sleek new stores easily persuaded customers to bypass traditional convenience stores. *Convenience Store News* reported that between 1984 and 1989, the number of convenience stores attached to gas stations almost doubled from 16,000 to 30,000. "There is no question that the line between the petroleum industry stores and the traditional stores is getting blurred," said Ms. Grondin of *Convenience Store News*.[154]

The oil companies planned to expand in 1989. With their abundant resources, many petroleum companies increased the size of their c-stores to make room for expansion into fast-food operations.[155] "All of our new capital investment is going into the AM/PM ARCO gasoline concept," said Scott Stanworth, V.P. of retail marketing for ARCO. ARCO even hired sports stars, such as hefty football legend William "Refrigerator" Perry, to plug its stores in television ads in the West.[156]

In 1989, Exxon also saw more stores in its future. "There is no question that substantial earnings are available from the convenience stores," said G. Thomas, Marketing V.P.[157] "But milk, hot dogs, and tapes are secondary to gasoline," said an Amoco spokesperson. "We are gas marketers selling a few impulse items."[158]

Emro Marketing Since 1987, no company, oil-based or traditional c-store retailer, rose faster than Emro Marketing. Its Speedway and Starvin' Marvin stores ranked third in 1989. Emro's evolution as a c-store operator was similar to that of other oil retailers; "There was no master plan to be a major c-store player, things just turned out that way."[159] "Since 1986, everything we have built and/or remodeled is a c-store/gas station property," stated Emro's president of marketing. "We remain gasoline sellers first, but we feel a rising degree of comfort running c-stores. Our operations expertise ranks with the best in the industry."[160]

Supermarkets In 1989, stiffer competition also came from supermarkets, many of which stayed open around the clock and were putting convenience store items near their checkout lines.[161]

FINANCE

Since 1983, Circle K demonstrated steadily increased growth in revenues and profits. General financial information is shown in Exhibit 5, while the financial statements for fiscal 1989 are in Exhibit 6. Revenues have increased anywhere from 9 to 64 percent (average 28.25 percent) from 1984–1988, and net income from 16 to 65 percent (average 32.25 percent).[162] Apparently, Eller's goal to "become a national chain just behind Southland's 7-Eleven" was well on its way to realization.[163]

However, far from achieving this lofty goal, Circle K instead earned the dubious distinction of being named among the ten worst performing stocks of 1989.[164] Signs of trouble appeared in fiscal 1988 when, although the company demonstrated a continued increase in bottom line income, operating profits decreased. This was followed by an extremely dismal performance in 1989, when the first operating loss ($5,542,000) in ten years appeared, and bottom line income plummeted 75 percent. Management attributed this to several factors.[165] First, merchandise margins decreased to 36.0 percent (compared to 37.5 percent and 36.6 percent in 1988 and 1987), resulting in a decline of $30.3 million in gross profit. These lower margins resulted from increased competition which forced Circle K to expand its promotional efforts and cease attempts to pass price increases on to its customers.[166] Second, unpredictable fluctuations in the gasoline market resulted in a temporary, but significant, decrease in gross margins on gas sales. Once again, Circle K was forced to accept these lower gross margins in order to remain competitive.[167] Finally, interest expenses increased 69.4 percent in fiscal 1989. The majority of this increase resulted from debt incurred to finance acquisitions, new store construction, and remodeling. However, $6.9 million of this increase resulted from an increase in the interest rates on the variable rate debt carried by Circle K.[168]

Circle K's financial struggles were reflected in the price of its stock. Upon removal of Circle K from the selling block, stock prices immediately fell to $7.75.[169] Stock prices continued to fall, and as of April 18, 1990, Circle K's stock was trading at 1 5/8.[170] (See Exhibit 7.)

As a result of the decreased 1989 earnings, Circle K was not in compliance with financial covenants on its $325 million Bank Credit Agreement and $200 million

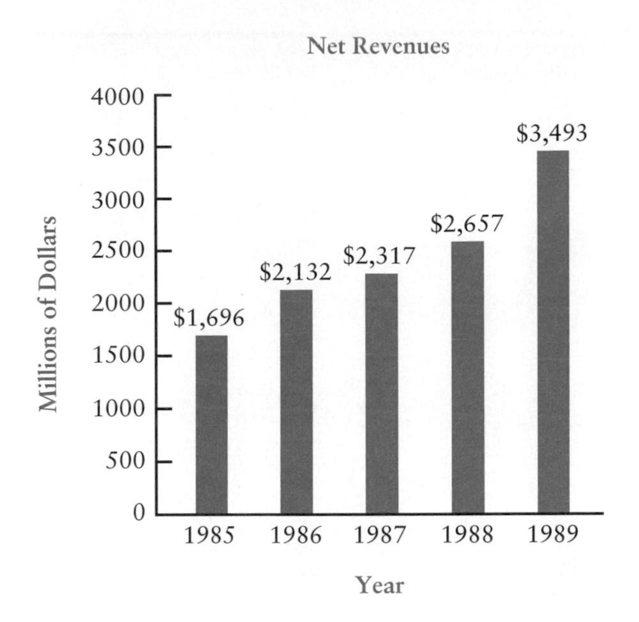

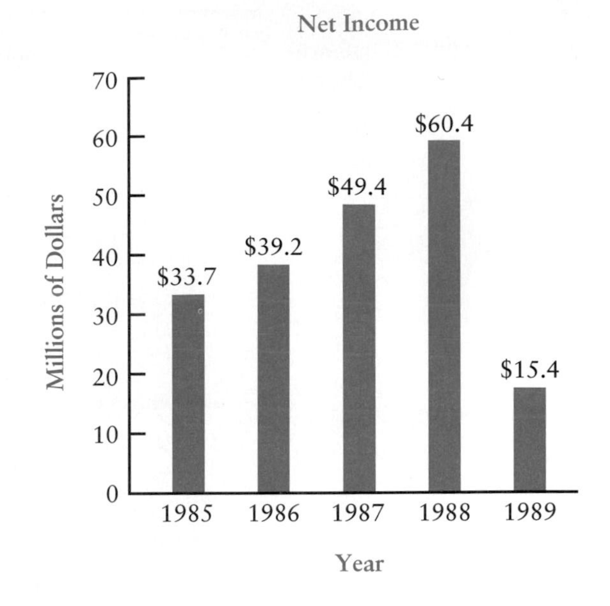

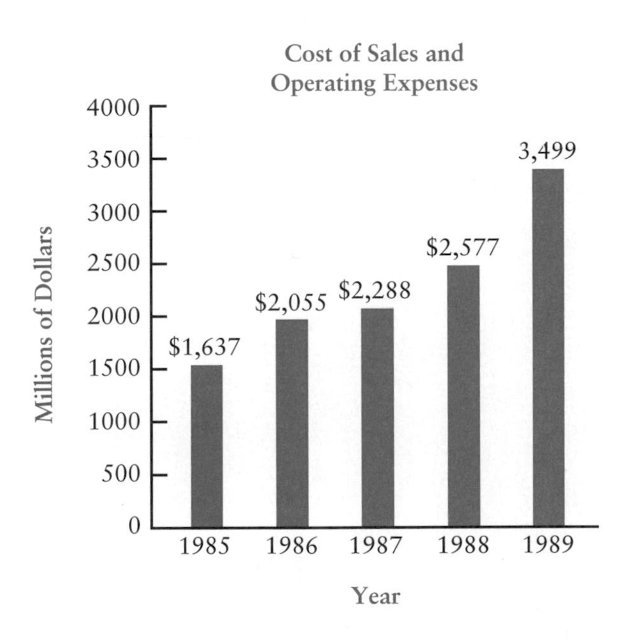

Source: Circle K 1989 Annual Report.

Exhibit 5
Circle K Corporation Financial Information: Fiscal Years 1985–1989

Senior Secured Notes Agreement. Initially, an agreement was reached with lenders, a syndicate of commercial banks, to waive the noncompliance until April 6, 1990, when $60 million of the bank borrowing would mature. Consent to an amendment of the required minimum fixed charge ratio was obtained from a syndicate of private investors which held the Senior Secured Notes. This amendment required Circle K to offer to repurchase $20 million of the notes on April 16, 1990, and to continue repurchasing $20 million quarterly until compliance was reached.[171]

Exhibit 6a
Consolidated Balance Sheets

The Circle K Corporation and subsidiaries

April 30:	1989	1988
Assets	(In thousands)	
Current assets:		
Cash and short-term investments	$38,488	$44,216
Receivables	36,265	34,446
Inventories	239,916	191,000
Properties held for sale	35,000	80,000
Federal income tax receivable	52,323	26,139
Prepaid expenses	7,018	3,712
Total current assets	409,010	379,513
Property plant and equipment	1,331,345	902,500
Less—Accumulated depreciation and amortization	262,856	194,186
Net property, plant and equipment	1,068,489	708,314
Deferred interest promissory note due from affiliate	—	35,289
Long-term receivables	64,237	65,193
Excess costs over acquired net assets, net	331,942	189,230
Favorable leases acquired, net	73,847	57,862
Other assets	97,415	100,383
	$2,044,940	$1,535,784

April 30:	1989	1988
Liabilities and stockholders' equity	(In thousands)	
Current liabilities:		
Due to banks	$91,000	$60,000
Accounts payable	134,944	112,144
Other current liabilities	124,501	108,463
Total current liabilities	350,445	280,607
Long-term debt	1,103,762	844,065
Deferred income taxes	93,045	38,133
Other liabilities	100,160	17,191
Deferred revenue	19,632	24,767
Commitments and contingent liabilities		
Mandatory redeemable preferred stock, at redemption value	47,500	47,500
Stockholders' equity:		
Series B preferred stock, at liquidation value	50,000	—
Common stock, $1 par value	50,402	50,003
Additional paid-in capital	168,018	165,040
Common stock warrants	2,300	2,300
Retained earnings	136,777	138,563
Equity adjustment from foreign currency translation	1,527	5,449
Less—Treasury stock at cost	(78,628)	(77,834)
Total stockholders' equity	330,396	283,524
	$2,044,940	$1,535,784

Exhibit 6b
Consolidated Statements of Earnings

The Circle K Corporation and subsidiaries

For the years ended April 30:	1989	1988	1987
	(In thousands, except per share amounts)		
Revenues:			
Sales	$3,441,384	$2,613,843	$2,289,444
Other	51,723	42,879	27,340
Gross revenues	3,493,107	2,656,722	2,316,784
Cost of sales and expenses:			
Cost of sales	2,580,398	1,893,058	1,649,496
Operating and administrative	729,306	561,894	485,694
Depreciation and amortization	93,033	65,659	51,680
Interest and debt expense	95,912	56,608	41,566
Total cost of sales and expenses	3,498,649	2,577,219	2,228,436
Operating profit (loss)	(5,542)	79,503	88,348
Gain on sale of assets	32,323	8,198	5,948
Earnings before federal and state income taxes and cumulative effect of accounting change	26,781	87,701	94,296
Federal and state income taxes	11,367	32,790	44,866
Net earnings before cumulative effect of accounting change	15,414	54,911	49,430
Cumulative effect on prior years of change in accounting for income taxes	—	5,500	—
Net earnings	$15,414	$60,411	$49,430
Earnings per common share before cumulative effect of accounting change:			
Primary	$0.21	$1.04	$0.93
Fully diluted	$0.20	$0.96	$0.85
Earnings per common share:			
Primary	$0.21	$1.15	$0.93
Fully diluted	$0.20	$1.04	$0.85
Cash dividends per common share	$0.28	$0.28	$0.28

It became clear by late March 1990, that Circle K was in no position to meet the terms of these agreements. A $28.1 million loss was posted for the third quarter, yielding a total loss of $25.5 million for the first nine months of fiscal 1990. The loss for this nine-month period occurred despite the fact that revenues were up 10 percent over the same period in 1989.[172]

On April 3, 1990, Circle K signed a tentative agreement with senior creditors and its largest shareholder, American Financial Corporation. The accord was subject to signing a definitive standstill agreement that would hold through the earlier of October 31, 1990, or completion of a financial restructuring. The tentative agreement deferred all principal and interest payments, and waived any

Exhibit 7
Circle K, Inc., Weekly Stock Closing Prices

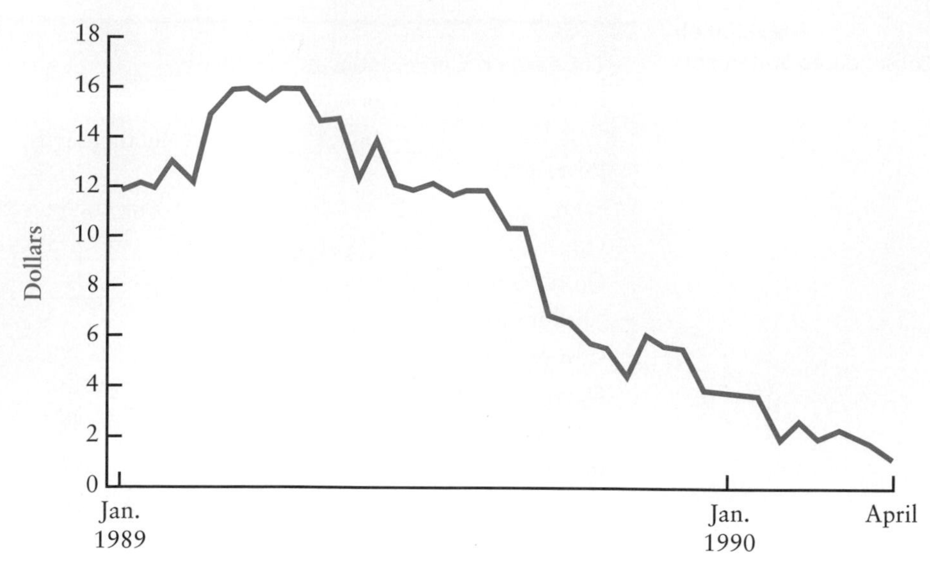

Source: *The Wall Street Journal,* March 28, 1990, p. A5, and April 5, 1990, p. B1.

existing defaults under then-current loan agreements. The standstill agreement required that Circle K acquire at least 90 percent of its subordinated debt by the end of October, 1990. The terms of any offer to subordinated holders had not been determined. The company hinted at an exchange of stock for subordinated debt and said it expected to file a registration statement with the SEC before May 15, 1990.[173]

The company hoped to accomplish a restructuring without seeking Chapter 11 Bankruptcy. Circle K officials claimed that the company had sufficient funds to meet trade obligations during the standstill period.[174] However, a Circle K spokesperson admitted, "If the company does not achieve a financial restructuring, it will not have adequate liquidity."[175]

Legal Issues

In addition to its financial woes, Circle K faced several shareholder lawsuits. In October, 1989, two unhappy shareholders filed a lawsuit against the company's Chief Executive Officer, Karl Eller, and Chief Operating Officer, Robert Reade.[176] The plaintiffs alleged breach of fiduciary responsibility and asked for an unspecified amount in damages. The suit claimed that the defendants should have known "that the possibility of a leveraged buyout or a financial restructuring or merger was highly improbable because Circle K was saddled down with debt and had poor prospects for improving operating results in the near term."[177]

The lawsuit also alleged that the company should have known early in 1989 that its fourth quarter reports would show more than $23 million in losses. The plaintiffs claimed that Circle K knew, ignored, or failed to disclose factors that hurt the company's financial performance.[178] In response, R. Cox, Senior Vice President of Corporate Affairs, stated that "Circle K has always been open and completely accurate in the stating of any financial information or condition of the company.[179] Circle K denied any merit in the lawsuit and planned to vigorously defend against it.[180].

CIRCLE K'S FUTURE

Industry analysts have reported that Circle K Corporation, after reporting a $28.9 million quarterly loss in March of 1990, may be in the position where it must seek Chapter 11 protection. In April of 1990, the company signed an agreement with its major creditors and Carl Lindner for a seven-month moratorium on debt and interest payments. With this agreement, Circle K narrowly avoided default on its $1 billion of debt created by acquisitions.[181] Mr. Franke, the director who along with Mr. Dearth is leading the negotiations with the banks, said his approach in dealing with lenders has been candor. He stated a surviving Circle K would probably be "a skinnied-down company stretching from California to Florida."[182]

As for management, one board member stated that a reorganization plan could mean an agreement for Eller to retire as Chairman of the Board. Eller, while maintaining that he remains in control, has talked about moving on. "I did the best I knew how. Somebody has to be the hero when you're doing good, and the fall guy when things are going bad. I deserve all the credit, and all the woes." Eller's son Scott, a successful Phoenix venture capitalist, said his father is enough of an entrepreneur to "think he can earn it all back again if he wants to."[183]

Endnotes

1. *Circle K Corporation 10-K Report,* Fiscal Year Ending April 30, 1989, p. 1.
2. Circle K News Bulletin, October, 1989.
3. Kathleen Kerwin and Zachary Schiller, "Can Carl Lindner Straighten Out Circle K?" *Business Week,* January 8, 1990, p. 39.
4. *Circle K Company 1989 Annual Report,* pp. 17–18.
5. Ibid., p. 17.
6. Ibid., p. 17.
7. Richard Stern, "Seems like Old Times," *Forbes,* December 5, 1983, p. 56.
8. *1989 Annual Report,* pp. 17–18.
9. Teresa Carson and Todd Vogel, "Karl Eller's Big Thirst for Convenience Stores," *Business Week,* June 13, 1988, p. 87.
10. Ibid., p. 86.
11. Kathleen Kerwin, "Troubled Circle K Is Turning This Way and That," *Business Week,* November 20, 1989, p. 80.
12. "Circle K Won't Buy or Build Stores in '90 Shareholders Are Told," *Wall Street Journal,* November 24, 1989, p. B4E.
13. Carson, "Karl Eller's Big Thirst," p. 86.
14. *1989 Annual Report,* pp. 17–18.
15. Ibid., pp. 17–18.
16. Carson, "Karl Eller's Big Thirst," p. 86.
17. *1989 10–K.*
18. *1989 Annual Report,* pp. 17–18.
19. Ibid., pp. 17–18.
20. Ibid., pp. 17–18.
21. Jeff Rowe, "Circle K Reports Creditors to Ease Terms of Accord," *Wall Street Journal,* December 18, 1989, p. A3.
22. Kerwin, "Can Carl Lindner," p. 40.
23. Kerwin, "Troubled Circle K," p. 80.
24. Kerwin, "Can Carl Lindner," p. 40.
25. Ibid., p. 40.
26. "Circle K to Sell Its 350 Stores to PC Ventures of Canada," *Wall Street Journal,* December 20, 1989, p. B2.
27. "Circle K Won't Buy or Build," p. B4E.
28. Charles Anderer, "Circle K Selling 375 Units," *Convenience Store News,* 26(1), January 15–February 11, 1990, p. 1.
29. Kerwin, "Can Carl Lindner," p. 40.
30. Roy Harris, Jr., "Karl Eller of Circle K Always Pushing Deals, May Have Overdone It," *Wall Street Journal,* March 28, 1990, p. A1.
31. Frank Victoria and Peggy Smedley, "Why Oil Marketers Have C-Store Chains Circling Their Wagons," *National Petroleum News,* September, 1989, p. 44.
32. Ibid., p. 44.
33. "Why the C-Store Image Race Could Lead to a 'Shakeout,'" *National Petroleum News,* September, 1987, p. 38.
34. Chris Ebel, "Unit Growth Outpaces Population," *Convenience Store News,* 25(14), November 13–December 5, 1989, p. 58.
35. Ibid., p. 58.
36. "C-Store Assessment 1988: Mixed Signals, Less Profit," *National Petroleum News,* July, 1989, p. 26.
37. Ibid., p. 26.
38. Claudia Deutsch, "Rethinking the Convenience Store," *New York Times,* October 8, 1989, p. 15.
39. Victoria, "Why Oil Marketers," p. 36.
40. Ibid., p. 36.
41. Deutsch, "Rethinking the Convenience Store," p. 15.
42. "Retailers Debate Impact of Minimum Wage Hike," *Convenience Store News,* 26(1), January 15–February 11, 1990, p. 1.

43. Ibid., p. 55.
44. *1989 Annual Report,* p. 2.
45. Eric C. Peterson, "Shopping Center Futures Recipes for New Sites," *Stores,* March, 1985, p. 70.
46. Andi Stein, "Coeds Voice Their Choice," *Convenience Store News,* 26(1), January 15–February 11, 1990, p. 87.
47. Victoria, "Why Oil Marketers," p. 44.
48. "Why the C-Store Image Race," p. 41.
49. Peggy Smedley, "How Jobbers 'Re-Image' to Boost Sales and Profits," *National Petroleum News,* May, 1989, 30.
50. "C-store Robberies Rose 16 Percent Last Year," *Convenience Store News,"* 25(13), October 16–November 12, 1989, p. 1.
51. Lisa Gubernick, "Stores for Our Times," *Forbes,* November 3, 1986, p. 42.
52. Deutsch, "Rethinking the Convenience Store," p. 15.
53. Ibid., p. 15.
54. Gubernick, "Stores for Our Times," p. 40.
55. Victoria, "Why Oil Marketers," p. 44.
56. Gubernick, "Stores for Our Times," p. 41.
57. Victoria, "Why Oil Marketers," p. 50.
58. Ibid., p. 43.
59. Andrew Glangola, "Foodservice vs. Labor Costs," *Convenience Store News,* 25(13), October 16–November 12, 1989, p. 40.
60. Joe Agnew, "Convenience Stores Testing Fast-Food Market," *Marketing News,* October 24, 1986, p. 10.
61. Glangola, "Foodservice vs. Labor Costs," p. 40.
62. Andrew Glangola, "Soft-Serve Frozen Yogurt Full of Promise," *Convenience Store News,* 26(2), February 12–March 4, 1990, p. 40.
63. Ibid., p. 40.
64. Ibid., p. 40.
65. Ibid., p. 40.
66. Agnew, "Convenience Stores Testing Fast-Food," p. 10.
67. Deutsch, "Rethinking the Convenience Store," p. 15.
68. Ibid., p. 15.
69. Charles Anderer, "Overseas Competition Heats Up," *Convenience Store News,* 25(12), September 26–October 15, 1989, p. 186.
70. Ibid., p. 186.
71. Ibid., p. 186.
72. Carson, "Karl Eller's Big Thirst," p. 86.
73. Gubernick, "Stores for Our Times," p. 40.
74. Harris, Jr., "Karl Eller Always Pushing Deals," p. A1.
75. Carson, "Karl Eller's Big Thirst," p. 87.
76. Stern, "Seems like Old Times," p. 57.
77. Al Neuharth, *Confessions of an S.O.B.* (New York: Bantam Doubleday Dell Publishing Group, Inc., 1989), p. 87.
78. Ibid., p. 86.
79. Ibid., p. 86.
80. Kerry Hannon, "Confessions of a Convenience Store Man," *Forbes,* October 16, 1989, p. 10.
81. Gubernick, "Stores for Our Times," p. 40.
82. Carson, "Karl Eller's Big Thirst," p. 87.
83. Harris, Jr., "Karl Eller Always Pushing Deals," p. A1.
84. Ibid., p. A5.
85. Carson, "Karl Eller's Big Thirst," p. 87.
86. Harris, Jr., "Karl Eller Always Pushing Deals," p. A1.
87. Barbara Grondin, "Circle K Ends Search for a Buyer," *Convenience Store News,* October, 1989, p. 1.
88. Neuharth, *Confessions of an S.O.B.,* p. 95.
89. Kenneth B. Noble, "Company Halting Health Plan on Some 'Life Style' Illnesses," *New York Times,* August 6, 1988, p. 1.
90. Glenn Huntley, "Firm Suspends Policy Excluding AIDS Claims," *Business Insurance,* August 15, 1988, p. 11.
91. Ibid., p. 12.
92. Harris, Jr., "Karl Eller Always Pushing Deals," p. A1.
93. Ibid., p. A1.
94. Hannon, "Confessions of a Convenience Store Man," p. 10.
95. Harris, Jr., "Karl Eller Always Pushing Deals," p. A1.
96. Kerwin, "Can Carl Lindner," p. 39.
97. Harris, Jr., "Karl Eller Always Pushing Deals," p. A1.
98. Kerwin, "Troubled Circle K," p. 78.
99. Grondin, "Circle K Ends Search," p. 1.
100. Kerwin, "Can Carl Lindner," p. 39.
101. Ibid., p. 40.
102. Ibid., p. 40.
103. "Circle K Corp. Names Robert A. Dearth, 45, to President's Post," *Wall Street Journal,* January 22, 1990, p. B4.
104. Grondin, "Circle K Ends Search," p. 1.
105. Harris, Jr., "Karl Eller Always Pushing Deals," p. A1.
106. 1989 Annual Report, p. 5.
107. Circle K News Bulletin, October, 1989.
108. 1989 Annual Report, p. 5.
109. Kerwin, "Troubled Circle K," p. 79.
110. *1989 Annual Report,* p. 5.
111. Barbara Grondin, "Circle K Vexes Vendors," Convenience Store News, 25(11), August 31–September 25, 1989, p. 6.
112. Ibid., p. 6.
113. "Why the C-Store Image Race," p. 40.
114. *1989 Annual Report,* p. 5.
115. Kerwin, "Troubled Circle K," p. 79.
116. Ibid., p. 79.
117. Ibid., p. 79.
118. *1989 Annual Report,* p. 4.
119. Carson, "Karl Eller's Big Thirst," p. 87.
120. Ibid., p. 87.
121. Deutsch, "Rethinking the Convenience Store," p. 15.
122. Barbara Grondin, "Eller Unveils Circle K's Future," *Convenience Store News,* 26(1), January 15–February 11, 1990, p. 65.
123. Ibid., p. 65.
124. Harris, Jr., "Karl Eller Always Pushing Deals," p. A1.
125. Ibid., p. A1.
126. Ibid., p. A1.
127. Agnew, "Convenience Stores Testing Fast-Food," p. 10.
128. Karen Bruno, "Dunkin' Donuts, Winchell's Team with C-Store Chains in Breakfast Drive," *Nation's Restaurant News,* July 25, 1988, p. 3.
129. Charles Bernstein, "Circle K Falls Short of Fast-Food Goals," *Nation's Restaurant News,* December 7, 1987, p. 1.
130. Andrew Glangola, "Chilled Food Adds New Dimension to Take-Out," *Convenience Store News,* 26(1), January 15–February 11, 1990, p. 16.
131. *1989 Annual Report,* p. 2.
132. Harris, Jr., "Karl Eller Always Pushing Deals," p. A1.
133. Smedley, "How Jobbers 'Re-Image,'" p. 28.
134. Deutsch, "Rethinking the Convenience Store," p. 15.
135. Rowe, "Circle K Creditors to Ease Terms," p. A3.

136. "Promo Review," *Convenience Store News,* 26(3), March 5–March 25, 1990, p. 78.
137. "Circle K Gives $1.1 Million in Donations to Charity," *Convenience Store News,* 26(4), March 26–April 15, 1990, p. 88.
138. "Why the C-Store Image Race," p. 44.
139. Bernstein, "Circle K Falls Short," p. 1.
140. Peterson, "Shopping Center Futures," p. 70.
141. Maria Halkias, "Southland Completes Sale of Interest in Citgo," *Dallas Morning News,* February 1, 1990, p. B1.
142. Ibid., p. B1.
143. Ibid., p. B1.
144. "Chapter 7-Eleven for Southland?" *Business Week,* April 16, 1990, p. 34.
145. Barbara Grondin, "Southland to Keep Distribution, Food Centers," *Convenience Store News,* 26(1), January 15–February 11, 1990, p. 8.
146. Ibid., p. 8.
147. Deutsch, "Rethinking the Convenience Store," p. 15.
148. "7-Eleven Battles Illiteracy," *Convenience Store News,* 26(1), January 15–February 11, 1990, p. 82.
149. Gubernick, "Stores for Our Times," p. 42.
150. Deutsch, "Rethinking the Convenience Store," p. 15.
151. Ibid., p. 15.
152. Charles Anderer, "CSNews' Top 50 Charts Trends," *Convenience Store News,* 26(1), January 15–February 11, 1990, p. 46.
153. Jan Paschal, "Circle K's Sphere of Influence Grows," *USA Today,* April 5, 1988, p. 3B.
154. Deutsch, "Rethinking the Convenience Store," p. 14.
155. Victoria, "Why Oil Marketers Have C-Store Chains Circling," p. 40.
156. Carson, "Karl Eller's Big Thirst," p. 86.
157. Deutsch, "Rethinking the Convenience Store," p. 14.
158. Ibid., p. 14.
159. Anderer, "CSNews' Top 50 Charts Trends," p. 46.
160. Ibid., p. 46.
161. Rowe, "Circle K Creditors to Ease Terms," p. A3.
162. *1989 Annual Report,* pp. 10–11.
163. "Eller Aims for a National Chain," *Business Week,* October 24, 1983, p. 52.
164. Karen Nickel, "The Best and Worst Stocks of 1989," *Fortune,* January 29, 1990, p. 114.
165. *1989 Annual Report,* p. 2.
166. Ibid., p. 5.
167. Ibid., p. 3.
168. Ibid., p. 6.
169. "Circle K Calls Off Search for Buyer, Suspends Dividends," *Wall Street Journal,* September 14, 1989, p. B2.
170. "New York Stock Exchange Composite Transactions," *Wall Street Journal,* April 18, 1990, p. C3.
171. *Circle K Second Quarter 1990 Report to Shareholders.*
172. "Circle K Posted $28.1 Million Loss for Its 3rd Quarter," *Wall Street Journal,* March 27, 1990, p. C9.
173. Frederick Rose, "Circle K Signs Tentative Pact with Creditors," *Wall Street Journal,* April 5, 1990, p. A3.
174. Ibid., p. A3.
175. "Circle K Seeking to Renegotiate Debt," *Dallas Morning News,* March 28, 1990, p. 4-D.
176. Barbara Grondin, "Circle K, Eller Sued by Shareholders," *Convenience Store News,* 25(14), November 13–December 15, 1989, p. 6.
177. Ibid., p. 6.
178. Ibid., p. 6.
179. Ibid., p. 6.
180. Ibid., p. 6.
181. Harris, Jr., "Karl Eller Always Pushing Deals," p. A1.
182. Ibid., p. A1.
183. Ibid., p. A1.

CASE

23 Electrimex*

Geraldo Ortiz, general manager of Electrimex, was frustrated and a little angry with his Mexican subordinates. Over and over again, the same pattern repeated itself: Geraldo would ask his managers to do something, they would agree, and when Geraldo checked on their progress, he found that they had done nothing. They usually offered a good excuse, but it was often embarrassing to Geraldo when they mysteriously failed to perform and left their boss struggling to explain to his U.S. counterparts. Meanwhile, the pressure increased as the U.S. parent company shifted new products to the Mexican plant, while at the same time they were expected to prepare for the comprehensive European quality management and quality systems guidelines known as ISO 9000. Management assigned "monumental importance" to ISO 9000 as a means of getting a foothold in Central and South America.

ISO 9000

The International Organization for Standardization is a worldwide federation of national standards bodies that drafts technical standards requiring at least 75 percent approval by its members. International Standard ISO 9000 was prepared by a technical committee on quality assurance in 1987 and includes requirements covering economics—operating quality costs and external assurance quality costs, marketing, design, procurement, production, product verification, control of measuring and test equipment, post-production functions, quality documentation and records, personnel (including training, qualification, and motivation), product safety and liability, and the use of statistical methods. (See Figure 1.)

BACKGROUND OF COMPANY

Electrimex was one of three Mexican factories that operated as wholly owned subsidiaries of a U.S. parent corporation that manufactured a wide range of household electrical products. The company had been in business for generations in the United States, but as competition from low-cost Asian sources

This case was prepared by Stephen Jenner, California State University-Dominguez Hills. Used with permission. This case was prepared as a basis for class discussion rather than to illustrate either effective or ineffective handling of administrative situations.

*The name of the real company that served as the basis for this case study is disguised, along with the names of the managers.

Figure 1
Quality Loop

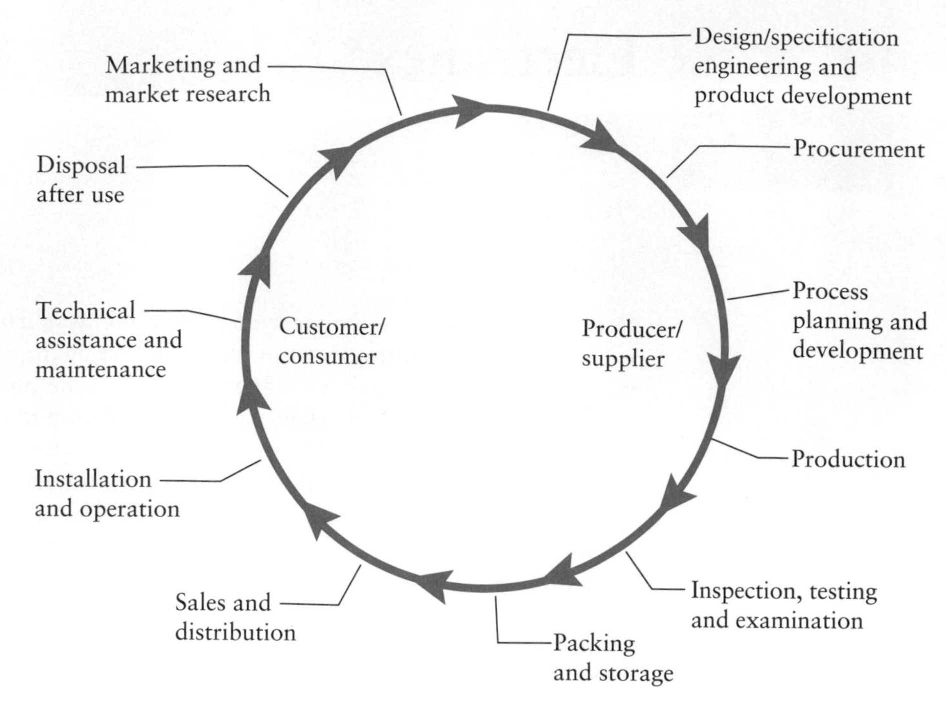

intensified, the relative unit labor costs for its unionized plants in the Northeast became a competitive disadvantage. Wages and benefits, plus payroll taxes and workers' compensation, were rising steadily and were not offset by increases in productivity or the depreciation of the U.S. dollar relative to the currencies of South Korea, Taiwan, Singapore, or Hong Kong. Meanwhile, entry level wages in Mexico were in the range of $1.20–$1.65 per hour, and the Mexican peso was depreciating steadily against the U.S. dollar. The Mexican government's "maquiladora/in-bond program" allowed U.S.-based companies to bring equipment and production inputs into Mexico as temporary imports free of duties, with the understanding that products would be exported back to the United States. This type of production-sharing arrangement between countries was also facilitated by U.S. government tariff policy which required U.S. companies to pay duty only on the value added abroad when the products returned. Lower-priced products assembled in Mexico were allowing the company to grow with major retailers such as Wal-Mart and Home Depot. The company claimed to have a product in virtually every American home in 1992.

Electrimex was established in Tijuana in January 1988 by Geraldo Ortiz, a U.S. national of Puerto Rican descent who was fluent in Spanish. Geraldo prepared a comprehensive plan to establish a plant in Tijuana, Baja California, which he implemented with great success, and Electrimex became the company's biggest plant worldwide. The family values of the parent corporation fit very well with Mexican culture—even before the plant was established, Geraldo was clear about the importance of corporate culture:

> To develop a healthy company culture at the plant level, the individual must feel that he/she has and is getting respect, objectivity and rewards for his/her contributions. We must undertake special care in Mexico not to develop a negative culture where

favoritism, alienation, and the "they and we" attitude prevails. We must foster the positive aspects of the Mexican idiosyncrasies, such as pride of workmanship, the hunger for recognition, the strong feelings for belonging and acceptance, strong family ties, and the desire to get ahead. Management must realize that it is not running a plant across a border but is instead a guest of a foreign country where a different culture and way of life, where difficult hardships tax the population. On the other hand, doing business in Mexico can be as easy or as difficult as one wants to make it. Progress, intelligently planned and managed, will add to the company culture positively since the Mexican national, with few exceptions, wants to learn and grow. The atmosphere we wish and should foster is one of problem solving, not blame placing, selling people on ideas, not ramming them down their throats, giving people the opportunity to learn from their mistakes, not threatening dismissal for failure.

DEVELOPING YOUNG MEXICAN MANAGERS

All of the managers and supervisors at Electrimex seemed to have a clear understanding of the parent company's objectives and expectations for Electrimex, as well as great respect for the general manager. (See Figure 2.) On a typical day, each of the eight top managers received as many as 100 messages from the United States in English through the electronic mail computer system ("E-mail"), as well as follow-up telephone calls. Many of the supervisors were unable to communicate in English and were spared this flood of communications; this created an additional burden for their managers who had to translate. However, even with all this direction, these young and relatively inexperienced people lacked the maturity and discipline to work effectively on their own. Electrimex employees were very young, as was the rest of the population. The average age

Figure 2
Electrimex de Baja California, S.A. de C.V., Plant Organizational Chart

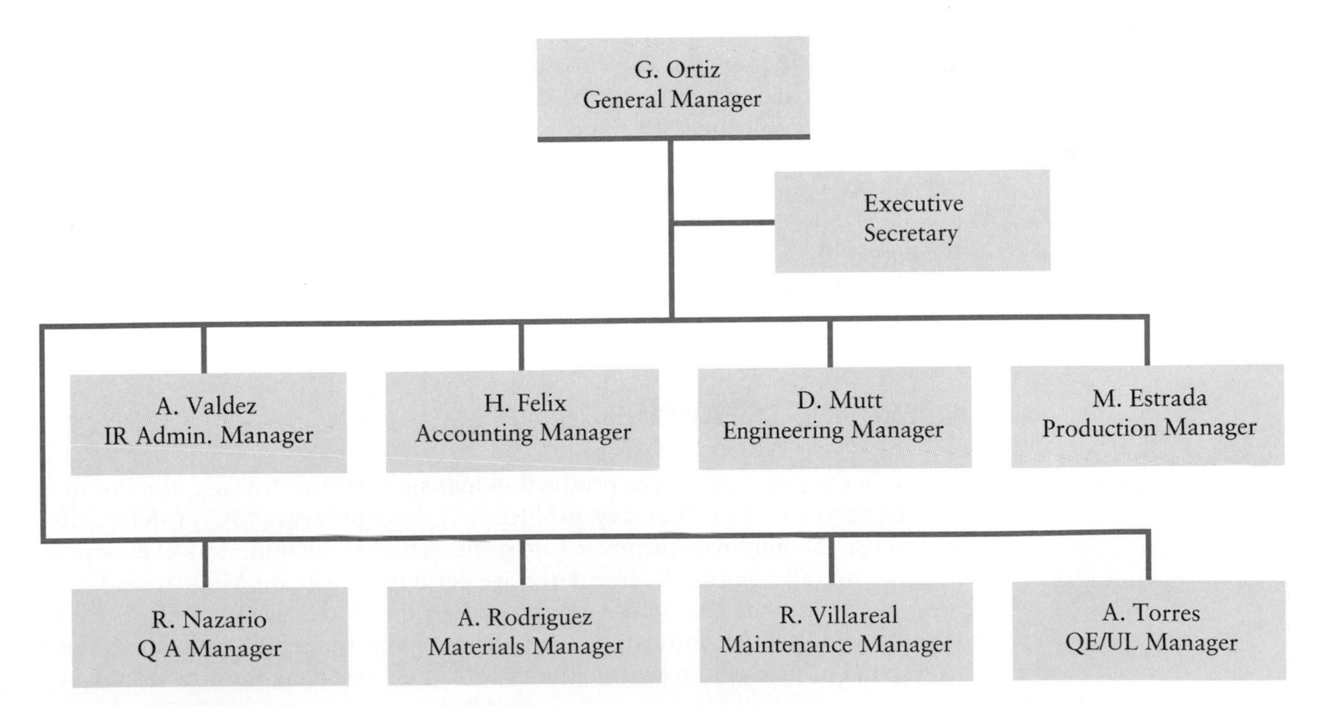

of Mexicans was 15 years, and two-thirds of the Mexican population was under the age of 25. The average age of Electrimex employees was 19, and most of the assembly line workers were teenage women.

Electrimex employee turnover was in the range of 7 percent per month, while the average for maquiladoras in the area was 11 percent per month. The cost of each employee turnover was estimated at $150, including indirect employees to recruit and interview new workers, compensation administration, the time required for inexperienced people to get down the learning curve, and the supervisors' time to train the new workers. At the rate of 7 percent per month and a total work force of 1,300, the cost of turnover was estimated to be $13,650 per month. Solutions proposed to overcome the employee turnover problem included better pay with more increases, better transportation service, child care, better facilities (work areas, bathrooms, cafeteria), and better supervisor relations. Some supervisors were responsible for 60 workers, but they had group leaders to help them manage each line of approximately 15 workers. One supervisor reported success in motivating workers with small gifts, such as pens and stamps. Another emphasized the need to "be nice," to laugh and be friendly and not strict all the time. There were cases of sexual harassment of young female workers by their male supervisors, some of whom demanded sexual favors during off-duty hours.

Overall, many of the management problems at Electrimex seemed to be related to the transition from an entrepreneurial, start-up organization in which Geraldo was the "Daddy," to a more mature and consolidated organization. Geraldo felt that Electrimex should try to preserve the positive aspects of the entrepreneurial organization while seeking to achieve some of the positive characteristics of a consolidated organization. (See Table 1.)

Young Mexican managers appreciated the confidence, respect, and trust of the general manager, but were stressed and frustrated by their own lack of skills and understanding of other functions. In the future, it was expected that different department managers would need to work together in "tiger teams" or "task forces" to solve problems that crossed departmental boundaries. Geraldo Ortiz knew that he had to accelerate the development of these young people as managers in order to cope with the continuing growth and vertical integration of Electrimex.

Geraldo wanted Electrimex to be the first plant in the company and in Tijuana certified under ISO 9000, and he wanted to begin manufacturing his own components in the near future. However, he was well aware of the problems, and he often listed them in his mind, department by department.

OPERATING DEPARTMENTS

Production

Based on the judgment of the production manager, Milton Estrada, the Production Department had three key problems: (1) inconsistent flow of defect-free materials, (2) employee turnover (often the actual headcount was even worse than the overall reported 7 percent average per month; e.g., on Monday at 7 A.M. there were fewer workers than at any other time of the week), and (3) weak supervisory skills. According to Milton, the general manager was sometimes slow to respond or unable to react to requests for help in resolving these problems.

Table 1
Electrimex: Stages of Organizational Growth and Structure

Pros	Cons
Start-up and Entrepreneurial Phase	
Entrepreneurial spirit Youth Enthusiasm	Lack of professionalism "Rookie errors" Fear of failure
Managers molded in the "Electrimex way"	High turnover of managers and supervisors
Informality	Lack of discipline: need to remind managers of deadlines and commitments
Strong technical skills	Weak managerial skills
Clear feedback from market	Little time to correct problems
High level of commitment	Long hours and much stress
Efficient in small groups	Not suitable to larger factories
Managers solve problems when told by general manager	Lack of assertiveness, independence
	Reactive "firefighting" and tendency to blame others versus proactive problem solving and "swimming upstream" to solve problems at source
Convergence and Consolidation Phase	
Greater stability Better documentation	More "red tape"
Division of labor	Limited horizons Lack of understanding
Lower costs due to scale Greater standardization	Greater potential for errors Need discipline for quality
More growth opportunities	Need better selection, training for people, and reward systems Lack of depth of "players"
Clearer objectives Greater emphasis on units day-to-day activities	Greater distance from corporate goals Greater risk of failure
Setting direction	

A key objective was to shift from batch to continuous flow production, including assembly and packaging. For the products recently transferred to Mexico, there was often a lack of good standards based on time and motion studies—many standards were estimated even though the standard operating procedure was to set new standards when transfers took place. The assembly work was very repetitive and characterized by very short cycle times (5–25 seconds).

Milton was generally accepted as the most likely successor to the general manager and was seen by Geraldo as someone who needed to be developed by increasing his responsibilities relative to both the U.S. parent company and the other departments at Electrimex. Specifically, Geraldo and the corporate vice president responsible for Mexico needed to help Milton to understand U.S. cost

accounting and how Electrimex performance was measured and allow him to be involved in the planning process. They also encouraged him to prepare and present more reports that better integrated information now maintained in separate departments. The strongest interrelationships existed between Production and Quality Engineering (and these two managers seem to be the leaders of the group of eight below the general manager), as well as Quality Assurance, Maintenance, Engineering, and Materials. Geraldo considered the possibility that there needed to be more separate meetings of these managers and key supervisors, without the general manager and the other departments.

Geraldo tried to focus on providing clear standards and coaching individuals, especially Milton. According to his boss, Milton tended to be too loyal to his subordinates and often lacked the patience to see alternatives. Like many bright young people, Milton tended to expect others to grasp ideas quickly and implement policies with little more than a request from their boss.

Materials

The purchasing function was previously managed by the human resources manager and was now an additional burden for the Materials Department, which seemed to be struggling as a department. The manager, Alejandro Rodriguez, was responsible not only for purchasing, but also for making sure that all materials arrived on time. Even though he was always busy and typically spent two hours per day working directly with Geraldo, there continued to be failures due to problems with suppliers, U.S. and Mexican Customs, and transportation.

Trained as an engineer specializing in computer systems, Alejandro was frustrated by Electrimex's two computer systems, each with its problems. Now dependent on the United States, he wanted to develop his own subsystem, complete with his own materials lists (with the correct part numbers and quantities). He also complained that frequent engineering changes often made materials obsolete. Electrimex E-mail could be politically embarrassing and was very time consuming (he reviewed 100 documents per day).

The dependence on the U.S. parent corporation could make the Materials Department look worse; for example, the dumping of rework of bad products led to more scrap, which made Electrimex's performance look bad. Inconsistent performance of this vital function seemed to be causing a lot of problems at Electrimex. In addition to Alejandro's complaints about having too much on his plate and the criticisms of his subordinates, Geraldo noted that Alejandro was often unaware of his subordinates' activities. Alejandro often thought about how much he would like more rest and vacation time.

Quality Engineering

Amilcar Torres managed the Quality Engineering Department very informally. There was little documentation of engineering, testing, and pilot runs, or of the history of equipment brought in from the United States. Due to a lack of planning, engineering projects were often rushed. There was no formal requisition process for equipment. Amilcar felt that since his subordinates lacked skills, he was unable to delegate. For example, Amilcar believed that he was the only person in the plant who could translate U.S. training videos. Amilcar also spent a lot of time learning the technical details of the Electrimex computer network, and people always came to him for help.

According to his boss, Amilcar was too dependent on his subordinates, so he needed to be coached frequently in this area.

Geraldo felt that there was also a need for better relations, linkages, and teamwork with other departments. Specifically, in order to maintain high quality, Geraldo believed that there was a need to build relationships at the supervisor level between departments, such as Materials and Production. Amilcar was concerned about the overreliance on quality data provided by Production.

Quality Assurance

In order to sell in Europe, Electrimex needed to achieve the ISO 9000 standards, and there would be visits by inspection teams in the near future to evaluate the plant. The quality assurance manager, Raul Nazario, believed that there was a critical need for training courses for supervisors in the area of statistical process control. Raul doubted that inspectors or workers were capable of understanding more than the detailed procedures of their own jobs since they lacked formal education. The Quality Assurance Department relied on on-the-job training and a library of English language references on statistical process control.

At the present time, people from Quality Assurance sampled and tested throughout the plant and relied on the Production Department for some of the data on rejects. Meanwhile, there was growing pressure from the marketplace; Electrimex needed to reduce customer complaints since only three mistakes were allowed by some key accounts. There had been major problems with different customer bar code systems causing confusion during the packaging process. Managers complained that the workers were insensitive to the importance of these mistakes and that there was no direct consequence for individual errors. Furthermore, even the customers were not sure what they wanted. After following many steps to ensure success and following the credo of positive reinforcement, Electrimex became the plant with the least errors in the company.

Raul was a first-time manager with a background in industrial engineering, and Geraldo felt that he needed both technical training and development as a manager. Raul described himself as "a volcano" with a quiet exterior but capable of an explosion.

Engineering

David Mutt, manager of the Engineering Department, had just lost four of the eight engineers in his department. Like many young Mexicans, the engineers left to become entrepreneurs; one of them claimed that he was making three times as much money selling clothing at the local swap meet. With little work experience, these people felt that they had nothing to lose. David was able to fill two of the positions by internal transfers from other departments, and he was looking for other candidates by networking with his friends at other maquiladoras and placing an advertisement in the local newspaper. Now he learned that his packaging manager was pregnant and planning to leave the company.

David felt that someone should be assigned primary responsibility for the complete process of certification for ISO 9000. Given the complexity and high volume of production of Electrimex, the documentation required was overwhelming since every piece produced needed to be tested or inspected. Language differences further complicated the situation since much of the existing documentation was in English. For example, the training course in methods time

measurement which was used to set production standards had never been translated into Spanish. Meanwhile, there were plans to bring new products and new production lines to Electrimex, and a new computer-aided design and manufacturing system was to be brought on-line in two months.

Maintenance

The manager of the Maintenance Department, Ramon Villareal, was strong technically but came up from a supervisor position and appeared to Geraldo to be struggling as a manager. His parents were tenant farmers in the interior of Mexico, and his level of intellectual development was remarkable considering his upbringing in rural poverty. However, Geraldo was concerned that there was a lack of delegation in this department, combined with a lack of clear orders. Ramon was prone to get angry at subordinates in front of their peers, which was very bad in the context of the Mexican culture.

Geraldo needed to know the cause of machine failures so that problems could be solved, instead of a maintenance policy of "fix it quick." Preventive maintenance was rare, and there was little documentation of machine history. Many people in this department did not identify with Electrimex's objectives, especially at the lowest level; there was an emphasis on pay rather than love of work or pride in productivity. There had been a lot of resentment since overtime was cut by Ramon.

Accounting

The Accounting Department and its manager, Humberto Felix, had the confidence of everyone and a reputation for making very few errors. However, Humberto was somewhat inflexible in Geraldo's opinion, and his department could have been more involved in supporting operational decision making by providing biweekly budgets for planning and control purposes. There had never been an internal audit of production, inventory, or human resources. There was no common standard for payroll and other accounting systems throughout the organization in the United States and Mexico. In Tijuana, six people worked full-time in the office to manually maintain records and process payroll.

No one at either Electrimex or the U.S. corporate office had any detailed knowledge of rapidly changing Mexican tax laws.

Industrial Relations/ Administration

Anacleto Valdez was the manager in charge of the Industrial Relations and Administration Department. This department allocated most of its resources to the classic functions of a traditional Personnel Department: compensation administration, entry and exit of workers, and social activities for employees outside the workplace. There were classes in beauty, basketball, English, computers, and primary education, in addition to soldering and bobbin winding. Anacleto and his seven subordinates provided data for the Accounting Department on vacation time and other payroll inputs. They organized social events like the all-important Christmas party and published a monthly newsletter. Anacleto's second in command spent his time visiting different parts of the plant to gauge morale.

Electrimex was located near the outskirts of the rambling and rapidly growing city of Tijuana on the old road to Tecate. In order to recruit new workers,

technicians, and managers, the Industrial Relations Department usually placed an advertisement in the local newspaper. Candidates responding to these ads were asked to complete application forms and sent home pending a decision by Electrimex to schedule an interview by someone from the Industrial Relations Department and perhaps a manager or supervisor from the department where they would be working. New employee orientation consisted of reviewing booklets entitled "The Employee's Manual" and "The Internal Work Rules of Electrimex."

RELATIONS WITH THE PARENT CORPORATION

In addition to the vertical reporting relationships through the general manager to the department managers in the United States, there were other "dotted line" reporting relationships. The Electrimex materials manager reported to the materials manager in the United States, and there were similar upward lines from quality assurance manager, accounting manager, and the other department managers in Tijuana. They were often accountable to corporate vice presidents of manufacturing or finance as well.

The Mexican managers were deeply concerned about the fate of U.S. employees, and they were affected by the low morale up North as plants were downsized, as well as by the lack of cooperation, coupled with dependence. They often received incomplete education from their U.S. counterparts. One manager stated, "They don't think we have the capacity, or they don't want to delegate." They needed help with administrative policies and paperwork. There were also cases of sabotage by U.S. employees who resented the shift of production to Mexico.

The weekly meals with the general manager and a few production workers were terrific. Geraldo Ortiz enjoyed asking a group of line workers for their concerns and suggestions and then dramatically calling his managers and office workers into the room and demanding that they immediately resolve these issues.

Geraldo also enjoyed dining with his group of eight managers, and he convened a weekly general information meeting on Wednesday mornings. He used the weekly meeting to keep his managers informed of what was happening throughout the company and to coach his department managers, who generally seemed prepared for their individual reports. There was humor and considerable explanation of U.S. parent company actions and vendor relationships. There seemed to be a clear understanding of Electrimex's objectives of rapid growth and vertical integration. However, the meeting was generally two hours long, and there was no shared written agenda, no visual aids, many interruptions from outside, and much defensiveness. It was not clear that the accounting and industrial relations managers needed to attend, and many of the details discussed were irrelevant to more than one or two departments.

Facilities were cramped and split into two different buildings, and there were stored materials around production lines, a variety of different worktables, not enough bathrooms, a cafeteria which was a constant source of complaints, and no child care center. Management was convinced that day care for children was not a viable option. Parking was cramped, and much time was wasted looking for people to move cars blocking someone from leaving. However, a new warehouse was in the final phase of construction.

GERALDO'S PHILOSOPHY OF BUSINESS

Geraldo strongly believed that "the ultimate management book" was a famous book of letters by an ancient Roman, Marcus Tullius Cicero, born January 3, 106 B.C. In *De Officiis,* Cicero instructed his son in the ways of the world as follows:

> Whatever is profitable must also be honest, and whatever is honest must also be profitable. The contrary opinion the greatest source of all wickedness. . . . To separate profit from honesty is to pervert the first principles of nature.

Geraldo wanted a cohesive group of managers and supervisors capable of accepting individual and collective responsibility for future planned expansions, coping with internal stresses so that they can work out their daily problems in a "win-win" ambiance, taking an assertive attitude when faced with a dilemma, and acting to meet mutually agreed upon due dates. He reflected upon the high "body count" of managers and supervisors during the first three years of operations, and the enthusiasm, youth, and lack of depth of his management team.

EPILOGUE

Geraldo recently became something of a corporate hero as the leader of the most successful company entity ever. The plant's scheduling performance soared to 99 percent from 65 percent in less than a year, and the customers' inventory fill rates reached 98 percent. Inventory accuracy of the Tijuana warehouse was 98.7 percent, the highest in the company worldwide. The output of the facility generated 20 percent of the company's total profit on a mere 2 percent of the product line.

There was more good news: a major U.S. corporation waging a life-or-death battle with several Japanese competitors asked Geraldo's plant to be considered as a supplier in volumes that would represent a significant fraction of Tijuana production. When Geraldo got approval to send them a copy of the Electrimex Quality Manual developed for ISO 9000, they were very impressed. During the casewriter's last visit to Geraldo's office, there was a telephone call from the highest level in the corporate headquarters, and the monologue of high praise was only briefly punctuated with Geraldo saying, "Well thank you. . . . That's very kind of you. . . . I have good people."

CASE

24 R. H. Macy & Co.: Another Miracle on 34th Street?*

Rowland H. Macy, a Nantucket whaling skipper, opened Macy's in 1858 on the corner of 14th Street and Sixth Avenue in New York City. Unlike most shop owners of the day, Macy refused to specialize. He instead sold an assortment of items to create New York's first modern department store. The store had annual sales of over a million dollars by 1870. When the city grew farther north, Macy's moved to Herald Square. This building remains the world's largest department store with over 2 million square feet of floor space.

Macy's never regarded itself as fashionable during its formative years. Instead, it succeeded primarily because of its reputation for economy, style, and quality. Macy's post-World War II principles of "upgrade, innovate, and renovate" resulted in growth during both good times and bad. Macy's expanded outside of Manhattan when the population began to move to the suburbs. Consistently the most profitable U.S. department store, it led the industry in such performance measures as sales per square foot, return on assets, and profitability. (See Tables 1 and 2.)

Edward Finkelstein was catapulted to president after he successfully transformed the dowdy flagship Herald Square store into a trendy avant-garde shopping experience during the mid-1970s. Macy's continued to pursue a high-risk strategy characterized by bold moves into new markets. Macy's began to lose talented middle management to competitors in 1985, and its profits dipped nearly 15 percent in the fiscal year ending August 1985. The growth rate of Macy's California, the most innovative of all its divisions, dropped by half. This slump was attributed to expansion and upgrading costs and did not necessarily reflect a trend. Nonetheless, competition was intense and the proliferation of price-cutting taught consumers to buy only what they absolutely needed. As a result, Macy's began to cut costs and halted proposed expansion. This caution adversely affected Macy's image as the leader in fashion. For instance, Macy's relied more on private labels and less on brand names to provide higher margins.

Finkelstein then gambled by heavily stocking popular brands that appealed to the widest possible audience. And while most other retail chains were eliminating buyers, Finkelstein increased the number of purchasers that searched the world for desirable goods. Macy's Corporate Buying Division supported each regional store group. It had a principal office in New York City and buying offices in nineteen foreign cities, as well as buying representatives in ten other foreign countries. Corporate Buying also employed designers and technical

*This case was prepared by Paul Miesing, State University of New York at Albany, and Debra L. Sottolano, State University of New York at Albany. This case is based on published information and public documents. It is intended to serve as the basis for class discussion rather than to illustrate either effective or ineffective handling of an administrative situation.

Table 1
Macy's Balance Sheet
(in Millions of Dollars)

	1980	1982	1984	1986
Cash	87	74	72	66
Accounts Receivable	32	60	58	70
Inventories	361	502	757	868
Other Current Assets	41	38	68	433
Total Current Assets	521	674	955	1,437
Gross Plant	990	1,135	1,412	n.a.
Accumulated Depreciation	346	395	468	n.a.
Net Plant	644	740	944	2,166
Other Assets	163	201	247	256
Total Assets	1,328	1,615	2,146	4,396
Accounts Payable	260	330	412	405
Debts Payable	6	6	12	n.a.
Other Current Liabilities	127	151	221	n.a.
Total Current Liabilities	393	487	645	n.a.
Long-Term Debt	165	150	132	2,872
Shareholders' Equity	594	801	1,169	n.a.
Other Debt	176	177	200	n.a.
Total Liabilities & Net Worth	1,328	1,615	2,146	4,396

teams that established specifications and ensured quality control of Macy's expanding "private label" business. Other specialized corporate staffs in New York City provided accounting, engineering and construction, finance, law and taxation, personnel and labor relations, operations, real estate, and store design services.

In 1986 Macy's operated eighty-seven stores in thirteen states. Its Properties Division owned and operated three regional shopping centers and had interests in six others. Between 1981 and 1986, Macy's stores (excluding divested Midwest stores) had average annual sales growth of 13.6 percent. Furthermore, stores that had been operating for at least two years grew an average of 10.4 percent per year. These stores were strategically located in both major cities and

Table 2
Macy's Income Statement
(in Millions of Dollars)

	1980	1982	1984	1986
Total Revenues	2,401	3,002	4,100	4,653
Cost of Goods Sold	1,648	2,053	2,745	} 4,054
Selling & Administrative Costs	492	598	817	}
Operating Income	261	351	538	599
Interest Expenses	62	87	100	120
Earnings Before Taxes	199	264	438	479
Taxes on Earnings	96	128	216	197
Net Income	103	136	222	282

suburban areas, with over three-fourths in major shopping centers. They were organized into four regional groups. Macy's New York consisted of twenty-one stores that had approximately 7.5 million square feet of store space in New York, Texas, Connecticut, and Florida. These stores accounted for a third of Macy's total floor space and sales. Bamberger's operated twenty-four stores in New Jersey, Pennsylvania, Maryland, New York, and Delaware. Its name was changed to Macy's New Jersey on September 4, 1986. These stores represented 6.5 million square feet and accounted for 30 percent of floor space and sales. Macy's California operated twenty-five stores in California and Nevada that accounted for one-fourth of floor space and sales. Macy's Atlanta operated fifteen stores with 3 million square feet in Georgia and South Carolina. This represented 10 percent of floor space and sales. Local management operated each store group under policies established by the principal corporate officers.

Macy's believed that its continued growth and profitability were the result of the successful execution of coordinated strategies in four key areas. The first was innovative merchandising. Sales in 1986 consisted of men's, women's, and children's clothing and accessories (69 percent) and home furnishings, furniture, and electronics (28 percent). However, Macy's had to maintain a wide assortment of medium- to higher-priced merchandise to remain "the place to be." The specialized attention Macy's provided to its wide line of merchandise enabled it to become closely identified with certain brands and exclusive labels. For instance, Macy's targeted its "store-within-a-store" concept, designed and staffed by Esprit, at the young, quality shopper. A highly aggressive pricing policy, with point-of-sale markdowns, conveyed a strong value image to the customer and enhanced its competitive position. Macy's Credit Corporation purchased and financed customers' deferred payment accounts of its retail store groups. In fact, credit sales under Macy's revolving credit plans represented approximately two-thirds of sales.

Another reason for success was an active store modernization and expansion program. During the early 1980s, Macy's spent $360 million to build seventeen new stores and another $510 million to upgrade existing stores. With over half of its sales coming from areas where it was a market leader, Macy's usually opened new stores in markets where it already had a strong identity. However, some expansion was also in new geographic markets where it believed it could capture significant market share, such as in densely populated Sun Belt areas. From the fall of 1984 to the spring of 1987, Macy's New York opened stores in Houston, a Houston suburb, and Dallas. Bamberger's opened two stores in Baltimore while expanding its Willowbrook (New Jersey) store by 96,000 feet. Macy's Atlanta opened stores in Cobb County (Georgia), New Orleans, and Birmingham; expanded one outside Atlanta by 88,000 square feet; and closed seventeen stores that totaled 2.5 million square feet. Macy's California opened stores outside of Sacramento and in Marin County. Each of the new stores was at least 120,000 square feet, and most were over 240,000 square feet. From 1987 to 1989, there were at least ten additional sites for new stores planned for Alabama, Connecticut, Florida, Louisiana, New Jersey and Virginia (District of Columbia).

A third reason for Macy's success came from productivity improvements. Macy's merged divisions, divested less profitable stores, and centralized such overhead functions as credit services, data processing and store planning, design and construction, and payroll. Management monitored operating expenses

through a detailed and systematic process of planning and evaluating customer service as well as sales-support activities. The following are examples of programs that controlled costs and increased productivity: merchandise handling improvements, modernization and automation of clerical areas, renovation and restoration of selling areas, efficient space allocation, and centralization of selected data processing. Macy's also devised sophisticated computer systems to provide current and detailed information to internal purchasing organizations. The timely analysis of this information, particularly in the fashion merchandise areas, permitted a combination of inventory and selling space that was the most responsive to consumer preferences.

A final reason for success was that Macy's firmly believed in management training and development. Its rigorous thirteen-week executive training program, known as the "Harvard of retail training programs," eschewed research, strategic planning, and rigid return on investment. Instead of "number-crunchers," the program turned out well-rounded, entrepreneurially minded executives capable of both operations and retailing. Retailers regarded Macy's "Executive Training Squad" as the finest in the industry. Nevertheless, there were signs of trouble.

THE U.S. RETAIL INDUSTRY

The history of U.S. retailing is one of continuous response to a growing nation. At each stage of economic and social development, retail operations emerged to meet new environmental demands. Early pioneer trading posts were forerunners of today's department stores. The Yankee peddler was the next participant in the retail evolutionary process, bringing in the goods necessary for survival in remote areas. In the early 1800s, as settlements matured into towns, the general store emerged as the principal retailing institution. As towns grew into cities, the general store was unable to meet distinctive needs of consumers. As a result, specialty stores emerged to meet changing lifestyles. Chain stores were introduced with the opening of the Great Atlantic and Pacific Tea Company (A&P) in 1859. Metropolitan areas grew after the Civil War. Ironically, land for locating stores became limited just when consumers began to demand a wide and diverse range of goods. Consequently, large retail department stores introduced the "all under one roof" concept. Such stores expanded rapidly during the 1870s to the 1920s. Peaking between 1918 and 1929, they enjoyed a monopoly in central downtown business districts for nearly a century. Nonetheless, the department store industry continued to expand at a rate well above the general economy.

The post-World War II baby boom was eventually followed by a baby bust. Discount houses became popular with their low prices, "no frills" service, convenient location, and sales promotions. Retailers were forced to reevaluate their position when mass migration occurred from inner cities to the suburbs. The "malling of America" began in the 1950s when families moved to the suburbs and continued through the 1970s when overall retail sales grew a healthy 8.6 percent annually. Discount stores became strong competitors as they filled gaps left by hesitant department stores. Prosperity came to those stores that opened branches in suburban shopping centers and malls. The number of shopping centers increased from approximately 100 in 1950 to more than 22,000 by 1980. New images were created to merchandise fashion in the 1960s and 1970s as

retailers catered to people under 25 years old. Consumer spending soared in the 1980s and peaked in 1987. It became possible to achieve a 25 percent return by investing in a mall, and developers offered incentives and subsidies to lure department stores as key tenants. Between 1986 and 1989, the number of malls increased 22 percent to 34,683, but the number of shoppers going to malls every month rose only about 3 percent. By 1990 overcapacity became a problem with over eighteen square feet of retail space for every man, woman, and child—more than double the 1972 figure. Worsening the situation is that there has been no slow down in the building of shopping centers. A counter trend in format, designed to bring back the customer, are smaller and more accessible groups of stores arrayed into a "town square" format.

Demographic forces shape retailing. The ages between 28 and 44 are typically the years of household development and high spending on department store merchandise. However, this generation has fewer children. Moreover, there has been a decline in the proportion of teenagers in the population. A number of trendy men's and women's chains depend on a huge teenage population as their core market. As the postwar babies mature, the teen market is being replaced by the baby "boomlet" as the large population of young adults forms its own families. At the other end of the age spectrum is the "greying of America" as the baby boom generation matures. With improving health and medical care, the number and proportion of senior citizens are continuing to grow. While senior citizens are somewhat more fashion conscious than earlier generations, they have neither the need nor interest to maintain expensive working wardrobes. So far, most conventional retailers have not been successful in marketing to this group. Finally, the workweek has been decreasing. This means more leisure time and a vast new retail market in sports, recreation, and hobbies.

An efficient distribution system means lower costs to consumers and higher profits for producers, wholesalers, and retailers. Traditionally, manufacturers enjoyed consumer franchises that gave them power over highly fragmented retailers. However, customer loyalty and market power began to shift when large retailers increased their purchases of private-label products. (Private label goods eliminate middlemen which can boost profit margins to as much as double those of brand-name goods.) The subsequent battle over shelf space allowed retailers to win discounts from manufacturers and to be more selective in choosing vendors. As profit pressures continue for retailers, one recourse will be to shift more costs to suppliers. For instance, some retailers have become notorious for coercing suppliers to pay for unauthorized invoice deductions and inflated advertising. Even large manufacturers of extremely popular items are not immune to such tactics. Some manufacturers may retaliate by opening their own high-quality specialty stores. Others may decide to develop closer relationships with retailers to share information, improve product coding, agree on promotions, and plan cost reductions.

Competitive Structure

The retailing industry consists of four major groups (see Figure 1). Given the different types of retail stores, each company must evaluate its particular strengths and weaknesses and devise its own strategy for the future. At one extreme are the high-price boutiques that offer true distinction that only a few can afford. These stores provide one-of-a-kind or unusual items. These free-standing stores are often privately held companies. They are far more exclusive than are the

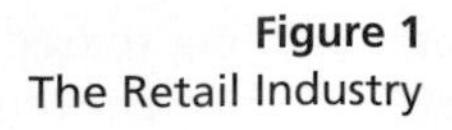

Figure 1
The Retail Industry

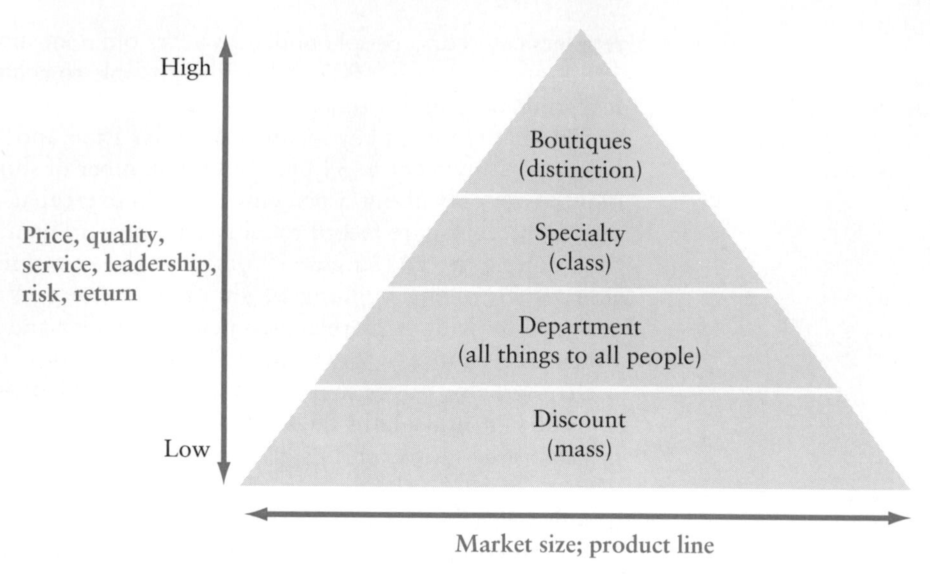

other types, catering to shoppers who disdain standard products. At the other extreme are the discount stores offering a price advantage on common items. Consumer spending is increasingly polarized between these high-price boutiques and low-margin, mass-volume discounters. While these traditionally represented extreme store types, a new phenomenon of "cross-shopping" refers to the tendency for the same customer to shop at both ends of the pyramid.

Specialty stores offer limited product lines to targeted population groups. These customers are willing to pay a higher price for quality, service, or image. By selling limited merchandise, these stores usually take high risks in anticipating trends. Nonetheless, the rewards are substantial if they are leaders in their markets, offer fashionable products, use innovative displays, and guess right. Specialty apparel stores swept the market as sales of retailers like The Limited (see Exhibit 1) and the Gap grew to a combined $100 billion in 1990. Since they sell an image, they must control product quality. Consequently, several stores integrate vertically from manufacturing to retailing. Additional examples of specialty stores include Pier 1 Imports, Radio Shack (Tandy Corporation), and Zales Jewelers. When these stores drew customers on their own, they took over the role of mall anchors traditionally held by large department stores. Demand for specialty stores is declining as today's middle-aged population is far less ego-involved with their purchases, the main appeal of many specialty shops. They also have had problems with product quality. As a result, this category of retailer is no longer gaining market share. "Category killer" chains also focus on one line of goods but draw customers with low prices and huge inventories. Examples of such "commodity retailing" include Herman's World of Sporting Goods, Home Depot, Petrie Shoes, S&K Famous Brands, Sound Warehouse, and Toys Я Us. Luring these consumers requires a low margin of error and strong cost controls.

Department stores are establishments that sell a full line of products. They significantly influenced the industry by catering to the middle-class population as "all things to all people." This was achieved by having many departments within one physical location. Department stores have a reputation for their wide assortment of general merchandise. The three primary merchandise categories are hard

Exhibit 1
The Limited

Leslie Wexner reinvented the specialty store business and made The Limited the nation's most successful specialty store merchant. The Limited's $400 sales per square foot are twice as much as department store averages. Wexner's strategy was to build private brands when some chains were dropping them. For instance, he spent over $10 million on an advertising campaign for Victoria's Secret. With seven specialty apparel store divisions, each with a different style and price range, he plans to double sales volume from $4.6 billion in 1989 to $10 billion by the mid-1990s. This was to be accomplished by increasing total selling space of The Limited to 2.5 million square feet in 1990 with the opening of as many as 250 superstores and major expansions of existing outlets. While he had previously attempted to acquire Federated, Macy's, and Carter Hawley Hale, Wexner lost interest in buying a department store chain. In fact, his sales increases were to come largely at the expense of struggling department stores.

Wexner's innovation was to make The Limited a cluster of specialty shops, with each division run as an independently competing company. Its store clusters made it the largest specialty store tenant in hundreds of malls, sometimes taking up to 25 percent of the mall space. This is larger than most department stores and enabled it to obtain such concessions as prime mall locations, cheaper rents, and even cash from developers. The Limited has the clout of a department store, but with few of the disadvantages, and is quicker at responding to fashion trends. According to Kenneth Gilman, executive vice president and CFO of The Limited, "You have to be expert in your product, understand your customer, and know how to add the most value to that combination."

goods (e.g., furniture, appliances, radios, and television sets), soft goods (e.g., apparel for men, women, and children), and dry goods (e.g., household linens). They retain a market share in such slow-growth businesses as apparel, fashion accessories, and cosmetics. To offset lower margins, department stores are attempting to maintain profits by increasing volume sales of soft goods and carrying fewer durable goods. In recent years these stores have strengthened their positions by developing a professional approach to marketing, emphasizing private label merchandise, and improving pricing policies. They also tried to attract younger consumers by becoming the primary outlet for moderately priced quality goods in convenient locations. Major restructuring took place as a result of intense competition. For instance, to cover all consumer segments, Associated Dry Goods purchased the Lord & Taylor specialty chain, Caldor discount stores, and Loehmann's off-price apparel stores. Later, May Department Stores purchased Associated Dry Goods. In the second quarter of 1986, there were thirty-eight retailing mergers amounting to a total of $2.6 billion (see Exhibit 2). In 1989, with the economy in a downturn, Hooker Corporation filed for Chapter 11 bankruptcy to shield its Bonwit Teller and B. Altman & Company from creditors. Other examples of department stores include Bloomingdale's, Filene's, Jordan Marsh, Macy's, J.C. Penney, and Sears, Roebuck. (See Table 3.)

Discount stores emerged in the 1960s. Not viewed initially as a challenge by traditional department stores, they eventually altered the industry's structure. Although both discount and department stores sell the same categories of goods, discounters sell both private labels and national brands at low prices. They avoid marking up prices as much as traditional retailers by purchasing merchandise in large volumes at wholesale rates. Nevertheless, all is not positive for the

Exhibit 2
Allied and Federated

Allied Stores Corporation and Federated Department Stores, Inc., were two of America's largest chains. Both were also victims of ongoing mismanagement. Allied included The Bon, Jordan Marsh, and Stern's; Federated owned Bloomingdale's, A&S, and Burdines. As their sales growth lagged the industry, Canadian real estate developer Robert Campeau—a 64-year-old, temperamental, high-risk-taking entrepreneur—acquired both for $11.3 million. He bought Allied in 1986 after it committed a $200 million blunder by purchasing nine bankrupt Gimbels stores and converting them to Stern's. Campeau purchased Federated in 1987 after winning a bidding war with Macy's. Federated's mistake was to pump too much money into its ailing MainStreet, Children's Pace, and Gold Circle divisions. It was also slow to move, lagging ten years behind competitors such as Macy's in eliminating bargain basements during the mid-1970s. Debates between division presidents and antiquated operations kept Federated's return on equity at a consistently lower level than its rivals. Under Campeau's more aggressive management, Federated consolidated back-office operations, cut 8,200 jobs, and was reportedly saving $330 million a year. Campeau planned to spend $250 million a year for store openings and remodelings. These stores needed to generate at least $1 billion in cash flow to cover operating costs and debt payments.

With nine store chains, Campeau hoped to wield mass purchasing clout that would translate into tremendous savings advantages over competitors. Federated and Allied used 400 key suppliers (down from 14,000) to provide 70 percent of all goods orders (up from 40 percent). Campeau planned to emphasize select name-brand suppliers as well as substantially increase private-label business. Federated tried to attract better salespeople by paying commissions to all floor managers and the existing sales staff of 29,500 people. Training programs and bonuses would cost as much as $1 million per store. Campeau was also known as a tough negotiator with mall developers, demanding and receiving equity stakes for no cash investments in exchange for promises to locate his stores as anchors. However, Campeau's strategies failed and he had to liquidate excess inventories through discount channels, forcing other department store chains to lower prices in order to stay competitive. His price cuts to raise cash flow started a price war that reduced profit margins for all department stores.

Campeau lost several key executives due to his inability to share control of his company with his management team. By late 1989 Campeau was scrambling to avoid a cash crisis. Olympia and York Developments, Ltd., owned by the Reichmann family of Toronto, granted Campeau an emergency loan of $250 million that bought him time. However, it was not enough. Campeau was ousted as CEO and several Allied and Federated divisions, including the flagship Bloomingdale's chain, were put on the block. Federated and Allied filed for Chapter 11 bankruptcy in early 1990. Sales for both chains slid, with Bloomingdale's alone losing almost $3 million that July. For all of 1991, Federated lost $967 million.

discount department store. Consumers continue to perceive these stores as selling poor-quality merchandise. With slow growth, these stores are successful if they have tight financial controls, plan inventories, accurately predict costs, and limit their promotional expenses. Examples of such stores include Alexander's, Bradlee's, Caldor, Jamesway, and Zayre's. The most successful two were KMart and Wal-Mart (see Exhibit 3), which earned $479 million and $602 million, respectively, in 1991.

Table 3
Department Store Chains

Chain	Annual Sales (in Billions of Dollars)	Stores
Sears	$28.0	747
J.C. Penney	12.0	1,283
May Department Stores	8.9	3,613
Federated Department Stores	6.9	220
R. H. Macy's	6.7	244
Dillard Department Stores	4.0	198
Nordstrom	3.2	68

A new marketing phenomenon is the off-price store, commonly referred to as a factory outlet. Brand-name manufacturers and upscale retailers can sell their surplus goods at these malls. In their search for value, some consumers are willing to shop in less lavishly decorated stores. Buying below wholesale prices and selling at 20 to 70 percent below retail, off-pricers operate on half the gross margin of department stores and still net 10 percent before taxes. This is possible by purchasing overruns, closeouts, off-season, and slightly irregular lots. In addition, inventory turnover rate is several times that of an ordinary retailer. An example is TJ Maxx, which offers brand-name merchandise at below specialty store prices. Department stores have responded in several ways, ranging from ignoring off-price outlets to opening their own. The most aggressive approach is to cut costs and offer customers prices that are comparable to the off-pricers. Until recently, only a minority of consumers were preoccupied with lower prices. Therefore, traditional retailers were able to maintain dominance in all categories of apparel and decorative home items.

Exhibit 3
Wal-Mart

Sam Walton founded Wal-Mart in rural Arkansas and grew it to a $50 billion (sales) mass merchant. It continues to grow far faster than the retailing industry. Its strategy is elementary: install electronic connections with all 5,000 suppliers (over half already receive point-of-sales data) and hope to eliminate most wholesalers. It is a major customer for such giant companies as Gitano, Haggar, Mr. Coffee, Procter & Gamble, Rubbermaid, Royal Appliance, and The Scotts Company. As a result, Wal-Mart is able to dictate such details as what to make, how much to ship, and when. Manufacturers feel compelled to deal with them, hoping that the large volume will compensate for the lower profit margins and rigorous dictates imposed by the powerful retailer.

Wal-Mart is forcing suppliers to rethink whom they sell to, how they price and promote their products, and even how they structure their own organizations. According to CEO David Glass, "We're probably in a better position to determine specifically what the customer wants to buy than is the manufacturer." Wal-Mart has managed to obtain so much power because of its sophisticated inventory management system, precise purchasing, and—above all—its competitive pricing. It prefers to offer "everyday low prices" and avoid price promotions.

Mail-order houses sell through catalogs and accept customer orders by telephone, mail, or in person. By using superior assortments at attractive prices, retailers have opened catalog showrooms to generate higher sales per square foot. Included in this category are both national department stores such as Bloomingdale's and J.C. Penney, as well as specialty stores such as L.L. Bean, Carroll Reed, and Talbots. Mail-order sales are growing twice as fast as general merchandise stores. Some analysts believe as much as one-half of purchases through the 1990s will come through catalogs with their increased convenience and better service. One reason for this trend is the increase in the number of time-constrained, two-wage earner families. Ordering by telephone and computer-based systems also reflects consumer interest in wide assortment, convenience, and fashion, as well as a growing dissatisfaction with sales assistance in retail stores.

Strategic Alternatives

Squeezed between the high-margin specialty and high-volume discount segments, department stores were forced to react in a variety of ways. Any attempt to increase market share probably will come at the expense of competitors. The market for new retail outlets is saturated and the costs of launching new brand names have skyrocketed. Fortunately, there were many high growth areas in the marketplace in spite of slow overall growth. Some retailers simply built new stores when the prime interest rate was low. In an industry where the store with the largest sales volume is very profitable while the fourth largest loses money, many retailers decided that acquiring the competition was the surest route to success. As a capital-intensive business, competitors will eventually grab the assets of troubled retailers. By using this strategy, retailers can offer an assortment of product lines through multiple channels of distribution. This in turn allows them to decentralize their organizational structure according to their lines of business and geography. Realizing that a substantial portion of growth will not come from expansion of stores or products, department stores must investigate whether or not to diversify into businesses with higher growth potential, such as Sears, Roebuck's entry into financial services. Department stores might have to look outside of their industry to continue to grow.

Profits no longer come automatically from opening a new outlet or expanding an existing product line. Market segmentation has become critical for implementing retailing strategy. Stores must position themselves to meet consumer needs. Those that are astute enough to find, exploit, and defend profitable niches will be successful in the future despite any general slowdown. Knowledge of various consumer segments is critical for retailers that remodel frequently and change their displays often. It is a competitive advantage to focus on a certain segment and formulate an appropriate combination of price, service, merchandise, and convenience.

Before World War II, the store buyer was often a department manager who concentrated on various aspects of merchandising and sales supervision. In this single store environment, the buyer often obtained knowledge through customer contact and personal observation. However, the establishment of branches in the postwar era forced stores to combine centralized buying with regional specialization. This system placed more importance on data gathering and reporting systems. Today, buyers and their assistants are responsible for vendor development, item selection, cost and shipping term negotiations, achievement of gross margin objectives, inventory planning and control, pricing, distribution, promo-

tion, presentation of merchandise, analysis of initial sales results, reorder, redistribution, and markdown of merchandise. These tasks are easier for specialty store buyers since they offer uniform merchandise to a narrow customer segment. Consequently, they can have almost total control over the merchandising function.

The environment is much more complicated for national department stores. Department store buyers must fill a variety of needs since they serve many markets. In addition, there is a greater internationalization of both buying and selling with 10 percent of all consumer goods sold in the United States now being imported from foreign suppliers. Moreover, sales of short life-cycle merchandise have grown steadily. Much of this merchandise cannot be reordered. Buyers must constantly replace styles, and often vendors. Finally, branches become important to buying. Although many new branches reach into market areas that are distant from the main store, buyers must balance the needs of the consumer with the directives of a centralized office. As a result, the buyer is frequently dependent on communication with branch managers. The limited merchandising responsibilities of branch executives, as well as the buyer's preoccupation with vendor contacts, often results in conflict between the buying and selling relationship. Successful department stores have emphasized shared responsibility, improvement in communication, and measurable performance standards.

Competition keeps downward pressure on prices. With heavy promotional pricing and limited growth, stores are emphasizing improved efficiency and productivity. Department stores have resorted to sophisticated sales forecasts and improved inventory controls. Some retailers sold off retail chains in those markets in which they no longer decided to compete; others eliminated marginal locations and product lines. Retail divestitures and leveraged buyouts were common. For instance, F. W. Woolworth's sacrificed $1 billion worth of sales by writing off its unprofitable Woolco department stores. This approach requires a strong chief executive, well-trained salesclerks, and appropriate employee compensation.

Most retail stores have a substantial inventory investment. Often the second largest asset on the balance sheet, inventory is exceeded only by plant and equipment. The use of credit cards has assisted buyers in targeting specific market segments. The information gleaned forms a database available for mailing lists, demographic data analysis, and assessing buying preferences. The effectiveness of this approach, however, depends on the company's management information systems. Most stores have computerized sales reports for all departments. An example is electronic point-of-sales (POS) equipment. By collecting information directly from the cash register, stores can anticipate trends, plan merchandise, improve sales clerk productivity, provide better customer service, verify credit, analyze price changes, monitor advertising effectiveness, obtain timely sales data, and reduce operating and transaction costs.

With fierce competition, many are looking for new distribution channels. Technological adaptation is just beginning in this industry. For example, today's technological equivalent of the mail-order catalog is the cable television shopping channel. Originally popular with small retailers, Sears initiated its own home shopping program, and J.C. Penney and Spiegel considered following suit. Just as is true with catalogs, these shows match consumers with merchandise. Most rely on impulse buying by presenting goods in 24-hour, game-show environments that give viewers several minutes to call in orders. The future may see televisions replace salespersons as the distribution link between manufacturers and consumers.

MACY'S GOES PRIVATE

Macy's top executives completed a $3.7 billion leveraged buyout (LBO) on July 15, 1986. This was then the largest retailing LBO in history, and the company changed its name to Macy's Merger Corporation. Finkelstein had invested $4.4 million of his own money to acquire 4.7 percent of the company. Many other executives purchased significant amounts of stock, with approximately 350 having a 20 percent stake in the company. Finkelstein attributed Macy's new entrepreneurial spirit to the LBO. Ownership and the reality of meeting fixed debt payments led to an intolerance of waste and had a positive effect on business. As part owners, Macy's loyal, energized staff now had stakes valued at millions that gave them considerable economic incentives to stay with the company. In addition, the sales force at older stores received commissions in order to boost their productivity. Macy's divisions also began working together much more effectively by sharing information and opportunities, communicating more frequently, and reducing the competitive attitude that previously had them working against each other. Macy's continued to market moderately priced to expensive merchandise, maintain flashy interiors, and sponsor elaborate events. They also kept developing their private labels which accounted for approximately one-fourth of sales. Finkelstein intended to open four to five stores each year (including some specialty stores) and diversify by selling private label brands to noncompeting retailers.

One reason for the buyout was to avoid having to account to stockholders in times of trouble. Moreover, a private company can take more risks, although the interest on the heavy borrowing needed to finance the purchase ties up much of the company's profits. Macy's major challenge in designing the LBO was to raise substantial funds yet have low interest obligations. Its unique solution was to use real estate to generate money for the LBO. Its 71 stores located in prime shopping malls enabled Macy's to acquire an $800 million, fifteen-year mortgage with minimum annual payments according to a formula based on sales and other factors. Macy's will make additional payments tied to volume increases. Regarding its ability to pay for this LBO, Macy's predicted that net retail sales for stores in operation at least two full years would increase $5.6 billion in 1987 and 1988, or 7.8 percent. Sales would then increase 8 percent per year through 1996 when they would hit $11.6 billion. Analysts predicted that earnings before depreciation, amortization, interest, and income taxes would increase 15 percent per year, reaching $377 million in 1996. Total assets would then be $5.4 billion, assuming that gross accounts receivable were 30 percent of net retail sales. Moreover, uncollectible accounts would have to represent no more than 3.6 percent of gross accounts receivable. Total inventory also must grow at the same rate as net retail sales and comprise 18 percent of net retail sales. Accounts payable and accrued liabilities should comprise no more than 10.6 percent of net retail sales.

The first year following the LBO, Macy's had sales of $5.2 billion, reduced its debt by $2.9 billion, and had losses of $14 million. Comparable store sales grew by 10 percent. Its $1.6 billion in junk bonds increased substantially in value. The Northeast, South, and California stores did well in 1987 despite the debt service. However, a year later in 1988, Standard and Poor's downgraded its outlook for Macy's as losses continued. That same year, Macy's unsuccessful bid to acquire Federated Department Stores cost it $90 million. Although Robert Campeau

won the bid, Macy's managed to obtain Federated's strong California chains of Bullock's and I. Magnin at a cost of $1 billion in additional debt. On September 18, 1989, Macy's released a letter to investors to assure its financial health, stating that its pretax earnings were up 10 percent to $925 million for the year ending July 29. As the 1989 Macy's Thanksgiving Day parade kicked off the Christmas season, Campeau's chains initiated drastic price cuts to move excess inventory that competitors were forced to match. The impact on industry gross margins was disastrous at a period when general merchandise retailers usually register up to one-third of their annual sales and one-half of their profits. Macy's rapidly evaporating earnings cushion threatened its ability to cover its annual interest expense. Investors were concerned that over the next two years, Macy's had to pay off or refinance $952 million in debt. It also needed to raise about $500 million of additional equity to have enough cash for Finkelstein to act aggressively and take market share away from troubled rivals.

Troubles Mount

Industry sales forecasts for 1990 were pessimistic and Macy's was not immune to this general pall over the $1.3 trillion retail industry. Although it began February 1990 with increased profits, by March bond traders were bidding Macy's junk debt down considerably in expectation that earnings would be severely lower than the previous year. Indeed, the company wound up reporting a $215 million loss for the year ended in July. Even after ridding itself of some $1.5 billion in debt by selling its credit card division to General Electric Credit Corporation, Macy's still had $4.8 billion in debts that carried $200 million in annual interest payments. According to Salomon Brothers' analyst Frederick Taylor, Macy's would probably need at least another $150 million in equity by 1993, just when the interest on a big zero-coupon bond issue would come due. Macy's needed to spend about $140 million–$160 million annually in capital expenditures to refurbish stores and keep them competitive. During October, Standard and Poor's (S&P) maintained Macy's CCC+ bond ratings but downgraded its outlook from stable to negative, citing "continuing operating weaknesses." Finkelstein intended to buy back some of Macy's deeply discounted debt to free up cash and reassure investors and vendors. (During this time, the confidence of its vendors continued to remain high.) To finance the buyback, Finkelstein issued $140 million in preferred stock.

By the end of 1990, Macy's was closing unproductive stores as well as reducing store inventories ($400 million–$650 million less inventory than the previous year) and would open no new stores until 1991. Finkelstein's $150 million advertising campaign to bring back shoppers failed and was considered a disastrous error by Wall Street. While company officials blamed the slumping economy in the Northeast for the reduced consumer spending, Finkelstein maintained that a strong consumer base would allow Macy's to survive the spending downturn and withstand poor Christmas sales. He argued that the LBO was solid and Macy's would not file for bankruptcy.

The Final Days?

Macy's began 1992 with further trouble by missing its January 10 deadline to make payments. While its suppliers granted an extension to January 25, the Prudential Insurance Company of America refused to accept a lower interest rate proposed for the retailer's bonds. The missed deadline prompted S&P to

downgrade Macy's bonds, and Macy's creditors were becoming skeptical and impatient. According to a Lehman Brothers' analysis, failure to make payments would result in no new goods being shipped and not enough spring sales to keep Macy's out of bankruptcy. Rumors of a prepackaged bankruptcy deal that would favor large debtholders and leave suppliers little say in the restructuring also threatened suppliers' shipments of goods. With $102.3 million in interest payments due on May 15, Goldman Sachs & Company—the firm that originally engineered the LBO—was developing a comprehensive plan to reduce Macy's $3.4 billion debt that would attempt to keep it out of Chapter 11. Macy's last hope of avoiding bankruptcy collapsed after Laurence Tisch backed out of a proposed $1 billion rescue. It filed for bankruptcy on January 27 and reported a record loss of $671.6 million for its second quarter ending February 1, 1992.

Macy's owed over $3.5 billion to bankers and creditors, listing $4.95 billion in assets and $5.32 billion of liabilities. According to J.P. Morgan bond analyst Michael Cha, Macy's could get about $350 million for its assets, but there might be few interested buyers because of the economic recession. It was expected that suppliers, whose claims ranked behind banks and mortgage lenders, would collect $275 million, which was less than half of their claims. Banks were forced to make loans of almost $600 million under previous commitments in order to provide a steady supply of new inventory to the once-proud retailer.

Macy's closed 57 specialty stores in March and laid off 1,000 of its workers. Outside directors were attempting to take over the board, and six of nine inside directors resigned. After months of rumors that the board wanted him out, Finkelstein resigned as CEO on April 25. Although Finkelstein was a strong merchant, Macy's could not afford his lack of financial insight, his huge ego, and his tendency to treat the company as his personal empire. Two men replaced him as co-chairs and co-CEOS. Mark Handler is a Finkelstein protege and will preserve relationships with vendors and employees. Myron Ullman III is Finkelstein's antithesis: a conservative, no-nonsense number-cruncher. Ullman long ago earned the trust of top board members. He has instituted computerized inventories, market research, and departmental profit and loss analyses at Macy's since 1988. He and his own hand-picked team of managers have cut expenses and improved Macy's inventory system. For instance, Ullman instituted the use of the Sabre Information System and developed the "Buyer-Planner-Store" which is a more efficient method of purchasing and distributing goods.

The pair has considered various merchandising strategies that might salvage Macy's future. One option is to have fewer discounts and sales promotions. In sharp contrast to Finkelstein's approach of private label goods, they will retain Macy's position as an upscale department store but will emphasize well-known, national brands. While these strategies are still indefinite, speculation is that Macy's will play down its fashion image. Wall Street is not waiting, however. Several directors holding preferred stock are considering purchasing Macy's bonds in the open market if prices start to fall so they can negotiate for ownership. Preferred shareholders may inject money directly into Macy's to help cut its $5.1 billion debt in exchange for a controlling equity stake. Other rumors include the possible sale of I. Magnin and Bullock's to a California retailer, such as Carter Hawley Hale. Spearheaded by Ullman, Macy's announced the closing of eight of its 120 department stores and opened a number of Macy's Close Out stores to reduce the amount of unsold merchandise. He also reevaluated the $30 million a year advertising budget.

Macy's has steadily lost money and key executives, many of whom were loyal to the ousted Finkelstein. Since it filed Chapter 11, Macy's reported a $225.9 million loss for the third quarter ending May 2. At its May 19 bankruptcy hearing, Macy's claimed it could not write a reorganization plan until it assesses its 1992 Christmas season. Its exclusive right to file a plan of reorganization was extended until February 1993. According to New York consultant Alan Millstein, "The motivating issue [for retailers] from now on will be price, not fashion and prestige." He expects more profit declines at the expensive department stores in the months ahead. In August senior executives previewed the outline of a business plan to creditors that would take effect February 1, 1993. This signaled that Macy's may be forced to operate under bankruptcy protection longer than expected. In September Macy's defaulted on its junk bonds. Some considered these to be a bargain since Macy's franchise value was greater than the prices reflected.

SECTION

C

Corporate Level: Domestic and Global Cases

CASE

25 Nucor

INTRODUCTION

Nuclear Corporation of America had been near bankruptcy in 1965, when a fourth reorganization put a 39-year-old division manager, Ken Iverson, into the president's role. Iverson began a process which resulted in Nucor, a steel mini-mill and joist manufacturer which rated national attention and reaped high praise.

In a 1981 article subtitled "Lean living and mini-mill technology have led a one-time loser to steel's promised land," *Fortune* stated:

> Although Nucor didn't build his first mill until 1969, it turned out 1.1 million tons of steel last year, enough to rank among the top 20 U.S. producers. Not only has Nucor been making a lot of steel, it's been making money making steel—and a lot of that as well. Since 1969, earnings have grown 31% a year, compounded, reaching $45 million in 1980 on sales of $482 million. Return on average equity in recent years has consistently exceeded 28%, excellent even by Silicon Valley's standards and almost unheard of in steel. The nine-fold increase in the value of Nucor's stock over the last five years—it was selling recently at about $70 a share—has given shareholders plenty of cause for thanksgiving.[1]

The Wall Street Journal commented, "The ways in which management style combines with technology to benefit the mini-mill industry is obvious at Nucor Corp., one of the most successful of the 40 or more mini-mill operators."[2] Ken Iverson was featured in an NBC special, "If Japan Can, Why Can't We?" for his management approach. As *The Wall Street Journal* commented, "You thought steel companies are only a bunch of losers, with stodgy management, outmoded plants and poor profits?" Well, Nucor and Iverson were different.

However, the challenges hadn't stopped. The economy made the 1980s a horrible time for the steel industry. All companies reported sales declines, most lost profitability and some, in both major and mini-mill operations, closed or restructured. Nucor's 30 percent plus return on equity hit 9 percent. Iverson, however, was one of 52 recipients of the bronze medal from *Financial World* in 1983 for holding onto profitability; they kept costs down but not at the expense of laying off their people—a near-religious commitment at Nucor.

By 1990 Nucor was the ninth largest steel producer in the U.S. and number 323 on the Fortune 500 list. But the easy gains scored by the new mini-mill operations over the integrated mills were over. The historical steel companies were

This case was prepared by Frank C. Barnes, University of North Carolina, Charlotte. Note: Many quotes by Ken Iverson are from prepared comments and speeches and are not footnoted. This case was prepared as a basis for class discussion rather than to illustrate either effective or ineffective handling of administrative situations.

1. Richard I. Kirkland, Jr., "Pilgrims' Profits at Nucor," *Fortune,* April 6, 1981, pp. 43–46.
2. Douglas R. Sease, "Mini-Mill Steelmakers, No Longer Very Small, Outperform Big Ones," *The Wall Street Journal,* January 12, 1981, pp. 1, 19.

arousing from their twenty-year slumber, adding modern technology, renegotiating with their equally aged unions, and closing some mills. They were determined to fight back. Mini-mill was fighting mini-mill, as well as imports, and a number had closed. Thus the industry faced a picture of excess capacity which would be the backdrop in the battle for survival and success over the next years.

Iverson and Nucor knew how to fight the battle. They invested $325 million in new processes in 1988. They went from $185 million in idle cash in 1986 to $180 million in debt by 1988. They had opened the first new fastener plant in the U.S. in decades, completed a joint venture with the Japanese to build a plant to make structural steel products, and built the first mini-mill in the world to make flat-rolled steel, the largest market and major business of the integrated producers. They had broken away from the other mini-mills and had at least a three-year headstart in taking a share of this market from the integrated mills. Iverson believed with their new products they should double sales, and probably earnings, by 1991. Analysts predicted a jump to 7th largest among mills and doubling or tripling share price in the immediate future.

BACKGROUND

Nucor was the descendant of a company that manufactured the first Oldsmobile in 1897. After seven years of success, R. E. Olds sold his first company and founded a new one to manufacture the Reo. Reo ran into difficulties and filed for voluntary reorganization in 1938. Sales grew 50 times over the next ten years, based on defense business, but declined steadily after World War II. The motor division was sold and then resold in 1957 to the White Motor Corporation, where it operates as the Diamond Reo Division. Reo Motors' management planned to liquidate the firm, but before it could do so, a new company gained control through a proxy fight. A merger was arranged with Nuclear Consultants, Inc., and the stock of Nuclear Corporation of America was first traded in 1955. Nuclear acquired a number of companies in high-tech fields but continued to lose money until 1960, when an investment banker in New York acquired control. New management proceeded with a series of acquisitions and dispositions: they purchased U.S. Semi-Conductor Products, Inc.; Valley Sheet Metal Company, an air conditioner contractor in Arizona; and Vulcraft Corporation, a Florence, South Carolina, steel joist manufacturer. Over the next four years, sales increased five times, but losses increased seven times. In 1965 a New York investor purchased a controlling interest and installed the fourth management team. The new president was Ken Iverson, who had been in charge of the Vulcraft division.

Ken Iverson had joined the Navy upon graduation from a Chicago-area high school in 1943. The Navy first sent him to Northwestern University for an officer training program but then decided it needed aeronautical engineers and transferred him to Cornell. This had been "fine" with Iverson, because he enjoyed engineering. Upon receiving his bachelor's degree in 1945 at age 20, he served in the Navy for six months, completing his four-year tour.

He wasn't too excited about an A.E. career because of the eight years of drafting required for success. Metals and their problems in aircraft design had intrigued him, so he considered a Master's degree in metallurgy. An uncle had

attended Purdue, so he chose that school. He married during this time, gave up teaching geometry so he could finish the program in one year, and turned down an offer of assistance toward a Ph.D. to "get to work."

At Purdue he had worked with the new electron microscope. International Harvester's research physics department had just acquired one and hired Iverson as Assistant to the Chief Research Physicist. Iverson stayed there five years and felt he was "set for life." He had great respect for his boss, who would discuss with him the directions businesses took and their opportunities. One day the Chief Physicist asked if that job was what he really wanted to do all his life. There was only one job ahead for Iverson at International Harvester and he felt more ambition than to end his career in that position. At his boss's urging, he considered smaller companies.

Iverson joined Illium Corporation, 120 miles from Chicago, as chief engineer (metallurgist). Illium was a 60-person division of a major company but functioned like an independent company. Iverson was close to the young president and was impressed by his good business skill; this man knew how to manage and had the discipline to run a tight ship, to go in the right direction with no excess manpower. The two of them proposed an expansion, which the parent company insisted they delay three to four years until they could handle it without going into debt.

After two years at Illium, Iverson joined Indiana Steel products as assistant to the vice-president of manufacturing, for the sole purpose of setting up a spectrographic lab. After completing this job within one year, he could see no other opportunity for himself in the company, because it was small and he could get no real responsibility. A year and a half later, Iverson left to join Cannon Muskegon as chief metallurgist.

The next seven years were "fascinating." This small ($5–6 million in sales and 60-70 people) family company made castings from special metals that were used in every aircraft made in the United States. The company was one of the first to get into "vacuum melting," and Iverson, because of his technical ability, was put in charge of this activity. Iverson then asked for and got responsibility for all company sales. He wasn't dissatisfied but realized that if he was to be really successful he needed broader managerial experience.

Cannon Muskegon sold materials to Coast Metals, a small, private company in New Jersey which cast and machined special alloys for the aircraft industry. The president of Coast got to know Iverson and realized his technical expertise would be an asset. In 1960 he joined Coast as executive vice-president, with responsibility for running the whole company.

Nuclear Corporation of America wished to buy Coast; however, Coast wasn't interested. Nuclear's president then asked Iverson to act as a consultant to find metal businesses Nuclear could buy. Over the next year, mostly on weekends, he looked at potential acquisitions. He recommended buying a joist business in North Carolina. Nuclear said it would, if he would run it. Coast was having disputes among its owners and Iverson's future there was clouded. He ended his two years there and joined Nuclear in 1962 as a vice-president, Nuclear's usual title, in charge of a 200-person joist division.

By late 1963 he had built a second plant in Nebraska and was running the only division making a profit. The president asked him to become a group vice-president, adding the research chemicals (metals) and contracting businesses, and to move to the home office in Phoenix. In mid-1965 the company defaulted

on two loans and the president resigned. During the summer Nuclear sought some direction out of its difficulty. Iverson knew what could be done, put together a pro-forma statement, and pushed for these actions. It was not a unanimous decision when he was made president in September 1965.

The new management immediately abolished some divisions and went to work building Nucor. According to Iverson, the vice-presidents of the divisions designed Nucor in hard-working, almost T-group-type meetings. Iverson was only another participant and took charge only when the group couldn't settle an issue. This process identified Nucor's strengths and set the path for Nucor.

By 1966 Nucor consisted of the two joist plants, the Research Chemicals division, and the Nuclear division. During 1967 a building in Fort Payne, Alabama, was purchased for conversion into another joist plant. "We got into the steel business because we wanted to be able to build a mill that could make steel as cheaply as we were buying it from foreign importers or from offshore mills." In 1968 Nucor opened a steel mill in Darlington, South Carolina, and a joist plant in Texas. Another joist plant was added in Indiana in 1972. Steel plant openings followed in Nebraska in 1977 and in Texas in 1975. The Nuclear division was divested in 1976. A fourth steel plant was opened in Utah in 1981 and a joist plant was opened in Utah in 1982. By 1984 Nucor consisted of six joist plants, four steel mills, and a Research Chemicals division.

In 1983, in testimony before the Congress, Iverson warned of the hazards of trade barriers, that they would cause steel to cost more and that manufacturers would move overseas to use the cheaper steel shipped back into this country. He commented, "We have seen serious problems in the wire industry and the fastener industry." *Link* magazine reported that in the last four years, forty domestic fastener plants had closed and that imports had over 90 percent of the market.

In 1986 Nucor began construction of a $25 million plant in Indiana to manufacture steel fasteners. Iverson told *The Atlanta Journal*, "We are going to bring that business back."[3] He told *Inc.* magazine, "We've studied for a year now, and we decided that we can make bolts as cheaply as foreign producers and make a profit at it."[4] He explained that in the old operation two people, one simply required by the union, made one hundred bolts a minute. "But at Nucor, we'll have an automated machine which will manufacture 400 bolts a minute. The automation will allow an operator to manage four machines." Hans Mueller, a steel industry consultant at East Tennessee State University, told the *Journal*, "I must confess that I was surprised that Iverson would be willing to dive into that snake pit. But he must believe that he can do it because he is not reckless."[5]

Before making the decision, a Nucor task force of four people traveled the world to examine the latest technology. The management group was headed by a plant manager who joined Nucor after several years experience as general manager of a bolt company in Toronto. The manager of manufacturing was previously plant manager of a 40,000-ton melt-shop for Ervin Industries. The sales manager was a veteran of sales, distribution, and manufacturing in the fastener industry. The plant's engineering manager transferred from Nucor R & D in Nebraska. The Touche-Ross accountant who worked on the Nucor account

3. Chris Burritt, "Foreign Steel Doesn't Scare Nucor's CEO," *The Atlanta Journal*, August 24, 1986, pp. 1M, 5M.
4. "Steel Man Ken Iverson," *Inc.*, April 1986, pp. 41–48.
5. Burritt, "Foreign Steel Doesn't Scare Nucor's CEO," pp. 1M, 5M.

joined the company as controller. The first crew of production employees received three months of in-depth training on the bolt-making machines, with extensive cross-training in tool making, maintenance, and other operations. By 1988, the new plant was operating close to its capacity of 45,000 tons.

In what *The New York Times* called their "most ambitious project yet," Nucor signed an agreement in January 1987 to form a joint venture with Yamato Kogyo, Ltd., a small Japanese steelmaker, to build a steel mill on the Mississippi River with a 600,000 ton per year capacity.[6] The $200 million dollar plant would make very large structural products, up to 24 inches. Structural steel products are those used in large buildings and bridges. Iverson noted, "These are now only made by the Big Three integrated steel companies." The Japanese company, which would own 49 percent of the stock, had expertise in continuous-casting in which Nucor was interested. Their 1985 sales totaled $400 million, with approximately 900 workers. They would provide the continuous casting technology while Nucor would provide the melting technology and management style. The mill was completed in 1988 at a cost of $220 million for 650,000 tons of capacity. By the end of 1988, the plant was operating at 50 percent of capacity.

In August 1986, Iverson told Cable News Network, "We are talking about within the next two years perhaps building a steel mill to make flat roll products; that would be the first time a mini-mill has been in this area."[7] It was expected that approximately $10 million would be needed to develop this process. The thin-slab would also produce feed stock for Vulcraft's 250,000 tons per year steel deck operation. Although the project was considered pure research at the time and projected for "late 1988," the Division Manager stated, "The more we look into it, the more we feel we'll be able to successfully cast those slabs." This process would be the most significant development in the steel industry in decades and would open up the auto and appliance businesses to the mini-mills. Then in January 1987 plans were announced to build the $200 million, 800,000 ton mill for the production of high-grade flat rolled steel by the first half of 1989. They stated, "We've tested numerous approaches . . . this one is commercially feasible. It's been tested and it can do the job."[8]

The flat rolled steel was the largest market for steel products at 40 million tons in 1988 and 52 percent of the U.S. market. This is the thin sheet steel used in car bodies, refrigerators, and countless products. Making flat rolled steel required casting a slab rather than a billit and had not been achieved in the mini-mill. Nucor had invested several million in research on a process but in 1986 chose to go with a technology developed by SMS, a West German company. SMS had a small pilot plant using the new technology and Nucor would be the first mini-mill in the world to manufacture flat rolled steel commercially.

The plant would be built in Crawfordsville, Indiana, with an April 1988 start-up. It was expected that labor hours per ton would be half the integrated manufacturer's 3.0, yielding a savings of $50 to $75 on a $400 a ton selling price. If the project were completed successfully, Nucor planned to have three plants in operation before others could build. Investment advisors anticipated Nucor's

6. "Nucor's Ambitious Expansion," *The New York Times*, June 30, 1986, pp. D1, D3.
7. "Inside Business," Interview with Ken Iverson, Cable News Network, August 17, 1986.
8. Jo Isenberg-O'Loughlin and Joseph J. Innace, "Full Steam Ahead on the Nucor Unlimited," *33 Metal Producing*, January 1986, pp. 35–50.

stock could increase to double or triple by the mid 1990s. In July 1989, when Nucor announced a 14 percent drop in 2nd quarter earnings due to start-up costs, its stock went up $1.62 to $63. Iverson stated, "We hope this will map out the future of the company for the next decade."

However, it would not be as easy as earlier ventures. In April 1989, *Forbes* commented "if any mini-mill can meet the challenge, it's Nucor. But expect the going to be tougher this time around."[9] The flat-rolled market was the last bastion of the integrated manufacturers and they had been seriously modernizing their plants throughout the '80s.

In December 1986 Nucor announced its first major acquisition, Genbearco, a steel bearings manufacturer. At a cost of more than $10 million, it would add $25 million in sales and 250 employees. Iverson called it "a good fit with our business, our policies, and our people." It was without a union and tied pay to performance.

In October 1988, Nucor agreed to sell its Chemicals Division to a New York company for a $38 million gain.

Nucor's innovation was not limited to manufacturing. In the steel industry, it was normal to price an order based on the quantity ordered. In 1984, Nucor broke that pattern. As Iverson stated, "Some time ago we began to realize that with computer order entry and billing, the extra charge for smaller orders was not cost justified. We found the cost of servicing a 20 ton order compared with a 60 ton order was about 35 cents a ton and most of that was related to credit and collection. We did agonize over the decision, but over the long run we are confident that the best competitive position is one that has a strong price to cost relationship." He noted that this policy would give Nucor another advantage over foreign suppliers in that users could maintain lower inventories and order more often. "If we are going to successfully compete against foreign suppliers, we must use the most economical methods for both manufacturing and distribution."

THE STEEL INDUSTRY

The early 1980s had been the worst years in decades for the steel industry. Data from the American Iron and Steel Institute showed shipments falling from 100.2 million tons in 1979 to the mid-80 levels in 1980 and 1981. Slackening in the economy, particularly in auto sales, led the decline. In 1986, when industry capacity was at 130 million tons, the outlook was for a continued decline in per-capita consumption and movement toward capacity in the 90–100 million ton range. The Chairman of Armco saw "millions of tons chasing a market that's not there; excess capacity that must be eliminated."

The large, integrated steel firms, such as U.S. Steel and Armco, which made up the major part of the industry, were the hardest hit. *The Wall Street Journal* stated, "The decline has resulted from such problems as high labor and energy costs in mining and processing iron ore, a lack of profits and capital to modernize plants, and conservative management that has hesitated to take risks."[10]

9. R. Simon, "Nucor's Boldest Gamble," *Forbes*, April 3, 1989, p. 122.
10. Sease, "Mini-Mill Steelmakers," pp. 1, 19.

These companies produced a wide range of steels, primarily from ore processed in blast furnaces. They had found it difficult to compete with imports, usually from Japan, and had given up market share to imports. They sought the protection of import quotas. Imported steel accounted for 20 percent of the U.S. steel consumption, up from 12 percent in the early 1970s. The U.S. share of world production of raw steel declined from 19 percent to 14 percent over the period. Imports of light bar products accounted for less than 9 percent of U.S. consumption of those products in 1981, according to the U.S. Commerce Department, while imports of wire rod totaled 23 percent of U.S. consumption. "Wire rod is a very competitive product in the world market because it's very easy to make," Ralph Thompson, the Commerce Department's steel analyst, told the *Charlotte Observer*.[11]

Iron Age stated that exports, as a percent of shipments in 1985, were 34 percent for Nippon, 26 percent for British Steel, 30 percent for Krupp, 49 percent for USINOR of France, and less than 1 percent for every American producer on the list. The consensus of steel experts was that imports would average 23 percent of the market in the last half of the 1980s.[12]

Iverson was one of very few in the steel industry to oppose import restrictions. He saw an outdated U.S. steel industry which had to change.

> About 12% of the steel in the U.S. is still produced by the old open hearth furnace. The Japanese shut down their last open hearth furnace about five years ago. . . .The U.S. produces about 16% of its steel by the continuous casting process. In Japan over 50% of the steel is continuously cast. . . .We Americans have been conditioned to believe in our technical superiority. For many generations a continuing stream of new inventions and manufacturing techniques allowed us to far outpace the rest of the world in both volume and efficiency of production. In many areas this is no longer true and particularly in the steel industry. In the last three decades, almost all the major developments in steel making were made outside the U.S. There were 18 continuous casting units in the world before there was one in this country. I would be negligent if I did not recognize the significant contribution that the government has made toward the technological deterioration of the steel industry. Unrealistic depreciation schedules, high corporate taxes, excessive regulation and jaw-boning for lower steel prices have made it difficult for the steel industry to borrow or generate the huge quantities of capital required for modernization.

By the mid 1980s the integrated mills were moving fast to get back into the game; they were restructuring, cutting capacity, dropping unprofitable lines, focusing products, and trying to become responsive to the market. The President of USX explained: "Steel executives, in trying to act as prudent businessmen, are seeking the lowest-cost solutions to provide what the market wants." Karlis Kirsis, Director of World Steel Dynamics at PaineWebber, told *Purchasing Magazine*, "The industry as we knew it five years ago is no more; the industry as we knew it a year ago is gone."[13]

Purchasing believed that buyers would be seeing a pronounced industry segmentation. There would be integrated producers making mostly flat-rolled and structural grades, reorganized steel companies making a limited range of products, mini-mills dominating the bar and light structural product areas, specialty

11. The *Charlotte Observer*, various issues.
12. "1985 Top 50 World Steel Producers," *Iron Age*, May 2, 1986, p. 48B1.
13. "Metals Report: Steel 1986," *Purchasing*, September 25, 1986, pp. 52–65.

steel firms seeking niches, and foreign producers. There would be accelerated shutdowns of older plants, elimination of products by some firms, and the installation of new product lines with new technologies by others. There would also be corporate facelifts as executives diversified from steel to generate profits and entice investment dollars. They saw the high-tonnage mills restructuring to handle sheets, plates, structurals, high quality bars, and large pipe and tubular products which would allow for a resurgence of specialized mills: cold-finished bar manufacturers, independent strip mills and mini-mills.[14]

Wheeling-Pittsburgh illustrated the change underway in the industry. Through Chapter 11 reorganization it had cut costs by more than $85/ton. They divided into profit centers, negotiated the lowest hourly wage rate ($18/hour) among unionized integrated steel plants, renegotiated supply contracts, closed pipe and tube mills, and shut 1.6 million tons of blast furnace capacity in favor of an electric furnace with continuous casting.

PaineWebber pointed out the importance of "reconstituted mills," which they called the "People Express" of the industry. These were companies which had reorganized and refocused their resources, usually under Chapter 11. These include Kaiser Steel, the Weirton Works, Jones and Laughlin, Republic, Youngstown, Wheeling, LTV, and others.

Joint Ventures had arisen to produce steel for a specific market or region. The Chairman of USX called them "an important new wrinkle in steel's fight for survival" and stated, "If there had been more joint ventures like these two decades ago, the U.S. steel industry might have built only half of the dozen or so hot-strip mills it put up in that time and avoided today's overcapacity." *Purchasing* observed, "The fact is that these combined operations are the result of a laissez-faire attitude within the Justice Department under the Reagan administration following the furor when government restrictions killed the planned USS takeover of National Steel (which later sold 50 percent interest to a Japanese steelmaker)."[15]

However, the road ahead for the integrated mills would not be easy. While it was estimated they would need $10 billion to improve their facilities, the industry had lost over $7 billion since 1982. *Purchasing* pointed out that tax laws and accounting rules are slowing the closing of inefficient plants. Shutting down a 10,000-person plant could require a firm to hold a cash reserve of $100 million to fund health, pension, and insurance liabilities. The Chairman of Armco commented: "Liabilities associated with a plant shutdown are so large that they can quickly devastate a company's balance sheet."[16]

The American Iron and Steel Institute (AISI) reported steel production in 1988 of 99.3 million tons, up from 89.2 in 1987, and the highest in seven years. As a result of modernization programs, 60.9 percent of production was from continuous casters. Exports of steel were increasing, 2 million tons in 1988 and forecast to 3 in 1989, and imports were falling, expected to be less than 20 percent in 1989. Some steel experts believed the U.S. was now cost competitive with Japan. Several countries did not fill their quotas allowed under the 5-year-old voluntary restraint agreements, which would expire in September 1989. The role of service centers in the distribution of steel continued with its fifth consecutive record year in 1988 of 23.4 million tons.

14. Ibid.
15. Ibid.
16. Ibid.

"If 1988 is remembered as the year of steel prosperity despite economic uncertainties, then 1989 is just as likely to go down as the year of 'waiting for the other shoe to drop,'" according to *Metal Center News* in January 1989.[17] The fears and the expectation of a somewhat weaker year arose from concerns of a recession, expiration of the voluntary import restraints, and labor negotiations schedules in several companies. Declines in car production and consumer goods were expected to hit flat-rolled hard. Service centers were also expected to be cutting back on inventories. AUJ Consultants told *MCN*, "The U.S. steel market has peaked. Steel consumption is tending down. By 1990, we expect total domestic demand to dip under 90 million tons."[18] Iverson expected 1989 to be mediocre compared to 1988.

THE MINI-MILL

A new type of mill, the "mini-mill," emerged in the U.S. during the 1970s to compete with the integrated mill. The mini-mill used electric arc furnaces to manufacture a narrow product line from scrap steel. In 1981 *The New York Times* reported:

> The truncated steel mill is to the integrated steel mill what the Volkswagen was to the American auto industry in the 1960's: smaller, cheaper, less complex and more efficient. Although mini-mills cannot produce such products as sheet steel [flat rolled] and heavy construction items, some industry analysts say it is only a matter of time before technological breakthroughs make this possible.[19]

Since mini-mills came into being in the 1970s, the integrated mills' market share has fallen from about 90 percent to about 60 percent, with the loss equally divided between mini-mills and foreign imports. While the integrated steel companies averaged a 7 percent return on equity, the mini-mills averaged 14 percent, and some, such as Nucor, achieved about 25 percent.

The leading mini-mills were Nucor, Florida Steel, Georgetown Steel (Korf Industries), North Star Steel, and Chaparral. Nucor produced "light bar" products: bars, angles, channels, flats, smooth round, and forging billets. It was beginning to make more alloy steels. Florida Steel made mostly reinforcing bar for construction (rebar) and dominated the Florida market. Korf Industries had two mini-mill subsidiaries which used modern equipment to manufacture wire-rod.

The mini-mills were not immune to the economic slump in the early eighties. Korf Industries, which owned Georgetown Steel, found its interest charges too large a burden and sought reorganization in 1983. In March of 1983, Georgetown followed the historic wage cutting contract between the United Steel Workers of America and the major steel companies and asked its union to accept reductions and to defer automatic wage increases. In 1982 Nucor froze wages and executives took a 5 percent pay cut. Plants went to a four-day schedule in which workers would receive only base rate if they chose to work a fifth day doing clean-up.

17. *Metal Center News*, January 1989.
18. Ibid.
19. "The Rise of Mini-Steel Mills," *The New York Times*, September 23, 1981, pp. D1, D6.

Florida Steel, with two-thirds of its sales in Florida, also felt the impact. At its headquarters in Tampa, a staff of over 100 handled accounting, payroll, sales entry, and almost all other services for all its facilities. Their division managers did not have sales responsibilities. Florida Steel experienced a sales decline for 1982 of 22 percent and an earnings drop from $3.37 per share to a loss of $1.40. The next year was also a year of losses.

Florida Steel employees had faced periodic layoffs during the recession. The firm was non-union (although the Charlotte plant lost an election in 1973) and pay was based on productivity. A small facility at Indian Town, near West Palm Beach, never became productive, even with personnel changes, and had to be closed. A new mini-mill in Tennessee was completed in late 1983.

Mini-mills had tripled their output in the last decade to capture 17 percent of domestic shipments. PaineWebber predicted the big integrated mills' share of the market would fall to 40 percent, the mini-mills' share would rise to 23 percent, "reconstituted" mills would increase from 11 percent to 28 percent, and specialized mills would increase their share from 1 percent to 7 percent. Iverson stated mini-mills could not go beyond a 35 percent to 40 percent share due to technical limitations; mini-mills could not produce the flat rolled sheet steel used in cars and appliances.

Iverson told *Metal Center News* in 1983: "We are very interested in the development of a thin slab, which would then allow mini-mills to produce plate and other flat rolled products . . . actually, the thinnest slab that can now be produced is about 6 inches thick. . . . (That results in a plant that is too large.) There are a number of people working to develop the process. . . . We have done some work, but our primary efforts at the moment are in connection with other people who are working on it. . . . The likelihood is it would be developed by a foreign company. There are more efforts by foreign steel companies in that direction than in the United States. . . . I'd say probably a minimum of three to five years, or it could take as much as 10 to achieve this."[20]

In 1983 Iverson described the new generation of mini-mills he foresaw: "If you go way back, mini-mills got started by rolling reinforcing bar. With the advent of continuous casting and improvements in rolling mills, mini-mills gradually got into shapes. Now they have moved in two other directions: one being to larger sizes, and the other being a growing metallurgical expertise for improved product quality and production of special bar quality in alloys. Both of these represent expansion of markets for mini-mills."

By 1986 the new competitive environment was apparent. Four mini-mills had closed their doors within the year and Iverson saw that more shutdowns were ahead. The overcapacity of steel bar products and the stagnant market had made it difficult for some companies to generate the cash needed to modernize and expand their product lines. "The mini-mills are going through the same kind of restructuring and rethinking as the integrated mill. They know the problem of overcapacity isn't going to go away quickly. And, for some of the remaining firms to survive, they will have to move into more sophisticated products like special quality and clean-steel bars and heavier structurals and, once the technology is perfected, flat-rolled products. You won't see the market growth by the mini-mills the way it was in the past until the overcapacity issue is resolved and the mills begin entering new product areas."

20. "Iverson Alloys Usher in New Era," *Metal Center News*, August 1987, p. 29.

ORGANIZATION

Nucor, with its 18-person corporate office located in Charlotte, North Carolina, had divisions spread across the United States. The 15 divisions, one for every plant, each had a general manager, who was also a vice-president of the corporation, directly responsible to Iverson and Aycock. (See Exhibit 1.) The divisions were of two basic types, joist plants and steel mills. The corporate staff consisted of single specialists in personnel and planning and a four-person financial function under Mr. Sam Siegel. Iverson, in the beginning, had chosen Charlotte "as the new home base for what he had envisioned as a small cadre of executives who would guide a decentralized operation with liberal authority delegated to managers in the field," according to *South Magazine*.[21]

Iverson gave his views on organization:

> You can tell a lot about a company by looking at its organization chart. . . . If you see a lot of staff, you can bet it is not a very efficient organization. . . . Secondly, don't have assistants. We do not have that title and prohibit it in our company. . . . In this organization nobody reports to the corporate office; the division managers report directly to me. . . . And one of the most important things is to resist as much as possible the number of management layers. . . . I've often thought that when a company builds a fancy corporate office, it's on its way down.
>
> Each division is a profit center and the division manager has control over the day-to-day decisions that make that particular division profitable or not profitable. We expect the division to provide contribution, which is earnings before corporate expenses. We do not allocate our corporate expenses, because we do not think there is any way to do this reasonably and fairly. We do focus on earnings. And we expect a division to earn 25 percent return on total assets employed, before corporate expenses, taxes, interest or profit sharing. And we have a saying in the company—if a manager doesn't provide that for a number of years, we are either going to get rid of the division or get rid of the general manager, and it's generally the division manager.

A joist division manager commented:

> I've been a division manager four years now and at times I'm still awed by it: the opportunity I was given to be a Fortune 500 vice-president. . . . I think we are successful because it is our style to pay more attention to our business than our competitors. . . . We are kind of a "no nonsense" company. That is not to say we don't have time to play, but we work hard when we work and the company is first and foremost in our minds. . . . I think another one of the successes of our company has been the fact that we have a very minimum number of management levels. We've been careful to avoid getting topheavy and so consequently we put a great deal of responsibility on each individual at each level. It has often been said, jokingly, that if you are the janitor at Vulcraft and you get the right promotions, about four promotions would take you to the top of the company.
>
> Mr. Iverson's style of management is to allow the division manager all the latitude in the world. His involvement with the managers is quite limited. As we've grown, he no longer has the time to visit with the managers more than once or twice a year. . . . Whereas in many large companies the corporate office makes the major decisions and the people at the operating level sit back to wait for their marching orders, that's not the case at Nucor. . . . In a way I feel like I run my own company because I really don't get any marching orders from Mr. Iverson. He lets you run the division the

21. Don Bedwell, "Nucor's Lean, Mean Management Team," *South Magazine*, August 1980, p. 50.

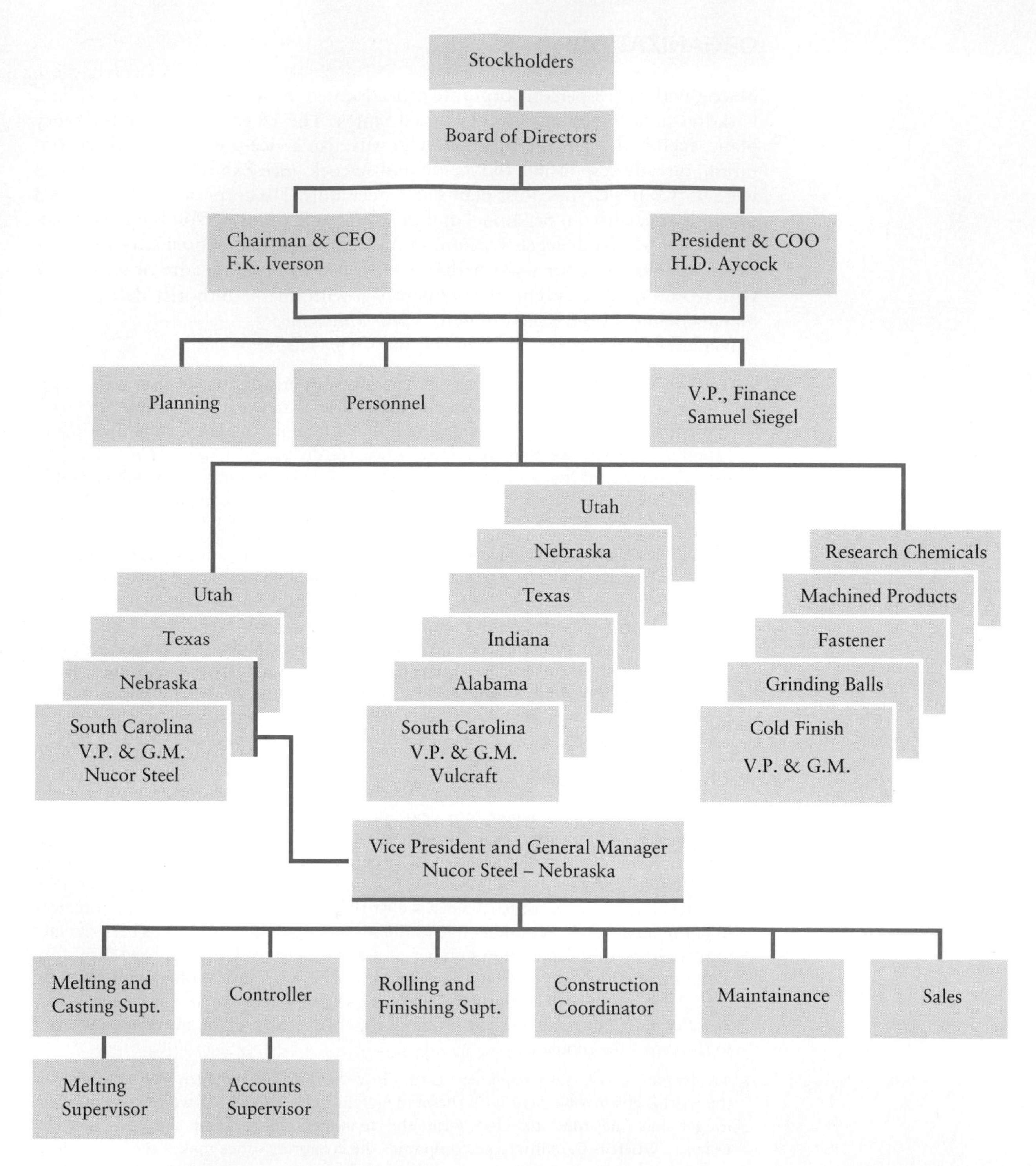

Exhibit 1
Nucor Organization Chart

way you see fit and the only way he will step in is if he sees something he doesn't like, particularly bad profits, high costs or whatever. But in the years I've worked with him I don't believe he has ever issued one single instruction to me to do something differently. I can't recall a single instance.

The divisions did their own manufacturing, selling, accounting, engineering, and personnel management. A steel division manager, when questioned about Florida Steel, which had a large plant 90 miles away, commented, "I really don't know anything about Florida Steel. . . . I expect they do have more of the hierarchy. I think they have central purchasing, centralized sales, centralized credit collections, centralized engineering, and most of the major functions." He didn't feel greater centralization would be good for Nucor. "The purchasing activity, for example, removed from the field tends to become rather insensitive to the needs of the field and does not feel the pressures of responsibility. And the division they are buying for has no control over what they pay. . . . Likewise centralized sales would not be sensitive to the needs of their divisions."[22]

South Magazine observed that Iverson had established a characteristic organizational style described as "stripped down" and "no nonsense." "Jack Benny would like this company," observed Roland Underhill, an analyst with Crowell, Weedon and Co. of Los Angeles; "so would Peter Drucker." Underhill pointed out that Nucor's thriftiness doesn't end with its "spartan" office staff or modest offices. "There are no corporate perquisites," he recited. "No company planes. No country club memberships. No company cars."[23]

Fortune reported, "Iverson takes the subway when he is in New York, a Wall Street analyst reports in a voice that suggests both admiration and amazement."[24] The general managers reflected this style in the operation of their individual divisions. Their offices were more like plant offices or the offices of private companies built around manufacturing rather than for public appeal. They were simple, routine, and businesslike.

In 1983, one of Iverson's concerns had been that as Nucor continued to grow they would have to add another layer of management to their lean structure. In June 1984 he named Dave Aycock President and Chief Operating Officer, while he became Chairman and Chief Executive Officer—they would share one management level. Aycock had most recently been Division Manager of the steel mill at Darlington. But he had been with the company longer than Iverson, having joined Vulcraft in 1955, and had long been recognized as a particularly valued and close advisor to Iverson.

Iverson explained: "The company got to the size that I just wasn't doing the job that I thought should be done by this office. I couldn't talk to the analysts and everyone else I have to talk to, put the efforts into research and development I wanted to, and get to all the units as frequently as I should. That's why I brought Dave in. And, of course, he has been with the company forever." In a February 1985 letter he told stockholders: "These changes are to provide additional emphasis on the expansion of the company's businesses."

"Dave is a very analytical person and very thorough in his thought process," another division manager told *33 Metal Producing*, a Mcgraw-Hill publication. "And Ken, to use an overworked word, is an entrepreneurial type. So, they complement each other. They're both very aggressive men, and make one hell of a good team."[25] Aycock stated: "I am responsible for the operations of all our divisions. To decide where we are going, with what technologies; what are our

22. Interviews conducted by Frank C. Barnes.
23. Bedwell, "Nucor's Lean, Mean Management Team," p. 55.
24. "Pilgrims' Profits at Nucor," *Fortune*, April 6, 1981.
25. Isenberg-O'Loughlin and Innace, "Full Steam Ahead on the Nucor Unlimited," pp. 35–50.

purposes. And what is our thrust. I help Ken shape where we are going and with what technologies. . . . I've been quite aggressive my whole career at updating, adapting, and developing new technology and new ideas in production and marketing. "Dave's the fellow who now handles most of the day-to-day operations," Iverson commented. "And he handles most of the employees who write to us"—about 10 to 15 percent of his time.[26]

DIVISION MANAGERS

The general managers met three times a year. In late October they presented preliminary budgets and capital requests. In late February they met to finalize budgets and treat miscellaneous matters. Then, at a meeting in May, they handled personnel matters, such as wage increases and changes of policies or benefits. The general managers as a group considered the raises for the department heads, the next lower level of management. As one of the managers described it:[27]

> In May of each year, all the general managers get together and review all the department heads throughout the company. We have kind of an informal evaluation process. It's an intangible thing, a judgment as to how dedicated an individual is and how well he performs compared to the same position at another plant. Sometimes the numbers don't come out the way a general manager wants to see them, but it's a fair evaluation. The final number is picked by Mr. Iverson. Occasionally there are some additional discussions with Mr. Iverson. He always has an open mind and might be willing to consider a little more for one individual. We consider the group of, say, joist production managers at one time. The six managers are rated for performance. We assign a number, such as +3 to a real crackerjack performer or a –2 to someone who needs improvement. These ratings become a part of the final pay increase granted.

The corporate personnel manager described management relations as informal, trusting, and not "bureaucratic." He felt there was a minimum of paperwork, that a phone call was more common and that no confirming memo was thought to be necessary. Iverson himself stated:

> Management is not a popularity contest. If everybody agrees with the organization, something is wrong with the organization. You don't expect people in the company to put their arms around each other, and you don't interfere with every conflict. Out of conflict often comes the best answer to a particular problem. So don't worry about it. You are always going to have some conflict in an organization. You will always have differences of opinion, and that's healthy. Don't create problems where there are none.

A Vulcraft manager commented: "We have what I would call a very friendly spirit of competition from one plant to the next. And of course all of the vice presidents and general managers share the same bonus systems so we are in this together as a team even though we operate our divisions individually." The general managers are paid a bonus based on a total corporate profit rather than their own divisions' profits. A steel mill manager explained:

26. "Ken Iverson," *33 Metal Producing*, p. 4.
27. All quotes are either from Ken Iverson or from interviews with Nucor managers conducted by Frank C. Barnes.

> I think it's very important for the general managers to be concerned with contributing to the overall accomplishment of the company. There is a lot of interplay between the divisions with a flow of services, products, and ideas between divisions. Even though we are reasonably autonomous, we are not isolated.... We don't like the division managers to make decisions that would take that division away from where we want the whole company to go. But we certainly want the divisions to try new things. We are good copiers; if one division finds something that works, then we will all try it. I think that's one of our strengths. We have a lot of diverse people looking at ways to do things better.

Iverson revealed his view of management in his disdain for consultants:

> They must have a specific job to do because they can't make your decisions.... The fellow on the line has to make decisions.... First he has to communicate and then he has to have the intestinal fortitude and the personal strength to make the decisions, sometimes under very difficult conditions.... A good manager is adaptable and he is sensitive to cultural, geographical, environmental, and business climates. Most important of all, he communicates.... You never know if someone is a good manager until he manages. And that's why we take people as young as we possibly can, throw responsibility at them, and they either work or they don't. In a sense it's survival of the fittest. But don't kid yourself; that's what industry is all about.

A steel division manager commented in comparing the Nucor manager to the typical manager of a large corporation:

> We would probably tend to have managers who have confidence in their abilities and, very importantly, have confidence in other people in their division. And people who are very sensitive to the employees of their division.... But I think if you saw four or five different division managers, you'd have four or five different decision-making styles.

A Vulcraft general manager in his early 40's who had been promoted to the division manager level nine years earlier said:

> The step from department manager to division manager is a big one. I can't think of an instance when a general manager job has been offered to an individual that it has been passed up. Often it means moving from one part of the country to another. There are five department heads in six joist plants, which means there are 30 people who are considered for division manager slots at a joist plant. Mr. Iverson selects the division managers.

His own experience was enlightening:

> When I came to this plant four years ago, we had too many people, too much overhead. We had 410 people at the plant and I could see, because I knew how many people we had in the Nebraska plant, we had many more than we needed. That was my yardstick and we set about to reduce those numbers by attrition.... We have made a few equipment changes that made it easier for the men, giving them an opportunity to make better bonuses. Of course the changes were very subtle in any given case but overall in four years we have probably helped the men tremendously. With 55 fewer men, perhaps 40 to 45 fewer in the production area, we are still capable of producing the same number of tons as four years ago.

The divisions managed their activities with a minimum of contact with the corporate staff. Each day disbursements were reported to Siegel's office. Payments flowed into regional lock-boxes. On a weekly basis, joist divisions reported total quotes, sales cancellations, backlog, and production. Steel mills reported tons-rolled, outside shipments, orders, cancellations, and backlog. Mr. Iverson graphed the data. He might talk to the division about every two weeks. On the other hand Iverson was known to bounce ideas off the steel division manager in Darlington with whom he had worked since joining the company.

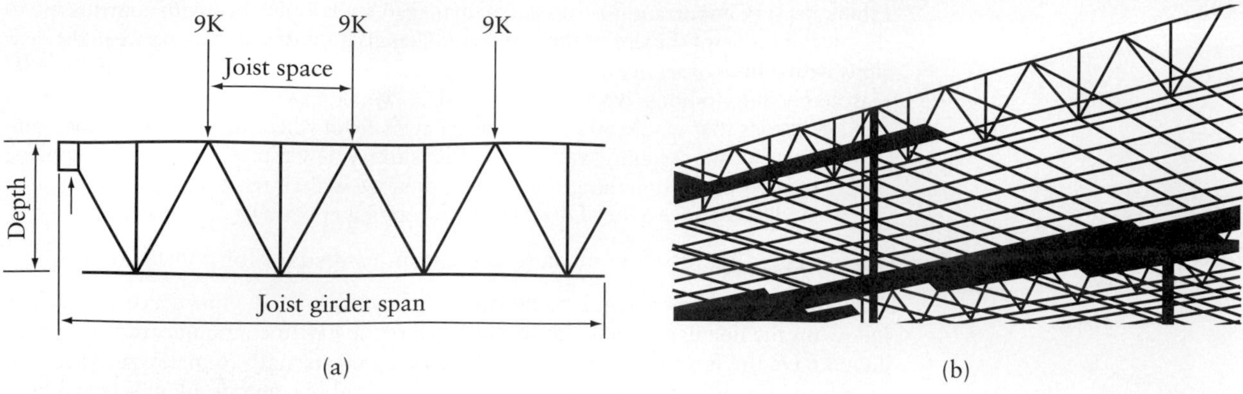

Exhibit 2
Illustration of Joists

The Vulcraft manager commented on the communications with the corporate office: "It's kind of a steady pipeline. I might talk to the corporate office once a day or it might be once a week. But it generally involves, I would not say trivial information, just mundane things. Occasionally I hear from Sam or Ken about serious matters."

Each month the divisions completed a two-page (11″ X 17″) "Operations Analysis" which was sent to all the managers. Its three main purposes were (1) financial consolidation, (2) sharing information among the divisions, and (3) Iverson's examination. The summarized information and the performance statistics for all the divisions were then returned to the managers.

VULCRAFT—THE JOIST DIVISIONS

Half of Nucor's business was the manufacture and sale of open web steel joists and joist girders at six Vulcraft divisions located in Florence, South Carolina; Norfolk, Nebraska; Ft. Payne, Alabama; Grapeland, Texas; St. Joe, Indiana; and Brigham City, Utah. Open web joists, in contrast to solid joists, were made of steel angle iron separated by round bars or smaller angle iron (see Exhibit 2).

These joists were costless and of lower greater strength for many applications and were used primarily as the roof support systems in larger buildings, such as warehouses and stores.

The joist industry was characterized by high competition among many manufacturers for many small customers. The Vulcraft divisions had over 3,000 customers, none of whom dominated the business. With an estimated 25 percent of the market, Nucor was the largest supplier in the U.S. It utilized national advertising campaigns and prepared competitive bids on 80 percent to 90 percent of buildings using joists. Competition was based on price and delivery performance. Nucor had developed computer programs to prepare designs for customers and to compute bids based on current prices and labor standards. In addition, each Vulcraft plant maintained its own Engineering Department to help customers with design problems or specifications. The Florence manager commented, "Here on the East Coast we have six or seven major competitors; of course none of them are as large as we are. The competition for any order will

be heavy, and we will see six or seven different prices."[28] He added, "I think we have a strong selling force in the marketplace. It has been said to us by some of our competitors that in this particular industry we have the finest selling organization in the country."

Nucor aggressively sought to be the lowest-cost producer in the industry. Materials and freight were two important elements of cost. Nucor maintained its own fleet of almost 100 trucks to ensure on-time delivery to all of the states, although most business was regional because of transportation costs. Plants were located in rural areas near the markets they served.

The Florence manager stated:

> I don't feel there's a joist producer in the country that can match our cost. . . . We are sticklers about cutting out unnecessary overhead. Because we put so much responsibility on our people and because we have what I think is an excellent incentive program, our people are willing to work harder to accomplish these profitable goals.

Production

On the basic assembly line used at Nucor, three or four of which might make up any one plant, about six tons per hour would be assembled. In the first stage eight people cut the angles to the right lengths or bent the round bars to desired form. These were moved on a roller conveyer to six-man assembly stations, where the component parts would be tacked together for the next stage, welding. Drilling and miscellaneous work were done by three people between the lines. The nine-man welding station completed the welds before passing the joists on roller conveyers to two-man inspection teams. The last step before shipment was the painting.

The workers had control over and responsibility for quality. There was an independent quality control inspector who had authority to reject the run of joists and cause them to be reworked. The quality control people were not under the incentive system and reported to the Engineering Department.

Daily production might vary widely, since each joist was made for a specific job. The wide range of joists made control of the workload at each station difficult; bottlenecks might arise anywhere along the line. Each work station was responsible for identifying such bottlenecks so that the foreman could reassign people promptly to maintain productivity. Since workers knew most of the jobs on the line, including the more skilled welding job, they could be shifted as needed. Work on the line was described by one general manager as "not machine type but mostly physical labor." He said the important thing was to avoid bottlenecks.

There were four lines of about 28 people each on two shifts at the Florence division. The jobs on the line were rated on responsibility and assigned a base wage, from $6 to $8 per hour. In addition, a weekly bonus was paid on the total output of each line. Each worker received the same percent bonus on his base wage.

The amount of time required to make a joist had been established as a result of experience; the general manager had seen no time studies in his fifteen years with the company. As a job was bid, the cost of each joist was determined through the computer program. The time required depended on the length, number of panels, and depth of the joist.

28. Interviews conducted by Frank C. Barnes.

Exhibit 3
Tons per Manhour, 52-Week Moving Average

Year	Tons per Manhour
1977	.163
1978	.179
1979	.192
1980	.195
1981	.194
1982	.208
1983	.215
1984	.214
1985	.228
1986	.225
1987	.218

Exhibit 4
A Sample of Percentage Performance, July 1982

		Line			
		1	2	3	4
Shift	1st	117	97	82	89
	2nd	98	102	94	107

At the time of production, the labor value of production, the standard, was determined in a similar manner. The general manager stated, "In the last nine or ten years we have not changed a standard." The standards list in use was over 10 years old. Previously, they adjusted the standard if the bonus was too high. He said the technological improvements over the last few years had been small. The general manager reported that the bonus had increased from about 60 percent nine years earlier to about 100 percent in 1982 and had stabilized at that point. Exhibits 3 and 4 show data typically computed on performance and used by the manager. He said the difference in performance on the line resulted from the different abilities of the crews.

"We don't have an industrial engineering staff. Our Engineering Department's work is limited to the design and the preparation of the paperwork prior to the actual fabrication process. Now, that is not to say that we don't have any involvement in fabrication. But the efficiency of the plant is entirely up to the manufacturing department. . . . When we had our first group in a joist plant, we produced 3½ tons an hour. We thought that if we ever got to 4 tons, that would be the Millennium. Well, today we don't have anybody who produces less than 6½ tons an hour. This is largely due to improvements that the groups have suggested."

Management

In discussing his philosophy for dealing with the work force, the Florence manager stated:[29]

> I believe very strongly in the incentive system we have. We are a non-union shop and we all feel that the way to stay so is to take care of our people and show them we care.

29. Interviews conducted by Frank C. Barnes.

> I think that's easily done because of our fewer layers of management.... I spend a good part of my time in the plant, maybe an hour or so a day. If a man wants to know anything, for example, an insurance question, I'm there and they walk right up to me and ask me questions which I'll answer the best I know how.... You can always tell when people are basically happy. If they haven't called for a meeting themselves or they are not hostile in any way, you can take it they understand the company's situation and accept it.... We do listen to our people.... For instance last fall I got a call from a couple of workers saying that people in our Shipping and Receiving area felt they were not being paid properly in relation to production people. So we met with them, discussed the situation and committed ourselves to reviewing the rates of other plants. We assured them that we would get back to them with an answer by the first of the year. Which we did. And there were a few minor changes.

The manager reported none of the plants had any particular labor problems, although there had been some in the past.

> In 1976, two years before I came here, there was a union election at this plant which arose out of racial problems. The company actually lost the election to the U.S. Steelworkers. When it came time to begin negotiating the contract, the workers felt, or came to see, that they had little to gain from being in the union. The union was not going to be able to do anything more for them than they were already doing. So slowly the union activity died out and the union quietly withdrew.

He discussed formal systems for consulting with the workers before changes were made:

> Of course we're cautioned by our labor counsel to maintain an open pipeline to our employees. We post all changes, company earnings, changes in the medical plan, anything that might affect an employee's job. Mr. Iverson has another philosophy, which is, "Either tell your people everything or tell them nothing." We choose to tell them everything. We don't have any regularly scheduled meetings. We meet whenever there's a need. The most recent examples were a meeting last month to discuss the results of an employee survey and three months before was held our annual dinner meetings off site.
>
> We don't lay our people off and we make a point of telling our people this.

"In the economic slump of 1982, we scheduled our line for four days, but the men were allowed to come in the fifth day for maintenance work at base pay. The men in the plant on an average running bonus might make $13 an hour. If their base pay is half that, on Friday they would only get $6–$7 an hour. Surprisingly, many of the men did not want to come in on Friday. They felt comfortable with just working four days a week. They are happy to have that extra day off." Recently the economic trouble in Texas had hurt business considerably. Both plants had been on decreased schedules for several months. About 20 percent of the people took the 5th day at base rate, but still no one had been laid off.

In April 1982 the executive committee decided, in view of economic conditions, that a pay freeze was necessary. The employees normally received an increase in their base pay the first of June. The decision was made at that time to freeze wages. The officers of the company, as a show of good faith, accepted a 5 percent pay cut. In addition to announcing this to the workers with a stuffer in their pay envelopes, meetings were held. Each production line, or incentive group of workers, met in the plant conference room with all supervision—foreman, plant production manager, and division manager. The economic crisis was explained to the employees by the production manager and all questions were answered.

STEEL DIVISIONS

Nucor had steel mills in five locations: Indiana, Nebraska, South Carolina, Texas, and Utah. The mills were modern "mini-mills," all built within the last 20 years to convert scrap steel into standard angles, flats, rounds, and channels using the latest technology. Sales in 1988 were 1.44 tons, a 10 percent increase over that of 1987. This figure represented about 70 percent of the mills' output, the remainder being used by other Nucor divisions. In recent years, Nucor has broadened its product line to include a wider range of steel chemistries, sizes, and special shapes. The total capacity of the mills reached 2.8 tons in 1988.

A casewriter from Harvard recounted the development of the steel divisions:

> By 1967 about 60% of each Vulcraft sales dollar was spent on materials, primarily steel. Thus, the goal of keeping costs low made it imperative to obtain steel economically. In addition, in 1967 Vulcraft bought about 60% of its steel from foreign sources. As the Vulcraft Division grew, Nucor became concerned about its ability to obtain an adequate economical supply of steel and in 1968 began construction of its first steel mill in Darlington, South Carolina. By 1972 the Florence, South Carolina, joist plant was purchasing over 90% of its steel from this mill. The Fort Payne plant bought about 50% of its steel from Florence. The other joist plants in Nebraska, Indiana and Texas found transportation costs prohibitive and continued to buy their steel from other steel companies, both foreign and domestic. Since the mill had excess capacity, Nucor began to market its steel products to outside customers. In 1972, 75% of the shipments of Nucor steel was to Vulcraft and 25% was to other customers.[30]

Iverson explained in 1984:

> In constructing these mills we have experimented with new processes and new manufacturing techniques. We serve as our own general contractor and design and build much of our own equipment. In one or more of our mills we have built our own continuous casting unit, reheat furnaces, cooling beds and in Utah even our own mill stands. All of these to date have cost under $125 per ton of annual capacity—compared with projected costs for large integrated mills of $1,200–1,500 per ton of annual capacity, ten times our cost. Our mills have high productivity. We currently use less than four manhours to produce a ton of steel. This includes everyone in the operation: maintenance, clerical, accounting, and sales and management. On the basis of our production workers alone, it is less than three manhours per ton. Our total employment costs are less than $60 per ton compared with the average employment costs of the seven largest U.S. steel companies of close to $130 per ton. Our total labor costs are less than 20% of our sales price.

In contrast to Nucor's less than four manhours, similar Japanese mills were said to require more than five hours and comparable U.S. mills over six hours. Nucor's average yield from molten metal to finished products was over 90 percent compared with an average U.S. steel industry yield of about 74 percent, giving energy costs of about $39 per ton compared with their $75 a ton. Nucor ranked 46th on *Iron Age*'s annual survey of world steel producers. They were second on the list of top ten producers of steel worldwide based on tons per employee, at 981 tons. The head of the list was Tokyo Steel at 1,485. U.S. Steel was 7th at 479. Some other results were: Nippon Steel, 453; British Steel, 213; Bethlehem Steel, 329; Kruppstahl, 195; Weirton Steel, 317; and Northstar Steel, 936. Nucor also ranked 7th on the list ranking growth of raw steel production. U.S. Steel was 5th

30. Harvard Intercollegiate Case Clearing House, Harvard Business School.

on the same list. U.S. Steel topped the list based on improvement in tons-per-employee, at 56 percent; Nucor was 7th with a 12 percent improvement.[31]

THE STEEL MAKING PROCESS

A steel mill's work is divided into two phases, preparation of steel of the proper "chemistry" and the forming of the steel into the desired products. The typical mini-mill utilized scrap steel, such as junk auto parts, instead of the iron ore which would be used in larger, integrated steel mills. The typical mini-mill had an annual capacity of 200–600 thousand tons, compared with the 7 million tons of Bethlehem Steel's Sparrow's Point, Maryland, integrated plant.

A charging bucket fed loads of scrap steel into electric arc furnaces. The melted load, called a heat, was poured into a ladle to be carried by an overhead crane to the casting machine. In the casting machine the liquid steel was extruded as a continuous red-hot solid bar of steel and cut into lengths weighing some 900 pounds called "billets." In the typical plant the billet, about four inches in cross section and about 20 feet long, was held temporarily in a pit where it cooled to normal temperatures. Periodically billets were carried to the rolling mill and placed in a reheat oven to bring them up to 2000°F at which temperature they would be malleable. In the rolling mill, presses and dies progressively converted the billet into the desired round bars, angles, channels, flats, and other products. After cutting to standard lengths, they were moved to the warehouse.

Nucor's first steel mill, employing more than 500 people, was located in Dar lington, South Carolina. The mill, with its three electric arc furnaces, operated 24 hours per day, 5½ days per week. Nucor had made a number of improvements in the melting and casting operations. The former general manager of the Darlington plant had developed a system which involved preheating the ladles, allowing for the faster flow of steel into the caster and resulting in better control of the steel characteristics. Less time and lower capital investment were required. The casting machines were "continuous casters," as opposed to the old batch method. The objective in the "front" of the mill was to keep the casters working. At the time of the Harvard study at Nucor each strand was in operation 90 percent of the time, while a competitor had announced a "record rate" of 75 percent which it had been able to sustain for a week.

Nucor was also perhaps the only mill in the country which regularly avoided the reheating of billets. This saved $10–12 per ton in fuel usage and losses due to oxidation of the steel. The cost of developing this process had been $12 million. All research projects had not been successful. The company spent approximately $2,000,000 in an unsuccessful effort to utilize resistance-heating. They lost even more on an effort at induction melting. As Iverson told *33 Metal Producing*, "That cost us a lot of money. Timewise it was very expensive. But you have got to make mistakes and we've had lots of failures."[32] In the rolling mill, the first machine was a roughing mill by Morgarshammar, the first of its kind in the Western Hemisphere. This Swedish machine had been chosen because of its

31. "1985 Top 50 World Steel Producers," *Iron Age*, May 2, 1986, p. 48B1.
32. Isenberg-O'Loughlin and Innace, "Full Steam Ahead on the Nucor Unlimited," pp. 35–50.

lower cost, higher productivity, and the flexibility. Passing through another five to nine finishing mills converted the billet into the desired finished product. The yield from the billet to finished product was about 93 percent.

The Darlington design became the basis for plants in Nebraska, Texas, and Utah. The Texas plant had cost under $80 per ton of annual capacity. Whereas the typical mini-mill cost approximately $250 per ton, the average cost of all four of Nucor's mills was under $135. An integrated mill was expected to cost between $1,200 and $1,500 per ton.

The Darlington plant was organized into 12 natural groups for the purpose of incentive pay: two mills, each had two shifts with three groups—melting and casting, rolling mill, and finishing. In melting and casting there were three or four different standards, depending on the material, established by the department manager years ago based on historical performance. The general manager stated, "We don't change the standards." The caster, the key to the operation, was used at a 92 percent level—one greater than the claims of the manufacturer. For every good ton of billet above the standard hourly rate for the week, workers in the group received a 4 percent bonus. For example, with a common standard of 10 tons per run hour and an actual rate for the week of 28 tons per hour, the workers would receive a bonus of 72 percent of their base rate in the week's pay check.

In the rolling mill there were more than 100 products, each with a different historical standard. Workers received a 4 percent to 6 percent bonus for every good ton sheared per hour for the week over the computed standard. The Darlington general manager said the standard would be changed only if there was a major machinery change and that a standard had not been changed since the initial development period for the plant. He commented that, in exceeding the standard the worker wouldn't work harder but would cooperate to avoid problems and moved more quickly if a problem developed: "If there is a way to improve output, they will tell us." Another manager added: "Meltshop employees don't ask me how much it costs Chaparral or LTV to make a billet. They want to know what it costs Darlington, Norfolk, Jewitt to put a billet on the ground—scrap costs, alloy costs, electrical costs, refactory, gas, etc. Everybody from Charlotte to Plymouth watches the nickels and dimes."[33]

The Darlington manager, who became COO in 1984, stated:

> "The key to making a profit when selling a product with no aesthetic value, or a product that you really can't differentiate from your competitors, is cost. I don't look at us as a fantastic marketing organization, even though I think we are pretty good; but we don't try to overcome unreasonable costs by mass marketing. We maintain low costs by keeping the employee force at the level it should be, not doing things that aren't necessary to achieve our goals, and allowing people to function on their own and by judging them on their results.
>
> To keep a cooperative and productive workforce you need, number one, to be completely honest about everything; number two, to allow each employee as much as possible to make decisions about that employee's work, to find easier and more productive ways to perform duties; and number three, to be as fair as possible to all employees. Most of the changes we make in work procedures and in equipment come from the employees. They really know the problems of their jobs better than anyone else. We don't have any industrial engineers, nor do we ever intend to, because that's a type of specialist who tends to take responsibility off the top division management and give them a crutch.

33. Interview conducted by Frank C. Barnes.

To communicate with my employees, I try to spend time in the plant and at intervals have meetings with the employees. Usually if they have a question they just visit me. Recently a small group visited me in my office to discuss our vacation policy. They had some suggestions and, after listening to them, I had to agree that the ideas were good."[34]

THE INCENTIVE SYSTEM

The foremost characteristic of Nucor's personnel system was its incentive plan. Another major personnel policy was providing job security. Also all employees at Nucor received the same fringe benefits. There was only one group insurance plan. Holidays and vacations did not differ by job. The company had no executive dining rooms or restrooms, no fishing lodges, no company cars, or reserved parking places.

Absenteeism and tardiness were not problems at Nucor. Each employee had four days of absence before pay was reduced. In addition to these, missing work was allowed for jury duty, military leave, or the death of close relatives. After this, a day's absence cost them bonus pay for that week and lateness of more than a half hour meant the loss of bonus for that day.

Employees were kept informed about the company. Charts showing the division's results in return-on-assets and bonus payoff were posted in prominent places in the plant. The personnel manager commented that as he traveled around to all the plants, he found everyone in the company could tell him the level of profits in their division. The general managers held dinners at least twice a year with their employees. The dinners were held with 50 or 60 employees at a time. After introductory remarks the floor was open for discussion of any work-related problems. The company also had a formal grievance procedure. The Darlington manager couldn't recall the last grievance he had processed.

There was a new employee orientation program and an employee handbook which contained personnel policies and rules. The corporate office sent all news releases to each division where they were posted on bulletin boards. Each employee in the company also received a copy of the Annual Report. For the last several years the cover of the Annual Report had contained the names of all Nucor employees. Every child of every Nucor employee received up to $1,200 a year for four years if they chose to go on to higher education, including technical schools.

The average hourly worker's pay was $31,000, compared with the average earnings in manufacturing in that state of slightly more than $13,000. The personnel manager believed that pay was not the only thing the workers liked about Nucor. He said that an NBC interviewer, working on the documentary "If Japan Can, Why Can't We," often heard, "I enjoy working for Nucor because Nucor is the best, the most productive, and the most profitable company that I know of.[35]

"I honestly feel that if someone performs well, they should share in the company and if they are going to share in the success, they should also share in the failures," Iverson stated.[36] There were four incentive programs at Nucor, one each for production workers, department heads, staff people such as accountants, secretaries, or engineers, and senior management, which included the division managers. All of these programs were on a group basis.

34. Ibid.
35. Ibid.
36. "Nucor's Ken Iverson on Productivity and Pay," *Personnel Administrator*, October 1986, pp. 46–108.

Within the production program, groups ranged in size from 25 to 30 people and had definable and measurable operations. The company believed that a program should be simple and that bonuses should be paid promptly. "We don't have any discretionary bonuses—zero. It is all based on performance. Now we don't want anyone to sit in judgment, because it never is fair...," said Iverson. The personnel manager stated: "Their bonus is based on roughly 90 percent of historical time it takes to make a particular joist. If during a week they make joists at 60 percent less than the standard time, they received a 60 percent bonus." This was paid with the regular pay the following week. The complete pay check amount, including overtime, was multiplied by the bonus factor. Bonus was not paid when equipment was not operating: "We have the philosophy that when equipment is not operating everybody suffers and the bonus for downtime is zero."[37] The foremen are also part of the group and received the same bonus as the employees they supervised.

The second incentive program was for department heads in the various divisions. The incentive pay here was based on division contribution, defined as the division earnings before corporate expenses and profit sharing are determined. Bonuses were reported to run as high as 51 percent of a person's base salary in the divisions and 30 percent for corporate positions.

Officers of the company were under a single profit sharing plan. Their base salaries were approximately 75 percent of comparable positions in industry. Once return-on-equity reached 9 percent, slightly below the average for manufacturing firms, 5 percent of net earnings before taxes went into a pool that was divided among the officers based on their salaries. "Now if return-on-equity for the company reaches, say 20 percent, which it has, then we can wind up with as much as 190 percent of our base salaries and 115 percent on top of that in stock. We get both."[38] In 1982 the return was 9 percent and the executives received no bonus. Iverson's pay in 1981 was approximately $300,000 but dropped the next year to $110,000. "I think that ranked by total compensation I was the lowest paid CEO in the Fortune 500. I was kind of proud of that, too."[39] In 1986, Iverson's stock was worth over $10 million. The young Vulcraft manager was likewise a millionaire.

There was a third plan for people who were neither production workers nor department managers. Their bonus was based on either the division return-on-assets or the corporate return-on-assets.

The fourth program was for the senior officers. The senior officers had no employment contracts, pension or retirement plans, or other normal perquisites. Their base salaries were set at about 70 percent of what an individual doing similar work in other companies would receive. More than half of the officer's compensation was reported to be based directly on the company's earnings. Ten percent of pretax earnings over a pre-established level, based on a 12 percent return on stockholders' equity, was set aside and allocated to the senior officers according to their base salary. Half the bonus was paid in cash and half was deferred.

In lieu of a retirement plan, the company had a profit sharing plan with a deferred trust. Each year 10 percent of pretax earnings was put into profit

37. Ibid.
38. Ibid.
39. Ibid.

sharing. Fifteen percent of this was set aside to be paid to employees in the following March as a cash bonus and the remainder was put into trust for each employee on the basis of percent of their earnings as a percent of total wages paid within the corporation. The employee was vested 20 percent after the first year and gained an additional 10 percent vesting each year thereafter. Employees received a quarterly statement of their balance in profit sharing.

The company had an Employer Monthly Stock Investment Plan to which Nucor added 10 percent to the amount the employee contributed and paid the commission on the purchase of any Nucor stock. After each five years of service with the company, the employee received a service award consisting of five shares of Nucor stock. Additionally, if profits were good, extraordinary bonus payments would be made to the employees. In December 1988, each employee received a $500 payment.

According to Iverson:

> I think the first obligation of the company is to the stockholder and to its employees. I find in this country too many cases where employees are underpaid and corporate management is making huge social donations for self-fulfillment. We regularly give donations, but we have a very interesting corporate policy. First, we give donations where our employees are. Second, we give donations which will benefit our employees, such as the YMCA. It is a difficult area and it requires a lot of thought. There is certainly a strong social responsibility for a company, but it cannot be at the expense of the employees or the stockholders.[40]

Nucor had no trouble finding people to staff its plants. When the mill in Jewett, Texas, was built in 1975, there were over 5,000 applications for the 400 jobs—many coming from people in Houston and Dallas. Yet everyone did not find work at Nucor what they wanted. In 1975, a Harvard team found high turnover among new production workers after start-up. The cause appeared to be pressure from fellow workers in the group incentive situation. A survival-of-the-fittest situation was found in which those who didn't like to work seldom stuck around. "Productivity increased and turnover declined dramatically once these people left," the Harvard team concluded. Iverson commented: "A lot of people aren't goal-oriented. A lot of them don't want to work that hard, so initially we have a lot of turnover in a plant but then it's so low we don't even measure after that."[41]

The Wall Street Journal reported in 1981:

> Harry Pigg, a sub-director for the USW in South Carolina, sees a darker side in Nucor's incentive plan. He contends that Nucor unfairly penalizes workers by taking away big bonus payments for absence or tardiness, regardless of the reason. Workers who are ill, he says, try to work because they can't afford to give up the bonus payment. "Nucor whips them into line," he adds. He acknowledges, though, that high salaries are the major barrier to unionizing the company.[42]

Having welcomed a parade of visitors over the years, Iverson had become concerned with the pattern: "They only do one or two of the things we do. It's not just incentives or the scholarship program; it's all those things put together that results in a unified philosophy for the company."

40. Ibid.
41. "A Calm Hand in an Industry Under the Gun," *The Business Journal*, September 5, 1986, p. 9.
42. Sease, "Mini-Mill Steelmakers," pp. 1, 19.

AS 1990 BEGAN

Looking ahead in 1984, Iverson had said: "The next decade will be an exciting one for steel producers. It will tax our abilities to keep pace with technological changes we can see now on the horizon." Imports didn't have to dominate the U.S. economy. He believed the steel industry would continue to play a pivotal role in the growth of American industry. He pointed out comparative advantages of the U.S. steel industry: an abundance of resources, relatively low energy costs, lower transportation costs, and the change in the government's attitude toward business.

The excitement he had predicted had occurred. Imports were a challenge for steel, just as for textiles, shoes, machine tools, and computers. The old steel companies were flexing their muscle and getting back into the game. Overcapacity hadn't left the mini-mill immune; there was no safe haven for anyone. Nucor was no longer a small company, David, with free shots at Goliath.

The honeymoon appeared over. Wall Street worried about what Nucor should do. Cable News Network posed the position of some on Wall Street: "They say basically you guys are selling to the construction companies; you are selling to some fairly depressed industries. They also say, Nucor, they were a specialized little niche company. They did what they did very well; but now all of a sudden, they are going out, building these big mills to make huge pieces of steel and they are talking casted cold, all that stuff. They're worried that you may be getting into deals that are a little too complicated from what they perceive you as being able to do well."[43]

The New York Times pointed out that expansion would certainly hurt earnings for the next several years. They quoted a steel consultant. "It is hard to do all that they are trying to do and keep profits up. With the industry in the shape it's in, this is not the time to expand beyond the niche they've established."[44]

When they were sitting with $185 million in cash, Iverson told *Inc.:* "It (going private) has been mentioned to us by a number of brokerage firms and investment houses, but we wouldn't even consider it. It wouldn't be fair to employees, and I don't know whether it would be fair to the stockholders.... You're going to restrict the growth opportunities.... You either grow or die.... Opportunities wouldn't be created for people within the company."[45]

Iverson told CNN: "We've decided that really we want to stay in that niche (steel). We don't want to buy any banks.... All of the growth of the company has been internally generated. We think there are opportunities in the steel industry today.... There are ample opportunities, although they are somewhat harder to find than they used to be."[46]

"Another of my strengths is the ability to stick to my knitting. The reason executives make a lot of mistakes is that sometimes they get bored—they think the grass is greener on the other side so they go out and buy a bank or an oil company or they go into business where they have no expertise.... I have never gotten bored with this company. I've done this job so long that I think I have

43. "Inside Business," Interview with Ken Iverson, Cable News Network, August 17, 1986.
44. "Nucor's Ambitious Expansion," *The New York Times*, June 30, 1986.
45. "Steel Man Ken Iverson," *Inc.*, April 1986, p. 48.
46. "Inside Business," Interview.

some insight into the needs and the capabilities of the company. I'm not misled into thinking we can do something that we can't."[47]

An economics professor and steel consultant at Middle Tennessee State University told the *Times*, "You're not going to see any growth in the steel market, so the only way to make money is to reduce costs and have new technology to penetrate other companies' business."[48]

The New York Times stated: "Critics question whether it is wise to continue expanding production capabilities, as Nucor is doing, when there is already overcapacity in the steel industry and intense competition already exists between the mini-mills." Iverson insisted the strategy would pay off in the long-term. He told the *Times*, "The company's strategy makes sense for us. To gain a larger share in an ever-shrinking market, you've got to take something from someone else."[49]

They had sold the Chemicals Division, gotten into the structural steel components business, into the fastener industry, and should soon be ready to go head-to-head with the major integrated producers for the lucrative flat-rolled market. Sales and earnings were projected to double in the next two years, as the stock price doubled or tripled.

Iverson's position was clear: "We're going to stay in steel and steel products. The way we look at it, this company does only two things well, builds plants economically and runs them efficiently. That is the whole company. We don't have any financial expertise, we're not entrepreneurs, we're not into acquisitions. Steel may not be the best business in the world, but it's what we know how to do and we do it well."

47. "A Calm Hand," p. 9.
48. "Nucor's Ambitious Expansion," June 30, 1986.
49. Ibid.

CASE

26 Hanson PLC

INTRODUCTION

Hanson PLC is one of the ten biggest companies in Britain, and its U.S. arm, Hanson Industries, is one of America's sixty largest industrial concerns. A conglomerate with over 150 different businesses in its portfolio, Hanson PLC has grown primarily by making acquisitions. By the end of 1989 the company had recorded twenty-six years of uninterrupted profit growth, cumulating in 1989 operating income of $1.61 billion on revenues of $11.3 billion and assets of $12.03 billion. The company's shareholders have been major beneficiaries of this growth. Between 1974 and 1989 the price of the company's shares on the London Stock Exchange increased eighty-fold, compared with an average increase of fifteen-fold for all companies quoted on the London Stock Exchange during this period.[1] Along the way, Hanson has gained a reputation for being one of the most successful takeover machines in the world. Its acquisitions during the 1980s included three American conglomerates (U.S. Industries, SCM Corporation, and Kidde) and three major British companies (London Brick, the Imperial Group, and Consolidated Gold Fields). So high is Hanson's profile that Oliver Stone, in his film *Wall Street*, reportedly used Sir Gordon White, head of Hanson Industries, as the model for the British corporate raider—the one who outmaneuvered the evil Gordon Gekko.

Despite this impressive track record, as Hanson enters the 1990s analysts increasingly wonder about the strategy of the company. There is speculation that the company may be on the verge of breaking itself up and returning the gains to shareholders. The age of the company's founders is fueling this speculation. The two men who built and still run the conglomerate, Lord Hanson and Sir Gordon White, are in their late sixties and both have promised to consider retiring when they are seventy. As one insider put it, "the guys that started it off will finish it off."[2] Another factor is that Hanson is now so big that it would take some spectacular deals to continue its historic growth rate. According to many, including Harvard Business School strategy guru Michael Porter, there simply are not that many obvious companies for Hanson to buy, thus "Even Hanson will be faced with poorer and poorer odds of maintaining its record."[3] On the other hand, at the end of 1989 Hanson had $8.5 billion in cash on its balance

This case was prepared by Charles W. L. Hill, University of Washington. The case was made possible by the generous assistance of Hanson Industries. It is intended as a basis for classroom discussion, rather than to illustrate either effective or ineffective handling of an administrative situation.

1. "The Conglomerate as Antique Dealer," *The Economist*, March 11, 1989, pp. 71–73.
2. Quoted ibid.
3. Quoted in John Byrne and Mark Maremont, "Hanson: The Dangers of Living by Takeover Alone," *Business Week*, August 15, 1988, pp. 62–64.

sheet. That, along with the billions it could borrow if need be (the company reportedly has a borrowing capacity of $20 billion), suggests that if Hanson and White should so wish, they could undertake an acquisition that would rival the RJR-Nabisco deal in size.

Other commentators question the long-term viability of the company. Some claim that Hanson PLC is little more than an asset stripper that in the long run will drive companies it manages into the ground. According to one investment banker, "I'm not convinced that Hanson runs companies any better than anyone else. But I certainly know it squeezes them for cash, sucking the life from them."[4] Similarly, one former executive noted that "Some of the incentive programs that they write for managers actually keep the company from growing.... They become so concerned with profit today that they don't re-invest for tomorrow."[5] The company disagrees. Sir Gordon White clearly sees Hanson PLC as reducing inefficiencies in the companies it acquires, not stripping assets. If anything is stripped away from acquisitions, according to White, it is unnecessary corporate bureaucracy, overstaffed head offices, and top-management perks, not assets; and he steadfastly maintains that the company treats all acquired businesses as if it were going to keep them.[6]

With these issues in mind, in this case we consider the growth and development of Hanson PLC. We review the administrative systems that the company uses to manage its ongoing businesses, and we look at two acquisitions and their aftermath in depth: the 1987 acquisitions of SCM Corporation and the Imperial Group.

HISTORY

The origins of Hanson PLC go back to the port city of Hull in Yorkshire, England, in the 1950s.[7] At that time, James Hanson was learning his family's transportation business (the family operated a fleet of passenger coaches) and Gordon White was selling advertising for Welbecson Limited, a magazine printing company owned by his father. James Hanson's brother, Bill, was White's closest friend, and when Bill died of cancer at twenty-nine, James and Gordon became close friends. In the late 1950s Hanson and White decided to team up in business. They formed Hanson White Ltd., a greeting card company. Although the company did well, the two soon became bored with the limited challenges and potential that the greeting card business offered, and in 1963 they sold out and began to look for acquisition opportunities.

Their first buy was Oswald Tillotson Ltd., a vehicle distribution company. This company was subsequently acquired by Wiles Group Ltd., a Yorkshire-based manufacturer of agricultural sacks and fertilizers. As part of the takeover deal Hanson and White were given a substantial ownership position in the Wiles

4. Quoted in Andrew Marton, "The Buccaneer from Britain," *Mergers and Acquisitions* (February 1987), 141–146.
5. Quoted in Byrne and Maremont, "Hanson: The Dangers," pp. 62–64.
6. Gordon White, "How I Turned $3,000 into $10 billion," *Fortune*, November 7, 1988, pp. 80–89.
7. The material in this section is based on the following sources: White, "How I Turned," pp. 80–89; Marton, "The Buccaneer from Britain," pp. 141–146; and Hope Lampert, "Britons on the Prowl," *The New York Times Magazine*, November 29, 1987, pp. 22–24, 36, 38, 42.

Group. Hanson and White soon gained management control of the Wiles Group, and in 1969, after deciding that James Hanson's name had a nicer ring to it than Gordon White's, they changed the name to Hanson Trust. Because of a series of small acquisitions, by the end of 1973 Hanson Trust owned twenty-four companies with combined sales of $120 million.

By 1973, however, the British economy was in deep trouble. The stock market had collapsed; the country was paralyzed by labor disputes; inflation was increasing rapidly, as was unemployment; and Prime Minister Edward Heath of the supposedly probusiness Conservative party had blasted conglomerate companies like Hanson Trust as representing "the unacceptable face of capitalism." All of this prompted Gordon White to rethink his future. As White put it, "I was disgusted with England at the time. Disgusted with socialism and unions and excessive, antibusiness government, disgusted with the way initiative was being taxed out of existence.... I'd done a lot of thinking. I told James (Hanson) that maybe we should call it a day. I thought I'd try America."[8] Hanson replied that there was no need to split up, and they agreed that Hanson would run the British operations while White tried to build operations in America.

White arrived in New York in the fall of 1973 in possession of a round-trip ticket, a one-year work visa, and $3,000 in travelers checks, which was the most the British currency controls permitted a U.K. citizen to take abroad at that time. Moreover, because of British exchange controls White could not gain access to Hanson's ample treasury without substantial penalties, and he had to struggle to convince banks that he was creditworthy. Despite this, in 1974 White managed to borrow $32 million from Chemical Bank to finance his first major U.S. acquisition, a friendly takeover of J. Howard Smith Company, a New Jersey–based processor of edible oils and animal feed that was later renamed Seacoast Products. The CEO of J. Howard Smith was David Clarke, whose family business it was. Clarke subsequently became White's right-hand man. He is now president of Hanson Industries and the most senior executive in the United States after White.

Over the next ten years White made another six major U.S. acquisitions, all of them friendly (these are listed in Exhibit 1). Then in 1984 White was ready for his first hostile takeover, the $532-million purchase of U.S. Industries (USI). USI was a conglomerate that had grown by acquisitions during the 1960s and 1970s. White became interested in the company when he read in a newspaper that management was putting together a leveraged buyout at $20 a share for a total purchase price of $445 million. He suspected that the company was worth more than that and quickly worked out how big a loan Hanson Industries could handle, using USI's projected cash flow to cover interest charges. To USI's pre-tax earnings of $67 million he added $40 million generated by depreciation and $24 million in savings that he thought Hanson could effect by removing USI's corporate headquarters. That yielded a total cash flow of $131 million, or more than $70 million after taxes. With interest rates running at 13 percent, White figured that Hanson Industries could afford a $544-million loan. In what was to become standard White thinking, he also reckoned that even with a worst-case scenario, he could recoup his investment by selling off the disparate pieces of the company.

Hanson Industries began to buy USI shares and by April 1984 held 5 percent of the company. Hanson then made a $19 per share bid for the company, which was quickly rebuffed by USI management. Three days later White increased Hanson's bid to $22 per share. USI's management, which had yet to raise the

8. White, "How I Turned," p. 81.

Exhibit 1
U.S. Acquisitions, 1974–1987

Acquisition		Cost (millions)	Businesses
1974	Seacoast	$32	Fish processing, pet food
1975	Carisbrook	$36	Textile manufacturing
1976	Hygrade	$32	Castings and casing units
1977	Old Salt Seafood	$2	Prepared foods
1978	Interstate United	$30	Food service management
1978	Templon	$7	Textile manufacturing
1981	McDonough	$185	Cement, concrete
1984	U.S. Industries	$532	33-company conglomerate
1986	SCM	$930	22-company conglomerate
1987	Kaiser Cement	$250	Cement plants
1988	Kidde	$1,700	108-company conglomerate
1990	Peabody	$1,230	Coal mining

Source: Adapted from Gordon White, "How I Turned $3,000 into $10 Billion," *Fortune*, November 7, 1988, pp. 80–89; and "Hanson PLC," *Value Line*, July 20, 1990, p. 832.

financing for its own proposed leveraged buyout, responded by increasing the purchase price to $24 per share. Hanson responded by initiating a tender offer of $23 per share in cash. For stockholders cash in hand at $23 per share was far more attractive than management's promise of $24 per share if financing could be arranged, and Hanson's bid quickly won the day.

After the acquisition was completed, Hanson Industries president David Clarke spent six months at USI's corporate headquarters reviewing operations. At the end of this period USI's corporate headquarters was closed down, the staff was laid off, and financial control was centralized at Hanson Industries' small headquarters. However, most of the operating managers in charge of USI's constituent companies stayed on, lured by Hanson's incentive pay scheme and the promise that they could run their own shows. In what was also typical Hanson fashion, nine of USI's operating companies were subsequently sold off to outside investors for a price of $225 million.

The acquisition of USI was followed by three other hostile takeover bids in the United States: for SCM Corporation, Kaiser Cement, and Kidde. Of these, the SCM bid was by far the most acrimonious. SCM took a poison pill and tried to protect its position through the law courts before Hanson finally won control over the company (the SCM takeover is discussed in detail later in the case).

While White was making these U.S. acquisitions, Hanson was not sitting idle in Britain. During the 1980s the company made a series of acquisitions in the United Kingdom. These are summarized in Exhibit 2. The most notable were the 1983 acquisition of London Brick, Britain's largest brick manufacturer, against vigorous opposition from London Brick's incumbent management; the £2.36–billion acquisition of Imperial, the largest tobacco company in Britain and the third largest in the world; and the £3.61–billion acquisition of Consolidated Gold Fields, the second largest gold-mining business in the world. The acquisitions of Imperial and Consolidated Gold Fields were the two largest takeovers ever undertaken in Britain (the Imperial takeover is discussed in detail later in this case).

Exhibit 2
U.K. Acquisitions During the 1980s

Acquisition		Cost (millions)	Businesses
1981	Ever Ready	£95	Dry cell batteries
1983	UDS	£250	Retail operations
1984	London Brick	£247	Brick manufacturer
1984	Powell Duffryn	£150	Engineering, shipping, fuel
1986	Imperial Group	£2,500	Tobacco, brewing, food
1989	Consolidated Gold Fields	£3,610	Gold mining, building aggregates

Source: Various press reports.

ACQUISITIONS PHILOSOPHY

Hanson PLC's acquisitions on both sides of the Atlantic are primarily overseen by Sir Gordon White. Lord Hanson is primarily responsible for the ongoing administration of the company. As Lord Hanson says of White, "He's the one with the gift for takeovers."[9] In turn, White says of Hanson, "James is a brilliant administrator and really knows how to run a company."[10] White claims that many of his acquisition ideas, including the USI deal, come from the newspapers. Others are suggested to him by contacts in the investment banking community, particularly Bob Pirie, president of the Rothschild investment bank, with whom White has lunch once a week.

Whenever possible, White avoids working at the office, opting instead to work from one of his houses. Unlike corporate raiders such as Saul Steinberg and Carl Icahn, White rarely reads annual reports or detailed stock reports on a target company, claiming that he can get all of the financial information that he needs from Standard & Poor's two page summaries. In addition, his three-man takeover staff distills reams of financial data on a target and provides him with a short memo on the target company. Says White, "I'm like Churchill, tell me everything you can tell me. On one page."[11]

Under White's leadership, one of the things that has distinguished Hanson PLC from many other acquisitive conglomerates is its distinctive acquisitions philosophy (which is in essence White's philosophy). This philosophy appears to be based on a number of consistent factors that are found to underlie most of Hanson's acquisitions.[12]

1. *Target characteristics* Hanson looks for companies based in mature, low-technology industries that have a less-than-inspiring record but show potential for improving performance. Normally the objective has been to identify a poorly performing target where the incumbent management team has gone some way toward improving the underlying performance but those efforts

9. Quoted in Lampert, "Britons on the Prowl," p. 36.
10. Quoted in White, "How I Turned," p. 81.
11. Quoted in Lampert, "Britons on the Prowl," p. 24.
12. The material in this section is based on the following sources: White, "How I Turned," pp. 80–89; Lampert, "Britons on the Prowl," p. 22–24, 36, 38, 42; and Mark Cusack, *Hanson Trust: A Review of the Company and Its Prospects* (London: Hoare Govett Limited, 1987).

have not yet been reflected in either the profit-and-loss account or, more importantly, the target's stock price.

2. *Research* Although White claims that he does little reading on takeover targets, his takeover staff does undertake detailed research into the potential of target companies before any bid is made. The staff routinely investigates companies undertaking leveraged buyouts.
3. *Risk assessment* One of White's most often quoted edicts is "watch the downside." What this means is that instead of considering the potential benefits of a deal, give consideration to what can go wrong and the likely consequences of a worst-case scenario. White will purchase a company only if he thinks that in a worst-case scenario he will be able to recover the purchase price by breaking the target up and selling off its constituent parts.
4. *Funding* White was one of the early pioneers of the highly leveraged takeover deal. All of the U.S. acquisitions have been financed by nonrecourse debt, secured on the assets of the target. This enabled White to engineer substantial acquisitions when Hanson Industries itself had a very small capital base. The British acquisitions have been funded by a mix of cash, equity, convertible securities, and loan stock.
5. *Disposals to reduce debt* After an acquisition has been completed, Hanson sends some of its own managers along with a group of external accountants to go through and audit the acquired business. After a thorough review, Hanson typically sells off the parts of the acquired company that cannot reach Hanson's stringent profitability targets. In the process, Hanson is able to reduce the debt taken on to fund the acquisition. The most outstanding example followed the purchase of SCM for $930 million. After the takeover Hanson sold off SCM's real estate, pulp and paper, and food holdings for a price of $964 million while holding on to SCM's typewriter and chemicals business, which in effect had been acquired for nothing. Thus, within six months of the takeover's being completed, Hanson was able to eliminate the debt taken on to finance the SCM acquisition. Similar, although less spectacular, disposals have characterized almost all of Hanson's major acquisitions on both sides of the Atlantic.
6. *Elimination of excess overhead* Another objective of Hanson's "housecleaning" of acquired companies is to eliminate any excess overhead. This typically involves closing down the corporate headquarters of the acquired company, eliminating some of the staff while sending other staff down to the operating level. Before Hanson took over, SCM had 230 people in its corporate office, USI had 180, Kidde had 200, and Hanson itself had 30. Today the total headquarters staff for all four is 120.

   Hanson also disposes of any management perks found either at the corporate or the operating level of an acquired company. For example, one of Kidde's operating companies had a collection of art and antiques, a hunting lodge, and three corporate jets. Hanson kept one jet and disposed of the rest, including the man at the top who had spent the money.
7. *The creation of incentives* Hanson tries to create strong incentives for the management of acquired operating companies to improve performance. This is achieved by (1) decentralization designed to give operating managers full autonomy for the running of their businesses, (2) motivating operating managers by setting profit targets that, if achieved, will result in significant profit enhancements, and (3) motivating managers by giving them large pay bonuses if they hit or exceed Hanson's profit targets.

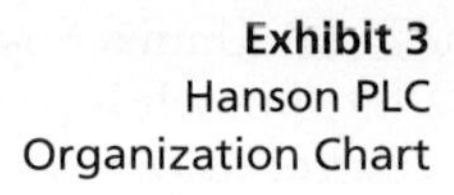
Exhibit 3
Hanson PLC
Organization Chart

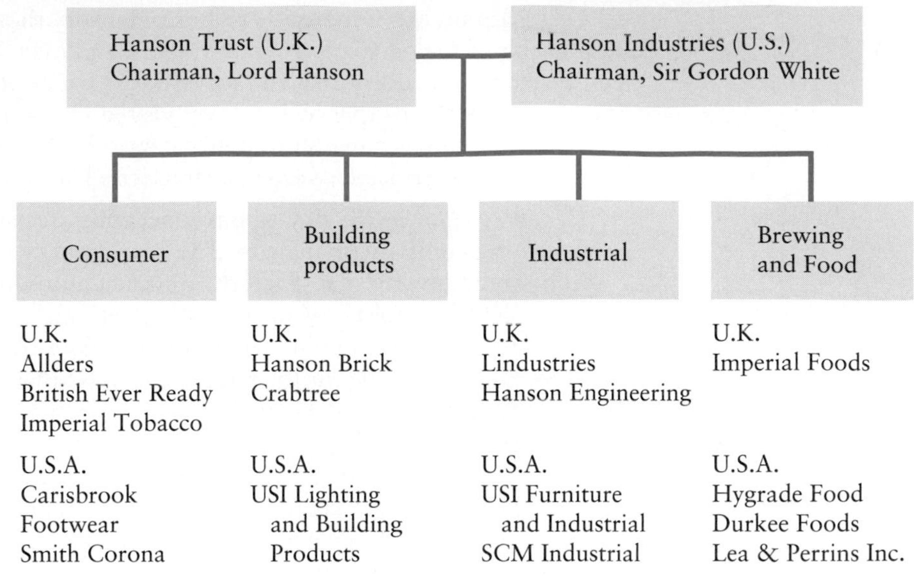

Source: Hanson Industries, *Annual Report*, 1986.

ORGANIZATION AND MANAGEMENT PHILOSOPHY

In addition to its acquisitions philosophy, Hanson is also renowned for its ongoing management of operating companies—of which there are over 150 in the corporate portfolio. Although Hanson does have some interests elsewhere, the strategic development of the group has centered on the United States and Britain, where a broad balance has tended to exist in recent years. Hanson PLC looks after the British operations, and Hanson Industries, the U.S. subsidiary, manages the U.S. operations. Each of these two units is operated on an entirely autonomous basis. Only one director sits on the board of both companies. Hanson PLC is headed by Lord Hanson; Hanson Industries is headed by Sir Gordon White.[13]

There are two corporate headquarters, one in the United States and one in Britain. At both locations there is a small central staff responsible for monitoring the performance of operating companies, selecting and motivating operating management, the treasury function (including acting as a central bank for the operating units), acquisitions and disposals, and professional services such as legal and taxation.

Below each headquarters are a number of divisions (see Exhibit 3). These are not operating companies. Rather, they are groupings of operating companies. In 1988 there were four U.S. divisions (consumer, building products, industrial, and food) and four British divisions (again, consumer, building products, industrial, and food). There are no personnel at the divisional level with the exception of a divisional CEO. Below the divisions are the operating companies. Each operating company has its own CEO who reports to the divisional CEO. The divisional

13. The material in this section is based on the following sources: Cusack, *Hanson Trust*; "The Conglomerate as Antique Dealer," pp. 71–73; Byrne and Maremont, "Hanson: The Dangers," pp. 62–64; and Gordon White, "Nothing Hurts More Than a Bogus Bonus," *The Wall Street Journal*, July 20, 1987, p. 18.

CEOs in Britain are responsible to Lord Hanson; those in the United States are responsible to David Clarke, White's right-hand man. White himself is primarily concerned with acquisitions and leaves most issues of control to David Clarke. Indeed, White claims that he has never visited Hanson Industries' U.S. corporate headquarters and as a matter of policy never visits operating companies.[14]

The following principles seem to characterize Hanson's management philosophy:

1. *Decentralization* All day-to-day operating decisions are decentralized to operating company managers. The corporate center does not offer suggestions about how to manufacture or market a product. Thus, within the limits set by centrally approved operating budgets and capital expenditures, operating management has unlimited autonomy. As a consequence, operating managers are responsible for the return on capital that they employ.
2. *Tight financial control* Financial control is achieved through two devices: (1) operating budgets and (2) capital expenditure policies. In a bottom-up process, operating budgets are submitted annually to the corporate center by operating company managers. The budgets include detailed performance targets, particularly with regard to return on capital employed (ROK). Corporate staff reviews the budgets and, after consultation with operating management, approves a budget for the coming year. Once agreed upon, the operating budget becomes "gospel." The performance of an operating company is compared against budget on a monthly basis, and any variance is investigated by the corporate center. If an operating company betters its projected ROK, the figure used as the base for next year's budget is the actual ROK, not the budgeted figure.

   Any cash generated by an operating company is viewed as belonging to the corporate center, not to the operating company. Capital expenditures are extremely closely monitored. All cash expenditures in excess of $3,000 (£1,000 in Britain) have to be agreed upon by corporate headquarters. Capital expenditure requests are frequently challenged by headquarters staff. For example, a manager who contends that an investment in more efficient machinery will cut labor costs must even provide the names of the employees that he or she expects to lay off to achieve the savings. According to company insiders, when justifying a request for capital expenditure, a manager must explain every possibility. In general, Hanson looks for a pre-tax payback on expenditures of three years. The quicker the payback, the more likely it is that an expenditure will be approved.
3. *Incentive systems* A major element of the pay of operating managers is linked directly to operating company performance. A manager can earn up to 60 percent of his or her base salary if the operating company exceeds the ROK target detailed in its annual budget. Bonuses are based strictly on bottom-line performance. As White puts it, "there are no bonuses for being a nice chap."[15] In addition, there is a share option scheme for the most senior operating company and corporate managers. Over 600 managers are members of the option scheme. The options are not exercisable for at least three years after they have been granted.
4. *Board structure* No operating company managers are ever appointed to the board of either Hanson PLC or Hanson Industries. The idea is to eliminate any conflicts of interest that might arise over budgets and capital expenditures.

14. White, "How I Turned," p. 81.
15. White, "Nothing Hurts More," p. 18.

Exhibit 4
SCM Divisional Results for Year to June 1985

Division	Revenues		Profits	
	$m	% change from 1984	$m	% change from 1984
Chemicals	539	+49%	73.7	–100%
Coatings and resins	687	+5%	49.9	–3%
Paper and pulp	362	+3%	23.1	+10%
Foods	422	+7%	23.0	+35%
Typewriters	176	–11%	(47.4)[a]	–200%

[a]Loss after a $35m charge for restructuring.

Source: Data from Hanson Industries, *Annual Report*, 1986.

5. *De-emphasizing operating synergy* In contrast to many diversified companies, Hanson has no interest in trying to realize operating synergy. For example, two of Hanson PLC's subsidiaries, Imperial Tobacco and Elizabeth Shaw (a chocolate firm), are based in Bristol, England, and both deliver goods to news agents and corner shops around Britain. However, Hanson prohibits them from sharing distribution because it reckons that any economies of scale that result would be outweighed by the inefficiencies that would arise if each operating company could blame the other for distribution problems.

THE SCM ACQUISITION

SCM was a diversified manufacturer of consumer and industrial products. SCM had twenty-two operating companies based in five industries: chemicals, coatings and resins, paper and pulp, foods, and typewriters.[16] Among other things, SCM was the world's leading manufacturer of portable typewriters (Smith-Corona typewriters), the world's third largest producer of titanium dioxide (a white inorganic pigment widely used in the manufacture of paint, paper, plastic, and rubber products), the sixth largest paint manufacturer in the world through its Glidden Paints subsidiary, and a major force in the U.S. food industry through its Durkee Famous Foods group (see Exhibit 4).

Attractions to Hanson

The SCM group was first brought to Gordon White's attention by Bob Pirie, president of Rothschild Inc. in New York. Pirie thought, and Hanson's research team soon confirmed, that SCM had a number of characteristics that made it a perfect Hanson buy.

1. *Poor financial performance* Summary financial data for SCM are given in Exhibit 5. Pre-tax profit had declined from a peak of $83.2 million in 1980 to $54.1 million in 1985. The 1985 return on equity of 7.7 percent was very poor by Hanson's standards, and earnings per share had declined by 19 percent since 1980.

16. Most of the detail in this section is drawn from two sources: Cusack, *Hanson Trust*; and Lampert, "Britons on the Prowl," pp. 22–24, 36, 38, 42.

Exhibit 5
Financial Data for SCM

	1980	1981	1982	1983	1984	1985
Net sales ($m)	1,745	1,761	1,703	1,663	1,963	2,175
Pre-tax profits ($m)	83.2	72.6	35.3	37.8	64.8	54.1
Earnings per share ($)—fully diluted	4.76	5.01	3.20	2.63	4.05	3.85
Return on equity (%)	12.4	12.0	5.80	4.90	8.0	7.70

Source: Data from Hanson Industries, *Annual Report*, 1986.

2. *Beginnings of a turnaround* There were signs that incumbent management was coming to grips with SCM's problems—particularly in the troubled typewriter operation, where the 1985 loss was due to a one-time charge of $39 million for restructuring. Financial performance had improved since the low point in 1983, but the benefits of this improvement were not yet reflected in the company's stock price.
3. *Mature businesses* SCM's presence in mature proven markets that were technologically stable fit White's preferences.
4. *Low risk* Some 50 percent of SCM's turnover covered products well known to the U.S. consumer (for example, Smith-Corona typewriters, Glidden paint, Durkee foods). White felt that there would be a ready market for such highly branded businesses if Hanson decided to dispose of any companies that did not meet its stringent ROK requirements.
5. *Titanium dioxide* Titanium dioxide was dominated by a global oligopoly. Hanson was aware of two favorable trends in the industry that made high returns likely: (1) worldwide demand was forecasted to exceed supply for the next few years, and (2) input costs were declining because of the currency weakness of the major raw-material source, Australia.
6. *Corporate overhead* A corporate staff of 230 indicated to White that SCM was "a lumbering old top-heavy conglomerate with a huge corporate overhead that was draining earnings."[17] He envisaged substantial savings from the elimination of this overhead.

The Takeover Battle

After reviewing the situation, in early August White decided to acquire SCM. He began to buy stock, and on August 21 Hanson Industries formally made a $60 per share tender offer for SCM, valuing the company at $740 million. SCM's top-management team responded on August 30 with its own offer to shareholders in the form of a proposed leveraged buyout of SCM. SCM's management had arranged financing from its investment banker Merrill Lynch and offered shareholders $70 per share. On September 4 White responded by raising Hanson's offer to $72 per share.

SCM's management responded to White's second offer by increasing its own offer to $74 per share. To discourage White from making another bid, SCM's management gave Merrill Lynch a "lock-up" option to buy Durkee Famous Foods and SCM Chemicals (the titanium dioxide division) at a substantial

17. White, "How I Turned," p. 84.

discount should Hanson or another outsider gain control. In effect, SCM's management had agreed to give its "crown jewels" to Merrill Lynch for less than their market value if Hanson won the bidding war.

White's next move was to apparently throw in the towel by announcing withdrawal of Hanson's tender offer. However, in contrast to normal practice on Wall Street, White went into the market and quickly purchased some 25 percent of SCM's stock at a fixed price of $73.5 per share, taking Hanson's stake to 27 percent. Furious at this break with convention, SCM's lawyers drafted a lawsuit against Hanson charging that White's tactics violated tender-offer regulations and demanding a restraining order prohibiting Hanson from making any further market purchases. Hanson quickly filed a counter suit, claiming that Merrill Lynch's "lock-up" option to buy the SCM divisions illegally prevented the shareholders from getting the best price.

Hanson lost both suits in federal court in New York. White immediately appealed and on September 30 a U.S. court of appeals ruled in Hanson's favor. This, however, was not to be the end of the matter. On October 7 Hanson spent another $40 million to increase its stake in SCM to 33 percent, thereby effectively stalling the leveraged buyout plan, which needed approval by two-thirds of the shareholders. The following day Hanson revised its tender offer to an all-cash $75 per share offer, subject to SCM dropping the "lock-up" provision. Merrill Lynch responded by indicating that it intended to exercise the "lock-up" option because the option had been triggered by Hanson's acquiring 33 percent of SCM.

Hanson's next move, on October 10, was to file a suit to prevent Merrill Lynch from exercising the right to buy SCM's crown jewels. On October 15 it followed this with a second suit against Merrill Lynch for conspiracy. A U.S. district court ruled on November 26 that the "lock-up" was legal and that Hanson had triggered its exercise by the size of its stake. Once again Hanson appealed to a higher court. On January 6, 1986, a U.S. court of appeals overturned the lower court ruling, granting to Hanson an injunction that prevented SCM from exercising the "lock-up" option. The following day Hanson Industries won control over SCM after further market purchases. The final purchase price was $930 million, which represented a price/earnings multiple of 11.5.

After the Acquisition

Having gained control of SCM, Hanson immediately set about trying to realize SCM's potential. Within three months, 250 employees were laid off, mostly headquarters staff, and the former SCM headquarters in New York was sold for $36 million in cash. At the same time, White and his team were using their new position as owners to thoroughly audit the affairs of SCM's operating companies. Their objective was to identify those businesses whose returns were adequate or could be improved upon and those businesses for which the outlook was such that they were unlikely to achieve Hanson's stringent ROK requirements.

At the end of this process, four businesses were sold off in as many months for a total amount that recouped for Hanson the original purchase price and left Hanson with the two best businesses in SCM's portfolio: Smith-Corona typewriters and the titanium dioxide business. In May 1986 SCM's paper and pulp operations were sold to Boise Cascade for $160 million in cash, a price that represented a price/earnings multiple of 29 and was 3 times book value. Hanson felt that the outlook for those operations was not good because of a depression

in paper and pulp prices. Boise Cascade obviously thought otherwise. Shortly afterward, Sylvachem, part of SCM's chemicals division, was sold for $30 million, representing a price/earnings multiple of 18.5.

In August 1986 Glidden Paints was sold to the British chemical giant and Europe's largest paint manufacturer, Imperial Chemical Industries PLC (ICI) for $580 million. This represented a price/earnings multiple of 17.5 and was 2.5 times book value. The purchase of this operation enabled ICI to become the world's largest paint manufacturer. A few days later Durkee Famous Foods was sold to another British firm, Reckitt & Colman PLC, for $120 million in cash and the assumption of $20 million in debt. This represented a price/earnings multiple of 17 and was 3 times book value. This disposal served to withdraw Hanson from an area that was subject to uncontrollable and volatile commodity price movements. For Reckitt & Colman, however, which was already one of the largest manufacturers of branded food products outside the United States, it represented an important strategic addition.

The four disposals amounted to $926 million and were accomplished at an average price/earnings multiple of 19.5. Having recovered 100 percent of the purchase price paid for SCM within eight months, Hanson had effectively acquired for nothing a number of businesses that were projected to contribute around $140 million to net pre-tax profit for their first full year under Hanson control.

Hanson held on to the titanium dioxide business for two main reasons. First, with the industry operating at close to 100 percent capacity and with projections indicating an increase in demand through 1989, prices and margins were expected to increase substantially. Although several companies had plans to expand global capacity, given the 3-to-4-year time lag in bringing new capacity on stream, this seller's market was likely to persist for a while. Nor did it look as if the additional capacity would outstrip the projected rise in demand. Second, two-thirds of world production of titanium dioxide is in the hands of global producers. SCM's business is ranked third with 12 percent of world capacity, behind Du Pont and Tioxide PLC. Given this oligopoly, orderly pricing in world markets seemed likely to continue.

Hanson also decided to hold on to SCM's typewriter business, despite the fact that in recent years it had been the worst-performing unit in SCM's portfolio. Hanson quickly realized that SCM management had in effect just completed a drastic overhaul of the typewriter businesses and that a dramatic turnaround was likely. In the two years prior to Hanson's acquisition, SCM's management had undertaken the following steps:

1. A new line of electronic typewriters had been introduced to match the increasingly sophisticated Japanese models.
2. Capacity had been reduced by 50 percent, and six U.S. production facilities had been consolidated into a single assembly plant and distribution center in New York to manufacture all electronic models.
3. As a result of automation, scale economies, and labor agreements, productivity at the New York plant had increased fourfold since 1984, and unit labor costs had declined by 60 percent.
4. The manufacture of electric models had been moved offshore to a low-cost facility in Singapore.
5. Smith-Corona had just introduced the first personal word processor for use with a portable electronic typewriter, and it retailed at just under $500.

Exhibit 6
Imperial Divisional Results for Year to October 1985

Division	Revenues		Profits	
	£m	% change from 1984	£m	% change from 1984
Tobacco	2,641	+7%	123.1	+11%
Brewing and leisure	974	+8%	97.0	+20%
Foods	719	+4%	33.0	+5%
Howard Johnson	617	+11%	11.1	–40%

Source: Data from Hanson Industries, *Annual Report*, 1986.

As a result of these improvements, the Smith-Corona business seemed ready to become a major profit producer. Hanson forecasted profits of $30 million for this business during 1986–1987, compared with an operating loss of $47.4 million in financial year 1985.

THE IMPERIAL ACQUISITION

On December 6, 1985, while still engaged in the SCM acquisition, Hanson opened another takeover battle in Britain by announcing a £1.5-billion offer for Imperial Group PLC.[18] Imperial Group was one of the ten largest firms in Britain. Imperial was Britain's leading tobacco manufacturer and the third largest tobacco company in the world. Its Courage Brewing subsidiary was one of the "big six" beer companies in Britain. Its "leisure" operations included 1,371 public houses (taverns), 120-plus restaurants, and over 750 specialized retail shops. Imperial manufactured over 1,000 branded food products (see Exhibit 6 for a breakdown of Imperial's divisional results). In September 1985 Imperial had sold its fourth business, the U.S. motel chain Howard Johnson, to Marriott. Howard Johnson had been purchased in 1980 and was widely regarded as on of the worst acquisitions ever made by a major British company.

Attractions to Hanson

Hanson's interest in Imperial was prompted by the news on December 2, 1985, of a planned merger between Imperial and United Biscuits PLC, a major manufacturer of branded food products. The financial press perceived this measure as a defensive move by Imperial. However, despite its well-documented problems with Howard Johnson, Imperial's financial performance was reasonably strong (see Exhibit 7). What factors made Imperial an attractive takeover target to Hanson? The following seem to have been important.

1. *Mature business* Like SCM's businesses, most of Imperial's businesses were based in mature, low-technology industries. There is little prospect of radically changing fashions or technological change in the tobacco, brewing, and food industries.

18. The material in this section is based on the following sources: Cusack, *Hanson Trust*; and Lampert, "Britons on the Prowl," pp. 22–24, 36, 38, 42.

Exhibit 7
Financial Data for Imperial

	1981	1982	1983	1984	1985
Revenues (£m)	4,526	4,614	4,381	4,593	4,918
Pre-tax profits (£m)	106	154	195	221	236
Earnings per share (pence)	12.8	16.4	18.0	20.3	22.4
Return on capital (%)	12.7	17.9	20.4	21.1	18.1

Source: Data from Hanson Industries, *Annual Report*, 1986.

2. *Low risk* Most of Imperial's products had a high brand recognition within Britain. Thus Hanson could easily dispose of those that did not stand up to Hanson's demanding ROK targets.
3. *Tobacco cash flow* Imperial's tobacco business was a classic cash cow. The company had 45 percent of the tobacco market and seven of the ten best-selling brands in 1985. Although tobacco sales are declining in Britain because of a combination of health concerns and punitive taxation, the decline has been gradual, amounting to 29 percent since the peak year of 1973. Given Hanson's emphasis on ROK and cash flow, this made Imperial particularly attractive to Hanson. Imperial had arguably squandered much of this cash flow by using it to underwrite unprofitable growth opportunities, particularly Howard Johnson.
4. *Failure of Imperial's diversification strategy* Imperial's recent track record with respect to diversification was poor. In 1978 it bought a construction company, J. B. Eastward, for £40 million. After four years of trading losses, Eastward was sold in 1982 for a total loss of £54 million. In 1979 Imperial paid $640 million for Howard Johnson, the U.S. motel and restaurant chain. In 1985, after six years of declining profits, this business was sold for $341 million. These losses suggested a fundamental weakness in Imperial's top management in an area in which Hanson was strong: diversification strategy. Moreover, the failure of Imperial's diversification strategy probably resulted in Imperial's shares being discounted by the stock market.
5. *Inadequate returns in brewing and leisure* Imperial's brewing and leisure operations earned a ROK of 9 percent in 1985. This return was considered very low for the brewing industry, which was characterized by strong demand and was dominated by a mature oligopoly that had engineered high prices and margins. Hanson thought that this return could be significantly improved.

The Takeover Battle

The planned merger between Imperial and United Biscuits PLC (UB), announced on December 2, 1985, gave rise to considerable concern among Imperial's already disgruntled shareholders. Under the terms of the proposed merger, UB, although contributing just 21 percent of net assets, would end up with a 42 percent interest in the enlarged group. The implication was that Imperial's shareholders would experience significant earnings dilution. In addition, it was proposed that the corporate management of the enlarged group would primarily

come from UB personnel. These factors prompted a reverse takeover by UB of the much larger Imperial group.

Hanson's interest was sparked by this controversy. Hanson's corporate staff had been tracking Imperial for some time, so when the "for sale" sign was raised over Imperial, Hanson was able to move quickly. On December 6, 1985, Hanson made a 250-pence per share offer for Imperial, valuing the group at £1.9 billion. This offer was rejected out of hand by Imperial's management.

The next major development came on February 12, 1986, when the British secretary of state of trade and industry referred the proposed Imperial/UB merger to the Monopolies and Mergers Commission for consideration. Britain's Monopolies and Mergers Commission has the authority to prohibit any merger that might create a monopoly. The referral was due to the recognition that an Imperial/UB group would command over 40 percent of the British snack-food market.

On February 17, Hanson took advantage of the uncertainty created by the referral to unveil a revised offer 24 percent higher than its original offer, valuing Imperial at £2.35 billion. On the same day, UB announced a £2.5-billion bid for Imperial and indicated that, if the offer was successful, Imperial's snack-food businesses would be sold, thus eliminating the need for a Monopolies and Mergers Commission investigation. Imperial's board duly recommended the UB offer to shareholders for acceptance.

Many of Imperial's shareholders, however, were in no mood to accept Imperial's recommendation. Under British stock market regulations, once the Imperial board accepted UB's offer, Imperial's shareholders had two months in which to indicate their acceptance or rejection of it. If the offer was rejected, then the shareholders were free to consider the hostile bid from Hanson. What followed was an increasingly acrimonious war of words between Hanson and Imperial. Hanson charged Imperial with mismanagement. Imperial responded by trying to depict Hanson as an asset stripper with no real interest in generating internal growth from the companies it owned. In the words of one Imperial executive during this period, Lord Hanson "buys and sells companies well, but he manages them jolly badly. He buys, squeezes and goes on to the next one. The only way to grow is by bigger and bigger acquisitions. Like all great conglomerate builders of the past, he's over the hill."[19]

Imperial's management failed to win the war of words. By April 17, UB had secured acceptances for only 34 percent of Imperial's shares, including 14.9 percent held by UB associates. The UB offer lapsed, leaving the way clear for Hanson. On April 18, Hanson secured acceptances for over 50 percent of Imperial's shares, and its offer went unconditional. At £2.5 billion, the takeover was the largest in British history; it implied a price/earnings multiple of 12.3 on Imperial's prospective earnings.

After the Acquisition

After the acquisition Hanson moved quickly to realize potential from Imperial. Of the 300 staff at Imperial's headquarters, 260 were laid off, and most of the remainder were sent back to the operating level. In July Imperial's hotels and

19. Quoted in Philip Revzin, "U.K.'s Hanson Trust Aims for Big Leagues in Takeovers," *The Wall Street Journal*, February 25, 1986, p. 30.

restaurants were sold to Trusthouse Forte for £190 million in cash, representing a price/earnings multiple of 24 on prospective earnings and amounting to 1.7 times book value. The sale was followed in September 1986 by the sale of the Courage Brewing operations, along with a wine and spirits wholesaler and an "off-license" chain (liqueur stores) to Elders IXL, an Australian brewing company, for £1.4 billion in cash. The price/earnings multiple for that deal amounted to 17.5 times prospective earnings and represented a premium of £150 million over book value. It was quickly followed by the sale of Imperial's Golden Wonder snack-food business to Dalgety PLC, a British food concern, for £87 million in cash, representing a price/earnings multiple of 13.5 over prospective earnings.

As a result of these moves, by the autumn of 1986 Hanson had raised £1.7 billion from the sale of Imperial's businesses. Effectively, Hanson recouped 66 percent of the total cost of its acquisition by selling companies that contributed to just over 45 percent of Imperial's net profit forecasted for the year to October 1986. The net cost of Imperial on this basis had fallen to £850 million, with a consequent decline in the price/earnings multiple on prospective earnings from 12.3 to 7.6.

This was followed in 1988 by the sale of Imperial's food businesses for £534 million, along with the sale of various other smaller interests for £56 million. By the end of 1988, therefore, Hanson had raised £2.26 billion from the sale of Imperial's assets. It still held on to Imperial Tobacco, by far the largest business in Imperial's portfolio, which it had in effect gained for a net cost of £240 million—this for a business that in 1988 generated £150 million in operating profit.

RECENT DEVELOPMENTS

Following the SCM and Imperial acquisitions, in 1987 Hanson acquired Kidde, a 108-company U.S. conglomerate, for $1.7 billion. Kidde seemed set for the "Hanson treatment." Its headquarters was closed within three months of the takeover, and a series of disposals were arranged. These were followed in 1988 by continuing disposals of operations acquired in the Imperial and Kidde acquisitions. In total, they amounted to $1.5 billion.

In mid 1989 Hanson embarked on its biggest takeover, the £3.61–billion ($4.8–billion) acquisition of Consolidated Gold Fields PLC (CGF). In addition to being the second largest gold-mining operation in the world, CGF also owns a large stone and gravel operation, ARC Ltd., with major holdings in Britain. CGF came to Hanson's attention following an abortive takeover bid for the company from South African–controlled Minorco.

Hanson bought Minorco's 29.9 percent minority stake in CGF and launched its own takeover bid in July 1989. After raising its bid, Hanson won control of CGF in August. CGF also seemed set to be broken up. About half of CGF's value consists of minority stakes in publicly quoted mining companies in the United States, South Africa, and Australia. These stakes range from 38 to 49 percent, enough to hold the key to control in many of the companies. Thus Hanson should be able to extract a premium price for them. Initial estimates suggest that Hanson should be able to raise $2.5 billion from the sale of CGF's minority

Income Data (Million $)

Year Ended Sep. 30	Revs.	Oper. Inc.	% Oper. Inc. of Revs.	Cap. Exp.	Depr.	Int. Exp.	Net Bef. Taxes	Eff. Tax Rate	[2]Net Inc.	% Net Inc. of Revs.
[3]1989	11,302	1,609	14.2	2,141	200	533	[1]1,718	23.6%	1,313	11.6
[3]1988	12,507	1,561	12.5	724	215	485	[1]1,488	23.2%	1,143	9.1
[4]1987	10,975	1,230	11.2	522	172	493	[1]1,217	22.8%	939	8.6
[4]1986	6,196	713	11.5	848	105	359	[1]667	22.5%	517	8.3
1985	3,771	477	12.7	84	74	172	356	23.5%	272	7.2
1984	2,930	303	10.3	61	55	119	208	25.7%	154	5.3
1983	2,226	207	9.3	59	47	81	137	30.2%	94	4.2
1982	1,952	NA	NA	NA	NA	NA	NA	NA	72	3.7
1981	1,549	NA	NA	NA	NA	NA	NA	NA	62	4.0

Balance Sheet Data (Million $)

Sep. 30	Cash	Assets	Curr. Liab.	Ratio	Total Assets	Ret. on Assets	Long-Term Debt	Common Equity	Total Inv. Capital	% LT Debt of Cap.	Ret. on Equity
1989	8,574	12,038	5,278	2.3	17,482	8.5%	8,028	1,689	10,683	75.1	47.6%
1988	6,527	10,413	4,165	2.5	13,210	9.4%	3,592	3,707	7,878	45.6	33.5%
1987	5,025	8,236	3,422	2.4	10,471	9.3%	2,837	2,841	6,151	46.1	37.5%
1986	2,509	7,977	3,572	2.2	9,577	7.6%	2,834	2,068	5,252	54.0	29.1%
1985	1,659	2,908	1,277	2.3	4,021	7.7%	903	1,376	2,563	35.2	27.7%
1984	641	1,775	925	1.9	2,638	9.0%	981	505	1,540	63.7	36.7%

Data as orig. reptd. prior to 1986 data as reptd. in 1985 Annual Report (prior to 1984 from Listing Application of Nov. 3, 1986), Conv. to US$ at year-end exch. rates. **1.** Incl. equity in earns of nonconsol. subs. **2.** Bef. spec. item(s) in 1989, 1988, 1986. **3.** Excl. disc. opers. and reflects merger or acquisition. **4.** Reflects merger or acquisition. NA-Not Available.

Source: Standard & Poor's, *Standard NYSE Stock Reports,* Vol. 57, No. 54, Sec. 12, p. 1096. Reprinted with permission.

Exhibit 8
Hanson PLC—
Financial Record

holdings.[20] Indeed, by February 1990 Hanson had reportedly recouped about one-third of the purchase price for CGF through disposals and was looking to sell additional operations while gold prices remained high.[21]

The CGF deal led to the June 1990 acquisition of Peabody Holdings Co., the largest U.S. coal producer, for a total cost of $1.23 billion in cash. CGF had a 49 percent stake in Newmont Mining Corp., the biggest U.S. gold-mining concern. In turn, Newmont owned 55 percent of Peabody. In April 1990 Hanson purchased the 45 percent of Peabody not owned by Newmont from three minority owners. Then in June it outbid AMAX Corporation for Newmont's stake in Peabody.

20. Mark Maremont and Chuck Hawkins, "Is Consgold Just an Appetizer for Hanson?" *Business Week*, July 10, 1989, pp. 41–42.
21. Joann Lubin, "Hanson to Buy Peabody Stake for $504 Million," *The Wall Street Journal*, February 16, 1990, p. A4.

The attraction of Peabody to Hanson lies in two factors: (1) the company owns large deposits of low-sulfur coal, which is increasingly in demand because of environmental concerns; (2) the company has recently invested heavily to upgrade its plant. As a result, in the past four years labor productivity has increased 50 percent.[22] In addition, analysts speculate that the deals, by improving Newmont's financial position (Newmont has used the cash to reduce its debt), may make it possible for Hanson to sell off its 49 percent stake in Newmont for a reasonable premium.

22. "Hanson PLC," *Value Line,* July 20, 1990, p. 832.

CASE

27

Ups and Downs at Kodak

It was time to prepare the 1990 Annual Report, and Kay Whitmore, the new chief executive officer of the Eastman Kodak Company, was reflecting on Kodak's situation. His predecessor, Colby Chandler, to lessen Kodak's dependence on the photographic products industry and to counter competition from other imaging techniques, had engaged in an ambitious program of diversification. Moreover, Chandler had taken steps to strengthen Kodak's position in its core business. This strategy had seemed to be working, for Kodak's sagging performance had picked up in 1987 and 1988 (see Exhibit 1), and optimism in the company had been high. However, 1989 had been a disastrous year with profits falling dramatically; and although things were looking a little better in 1990 after the latest round of cost containment efforts and restructuring, it was unclear whether this improvement was a short-term phenomenon or a sign of good times ahead. Was Kodak's new strategy working, Whitmore wondered, and what could be done? If a turnaround did not happen soon, the prospect of corporate raiders dismantling the company (which was valued at a far higher figure than its stock price) would increase. Whitmore wondered how he could solve Kodak's problems.

KODAK'S HISTORY

Eastman Kodak Company was incorporated in New Jersey on October 24, 1901, as successor to the Eastman Dry Plate Company, the business originally established by George Eastman in September 1880.[1] The Dry Plate Company had been formed to develop a dry photographic plate that was more portable and easier to use than other plates in the rapidly developing photography field. To mass-produce the dry plates uniformly, Eastman patented a plate-coating machine and began to manufacture the plates commercially. Eastman's continuing interest in the infant photographic industry led to his development in 1884 of silver halide paper-based photographic roll film. Eastman capped this invention with his introduction of the first portable camera in 1888. This camera used his own patented film, which was developed using his own proprietary method. Thus Eastman had gained control of all the stages of the photographic process. His breakthroughs made possible the development of photography as a mass leisure activity. The popularity of the "recorded images" business was immediate, and sales boomed. Eastman's inventions revolutionized the photographic

This case was prepared by Gareth R. Jones, Texas A&M University. This case was prepared as a basis for class discussion rather than to illustrate either effective or ineffective handling of administrative situations.

1. "Eastman Kodak Co.," *Moody's Industrial Manual*, 1 (1986), 3016.

Exhibit 1
Summary of the Year in Figures

Eastman Kodak Company and subsidiary companies

	1989	1988**	Change
	(Dollar amounts and shares in millions, except per share figures)		
Sales	$18,398	$17,034	+8%
Earnings from operations	1,591*	2,812***	–43%
Net earnings	529*	1,397	–62%
—percent of sales	2.9%	8.2%	
—per common share	$1.63	$4.31	
Cash dividends declared	$649	$616	
—per common share	$2.00	$1.90	
Average number of common shares outstanding	324.3	324.2	
Shareowners at close of year	171,954	174,110	
Total net assets (shareowners' equity)	$6,642	$6,780	–2%
Additions to properties	$2,118	$1,914	+11%
Depreciation	$1,181	$1,057	+12%
Wages, salaries, and employee benefits	$5,877	$5,469	+7%
Employees at the close of year			
—in the United States	82,850	87,900	–6%
—worldwide	137,750	145,300	–5%

*After deduction of $875 million of restructuring costs ($549 million after-tax).
**Sales, earnings, assets, and employment data include Sterling Drug Inc. since the date of acquisition (February 23, 1988).
***Restated to reflect Goodwill amortization in Cost of Goods Sold.
Source: Eastman Kodak Company, *Annual Report*, 1989.

industry, and his company was uniquely placed to lead the world in the development of photographic technology.

From the beginning, Kodak focused on four objectives to guide the growth of its business: (1) mass production to lower production costs, (2) maintaining the lead in technological developments, (3) extensive product advertising, and (4) the development of a multinational business to exploit the world market. Although common now, those goals were revolutionary at the time. In due course, Kodak's yellow boxes could be found in every country in the world. Preeminent in world markets, Kodak operated research, manufacturing, and distribution networks throughout Europe and the rest of the world. Kodak's leadership in the development of advanced color film for simple, easy-to-use cameras and in quality film processing was maintained by constant research and development in its many research laboratories. Its huge volume of production allowed it to obtain economies of scale. Kodak was also its own supplier of the plastics and chemicals needed to produce film, and it made most of the component parts for its cameras.

Kodak became one of the most profitable American corporations, and its return on shareholders' equity averaged 18 percent for many years. To maintain

its competitive advantage, it continued to invest heavily in research and development in silver halide photography, remaining principally in the photographic business. In this business, as the company used its resources to expand sales and become a multinational enterprise, the name Kodak became a household word signifying unmatched quality. By 1990, approximately 40 percent of Kodak's revenues came from sales outside the United States.

Starting in the early 1970s, however, and especially in the 1980s, Kodak ran into major problems, reflected in the drop in return on equity shown in Exhibit 1. Its pre-eminence has been increasingly threatened as the photographic industry and industry competition have changed. Major changes have taken place within the photography business, and new methods of recording images and memories beyond silver halide technology have emerged.

THE NEW INDUSTRY ENVIRONMENT

In the 1970s Kodak began to face an uncertain environment in all its product markets. First, the color film and paper market from which Kodak made 75 percent of its profits experienced growing competition from the Japanese when, led by Fuji Photo Film Co., they entered the market. Fuji invested in huge, low-cost manufacturing plants, using the latest technology to mass-produce film in large volume. Fuji's low production costs and aggressive, competitive price cutting squeezed Kodak's profit margin. Finding no apparent differences in quality and obtaining more vivid colors with the Japanese product, consumers began to switch to the cheaper Japanese film, and this shift drastically reduced Kodak's market share.

Besides greater industry competition, another liability for Kodak was that it had done little internally to improve productivity to counteract rising costs. Supremacy in the marketplace had made Kodak complacent, and it had been slow to introduce productivity and quality improvements. Furthermore, Kodak (unlike Fuji in Japan) produced film in many different countries in the world, rather than in a single country, and this also gave Kodak a cost disadvantage. Thus the combination of Fuji's efficient production and Kodak's own management style allowed the Japanese to become the cost leaders—to charge lower prices and still maintain profit margins.[2]

Kodak was also facing competition on other product fronts. Its cameras had an advantage because of their ease of use as compared with complex 35mm single-lens reflex models. They were also inexpensive. However, the quality of their prints could not compare with those of 35mm cameras. In 1970 Kodak had toyed with the idea of producing a simple-to-use 35mm camera but had abandoned it. In the late 1970s, however, the Japanese did develop an easy-to-use 35mm pocket camera featuring such innovations as auto flash, focus, and rewind. The quality of the prints produced by these cameras was far superior to the grainy prints produced by the smaller Instamatic and disc cameras, and consumers began to switch to these products in large numbers. This shift led to the need for new kinds of film, which Kodak was slow to introduce, thus adding to its product problems.

2. Thomas Moore, "Embattled Kodak Enters the Electronic Age," *Fortune*, August 22, 1983, pp. 120–128.

Shrinking market share due to increased competition from the Japanese was not Kodak's only problem. In the early 1980s Kodak introduced several less-than-successful products. In 1982 Kodak introduced a new disc camera as a replacement for the pocket Instamatic. The disc camera used a negative even smaller than the negative of the Instamatic and was smaller and easier to use. Four and a half million units were shipped to the domestic market by Christmas, but almost a million of the units still remained on retailers' shelves in the new year. The disc cameras had been outsold by pocket 35mm cameras, which produced higher-quality pictures.[3] The disc camera also sold poorly in the European and Japanese markets. Yet Kodak's research showed that 90 percent of disc camera users were satisfied with the camera and especially liked its high "yield rate" of 93 percent printable pictures, compared with 75 percent for the pocket Instamatic.

A final blow on the camera front came when Kodak lost its patent suit with Polaroid Corp. Kodak had foregone the instant photography business in the 1940s when it turned down Edwin Land's offer to develop his instant photography process. Polaroid developed it, and instant photography was wildly successful, capturing a significant share of the photographic market. In response, Kodak set out in the 1960s to develop its own instant camera to compete with Polaroid's. According to testimony in the patent trial, Kodak spent $94 million perfecting its system, only to scrub it when Polaroid introduced the new SX-70 camera in 1972. Kodak then rushed to produce a competing instant camera, hoping to capitalize on the $6.5 billion in sales of instant cameras. However, on January 9, 1986, a federal judge ordered Kodak out of the instant photography business for violating seven of Polaroid's patents in its rush to produce an instant camera. The estimated cost to Kodak for closing its instant photography operation and exchanging the 16.5 million cameras sold to consumers was expected to reach $800 million. In 1985 Kodak reported that it had exited the industry at a cost of $494 million.[4] However, the total costs of this misadventure were finally realized on July 15, 1991, when Kodak agreed to pay Polaroid a sum of $925 million to settle out of court a suit that Polaroid had brought against Kodak for patent infringement.[5]

On its third product front, photographic processing, Kodak also experienced problems. It faced stiff competition from foreign manufacturers of photographic paper and from new competitors in the film-processing market. Increasingly, film processors were turning to cheaper sources of paper to reduce the costs of film processing. Once again the Japanese had developed cheaper sources of paper and were eroding Kodak's market share. At the same time many new independent film-processing companies had emerged and were printing film at far lower rates than Kodak's own official developers. These independent laboratories had opened to service the needs of drugstores and supermarkets, and many of them offered twenty-four-hour service. They used the less expensive paper to maintain their cost advantage and were willing to accept lower profit margins in return for a higher volume of sales. As a result, Kodak lost markets for its chemical and paper products—products that had contributed significantly to its revenues and profits.

3. "Kodak's New Lean and Hungry Look," *Business Week*, May 30, 1983, p. 33.
4. Charles K. Ryan, *Eastman Kodak, Company Outline*, Merrill Lynch, Pierce, Fenner & Smith Incorporated, May 7, 1986.
5. Press release, Eastman Kodak Company, July 15, 1991.

The photographic industry surrounding Kodak had changed dramatically. Competition had increased in all product areas, and Kodak, while still the largest producer, faced increasing threats to its profitability as it was forced to reduce prices to match the competition. To cap the problem, by 1980 the market was all but saturated: 95 percent of all U.S. households owned at least one camera. Facing increased competition in a mature market was not an enviable position for a company used to high profitability and growth.

The second major problem that Kodak had to confront was due not to increased competition in existing product markets but to the emergence of new industries that provided alternative means for producing and recording images. The introduction of videotape recorders, and later video cameras, gave consumers an alternative way to use their dollars to produce images, particularly moving images. Video basically destroyed the old, film-based home movie business of which Kodak had a virtual monopoly. Since Sony's introduction of the Betamax machine in 1975, the video industry has grown into a multi-billion-dollar business.[6] VCRs and 16mm video cameras are increasingly hot-selling items as their prices fall with the growth in demand and the standardization of technology. More recently, 8mm video cameras have been emerging—obviously, much smaller than the 16mm version. The introduction of laser and compact discs has also been a significant development. The vast amount of data that can be recorded on these discs gives them a great advantage in reproducing images through electronic means, and it may be only a matter of time before compact disc cameras become available. It increasingly appears as though the whole nature of the recording industry is changing from chemical methods of reproduction to electronic methods. This transformation, of course, will undermine Kodak's edge in the market because its technical pre-eminence is based on silver halide photography.

Changes in the competitive environment have caused enormous difficulties for Kodak. Between 1972 and 1982 profit margins from sales declined from 15.7 percent to 10.7 percent.[7] Kodak's glossy image lost its luster. It was in this declining situation that Colby Chandler took over as chairman in July 1983.

KODAK'S NEW STRATEGY

Chandler saw the need for dramatic changes in Kodak's businesses and quickly pioneered four changes in strategy: (1) he strove to increase Kodak's control of its existing chemical-based imaging businesses; (2) he aimed to make Kodak the leader in electronic imaging; (3) he spearheaded attempts by Kodak to diversify into new businesses to create value; and (4) he embarked on major efforts to reduce costs and improve productivity. To achieve the first three objectives, he embarked on a huge program of acquisitions, realizing that Kodak did not have the time to venture new activities internally. Because Kodak was cash rich and had low debt, financing these acquisitions was easy.

6. John Greenwald, "Aiming for a Brighter Picture," *Time*, January 9, 1984, p. 49.
7. Barbara Buell, "Kodak Is Trying to Break Out of Its Shell," *Business Week*, June 10, 1985, pp. 92–95.

Imaging	Chemicals	Health	Information systems
Photographic products group	**Eastman Chemical Company**		**Commercial systems group**
Consumer Imaging Division	Chemicals	Sterling Drug Inc.	Copy Products Division
Consumer Services Division	Plastics	Health Sciences Division	Customer Equipment Service Division
Motion Picture and Television Products Division	Fibers	Clinical Products Division	Graphics Imaging Systems Division
Professional Photography Division		Lehn & Fink Products	Kodak Apparatus Division
			Imaging information systems group
			Business Imaging Systems Division
			Federal Systems Division
			Image Acquisition Products Division
			Integration and Systems Products Division
			Mass Memory Division
			Printer Products Division

Source: Eastman Kodak Company, *Annual Report*, 1989.

Exhibit 2
Kodak's Product Groups

For the next six years, Chandler acquired businesses in four main areas, and by 1989 Kodak had been restructured into four main operating groups: Imaging, Information Systems, Health, and Chemicals. In a statement to shareholders at the annual meeting in 1988, Chandler announced that with the recent acquisition of Sterling Drug for $5 billion, the company had achieved its objective: "With a sharp focus on these four sectors, we are serving diversified markets from a unified base of science and manufacturing technology. The logical synergy of the Kodak growth strategy means that we are neither diversified as a conglomerate nor a company with a one-product family."[8]

Exhibit 2 summarizes the four groups and their activities. The way these operating groups emerged over time is described below.

The Imaging Group

Imaging contains Kodak's original businesses, including consumer products, motion picture and audiovisual products, photofinishing, and consumer electronics. The unit is responsible for strengthening Kodak's position in its existing businesses. Kodak's strategy in its photographic imaging business has been to fill gaps in its product line by introducing new products either made by Kodak or bought from Japanese manufacturers and sold under the Kodak name. For example, in attempting to maintain market share in the camera business, Kodak introduced a new line of disc cameras to replace the Instamatic lines. However, in addition, Kodak entered into an agreement with Chinon of Japan to produce a range of 35mm automatic cameras under the Kodak name. This arrangement

8. Eastman Kodak Company, *Kodak Highlights, First Quarter*, 1988, p. 7.

would capitalize on the Kodak name and give Kodak a presence in this market to maintain its camera and film sales. That venture has succeeded; Kodak has sold 500,000 cameras and has 15 percent of the market.

In addition, Kodak has developed a whole new range of "DX" coded film to match the new 35mm camera market—film that possesses the vivid color qualities of Fuji film. Kodak had not developed vivid film color earlier because of its belief that consumers wanted "realistic" color.

Kodak also entered the electronic imaging industry through a joint venture with Matsushita. Matsushita produced a range of 8mm video cameras under the Kodak name. However, sales of these cameras never took off (some blame the outdated design of the camera), and in 1987 Kodak announced that it was withdrawing from the market.

Kodak has made major moves to solidify its hold on the film-processing market. Kodak has attempted to stem the inflow of foreign photographic paper by gaining control over the processing market. In 1986 it acquired Texas-based Fox Photo Inc. for $96 million, becoming the largest wholesale photograph finisher. In 1987, it acquired the laboratories of American Photographic Group. In 1989, it solidified its hold on the photofinishing market by forming a joint venture between its operations and the photofinishing operations of Fuqua Industries. The new company, Qualex Inc., has ninety-four laboratories nationwide. These acquisitions provide Kodak with a large, stable "captive" customer for its chemical and paper products as well as control over the photofinishing market. Also, in 1986 Kodak introduced new, improved one-hour film-processing labs to compete with other photographic developers. To accompany the new labs, Kodak popularized the Kodak "color watch system," which requires these labs to use only Kodak paper and chemicals.[9] Kodak hoped that this would stem the flow of business to one-hour mini-labs and also establish the quality standards of processing.

As a result of these moves, Kodak gained strong control over the processing end of the market and has made inroads into the film and camera end as well. In 1988, Kodak earnings were helped by the decline in value of the dollar, which forced Fuji Photo, its main competitor, to raise its prices. Consequently, Kodak was able to increase its prices. All these measures increased Kodak's visibility in the market and allowed it to regain strength in its existing businesses.

New and improved film products, including Kodak Gold Label film and Ektachrome film, were announced during 1988. Similarly, new types of 35mm cameras, some of which Kodak intends to make in its Rochester plant, were announced. Kodak also formed a battery venture with Matsushita. Matsushita produces a range of alkaline batteries for Kodak, and a gold-top battery is being extensively advertised in opposition to Duracell's copper-top battery. In 1988, Kodak announced the introduction of new and improved Kodak Supralife and Ultralife batteries to be produced in a joint venture with Matsushita at a new battery-manufacturing facility built in Georgia, where production began in 1989. Moreover, Kodak internally ventured a new lithium battery, which lasts six times as long as conventional batteries. This was an opportunity for future growth because of the extensive use of the battery in cameras.

Kodak also engaged in a massive cost-cutting effort to improve the efficiency of the photographic products group. For the last six years it has introduced more and more stringent efficiency targets aimed at reducing waste while increasing

9. Taylor, "Kodak Scrambles," pp. 34–38.

productivity. In 1986, it established a baseline for measuring the total cost of waste incurred in the manufacture of film and paper throughout its worldwide operations. By 1987 it had cut that waste by 15 percent, and by 1989 it announced total cost savings worth $500 million annually.

Despite these strategic moves, the net earnings of Kodak's photographic business dropped dramatically in 1989. Although Kodak's volume and sales of its products were up, profit margins were down. Polaroid with its new One Film product was advertising aggressively to capture market share. Fuji, realizing the strong threat posed by Kodak's reassertion of industry control, responded with an intense competitive push. Both Fuji and Kodak were spending massive amounts to advertise their products in order to increase market share. Kodak had 80 percent of the $7 billion film market in 1989 and Fuji had 11 percent, but Fuji increased its advertising budget by 65 percent in 1989 to increase its market share and simultaneously offered discount coupons on its film products. Moreover, Fuji announced plans for a major new film-making plant in Europe—a plant the size of its Japanese plant, which by itself can produce film for one quarter of the world market. The result has been a huge amount of excess capacity in film production, which raises costs and encourages competition. Fighting back, Kodak announced a fifteen-year agreement with the Walt Disney Company to use Disney characters in its advertising. Kodak also announced new multipacks and discounts on its products. However, these moves were very expensive for Kodak and cut into profits. They offset some of the prospective benefits from Kodak's cost-cutting efforts and led to the poor earnings results (see Exhibits 3 and 4). Thus growth in Kodak's photographic imaging business has been slow.

It was because of this slow industry growth that Chandler saw the need for diversification. Because sales increase only 5 percent a year and Kodak already has 80 percent of the market, Kodak was tied to the fortunes of one industry. This fact, plus the increase in the use of other imaging techniques, led to Chandler's second strategic thrust: an immediate policy of acquisition and diversification into the electronic imaging business with the stated goal of being "first in both industries."[10]

The Information Systems Group

In 1988, when Sony introduced an electronic camera that could take still pictures and then transmit them back to a television screen, it became increasingly obvious that the threat to Kodak from new electronic imaging techniques would continue to increase. Although the pictures could not match the quality achieved with chemical reproduction with video film, the advent of compact discs offered the prospect of an imaging medium that could meet such standards in the future. To survive and prosper in the imaging business, Kodak realized that it required expertise in a broad range of technologies to satisfy customers' recording and imaging needs. Furthermore, it saw the electronic imaging business increasing and a large number of different types of markets emerging, including business and industrial customers. Electronic imaging had become important in the medical sciences and in all business, technical, and research activities, especially since the advent of the computer. Thus, Kodak began targeting electronics, communications, computer science, and various hard-copy-output technologies as being increasingly important to its future imaging products. To buy time until it could

10. Eastman Kodak Company, *Annual Report*, 1989.

Exhibit 3
Consolidated Statement of Earnings

Eastman Kodak Company and subsidiary companies

	1989	1988	1987
	(in millions, except per share data)		
Sales			
Sales to: Customers in United States	**$10,302**	$9,554	$7,611
Customers outside the United States	**8,096**	7,480	5,694
Total sales	**18,398**	17,034	13,305
Costs			
Cost of goods sold	**11,075**	9,727*	8,037*
Sales, advertising, distribution, and administrative expenses	**4,857**	4,495	3,190
Restructuring costs	**875**	—	—
Total costs and expenses	**16,807**	14,222	11,227
Earnings			
Earnings from operations	**1,591**	2,812	2,078
Investment income	**148**	132	83
Interest expense	**895**	697	181
Other income (charges)	**81**	(11)*	4*
Earnings before income taxes	**925**	2,236	1,984
Provision for United States, foreign, and other income taxes	396	839	806
Net earnings	**$529**	$1,397	$1,178
Average number of common shares outstanding	**324.3**	324.2	334.7
Net earnings per share	**$1.63**	$4.31	$3.52

*Goodwill amortization has been reclassified from Other Income (Charges) to Cost of Goods Sold.

Source: Eastman Kodak Company, *Annual Report*, 1989.

produce its own products, Kodak marketed the products of others under its own famous brand name. Among recent products is an electronic publishing system for corporate documents and an automated microfilm-imaging system.

Kodak's goal of reinvesting profits to build and extend its businesses could be seen in its move toward acquisitions and joint ventures. Growth of the Information Systems group has been due to several acquisitions, including Atex Inc., Eikonix Corp., and Diconix Inc. Atex, acquired in 1981, makes newspaper and magazine publishing systems.[11] It sells versatile electronic publishing and text-editing systems to newspapers and magazines worldwide as well as to government agencies and law firms. Its list of customers include leading newspapers in such cities as Boston, Chicago, Dallas, Houston, Miami, New York, and Philadelphia; national magazines such as *Time, Newsweek, U.S. News & World Report, Forbes, Reader's Digest,* and *National Geographic;* and government customers such as the U.S. Supreme Court and the U.S. Government Printing Office.

11. Taylor, "Kodak Scrambles," pp. 34–38.

Exhibit 4
Consolidated Statement of Retained Earnings

Eastman Kodak Company and subsidiary companies

	1989	1988	1987
	(in millions, except per share data)		
Retained earnings			
Retained earnings at beginning of year	$7,922	$7,139	$6,533
Net earnings	529	1,397	1,178
Total	8,451	8,536	7,711
Less: Cash dividends declared at $2.00 per share ($1.90 in 1988; $1.71 in 1987)	649	616	572
Add: Income Tax Benefit—KESOP	—	2	—
Retained earnings at end of year	$7,802	$7,922	$7,139

Source: Eastman Kodak Company, *Annual Report*, 1989.

Eikonix Corp. is a leader in the design, development, and production of precision digital imaging systems. Included in its range of commercial products are devices that scan and convert images into digital form and equipment to edit and manipulate color photographs and transparencies to produce color separations for printing and graphic arts applications. The Eikonix Designmaster 8000 allows users to proceed directly from artwork to printing plates with unmatched quality and flexibility.

Further growth within the Information Systems group came with the development of the Ektaprint line of copier-duplicators. The copiers achieved good sales growth and reached new standards for quality, reliability, and productivity in the very competitive high-volume segment of the copier marketplace. In 1988, Kodak announced another major move into the copier service business. It purchased IBM's copier service business and copier sales agreements in the United States. Kodak also announced that it would market copiers manufactured by IBM while continuing to market its own Ektaprint copiers. This service agreement was eventually extended to sixteen countries outside the United States.[12]

Kodak further enhanced its position in imaging with the announcement of two new image management packages: the Kodak Ektaprint Electronic Publishing System (KEEPS) and the Kodak Imaging Management System (KIMS). KIMS electronically scans, digitizes, and stores film images and transmits image information electronically. The system enables users with large, active databases to view and manipulate information stored on microfilm and magnetic or optical disks.[13] Presently, KIMS is being marketed by Digital Equipment Corporation in a joint venture. KEEPS is designed for use where there is a need for high-quality documents formed from text, graphics, and other images. The documents are reproduced by software designed specifically for electronic publishing. KEEPS has the ability to edit, print, and update text and graphics for publications. The computer comes from Sun Microsystems Inc. The software, enhanced by Kodak, is produced by Interleaf Inc., and the printer is manufactured by Canon (one of

12. Eastman Kodak Company, *Kodak Highlights, Third Quarter,* 1988, p. 9.
13. Eastman Kodak Company, *Annual Report,* 1985, p. 5.

Kodak's Japanese competitors).[14] Kodak has also announced a new $500,000 imaging system that locates microfilm and scans it for computer use. This product is directed at the banking and insurance company markets. In 1988, Kodak announced that it would begin marketing a "VY-P1" printer developed in a joint venture with Hitachi. This printer can make high-quality still images from VCRs and camcorders.

With these moves, Kodak extended its activities into the electronic areas of artificial intelligence, computer systems, consumer electronics, peripherals, telecommunications, and test and measuring equipment. Kodak hoped to gain a strong foothold in these businesses to make up for losses in its traditional business. Kodak purchased companies that made products as diverse as computer workstations and floppy disks. It aggressively acquired companies to fill in its product lines and obtain technical expertise in information systems. After taking more than a decade to make its first four acquisitions, Kodak completed seven acquisitions in 1985 and more than ten in 1986. Among the 1985 acquisitions—for $175 million—was Verbatim Corporation, a major producer of floppy disks. This acquisition made Kodak one of the three big producers in the floppy disk industry.

Entry into the information systems market, like the expansion in its core photographic products business, produced new competitive problems for Kodak. In entering office information systems, Kodak entered areas where it faced strong competition from established companies such as Digital and IBM.[15] The Verbatim acquisition brought Kodak into direct competition with 3M. Entering the copier market brought Kodak into direct competition with Japanese firms like Canon, which competitively market their own lines of advanced, low-cost products. Kodak was entering new businesses where it had little expertise, where it was unfamiliar with the competitive problems, and where there was already strong competition.

Kodak was forced to retreat from some of these markets. In 1990, it announced that it would sell Verbatim to Mitsubishi. (Mitsubishi was immediately criticized by Japanese investors for buying a company with an old, outdated product line!) Kodak has withdrawn from many other areas of business by selling assets or closing operations and taking a write-off. For example, to reduce costs, it sold Sayett Technology, Kodak Video programs and videocassettes, and Aquidneck Data Corporation. The decline in the performance of the Information Systems group, attributed to increased competition, a flat office systems market, and delays in bringing out new products, reduced earnings from operations from a profit of $311 million in 1988 to a loss of $360 million in 1989.

The Health Group

Kodak's interest in health products emerged from its involvement in the design and production of film for medical and dental x-rays. The growth of imaging in medical sciences offered Kodak an opportunity to apply its skills in new areas, and it began to develop such products as Kodak Ektachem—clinical blood analyzers. It developed other products—Ektascan laser imaging films, printers, and accessories—for improving the display, storage, processing, and retrieval of diagnostic images. However, Kodak did not confine its interests in medical and health matters to imaging-based products.

14. Barbara Buell, "Kodak Scrambles to Fill the Gap," *Business Week,* February 8, 1986, p. 30.
15. "Kodak's New Image: Electronic Imaging," *Electron Business*, January 1986, 38–43.

In 1984, it established within the Health group of a Life Sciences division to develop and commercialize new products deriving from Kodak's distinctive competencies in chemistry and biotechnology. One of the division's objectives was to focus on product opportunities in markets with relatively few competitors and high profit potential—products such as nutritional supplements that can be delivered orally or intravenously, as well as nutrition products for sale over the counter to consumers. Another objective was to develop innovative ways to control the absorption of pharmaceutical drugs into the body so that a drug remains therapeutically effective for the optimum amount of time. A third objective involved developing new applications for existing products and processes. Kodak has in its files about 500,000 chemical formulations on which it can base new products.

Within Life Sciences was the Bio-Products division, which engaged in joint research with biotechnology companies such as Cetus Corporation, Amgen, and Immunex. Bio-Products pursued an aggressive strategy to scale up and commercialize products based on biotechnology derived from in-house as well as outside contract research. Ventures entered into by the Bio-Products division included an agreement with Advanced Genetic Sciences for the commercial production of SNOWMAX, a product useful in making artificial snow for ski areas.[16]

Kodak began to enter into joint ventures in the biotechnical industry, both to build its business and to enter new businesses. In April 1985 Kodak and ICN Pharmaceuticals jointly announced the formation of a research institute that will explore new biomedical compounds aimed at stopping the spread of viral infections and slowing the aging process. Kodak and ICN will invest $45 million over six years to form and operate the Nucleic Acid Research Institute, a joint venture located at ICN's Costa Mesa, California, facility. The institute will dedicate much of its research exclusively to preclinical studies of new antiviral and antiaging substances.

However, these advances into biotechnology proved expensive, and the uncertainty of the industry caused Kodak to question the wisdom of entering this highly volatile area. In 1988, to reduce the costs of operating the Bio-Products division, a joint venture incorporating Bio-Products was formed between Kodak and Cultor Ltd. of Finland, and Kodak essentially left the market. The remaining parts of the Life Sciences division were then folded into the Health group in 1988, when Chandler completed Kodak's biggest acquisition, the purchase of Sterling Drug for over $5 billion.

The Sterling acquisition once again totally altered Kodak's strategy for the Health Group. Sterling Drug is a worldwide manufacturer and marketer of prescription drugs, over-the-counter medicine, and consumer products. It has such familiar brand names as Bayer aspirin, Phillips' milk of magnesia, and Panadol. Chandler thought this merger would provide Kodak with the marketing infrastructure and international drug registration that it needed to become a major player in the pharmaceuticals industry. With this acquisition Kodak's Health group became pharmaceutically oriented, its mission being to develop a full pipeline of major prescription drugs and a world-class portfolio of over-the-counter medicines.[17]

16. Eastman Kodak Company, *Annual Report,* 1986, p. 24.
17. Eastman Kodak Company, *Kodak Highlights, Third Quarter,* 1988, p. 5.

Analysts, however, questioned the acquisition. Once again Chandler was taking Kodak into an industry where competition was intense and the industry itself was consolidating because of the massive cost of drug development. Kodak had no expertise in this area, despite its forays into biotechnology, and the acquisition was unrelated to the other activities of the Health group. Some analysts claimed that the acquisition was aimed at deterring a possible takeover of Kodak and that it was too expensive.

The acquisition of Sterling dramatically increased the sales of the Health group but dampened Kodak's earnings and helped lead to a reversal in profits in 1989. Moreover, by purchasing Sterling, Kodak had obtained Sterling's Lehn & Fink products division, which produced products as diverse as Lysol and Minwax wood-care products. Far from wishing to sell this division, Kodak believed that this acquisition would lead to long-term profits. Analysts asked whether this was growth without profitability.

The Chemicals Group

Established more than sixty-five years ago as a supplier of raw materials for Kodak's film and processing businesses, the Eastman Chemical Company is responsible for developing many of the chemicals and plastics that have made Kodak the leader in the photographic industry. The company is also a major supplier of chemicals, fibers, and plastics to thousands of customers worldwide. Kodak is enjoying increased growth in its plastic material and resins unit because of outstanding performance and enthusiastic customer acceptance of Kodak PET (polyethylene terephthalate), a polymer used in soft-drink bottles and other food and beverage containers. The growth in popularity of 16-ounce PET bottles spurred a record year for both revenue and volume in 1985. Kodak announced the opening of a major new PET facility in England in 1988. In 1986, three new businesses were established within the Chemicals group: Specialty Printing Inks, Performance Plastics, and Animal Nutrition Supplements. They all share the common objective of enabling Chemicals to move quickly into profitable new market segments where there is the potential for growth.[18]

In its chemical business, too, Kodak has run into the same kinds of problems experienced by its other operating groups. There is intense competition in the plastics industry, not only from U.S. firms like Du Pont but also from large Japanese and European firms like Imperial Chemical Industries PLC and Hoech, which compete directly with Kodak for sales. In specialty plastics and PET, for example, volume increased but Kodak was forced to reduce prices by 5 percent to compete with other firms in the industry. This squeeze in profit margins also contributed to the reversal in earnings in 1989.

Logical Synergies?

With the huge profit reversal in 1989 after all the years of acquisition and internal development, analysts were questioning the existence of the "logical synergy" that Chandler, in 1988 address to shareholders, claimed for Kodak's businesses. Certainly, the relative contributions of the various operating groups to Kodak's total sales differed from the past, and Kodak was somewhat less dependent on the photographic industry. But was Kodak positioned to compete successfully in

18. Eastman Kodak Company, *Annual Report*, 1986, p. 19.

the 1990s? What was the rationale for Kodak's entry into different businesses; what were the synergies that Chandler was talking about? Wasn't the improvement on profits in 1990 due to corporate restructuring to reduce costs?

CORPORATE RESTRUCTURING AND COST REDUCTION

As Chandler tackled changes in strategy, he also directed his efforts at reshaping Kodak's management style and organizational structure to (1) reduce costs and (2) make the organization more flexible and attuned to the competitive environment. Because of its dominance in the industry, in the past Kodak had not worried about outside competition. As a result, the organizational culture at Kodak emphasized traditional, conservative values rather than entrepreneurial values. Kodak was often described as a conservative, plodding monolith because all decision making had been centralized at the top of the organization among a clique of senior managers. Furthermore, the company had been operating along functional lines. Research, production, and sales and marketing had operated separately in different divisions. The result of all these factors was a lack of communication and slow, inflexible decision making that led to delays in making new product decisions. When the company attempted to transfer resources between divisions, the separate functional operations also led to poor interdivisional relations, for managers protected their own turf at the expense of corporate goals. Moreover, there was a lack of attention to the bottom line, and management failed to institute measures to control waste.

Another factor encouraging Kodak's conservative orientation was its promotion policy. Seniority and loyalty to "mother Kodak" counted nearly as much as ability when it came to promotions. The company had been led by only twelve presidents since its beginnings in the 1880s.[19] Long after George Eastman's suicide in 1932, the company followed his cautious ways: "If George didn't do it, his successors didn't either."[20]

Kodak's technical orientation also contributed to its problems. Traditionally, its engineers and scientists had dominated decision making, and marketing had been neglected. The engineers and scientists were perfectionists who spent enormous amounts of time developing, analyzing, testing, assessing, and retesting new products. Little time, however, was spent determining whether the products satisfied consumer needs. As a result of this technical orientation, management passed up the invention of xerography, leaving the new technology to be developed by a small Rochester firm named Haloid Company (later Xerox). Similarly, Kodak had passed up the instant camera business. Kodak's lack of a marketing orientation allowed competitors to overtake it in several areas that were natural extensions of the photography business, such as 35mm cameras and video recorders.

Kodak's early management style, while profitable throughout the 1960s because of the company's privileged competitive position, was thus creating difficulties. With its monopoly in the photographic film and paper industry gone,

19. Barbara Buell, "A Gust of Fresh Air for the Stodgy Giant of Rochester," *Business Week*, June 10, 1985, p. 93.
20. Moore, "Embattled Kodak," p. 120.

Kodak was in trouble. Chandler had to alter Kodak's management orientation. He began with some radical changes in the company's culture and structure.

Firmly committed to cost cutting, Chandler orchestrated a massive downsizing of the work force to eliminate the fat that had accumulated during Kodak's prosperous past. Traditionally, Kodak had prided itself on being one of the most "Japanese" of all U.S. companies, hiring college graduates and giving them a permanent career. Now it had to go against one of its founding principles and reduce its work force. Kodak's policy of lifetime employment was swept out the door when declining profitability led to a large employee layoff.[21] Chandler instituted a special early retirement program, froze pay raises, and made the company's first layoffs in more than a decade. By 1985 the "yellow box factory" had dropped 12,600 of its original 136,000 employees. To further reduce costs in 1986, divisions were required to cut employment by an additional 10 percent and to cut budgetary expenditures by 5 percent. These measures helped, but because of Kodak's deteriorating performance, new rounds of cost cutting came in 1988 and 1989. Additional 5 percent reductions in employment aimed at saving $1 billion. The effect of these huge cuts was seen in 1990 when profits rebounded; however, it was not clear whether their effect on earnings would be short run or long run.

Although these measures had an effect on Kodak's culture, Chandler still needed to reshape Kodak's structure. In 1985 he began by shedding the old, stratified corporate structure for what he called an "entrepreneurial" approach. The first step was to reorganize the Imaging group into seventeen operating units. Each of the seventeen line-of-business units now contains all the functions necessary for the success of the enterprise, including marketing, financial, planning, product development, and manufacturing. Each unit is treated as an independent profit center and managed by a young executive with authority over everything from design to production. All units have a common goal of improving quality and efficiency and eliminating problems in the transfer of resources and technology among operating groups. The purpose behind this change was to eliminate the old divisional orientation, which had led to competition and reduced integration within the company. Chandler hoped that the changes in organizational control and structure would promote innovation, speed reaction time, and establish clear profit goals.[22] With this restructuring, Chandler also reduced Kodak's top-heavy management in order to decentralize decision making to lower levels in the hierarchy. This reorganization was a sign that the company was at last shedding its paternalistic approach to management.[23]

In further attempts to bring costs more into line with those of foreign competitors who benefit from lower wage rates, favored government treatment, and currency advantages, Kodak instituted new control systems. In February 1986 operating groups were directed to reduce operating and expense budgets. In the move to maintain quality while keeping costs low, manufacturing plants have introduced stringent specifications that have improved both quality and efficiency. To compete effectively in a global marketplace, Kodak uses quality as the yardstick to measure its success.[24]

21. Buell, "A Gust of Fresh Air," p. 93.

22. Ibid.

23. "Yellow at the Edges," *The Economist*, December 7, 1984, p. 90.

24. Eastman Kodak Company, *Annual Report*, 1985, p. 12.

Relying on its new risk-taking attitude, Kodak also attempted to create a structure and culture to encourage internal venturing. It formed a "venture board" to help underwrite small projects and make conventional venture capital investments. In addition, the company created an "office of submitted ideas" to screen outside projects. Kodak received more than 3,000 proposals, although only 30 survived the screening process.[25] This aggressive research program led to a breakthrough in tubular silver halide grains, which improve the light-gathering capability of film. The discovery resulted in the new line of 35mm products.

However, Kodak's attempts in intrapreneurship have generally been unsuccessful. Of the fourteen ventures that Kodak created, six have been shut down, three have been sold, and four have been merged into the company; only one still operates independently.[26] One reason for this failure was that Kodak did not give managers an equity stake in the new ventures, so they felt that they had no stake in the ventures' success.

Having learned its lesson, Kodak recently announced that throughout the company pay would be more closely related to performance. For example, in 1989 as much as 40 percent of a manager's annual compensation was to be based on corporate performance. Even at the middle-manager level, 15 percent of compensation was to be linked to company results. Finally, at the level of wages, Kodak announced that it would link dividends paid to ordinary workers to the company's return on assets. It hopes by these measures to make the company more entrepreneurial and to move it along the cost reduction path. However, cost cutting will not be enough to turn Kodak around if its businesses do not generate increased revenues and achieve their profit potential.

Kodak also reorganized its worldwide facilities to reduce costs. International divisions were turning out identical products at higher cost than their counterparts in the United States. In a plan to coordinate worldwide production to increase productivity and lower costs, Kodak streamlined European production by closing duplicate manufacturing facilities and centralizing production and marketing operations, and it also brought some foreign manufacturing home. As a result, Kodak gained $55 million in productivity savings. However, the rise of the dollar boosted the cost of export products to foreign customers; thus export expenses offset most of the gains.[27] Now that the dollar has fallen, these problems have been reversed, and profits from foreign operations are helping Kodak's earning figures as Kodak's international operations have regained their profitability. However, Fuji's new European facility will pose a severe challenge. Starting from scratch and employing production techniques learned from low-cost Japanese operations, Fuji will squeeze Kodak's profit margins and cause further changes in its European operations. In 1989, Kodak moved its international headquarters to London to decentralize authority to managers on the spot.

25. Taylor, "Kodak Scrambles," pp. 34–38.
26. James S. Hirsch, "Kodak Effort at 'Intrapreneurship' Fails," *The Wall Street Journal*, August 17, 1990, p. 32.
27. Eastman Kodak Company, *Annual Report,* 1985.

KODAK'S FUTURE

Whether Kodak has succeeded in its efforts to reorganize its strategy and structure has yet to be seen. Some analysts, pointing to the recent upswing in profits, are confident that the changes already made will restore Kodak's profitability. Others think that Kodak has done too little too late, that it has not achieved a clear rationale for its pattern of acquisitions, and that it still has many problems to deal with. They claim that Kay Whitmore needs to take a close look at Kodak's acquisitions and decide whether mistakes have been made and, if necessary, to divest acquisitions. On the other hand, given the investment in Sterling Drug and in other product lines, Whitmore needs to consider whether Kodak should make additional acquisitions to strengthen its stake in these new businesses so that it can deal with the fierce competition in the new product markets. Are there synergies to be achieved between operating groups? If there are, is the right structure in place to achieve them?

Kodak faces challenges with managing its new businesses. Given the failure of its intrapreneurship program, managing these ventures with a new entrepreneurial style rather than through the centralized, conservative approach of the past will not be easy. Already, difficulties have crept in. One example is Kodak's managing of Atex Inc., the manufacturer of desk-top publishing systems that Kodak bought in 1981. Because of Kodak's overbearing management style, the top executives and employees of Atex resigned, creating serious management problems for Kodak. The Atex executives claimed that Kodak executives were hard working but bureaucratic and did not understand the competitive nature of computer technology. Kodak managers should have been reacting to the computer marketplace weekly. They did not, and Atex executives could not handle Kodak's slow pace.[28]

What effects the reorganization of Kodak into four operating groups will have on performance remains to be seen. Even with reorganization, however, Kodak has moved into some uncertain environments in which the company has little experience and faces formidable rivals. Kodak faces competition from RCA and GE in consumer electronics, IBM and DEC in office systems. It must combat foreign competition from Fuji, Konica, Nikon, Canon, and Minolta in still cameras and copiers. It has already lost the battle with Matsushita, Sony, and Toshiba in video cameras and recorders and videotapes. Kodak also has the problem that entry into new businesses means lower profit margins. Ventures such as electronic imaging, magnetic tape, and floppy disks were in highly competitive industries that traditionally have lower profit margins than does chemical photography. Besides, new businesses are very expensive to enter, and Kodak's long-term earnings are heavily dependent on the future growth of these industries and on its ability to profit from this growth.

Venturing into the volatile biotechnology, pharmaceuticals, and office information systems business was obviously a gamble. However, Kodak had little choice because its existing business is mature and amateur and professional photography was a saturated market. Nevertheless, some analysts claim that Kodak

28. Moore, "Embattled Kodak," pp. 120–128.

should have stayed inside the imaging businesses and kept its activities closely aligned to its core skills. They argue that Kodak is still a one-business company and that its recent activities only disguise that fact. In fact, they view the whole acquisition process over the last ten years as a way of fending off takeover attempts by companies competing for Kodak's huge cash flow. In 1990, they pointed to Kodak's creation of "tin parachutes" as yet one more way in which the company is fighting to maintain its independence. In the event of a takeover, Kodak has guaranteed all its employees large severance pay and other benefits. This plan makes Kodak a very expensive takeover target. Whether a takeover will occur depends on the outcome of the litigation with Polaroid. The amount of the settlement has yet to be announced. As soon as it is, analysts claim that takeover is a distinct possibility. Already a friendly takeover of Kodak by the Walt Disney Company has been suggested because of their fifteen-year marketing agreement. Would this add value to Kodak or to Disney? What should be done?

Can Kodak learn to play a different and tougher competitive game, or will it be taken over? The market has changed, and Kodak must play in businesses where it is no longer a worldwide leader and where it has neither a technological advantage nor a significant cost advantage. The question now is whether Kodak's moves under Whitmore can make Chandler's acquisition strategy bear fruit and whether Kodak can manage its new strategy and structure to fight off a takeover attempt. Financially, Kodak is still one of the top twenty-five U.S. companies. It is financially sound, with total assets of $25 billion. Kodak's brand name is also a major asset: it is one of the most recognized in the world. Can Kodak utilize these assets in the new competitive environment, or is it too late?

The Eastman Kodak Company and subsidiary companies' consolidated statements are summarized in Exhibits 5, 6, and 7.

Exhibit 5
Consolidated Statement of Financial Condition

Eastman Kodak Company and subsidiary companies

	Dec. 31, 1989	Dec. 25, 1988
	(in millions)	
Assets		
Current assets		
Cash and cash equivalents	$1,095	$848
Marketable securities	184	227
Receivables	4,245	4,071
Inventories	2,507	3,025
Deferred income tax charges	306	272
Prepaid charges applicable to future operations	254	241
Total current assets	8,591	8,684
Properties		
Land, buildings, machinery, and equipment at cost	16,774	15,667
Less: Accumulated depreciation	8,146	7,654
Net properties	8,628	8,013
Other assets		
Unamortized goodwill	4,579	4,610
Long-term receivables and other noncurrent assets	1,854	1,657
Total assets	$23,652	$22,964
Liabilities and shareowners' equity		
Current liabilities		
Payables	$6,073	$5,277
Taxes—income and other	338	411
Dividends payable	162	162
Total current liabilities	6,573	5,850
Other liabilities and deferred credits		
Long-term borrowings	7,376	7,779
Other long-term liabilities	1,371	990
Deferred income tax credits	1,690	1,565
Total liabilities and deferred credits	17,010	16,184
Shareowners' equity		
Common stock, par value $2.50 per share 950,000,000 shares authorized; issued 373,581,604 in 1989 and 373,421,584 in 1988	934	934
Additional capital paid in or transferred from retained earnings	6	1
Retained earnings	7,802	7,922
Accumulated translation adjustment	(41)	(81)
	8,701	8,776
Less: Treasury stock at cost at December 31, 1989—49,004,563 shares at December 25, 1988—49,007,304 shares	2,059	2,059
Total shareowners' equity	6,642	6,780
Total liabilities and shareowners' equity	$23,652	$22,964

Source: Eastman Kodak Company, *Annual Report,* 1989.

Exhibit 6
Consolidated Statement of Cash Flows

Eastman Kodak Company and subsidiary companies

	1989	1988 (in millions)	1987
Cash flows from operating activities			
Net earnings	**$529**	$1,397	$1,178
Adjustments to reconcile net earnings to net cash provided by operating activities:			
Depreciation and amortization	**1,326**	1,183	995
Provision for deferred taxes	—	160	193
Retirement of properties	**322**	265	303
Increase in receivables	**(174)**	(503)	(535)
Decrease (increase) in inventories	**518**	(507)	(106)
Increase in liabilities excluding borrowings	**334**	10	606
Other items, net	**(236)**	(694)	(350)
Total adjustments	**2,090**	(86)	1,106
Net cash provided by operating activities	**2,619**	1,311	2,284
Cash flows from investing activities			
Additions to properties	**(2,118)**	(1,914)	(1,652)
Acquisitions—net of cash acquired	—	(4,781)	—
Marketable securities—purchases	**(356)**	(329)	(394)
Marketable securities—sales	**406**	684	288
Other items, net	**10**	16	22
Net cash used in investing activities	**(2,058)**	(6,324)	(1,736)
Cash flows from financing activities			
Net increase (decrease) in short-term borrowings	**482**	413	(178)
Proceeds from long-term borrowings	**762**	5,432	1,537
Repayment of long-term borrowings	**(878)**	(71)	(132)
Dividends to shareowners	**(649)**	(600)	(568)
Treasury stock purchases	—	—	(978)
Other items, net	**5**	2	(3)
Net cash provided by (used in) financing activities	**(278)**	5,176	(322)
Effect of exchange rate changes on cash	**(36)**	(17)	40
Net increase in cash and cash equivalents	**247**	146	266
Cash and cash equivalents, beginning of year	**848**	702	436
Cash and cash equivalents, end of year	**$1,095**	$848	$702

Source: Eastman Kodak Company, *Annual Report,* 1989.

Exhibit 7 Kodak in Review

Eastman Kodak Company and subsidiary companies

	1989	1988	1987	1986	1985
	(Dollar amounts and shares in millions except per share figures)				
Management's discussion and analysis					
Sales	**$18,398**	$17,034	$13,305	$11,550	$10,631
Earnings from operations[(1)]	**1,591***	2,812	2,078	724**	561***
Earnings before income taxes	**925**	2,236	1,984	598	530
Net earnings	**529***	1,397	1,178	374**	332***
Earnings and dividends					
Net earnings—percent of sales	**2.9%**	8.2%	8.9%	3.2%	3.1%
—percent return on average shareowners' equity	**7.9%**	21.8%	19.0%	5.8%	4.8%
—per common share[(2)(3)]	**1.63**	4.31	3.52	1.10	.97
Cash dividends declared					
—on common shares	**649**	616	572	551	553
—per common share[(3)]	**2.00**	1.90	1.71	1.63	1.62
Common shares outstanding at close of year	**324.4**	324.2	324.1	338.7	338.5
Shareowners at close of year	**171,954**	174,110	168,517	172,713	184,231
Balance sheet data					
Current assets	**$8,591**	$8,684	$6,791	$5,857	$5,677
Properties at cost	**16,774**	15,667	13,789	12,919	12,047
Accumulated depreciation	**8,146**	7,654	7,126	6,643	6,070
Total assets	**23,652**	22,964	14,698	12,994	12,142
Current liabilities	**6,573**	5,850	4,140	3,811	3,325
Long-term obligations	**7,376**	7,779	2,382	981	988
Total net assets (shareowners' equity)	**6,642**	6,780	6,013	6,388	6,562
Supplemental information					
Sales—Imaging[(4)]	**$6,998**	$6,642	$6,206	$8,352	$8,531
Information systems	**4,200**	3,937	3,494		
Chemicals[(4)]	**3,522**	3,123	2,635	2,378	2,348
Health[(4)]	**4,009**	3,597	1,206	1,056	
Research and development expenditures	**1,253**	1,147	992	1,059	976
Depreciation	**1,181**	1,057	962	956	831
Taxes (excludes payroll, sales, and excise taxes)	**551**	973	911	329	297
Wages, salaries, and employee benefits	**5,877**	5,469	4,645	4,912	4,482
Employees at close of year					
—in the U.S.	**82,850**	87,900	81,800	83,600	89,200
—worldwide	**137,750**	145,300	124,400	121,450	128,950
Subsidiary companies outside the U.S.					
Sales	**$8,391**	$7,748	$5,572	$4,387	$3,429
Earnings from operations[(1)]	**771**	977	779	400	169

(1) Data for 1988 and 1987 restated to reflect Goodwill amortization in Cost of Goods Sold.
(2) Based on average number of shares outstanding.
(3) Data for 1985 and 1986 have been restated to give effect to the 3-for-2 partial stock split in 1987.
(4) Data for 1988 and 1987 restated for change from three to four segments.
*After deducting restructuring costs of $875 million which reduced net earnings by $549 million.
**After deducting unusual charges of $520 million and certain other special charges of $134 million which in total reduced earnings from operations by $654 million. Net earnings were reduced by $373 million because of all special charges and an additional $50 million from the retroactive repeal of the U.S. investment tax credit as a result of the 1986 tax law change.
***After deducting unusual charges of $563 million which reduced net earnings by $302 million.

Source: Eastman Kodak Company, *Annual Report*, 1989.

Eastman Kodak Company and Subsidiary Companies Summary of Operating Data

Eastman Kodak Company and subsidiary companies

	1992	1991	1990	1989	1988
	(Dollar amounts and shares in millions except per share figures)				
Sales	**$20,183**	**$19,419**	**$18,908**	**$18,398**	**$17,034**
Earnings before income taxes	**1,601**(1)	**11**(3)	**1,257**(4)	**925**(5)	**2,236**
Net earnings	**1,146**(1)(2)	**17**(3)	**703**(4)	**529**(5)	**1,397**
Earnings and Dividends					
Net earnings—percent of sales	5.7%	0.1%	3.7%	2.9%	8.2%
—percent return on average shareowners' equity	18.1%	0.3%	10.5%	7.9%	21.8%
Primary earnings per share(6)	3.53	.05	2.17	1.63	4.31
Cash dividends declared—on common shares	650	649	649	649	616
—per common share	2.00	2.00	2.00	2.00	1.90
Common shares outstanding at close of year	325.9	324.9	324.6	324.3	324.2
Shareowners at close of year	166,532	169,164	168,935	171,954	174,110
Statement of Financial Position Data					
Current assets	$7,405	$8,258	$8,608	$8,591	$8,684
Properties at cost	19,840	19,034	17,648	16,774	15,667
Accumulated depreciation	10,005	9,432	8,670	8,146	7,654
Total assets	23,138	24,170	24,136	23,652	22,964
Current liabilities	5,998	6,899	7,163	6,573	5,850
Long-term borrowings	7,202	7,597	6,989	7,376	7,779
Total net assets (shareowners' equity)	6,557	6,104	6,748	6,642	6,780
Supplemental Information					
Sales—Imaging	$7,415	$7,075	$7,128	$6,998	$6,642
Information	4,063	3,968	4,140	4,200	3,937
Chemicals	3,927	3,740	3,588	3,522	3,123
Health	5,081	4,917	4,349	4,009	3,597
Research and development costs	1,587	1,494	1,329	1,253	1,147
Depreciation	1,393	1,329	1,168	1,181	1,057
Taxes (excludes payroll, sales, and excise taxes)	784	165	719	551	973
Wages, salaries, and employee benefits	6,293	6,105	5,783	5,877	5,469
Employees at close of year—in the U.S.	77,100	76,900	80,350	82,850	87,900
—worldwide	132,600	133,200	134,450	137,750	145,300
Subsidiary Companies Outside the U.S.					
Sales	$9,353	$9,011	$8,668	$8,391	$7,748
Earnings from operations	673	670	1,150	771	977

(1)After deducting $220 million of restructuring costs which reduced net earnings by $141 million.
(2) Net earnings for 1992 benefited by $152 million from the cumulative effect of adopting SFAS No. 109, Accounting for Income Taxes.
(3) After deducting $1,605 million of restructuring costs which reduced net earnings by $1,032 million.
(4) After deducting $888 million for the litigation judgment including post-judgment interest which reduced net earnings by $564 million.
(5) After deducting restructuring costs of $875 million which reduced net earnings by $549 million.
(6) Based on average number of shares outstanding.

Source: Eastman Kodak Company, *Annual Report*, 1992.

Eastman Kodak Company and Subsidiary Companies Consolidated Statement of Earnings

	1992	1991	1990
	(In millions, except per share data)		
Revenues			
Sales	$20,183	$19,419	$18,908
Earnings from equity interests and other revenues	394	255	289
Total revenues	20,577	19,674	19,197
Costs			
Cost of goods sold	10,392	9,985	9,637
Marketing and administrative expenses	5,869	5,565	5,098
Research and development costs	1,587	1,494	1,329
Interest expense	813	844	855
Restructuring costs/Litigation judgment	220	1,605	888
Other charges	95	170	133
Total Costs	18,976	19,663	17,940
Earnings before income taxes	1,601	11	1,257
Provision (benefit) for income taxes	607	(6)	554
Earnings before cumulative effect of change in accounting principle	994	17	703
Cumulative effect of change in accounting principle	152	—	—
Net earnings	$1,146	$17	$703
Primary earnings per share before cumulative effect of change in accounting principle	$3.06	$.05	$2.17
Cumulative effect of change in accounting principle	.47	—	—
Primary earnings per share	$3.53	$.05	$2.17
Fully diluted earnings per share before cumulative effect of change in accounting principle	$2.98	$.05	$2.16
Cumulative effect of change in accounting principle	.43	—	—
Fully diluted earnings per share	3.41	$.05	$2.16

Eastman Kodak Company and Subsidiary Companies Consolidated Statement of Retained Earnings

	1992	1991	1990
	(In millions, except per share data)		
Retained earnings			
Retained earnings at beginning of year	$7,225	$7,859	$7,802
Net earnings	1,146	17	703
Cash dividends declared ($2.00 per share)	(650)	(649)	(649)
Other changes	—	(2)	3
Retained earnings at end of year	$7,721	$7,225	$7,859

Source: Eastman Kodak Company, *Annual Report*, 1992.

Eastman Kodak Company and Subsidiary Companies Consolidated Statement of Cash Flows

	1992	1991 (In millions)	1990
Cash flows from operating activities:			
Net earnings	$1,146	$17	$703
Adjustments to reconcile net earnings to net cash provided by operating activities:			
Depreciation and amortization	1,539	1,477	1,309
Provision (benefit) for deferred taxes	1	(153)	(192)
Loss on sale and retirement of properties	148	131	154
Decrease (increase) in receivables	216	(15)	(88)
(Increase) decrease in inventories	(150)	114	82
Increase in liabilities excluding borrowings	271	755	414
Cumulative effect of change in accounting	(152)	—	—
Other items, net	347	145	35
Total adjustments	2,220	2,454	1,714
Net cash provided by operating activities	3,366	2,471	2,417
Cash flows from investing activities:			
Additions to properties	(2,092)	(2,135)	(2,037)
Proceeds from sale of investments	189	33	10
Proceeds from sale of properties	85	53	83
Marketable securities—purchases	(159)	(60)	(128)
Marketable securities—sales	114	102	126
Other items	3	16	90
Net cash used in investing activities	(1,860)	(1,991)	(1,856)
Cash flows from financing activities:			
Net (decrease) increase in commercial paper borrowings of 90 days or less	(629)	(111)	114
Proceeds from other borrowings	549	1,535	1,691
Repayment of other borrowings	(1,184)	(1,207)	(2,102)
Dividends to shareowners	(650)	(649)	(649)
Other items	16	2	1
Net cash used in financing activities	(1,898)	(430)	(945)
Effect of exchange rate changes on cash	(17)	(2)	24
Net (decrease) increase in cash and cash equivalents	(409)	48	(360)
Cash and cash equivalents, beginning of year	783	735	1,095
Cash and cash equivalents, end of year	$374	$783	$735

Source: Eastman Kodak Company, *Annual Report*, 1992.

Eastman Kodak Company and Subsidiary Companies Consolidated Statement of Financial Position

	December 31, 1992	1991
Assets	(In millions)	
Current Assets		
Cash and cash equivalents	$374	$783
Marketable securities	186	141
Receivables (net of allowances of $198 and $200)	3,984	4,348
Inventories	2,379	2,311
Deferred income tax charges	244	421
Other	238	254
Total current assets	7,405	8,258
Properties		
Land, buildings, and equipment at cost	19,840	19,034
Less: Accumulated depreciation	10,005	9,432
Net properties	9,835	9,602
Other Assets		
Unamortized goodwill (net of accumulated amortization of $697 and $551)	4,273	4,349
Long-term receivables and other noncurrent assets	1,625	1,961
Total assets	$23,138	$24,170
Liabilities and Shareowners' Equity		
Current Liabilities		
Payables	$3,594	$3,835
Short-term borrowings	1,736	2,610
Taxes—income and other	505	292
Dividends payable	163	162
Total current liabilities	5,998	6,899
Other Liabilities		
Long-term borrowings	7,202	7,597
Other long-term liabilities	2,312	2,080
Deferred income tax credits	1,069	1,490
Total liabilities	16,581	18,066
Shareowners' Equity		
Common stock, par value $2.50 per share 950,000,000 shares authorized; issued 374,479,114 in 1992, 373,785,298 in 1991 and 373,638,981 in 1990	936	934
Additional capital paid in or transferred from retained earnings	26	9
Retained earnings	7,721	7,225
Accumulated translation adjustment	(85)	(12)
	8,598	8,156
Less: Treasury stock shares at cost 48,562,835 shares in 1992, 48,852,102 shares in 1991 and 49,001,140 shares in 1990	2,041	2,052
Total shareowners' equity	6,557	6,104
Total Liabilities and Shareowners' Equity	$23,138	$24,170

Source: Eastman Kodak Company, *Annual Report*, 1992.

CASE

28 Philips NV: Organizational and Strategic Evolution

INTRODUCTION

Established in 1891, the Dutch company Philips NV is one of the world's largest electronics enterprises. Its businesses are grouped into four main divisions: lighting, consumer electronics, professional products (computers, telecommunications, and medical equipment), and components (including semiconductor chips). In each of these areas it ranks alongside the likes of Matsushita, General Electric, Sony, and Siemens as a global competitor. By the early 1990s the company had several hundred subsidiaries in 60 countries. It operated manufacturing plants in more than 50 countries, manufactured thousands of different products, and employed 250,000 people worldwide (down from 350,000 a decade earlier). However, despite its global reach, by the early 1990s Philips was a company in deep trouble. After a decade of deteriorating performance, in 1990 Philips lost $2.4 billion on revenues of $33 billion (see Exhibit 1 for financial data). Although the company returned to profitability in 1991, 1992 brought a loss of $489 million on sales of $31.8 billion. The company attributed this loss to weak markets in Europe, where it generates just about half of its annual sales, and to a $652 million restructuring charge to cover planned layoffs.

EARLY HISTORY AND ORGANIZATION

Philips was founded in 1891 by Gerard Philips. Gerard, an electrical engineer, had developed an inexpensive process to manufacture incandescent lamps. He was later joined by his brother, Anton. While Gerard focused on technical matters, Anton became responsible for the commercial side of the business, particularly sales. From this arrangement was born the *duumvirate* form of management which came to characterize Philips for much of its history. Under this arrangement, which was found throughout the company, top management responsibility and authority was shared by two managers—one who was responsible for "commercial affairs" and another who was responsible for "technical activities." Thus most of Philips' 60 or so national operations were headed not by one individual, but by two. Indeed, in the case of many national organizations the technical and commercial managers were joined by a third individual, a financial manager, to form a triumvirate leadership committee. One consequence of this arrangement was that throughout the organization there was an informal competition between the technical and commercial managers, with

This case was prepared by Charles W. L. Hill, University of Washington. This case was prepared as a basis for class discussion rather than to illustrate either effective or ineffective handling of administrative situations.

Income Data (Million $)

Year Ended Dec. 31	Revs.	Oper. Inc.	% Oper. Inc. of Revs.	Cap. Exp.	Depr.	Int. Exp.	[3]Net Bef. Taxes	Eff. Tax Rate	[4]Net Inc.	% Net Inc. of Revs.	Cash Flow
[1,2]1992	32,178	2,976	9.2	1,831	1,891	1,065	[d]292	NM	[d]495	NM	1,396
[1]1991	33,274	3,614	10.9	1,191	1,914	1,217	965	26.4%	573	1.7	2,487
[1]1990	33,018	3,566	10.8	1,941	2,319	1,297	[d]2,380	NM	[d]2,680	NM	[d]361
[1]1989	29,985	2,869	9.6	2,141	1,802	1,012	763	35.8%	[d]415	1.4	2,217
1988	28,011	2,663	9.5	1,989	1,680	1,047	466	33.9%	265	0.9	1,945
1987	29,831	2,865	9.6	2,525	1,813	1,041	599	19.7%	458	1.5	2,271
1986	25,334	2,559	10.1	2,101	1,439	814	903	42.1%	[d]441	1.7	1,880
1985	21,802	2,257	10.4	1,603	1,269	833	658	39.4%	356	1.6	1,625
[2]1984	15,167	1,614	10.6	1,119	775	600	572	36.2%	314	2.1	1,089
1983	15,102	1,541	10.2	809	691	602	469	45.0%	212	1.4	903

Balance Sheet Data (Million $)

Dec. 31	Cash	Assets	Curr. Liab.	Ratio	Total Assets	% Ret. on Assets	Long Term Debt	Common Equity	Total Inv. Cap.	% LT Debt of Cap.	% Ret. on Equity
1992	912	15,408	10,269	1.5	26,856	NM	5,510	4,987	11,843	46.5	NM
1991	1,129	15,683	11,484	1.4	29,087	1.9	6,519	6,735	14,240	45.8	8.5
1990	1,488,	15,898	11,752	1.4	30,549	NM	6,966	6,611	14,792	47.1	NM
1989	809	15,415	11,213	1.4	28,809	1.5	5,230	8,849	15,243	34.3	4.7
1988	712	14,168	9,633	1.5	26,398	1.0	4,969	8,262	14,356	34.6	3.1
1987	1,020	15,069	10,522	1.4	28,260	1.7	4,894	8,779	14,974	32.7	5.5
1986	590	12,578	8,494	1.5	23,305	2.1	4,065	7,299	12,505	32.5	6.6
1985	630	11,173	7,151	1.6	19,202	2.0	3,299	5,864	10,045	32.8	6.5
1984	449	9,011	5,576	1.6	15,373	2.0	2,682	4,783	8,220	32.6	6.7
1983	552	9,243	5,756	1.6	15,617	1.3	2,434	4,498	8,269	29.4	4.4

Data as orig. reptd.; translated at period-end exchange rates; based on Netherlands GAAP. 1. Refl. merger or acq. 2. Refl. acctg. change. 3. Incl. equity in earns. of nonconsol. subs. 4. Bef. spec. items. d-Deficit. NM-Not Meaningful.

Exhibit 1
Financial Data

both attempting to outperform the other. This was generally viewed as being beneficial. As Anton once noted:

> [T]he technical management and the sales management competed to out-perform each other. Production tried to produce so much that sales would not be able to get rid of it; sales tried to sell so much that the factory would not be able to keep up.[1]

Perhaps reflecting the competition between commercial and technical management, sales volume, as opposed to profit, was the traditional measure of success at Philips—the belief being that so long as sales continued to grow, profits would automatically follow.

Up until World War II the foreign activities of Philips were run out of its head office in Eindhoven. During World War II, however, the Netherlands were

1. Quoted in "The Philips Group: 1987," Harvard Business School Case #388–050. Cambridge, Mass, 1987.

occupied by Germany. Cut off from their home base, Philips' various national organizations began to operate independently. In essence, each major national organization developed into a self-contained company with its own manufacturing, marketing, and R&D functions.

Following the war, top management felt that the company could be most successfully rebuilt through its national organizations. There were several reasons for this. First, high trade barriers made it logical that self-contained national organizations be established in each major national market. Second, it was felt that strong national organizations allowed Philips to be responsive to local demands in each country in which it competed. And third, given the substantial autonomy that the various national organizations had gained during the war, top management felt that reestablishing centralized control might prove difficult and yield few benefits.

At the same time, top management felt the need for some centralized control over product policy and R&D in order to achieve some coordination among national organizations. The response was to create a number of worldwide product divisions (of which there were 14 by the mid 1980s). In theory, basic R&D and product development policy were the responsibility of the product divisions, whereas the national organizations were responsible for day-to-day operations in a particular country. Product strategy in a given country was meant to be determined jointly by consultation between the responsible national organization and the product divisions. It was the national organizations that implemented strategy.

The top decision-making and policymaking body in the company was a 10-person board of management (which was distinct from the board of directors). While board members all shared general management responsibility, they typically maintained a special interest in one of the functional areas of the company (e.g., R&D, manufacturing, marketing). Traditionally, most of the members of the management board were Dutch and most had come up through the Eindhoven bureacracy. However, most did have the benefit of extensive foreign postings, normally as a top manager in one of the company's national organizations. Most top managers within Philips were also long-time company men, the majority having joined the company in their early 20s.

One of the key roles of the management board was to act as an arbitrator of negotiations between the highly autonomous national organizations and the product divisions. The negotiations embraced a whole range of issues, from setting sales targets for the coming year to getting a national organization to adopt a new product developed by one of the divisions. The fact that the product divisions did not always get the upper hand in these negotiations was graphically illustrated in the mid 1970s when Philips' U.S. national organization decided not to adopt the videocassette recorder format developed by Philips, the V2000 format. Instead the U.S. national organization adopted the VHS format that was being marketed by Philips' global rival, Matsushita. As it turned out, this decision was the correct one, for the VHS format became the dominant design in the videocassette industry, while Philips' V2000 format faded into obscurity.

The management board was supported in its tasks by a substantial Eindhoven-based corporate staff. The staff, which was often compared to a government civil service, performed a wide range of technical, general, and commercial services. These included building design and plant engineering; industrial coordination; financial, legal, and accounting services; management development; strategic planning; and advertising. Like the top managers, most of the corporate staff

were Dutch, and most had spent their whole careers at Philips. By the end of the 1980s this staff still numbered over 3,000. In addition, the Eindhoven-based product divisions had their own staff, which numbered around 2,500. As for Eindhoven itself, in many respects this was (and still is) the archetypal company town with its Philips theater, Philips library, and Philips museum. Indeed, even the local soccer team, PSV Eindhoven (one of Europe's best soccer clubs) was sponsored by Philips.

ENVIRONMENTAL CHANGE

From the 1960s onward a number of significant changes took place in Philips' competitive environment that were to affect the company profoundly. First, due to the efforts of the General Agreement on Tariffs and Trade (GATT), trade barriers fell worldwide. In addition, in Philips' home base, Europe, the emergence of the European Economic Community, of which the Netherlands was an early member, led to a further reduction in trade barriers among the countries of Western Europe.

Second, during the 1960s and 1970s a number of new competitors emerged in Japan. Taking advantage of the success of GATT in lowering trade barriers, the Japanese companies produced most of their output at home and then exported to the rest of the world. The resulting economies of scale allowed them to drive down unit costs below those achieved by Western competitors, such as Philips, which manufactured in multiple locations. This significantly increased competitive pressures in most of the business areas where Philips competed.

Third, due to technological changes, the cost of R&D and manufacturing increased rapidly. The introduction of transistors and then integrated circuits called for significant capital expenditures in production facilities, often running into hundreds of millions of dollars. To realize scale economies, substantial levels of output had to be achieved. Moreover, the pace of technological change was declining and product life-cycles were shortening. This gave companies in the electronics industry less time to recoup their capital investments before new-generation products came along.

Finally, as the world moved from a series of fragmented national markets toward a single global market, uniform global standards for electronic equipment began to emerge. This showed itself most clearly in the videocassette recorder business where three standards initially battled for dominance—Sony's Betamax standard, Matsushita's VHS standard, and Philips' V2000 standard. In the event, the VHS standard was the one most widely accepted by consumers, and the others were eventually abandoned. For Philips and Sony, both of which had invested substantially in their own standard, this was a significant defeat.

ORGANIZATIONAL AND STRATEGIC CHANGE

By the early 1980s Philips realized that if it was to survive it was going to have to radically restructure its business. Its cost structure was high due to the amount of duplication across national organizations, particularly in the area of

manufacturing. Moreover, as the V2000 incident demonstrated, the company's attempts to compete uniformly across the globe were being hindered by the strength and autonomy of its national organizations. From 1982 onward Philips began to attempt to change its organization. The various changes were associated with three successive CEOs, Wisse Dekker, Cor van de Klugt, and Jan Timmer.

Wisse Dekker, 1982–1986

The first attempt at change came in 1982 when Wisse Dekker was appointed CEO. Dekker quickly pushed for manufacturing rationalization, creating international production centers that served a number of national organizations and closing many small inefficient plants. He also pushed Philips to enter into more collaborative arrangements with other electronics firms to share the costs and risks of developing new products. In addition, Dekker accelerated a trend that already had begun within the company to move away from the dual leadership arrangement within national organizations (commercial and technical), replacing this arrangement with a single general manager. Furthermore, Dekker tried to "tilt" Philips' matrix away from national organizations by creating a corporate council where the heads of product divisions would join the heads of the national organizations to discuss issues of importance to both. At the same time, he gave the product divisions more responsibility to determine company-wide research and manufacturing activities.

Van de Klugt, 1986–1990

In 1986 Dekker was succeeded by Cor van de Klugt. One of van de Klugt's first actions was to specify that profitability was to be the central criterion for evaluating performance within Philips. The product divisions were given primary responsibility for achieving profits. This was followed in late 1986 by his termination of the U.S. Philips trust, which had been given control of Philips' North American operations during World War II and still maintained them as of 1986. By terminating the trust, in theory, van de Klugt reestablished Eindhoven's control over the North American subsidiary.

In May 1987 van de Klugt announced a major restructuring of Philips. He designated four product divisions—lighting, consumer electronics, electronic components, and telecommunications and data systems—as "core divisions," the implication being that other activities would be sold off. Lighting was designated a "stand-alone" product division, while technical linkages between the other three divisions were emphasized. The non-core product divisions included domestic appliances and medical systems. In 1987 Philips pooled its domestic appliances business in a joint venture with Whirlpool. In the same year Philips reached an agreement to merge its medical systems business into a joint venture with the General Electric Company of Britain (which has no link to the U.S. General Electric Company). This decision was welcomed by the management of the medical systems division, which had been increasingly frustrated in its attempts to compete globally by the necessity of having to "persuade" the general managers of national organizations to adopt certain products. Moreover, the rapidly developing medical systems business demanded that large investment decisions be made on a worldwide basis. The managers of Philips' medical division felt that their ability to make such decisions was compromised by a need to coordinate investments with the managers of national organizations, not all of whom had the same priorities as the medical division.

Van de Klugt also reduced the size of the management board. Its policymaking responsibility was devolved to a new group management committee, comprising the remaining board members plus the heads of the core product divisions. No heads of national organizations were appointed to this body.

Under van de Klugt, Philips closed or merged 75 of its 346 manufacturing plants spread over 50 countries. It also shed some 38,000 employees (17,000 by selling businesses to other companies out of a total of 344,000 in 1986).

Two of the four core product divisions appeared to respond positively to these changes. Philips' biggest success story was its lighting division. Number one in the world market, with a global market share of 30 percent, in 1989 the lighting division accounted for only 13 percent of the company's sales but more than 30 percent of its profits. The other division that did well was Philips' consumer products division. Although this division produces everything from compact discs (a technology pioneered by Philips) to electric tin openers, its star business during the late 1980s was the recording label, Polygram. Under the leadership of Jan Timmer, Polygram had expanded rapidly in the 1980s by aggressively purchasing smaller recording labels with star talent such as U2, Janet Jackson, and Luciano Pavarotti. Timmer subsequently was appointed by van de Klugt to head the consumer products division. Under Timmer's leadership, the division streamlined its structure, improved its marketing (which historically had been weak), and invested in several next generation consumer technologies, including an interactive compact disc system, a recordable digital compact cassette system, and high-definition television.

Despite these bright spots, Philips' competitive position continued to deteriorate under van de Klugt's tenure. The problem areas were the telecommunications and data systems division and the components division. In the telecommunications and data systems division, Philips suffered badly from its failure to anticipate the shift in computers away from the minicomputers that Philips manufactured and toward personal computers. As a result, by 1989 Philips had only a 1 percent share of the European computer systems market. In the electronic components business, Philips made a mistake when it decided to focus on the high-volume "commodity end" of the business, such as DRAM chips, where it was at a cost disadvantage vis-à-vis its Japanese and U.S. rivals. As a result of these strategic missteps, in 1990 Philips took a $718 million write-off on its inventory of unsold computers and chips, scrapping thousands of minicomputers that were never sold.

Many outside observers attributed these strategic failures to the dead hand of the huge head office bureaucracy at Eindhoven. They argued that while van de Klugt had changed the organizational chart, much of this change was superficial. Real power, they maintained, still lay with the Eindhoven bureaucracy and its allies in the national organizations. In support of this view, they pointed out that since 1986 Philips' work force had declined by less than 10 percent, instead of the 30 percent reduction that many analysts were calling for.

Jan Timmer, 1990–1994

Alarmed by a 1989 loss of $1.06 billion, the board of directors forced van de Klugt and half of the management board to resign in May 1990. Van de Klugt was replaced by Jan Timmer, who had made a reputation for himself as a tough cost-cutter while head of Philips' consumer electronics division. Timmer quickly announced that he would cut Philips' worldwide work force by 10,000 to

283,000 and launch a $1.4 billion restructuring. Investors were unimpressed—most of them thought that the company needed to lose 40,000–50,000 jobs—and reacted by knocking down the share price 7 percent.

Stung by the negative reaction to his early layoff announcements, Timmer went back to the drawing board and in September 1990 came up with a new plan, which he dubbed "Operation Centurion." Timmer's plan called for laying off 55,000 employees, the divestiture or closure of unprofitable businesses, and the aggressive pursuit of new product opportunities.

Philips' ability to quickly push through the planned layoffs was limited by Dutch law, which requires that a company pay 15 months' severance pay to any laid-off workers. As a consequence, the first 10,000 layoffs cost Philips' $700 million and took 18 months to execute. Given such cost, Philips was forced to spread out the financial pain over a number of years. Still, by 1993 the company had reduced its work force to 250,000, and it had plans to cut another 10,000–15,000 employees by mid 1994.

Timmer was reasonably successful in closing down or divesting several of Philips' money-losing operations. In September 1990 he canceled production of a key semiconductor chip in which the company had invested over $500 million since the mid 1980s. In mid 1991 he sold off Philips' minicomputer division—which at the time was losing $1 million per day—to Digital Equipment for around $300 million. This was followed by the sale to Whirlpool for $175 million its stake in the domestic appliance joint venture between the two companies. Then in May 1993 Philips sold its 35 percent stake in a chip-making joint venture with Matsushita to the Japanese company for a price of $1.6 billion. Despite these divestitures, as of late 1993 Philips still found itself with several big money losers. For example, Philips' PKI cellular telephone business reportedly lost a small fortune between 1991 and 1993. While the company was looking for a buyer in 1993, it was having difficulty finding one.

As for new product opportunities, here Philips under Timmer is gambling heavily upon a limited number of risky, but potentially very profitable, ventures. The main focus of new product opportunities is the consumer electronics division, Timmer's old charge, which in 1993 still accounted for one-third of Philips' sales. As of late 1993 Philips had two major new products, both of which could be potential blockbusters, but which could turn out to be costly failures.

The first of these is the so-called Imagination Machine. Introduced in the United States in late 1991, and Europe in late 1992, the Imagination Machine is an interactive compact disc technology (CD-I) that hooks into an ordinary television set and uses compact discs to reproduce sound and pictures. Viewers may interrupt at any time to explore a subject in greater depth. So far, however, the Imagination Machine has delivered nothing but promise. Philips' ability to market the CD-I hardware has been limited severely by the lack of available software.

Philips' second major new product is the digital compact cassette (DCC). The DCC reproduces the sound of a compact disc on a tape. The DCC's great selling point is that the buyer will be able to play their old analog tape cassettes on the new system. The DCC's chief rival is a portable compact disc system, called the mini disc, from Sony. Many observers see a replay of the classic battle between the VHS and Betamax video recorder standards in the coming battle between the DCC and the mini disc. If the DCC wins, it could be the remaking of Philips. As of late 1993, however, neither the DCC nor Sony's mini disc had taken the market by storm.

In Philips' apparent failure to exploit the superior technology in both the CD-I and the DCC, observers see a replay of an old Philips' story—great technology but poor marketing. Among other things, Philips played a major role in the development of the compact disc, the videocassette recorder, and the laser disc. Yet with the exception of the compact disc, where it struck up a very successful alliance with Sony to market the product worldwide, Philips never really profited from any of these innovations.

References

Aguilar, F. J., and M. Y. Yoshino. "The Philips Group: 1987," Harvard Business School Case #388–050. Cambridge, Mass.

Bartlett, C. A., and R. W. Lightfoot. "Philips and Matsushita: A Portrait of Two Evolving Companies," Harvard Business School Case #9–392–156. 1993, Cambridge, Mass.

Bartlett, C. A., and S. Ghoshal. *Managing Across Borders: The Transnational Solution,* Boston, Mass.: Harvard Business School Press, 1989.

"Brighter Spark," *The Economist*, August 21, 1993, p. 51.

Cohen, R. "Two European Giants Fail to Stop Their Slides," *The New York Times*, March 5, 1993, p. C1.

Echikson, W. "How Hard It Is to Change Culture," *Fortune*, October 19, 1992, p. 114.

Kapstein, J., and J. Levine, "A Would-Be World-Beater Takes a Beating," *Business Week*, July 16, 1990, pp. 40–41.

Levine, J. "Philips' Big Gamble," *Business Week*, August 5, 1991, pp. 34–36.

"Philips Fights the Flab," *The Economist*, April 7, 1992, pp. 73–74.

CASE

29

Philips NV and Sony: The Digital Compact Cassette versus the Mini Disc

INTRODUCTION

The digital compact cassette (DCC) uses digital technology to reproduce the high-fidelity sound associated with the compact disc on a recordable audiotape. The technology was developed by Philips NV's consumer division during the late 1980s and early 1990s (Philips' consumer division also developed the original compact discs). After some delay, the first of Philips' DCC machines hit the marketplace in November 1992. One month later Philips' global rival, Sony, introduced its own recordable digital audio system—the mini disc. Sony's mini disc system is based on a different technology—a 2.5 inch recordable optical disc. With the near simultaneous introduction of two different technologies for digital audio recording, observers believe that the consumer electronics industry may be about to witness a "winner-takes-all" worldwide battle to establish a new technological standard in consumer electronics. Either one of these technologies may ultimately replace the existing analog cassette player technology, much as the CD has replaced analog record players. At stake is a potentially huge market. In 1991 analog cassette player sales in the United States amounted to about $2 billion, while sales of prerecorded and blank tapes claimed $3.2 billion. Both companies also have a considerable investment at stake. Philips spent at least $50 million developing the DCC, and some reports suggest that Sony has spent $100 million developing the mini disc.

PRECEDENTS

There are precedents in the consumer electronics industry for the kind of competition that Sony and Philips are involved in. Two of the most interesting, both of which contain important lessons for Sony and Philips, are the competition between Sony and Matsushita in the videocassette recorder (VCR) business and Sony's failed attempt to establish digital audiotape (DAT) as an alternative audio technology in the late 1980s.

This case was prepared by Charles W. L. Hill, University of Washington. This case was prepared as a basis for class discussion rather than to illustrate either effective or ineffective handling of administrative situations.

The VCR Business

To many, the emerging competition between Philips and Sony seems reminiscent of the competition between Sony and Matsushita in the late 1970s and early 1980s to establish a dominant standard for videocassette recorders. At that time, Sony championed the Betamax format, while Matsushita championed the VHS format. In the event, although the Betamax format was widely viewed as being technologically superior, it was the VHS format that won out. Although the Betamax format was the early leader, accounting for over 50 percent of all videotapes and machines sold in 1976, by the end of 1978 the VHS format was outselling the Betamax format by 3 to 2, and by 1988 the VHS format accounted for 95 percent of world sales of videocassette recorders.

Matsushita's success can be attributed to a number of factors. First, despite its technological appeal, Sony's Betamax was hurt by a one-hour limit on its recording time. In contrast, the rival VHS format delivered up to three hours of recording time. Second, Matsushita and its subsidiary company, JVC, which actually developed the VHS technology, adopted a very aggressive policy in licensing its VHS technology to other manufacturers, signing up companies such as Hitachi, Sharp, Mitsubishi, and, later, Philips. In addition, an aggressive original equipment manufacturing (OEM) policy ensured that companies such as GE, RCA, and Zenith were also locked into the VHS format. By building "format volume" more rapidly than Sony, which did not pursue the same licensing and OEM agreements, Matsushita was better able to establish its VHS format as the dominant technology in the industry. Third, Matsushita invested in the manufacturing capacity required to serve a world market and then priced aggressively to build volume as rapidly as possible. Fourth, as the VHS format gained share against the Betamax format, more prerecorded tapes were issued in the VHS format than the Betamax format. As a result, by the early 1980s most videocassette stores stocked far smaller inventories of Betamax tapes than VHS tapes. Once this became apparent, sales of Betamax machines plummeted.

Digital Audiotape (DAT)

A second precedent for what may happen with regard to recordable digital audio technology can be found in the case of DAT technology. DAT technology was developed by Sony, which introduced it in Japan in 1987 and the United States in 1990. It proved to be a market flop and has now been superseded by Sony's recordable mini disc.

Technologically, DAT looks very appealing. Using the same digital format as compact discs—a continuous stream of zeros and ones—DAT technology captures crystal-clear, noise-free sound on tape. Hooked up to a CD player with a fiber optic cable, a DAT machine can make a flawless bit-for-bit copy of a CD. However, the ability of DAT technology to gain market share was limited by a number of problems.

First, the introduction of DAT technology into the United States, the world's largest potential market, was delayed by a threatened lawsuit from the Recording Industry Association of America (RIAA). The RIAA was concerned that bootleggers could use a DAT machine to roll out perfect copies of the music on CDs, in the process hurting sales of CDs. Eventually, Sony agreed to add a chip that allows only one digital copy at a time to be made from a CD or prerecorded DAT, and none from a DAT copy. This slows the copying process enough to make it commercially unattractive.

Even with this chip in place, most major recording companies decided not to produce prerecorded DATs. Part of the reason can be traced to basic economics.

Record companies spend only about 90 cents to make a CD. DATs cost 10 times that much and sell for around $25—roughly twice the price of CDs. The higher costs and lower margins make DATs unattractive to record companies. Indeed, the only major record company to back the DAT format was CBS Records, which is owned by Sony. And even CBS issued only a few dozen classical and jazz titles. If the lack of a library of prerecorded DATs was not enough to deter customers from purchasing a DAT machine, the price probably was. Sony's DAT recorders listed for $850–$950, and a blank two-hour tape retailed at $13.

Another reason for the failure of DAT to build market share was that many consumers apparently perceived the technology to be redundant. Having recently invested in CD players, most consumers were unwilling to undertake an additional investment in yet another digital technology. Besides, with CD players beginning to appear in cars, and with Sony itself offering a portable CD player (the Discman), it was difficult to see what need DAT would serve that was not already being served by CD technology (with the exception of recordability).

Sony initially projected first-year U.S. sales of 100,000 DAT machines but later acknowledged that sales fell far short of that number. Consumer electronics and record stores that invested in DAT inventory were disappointed by the lack of sales, and most quickly pulled out of the market. The result: the DAT technology never really got off the starting block.

PHILIPS' DCC SYSTEM

Philips' DCC technology represents one of the great new product hopes for a company that has seen better days (for more details on Philips, see Case 28). One of the world's largest electronics companies, in recent years Philips has been stung by a series of heavy losses, including one of $489 million on revenues of $31.8 billion in 1992. In the past decade Philips has cut its employment by almost 100,000 to 250,000. One of its major problem areas is its consumer electronics division, where a global recession has been translated into flat sales and heavy losses. Philips' consumer electronics division badly needs a new product success, and the company hopes that the DCC technology is it. Like Sony's DAT technology, Philips' DCC System is a recordable digital audiotape technology. There are, however, a number of crucial differences, both from a technological perspective and from a strategic perspective.

Technology

Philips DCC technology is meant to replace existing analog audiocassettes, much as the CD replaced old line recordplayers and vinyl records. Like existing audiocassette technology, it is a recordable technology. To limit copying of CDs onto DCC tapes, the DCC technology incorporates the same chip and code as the later DAT technology. This allows copying only from an original CD or pre-recorded DCC to a DCC. Music copied onto a DCC tape cannot then be transferred to another DCC tape (i.e., second-generation copying is not possible).

Philips modeled its DCC technology on existing audiocassette decks. DCC tapes are the same size as old audiocassette tapes, and they utilize the same basic drive mechanism. Consequently, the cost of producing a DCC player will be significantly less than that of a DAT player. Moreover, because the DCC tapes are

the same size as existing standard cassettes, the DCC player can play ordinary cassettes as well as DCC cassettes. This fact should have great appeal to the consumer, since the average household owns 60 ordinary music cassettes; consumers will not have to write off their existing investment in cassette tapes when they purchase a DCC system. The decision also appeals to record stores, which will not have to retool their display bins.

The DCC design does have its limitations, however. The fixed tape head and straight line recording format used in traditional cassette decks, and now in the DCC system, cannot lay down as much information per second as a DAT machine. In theory, this limits the ability of the DCC technology to replicate musical sound perfectly. Instead of trying to replicate every sound that a musical instrument makes, Philips conducted psychoacoustic research to determine which sounds the human ear registers. The DCC system ignores sounds at a volume below the threshold of human hearing, or those masked by louder tones of roughly the same frequency. The result, according to Philips, is that the DCC system can reproduce the sound of a CD system while only using one quarter of the bits (zeros and ones) a DAT machine uses to slavishly record everything. Listening tests by audiophile reviewers suggest that Philips' claims are valid. In a series of tests the reviewers could not distinguish between a CD, a DAT, and a DCC.

Strategy To produce and market the DCC, Philips entered into a strategic alliance with its global competitor, Matsushita. The deal allows Matsushita to produce DCC machines and tapes under license, marketing them under its Panasonic and Technics brand names. In addition, JVC, which is partly owned by Matsushita, will produce DCC machines and tapes under license, as will Tandy. Philips, of course, also will sell the DCC machines and tapes under its own brand name.

To ensure adequate support from record companies, early on Philips began to line up record companies to issue prerecorded DCC tapes. In early 1992 PolyGram Records, which is 80 percent owned by Philips, identified 150 artists, bands, and orchestras from the various labels that it owns and distributes whose releases would be available when the DCC hit the market. The lineup included big sellers such as U2, Van Morrison, Bryan Adams, and Pavarotti. The DCC format got another software boost from Matsushita's MCA, Inc., subsidiary. MCA, which along with PolyGram is one of the world's big six recording companies, announced that it too would launch a wide range of titles to coincide with the introduction of DCC tape decks sold under the Panasonic and Technics brand names. Further support came from EMI Music Group and Warner Music Group, both of which announced that they too would issue prerecorded DCC tapes. In something of a coup, CBS Records, which is owned by Sony, also announced that it would issue prerecorded DCC tapes.

SONY'S MINI DISC SYSTEM

Like Philips, Sony is one of the world's largest consumer electronics companies. Although Sony has had some big failures in the consumer electronics business, including Betamax and DAT, it also has had some big winners, including the Sony Walkman and the compact disc (which was developed jointly with Philips).

Like Philips, Sony is also a company in trouble. Although it is still making money, its profits came under pressure in the early 1990s. In fiscal 1991–1992 Sony reported a 44 percent drop in profits. This was followed by a 45 percent drop in fiscal 1992–1993. There are several reasons for Sony's profit slump, including a worldwide consumer electronics recession (which has been particularly severe in Japan), the high value of the yen (which is making Sony's exports expensive), and the general maturing of many of Sony's existing product lines—including the Walkman and the CD.

Technology

Sony's mini disc is based on an innovative optical disc digital recording technology. In essence, the mini disc is a shrunken CD, but with the added twist that it can prerecord sounds on blank discs by using a laser-based device. In a traditional compact disc the zeros and ones of digitized sound are represented by a pattern of pits on the underside of the disc. Once these pits are embedded in a CD they cannot be changed. The mini disc, however, is covered with a magnetic film, and the pits are replaced by magnetic patterns analogous to the north and south poles of a magnet (north is a zero and south is a one). These patterns can be changed, allowing the disc to be rerecorded. To achieve this trick, a laser is used to heat each segment of the disc, "softening" the surface film so that its magnetic pattern can be rearranged. After the disc is heated by a laser, a magnetic head reads the incoming signal and records the desired north or south polarity. (As with the DCC, second-generation recording from the mini disc is not possible.)

A mini disc is only 2.5 inches across, half the size of a conventional CD, but it can still store the same amount of data (i.e., 74 minutes of music). It is more durable than tape and like conventional CDs it allows for quick movement between tracks (a feature that the DCC does not have). Moreover, unlike a CD, a mini disc will not skip if bumped. To achieve this feature, Sony added a computer memory to the system that stores up to three seconds of music before passing it to the listener. Because of this lag, a bump will not be noticed; before the memory buffer is depleted the laser returns to the correct spot. According to Sony, this feature makes the mini disc portable and an ideal replacement for the Walkman and Discman.

Strategy

Like Philips, Sony has made efforts to line up alternative hardware suppliers for its mini disc. By mid 1993 Sony had licensed the mini disc technology to Sharp, Sanyo, JVC, and Mitsubishi, among others. In addition, Sony has actively sought out record label support, although it has been somewhat less successful than Philips. Sony's own CBS label planned an initial release of 500 titles on the mini disc. In addition, Warner Music Group and EMI have both committed themselves to publishing titles on the mini disc. However, Sony does not have the support of PolyGram or MCA.

Building on the mini disc's small size and portability, Sony has initially positioned the mini disc as a replacement for the Walkman and Discman. Three of Sony's first four mini disc models were portables, while the fourth was a car stereo. This positioning strategy had led to fears that the mini disc may cannibalize sales of the Walkman and Discman, both of which are currently very profitable.

Table 1
Basic Features of the DCC and Mini Disc

	DCC	Mini Disc
Launch	November 1992 for home decks; fall 1993 for portable models	December 1992 in portable format; spring 1993 for car and home models
Technology	Hiss-free digital audiotape with CD sound quality	First recordable optical disc; close to CD sound quality
Major Hardware Supporters	Philips, Panasonic & Technics, Tandy, JVC	Sony, Sharp, Sanyo, JVC, and Mitsubishi
Record Label Support	Bertelsmann Music Group, EMI, PolyGram, MCA, Warner, Sony	Sony Music (CBS), Warner, EMI
Suggested Retail Price	$700–$1,000 for home decks; $550 for portables	Portables, $550–$750; car units, $980; home decks, $1,000
U.S. Sales to July 1993	Fewer than 20,000 units	More than 40,000 units

THE FIRST YEAR

Table 1 summarizes the basic features of the DCC and the mini disc. As can be seen, a crucial positioning difference emerged early on. Philips entered the market with home decks of the DCC, while Sony initially focused on portable models of the mini disc. By late 1993, however, both companies expect to have a fuller range of models on the market. The initial sales of both the DCC and mini disc have been disappointing. In total, probably no more than 60,000 units had been sold in the United States by July 1993, with Sony's mini disc reportedly outselling the DCC format by 2 to 1. Both companies agree, however, that it is too early to draw any conclusions. A clearer picture could emerge in 1994. For now, however, it seems that the relatively high price of both the DCC and mini disc system has held back sales. The introduction of both products in the middle of a deep recession did not help matters. Moreover, sales may have been hurt by confusion among consumers as to the potential benefits of the competing technologies.

Philips had admitted publicly that it may have mishandled its initial launch of the DCC. According to the company, because of a software problem that took time to correct, Philips was forced to enter the market with its easier to develop home deck DCC systems, rather than a portable. As a result, the DCC came across as an up-market niche product, rather than the mass-market product that Philips hopes it will become. The first portable DCC players became available in small quantities in Japan in June 1993, but the main product launches are scheduled for September 1993 in the United States and Europe. Philips plans to start selling DCC models for cars at prices ranging from $886 to $1,181, and portable models for about $550. As with most consumer products, the company aims to cut prices as sales build and unit production costs fall.

Philips has come under fire from retailers and record companies for its poor initial advertising campaign, which failed to show the product and left viewers

confused. Moreover, the campaign failed to make clear one of DCC's best features, its ability to play analog tapes as well as DCC tapes. In contrast, Sony received high marks for an initial advertising campaign that stressed the mini disc's portability and CD-like sound quality.

To correct the problems with the initial launch, both Philips and Matsushita are planning new and separate campaigns in late 1993. However, Philips may already have an uphill battle to fight. Many retailers are already backing away from the technology. To quote a manager of Dow Stereo/Video, Inc., a chain of eight superstores in San Diego and one of the first stores to carry the DCC: "We haven't sold a single DCC unit in the last two months. There is no way we are going to order more."*

Meanwhile, in September 1993 Sony announced two new portable mini disc models. The new models are 40 percent smaller and 45 percent lighter than the original portables and have a longer battery time. However, the models are still bigger than the Walkman, which the mini disc in meant to replace. Moreover, at $525 and $715, respectively, the two new portable models remain expensive compared to the Walkman, which retails for less than $100. At the same time, Sony announced that it had shipped 300,000 units worldwide between November 1992 and August 1993, and the company still hopes to sell 10 million mini discs annually by 1996.

*Quoted in Patrick M. Reilly, "Sony's Digital Audio Format Pulls Ahead of Philips's," *The Wall Street Journal*, August 6, 1993, p. B1.

References

Bryant, A. "Coming Soon: New Tapes and CDs," *The New York Times*, June 17, 1992, p. C5.

"Double or Quits," *The Economist*, May 30, 1992, p. 67.

Hudson, R. L. "Philips' Official Calls DCC Launch Flawed, Vows Division Comeback," *The Wall Street Journal*, August 19, 1993, p. A7.

Kupfer, A. "The Next Wave in Cassette Tapes," *Fortune*, June 3, 1991, pp. 153–158.

Reilly, P. M. "Sony's Digital Audio Format Pulls Ahead of Philips's, but Both Still Have Far to Go," *The Wall Street Journal*, August 6, 1993, p. B1.

Schlesinger, J. M. "Sony Introduces Next Generation of MiniDisc Models," *The Wall Street Journal*, September 30, 1993, p. B16.

"Sounding Off," *The Economist*, November 7, 1992, p. 90.

Therrien, L., and N. Gross, "The Sound and the Fury at Sony and Philips," *Business Week*, June 15, 1992, p. 42.

Yoffie, D. B. "The World VCR Industry," Harvard Business School Case #9–387–098, 1988, Cambridge, Mass.

CASE

30 The China Strategy: A Tale of Two Firms

> Political patronage created the Taibao venture; but not only was it unable to ensure the ultimate success of the project, it appears to have contributed significantly to its failure. Our *guanxi* with the central leadership in China didn't automatically lead to cooperation at the local level and we paid heavy prices for that.—Ray Schon, Chairman, Western Energy, Inc.

> The heart of our success lies at our willingness to work with local suppliers, ensure quality standards, and support a nationwide dealer network in China.—John White, Vice President, International Operations, American Copier Co.

"I am very sorry to hear about the tragedy of Mr. Arnold Tanner. We have been friends for years." In September 1990 on a plane to China, John White, vice president of international operations of American Copier Co. (ACC), happened to sit next to Ray Schon, chairman of Western Energy, Inc. (WEI), and they compared notes on their firms' experiences in China.

White was a good friend of Arnold Tanner, then chairman of WEI, who suddenly passed away at the age of 85. Schon was Tanner's successor. One of his first priorities was to terminate a deal—the Taibao coal mine—that Tanner struck with the Chinese. The $700 million joint venture was plagued by a host of problems almost from the time the contract was signed in 1982. But the personal commitment of Tanner and China's supreme leader Deng Xiaoping, which elevated the venture into a symbol of China's "open door" policy, kept the project going while Tanner was still alive. Schon clearly lacked this political commitment and intended to withdraw from this unprofitable deal as part of the new restructuring program at WEI.

White was surprised to hear Schon talk about WEI's intended withdrawal from China. He himself was flying to China to visit with ACC Shanghai, to celebrate its third anniversary and to review ACC's China strategy with the joint venture's resident managers. Formed in late 1987, the $30 million ACC Shanghai joint venture already was number one in China's expanding copier market and planned to capture even greater market share. Recalling his first trip to China in 1983, which was encouraged by his friend Tanner, White began to think why ACC successfully stayed in China while WEI had to pull out.

Mike W. Peng of the University of Washington prepared this case as a basis for class discussion rather than to illustrate either effective or ineffective management practice.

ARNOLD TANNER, WESTERN ENERGY, INC., AND CHINA

Background

Primarily an oil company, Western Energy, Inc., conducted business in more than 100 countries and employed more than 78,000 people worldwide. With annual sales around $10 billion in the 1980s and the early 1990s, WEI was among the top ten major energy firms in the United States. WEI consisted of one of the world's largest petroleum (oil and gas) operations, a growing chemical business, a coal exploration business, and a nationwide retailing operation in the United States. Its strategy emphasized foreign production, and the firm had production facilities in Argentina, Bolivia, Canada, Ecuador, Malaysia, Pakistan, the Philippines, Syria, and the U.K. North Sea as well as the United States when it entered China in 1980. (See Table 1 for a five-year summary of selected financial data for WEI.)

From 1962 to 1990, Arnold Tanner was first the CEO and then chairman of the San Francisco–based firm. Before becoming the CEO in 1962, he worked for WEI for 25 years in various capacities. His long years of service at WEI and his leadership role made an enormous impact on WEI. Tanner was well respected as a dynamic and charismatic leader in the industry. Moreover, Tanner's foresights on business opportunities led his firm actively to seek opportunities in the Eastern Bloc. His legendary achievements included striking one of the first deals between a Western businessman and the Soviets in the 1930s, supplying the Soviets during World War II, and trading with Eastern Europe since the détente in the 1970s. As a result, his name was well recognized in many quarters of the Eastern Bloc. When China started its open door policy in 1979, China's political leaders naturally looked upon Tanner for his initiatives.

Tanner responded to the Chinese inquiry with enthusiasm. His first visit to China was in 1979 and he later became a frequent flyer to Beijing. As always, he took a high-profile approach and befriended China's supreme leader Deng Xiaoping. In the early 1980s China desperately needed to prove to a suspicious West that its open door policy was credible and that direct investment from

Table 1
Western Energy, Inc., Five-Year Summary of Selected Financial Data

Calendar Years	1991	1990	1989	1988	1987
(I) Operations (in $ millions)					
Revenues	$10,096	$11,509	$10,939	$10,351	$9,415
Operational income (loss)	379	(1,715)	247	295	102
Net income (loss)	460	(1,695)	293	316	220
(II) Financial Position (in $ millions)					
Total assets	$16,115	$18,619	$19,557	$19,533	$16,861
Total debt	5,546	7,425	7,738	7,227	5,925
Stockholders' equity	4,340	4,114	5,901	6,218	5,144
(III) Per Share Data					
Earnings (loss) per share from operations	$1.25	$(5.89)	$0.89	$1.19	$0.39
Earnings (loss) per share	1.52	(5.82)	1.06	1.27	0.96

abroad was genuinely welcome. Well respected both in the West and in the Eastern Bloc, Tanner became an ideal candidate to bridge the gap between China and the outside world. Of course Tanner did not respond to the Chinese interest with goodwill only. Earnings of WEI were flat in the late 1970s and Tanner was exploring new avenues in foreign exploration and production for growth of sales and earnings. Tanner sensed that if WEI penetrated China early, it might be able to capitalize on some first mover advantages[1] like preempting rival Western firms in the acquisition of China's energy resources.

In short, China's new open door, its drive for modernization, Tanner's longtime interest in doing business with the Eastern Bloc, and WEI's desire to expand its global operations into a new market made WEI a pioneering American firm entering China.

Politics and the Taibao Coal Mine

Since the initiation of the open door policy in the late 1970s, developing the energy sector to support industrial development has become a priority goal of the Chinese government. Among various energy resources, coal is the most important to China as three-quarters of the country's energy demand is met by coal. China's proven coal reserves exceed 900 billion tons, behind only the Soviet Union and the United States. Total estimated reserves, however, are in the neighborhood of 2 trillion tons; at current production levels it would take 2,000 years to exhaust the total supply.[2]

Despite the abundance of coal supply, the lack of capital and technology to effectively exploit the coal in sufficient amount to meet energy needs led to a national headache in the 1980s. In many parts of China, factories had to shut down for one or two days a month due to energy shortages; at one time Shanghai had only two days' worth of coal reserves on hand for power generation. It is evident that without the development of its energy sector, China's goal of modernization will not be realized. Therefore, seeking foreign partners to help develop China's energy resources became an important part of its policy.

In 1980 China opened its premier coal mine—the Taibao coal mine in Shanxi Province of northern China—to international bidding and sought a foreign partner. One of the largest open-pit coal mines in the world, the Taibao mine became the largest energy project in China ever opened to foreign firms at that time. Eight Western firms participated in the bidding, including three from the United States, two from Germany, and one each from France, Japan, and the United Kingdom. Not surprisingly, Tanner's WEI beat out all the competitors.

Politics was instrumental in this process and China's central leadership was heavily involved in this "pet project." Politically, China preferred having a major U.S. company as its partner as an unambiguous signal to American investors that the open door policy was for real. Unlike European and Japanese companies which had been doing business with China for years, the United States had virtually no business with China until 1979, when the two countries normalized their diplomatic relations. Decades of hostility between the two countries made American investors especially suspicious at that time. However, China sensed that the United States possessed more advanced technologies and more

1. M. B. Lieberman and D. B. Montgomery, "First Mover Advantages: A Survey," *Strategic Management Journal*, 9 (Summer Special Issue), 1988, pp. 41–58.
2. J. P. Huang, "Fueling the Economy," *The China Business Review,* March–April 1991, p. 22.

Table 2
Partners and Finances of the Taibao Mine Venture

United States (50 percent share)	China (50 percent share)
Western Energy, Inc. (responsible for $200 million initial capital)	China National Coal Corp. China Coal Import/Export Corp. China International Trust & Investment Corp. Province of Shanxi (Chinese partners responsible for $200 million of initial capital)
$300 million loan syndicated by 39 international banks (each side guarantees 50 percent of the loan)	

abundant capital and that courting American investment would be of strategic importance to its policy.[3] Among the three American firms that entered the bidding, WEI was better respected and financially stronger. Moreover, Tanner's assiduous cultivation of developing *guanxi* (connections)[4] with Chinese leaders, especially Deng Xiaoping, and previous contacts throughout the Eastern Bloc played an important role in China's selection of WEI as its sole foreign partner.

The Economics of the Taibao Joint Venture

Upon winning the bid, Western Energy, Inc., became the foreign partner in this 50–50 equity joint venture, which was incorporated as the Taibao Mine Group in China in 1982.[5] A 30-year, renewable joint-venture contract was signed. The Chinese partners included a consortium of Chinese organizations led by China National Coal Corp., the country's leading coal producer. The venture called for $700 million in capital endowment, with each side contributing $200 million and the remaining $300 million syndicated by 39 international banks (see Table 2). At full capacity, the mine should produce 12 million tons a year and employ 3,000 workers, 20–30 of whom would be WEI expatriates.

In the initial courtship during 1980–1982, WEI responded to Chinese interest with a number of extravagant promises, ranging from the scale of mine to Chinese workers' salaries to the amount of coal it could export. It agreed to export 75 percent of total output and to assume complete responsibilities of marketing the coal in the export market. Noted for their preference for "general principles" in the negotiations, the Chinese were serious about those promises and treated them as a foundation upon which details could be worked out later with WEI.

However, by the time the joint venture contract was signed and the feasibility study began, the economics of the project already were shaky in light of falling world coal prices. WEI was forced to hedge its earlier promises and began to pressure the Chinese side to grant it various concessions. For instance, WEI tried to make China Coal Import/Export Corp., one of the Chinese partners, buy WEI's share of the export coal at prevailing international prices, thus completely retreating from its earlier promise to market the coal itself in the international

3. B. S. Chen, "Economic Development Strategy for China's Coastal Areas and U.S. Investment in China," *Meiguo Yanjiu* (Journal of American Studies, Beijing, China) 2(3), 1988, pp. 7–25.
4. See Appendix 2 for a description of *guanxi* in China.
5. See Appendix 1 at the end of this case for a summary of China's joint venture law.

market. The Chinese negotiators were surprised, and intense arguments between the two sides ensued. On several occasions during the negotiations, disputes at the working level came close to derailing the project. But Tanner and the Chinese political leadership always intervened to enforce a solution. Numerous public ceremonies throughout the negotiation phase bound the prestige of Tanner and the Chinese leadership even more tightly to the consummation of the project. Eventually, WEI won several concessions from the Chinese side in 1985, including shifting the responsibilities of export marketing to China Coal Import/Export Corp.

Operational Problems: Central versus Local *Guanxi*

The operational phase of the Taibao venture since 1986 proved to be even more problematic than the negotiation phase. Although getting the mine up and running was undeniably a major achievement, the project, as of September 1990, still was not certified as "complete," despite being operational for four years. In 1990, its best year in terms of production, it produced only three-quarters of its 12-million-ton capacity and suffered a $31 million loss. Exports were probably less than half of the 8–9 million tons WEI originally anticipated.

Four sources of problems contributed to the venture's lackluster performance. First, continuing low world coal prices prevented the venture from earning the foreign exchange necessary to break even. Second, lower-than-expected coal quality, with high sulfur content in one seam and high ash content in another, further depressed the marketability of the coal produced at Taibao. Technical problems like defective equipment and the workers' lack of training consisted of the third source of problems. The largest source of problems came from the lack of cooperation between WEI and its local partners, despite its influential *guanxi* with the central leadership.

Tanner was very skillful in cultivating *guanxi* with the central leadership in Beijing and was able to use his central *guanxi* influence to make his Chinese partners grant him concessions. However, WEI failed to develop close *guanxi* relations with local partners, which caused many problems. Many WEI managers reported that disputes over production and marketing strategies were common among partners. For instance, the Americans wanted to decrease the production of high-sulfur coal, which could be sold only on the domestic market for local currency, and to increase the production of low-sulfur coal for the export market. The Chinese insisted that due to the depressed export market, producing a large amount of low-sulfur coal would result in large inventories, thus further hampering the venture's already bad cash flow situation.

Instead of working together, both sides seemed to develop an appetite to blame the other for whatever problems occurred. On another occasion, WEI accused the China Coal Import/Export Corp. of failing to market the coal aggressively in the export market. In response, the Chinese managers pointed out the insincerity on WEI's part by retreating from its earlier promises and relinquishing the entire responsibility of international marketing. Due to political pressure from China's central leadership, China Coal Import/Export Corp. reluctantly assumed the exporting functions for the Taibao venture in 1985. Now a depressed world market and the less-than-expected coal quality gave the reluctant Chinese partner an excuse for not living up to its promises. Many WEI officials believed that their Chinese partners deliberately exacerbated these problems in spite of the political pressures that forced them to make concessions to WEI in the first place.

Still More Politics

In June 1989 the Tiananmen incident in Beijing shocked the world. Foreign businesspeople were pulling out of China immediately following the incident, and international investors led by the World Bank became hesitant to commit further funds to China. The Chinese leadership desperately needed to prove to the world that despite all the tragedies, China's ten-year-old open door policy would continue. As the government's credibility declined to a record low, it needed a live example to convince the West it was sincere about its policy. Once again, the Taibao venture played into the hands of the Chinese leadership. In spite of internal disagreement at WEI, in late 1989 Arnold Tanner went back to China in a "business as usual" fashion to meet with the Chinese leaders, who promptly used this visit by an "old friend" as a photo opportunity to appease the West.

Inside WEI, as the company's financial situation worsened in the late 1980s with increasing debts, discussions of withdrawing from the Taibao venture became more frequent and intense. In a manner similar to how Deng Xiaoping ruled China, Tanner dismissed such ideas and urged for a "long-term" perspective. The Chinese leadership, on the other hand, had the strong desire to save its political face and to avoid the failure of a flagship project. Therefore, despite huge financial losses which depleted WEI's cash flow, the Taibao venture continued until Tanner's sudden death in August 1990.

Exit?

Within weeks of becoming WEI's new chairman, Ray Schon reassessed the company's overall strategic position and concluded that "the business climate of the 1990s is vastly different from that of the 1980s." To him, the 1990s seemed to be defined by lack of liquidity in financial markets, recessionary pressure on global economies, increasing volatility in energy prices, and chronic instability in world markets. The year 1990 left the company with a net loss of $1.7 billion (see Table 1). In response, Schon started a major restructuring and divestiture program aimed at "building on proven strengths and having the operational and financial flexibility to respond in a timely manner to unpredictable markets." Specifically, this program would sell off unprofitable lines of business to reduce debt, which was running at $7.4 billion in 1990, and would focus WEI's resources on those businesses in which it already excelled—oil, natural gas, and chemicals.

The changes in corporate strategy decided the fate of the Taibao venture. In his announcement to start the restructuring program, Schon publicly announced his intention to withdraw WEI from the unprofitable project, which was Tanner's favorite project but never part of WEI's core business. To do that, WEI would have to write off $200 million in unprofitable investment but would be relieved of $150 million in loan guarantees. WEI would have two options: (1) to sell its share to its Chinese partners or (2) to sell to another foreign investor. One way or the other, Ray Schon understood that his trip to China would be a stormy one.

Schon told White on the plane:

> Political patronage created the Taibao, but not only was it unable to ensure the ultimate success of the project, it appears to have contributed significantly to its failure. Contrary to our expectations, our *guanxi* connections with the central leadership didn't automatically lead to cooperation at the local level and we paid heavy prices for that. The business in the 1990s simply won't be the same as when Tanner was around; we can no longer afford to support such an unprofitable business.

AMERICAN COPIER CO. IN SHANGHAI

Unlike Western Energy, Inc.'s approach in China, characterized by early entry, high profile, and central *guanxi*-developing, American Copier Co.'s (ACC) China strategy was markedly different: it was cautious, low profile, and aimed at building cooperative relations with local partners. It took about four years (1983–1987) of long negotiations for ACC to set up its Shanghai joint venture, but the project was apparently worth waiting. For ACC, China proved a good match, offering both low-cost design and labor and a growing market for copier machines and products. Formed in late 1987, the $30 million ACC Shanghai became number one in China's growing copier market by 1989 and planned to capture even greater market share.

Choosing Joint Venturing in Shanghai

With annual sales in the neighborhood of $10 billion throughout the 1980s, ACC is a global company serving the worldwide document processing markets. (See Table 3 for a five-year summary of ACC's selected financial data.) Its activities encompassed developing, manufacturing, marketing, servicing, and financing a wide range of document processing product and service offerings. Its copiers, duplicators, production publishers, electronic printers, facsimile products, scanners, and computer products were marketed in over 130 countries. In addition to a worldwide network of dealers and distributors, ACC maintained research and development (R&D) facilities in Canada, Great Britain, Japan, and the United States. Moreover, before joint venturing with the Chinese, ACC already had substantial experience from its joint venture operations in Australia, Brazil, Germany, Great Britain, India, and Japan.

When ACC entered China in the early 1980s through exporting, the copier market in China was dominated by Japanese makers, including Canon, Minolta, Ricoh, and Toshiba. Many of these companies had a longer history of serving

Table 3
American Copier Company, Five-Year Summary of Selected Financial Data

Calendar Years	1991	1990	1989	1988	1987
(I) Operations (in $ millions)					
Revenues	$12,869	$12,692	$11,720	$11,152	$10,438
Operational income	454	605	653	347	542
Net income	454	243	704	388	578
(II) Financial Position (in $ millions)					
Total assets	$31,658	$31,635	$30,088	$26,441	$22,450
Total debt	9,886	10,579	10,754	7,874	5,722
Stockholders' equity	5,140	5,051	5,035	5,371	5,105
(III) Per Share Data					
Earnings per share from operations	$3.91	$5.51	$6.05	$3.09	$4.94
Earnings per share	3.91	1.66	6.56	3.49	5.30

Table 4
Partners and Finances of the Shanghai Venture

United States (51 percent share)	China (49 percent share)
American Copier Co. (responsible for $15 million initial investment)	Shanghai Photo Industry Co. (holding 44 percent share and contributing plants and labor, assessed at $5 million)
	Bank of China (holding 5 percent share and responsible for $10 million investment)

the China market, but ACC was the only copier producer thus far to establish a joint venture in the country. Though it would take ACC significantly longer than its competitors (some of which signed technology transfer agreements with Chinese firms) to show a return on its $15 million investment, the company's dominant position in a restricted-size market undoubtedly reflected greater official support for the joint venture than for its competitors.

ACC's initial exports to China in the early 1980s were considered moderately successful. In order to capture a larger share of the growing market, ACC initially considered a technology transfer agreement in 1983. But it soon decided to pursue a joint venture instead due to considerations of China's underdeveloped intellectual property protection regime. Numerous sites were considered for the venture, and all the local authorities that learned of ACC's interest courted ACC for its investment. ACC avoided being too involved with local Chinese politics and did not provide vague promises or agree on "general principles" which the Chinese wanted to hear. Eventually, ACC settled on Shanghai due to the large concentration of components suppliers and the number of skilled labor in the area.

ACC's Shanghai venture partners included Bank of China, which held 5 percent of the venture and provided for $10 million of investment, and the Shanghai Photo Industry Co., which held 44 percent of the share and contributed existing plants, equipment, and some personnel assessed at $5 million. ACC held the remaining 51 percent of the venture and invested $15 million (see Table 4). Signed in 1987, ACC Shanghai has a 30-year, renewable joint venture contract and a 10-year renewable technology license for production of desktop copiers and accessories and other copier products. The license gave ACC Shanghai the right to use ACC's desktop office copier technology. ACC Shanghai was designed to produce low-end and mid-range copiers suitable for the China market and was capable of switching to produce more advanced designs. At full capacity, which should be reached in 1994, ACC Shanghai will be capable of producing 40,000 units annually and will employ 900 workers. In September 1990 ACC Shanghai employed more than 600 people, six of whom were expatriates.

Localizing Production

Despite the Chinese preference of having a high percentage of the venture's output exported, the ACC negotiation team, led by John White, managed to persuade the Chinese that the models ACC would introduce to China would be mid-range to low-end ones suitable for China and the focus should be on the domestic market. In return, ACC accepted a stipulation insisted on by the

Chinese that 70 percent of the venture's components would be sourced locally by the end of 1992. To date, ACC managers claim that the venture is on track to achieve this goal, though the process is difficult since none of the local suppliers initially had the technical expertise or equipment necessary to produce the quality components needed by ACC Shanghai.

To overcome these obstacles, ACC heavily engaged in "vendor development" in the United States. ACC, through its Shanghai venture, either transferred technology or provided technical support to approximately 60 suppliers, mostly in Shanghai. Aside from training the suppliers on how to use the technology or equipment transferred, ACC coached them in materials management and handling, as well as in accounting. Moreover, ACC Shanghai developed close working relations with the Shanghai Foreign Investment Commission, which provided funding to local companies to enable them to upgrade their plants and purchase the new technology.

ACC estimated that it spent several million dollars in training, support, and monitoring of Chinese suppliers to ensure consistent quality and delivery. Some of these development costs were charged to the suppliers, and the rest was absorbed by ACC Shanghai. While the training did pay off in improved quality of locally supplied components over the past few years, Chinese components still tended to be produced at above world market prices, thus forcing up the final cost of ACC Shanghai copiers. By company estimates, locally sourced components cost on average 10–20 percent more than imported ones.

Ensuring Quality

ACC was renowned throughout the world for its quality products. All components used by ACC Shanghai were subject to quality standards established by ACC. The parent company also instituted its corporate quality control culture in the venture to ensure that ACC Shanghai's output was on par with ACC products manufactured in other countries. ACC attempted to reinforce the concept of quality at all levels, not just in interaction with the end user. The company's LUTI system—learn, use, teach, and inspect—was ongoing, with each management level teaching it to the level below, as well as to new employees.

A Customer Satisfaction Review Board, which met on a monthly basis, was established by ACC Shanghai to ensure the reputation of its products. The board, composed of representatives from the venture's marketing, service, distribution, management, engineering, and quality control departments, examined complaints and conducted customer surveys to determine where improvement was needed. The results from the first survey, conducted in 1989, one year after the first copier rolled off the production line, indicated 90 percent customer satisfaction with the venture's products. Further proof of ACC Shanghai's success in attaining high quality came from the Shanghai municipal government, which awarded the venture the Shanghai Quality Award in 1989 and 1990, and from the parent company, which awarded the venture an in-house quality award in 1990.

Capturing the Market

The first ACC Shanghai 2020 copier was produced in October 1988, little more than a year after the joint-venture contract was signed. A mid-range model, the 2020 did not incorporate the latest technology, but its reliable, sturdy operation was very suitable for China.

In order to meet demand outside the Shanghai area, ACC Shanghai—with help from its partner Shanghai Photo Industry Co.—established a nationwide distribution, sales, and service network in China. The network included over 100 dealers throughout China, all of whom were trained by ACC Shanghai. Three ACC representative offices—in Beijing, Guangzhou, and Shanghai—provided additional dealer support in such areas as training, inventory, and advertising.

In 1987 a vigorous advertising campaign was launched through television and newspaper media in China to increase the publicity of ACC Shanghai. Competing against Japanese brands like Canon, Minolta, Ricoh, and Toshiba, ACC Shanghai skillfully named its products "Shang Am" ("Hu Mei" in Mandarin Chinese pronunciation), which stands for "Shanghai Beauty."[6] American name brands usually carry a premium among Chinese customers, and products from Shanghai are renowned for their high quality in China. Thus the eye-catching name "Shanghai Beauty," which highlighted the combination of American technology and Shanghai production, created an attractive and trustworthy image among Chinese users. Moreover, despite the high components costs, ACC Shanghai competitively priced its copiers to be within the range of Japanese offerings.

Vigorous quality standards, extensive dealer networks, and an aggressive and skillfully executed advertising campaign accompanied with reasonable prices led ACC Shanghai to become the number-one copier seller in China. In 1989 ACC Shanghai gained 32 percent of the Chinese desktop copier market and around 45 percent by late 1990.

Problems

As expected, the China market was full of problems, some of which were anticipated and some not. The original feasibility study proved to be overly optimistic in its assumptions of production costs and size of the copier market in China. "These miscalculations were perhaps unavoidable," John White said to a frustrated Schon on the plane, "given the unforeseen nature of some of the factors that have affected ACC Shanghai's performance."

Besides high costs of locally sourced components produced in China, the devaluation of the Chinese yuan against the U.S. dollar in the mid 1980s resulted in higher costs of imported components to the venture. Perhaps more important, the introduction of government purchase controls as part of the government's austerity policy begun in 1988 led to a far smaller market than ACC had originally envisioned. In order to purchase a copier, a prospective buyer first had to obtain permission from several government agencies. This market-restricting policy was further strengthened in the post-Tiananmen implementation of the government's austerity program. This system seriously inhibited market forces; ACC estimated the real market in China to be five times its present size.

Despite the government's austerity program, the general open door policy was to continue, and the policy to support joint venture companies was unchanged. In this difficult situation, ACC's joint-venture strategy paid off since government agencies were more likely to approve the purchase of a domestically produced, reasonably priced copier like "Shang Am" than to buy an imported model, even when the two models were of the same performance and price. Thus ACC

6. "America" ("Mei Guo"), when pronounced in Mandarin Chinese, China's official language, stands for "beautiful country."

Shanghai was able to receive greater official support though it did not deliberately cultivate *guanxi* with the government.

Problems unrelated to the macroeconomic environment also confronted ACC Shanghai. For instance, the paper feeders initially produced by the venture malfunctioned due to the poor quality of Chinese paper. The feeders were redesigned by ACC Shanghai to handle the low-grade paper used in most Chinese offices and were reportedly functioning well.

Future Prospects

In September 1990 ACC Shanghai was approaching its third year of operations and John White was going to review the parent company's China strategy with the joint venture's resident managers. He envisioned that in the immediate future ACC Shanghai would focus on designing two new products—a low-end model for developing segments in the China market and a more sophisticated, high-end model for the upper-stream segments. ACC Shanghai engineers initially worked in conjunction with ACC corporate engineers to develop the prototypes for the two models, but total design responsibility was recently turned over to ACC Shanghai. The first model of the low-end copier, which was expected to become a major product line in China, was scheduled to enter the China market in 1992. According to a similar plan, small volumes of the high-end model would hit the market in 1993.

Looking several years ahead, with the existing 2020 mid-range model, ACC Shanghai will have three models each concentrating on the low-end, mid-range, and high-end segments of the China market. Whether other new product lines will be manufactured by ACC Shanghai is undetermined as of yet. White explains:

> My inclination is to continue the three-model operations with ACC Shanghai for a few more years. We have built up a vendor base there and have spent a long time training people in quality control and other areas. But starting a new product line is very taxing—I wouldn't let our joint ventures in India and Brazil, for example, even contemplate it. While there are advantages to keep everything in one organization, it could be too much for a young venture like the one we have in Shanghai. I want to make sure that ACC Shanghai continues to operate on a sound financial footing. This venture is already ahead of where our first venture in Japan was at the equivalent time. Eventually, I'd like to see it become like ACC Japan or ACC UK, a stand-alone operation with its own product lines.

White noted that whether ACC Shanghai could meet such lofty aspirations would depend on two factors. First, the market would have to expand, which would require the abolition or liberalization of the government purchase-control system. However, the Chinese government did not seem to be willing to liberalize its stringent purchase-control policy, and ACC found it had little influence on the government. To expand customer bases (and to project a good corporate image), ACC Shanghai recently started a school program to give selected high schools in China a gift package consisting of copiers and accessories. Second, costs would have to come down, which would require further improvements in the local supplier network. Given existing good *guanxi* with the local suppliers built up on years of cooperative working relations, ACC Shanghai felt confident it could overcome the components cost problems and could bring the costs of locally sourced components on par with international levels in a few years.

EPILOGUE

As the plane landed in Shanghai, John White shook hands with Ray Schon, wished Schon "good luck," and then stepped out of the plane. Though the future was still daunting, he was delighted with ACC Shanghai's past three years and had strong hope that the Shanghai venture would turn out to be a successful one for his company.

After a two-hour stop, the plane continued its journey to Beijing. Schon, already exhausted, decided not to stop in Beijing to meet Tanner's "old friends" in the Chinese leadership; instead, he made up his mind to go directly to Shanxi to terminate the Taibao venture as soon as possible.

APPENDIX 1

Summary of the Law of the People's Republic of China on Joint Ventures Using Chinese and Foreign Investment (adopted in 1979 at the Second Session of the Fifth National People's Congress)

1. Foreign companies and individuals within the territory of the People's Republic of China (PRC) may incorporate themselves into joint ventures with Chinese companies or other Chinese entities with the objective of expanding international economic cooperation and technological exchange.

2. The Foreign Investment Commission must authorize joint ventures, and if approved, ventures are required to register with the General Administration for Industry and Commerce of the PRC, which will then issue a license within three months.

3. Joint ventures shall have limited liability and the foreign parties will contribute not less than 25 percent of the registered capital.

4. The participants will share profits, risks, and losses of the joint venture in proportion to their capital contributions.

5. The equity of each party may be capital goods, industrial property rights, cash, and so on, in the ventures.

6. The contributors of technology or equipment run the risk of forfeiture or damages if the technology or equipment contributed is not truly advanced and appropriate for Chinese needs. If losses are caused by deception through the intentional provision of outdated equipment or technology, compensation must be paid for the losses.

7. Investments by the Chinese participants may include the right of use of a site but it shall not constitute a part of the investment as the joint venture shall pay the Chinese government for its use.

8. A joint venture will have a board of directors and the chairman of the board is to be appointed by the Chinese participants. The Foreign parties may appoint two vice presidents. They do not necessarily have to be Chinese but must be approved by the partners of the joint venture.

9. A joint venture agreement must stipulate procedures for the employment and discharge of the workers and staff members and comply with Chinese laws.

10. The net profit of a joint venture shall be distributed in proportion to the parties' respective investment shares after deductions for reserve funds. Bonuses and welfare funds for the workers, the expansion funds of the venture, and the profits or losses shall be in accordance with the capital investment of the parties involved and be subject to the tax laws of PRC and expatriation.
11. Joint ventures must maintain open accounts in a bank approved by the Bank of China.
12. All foreign exchange transactions shall be in accordance with the foreign exchange regulations of the PRC.
13. Joint ventures may borrow funds directly from foreign banks. Appropriate insurance will be provided by Chinese insurance companies. A joint venture equipped with up-to-date technology by world standards may apply for a reduction of or an exemption from income tax for the first two or three profit-making years.
14. A joint venture is encouraged to market its products outside China through direct channels, its associated agencies, or Chinese foreign trade establishments. Its products also may be distributed in the Chinese market.
15. The contract period of a joint venture must be agreed upon by both parties and may be extended subject to authorization by the Foreign Investment Commission.
16. Disputes that cannot be settled through consultation between partners may be settled through consultation or arbitration by a Chinese arbitral body or an arbitral body agreed upon by the parties involved.

APPENDIX 2

The Importance of *Guanxi* (Connections) in China

Guanxi is the word that describes the intricate, pervasive network of personal relations which every Chinese cultivates with energy, subtlety, and imagination. It is a relationship between two people or organizations containing implicit mutual obligation, assurances, and understanding and governs Chinese attitudes toward long-term social and business relationships. If a *guanxi* relationship of trust and mutual benefits is established, an excellent foundation will be built to develop future relationship. *Guanxi* ties also may be helpful in dealing with the Chinese bureaucracy as personal interpretations are often used in lieu of legal interpretations.

Though the use of *guanxi* networks have mushroomed during the reform in China since 1979,[7] *guanxi* has much stronger and deeper roots embedded in the Chinese society. Traditionally, the strong value of family ties has placed an emphasis on getting things done through who you know. One of the most important aspects of the *guanxi* network is that it is neither officially

7. M. W. Peng, "A Process Model of Governance Transformation for Planned Economies in Transition," Working Paper, University of Washington, Seattle, 1992.

acknowledged nor written down. Members of *guanxi* networks highly value reciprocity, trust, and the implicit understanding between the two parties involved (i.e., "I give you a favor now and I believe that you will return a favor to me in the future whenever I need it"), thus reducing the need to write everything down.

Due to cultural differences and language barriers, the visitors to China are not in a position to cultivate *guanxi* with the depth possible between two Chinese. Nevertheless, *guanxi* is an important aspect of social life in China and deserves attention so that good relations may be developed and things can get done. If a foreigner seeks to develop *guanxi* with the Chinese, he or she should be pleased when being called by the Chinese as an "old friend." Among American dignitaries, Richard Nixon, Henry Kissinger, and Jimmy Carter who brought diplomatic relationships with China in the 1970s enjoy the "old friend" status.

CASE

31 The Ito-Yokado Company, Ltd., Takes Over 7-Eleven

In mid-March 1991, Masanori Takahashi, a senior strategy analyst for Ito-Yokado Company, Ltd., was preparing to depart for Dallas, Texas. Once there, he would be leading a team of Japanese and American managers responsible for establishing transitional and long-term strategies for the Southland Corporation. Southland had been acquired by Ito-Yokado on March 5, 1991. The acquisition had taken almost an entire year of intense bargaining and negotiation with Southland and its creditors.

As Takahashi left his Tokyo office, he could not help but feel both excitement and apprehension. He had gained confidence while involved with Ito-Yokado's successful Operation Reform Project. But this experience might or might not prove to be useful with respect to Southland.

COMPANY BACKGROUND

Ito-Yokado's founder, Masatoshi Ito, was born in 1924 and graduated from a commercial high school in Yokohama. He worked for a brief while at Mitsubishi Heavy Industries before joining Japan's war effort in 1944. After World War II, he worked with his mother and elder brother at the family's 66 square foot clothing store in Tokyo.[1] The store was incorporated as Kabushiki Kaisha Yokado in 1958. By 1960 Ito was in sole control of the family business. During that same year he made his first visit to the United States.

In 1960 Ito visited National Cash Register (NCR) in Dayton, Ohio.[2] While in the United States, Ito was introduced to terms such as "supermarkets" and "chain stores" by NCR, which was interested in selling cash registers to Japanese retailers. In Japan, retailing was dominated by mom-and-pop stores and a handful of venerable department stores, with few types of retail outlets in between. Ito began to see the possible role of mass merchandisers in a society becoming "mass-oriented."

This case was written by M. Edgar Barrett, Distinguished Professor of International Policy and Control at the American Graduate School of International Management (Thunderbird Campus), and by Christopher D. Buehler, Research Assistant at the same institution. The data shown in the first two paragraphs (and the last paragraph) of the case are purely fictional. Data provided elsewhere are drawn from public sources. The case was prepared as a basis for class discussion rather than to illustrate either effective or ineffective handling of an administrative situation.

1. Andrew Tanzer, "A Form of Flattery," *Forbes*, June 2, 1986.
2. Jim Mitchell, "Southland Suitor Ito Learned from the Best," *The Dallas Morning News*, April 1, 1990.

Ito soon opened a small chain of "superstores" in the Tokyo area. These stores carried a large selection of household goods, food, and clothing of generally lesser quality and lower price than either the mom-and-pop or department stores.[3] By 1965, Ito had opened eight superstores. In the same year, the name of the chain was changed to Ito-Yokado.

The Growth of Ito-Yokado As a Superstore

Ito's concept for the superstores was centered on having the rough equivalent of several types of retail stores contained within one, multistory superstore. The initial stores were located near population centers and railroad stations in the Tokyo area.[4] Often, several stores were located in close proximity to achieve "regional dominance."[5] The results were high name recognition, reduced distribution costs, and the effective squeezing out of competition.

Ito soon realized that social changes in Japan could create new opportunities for his retailing ideas. Younger and more mobile Japanese appeared to be less willing to spend a great deal of time shopping at numerous mom-and-pop stores. Also, the Japanese society was experiencing increased suburbanization. Ito decided to locate stores in suburban prefectures. There are 47 prefectures, or provinces, in Japan.

One reason for locating stores in suburban areas was the lower cost of real estate. This allowed Ito-Yokado to open larger stores with more parking spaces than competitors located in congested urban areas. Ito continued to use a strategy of "regional dominance" with these new openings, most of which were concentrated in the greater-Kanto district, which consists of the Tokyo metropolitan area and surrounding cities. By the early 1970s, Ito-Yokado stores were opening at the rate of four or five per year. By the late 1970s, nine or 10 new stores were opened annually.[6] In early 1987, 101 of 127 Ito-Yokado superstores were located in the greater-Kanto district.

Ito also adopted a strategy of leasing some properties for new stores. As of the mid-1980s, over 87 percent of Ito-Yokado's aggregate sales floor space, 10 of the company's 11 distribution centers, and the company headquarters in Tokyo were all leased.[7] Often, property prices were astronomical, or the owners of well-located sites would not part with their property for any price.

Constraints on Growth

The initial success of Ito-Yokado and the other superstores soon resulted in retaliatory action by a powerful competitor: the mom-and-pop store owners. These small retailers were said to "pull the strings of Liberal Democratic Party politicians at the local level."[8] The action initiated by the small retailers resulted in the 1974 Large Store Restriction Act, which subsequently was strengthened in 1979. The original act restricted the opening of stores with sales areas of over 1,500 square meters (16,500 sq. ft.). The act also restricted the hours of operation of new and existing "large" stores. A series of changes in 1979 added

3. Ito was not the first to open this type of retail outlet. Isao Nakauchi opened the first Daiei superstore in the Osaka area a few years before the first Ito-Yokado store was opened. In 1990 Daiei was Japan's largest retailer in terms of gross sales.
4. Mitchell, op. cit.
5. Hiroshi Uchida, *First Boston/CSFB Report on Ito-Yokado, Ltd.,* April 20, 1988, p. 7.
6. Ibid., p. 6.
7. Ibid., p. 7
8. Tanzer, op. cit.

restrictions on stores with sales areas greater than 500 square meters (5,500 sq. ft.). A Commerce Coordination Committee was established in each area to set policy regarding large store openings and hours of operation. The committees were effectively controlled by the small retailers. By the early 1980s, Ito-Yokado was opening only four or five new stores annually.[9]

Factors other than the Large Store Restriction Act also adversely affected Ito-Yokado. Japanese consumers' real disposable income decreased by a little over 1 percent during 1980–1981.[10] Japan experienced a general economic downturn in the early 1980s, as did the rest of the world, again serving to limit consumer purchasing power. Net income for Ito-Yokado—which had grown almost 30 percent per year between 1976 and 1981—grew by 9.7 percent in 1982 and by 0.9 percent in 1983.[11]

Ito-Yokado as a Parent Company

During the early 1970s, Ito began pursuing new retailing interests. In 1972 he approached Dallas-based Southland Corporation in an attempt to secure a license to operate 7-Eleven stores in Japan. He was rebuffed.[12] He made a similar attempt in 1973 with the aid of a Japanese trading company, C. Itoh & Co., and was successful in obtaining the license. Concurrently, Ito was pursuing another American firm, Denny's Restaurants, in an attempt to obtain rights for opening Denny's Restaurants in Japan. Both subsidiaries, Denny's Japan and 7-Eleven Japan (originally called York Seven but renamed 7-Eleven Japan in 1978), were established in 1973. The first 7-Eleven and the initial Denny's in Japan were both opened in 1974. Stock for each of the two majority-owned subsidiaries was traded independently on the Tokyo Stock Exchange. Both subsidiaries became profitable around 1977.[13]

ITO-YOKADO IN THE 1980s

The Ito-Yokado group consists of three business segments: superstores and other retail operations; restaurant operations; and convenience store operations. The convenience store operations segment is made up of 7-Eleven Japan. The restaurant operations segment consists of Denny's and Famil Restaurants. Ito-Yokado superstores, Daikuma discount stores, two supermarket chains (York Mart and York-Benimaru), Robinson's Department Stores, and Oshman's Sporting Goods Stores make up the superstores and other retail operations segment.

Superstores and Other Retail Operations

York Mart and York-Benimaru York Mart was a 100 percent owned subsidiary. It was established in 1975. In 1990 it operated 40 supermarkets located primarily in the Tokyo area.[14] These stores sold mainly fresh foods and packaged goods, and competition was high in this geographic and retail area.

9. Uchida, op. cit., pp. 7–8.
10. Ibid.
11. Ibid. p. 8.
12. Mitchell, op. cit.
13. Uchida, op cit., p. 8.
14. Ibid., p. 8; and *Moody's Industrial Manual,* 1990, Vol. I, p. 1275.

York-Benimaru was a 29 percent owned affiliate of Ito-Yokado and was an independently managed regional supermarket chain. York-Benimaru operated 51 stores as of 1988. The stores were located in the Fukushima Prefecture of Koriyama City in northern Japan.[15] Like York Mart, York-Benimaru operated with a higher profit margin than the supermarket industry as a whole. Ito-Yokado's share of this profit was the major contribution to the "equity in earnings of affiliates" portion of Ito-Yokado's income statement.[16]

Daikuma Daikuma discount stores were consolidated into the Ito-Yokado group in 1986, when Ito-Yokado's ownership of Daikuma increased from 47.6 percent to 79.5 percent.[17] In 1990 Daikuma was one of the largest discount store chains in Japan with 14 stores. While Daikuma was popular among young Japanese consumers, the discount stores attracted the critical attention of competing small retailers. Since the discount stores were regulated by the Large Store Regulation Act, intensive effort was required to open new stores. Despite these circumstances and increasing competition, Daikuma opened two discount stores in 1989.[18]

Robinson's Department Stores In 1984, the Robinson's Japan Company was established to open Robinson's Department Stores in Japan. The Robinson's name was used under the terms of a license granted by the American store of the same name. The Japanese company was 100 percent owned by Ito-Yokado, and the first Robinson's Department Store in Japan was opened in November 1985 in Kasukabe City of Saitama Prefecture.[19] This was a residential community north of Tokyo and was a rapidly growing area. Although an Ito-Yokado superstore was located nearby, Ito-Yokado's management believed that a niche existed for a slightly more upscale retail store. Ito-Yokado had "shattered traditional wisdom by opening up a department store in the suburbs, not in the center of Tokyo."[20] The location was expected to serve a population area of over 600,000 residents and offer a broad selection of consumer goods at prices higher than superstores yet lower than the downtown Tokyo department stores.

Many of the strategies employed by Ito-Yokado in opening its Robinson's Department Stores followed similar strategies employed in its superstores. The land was leased (in a suburb). Instead of purchasing goods on a consignment basis as most other department stores did, Robinson's managers were made responsible for the outright purchase of goods from suppliers. This allowed Robinson's to purchase goods at a significantly reduced price. Robinson's reported its first profit in fiscal year 1989, approximately four years after opening.[21] In contrast, most Japanese department stores operate approximately 10 years before reporting a profit.[22] The single Robinson's location grossed about 28 billion yen ($220 million) in fiscal 1989.[23] The second Robinson's Department

15. Uchida, op. cit., p. 8.
16. Ibid.
17. Ibid.
18. *Moody's Industrial Manual*, op. cit., p. 1275.
19. Uchida, op. cit., p. 10.
20. Ibid.
21. *Moody's Industrial Manual*, op. cit., p. 1275.
22. Uchida, op. cit., p. 10.
23. *Moody's Industrial Manual*, op. cit., p. 1275.

Store was scheduled to open in late 1990 in Utsunomiya, about 100 kilometers (60 miles) north of Tokyo.

Oshman's Sporting Goods Ito-Yokado licensed the Oshman's Sporting Goods name from the Houston, Texas, parent company in 1985. In 1985 two stores were opened. One of the stores was located inside the original Robinson's Department Store.

Restaurant Operations

Famil The Famil restaurant chain was started in 1979 as an in-store restaurant to serve customers at Ito-Yokado superstores. It had, however, expanded to 251 locations by 1988.[24] The Famil chain did not record its first positive earnings until 1986. In Famil's recent attempts to expand operations, the company had emphasized its catering business.[25] By 1990 the in-store operations (those located in Ito-Yokado superstores) accounted for 45 percent of Famil's sales, the catering business accounted for 32 percent of sales, and free-standing stores accounted for 23 percent of sales.[26]

Denny's Japan Ito-Yokado opened the initial Denny's (Japan) Restaurants in 1974 with a license from Denny's, Inc., of La Mirada, California. Ito-Yokado tailored the American family restaurant to the Japanese market, and Denny's Japan became profitable around 1977. By 1981, 100 Denny's Japan restaurants had been established,[27] and in 1990 there were 320 such restaurants operated by Ito-Yokado.[28] In 1990, Ito-Yokado controlled 51 percent of Denny's Japan stock. In the early 1980s, Ito-Yokado decided that Denny's Japan should purchase all rights to the Denny's name in Japan. The purchase was made in 1984, and royalty payments to the American parent were thereby discontinued.[29] In fiscal year 1990 (March 1989 to February 1990), Denny's Japan reported a net annual sales increase of 10.9 percent, as compared to the 4.9 percent Japanese restaurant industry sales increase for the same period.[30] In 1988 Denny's Japan began using an electronic order-entry system, which allowed managers of individual restaurants to order food supplies quickly based on trends in their own restaurant. It also allowed for the periodic updating of menus to reflect new food items.

Convenience Store Operations

7-Eleven Japan Since the opening of the first 7-Eleven store in 1974, the chain had grown to over 4,300 stores located in virtually all parts of Japan by February 1990.[31] At that time, about 300 new stores were being opened annually.[32] Ito-Yokado owned approximately 50.3 percent of 7-Eleven Japan in 1990.

24. Uchida, op. cit., p. 10.
25. Ibid.
26. *Moody's Industrial Manual,* op. cit., p. 1275.
27. Ibid.
28. Yumiko Ono, "Japanese Chain Stores Prosper by Milking American Concepts," *The Asian Wall Street Journal*, April 2, 1990.
29. Ibid.
30. *Moody's Industrial Manual,* op. cit., pp. 1275–1276.
31. James Sterngold, "New Japanese Lesson: Running a 7-11," *The New York Times*, May 9, 1991, p. C1.
32. Ono, op. cit.

Originally, young urban workers represented the primary customer base. As 7-Eleven penetrated the Japanese market, however, almost everyone became a potential customer. In Tokyo, for example, one could pay one's utility bills at the chain's stores.[33]

The 7-Eleven stores were small enough, with an average of only 1,000 square feet, to effectively avoid regulation under the Large Store Regulation Act. This allowed 7-Eleven to compete with the mom-and-pop retailers on the basis of longer hours of operation and lower prices. Faced with this competition, many of the small retailers joined the ranks of 7-Eleven. By converting small retailers to 7-Eleven stores, Ito-Yokado was able to expand rapidly and "blanket" the country.[34]

7-Eleven Japan pursued a strategy of franchising stores instead of owning them. The franchise commission for 7-Eleven stores was approximately 45 percent of the gross profit of the store (the commission was 43 percent for 24-hour stores). Ito-Yokado provided most of the ancillary functions for each store (e.g., administration, accounting, advertising, and 80 percent of utility costs). In 1987, 92 percent of all 7-Eleven stores in Japan were franchised,[35] and by 1990 only 2 percent of the 7-Elevens were corporate owned.[36]

Within the Ito-Yokado group, 7-Eleven contributed 6.8 percent of revenues in 1990. With this relatively small portion of overall corporate revenues, however, 7-Eleven Japan contributed over 35 percent of the group's profit. Under its licensing agreement, 7-Eleven Japan paid royalties of 0.6 percent of gross sales to the Southland Corporation. In 1989 and 1990, 7-Eleven Japan paid royalties of about $4.1 million and $4.7 million, respectively.

Operation Reform Project

Ito-Yokado implemented the Operation Reform Project in late 1981 in a retail industry environment punctuated by reduced consumer spending and decreasing margins. The goals of the project were to increase efficiency and boost profitability by increasing the inventory turn while avoiding empty store shelves. The plan was originally implemented in the Ito-Yokado superstores and the 7-Eleven Japan convenience stores.

The implementation of the project involved a coordinated effort of catering to often rapidly changing consumer preferences while, simultaneously, monitoring merchandise flow more closely. This coordination was accomplished by making individual store managers more responsible for such decisions as what merchandise was to be stocked on store shelves, thus allowing managers to tailor merchandise selection in their individual stores to local preferences. Top Ito-Yokado regional managers held weekly meetings with store managers to monitor the implementation of the project. As late as 1988, these meetings were still held on a weekly basis.[37]

In order to avoid depletion of store stocks, Ito-Yokado established an on-line ordering system with vendors. In 1982 the ordering system reached only 400 vendors. By 1988, however, the system linked Ito-Yokado with 1,860 vendors.[38]

33. Ibid.
34. Tanzer, op. cit.
35. Uchida, op. cit., p. 13.
36. *Moody's Industrial Manual,* op. cit., p. 1276.
37. Hiroaki Komatsu, *Nomura Securities Report on Ito-Yokado Co., Ltd.,* June 7, 1988, p. 4.
38. Ibid.

Point-of-Sale System[39] As implementation of the Operation Reform Project began, Ito-Yokado paid increased attention to the importance of obtaining information regarding the flow of merchandise through individual stores. The tool chosen to accomplish this task was the point-of-sale (POS) system. POS system usage was increasing in the United States in the early 1980s, but the systems were used primarily to increase productivity at the cash register.[40] In contrast, Ito-Yokado used similar systems as a part of the project by monitoring specific merchandise flow. As of the late 1980s, many retailers in the United States had begun utilizing POS in similar capacities, and some had begun to use POS to track the purchases of individual consumers.[41]

The first use of POS systems in Japan came in 1982, when 7-Eleven Japan began installing them in its stores. By 1986 every 7-Eleven store in Japan was equipped with such a system.[42] The systems available were sophisticated enough to monitor the entire stock of merchandise in a typical convenience store having about 3,000 items.[43] The systems could monitor the flow of every item of merchandise through the purchase, inventory, sale, and restocking stages.

In late 1984 Ito-Yokado decided to install POS systems in the superstores. The sophistication of those systems installed in convenience stores, however, was not adequate to handle the merchandise flow of a superstore, which could stock up to 400,000–500,000 items.[44] New POS systems were developed in a coordinated effort by Ito-Yokado, Nippon Electric, and Nomura Computer Services.

The installation of POS systems in the existing superstores was completed in November 1985, with over 8,000 POS registers installed in 121 stores.[45] With 138 stores in 1990, Ito-Yokado had an estimated 9,000 POS registers in the superstores alone. In 1986, after the systems had been installed in all superstores and 7-Elevens, Ito-Yokado accounted for about 70 percent of the POS systems in use in Japan.[46] As of 1988, 7-Eleven Japan was the only major convenience

39. POS systems are computer-based merchandise control systems. They can provide a variety of functions such as inventory monitoring, price identification and registering, and—in some circumstances—merchandise ordering.

    The implementation of POS systems became a reality in the early 1970s, when IBM announced the creation of a merchandise system which later became the Universal Product Code (UPC). In 1974 Marsh Supermarkets became the first retail store to utilize UPC-based POS systems. Also in 1974, the European Article Number (EAN) system, which virtually is a superset of the UPC, was introduced in Europe. The EAN system was adopted by 12 European nations in 1977. In 1978 Japan joined the EAN Association (EANA). By 1989, 40 total countries were members of the EANA.

    The Japanese domestic market utilizes the same bar-code system used in the United States and Europe for product marking under the EAN guidelines for product marking. The Japanese coding system for consumer goods is called Japanese Article Numbering (JAN). A similar system for product marking used by wholesalers and distributors in Japan is the Value Added Network (VAN). The first product utilizing the JAN code was introduced in Japan in 1978. (Sources: Ryosuke Asano, "Networks Raise Efficiency. . . ," *Business Japan,* October 1989, pp. 45–52; Radack et al., *Automation in the Marketplace*, March 1978; "Pointing out Differences in Point-of-Sale . . . ," *Chain Store Age Executive*, October 1990, pp. 16B–17B.
40. Tanzer, op. cit.
41. For an example of one such application, see Blake Ives et al., *The Tom Thumb Promise Club*, Edwin L. Cox School of Business, Southern Methodist University, 1989.
42. Hiroaki Komatsu, *Nomura Securities Report on Seven-Eleven Japan*, March 15, 1988, p. 4.
43. Uchida, op. cit., p. 13.
44. Ibid.
45. *Moody's Industrial Manual*, op. cit., p. 1275.
46. Tanzer, op. cit.

store chain in Japan to have installed POS systems.[47] By August 31, 1989, Japan had 119,137 POS scanner-equipped registers in 42,880 stores, making it the country with the most POS systems in use.[48]

The POS systems used by 7-Eleven and Ito-Yokado superstores were upgraded in 1986 to add a new dimension to Ito-Yokado's Operation Reform Project.[49] The upgraded systems allowed for bidirectional communication with company headquarters. This feature essentially allowed information to flow not only from individual stores to a central location but also from the central location back to individual stores. By linking the central system to other computer systems, more information than just sales of retail items could be transmitted. This capability allowed Ito-Yokado to increase the efficiency of deliveries by centralizing some orders. By increasing the total size of orders, Ito-Yokado increased its bargaining position with distributors. One result of this bargaining strength was more frequent deliveries of smaller volume. From 1987 to 1988 deliveries increased from one to three per week for stores in many regions of Japan, notably the Tokyo, Hokkaido, and Kyushu areas.

Using the POS systems, 7-Eleven began to offer customers door-to-door parcel delivery in conjunction with Nippon Express. In addition, some POS terminals were being used to issue prepaid telephone credit cards.[50] Since October 1987, Tokyo area customers have been able to pay their electric bills at 7-Eleven; since March 1988, they have been able to pay their gas bills.[51] Since women traditionally manage household finances in Japan, these services were designed to attract more women customers to the convenience stores.

Results For the Ito-Yokado superstores alone, average days of inventory decreased from 25.8 in 1982 to 17.3 in 1987. By 1990 it was estimated to be 13 days.[52] The effect on operating margins and net income for the entire Ito-Yokado corporation was equally dramatic. In 1982 the company's operating margin stood at 5.1 percent. It had increased to 8.1 percent by 1987. By 1990 the operating margin had climbed to 10.5 percent. Net income for the corporation increased from 14,662 million yen in 1982 to 34,649 million and 58,465 million yen in 1987 and 1990, respectively.[53]

7-Eleven Japan recorded similar increases in operating margins and net income during the same period. In 1982, 7-Eleven Japan's operating margin was 20.7 percent. It had increased to 34.6 percent by 1987. Net income from the 7-Eleven operations increased from 7,837 million yen in 1982 to 33,000 million yen in 1987.[54]

As of 1990 the Ito-Yokado corporation was the second largest retailer in Japan, with 1,664,390 million yen of annual gross sales. The leading retailer was Daiei, with 2,114,909 million yen of revenues. Ito-Yokado was, however, the most profitable retailer in Japan, with net income of 58,465 million yen. In comparison, Daiei recorded net income of only 9,457 million yen for 1990.

47. Komatsu, op. cit., p. 4.
48. *Business Japan*, October 1989, p. 51.
49. Komatsu, op. cit., p. 5.
50. Ibid.
51. Ibid.
52. Uchida, op. cit., pp. 12, 22; and *Moody's Industrial Manual*, op. cit., p. 1276.
53. Ibid.
54. Ibid.

THE SOUTHLAND CORPORATION

The Southland Corporation[55] began in Dallas, Texas, in 1927. Claude S. Dawley consolidated several small Texas ice companies into the Southland Ice Company. This new company was under the direction of 26-year-old Joe C. Thompson, Sr. Under Thompson's guidance, Southland began to use its retail outlets (curb service docks) to sell products other than ice, such as watermelon, milk, bread, eggs, and cigarettes. With the addition of these products, the concept of the "convenience store" was born. By 1986 the company had four operating groups: the Stores Group, the Dairies Group, the Special Operations Group, and the Gasoline Supply Division.

The Stores Group represented the largest of the operating groups in terms of sales through the 1980s. The group was responsible for the operating and franchising of convenience stores. At the end of 1985, there were 7,519 7-Eleven stores in most of the United States and five provinces of Canada. This group was also responsible for 84 Gristede's and Charles & Company food stores; 38 Super-7 outlets; and 7-Eleven stores operated under area licensees in the United States, Canada, and several Pacific Rim countries, including Japan.

The Dairies Group was one of the nation's largest dairy processors in 1986 and served primarily the Stores Group, although aggressive marketing in the 1980s targeted serving institutional dairy needs. This group operated in all of the United States and parts of Canada. The Special Operations Group consisted of Chief Auto Parts (acquired in 1979); Pate Foods (a snack food company); Reddy Ice (the world's largest ice company); and Tidel Systems (a manufacturer of cash dispensing units and other retailer equipments). The Gasoline Supply Division was formed in 1981 to serve the gasoline requirements of the over 2,800 7-Eleven stores handling gasoline. This division's history was punctuated by the 1983 acquisition of Cities Service Refining, Marketing, and Transportation businesses (CITGO) from Occidental Petroleum.

Southland's Recent Activities

Southland's dramatic growth and diversification during the 1970s and early 1980s resulted in 7-Eleven having a dominant position in the convenience store industry. Despite this position and diversity, however, circumstances since the mid-1980s had greatly eroded 7-Eleven and Southland's strengths.

The oil price collapse of early 1986 was the sharpest drop of crude oil prices in history. The instability of crude oil and wholesale refined products, coupled with CITGO's inventory methods and various write-downs, resulted in only modest income for a previously very profitable company. The volatility of CITGO's financial position greatly affected Southland's earnings. Southland's equity interest in CITGO contributed a $52 million loss to the corporation in 1986. In order to reduce the impact of an unstable crude oil market and the accompanying volatility of CITGO's earnings, Southland entered into a joint venture with Petroleos de Venezuela (PDVSA) in late 1986.

A takeover attempt of Southland occurred in April 1987. Canadian financier Samuel Belzberg approached the Southland board of directors with an offer of $65 per share of common stock. Unwilling to relinquish control of Southland, the Thompson family tendered $77 per share for two-thirds of the outstanding

55. A more detailed history of Southland can be found in M. Edgar Barrett, *The Southland Corporation (A)*, 1983, and *The Southland Corporation (B)*, 1991.

shares in July 1987. The other third of the shares would be purchased at $61 per share (plus $16 per share of new preferred shares) by the would-be private Southland Corporation.

Financing for this acquisition came from $2 billion in loans from a group of banks and a $600 million bridge loan from Goldman Sachs and Salomon Brothers. An additional $1.5 billion was generated by the issue of subordinated debentures (junk bonds) in November 1987. This occurred after the stock and "junk bond" markets crashed in October 1987. Southland's investment bankers had to sell the bonds at a blended rate of almost 17 percent, instead of the anticipated rate of 14.67 percent. The Thompson family came out of the buyout owning 71 percent of Southland at a total cost of $4.9 billion.

Paying the High Costs of a Leveraged Buyout (LBO)

After Southland was taken private, significant changes occurred in both Southland and 7-Eleven operations. Southland was restructured, with the elimination of two levels of middle managers. During this time, Southland began selling more 7-Eleven stores than it opened in the United States and Canada. Due to the increased number of licensees opening stores overseas, however, the total number of stores worldwide continued to increase. 7-Eleven Japan was primarily responsible for this increase, with the opening of 340 and 349 stores in 1988 and 1989, respectively. Southland also divested itself of many large assets in the 1988 to 1990 period (see Exhibit 1). Significant in this group of divestments were the entire Dairy Group, over 1,000 7-Eleven stores in the continental United States, Southland's remaining interest in CITGO (sold to PDVSA), and 7-Eleven Hawaii (purchased by 7-Eleven Japan).

As of December 31, 1990, Southland operated 6,455 7-Eleven convenience stores in the United States and Canada, 187 High's Dairy Stores, and 63 Quik Mart and Super-7 stores. Southland owned 1,802 properties on which 7-Eleven stores were located. Another 4,653 7-Eleven stores in the United States and Canada were leased.[56]

Three of Southland's four food processing facilities were owned (the other was leased). The company also owned six properties in the United States on which distribution centers were located. Five of the six distribution centers were company-owned. The company also owned its corporate headquarters (called "Cityplace") located near downtown Dallas.[57]

THE PURCHASE OF SOUTHLAND BY ITO-YOKADO

The divestments of 1988, 1989, and 1990 constituted attempts by Southland to generate sufficient cash to service the massive debt incurred from the LBO of 1987. By early 1990, however, it was apparent that the cash generated from these divestments and Southland's operations was not sufficient to cover its interest expense. Some experts estimated that Southland's cash shortfalls would reach $89 million in 1990 and over $270 million in 1991.[58] Southland's long-

56. The Southland Corporation, 1990 Form 10-K, pp. 21–23.
57. Ibid.
58. Linda Sandler, "Southland's Junk Bonds Face Trouble," *The Wall Street Journal*, September 7, 1989.

Date Announced	Asset	Buyer	Amount
January 1988	Tidel Systems	D. H. Monnick Corp.	Undisclosed
February 1988	Chief Auto Parts	Management and Shearson Lehman	$130 million
March 1988	Movie Quik	Cevax U.S. Corp.	$51 million
March 1988	Reddy Ice	Reddy Ice, Ltd.	$23 million
April 1988	402 properties including 270 Houston-area 7-Elevens	National Convenience Stores, Inc.	$67 million plus $13 million for related inventories
April 1988	473 7-Eleven stores in 10 states	Circle K	$147 million
April 1988	Southland Dairy Group	Morningstar Foods	$242.5 million
July 1988	Snack Foods Division	Undisclosed	$15 million
November 1988	79 San Antonio-area 7-Elevens	National Convenience Stores, Inc.	Undisclosed
July 1989	184 7-Elevens in three states	Ashland Oil et al.	Undisclosed
October 1989	50 percent of CITGO	Petroleos de Venezuela, S.A. (PDVSA)	$661.5 million
November 1989	58 7-Elevens in Hawaii, plus other properties	7-Eleven Japan	$75 million
April 1990	56 Memphis-area 7-Elevens	Undisclosed	$12.9 million
August 1990	28 7-Elevens in Florida, plus other properties	Undisclosed	$7.5 million
December 1990	Cityplace land in Dallas	Oak Creek Partners, Ltd.	$24 million

Sources: *The Dallas Morning News*, November 15, 1989, p. D-1.
The Dallas Morning News, October 10, 1988, p. D-1.
Automotive News, February 8, 1988, p. 108.
The Wall Street Journal, February 19, 1988.
The Wall Street Journal, January 28, 1988.
The Wall Street Journal, March 4, 1988.
The New York Times, March 4, 1988.
The Southland Corporation, 1990 Form 10-K.

Exhibit 1
Asset Divestitures of Southland from 1988 to 1990

term debt still totaled about $3.7 billion, and interest expense alone in the first three quarters of 1989 was almost $430 million.[59] In March 1990 Southland announced that it was seeking "rescue" by Ito-Yokado.[60]

Proposed Acquisition of Southland by Ito-Yokado

Southland had "looked at possibilities of receiving assistance from other American companies, but decided that [Ito-Yokado was the best potential partner]."[61] The original proposal would have resulted in Ito-Yokado receiving 75 percent ownership of Southland for $400 million. This proportion of Southland would be split between Ito-Yokado and 7-Eleven Japan, with 7-Eleven Japan obtaining two-thirds of the 75 percent share.

59. Richard Alm, "Southland Seeks Rescue by Japanese Firm," *The Dallas Morning News*, March 23, 1990.
60. Ibid.
61. Karen Blumenthal et al., "Japanese Group Agrees to Buy Southland Corp.," *The Wall Street Journal*, March 23, 1990.

The deal was contingent on Southland's ability to swap its outstanding publicly traded debt for stock and zero-coupon (non-interest bearing) bonds. The publicly traded debt amounted to approximately $1.8 billion. There were five classes of public debt, ranging in classification and interest paid. The interest rate of these bonds varied from 13.5 percent to 18 percent. Ito-Yokado's offer was also contingent on 95 percent of all bondholders of each public debt issue accepting the swap. Under this original proposal, the Thompson family would retain a 15 percent stake in Southland, and the remaining 10 percent of the company would be held by bondholders.

Revisions to the Proposed Buyout

Southland did not make a scheduled interest payment due on June 15. This meant that, at the end of a 30-day period, unpaid bondholders could try to force Southland into bankruptcy court.[62] Bondholders, meanwhile, had shown little regard for the original deal struck between Ito-Yokado and Southland.

Three more revisions of the proposed debt restructuring and terms for the buyout were submitted between mid-June and mid-July 1990. In each revision, either Ito-Yokado's or the Thompson family's stake in Southland was reduced and the share of stock offered to bondholders increased. With each revision came increased bondholder support, yet this support was far short of either the two-thirds majority (as required in Chapter 11 restructuring cases) or the 95 percent acceptance rate dictated by Ito-Yokado. As revisions were submitted, the expiration dates of the debt restructuring and stock purchase by Ito-Yokado were extended.

On July 16 a bondholder filed suit against Southland for failure to pay interest on June 15.[63] By September 12 a majority of bondholders had tendered their notes.[64] This majority was still far short, however, of the 95 percent swap requirement dictated by Ito-Yokado. The deadlines were extended to September 25 for both the debt swap offer by Southland and the stock purchase offer by Ito-Yokado.[65] As Southland was apparently headed for involuntary bankruptcy filing under Chapter 11, the proposal again seemed in jeopardy.

Acceptance of the Proposed Buyout

The deadline for Southland's debt swap offer was again extended. Bondholder approval was finally obtained in late October. Ito-Yokado's offer to buy out Southland was extended to March 15, 1991, pending court approval of the prepackaged bankruptcy deal.[66] The bankruptcy court petition for approval of the prepackaged debt restructuring was filed on October 24, 1990.[67]

Although Southland did not have sufficient bondholder approval as dictated by Ito-Yokado, the bankruptcy court proceedings were swift. The last few bondholders who held out were placated in January when the Thompsons relin-

62. Karen Blumenthal, "Southland Approaches Two Crucial Dates in Plan to Rearrange $1.8 Billion in Debt," *The Wall Street Journal*, April 1990.
63. Ibid.
64. Kevin Helliker, "Southland May Be Considering Seeking Chapter 11 Status, Thus Risking Bailout," *The Wall Street Journal*, September 14, 1990.
65. Ibid.
66. Kevin Helliker, "Southland Says Reorganization Clears Hurdle," *The Wall Street Journal*, October 24, 1990.
67. "Southland Chapter 11 Plan Needs Approval from SEC," *The Wall Street Journal*, December 6, 1990.

Exhibit 2
Southland Corporation's Debt Restructuring: Terms for $1,000 Principal Debt of Various Classes (as Accepted by Bondholders on February 21, 1991)

	13.5% Senior	15.75% Senior	16.5% Senior	16.75%	18% Junior
Principal Retained	$450	300	255	200	95
Interest Rate of New Debt	12%	5	5	4.5	4
# Shares of Common Stock Received	86.5	40.5	35	28	11
# Stock Warrants Received	1	7.5	6.5	6	6

Notes:
- "Principal retained" was in the form of newly issued bonds bearing interest as shown.
- Holders of 13.5% Senior Notes also received $57 cash per $1,000 principal of old debt.
- Holders of 16.75% Notes may have received $250 of 12% Notes with no stock warrants instead of $200 of 4.5% Notes and 6 stock warrants (per $1,000 principal of old debt). In either case the holder would have been entitled to 28 shares of common stock.
- Stock warrants gave the holder the option to purchase one share of common stock per warrant for $1.75 per share from June 5, 1991, to February 23, 1996.

Source: The Southland Corporation, 1990 Form 10-K.

quished warrants for half of their 5 percent stake of Southland's stock.[68] On February 21, 1991, the U.S. bankruptcy court in Dallas approved the reorganization of Southland.[69] At that time, at least 93 percent of the holders of each class of debt issued by Southland had approved the reorganization.[70] On March 5, 1991, Ito-Yokado purchased 71 percent of Southland's stock for $430 million.[71] Two-thirds of this stock was purchased by 7-Eleven Japan and the other third purchased directly by Ito-Yokado. The terms of the accepted debt restructuring agreement between Southland and its bondholders are shown in Exhibit 2.

THE CONVENIENCE STORE INDUSTRY IN THE UNITED STATES

The convenience store industry in the United States changed dramatically during the decade of the 1980s. The number of convenience stores in the United States, the gross sales of these stores, and the gross margins all increased during this time period. The net income of convenience stores, however, decreased significantly. This outcome was largely the result of the rapid expansion of several chains of convenience stores and the increased number of convenience stores opened by oil companies.

Aggregate Measures of the Industry

The number of convenience stores grew from about 39,000 in 1982 to over 71,000 in 1990. From 1985 to 1990 industry sales increased from $51.4 billion to $74.5 billion, an increase of 7.5 percent per year. Gross margins increased

68. David LaGeese, "Judge Approves Southland's Reorganization," *The Dallas Morning News*, February 22, 1991, p. 1D.
69. Ibid.
70. Ibid.
71. "Southland Sells 70% Stake, Completing Reorganization," *The Wall Street Journal*, March 6, 1991, p. A2.

Exhibit 3
Industry-wide Convenience Store Performance, 1985–1989

Industry Indicator	1985	1986	1987	1988	1989	1990
Number of stores	61,000	64,000	67,500	69,200	70,200	71,200
Gross revenue (in $ billion)	51.4	53.9	59.6	61.2	67.7	74.5
Net income (in $ billion)	1.39	1.40	1.31	1.16	0.271	(0.149)
Average per-store profit before tax (in $ thousand)	22.8	21.9	19.2	16.8	3.9	(2.1)

Source: National Association of Convenience Stores (NACS), *State of the Convenience Store Industry*, various issues.

from 22.8 percent in 1985 to 26.2 percent by 1988, but had fallen to 20.7 percent in 1990. Despite such growth, convenience store operations experienced a decrease in net profit in the late 1980s. The total industry pretax profit peaked in 1986 at $1.4 billion, fell to $271 million in 1989, and in 1990 the industry experienced a pretax loss of $149 million. Some trends are shown in Exhibit 3.[72]

The expansion of convenience stores in the 1980s was led by large convenience store chains and oil companies. In addition to the growth experienced by the Southland Corporation's 7-Eleven, Circle K, a Phoenix-based convenience store chain, expanded from 1,200 stores in 1980 to 4,700 stores in 1990.

The Role of the Oil Companies

The impact of oil companies on the convenience store industry had been significant. Virtually all of the major U.S. oil companies began combining convenience store operations with gasoline stations in order to boost profits. In 1984 Exxon opened its first convenience store/gas station. By 1990 it had 696. The Atlantic Richfield Company (ARCO) operated approximately 750 am/pm Mini Markets in 1990. Texaco operated a combined total of 1,321 Star Marts and Food Marts in the same year. There was, however, a total of about 6,800 direct and marketer-supplied convenience stores with the Texaco name in 1990.[73] From 1984 to 1989 the number of convenience stores operated by oil companies increased from 16,000 to 30,000.[74]

Since gasoline sold at a lower margin (about 6 percent in 1984) than non-gasoline convenience store products (32 percent in the same year), the sale of convenience store items presented an opportunity for those gas stations with good locations (i.e., street corners) to increase profits. In order to capitalize on the potential for higher profits in retailing, the major oil companies boosted their marketing expenditures. In 1979 the petroleum industry spent about $2.2 billion for their marketing efforts. By 1988 these expenditures were almost $5 billion.[75]

72. This information is drawn largely from National Association of Convenience Stores (NACS), *State of the Convenience Store Industry*, various issues.
73. *National Petroleum News*, September, 1991, p. 37.
74. Claudia H. Deutsch, "Rethinking the Convenience Store," *The New York Times*, October 8, 1989.
75. NACS, *Challenges for the Convenience Store Industry in the 1990's, A Future Study*, p. 194.

The convenience stores operated by oil companies were growing in both number and size. In 1986 only about 20 percent of the oil company convenience stores were 1,800 or more square feet in size (the size of about 90 percent of traditional convenience stores). By 1990, however, over 50 percent of the oil company convenience stores were between 1,800 and 3,000 square feet in size.[76]

Merchandise Trends for Convenience Stores

Due to the intensified retailing efforts of oil companies and large convenience store chains, some trends (other than those mentioned above) evolved. In 1985 gasoline accounted for 35.4 percent of convenience store sales. By 1990 gasoline accounted for 46 percent of sales.[77] The gross margin for gasoline sales had increased from 7.3 percent in 1985 to 11.7 percent in 1989 and was 10.4 percent in 1990.[78] Of the 61,000 convenience stores in the United States in 1985, 55 percent sold gasoline, and in 1990, 66 percent of the 71,200 convenience stores sold gasoline. In 1990, 85 percent of new convenience stores built were equipped to sell gasoline.[79]

As gasoline sales and margins became an increasingly significant contributor to convenience store revenues, revenue contribution from other merchandise stagnated. In 1985 merchandise (other than gasoline) sales for the convenience store industry amounted to $33.2 billion. In 1990 sales of non-gasoline merchandise were $40.4 billion.[80] This increase in merchandise sales, however, was offset by the large number of store openings. In 1985 the average yearly merchandise sales per store were $544,000. This number increased to only $568,000 in 1990.[81]

The Setting

While flying from Japan to the United States, Takahashi reflected on the success that both Ito-Yokado and 7-Eleven Japan had enjoyed over the course of many years. These achievements were the result of long-term strategies which were carefully tailored to the Japanese market. Could these same, or similar, strategies be the foundation for making Southland financially successful again? He realized that the convenience store industry in the United States was vastly different than that of Japan. Nevertheless, he was confident that, through careful and thorough planning, the goal of making Southland profitable could be achieved.

76. Ibid., p. 198.
77. NACS, *1991 State of the Convenience Store Industry*, p. 5.
78. Ibid., p. 7
79. Ibid., p. 27.
80. Ibid., p. 5.
81. Ibid., p. 1.

Index